T0246699

JIM MURRAY'S
WHISKEY BIBLE
2024

This 2024 edition of Jim Murray's Whiskey Bible
is dedicated with affection to the memory
of
John Berylson
(1953-2023)
He liked us. And he cared.

לזכרון של נרצחים ז"ל, ע"י המחבלים, בישראל
ב -7 באוקטובר תשפ"ד.
ינוח על משכבם בשלום

This edition first published 2023 by Dram Good Books Ltd

10 9 8 7 6 5 4 3 2 1

The "Jim Murray's" logo and the "Whiskey Bible" logo are trade marks of Jim Murray.

Text, tasting notes & rankings, artwork, Jim Murray's logo and the Whiskey Bible logo copyright
© Jim Murray 2023

Design copyright © Dram Good Books Ltd 2023

For information regarding using tasting notes from Jim Murray's Whiskey Bible contact:
Dram Good Books Ltd, Unit 2, Barnstones Business Park, Litchborough, U.K., NN12 8JJ
Tel: 44 (0)117 317 9777. Or contact us via www.whiskybible.com

This book is sold subject to the condition that it shall not, by way of trade or otherwise, be lent, re-sold, hired out or otherwise circulated without the author's prior consent in any form of binding or cover other than that in which it was published and without a similar condition including this condition being imposed on any subsequent purchaser.

All rights reserved. No part of this publication may be reproduced, stored in a retrieval system, or transmitted in any form or by any means, electronic, mechanical, photocopying, recording or otherwise, without the prior permission of the copyright owner and the publishers.

CIP catalogue record for this book is available from the British Library

ISBN: 978-1-8383207-7-5

Printed in Belgium by Snel.

Written By: Jim Murray
All Whiskies Tasted By: Jim Murray
Edited by: David Rankin, George Dearsley and Peter Mayne
Design: Jim Murray, Vincent Flint-Hill, James Murray and Dean Richards
Maps: James Murray, Rob-indesign, Vincent Flint-Hill and Dean Richards
Sample Research: Vincent Flint-Hill, Cole Tomberlain, Brendan Leahy, Polly Spokes, Birgit Bornemeier, Jane Garnett and Charlie Jones.
Sales: info@whiskybible.com
PA to Jim Murray: Jane Garnett
European Dictionary: Julie Nourney, Tom Wyss, Mariette Duhr-Merges, Stefan Baumgart, Erik Molenaar, Jürgen Vromans, Henric Molin and Kalle Valkonen.

Author's Note
I have used the spelling "whiskey" or "whisky" depending on how the individual distillers prefer. All Scotch is "whisky". So is Canadian. All Irish, these days, is "whiskey", though that was not always the case. In Kentucky, bourbon and rye are spelt "whiskey", with the exception of the produce of the early Times/Old Forester Distillery and Maker's Mark which they bottle as "whisky". In Tennessee, it is a 50-50 split: Dickel is "whisky", while Daniel's is "whiskey".

JIM MURRAY'S
WHISKEY
BIBLE
2024

DRAM GOOD BOOKS

Contents

Introduction

Was it really 20 years ago that the first-ever Jim Murray's Whisky Bible hit the book-shelves – and became an instant bestseller? Well, apparently it was.

That was a time when most Independent bottlers still coloured their single malts with caramel, many having no idea of the damage it inflicted on the taste. Few cask strength bottlings were on the market. And single malt lovers around the world stuck to Scotch, not yet trusting the quality of Japanese or from anywhere else from outside Scotia's shores. It was, in short, a very different world: one today's whisky lovers would barely recognise. Indeed, the first-ever Jim Murray's Whisky Bible, published in 2003, contained the delights of 12 other countries outside of Scotland, Northern Ireland, The Irish Republic, USA, Canada and Japan. This year, there are over 30. And of those, English and Welsh – neither of which existed 20 years ago – are so good now they demand a chapter all their own in these now famous pages.

Just six years before I began work on the Whisky Bible, I had published another bestseller: Jim Murray's Complete Book of Whisky, where I had travelled to every single working distillery in the world. Twenty-five years on from my Complete Book of Whisky, such an undertaking is impossible now: there are so many whisky distilleries in operation, that my entire life would be consumed in trying to travel to them all.

Since I took the momentous decision to create and write the Whisky Bible each year – a decision which I knew would be a life-changing one with my shutting myself off for a least four months every year to complete – I have tasted almost 25,000 different whiskies for this book alone. But been gratified to see sales of over a million copies, thus introducing so many people to the possibilities of all the world's whiskies.

From the very first moment I conceived the idea of the Whisky Bible, I was determined to remain fiercely independent: not a single advertisement has ever been found in its pages or on our website. And if I upset distillers by criticising a famous brand, then so be it. The book was designed to inform and help the consumer, the natural instincts of a former national newspaper journalist. And the Bible Thumping section has always been a campaigning piece fighting for those vital souls who open their wallets and keep the whisky industry thriving.

But I also decided to give discretionary awards to those distillers I believed deserved praise. In life, I have always believed in meritocracy: I do not care which sex, colour or religion a person is: it is their excellence that should be acknowledged. The cream should rise to the top. So, too, with whisky. Whichever the distiller, big or small, from whichever country, the better whiskies will be praised and the poorer ones constructively criticised. And as more and more brave people around the world decided to put their houses up as security to pursue the dream of producing a distillery, then so I have widened the awards. Having built this Whisky Bible up entirely on my own and starting without any cash reserves, I know only too well the painful sacrifices that have to be made make the seemingly impossible happen. Equally, I do not believe in positive discrimination: not least because it is a form of discrimination, something I abhor. So I have never given extra marks to a distiller because they are new: every point in the Whisky Bible has to be earned.

For that reason, I have decided, from this 20th Anniversary edition onwards, that I will radically widen the awards section. Every country covered now will get its own award. And every State in the US where I have tasted a new whiskey in the preceding year will likewise see the top bottling receive a gong. It means an extra two weeks' judging and writing. But it is a fantastic way of repaying those who have helped widen the whisky world as we know it. Certainly, there is no doubt that it takes longer now to write Jim Murray's Whisky Bible than it did 20 years ago. That has nothing to do with me being 20 years older. But has everything to do with most whiskies sent to me now being cask strength, when for the first decade it was only a fraction of the whiskies available. Also, 20 years ago most whiskies outside the US were dumbed down in both taste and aroma by caramel. Not now. Which means that it takes longer to get to the overall picture of a whisky – especially with the Murray Method being deployed. Great news for the consumer. The proof of that came with the quickest whiskies of all to taste this year were the standard Scotch single malts and blends, not all of which are naturally coloured. Even after 20 years, some things never change...

However, writing this book is not all about whisky. It is very much about people, too. I may be about to complete 25,000 whiskies tasted for the Whisky Bible, but it seems as though I've met double that number people in that time and forged lifelong friendships with those who appear to appreciate the work I do. Indeed, some of the most wonderful people I have ever met in my life are as a result of spending over 30 years in this industry as a writer, a blender, a consultant, and a presenter. And the Whisky Bible has played a big part of that because I when I meet someone for the first time, it feels that we have already forged a bond through common language and understanding. It is, in many ways, the most enjoyable aspect of producing this book: meeting kindred souls throughout the world, men and women, old, middle-aged and young, who are so fascinated in expanding their knowledge and understanding of the greatest spirit on God's earth...

I had probably never fully appreciated how much I and this book meant to people until it became apparent three years ago that certain unpleasant forces, resentful of its power and popularity, were at work hell-bent on destroying both me and the Whisky Bible. The love and support I received from so many male and female distillers and consumers alike, and still do to this day, is testament to the place in people's hearts this book has found over the last two decades.

Both the industry and its consumers need a clear, unbiased and fearless champion. For the last 20 years, Jim Murray's Whisky Bible has been just that. And shall continue to be...

Jim Murray
Deepest and remotest Northamptonshire
September 2023

How to Read The Bible

The whole point of this book is for the whisky lover – be he or she an experienced connoisseur or, better fun still, simply starting out on the long and joyous path of discovery – to have ready access to easy-to-understand information about as many whiskies as possible. And I mean a lot. Thousands.

This book does not quite include every whiskey on the market... just by far and away the vast majority. And those that have been missed this time round – either through accident, logistics or design – will appear in later editions once we can source a sample.

WHISKEY SCORING

The marking for this book is tailored to the consumer and scores run out just a little higher than I use for my own personal references. But such is the way it has been devised that it has not affected my order of preference.

Each whisky is given a rating out of 100. Twenty-five marks are given to each of four factors: nose (n), taste (t), finish (f), balance and overall complexity (b). That means that 50% of the marks are given for flavour alone and 25% for the nose, often an overlooked part of the whisky equation. The area of balance and complexity covers all three previous factors and a usually hidden one besides:

Nose: this is simply the aroma. Often requires more than one inspection as hidden aromas can sometimes reveal themselves after time in the glass, increased contact with air and changes in temperature. The nose very often tells much about a whisky, but – as we shall see – equally can be quite misleading.

Taste: this is the immediate arrival on the palate and involves the flavour profile up to, and including, the time it reaches maximum intensity and complexity.

Finish: often the least understood part of a tasting. This is the tail and flourish of the whisky's signature, often revealing the effects of ageing. The better whiskies tend to finish well and linger without too much oak excess. It is on the finish, also, that certain notes which are detrimental to the whisky may be observed. For instance, a sulphur-tarnished cask may be fully revealed for what it is by a dry, bitter residue on the palate which is hard to shake off. It is often worth waiting a few minutes to get the full picture of the finish before having a second taste of a whisky.

Balance: This is the part it takes a little experience to appreciate but it can be mastered by anyone. For a whisky to work well on the nose and palate, it should not be too one-sided in its character. If you are looking for an older whisky, it should have evidence of oak, but not so much that all other flavours and aromas are drowned out. Likewise, a whisky matured or finished in a sherry butt must offer a lot more than just wine alone and the greatest Islay malts, for instance, revel in depth and complexity beyond the smoky effects of peat.

Each whisky has been analysed by me without adding water or ice. I have taken each whisky as it was poured from the bottle and used no more than warming in an identical glass to extract and discover the character of the whisky. To have added water would have been pointless: it would have been an inconsistent factor as people, when pouring water, add different amounts at varying temperatures. The only constant with the whisky you and I taste will be when it has been poured directly from the bottle.

Even if you and I taste the same whiskies at the same temperature and from identical glasses – and even share the same values in whisky – our scores may still be different. Because a factor that is built into my evaluation is drawn from expectation and experience. When I sample a whisky from a certain distillery at such-and-such an age or from this type of barrel or that, I would expect it to offer me certain qualities. It has taken me 30 years to acquire this knowledge (which I try to add to day by day!) and an enthusiast cannot be expected to learn it overnight. But, hopefully, Jim Murray's Whisky Bible will help...!

SCORE CHART

Within the parentheses () is the overall score out of 100.

0–50.5 Nothing short of absolutely diabolical.

51–64.5 Nasty and well worth avoiding.

65–69.5 Very unimpressive indeed.

70–74.5 Usually drinkable but don't expect the earth to move.

75–79.5 Average and usually pleasant though sometimes flawed.

80–84.5 Good whisky worth trying.

85–89.5 Very good to excellent whiskies definitely worth buying.

90–93.5 Brilliant.

94–97.5 Superstar whiskies that give us all a reason to live.

98–100 Better than anything I've ever tasted!

KEY TO ABBREVIATIONS & SYMBOLS

% Percentage strength of whisky measured as alcohol by volume. **b** Overall balance and complexity. **bott** Date of bottling. **nbc** No bottling code. **db** Distillery bottling. In other words, an expression brought out by the owners of the distillery. **dist** Date of distillation or spirit first put into cask. **f** Finish. **n** Nose. **nc** Non-coloured. **ncf** Non-chill-filtered. **sc** Single cask. **t** Taste. ◇ New entry for 2024. ⊙ Retasted – no change. ⊙ ⊙ Retasted and re-evaluated. **v** Variant
🏆 2024 Category Winner. 🏆 2024 Category Runner-up.

Finding Your Whisky

Worldwide Malts: Whiskies are listed alphabetically throughout the book. In the case of single malts, the distilleries run A–Z style with distillery bottlings appearing at the top of the list in order of age, starting with youngest first. After age comes vintage. After all the "official" distillery bottlings are listed, next come other bottlings, again in alphabetical order. Single malts without a distillery named (or perhaps named after a dead one) are given their own section, as are vatted malts.

Worldwide Blends: These are simply listed alphabetically, irrespective of which company produces them. So "Black Bottle" appears ahead of "White Horse" and Japanese blends begin with "Ajiwai Kakubin" and end with "Za". In the case of brands being named after companies or individuals the first letter of the brand will dictate where it is listed. So William Grant, for instance, will be found under "W" for William rather "G" for Grant.

Bourbon/Rye: One of the most confusing types of whiskey to list because often the name of the brand bears no relation to the name of the distillery that made it. Also, brands may be sold from one company to another, or shortfalls in stock may see companies buying bourbons from another. For that reason all the brands have been listed alphabetically with the name of the bottling distiller being added at the end.

Irish Whiskey: There are four types of Irish whiskey: (i) pure pot still; (ii) single malt, (iii) single grain and (iv) blended. Some whiskies may have "pure pot still" on the label, but are actually single malts. So check both sections.

Bottle Information

As no labels are included in this book I have tried to include all the relevant information you will find on the label to make identification of the brand straightforward. Where known I have included date of distillation and bottling. Also the cask number for further recognition. At the end of the tasting notes I have included the strength and, if known, number of bottles (sometimes abbreviated to btls) released and in which markets.

PRICE OF WHISKEY

You will notice that Jim Murray's Whisky Bible very rarely refers to the cost of a whisky. This is because the book is a guide to quality and character rather than the price tag attached. Also, the same whiskies are sold in different countries at varying prices due to market forces and variations of tax, so there is a relevance factor to be considered. Equally, much depends on the size of an individual's pocket. What may appear a cheap whisky to one could be an expensive outlay to another. With this in mind prices are rarely given in the Whisky Bible.

Bible Thumping
The Evils of Colour
Prejudice Revisited

When Jim Murray's Whisky Bible 2004 hit the shelves 20 years ago, it caused a little bit of a stir, to put it mildly. And in some places quite dark mutterings.

Not only did it have the audacity to pit Scotch whisky with other malts from around the globe, but it shared the same book covers as Bourbon, rye, Irish pot still and Canadian, too. That was considered bad form, a whisky blasphemy, by some...and in some quarters, I regret, it still is. However, what really raised hackles highest in the industry was my first-ever Bible Thumping. In it I tore into the usage of caramel to change the colour, flavour, aroma, consistency and overall perception of whisky, something then vehemently denied by both the Scotch and Irish whisky industries. But today entirely accepted as fact. Even to the extent that many brands make a point of boasting that no colour is added.

It is the fact that the vast majorities of whiskies are today naturally coloured that it now makes it so much longer to write the Whisky Bible than was originally the case. In the early days, the caramel blanketed out the more complex tones and gave a more uniform personality. Or, when the caramel was overdone, no personality whatsoever. Thus, even when using the Murray Method to shift the temperature and stir those hidden molecules, too often the caramel was too dense to see any great change. So to nose and taste a whisky now takes probably three or four times the length of time than when caramel was omnipresent..... because now we can see whiskies in all whatever glory they may have. And by using the Murray Method almost in three dimensions.

This year it was particularly noticeable which whiskies least troubled my tasting schedule. And, sad to relate, it was, as in the old days, the malts from some of the bigger distilleries in Scotland. After a period of cutting down on caramel, it is clearly moving back into circulation. Doubtless this is because some of the non-age statement malts are a little younger than was once the case and the marketing types want to see a more substantial degree of colour to enhance its looks and blunt its youthful sharpness: to tone down slightly the new-makey qualities that might otherwise be obvious.

For me, it is sad that these whiskies (which you will easily recognise from my tasting notes) have been treated in this way. So it no surprise that an Ardbeg – unencumbered by caramel and just wonderfully carefree and vibrant on the palate – not only picked up Scotch of the Year, but registered as the second best whisky I had tasted this year. A dollop of caramel would have been enough to obscure the brilliance that made it so special.

It takes only a fraction too much caramel or oak or sherry to stand between greatness and something a little less. Such an example came this year with the extraordinary Belgrove Rye 8 Years Old from Australia. A few months before they bottled it I was sent a sample from an unbottled cask which had not been vigorously shaken as the whisky thief did its job. The result was a rye of such incredible delicacy and such purity of grain flavour that a potential World top three might well have been on the cards. By the time the whiskey was dumped and all the heavier oak sediment had been stirred into the mix we had a subtly different whisky: darker in colour, still astonishing in its beauty, but now lacking that unique clarity of nose and taste which set it apart. It still ended up as the Fourth best whisky I tasted in the world this year, but so little can determine so much. Imagine, then, what as alien addition like burnt sugar can do to a whisky...

It is because I have noticed a worrying trend for some distilleries to reintroduce greater levels of caramel, I have decided to re-run the first ever Bible Thumping from the 2004 edition. For those of a pathetically Wokey disposition, look away now, as it contains a very old Scottish joke I have been told more times than I've had plates of haggis and neeps. But that old Bible Thumping rings as true today as it did 20 years ago when the wider whisky world – including, in those days, independent bottlers - had still to wake up to how they were damaging their own brands and pointlessly undermining some truly magnificent whisky. It is a message some need, sadly, to take onboard a whisky generation on.

So, for the next two pages, enjoy a blast from the past...

Admit it: it's happened to you, hasn't it. You know that feeling. You grab a new bottle of one of your favourite whiskies, one you haven't tasted for a while. In your mind are memories of great moments of just you, a glass, the whisky. Kids listening to music upstairs, your partner on the phone or computer. It's just the three of you to resume that sacred trinity. But before you open it you can't help just looking a second time at the colour of the whisky. Your brow furrows slightly. It seems darker than how you remember it. But you don't worry. It simply means that they are using more sherry than before, right?

You pour. Yes, it's definitely a shade darker. Then you nose - aaahhh there's those deep orangey notes, but the barley - where's the barley? And there's no evidence of sherry - what's going on? You are not salivating like you used to - you taste, first a sip then a real mouthful. There's a tingling sensation, the malt arrives to sing to your tastebuds and now you swallow and wait for the big finish which doesn't come. Where has it gone? Where are those high notes you remember that made your nerve-ends tingle? Why has most of the flavour already vanished? You take another mouthful - the same thing happens - no, the finish is even shorter this time. You look at the bottle with suspicion... yep, it's definitely the same whisky you drank two years ago - even the label's the same. Yet it is different. It is darker. It is duller - it's been caramelised!!!

It's happened to you. It's happened to me - oh, how it's happened to me.

Too often in recent years. And particularly in the last six months. To the point where you have reached that certain moment when you know you have to have a rant. It is one of those things that come over you and nothing short of being hit by a rampaging elephant will stop you from having your say.

For this book it happened when I was about a quarter of the way through all those tasting notes. I was trying to run a tight schedule but I had to quit for the day about four hours early. The reason? I had tasted so much caramel in the whiskies I had been analysing that the build up was dulling my tastebuds sample by sample. I could no longer trust what my senses were telling me.

Now how can this be? Listen to the average marketing guy and he will tell you that caramel is purely a colouring agent and doesn't have a single say in the smell or taste of whisky. In fact, it's not just the marketing men. I know a blender or two who reckon exactly the same thing.

It's all our fault

Frankly, I don't think anyone could be wider of the mark. Caramel, when overused, can kill a whisky dead. Even in moderate amounts it can clip a whisky's wings to dramatic effect: instead of soaring it will crash towards the finish. When you look through this book you will see which brands have been marked down for excessive caramel use: look for the term "toffee". True, a whisky can pick up natural caramel notes from the oak. But they usually (though not, admittedly, always) tend to blend and balance in. And when they've been heavy-handed on the caramell the bottling hall, toffee is the finish you often get instead of the more complex tones that should herald the finale of decent whisky.

In fairness to the industry, we can easily understand why caramel is used. It's our fault. It's the trait of the consumer that he wants to see every whisky look exactly the same: if two bottles of the same brand have a fractionally different colour, then surely there is something wrong with one of them. We have been brought up on a diet of sameness. When just a fraction of caramel is added simply as a way of guaranteeing colour consistency, often the effect is negligible. Though, of course, that depends on the kind of whisky. If it is light in character then its tolerance to caramel is less. Sadly, the suspicion is there that caramel is added to give some whiskies that older look. Or more powerful. How many times have you been at a tasting or in a bar and seen someone hold a dark whisky to the light and tell his friend sitting next to him: "Wow, that looks strong"? When in fact it is just a coloured dram at 40% while a cask strength Islay sitting next to it is gives the insipid appearance of Riesling yet is ready to blow the guy's socks off.

Perhaps that's one of the factors as to why I enjoy bourbon and rye so much. Talk about "here's looking at you, kid." The beauty of bourbon is that what you see is, roughly, what you get. It's the law: no additives. Sure, they have filtration. But just looking at a bourbon tells you much about its history: the darker it is the more action the whiskey is likely to have seen inside the barrel. A lighter bourbon may not be younger: it could have been lurking in the lower reaches of the warehouse keeping away from the heat and be lighter in colour and character than something a few years younger but merrily broiling away beside the rafters.

But with whisky from elsewhere, you never quite know Unless the label specifies that you are dealing with something uncoloured. Or you are in an enlightened country that decrees that if a whisky includes caramel that should be stated on the label.

There will be those in the industry who will be shaking their head disagreeing with every word I have written here. I can hear their voices now: "Listen, they have been using caramel in whisky since the year dot. It doesn't make a bit of difference to the taste of the whisky. You are talking out of your arse, Jim." It has been said to me by one or two already.

Interestingly, one who said it to me a little more courteously executive changed his tune when I got him inside a lab and started adding caramel to the base whisky before it was bottled and got him to taste it at five different colour levels.

And if caramel really makes no difference, explain this. When I blend rum, to give it a specific "Naval" style I add caramel. Without it, it would just be golden in colour. But not only does the colour change, so too does the entire flavour make-up. This happens even when dealing with high-ester rums of massive character.In the old Naval dockyards of Deptford caramel was always added to British naval rum. And as caramel is made from sugar in the first place, it tends to sit quite naturally with rum which is distilled from the same substance.

Just the other month, I was reading somewhere some rubbish to the effect that if a rum is dark then it is aged. This, of course, is nonsense: there are any number of dark rums around which is basically new crop (rum from straight off the still and never seen the inside of a barrel) sent over to Europe in stainless steel or plastic drums and then mixed with caramel. Likewise, it was common practice in Guyana to pre-colour some of their Demerara rum. In other words caramel is put into the barrel along with new spirit and then left to age. The difference in both colour and flavour between pre-coloured rum and identical spirit left to mature in an identical cask without caramel is stark and dramatic.

So if it can have this effect on rum, why not whisky - which is made from grain, not sugar? Of course the answer is that it does. For that reason I never use caramel when working with whisky. I don't want to do anything that subtracts from the natural charisma of the whisky, which caramel invariably does. It dulls. It blunts.

That is one of the reasons I was so taken with a new vaned malt called Six Isles. The fact there was no colouring absolutely screamed at you; the flavours are natural, fresh and unhindered. Of course when it enters the Far Eastern markets, especially Taiwan, the pressure will be on for the company to add some caramel and colour it up. Well, I'm praying they don't. I have already done that in my lab to see what happens and the result is something markedly inferior.

Of course the marketing guys will point out, with some justification, that if that is what a specific market wants, then that is what they should get. But wouldn't it be great to see a company stand its ground and say: "this is the way we present our whisky: totally natural and in peak condition. Now you learn to appreciate it."

It all comes down to education. I like to feel I do my bit when giving tastings, but I can't be everywhere or hope I will convert all I meet. Which is why I mention it here: it is a topic in need of a good crusade.

The distillers must have the confidence to go for it, too. They can take a leaf out of the book of those independent bottlers who are going down the uncoloured, unchill-filtered route. They, in turn, had followed the example set by Springbank and you don't hear many calls to add caramel to that. One of those independents, Whisky Galore, launched their range a year or two ago with a disastrous bunch of frankly uninspiring, caramel-flavened malts. They soon discovered their mistake and now their natural coloured range is as good as any around and even contains a true classic or two.

No spirit, it seems to me, is more natural or as indicative of its environment than whisky, nor so delicate and fragile. Perhaps now it is time for some bravery from the big boys. And not just in Scotland, but worldwide.

We all know the old Scottish joke that a Scotsman likes his whisky the same way he likes his women: naked. Here's praying it won't be too long before that means without caramel, as well as water.

Looking to Book Jim Murray?

Jim Murray hosts a wide range of private, corporate and training events around the globe.

To speak to us about booking Jim Murray for your event, please contact:

info@whiskybible.com

Tel: +44 117 317 9777

How to Taste Whisky

I t is of little use buying a great whisky, spending a comparative fortune in doing so, if you
don't get the most out of it.

So when giving whisky tastings, no matter how knowledgeable the audience may be I take them
through a brief training schedule in how to nose and taste as I do for each sample included in
the Whiskey Bible.

I am aware that many aspects are contrary to what is being taught by distilleries' whisky
ambassadors. And for that we should be truly thankful. However, at the end of the day we all find
our own way of doing things. If your old tried and trusted technique suits you best, that's fine by
me. But I do ask you try out the instructions below at least once to see if you find your whisky is
talking to you with a far broader vocabulary and clearer voice than it once did. I strongly suspect
you will be pleasantly surprised – amazed, even - by the results.

Amusingly, someone tried to teach me my own tasting technique some years back in an hotel
bar. He was not aware who I was and I didn't let on. It transpired that a friend of his had been to
one of my tastings a few years earlier and had passed on my words of "wisdom". I'd be lying if I
said I didn't smile when he informed me it was called "The Murray Method." It was the first time
I had heard the phrase... though certainly not the last!

"THE MURRAY METHOD"

1. Drink a black, unsweetened, coffee or chew on 90% minimum cocoa chocolate to cleanse
the palate, especially of sugars.

2. Find a room free from distracting noises as well as the aromas of cooking, polish, flowers
and other things which will affect your understanding and appreciation of the whisky.

3. Make sure you have not recently washed your hands using heavily scented soap or are
wearing a strong aftershave or perfume.

4. Use a tulip shaped glass with a stem. This helps contain the alcohols at the bottom yet
allows the more delicate whisky aromas you are searching for to escape.

5. Never add ice. This tightens the molecules and prevents flavours and aromas from being
released. It also makes your whisky taste bitter. There is no better way to get the least from your
whisky than by freezing it.

6. Likewise, ignore any advice given to put the bottle in the fridge before drinking.

7. Don't add water! Whatever anyone tells you. It releases aromas but can mean the whisky
falls below 40%... so it is no longer whisky. Also, its ability to release flavours and aromas
diminishes quite quickly. Never add ridiculous "whisky rocks" or other supposed tasting aids.

8. Warm the undiluted whisky in the glass to body temperature before nosing or tasting. Hence
the stem, so you can cradle in your hand the curve of the thin base. This excites the molecules
and unravels the whisky in your glass, maximising its sweetness and complexity.

9. Keep an un-perfumed hand over the glass to keep the aromas in while you warm. Only a
minute or two after condensation appears at the top of your glass should you extend your arms,
lift your covering hand and slowly bring the glass to your nose, so the alcoholic vapours have
been released before the glass reaches your face.

10. Never stick your nose in the glass. Or breathe in deeply. Allow glass to gently touch your
top lip, leaving a small space below the nose. Move from nostril to nostril, breathing normally. This
allows the aromas to break up in the air, helping you find the more complex notes.

11. Take no notice of your first mouthful. This is a marker for your palate.

12. On second, bigger mouthful, close your eyes to concentrate on the flavour and chew the
whisky - moving it continuously around the palate. Keep your mouth slightly open to let air in
and alcohol out. It helps if your head is tilted back very slightly.

13. Occasionally spit – if you have the willpower! This helps your senses to remain sharp for
the longest period of time.

14. Look for the balance of the whisky. That is, which flavours counter others so none is too
dominant. Also, watch carefully how the flavours and aromas change in the glass over time.

15. Assess the "shape" and mouthfeel of the whisky, its weight and how long its finish. And
don't forget to concentrate on the first flavours as intensely as you do the last. Look out for the
way the sugars, spices and other characteristics form.

16. Never make your final assessment until you have tasted it a third or fourth time.

17. Be honest with your assessment: don't like a whisky because someone (yes, even me!), or
the label, has tried to convince you how good it is.

18. When you cannot discriminate between one whisky and another, stop immediately.

Immortal Drams:
The Whisky Bible
Winners 2004-2023

	World Whisky of the Year	Second Finest Whisky of the Year	Third Finest Whisky of the Year
2004/5	George T Stagg	N/A	N/A
2006	George T Stagg	Glen Moray 1986	N/A
2007	Old Parr Superior 18 Years Old	Buffalo Trace Twice Barreled	N/A
2008	Ardbeg 10 Years Old	The Ileach Single Islay Malt Cask Strength	N/A
2009	Ardbeg Uigedail	Nikka Whisky Single Coffey Malt 12 Years	N/A
2010	Sazerac Rye 18 Years Old (bottled Fall 2008)	Ardbeg Supernova	Amrut Fusion
2011	Ballantine's 17 Years Old	Thomas H Handy Sazerac Rye (129 proof)	Wiliam Larue Weller (134.8 proof)
2012	Old Pulteney Aged 21 Years	George T Stagg	Parker's Heritage Collection Aged 10 Years
2013	Thomas H Handy Sazerac Rye (128.6 proof)	William Larue Weller (133.5 proof)	Ballantine's 17 Years Old
2014	Glenmorangie Ealanta 1993	William Larue Weller (123.4 proof)	Thomas Handy Sazerac Rye (132.4 proof)
2015	Yamazaki Single Malt Sherry 2013	William Larue Weller (68.1 abv)	Sazerac Rye 18 Years Old (bottled Fall 2013)
2016	Crown Royal Northern Harvest Rye	Pikesville 110 Proof Straight Rye	Midleton Dair Ghaelach
2017	Booker's Rye 13 Years, 1 Month, 12 Days	Glen Grant 18 Year Old	William Larue Weller (134.6 proof)
2018	Colonel E.H. Taylor 4 Grain Aged 10 Years	Redbreast Aged 21 Years	Glen Grant 18 Year Old
2019	William Larue Weller (128.2 proof)	Glen Grant Aged 18 Years	Thomas Handy Sazerac Rye (127.2 proof)
2020	1792 Full Proof Kentucky Bourbon	William Larue Weller (125.7 proof)	Thomas Handy Sazerac Rye (128.8 proof)
2021	Alberta Premium Cask Strength Rye	Stagg Jr Barrel Proof	Paul John Mithuna
2022	George T Stagg	Thomas Handy Sazerac Rye	Glen Grant Aged 18 Years
2023	Thomas Handy Sazerac Rye	William Larue Weller	Glen Grant Aged 15 Years

Jim Murray's Whisky Bible Awards 2024

Talk about making up for lost time! Last year, Buffalo Trace decided their George T Stagg wasn't quite up to snuff: so snuffed it out for a year rather than launch what they believed would have been a sub-standard bottling. Now that's what I call classy.

Classier still, on relaunch, not only was it up to the exacting standards expected of the brand, it was easily the best whiskey I tasted in the entirety of the year....and thus became Jim Murray's Whisky Bible World Whisky of the Year 2024. That is now the 5th time it has landed the Bible's World Whisky of the Year title...remarkably last doing so in 2022...the last time it was bottled before its enforced absence. When Stagg hits the heights, absolutely nothing yet can match it for poise, power and panache: it really is a force of its own.

The only whisky from outside Frankfort to get close this year was Ardbeg Corryvreckan, with by far the best of this resoundingly peaty dram I have tasted in a very long while. Indeed, this was the finest Ardbeg I had encountered since 2010 when its Supernova also picked up the runners-up spot with a similar magnificently multi-layered and memorably intense bottling. Buffalo Trace and Ardbeg leading the world in their whiskies: just like old times.

Most years sees a surprise: a whisky springing up from nowhere and climb to the very highest peaks to the rarefied atmosphere of the World's top five whiskies. Well, in this 20th Anniversary edition, we actually have two. In fourth place came an extraordinary rye whisky from Australia that will shock some distillers in Kentucky who would kill to produce something this bold and breath-taking. The Belgrove Rye 8-y-o from Tasmania redefines rye whisky from outside of North America. And will cause a few shockwaves in it. Remarkably, I had tasted the same whisky when it was a little younger and pre-bottled...and that would have been good enough to seriously challenge for third spot Kentucky's Premier rye, Thomas Handy Sazerac. Is it possible Australia will one day provide World Whisky of the Year? On this evidence, it is by no means out of the question.

And the other surprise? Well, that arrived via Denmark with Mosgaard Organic Peated Single Malt. Denmark is very much an agricultural country and there is plenty of farmyard freshness about this bottling, the type that will make peat lovers swoon.

Like the rye from Belgrove, the whisky perfectly encapsulates the progress in the whisky would that has been seen in the 20-year-lifetime of Jim Murray's Whisky Bible. Back in 2003, when the 2004 edition was being put to bed, was it likely that Australia would produce a rye better than most today found in Kentucky? No. Was it likely that Denmark – then not even a whisky producing nation – would create a peated whisky worthy to sit alongside Scotland's finest? Again, no.

This is how far we have progressed. And now, already, I am wondering what surprises there are in store for me while tasting for the 2025 edition. That is the fun and mystique of whisky....

2024 World Whiskey of the Year
George T Stagg

Second Finest Whiskey in the World
Ardbeg Corryvreckan

Third Finest Whisky in the World
Thomas Handy Sazerac

Fourth Finest Whiskey in the World
Belgrove Rye 8 Years Old

Fifth Finest Whisky in the World
Mosgaard Organic Peated Single Malt

SCOTCH

Scotch Whisky of the Year
Ardbeg Corryvreckan
Single Malt of the Year (Multiple Casks)
Ardbeg Corryvreckan
Single Malt of the Year (Single Cask)
King of IB Aultmore 40 Years Old
Scotch Blend of the Year
Chivas Regal 13
Scotch Grain of the Year
Valour Blended Grain 35 Years Old
Scotch Vatted Malt of the Year
Shackleton

Single Malt Scotch

No Age Statement
Ardbeg Corryvreckan
10 Years & Under (Multiple Casks)
Ardbeg Guaranteed 8 Years Old For Discussion
10 Years & Under (Single Casks)
Kingsbury Gold Caol Ila 9 Years Old
11-15 Years (Multiple Casks)
Jura 12 Years Old
11-15 Years (Single Cask)
Valour Glentauchers 15
16 - 21 Years (Multiple Casks)
Glenmorangie 18
16-21 Years (Single Cask)
Kingsbury Gold Bunnahabhain Aged 17
22-27 Years (Single Cask)
Valour Auchentoshan 27
28-34 Years (Single Cask)
Vintage Bottlers Islay 32
35-40 Years (Single Cask)
King of IB Aultmore 40

Blended Scotch

No Age Statement
Johnny Walker Red
Age Stated
Chivas Regal 13

IRISH WHISKEY

Irish Whiskey of the Year
Natterjack Irish Whiskey Cask Strength
Irish Pot Still of the Year
Blackwater Dirtgrain Mash Bill 15
Irish Single Malt of the Year
Hyde No 11 The Peat Cask 1949
Irish Blend of the Year
Natterjack Irish Whiskey

CANADIAN WHISKY

Canadian Whisky of the Year
Sons of Vancouver 4
Canadian Rye of the Year
Sons of Vancouver 4
Canadian Single Malt of the Year
Glen Breton 16 Years Old

AUSTRALIAN

Australian Whisky of the Year
Belgrove Rye 8 YO
Runner-up
Belgrove Sheep Shit
Australian Single Malt of the Year
Adams Tasmanian Peated
Tasmanian Single Rye of the Year
Belgrove Rye

Australian Vatted of the Year
Tasmanian Ind Bottlers The Blend

JAPANESE WHISKY

Japanese Whisky of the Year
The Matsui Singla Malt Sakura Cask
Japanese Single Malt of the Year
The Matsui Singla Malt Sakura Cask
Japanese Vatted Malt of the Year
The Kurayoshi Pure Malt Aged 18 Years
Japanese Blended Whisky of the Year
The Kyoto Black Label

ENGLISH & WELSH WHISKY

Whisky of the Year
Penderyn Ex-Rye Cask 6 Years Old
English Whisky of the Year
Cotswolds Charred Virgin Oak
Welsh Whisky of the Year
Penderyn Ex-Rye Cask 6 Years Old

EUROPEAN MAINLAND

European Whisky of the Year
Mosgaard Organic Single Malt Peated Bourbon Cask
Runner-up
Belgian Owl Intense Cask Strength

India

Indian Whisky of the Year
Paul John Classic
Runner Up
Amrut Peated

New Zealand

New Zealand Whisky of the Year
Cardrona Growing Wings Single Malt

South America

South American Whisky of the Year
Lamas The Dog's Bollocks II Single Malt

AMERICAN WHISKEY

Whiskey of the Year
George T Stagg
Bourbon of the Year Multiple Barrels (no age statement)
George T Stagg
Bourbon of the Year Multiple Barrels (with age statement)
1792 Aged 12 Years
Bourbon of the Year Single Barrel
Blanton's Straight From The Barrel
Rye of the Year Multiple Barrels (no age statement)
Thomas H. Handy Sazerac
Rye of the Year Multiple Barrels (with age statement)
Sazerac 18
Rye of the Year Single Barrel
Wilderness Trail Single Barrel Cask Strength Rye Aged 4 Years 8 Months Barrel no 751783
Micro distillery Whiskey of the Year Multiple Barrels
Garrison Brothers Cowboy Bourbon 2022
Micro distillery Whiskey of the Year SC
OCD #5 Premium Kentucky Bourbon

*Overall age category and/or section winners are presented in **bold**.*

The Whisky Bible Liquid Gold Awards (97.5-94)

Jim Murray's Whisky Bible is delighted to again make a point of celebrating the very finest whiskies you can find in the world. So we salute the distillers who have maintained or even furthered the finest traditions of whiskey making and taken their craft to the very highest levels. And the bottlers who have brought some of them to us.

After all, there are over 4,100 different brands and expressions listed in this guide and from every corner of the planet. Those which score 94 and upwards represents only a very small fraction of them. These whiskies are, in my view, the élite: the finest you can currently find on the whisky shelves of the world. Rare and precious, they are Liquid Gold.

So it is our pleasure to announce that all those scoring 94 and upwards automatically qualify for the Jim Murray's Whisky Bible Liquid Gold Award. Congratulations!

97.5

Scottish Single Malt
Gordon & MacPhail Speyside Glen Grant 1948
Glenmorangie Ealanta 1993 Vintage
Old Pulteney Aged 21 Years
Scottish Blends
Ballantine's 17 Years Old
Irish Pure Pot Still
Midleton Dair Ghaelach Grinsell's Wood Ballaghtobin Estate
Bourbon
1792 Full Proof Kentucky Straight Bourbon
Colonel E.H. Taylor Four Grain Bottled in Bond Aged 12 Years
George T. Stagg
Stagg Jr Barrel Proof
William Larue Weller 125.7 proof
William Larue Weller 128.2 proof
William Larue Weller 135.4 proof
American Straight Rye
Booker's Rye 13 Years, 1 Month, 12 Days
Pikesville Straight Rye Aged at Least 6 Years
Thomas H. Handy Sazerac Straight Rye
Thomas Handy Sazerac Rye
Canadian Blended
Alberta Premium Cask Strength Rye
Crown Royal Northern Harvest Rye

97

Scottish Single Malt
Ardbeg 10 Years Old
Bowmore Aged 19 Years The Feis Ile Collection
Glenfiddich 50 Years Old
Glen Grant Aged 15 Years Batch Strength 1st Edition bott code: LRO/HI16
Glen Grant Aged 18 Years Rare Edition
Glen Grant Aged 18 Years Rare Edition bott code. LRO/EE04
Glen Grant Aged 18 Years Rare Edition bott code: LRO/EE03
Gordon & MacPhail Mr George Centenary Edition Glen Grant 1956
The Macphail 1949 China 70th Anniversary Glen Grant Special Edition 1
The Last Drop Glenrothes 1970
Scottish Grain
The Last Drop Dumbarton 1977
Scottish Blends
Compass Box The Double Single
The Last Drop 1971 Blended Scotch Whisky
Irish Pure Pot Still
Redbreast Aged 21 Years
Bourbon
Colonel E H Taylor Small Batch Straight Kentucky Bourbon Bottled In Bond
Elmer T. Lee 100 Year Tribute
Old Forester
William Larue Weller 128 proof
William Larue Weller
American Straight Rye
Thomas H. Handy Sazerac 125.7 proof

Thomas H. Handy Sazerac 127.2 proof
Thomas H. Handy Sazerac 128.8 proof
Canadian Blended
Canadian Club Chronicles: Issue No. 1 Water of Windsor Aged 41 Years
Crown Royal Northern Harvest Rye
Indian Single Malt
Paul John Mithuna

96.5

Scottish Single Malt
The Perfect Fifth Aberlour 1989
Annandale Man O' Sword Smoulderingly Smoky
Ardbeg 20 Something
Ardbeg 21 Years Old
Berry Bros & Rudd Ardmore 9 Years Old
Bowmore Black 50 Year Old
Octomore Edition 10.3 Aged 6 Years
Dramfool Port Charlotte 2002 16 Years Old
Old Malt Cask Bunnahabhain Aged 27 Years
Caol Ila 30 Year Old
Convalmore 32 Year Old
Glencadam Aged 18 Years
Glenfiddich 30 Years Old
Glen Grant Aged 15 Years Batch Strength 1st Edition bott code: LRO/FG 19
Glen Grant Aged 15 Years Batch Strength 1st Edition bott code LRO/JH03
Glen Grant 18 Years-Old Rare Edition
The Glenlivet Cipher
Golden Glen Glenlossie Aged 22 Years
Highland Park 50 Years Old
The Perfect Fifth Highland Park 1987
Gordon & MacPhail Private Collection Inverleven 1985
Berry Bros & Rudd Arran 21 Years Old
Kilchoman Private Cask Release
Knockando Aged 21 Years Master Reserve
AnCnoc Cutter
AnCnoc Rutter
Laphroaig Aged 27 Years
Kingsbury Sar Obair Linkwood 30 Year Old
Loch Lomond Organic Aged 17 Years
The Whisky Agency Lochside 1981
The First Editions Longmorn Aged 21 Years
Port Ellen 39 Years Old
Gleann Mór Port Ellen Aged Over 33 Years
Talisker Aged 25 Years
Valour Whisky Ledaig Aged 15 years
Tomatin 36 Year Old American & European Oak
Tullibardine 1970
Arcanum Spirits TR21INITY Aged Over 21 Years
Glen Castle Aged 28 Years
Whisky Works 20 Year Old Speyside 2019/WV02./CW
Scottish Grain
Berry Bros & Rudd Cambus 26 Years Old
The Perfect Fifth Cambus 1979
The Whisky Barrel Dumbarton 30 Year Old
Scottish Blends
The Antiquary Aged 35 Years

Dewar's Aged 18 Years The Vintage
Dewar's Double Double Aged 27 Years Blended Scotch Whisky
Johnnie Walker Blue Label The Casks Edition The Last Drop 1965
The Last Drop 56 Year Old Blend
Royal Salute 32 Years Old
Teacher's Aged 25 Years

Irish Pure Pot Still
Midleton Barry Crockett Legacy
Redbreast Aged 32 Years Dream Cask

Bourbon
1792 Aged 12 Years
Blanton's Uncut/Unfiltered
Bulleit Bourbon Blender's Select No. 001
Colonel E.H. Taylor 18 Year Marriage BiB
Colonel E H Taylor Single Barrel BiB
George T. Stagg 116.9 proof
George T. Stagg 129.2 proof
George T. Stagg 144.1 proof
Michter's 20 Year Old Kentucky Straight Bourbon batch no. 18I1370
Michter's 20 Year Old Kentucky Straight Bourbon batch no. 19H1439, bott code: A192421439

American Straight Rye
Buffalo Trace Kosher Kentucky Straight Rye
Knob Creek Cask Strength
Sazerac 18 Years Old Bottled Summer 2021
American Microdistilleries
Glenns Creek OCD 5 Kentucky Bourbon Aged At Least 36 Months
Garrison Brothers Balmorhea Texas Straight Bourbon Whiskey
Garrison Brothers Balmorhea Texas Straight Bourbon Whiskey dist 2014
Garrison Brothers Balmorhea Texas Straight Bourbon Whiskey dist 2015
Woodinville Straight Bourbon Whiskey Private Select

American/Kentucky Whiskey Blends
Michter's Celebration Sour Mash Whiskey Release No. 3
Whiskey Distilled From Bourbon Mash
Knaplund Straight Bourbon Whiskey Atlantic Aged
Canadian Blended
Canadian Club Chronicles Aged 42 Years
Japanese Single Malt
Nikka Whisky Single Malt Yoichi Apple Brandy Wood Finish
English Single Malt
The English Single Malt Aged 11 Years
The Norfolk Farmers Single Grain Whisky
The Norfolk Single Grain Parched
Welsh Single Malt
Penderyn Icons of Wales No 5 Bryn Terfel
Penderyn Madeira Malvasia Single Cask
Penderyn Rhiannon
Penderyn Single Cask no. 182/2006
Penderyn Single Cask 15-Year-Old Bourbon Cask
Belgian Single Malt
Belgian Owl 12 Years Vintage No. 07 First Fill Bourbon Single Cask No 4275925
Belgian Owl Single Malt The Private Angels 60 Months
Belgian Owl 11 Years Old Eau-de-vie de Safran Cask Finish
Braeckman Belgian Single Grain Whiskey Single Barrel Aged 10 Years
Danish Single Malt
Thy Whisky No. 9 Bøg Single Malt
Italian Single Malt
PUNI Aura Italian Single Malt
Indian Single Malt
Paul John Single Cask Non Peated #4127

Taiwanese Single Malt
Kavalan 40th Anniversary Single Malt Selected Wine Cask Matured Single Cask
Nantou Distillery Omar Cask Strength

96
Scottish Single Malt
Annandale Vintage Man O'Words 2015
Ardbeg 1977
Ardbeg Provenance 1974
The Balvenie The Week of Peat Aged 14 Years
Octomore 71 5 Years Old
Glenwill Caol Ila 1990
Gordon & MacPhail Connoisseurs Choice Caol Ila Aged 15 Years
Gordon & MacPhail Private Collection Dallas Dhu 1969
The Dalmore Candela Aged 50 Years
Gordon & MacPhail Glen Albyn 1976
Cadenhead's Cask Strength Glendronach Aged 30 Years
Cadenhead's Cask Strength Glenfarclas Aged 17 Years
Glenfiddich Fire & Cane
Glen Grant Aged 10 Years
Glen Grant Rothes Chronicles Cask Haven First Fill Casks bott code: LRO/FG 26
Glen Grant Rothes Chronicles Cask Haven Chapter 7 Glen Grant 1998
The Macphail 1949 China 70th Anniversary Glen Grant Special Edition 2
Glen Scotia 45 Year Old
Cadenhead's Cask Strength Glentauchers Aged 41 Years
The Glenturret Fly's 16 Masters Edition
The Perfect Fifth Glenlivet 40 Year Old
Highland Park Loki Aged 15 Years
Highland Park Aged 25 Years
Highland Park 2002
Highland Park Sigurd
Kilchoman 10 Years Old
Lagavulin Aged 12 Years
Lagavulin 12 Year Old
Cadenhead's Lagavulin 11 Year Old
Laphroaig Lore
Laphroaig PX Cask
Laphroaig Quarter Cask
Loch Lomond 10 Year Old 2009 Alvi's Drift Muscat de Frontignan Finish
G&M Private Collection Longmorn 1966
Port Ellen 9 Rogue Casks 40 Year Old
Old Pulteney Aged 25 Years
Artful Dodger Springbank 18 Year Old 2000
The Perfect Fifth Springbank 1993
Ledaig Dùsgadh 42 Aged 42 Years
Tomatin Warehouse 6 Collection 1977
Compass Box Myths & Legends I
Glen Castle Islay Single Malt 1989 Vintage Cask 29 Years Old
Abbey Whisky Anon. Batch 3 Aged 30 Years
Whiskey Bottle Company Cigar Malt Lover Aged 21 Years
Scottish Vatted Malt
Compass Box The Spice Tree
Glen Castle Blended Malt 1992 Sherry Cask
Glen Castle Blended Malt 1990 Sherry Cask Matured 28 Years Old
Scottish Grain
SMWS Cask G14.5 31 Year Old
Single Cask Collection Dumbarton 30 Years Old
The Cooper's Choice Garnheath 48 Year Old
Port Dundas 52 Year Old
The Sovereign Blended Grain 28 Years Old
Scottish Blends
Ballantine's Aged 30 Years
Ballantine's Finest
Ballantine's Limited release no. A27380

Dewar's Aged 25 Years The Signature
Grant's Aged 12 Years
Islay Mist Aged 17 Years
Johnnie Walker Blue Label Ghost & Rare
Oishii Wisukii Aged 36 Years
Royal Salute 21 Years Old
Whyte & Mackay Aged 50 Years

Irish Pure Pot Still

Method and Madness Single Pot Still
Powers Aged 12 Years John's Lane Release
Redbreast Aged 12 Years Cask Strength
batch no. B1/18
Redbreast Dream Cask Aged 28 Years

Irish Single Malt

The Whisky Cask Company The Ash Tree 1989

Bourbon

1792 Full Proof Kentucky Straight Bourbon
Ancient Ancient Age 10 Years Old
Bib & Tucker Small Batch Aged 6 Years
Cadenhead's World Whiskies Heaven Hill
Aged 23 Years
Colonel E.H. Taylor Barrel Proof
Eagle Rare 17 Years Old Summer 2021
Elijah Craig Barrel Proof Kentucky Straight
Bourbon Aged 12 Years
Elijah Craig Toasted Barrel Kentucky Straight
Bourbon
Harding's Creek Kentucky Straight Bourbon
184 Months
John J Bowman Pioneer Spirit Virginia Straight
Bourbon Cask Strength 10 Years Old Batch 1
Michter's Single Barrel 10 Year Old Kentucky
Straight Bourbon barrel no. 19D662
Old Grand-Dad Bonded 100 Proof
Pappy Van Winkle 15 Years Old
Pappy Van Winkle Family Reserve Kentucky
Straight Bourbon Whiskey 15 Years Old
Stagg Jr
Very Old Barton 100 Proof
William Larue Weller

American Straight Rye

Colonel E.H. Taylor Straight Rye BiB
J Mattingly House Money Small Batch Rye
Whiskey Aged 4 Years
Michter's 10 Years Old Single Barrel Kentucky
Straight Rye barrel no. 19F965
Sazerac Rye
Sazerac 18 Years Old bott Summer 2018
Sazerac 18 Years Old bott Summer 2019
Smooth Ambler Old Scout Rye Single Barrel
4 Years Aged
Van Winkle Family Reserve Kentucky Straight
Rye Whiskey 13 Years Old No. 99A
Wild Turkey Master's Keep Cornerstone Aged
a Minimum of 9 Years
Wilderness Trail Small Batch Kentucky
Straight Rye Bottled in Bond

American Microdistilleries

Balcones Peated Texas Single Malt Aged 26
Months in American Oak
291 Barrel Proof Aged 2 Years
Glenns Creek OCD 5
Garrison Brothers Balmorhea Texas
Straight Bourbon Whiskey 2021 Release
Garrison Brothers Cowboy Bourbon Barrel
Proof Aged Four Years
Grand Traverse Michigan Wheat 100% Straight
Rye Wheat Whiskey Bottled in Bond
Rock Town Single Barrel Rye Whiskey Aged
32 Months
The Notch Single Malt Whisky Aged 15 Years
Woodinville Bottled-in-Bond Straight
Bourbon Whiskey Pot Distilled

Canadian Blended

Crown Royal Noble Collection 13 Year Old
Bourbon Mash
Crown Royal Special Reserve
Heavens Door The Bootleg Series Canadian
Whisky 26 Years Old 2019

J. P. Wiser's 35 Year Old
Lot No. 40 Rye Whisky

Japanese Single Malt

Chichibu 2012 Vintage
The Hakushu Paul Rusch 120th Anniversary
Nikka Coffey Malt Whisky
ePower Komagatake
The Matsui Single Cask Mizunara Cask
The Yamazaki Single Malt Aged 18 Years

English Single Malt

Cotswolds Single Malt Whisky Peated Cask
Batch No. 01/2019
The English Single Malt Whisky Small Batch
Release Heavily Smoked Vintage 2010
The English Single Malt Triple Distilled

Welsh Single Malt

Penderyn Ex-Rum Single Cask 7 Years Old
Penderyn Portwood Single Cask 12 Year Old
Penderyn Single Cask Ex-Bourbon cask no.
195/2007

Australian Single Malt

Adams Tasmanian Single Malt Peated Sherry
Callington Mill Entropy Single Malt
Launceston Distillery Cask Strength Bourbon
Cask Tasmanian Single Malt
Tasmanian Heartwood The Angel of
Darkness Cask Strength
Iniquity Anomaly Series Flustercluck

Austrian Single Malt

Weidenauer Hafer Whisky Tawny Port Finish

Belgian Single Malt

Belgian Owl Single Malt 12 Years Vintage No
6 Single First Fill Bourbon Cask No 4018737
Belgian Owl Single Malt 12 Years Single Cask
No 14018725
Belgian Owl Single Malt Aged 15 Years First
Fill Bourbon cask

Czech Republic Single Malt

Prádlo 18 Years Old Czech Single Malt
Gold Cock Single Malt 2008 Virgin Oak

Danish Single Malt

Copenhagen Single Malt First Edition
Mosgaard Organic Single Malt Black Peat
Stauning Kaos
Thy Danish Whisky No. 12 Kornmod Aged
3 Years

French Single Malt

Kornog Single Malt Oloroso Finish 2019

German Single Malt

Oloroso 21 DM
Feller Single Malt Valerie Madeira
Hercynian Willowburn Exceptional Collection
Aged 5 Years Single Malt

Swedish Single Malt

Mackmyra Svensk Single Cask Whisky
Reserve The Dude of Fucking Everything
Smögen 100 Proof Single Malt Whisky

Swiss Single Malt

Langatun Old Woodpecker Organic

Indian Single Malts

Paul John Kanya

Paul John Tula

95.5

Scottish Single Malt

Ardbeg An Oa
Ardbeg Grooves Committee Release
Balblair 2000 2nd Release
Ben Nevis 32 Years Old 1966
The BenRiach Aged 12 Years Matured In
Sherry Wood
Benromach 30 Years Old
Benromach Organic 2010
Octomore Edition 10.4 Aged 3 Years
The First Editions Bruichladdich Aged 28
Years 1991
Caol Ila Aged 25 Years
The Dalmore Visitor Centre Exclusive

Abbey Whisky Glendronach 1993
Glenfarclas 105
Glenfarclas The Family Casks 1979 W18
Glenfarclas The Family Casks 1989 W18
Glenfiddich Aged 15 Years Distillery Edition
Glenfiddich Project XX
Glengoyne 25 Year Old
Glen Grant Aged 10 Years bott code: LRO/GE01
Gordon & MacPhail Private Collection Glen Grant 1948
The Glenlivet Archive 21 Years of Age
The Whisk(e)y Company The Spirit of Glenlossie Aged 22 Years
Glenmorangie 25 Years Old
Glenmorangie Private Edition 9 Spios
Glen Moray Chardonnay Cask 2003
The Singleton of Glen Ord 14 Year Old
The Singleton Glen Ord Distillery Exclusive
The Last Drop Glenrothes 1970
Whisky Illuminati Glentauchers 2011
G&M Rare Old Glenury Royal 1984
Highland Park Aged 18 Years
Fadandel.dk Orkney Aged 14 Years
AnCnoc 1999
Lagavulin Aged 8 Years
Loch Lomond The Open Special Edition Distiller's Cut
The Macallan Fine Oak 12 Years Old
Cadenhead's Whisky & More Baden Miltonduff 10 Year Old
Old Pulteney Aged 15 Years
Gordon & MacPhail Connoisseurs Choice Pulteney Aged 19 Years
Rosebank 21 Year Old
William & Co Spirits Speyside 27 Years Old
Springbank 22 Year Old Single Cask
Kingsbury Sar Obair Springbank 28 Year Old
Tomatin Warehouse 6 Collection 1975
Tullibardine The Murray Double Wood Edition
Wolfburn Latitude
Port Askaig Islay Aged 12 Years Spring Edition
Arcanum Spirits Arcanum One 18 Years Old
Compass Box Myths & Legends III
Whisky Illuminati Artis Secretum 2011

Scottish Vatted Malt
Compass Box The Lost Blend
Chapter 7 Millenium 2010 Aged 9 Years
Wemyss Malts Spice King Batch Strength

Scottish Grain
Whisky-Fässle Invergordon 44 Year Old

Scottish Blends
Artful Dodger Blended Scotch 41 Year Old
Ballantine's Aged 30 Years
The Chivas 18 Ultimate Cask Collection First Fill American Oak
Chivas Regal Aged 25 Years
James Buchanan's Aged 18 Years
Johnnie Walker Black Label 12 Years Old
Royal Salute 21 Year Old The Lost Blend
Royal Salute 62 Gun Salute

Irish Pure Pot Still
Redbreast Aged 12 Years Cask Strength batch no. B2/19

Irish Single Malt
Bushmills Aged 21 Years
Bushmills Port Cask Reserve
The Irishman Aged 17 Years
J. J. Corry The Flintlock No. 1 16 Year Old
Kinahan's The Kasc Project M
Kinahan's Special Release Project 11 Year Old

Bourbon
Blade and Bow 22 Year Old
Buffalo Trace Kosher Kentucky Straight Bourbon Rye Recipe
Buffalo Trace Single Oak Project Barrel #27
Buffalo Trace Single Oak Project Barrel #30
Eagle Rare Aged 10 Years
Elmer T Lee Single Barrel Kentucky Straight Bourbon Whiskey

Frankfort Bourbon Society Elijah Craig Small Batch Serial No 4718833
Knob Creek Aged 9 Years
Michter's 25 Year Old
Michter's Single Barrel 10 Year Old Kentucky Straight Bourbon barrel no. 19D625
Old Forester 1920 Prohibition Style
Pappy Van Winkle Family Reserve Kentucky Straight Bourbon Whiskey 23 Years Old
Parker's Heritage Collection 24 Year Old Bottled in Bond Bourbon
Rock Hill Farms Single Barrel Bourbon
Weller Antique 107
Weller C.Y.P.B Wheated Straight Bourbon
Wild Turkey Rare Breed Barrel Proof
Wilderness Trail Small Batch Kentucky Straight Bourbon Bottled in Bond
William Larue Weller 135.4 proof

Tennessee Whiskey
Uncle Nearest 1820 Aged 11 Years

American Straight Rye
Knob Creek Rye Single Barrel Select
Michter's US*1 Single Barrel Strength Kentucky Straight Rye
Wild Turkey 101 Kentucky Straight Rye

American Microdistilleries
Rock Town Chocolate Malt Straight Bourbon Whiskey Single Barrel No. 21 Aged 34 Months
Horse Soldier Reserve Barrel Strength Bourbon Whiskey
Balcones ZZ Top Tres Hombres Texas Whisky
Garrison Brothers Single Cask 2016
Burns Night Single Malt
Balcones FR.OAK Texas Single Malt Whisky Aged at least 36 Months in Oak
Corsair Dark Rye American Rye Malt Whiskey Aged 8 Months
Koval Single Barrel Rye Barrel 6249
Garrison Brothers Cowboy Bourbon Barrel Proof Aged Five Years
Garrison Brothers Cowboy Bourbon Texas Straight Bourbon Whiskey 2020 Release
Garrison Brothers Laguna Madre Texas Straight Bourbon Whiskey 2020 Release
Cadenhead's Garrison Brothers 2014
Laws Whiskey House Four Grain Straight Bourbon Whiskey Barrel Select Aged 3 Years
Woodinville Cask Strength Straight Bourbon

Canadian Single Malt
Lohin McKinnon Peated Single Malt Whisky
Forty Creek Copper Pot Reserve
Canadian Rockies 17 Years
Shelter Point Single Cask Virgin Oak Finish

Canadian Blended
Crown Royal Northern Harvest Rye
Gibson's Finest Rare Aged 18 Years

Japanese Single Malt
The Matsui Single Malt Sakura Cask

Japanese Vatted Malt
Nikka Taketsuru Pure Malt
The Kurayoshi Pure Malt Whisky Aged 18 Years

Japanese Single Grain
Makoto Single Grain Whisky Aged 23 Years
Nikka Coffey Grain Whisky

English Single Malt
Bimber Distillery Single Malt London
Cotswolds Single Malt Whisky Founder's Choice STR
The English Single Malt Whisky 'Lest We Forget' 1914 - 1918
The English Single Malt Whisky Small Batch Release Triple Distilled

English Single Malt
Cotswolds Bourbon Cask Single Malt The English Single Malt Smokey Virgin

Welsh Single Malt
Penderyn Celt
Penderyn Legend

Penderyn Madeira Finish
Penderyn Myth bott code 200292
Penderyn Ex-Tawny Port Single Cask
Penderyn Single Cask 13 Year Old Rich Oak Cask
Australian Single Malt
Bakery Hill Peated Malt Cask Strength Single Malt Whisky
Cadenhead's World Whiskies Cradle Mountain Aged 24 Years
Heartwood Night Thief
Limeburners Western Australia Single Malt Whisky Port Cask Cask Strength
Australian Vatted Single Malt
Heartwood 2nd Moment of Truth
Austrian Single Malt
J.H. Original Rye Whisky 6 Jahre Gelagert
Belgian Single Malt
Belgian Owl Intense Single Malt
Belgian Owl Intense 45 Months cask 7016932
Braeckman Belgian Single Grain Whisky Single Barrel Aged 12 Years
Corsican Single Malt
P & M Aged 13 Years Corsican Single Malt
Danish Single Malt
Mosgaard Organic Single Malt Palo Cortado
Stauning Peat
Stauning Rye The Master Distiller
French Single Malt
Eddu Gold
Kornog Single Malt Sant Erwan 2021
German Single Malt
Feller New Make Barley Malt Peated
St Killian Single Malt Signature Edition "Eight"
Slovakian Single Malt
Nestville Master Blender Aged 13 Years Limited Edition 2022
Swedish Single Malt
High Coast Distillery Visitor Center Cask
Mackmyra Brukswhisky art nr. MB-003
Mackmyra Brukswhisky art nr. MB-004
Mackmyra Single Cask 2nd Fill ex-Bourbon Cask Fat Nr 11638
Mackmyra Svensk Moment 22
Smögen Primör Revisited Single Malt 2019
Swiss Single Malt
Langatun 10 Year Old Chardonnay
Langatun Cardeira Cask Finish Single Malt
Langatun Single Malt Old Crow
Brazilian Single Malt
Lamas Nimbus Robustus Single Malt
Indian Single Malt
Amrut Greedy Angels Peated Rum Finish Chairman's Reserve 10 Years Old
Amrut Peated Port Pipe Single Cask
Amrut Single Malts of India Kurinji
Paul John Christmas Edition
Paul John Christmas edition 2022
The Cyprus Whisky Association Paul John Single Malt

95 (New Entries Only)
Scottish Single Malt
Valour Whisky Auchentoshan 27 Years Old
Kingsbury Gold Caol Ila Aged 9 Years
Glenmorangie Barrel Select Release Amontillado Finish Aged 12 Years
Glenmorangie The Quinta Ruban Aged 14 Years
Glenmorangie Signet
Art Edition No 5 Glentauchers Aged 13 Years
Wolfburn Morven Lightly Peated
Scottish Vatted Grain
Valour Whisky Blended Grain 35 Years Old
Scottish Blend
Chivas Regal Extra Aged 13 Years
Bourbon
Bardstown Bourbon Company Discovery Series No 5
Booker's Aged 7 Years 4 Months 14 Days

Colonel E. H. Taylor Four Grain Straight Kentucky Bourbon Bottled In Bond
Door Knocker Kentucky Straight Bourbon 5 Years 4 Months Double Barreled
Eagle Rare Aged 10 Years
Old Forester 100 Proof
Penelope Architect Build No 6 Straight Bourbon Age: 4 Years
Straight Rye
Knaplund Rye Whiskey Atlantic Aged 6 Years
Pikesville 110 Proof Straight Rye Aged At Least 6 Years
Wild Turkey Rare Breed Barrel Proof Rye
American Microdistilleries
Spirit Hound Straight Malt Whisky Cask Strength Single Barrel 3 Years Old
Whiskey Thief Kentucky Straight Bourbon Aged 6 Years
Whiskey Thief Kentucky Rye Aged 5 Years
McKenzie Small Batch Straight Bourbon 4 Grain Aged A Minimum of 4 Years
Oregon Spirit Single Barrel Bottled In Bond Wheat Whiskey Aged 5 Years
Garrison Brothers Balmorhea Bourbon 2023
Irish Pot Still
Blackwater Dirtgrain Mash Bill 15
English Single Malt
Cotswold Hearts & Crafts Banyuls Cask
The English Sherry Butt Heavily Smoked Small Batch Single Malt
Sacred Peated English Whisky
White Peak Wire Works
Welsh Single Malt
Penderyn Amontillado
Penderyn Peated
Penderyn Tawny Port Small Batch
Australian Single Malt
Kinglake Full Noise Single Malt
Limeburners Port Cask Single Malt
Limeburners Tigersnake Mixed Grain
Austrian Single Malt
Broger Burn Out heavily peated malt whisky
Belgian Single Malt
Belgian Owl Passion Aged for 42-47 Months
Belgian Owl Intense Cask Strength Aged for 36-60 Months
Danish Single Malt
Trolden Nimbus Stratus Single Malt Peated Batch No 1
German Single Malt
Feller Signature 12 Single Malt Amarone Cask
Hercynian Emporer's Way Peated Single Malt
MEW Rare Cask Mizunara Oak
Italian Single Malt
Retico Finest Italian Single Malt Aged 7 Years
Swiss Single Malt
Säntis Malt Single Malt Edition Dreifaltigkeit lot No 9
Brazilian Single Malt
Lamas The Dog's Bollocks II Single Malt
Indian Single Malt
Amrut Single Malt Cask Strength
Goalong Single Malt Whiskey Small Batch Bourbon & Brandy Cask Aged 5 Years
Paul John Bold
Paul John Peated

94.5 (New Entries Only)
Scottish Single Malt
Annandale Founder's Selection Man O' Swords Smoulderingly Smoky
Ardbeg Guaranteed 8 Years Old
Ardbeg Guaranteed Ten Years Old
Glenmorangie The Original Aged 10 Years
Oban 14
Wolfburn Langskip
Vintage Bottlers Secret Series 2 Speyside
Scottish Blend
Johnnie Walker Red Label

Bourbon
 1792 Bottled In Bond
 1792 Small Batch
 Blanton's Gold Edition
 Buffalo Trace Kosher Bourbon Rye Recipe
 Bulleit Bourbon
 Door Knocker Kentucky Straight Bourbon 5 Years Old
 Maker's Mark Wood Finished Series 2022 Limited Release 10
 Old Pepper Straight Bourbon Bottled In Bond
 Wilderness Trail Family Reserve Cask Strength Bourbon Aged 8 Years

American Microdistilleries
 Los Angeles L.A. Beach Hi-Wheat Straight Bourbon Bottled In Bond Single Barrel 5 291 E13 Colorado Single Malt Whiskey Aged For 1752 Days
 Louisiana Aged A Minimum Two Years
 Iron Smoke Straight Bourbon Casket Strength
 Fox and Hare Single Barrel Straight Rye Aged At Least 4 Years
 Garrison Brothers Small Batch Bourbon 2023 Release Aged 3 Years
 Copperworks American Single Malt No 47
 Woodinville Cask Strength Straight Bourbon

Canadian Single Malt
 Glen Breton Rare Single Malt Aged 14 Years
 The Liberty Distillery Trust Whiskey

Irish Pot Still
 Curraghmore First Release

English Single Malt
 Cotswold Single Cask Charred Virgin Oak

Welsh Single Malt
 Penderyn Madeira Finish
 Penderyn Rich Oak

Australian Single Malt
 Adams Tasmanian Single Malt Original Peated Sherry
 The Aisling Boilermaker Series 2 Apera Cask
 The Aisling Whiskycrafter Preimhe Shiraz Baraille Royalty Special Edition
 Coburns Calliope
 Coburns Zeus
 Deviant Heavily Peated Single Malt
 Iniquity Gold label batch 007

Austrian Single Malt
 Broger Hoamat Gerste bott code LGE-15
 Broger Jubiliaums Edition 30 Jahr Brennerei 15 Jahre Whisky

Belgian Single Malt
 The Bassets Craft Distillery Cigar Malt 2023
 Belgian Owl Evolution Aged for 48-59 Months
 Belgian Owl Thematic Series: Coffee 5 Years

Czech Single Malt
 Old Well Czech Single Malt Lightly Peated

Faroe Island Single Malt
 Einar's Single Malt Cask Strength Batch 10
 Einar's Single Malt Cask Strength Batch 12

German Single Malt
 Doinich Daal Black Forest Single Malt Pfaffarauscher Batch No 07
 Hercynian Elsburn Wayfare Single Malt
 Hercynian Elsburn Single Malt Aged 11 Years
 Moonshine Single Still Whisky Ex-Bourbon Barrel Vol. 3

Slovenian Single Malt
 Broken Bones Single Malt Peated 4 Years

Swiss Single Malt
 Johnett Single Malt Single Cask No 113

New Zealand Single Malt
 Pokeno Prohibition Porter Single Malt

94 (New Entries Only)

Scottish Single Malt
 Art Edition No 4 Bunnahabhain Aged 13 Years
 Kingsbury Gold Staoisha Bunnahabhain Aged 8 Years
 Valour Whisky Bunnahabhain 30 Years Old

 Glenmorangie The Cadboll Estate Single Barley Aged 15 Years
 Kilchoman Fino Sherry 2023 Edition
 Wolfburn 10 Years Old
 Ferg & Harris Speyside Aged 12 Years

Bourbon
 McAfee Brothers Benchmark Single Barrel
 Rock Town Column Still Collection Single Barrel Bourbon Whiskey Cask No 6
 Weller Antique 107
 Wilderness Trail Bourbon On The Banks

Straight Rye
 Colonel E. H. Taylor Straight Kentucky Rye Bottled In Bond

American Microdistilleries
 Whisky On Tap The Golden Promise American Single Malt
 Koval Single Barrel Bourbon
 Whiskey Thief Riders On The Storm
 Grand Traverse Hand Selected Bourbon Single Barrel
 John Myer New York Straight Bourbon
 Copperworks American Single Malt Craft Malt Week 2022

Whiskey Distilled From Bourbon Mash
 Bhakta Armagnac Cask Finish Bourbon Distilled 2013
 World Whisky Society Classic Collection Cognac Edition Number 14 Aged 10 Years

Canadian Single Malt
 Canadian Rockies 28 Years Old

Japanese Single Malt
 The Matsui Single Malt Mizunara Cask
 Akashi Cask Strength Bourbon Cask 2010

Japanese Blended
 The Kyoto Black Label

English Single Malt
 The English Virgin Oak Small Batch Single Malt
 The Norfolk Popcorn Single Grain Whisky Vintage Cask Vatting

Welsh Single Malt
 Penderyn Celt
 Penderyn Madeira Finish
 Penderyn Portwood

Australian Single Malt
 Coburns Cybele
 Coburns Perseus
 Enchantress Rebis Release

Belgian Single Malt
 Belgian Owl New Make Barley Spirit

Danish Single Malt
 Mosgaard Organic Single Malt Amontillado Cask
 Trolden Nimbus Cumulus VII Single Malt Peated Edition

Finnish Single Malt
 Kyro Wood Smoke

German Single Malt
 Destillerie Rieger and Hofmeister Schwabischer Malt Rauchmalzwhisky
 Derrina Einkorn Single Grain
 Blaue Maus Jubilaums-Abfullung 2023 Single Cask Malt 30 Years Old

Slovakian Single Malt
 Nestville Aged 12 Years Reminiscence of Vanilla

Sweden Single Malt
 Granum Single Grain

Swiss Single Malt
 Säntis Malt Single Malt Edition Himmelberg
 Johnett Single Malt Single Cask No 132

Brazillian Single Malt
 Lamas Sassafras Single Malt

Indian Single Malt
 Paul John Brilliance

New Zealand Single Malt
 Pokeno Revelation Single Malt

American Whiskey

The year 2022 marked not only the publication of the 20th edition of the Whisky Bible but also the 30th anniversary of my moving from part-time to full-time whiskey writing – the first person in the world ever to dedicate his life to writing about this singular spirit.

Friends of mine working at various Kentucky distilleries questioned my decision. In 1992 both bourbon and rye were in decline. And after so many years of setbacks and witnessing the pain of shrinking markets, they could not see why I would go gung-ho on a spirit they believed was going rapidly out of fashion.

Yes, they witnessed with more weary than envious eyes that things were happening in Scotland, especially in view of the work Michael Jackson and I were doing to wake people up to the still largely undiscovered mysteries of single malt.

But bourbon? Rye….!!!! To Kentuckians that one was going the way of the dodo, holding up in a few shrinking markets to the east.

That was then. This is now. And now has never looked better for American whiskey since prohibition reared its ugly head.

What 30 years ago was sleepy Ancient Age distillery, making small amounts of outstanding bourbon on the banks of the Kentucky River, has led the way back. And though its buildings singularly defined Kentucky's distilling past, then there appeared to be no future. Today, the finishing touches have been made to actually double capacity, an absolutely huge undertaking. And land is being fought over in the courtrooms for warehouses.

Down the road at Danville, it was once a matter of driving around seeking out the industrial archaeology of an extinct distilling town. Not today. On one side of the old road out to Lebanon in their gorgeous yellow and black livery meadowlarks sing sweetly and flutter around in the long summer grasses, as they have done for thousands of years. While on the other side of the pavement a huge new distillery hisses out its new make and rumbles and clangs this now oak-caged spirit into vast buildings in which they will be housed, all the time people coming and going keen to witness the new age of bourbon. More remarkable is that the Wilderness Trail, a distillery which didn't exist a dozen years ago, is now making a whiskey which is literally world-class – able to stand up to comparison with anything made anywhere. Especially its rye, which a generation of distillers ago, was being written off as a soon-to-be lost style.

Yes, Kentucky is rocking.

And in other States, too, enormous work has been going on in producing high class bourbons, ryes and malt. So much so that it I will now be having to spend even more time in the US to keep up with all the developments there.

It also means that from now on, Jim Murray's Whisky Bible will each year be giving awards to be best whiskeys to be found made in each State. Because these remarkable people who have invested so much need to be recognised for their bravery, vision and efforts. And, when appropriate, excellence.

Jim Murray's Whisky Bible 2023 American Whiskies of the Year	
Whiskey of the Year	George T Stagg
Rye of the Year	Thomas H. Handy Sazerac
US Micro Whisky of the Year	Glenns Creek OCD Premium

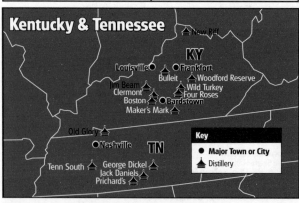

Bourbon Distillery List

Bardstown	Lexington	
Barton 1792	Barrel House	Jim Beam Urban Stillhouse
Rebell Yell	Bluegrass	Kentucky Peerless
Willett Distillery	James E. Pepper	Michter's Fort Nelson
	Town Branch	Michter's Shively
		Old Forester
	Louisville	Rabbit Hole
	Angel's Envy	Stitzel Weller
Frankfort	Bernheim.	
Buffalo Trace	Evan Williams	**Shelbyville**
Castle & Key	Heaven Hill Bernheim	Bulleit Distilling Co.
Glenns Creek		Jeptha Creed

Bourbon Distilleries

Bourbon confuses people. Often they don't even realise it is a whiskey, a situation not helped by leading British pub chains, such as Wetherspoon, whose bar menus list "whiskey" and "bourbon" in separate sections. And if I see the liqueur Southern Comfort listed as a bourbon one more time I may not be responsible for my actions.

Bourbon is a whiskey. It is made from grain and matured in oak, so really it can't be much else. To be legally called bourbon it must have been made with a minimum of 51% corn and matured in virgin oak casks for at least two years. Oh, and no colouring can be added other than that which comes naturally from the barrel.

Where it does differ, from, say Scotch, is that the straight whiskey from the distillery may be called by something other than that distillery name. Indeed, the distillery may change its name which has happened to two this year already and two others in the last three or four. So, to make things easy and reference as quick as possible, I shall list the Kentucky-based distilleries first and then their products in alphabetical order along with their owners and operational status.

Jim Murray's Whisky Bible 2024 United States Micros State Awards	
Arkansas	Rock Town Single Barrel Arkansas Straight Bourbon Cask No 912 Aged 41 Months
Arizona	John Shaw Single Malt Whisky Mesquite Smoked Whisky Aged At Least 2 Years
California	Stark Whisky On Tap The Golden Promise Aged 7 Winters and 6 Summers
Colorado	291 XI Barrel Proof Single Barrel Colorado Whiskey 291 Anniversary
Florida	Kozuba High Wheat Rye Whiskey 7 Years Old
Illinois	Koval Single Barrel Bourbon Barrell No 4351
Kentucky (micro)	OCD #5 Premium Kentucky Bourbon Barrel 7
Louisiana	Louisiana Single Malt Aged A Minimum Two Years
Michigan	Grand Traverse Michigan Wheat 100% Straight Wheat Whiskey Bottled In Bond
Montana	Montgomery Sudden Wisdom Straight Rye Aged 3 Years
New York	Iron Smoke Straight Bourbon Bottled In Bond Aged 8 Years
Oregon	Oregon Single Barrel Bottled In Bond Wheat Whiskey Aged 5 Years
Texas	Garrison Brothers Cowboy Bourbon 2022 Release
Washington	Woodinville Cask Strength Straight 100% Rye
West Virginia	Smooth Ambler Founders' Cask Strength Series Straight Bourbon 2022 Aged 6 Years
Wyoming	Wyoming Whiskey Single Barrel Straight Bourbon

23

Bourbon

◈ **1792 Aged 12 Years** bott code L22168 db **(96.5) n24** textbook small grain involvement so far bourbon is involved. There is a flickering of what seems spiciness, but actually isn't. Well, there is, but that is only half of the story and 50% of the stimulus. It is that flickering rye while sitting on a velvet cushion, the corn oils, cocoas and red liquorice forming its satin-like home, which quietly blows the mind; **t24** and now the finest mouth feel of the year. By far the biggest lashing of ulmo honey or any whiskey this year, supported by the corn oils and other, slightly toastier vanillas. A little black cherry moves through the middle; **f24** a fade of playfully bittering kumquat, yet more buzzing small grains and a gloriously silky chocolate-liquorice finale... And it is one very long fade....; **b24.5** oh, hello! I may just have found some kind of award-winner. This is the best bourbon I have tasted so far this year. But I still have some crackers to open in my tasting rooms yet. For those able to track down this batch of a consistently excellent bourbon, just use the Murray Method and give yourself half an hour minimum. And then prepare to be seduced. As well as quite amazed...Oh, and to fall in love a bit... *48.3% (96.6 proof)*

◈ **1792 Bottled In Bond** bott code L23180 db **(94.5) n23** gorgeously nutty. Starts out as light roasted chestnut and slowly transforms into praline...; **t24** one moment you are marvelling at the depth of the corn oil, the next you are rocked off your seat by the startling intensity of the chocolate mousse. If that isn't enough, there is even a polished honey tone to the more muscular oak moments. The spices are just so delicate and well-mannered; **f23.5** the chocolate caramel fade: do you drink it or eat it...? **b24** this is 1792 shewing real panache. It sets out its chocolatey intent early and sticks to it, despite going through a few nutty and occasionally honeyed byways. Simply delicious very high-class bourbon. *50% (100 proof)*

◈ **1792 Full Proof** bott code L22067 db **(96) n23.5** some upstart nibbling kumquat is soon put in its place by a volley of small grains, rye in particular, and a thick coat of chocolate cake mix; **t24.5** the clock has just stopped. It needed to, because I'm not sure there is enough time in the day to really get to the bottom of this extraordinary work of art that has been hung all around your palate. The interplay between red and black liquorice is sublime, as is the mildly minty chocolate middle. The kumquat returns, accompanied now by a fruit-edge to the rye grains which somehow manage to send the salivation levels skyrocketing. The caramel begins dense, but hits a thick layer of butterscotch even before the finish. But compressed between all these flavour seams is heather honey, squelchy and immediately melting...; **f24** so soft and really underscoring that cocoa-liquorice theme that seems to be melting into the honey-tinted vanilla; **b24** this is faultless whiskey. 1792 will be fighting it out with two world-class whiskeys for some kind of recognition in the 2024 Bible. And this consistency of imperious bourbon from 1792 rather does suggest that we are now talking one of the top six distilleries in the world at this moment... *62.5% (125 proof)*

◈ **1792 Single Barrel** bott code L21217 db **(90) n22.5** the lightest liquorice mingles with even lighter vanillas. Decent spice prickle and citrus...; **t23** early silky corn oil and red liquorice, then the small grain explosion that has been a marker for this distillery for the last 30 years at least; **f22** something is telling me that the slight bittering I am getting is not unknown on their single cask bottlings. But the excesses are pleasantly countered by the intense vanilla and whittling small grains; **b22.5** for me, Single Barrel is, despite its strength, always the friendliest of the 1792 range. There is nothing here to overturn that observation. *49.3% (98.6 proof)*

◈ **1792 Small Batch** bott code L23037 db **(93.5) n23** the small grains have gone bananas. And the bananas have gone all grainy...a complex, bitty, vaguely vanilla-fruity composition; **t24** magnificent silk caresses the palate on entry while liquorice grows from that persistent vanilla; **f23** here we go again: the small grains are in hyperactive mode again and ping around the palate like a pinball...; **b23.5** further proof, were it needed, that 1792 has become a by-number for bourbon brilliance. Such a complex offering. *44.85% (93.7 proof)*

◈ **1792 Small Batch** bott code L231501522365 db **(94.5) n23.5** must qualify as one of the busiest small grain noses in existence: there are so many points and counter points rumbling around, and so difficult to pinpoint, it's easy to forget to actually get round to tasting the whiskey...; **t23.5** a supremely well-balanced delivery which makes you simply sigh with pleasure. There is an unusually early flash of something chocolate-related which vanishes as the corn and spices take control; **f23.5** the build of cocoa, topped by rye and growing spice, is unique...and so delicious...; **b24** proof yet again that Small is beautiful... *46.85%*

American Eagle Tennessee Bourbon Aged 4 Years bott code: L927704 db **(91) n22.5 t23 f22.5 b23** An attractive bourbon very much of the hickory persuasion. Enticing, soft, good corn involvement and well distributed spice. A very sound whiskey. *40%*.

American Eagle Tennessee Bourbon Aged 12 Years bott code: L9053HA12 db **(84.5) n21 t22 f20 b21.5** When I tasted this earlier in the year, I was quite impressed. This bottling seems to have dropped a notch. The nose warns of an unhappy alliance between the spirit and oak. The unhappy finish confirms it dramatically. *43%*.

American Rockies Small Batch Bourbon Whiskey (76) n19 t22 f17 b18 Sweet, soft, fruity and rounded. But very dull. With an unattractive furry finish to boot. Just not sure what all these fruit notes are doing in a bourbon. 44% (88 proof).

Ancient Age Kentucky Straight Bourbon bott code: L190240120:254 **(93) n23 t23 f23.5 b23.5** Very similar to the bottling code above One very slight difference here is just a slight downturn in the intensity of the honey while the spices, perhaps with a fraction less to counter it, have a marginally louder voice. Perhaps not quite the same balance, but the finish goes on so much longer. 40% (80 proof).

Ancient Age Kentucky Straight Bourbon db **(91.5) n22 t23 f23 b23.5** Even at a placid 80 proof, this bourbon just gets the taste buds so excited. So much going on beneath the seemingly gentle surface. Such effortless elegance, it is almost obscene...the old AA was never quite this good. 40% (80 proof)

Ancient Ancient Age 10 Years Old (96) n23.5 t24 f24 b24.5. This whiskey is like shifting sands: same score as last time out, but the shape is quite different again. Somehow underlines the genius of the distillery that a world class whiskey can reach the same point of greatness, but by taking two different routes...However, in this case the bourbon actually finds something a little extra to move it on to a point very few whiskeys very rarely reach... 43%

Ancient Ancient Age 10 Star (94.5) n23 t24 f23.5 b24. A bourbon which has slipped effortlessly through the gears over the last decade. It is now cruising and offers so many nuggets of pure joy this is now a must have for the serious bourbon devotee. Now a truly great bourbon which positively revels in its newfound complexity: a new 10 Star is born... 45%

Ancient Age 10 Star Kentucky Straight Bourbon bott code: L182010116 **(94) n22.5 t23.5 f24 b24** A bourbon which had lost its way slightly in recent years. And though it still splutters about a bit for identity and rhythm on the nose, there is no doubting it is right back on track with some taste-bud catching moments. It is at times, monumental. 45% (90 proof).

◈ **Ancient Age 90** bott code L22333 db **(88.5) n22 t22.5 f22 b22** Huge toffee and Worthers Originals on both nose and delivery with a side dish of soft heather honey. Ultra-easy drinking, super-soft from nose to finale and with far more complex oak layering than might be given credit for. 45% (90 proof)

◈ **Baker's Single Barrel Minimum 7 Years barrel age 8 yrs 2 mos** date barrelled 02-2014 warehouse CL-Hott code L2228CLN serial no 200374 db **(91) n23.5** jaw-dropping chunky liquorice. Dry and toasty; **t23** huge corn oil delivery but then a avalanche of small grains which finishes off the taste buds which aren't already salivating; **f22** a little bitterness travels through as does a hint of kumquat citrus; **b22.5** starts like a formula one car racing off the grid with engine at full revs. Finishes, however, far from full throttle with a bit of bitter smoke issuing from the exhaust. Still, plenty to lap up... 53.5%

◈ **Bardstown Bourbon Company Discovery Series No 5** db **(95) n23.5** lovely corn oil carpeting of the nose allowing the small grains – the ryes especially – to dance and sparkle. So rare to find the spices fitting in as though made to measure. Amazingly alive...; **t24** absolutely brilliant: massively mouth-watering delivery of near incomprehensible layering. As on the nose, the rye positively shimmers while a delicate liquorice daubed with light heather honey strata denotes some impressive are working its charms; **f23.5** perhaps a slight bitterness, but it's very short lived as those ancient corn oils carry on their work of relaying the oak-honey across the palate, now with a frail spiced butterscotch sign off; **b24** one of the most complex bourbons I've found this year. The small grains are intense and have so much to say they are telling the most intricate and charming of tales... 52.35%

◈ **Bardstown Bourbon Company Fusion Series No 9** db **(89) n22** a little off-balance with the ryes just outpointing the vanillas and shewing off a little too eagerly. The corn oils appear but seems strangely detached; **t23** much better! Works in a way the nose doesn't quite achieve with the grains more integrated. The sugars are even then spread towards a more rye-fruity muscovado style. Spices already plucking away while the vanillas, like the sugars keep an even tempo; **f22** quietens down surprisingly before bittering out slightly; **b22** very high rye personality but just never seems to get the balance right. That said, intermittently a pretty delicious experience when the rye does get a clear run. 48.4%

◈ **Basil Hayden** bott code 301B20445 db **(88.5) n22.5 t22 f22 b22** A gentle tease of a bourbon playing heavily on a toffee and light hickory which accentuates a sweet and bitter persona. 40% (80 proof)

Basil Hayden Kentucky Straight Bourbon bott code: 159B20317 db **(84) n21 t21.5 f20.5 b21** Never quite gets off the ground. Citrussy and tangy. 40% (80 proof)

◈ **Basil Hayden Subtle Smoke** finished in hickory smoked new oak barrels bott code L202084 db **(90) n22.5** the smoke plays soothing little games on the nose reducing the sugar bite...; **t23** a very sweet delivery with a light maple sweetness joining the obvious hickory and caramel body; **f22** light spices on the short finish with the last of the phenols still just about clinging on **b22.5** they aren't lying: there is subtle smoke which flickers on the nose and plays out almost apologetically throughout the palate. Even had they beefed up the strength it still would have been a subtle but more flavoursome experience as this would doubtless benefit from a few extra oils. 40% (80 proof)

Blade & Bow batch SW-B1 (**84**) **n21.5 t21.5 f20 b21**. A simple, if at times massively sweet, offering which minimises on complexity. 45.5%

Blade and Bow 22 Year Old (**95.5**) **n24 t24 f23.5 b24** This may not be the oldest bourbon brand on the market, but it creaks along as though it is. Every aspect says "Old Timer". But like many an old 'un, has a good story to tell... in this case, exceptional. 46% (92 proof)

Blade & Bow DeLuxe batch WLCFSS-2 (**88.5**) **n22.5 t22.5 f21 b22.5** A steady ship which, initially, is heavy on the honey. 46%

Blaize & Brooks Kentucky Straight Bourbon batch "Homesick" (**92**) **n23 t22.5 f23.5 b23** For the second time today I am nosing and tasting the past. Absolutely superb Old Timer style bourbon, cutting out all the fancy stuff and concentrating on all the good bits: like hickory, corn and spice. The easiest of easy drinking. 50% (100 proof)

⟨⟩ **Blanton's Gold Edition** dumped 5-10-23 barrel 946 Rick No 29 Warehouse H db (**94.5**) **n23.5** one of those deceptive noses where far more is happening than you might believe. Peer through the caramel and locate those deft spices, that apple pie, the custard and rhubarb crumble. Mesmeric...; **t23.5** some sharp rye notes surprise on delivery, before they fall back into place behind the vanilla-smeared corn oil. The result is a slightly eye-watering salivating opening to proceedings. The midpoint is alive with small grain activity and controlled spices; **f23.5** so much caramel. Such intense vanilla. Such melting sweetened corn flower...; **b24** the last time I tasted a Blanton's Gold, I had one of the best single barrel Buffalo Trace experiences of my life. And seeing that I've been at their casks for the last 30 years, that is saying something. For that reason I chose this bottling to represent the 600th of the 750 whiskeys I'll be tasting this year. This doesn't have the vivacity and honeyed glory of that last Blanton's Gold. Instead, this embarks on a more conservative and in some ways subtle but, ultimately, less memorable course of action. Still a belter, though... 51.5% (103 proof)

⟨⟩ **Blanton's The Original Single Barrel Bourbon** dumped 3-8-23 barrel 946 Rick No 49 Warehouse H db (**91**) **n22.5** compared to barrel 2062, this is a much more basic nose, with the red liquorice much happier to shew muscle. The caramels are pretty hefty, too...; **t23** serious display of intense toffee punctuated by busy spice; **f22.5** takes its foot off the pedal to freewheel downhill with the caramels; **b23** an untaxing, toffee intense bourbon designed for easy drinking. 46.5% (93 proof)

⟨⟩ **Blanton's Straight From The Barrel Bourbon** dumped 6-9-23 barrel 2062 Rick No 41 Warehouse H db (**96**) **n23.5** not often you find kumquats bursting out of a Blanton's, but it certainly is here: wonderfully fruity, but not short on budding liquorice, either. Oh, and those spices....; **t24.5** massive. Yet simultaneously controlled. Just sit back and let the taste buds soak up those intense corn oils studded with hickory and black peppers. While the heather honey glides almost beneath the radar to ensure the most delicate of countering sweetness. Indeed, that honey slightly alters the mouth-feel, adding a waxy depth to something already magnificently intense; **f24** long, naturally. That wax, that corn oil, those deep oaky vanilla tones.... just rumbles on with an ulmo honey edge; **b24** that Buffalo Trace is the producer of the best whisk(e)y in the world is currently beyond dispute. The fact you can open a bottle of a single cask produced from there and be faced with something this sublime is almost unnerving. It is not just the flavours, it is its structure, comportment, pace of delivery...just all-round mmmmmph! And this thoroughbred has it in effortless spades. Frankly, if all whiskeys I taste for the Bible were this deep and complex, then the book would never get finished. It has taken the best part of an hour to thoroughly unravel the meaning of this bourbon. Which, for a single cask, makes it among the top 1% in complexity... Salivating...soothing...stimulating...all in one. 62.2% (124.4 proof)

Blanton's Uncut/Unfiltered (**96.5**) **n25 t24 f23.5 b24.** Uncut. Unfiltered. Unbelievable. 65.9%

Bondi Bourbon Whiskey Aged 4 Years (**85**) **n20.5 t21.5 f21.5 b21.5** Rammed full of varied honey notes, the feintiness on both the nose and delivery can't be entirely ignored. Still. Chewy and attractive late on. 40% (80 proof).

Bondi Bourbon Whiskey Aged 4 Years db (**89.5**) **n22 t22.5 f22 b23** My first-ever whiskey from Minnesota...and I'm genuinely a happy bourbon lover. Has many Kentuckian qualities, especially the evenness of the sugar to tannin levels. Sits on the palate with a degree of grace and sings all the right tunes. A distillery to watch, especially when they have fully learned the strengths and weaknesses of their stills. 40%

Booker's 6 Years 6 Months 12 Days batch 2021-04db (**92.5**) **n23 t23.5 f23 b23** A moody bourbon that isn't afraid to reveal its age. 62.2% (124.4 proof).

⟨⟩ **Booker's Aged 7 Years 4 Months 14 Days** batch 22-03db (**95**) **n23.5** the nose is concocted in massive liquorice-hickory with a light heather honey counter backup...; **t24.5** immense. And just about perfect so far as traditional bourbon goes. There is a concentrated blueberry fruitiness followed by a molasses-rich liquorice note which is soon hijacked by spice; **f23** the vanilla and ulmo honey cascades down for a much softer finale than the muscular bourbon start; **b24** just lavishes you with liquorice. This is hard-nosed traditional bourbon. Wear spurs and demand in a dirty glass; it doesn't come much more original than this. A true and authentic bourbon experience. *63.25%*

Booker's Kentucky Straight Bourbon Aged 6 Years, 6 Months, 19 Days batch no. 2019-04 db **(95) n23.5 t24 f23.5 b24** Huge! Not a bourbon to be trifled with. And you will note that despite its enormity there is not a single off-key moment, not a single false step. *63.5%*

Bower Hill Barrel Reserve Kentucky Straight Bourbon Small Batch bott code T269190640 db **(84.5) n21 t21.5 f21 b21** An odd juniper-type note appears to have hijacked the nose and delivery. From then on, with all the abounding toffee, it is hard to dislodge it from either the palate or brain. *43% (86 proof) selected and bottled by Bower Hill Distillery Silverton, Ohio*

Boone County Pot Still Kentucky Straight Bourbon Made Spring 2016 Bottled Spring 2022 db **(82) n22.5 t21.5 f18 b20** Carries all the hallmarks of a new distillery coming to terms with its apparatus. The cut points haven't quite been struck in the sweet zones yet and so we lurch from a hefty but attractively characterful nose to the crashlanding of a feinty finish. But the corn oils and virgin oak have managed to weave some magic of their own and a few heather honey and liquorice high points are to be had. Not great, but I see this as a historic bottling, so an honour to taste. *474% (94.8 proof). distilled aged and bottled by Boone County Distilling*

Bourbon30 Small Batch Bourbon (86) n22.5 t23 f19.5 b21 An odd bottling, this. There is an aggressive, non-spiced burn late on which undoes some of the earlier charm. It comes as a surprise as, until then, this is a neat and tidy offering comfortable in its pleasantly manicured toffee. *45% (90 proof)*

Bourbon30 Small Batch Bourbon (92) n23.5 t23.5 f22 b23 Been hearing positive things about blender Jeff Mattingley's work over at Georgetown, and with good reason. This is a delightfully weighted bourbon which enjoys reaching certain points of intensity and then applying the brakes, going no further. Big whiskey, yet suitably restrained, too. *50% (100 proof)*

Bowman Brothers Small Batch Virginia Straight Bourbon bott code: L183540513 **(93) n23.5 t23 f23 b23.5** A significant improvement on the last Small Batch I encountered with much more confidence and depth on the finish. The coffee note hangs around wonderfully... *45% (90 proof).*

Bowman Brothers Virginia Small Batch bott code: 71600080ASB08:22 **(88.5) n22 t23 f21.5 b22** A lovely bourbon, though the sugars are thinly spread. *45% (90 proof)*

Buffalo Trace bott code L21084 **(92.5) n23t23.5 f23 b23** The first thing to hit me about this bottling was how the oils and lingering richer notes were a little duller. So, after nosing I checked the bottle. And sure, enough, the strength had been dropped from 45% to 40%, a whopping drop of 10 proof. That is a significant change and will mean the finishes will never quite linger as they once did due to the oil being broken. However, in the case of this bottling, richness of texture has given way to elegance. *40%*

Buffalo Trace bott code: L21 327 db **(93.5) n23.5 t23.5 f23 b23.5** I had never seen BT's standard bourbon in a 1.75 litre bottle before...not least because stocks were so scarce, you did well sometimes to find it in a standard bottle. But no.... no reduction in quality here. Warming with caramel and light liquorice, the mouthfeel remains its usual sensual, improbably complex self and the spices are seemingly hand-picked for balance. A Kentucky bourbon standard bearer, no matter what size bottle it comes in. *45% (90 proof)*

Buffalo Trace db **(94) n23.5; t23 f23.5 b24** This is Buffalo Trace showing off. Always a class act, here it reveals the range of its complexity with delightful cameo performances of little aroma and flavour profiles sometimes, but by no means always, seen in their usual bottlings. Classic. *45% (90 proof) Frankfort Bourbon Society*

◈ **Buffalo Trace Kosher Straight Bourbon Rye Recipe** bott code L22078 db **(94.5) n23.5** that there is rye on hand there is no doubt: it punches, nips and bites with a disguised hardness at the softer underbelly of the corn-oil vanilla; **t24** I was expecting the rye to continue its great work on the nose. And it does. After a while it buckles slightly under the weight of the corn and only re-establishes itself beyond the hallway mark working in tandem with some endearing spices. Even so, the complexity levels will require a new complexometer fitted...; **f23** the liquorice is now in a league of its own... **b24** As it happens, I was, about 20 years ago, in the bottling hall in to the see the world's first-ever kosher whisky bottled. Two rabbis were on hand to oversee this historic moment and when I asked them what set kosher whisky apart from gentile whisky, they told me it was the lack of use of sherry casks, or others that had held wine. "They are unclean" they declared...and in light of what happened with the sulphur treatment of virtually all the world's sherry butts used in the making of whisky, it was hard to disagree with them. Now, as it happens, one of my dearest and most loved friends is a rabbi. And he tells me this is no longer the case: wine casks can be kosher. Confused...? Well, even if you are, these bourbon bottlings from BT make life a lot easier. 100% toasted virgin oak and not a single wine cask in sight. Thank God.... Oh, and for the whiskey.... possibly the most beautifully weighted and complex standard bourbons I have encountered this year. 47% (94 proof)

Buffalo Trace Kosher Kentucky Straight Bourbon Wheat Recipe bott code: L211110117:01a db **(93.5) n23.5 t23.5 f23 b23.5** It is though these Kosher BTs are happy to be extended versions of their usual selves: the rye recipe has that grain in concentrate and at its most clearly defined. While this wheated version has turned up the spices to max volume, as though proving a point. Just so remarkable...and simply the most profound difference in a grain recipe I have ever seen brought out by a single distillery. Oh, and by the way: this outstanding whiskey was bottled for Passover. However, it is not to be passed over... 47% (94 proof)

⬧ **Buffalo Trace Kosher Straight Bourbon Wheat Recipe** bott code L22131 **(95.5) n24** a spiced bready aroma occasionally morphs into my old mum's bread pudding, though with a little less fruit. It is the kind of nose that makes not taking a follow-up mouthful an utter impossibility; **t24** I really don't want to write the tasting notes...I just want to sit with a glass of this nectar and enjoy its every nuance. And are there a lot of nuances...! **f23.5** the main theme on delivery had been that unique red liquorice, spiced chocolate thread. All integrated with the richest corn oil known to mankind. Well, here it is much the same, except the spices have upped a notch while the oils have receded; **b24** when Frankfort's excellent new bourbon venue, The House of Commons, on the corner of St Clair and West Main, opened its doors for the very first time I had the honour of being there as a guest. The first two whiskeys I drank there were BT Kosher Bourbon Rye Recipe, followed by the Wheat Recipe. I was a little surprised to find that the Wheat outpointed the rye recipe handsomely – not what I had previously experienced. I don't know if these were from the same batches, but the same thing has happened again. Either way, the BT Kosher bottlings really are bourbons very much out of the top drawer. As for this particular batch, simply dazzling. The palate barely has enough nerve endings to cope with what is thrown at it. 47% (94 proof)

Buffalo Trace Single Oak Project Barrel #132 (r1yKA1 *see key below*) db **(95) n24 t23.5 f23.5 b24.** This sample struck me for possessing, among the first batch of bottlings, the classic Buffalo Trace personality. Afterwards they revealed that it was of a profile which perhaps most closely matches their standard 8-year-old BT. Therefore it is this one I shall use as the tasting template. 45% (90 Proof)

Key to Buffalo Trace Single Oak Project Codes

Mash bill type: r = rye; w = wheat
Tree grain: 1 = course; 2 = average; 3 = tight
Tree cut: x = top half; y = bottom half
Warehouse type: K = rick; L = concrete

Entry strength: A = 125; B = 105
Seasoning: 1 = 6 Months; 2 = 12 Months
Char: All #4 except * = #3

Buffalo Trace Single Oak Project Barrel #1 (r3xKA1*) db **(90.5) n22 t23 f23 b22.5.** 45%
Buffalo Trace Single Oak Project Barrel #2 (r3yKA1*) db **(91.5) n23 t23 f22.5 b23.** 45%
Buffalo Trace Single Oak Project Barrel #3 (r2xKA1) db **(90.5) n22.5 t23 f22.5 b22.5.** 45%
Buffalo Trace Single Oak Project Barrel #4 (r2yKA1) db **(92) n23 t23 f23 b23.** 45%
Buffalo Trace Single Oak Project Barrel #5 (r2xLA1*) db **(89) n23 t22.5 f21.5 b22.** 45%
Buffalo Trace Single Oak Project Barrel #6 (r3yLA1*) db **(90) n22.5 t22 f23 b22.5.** 45%
Buffalo Trace Single Oak Project Barrel #7 (r3xLA1) db **(90.5) n23 t22.5 f22.5 b22.5.** 45%
Buffalo Trace Single Oak Project Barrel #8 (r3yLA1) db **(92.5) n23 t23 f23.5 b23.** 45%
Buffalo Trace Single Oak Project Barrel #9 (r3xKA2*) db **(90) n22 t22.5 f23 b22.5.** 45%
Buffalo Trace Single Oak Project Barrel #10 (r3yKA2*) db **(93) n23.5 t23.5 f22.5 b23.5.** 45%
Buffalo Trace Single Oak Project Barrel #11 (r3xKA2) db **(94.5) n23 t24 f23.5 b24.** 45%.
Buffalo Trace Single Oak Project Barrel #12 (r3yKA2) db **(92) n24 t23 f22.5 b22.5.** 45%
Buffalo Trace Single Oak Project Barrel #13 (r3xl A2*) db **(89.5) n22 t23 f22 b22.5.** 45%.
Buffalo Trace Single Oak Project Barrel #14 (r3yLA2*) db **(95) n24 t24 f23 b24.** 45%
Buffalo Trace Single Oak Project Barrel #15 (r3xLA2) db **(90.5) n22.5 t23 f22 b23.** 45%.
Buffalo Trace Single Oak Project Barrel #16 (r3yLA2) db **(91.5) n22.5 t23.5 f22.5 b23.** 45%.
Buffalo Trace Single Oak Project Barrel #17 (r3xKB1*)db **(88.5) n21.5 t22.5 f22.5 b22.** 45%
Buffalo Trace Single Oak Project Barrel #18 (r3yKB1*) db **(92.5) n23 t23 f23.5 b23.** 45%
Buffalo Trace Single Oak Project Barrel #19 (r3xKB1) db **(93) n23 t23.5 f23 b23.5.** 45%.
Buffalo Trace Single Oak Project Barrel #20 (r3yKB1) db **(95) n23.5 t24 f23 b23.5.** 45%
Buffalo Trace Single Oak Project Barrel #21 (r3xLB1*) db **(92) n23 t23 f23 b23.** 45%
Buffalo Trace Single Oak Project Barrel #22 (r3yLB1*) db **(91) n22 t23.5 f22.5 b23.** 45%.
Buffalo Trace Single Oak Project Barrel #23 (r3xLB1) db **(89) n21 t22.5 f22.5 b23.** 45%.
Buffalo Trace Single Oak Project Barrel #24 (r3xLB1) db **(90) n22 t23 f22.5 b22.5.** 45%
Buffalo Trace Single Oak Project Barrel #25 (r3xKB2*) db **(90.5) n22.5 t23 f22.5 b22.5.** 45%

Buffalo Trace Single Oak Project Barrel #26 (r3yKB2*) db (89.5) n22 t23.5 f22 b22. 45%
Buffalo Trace Single Oak Project Barrel #27 (r3xKB2) db (95.5) n23 t24 f24.5 b24. 45%
Buffalo Trace Single Oak Project Barrel #28 (r3yKB2) db (94.5) n23 t24 f23.5 b24. 45%
Buffalo Trace Single Oak Project Barrel #29 (r3xLB2) db (91) n23 t22.5 f23 b22.5. 45%
Buffalo Trace Single Oak Project Barrel #30 (r3yLB2*) db (95.5) n23.5 t24 f24 b24. 45%
Buffalo Trace Single Oak Project Barrel #31 (r3xLB2) db (87.5) n22 t22 f21.5 b22. 45%
Buffalo Trace Single Oak Project Barrel #32 (r3yLB2) db (90.5) n23.5 t23 f21.5 b22.5. 45%
Buffalo Trace Single Oak Project Barrel #33 (w3xKA1*) db (94.5) n24 t23.5 f23 b24. 45%
Buffalo Trace Single Oak Project Barrel #34 (w3yKA1*) db (90) n21.5 t23.5 f22.5 b22.5. 45%
Buffalo Trace Single Oak Project Barrel #35 (w3xKA1) db (89.5) n22 t22 f23 b22.5. 45%
Buffalo Trace Single Oak Project Barrel #36 (w3yKA1) db (91.5) n23 t23 f23 b22.5 b23. 45%
Buffalo Trace Single Oak Project Barrel #37 (w3xLA1*) db (90) n21 t23 f22 b22. 45%
Buffalo Trace Single Oak Project Barrel #38 (w3yLA1*) db (87.5) n22 t23.5 f20.5 b21.5. 45%
Buffalo Trace Single Oak Project Barrel #39 (w3xLA1) db (87) n21.5 t22 f21.5 b22. 45%
Buffalo Trace Single Oak Project Barrel #40 (w3xLA1) db (93) n23 t23 f23.5 b23.5. 45%
Buffalo Trace Single Oak Project Barrel #41 (w3xKA2*) db (92.5) n22 t23 f23.5 b24. 45%
Buffalo Trace Single Oak Project Barrel #42 (w3yKA2*) db (85.5) n22 t21.5 f21 b21. 45%
Buffalo Trace Single Oak Project Barrel #43 (w3xKA2) db (89) n22 t23 f22 b22. 45%.
Buffalo Trace Single Oak Project Barrel #44 (w3yKA2) db (89) n23 t23 f21 b22. 45%
Buffalo Trace Single Oak Project Barrel #45 (w3xLA2*) db (87) n23 t22 f21 b21. 45%.
Buffalo Trace Single Oak Project Barrel #46 (w3yLA2*) db (88) n21.5 t22 f22.5 b22. 45%
Buffalo Trace Single Oak Project Barrel #47 (w3xLA2) db (88.5) n22.5 t22 f22 b22. 45%.
Buffalo Trace Single Oak Project Barrel #48 (w3yLA2) db (90.5) n22 t23 f22.5 b23. 45%.
Buffalo Trace Single Oak Project Barrel #49 (w3xKB1) db (93) n24 t23 f23 b23. 45%
Buffalo Trace Single Oak Project Barrel #50 (w3yKB1*) db (88) n21.5 t23 f21.5 b22. 45%
Buffalo Trace Single Oak Project Barrel #51 (w3xKB1) db (89.5) n23 t23 f21.5 b22. 45%
Buffalo Trace Single Oak Project Barrel #52 (w3yKB1) db (87.5) n21.5 t22 f22 b22. 45%
Buffalo Trace Single Oak Project Barrel #53 (w3xLB1*) db (91) n22 t23 f23 b23. 45%
Buffalo Trace Single Oak Project Barrel #54 (w3yLB1*) db (89) n22 t23 f22.5 b22.5. 45%
Buffalo Trace Single Oak Project Barrel #55 (w3xLB1) db (89) n22 t23 f22 b22. 45%.
Buffalo Trace Single Oak Project Barrel #56 (w3yLB1) db (91) n24 t22.5 f22 b22.5. 45%
Buffalo Trace Single Oak Project Barrel #57 (w3xKB2*) db (94) n23 t23.5 f23.5 b24. 45%
Buffalo Trace Single Oak Project Barrel #58 (w3yKB2*) db (90.5) n22.5 t23 f22.5 b22.5. 45%
Buffalo Trace Single Oak Project Barrel #59 (w3xKB2) db (92) n22 t23.5 f23 b23.5. 45%
Buffalo Trace Single Oak Project Barrel #60 (w3yKB2) db (87.5) n22.5 t22.5 f21 b21.5. 45%
Buffalo Trace Single Oak Project Barrel #61 (w3xLB2*) db (94.5) n24 t23 f23.5 b24. 45%
Buffalo Trace Single Oak Project Barrel #62 (w3yLB2*) db (88) n22 t22.5 f21.5 b22. 45%
Buffalo Trace Single Oak Project Barrel #63 (w3xLB2) db (95.5) n24 t23 f24 b24.5. 45%
Buffalo Trace Single Oak Project Barrel #64 (w3yLB2) db (91) n22.5 t23.5 f22.5 b23. 45%
Buffalo Trace Single Oak Project Barrel #65 (r2xKA1) db (91) n23.5 t22 f23 b22.5. 45%
Buffalo Trace Single Oak Project Barrel #66 (r2yKA1*) db (88.5) n22.5 t22.5 f21.5 b22. 45%
Buffalo Trace Single Oak Project Barrel #67 (r2xKA1) db (89.5) n22 t23 f22 b22.5. 45%
Buffalo Trace Single Oak Project Barrel #68 (r2yKA1) db (92) n22.5 t23 f23.5 b23. 45%
Buffalo Trace Single Oak Project Barrel #69 (r2xLA1*) db (94.5) n23 t24 f23.5 b24. 45%
Buffalo Trace Single Oak Project Barrel #70 (r2yLA1*) db (91.5) n22.5 t23 f23 b23. 45%
Buffalo Trace Single Oak Project Barrel #71 (r2xLA1) db (92) n22.5 t23 f23.5 b23. 45%
Buffalo Trace Single Oak Project Barrel #72 (r2yLA1) db (89) n22.5 t23 f21.5 b22. 45%
Buffalo Trace Single Oak Project Barrel #73 (r2xKA2*) db (87.5) n21.5 t22 f22 b22. 45%
Buffalo Trace Single Oak Project Barrel #74 (r2yKA2*) db (88) n22 t22 f22 b22. 45%
Buffalo Trace Single Oak Project Barrel #75 (r2xKA2) db (91.5) n23 t22.5 f22 b23. 45%.
Buffalo Trace Single Oak Project Barrel #76 (r2yKA2) db (89) n22.5 t22.5 f22 b22. 45%
Buffalo Trace Single Oak Project Barrel #77 (r2xLA2*) db (88) n22 t23 f21 b22. 45%.
Buffalo Trace Single Oak Project Barrel #78 (r2yLA2*) db (89) n22.5 t22 f22.5 b22. 45%
Buffalo Trace Single Oak Project Barrel #79 (r2xLA2) db (93) n23 t23.5 f23 b23.5. 45%.
Buffalo Trace Single Oak Project Barrel #80 (r2yLA2) db (91.5) n23 t22.5 f23 b23. 45%.
Buffalo Trace Single Oak Project Barrel #81 (r2yKB1*) db (94) n23 t23 f24 b24. 45%
Buffalo Trace Single Oak Project Barrel #82 (r2yKB1) db (91.5) n22.5 t23.5 f22.5 b23. 45%
Buffalo Trace Single Oak Project Barrel #83 (r2xKB1) db (92) n22.5 t23 f23.5 b23. 45%.
Buffalo Trace Single Oak Project Barrel #84 (r2yKB1) db (94) n23.5 t24 f23 b23.5. 45%.
Buffalo Trace Single Oak Project Barrel #85 (r2xLB1*) db (88.5) n21.5 t22.5 f22 b22.5. 45%
Buffalo Trace Single Oak Project Barrel #86 (r2yLB1*) db (90) n22.5 t22 f23 b22.5. 45%
Buffalo Trace Single Oak Project Barrel #87 (r2xLB1) db (93.5) n22.5 t23.5 f23.5 b24. 45%.
Buffalo Trace Single Oak Project Barrel #88 (r2yLB1) db (89) n23.5 t22 f21.5 b22. 45%
Buffalo Trace Single Oak Project Barrel #89 (r2xKB2*) db (89.5) n22 t22.5 f22 b22.5. 45%
Buffalo Trace Single Oak Project Barrel #90 (r2yKB2*) db (94) n23.5 t24 f23 b23.5. 45%

Bourbon

Buffalo Trace Single Oak Project Barrel #91 (r2xKB2) db (86.5) n21.5 t22 f21.5 b21.5. 45%
Buffalo Trace Single Oak Project Barrel #92 (r2yKB2) db (91) n22 t23 f23 b23. 45%
Buffalo Trace Single Oak Project Barrel #93 (r2xLB2*) db (89) n22.5 t22 f22 b22.5. 45%
Buffalo Trace Single Oak Project Barrel #94 (r2yLB2*) db (92.5) n23 t24 f23 b23. 45%
Buffalo Trace Single Oak Project Barrel #95 (r2xLB2) db (94) n23 t23.5 f23.5 b24. 45%
Buffalo Trace Single Oak Project Barrel #96 (r2yLB2) db (89) n22 t23.5 f21.5 b22. 45%
Buffalo Trace Single Oak Project Barrel #97 (w2xKA1*) db (87) n22.5 t22 f21.5 b21.5. 45%
Buffalo Trace Single Oak Project Barrel #98 (w2yKA1*) db (93) n22 t23.5 f23 b23.5. 45%
Buffalo Trace Single Oak Project Barrel #99 (w2yKA1) db (86.5) n22 t22 f21 b21.5. 45%
Buffalo Trace Single Oak Project Barrel #100 (w2yKA1) db (94) n23 t23.5 f23.5 b24. 45%
Buffalo Trace Single Oak Project Barrel #101 (w2xLA1) db (96) n23.5 t24 f23.5 b25. 45%
Buffalo Trace Single Oak Project Barrel #102 (w2yLA1*) db (88.5) n22 t22 f22.5 b22. 45%
Buffalo Trace Single Oak Project Barrel #103 (w2xLA1) db (89) n22.5 t22 f22 b22.5. 45%
Buffalo Trace Single Oak Project Barrel #104 (w2xLA1) db (91) n23 t23 f22.5 b22.5. 45%
Buffalo Trace Single Oak Project Barrel #105 (w2xKA2*) db (89) n22.5 t22 f22.5 b22. 45%
Buffalo Trace Single Oak Project Barrel #106 (w2yKA2*) db (92.5) n24 t23 f23 b23.5. 45%
Buffalo Trace Single Oak Project Barrel #107 (w2xKA2) db (93.5) n23.5 t23 f23 b24. 45%.
Buffalo Trace Single Oak Project Barrel #108 (w2yKA2) db (94) n22.5 t24 f23.5 b24. 45%
Buffalo Trace Single Oak Project Barrel #109 (w2xLA2*) db (87.5) n21.5 t23.5 f21 b21.5. 45%.
Buffalo Trace Single Oak Project Barrel #110 (w2yLA2*) db (90) n22 t22.5 f22 b23. 45%
Buffalo Trace Single Oak Project Barrel #111 (w2xLA2) db (89) n22.5 t22.5 f22 b22. 45%.
Buffalo Trace Single Oak Project Barrel #112 (w2yLA2) db (90) n21.5 t23 f22.5 b23. 45%.
Buffalo Trace Single Oak Project Barrel #113 (w2xKB1*) db (88) n22.5 t22 f22 b21.5. 45%
Buffalo Trace Single Oak Project Barrel #114 (w2yKB1*) db (90) n22 t23 f22 b23. 45%
Buffalo Trace Single Oak Project Barrel #115 (w2yKB1) db (88.5) n22 t22.5 f22 b22. 45%.
Buffalo Trace Single Oak Project Barrel #116 (w2yKB1) db (90.5) n22 t22 f23.5 b23. 45%
Buffalo Trace Single Oak Project Barrel #117 (w2xLB1*) db (82.5) n20 t20.5 f22 b20. 45%
Buffalo Trace Single Oak Project Barrel #118 (w2yLB1*) db (86) n20.5 t21.5 f22 b22. 45%
Buffalo Trace Single Oak Project Barrel #119 (w2xLB1) db (93.5) n22.5 t24 f23.5 b23.5. 45%.
Buffalo Trace Single Oak Project Barrel #120 (w2xLB1) db (89.5) n23 t22 f22.5 b22. 45%
Buffalo Trace Single Oak Project Barrel #121 (w2xKB2*) db (89) n22.5 t23 f21.5 b22. 45%
Buffalo Trace Single Oak Project Barrel #122 (w2yKB2*) db (93) n22 t23.5 f23.5 b24. 45%
Buffalo Trace Single Oak Project Barrel #123 (w2xKB2) db (85.5) n21 t22 f21 b21.5. 45%
Buffalo Trace Single Oak Project Barrel #124 (w2yKB2) db (90.5) n22.5 t23 f22.5 b22.5. 45%
Buffalo Trace Single Oak Project Barrel #125 (w2xLB2*) db (93) n24 t22 f22.5 b22.5. 45%
Buffalo Trace Single Oak Project Barrel #126 (w2yLB2*) db (90) n22 t23 f22.5 b22.5. 45%
Buffalo Trace Single Oak Project Barrel #127 (w2xLB2) db (85.5) n21.5 t22 f21 b21. 45%.
Buffalo Trace Single Oak Project Barrel #128 (w2yLB2) db (89) n21.5 t22 f22.5 b22.5. 45%
Buffalo Trace Single Oak Project Barrel #129 (r1xKA1*) db (88) n22.5 t22 f22 b22. 45%
Buffalo Trace Single Oak Project Barrel #130 (r1yKA1*) db (92.5) n22 t23.5 f23 b24. 45%
Buffalo Trace Single Oak Project Barrel #131 (r1xKA1) db (92.5) n23 t23 f23.5 b23. 45%
Buffalo Trace Single Oak Project Barrel #132 *See above.*
Buffalo Trace Single Oak Project Barrel #133 (r1xLA1) db (89) n22.5 t23 f21 b22.5. 45%
Buffalo Trace Single Oak Project barrel #134 (r1yLA1*) db (91.5) n22 t23.5 f23 b23. 45%
Buffalo Trace Single Oak Project Barrel #135 (r1xLA1) db (92.5) n23 t23 f23.5 b23. 45%
Buffalo Trace Single Oak Project Barrel #136 (r1yLA1) db (92) n23.5 t22.5 f23 b23. 45%
Buffalo Trace Single Oak Project Barrel #137 (r1xKA2*) db (90.5) n22 t23.5 f22 b23. 45%
Buffalo Trace Single Oak Project Barrel #138 (r1yKA2*) db (87) n22.5 t21.5 f21.5 b21.5. 45%
Buffalo Trace Single Oak Project Barrel #139 (r1xKA2) db (88) n22.5 t22 f21.5 b22. 45%
Buffalo Trace Single Oak Project Barrel #140 (r1xKA2) db (93) n23 t24 f23 b23. 45%
Buffalo Trace Single Oak Project Barrel #141 (r1xLA2*) db (90) n23.5 t22 f22.5 b22. 45%
Buffalo Trace Single Oak Project Barrel #142 (r1yLA2*) db (89.5) n22.5 t22.5 f22 b22.5. 45%
Buffalo Trace Single Oak Project Barrel #143 (r1xl A2) db (88.5) n22.5 t22.5 f21.5 b22. 45%.
Buffalo Trace Single Oak Project Barrel #144 (r1yLA2) db (91) n23 t23 f22.5 b22.5. 45%
Buffalo Trace Single Oak Project Barrel #145 (r1xKB1*) db (91) n22.5 t22 f23.5 b23. 45%
Buffalo Trace Single Oak Project Barrel #146 (r1yKB1*) db (93) n23 t24 f22 b24. 45%
Buffalo Trace Single Oak Project Barrel #147 (r1xKB1) db (93) n23.5 t23 f23.5 b23. 45%.
Buffalo Trace Single Oak Project Barrel #148 (r1yKB1) db (94) n22.5 t24 f23.5 b24. 45%
Buffalo Trace Single Oak Project Barrel #149 (r1xLB1*) db (92) n22.5 t23.5 f23 b23. 45%
Buffalo Trace Single Oak Project Barrel #150 (r1yLB1*) db (93) n23 t23.5 f23 b23.5. 45%
Buffalo Trace Single Oak Project Barrel #151 (r1xLB1) db (91.5) n22 t23 f23.5 b23. 45%.
Buffalo Trace Single Oak Project Barrel #152 (r1xLB1) db (81.5) n21 t20.5 f20 b20.5. 45%
Buffalo Trace Single Oak Project Barrel #153 (r1xKB2*) db (94) n23.5 t23.5 f23 b24. 45%
Buffalo Trace Single Oak Project Barrel #154 (r1yKB2*) db (92) n22.5 t23 f23 b23.5. 45%

Buffalo Trace Single Oak Project Barrel #155 (r1xKB2) db (93) n23 t24 f22.5 b23.5. 45%
Buffalo Trace Single Oak Project Barrel #156 (r1yKB2) db (85.5) n22 t21 f21.5 b21. 45%
Buffalo Trace Single Oak Project Barrel #157 (r1xLB2*) db (84.5) t21 t21.5 f20.5 b21. 45%
Buffalo Trace Single Oak Project Barrel #158 (r1yLB2*) db (88) n22 t22 f22 b22. 45%
Buffalo Trace Single Oak Project Barrel #159 (r1xLB2) db (88) n20.5 t22.5 f22 b22.5. 45%
Buffalo Trace Single Oak Project Barrel #160 (r1yLB2) db (92.5) n23.5 t23 f22 b23. 45%
Buffalo Trace Single Oak Project Barrel #161 (w1xKA1*)db (87) n21 t22 f22 b22. 45%
Buffalo Trace Single Oak Project Barrel #162 (w1yKA1*) db (88.5) n22 t22 f22.5 b22. 45%
Buffalo Trace Single Oak Project Barrel #163 (w1xKA1) db (90) n23 t22.5 f22 b22.5. 45%
Buffalo Trace Single Oak Project Barrel #164 (w1yKA1) db (94.5) n23.5 t23 f24 b24. 45%
Buffalo Trace Single oak Project Barrel #165 (w1xLA1*) db (91.5) n22.5 t23 f23 b23. 45%
Buffalo Trace Single Oak Project Barrel #166 (w1yLA1*) db (91) n22 t22 f23 b23. 45%
Buffalo Trace Single Oak Project Barrel #167 (w1yLB1) db (94) n23.5 t23.5 f23 b24. 45%
Buffalo Trace Single Oak Project Barrel #168 (w1xLA1) db (89.5) n22 t23 f22 b22.5. 45%
Buffalo Trace Single Oak Project Barrel #169 (w1xKA2*) db (94) n23.5 t23.5 f23 b24. 45%
Buffalo Trace Single Oak Project Barrel #170 (w1yKA2*) db (92.5) n22.5 t23 f23.5 b23.5. 45%
Buffalo Trace Single Oak Project Barrel #171 (w1xKA2) db (88.5) n22 t23 f21.5 b22. 45%
Buffalo Trace Single Oak Project Barrel #172 (w1yKA2) db (90.5) n22.5 t23 f22.5 b22.5. 45%
Buffalo Trace Single Oak Project Barrel #173 (w1xLA2*) db (91) n23.5 t23 f22 b22.5. 45%
Buffalo Trace Single Oak Project Barrel #174 (w1yLA2*) db (89) n22 t22.5 f22.5 b22. 45%
Buffalo Trace Single Oak Project Barrel #175 (w1xLA2) db (91.5) n21.5 t23 f24 b23. 45%
Buffalo Trace Single Oak Project Barrel #176 (w1yLA2) db (89) n21.5 t22.5 f22.5 b22.5. 45%.
Buffalo Trace Single Oak Project Barrel #177 (w1xKB1*)db (87) n21.5 t22 f22 b21.5. 45%
Buffalo Trace Single Oak Project Barrel #178 (w1yKB1*) db (88.5) n22.5 t23 f21.5 b21.5. 45%
Buffalo Trace Single Oak Project Barrel #179 (w1xKB1) db (88) n21 t22 f22.5 b22.5. 45%
Buffalo Trace Single Oak Project Barrel #180 (w1yKB1) db (92) n22 t23.5 f23 b23.5. 45%
Buffalo Trace Single Oak Project Barrel #181 (w1xLB1*) db (94.5) n22.5 t24.5 f23 b23.5. 45%
Buffalo Trace Single Oak Project Barrel #182 (w1yLB1*) db (86) n21.5 t21.5 f22 b21. 45%
Buffalo Trace Single Oak Project Barrel #183 (w1xLB1) db (95.5) n24 t24 f23.5 b24. 45%.
Buffalo Trace Single Oak Project Barrel #184 (w1yLA1) db (93) n23.5 t23 f23 b23.5. 45%
Buffalo Trace Single Oak Project Barrel #185 (w1xKB2*) db (92.5) n23 t23.5 f23 b23. 45%
Buffalo Trace Single Oak Project Barrel #186 (w1yKB2*) db (90) n23 t22.5 f22 b22.5. 45%
Buffalo Trace Single Oak Project Barrel #187 (w1xKB2) db (88) n22 t22 f22 b22. 45%
Buffalo Trace Single Oak Project Barrel #188 (w1yKB2) db (90) n21.5 t23.5 f22.5 b22.5. 45%
Buffalo Trace Single Oak Project Barrel #189 (w1xLB2*) db (88.5) n24 t22 f21 b21.5. 45%
Buffalo Trace Single Oak Project Barrel #190 (w1yLB2*) db (94) n23.5 t24 f23 b23.5. 45%
Buffalo Trace Single Oak Project Barrel #191 (w1xLB2) db (94.5) n23 t23.5 f24 b24. 45%
Buffalo Trace Single Oak Project Barrel #192 (w1yLB2) db (94.5) n23 t24 f23.5 b24. 45%

⟨ **Bulleit Bourbon** bott code L22532ZB002 db (94.5) n23.5 crisp, with superb small grain busy-ness. The Demerara sugars positively crunch if you sniff too hard; t23.5 and there we go again: just as on the nose, a rock hard grain surge establishes its credential and allows the red liquorice, spices and Demerara sugar to grow at its own pace; f23.5 long and spicy but with just enough soft oil to lengthen out the sugars; b24 a marvellously consistent and underrated bourbon which is now just revelling in its crunchiness. 40%

Bulleit Bourbon Frontier Whiskey bott code: L1166ZB001 (94.5) n23.5 t23.5 f23.5 b24 Reading my tasting notes from last year, very little to add or take away. Except this bottling has a subtle extra degree of spice and chocolate, finishing with extra depth and a flourish. Another Bulleit which impressively hits the target. 45%

Bulleit Straight Kentucky Bourbon Single Barrel bottle no L0066ZE008202933 db (93) n23 t23.5 f23 b23.5 typical Bulleit: unerringly straight, brittle and on target. 52% (104 proof)

Bulleit Bourbon 10 Year Old (90) n23 t22.5 f22 b22.5 Not remotely spectacular. But does the simple things deliciously. 45.6% (91.2 proof)

⟨ **Bulleit Bourbon Single Barrel** barrel no 1-B3-0575 db (92.5) n24 delves deep into the caramel but offers a light liquorice depth also. Some unexpected coconut and delicate marzipan; t23 mouth-filling but the sugars are overly excited, too, which rather clashes with the balance. As tart as it is salivating; f22.5 big spice before multiple layers of vanilla...all of them simple...; b23 a sweet, caramel intense but lively bourbon. Indeed, though excellent, a little too sweet for greatness. The nose, however, is something else entirely... 52% (104 proof)

Bushwood Front 9 Premium Kentucky Straight Bourbon Single Barrel Aged 6 Years db (86) n22.5 t22.5 f20 b22 The nose is light for all the gentle hickory and intricately spiced, while on delivery the corn oils make an early start, bringing in just-so quantities of toffee and vanilla, as well as barley sugars. The finish, sadly, is just a little thin, warm and austere. This could hardly be more different from their Long Ball bottling. That's all about lush honey. This is far more concentrating on the intrinsic busyness of the small grains. Intriguing. 50.5% (101 proof)

⟜ **Colonel E. H. Taylor Barrel Proof** bott code L23142 db **(95.5) n23.5** very crisp with the small grains having a bigger say than the recipe suggests they should have. A seemingly light toffee mint note grows in significance...; **t24** a powerful delivery taking full advantage of the massive creamy caramel which have been dredged from the oak and blended with the profound corn oils. By the midpoint we are in handsome liquorice territory as the roastiness gains in significance. However, rather than the expected molasses the sweetness is provided by a more delicate manuka honey-hickory combination which injects a degree of fragility into something that before stormed all before it; **f24** that hickory note is now a drying force, linking in with a more sawdusty vanilla. Ridiculously genteel late on...; **b24** huge, as you might reasonably expect from a bourbon that's built like a tank. But this isn't all about the strength: if there was no meat to magnify, you'd still end up with a poor meal. Here the strength takes full advantage of a bourbon that is already packed to the gunnels with personality. It is then topped off by an improbably elegant finish to such a colossal whiskey. This bottling is a whiskey event in its own right.... *65.55% (131.1 proof)*

⟜ **Colonel E. H. Taylor Four Grain Straight Kentucky Bourbon Bottled In Bond** bott code db **(95) n23.5** one of those noses where it is difficult to know where to start: varying aromas appear to be heading in different directions. For a seemingly big whiskey most of the impact on the nose is delicate to the point of teasing. Likewise, the deft honey tones appear to thin the doubtless intense tannin. All is contradictory...; **t24** the corn oil had been aloof on the nose. Not so now. For a moment vanilla ice cream with a fruit syrup, as the rye and light maple combine to take on the oak. The spices are pitter-pattering like mad and eventually build up some heat. All the time a blend of ulmo and heather honey keeps the sweetness at its optimum level while liquorice reminds you that the deeper, age-exposed tannins are busy, too...; **f23.5** the small grains still rumble, the liquorice still grumbles. The surprise finale is surprisingly tart, not unlike un-sugared rhubarb pie...; **b24** Four Grain Colonel Taylor is always synonymous with complexity. And no change here as the small grains again go into overdrive. This time ably assisted by a generous dollop of heather honey. A fascinating, unpredictable and massively entertaining bourbon. *50% (100 proof)*

⟜ **Colonel E. H. Taylor Single Barrel Straight Kentucky Bourbon Bottled In Bond** bott code L20097 db **(89) n23** toffee nut and mint...with the emphasis very much on the toffee...; **t23** if there is a patent for this degree of natural caramel and vanilla extracted from a cask and blended so perfectly with corn oils, then this bottling should have it. The real treat comes in the second half, when dried dates, diced Brazil nuts and molasses combine for something rather out of the ordinary...; **f21** the finish is mostly a continuation of the main body of the work. Except the spices are now elevated to sub-frenzy mode...and a degree of bitterness is finding its way off the oak...; **b22** the epitome of cream toffee. But a nagging late bitterness slightly undermines the earlier excellence.... *50% (100 proof0*

Colonel E H Taylor Small Batch Straight Kentucky Bourbon Bottled In Bond bott code: L22087 db **(97) n24.5 t24 f24 b24.5** It is bourbon like this which confirms Buffalo Trace as the greatest distillery in the world right now in terms of high-quality output. Another, frankly, gloriously complex and mesmerising bottling which is the epitome of truly great bourbon. Indeed, this bourbon is the definition of understated whiskey elegance. Oh, and if you want to up the spice level a notch or two, just deploy the Murray Method... *50% (100 proof)*

⟜ **Coopers' Craft Barrel Reserve 100 Proof** nbc db **(92.5) n23** sticks to the same classic aroma I found last time out. Plenty of polished oak, a subtle liquorice/hickory blend and a subtle sub-current of banana split dessert; **t23.5** fascinating: the char is causing something akin to a phenolic smokiness to the bourbon but balanced out by a complex display of Demerara and muscovado sugar notes. The mid-ground moved back towards of darker, heavier liquorice tones; **f23** the corn oils had always been busy lurking but for the adieu it's here ensuring a light coating on which the spices can work; **b23** hard not to taste this and not think of Louisville City, the top soccer club in Kentucky. At the moment, this has far more in attack than misfiring LouCity and much more intricate approach play, too. I think last year I made a plea for Brian Ownby to join Millwall in England. But I get the feeling that Louisville without him now would be like this bourbon without the Coopers' craft... Classic bourbon. *50%*

Coopers Craft Kentucky db **(89) n22 t22.5 f22 b22.5** Superb everyday bourbon with no weaknesses. *41.1% (82.2 proof)* Brown-Foreman

David Nicholson 1843 Kentucky Straight Bourbon bott code: 1201752 **(87) n22 t22.5 f21 b21.5** A much sweeter bourbon than when I last tasted this brand. Toffee dominates, though on delivery there is a malty, molassed wash of something charmingly mouth-watering. The finish, however, is a little less accommodating and tends to a degree of hotness and a late bitterness. *50% (100 proof)*

David Nicholson Reserve Kentucky Straight Bourbon bott Code 112 **(83.5) n22.5 t22 f19 b20** More classic bourbon characteristics found here than its sister 1843. However, there is also an unusual nuttiness at work, which becomes evident after the early sweetened hickory delivery. This also mysteriously warms and then bitters out towards the finish. *50% (100 proof)*

Deadwood Tumblin' Dice 6 Year Old Single Barrel Straight Bourbon barrel entry 7/17/15 bottled 8/19/21 heavy rye mashbill (84) n22.5 t21.5 f19 b20 They aren't joking about the rye: the fruitiness and firmness of the grain fair pings at you, especially on the nose. However, after an initial rush of lightly honeyed corn there appears to be an innate bitterness which knocks the bourbon off its stride, despite a late spiced mocha intervention. These dice, sadly, have rolled nothing but ones and threes... *58.5% (117 proof)*

 Doc Holliday Straight Bourbon Aged 8 Years barrel no 980 (95.5) n23.5 quintessential bourbon. The hickory and liquorice do battle with a sweetening heather honey-molasses note... though both ensure an impressive weight. The acidity to the char burns through for extra good measure. Fabulous, ultra-old-fashioned bourbon nose...; t24 absolutely hits the spot with a near perfect display to corn oil formulating with spoon-stirringly thick liquorice. The honey is dense and mingles with the eye-watering spices to perfection. Some chocolate-hickory runs back through the middle; f24 long, lush, with dollops of heather honey which fades with a slightly dirty, but in this case perfectly in tune, degree of oils off the still. Magnificent...; b24 like a number of Doc Holliday's victims, I'm just blown away. If they don't serve this in a dirty glass at The Crystal Palace at Tombstone, then they are missing a trick. Brilliantly distilled with just enough greasy bite to remind you of the old days. One of the best and most satisfying whiskies I have tasted so far this year. I would keep a bottle of this at home any day... *63% sc 144 bottles World Whiskey Society*

Door Knocker Kentucky Straight Bourbon barrels V and VI (94.5) n23.5 t23.5 f23.5 b24 well blended barrels of high grade Three Boys makes for quite a complex and elegant bourbon which charms with its reserved two-tone sweetness. *60% (125.3 proof)*

Door Knocker Kentucky Straight Bourbon barrel VII (93) n23 t23.5 f23 b23.5 one of those excellent bourbons that is bold and assertive without ever being aggressive. The entire flavour profile is vivid and profound. The weight and shape always showing control. So enjoyable. *67.5% (135 proof)*

Door Knocker Kentucky Straight Bourbon barrel XIII (81) n20 t22 f19 b20 Well, that was different. One of those experiences I can neither say I disliked or enjoyed. But it was fascinating being aware that this has ridiculously high corn content and the malted barley has been roasted. The result is a nose that, well...just doesn't seem like bourbon, with a massive grassiness to it. Certainly, the yeast and what happened in the fermenters is playing a massive part in this whiskey's profile. The delivery is soft and sweet...maybe a little too sweet as it accentuates the late bitterness on the creamy finish. *44.5% (89 proof)*

Door Knocker Kentucky Straight Bourbon barrel XV (85) n21 t22.5 f20 b21.5 Another in the same mould as barrel XIII. But this one at least takes off on delivery injecting a honeyed red liquorice bourbon fingerprint. But still a little too tangy and untidy for greatness. *(121 proof)*

 Door Knocker Kentucky Straight Bourbon 5 Years 4 Months Double Barreled batch XII (95) n23.5 this has been double barreled...but had it spent time in a maple cask some of the results would have been similar. The stark contrast between the heady liquorice/heavy roast Java coffee against the bright, syrupy sugars is truly startling...; t24 after all the enormity on the nose and the muscular tannins on the very first arrival, the following waves of pillow-soft vanilla come directly from leftfield. Such a ridiculous contrast after a tannin attack of Biblical proportions; f23.5 we are back now to that slight maple syrupy pose. Among my myriad flavour experiments over the last 40 years I have tried powerful high roast coffee sweetened with maple syrup...and it's not a million miles from this finale...; b24 the sharp intensity of the tannin is such that it feels like the tastebuds are being pulled from the palate by the roots, in the same way a digger pulls a giant tree stump from out of the ground. A sensational bottling where the double barreling equates to doubling the intensity. And possibly double the dark sugars... Fabulous! And not for the faint-hearted. *53% (106 proof) distilled at Whiskey Thief Distillery*

 Door Knocker Kentucky Straight Bourbon 5 Years Old batch XIV new #4 char barrel (94.5) n23 the toast is burning in the kitchen. While someone's dropped the jar of molasses...; t24 what a complete delivery: caramel, vanilla, delicate spice, and varied sugars, but all heavily on the dark. Curiously, the midpoint is quite dry, though, as the hickory kicks in; f23.5 long and with the molasses back in harness. Even the vanilla has a burnt edge to it while the mallows have just been rescued from the fire...; b24 a kind of anthem to toasty whiskey. But to make it work they appear to have included every kind of dark sugary note they are able to find. Kind of youthful. Kind of old. Kind of delicious. *59% (118 proof) distilled at Whiskey Thief Distillery*

 Eagle Rare Aged 10 Years bott code L23165 db (95) n24 the take-off of the liquorice if just so elegant. Burnt fudge and hickory are not far behind: this is substantial, solid and very serious whiskey all the better for the molasses and spice base; t23.5 the darker sugars are ahead if the game, the spices not far behind. But the real weight doesn't drop into place until the oaky liquorice and the intense corn oil meet head on....; 23.5 wow, that corn oil lingers for longer than any bourbon has a right to expect. While it sings its silky song, the liquorice-hickory tones offer impressive depth and anchorage **b24** when Eagle Rare was first launched I felt for the first two or three years there was some groping around looking for the angle, the key components to make this something different. There is no doubt that they have settled on its personality. For the last half dozen years it has been consistent, but always increasing on the weight. Here you get the feeling they have reached something close to their zenith where the weight is so brilliantly distributed. Most birds this size don't fly. This one soars... 45% (90 proof)

Eagle Rare Aged 10 Years Single Barrel (89) n21.5 t23 f22 b22.5. A surprising trip, this, with some dramatic changes en route. 45%

Eagle Rare Aged 10 Years Kentucky Straight Bourbon Single Barrel Select bott code: db **(94) n23 t23.5 f23.5 b24** Not often a single cask outperforms a standard vatting. But certainly has in the two Eagle Rares I have officially tasted this year. Whoever picked this cask knew what they were doing. 45%

Eagle Rare 17 Years Old bott Summer 2019 db **(95) n24 t23.5 f23.5 b24** The rich caramel thread found in this whiskey could so easily become its tomb, as with many bourbons that toffee note strangles the life out of all development. Not here: the hickory and spice in tandem produce some truly wonderful moments. 50.5% (101 proof).

Eagle Rare 17 Years Old bott Summer 2020 db **(94) n24 t23.5 f23 b23.5** This has to be one of the more evenly weighted Eagle Rares, certainly shewing dexterity early on which was not present four or five years ago. Only the finish, perfectly acceptable by usual standards, fails to stand up to the pedigree. 50.5% (101 proof).

Eagle Rare 17 Years Old Summer 2021 (96) n24 t24.5 f23.5 b24 ER at its toastiest and almost pompously bourbon, offering a mix of hickory and liquorice that is quite divine. But maybe it is the often under-the-radar part played by the balancing molasses which deserves a display of celebratory fireworks to mark its brilliance. Probably the best Eagle Rare ever... 50.5% (101 proof)

⟨⟨ **Eagle Rare 17 Years Old Fall 2022** db **(95.5) n24** the relaxed way the liquorice and molasses combine and reverberate about the nose is reminiscent of a master craftsman deftly but confidently chiselling a figure into faultless shape. The brittleness of the small grains is the perfect counterweight to the subtle oils while the spices are determined to prickle...; **t24** for all the surprising firmness, it is the layering which grabs the attention. The sugars, dark and lush, are propelled forward ahead of the deeper liquorice ad light hickory oaky tones but they quickly make up lost ground. There is a surprise walnut cake thrust to the middle, creamy with the corn oils; **f23.5** a slightly shorter finale than usual for the ER, with coffee replacing the usual hickory but the liquorice standing its ground. Again, the small grains chip in with a crunchy Demerara sweetness which is soon swallowed by the late, intense vanilla; **b24** a little thinner in body than usual, this ER still boasts personality in abundance. Most impressive is the restrained, effortless transition through the gears of intensity. Delightfully restrained. 50.5% (101 proof)

Early Times Kentucky Straight Bourbon Bottled-in-Bond bott code: 1721205035113 db **(88.5) n21.5 t23 f21.5 b22.5** For a BiB, this one takes its foot off the gas and cruises from first sniff to last, delicate fade. Perhaps a little spice burn out of keeping with the overall picture brings the score down a notch. But this is easy-drinking, black liquorice-oriented bourbon that gets the midpoint vanillas and dark sugars spot on. 50% (100 proof)

Easy Rider Kentucky Straight Bourbon Aged 4 Years (88.5) n22.5 t22.5 f21.5 b22 One of the increasingly rare 80 proof bourbons doing the rounds these days. But has loads of old-fashioned charm and I just love the lightly minted hickory with a vague spiced molasses hook. The same delicate attributes are found at various stages around the delicate palate. Easy riding indeed! 40% (80 proof)

⟨⟨ **Elijah Craig Barrel Proof Aged 11 Years 5 Months** batch No 8523 db **(91) n22** fresher than its years. Some fascinating banana notes mixing in with the thick vanilla and red liquorice..; **t23.5** wow! Didn't expect that early rye spike on delivery which comes with some sensual heather honey! Quite waxy in part with the tannins building almost surreptitiously. The sweetened vanillas are pretty full on; **f22.5** light coffee/mocha trace, though that coffee is a bit heavy on the high roast bitterness late on; **b23** an elegant bourbon which reveals its age in occasional fits and starts. The journey ends here for those looking for a big vanilla bourbon. 62.1%

Elijah Craig Small Batch Kentucky Straight Bourbon db **(89.5) n22.5 t22.5 f22 b22.5** About as quiet and understated as Elijah Craig ever gets. 47% (94 proof).

Elijah Craig Small Batch bott code: A34811741 db **(88.5) n22 t22.5 f21.5 b22.5** Stays true to form as the least demanding of all the Elijah Craigs out there. A lovely standard Kentucky bourbon determined to do as little as possible to draw your attention away from the corn-tannin harmony which provides a buttery toastiness. As gentle and pleasant as a morning stroll through downtown Bardstown on an early spring day. 47% (94 proof)

Elijah Craig Toasted Barrel Kentucky Straight Bourbon finished in toasted new oak barrels, bottle code: A20702146 db **(96) n24 t24 f23.5 b24.5** This is bourbon squared. Bourbon concentrate. Bourbon max. Bourbon, taken out of bourbon casks and then put back into virgin oak again. It is like shoving a 7-litre engine beside the 5 litre one already in our car. It is for those who think great straight bourbon isn't quite enough. The colour is Mahoney, and the nose and flavour is festooned with splinters. Only at the very death does it slightly come off the rails when the tannins have herded up a few too many bitter notes. But that apart, for those who like to take their bourbon pure.... One of the best things to come from Heaven Hill in my lifetime... 47% (94 proof).

E J Curley Kentucky Straight Bourbon Small Batch db **(92.5) n22.5 t23.5 f23 b23.5** anyone who remembers the classic everyday bourbon of 30 years ago will immediately recognise this classic style – but with one difference. These bourbons poured from the bottle at 80 proof. This is at 95...and that makes one hell of a difference. A true go to daily bourbon...with a touch of quiet class. 47.5% (95 proof)

Evan Williams Bottled-in-Bond bott code M05520522 db **(89) n22 t22.5 f22 b22.5** a whiskey I rather love for its simplicity. Just does the basic things well and ticks the right boxes in mainly the right order. Truly easy-drinking and one of the sweeter Kentuckians. 50% (100 proof)

⟫ **Evan Williams Bottled-In-Bond** bott code M10131912 db **(93.5) n23** a fresh, simple aroma relying heavily on heather honey topped with liquorice; **t23.5** a super-salivating delivery with the spices up front and early...and determined to linger; **f23.5** a satisfying corn oil lick which does nothing to diminish the good work of those spices or deter the late, light, toasty molasses; **b24** a serious step up from the last time I tasted this. A few honey barrels found their way into this dumping. The complexity of the spices is on a different level altogether. Excellent. 50%

⟫ **Evan Williams Single Barrel Vintage Put In Barrel 2015** barrel no 11 barreled 12.17.12 bottled 3.31.23 db **(87.5) n22 t22 f21.5 b22** Wallows in its toffee softness. But badly needs a secondary profile for contrast. Perhaps could have done with being another 10 proof stronger to really extract the deeper tannins. 43.3%

Ezra Brooks Cask Strength Single Barrel barrel no 7700079 filed 5/15/17 **(94.5) n23.5 t23.5 f23.5 b24** The mahogany colour to the bourbon suggests it has seen plenty of heat in the last four years and this is matched by the intensity of not just the tannin but the roastiness of the grains. Glorious bourbon with Heaven Hill-style in top form. 60% (120 proof) Selected by Capital Cellars, Frankfort, Ky. Distilled and Aged in Kentucky for Lux Row

⟫ **Four Roses** bott code 08223 db **(88) n22 t22 f21.5 b22.5** They are definitely saying it with flowers here. And that is Four Roses standard bottling is staying on its light-even course and away from the weightier course of a few years back. Attractive, friendly and piles on the ulmo honey and vanilla in droves. Perhaps could do with the odd prickle, but if it's super-soft you want....then you've found it. 40%

Four Roses Bourbon bott code: 2018/11/20 db **(88) n24 t22.5 f20 b21.5** After a few years with a little extra weight behind it, the standard Four Roses has reverted back to a light and flimsy style recognisable to those of us who encountered it between the 1970s and late 1990s. One of the most fragile Kentucky bourbons in the market place, but profiting from a sublime nose. 40%.

Four Roses Single Barrel 100 Proof warehouse KE barrel no 82-1Fdb **(92) n23 t23.5 f23 b23.5** Of all Kentucky's bourbon distilleries, none make theirs as clean, crisp and sometimes aloof as Four Roses. This gently honeyed bottling is a very good example of the distillery looking tough...but being a real sweetie. 50% (100 proof)

⟫ **Four Roses Single Barrel** warehouse ME Barrel 84-10 db **(95.5) n23.5** brilliantly flinty nose with the Demerara sugars positively crunching under the sniff. Light golden syrup fits the bill perfectly; **t24** an immediate small grain explosion of the very highest calibre. Adorable spices wade into the sugary mix. Though there, the liquorice-hickory combination is happy to take a back seat to the heather honey; **f24** can't get enough of that developing chocolate; **b24** the best Four Roses I have tasted for a very long time. Complexity levels are off the charts and the sugar-spice balance just can't be bettered. As breath-taking as it is majestic. 50%

Four Roses Small Batch bott code: 1311047220 db **(92) n22.5 t23 f23 b23.5** One of the more fragile Kentuckians... 45% (90 proof)

Four Roses Small Batch Select bott code: 104406022143db **(87) n22 t22 f21 b22** The nose is a little astringent as the spices nip and corn goes into hiding. Definitely setting out to make a dent on the palate. The small grains steam in to claim the high ground. Demerara sugars try to mediate...but fail... while the finish is slightly bitterish. For those who find the standard Small Batch a little too slight and perhaps inconsequential, here is it's 6' 6" big brother. Trouble is, it doesn't have anything like the same elegance and class. A few unsympathetic barrels lumped together here. 52% (104 proof) ncf

⟫ **Four Roses Small Batch** bott code 34722 db **(86.5) n21.5 t22 f21.5 b21.5** Disappointingly bland. The vanilla is overwhelming, even forcing the spices to wave the white flag. A late-night bourbon if there ever was: it certainly sent me to sleep. 45%

⟫ **Four Roses Small Batch Select** bott code 20722 db **(93) n22.5** some bubbling vanilla works well with the liquorice; **t24** eye-wateringly sharp small grain delivery is spellbinding and keeps you fixed in its grasp like a possum in your full beam headlights. The blend of liquorice and heather honey is sublime; f23 reverts to a softer vanilla fade. Though the spices keep track; b23.5 this really is the epitome of understated, mouth-watering bourbon. Hits the bullseye with every flavour shot. *52% ncf*

George T. Stagg db **(96)** n24 t24.5 f23.5 b23.5 As a George T Stagg goes, this is a bit of a wimp: some 20 proof weaker than some of its incarnations. So for those of you of a delicate disposition, you might be able to tackle this tamed monster for once. *62.45% (124.9 proof).*

George T. Stagg db **(96.5)** n24 t24 f24.5 b24 On nosing this I did the kind of double take James Finlayson would have been proud of in a Laurel and Hardy film. Stagg...at this strength? I was expecting the usual low 70% abv or high 60s, perhaps. But less than 60%....? A very different George T Stagg to what we have seen over the years. But the pedigree remains... *58.45% (116.9 proof).*

George T. Stagg db **(97.5)** n24.5 t24.5 f24 b24.5 Stagg hovering around about its ultimate. And we know what that means: one of the greatest whiskey experiences of your life. This is one of those whiskies where it is a case of not whether it is good enough for you? The question is whether is, are you good enough for it...? Staggering. Quite literally. *65.2% (130.4 proof).*

⬧ **George T. Stagg** db **(97.5)** n24.5 when on form, a George T Stagg nose is the very epitome of truly great straight bourbon. And this is very much on form... The layering is insane with extra fruity tones piling into the sweet hickory and drier black liquorice as the tannins mount up into something significant. The heather honey and maple syrup blend beautifully. It is like exploring mountain tracks, each one leading to a beautiful view from an aromatic outcrop...; t24.5 the corn oils wash over the palate like freak waves. But not so powerful that they leave nothing behind, for the intense small grain, busy and constantly working on the salivation levels, refuse to be daunted. As this builds to a crescendo, those heavier tannins strike their claim, bringing the liquorice into position and the spices bounding energetically about the palate. The molasses melts into the deeper tannins to produce a deeply toasted, vaguely burned, sweetness; f24 the genteel elegance makes a mockery of this bourbon's immense strength. b24.5 who needs sherry casks, when the magical combination of virgin oak, corn, rye and malted barley can conjure up moist dates and even Melton Hunt cake oozing in extra molasses? This is a whiskey which makes a mockery of its high strength: so absorbed are you in the depth of intrigue you don't for a moment think about alcoholic content. This takes you on to another level of organoleptic ecstasy altogether... *69.35% (138.7 proof0*

Green River Kentucky Straight Bourbon Whiskey aged 3 years 9 months, db **(94.5)** n24 t23.5 f23.5 b23.5 For a barrel under four years, this is outrageously good. Must have come from the very top story of a warehouse as this has matured way beyond its tender years. Rich and ticks every box under the sun. Plus a few more besides. This is some hell of a barrel pick. *(117 proof)*

Green River Kentucky Straight Bourbon bott code: L12022/011/1992222 db **(89.5)** n22 t23 f22 b22.5 a thoroughly enjoyable character bourbon with many contrasting features *45% (90 proof) Green River Distillery, Owensboro.*

Gold Boot The Crux Cask Strength Single Barrel Kentucky Straight Bourbon William Larue Weller (89) n22 t21.5 f23 b22.5 Wow! This gold boot gives the tastebuds a really good kicking with this uncompromising beast of a bourbon. Full-bodied, perhaps from new stills, or some new apparatus as extra copper has leached into this from somewhere which, when mingling with the honey, gives this bourbon a muscular richness. Size 14. *61.21% (122.4 proof)*

Harding's Creek Kentucky Straight Bourbon 184 Months aged bott code: 503861223 db **(96)** n24.5 t24 f23.5 b24 For those without a calculator to hand, this is 15 years 4-month-old Jim Beam. And, ladies and gentlemen, I present to you a truly classic bourbon. A standing ovation to the blenders, as creating this degree of complexity with zero scarring amid such an old bourbon is no mean achievement. *54% (108 proof) 750bottles*

High West Whiskey American Prairie Bourbon batch no. 20B11 **(90.5)** n22.5 t23 f22 b23 An usually high corn oil statement gives this bourbon a soft and long tenure. The sweeter tones keep the hickory straight. A little unusual. But satisfying, nonetheless. *46% (92 proof). nc ncf. A blend of straight bourbon whiskies.*

⬧ **I-Bourbon (90.5)** n23 sensuous small grain persona with a buzzing spiciness which dovetails elegantly with the hickory and vanilla; t22 and that vanilla really does take off early and keep on flying. Light ulmo honey ushers in the required sweetness; f22.5 just like the nose we are back into complexity mode. The vanillas have faded slightly and these darting, bitty elements of the grains, working in tandem with residual corn oil and a delicate nuttiness make for a charming fade; b23 well, the design of the bottle may be minimalist, but the same can't be said for certain aspects of this bourbon. Very light, but never loses its elegance and allows the smaller grains used in the recipe to really make their moves. Charming. And complex. *43% (86 proof) Distilled in Tennessee*

I.W. Harper Kentucky Straight Bourbon db (81) n21.5 t22 f18 b19.5 An unusually hot bourbon where the spices have a slightly malevolent input. The usual molassed richness has a degree of prune fruitiness, too. Pleasant early on, but a little too aggressive. 41% (82 proof)

J Mattingly Gays Hops-N-Schnapps Private Barrel select Small Batch Bourbon **(91.5)** n22.5 t23.5 f22.5 b23 A really bouncy bourbon that makes maximum play from the rich corn oils and telling honey. Just love this. 58% (116 proof)

J Mattingly Honey I'm Home Private Barrel Select Small Batch Bourbon (90.5) n22.5 t23.5 f22 b22.5 Distilled by bees. Blended by drones. Approved by Ralph Kramden, Lucille Ball and Dick van Dyke. 58.5% (117 proof) Distilled in Kentucky 108 bottles

J Mattingly Privately Selected by Pattison Brothers Distillery Small Batch Bourbon **(91.5)** n23 t23 f22.5 b23 One of the guys at Bourbon30 told me that a particular bourbon of theirs had coconut as one of its characteristics. I thought maybe he had put the wrong kind if sunscreen on that day. But, as it happens, he was spot-on: the rare experience of finding coconut notes in a bourbon. And it does no damage at all. Rather lovely fare. 53% (106 proof) 200 bottles

James E. Pepper 1776 Straight Bourbon Whiskey Aged Over 3 Years (91.5) n23 t23 f22.5 b23 Beautiful old school bourbon. 50% (100 proof). ncf.

⬥ **Jim Beam** bott code L3061FFE521721040 db **(88.5)** n22 t22 f22 b22.5 A conservative, undemanding marriage of hickory and vanilla which cruise on the silky corn oils. Quietly delicious, but happy to set its development limits. On this evidence a criminally under-rated bourbon. 40%

Jim Beam Black Double Age Aged 8 Years (93) n23 t24 f22.5 b23.5. Rather than the big, noisy, thrill-seeking JB Black, here it is in quiet, reflective, sophisticated mode. Quite a shift. But no less enjoyable. 43% (86 proof)

⬥ **Jim Beam Black Extra-Aged** bott code L2271CLH db **(90.5)** n22.5 toasty liquorice with layered hickory; t22.5 light spices billow before the corn oils lift. Salivating Demerara sugars; moves slickly into standard Jim Beam mode with a creamy hickory layering; f23 elegant, vanilla and hickory in melt-in-the-mouth mode; b23 for all the extra aging, the yield on that lovely vanilla-hickory thread remains undiminished. Gently elegant. 43%

Jim Beam Bonded 100 Proof bott code: L8 305 **(90)** n22.5 t23 f22 b22.5 Satisfyingly salivating with lots to chew on here and offers some truly classical moments. That said, thins out late on as a younger style takes control... 50% (100 proof).

⬥ **Jim Beam Double Oak Twice Barreled** bott code L2342CLH db **(92)** n23 outstanding silky liquorice on toast – but younger than I remember this; t23 chewy delivery with the oak up front but the corn oils not far behind. The thin hickory and ulmo honey is teasingly understated; f23 although the tannins have grown, there is still a dramatic understatement; b23 no longer making a point of an 8-year-old statement, this doesn't even try to make the tannins the central element. Very much in the present Jim Beam style, we are talking soft hickory/vanilla as a base...here with limited extra toastiness. The balance, though, is always charming. 43%

Jim Beam Single Barrel Kentucky Straight Bourbon barrel no JB6378 db **(85)** n21.5 t22 f20.5 b21 Surprised by this bottling. Jim Beam have warehouses full of astonishingly good bourbon. So why they have picked one with an untidy, bitter finish is beyond me. The tight nose suggests we might be in trouble later down the line. And after a beautifully blossoming start of cottonwool-like vanilla and Demerara sugars, it starts heading south soon after. 47.5% (95 proof)

Jim Beam Signature Craft Bourbon Aged 12 Years db (88) n21.5 t23 f21.5 b22 a cranky JB trying hard not to be JB. 43% (86 proof)

John E. Fitzgerald Very Special Reserve Aged 20 Years (93) n22.5 t24 f23 b23.5 A bourbon lover's bourbon! 45% (90 proof)

John J Bowman Pioneer Spirit Virginia Straight Bourbon Single Barrel db **(94)** n23.5 t24 f23 b23.5 While the Bowman Small Batch may be simplistically attractive, this takes the whiskey up several further levels, especially with the liquorice and honey beating their chests. For those who drink only straight Kentucky Bourbon (and I have met a staggering number who do), this might be worth crossing a State line or two to have a look at. I defy you to tell the difference... 50% (100 proof)

John J Bowman Pioneer Spirit Virginia Straight Bourbon Small Batch db **(88)** n21.5 t22.5 f22 b22 Virginia Sticky Toffee Pudding...in a glass. 45% (90 proof)

⬥ **J.T.S Brown Bottled 100 In Bond** bott code B2560511 db **(92.5)** n23 toasted brown bread with a light manuka honey and liquorice spread; t23 big, juicy delivery with a tang kumquat and red liquorice interplay; f23 dries beautifully, lifts off wonderfully on that drier hickory signature with the spices warming things subtly; b23.5 a real old-fashioned bourbon of the style you would have enjoyed 30 or 40 years ago. Absolutely packed with rich flavours, a sturdy body and entangled with all kinds of tannin tones. An all-day-every-day kind of bourbon. 50%

Kentucky Owl Bourbon Whiskey batch no. 9 **(90.5)** n23 t23 f22 b22.5 If, like me, you are a pretty serious birdwatcher then you know just how captivating the sight of an owl in full swoop can be. Trust me: despite those extra oils, this will captivate you... 63.8% (1276 proof). 11,595 bottles.

Bourbon

Kentucky Owl Confiscated bott code: 3158860834 **(80) n19 t22 f19 b20** From the moment the boiled cabbage nose hits you, this is one very disappointing whiskey. Stands up to scrutiny on delivery, where the intense caramels and vanillas combine rather well. But the dirty, buzzy finale is also a let down. Not a bourbon, in this form, I could give two hoots about, to be honest. 48.2% (96.4 proof).

Knaplund Wheated Straight Bourbon Whiskey Atlantic Aged batch no.01 **(95) n24 t23.5 f23.5 b24** Quite literally, a winner by a nose. This is a bourbon that just exudes complexity. A 20-minute whiskey...and that's just to sniff at. My god, this is serious stuff...! 50% (100 proof) Distilled in the US, aged at the Atlantic Sea and bottled in Denmark by Knaplund Distillery.

⬧ **Knaplund Wheated Straight Bourbon Whiskey Aged 5 Years** batch 02 **(96) n24** by far the saltiest bourbon nose you will ever encounter; the layering and varied intensities of the vanilla is not something you are likely to encounter often, also. Hickory is there, but aloof. As it warms, the spices move from the slumbering position to wide-awake wheated mode. Most breath-taking, though, is the labyrinthine layering and overall gentleness...; **t24** is it the saltiness which is lifting the vanillas into something a little sharper and succulent. No doubting something different is happening with the corn oils seemingly much more integrated with the oak than is normally found in Kentucky. Red liquorice offers a restricted sweetness which that usual exclamation of a base sugars or honey found in most bourbon is missing, doubtless the victim of the delicate merging of the tannins. The feeling of the taste buds being softly caressed compensates for drama, though a most delicate hint of heather honey does start to wander across the palate; **f23.5** sensually soft with the vanillas still revelling in their salty glow...; **b24.5** the succinct blurb on the front label says it all: Distilled in the USA. Aged at the Atlantic Sea. Bottled by hand in Denmark. To be enjoyed by good people." That's right: bad people need not apply. A whiskey this rare and this mind-bogglingly complex should be exclusively for the glasses of good guys and gals: we've deserved it. This was a magnificent bourbon last time I tasted it; it is no less magnificent now: indeed, this is a significant step up. 50%

Knaplund Handcrafted Small Batch Whiskey blend of American and Danish whiskey, bott 10/6/21 **(94) n23.5 t23.5 f23b24** If you're looking for complexity, I think you've just found it.... 50% (100 proof) Aged in the Atlantic Sea then blended and bottled in Denmark by Knaplund Distillery

Knob Creek 100 Proof Small Batch bott code:: L9/55 CLH290 **(89) n22.5 t22.5 f21.5 b22.5** "Since 1992" chirps the label. But if you tasted that original Knob Creek against this, you might have a few problems spotting the relationship. This is the lightest of the Knob Creeks I have ever encountered, with a youthful zestiness to where you would normally find heady, rumbling dark sugars and tannin. Enjoyable, drinkable bourbon? Of course. But a chest-hair curling Knob Creek to chew on until your jaw drops, as of old? Nope. 50%.

Knob Creek Aged 9 Years bott code L1099CLA db **(89) n22.5 t22.5 f22 b22** had I blind tasted this I would never have recognised this as Knob Creek in a month of Sundays. For all its pyrotechnics on delivery, it's still a disappointing experience. 50% (100 proof)

Knob Creek Aged 9 Years bott code: L2047CLJ db **(94) n23.5 t23 f24 b23.5** this bottling is far truer to the Knob Creek cause: everything is muscular and tends to shout its point across. Normal service has been restored. 50% (100 proof)

Knob Creek Aged 12 Years bott code: L9252CLA db **(93.5) n23.5 t23.5 f23 b23.5** Needs the full Murray Method of tasting to really get this engine to fire up. Too cool and the caramels swamp everything. When warmed slightly, the small grains go into complexity overdrive. 50% (100 proof).

Knob Creek Single Barrel db **(93) n23 t23.5 f23 b23.5** far more intense Knob Creeks than this. But have to say that the combination of extra copper and counter corn is a treat. The balance of sugar to mocha is also a treat... 60% (120 proof). Frankfort Bourbon Society.

Knob Creek Small Batch db **(88) n22.5 t22 f21.5 b22** not often a single barrel outperforms a small batch. But certainly the case here, as it struggles to land the craft evenly, making a few bounces before touching down. 50% (100 proof) Frankfort Bourbon Society.

Larceny Small Batch Kentucky Straight Bourbon wheated bourbon mashbill bott code: M04220530 **(91.5) n23 t23.5 f22 b23** superbly rounded and, at times, almost puckering. This is a bourbon which revels in its almost onion-like layering with spices found in every rung. Excellent. 46% (92 proof). bottled by Old Fitzgerald Distillery, Bardstown, Ky.

Lexington Kentucky Bourbon bott code: 12219D0957 **(88.5) n22 t22 f22.5 b22** Attractive and revels in its simplicity. Plenty of toffee and corn oil. The spices maketh the finish. Salivating in all the right places showing good small grain involvement. 43% (86 proof)

Luca Mariano Kentucky Straight Bourbon 7 Years Old barrel no 1 **(92) n22.5 t23 f23 b23.5** early Wilderness Trail whiskey in all its finery. The copper peaks suggest a still not long in action. And action is certainly what you get in the glass. Excellent. 51.5% (103 proof). 211 bottles

Lucky Seven The Hold Up Aged 12 Years batch no. 1 **(93.5) n24 t23 f23 b23.5** A big bourbon which never bullies. The chocolate from the midpoint onwards will sate the most voracious of chocoholics. 50% (100 Proof).

Lucky Seven The Holiday Toast double oak finished in new American oak barrels, batch no.01 **(95) n23.5 t24 f23.5 b24** When I see that a straight bourbon has been finished in a fresh virgin oak cask, and at full strength for good measure, I strap myself in for the tannin attack that is to follow. And the question I ask, even before nosing: have they overcooked it....? No, they certainly haven't. If anyone else is considering treating their bourbon this way, they could do worse than to use this as a blueprint. *57.5% (115 proof)*

Lucky Seven The Jokester Aged 6 Years batch no. 1, bott code: 19339SS11235 **(89.5) n22.5 t22.5 f22 b22.5** Not a bourbon that tries to wow you with a dazzling degree of complexity. Instead, ensures good traditional hickory themed solidity and a subtle change in sugar levels does the trick. *47.5% (95 Proof).*

Lucky Seven The Jokester Kentucky Straight Bourbon Aged 6 Years Final Batch batch no 6. db **(78.5) n22 t22.5 f16 b18** I came in at the start of the show last year, tasting batch no 1. And now I'm leaving with their final performance, having missed the four intervening appearances. But what has happened in the intervening time? After the pure velvet on nose and delivery, the lumpy and unpleasantly hot finish comes as a blow to the solar plexus. Not what I was expecting. *47.5% (95 proof)*

Lucky Seven The Proprietor Aged 12 Years barrel no. 7, bott code: 19339SS11446 **(94) n23 t23.5 f23.5 b24** I have no idea what kind of strange alchemy has been going on here. But this is almost identical to Lucky Seven's Hold Up...except everything is back to front, or the wrong way round...the flavours and development coming in reverse order, the early mouth-watering character apart. Fun and fascinating. In 30 years, I cannot remember this happening before...! You really have to track down both bottlings to see exactly what I mean... Anyway, magnificent, hairs-on-chest bourbon. *59.15% (117.3 Proof). sc.*

◈ **Maker's Mark** bott code L3076MNA db **(92.5) n23** such a delightful mix of fresh brown wholemeal loaf, demerara sugars and spices. Not a missed beat; not an atom out of place...; **t23** the sugars promised on the nose are upfront early, present and correct. Just a vaguest hint of ginger arrives and vanishes in a flash as a creamy hickory note takes over. The layering here ridiculously delicate; **f23** a late accumulation of corn oil and delicate vanillas remain warmed by the gentle spice; **b23.5** one of the best-layered Maker's I've encountered for a while. Everything is super-soft and genteel: has all the threat of an Edwardian spinster on her evening walk. *45%*

◈ **Maker's Mark No 46 French Oak Cask Strength** batch 23-02 db **(89.5) n22.5** almost saccharine sweet in part; the spices look shell-shocked; some fruity muscovado sugars floating around, too...; **t23** huge sugar delivery, all backed by a big wheaty second wave. The spices can barely get a word in, but the wheat-hickory middle is very much intact and sticking to the distillery-style softness; **f22** often high early sugars underline the bitterness at the death, and there is no change here; **b22** Maker's as once would have been considered unimaginable. However, the virgin French oak staves appear to have injected a fair degree of intense sugars which have slightly impacted on balance. A lovely bourbon but for a Maker's certainly one that has its feathers ruffled. *55.05%*

◈ **Maker's Mark Wood Finished Series 2022 Limited Release 10** virgin toasted American oak staves finish batch code BRT-01 db **(94.5) n23** all Maker's usual features....on steroids. The usual peppers are really nipping...; **t24** just so salivating. The small grains are on a march here with a bodyguard of light molasses and hickory by its side. The spices, just as on the nose, are not going to be ignored here...; **f23.5** such a classy fade. As though it has moved all its earlier shape and features into now a smaller, quieter version of its previous self, only with the spices upping their game: superb...; **b24** this is Maker's shewing all its unique fingerprints in neon. Huge by this distillery's standards but magnificently, keeping its personality and definition focussed and in full. *54.7%*

Mayor Pingree Aged 7 Years Straight Bourbon Whiskey batch no. 4 db **(94.5) n24 t23.5 f23.5 b23.5** Distilled in Lawrenceburg, Indiana, the label confirms. The announcement had already been made on the nose... Casks almost certainly picked from the higher points of the warehouse. *59% (118 proof). ncf sc.*

◈ **McAfee's Benchmark Old No 8 Brand** bott code 1722113 db **(87.5) n22 t22 f21.5 b22** It is strange that I find it almost impossible to lose myself in a glass of this and not be taken back some three decades to the old Ancient Age white label brand which had near identical attributes with its drawling caramels and lazy, half-awake spices. This forthcoming year, 2024, marks the 30th anniversary of my arriving in Kentucky, having loved bourbon long before then from afar, especially Maryland. So it is quite wonderful that a bourbon exists today that is so effortlessly capable of winging me back in time to a flavour profile that has barely changed an atom. A Benchmark, indeed... *40% (80 proof)*

◈ **McAfee Brothers Benchmark Single Season Bonded** aged 4 years bott code 1722113 db **(93) n23** when gently warmed, the spices need no second encouragement to puncture the super-soft toffee and vanilla duvet which is spread across the light lemon honey; **t23** salivating, still mildly youthful small grain complexity developing towards a far more cocoa enriched middle; **f23** just love this finish of bouncing small grains, light spices, chocolate fondant and deepening molasses: classy...; **b23.5** no-one does rich corn oils quite like Buffalo Trace distillery and here the way they use it to offer such a luxuriating feel to this bourbon is textbook. The later chocolate development is such a bonus. This is remarkable trade up from the standard Benchmark. *50% (proof)*

⬦ **McAfee Brothers Benchmark Full Proof** bott code L22361 db **(95.5) n23.5** there is a rawness to this nose which just excites. Perhaps it is the youthful freshness at odds with the massive Demerara sugar and molasses depth which suggests something a little older. The spices, like the small grains, which are clean but jagged. This is a pulse-racing nose...; **t24** no surprises on the delivery with its incredible ability to salivate. The Demerara sugars are now in full flow, quickly sweetening the mocha which has built around the midpoint. The corn oils shew such great depth, clarity and the lightest layering of ulmo honey; **f24** improbably long. The mocha has no intention of quitting any time soon or the corn oil from ending its sticky caressing of the palate. It is almost showing off having so much flavour hanging around for so long...and all of it harmonising...; **b24** the story of the McAfee brothers is writ large in the hearts and minds of all of lucky enough to spend time in Kentucky, the Frankfort area in particular. When they explored territory previously unseen by European eyes they encountered a land and nature at its wildest, at its most virginal. That is almost how you feel when face to face this bourbon. There is something young and fresh about it, a bit like the undergrowth they would have had to overcome, but a part of something much wilder, much older and still untamed. This is easily one of the most flavoursome bourbons of the year, the layering and depth as labyrinthine as a any ancient Kentucky forest. Masterful. Probably the best screwcap bourbon on the planet. *62.5% (125 proof)*

⬦ **McAfee Brothers Benchmark Single Barrel** bott code 1722109 db **(94) n23** fragile, with a youthful citrus tone. The caramel and vanilla notes are outdoing the other trying not to dominate. At times each fail...; **t23.5** salivating and almost gristy sugary on delivery, in the style of a single malt. Powdery vanilla off the oak continues a simplistic, though very pleasing start. Suddenly it ramps up a couple of gears to display a layered vanilla topped with a chocolate wafer; **f23.5** after a continuation of the wafer-thin chocolate, the finale reverts to a thinner vanilla tone; **b24** a sublimely complex bourbon which handsomely rewards patience. If some points were more understated, they'd actually be invisible. A bourbon for quiet reflection. And even quieter exploration. Excellent. *47.5% (95 proof0*

⬦ **McAfee Brothers Benchmark Small Batch** bott code L23095 db **(88) n22 t22.5 f21.5 b22** Such a big caramel and vanilla double whammy on the nose of this one, though on delivery the silky corn oils make it easy for the muscovado sugars to dominate. The spices arrive but hardly have their hearts in it. However, just a little bitterness has crept into this one despite the big vanilla presence. A little lemon blossom honey tries to repair the mild damage. *45% (90 proof)*

⬦ **McAfee Brothers Benchmark Top Floor** bott code L22251 db **(93) n22.5** an impressive cocktail of firm, toasty vanillas - even a hint of toasted mallow – among spices, light molasses and chestnut... all soothed by light hickory; **t23** much more corn oil apparent early on than the nose, so a surprise. The vanilla-butterscotch intermediate phase is soon met by thinned molasses and burgeoning spice; **f24** a chocolate/liquorice intensity builds, along with a much drier, chalkier oak input. The spices and a secondary Demerara sweetness ensure balance; **b23.5** I remember a great many years ago a certain legendary Kentucky blender, no longer with us, telling me you should never take all your barrels from the top of the warehouse, unless it can't be avoided. The reason: you are far too likely to get an overburden of caramel if young, overpowering toastiness of old. So, of all the 750 whiskeys tasted for the 2024 Whiskey Bible, this was bar far the most intriguing. And does it work? Yep! *43% (86·proof)*

Michter's 20 Year Old Kentucky Straight Bourbon batch no. 18I1370, bott code: A182681370 **(96.5) n24 t24 f24 b24.5** When people ask me why I think that bourbon has the edge over Scotch at the moment, perhaps I should point them in the direction of a bottling like this to give them some understanding as to why... One of the best 20+ year-old bourbons I have ever encountered. *57.1% (114.2 proof). 463 bottles.*

Michter's 20 Year Old Kentucky Straight Bourbon batch no. 19H1439, bott code: A192421439 **(96.5) n24.5 t24 f23.5 b24.5.** When this bourbon was distilled, it was unlikely a barrel could reach this degree of antiquity and still taste as wonderfully complete as this. Then, if a bourbon reached its second decade, it was one that had slipped through the net and had not been especially cared for. Meaning, nearly always, they were too old and clogged with oak. Not this fellow. This is an old timer all right. But beautifully manicured and more beautiful now than at any previous time in its life. A privilege to taste. *57.1% (114.2 proof). 440 bottles.*

Michter's 25 Year Old Kentucky Straight Bourbon batch no. L20I2076, bott code: A202512076 **(95.5) n24 t24.5 f23 b24** It is not only the age which is jaw-dropping: the fact that after all these years a bourbon can offer so many untarnished gems...! The midground is fascinating with wonderful mix of dark chocolate mousse and bourbon, one of my favourite combinations. Here it comes with cobwebs. And they only seem to intensify the experience further. Amazingly, the elegance has not been compromised any way shape or form. Simply majestic! *58.1% (116.2 proof). sc. 348 bottles.*

Michter's Single Barrel 10 Year Old Kentucky Straight Bourbon barrel no. 19D625, bott code: A19095625 **(95.5)** n24.5 t23.5 f23.5 b24 An incredibly beautiful whiskey. A contender for the single barrel of the year, for sure... *47.2% (94.4 proof). sc*

Michter's Single Barrel 10 Year Old Kentucky Straight Bourbon barrel no. 19D662, bott code: A19099662 **(96)** n24 t24 f23.5 b24.5 A classic top quarter of warehouse 10-year-old (barrel 625, above, was much nearer midpoint) which has seen some heat action and ensures maximum depth and entertainment for its age. Beautifully made, too...! *47.2% (94.4 proof). sc.*

Michter's Small Batch Kentucky Straight Bourbon batch no. L18F873, bott code: A8172873 **(87.5)** n22 t22.5 f21 b22 An attractive, slightly minty and ungainly offering with extra bitterness to the toastiness, especially at the death. Some subtle orange blossom honey aids the sweetness. *45.7%*

Michter's Small Batch Kentucky Straight Bourbon batch no. 20C430, bott code: A200830430 **(92)** n23 t23.5 f22.5 b23 A deceptively weighty bourbon which is an essay in genteel understatement. Complex and fascinating, especially in the many guises the cocoa creates. *45.7%*

Michter's Small Batch Original Sour Mash batch no. L18V1608, bott code: A183041608 **(92)** n23.5 t23 f22.5 b23 One of the weaker Michter's by strength, but lacks nothing in subtlety. *43%*

⁂ **Michter's Small Batch Kentucky Straight Bourbon** batch 23A0117 db **(89.5)** n22 a reserved, conservative vanilla nose with a hint of grapefruit; t23 so easy and understated...so relaxed it almost forgets to take off. The creamed hickory is most attractive, though...; f22 the small grains break through at last offering a tart fruitiness to the finale; b22.5 good, but perhaps not fully shewing the Michter's solidity and sophistication I have usually come to expect. *45.7%*

Monk's Road Fifth District Series Aged 6 Years barrel no 80 db **(92.5)** n22.5 t23 f23.5 b23.5 A sweet, crunchy and unfailingly harmonious bourbon. *50% (100 proof)*

Nashville Barrel Company Straight Bourbon Texas Cask Strength (94) n23 beautifully firm with the small grains busy and complex and confined hickory growling on a chain...; t24 that is a superb delivery. The corn oils are seismic, yet brilliantly controlled by the tightness of the smaller grains, the crispness of the sugars and the intensity of the heather honey-sweetened hickory. The pace and depth are first class...; f23 buttery hickory and spices. The layering of the oaky vanilla is snowflake delicate; b24 *59.31% (114.62 proof) distilled in Indiana*

New Riff Backsetter Bourbon Bottled in Bond db **(87)** n22.5 t22 f21 b21.5 One of the sweetest bourbons I've encountered for a little while: the expected liquorice and toasty molasses making way for an infinitely more honeyed style with a heather honey forging ahead of the later maple syrup. Strangely tangy, though: a bit like particularly virile marmalade. *50% (100 proof). ncf.*

New Riff Single Barrel Kentucky Bourbon Barrel no 16-7733 dist 1.5.16 bott 5.19.20 db **(91)** n23 t23 f22 b23 a beautiful, buttery bourbon true to the lighter Kentucky tradition. Quietly impressive. *56.1% (112.2 proof). East Texas Whisky Club.*

New Riff Single Barrel Kentucky Straight Bourbon Whiskey barrel no. 15-6995, dist Fall 2015, bott Fall 2019 db **(89)** n22.5 t22.5 f21.5 b22.5 Maybe a little too much extracted from the still by this distillery's usually high standards. *56.75% (113.5 proof). ncf sc.*

New Riff Single Barrel Kentucky Straight Bourbon Whiskey barrel no. 16-7128, dist Spring 2016, bott Spring 2020 db **(92)** n22.5 t23.5 f22.5 b23.5 A rich, sweet and satisfying bourbon. *56.6% (113.2 proof). ncf sc.*

Noah's Mill batch no 21-63 db **(94)** n23.5 t23.5 f23.5 b24 this isn't a five-minute bourbon. Unless you have a good half hour to spend exploring this, probably not worth bothering. An exhibition of complexity and guile. *57.15% (114.3 proof). distilled, aged and bottled by Willett Distillery, Bardstown, Ky*

Old Bardstown Bottled In Bond Kentucky Straight Bourbon db **(94.5)** n23 t24 f23.5 b24 textbook Bardstown: a classic old brand in truly classic form. Beautiful. *50% (100 proof). Distilled and bottled by Willett Distillery, Bardstown*

⁂ **Old Carter Straight Bourbon** batch 14 **(92)** n23.5 mega toasty. The peel of kumquats tries to diffuse the enormity of that toasty oak but has only so much success. Some toasted cocoa notes here, too...; t23 well, that nose doesn't lie! From the first moment the tannins gush like the Kentucky in full spate. Some deep molasses offers a degree of balance and control. The first and second flavour waves are the peak of this whiskey with a short spasm of liquorice hitting just the right spot; f22.5 again the nose doesn't lie...! This time that cocoa note comes to pass...; a dry finish with some late oils softening things at the very death; b23 for those who like a heavy char to their bourbon this is a thoroughbred. A deep, toasty and substantial bourbon. *58.7% (117 proof) nf 3,046 bottles*

Old Charter 8 bott code: B170871 10:094 **(91)** n22.5 t23 f22.5 b23 A wonderfully oily affair which sticks to the palate like a limpet. From taste alone, appears no longer to be an 8-year-old but has retained the number 8. Probably a mix of years as the layering and complexity is significant. *40% (80 proof)*

Old Charter 8 Kentucky Straight Bourbon bott code: L183420122 (92) n22.5 t23.5 f22.5 b23.5 Very similar to the bottling above, except here the sugars, up in attack earlier, gleam and sparkle while the later spices bristle a little more aggressively: slightly more polarisation, but more polish, too. Such great stuff! 44% (88 proof).

Old Carter Straight Bourbon Barrel Strength Batch 1 (91.5) n22 t23.5 f23 b23 The nose may be slightly cumbersome and plodding, like the horse on the label, but as soon as it hits the palate you know you are backing a winner. 54.45% (108.8 proof). 1567 bottles.

⬨ **Old Crow** bott code L3021 db (87.5) n22 t21.5 f22 b22 A much younger bird than was once proudly the case. This one has barely left the nest; it certainly isn't in full breeding plumage. Soft hickory and a light layering of Demerara sugars is the best you'll get. 40%

Old Ezra Aged 7 Years Kentucky Straight Bourbon bott code: LF4227 (92) n22.5 t23.5 f23 b23 Essentially, a light and complex bourbon with, presumably, the majority of barrels gleaned from the lower floors. 50.5% (101 proof).

Old Fitzgerald Bottled-in-Bond Aged 9 Years Fall 2018 Edition made: Fall 2008, bott 05/23/2018 db (93.5) n23.5 t23.5 f23 b24 Middle aged wheated bourbon at its deliciously complex best. 50% (100 proof).

Old Fitzgerald Bottled-in-Bond Aged 9 Years Spring 2020 Edition made: Spring 2011, bott Spring 2020 db (91.5) n22.5 t23 f23 b23 As the spices kick in there is the effect of good old fashioned British Bread Pudding. Not as good as that my old mum used to make...nothing ever could be! But one of the things I love about Old Fitz is that you never quite know where this brand will take you next. Also, a very sweet version, too... 50% (100 proof).

Old Fitzgerald Bottled-in-Bond Aged 13 Years Spring 2019 Edition made: Fall 2005, bott 01/30/2019 db (95) n23.5 t24 f23.5 b24 A very different animal to their 9-year-old offering, which is tighter and with a more precise game plan. By contrast, this drifts and is less attentive to the wheat...though you never lose sight of it. 50% (100 proof).

Old Fitzgerald Bottled-in-Bond Aged 14 Years Fall 2020 Edition made: Fall 2005, bott Fall 2020 db (94) n23.5 t23.5 f23 b24 A serious, weighty bourbon with a sweet tooth. Carries its years effortlessly. 50% (100 proof).

Old Fitzgerald Bottled-in-Bond Aged 15 Years Fall 2019 Edition made: Fall 2004, bott Fall 2019 db (89) n23 t22 f22 b22 Old Fitz is feeling his years in this one... 50% (100 proof).

⬨ **Old Fitzgerald** bott code B03131027 db (93) n23 huge character here with a lovely, diced apple freshness; t23.5 that is a stunning delivery: the balance between the corn oils and the light molasses is classic, especially when the hickory moves into view; f23 long, sophisticatedly dry thanks to light grizzling of the spices and growing of the vanillas. That said, still enough light molasses to cover to the end; b23.5 for an everyday whiskey this remains damned fine bourbon. Seriously complex and satisfying. 40%

⬨ **Old Forester 100 Proof** bott code A3552216413156078 db (95) n23.5 such a lovely, tart, brown-sugared overture the arrival of the liquorice is inevitable...; t23.5 molasses and corn oil are in a loving embrace here. The spices, headier vanillins including liquorice and hickory as well as spices hide behind a curtain until the fling has finished...; f24 this is such a long experience, when the liquorice does arrive it has time to flex its muscles and make a small speech before the corn oils move back into the scene. The spices now bristle while the hickory sings...; b24 this is such a classic, timeless style of bourbon I could drink this any time of the day in any situation. It is as though time has stood still here in Kentucky. One of the greatest screwcap whiskies in the world. 50%

⬨ **Old Forester 1870 Original Batch** bott code L1872121111 db (91) n22.5 an unusual combination of mint and dark fudge; t23 a salivating amalgamation of dark sugars – mainly molasses and muscovado – building into a much oakier theme. The liquorice is inevitable, but the lack of spices is a surprise; f22.5 back towards a chocolate mint fade with the spices now picking up. Slightly out of alignment late on, for all that..; b23 Old Forester played in a slightly different key with the trademark liquorice and/or hickory much more subdued and a more minty vanilla style dominating in its place... 45%

⬨ **Old Forester 1897 Bottled In Bond** bott code F264221600712549 db (92.5) n23 the crunchier sugars are certainly in crunch mode: there is a distinctive brittleness which refuses to give way to the corn oils; t23 the rye grains pings around the tastebuds and teeth like pinball. The vanillas finally make their mark...; f23.5 complex and balanced, there is a wonderful interplay between yielding and crisp, salivating ad drying...; b23 always worth tasting this against the standard OF 100 proof. Two very different whiskeys, this one not quite displaying the recognisable Forester flag... 50%

⬨ **Old Forester 1910 Old Fine Whisky** bott code L312211418 db (95.5) n23.5 just love the crisp rye moulding into the liquorice. As well as the dappled maple syrup...; t24.5 a near perfect marriage between high char liquorice and molasses with a smoked, lightly phenolic vanilla. The interplay is astonishing. As is the shy delivery of the years. The slow rising of the hickory is a thing of improbable beauty...; f23.5 slightly lighter now with much more emphasis on those spices; **b24** not sure how much time you have in the day. But anyone with less than 20 minutes to spare shouldn't even think about starting on this one. Easily one of the most complex and deeply satisfying bourbons out here... 46.5%

⟨⟨⟨ **Old Forester 1920 Prohibition Style** bott code L256210952 db **(89) n22** an abrasive nose: some real attitude here... and we are not talking alcohol. Curious cocoa kick on the rye...; **t23** picks up impressively with an immediate praline caress and vanilla follow through. The spices and small grains form a playful, though muscovado sweet, middle; **f21.5** rich, but just a little bit of trailing bitterness at the death detracts from the vanillas a little; **b22.5** a bourbon with some momentous moments but some phases that don't exactly work, either. That said, there is a lot of bourbon here. 57.5%

Old Forester Statesman bott code F068220932710596 db **(92.5) n22.5** weighty and pleasing, the liquorice shows early and has plenty of molasses in tow to accompany the earthier tannins; **t23.5** typically busy Forester; on one hand throwing weight about, but then seducing you with a beguiling level of small grain activity. Salivating and sharp, this is so lip-smacking; **f23** the spices fizz to the end, though without aggression. A little maple syrup softens the liquorice; **b23.5** there is something riveting about the quiet complexity of this bottling: the weight ration and length of each phase is spot on. Charming. 47.5% (95 proof)

Old Grand-Dad (90.5) n22 t23 f23 b23.5. This one's all about the small grains. A busy, lively bourbon, this offers little to remind me of the original Old Grand-Dad whiskey made out at Frankfort. That said, this is a whisk(e)y-lover's whiskey: in other words the excellence of the structure and complexity outweighs any historical misgivings. Enormously improved and now very much at home with its own busy style. 43%

Old Grand-Dad 80 Proof bott code: L7119FFB140640030 **(87) n21.5 t22.5 f21 b22** Steady and pretty light weight. Doesn't have quite the same backbone as the 43%. But who cannot fall for the charm of delicate citrus and chalky vanillas? Just enough liquorice and rye juiciness to lift it into the easy drinking category. 40% (80 proof).

⟨⟨⟨ **Old Grand-Dad Bonded At Least Four Years Old** bott code 220820953 db **(91.5) n22.5** a drier than of old nose, with not quite the sugars leeched out of the oak as was once the case. A little liquorice offers a degree of gravitas; **t22.5** light Demerara with an oily twist of liquorice; **f22.5** the corn oils stay the course; **b23** like Old Crow, the years don't seem to have accumulated as they once did. Indeed, this Old Grand-Dad has virtually no grey hairs at all. Even so, beautifully made if only half-heartedly matured. Still lovely chewing whiskey. 50%

Old Medley 12 Years Old Kentucky Straight Bourbon bott code: L4340-120915 db **(94) n23** toasted almonds and honey. Beautifully brittle; **t23.5** one of those super-salivating deliveries as the small grains go ape. The vanillas are mainly of the custardy variety and allow their full share of molasses and manuka honey to take their place; **f23.5** light liquorice joins the vanilla; **b24** just magnificently complex. Medley by name, medley by nature... 43.4% (86.8 proof)

⟨⟨⟨ **Old Pepper Straight Bourbon Bottled In Bond** batch S2019 **(94.5) n23.5** really makes a big play of small grain activity amid the soaring tannin. Truly classic bourbon aroma with no intention of holding back...; **t23.5** the spirit certainly saw a lot of the barrel because the tannins leap around the palate. Even by the midpoint all kinds of intense chocolate tones are cascading down, the spices right behind them; **f24** slightly more mocha to shew now. Creamier at this juncture with the corn oils now making their mark. Incredibly lengthy and satisfying; **b24** Pepper by name, pepper by nature.... A classic Kentucky bourbon, especially when that chocolate and spice starts jamming. Absolutely love it! Pure quality. 50% (100 proof)

Old Rip Van Winkle Aged 10 Years bott code: B1705307:267 db **(93.5) n24 t23 f23 b23.5** There is something of the old Ancient Age 10 in this, you know... 53.5% (107 proof).

⟨⟨⟨ **Old Scout Straight Bourbon Aged 7 Years** barrel no 37444 **(93) n23** a pleasing mix of red and black liquorice with a spicy jolt in there, too; **t23.5** superb delivery: just the right bite followed by an oozing of molasses plus tannin and then rich corn oil; **f23** it's that corn oil now having the last word, though the vanillas are pretty worthy, too; **b23.5** a softie of a bourbon despite its pretty high strength. The corn oils and spices work particularly well on this one. High grade stuff from what once would have been labelled Smooth Ambler. 56.2% Distilled in Indiana.

Old Tub Kentucky Bottled in Bond Aged 4 Years Straight Bourbon bott code; L4349CLK020570837 db **(93) n23** Jim Beam as it used to be: the tannins making just the right degree of noise as the sugars and light liquorice work overtime; **t23.5** spot on. Corn oils and light spices enter early. Delicate mocha and hickory notes caress; **f23** more liquorice and molasses before butterscotch makes a definitive entry; **b23.5** truly excellent, good honest bourbon recognisable from a lifetime ago. A brilliant go-to whiskey. 50% (100 proof) Jim Beam

Old Virginia Kentucky Straight Bourbon Aged 6 Years bott code: L833901B **(91.5) n23 t22.5 f23 b23** The kind of old-fashioned style bourbon I fell in love with over 40 years ago... 40%.

Orphan Barrel Rhetoric Aged 24 Years bott code: L8059K1002 **(95) n24 t24 f23.5 b23.5** An unusual bourbon for this kind of great age. Usually they head down a heavy duty tannin route.

Bourbon

Instead this one almost drowns in natural creamy caramels. Almost as meek as Theresa May when facing the EU bully boys though, of course, nothing on the planet is that pathetic. *45.4%*

Paul Sutton Kentucky Straight Bourbon Small Batch Hand Drawn Blend batch 51 date 3/22 db **(87) n21.5 t22 f21.5 b22** Decades ago I was taught by a Kentucky distiller about "smoky" bourbons; those with a distinct heavy earthiness to their character. I encounter them rarely, but here is one. It means it is weighted with character, on the nose almost a bacon saltiness amid the hickory. The delivery is far more routine, with lashings of toffee engaging the vanilla and acacia honey. Then we are back to that smokiness on the finish. Those looking for bourbon with its own unique and not unattractive personality might look this one up. *50% (100 proof)*

Pappy Van Winkle Family Reserve 15 Years Old bott code: L172520110-237 **(96) n24 t23.5 f24 b24.5** Weller Antique fans will possibly find a closer match here structure-wise than the 10-year-old. While those in pursuit of excellent bourbon should just linger here awhile. Anyone other than true bourbon lovers need not sample. But there again... *53.5%*

Pappy Van Winkle Family Reserve Kentucky Straight Bourbon Whiskey 15 Years Old bott code: L181340105:017 db **(96) n24 t24.5 f23.5 b24** Usually I spit everything I taste. I accidentally found myself swallowing a drop of this without thinking. A bourbon-lover's bourbon... *53.5% (107 proof).*

Pappy Van Winkle's Family Reserve 20 Years Old bott code: L172640108:18N **(95) n24 t22.5 f24.5 b24** An ancient bourbon, so should be a flavour powerhouse. But this is all about understatement and complexity. *45.2% (90.4 proof).*

Pappy Van Winkle Family Reserve Kentucky Straight Bourbon Whiskey 20 Years Old bott code: L18233C10723N db **(85.5) n21 t22.5 f21 b21** Some profound vanilla and citrus moments on delivery. But the nose tells you things aren't as they should be and the finish confirms it. One or two casks used here that have gone through the top, bringing out some pretty tired notes from the oak. Just never comfortable in its own skin. *45.2% (90.4 proof).*

Pappy Van Winkle Family Reserve Kentucky Straight Bourbon Whiskey 23 Years Old bott code: L180590111:08N db **(95.5) n24 t24 f23.5 b24** One of the holy grails of bourbon is to produce consistently a 23- to 25-year-old which is still sweet and not tannin dominated: no easy ask. This has certainly moved a little way towards that, shewing some of the character of the last bottling I tasted, although this is unquestionably drier. At least on the nose a decisive sweetness I detected and there are still sugars enough to give some fabulous moments on the palate. The tannins do, though, still have the biggest say. But remember: this whiskey has matured for a very long time. In the glass it takes well over an hour to get the best out of it: the secrets of such an ancient bourbon are always revealed tantalisingly slowly... *47.8% (95.6 proof).*

◇ **Penelope Architect Build No 6 Straight Bourbon Age: 4 Years** finished with French oak staves **(95) n23.5** mon dieu! Le volume is at full blast for tannin, liquorice in particular: fortunately there are some molassed nose plugs to tone down the toasty onslaught: together it works rather well. The spices have decided to take no prisoners...; **t23.5** magnifique! The corn oils form the perfect conductor to comfortably take on board the weight of the liquorice and burnt toast as well as balancing manuka honey. Spices, though behaved, pepper the taste buds; **f24** sacre bleu! Wonderfully long and happy to keep the tastiness going, seemingly aware that the balancing mix of light molasses and muscovado sugars are equal to the continuing tasty layering; **b24** voila! French oak staves doing what French oak staves do: ramp up the tannins and oak content by some margin. Have to say that for all its je ne sais quoi, it blends in with the sturdiness of the bourbon exceptionally well. Formidable! Le magic...! *52% (104 proof) ncf distilled in Indiana*

◇ **Penelope Barrel Strength Four Grain Straight Bourbon** corn, rye, wheat, malted barley batch 13 **(88) n22 t23 f21 b22** Bit of a Russian Roulette bourbon this four-grain chappie from Penelope. Initially thought this might be one of the better exponents, but the bitterness vaguely noticeable on the nose catches up with it on the finish. Some lovely, sweet vanilla and hickory moments early on, though. *56% (112 proof) ncf distilled in Indiana*

◇ **Penelope Toasted Series Straight Bourbon Age 5 Years** batch 23-301 **(92) n23** impressive nuttiness melts effortlessly into a spiced corn oil and deft liquorice. The toastiness, though holding back, is supercharged, like lightning about to strike; **t23.5** wow! Lots of ordinary plain, granulated white sugar blended in with muscovado. And then, crack! The midpoint takes the brunt of the oak, though those myriad sugars were always going to take the weight; **f22.5** still sticky with sugar – a kind of treacle pie. The roastiness is upping the amps by the second; **b23** if you are looking for a bourbon that has extracted maximum sugars from the oak but still retains a darker, toasty persona, then here's your bourbon. *50% (100 proof) distilled in Lawrenceburg Indiana*

Quarter Horse Kentucky Bourbon Whiskey Aged a Minimum of 1 Year in New Oak (87) n21.5 t23 f21.5 b21.5 An intriguing whiskey which simultaneously shews its youth and the spirit and maturity from the cask. The creamy toffee notes on delivery and follow through are superb. For a Quarter Horse it's not half bad... *46% (92.*

◈ **Ramspring Single Barrel Reserve Kentucky Straight Bourbon Age 6** barrel B6 **(92)** **n23** delightful toffee-mint with a pleasing undercurrent of treacle and ulmo honey; **t22.5** the landing on the palate is that soft it is hard to know which flavour profile is in the saddle. However, there is a juicy element striking quite quickly, this bringing into play the sweeter tones – always subtly from a darker, molasses-style sugar - made all the sharper by some dovetailing drier oak; **f23** the spices have taken their time to press the play button, but they are at work now. Just. No sooner to they get going but the corn oils go into overdrive really thickening up that toffee and giving a delicate sheen to some cocoa-liquorice; **b23.5** a bourbon which has gently leached the natural caramels from the oak and used the charms of the corn oil to give it extra creaminess and length. A most genteel bourbon. *45% distilled at Whiskey Thief Distillery*

Rare Character Presents Single Barrel Series Selected By Eureka! Straight Bourbon Age 4 Years 9 Months barrel no I21-15 distilled 7/2017 bottled 4/2022 mashbill: 75/21/4 **(91.5)** **n22.5 t23.5 f22.5 b23** you don't need the mashbill to know this is a high corn bourbon. The evenness of the experience and the barely noticeable changes through the gears underlines that. Trades off more demanding complexity for voluptuous charm... *58.93% (117.86 proof)* *Distilled and Aged in Indiana*

Rebel Yell Small Batch Reserve Kentucky Straight Bourbon Whiskey (94.5) n23.5 t24 f23 **b23.5** A full on, toasty bourbon making the most of the ample spices on hand. *45.3% (906 proof).*

Redemption High Rye Bourbon Aged No Less Than 2 Years batch no. 122, bott code: L9262600:23 **(91)** n22.5 t23 f22.5 b23 So much better than the last Redemption High Rye I encountered. Surprisingly well spiced for a bourbon sporting a rye content weighing at a hefty 38% of the mash bill. *46% (92 proof).*

Redwood Empire Pipe Dream Bourbon Whiskey Aged at least 4 Years bott code: L19 1760 **(91.5)** n23 t23 f22.5 b23 For a whiskey of this age, the hickory content is high. And a very sweet hickory at that. Very distinctive bourbon. *45%.*

Rock Hill Farms Single Barrel Bourbon bott code: B1717118:40K **(95)** n24 t24 f23.5 b24 Almost impossible to find fault with this. Anyone who loves whisky, bourbon in particular, will simply groan in pleasure in the same way your leg might jolt out when the knee is tapped. The only fly in the ointment is that I cannot tell you the barrel or bottling, because it isn't marked on the bottle. This really is bourbon at it sexiest. *50% (100 proof)*

Rock Hill Farms Single Barrel Bourbon bott code: L18102010829K **(95.5)** n24 t24 f23.5 b24 Take a bet on this and you are likely to be a winner. A true bourbon connoisseur's favourite... *50%*

◈ **Rock Town Column Still Collection Single Barrel Bourbon Whiskey Cask No 4 Aged 36 Months (87)** n22 t22 f22 b21 A little gingerbread geeing up the tannins on the nose and warning of things to come. On delivery again the oak really has little holding it back: the tannins and accompanying spices are everywhere and trample roughshod over the grains, as though they didn't exist. A little maple syrup tries to keep matters in hand, but it is an uphill battle against the aggressively warming oak. *60% (120 proof) mash bill 78% corn 13% malted barley 8% wheat distilled in collaboration with Bardstown Bourbon Company*

◈ **Rock Town Column Still Collection Single Barrel Bourbon Whiskey Cask No 6 Aged 36 Months (94)** n23 unlike in barrel 4, the corn oil here takes a salute, though the oak still ensures there is a nip in the air...; **t24** I really wasn't expecting a delivery of such style and panache after experiencing barrel number 4. The corn oils take no time in making their mark. But it is the fabulous layering of the tannin – and different levels of intensity is almost incalculable. Better still, the honey is in complete harmony: mainly manuka but some gorgeous ulmo (from Chile) in there for good measure. The middle is also nutty – a kind of Brazil nut concentrate – which works so well with the developing cocoa; **f23** the corn oil is dripping around the palate still, as is a little Indian medium roast cocoa; **b24** now that's entertainment...just an insane depth to the complexity. It feels as though I have just been to a display of world chocolate. *61% (122 proof) mash bill 78% corn 13% malted barley 8% wheat distilled in collaboration with Bardstown Bourbon Company*

◈ **Rock Town Column Still Collection Small Batch Straight Bourbon Whiskey Batch No 2 Aged 34 Months (93)** n22.5 highly attractive praline with a gentle, blunting buttery edge to the spices; **t23** the sugars are more readily identifiable early on here than has been the case with their single casks, ensuring a salivating delivery. The vanillas are doing a great job ensuring is a softer underbelly to this, though a little red liquorice and hickory fill in an open ground; **f23.5** much drier with the tannins dominant, though the vanilla is closely linked to the grumbling spices. Some lovely mocha mops up the finish; **b24** elegant, understated and unashamed of its vanilla base and spine, there are enough sub contexts to ensure highly attractive complexity, especially with the busy small grains. An impressive old-fashioned style. *46% (92 proof) mash bill 78% corn 13% malted barley 8% wheat distilled in collaboration with Bardstown Bourbon Company*

◈ **Rock Town Column Still Collection Toasted French Oak Single Barrel Finish Straight Bourbon Aged 36 Months (88)** n21.5 t24 f21 b21.5 The nose suggests this will be in some ways a challenge with a strained, milky touch to the vanilla. It certainly recovers with aplomb on delivery, the molasses sitting prettily with the vanillas and generates one of the sharpest, eye-watering midpoints of any whisky this year: quite wonderful. But often, if the nose isn't quite right, nor will be the finish further down the line. And it is true here, as balance is compromised on the milky finish. But that delivery: the stuff of legends! *50.8% (101.6 proof) mash bill 78% corn 13% malted barley 8% wheat distilled in collaboration with Bardstown Bourbon Company*

Rowan's Creek Straight Kentucky Bourbon batch no 21-20 db **(87) n22 t22.5 f21 b21.5** Perhaps a little too flinty and sweet for bourbon greatness. The slight bitterness is also very un-Willett-like, too. *50.05% (100.1 proof) distilled, aged and bottled by Willett Distillery, Bardstown, Ky*

Russell's Reserve 6 Years Old Kentucky Straight Bourbon db **(88.5) n21.5 t22.5 f22 b22.5** Super-relaxed and toffee-laden, the spices take their time to kick through. The corn oil has a big hand in this. *45% (90 proof)*

Russell's Reserve Kentucky Straight Bourbon 10 Years Old bott code: LL/GI210755 db **(92.5) n23 t23 f23 b23.5** One of the softest decade-old bourbons I have tasted in a very, very long time. *45% (90 proof).*

Russell's Reserve 10 Years Old Kentucky Straight Bourbon db **(91) n21.5 t23.5 f23 b23** a classic case of the taste bearing no relation to the nose. Pity this isn't Jimmy's preferred strength of 101, though... *45% (90 proof)*

⬙ **Russell's Reserve Single Barrel** bott code 2022/06/22 db **(91.5) n22** a dry, dusty offering; **t23.5** ups its game with a soft coating of waxy heather honey. The corn oil is voluptuous, the spices teasing, playful and salivating; **f23** really does keep churning out the custardy vanillas enlivened by black pepper; **b23** the waxy honey is a heart-winner. Superb layering and fascinating battle between sweet and dry where clearly no winner emerges. *55% ncf*

Russell's Reserve 2020 db **(94.5) n23.5 t23.5 f23.5 b24** commendable guile throughout. This bourbon is an object lesson in understatement and balance. A treat.. *Frankfort Bourbon Society.*

Seven Devils Straight Bourbon Whiskey (82.5) n20 t21.5 f20.5 b20.5 Nutty, caramel-laden and sweet, there is a buzz on the palate to this which suggests the distillate has not been quite as well made as it could be. Doesn't sit right, despite (or maybe because of) the praline. *45% (90 proof). Bottled by Koenig Distillery*

Shenk's Homestead Kentucky Sour Mash 2019 Release batch no. 19GI139, bott code: A191861139 **(88) n22.5 n22.5 t22 f21.5 b22** Exceptionally gentle whiskey boasting modest but important kumquat note on both nose and body and a shimmering, slightly metallic heather honey sweetness. A tad bitter late on. *45.6% (91.2 proof). 2,882 bottles. Bottled by Michter's Distillery.*

⬙ **Smooth Ambler Contraction Bourbon A Blend of Straight Bourbon Whiskies** batch no 511 **(86.5) n22 t22.5 f20.5 b21.5** Incredibly intense toffee at work here. There are some major oils at play also – and I mean beyond those from the corn – and they are not helping on the complexity front. The slightly bitter finish does little to find the whiskey's mojo, either. Not quite the excellent bourbon it once was, but might be again if they could control the tanginess of the oily input. *46% (92 proof) ncf distilled in West Virginia, Tennessee and Indiana.*

Smooth Ambler Old Scout Aged 5 Years Bourbon barrel no. 28092 **(95) n23.5 t24 f23.5 b24** A truly wonderful barrel plucked, most likely, from the upper stories of the warehouse, as this has the personality of a standard bourbon twice its age. The secret of its greatness, however, is the balance of its controlled intensity. A bourbon lover's bourbon... *59.1% SC Distilled in Indiana*

Smooth Ambler Old Scout Straight Bourbon batch No 55 distilled in Indiana **(92) n23 t23 f22.5 b23.5** Non-spectacular but thoroughly enjoyable bourbon that wears its excellence well. *49.5% (99 proof).*

Smooth Ambler Old Scout Straight Bourbon batch no. 80 **(92) n23 t23 f22.5 b23** An interesting variant on the last batch I tasted with the hickory now restricted to the nose. A very relaxed, high-grade bourbon. *49.5% (99 proof) Distilled in Indiana*

Stagg Jr bott code: B1707310457 **(96) n24 t24.5 f23.5 b24** I well remember the first Stagg Junior I encountered. Which though truly excellent, skimped a little too much on the sugars and struggled to find its balance and, thus, full potential. Certainly no such worries with this bottling: indeed, the honey is remarkable for its abundance. Staggering!.. *64.75% (129.5 proof)*

Stillwater Rye Black Label Batch 1 Premium Straight Rye Whiskey Single Barrel db **(92.5) n23 t23 f23 b23.5** well-made and single-minded rye which eschews complexity for intensity. This Stillwater certainly runs deep... *47.5% (95 proof)*

Timber Craft Ninety-Eight Indiana Straight Bourbon bott code: LB1124020 **(93) n23 t23.5 f23 b23.5** in nearly 50 years of tasting bourbon, this is probably the first 49% abv version I have ever found! And this massively flavoured bourbon was certainly worth waiting for... *49% (98 proof)*

Three Chord Blended Bourbon Private Barrel Pick Honey Cask Finish db **(87.5) n22.5 t21 f22.5 b21.5** The buzz around Frankfort was that a unique whiskey had arrived in town: a specially bottled bourbon that had been finished in a barrel previously treated with real honey. So, having combed the area and found out where it was, I made a bee-line to the store and was stung for a few bucks as I bought the bottle. You'll not be surprised that this is one for liqueur lovers – the delivery sweet enough to induce an instant toothache. But I have to admit the mouthfeel is sensual to the point of being a bit sexy...hang on, am I droning on...? Well, I can certainly wax lyrical about the finish which has just the right amount of countering spices. Gentleman: come Mother's Day, this is the perfect gift for the queen bee in your life. (copyright 2022 "Sexist and Misogynist" Whisky Writers Inc). *58.1.% (116.2 proof). Barrel pick for Capital Cellars, Frankfort, Ky.*

Three Keys Distillery Kentucky Straight Bourbon Small Batch Aged 2 Years 11 Months Barrel No 18 bottled 6/2021 Mashbill: 70% Kentucky corn, 21% rye 9% malted barley **(92.5) n23 t23.5 f23 b23** high rye Owensboro bourbon showing at its very best. Impressive. *50.5% (101 proof) Distilled and Aged in Owensboro, Ky, for Three Keys*

Treaty Oak Distilling Red Handed Bourbon Whiskey db **(90) n22 t23 f22.5 b22.5** As thick cut as a Texas steak.....and no less juicy! *47.5% (95 proof).*

Van Winkle Special Reserve 12 Years Old Lot "B" bott code: L172550110:147 **(93.5) n23 t23 f24 b23.5** Those looking for comparisons between certain Weller products and Van Winkle's might find this particular bottling a little better weighted, less forthright and more complex. *45% (90 proof)*

Van Winkle Special Reserve 12 Years Old Lot "B" Batch Bourbon Whiskey bott code: L181300112 **(94.5) n23.5 t23.5 f23 b23.5** Roughly consistent in quality to the bottling above, but better here and takes a slightly different route - by putting its foot on the toastiness and steering by some very impressive waxy Manuka honey. For those who like their bourbon hairy, bristling with spice, honey and big oak interaction. *45.2% (90.4 proof).*

Very Old Barton 6 bott code: 907:104 **(93) n22 t24 f23.5 b23.5** The VOB 6, when the number stood for the years, has for the last quarter of a century been one of my bourbons of choice: an understated classic. This version has toned down on the nose very slightly and the palate underlines a far less definite oak-to-grain parry and counter-thrust. That said, still a bourbon which mesmerises you with its innate complexity and almost perfect weight and pace on the palate. One that has you instinctively pouring a second glass. *45% (90 proof)*

Very Old Barton 90 Proof Kentucky Straight Bourbon bott code: L181370113 **(92) n22.5 t23.5 f23 b23** Gorgeous whiskey, though not perhaps the tour de force of previous bottlings. *45% (90 proof).*

Very Old Barton 100 Proof bott code: L17/640102:074 **(96) n23.5 t24.5 f23.5 b24.5** Here's a challenge for you: find fault with this whiskey... Brilliant bourbon of the intense yet sophisticated variety. *50% (100 proof)*

Very Old Barton Kentucky Straight Bourbon bott code: 3820123 **(87.5) n22 t22 f21.5 b22** A consistent bourbon (just noticed I have marked it identically to the last bottling!) giving a limited but delightful account of the VIB brand, ensuring the busy small grains keeps on scrambling around the palate and just enough liquorice and hickory meets the onrushing caramel and praline. Deceptively delicious. *40% (80 proof).*

Virginia Gentleman (90.5) n22 t23 f23 b23.5. A Gentleman in every sense: and a pretty sophisticated one at that. *40% (80 Proof)*

◈ **Weller Aged 12 Years** bott code L22090 db **(86) n21 t22.5 f21 b21.5** A strangely lacklustre, unbalanced version of a usually trustworthy brand. The nose is immediately out if its usual alignment and though the wheated component is sailing full speed ahead, other elements are sinking fast. *45% (90 proof)*

◈ **Weller Antique 107** bott code L23034 db **(94) n23** such an attractive amalgamation of heather honey and freshy baked bread. The spices are at their prickly best; **t23.5** a delicate acacia honey note trickles out, giving the appearance a slightly overcooked Belgian waffle on delivery. The spices pitter-patter deliciously and as the perfect foil to the dominating sweetness; **f23.5** long, increasingly toasty, and never any less tasty. The elegant battle between honey and pepper remains a delightful and unresolved constant; **b24** that's more like it! After the disappointment of the 12-y-o, the 107 is flying the Weller flag high and proudly. Quite lovely. *53.5% (107 proof)*

Weller C.Y.P.B Wheated Kentucky Straight Bourbon bott code: L18163011042N **(95.5) n24 t24 f23.5 b24** Has all the chutzpah of a wheated bourbon that knows it's damn good and goes out to shock. Enjoy the myriad little favour and spice explosions. And the deceptive depth.... *47.5% (95 proof).*

◈ **Weller Full Proof** bott code L23138 db **(95.5) n23.5** a richer, fuller nose than previous recent Wellers where the corn oil holds court while the wheat plots and menaces in the background; **t24.5** the house style honey explosion is no way contained: every section of the palate is enriched by a blend of heather and ulmo honey. In some ways startling, in every way delicious. The midpoint is an intriguing marriage between crusty brown bread and ginger cake... with those trusty honey and spices adding to the depth; **f23.5** a more delicate experience now with the honey reduced and layering thinner, busier and more convoluted as the small grains really begin shuffling the pack. The lightest hickory tone underlines the serious maturation here;

Bourbon

b24 for all the seemingly simplistic honeys doing the rounds, this is a highly complex whiskey. As ever, the Buffalo Trace wheated bourbon has a life of its own and one quite like any other. I doubt any whiskey on the planet has quite the wide range of honeys either in texture or variance of sweetness. Of its type an undeniable, unalienable classic. *57% (114 proof)*

⬩ **Weller Single Barrel** bott code 32033072621 db **(92.5) n22.5** a dark, combustible aroma with the spices seemingly about to explode at any moment. As is the house style, we have freshly baked grainy loaves cooling. Being Weller, some spiced sugars are on full lurk and ready to pounce...; **t24** the corn oils ensure a silky disposition; the molten muscovado sugars offer a vaguely toasty sweetness; **f23** continues with the while flag. No meaningful spices but plenty of mouth-kissing sugars of a honeyed varietal. A little age kicks in late on as soft hickory begins to gather...; **b23** Weller at its most laid back and positively supine. The spices, beyond the nose, have taken a day off and allowed the sugars and playful hickory control instead... *48.5% (97 proof)*

Weller Special Reserve bott code: L172080115:014 **(93) n23 t23.5 f23 b23.5** Imperiously excellent, yet somehow given to understatement. *45% (90 proof)*

Weller Special Reserve Kentucky Straight Bourbon bott code: L19018 0118 **(94) n23 t23.5 f24 b24** Almost too soft and easy to drink. A thousand kisses in a glass.. *45% (90 proof).*

Weller Special Reserve db **(94) n23 t23.5 f23.5 b24** if I remember correctly, the last time I officially tasted this for the Bible, I said that there were 1,000 kisses in a glass. I forgot caresses, too... *45% (90 proof)*

Western Gold 6 Year Old Bourbon Whiskey (91.5) n22 t23 f22.5 b23 Taken from barrels sitting high in the warehouse, that's for sure. You get a lot for your six years... *40%.*

The Whisky Cask Company Heaven Hill 2009 Kentucky Straight Bourbon Whiskey American white oak casks, dist Aug 2009, bott Sep 2019 **(87.5) n22 t22 f21.5 b22** Both nose and delivery are heavy on the hickory. A little golden syrup runs off with the corns oils. A tad bitter on the finish but compensated for by the delicate late vanillas. *58.2% 296 bottles*

The Whisky Shop Maker's Mark batch no. 002, oak staves with barrel finish **(94.5) n23.5 t24 f23 b24** So rare to find Maker's Mark at this strength. The kind of whisky that give wheated bourbon lovers a little stiffy... *54.95%.*

Widow Jane Straight Bourbon Whiskey Aged 10 Years barrel no. 1785, bott 2018 **(95) n23.5 t23.5 f24 b24** This is one very passionate Widow... *45.5% (91 proof). sc.*

Wilcox Bourbon Whiskey (73.5) n19 t19 f17.5 b18 When you buy a bourbon whiskey, you have in your mind a clean, complex Kentuckian. Not sure who made this, but far too feinty for its own good with none of the liquorice and honey notes you should rightfully expect. A very poor representation of bourbon, and not remotely in the true Kentucky style. *40% (80 proof).*

⬩ **Wild Turkey Aged 12 Years** bott code: LL/JL021145 db **(91) n22.5** a leisurely mix of red and black liquorice with a light muscovado sugar and butterscotch accompaniment; **t23** elegant delivery and goes through the gears without missing a beat. As usual, the honey centre stage, and again it's heather honey in the driving seat. But the tannins are drier and even try to bitter early, but fail; **f22.5** genteel spices and the late trademark waxiness; **b23** such a gorgeously layered whiskey, the emphasis still on the waxy honey though the oak has a degree of grouchiness about it. *50.5%*

Wild Turkey 81 Proof bott code: LL/DF291109 db **(91.5) n23 t23 f22.5 b23** A much sweeter, more relaxed bottling than the old 40% version, gathering up honey notes like a wild turkey hoovering up summer berries. *40.5% (81 proof).*

Wild Turkey 81 Proof bott code: LL/HA040353 db **(92) n22.5 t23.5 f22.5 b23** More oak interaction with this feller than any other 81 proof I've encountered. Lays on the hickory with a trowel: delicious! *40.5% (81 proof).*

Wild Turkey 101 Proof bott code: LL/HH300747 db **(93) n23.5 t23.5 f23 b23** The astonishing overall softness on the palate is counterintuitive to the slight aggression on the nose. I've been savouring this whisky for over 30 years. And still it has the ability to surprise. *50.5% (101 proof).*

Wild Turkey 101 bott code LL7JD071129 **(88) n22 t22.5 f21 b22** Not often I feel that Wild Turkey 101 isn't quite on the ball. But that is certainly the case here. The red liquorice and rye-rich nose, attractive as it is, seems a little off the pace. Further, the corn oil dominated delivery, plus the imprecise hickory is loose in its construction. The prevailing bitterness to the sugary finish almost comes as no surprise. Doubt you'd say no to a second glass offered, as there is still plenty to enjoy. But by WT101 usually very high standards, it's a bit of a turkey. *50.5%*

Wild Turkey 101 Kentucky Straight Bourbon bott code: 268H11006 db **(92) n23.5 t23.5 f22 b23** it is now over 30 years since Jimmy Russell first personally introduced me to his favourite of all the whiskeys he was responsible for distilling. Not just that 101 was his preferred choice of strength, but I remember he particularly adored the nuanced honeyed tale that unravels on this whiskey. "Like the Kentucky River, Wild Turkey 101 is mighty, bold, and it takes its own time," quoth Jimmy on the back label. While I look out onto the Kentucky River from the tasting room of my home, it is anything but bold after a week of near 100 degree temperatures, slouching along northwards as the banks dry and become more exposed. But there is a timeless elegance to that ol' River, just as there is to this whiskey. Technically, made in a different distillery, maybe, to the one Jimmy first showed me proudly around it has certainly lost none of its old charm and quiet charisma. Just lovely stuff... *50.5% (101 proof).*

Wild Turkey Kentucky Spirit Single Barrel barrel no. 0401, warehouse A, rick no. 6, bott 01/14/19, bott code: LL/HA152135 db **(89) n22.5 t23 f21.5 b22** A real enjoyable softie if, perhaps, a tad one dimensional. *50.5% (101 proof). sc.*

Wild Turkey Longbranch oak and Texas mesquite charcoal refined bott code: LL/GI180207 db **(91.5) n23 t23 f22.5 b23** Mesquite must be America's answer to peat: here there is a just a light touch, barely noticeable until the finish, and emphasised by the very late warmness to the finale itself. *43% (86 proof).*

Wild Turkey Longbranch bott code: LL/HD261325 db **(92.5) n23 t23 f23 b23.5** "Mesquite must be America's answer to peat" I thought as I nosed and tasted this. "Have I written that before about this?" I mused. I had. And it is... *43% (86 proof).*

Wild Turkey Longbranch Kentucky Straight Bourbon oak and Texas mesquite charcoal refined db bott code: 29/01/2022 **(88) n22.5 t22 f21.5 b22** Some folk tell me they can never find the mesquite influence in this brand. Well, they should certainly take a look at this bottling, because its bite on both the nose and finish is far from shy. That said, you get the feeling this is a bourbon that is about 7%abv under par because the toffee really is a little too monosyllabic and the small grains a little too frugal. Still worth a second pour, though. *43%*

Wild Turkey Rare Breed Barrel Proof bott code: LL/GD020831 db **(95.5) n23.5 t24 f24 b24** A clever glass bottle, its roundness reinforcing the mouthfeel and character of the bourbon itself: one of the most rounded in all Kentucky. In some ways this whiskey is the blueprint for bourbon: its characteristics embrace what we mentally define as bourbon. *58.4% (116.8 proof).*

Wild Turkey Rare Breed Barrel Proof bott code: LL/HA140731 db **(94.5) n23.5 t24 f23 b24** Hickory is all the rage with Wild Turkey this year: another bottling that is leading with that delightful trait. However, have noticed the honey level has receded slightly. *58.4% (116.8 proof).*

◇ **Wild Turkey Rare Breed Barrel Proof** bott code 22/05/10 db **(86.5) n22 t23 f19 b21.5** The last one I had of these, it had me on my knees in worship of it. Not this time, sadly. Beyond the trademark honey notes just too much monosyllabic vanilla for greatness. Lots of spices, but finding that finish odd, synthetic and problematic. *58.4% 116.8 proof*

◇ **Wilderness Trail Bourbon On The Banks** batch no BOTB-4G db **(94) n23** could be so easy just to say this is a caramel fest...but look deeper and there's a little mint pitching up with some assertive spice; **t23.5** gosh...and it's really that spice which has a massive say in directing operations. This is warming, with all kinds if small grains complexity; **f23.5** unusually pithy for a WT, with some surprise late kumquat kicking in...; **b24** this is bourbon that doesn't sit on the fence, or happy to be pigeonholed. A shape-shifting bourbon if ever there was one... *55.5% (111.01 proof)*

◇ **Wilderness Trail Family Reserve Cask Strength Bourbon Aged 4 Years 8 Months** mashbill: corn, wheat, malted barley batch no MDS-BW-02 db **(92) n23** you don't have to look at the label to see the mashbill here: peppers and wheat are pouring from the glass. Bourbon born and bread...literally! **23.5** such a pleasing delivery. The high salivating levels confirm a bourbon still relatively young, though not lacking depth and character for that. The spice and honey main thread is sublime while the corn is accommodating in transporting the gorgeous mix to every crevice; **f22.5** pleasing liquorice-hickory fade...with spices, of course...; just a little late bitterness; **b23** a typical Wilderness trail offering where the taste buds near collapse with exhaustion. *55.4% (110.8 proof)*

◇ **Wilderness Trail Family Reserve Cask Strength Bourbon Aged 8 Years** mashbill: corn, wheat, malted barley batch no LF19A db **(94.5) n23.5** just a cursory hint at outline clove, with the peppers matching the liquorice atom for atom...; **t23.5** mmmm...superb corn oil bathed in a deft marzipan and clementine sweetness before the inevitable spice buzz strikes; **f23.5** those citrus notes are in no hurry to go away. The liquorice sticks as do a coffee and brown bread depth. Pleasingly busy and tangy...; **b24** a new distillery proving that its bourbon can get old gracefully. Rich, deep and doubtless, would have travelled for many more years yet...

◇ **Wilderness Trail Family Reserve Cask Strength Bourbon Bottled In Bond** mashbill: corn, wheat, malted barley batch no 31E23A db **(88.5) n22.5 t22.5 f21.5 b22** Rather flat by WT standards with the corn oils rather too full of itself. There are some decent citrus and hickory tones that do ensure depth on the full-flavoured delivery, thought the sweetness is a tad too syrupy and the finish is tending towards bitterness. *50% (100 proof)*

◇ **Wilderness Trail Family Reserve Cask Strength Bourbon Bottled In Bond** mashbill: corn, rye, malted barley batch no 22E23A db **(91) n22.5** loads of small grains at work here – and not just the rye. Youthful, busy and injecting a little kumquat into the vanilla; **t23** big flavours on delivery to match the sensuous oiliness. Ulmo honey abounds with the tannin-led spices rising in slow motion; **f22.5** so much molasses and vanilla doing battle on the thick finale; **b23** a chewing bourbon with a bigger and far more significant age-feel than your normal BIB. A very complete bourbon. *50% (100 proof)*

⬦ **Wilderness Trail Family Reserve Single Barrel Cask Strength Bourbon Aged 4 Years 2 Months** mashbill: corn, rye, malted barley barrel no 767757 db **(96.5) n24** for a 4-year-old, the nose is nigh unbelievable. Pure chocolate meets pure liquorice meets pure blood orange peel meets cowering spices...; **t24** what can you say about that marriage between intense chocolate and mouth-tingling spice...except "more, please!" The mildness of the molasses is simply mind-blowing...; **f24** still those spices prickle away. Still that chocolate meanders around the palate, still the molasses politely sees off any possibility of encroaching bitterness, still the corn oils kiss and bathe the taste buds with an endearing buttery depth; **b24.5** no-one will convince me that this hasn't been plucked from the very top of a warehouse. This may be a bourbon of barely four years, but its richness suggests something nearly three times that. A phenomenal cask of great integrity and complexity. Which shews exactly why a great deal of money was recently handed over to grab ownership of this distillery.... And one of the finest single barrel whiskeys bottled anywhere in the world this year. And among the 4-year-olds and under...only a super-delicate malt from Slovenia of all places gives it a run for its money...!!! *57.41% (114.83 proof)*

⬦ **Wilderness Trail Settlers Select Rye Single Barrel** barrel no 17D03-11 db **(86) n21.5 t22 f21 b21.5** Having tasted a fair bit of Wilderness Trail rye of late, the nose here came across offering a style I hadn't quite seen before. I certainly don't recognise the tightness to the grain which appears to restrict is usual freshness and depth. For a moment or two on delivery it looks as though those grains might break free, but no dice. A shackled bottling, even slightly bitter on the finish. Odd. *50.48%*

Willett Pot Still Reserve Straight Bourbon batch no 19A1 db **(89) n22.5 t23 f21.5 b22** been quite a while since I last sampled a batch of this. Something timeless about both the nose and delivery. *47% (97proof)*

William Dalton Wheated Indiana Straight Bourbon Bottled in Bond Aged 4 Years mashbill 78% corn 28% wheat 10% malt db **(89.5) n22 t23.5 f21.5 b22.5** big flavoured and commanding, this at times hits great heights, allowing the wheat full scope to do its own considerable thing. A slightly untidy finish hardly diminishes the overall excellence. *50% (100 proof) Spirits of French Lick*

William Larue Weller db **(97.5) n24 t25 f24 b24** ...The most delicious lesson in whiskey structure imaginable. This was my 1,263rd and final new whiskey for the Jim Murray Whisky Bible 2019. Did I leave the very best until last....? *64.1% (128.2 proof).*

William Larue Weller db **(97.5) n25 t24.5 f23.5 b24.5** I have before me a glass of whiskey. It is pure amber in colour and has won more top honours, including World Whisky of the Year, in Jim Murray's Whisky Bible than any other brand. For that reason the sample before me is, as I nose and taste it on the evening of 26th August 2019, the 20,000th whisky I have specifically tasted for this book since it was first published in 2003. There really could be no other I could possibly bestow this personal honour upon. It is a landmark whiskey in every sense... Oh, once again, I have not been let down. I will have to wait to see if this is World Whisky of the Year once more: on the evidence before me it will be close. But I do know no whiskey will better its truly perfect nose... *62.85% (125.7 proof).*

William Larue Weller db **(96.5) n24 t24.5 f24 b24** Another blistering, palate-seducing chunk of whiskey genius from Weller which, perhaps with Glen Grant, is the most consistent whiskey in the universe. Certainly, on this planet. There are always fine lines between each year's bottling. This one is perhaps defined by the determination of the spice and the unrelenting toastiness. Most previous bottlings have had a thin layer of delicate, sweetening sugars which cannot be found here. So, this is more business-like and intense. It sorts out the men from the boys...sorry, I mean the adults from the children. But it remains, unquestionably, whiskey gold of the very purest quality... *67.25% (134.5 proof).*

William Larue Weller db **(97) n24 t24.5 f24 b24.5** strap yourself in for a ride, at warp speed, into bourbon heaven. My word, I've tasted a lot of super high-class bourbon this year. Anything better than this? Probably not. *62.65%*

⬦ **William Larue Weller** db **(96.5) n24** perhaps the nuttiest Weller I have encountered yet: almost like a high strength healthy breakfast cereal with freshly toasted almonds and a heather honey accompaniment. The lightest smearing of hickory adds a degree of phenolic depth. Curiously, also one of the lightest noses in body for a Weller for a while, too, with the corn oils present but in no significant depth...; **t24.5** that thinner body is markedly noticeable as the immediate launch of the joint oak and eye-wateringly tart, small grain intensity is something to behold. The spices are up early but relatively behaved, the vanillas dry and reserved. After that early crescendo, however, at the midpoint the complexity has nowhere to hide: the interplay between the grain and tannins is some spectacle. And the taste buds are lapping up every complex moment. However, for all its oddity the intensity and overall deliciousness is off the scales....; **f23.5** that lack of oil cover means a shorter finish. But they honey is back on the scene weighted down by a little liquorice and warmed by residual spice; **b24.5** Weller as I don't quite remember seeing it before. Vividly alive and boldly punctuated with the smaller grains, the wheat especially, this honeyed beauty takes full advantage of a lull in the usual corn oil richness to offer something almost three dimensional on the palate, rasping and crackling on the palate like a supercharged V8 engine. Strap yourself in and enjoy the ride...if you know how to handle it. *62.35% (124.7 proof)*

The Wiseman Kentucky Owl Straight Bourbon db **(86.5) n22 t22 f21 b21.5** A well-oiled, corn-rich bourbon still a little on the young side. Limited sugar development, other than custardy vanilla. The finish is a little thin. *45.4%*

⬧ **Woodford Reserve Double Oaked** bott code L069311157IA db **(88.5) n23** just love that liquorice layer which gives backbone to the yielding vanillas; **t22.5** huge vanilla and molasses on delivery. The small grains bounce around a bit to let you know they are there. But the buttery cake mix is very different; **f21** soft mocha but a surprising late juiciness as the rye tones re-emerge. The cut appears marginally wide on this one.; **b22** perhaps not technically perfect but a meandering bourbon full of surprises, nonetheless. More peek-a-boo sugar tones than you can shake a whiskey thief at... *45.2%*

⬧ **Woodford Reserve Master's Collection Batch Proof** bott code L102212051 db **(95.5) n23.5** ultra-toasty, with a toffee apple freshness and a spectacular array of perfectly weighted spices; **t24** simply magnificent. Huge tannins rise and spices with them. Then they lower as silky vanillas make their elegant entrance. But even through the midpoint the spices are lingering and complex; **f24** a fittingly long fade with the dominant vanillas, butterscotch, liquorice and molasses in near perfect harmony...just wow! **b24** probably the best bourbon bearing the Woodford Reserve name I have ever tasted. A masterpiece. *459.2%*

⬧ **Woodford Reserve label batch 3157** db **(86) n22 t22 f20.5 b21.5** Supremely soft with a huge spread of vanilla and muscovado sugars. Tangy towards the finish and ultimately unacceptably bitter. *45.2%*

Yellowstone Hand Picked Collection Kentucky Straight Bourbon Single Barrel single barrel No 7772660 barreled /5/2017 selected Fall 2021 db **(92) n22.5 t23 f23 b23.5** the generous use of sugars from both the oak and the small grains would have made this barrel a difficult one not to pick. Refreshing yet bold. *54.5% (109 proof). Frankfort Bourbon Society*

Tennessee Whiskey

⬧ **Big Moustache** bott 7/12/2022 **(89.5) n22.5 t23 f21.5 b22.5** A beautifully big, hickory-laden Tennessee, well backed up with pounding spiced demerara and molasses. The oils are something else, though that something else should be something else when it comes to finish which reveals the tang of the wider cut. That besides, this is a full-on mouth-filler just bristling with flavour and personality. *50% (100 proof) ncf BBC Spirits*

Heaven's Door Tennessee Bourbon Whiskey 10 Year Old bott code: 10/25/18 **(85) n21.5 t22.5 f20 b21** I'm knock-knock-knocking this Heaven's Door: far too heavy, I'm afraid. But, wow! What a delivery...!!! *50% (100 proof).*

Heaven's Door Tennessee Bourbon Whiskey Aged for a Minimum of 7 Years bott code: 2019/04/120555 **(94) n23 t24 f23.5 b23.5** Another bewildering whiskey type to contend with in the USA. Now it is Tennessee Bourbon. I presume that is a bourbon whiskey made in Tennessee but without deploying the charcoal mellowing process. Whatever, it is quite Heavenly.... *45% (90 proof).*

Joe Got A Gun Single Barrel No 4 Three Years Old db **(90.5) n22.5 t23.5 f22 b22.5** has returned to its hickory and citrus roots of its first bottling. A superb Tennessee carrying a little extra weight this time. Joe's gun certainly isn't firing blanks. *45%*

Obtainium Tennessee Rye db **(83) n21 t21.5 f20 b20.5** Far too dependent on the blood orange core. Sharp, fruity, ultimately bitter and, overall, just awry with the rye... *578%.*

Peg Leg Porker Tennessee Straight Bourbon Whiskey (91.5) n22.5 t23 f22.5 b23.5 Still generally has the awkward gait of youth but is old enough to unveil sufficiently luminous sugar to perfectly match the surprising intensity to the spice. Some enjoyable late cocoa towards the death lifts the whole piece considerably. The lushness of the corn oil is exhibition quality; and unlike the 8- and 12-year-old is hickory free. Incidentally, this is a bourbon which benefits massively by the Murray Method...by over five points, no less. You could say it saves its bacon... *45% (90 Proof)*

Peg Leg Porker Tennessee Straight Bourbon Whiskey Aged 8 Years (91) n22.5 t23.5 f22 b23 Deeply attractive, straight as a die bourbon with a decidedly hickory-rich bent on the nose and sturdy corn oils to ensure a rich texture and a generous spreading of muscovado sugars.

One of those delightful bourbons where the actual mouth feel is as enjoyable of the flavours themselves. The midground to finish is a glorious exhibition of light ulmo honey and deep vanilla, the spice being the flag planted on the top of the pile. 45% (90 Proof)

Peg Leg Porker Tennessee Straight Bourbon Whiskey Aged 12 Years (87.5) n22 t22.5 f21 b22 an interesting bourbon, not least because the distillate does not seem to be as such high class as their No Age Statement and 8-year-old versions. This is vaguely fruitier, more meandering and less precise. A kind of bourbon that keeps standing at the edge of a road and is not sure whether to cross or not. This hesitancy is particularly noticeable on the uneven finish. But, again, the corn oils are simply brilliant; the slow leakage of cocoa into the system delightful and, for its obvious weaknesses, the overall experience is enjoyable 45% (90 Proof)

Peg Leg Porker Tennessee Straight Bourbon Whiskey Aged 15 Years batch no. 1 (84.5) n22 t21.5 f20 b21 This wouldn't have been the finest white dog you would have found in Tennessee when it was made 15 years ago. The years in cask has helped for sure, injecting plenty of sugars from the oak which proffers respectability. But there is no escaping the vegetable tones which point towards a fermentation problem and/or an early lack of copper in the system. 45% (90 Proof). 2,500 bottles

Pritchard's Tennessee Whiskey (89) n22 t22.5 f22 b22.5 An enjoyable, solid and simplistic Tennessee which has a seemingly youthful air. Firm, with a good hickory-led swagger. 40%

Uncle Nearest 1820 Premium Whiskey Aged 11 Years Nearest Green Single Barrel barrel no. US-1 (94.5) n23 t24 f23.5 b24 A real roller coaster of a ride. Let's get back on again... 57.6%

Uncle Nearest 1820 Premium Whiskey Aged 11 Years Nearest Green Single Barrel barrel no. US-2 (92.5) n23 t23 f23 b23.5 Have to applaud the delicate nature of this whiskey and its superior layering. Just too easy to enjoy. 55.1% (110.2 proof). 146 bottles.

Uncle Nearest 1856 Premium Whiskey (89.5) n22 t22.5 f22.5 b22.5 No bells and whistles. Just a slow radiating of gentle sugar and tannin tones. Easy sipping. 50% (100 proof).

Uncle Nearest 1856 Premium Whiskey bott code: 192451651 (91.5) n23 t23 f22.5 b23 A busier incarnation than the last bottling of 1856 I encountered. Thoroughly enjoyable. 50% .

Uncle Nearest 1884 Small Batch Whiskey bott code: 10/29/20191007 (90.5) n22.5 t22 f23 b23 Perhaps noticeable for its significant lack of corn oils. Delicate and leans towards a hickory persona. A covertly complex and delightful Tennessee. 46.5% (93 proof).

GEORGE DICKEL

George Dickel Aged 17 Years bott code: L6154K1001 db (94) n24 t24 22.5 b23.5 The oldest George Dickel I have ever encountered has held its own well over the years. A defiant crispness to the piece makes for memorable drinking, though it is the accommodating and comfortable nose which wins the greatest plaudits... 43.5% (87 proof).

George Dickel Barrel Select (90.5) n21 t23 f23.5 b23 The limited nose makes the heart sink. What happens once it hits the palate is another story entirely. Wonderful! 43%

George Dickel Distillery Reserve Collection 17 Year Old (91.5) n23.5 t23.5 f21.5 b23 Outside of a warehouse, I'm not sure I've encountered a Tennessee whiskey of this antiquity before. I remember one I tasted some while back, possibly about a year older or two older than this, was black and like tasting eucalyptus concentrate. This is the opposite, showing extraordinary restraint for its age, an almost feminine charm. 43.5%

George Dickel No. 12 bott code: L7034R60011402 db (89) n21.5 t23.5 f22 b22 In a way, a classic GD where you feel there is much more still in the tank... 45% (90 proof).

JACK DANIEL

Jack Daniel's 120th Anniversary of the White Rabbit Saloon (91) n22.5 t23.5 f22 b23 On its best-behaved form. After the delivery, the oils are down a little, so not the usual bombastic offering from JD. Nonetheless, this is pure class and the clever use of sugars simply make you drool... 43%. Brown-Forman.

Jack Daniel's Gentleman Jack bott code: 141734518B db (90.5) n22.5 t22.5 f22.5 b23 A Jack that can vary slightly in style. A couple of months back I included one in a tasting which was much fuller bodied and dripping in maple syrup. This one is infinitely more laid back. 40% (80 proof).

Jack Daniel's Old No 7 Brand bott code: L214734202 (92) n22.5 t23 f23 b23.5 This is JD wearing its best bib and tucker: rarely have I seen it quite so well behaved. It is as though someone has got that doubler up and working properly, because this is a much cleaner whiskey than when I last tasted it a couple of years back: a kind of a halfway house between Gentleman Jack and the original Ol' No 7. Refined, elegant and pretty classy. 40%.

Jack Daniel's Master Distiller Series No 1 db (90.5) n24 t22 f22 b22.5 no mistaking the JD pedigree. Just a few telling extra degrees of fruit. 43%

Jack Daniel's Straight Rye Whiskey bott code: L184601033 db (87.5) n21.5 t23 f21.5 b21.5 For some reason the rye refuses to take pole position and is lost behind a series of pretty ordinary corn and oak-vanilla notes, though the cool mintiness is a classy touch. Pleasant and plodding without being in any way - well, except minty moments - exciting or stimulating...as a good rye should always be! 45% (90 proof).

Jack Daniel's Tennessee Straight Rye bott code 208821212 db (86.5) n22.5 t22 f21 b21 I dunno! They've had so long to get their rye right by now, but still, after all these years, it remains off kilter and refuses to sing true. The nose has improved for sure, which had me hoping for the best as the grain certainly makes its mark there. But it doesn't quite lead on as hoped, so all is a bit murky and untidy still. 45% (90 proof)

Corn Whiskey

Obtainium Kentucky Corn Whiskey db (92.5) n23 t23.5 f23 b23 Now that's pretty good corn whiskey! Beautifully made and matured. 63.1% (126.2 proof).

Straight Rye

Big Moustache Rye bott 7/22/2022 (87.5) n21 t22.5 f22 b22 Talk about a clipped moustache...! This is such a strange rye – mainly because the usual characteristics for the grain are so limited here. Yet this is perfectly pleasant whisky and would have scored more had I not been judging it as a rye. A little of the grain's fingerprint is noticeable on the nose, though mainly it is the oak doing the talking, plus a little ripe tomato. Big fat and chewy on delivery and it is here the rye has a brief, vaguely crisp fling. But it is quite content to hide behind a curtain of vanilla. Salivating in all the right places. 45% (90 proof) ncf BBC Spirits

Buffalo Trace Kosher Straight Rye bott code L23130 db (89.5) n23 a vague tobacco note mingles with a the much sturdier rye...; t23.5 altogether sharper and more focussed on is purpose than the nose. At times quite eye-watering. There is the odd eucalyptus note entering the fray, but an outbreak of intense vanilla soon puts an end to that. The spices rise...and continue rising. At its very best a sherry trifle note comes into play, the rye offering the fruit...; f21 just a little bitterness creeps into the mix. Unexpected. Struggles to keep the balance as it should be...; b22 a big rye, but not quite in the same league as the last bottling of this I encountered. Much more muffled and diffused, too, which was only outperformed by the Thomas Handy Rye...which happened to pick up my World Whisky of the Year for 2023. As attractive as this whiskey may be, this bottling is a long way off those heady expectations... 47% (94 proof)

Bulleit 95 Rye Frontier Whiskey bott ode: L9145R60011708 (86.5) n21.5 t23 f20.5 b21.5 An upgrade on the last bottling, but still that mysterious tobacco note issuing from an Indiana distillery which was once the byword for pristine, super-pure nosing and tasting rye. When the grain does burst through it is sharp, salivating and full of its old Demerara sugar crispness. Lots of chocolate to be had, too, even if there is a strange buzz to the finish. And if you are into tobacco, this Bulleit's got your name on it. 45% (90 proof).

Bulleit 95 Rye Frontier Whiskey Straight American Rye Mashbill: 95% rye bott code: L0346ZB001175651 (81) n21 t22 f19 b19 What on earth is this? Unrecognisable as a Bulleit rye. Tobacco on the nose and syrupy and disjointed on the finish – further weakened by a bitter tang - this is all over the place. Only the intense rye and honey on delivery lives up to expectation... and even that is all too brief. 45% (90 proof)

Colonel E. H. Taylor Straight Kentucky Rye Bottled In Bond bott code L21280 db (96) n24 such a hefty aroma with age pecking away at the grain from every angle. The unique fruity edge of the rye combines with the oak to generate a delicate clove and eucalyptus groundswell, under which the rye itself dazzles with a Demerara-sweet crispness; t24.5 what a delivery....! Perfection! The vanillas off the oak are the perfect buffer for the eye-watering, teeth-cracking rye. Backed up immediately by a ulmo honey and molten Demerara sugar sub-plot the salivation levels are at maximum despite the heartier, toastier tannins; f23.5 for the first time the rye is subdued by the oak, where hickory and cocoa dominate; b24 if it was possible to award 100 out of 10 for mouthfeel alone, then this rye'd be there. Ditto grain delivery on both nose and palate. Faultless. The clove on the nose occasionally forewarns of overexuberance of tannin late on. Not here, though. That said, the oak plays a big enough role to momentarily silence the rye itself, which is some achievement. But it does so without resorting to over violence on the palate or the dark arts of excessive toastiness. Magnificent whiskey of the most complex and satisfying kind. Or, as they say on the label: "of topmost class"..... 50% (100 proof)

Colonel E. H. Taylor Straight Kentucky Rye Bottled In Bond bott code L22326 db (94) n23.5 very quiet interplay between rolling toffee and firmer clean rye. The grain, however, is barely fighting its corner...; t24 the rye has a far bigger say on delivery, teaming up with the spices to make further impact. The chocolate-raisin middle as not expected...; f23 the lighter oils at this point allows a layering of the rye, though it is far more whispered than proudly sung. At least the late cocoa is a constant...; b23.5 quite fascinating and an incredibly rare insight into comparing this rare rye from two bottlings just over a year apart... The result is two very different styles. These are more cousins than brothers and this rye is very much at the other end of the spectrum to the ultra-intense L21280 bottling. Both things of beauty in their own ways, this bottling is using far less tannin so offers an unexpected lightness which the rye grain is utilising for its own ends, but not enough to match the all-round depth and complexity of the above bottling.... 50% (100 proof)

Elijah Craig Kentucky Straight Rye Whiskey first to char oak barrels, bott code: A35292135 db **(94.5) n23 t24 f23.5 b24** Superbly made. And as relaxed yet beautifully busy as ol' Earl Scruggs on his banjo. And just as note perfect... 47% (94 proof).

Ezra Brooks Kentucky Straight Rye Whiskey bott code: A129171852 **(91.5) n23 t23.5 f22 b23** Pretty classic rye of the old school. Go back 25 years, pick a rye up off the shelf...and here you go! 45% (90 proof).

Frankfort Bourbon Society Knob Creek Single Barrel Select Rye Barrel No 7540 bott Fall 2018 **(88.5) n22 t23 f21.5 b22** One of the spicier rye whiskeys you are likely to encounter. Pleasant, but the inert nature of the vanilla and the rapid loss of sugars make this a bit of an also ran in Knob Creek terms. 57.5% (115 proof).

High Plains Rye db **(90) n22.5 t22.5 f22 b23.** The creator of this rye, Jim Rutledge, and I go back nearly 30 years and learned our blending from the same school. When at Four Roses Jim was determined to move it away from its ultra-clean, safe and non-committal style towards something with far more weight, substance and complexity – and not simply from cask choice alone. And he did, quite frankly, a brilliant job there, taking the distillery into a different stratum. This spirit isn't of the same quality and on nose and delivery I feared the worst. 48.5%

Highspire Whiskey 100% Rye Grain Aged 4 Months oak, finished with oak staves, batch no 3 **(73.5) n18.5 t19 f18 b18** Youthful and a rather feinty. Both the rye and tannin are there in spades, but with little integration; some hefty flavours, especially on the oak side which somehow over-dominates the grain. An interesting young whiskey, but the oak seems forced and at no times forms an attractive allegiance with the rye. I think they need to go a little gentler on this one. 40% (80 proof). Distilled by Kindred Distilled Spirits Crestwood, Ky.

High West Whiskey Double Rye! batch no. 20B11 **(86) n21 t22.5 f21 b21.5** Mouth filling and chewy, the rye grain doesn't really get into its stride until we are on the second or third major flavour wave, when the bristling fluty, fruitiness catches hold. The fact there is a little tobacco on the nose and distinct oily earthiness on the finish suggests that one of the ryes used came from an undistinguished cut. A pity, as it was obvious there was massive potential otherwise. 46% (92 proof). nc ncf. A blend of straight rye whiskies.

High West Whiskey Rendezvous Rye batch no. 19K12 **(93.5) n23.5 t23.5 f23 b23.5** One of those ryes where you find yourself slapping the back of your head to overcome the eye-watering sharpness of the grain. 46% (92 proof). nc ncf. A blend of straight rye whiskies.

J Mattingly House Money Small Batch Rye Whiskey Aged 4 Years (96) n23.5 t24 f24.5 b24 If you see the magic words "Distilled in Indiana" attached to any rye whiskey, then you know there is a high possibility that you are in for something world class. Only Lawrenceburg Indiana produces a rye that can give Buffalo Trace a run for its money...and here you can see exactly why. The grain itself takes first, second and third position on both nose and delivery before the softer and beautifully balancing chocolate mousse accepts a humble but vital position of second in command. The spices are far more restrained than most ryes, but still make a telling contribution as they represent their tannins in their splendidly refined and elegant pose. Added to this, there is a concentrated rye Demerara sugar crispness to the very end which melds with unbelievable finesse with the mocha. Fantastic rye of the very highest calibre: unquestionably the finest made anywhere in the world outside Kentucky. 57% (114 proof) distilled in Indiana.

J Mattingly Racing Rye Small Batch Straight Rye Whiskey (79) n20.5 t21.5 f18 b19 An odd rye, this. The grain itself retains a pristine quality jutting out from all around it. However, there is a strange, hard-to-define murkiness which is at odds with the grain itself. The finish spins off the track and burns...literally. 57% (114 proof)

James E. Pepper 1776 Straight Rye Whiskey (88.5) n22 t22.5 f21.5 b22.5 Not technically quite on the ball, but the intensity of the rye deserves a standing ovation. 50% (100 proof). ncf

James E. Pepper 1776 Straight Rye Whiskey Barrel Proof (87.5) n22 t22 f21.5 b22 On the nose, delivery and finish there is evidence of a wider than normal cut here, giving the whisky a slightly murky feel. Great rye contribution and spices. But the oils are a bit OTT. 57.8% (115.6 proof). ncf

Jim Beam Rye Pre-Prohibition Style Kentucky Straight Rye bott code: 411560842 db **(95) n23.5 t24 f23.5 b24** Jim Beam Rye back to - and even beyond - its old glory. Just stupendous! Wow! 45% (90 proof)

Kentucky Owl Aged 10 Years Kentucky Straight Rye bott Nov 18 **(90.5) n22.5 t23.5 f21.5 b23** Unlike their pretty poor bourbon offering, this rye is more Owl than Owl! 57% (114 proof).

◇ **Knaplund Rye Whiskey Atlantic Aged 6 Years** batch 01/23 **(95) n23** Knaplund usually equates to super-softness, but when nosed cool, this rye has teeth: spicey sugars buried into chocolate; **t24.5** oh...my.....word! One of the great flavour arrivals of the 2023 Whisky Bible. I cannot believe what I am tasting here: Demerara sugar, Lubec marzipan and heather honey joining forces to form a succulent mix which slowly transforms into a light chocolatey Swiss Roll. What really knocks you out is the softness and measured building of the flavour profile, seemingly atom by atom,...as though everything is acted out on your tastebuds in slow motion; **f23.5** the saltiness breaks through here as the tannins become more assertive – in their own powder-puff way – infusing a delicate liquorice tone to the proud and persistent rye...; **b24** thank God not all whiskies are as complex and time-consuming to negotiate, understand and appreciate as the Knaplunds, especially this one. It has taken me over an hour to get anywhere near mastering this one. And if all whiskies were this complex, the Whisky Bible would never be completed.... As for the whiskey itself....the delivery is toying with perfection....both in texture and flavour. 50%

Knob Creek Cask Strength warehouse A, barreled 2009, 2018 release, bott code: L8106CLA **(96.5) n24 t24 f24 b24.5** Knob Creek rye has always been excellent, but having tasted Jim Beam's rye output for some 40 years I always thought it delivered within itself. Now this one is much closer to what I had been expecting. Brilliant! And the first rye to give the great rye of Buffalo Trace a serious run for their money. Indeed; this is going for a head to head... 59.8% (1196 proof).

Knob Creek Cask Strength Rye db **(95) n24 t24 f3.5 b23.5** Another unforgettable rye from Knob Creek, not least for the amount of hairs you'll find on your chest the next day. This is uncompromising in every sense of the word, but scores a little lower than last year's award winner as the tannin just seems a little tighter and less willing to give the grain full scope. The delivery, though...just rye-t on...!!! 63.1% (126.2 proof).

Knob Creek Rye Single Barrel Select barrel no. 7809 **(95.5) n23.5 t24 f23.5 b24.5** A cleverly selected bottle by Kelly May, who appears to have eschewed the usual pile-driver Knob Creek style for a nuanced and satisfying rye where both the barrel and grain appear to have an equal say. Stunning stuff! Just hope you can get to their bar before this little classic runs out! Certainly one of my favourite ryes for 2019 and unquestionably one of the most enigmatic... 57.5% (115 proof). *Selected by Kelly May of Bourbon on Main, Frankfort, Ky. sc.*

Knob Creek Straight Rye Whiskey (92.5) n23.5 t23.5 f22.5 b23 a slightly more genteel rye than I expected, if you compare standard Knob Creek to their usual bourbon. 50% (100 proof).

Knob Creek Straight Rye Whiskey batch L5349CLA **(92.5) n23.5 t23.5 f22.5 b23** Curious: just checked: I scored a batch from last year at 92.5 also. Can't say this isn't consistent quality...! 50%

Michter's 10 Years Old Single Barrel Kentucky Straight Rye barrel no. 19F965, bott code: A19156965 **(96) n24.5 t24 f23.5 b24** Interesting how the rye itself takes a back seat and intervenes only when the chocolate richness of the oak becomes slightly too dominant. Doesn't possess the obvious rye-rich traits of their barrel 19H1321, but the whole works far, far better. 46.4% (92.8 proof). sc.

Michter's 10 Years Old Single Barrel Kentucky Straight Rye barrel no. 19H1321, bott code: A192341321 **(93.5) n24 t23.5 f22.5 b23.5** Radiates great age. Wears its vintage well and with great pride. 46.4% (92.8 proof). sc.

⬧ **Michter's Single Barrel Kentucky Straight Rye** barrel no. 2312137 db **(93.5) n23** a clean mingling of apples, Demerara sugar and intense rye; **t23.5** the mouth is cleansed by a salivating wash of sugar-rich rye. A secondary wave of vanilla makes maters a little les vivid; **f23** apple pie... with the uncooked cooking apple...; **b24** a very precise, fruity rye with more than a little apple in its make up. Refreshing. 42.4%

Michter's US*1 Single Barrel Strength Kentucky Straight Rye charred white oak barrel, barrel no: L21B478, db, **(95.5) n24 t24 f23.5 b24** Some rye whiskey seems to bask in a Demerara crispness. Michter's appear to prefer a black cherry countenance. And there are no complaints here, not least because we are up there with the truly great rye whiskeys. 55.6% (111.2% Proof) sc

Nashville Barrel Company Straight Rye Texas Cask Strength db **(90.5) n22** two-toned with, on one hand, intense though not overly clean rye. The other just a heady tobacco note; **t23.5** enormous. The rye seems to grow in the mouth, both in specific grain intensity and eye-watering sharpness. Light molasses mingle with a creamy mocha, too; **f22** a tad untidy and oily, though rye waves continue to roll alongside the spices...; **b23** as the scores tell, this is bursting with rich and delicious rye-ness. But it has been a while since I've seen that famous old Indiana sparkle. Heavy and at times cumbersome. 58.37% (116.74 proof) distilled in Indiana

New Riff Backsetter Rye Bottled in Bond db **(86) n21 t22.5 f21 b21.5** Well, that was an experience! The nose works you hard to find the rye. The flavours are flowing and full on. But, again, in a very idiosyncratic style. Pleasant enough, but not exactly what I look for in a classic rye style. Still, the acacia honey middle works well with the oaky vanillas. But not a patch on New Riff's straight rye. 50% (100 proof). ncf.

New Riff Balboa Rye Whiskey Bottled in Bond dist Jun 14, bott Nov 19 db **(94) n24 t23.5 f23 b23.5** A good old-fashioned 4-year-old rye very much in the Kentucky tradition. Quite beautifully distilled – as clean and technically excellent as any outside the Kentucky and Indiana big boys.

One of those stunners that is all about crisp grain and molten Demerara. Lip-smacking and enough sweetness and chocolate to make up for the late oils on the finale. *50% (100 proof). ncf.*

<> **Old Pepper Straight Rye Bottled In Bond** batch S2019 db **(92.5) n22** slightly musty as the vanilla-led oak takes a little bit of polish off the otherwise healthy rye nip; **t23.5** takes its time getting its feet under the table but slowly begins concocting an understatedly rich story. The grain begins falteringly, but wave after wave of ever clearer rye brings it into meaningful discourse with the vanilla and liquorice-led oak; **f23.5** just as with the case of the bourbon a chocolate/mocha finale begins to take delicious shape, though with less oil to spread the intensity around. The spices are slower off their marks and finally let loose towards the end of the middle and especially at the start of the finish; **b23.5** a fascinating rye uncannily very much in the style of Wild Turkey's from 25-30 years ago. *50% (100 proof)*

<> **Pikesville 110 Proof Straight Rye Aged At Least 6 Years** bott code A32721213 db **(95) n24.5** this is the definition of clean, ultra-crisp rye. The aroma ranges from Demerara sugars through to sweetened eucalyptus...; **t24** so fresh...so clean...confident...so layered.... The delivery is the kind of experience rye lovers pray for. Especially with the texture being perfectly weighted between chewy and refreshing...; **f23** the ryes move towards a more acacia honey mode... but the sweetness also highlight a nagging bitterness...; **b23.5** it's been a few years since I last encountered this and delighted to report that it remains one of the greatest whiskey experiences on the planet. Only a slight bitterness off the oak towards the very finish prevents this from a major Whisky Bible 2024 award. But still a rye of extraordinary excellence. And if there was an award just for the most salivating delivery of any whiskey, then this would win hands down... *55%*

Rebel Yell Small Batch Rye Aged 24 Months bott code: A075181421 **(83.5) n21.5 t21.5 f21.5 b19** Normally ryes coming out of Indiana score highly, as they should because with Buffalo Trace the output from there represents, on their day, the best rye in the world. However, this is a classic example of when a whiskey is undercooked; it is way too young in that the grain and tannin are barely on speaking terms. Negligible balance, though the light liquorice note early on in delivery and late spices do salvage something. *45% (90 proof).*

Redemption Riverboat Rye (78) n19 t21 f19 b19. Dry, weirdly off key and oily – and holed below the water line. *40%*

Redemption Rye (85.5) n22 t22.5 f20 b21. The tobacco nose is a bit of a poser: how did that get there? Or the spearmint, which helps as you try to chew things over in your mind. The big rye wave on delivery is supported by mixed dark sugars yet something ashy about the finish. *46%*

Redemption Rye Aged No Less Than 2 Years batch no. 259, bott code: L9169607:27 **(86.5) n22 t23 f20 b21.5** Bright, brittle rye but always with a feintiness lurking in the wings. The delivery, though, is rye at its most beautifully intense and pure. *46% (92 proof).*

Redwood Empire Emerald Giant Rye Whiskey Aged at least 3 Years bott code: L19 1490 **(86) n22 t21.5 f21 b21.5** While the grain may be stark, the tobacco note tends to knock this whiskey sygogglin, as the moonshiners of the south Appalachians might say. Never seems to be on an even keel, thought the odd sharp note is more than attractive. *45%.*

<> **Russell's Reserve Kentucky Straight Rye Single Barrel** bott code 06/21 db **(92.5) n23.5** spicy, waxy light honey with the rye grain elbowing in almost as a sharp reminder of purpose; **t23.5** lashing of vanilla and light oils. Ulmo honey gives way to those sharp, brittle rye grains. A little Demerara adds to the overall juiciness; **f22.5** warming and brittle to the end despite the vanilla carpeting; **b23** quite a vivid rye which never seems to settle into a happy rhythm. Tart and juicy at varying points, this is not a whiskey you settle down with for a relaxing experience. *52% ncf*

Sagamore Spirit Straight Rye Whiskey batch no. 7C **(90.5) n23.5 t23 f21.5 b22.5** Very attractive rye, but seems underpowered and slightly lacking in the oils required for the expected rich finish. *41.5% (83 proof).*

Sagamore Spirit Straight Rye Whiskey Barrel Select Aged 6 Years barrel no. 2, floor 3, rack 2, new charred oak barrels **(94.5) n23.5 t24 f23 b23** When top form Indiana rye is at work, what's not to like...? Oh, and one of those rare whiskies at its best when at ambient room temperature than slightly warmed. *55% (110 proof). sc. Bottled for Ryeday 13.*

Sagamore Spirit Straight Rye Whiskey Cask Strength batch no. 4A **(95) n24 t24 f23.5 b23.5** Wow! What a way to start another Whisky Bible tasting day...!!! *56.1% (112.2 proof).*

Sagamore Spirit Straight Rye Whiskey Double Oak batch no. 2C **(91) n24 t23 f21.5 b22.5** Beautiful in part but a little too intense with the oak late on. *48.3% (96.6 proof).*

Sagamore Spirit Straight Rye Whiskey Double Oak batch no. 4A, new charred oak barrels **(95) n23 t24 f24 b24** It may sound strange but there is a distinctive bourbon type feel to the rye, perhaps from the ratio of tannin to grain. A serious mouthful just laden with flavours. Superb. *48.3% (96.6 proof).*

Sazerac Rye bott code: L22159011321B db **(95) n24 t24 f23 b24** as a standard rye, Sazerac ploughed a lone furrow. Until now. As excellent as this rye remains, it has been eclipsed by its

Kentucky stablemate BT Kosher Rye, which is, quite simply, more fully flavoured. Hard to believe, I know. But there it is... 45% (90 proof)

Sazerac 18 Years Old bott Summer 2020 db (89.5) n22.5 t23.5 f21 b22.5 Right. Where do I start? A lovely whiskey with so many characteristics to fully enjoy. But... Both Elmer T Lee and I had a little say in how this whiskey was shaped at its conception. And this wasn't it: this is not what we signed off on. There is dullness here which is in stark contrast to the Sazerac which has been acknowledged across the globe as the blueprint for sensational rye. Many companies would die for a whisky this tasty. But.... 45% (90 proof).

Sazerac 18 Years Old Bottled Summer 2021 db (96.5) n24 t24 f24 b24.5 age has never been more apparent on a Sazerac Rye than this bottling. The tannins even have the effrontery to at times outrank the rye itself: unheard of. But that noble grain doesn't go down without a fight and it elegantly sweeps back around the palate restoring a cut-glass quality as soon as it is able. What class...! 45% (90 proof)

◈ **Sazerac 18 Years Old Fall 2022** db (96.5) n25 possibly the most complete Sazerac 18 nose for four or five years. The intense oak and grain are on totally equal footing with a minty mocha note as the buffer between the two. The nose is thick and singular and the more you home in on the rye, the broader becomes the fruity spectrum, especially the blood orange end of it. Look further and a lighter mango sweetness chimes with the Demerara sugars. Meanwhile the oak offers not just a subtle beat of spice but a deeper, anchoring grumble. Such is the weight, layering, subtlety and complexity it is truly the perfect straight rye nose; t24 while the oak and grain are neck and neck on the nose, the tannins are first and second to show on delivery. Indeed, compared to the nose it appears to have a lumbering gait with the tannins keeping the more angular notes of the rye in check for a while, though they break through at about the eighth or ninth attempt: that's when the juices start flowing. That is the prelude to the mocha, so handsomely played on the nose, arriving in equally impressive fashion on the palate. The spice buzz is so beautifully engineered, the secondary vanillas soothing and a soft counter to the harder rye...; f23.5 just a little shorter than some Sazerac 18s, and a tad more bitter, too. That's the oak at work, mainly, but also a revert to the blood orange – in this case orange peel – that gave a sweeter performance on the nose. Still the complexity refuses to let up, though the burnt sugars do dominate late on; b24 it is quite likely that nosing this for five or ten minutes and follow that up by taking a mouthful of the Thomas Handy Sazerac 64.45% will offer you one of the greatest olfactory experiences of your life. A truly faultless aroma though for once the experience on the palate doesn't quite live up to it. But then, how do you live up to perfection? 45% (90 proof)

◈ **Smooth Ambler Contraction Rye A Blend of Straight Rye Whiskies** batch no 64 (87.5) n22 t23 f21 b21.5 It was doing ok until the off-key finale kicked in. A quirky and haphazard rye with no apparent gameplan or roadmap. But enough crucial moments of joy, especially with its curiously minty intervals, to make it worth investigating. 52.5% (105 proof) ncf distilled in West Virginia, Tennessee and Indiana

◈ **Smooth Ambler Single Barrel Old Scout Straight Rye Aged 6 Years** barrel no 16930 (91.5) n22 a little unbalanced here with the barrel going through a phase where the more striking rye and the tannins have come to a bit of an impasse. It is the sharper rye notes, though muffled, which just about dominate; t24 wow! Does this whiskey correct itself once on the palate, though! Molten muscovado sugars sip into every crevice. This is in danger of becoming overly sweet, but the tannins come to the rescue thanks to a series of spice and vanilla cream moments. However, it is concentrated rye which concentrates the mind...and waters the eyes...; f22.5 the spices have their say and are well silhouetted against the lingering sugars; b23 a day or two back I made a liquid to keep my hummingbirds at my old Kentucky home happy, melting a glass of sugar into four glasses of warm water. The friendly sweetness on delivery for some reason reminded me of that hummingbird nectar, though they won't be lucky enough to also enjoy those salient spices and eye-watering rye tones... 58.9% distilled in Indiana

Thomas H. Handy Sazerac db (97) n24.5 t24.5 f24 b24 I am often asked by those unable to track down either Sazerac or, at best, just one: "what is the difference between these two whiskeys?" The grains are jagged and crisp...shards of rye that cut deep. A light floral edge accompanies the vivid fruit. This is sharp and delectable. Rye with a three dimensional firmness; one of the deliveries of the year. As near as damn it getting a 25 for its intensity and elan. Rich chocolate, black cherry... and yet more and more insistent, relentless, rye...;62.85% (125.7 proof).

Thomas H. Handy Sazerac Straight Rye (97.5) n24 t24.5 f24.5 b24.5 This was World Whisky of the Year last year and anyone buying this on the strength of that will not be disappointed. Huge whiskey with not even the glimmer of a hint of an off note. Magnificent: an honour to taste and rye smiles all round... 66.2%. ncf.

Thomas H. Handy Sazerac Straight Rye (95.5) n24 t24 f23.5 b24 Perhaps because this has become something of a softie, without all those usual jagged and crisp rye notes, it doesn't quite hit the spot with quite the same delicious drama. Still a beauty, though. 64.6%

Thomas H. Handy Sazerac db (97) n24 t24.5 f24 b24.5 Rye whiskey par excellence. How can one grain do so much to the taste buds? As bewildering as it is beautiful. 64.4% (128.8 proof).

Thomas H. Handy Sazerac db (97.5) n24.5 t24.5 f24 b24.5 Truly breathtaking! What a joy! What a rye! What a winner...!!! 64.5% (129 proof).

Thomas Handy Sazerac Rye db (97.5) n24 t25 f24 b24.5 intense. In igloos. In houses. In bars. It doesn't matter where you drink this: you are in for one hell of a treat. And journey. Enormous whiskey and glorious rye in its most naked form. 64.75% (129.5 proof)

⬧ **Thomas H Handy Sazarac** bott code db (97) n24 not for the first time when it comes to Handy, one takes a sniff of this and then simply marvels at the scope and richness this grain, when distilled to perfection, brings. The Sazerac 18 this year has the wider range so far as aroma is concerned. But the Handy here appears to be concentrating on purity and intensity on the rye grain itself, whipping it into such a tight corridor of intensity that it appears to burn laser-like through the oak. And the tannins are hardly playing games with a marvellous sweetened eucalyptus tone emphasising some serious aging; t25 it is hard to write when you are mentally speechless. Such is the sheer perfection of this delivery it takes a little while to gather your thoughts and then then study an action replay on the palate to try and understand what you have just tasted and just why it impacted so spectacularly all other thought processes were lost for a while. Firstly, it has to be the clarity of the estery rye, then followed by the continuous multiplication of its, literally, pure intensity: layer, after layer after layer....; f24 long, with the oak sufficiently confident now to add some spices into the mix. Remarkably, the mix of spice and rye-rich remnants are enough to keep the salivation levels high even this very late on. Usually, coffee comes into the equation and of you are patient, it does so here...though a little later than usual. Less the usual Blue Mountain but here a moderately high roast Java; b24 for the second year running Thomas Handy provides the most impressive delivery and follow through - indeed, the tastiest delivery - of any whiskey on the planet. Professionally, I spit every single mouthful of whiskey I taste. After this delivery, though I spat as usual, it was not an easy thing to do: it seemed like an act against nature. 64.45% (130.9 proof)

⬧ **Three Chord Amplify Rye** batch no. 11 (87) n21 t23 f21 b22 If this rye was all about the delivery there'd be no problem: the intensity and denseness of the grain is beyond reproach. But the nose suggests we might be in for a stormy finish, and so it proves. One of the distillery's cuts wasn't perhaps where it should have been. The oils at the end are furry, off key, tangy and take no prisoners. A bipolar whiskey. 47.5% (95 proof) distilled in Kentucky and Indiana

Van Winkle Family Reserve Rye 13 Years Old batch Z2221 (90) n22.5 t23.5 f22 b22 A hard-as-nails, uncompromising rye with a slightly tangy finale. A whiskey to break your teeth on... 47.8% (95.6 proof)

Van Winkle Family Reserve Kentucky Straight Rye 13 Years Old No. 99A bott code: L180400107:23N db (96) n24.5 t24 f23.5 b24 Quite simply, textbook rye whiskey... 47.8%

Wild Turkey Master's Keep Cornerstone Aged a Minimum of 9 Years batch no. 21587, bott code: LLJHE301949 db (96) n23.5 t24 f24 b24.5 Easily the most profound rye whiskey I have ever seen carrying the Wild Turkey name. Easy for the chocolate off the oak to overwhelm the rye and the rye to also for an imbalance with the chocolate. Instead, they support each other magnificently. 54.5% (109 proof).

⬧ **Wild Turkey Rare Breed Barrel Proof Rye** bott code LL/JJ011155 db (95) n23 the grains shine brightly and confidently and precisely burn through the house waxy honey trademark sweetness; t24 faultless delivery with both the rye an heather honey joined in a mouth-watering embrace and simply flying off the roof with full flavours at full attention. The secondary laying of ulmo honey is perfect; f24 the spices had begun quietly earlier on. Now they are in control, but ensuring a waxy rye note still makes its brittle mark. The late chocolate mousse is a magnificent bonus; b24 this is rye whiskey of the very highest quality where the grains have been polished in honey and the spices constantly peppering away for balance. Just a single pour of this is simply not an option... 56.1%

Wild Turkey Rye bott code: 194712P22:59 db (91.5) n23 t23 f22.5 b23 A perfectly graceful, well-made rye. But at this strength a bit like Rolls Royce powered by a lawnmower engine. 40.5% (81 proof).

Wild Turkey Rye 81 Proof bott code: LL/GE250429:59 db (92.5) n23.5 t23 f22.5 b23.5 A greatly improved rye than in recent years, here really displaying the grain to excellent effect. The finish has a slight tang, but, that apart, spends its time moulding the mint to the sugars. One characterful whiskey... 40.5% (81 proof).

Wild Turkey 101 Kentucky Straight Rye bott code: LL/GH130429 db (95.5) n23.5 t24 f23.5 b24.5 Simply magnificent. The kind of whiskey, when you spot in the bar, it is almost impossible not to order. 50.5% (101 proof)

Wild Turkey 101 Kentucky Straight Rye db (92) n22.5 t23.5 f23 b23 looks as though 101 suits WTs rye as well as their bourbon. Delicious! 50.5% (101 proof)

Woodford Reserve Master's Collection New Cask Rye ref: 0f 21960db **(94) n23 t23.5 f24 b23.5** a majestically celebrated rye 46.2% (92.4 proof)

⟐ **Wilderness Trail Small Batch Rye Bottled In Bond** batch no 18E23A db **(92.5) n23** fruity, diced fresh apple; **t23** the nose didn't suggest there would be this overall fatness to the mouth feel. The corn has a lot to say here and talks up the vanillas from the oak as effectively as it can. It means the poor old rye can't get a word in edgeways...; **f23** the spices, gagged until now, erupt; **b23.5** this is a such an enjoyable whiskey. But, as a rye, it is a little underwhelming as the grains aren't broadcasting as you might come to expect. Somewhat enigmatic... 50% (100 proof)

⟐ **Wilderness Trail Small Batch Rye Bottled In Bond Aged 7 Years** batch no 27C23A db **(96.5) n24** good age here with a light eucalyptus note amalgamating with the sturdier sugars. The spices mean business and pulse with warm intent; **t24** that wasn't the delivery I was expecting: the nose shewed much wrinkly skin, but the first notes to hit the palate were infinitely more alert and youthful. However, by the time we get to the sixth or seventh flavour waves, the rye has again taken on a far more aged persona with cloves hankering down with the more intense, vaguely spiced grain; **f24** the layering on the finish is exemplary. And virtually every avenue leads to statements of grand age – far older than its seven years - and rye grain at its most complex and complete. The chocolate mousse (with a rich rye addition) is almost the perfect sign off...; **b24.5** this is one of those whiskeys which if you didn't take time and care you could just overlook as being a pretty decent offering. However, give it the Murray Method plus an hour of your time and you will unearth one of the great rye whiskies of 2023. A masterpiece of a rye which will be going head-to-head with Buffalo Trace's finest to see who has produced the rye of the year. It will be close... 50% (100 proof)

⟐ **Wilderness Trail Single Barrel Cask Strength Rye Aged 4 Years 8 Months** barrel no 751783 db **(96) n24** anyone who doesn't get excited about the marriage between the pulsating grain and the more delicate heather honey shouldn't be reading this book. Indeed, they should stick to Cognac...; **t24** here we go again: the delivery is rye – crisp, salivating and tantalisingly alive with spices - on steroids and is quite sublime. The light coating of corn oil is balm...rich; **f24** textbook rye finale with the grain still pulsating its crisp, green message, the dignified and brittle to the very last...and the pulsing spices now joined with light mocha...; **b24** if anyone is studying the making of rye and needs some blueprints, just scurry off to Buffalo Trace and Wilderness Trail and grasp some top-ranking examples. This barrel will be among them. Sublime. 59% (118 proof)

Straight Wheat Whiskey

Bernheim Original Kentucky Straight Wheat Whiskey db **(92) n22.5 t23 f23.5 b23.5** as wheat whiskey so often can, just gets better and better. Not as spicy as some previous bottlings, just still lost none of its allure. 45% (90 proof)

American Microdistilleries
Alabama
JOHN EMERALD DISTILLING COMPANY Opelika, Alabama.

John's Alabama Single Malt Aged Less Than 4 Years batch no. 103 db **(89) n22.5 t22.5 f22 b22** A little extra thrust from the delicate smoke makes a huge difference. 43%.

Alaska
ALASKA DISTILLERY Wasilla, Alaska.

Alaska Proof Bourbon db **(86) n22 t22.5 f20 b21.5**. It must be Alaska and the lack of pollution or something. But how do these guys make their whiskey quite so clean....? For a rugged, wild land, it appears to concentrate on producing a bourbon which is borderline ethereal and all about sugary subtlety. The downside is that such lightness allows any weakness in the wood or distillation to be flagged up, though with nobody saluting. 40% (80 proof)

Arizona
CANYON DIABLO DISTILLERY, Flagstaff, Arizona

⟐ **John Shaw Single Malt Whisky Mesquite Smoked Whisky Aged At Least 2 Years** db **(89) n21.5** the odd feint doing the rounds, but the mesquite is an interesting distraction; **t22.5** now that is impressive – and after the nose, surprisingly so. The malt really does have a voice, which is deep and purposeful. The barley sugar notes are intense and infuse an impressive degree of sugar, The mesquite hasn't yet really made its mark...; **f22** ...though it has now. And some...! The spices offer a lovely hot and sweet number; the feints stir up the oils but again the mesquite ruthlessly deals with it...; **b23** in some 35 years writing about whisky, I'd like to congratulate the people of Canyon Diablo for coming up with the best rear label story I have ever read on any whisky bottle. Brilliantly and concisely written, it gives no insight into the John Shaw brand, in as to why it is a single malt and not bourbon and why it is mesquite smoked: none whatsoever. Instead, you read enthralled, barely waiting to get some of the whisky inside you. Perhaps for the first time in the 20 years I have been writing this book I shall chance my arm with the copyright laws and treat you to the back label in its entirety: "John Shaw & partners entered a saloon, ordered a whisky, drew their guns, robbed a poker game & escaped without drinking their shots. The sheriff pursued them to Canyon Diablo & in a shootout Shaw met his demise. Later, as the saloon patrons learned of the tale & untouched whisky, several headed to Canyon Diablo. There they dug up his stiff corpse & indulged him his last whisky, pouring it down the dead man's throat." If the whisky was as good as those perfect prose, we'd be celebrating World Whisky if the Year. However, we'll have to satisfy ourselves with this lightly flawed (a bit like John Shaw) but ultimately highly enjoyable offering, *45% (90 proof)*

GRAND CANYON DISTILLERY Williams, Arizona.

Grand Canyon Star Shine American Single Malt aged 18 months in new American oak barrels, db **(93) n23.5 t23.5 f23 b23** Forget about the maturation under the twinkling firmament. It is one particular star that has cosmic effect on this, and all of it for the good. This is heavenly whisky 46%

HAMILTON DISTILLERS Tuscon, Arizona.

Whiskey Del Bac Dorado Mesquite Smoked Single Malt batch MC16-1, bott 29 Feb 16 db **(94) n23 t23.5 f24b23.5** Dang! I'd sure like to see a bottle of this come sliding up to me next time I'm-a-drinkin' in the Crystal Palace Saloon Bar in Tombstone, yesiree! And I'd take my own dirty glass – one smoked with mesquite!! *45% (90 proof). ncf.*

SANTAN SPIRITS Chandler, Arizona.

Sacred Stave American Single Malt Whiskey finished in American red wine barrels db **(85.5) n20.5 t22.5 f21 b21.5** A bit of a wide cut here which has a few problems gelling with a fruit influence so far as harmony is concerned. But plenty to enjoy of the creamy crescendo just after delivery when the malt's sharper, more vivid qualities take on a purer form. *45% (90 proof).*

Arkansas
ROCK TOWN DISTILLERY Little Rock, Arkansas.

⬥ **Rock Town Single Barrel Arkansas Straight Bourbon Cask No 520 Aged 80 Months** db **(93) n23** the wheat comes through louder and clearer than the 9% mash bill content suggests. Freshly baked wholemeal bread...; **t23.5** beautifully distilled with a rich copper spine from which the spices, barley sugars and liquorice hang so elegantly; **f23** now the corn makes its mark – and how! - with some sublime ulmo honey and waxy oils. The spices at times are just wonderfully silly in their gung-ho attack. That fresh "Hovis" brown bread signature is still hanging on in there; **b23.5** for such a corn monster, the small grains play a bit of a David and Goliath act here. The wheat in particular pings about the palate and even has time for a brown bread cameo. Just lovely: a corn-ucopia of life-affirming flavours...! *60.4% (120.8 proof) mash bill 82% corn 9% malted barley 9% wheat*

⬥ **Rock Town Single Barrel Arkansas Straight Bourbon Cask No 912 Aged 41 Months** bott code db **(95) n23.5** this may have the intense rumblings of a still youngish bourbon but the level of peppery, wheat-rich interaction is off the scale. The tannins add only a degree of sweet vanilla as a counter measure. ...; **t24** a surprise pulse of sweetish marzipan before the inevitable explosion of souped-up spices. A lovely liquorice, molasses and mocha middle; **f23.5** there is now even a creaminess to that mocha, the corn oils deciding now to kick in. The spices may be rabid, but with this sweetened cocoa development at least they are muzzled; **b24** are they sure about that 9% wheat content? This flavour bomb is like old time Old Charter on steroids... If the spices were aligned to nuclear reactor, all kinds of red bulbs would be flashing and alarm bells ringing off the wall... *62.5% (125 proof) mash bill 82% corn 9% malted barley 9% wheat*

⬥ **Rock Town 12th Anniversary Arkansas Single Malt Finished in a Sherry Butt** aged 2 years in ex-bourbon and 34 month in sherry cask db **(86) n20.5 t23 f21.5 b21** The caramel malt lies up to its name as toffee is at work from the moment this whiskey enters the palate. Annoyingly, there is a slight butyric note on both the nose and later stages which costs a few points. But for its obvious faults, the level of intensity of the positive flavours is also quite remarkable, especially the spices. As for the sherry butt: no negative contribution on this occasion, but very little on the fruit front, either. *50% (100 proof) mash bill 85% pale malt 11% caramel malt 4% brown malt*

California
10TH STREET DISTILLERY San Jose, California.

10th Street American Whisky Single Malt bourbon casks db **(94) n24 t23.5 f22.5 b24** don't make the mistake of having a single glass of this. That will only allow you to set your sights. To understand this whisky, the Murray Method is essential as the layering this unearths is wonderful. One of the closest American whiskies to Scotch I have ever tasted. *46% (92 proof). ncf.*

ALCHEMY DISTILLERY Arcata, California.

◈ **Boldt Straight Corn Whiskey Aged 4 Years Bottled In Bond** batch 49 db **(89)** n21.5 slightly feinty for sure, but the senses are diverted by the liveliness of the tannins; t23 gorgeous mouth feel with those oils being absolutely on the money. The mid-ground is occupied by combating forces of caressing ulmo honey, and almost a Maryland cookie style chocolate and nut sweetness. The spices dig deep to lift this to a level it may not quite deserve...; f22 much drier as the oils reassert themselves. Enormous vanilla at the very death; b22.5 a dense corn whiskey defined in many ways by the overexuberance of the cut. But, that apart, it is also quite a flavour-revelling little number that demands the drinker should get their teeth into. *50% (100 proof)*

◈ **Boldt Straight Rye Whiskey Aged 4 Years Bottled In Bond** batch 51 db **(91.5)** n22.5 the rye has no intention of mucking about: it is in there dealing out an intriguing mix of firm fruity tones amid the predictable (and necessary) peppery spices; t23 unusually fat for a rye, but the cut has done no damage to the structure of the grain or the dexterity of the alternating crisp and molten muscovado sugars in tandem with those peppers; f22.5 much spicier now, though that mocha finally has come out of the left field...; b23.5 a Boldt upright rye whiskey citizen! *50% (100 proof)*

GRIFFO DISTILLERY Petaluma, Sonoma Co

◈ **Griffo Stony Point Whiskey** batch no 15 db **(89.5)** n22.5 makes a point in dealing out the corn oils as thickly as possible. A little demerara sugar and light spices season it delicately; t23 a much more lively and uplifting delivery than expected with the sugars now having switched from Demerara to something more along the muscovado and thinned molasses line; f21.5 just a tad untidy and tangy with the tannins not dissimilar to tea; b22.5 an endearingly soft whisky which has cheerfully extracted as much sugar out of the local and French casks used during maturation. *47% (94 proof)*

◈ **Griffo Stout Barreled Whiskey** batch no 13 db **(88)** n20 t23 f22 b23 Not a great fan of the hop note picked up on the nose, which plays with my mind thereafter. However, no faulting the beautiful spice buzz as it delves into the rich corn oils while the milky chocolate towards the middle and finish – deepened in flavour by molasses. The very finish, like the nose, is out of keeping with the spectacular middle but there is no lasting damage. A very different whiskey which would have scored highly had it not been for that niggling hop! *45% (90 proof)*

LOS ANGELES DISTILLERY Los Angeles, California.

◈ **Los Angeles High Tide Straight Rye Single Barrel Bottled In Bond** all rye, all malted batch/cask 51/3 db **(90.5)** n22.5 thick to the point of a slight feintiness. But this is malted rye, so that note doesn't have too long to register before the vaguely fruity intensity of the grain takes over, all fortified by a dense oakiness, too; t23 outside of peated malt, malted rye has the biggest flavour profile of any whiskey on the planet. And this underlines that fact with the most intense and intrepid rye delivery you can imagine. At times the expected fruit note takes on an unexpected tangy citrus hue; f22 that wide cut gathers up the oils and gives a furriness to the spiced vanillas; b23 most malted ryes have a firmness to match the intense grain. Because of that generous cut, the oils make that a much softer scenario and while perhaps not technically entirely tickety-boo, that astonishing intensity and richness on delivery is worth the entrance money alone... Incidentally, it is so strange that I should randomly open a box and out pops a whisky from Culver City. You see, today is July 5th and earlier today I quietly marked the sixth anniversary of the death of my old mum (it was, coincidentally, on her 96th birthday). I was thinking about some of the funny times we had together and one included a previous birthday I took her out to dinner, telling her she would, as a widow, be having a special guest. And there, when we arrived was the place marked for the mystery diner...who I brought in shortly after: it was the mannequin used by Gene Kelly for the film "Singing in the Rain" on which all his clothes for the film were fitted and hung. So mum's birthday guest was the essence of her screen hero and it was a silly and fun evening she never forgot. Oh, and on the mannequin was stencilled Gene's name and attacked to it was a brass plate explaining it had been sold at auction by MGM studios, Culver City, in 1970. And today, of all days, the anniversary of that event, comes the first whiskey I have ever tasted from there. Spooky, eh...? *50% (100 proof)*

◈ **Los Angeles L.A. Beach Hi-Rye Straight Bourbon Bottled In Bond Single Barrel 5 Yrs** nbc db **(87.5)** n20.5 t23 f22 b22 Bit of an untidy whiskey, this, truth be told. There is a niggardly (and no: that one hundred percent is not a racist word!) note on the nose which undermines the clarity of the rye tones. And though it peps up considerably on the palate and at times behaves more like a rye than a bourbon, there is always that slightly muffled note of compromise. So close to being a real treat... *50% (100 proof)*

⟐ **Los Angeles L.A. Beach Hi-Wheat Straight Bourbon Bottled In Bond Single Barrel 5 Years Old** 52% corn 48% malted wheat batch/cask 36/3 db **(94.5)** n23 apart from a Jamaican high ester rum note – which is not at all unattractive – the main thrust is that wheat included in the mashbill, which certainly isn't afraid of pursuing its own tantalising agenda; **t24** whoomph! And there it is again, bang on delivery. A mix of bready and toasty tones, immediately armed by some certifiable spices which rip into the palate...in a very naughty but nice kind of way. As I write this I have just spotted the mash bill on the bottle...now that explains so much...! Oh, best not to ignore the tannins, which also dig in deep here...; **f23.5** long with the corn oils being hijacked by the wheat (no surprise there) to further their total overthrow of your taste buds. Plenty of muscovado sugars indulge, too, giving a surprising degree of juiciness right to the very spicy end...; **b24** a very serious bit of bourbon making. The wheat grain influence is astonishing and gives the whiskey an impressive overall sugar/pepper lustre. Great stuff. No, make that fabulous... *50% (100 proof)*

⟐ **Los Angeles L.A. Beach Straight Bourbon Bottled In Bond Single Barrel 5 Years Old** 51% corn 49% malted barley batch/cask 50/7 db **(87.5)** n21 t22 f22.5 b22 Now that's odd! Almost a complete re-run as their Hi-Rye bourbon, in that the weakness and strengths appear to be at the very same junctures. Not sure I've ever encountered that before, after nearly 25,000 whiskies tasted for this book. The barley really does offer a disarming juiciness which lasts the entire length of the tasting experience, and some attractive cocoa at the death. And, again, the tannins are punchy and proud. I really must talk to the guys at Los Angeles Distillery: I am truly intrigued... I've not had time to do it yet but would love to experiment by leaving both in warm water for a good half hour to see what happens. My guess is that they will both improve. *50% (100 proof)*

⟐ **Los Angeles Glen L.A. Double Cask Tokaji Cask Single Malt Bottled In Bond Single Barrel** cask 1 new oak 7 yrs, cask 2 Tokaji aszu cask 7 yrs batch# 17.17 db **(86.5)** n25 t22 f20.5 b21.5 It's not the first time I've encountered freshly-sliced cucumber on a whisky nose, but certainly the first for a while. As the glass warms, though, the grape dominates. Lots of vanilla and caramel washing over the fruit influence. Sadly, nearly all Tokaji casks were heavily sulphur-treated before being packed off from Hungary. This one isn't anything like so bad as many. But there is a distinct furry-bitter weakness on the finish. *50% (100 proof)*

⟐ **Los Angeles Glen L.A. Single Cask Tokaji Cask Single Malt Bottled In Bond Single Barrel** matured in Tokaji aszu cask 7 yrs batch# 19 db **(89.5)** n22 well, yes: untidy it may be but there is some decent bitter lemon to stir the nose into action; **t23** salivating delivery, indeed captivating, with a grassy, malty undercurrent. The spices, though there, are a tad constrained. Grapefruit juice gathers at the midpoint; **f22** it's what's not happening here, rather than what is that's impressing me: no sulphur off notes early on the finish (though you will spot a few after you've put the glass down). Lots of tangy vanilla instead; **b22.5** ah, that rarest of beasts; a Tokaji cask which has escaped the really heavy sulphur treatment. Well, if you on for some chirpy, at times tart, fruitiness then here's your tipple. Very pleasantly surprised... *50% (100 proof)*

⟐ **Los Angeles Glen L.A. Triple Cask Tokaji Cask Single Malt Bottled In Bond** Single cask 1 new oak 7 yrs, cask 2 Bordeaux wine 7 yrs, cask 3 Tokaji aszu cask 7 yrs batch# 17.13.17 db **(87)** n22 t22.5 f20.5 b22 In the 30 years I have been doing this job, I cannot quite remember an experience where the three individual characteristics of the actual barrels used were so easily spotted...and working aloof of the other. Well, that certainly happens here when within seconds of the whiskey hitting the tastebuds there are three quite separate explosions. The first to shew is the tannin: a beast of bristling sap and vanilla. Next comes a forthright essay of grapiness. Next comes – and those who are familiar with ultra-sweet PX casks will recognise the signs – of furrows being filled and ridges flattened by the sugary grape. Best when tasted at its coolest: the vanilla becomes a little too overpowering if warmed, though it does help distract from the late niggle on the finish. *50% (100 proof)*

MOYLAN'S DISTILLING COMPANY Petaluma, California

Moylan's Bourbon Whisky Cask Strength batch B-7 db **(93.5)** n23 t24 f23 b23.5 This is a bourbon that just screams "small stills: and "copper" at you. Metallic, intense and, at times, a real dip into the old days. Certainly not dissimilar to some of the old honey casks I discovered at the long-lost Heaven Hill distillery back in the 1990s. There is a slight blot on the copybook with vague feint lines appearing on both nose and finish. But I'd still like to meet whoever distilled this and shake his or her hand. *56.3% (112.6 proof) Blended and Bottled by Moylan's*

SONOMA DISTILLING COMPANY Rohnert Park, California.

⟐ **Sonoma Black Truffle Rye Aged A Minimum Three Years Lott 2022** db **(88)** n21 t22 f23 b22 Of course this isn't a whiskey and shouldn't be in the Bible at all. But...truffles!!! One of my most favourite things in the world...how could I just ignore it. It is a pity that the cut is a bit wide on this as the nose doesn't let much get through other than an intense rye tone. However, as the spirit meanders around the palate, getting softer every second, the breakthrough comes on that special period just beyond the middle and on the cusp of the finale...and then the truffle certainly gets through and makes for the most delicate moments, seemingly tiptoeing across the tongue with a chocolatey accompaniment. What else that has gone on before doesn't really matter: it is that magic moment which counts... *47.5% (95 proof) straight rye with French black truffles*

⬩ **Sonoma Black California Wheat Aged A Minimum Three Years Lott 2022** db (93) n22.5 digestive biscuit in tandem sharp, spicy, fruit rye...wow! t24 the oiliness present here works in its favour as the coating around the palate is immediate and effective. A few moments later heather honey has interlocked with eye-watering rye as the flavour intensity soars to the point of reaching red on the sensory dial...; f23 oils and light spices galore. A little cocoa, but still more lingering honey; b23.5 beautifully distilled whiskey with barely a feint in sight. Not only a massive flavour profile at work here, but a unique combination of flavours leaving no tastebud unturned... *46% (92 proof) made from wheat and malted rye and matured in used whiskey and cognac barrels*

⬩ **Sonoma Black Straight Bourbon Aged A Minimum Two Years Lott 2022** db (90.5) n22 a little heady on the oils for certain there are smoky tannins at play here making the heaviness even greater; t23 good heavens! A truly unique flavour profile on delivery (something this distillery makes a point of!). It is as though a treacle tart has been taken with a mouthful of peated malt, then manuka honey is added to the mix. Meanwhile much drier vanillas and trace cocoa powder are keeping things balanced; f22.5 right, those coco powders are now more than trace. The oils are considerable but clean; b23 another huge-flavoured contribution from Sonoma. Unlike their ryes, they have got the cuts far closer to where they should be here. And though not perfect, the overall charm and enormity of the bourbon is not ultimately compromised. Big and lip-smackingly chewy. *46% (92 proof) made with cherrywood smoked malted barley*

⬩ **Sonoma Black Straight Rye Aged A Minimum Two Years Lott 2022** db (87) n22 t22 f21 b22 Initially, a disappointing whiskey because having tasted their rye before I thought by now they might have learned from previous errors and made their cuts that much cleaner. Instead, they have gone the other way and the feints are even more profound. A charge of lack of personality can't be raised against this whiskey and I have certainly seen what is capable of if you sit the glass in very warm water for fifteen minutes to evaporate the excess oils. Then the rye comes to life with intense, laser-sharp, eyewatering blasts of grain followed by a much friendlier, oily cocoa tone. In that shape it scores over 90. But, for scoring, I must judge it how it arrives in the bottle. Still, keep the hot water close by and prepare yourself for a secret treat. *46.5% (93 proof) made with cherrywood smoked malted barley*

⬩ **Sonoma Bourbon Whiskey** nbc (88) n23 t22 f21 b22 Bit of a shame, this. The nose, just filled with all kinds of mint and hickory delights promises so much. But halfway through the delivery light feints take hold and refuses to let go. Despite that weakness, there is absolutely no faulting the glorious intensity of the molasses and spices. A cleaner cut would have brough a very decent score. *46% (92 proof) 70% corn, 25% wheat, 5% malted barley*

⬩ **Sonoma Straight Bourbon Finished in Wine barrels** barrel no DFS01, dist 2018 (88.5) n22 t22.5 f22 b22 Technically, this was by far the best of the three Sonomas I tasted this year. Free from feints, this bourbon is clearly rich, confident and belting out some wonderful liquorice tones. The wine barrel is likewise of decent quality and does offer a fruity gloss. Sadly, the wine casks also negate the high points of the bourbon, making it all just a little too silky and, spices apart, monosyllabic. A pity they didn't use the straight bourbon here for their bourbon bottling... *46% (92 proof) 70% corn, 25% wheat, 5% malted barley*

⬩ **Sonoma Rye** nbc (86.5) n22 t23 f20.5 b21 Such a frustrating whiskey. There are so many good things going on thanks to the pure intensity of the rye itself that if you shut your mind off to its faults, you'd just adore it. Sadly, I must address those weaknesses, which I suspect arise from the nature of the cut itself for there are feints at play. And there I also some strange, boiled sugar candy fruits afoot which goes against the grain. Literally. The delivery, though, is quite something with the rye flying at you from all directions. *46.5% (93 proof) 80% rye, 20% malted rye*

SPIRIT WORKS DISTILLERY Sebastopol, California.

⬩ **Spirit Works Four Grain Bourbon Whiskey** batch 009 db (88) n23 t22.5 f20.5 b22 Now this is a curious whiskey. Although undoubtedly a bourbon, most of the signatures are not those you would necessarily associate with at that particular whiskey style. The nose does offer some strained kumquat peel and liquorice but once it hits the palate we are talking a delicate, complex whiskey not of bourbon character but still offering bitter-sweet complexity of an enjoyable depth. The bitter finish is a bit all over the place, admittedly, but still the sweetened, spicy, buttery middle can be thoroughly enjoyed. *45% (90 proof)*

⬩ **Spirit Works Straight Rye Whiskey** batch 032 db (90.5) n22.5 attractive: the usual slightly wider than usual cut that seems de rigeur for rye. But under that slight grime is a penetrating degree of raw rye which triggers both the spicy and fruity elements demanded; t23 full-bodied with an early muscovado sugar volley to keep the vanillas on their toes; f22 layered though gentle spices pucker. The heavier oils return; **b23** sticks very true to the spirit of rye. Clean and flavoursome. 45% (90 proof)

◈ **Spirit Works Straight Wheat Whiskey** barrel no 024 db **(95.5) n23.5** truly classic wheat whiskey aroma with a glorious mix of spice, freshly roasted brown bread, topped with a light French toast sweetness; **t24** the oils here are textbook and not only lightly coat the mouth but hold together the complex fault lines between the bold, crunchy dark sugars and the nibbling spices; **f234** a lovely bread pudding finale my dear old mum would have been proud of..; **b24** beautifully distilled, immaculately matured, this shows exactly how that delicate interplay between dark, toasty sugars and spices should be when wheat is so heavily involved. Top grade for its style... indeed, of the 20 whiskies I have tasted today, this is top dog. And by some distance. 45% (90 proof)

ST GEORGE SPIRITS Alameda, California.
◈ **St George Baller Single Malt Whisky Aged 3 Years** db **(95.5) n24** that singularly sexy, ultra-fresh, diced apple clarity sets the senses ready for a jolly good time. This has a delicate smokiness I don't remember from the old days, but it serves as the flimsiest of anchors. The near perfect pre-prandial sniff to get your taste buds awake and ready..; **t23.5** as ever, beautifully distilled. Despite the intense gristiness of that malt, there is a lightness to the oils which reveals they have got their cuts just about perfect here: light oils and absolutely no feints is the bullseye on the target of every distiller. This is the golden shot...; **f24** those oils guarantee length and here no refunds are necessary. The malt heads through a cabaret of delicate performances, ranging from further intensity of the grist to a fragile Brazil nut oiliness as well as a charming and exquisitely elegant unfurling of vanillas and butterscotch. When the Murray Method is gently applied, magically a high-end mocha wafer melts in the mouth...sensational...literally! **b24** it is over 25 years since St George became the second small batch independent distillery I located and visited in the US, Old Potrero in San Francisco being the first. I remember vividly to this day the apple freshness of their young malts the other side of the Bay in Alameda. And it is almost a journey back in time by nosing this: very little has changed, except they have now so perfected their style that of their type they are perhaps unparalleled in the United States. Even from the labels it's obvious that the distillery's driving force, Lance Winters, has lost none of his humour and quirkiness over the passing quarter if a century. Note to Lance: nor have I, mate! 47% (94 proof)

◈ **St George Single Malt Whisky batch SM022** db **(87.5) n22 t23 f21 b21.5** Less of the house style fresh apple and far more heady oiled up barley, which is huge on delivery. Some dappled tannin barley on both nose and body. Altogether a much more muscular style of malt than their mind-blowing Baller. This one lays the malt on with an oily trowel but struggles to lose a nagging bitterness. 43% (86 proof)

STARK DISTILLERY Pasadena, California.
◈ **Whisky On Tap The Golden Promise Aged 7 Winters and 6 Summers** batch one db **(95.5) n24** one of those bemusing, faultless noses where, despite the incessant onslaught of oak, the malt combines with the more sugary aspects of the tannins to offer the perfect reposte. This is dark and deep and delightfully integrated; **t24** for all its strength, for all those highly active spices, this is beautifully rounded and stretching the heather honey until it is about to crack. The inhouse toasty phenol note sits so comfortably with it while the spices buzz on delivery; **f23.5** long, molassed and elegantly toasty: a lingering, layered fade where the malt more than holds its own. The taut interplay between the natural caramels and rampant barley is as fascinating as it delicious; **b24** I remember the days when old Highland Park used to offer this type of honey profile. Not only a big whiskey, but one where the mouthfeel perfectly matches the complex flavour storyline. And anyone into naturally honey-rich whiskeys will get a hell of a buzz out if this. On the evidence of this, I think we have a new absolutely top dollar distillery on our hands... 64.23% (128.46 proof) 92 bottles

◈ **Whisky On Tap The Golden Promise American Single Malt** dist summer 2016 bott winter 2022 batch WOT016 db **(94) n23** there is a faux smokiness to this, perhaps a by-product of some serious charring: certainly anyone who has smelt charcoal being made will recognise some of the more acidic aspects of this aroma; **t23.5** full bloodied maple-type sugars from the oak bleed into the more accommodating barley tones. The result is eye-watering, sharp and lively: indeed, the clarity of the malt is profound; **f23.5** surprising oils hold on and even make room for some melt-in-the-mouth ulmo honey; **b24** lively and lovely, huge yet delicate, the Hungarian casks involved are being put to good use here and thumping out some crisp and meaningful sugars. But, above all, the original distillate was made to a very high spec. Impressive. Yet more excellence from California: this Golden Promise has delivered... 61.17% (122.34 proof) 133 bottles

Colorado
AXE AND THE OAK Colorado Springs, Colorado.
Axe and the Oak The First Stake Cask Strength Bourbon Whiskey Aged 3 Years batch 3 db **(95) n23 t24.5 f23.5 b24** If anyone says that it is sexist to say that a whiskey is sensual and

sexy, they seriously want certifying. Taste this and tell me it is neither. You simply wouldn't be able to. The best whiskey from Axe and the Oak I can remember in a very long time, if not ever. Sexy and sublime. And, I admit, quite some surprise... 59% (118 proof) 1,000 bottles

BLACK BEAR DISTILLERY Green Mountain Falls, Colorado.

Black Bear Bourbon Irish Style Colorado Whiskey finished in sherry casks db (88) n21.5 t22.5 f22 b22 Quite a bulky whiskey, with the additional fatness of the grape adding to the oils from the generous cut. Technically, doesn't pull up any trees. But it is impossible not to be drawn towards the delicious mix of blackcurrant pastel candy and mocha. Genuinely tasty whiskey and great fun. Oh, and lip-smackingly salivating to boot. 45% (90 proof).

BRECKENRIDGE DISTILLERY Breckenridge, Colorado.

Breckenridge Colorado Whiskey Powder Hound batch no. 1 db (91) n22 t23.5 f22 b23.5 Despite a slight blemish at the death, this is probably the most complex and well balanced whiskey I have yet seen from this distillery. 45% (90 proof).

DEERHAMMER DISTILLING COMPANY Buena Vista, Colorado.

Deerhammer American Single Malt Whiskey virgin oak barrel #2 char, batch no. 32 db (87.5) n21.5 t23.5 f20.5 b22 This, like most Colorado whiskeys, is huge. Had the cut been a little less generous, the oils a little less gripping and tangy, this would have scored exceptionally highly. For there is no doubting the deliciousness of the big toasted malt, the kumquat citrus element, the moreishness of the heavyweight dark fudge and the magnificent Java coffee. All these make a delivery and follow through to remember. I look forward to the next bottling where hopefully the cut is a little more careful: a very significant score awaits as this is borderline brilliant... 46% (92 proof). 870 bottles.

DISTILLERY 291 Colorado Springs, Colorado.

◇ **291 Bad Guy Proof Single Barrel Colorado Bourbon Whiskey** batch no 8 db (95.5) n23.5 heady and thick set, it has escaped the heavier oils and instead concentrates on a surprisingly delicate chocolate mosaic, with diced walnut for company; t24.5 vroom! The spices spark off immediately. But the sugary volley of muscovado with ulmo and heather honeys. A superb black and red liquorice interplay guarantees oaky depth...but all the while chocolate and then mocha note takes turns making their marks; f23.5 long and now a light spiciness acts like a spur to pep life back to bourbon that was thinking of becoming a little too comfortable. But that chocolate: a kind of Venezuelan, lightly oiled, siting so prettily with the butterscotch offered by the malt is memorable; b24 the Bad Guy has turned into the Good Guy this time out, after last year's naughty performance. This is a clean whiskey you pour into a dirty glass. And then lean on that bar and allow the most gloriously intense chocolate mousse slip down your throat. "Fabulous" doesn't do it justice. 59.6% (119.2 proof) 1,294 bottles

◇ **291 All Rye Colorado 100% Rye Malt Whiskey** batch no 1 db (89) n21 the grain is curiously mossy and tight. The oak notes are brief and clipped; t22.5 that's better...after a massive spice thrust on delivery, the sugars begin to filter down – especially muscovado which takes the starring role. Juicy, though still quite odd...; f23 the honeyed chocolate adds a distraction to the peculiar light tang; b22.5 a singular style of whiskey which has massive entertainment value but has the odd nose and taste glitch. A work in progress, as they say... 66.3% (132.6 proof) 1,303 bottles

◇ **291 Barrel Proof Single Barrel Colorado Rye Malt Whiskey** distilled from a rye malt mash, barrel no 951 db (91) n23 a full-frontal assault by the rye grain leaving you in no doubt that this is the malted variety to max out the grain's aromatic output. Just a hint of tobacco...; t23 flat out on the full fat body, there is a remarkable mouth-watering statement going on here, too. Toasted honeycomb combines with the fruitier aspect of the grain. One if the most intense pure rye cries on the palate this year; f22 still very toasty and nutty now, too. And a little oil deposit, giving the rye a dappled effect; b23 had the cut just been a little less clumsy and the fragrances and flavours far purer, this might have been on the way to an award. As it is, just wallow in its intensity... 64.4% (128.8 proof) 47 bottles

◇ **291 Barrel Proof Single Barrel Colorado Bourbon Whiskey** barrel no 1028 db (91) n22.5 a pretty chunky cut at work here which takes some of the gloss off the nutty, leathery thrust; t23 fat and jaw-achingly chewy. Spicy, too, with the depth of the hickory helped along by that slightly wide cut; f22.5 slightly burnt toast with the thinnest layer of praline; b23 my first 291 whiskey of the year: why is it whenever I pick up a glass of this stuff I sink five or six inches into the chair, as though snuggling into position to watch a favourite old movie. 63% (126 proof) 50 bottles

◇ **291 Small Batch Colorado Bourbon Whiskey** batch no 44 db (90) n22.5 again, a generous cut but there is also some pleasing small grain bittiness; t22 every bit as chewy as the nose forecasts. Enormous degree of caramel extracted from the oak which ties in with the corn and distillation oils to make this a stand your spoon in whiskey; **f23** the spices rumble gently but do nothing to ward off that delicious chocolate nougat fade; **b22.5** the biggest chocolate nougat kick I've encountered so far this year...a super-delicious meeting of imperfect personalities. *50% (100 proof) 1277 bottles*

291 Small Batch Colorado Rye Whiskey batch no 15 db **(84.5) n21 t21 f21.5 b21** That tobacco note I picked up on in the corresponding bottling last year hasn't gone away any. Indeed, it is now a little more pronounced. Elsewhere, there is a puckering sharpness as the grains battle to get fully into stride. A shame, because further down the line there is a rally inspired by the tannins. But even that veers off course. *50.8% (101.7 proof)*

291 E Colorado Bourbon Whiskey batch no 11 bott 11-11-22 db **(92) n23** tannins have been driven into the corn oil to make for an insanely peppery aroma. Red liquorice on heat...; **t22.5** yikes, this is aggressive! Even the Murray Method can't calm this one down. Below the warmth comes a mix of intense vanilla and outline, forever drying hickory; **f23** the hickory keeps its place though sugars are a rarity this is dry, even as the cocoa mounts; **b23.5** the least oily 291 I have tasted for quite a while. Once it is over its peppery onslaught the depth of dryness, and the rise of the cocoa tone, is truly remarkable. *64.9% (129.9 proof)*

291 E Colorado Wheated Bourbon Whiskey Aged For 724 Days batch no 12 db **(90) n22** wow! That tannin doesn't half have something to say for itself. And is pretty shrill when doing so; **t23** a gorgeous soft wave of corn oil bathes the taste buds, lulling them into a false sense of security before the wheat-driven spices strike. It isn't long before the muscular tannin weighs in also. Light molasses does its best to soften the blows; **f22.5** the house style of liquorice and chocolate are doing their best but have to wave the white flag as those tannins bite hard and deep; **b22.5** there are times when the tannins can just be a little too tart for their own good, and here is such a case. When the tannin is this sharp, it is hard to concentrate on other aspects of the whiskey. Enjoyable and hardly short of some character. *60.8% (121.6 proof)*

291 E13 Colorado Single Malt Whiskey Aged For 1752 Days db **(94.5) n23** would have been all too easy for the tannins to overstretch the mark here – but they haven't. Just the very lightest touch of butyric drops half a point...but so much has happened over the six or so Colorado summers since this was made, it barely matters; **t23** like the nose there is the odd uncomfortable hurdle to clear, with some harrowing spices - though this is confined to very early on when cool: the Murray Method virtually eradicates the false steps and brings out the silky ulmo honey and vanillas to their best profile; **f24.5** now we have a delightful meeting of still intense barley with the most layered oak imaginable – and you'd be right for guessing may be involved somewhere down the line. The mocha tones are sensationally soft and involved with an almost choreographed tapering of the cocoa and upping of the coffee; **b24** one of the best finishes you'll encounter anywhere in the world this year. It took just over 45 minutes to get a handle on this malt. If all whiskeys were this challenging and complex, this book would never get even close to finishing... *65.1% (130.2 proof)*

291 HR Colorado Bourbon Whiskey Aged For At Least One Year batch no 26 db **(88.5) n21.5 t23.5 f21.5 b22** HR stands for "High Rye content", and there is no doubting their word. Lots of flavour, but things are a tad haphazard and struggles for equilibrium. The nose is crowded by heavy tannin which doesn't appear fully settled and relaxed. The delivery is a treat, for sure: warming and chewy with a wonderful red liquorice theme which settles down into muscovado sugars and small grain juiciness. But the finish is a tad tangy and bitter. An enjoyable whiskey but one that seems to be living on its nerves. *63% (126.1 proof)*

XI Barrel Proof Single Barrel Colorado Whiskey 291 Anniversary batch no 220911 db **(96) n23.5** a whiskey determined to get its money's worth out if the oak but arrests the progress with a chocolate and liquorice double act. Quite curiously salty...; **t24** yep, that tannin really does rule the roost early on, and the spices come with a cutlass between the teeth. But the measured molasses blunts their cutting edge; **f24** this distillery really does do chocolate liqueur a lot better than most and here it gives a masterclass...; **b24.5** a whiskey which is the definition of controlled aggression. It is also an exhibition of balance – which is some achievement when certain aspects of this flavour profile is exploding off the charts. Here they have struck gold by finding exactly the right rhythm and density for the sugars and cocoa to compensate for the heftier tannins. It means your taste buds are exhausted by the end of your glass: they have had to work non-stop to fully compute the stunning data they are being presented with. Happy Anniversary 291, one of America's truly great distilleries. And congratulations on producing one of the whiskeys of the year to celebrate it! *68.7% (137.5 proof)*

DOWNSLOPE DISTILLING Centennial, Colorado.

Downslope Double Diamond Whiskey Bottled In Bond 2022 release, tawny port finish db **(92) n22.5 t23.5 f22.5 b23.5** There was an old British lager called Double Diamond which famously, so the advert ditty went, "worked wonders". I remember the last time I tasted this a couple of years back, this certainly didn't. Well, it does now! This is a huge whisky wallowing in its malt and rye mix and topped off with a tawny Port cask that must have still been dripping wet with the wine when filled. Certainly the aroma of the Port fills the glass, along with some accompanying light spices. The lushness of the delivery is astonishing – not unlike a cream sherry. But the spices and rye notes are picking up here to make for serious juiciness amid the cream. The finish is also rich and silky but with a little bitter orange creeping in late on, as well as toffee raisin. Incidentally, I was tasting this outside in the cool of a still English evening after a scorching hot day...and as I tasted the tawny port, a tawny owl was calling from less than hundred yards away... *50% (100 proof)*

⬦ **Downslope American Single Malt Cherry Port Finish 2023** release db **(90) n22.5 t23 f22 b22.5** The Port cask at work here is determined to make its mark – and does so to mixed effect. Certainly on the nose it stamps its authority with a spicy buzz while it takes the delivery by the scruff of the neck to blast out some eye-wateringly tart plum tones. The tannins off the oak are also in on the act, doubling up to ensure satisfying complexity. The oil level is spot on, allowing a certain glistening to that persistent fruit. Just a little bitterness from the oak at the death is the only weakness. Quite a mouthful... *45% (90 proof)*

⬦ **Downslope American Single Malt Wine Barrel Finish** db **(92.5) n23 t23 f23 b23.5** Well, they must have found some peat in Colorado, because if those aren't phenols I'm detecting on both the nose and delivery, then I'm the Prince of Canada. Have to say this really is excellently portrayed peat because it has been outlined in this distillery's unique pastel shade of subtlety and softness. The wine cask selected here is a bit of gem, too. Offering the same degree of clarity as the high quality distillate. The fruit isn't in any way overbearing but has enough weight and stamina to give a vaguely fruity hue to the grist. So enjoyable. *45% (90 proof)*

⬦ **Downslope Rye Whiskey Wine Barrel Finish** db **(88.5) n22 t22.5 f22 b22** When I think of Downslope, my usual reaction is: "Ah, that's the distillery that makes really gentle whiskeys." And there is nothing about this that shakes that assertion. The spice prickles very well on the nose and gives the grain ample opportunity to display its sharper tongue, which it does with a degree of reticence. The delivery is at first a little feeble, but slowly confidence grows as does a really delightful rye and vanilla double-header. The slightly oily tang on the fade is brief while the grain clings on. Pleasant though makes a point of pulling up no trees. *40% (80 proof)*

⬦ **Downslope Straight Bourbon 2nd Release 2023** release db **(89) n22 t22.5 f22 b22.5** Definitely a bourbon that repays a visit. At first glance, pretty standard fare. However, the Murray Method helps this blossom into a charming hickory and Demerara affair with oils in all the appropriate places. Seems definitely a tad underpowered, though, especially when I remember their last bourbon that I encountered which had some powerful legs and allowed a deeper honey note than can be found here. A real easy-going Colorado. *45% (90 proof)*

LAWS WHISKEY HOUSE Denver, Colorado.
Laws Whiskey House Henry Road Straight Malt Whiskey Bonded 4 Years Old batch no. 1 db **(93) n23 t23.5 f23 b23.5** If this is Batch One, I can't wait for the next ones. Congratulations to all at Laws for producing such an outstanding malt whiskey first time out. *50% (100 proof).*

LEOPOLD BROS Denver, Colorado.
Leopold Bros Straight Bourbon Cask Select barrel no. 135, bott 11 Mar 19 db **(87.5) n22 t22.5 f21 b22** Really interesting here how the rye plays such a significant role in the flavour personality of this bourbon. The given mash bill reveals 17% malted barley to 15% rye, yet it is that latter grain that can be found in all the highlights. Especially on the nose and eye-watering delivery. Good spice, but just need to get the feints down a little to make the most of the growing honey tones. Seriously promising. *50%. sc.*

SPIRIT HOUND DISTILLERS Lyons, Colorado.
⬦ **Spirit Hound Straight Malt Whisky Bottled In Bond Aged 4 Years** barrel 187 db **(93.5) n22.5** on that delightful cusp between retained youth and the first grey hairs: fresh-faced malt all the way when cool and an oaky indulgence when warmed slightly; **t24** beautifully melodious and the most scintillating delivery of any Spirit Hound I've ever experienced. As well as concentrated malt there is the most sublime eruption of spiced maple and heather honey. When this calms, the midpoint is a complex interwangling of varied vanilla and barley tones; **f23** the excellent distillation means oils, though at a premium, aren't quite extinct. This allows the barley sugars to maintain their position and see off a very slight late bitterness; **b24** disarmingly complex and not unhappy to shew its sweet side. *50% (100 proof) Exclusively bottled for The Stanley*

⬦ **Spirit Hound Straight Malt Whisky Aged 2 Years** barrel 305 db **(91.5) n22.5** that's a youthful way to start my tasting day with some sharp lemon drops amid the healthy barley; **t23.5** the nose announces a salivating freshness and the delivery confirms it beyond doubt. Huge gristy malt surge makes for a lip-smacking experience; **f22.5** simplistic citrusy lemon curd tart working in tandem with a soft powdering of oaky vanillas; **b23** a young puppy of a Spirit Dog, this, which is yet to develop a gruff bark. An excellent pre-prandial malt which gets the juices flowing, or as a refreshing dram capable of cutting through the muggiest of summer days. The clarity of the gristy barley underlines just how technically excellent the original distillate is. *45% (90 proof)*

⬧ **Spirit Hound Straight Malt Whisky Cask Strength Single Barrel 3 Years Old** barrel no 287 db **(95) n23.5** the natural caramels leeched from the barrel sits comfortably with the malt concentrate. A splendid toffee apple freshness, too, with the spices, though there, holding back...; **t24** ah! That is quite beautiful. Just a re-enactment of the nose, though now in a far more intense format. Astonishingly, there is no aggression whatsoever, despite the spices now coming out of its shell and forming a fabulous counterpoint to the heather honey which binds together the malt and vanillas; **f23.5** much easier now: with the spices spent, this is a nutty vanilla fest if the most elegant and relaxed type...; **b24** this is top rank distilling and really excellent maturation. The result is silky but intense malt which just never lets up in promoting its way above average riches. *62.88% (125.76 proof)*

VAPOR DISTILLERY Boulder, Colorado.

Boulder Spirits American Single Malt Bottled In Bond aged no less than 4yrs, 53 gall level 3 char cask, db **(94) n22.5 t24 f23.5 b24** Damn! This distillery knows how to distil high quality whiskey! This is stunning! *50% (100 proof)*

Boulder Spirits American Single Malt Sherry Cask Finish aged 3yrs 6 mo, 53 gall level 3 char cask, 6 months in sherry cask db **(87) n22.5 t23 f20 b21.5** Silky and voluptuous to start with, there is more than a hint of sherry trifle on delivery. The finish, however, is a little dry and tangy. *47% (94 proof)*

Boulder Spirits Straight Bourbon aged no less than 3yrs, 53 gall level 3 char cask, db **(87.5) n22.5 t21.5 f22 b21.5** From the attractive, honey-ringed nose it drops in sweetness on delivery and, for a bourbon, becomes quite remarkably dry. Readjusts about two thirds of the way in as the vanillas gather and the spices rise. *42% (84 proof)*

Boulder Spirits Straight Bourbon Bottled In Bond mashbill: 51% corn 44% malted barley 5% rye db **(89.5) n22 t22.5 f22.5 b22.5** from an indifferent start on the nose, this grows into something worth investigating. Some ultra-high malt mashbills I've encountered in the past haven't ended well. But this doesn't have a hybrid feel: though the corn oils are scarce, this is chewing bourbon all the way. *50% (100 proof)*

Boulder Spirits Straight Bourbon Sherry Cask Finish aged 3yrs 6 months, 53 gall level 3 char cask, 6 months in sherry cask db **(85.5) n22.5 t23 f19 b21** It is fascinating how the fruit influence of the sherry cask has turned what was originally a straight bourbon into something nosing far more along the lines of a rye! The delivery boasts a real cream sherry feel, despite only a six month stint with the wine cask. Again, the finish is dull, a tad furry and bitter. Up to that point we had been treated to a moist fruitcake with a fair dose of golden syrup. *47% (94 proof)*

WOOD'S HIGH MOUNTAIN DISTILLERY Salida, Colorado.

Wood's Tenderfoot American Malt Whiskey Aged 18 Months batch no. 66 db **(88) n21.5 t22 f22.5 b22** A cleaner distillate than the 4-year-old means the grain here piles in at its most juicy and grassy. More melt-in-the mouth sugars, too, and though the house cocoa turns up towards the end as expected, there is far more layering from the grain now. *45% (90 proof)*.

Florida
FLORIDA FARM DISTILLERS Umatilla, Florida.

Palm Ridge Golden Handmade Micro Batch Wheated Florida Whiskey nbc db **(92) n22.5 t23f23.5 b23** A massive personality and an exhibition of controlled sugars. *45% (90 proof). ncf.*

KOZUBA & SONS DISTILERY St. Peterburg, Florida

⬧ **Kozuba High Wheat Rye Whiskey 7 Years Old** 65% rye 35% wheat nbc db **(91.5) n22.5** a soft, bready countenance keeps the clipped Demerara-sweetness in check. The spices are almost mesmerising in their busy-ness; **t23** such a silky delivery. Though the rye is the main ingredient, early on it is the wheat which shapes the direction of its on-palate personality. Slowly, though, the abrasiveness of the rye begins to battle through and the sharpness takes an upward trajectory; **f23** tangy and vibrant, some citrus tones filter through amid the spices and growing vanillas; **b23** extremely well-made whiskey with an impressive clarity. The wheat, as so often the case when mixed in with rye, adds spice but does reduce slightly in the rye's ability to sparkle on the palate, but I think that was intended here. The overall feel is a rye of unusual softness. *45% (90 proof)*

⬧ **Kozuba High Wheat Rye Whiskey Family Selection 7 Years Old** 65% rye 35% wheat nbc db **(88) n22** that attractively sluggish wheat involvement seems to make everything move in slow motion: delicate with unhurried, easy-going spices; t23 a complex delivery with a two-toned texture: on one hand a chewy, bready depth, on the other a thinner, far more biting, bitter-lemon contrast; f21 tangy citrus and warming spice; b22 a very different rye with a flavour profile unique to this distillery. Perhaps not technically perfect but fascinating: poles apart from any other rye on the market... *53.8% (1076 proof)*

⬥ **Kozuba Straight Rye Double Oaked** 100% malted rye nbc db (**84**) n21 t21.5 f21 b20.5 Well, for a start, the fact it has been finished in ex-Cognac casks means this is no longer straight rye...I need to clear that as it is causing so much confusion among people new to whiskey. As for this particular version: can't say it works for me, brandy cask or no. Simply too aggressively sharp with the butyric-type note thrown in for good measure, *55% (110 proof) Three years in American oak followed by in two years ex-brandy European oak casks.*

⬥ **Kozuba Straight Rye Small Batch** 100% malted rye nbc db (**86.5**) n22 t22.5 f20.5 b21.5 A seemingly youthful rye which puts the accent of the whiskey very much on a fresh citrus-led tang. Eye-watering sharp in places, the salivating qualities on delivery are rather lovely. The finish needs a little bit of attention as the untidiness fails to live up to the earlier promise. *45% (90 proof)*

MANIFEST DISTILLING Jacksonville, Florida.
Manifest 100% Rye Batch 1 db (**86.5**) n20.5 t21.5 f23 b21.5 A very untidy rye, not least with a bitter-ish tobacco note on the nose and very little structure to the delivery. However, at around the midpoint it throws off its shackles and displays both the grain and a gorgeous chocolate milkshake note off to superb effect, the sparkling Demerara on the finale rounding things off superbly. Worth investigating just for that dreamy finish. *50% (100 proof).*

Georgia
ASW DISTILLERY Atlanta, Georgia.
Burns Night Single Malt db (**95.5**) n24 t24 f23.5 b24 I tasted this after their Tire Fire, as this contained the feints from that distillate...so one must assume there was a lot, as Tire Fire is so clean. I suspect this is better quality whiskey than Rabbie Burns ever got his lips around... This will be in the running for micro-distillery whiskey of the year for certain... Magnificent: such a classy, classy act... *46% (92 proof).*

SWAMP FOX DISTILLING CO. Buena Vista, Georgia.
Swamp Fox Distilling Co. Will O' The Wisp White Whiskey Aged 3 Months Minimum nbc db (**84**) n20.5 t21.5 f21 b21 This young whiskey is vibrant and bursting at the seams with busy sugars and complex compound grains. It is undone, though, by the tobacco notes from the distillation which undermines both the nose and finish in particular. *50% (100 proof).*

Illinois
BLAUM BROS Galena, Illinois.
Blaum Bros Straight Rye Whiskey 4 Years Old db (**90.5**) n23 t23 f22 b22.5 A sturdy and steady rye with just the right degree of brittleness. *50% (100 proof).*

FEW SPIRITS DISTILLERY Evanston, Illinois.
FEW Bourbon Whiskey batch no. 18K14, bott code: 318 347 1555 db (**95**) n23.5 t24 f23.5 b24 This distillery has moved a long way in a relatively short space of time. A real force for quality now on the US whiskey scene. *46.5% (93 proof).*

KOVAL DISTILLERY Chicago, Illinois.
⬥ **Koval Single Barrel Bourbon** certified organic, barrel no. 4351 db (**94**) n23.5 one of those bourbons where the small grains appear to lord it over the corn....and even tannin. Busy, and beautifully balanced...not least thanks to the deft Manuka honey; t23.5 excellent red and black liquorice interplay, all played out on the silkiest corn oil imaginable, sweetened further by ulmo honey. At about the midway mark those small grains come back into action – you'll know because your tongue will suddenly start thrashing around your palate to greet them...; f23 light mocha to join the black liquorice....; b24 I have to say that this distillery does bourbon rather well...and consistently well at that. *47% (94 proof)*

⬥ **Koval Single Barrel Millet** 100% millet barrel no. 6796 db (**92.5**) n22.5 ticks all the classic millet whiskey boxes, especially with the intensity of the grain, which in itself is neither sweet nor dry. But there are oaky influences upping the sweetness levels considerably. It is the spices, though, which really has its say...; t23.5 that is rather beautiful distillation, with the cuts on point to absolutely make the most of the flavours and natural oils of the grain. Plenty of toffee mixing in with this, though the one surprise is reticence of the spices to get too deeply involved; f23 long, with the spices at last waking up. Light manuka honey sits well with the butterscotch tart and vanilla; **b23.5** now here's a whiskey my parrot, Percy, would be deeply interested in....enough for him to even turn beak up at the three grain. Sadly for him, he's at my home in England...while I'm tasting this at my home in Kentucky. Millett, for those new to this grain, tends to offer a deeply intense persona with flavour you need to cut with a knife. This is a very good representation, though sweeter than most. *55% (110 proof)*

⟐ **Koval Single Barrel Rye Bottled In Bond** 100% rye, certified organic, barrel no. MU6X66 db **(93)** **n23.5** rye at its most toasty. Rather than the usual display of crisp grain, the tannins have taken control here for a more earthy, weighty and even slightly salty slant. The rye chips in with its customary firmness; **t23** salivating and acidic, the vanillas really do pile in here in a way not for a moment forecast on the nose. The midground returns to that heavier, saltier tannin, to keep the juices flowing; **f23** long with attractive, meandering milky coffee tones, delicately sweetened with Demerara, keeping a lid on the spices; **b23.5** a very entertaining take on a BIB rye, with the tannins have an ever bigger say than the grain – never a straightforward achievement when it comes to rye. *50% (100 proof)*

⟐ **Koval Single Barrel Rye Amburana Barrel Finished** barrel no.717AS3 db **(84.5)** **n21.5** **t22.5** **f20** **b20.5** An individual's take on this one will be on how you feel an amburana wood. I first came across it many, many years ago in Brazil...and it reminded me of cookies that my Brazilian then girlfriend used to make. While attractive in its own right, it doesn't much help in a whiskey achieving balance – without which great whiskey can never be achieved. Take the nose: the rye characteristic has been obliterated. And when I pour a rye I rather want to see that grain in action. The main thrust on the palate is silky - creamy, even - sweet and pleasant enough. But still displaying so much of the ultra-sweet amburana nature, again the grain is lost until towards the very end. That said, I really do like the sweet/spice balance which works well. But the finish is just a shade too short with the grain now obliterated from view. I know some people are gushing over this type of wood interference, the latest fad to hit whiskey. I'm afraid I'm not one of them. *50% (100 proof)*

⟐ **Koval Single Barrel Rye Maple Syrup Cask Finish** 100% rye barrel no. &Q9W1S db **(93.5)** **n23** just love the way the prickly spices play their part here, acting as the perfect foil to the dominating honeyed sweetness. Almost a Port Morant Demerara rum-like quality to this, too...; **t23.5** silky, elegant and eloquent, the sugars build early and for a moment look as though they will become too dominant. But a wonderful vanilla and tannin surge causes restraint, though the spices nibble pleasantly; **f23** spiced treacle tart; **b24** the maple syrup cask in North America's answer to Europe's PX wine cask. The sugary nature of the rye responds positively to the maple influence of the wood. It makes for not just lush whiskey but a very sweet and sharp one which keeps the taste buds hopping from one moment to the next. Rather lovely. *50% (100 proof)*

⟐ **Koval Single Barrel Three Grain Whiskey** mashbill: rye, oat, millet, certified organic, barrel no. 3926 db **(89)** **n22** quite acidic and tart; **t23** massive and unique flavour explosion on delivery. It is though the grains hit the palate and then go their separate ways around the taste buds, leaving a void into which spices, toffee and heather honey falls; **f21.5** not so sure about the finale which return to that tart nose and even offers a mildly puckering quality. The tannins when they arrive are pretty full frontal...; **b22.5** if you want to take your taste buds to the gym and put them through their paces, grab a bottle of this. Nothing on the planet quite matches the mouth-watering mild insanity of this flavour profile. *55% (110 proof)*

WHISKEY ACRES DISTILLING CO. DeKalb, Illinois.

Whiskey Acres Distilling Co. Straight Rye Whiskey Aged at Least 2 Years db **(92)** **n23.5** **t23** **f22.5** **b23** An incredibly tasty rye where the flavours are impossible to tame. Rich and vibrating with rye intensity. Again, a slightly cleaner cut and we'd be talking top drawer whiskey. *43.5%*

Indiana
HARD TRUTH DISTILLING CO Brown County, Indiana.

Hard Truth Sweet Mash Straight Rye Aged over 2 years batch no 3, size 30 barrels, dumped 2/16/22 rackhouse no. 1; mash bill 1; db **(94.5)** **n23** **t24** **f23.5** **b24** well, I certainly warmed to this distillery the moment I saw its name. But I positively embraced them with pure love when I tasted this stupendous rye. My word: there is no getting away from The Truth that they have hit the ground running. They have no right to have produced something this good so early in their lifetime. This is complex rye, true and hard-hitting. But always with a kind softness lurking somewhere about the nose and palate. And though the Truth may sometimes hurt, this most certainly doesn't... *57.65% (155.3 proof). cs nf*

SPIRITS OF FRENCH LICK West Baden Springs, Indiana.

Lee W Sinclair Four Grain Bourbon Aged At Least 4 Years Bottled In Bond recipe: corn, wheats, oats, barley bott code 21234 db **(87.5)** **n22** **t22.5** **f21** **b22** Even before I checked the mashbill on this I was thinking: "porridge!" Both on nose and delivery. Oats can have a disproportionate effect on a whiskey, and this is certainly the case here...giving it a doughy quality found in certain Austrian whiskies. The nose and finish testify to some looseness so far as feints are concerned. But there is no faulting the powerful character and delicious nature of this bourbon, especially on the magnificent delivery which is at times a festival of ulmo honey. The tannins work superbly and there is, at times, a seasoned citrus element. The spices, if anything, are a little too lively on the finish. However, this is obviously a bourbon on a mission and sets out on its own trail. It is certainly an interesting and enjoyable one. *50% (100 proof). Distilled and Bottled by Spirits if French Lick, West Broch Springs Indiana*

⬧ **The Mattie Gladden Indiana Straight Bourbon Aged 5 ½ Years** barrel no 519 55% corn 35% rye 18% malt db **(86) n21.5 t22 f21 b21.5** OK, I'm getting confused here. Having been pointed in the direction of this brand by people whose understanding of bourbon I trust and respect, last year I tasted something which rather disappointed me. So I have gone again, reassured by my friend that all is now well. And still, just like last year, a feintiness from the wayward cut has undone its limited charms. Next year, perhaps...? Best of five...? *52% (104 proof) Selected by Frankfort Bourbon Society.*

⬧ **Lee W. Sinclair Barrel Series Indiana Straight Bourbon** barrel no 718 db **(89.5) n22.5** highly attractive caramel gleaned off very high-quality oak. The sugar and spices square up to each other as equals. A tad hot from non-spice influences and the oils could do with trimming. But deeply attractive for all that...; **t22** wow! Hot as Hades, and spices from the oak haven't even entered the fray yet. But when it settles there is a small grain explosion which is highly salivating while the corn oils and vanillas form a rich backdrop; **f22.5** so much vanilla and caramel. A real crème brûlée statement made here as at last a genteel softness is at last allowed to dominate; **b22.5** now that's more like it. Still a long way from technical excellence, though there is a little way to go). However, someone should spare the whip so far as the stills are concerned. This needs kinder distillation. *52.9% (105.9 proof) Selected by Frankfort Bourbon Society.*

⬧ **Hoosier Homestead Rye Aged 5 ½ Years 100% Indiana Rye** barrel no 463 db **(87) n21.5 t22 f21.5 b22** Despite the light feints at play here we still have a rye which is punching out grains like there is no tomorrow. The big heat confirms yet again that those stills were positively hissing when his rye was made. The result is a far thinner whiskey than it should be as the poor old copper has been flashed by, rather than hugged and loved. A little hickory and clove works wonders on installing depth and there is much here to savour. But an equal amount to regret. *51.45% (102.9 proof)*

⬧ **The Lost River Indiana Straight Bourbon Aged 6 ½ Years** db **(87) n22 t21.5 f22 b21.5** On the nose there is excellent interplay between rich caramels, and toasty liquorice;. In the background the oxyacetylene torches have been ignited. Which results in ridiculously warming on delivery, but after the heat ray has been switched off we have a really gorgeous vanilla and red liquorice massage of the palate. Yay! A French Licks whiskey free from any feinty weakness. But still marked down because those stills were run like the end of the world was nigh. Please don't confuse spice with heat off the still. Had this been naturally spiced, rather than raced, this would have been one hell of a bourbon whiskey. *57.1% (114.2 proof)*

⬧ **Hindostan Falls Barrel Series Aged 4 ½ Years** heirloom corn rye, malt. barrel no 915 db **(86) n22.5 t22 f20.5 b21** This has to be among the most aggressive whiskeys in the US, if not the world. At first it gaslights you into thinking all is well: on the nose is the cream toffee with a rye guest appearance just giving things a fresh green apple element, indeed something of a toffee apple demeanour. And once the searing heat of delivery subsides we can get on with the more approachable hickory-kissed vanilla. But soon we are back to the toffee again and even more explosive fireworks that take a layer or two of skin off the palate. Yikes! *50.7% (10.7 proof)*

OLD 55 DISTILLERY Newtown, Indiana.

Old 55 Single Barrel Bourbon batch 18D4A db **(90.5) n23 t23 f22 b22.5** OK, now I'm confused! No, make that bewildered... How can a distillery which made and matured this be responsible for their bizarre 100% sweet corn above. I am genuinely scratching my head to remember the last time I encountered two polar-opposites in quality from the same distillery. Please note and mark it vividly in your diary: this is delicious and quite faultless, super-rich bourbon. *54.8%*

Iowa
CAT'S EYE DISTILLERY Bettendorf, Iowa.

Cat's Eye Distillery Essence of Iowa db **(87) n21.5 t22 f21.5 b22** Ah! So this is what Iowa smells like, is it? Well, for those who have never been there, let me tell you it has a distinctive citrus lightness to the aroma, though at times it can come through quite sharply. Strange, as I always though Iowa smelt like cheese. To taste, there is a very sweet vanilla lead, the corn oils filling the palate to generate a lush and friendly mouthfeel. Perhaps a little tangy at the death. But, in essence, Iowa is a very friendly place, indeed. *40% (80 proof)*.

CEDAR RIDGE Shwisher, Iowa
No 9 Slipknot Iowa Corn Whisky Aged 3 Years db **(91)** n22.5 t23.5 f22 b23 Pretty classic corn oil, not one of the easier American whiskies to get right. No shortage of acacia honey to aid the enjoyment. Iowa is one of the few States in the US I have yet to visit. This distillery gives me reason enough to put that right. *45% (90 proof)*

Kentucky
CASTLE AND KEY Millville, Kentucky
⬥ **Castle & Key Small Batch Kentucky Straight Bourbon Aged 4 Years Released in 2023** batch no 1 db **(88)** n22 t23 f21.5 b21.5 Such an improvement on last year's offering which represented one of the disappointments of 2022. No feints at work here, though you still get the feeling that this is a bourbon continuing to find both its feet and identity. Structurally sound now, you still get the feeling that this was extracted from the warehouse at a time it wasn't quite ready. There is a vague bitterness to both the nose and finish, though the sprightly – almost sneeze-inducing - black peppers on the aroma compensates. Decent vanillas wallow but the liquorice note it was building up to hasn't quite developed. Off-balance but promising. *50% (100% proof)*

⬥ **Castle & Key Small Batch Wheated Kentucky Straight Bourbon Aged 5 Years Released in 2023** batch no 1 db **(91.5)** n22.5 prickly spices sidestep a mild vegetable note. But a little marzipan-sweetened hickory works wonders; t23 and there is that hickory note again, flying proud on delivery. The sugars are granular and so, curiously, are the vanilla notes. The corn oils impressively do their job; f23 lots of molasses-darkened custard at play here, though the oak interference does start to make the finish unusually dry. Those spices are persistent to say the least. Some very late mocha is a surprise; b23 by far and away the best bourbon I have seen yet from the Castle and Key and hope this is an indicator of things to come. So attractively but understatedly complex. And well made, too... *45% (90% proof)*

⬥ **Castle & Key Restoration Kentucky Straight Rye Aged 3 Years Released in 2022** batch no 3 db **(87)** n22 t22.5 f21 b21.5 As well as whiskey, McCracken Pike, where this distillery is located and where for two decades I had a home, over the years had its share of tobacco barns, too. And it was there the leaves would be laid out to dry. So no little irony that there is an intriguing battle between rye and tobacco notes starting on the nose and finishing at the very end. If you are smoker, you might just adore this. If, like me you aren't and never have been. it will be a bit more of a challenge. Got to say, though, that the delivery, where the rye notes are at their clearest and most intense, is rather lovely. *53% (106% proof)*

GLENNS CREEK DISTILLERY Frankfort, Kentucky.
⬥ **Glenns Creek A-Maize-ing C.O.B. Kentucky Bourbon Whiskey Aged At Least 33 Months** recipe 100% corn; barrel no 6 db **(93)** n24 corn plus heather honey plus vanilla; t23.5 corn plus vanilla plus heather honey; f22.5 vanilla plus corn plus heather honey; b23 just a reminder: C.O. B. stands for Corn Only Bourbon. And this is certainly a cornucopia of maizey intent. It was just over a year ago I last tasted another sample of this, and this bottling is correspondingly containing whiskey at least nine months older. The result is just as slick as the last bottling, with corn oils by far the most dominant and prevailing force. But here some heather honey and vanilla notes have been etched into the picture. While the finish may just have a faint echo of something a little bitter, the nose is stunningly sexy: positively cornographic.... *52% (104% proof)*

⬥ **Glenns Creek Café Ole Kentucky Bourbon Whiskey Aged At Least 47 Months** barrel no 19 db **(84)** n20 t21 f22 b21 Now, I'm not sure they really intended this. It is so very different to the last bottling as to be unrecognisable. It has snagged on a mild butyric note which has thrown the nose and delivery right out of line. Once it corrects its wobble it re-finds those remarkable mocha notes but seems a bit wary afterwards. By the way, the molasses now running through it really is a remarkable force for the good. *54.5% (109% proof)*

⬥ **Glenns Creek !Cuervito Vivo! Kentucky Bourbon Whiskey Aged At Least One Year** barrel no 2 db **(92)** n22 very young but some budding if untidy hickory notes intrigue; t23.5 ooh, I just so love that! I mean, really love it! The marriage of hickory and black liquorice here just squawks "bourbon" at you. Incredibly dry in the very places you'd expect sweetness, though some molasses notes roll in as brooding as a thundercloud...; f23 long, still remarkably dry despite a whole volley of vanilla tones. But the hickory still beats, though now joined by a little mocha...; b24 Caw! That was excellent! And just so complex, too. There is something almost disconcertingly timeless about this. I wouldn't mind wagering that old Dr James Crow tasted something not unlike this on Glenns Creek when he was setting up his fledgling wilderness distilleries on beautiful Glenns Creek in the 1830s and '40s. Probably best served in a dirty glass... *52.4% (104.8% proof)*

⟐ **Glenns Creek OCD #5 Kentucky Bourbon Whiskey Aged At Least 43 Months** barrel no 103 db **(91.5) n23** that uniquely fruity #5 years strain is back at work as last year, though this time with a little extra hickory to contend with. Huge esters present, but the trademark lemon blossom honey is there is force, also, alternating between waxy and dry and occasionally sweeter. The spice prickle is insistent, but controlled. Like the Swheat, this is super-dense...; **t23** typical knife and fork delivery: this is so dense with the tannins delving deeply into the corn oils. The liquorice is subdued and is more intent into moving into a more praline-style tannin; **f22.5** the hickory faces stiff competition from the corn. Buttery and ridiculously soft, but slightly bitter late on, too...; **b23** last year the standard OCD #5 was able to see off their Premium version. And all other whiskeys from the micro distilleries from the US. Not this time: the Premium Barrel number 7 below is on a different level. *52% (104% proof)*

⟐ **Glenns Creek OCD #5 Premium Kentucky Bourbon Whiskey** barrel no 7 db **(96.5) n24** how loquacious is that liquorice? How hunky is that hickory? How magnificent is that mocha? How meaningful are those molasses? How spectacular are those spices...? **t24** off the charts layering. You'll find limestone cliffs on the Kentucky river with fewer layers visible than this...The leading hickory is given a softening by the all-prevailing corn oils and simply melts in the mouth. Its place is soon taken by a mewing ulmo honey and vanilla middle before the spices begin to quietly congregate and a succession of still vaguely juicy, vividly crisper rye notes strike; **f24** this is insane! This should be getting simpler, but those layers just keep on coming, the most impressive offering a vanilla and mocha wafer effect. The rye stick has a presence while the hickory/ liquorice note remains muffled by those irrepressible corn oils; **b24.5** just so many flavours, just so few million taste buds to cope with them... What is remarkable about this bourbon is that it is huge, yet the dampening effect of the corn oils – practically unique to this distillery – means that as large as they are, they are always within scale of the whole. The result is a bourbon that you can chew for seemingly hours on end, and no matter how complex the flavour pattern, how big the principal players, it just never gets too much. Remarkable whiskey from Glenns Creek... again! *55.5% (111% proof)*

⟐ **Glenns Creek OCD #5 Premium Kentucky Bourbon Whiskey** barrel no 8 db **(93.5) n23.5** this one is far happier to concentrate on the liquorice side of things, with some heather honey thrown in as a sweetener and rye as a fruitier counterweight...; **t24** far more up-front flavours than barrel no 7. Much more small grain oriented. The oils are not so intense, so there is a crunchy sharpness at work here. But the liquorice has a briefer life span; **f23** slightly bitter at the death, though that doesn't deter the mocha in any way; **b23** shews you how good barrel No 7 was when this, as excellent as it is, is dwarfed in brilliance by its predecessor. *56.8% (113.6% proof)*

⟐ **Glenns Creek Swheat Kentucky Bourbon Whiskey** barrel no 11 db **(95.5) n23.5** exhibition wheated bourbon. There is something of digestive biscuit dunked in molasses-sweetened coffee about this aroma. And trust me, when I'm back in England I will be buying a pack of McVitie's and dunking them into a lightly molassed drop of Javan...; **t24.5** a truly perfect delivery. The corn oils are sublime, of an important weight...and determined to ensure that every atom of wheatiness is placed on full display. So thick, you could stand a spoon up in this. But, even so, the slow arrival of that red and black liquorice, those ever-warming spices, the muscovado sugar...and all the while the creaminess of the corn...; **f23.5** long, with the wheated tones having a longer, sophisticatedly drier say and we are back to cookies again here...and residual coffee. The sweet-dry ratio cannot really be bettered; **b24** would the real barrel number 11 please stand up! Last year, I marked the sample I tasted was from barrel 11. It wasn't: it was from barrel 10. That was very, very good. This effort, one of the densest bourbons you will ever encounter, is even better. Just so beautifully made and the wheat really does do a star turn here offering even more than you might reasonably dare hope for. Quite unique. 53% (106% proof) ncf

LOG STILL DISTILLERY Gethsemane, Kentucky

Monk's Road Fifth District Series Aged 6 Years series 01 barrel no 38 db **(94.5) n23.5 t23.5 f23.5 b24** Not sure you can find a more classic Kentucky 6-year-old than this. The balance between toasted oak and busy grains is exemplary. A bourbon lover's bourbon. Especially those who appreciate the old school... *50% (100 proof)*

KENTUCKY ARTISAN DISTILLERY Crestwood, Kentucky

Cream of Kentucky Straight Rye Whiskey Bottled in Bond db **(81.5) n19 t20 f21.5 b21** On the nose, the minty rye has much to say, but so have the oils from the overgenerous cut. Too feinty on delivery, equally, but this dies off as the grain kicks up a serious head of juicy steam. Toffeed, yet teasing by the mid-ground and for a moment looking confident, thanks especially to the massive injection of spiced muscovado sugars. The oils hanging limpet-like to the palate cling to the spices and sugars with the same determination. The grain at last firms up, as do the cocoa tones which manifest as a full-on chocolate Swiss roll with fondant. Long and, indeed, very creamy.... A rye, then, which takes liberties on the width of the cut, but late on mildly benefits from them: cream, indeed! *50%*

RD ONE DISTILLERY Lexington, Kentucky.

⬩ **RD One Small Batch Kentucky Straight Bourbon Aged 4+ Years** db **(90) n22.5** a nose not to be sneezed it...or maybe it is. This is about as peppery as it gets...; **t23** an astonishing delivery, unique to Kentucky this year. Because of the low corn oil present early on heather honey rises distinctly and catches the spices just as they are about to lift off. Finally, the corn arrives, as does the vanillas changing both the texture and flavour profile into something deeper and chewier; **f22** just a little nagging burnt toast bitterness on the finish, though the sugars and peppers continue to have much to say...; **b22.5** distilled by Dr Pepper...? The spices on here, especially the nose, aren't playing games, and certainly not early on. A full-flavoured bourbon with a degree of distinctive quirkiness, too. Though the passing mocha is relatively standard by this bottling's norm... *49% (98 proof)*

⬩ **RD One Kentucky Straight Bourbon Double Finished In Oak and Maple Barrels** db **(92) n22** maple. With a subtext of maple. And if you look even more carefully you'll find...maple...; **t23.5** wow...I just have to say that the texture is exemplary. The corn oil has blended in with the sticky maple syrup extracted from the wood and formed a mouth feel which is, frankly, perfect. The sugars are at times a little overwhelming, but the natural liquorice off the oak counters brilliantly; **f23** the maple is at last tamed by the vanillas which gang together to ringfence the sanctity of whiskey. The final moments though, where the spices, liquorices, maple and corn oils have their final parting waves is an eye-opener; **b23.5** I have rarely tasted a whiskey finished in a maple cask where I have wondered if a visit to the dentist will soon be required. Here is another example. Though you'd have to be incapable of the joys of life if you didn't fancy at least a second glass of this flavour bomb...Perhaps the most beautifully balanced of maple-derived whiskey signatures I have yet encountered...and certainly one of the surprise packages of the year. *49.95% (99.9 proof)*

⬩ **RD One Kentucky Straight Bourbon Finished With French Oak** db **(92.5) n23** there is enough oak on this for Henry VIII to have built three navies...Intense. Or perhaps In tents...oak ones...; **t23** the nose was spattered with darting peppers. So, too, is the delivery. Though unlike on the nose, there is soon a veritable warehouse of varied sugars and honeys, ranging from vanilla-rich ulmo to a controlled manuka honey-molasses mix. In fact, everything except maple...which perhaps they should leave for another bottling...; **f23** the sugars have worked so hard at the midpoint, the finish is like hummingbird sitting on a branch having had its sucrose-rich fill. Time for some tannin...; **b23.5** something I certainly can't find RD One guilty of is producing identikit whiskey: all their bottlings seem to have a truly unique fingerprint. And this is certainly no exception. *50.5%*

⬩ **RD One Kentucky Straight Bourbon Finished In Brazilian Amburana Barrels** db **(84) n21 t21 f21 b21** It is like a whiskey that has been coercively controlled by a dominant partner. All its original character is wiped away and the odd spice note which you feel might lead to something along a bourbony line is no more than a bit of gaslighting on the drinker. I was told that "experts" reckon this is the new way American whiskey is going. God spare us from "experts". And non-oak. And passing fads. Still, for those who like this style, well I have yet to find anything purer and truer to type. Viva bourbon! *55% (110 proof)*

WHISKEY THIEF DISTILLERY Frankfort, Kentucky.

⬩ **Whiskey Thief Kentucky Straight Bourbon Aged 5 Years** cask B2.2 corn 65% rye 20% malted barley 15% db **(93) n23** pretty well spiced up for a five-year-old with the oak offering hefty weight against the kumquat; **t23.5** confirmation of that spice takes no time in arriving, but nor does a soothing heather honey tone. There is a light hickory buzz working well in tandem with that almost earthy tannin. The soft and shy background of butterscotch and vanilla is so impressively delicate; **f23** amid the light toast the corn oils bid a buttery farewell; **b23.5** this distillery does elegance ridiculously well and doesn't even break sweat to achieve it. *54.4% (108.8% proof)*

⬩ **Whiskey Thief Kentucky Straight Bourbon Aged 6 Years** cask B1 corn 70% rye 20% malted barley 10% db **(95) n23.5** lively spices and lovely liquorice: quite a toasty combination...; **t24** you cannot ask for more from a delivery: both the texture and honey-spangled red liquorice are nigh on perfect. A stunning ulmo and heather honey mix fills the midground; **f23.5** a fabulously long finish, and ridiculously salivating to boot. The spices still simmer, the corn oils caress the taste buds with gentle Demerara sugars and vanilla. While the oak throbs out a statement of good age; **b24** a magnificent bourbon which could not be more comfortable in its own skin. Everything it does is achieved with panache; every beat of flavour seems impeccably timed; every delivery of sugar and honey is met by a countering form of tannin. Even if someone offered you vast amounts of money to dislike this bourbon, you'd simply fail. Miserably. *60.6% (121.2% proof)*

⬩ **Whiskey Thief Kentucky Straight Bourbon Aged 6 Years** cask B2 corn 72% rye 18% malted barley 10% db **(90.5) n23** originally trace mocha, but amid the corn oils it begins to grow in importance; **t23.5** rumbling and rambling oakiness here but always made friendlier by the light golden syrup; **f21.5** the small grains play a surprising degree of importance here, but the tannins are bittering slightly, tool; **b22.5** a generally soft bourbon that one feels is currently transitioning and at a point where although the flavour profile is excellent, there is a slight degree of randomness, also... *57.7% (115.4% proof)*

⌘ **Whiskey Thief Kentucky Straight Bourbon Aged 6 Years** cask B2.2 corn 55% smoked rye 30% malted barley 5% db **(96) n24** well, that's different! It is unlikely you will find a more laid-back, now-you-see-it-now-you-don't smokiness to any whisky on the planet this year. It is fascinating, because the rye sports a delightful muscovado sugar sharpness while an apologetic phenol note tries to quieten it...unsuccessfully, as it happens; **t24** again the rye, uncluttered by smoke, is first to hit home. A light phenol note tucks in rather charmingly with a more delicate tannin and then the spices get moving, slowly at first and then with a far greater pulse; **f24** those spices work beautifully in tandem with some incredibly persistent Demerara. Trace corn oil does offer a degree of stickiness, but the late vanillas are far more confident; **b24** if you are looking for a bourbon that just refuses to step down the well-trodden flavour path, then here it is. And, on the subject of flavours, few whiskeys this year will be offering so many in such a kaleidoscopic format. Wonderful. Breath-taking. Unique. And a genuine whiskey experience. *54.3% (108.6% proof)*

⌘ **Whiskey Thief Kentucky Straight Bourbon Aged 6 Years** cask B4 corn 77% rye 15% malted barley 8% db **(91) n22.5** quite a corn fest, this, with only a little tannin and a half-hearted citrus note as a very effective back up; **t23.5** soft, silky, buttery and then a sweet sheen of golden syrup; some good spices through the middle as the oak gets in the act; **f22.5** corn oils and vanilla in concentrate; **b22.5** perhaps not the most complex Whiskey Thief out there, but what it does it ensures is carried out with genteel aplomb *58.5% (117% proof)*

⌘ **Whiskey Thief Kentucky Straight Bourbon Aged 7 Years** cask B3 corn 72% rye 18% malted barley 10% db **(92.5) n23.5** the rye stomps about as though in hobnail boots, ensuing it is noticed. But it also provides structure. Elsewhere, a surprising coffee note can be detected; **t23** lashings of toffee briefly punctuated by spice. The cocoa and vanilla give this a delicious molten Milky Way candy persona; **f23** the rye returns at the death for a much crunchier finale. Still creamy in part with the tannins giving extra depth to the chewiness; **b23** a very stylistic bourbon which confounds you by displaying its small grain charms at the beginning and end, yet managing to lose them entirely throughout the middle. Perhaps the definition of easy drinking. *59.8% (119.6% proof)*

⌘ **Whiskey Thief Kentucky Straight Bourbon Aged 7 Years** cask B3.2 corn 80% rye 8% malted barley 12% db **(94.5) n23.5** a real classic old corn whiskey nose: heady, oily, soft and rich with red liquorice; **t23.5** that is a highly sensual delivery: the taste buds have the softest and sleekest body being run over it. Both molasses and Demerara sugar play key roles in upping the sweetness levels, to the extent that the whiskey becomes momentarily juicy...; **f23.5** superb chocolate mint finale as the spices a last find their trilling voice – and so silky with it...; **b24** more corn here than one of my jokes. A bewildering degree of complexity for a whiskey geared up to be relatively monolithic. No such thing as a sexy whiskey, eh? Then taste this and think again... *60.4% (120.8% proof)*

⌘ **Whiskey Thief Kentucky Straight Bourbon Aged 7 Years** cask B4 corn 80% rye 8% malted barley 12% db **(88) n22 t22.5 f21.5 b22** Now, how curious is this? Two casks with same age and mashbill (see cask 3.2 directly above) – and yet two very different results. Whereupon 3.2 is a tapestry of complex flavours woven into the corn-rich fabric, this is a much more monosyllabic interpretation...and it must be down to the virgin oak cask. There is nothing not to enjoy about this whiskey, as there are no off notes and all hangs together in a friendly and amiable way. But the small grains here are not attempting their magic and the oak has provided next to nothing in the way of spices or complex cocoa tones. This is much more down the corn whiskey side of the whiskey family than bourbon...and seems excessively proud of it. *60.7% (121.4% proof)*

⌘ **Whiskey Thief Kentucky Rye Aged 5 Years** cask R1 rye 65% malted rye 30% barley 5% db **(95) n23.5** so rare: a new distillery that gets their cuts spot on from the very go: you can almost sniff the outline and shape of the grain itself, so distinct is it. The spices harmonise impressively; **t24** what a delivery! Again, the principal grain is super crunchy, but the malted grains back it up with a sublime wave of salivating, improbably intense spiced muscovado sugars, perfectly backed by some pretty deep tannins; **f23.5** the oaky influence here manifests more in the late spice explosion, level the rye to keep the juicy, salivation levels improbably high for a very long time. A little mocha late on at last offers a deserved softening to the very finale; **b24** when I visited – on more than one occasion – what was then the Three Boys Distillery and now Whiskey Thief, there was none of their rye available to sample. This time my cup overfloweth and there were two. To be honest, I wasn't expecting too much because rye often proves to be the Achilles heel of some of the best bourbon makers. How silly was I to doubt their ability. This is very high class, clean and beautifully defined rye. Bravo....and a whiskey well worth stealing... *57.4% (115.8% proof)*

⚜ **Whiskey Thief Kentucky Rye Aged 5 Years** cask R1.2 rye 65% malted rye 30% barley 5% db (88) n22 t22.5 f21.5 b22 This is a duskier, flatter version of the same rye recipe as above.... and even at an identical strength. More toffee has equated to a calmer, more conservative experience until the slightly bitter finale. Pleasant enough but lacking the nerve-tingling thrills of cask R1. *574% (115.4% proof)*

⚜ **Whiskey Thief Riders On The Storm Aged 7 Years** nbc db (94) n23 something of the old-fashioned candy store with this one, boiled fruit sweet jar open; t23.5 a vivid delivery, the small grains taking no time in not only making their "'ow do"s. Red liquorice melds with blueberry pie with molten icing sugar giving a finishing glaze. On a deeper level the oak is forever enriching, outwardly with intense vanilla. But, on a micro-level, a cluster of deftly spice toasty, sugar notes begin pulsing...; f23.5 the buttery corn oils allows myriad waves of spices and more intrinsic dark sugar tones to play off against the other seemingly indefinitely; b24 such a neat and tidy bourbon, bristling with small grain activism. Sometimes too subtle for its own good, it vastly repays reinspection. One of the most intricate and complex offerings from this magnificent distillery yet. *53.25% 106.5 proof*

⚜ **Whiskey Thief Rain Fall Down Aged 6 Years** nbc db (96) n23.5 the marriage between cocoa and spice here could be the subject for a PhD dissertation.... The nip, the nibble, the kiss, the caress. Or, failing that, a raunchy sex novel...; t24 what a delivery...just what a delivery! The corn oils are so ridiculously accommodating: it is the dais from which the molasses makes its seductive speech, from which the spices fire their unerring shots and where that milk chocolate fondant smothers you and then reduces your taste buds to a quiet frenzy...; f24 just more and more of the same, again with the spices and small grains in a never-ending swirl of activity and the chocolate mousse refusing to let go until you have caved in to its charms entirely...; b24.5 did someone throw some chocolate malt into this by accident? Or is this just distilled chocolate? Simply one of the best bourbons I have tasted this year: made and matured to spitting distance from perfection... Or, preferably, swallowing distance... *58.3% 116.6 proof*

Louisiana
ATELIER VIE PLC New Orleans, Louisiana.
⚜ **Louisiana Single Malt Aged A Minimum Two Years** nbc db (94.5) n23.5 just checked the label: it says nothing about smoke being on this malt...but it's there and make no mistake! Glorious phenols of the most understated and, frankly, sexy kind...; t23.5 the delivery is slightly more than speckled in peat. Light demerara sugars merge into the phenols and spices are the inevitable consequence; f23.5 long, beautifully made with a fabulous clarity to the vanilla which is still haunted by the lingering smoke...; b24 a bewilderingly beautiful malt whisky, the particular style of which I have never before encountered from an American distillery. The smoke on this is just so understated yet effective, one cannot but simply admire and enjoy for all it is worth... I need to get back to New Orleans as I have not been there since pre-Covid: this is astonishing. Singularly the most Scottish style of single malt currently produced in the USA. Indeed, on a blind tasting, were it not for the intensity of the sugars, I would have mistaken this for Scotch every time... *47% (94 proof)*

Maine
WIGGLY BRIDGE DISTILLERY York, Maine.
Wiggly Bridge Small Barrel Bourbon Whisky Aged Under 4 Years in New Small American Oak Barrels db (86) n21 t22 f21.5 b21.5 Though many sugars work overtime to impress, doubtless drawn from the small barrels used, the feints apparent from nose to finish do distract and subtract. The distillers are on the right track, for sure, as a degree of liquorice is to be had. But, hopefully, future bottlings will show a greater understanding of the demands of the stills and the precision required for a clean cut....a bridge, Wiggly or not, that needs crossing. That said, genuinely enjoyed the consistent stratum of molassed toffee buoyed by fine corn oils. *43% (86 proof)*

Maryland
OLD LINE SPIRITS Baltimore, Maryland.
Old Line American Single Malt Whiskey Double Cask aged 3.5 years, Port cask, id: 2102ASM.PCF375 (92.5) n22.5 t23.5 f23 b23.5 It is now fair to say that Old Line have developed their own unique stye of whiskey different to anything else on the planet. It is certainly, for me, the most confusing. Because there is an all-consuming silkiness to their whiskies which are always borderline: when fruit takes over and the malt is lost, does it then cease to be a whisky? I think Old Line has given me more cause for lost sleep, more re-visits to my tasting lab than any other distillers for the last year or two because I keep asking myself: do I love this or am I disappointed by its incredibly linear personality? Then you taste a whiskey like this, watch the atom-by-atom development of the chocolate, as though in super slow motion and you conclude: hell! How can you not love this...? *61.8%*

Massachusetts
TRIPLE EIGHT DISTILLERY Nantucket, Massachusetts.

The Notch Single Malt Whisky Aged 15 Years batch no. 001, dist 2002, bott 2018 db **(96)** n24 t23.5 f24 b24.5 Unquestionably one of the great island malt whiskies outside Scotland. Exudes class from first sniff to last, fading salty signal. Truly brilliant. 48% (96 proof).

Michigan
GRAND TRAVERSE DISTILLERY Traverse City, Michigan.

⬩ **Grand Traverse Double Barrel Ole George 100% Straight Rye** nbc db **(93.5)** n23.5 a small scattering of black peppers seasons up the crisp but otherwise well-behaved intricate rye notes; t23.5 the delivery jolts you back in your chair: the rye is huge, green, grassy and immediately salivating, the peppers joining in quickly add to the delicious carnage on the palate. A breezy series of Demerara sugar notes keep the salivation levels at maximum; f23 a much duller period now as the oak takes command, although those spices are happy to make guerrilla attacks... b23.5 a sturdy, whiskey, with quite beautiful strata, which keeps rye and its accompanying sugars briskly on track. Attractive, no-nonsense, massively flavoured fayre. 46.5% (93 proof)

⬩ **Grand Traverse Double Barrel Ole George 100% Straight Rye** nbc db **(90.5)** n22.5 mildly dusty from the oak unput, the rye has its moment or two of sharp, fruity passion. But they are brief and subdued; t23 an attractive, juicy blast off and fragments of crisp rye scatter across the palate. But a thick toffee-vanilla cloud descends...; f22 the odd echo of rye. But all rather flat and vanilla heavy; b23 a slightly oilier and more vanilla-led version where the rye has far less to say. Which is a bit of a pity, because when it does speak it does so rather eloquently... 50% (100 proof)

⬩ **Grand Traverse Hand Selected Bourbon Single Barrel** barrel no. 632 db **(94)** n24 wonderfully nutty, including roast chestnut. Sits prettily with the polished leather. Some classic light red liquorice and heather honey tones; t23 again, we are back on the trail of chestnut puree. The spices strike early and decisively, interrupting the gathering small grain sweetness; f23 lots if natural toffee, lingering spices and soothing vanillas; b24 there is something noble about the simplicity of this bourbon. It has decided a path, sticks to it and ensures quiet bourbon notes tumble one after the other. Beautiful. 54.45% (108.9 proof)

⬩ **Grand Traverse Single Barrel Ole George Straight Rye** barrel no. 761 db **(89)** n23 t22.5 f21.5 b22 the crisp rye is graphic, the tannins quietly assertive; t22.5 incredibly intensive rye – truly in concentrate form. But there is also a niggling oily note, too; f21.5 clumsy finish with that rye still with its foot flat on the floor; b22 a mind-blowing rye with more grain on shew than I have ever before seen. But there is a nagging off-key note, too, which undoes some of the amazing work. Still have to say that you must ride this one just for the experience. 64.55% (129.1 proof)

⬩ **Grand Traverse Solera Ole George Rye Finished In Cognac Barrels** nbc db **(88.5)** n22 t22.5 f22 b22 Loads of toffee apple here – though for apple read rye. Unbelievably even, though the spices are a tad out of proportion and the toffee a bit on the over enthusiastic side, too. That said, quite wonderfully distilled. 50% (100 proof)

⬩ **Grand Traverse Michigan Wheat 100% Straight Wheat Whiskey Bottled In Bond** nbc db **(95.5)** n24 you almost have to laugh as the spices from the wheat arrive early and in force and demand your attention. In the background, you might well be in a European bakery with bread and savouries in the ovens... But there are sugars and here they are pretty crisp and of the muscovado variety; t24 just about the perfect arrival on the palate: multi-layered and multi-toned. The sharpness of the wheat is equalised by the yielding vanillas, the spices met head on by the oscillating Demerara and delicate molasses sugars; f23.5 the thick vanillas are left to guide the whiskey home, the spices at last mostly, though not entirely, a spent force and just a hint of praline towards the very end; b24 a fabulous wheat whiskey, still on the same dream-like level as when I last tasted this, with the spices here being slightly more detached than they were previously. This is superbly - indeed, quite faultlessly - distilled and matured and a whiskey required the full Murray Method to get to the bottom of...and then savoured all the way. Spellbinding. 50% (100 proof)

JOURNEYMAN DISTILLERY Three Oaks, Michigan.

Journeyman Last Feather Rye Whiskey batch 72 db **(91)** n22.5 t23.5 f22 b23 Truly a unique rye whiskey profile and one, that despite the odd fault, literally carries you on a delicious journey. 45% (90 proof).

NEW HOLLAND BREWING COMPANY Holland, Michigan.

⬩ **Dragon's Milk Beer Barrel Bourbon** bourbon finished in Dragon's Milk Stout barrels nbc db **(87)** n21 t22 f22 b22 A silky whiskey typical of a cream stout cask in action. I have a slight problem with the hop on the nose (as I always do). But beyond that this is super-easy going with molten Demerara working well with the untaxing vanillas. 40% (80 proof)

◇ **Dragon's Milk Origin Straight Bourbon Aged 5 Years** bott code B243 db (**91**) n22.5 delicate ginger nibbling on the lightest liquorice. Busy, with a gentle sweet curve of molasses and the small grains bubbling away endearingly; **t23** immediately salivating and hits its stride early on with an decent manuka honey and liquorice double act before lashings of vanilla makes its mark; **f22.5** attractive late liquorice-hickory voluntary; **b23** takes a little bit of time to tease this bourbon into action but well worth the wait. Especially when those small grains get going. 47.5% (95 proof). 502 243 5073

Minnesota
DU NORD CRAFT SPIRITS Minneapolis

◇ **Du Nort Mixed Blood Whiskey** "homegrown mash blended with whiskeys of other houses" nbc db (**86**) n22 t22.5 f20 b21.5 No, I have no idea what that blurb on the label means, either. As they are distillers, I gave them the benefit of the doubt and their own entry, rather than just placing in American Blends. My eyebrows raised when I found a peaty phenolic glint to the nose which is not at all unattractive, while that smoke also plays a key role in the arrival an early development. Just turns a little too thin towards the finish, as does the oak content, though the silky texture is maintained. Very much American blend in nature, but with some early charm. 40% (80 proof)

Montana
MONTGOMERY DISTILLERY Missoula, Montana.

◇ **Mama Tried High-Rye Bourbon** nbc db (**87.5**) n21.5 t23 f21 b22 Not all quite technically present and correct, as the nose and finish testify. But there is no faulting the delivery which really does make a thing about the high rye included in the mashbill, for it's this grain which dominates quite spectacularly, on the flavour profile. Thumping Demerara sugars and spices combine with a gorgeous degree of thick vanilla. For good measure. The dry, bitter-ish and tangy finish can't quite keep pace, but worth finding for the delivery alone. 45% (90 proof)

◇ **Mama Tried Wheated Bourbon** nbc db (**88.5**) n21.5 t22.5 f22 b22.5 A pleasant, ambling bourbon where the spices off both the wheat and oak make by far the biggest impact. The sub-current of amiable vanilla carries just enough liquorice to give this the bourbon weight required for attractive drinking. Salivating throughout... 45% (90 proof)

◇ **Montgomery American Single Malt 5 Years Aged** dist 2017 wheat nbc db (**84.5**) n20.5 t22 f21 b21 One of the most malty, most gristy whiskeys made in the USA. The aroma is perhaps not the greatest advertisement for it, displaying the odd butyric note or two, but it gamely rallies on the palate with a welter of sugary blows which beats the taste buds into submission. The milky coffee tone at the death is quite intriguing. 45% (90 proof)

◇ **Sudden Wisdom Straight Rye Aged 3 Years** 100% rye nbc db (**91**) n23 now, I do like that...! Just adore that sprig of mint adorning the freshly shelled peas and crunchy citrus. Unmistakably rye, and Montgomery have set about giving their own unique aromatic fingerprint; **t23** what an impressively precise delivery: the rye is given free rein to display its mouth-watering wares, the sweetness is shaped by a wonderful mix between Demerara sugars and melon-blossom honey. The spices start slowly but grow dramatically; **f22** so impressed with the oil content here which is enough to really extract every last nuance from the grain. Remains refreshing and lively to the very end, even when some delicate vanillas come into play; **b23** could be the distillery has found its niche. Fabulous texture, they have found their cuts here and the secret of extracting every last nuance from their grain. Big-flavoured, statement-making, entertaining rye. Love it. 45% (90 proof)

New England
SONS OF LIBERTY Rhode Island, New England.

Battle Cry American Single Malt Whiskey db (**77.5**) n19 t21 f18 b19.5 A sweet, nutty whiskey weakened by the butyric-like off notes. 46% (92 proof).

New York
BREUCKELEN DISTILLING Brooklyn, New York.

77 Whiskey Bonded Rye & Corn Aged 4 Years American oak barrels db (**95**) n23.5 t24 f23.5 b24 There you go: Breuckleyn back on track with a spot edition of their signature brand. Sings from the glass like a barber-shop quartet. 50% (100 proof).

CATSKILL PROVISIONS DISTILLERY Long Eddy NY

◇ **Pollinator Spirits Bonfire Rye** batch no 10 db (**87**) n22 t22 f21 b22 not quite technically perfect but there is a minty swirl to the fruitier rye tones here. The citrus and vanilla are evenly matched. A faltering start on the palate maybe, but you have to doff your hat to the sheer determination of that rye grain to make its mark. However, the clumsy oils are just too persistent on the finish. 50% (100 proof)

⟨⟩ **Pollinator Spirits Bourbon Finished In Maple Syrup Barrels** batch 10 db **(88.5)** n22 t22 f22.5 b22 This is an attractive, supremely soft whiskey having the same done to it as many single malts in Scotland when matured in PX sherry. The sugars are so profound and the lush that they even out the hills and valleys of the flavour profile to present a flat landscape on the nose and palate. It inhibits complexity, but here the trade-off is a lovely interplay between the richer, darker tones of the maple syrup and the myriad spices. Meanwhile, what was once the bourbon has vanished. Still, if you are looking for a gentle, liqueur-ish whiskey, you have just found it. 40% (80 proof) 900 bottles

⟨⟩ **Pollinator Spirits Rye Finished In Honey Barrels** batch 43 db **(85.5)** n21 t23 f20.5 b21 This is not the first whisky I have encountered in the world matured in honey barrels. But it is certainly the first rye so treated. The result is, I admit, an entirely new flavour map for me, though it is only too easy to veer off course. This is not helped by a fustiness to the rye which dominates the nose and finish. However, when the sugars make a beeline for the mid-ground, they take with them some short-lived but effective spices and neutralise the quirkier notes of the rye, allowing the grain a moment or two of charm. Some brief excellence here. 40% (80 proof)

COOPERSTOWN DISTILLERY Cooperstown, New York.
Cooper's Legacy Bourbon Whiskey Grant's Recipe bott code. 147 02 db **(95)** n23.5 t24 f23.5 b24 I'd like, with this exceptional bourbon, to raise a toast to my son, James', new (indeed, first) dog: Cooper. Named, naturally, after Dale Cooper of Twin Peaks fame. Dale whippet. Dale bourbon. 50% (100 proof).

FINGER LAKES DISTILLING Burdett, New York.
⟨⟩ **McKenzie Bottled In Bond Straight Bourbon Aged Minimum of 4 Years** nbc db **(92)** n23 a sharp almost acidic nip to the liquorice. Light molasses, but does nothing to reduce the toasty timbre; t23.5 boy, does this one shake up the taste buds. Incredibly alive, tart, and juicy the black liquorice is almost three dimensional in its complex structure. Light corn oils through the middle; f22.5 bitters very slightly towards the end. But the toastiness never wavers. Delicate hickory towards the death; b23 one of the tarter bourbons doing the rounds. But certainly doesn't stint on the classic bourbon characteristics. Confident stuff and highly impressive, indeed. 50% (100 proof) ncf; a wheated bourbon

⟨⟩ **McKenzie Empire Rye Straight Rye Aged Minimum of 4 Years** 80 rye 20% malted barley nbc db **(92.5)** n23.5 clean rye which builds in its intensity with a spicy elegance; t24 the brittleness of the rye generates a wonderfully salivating scene, with spices quickly out of the blocks before being recalled for a false start. Absolutely classic rye fruitiness, this time sharp and uncompromising, the Demerara sugars sweet enough to cope with any excesses: simply fabulous...; f22.5 the oak feels a bit strained towards the end while lime peel keeps the fruity sharpness very much alive; b23.5 a testament to the high distilling practices carried out at Finger Lakes, this is one of the very few independent whiskey producers who make their rye without any hint of feints spoiling the fun. High rye content and very high-quality whiskey – as one now comes to expect from the McKenzie brand. 45.5% (91 proof) ncf

⟨⟩ **McKenzie Pure Pot Still Whiskey Aged Minimum of 6 Years** nbc db **(92)** n23.5 a distinctive semi-gristy and meal flour nose, retaining a clipped, clean acacia honey sweetness. The vanillas are light a mildly aloof; t23.5 mmmm! What a delicious mouthfeel on delivery. Silky texture – no doubt thanks to the tell-tale oat involvement (and good luck to them on cleaning out their equipment after making this!) – with a flavour profile of golden syrup stirred into porridge and firmer, sharper tone as the mouth feel firms up and becomes almost eye-watering; f22 just a degree of unkempt and unwanted tartness towards the finale; b23 from its personality and colour it appears that this whiskey has been matured in used bourbon casks: a very wise choice for retaining and maximising the character of the grain. Further evidence, not that it was needed, that these people really know what they are doing. 40% (80 proof) ncf distilled from barley and oat mash

⟨⟩ **McKenzie Small Batch Straight Bourbon 4 Grain Aged A Minimum of 4 Years** nbc db **(95)** n23.5 they make play on the label about the four grains and that is interesting: because the first time I spotted that I had already nosed this and was astonished by the small grains complexity which has replaced the normal liquorice as leading the aromatic charge. The sugars are demure and weighted towards Muscovado. The liquorice is about, of course, alongside a subtle degree of hickory; t24 those bitty small grains are straight into action on delivery. The sugars are so clean and fruity it takes a while before they begin to take on a more classical dark hue. The corn oils are elegant and precise, the spices ridiculously polite and controlled; f23.5 long, languid and just layering on the vanilla, butterscotch and heather honey to a delightful degree. Look carefully and that liquorice is, of course, still doing the rounds; b24 of the three McKenzie bourbons, this one enjoys star billing. The complexity of this bourbon is exhilarating and shews such a high degree of bourbon craftsmanship. A bourbon I'd happily enjoy any day of the week... even in Kentucky. This is a big whiskey, though first you wouldn't know, so complex are the myriad influences that make up this ultra-sophisticated bourbon. The closest I can recall in style to this was when pre-Sazerac owned Barton Distillery made their sublime 6-year-old some 25 years ago... What a shame there is no batch or bottling code to this... 48% *(96 proof) ncf*

⬧ **McKenzie Straight Bourbon Aged A Minimum of 4 Years** nbc db **(93.5)** n23 a lovely honeydew melon sweetness tops of the more brooding house style liquorice; **t23.5** beautifully vivid on the palate, the delivery offers a friendly exchange between Demerara and molasses while the oak builds slowly but surely in its toastiness. Spices are sprinkled through the mid-point but are never more than gentle; **f23** back to the liquorice again, a pleasing combination of back and red with a little hickory building for good effect; **b24** beautifully distilled bourbon. The cuts on here are just about perfect and while the harmony between the oak-unleashed sugars and resident corn oils work beautifully. Another impressive bourbon from this solid and honest distillery. 50% *(100 proof) ucf high rye bourbon*

⬧ **McKenzie Straight Malt Whiskey Aged Minimum of 10.5 Years** nbc db **(81)** n20.5 t22 f18.5 b20 On my flight to Kentucky from London to taste these American whiskeys, I watched (for the third time in my life) the film "Contact". I remember the first time: I was flying to the West Indies in the late 1990s, at the time of the film's release, to create a pot still rum blend. The film starts with radio and television waves being broadcast from this planet inadvertently outwards towards the solar system. The further you travelled in distance, and therefore time, the older the programmes and the less sophisticated they became. It strikes me as the perfect metaphor for whiskey, especially that made by the small independent distillers who in their early days had to learn by trial and error. So, when I see a whiskey produced by anyone with considerable great age to what they are bottling today, I expect it to be faulty and unsophisticated; almost certainly feinty. Well, as some distilleries go, the feints on this aren't too bad. But they are big enough – and a few other technical frailties - to make this malt fly off kilter too many times to count. Not the greatest whiskey you'll ever experience. But, personally, I have always found history fascinating. 43% *(86 proof) ucf*

IRON SMOKE WHISKEY Fairport, New York.

⬧ **Iron Smoke Straight Bourbon Bottled In Bond Aged 8 Years** nbc db **(95.5)** n24 so toasty... and more. The sweetness is not unlike French toast, though with a little maple syrup finding its way into the recipe, also. But these strands of dark sugars and slightly burned toast are incessant...; **t24** the blend of hickory and black liquorice needs a carefully monitored dose of molasses for perfect balance. And it gets it...; **f23.5** the corn oils at last spilling out to soften things a little and add length. But you know those liquorice tones will return despite the prevailing sugars...and they do...; **b24** I've just crumpled into a whimpering heap with this display of complex toasty tones which hits the nose and massages the palate like a bourbon greatest hits playlist; this is simply outstanding bourbon. And make no bones about it... 50% *(100 proof) 1866 bottles*

⬧ **Iron Smoke Straight Bourbon Four Grain** bott 4.21.23 batch 66 db **(90.5)** n23 hang on... is that apple wood (a quick reference to the bottle is required....please hold on, dear reader)....? Ah, yes it is..! Now that's not something I've encountered for three or four years..; **t22.5** super soft delivery (which may be accounted for that of the whiskeys I have tasted today, this is the only one at the old-fashioned 40%...!) with corn oil bathing the taste buds with sweet vanillas while the more assertive sugars and smoke take a more forceful line; **f22** surprisingly sharp, almost malty in style, and salivating at the death; **b23** a malt that will kill you with gentle kindness. 40% *(80 proof)*

⬧ **Iron Smoke Straight Bourbon Casket Strength** bott 6.9.22 batch 10 db **(94.5)** n23.5 silky hickory enjoys the punchy spices. A little pear drop sharpness works well here, too...; **t23.5** the corn oil fattens and caresses. But then the spices blaze away until the house-style liquorice and hickory dual act ensure the right degree of toastiness. Vanillas from the oak are also pretty full on, as are the Demerara sugars; **f23.5** light manuka honey stays the course, offering an extra waxy dimension. The spices continue their warming work but the butterscotch and vanillas ensure this turns into some kind of treacle tart with attitude; **b24** got to say that although they have been carrying the "Casket Strength" line for a good number of years (their motif is a skull smoking a pipe), amid all the po-faced, Woke, humourless misery that is engulfing the world, it was wonderful to see the great distillers at Iron Smoke carry on with their amusing brand: indeed, it made me laugh out loud to see it again. So, to honour these people who not only make great whiskey but have retained their sense of humour, I made this my 500th whisky tasted for this the 2024 Whisky Bible. Oh, and as for the whiskey itself: you can shove a bottle of this in my casket when the time comes... 60% *(120 proof)*

KINGS COUNTY DISTILLERY Brooklyn, New York.

Kings County Distillery Peated Rye Aged 2 Years or More batch no. 2 db **(94)** n23 t24 f23 b24 From those who brought you Peated Bourbon, Kings Country now offer their Peated Rye version. It takes a while or the palate to adjust to these unusual signals, but once it does it is a joy all the way... Brilliant! 45% *(90 proof)*.

LAST SHOT DISTILLERY Skaneateles, NY

◈ **Last Shot Bourbon Small Batch Single Barrel** barrel no. 68 db **(88.5) n22 t22 f22 b22.5** Big on the hickory and molasses, it still somehow has a truly singular bourbon style. Indeed, anyone who remembers Bowmore from 20 years ago will pick up a particular Victory V cough sweet style. Love the spices on this which takes on the sugars head-to-head, while the soft vanillas make for the most gentle of landings. A distillery which has certainly forged its very own signature. 42% *(84 proof)*

◈ **Last Shot Skaneateles Whisky Distiller's Reserve** distilled from corn, wheat and tritical bott code 25622 db **(86) n20.5 t22 f21.5 b22** Struggles from the start to find a particular rhythm. Tritical is used by a few European distillers and most find a problem controlling its occasionally bitter output. The nose apart, the distillers appear to have overcome that challenge, and well done them. The avalanche of Demerara sugars helps no end. 46% *(92 proof)*

MYER FARM DISTILLERS Ovid, NY

◈ **John Myer New York Straight Bourbon Single Barrel** batch/year 23/2022 db **(94) n23** impressive degree of toffee and nut. The leather and red liquorice polishes its bourbony credentials; **t23.5** cripes! One of the crisper bourbons on shew – these sugars really rattle your back teeth. The small grains strafe the taste buds and a lot of salivating results. Again, red liquorice dominates, though a little molasses rows into the moment; **f23.5** just so beautifully busy with those toasty, lightly molasses-rich moments ensuring the big flavours expound – and expand - to the very end; **b24** I suspect this may be the first whiskey I've ever sampled from this distillery and to say I'm pleasantly surprised is an understatement. Just so beautifully crafted. 45% *(90 proof)*

◈ **John Myer New York Straight Four Grain Whiskey Single Barrel Aged 8 Years** batch/year 1/2023 db **(85.5) n20.5 t22.5 f21 b21.5** There is an overwhelming feeling that the stills had not been cranked up that often when they got around to distilling this. Certainly, they had quite got the cuts (and possibly even fermentation) right and, so far as the nose was concerned, there was no correcting that. It is also a nose reminiscent of some peated malt at a famous distillery in Scotland that didn't quite go the way intended and a kind of boiled tomato note was the result. Once on the palate, though the journey is a unique one it is pleasant enough and at times quite attractive. The spices keep pace throughout and the icing sugar can be a little gung-ho here and there. It has ended up with a far higher rating than the nose suggested was possible, but then it possesses far more charm than you might originally think, too. 45% *(90 proof)*

◈ **John Myer New York Straight Rye Single Barrel** batch/year 13/2022 db **(89) n22** attractively minty. A little oily, but the Demerara sugars and thin grapefruit juice adds the balance; **t23** now the rye gets a clear road to do its thing – and grabs the chance with both hands. Quite acidic, sharp and uncompromising in its rye-rich tartness; **f21.5** settles down into a more sombre vanilla-rich mood; **b22.5** the odd technical glitch apart, this rye is an up and in-your-face extrovert...until its collapses exhausted at the end. 45% *(90 proof)*

NEW YORK DISTILLING COMPANY Williamsburg, Brooklyn

◈ **Ragtime Rye New York Straight Rye Whiskey Aged 8 Years** nbc db **(83) n21.5 t21 f20 b20.5** I get the feeling that the distillery was still just finding its feet when this rye was distilled. Harsh, hard and hot. Too many non-sequiturs on the palate to be true. Lots of caramel blots the most excessive of the plaque-dissolving heat from the stills and even allows the grain to occasionally raise its unsullied head above the parapet. But these stills shouldn't be driven like a Formula 1 racing car: the foot needs to come off the pedal. 56% *(112 proof)*

TACONIC DISTILLERY Stanfordville, New York.

◈ **Fox and Hare Single Barrel Straight Rye Aged At Least 4 Years** nbc db **(94.5) n23.5** this is a cracking rye aroma: so clean, allowing the grain to fully expand and tap out its incredible brittle fruity-Demerara sharpness: textbook....; **t24** oh...my...word! The rye is so firm I feel my teeth will be chipped as the two make contact. There is some amazing under-ripe grape and Chinese gooseberry moments giving a shrill sharpness to the already crunchy and super-sharp grain...; **f23** the vanillas flood in like an incoming tide. Yet those granite-like rye tones refuse to be swept away. Just a light oak-induced soapiness late on...; **b24** one of the best and most flavour-studded ryes I have encountered from outside Kentucky for quite some while, even taking into account its last moment flaw (which was pre-warned on the nose as a potential tired cask) .... A brilliantly distilled classic. 62.5% *(125 proof)*

◈ **Horse and Jockey Single Barrel Straight Bourbon Aged At Least 4 Years** nbc db **(92.5) n23** lots of spices join the caramelised cookie thread to make this quite a blistering nose; **t23.5** a gripping delivery which is sharp and eye-watering - and in a way that has nothing to do with the strength. This is about the grains, the small guys in particular, and the way the make the most of their refreshing and salivating nature. Next up are a succession of juicy, crunchy Demerara tones, with a red liquorice follow through. The fat corn oil builds to excellent effect; **f22.5** bitters slightly despite the raging vanillas and persistent spices; **b23.5** fascinating bourbon. The nose is spicy enough to be wheat recipe, the delivery juicy and brisk enough to be a rye one. The only thing I think the distillery can improve upon is giving some kind of barrel, batch or bottling code. There is a number 14 on the mounted racehorse on the label. Whether that is a hint, I really don't know. 62.5% (125 proof)

⟡ **Taconic Single Malt Aged A Minimum of Two Years** nbc db **(80.5)** n19 t21 f20 b20.5 Nope. 43% (86 proof)

⟡ **Taconic Straight Bourbon Bottled In Bond** nbc db **(93)** **n23.5** so much copper punching through – it is even noticeable despite the impressive black liquorice belting out from the oak. The spices ping with intent; **t23.5** heather honey and liquorice combine for a full-bodied delivery while the small grains nibble...as they should; **f23** a little tangy with the copper still doing the rounds. But a light hickory and honey fade ticks the right boxes; **b23** when you get this degree of copper coming through on both nose and taste, it has either been very slowly distilled or some new equipment was being used. Either way, that metallic kick works so well with those classic bourbon signatures. Delightfully flavoursome and had you been told this was Kentucky bourbon, you'd believe it without demur. 50% (100 proof)

⟡ **Taconic Straight Bourbon Dutchess Private Reserve** nbc db **(91)** **n22.5** enough vanilla for an ice cream daubed in bourbon source...; **t23** the molasses is an early arrival, as are the spices. Corn oils drifts about the palate upping the vanillas by the second; **f22.5** so slow and laid-back in its vanilla and toffee, it almost has a Kentucky drawl...; **b23** these guys really do make the most Kentucky-style bourbon outside of Kentucky: so impressed. This one is shifting the emphasis onto vanilla and spice. 45% (90 proof)

North Carolina
BLUE RIDGE DISTILLING CO. Bostic, North Carolina.

⟡ **Defiant American Single Malt Whisky** bott code 186/22 db **(82)** n19 t21 f21 b21 Defiant by name and nature. Still their whisky displays an incredibly feinty personality, which I know they have been long more than aware of. I suspect they just like it that way! Certainly malty, too. 41% (82 proof)

⟡ **Defiant Patriot American Single Malt** bott code 187/22 db **(80)** n18 t22.5 f19.5 b20 The most peculiar thing about this whisky is that despite the disastrous, feinty nose, the actual intensity of the malt itself once it hits the palate is compelling. It is incredibly rare to find such a disconnect between aroma and immediate delivery. This is technically a nightmare, certainly. Equally, I have to doff my hat and acknowledge that the mix of golden syrup an concentrated barley on delivery has something going for it. But the beauty is all too brief. 50% (100 proof)

⟡ **Defiant Rye** bott code 188/22 db **(87)** n20.5 t22.5 f21.5 b22.5 This is so far ahead of their single malt bottlings, it's hard to imagine it came from the same distillery. Of course, there is the odd technical fault here involving the cuts. And the Murray Method doesn't help, either. But this is much nearer the mark as to where it should be. While the rye offers a dazzling degree of intensity. Wow! If these guys could just get their cuts right and to allow this rye to display its charms without all the baggage, they'd really be on to something. 46% (92 proof)

⟡ **Defiant Patriot American Single Malt** batch no. 1586 db **(76)** n18 t20 f19 b19 Feinty and never gets off the ground for all the big caramel surge. 46% (92 proof)

Ohio
AMERICAN FREEDOM DISTILLERY Columbus, Ohio
Horse Soldier Reserve Barrel Strength Bourbon Whiskey db **(95.5)** n23.5 t24.5 f23.5 b24 Uncannily beautiful. 58.45% (116.9 proof).

Oregon
CLEAR CREEK DISTILLERY Portland, Oregon.
McCarthy's Oregon Single Malt Aged 3 Years batch W16-01, bott 6 May 16 db **(88.5)** n22 t23 f21.5 b22 For the first time since I tasted their first bottlings – in the days when my beard was still black - this whiskey has changed. Appears to have far less copper in the system to give the normal all-round richness; this is quite apparent on the nose and finish in particular. But they appear to have upped the peat ratio to good effect. 42.5% (85 proof)

OREGON SPIRIT DISTILLERS Bend, Oregon.
⟡ **Oregon Spirit Single Barrel Bottled In Bond Bourbon Aged 4 Years** barrel no. 190223/07 db **(90.5)** n22 rock hard, unyielding (even after applying the Murray Method) but

impressively nutty; **t22.5** a devout rigidity means there is little moving off its plotted source of liquorice and tamed molasses; **f23** ah, relaxes to quietly warble a charming mocha tune; **b23** one of the nuttier bourbons you'll find on the shelves. The corn oils have only limited impact on the mouth feel as this has a rare crispness throughout which generates a degree of mouth-watering solidity – not unlike boiled candy – but with only limited sweetness: that being provided by the molasses. Really do enjoy that late, understated mocha at the conclusion. *50% (100 proof)*

⬩⬩⬩ **Oregon Spirit Single Straight American Bourbon Aged 4 Years** barrel series no. 190216 db **(89.5) n22** sticks rigidly to the rigid house style...and heroically nutty, too; **t23** ah, the corn oils, missing on the single barrel, are up early and bring with them a series of vanilla and toffee notes; **f22** back to a more urbane nuttiness; **b22.5** a more two-toned textured narrative than the single barrel with a greater corn input, but more toffee-nut, too. *47% (94 proof)*

⬩⬩⬩ **Oregon Spirit Single Barrel Bottled In Bond Bourbon Aged 4 Years** barrel no. 180222/02 db **(89) n21.5** wow! This must be high rye content rye because that grain, helped by a generous cut on the still, occupies the nose with singular determination; **t23** ....and if you think the nose is big on the rye, just wait until it launches onto your palate. The cut really is as wide as it can handle, but this seems to help ladle out a custardy vanilla off the oak...though the brisk rye is interwoven into the framework; **f22** the oils force a degree of bitterness, but the rye defiantly thumps out a faux-fruity message; **b22.5** there is no mistaking the grain in question here: rye is involved with every atom of flavour here. However, the cut is perhaps a little too generous, allowing a degree of oily drift. *50% (100 proof)*

⬩⬩⬩ **Oregon Spirit Single Straight American Bourbon Aged 4 Years** barrel series no. 180123 db **(92) n23** love it! A much crisper and cleaner rendition with the rye pinging off some dank Demerara. A little spiced toffee off the oak, too...; **t23.5** brilliant delivery. Brittle rye offers a sharp, salivating front to the much gentler toffee. The spices really do wake up now and fizz a bit. A lovely molasses and Demerara blend helps brings out the full depth of the grain; **f22.5** long with a easy-going vanilla fade; **b23** a much better cut here allows the rye to show its charisma and charm without oily molestation. After giving it the full MM treatment, at its keenest when at cooler room temp where the rye positively sings. *45% (90 proof)*

⬩⬩⬩ **Oregon Spirit Single Barrel Bottled In Bond Wheat Whiskey Aged 5 Years** db **(95) n24** fabulous, even textbook, nose. A form of spiced toasted brown bread. A little ulmo honey is spread onto it...; **t24** best delivery I have tasted so far this week! The oils are faultless and imbued with just enough ulmo honey to ensure that the spices are met with a perfect level of sweetness. On an entirely different plane, the wholemeal bread is doing fine and toasting up rather nicely. Toffee and butterscotch, both oak-derived, fill the middle ground; **f23** just a hint of bitterness doing away with half a point. But the light spice and doughy grain still impress, especially with that late molasses arriving for company; **b24** one of the things I most admire about this distillery is their no-nonsense approach to whiskey. They make a whiskey, call it exactly what it is on the label – stating age and strength - and then bottle it. That's it! It is a form of old-fashioned simplicity. I had hoped I could reward their simple honesty with a high score...and now I can. Quite beautifully distilled and plucked from the warehouse at its peak time. Make no mistake: this is very high-grade Wheat Whisky – the best you'll currently find outside Kentucky. *50% (100 proof)*

⬩⬩⬩ **Oregon Spirit Single Straight American Wheat Whiskey Aged 5 Years** db **(88) n22.5 t22.5 f21 b22** Pleasant, flavoursome and chewy enough but disappointingly bitter late on. And though I love the sough dough on the nose, which fits in with the whole grain loaf on the palate, nothing like so charismatic and heart-wining as the single barrel incarnation... *45% (90 proof)*

Pennsylvania
DAD'S HAT RYE DISTILLERY Bristol, Pennsylvania.
Dad's Hat Pennsylvania Straight Rye Whiskey Aged Minimum 3 Years db **(91.5) n23 t23.5 f22 b23** The truest rye I have seen from you yet: I take my hat off to you guys...quite literally...! *47.5%*

South Carolina
PALMETTO DISTILLERY Anderson, South Carolina.
⬩⬩⬩ **Palmetto S C Whiskey** nbc db **(84) n21 t22.5 f19.5 b21** Well, I certainly have to give Palmetto top marks for consistency. I thought they may have just tidied up that harsh and tangy finale since I last tasted this two or three years ago, but they decided to carry on with that style. There is much more emphasis on their soft crème brulée which gives a moment or two of deliciousness. But that nose and finish needs some work. *44.65% (89.3% proof)*

Tennessee
CORSAIR ARTISAN DISTILLERY Nashville, Tennessee.
Corsair Triple Smoke American Single Malt Whiskey Aged 8 Months batch no. 319 db **(92.5) n24 t22.5 f23 b23** Bottled a tad too young, despite the high pleasure value. Even so, a very complex offering. *40% (80 proof). 252 bottles.*

Texas
BALCONES DISTILLERY Waco, Texas.

Balcones ZZ Top Tres Hombres Texas Whisky batch ZZ22-1 db **(95.5) n24 t24 f23.5 b24** now, had I tasted this in England I would have called this 'Zed Zed' Top. But here in Texas one automatically says 'Zee Zee': it's easy. And if they were looking for harmony with this whisky, then they found it. I have never knowingly listened to ZZ Top (sorry, guys!) but if their music is as melodic and pleasing as this gloriously blended creation by Balcones, then I had better give them a listen...because this is gold disc standard. *50%*

CROWDED BARREL Austin, Texas

◈ **Whisky Tribe Single M.O.M Single Malt of Magnificence 3 Years Old** bott code db **(90.5) n23** gentle smoke backed up by some attractive spice nip; **t23** no doubting the youth: this has a deliciously salivating entry. The smoke holds its ground despite the firmness of the grain itself, the phenols acting like a softening blanket. The gristy early sweetness is joined by a more relaxed thin molasses; **f22** a little out of harmony but helped by light mocha; **b22.5** always a rarity to find a peated whiskey distilled in the US. Even rarer to discover that the peated malt actually came from Ireland....! A very firm malt which carries the smokiness with aplomb. *58.1%.*

DALLAS DISTILLERIES Garland, Texas.

Herman Marshall Texas Bourbon batch 18/12 **(90.5) n22.5 t23 f22.5 b22.5** A very confident and beautifully-made Texan which never sits still. *46% (92 proof).*

FIVE POINTS DISTILLING Forney, Texas.

Lone Elm Single Barrel Texas Straight Wheat Whiskey 2017 barrel no 811, barrelled 09/17 db **(92.5) n23 t23 f23 b23.5** a big, straight wheat whiskey, not quite as relaxed as barrel 770 but with much more muscle and the odd surprise turn. Delightful. *62.6% (125.2 proof)*

GARRISON BROTHERS Hye, Texas.

◈ **Garrison Brothers Balmorhea Bourbon 2023 Release** db **(95) n23.5** the spice tingle is playful, the corn oils luxuriant, the Demerara sugars happily on top of the broader toasty charcoal notes; **t24** ever been in a 747 and the pilot has landed the beast so deftly you hardly felt the touchdown? I remember it happened to me in Tokyo once...when I was still waiting for the bump... and it never arrived. We had made contact with the Earth seamlessly it seemed, as if absorbed into the tarmac. Well, that's probably the best way of describing the arrival on the palate of this giant. A gossamer soft contact of corn oil and mocha...then a slow unravelling of toasty tannins and countering sugars...very much in the house style. No bump, no explosion....other than a fabulous salivating taste burst of toasted honeycomb..; there are other honey notes at work, too, mainly ulmo, giving the powerful vanilla a sweet glossiness; **f23.5** by no means as long as some previous Balmorheas I have tasted over the years, this concentrates primarily on the molten Demerara and lingering vanillas; **b24** when you get a whiskey which noses like a distilled bourbon barrel, you know you are in for something special. It is simply too easy to over-age any whisky – in other words allow the tannins to dominate to the degree that balance is seriously compromised, if not lost altogether. Which is why Balmorhea each year confounds. Twice matured in virgin oak, this should be way over the top. But it isn't: that is because just the right amount of sugars have been captured and within the piece countless personality traits can be defined. But it takes time, patience and the Murray Method to unlock this challenging but ultimately rewarding bourbon. As always, sampling this is one of the highlights of my Whisky Bible tasting year and this one throws up a bit of a surprise with its overall lightness of touch. *57.5% (115 proof)*

◈ **Garrison Brothers Cowboy Bourbon 2022 Release** aged in oak, dist and barrelled 2014 db **(96) n24** gosh! Seek and yea shall find. Red liquorice leads the way, certainly (which is perhaps fitting, seeing as the colour of this bourbon must have made them tempted to call it "Prince Harry"). The oak is both dry and in concentrate form, yet seemingly offering enough molasses for exquisite balance. The hickory is stop-start while polished leather abounds...; **t24** amazingly, it's the oils which grab your attention. Not because there is too little, or too much. But because it is precise and perfect. This allows the corn juice to saunter about briefly...before wave upon wave of intense but perfectly sweetened oaky tones caress the mouth, again with the red liquorice leading the way. The dark liquorice builds in intensity, alongside manuka honey and as equilibrium is reached the intensity fades and the component parts form the most gorgeous mosaic; **f24** after the intensity of before, the fade of the finish is like birdsong on the setting sun. All the flavours found on delivery are, thanks to those oils, still present and correct at the very end, though now in the most elegant and soothing form...that red liquorice note fading like a Rick Wright keyboard note on a classic piece of Floyd...; **b24** this Cowboy just rounds you up and lassoes you in until there is no escaping. A tad fatter than some previous years which has allowed the enormity of the whiskey to be more evenly spread and more easily managed. When cool this is a challenge. Gentle application of the Murray Method though turns a cougar into a playful pussy. *674% (134.8 proof)*

◇ **Garrison Brothers Guadalupe Bourbon 2023 Release** Port cask finished db (**93**) **n23** the wine cork kick carries a top Bordeaux-style bite, which was so unexpected. There is a dry and dusty grape echo, powerful enough to subdue the more muscular moments from the bourbon-type tannins; **t23.5** that Bordeaux bite is repeated on delivery – which is as surprising as the nose. Dark liquorice keeps the bourbon end up. It is the mix of black peppers and molasses which works best through the middle, though, with only a slight nod towards blackcurrant jam at the midpoint. However, the overall creamy texture is a bit of a surprise; **f23** long with a fruit pastel sweetness attaching to the spicier, drier oaks; **b23.5** the wine cork kick coming off this is a real shock to the system after solidly nosing and tasting straight Garrison Brothers bourbon for four hours! This is a bolder and much more interesting Guadalupe than I was anticipating, having carefully created its own personality. *53.5% (107 proof)*

◇ **Garrison Brothers Laguna Madre Bourbon 2022 Release** aged in oak db (**92.5**) **n23.5** exceptionally crisp nose as though some rye grain has got in and made a stand. Light red liquorice tones work well with a slightly more leathery moment or two; **t23.5** really pleasing intertwangling between light and heavy here with the top notes shewing a distinctly seedcake quality, the sugars glistening from the crust. Meanwhile denser tannins groan mildly under their own weight and offer the perfect anchor; **f22.5** when you get a surging sweetness early on, very often a vague bitterness follows...and this is no exception on the unusually short finish for a Garrison offering; **b23** by far the sweetest of the Garrison range this year boasting an extraordinary preponderance of Demerara-stye sugars. Alternating between light and lofty, ultimately it plumps for light... *50.5% (101 proof)*

◇ **Garrison Brothers Single Barrel Cask Strength Bourbon** aged 3 years, cask no 16081, dist and barrelled Apr 2017 barrel db (**96**) **n24** where do you start? Dark cherries? Mildly burnt plum pudding? Spiced liquorice? Molasses melting in mocha...? Smoking charcoal...? Overcooked toffee pie...? **t24** youthful, for all the obvious roastiness on the nose while the signature of that corn oil is, frankly, sensational. As on the nose, there is a black cherry thread while the spices should be searing, they are instead compact and friendly, working in tandem with a slightly salty element. The molasses are a little detached at first, but re-join the throng as the vanilla goes into overdrive. Wow, the structure of this is really something else...; **f24** how could this ever be less than incredibly long? a meandering pathway through at times, it seems, burnt forest with so much lingering dark liquorice and spent cocoa. But the most extraordinary trick is the fortitude of the lingering dark sugars, equally singed and toasty but pulsing out as a remarkable retort to those drier elements. The resulting balance and complexity so late on seem highly unlikely...but your mesmerised taste buds confirms it is happening...; **b24** if I'm presented with a better young single bourbon barrel for this year then miracles are in abundance at the moment; indeed, it is the only contender the older OCD Premium at the moment. I humbly suggest you use the Murray Method but pause at regular intervals or slight temperature changes as each have incredibly subtlety. I have driven from Texas to Kentucky – a 1,000 mile hike – in massive old pick-ups over the years or covered the journey in sprightly sports cars. The traverse over the palate of this whiskey appears to be a mixture of those two modes of transport: a giant with a powerful engine, but with an amazing niftiness and dexterity making for a dream drive. Make no mistake, this is not a big whiskey: it's epic...absolutely gargantuan. And I don't just mean from the strength. Ye-harr...! *70% (139.9 proof)*

◇ **Garrison Brothers Small Batch Bourbon 2023 Release Aged 3 Years** db (**94.5**) **n23** one of the friendliest Garrison aromas of all time: corn oil and vanilla in just about equal portions...; **t24** just so ridiculously soft! There is a butteryness to the rampant corn oil which sits so comfortably with the wonderfully pure vanilla which slowly oscillates with the ulmo honey to create the most silky layering. The key to the complexity, however, are the spices which are almost too delicate to be noticed, but in fact offer just the right degree of genteel intensity; **f23.5** long, with that corn oil really sticking like paste. But it's the vanilla in tandem with light ulmo honey which gets the kudos; **b24** a remarkable bourbon: the flavours appear to be released and move around the palate as though in slow motion. Seductively sweet and alluring, this is a real ramp up in quality from their last small batch, which itself was no mug. *47% (94 proof)*

TREATY OAK, Dripping Springs, TX

◇ **Treaty Oak The Day Drinker Texas Bourbon Aged At Least 12 Months** nbc db (**87**) **n22 t22 f21.5 b21.5** A young punk of a bourbon. If this was capable of wearing a hat, it'd be a baseball cap back to front. I never use the word "unpretentious" when describing a whisky. So here I'll settle for non-pretentious. Has plenty of youthful charm and buzz on both the nose and delivery, though it has exhausted its welcome by the time it reaches its thin finish. Light hickory arrives after the huge surge of unbalanced tannins on delivery. Just a fun bourbon...providing you don't think about it too much... 40% (80 proof)

⬦ **Treaty Oak Ghost Hill Texas Bourbon Aged 2 Years** nbc db **(93)** n23 this has gone up in the world: absolutely classic bourbon nose, whether from Texas or Kentucky. The liquorice is solid while the softer elements appear to drift from heather honey; t23.5 like the nose, rock-hard. And again, the black liquorice holds its ground while the spices fizz as though they mean it; f23 long with lots more liquorice – and yes, a touch of hickory – on the fade. But plenty of butterscotch, too; b23.5 this whiskey was made since the last time I met the lovely folk of Treaty Oak. And I have to say it has improved in that time. Some of their previous bottlings contained a Victory V cough sweet hickory thread, and while hickory is excellent in a bourbon, that cough sweet style weakens it somewhat. No such problems here: this is better fermented and distilled...and can't much fault the maturation, either. The fact they are using the exact same mashbill of 57% Yellow Dent No 1 corn, 32% Texas wheat and 11% American (not Texas, mind) malted barley underscores their better understanding of how to create excellent bourbon. 47.5% (95 proof)

YELLOW ROSE DISTILLING Houston, Texas.

Yellow Rose Straight Bourbon 10th Anniversary Special Edition 24 Months Old db **(89)** n23 t22.5 f21.5 b22 this is a young whiskey in character despite the opaque darkness which matches the night-time Texas sky under which these notes are written. Quite a stark whiskey and though the finish fails to impress, there's enough on the nose and delivery to join in the celebration of this distillery's 10th anniversary... 62.65% (125.3 proof). 2,700 bottles.

Virginia
CATOCTIN CREEK DISTILLERY Loudoun County, Virginia.

Catoctin Creek Roundstone Single Barrel Virginia Rye Whiskey batch no. 19A01 db **(88)** n19.5 t23 f22.5 b23 Again, the wide cut acts as a bit of a ball and chain around this whiskey. But when it gets rolling, the salivating qualities of the crisp rye and then chocolate and honey notes are really impressive. Most enjoyable. 40% (80 proof). ncf sc.

VIRGINIA DISTILLERY CO. Lovinston, Virginia.

Virginia Distillery Co. Courage & Conviction Prelude American Single Malt Whisky db **(88)** n22 t22.5 f21.5 b22 Everything about this youthful single malt screams "new distillery!". And what a gorgeous distillery this is, located in the stunning highlands of Virginia, close to the Blue Ridge Mountains. Even if the Scotch Whisky Association arrogantly believe that only Scotland possesses such things as highlands and litigiously and ridiculously claim otherwise should any distillery in the world dare mention the fact. Virginia has them also. There's a little feint on the early nose, but this soon burns off with a little Murray Method handling, then an overriding degree of copper and light vanilla. But the nose is ostensibly buttered up new make – and from new stills. The flavour profile is rich from the wide cut but then increasingly, and deliciously, malty. Fascinating! I have seen some of what is coming further down the line. It is ,technically better than this, as you would expect from a fledgling copper pot still distillery, And promising some glorious days ahead. 46% (92 proof).

Washington
CHAMBERS BAY DISTILLERY University Place, Washington.

Chambers Bay Straight Bourbon Whiskey Bourbon Boathouse-Aged a minimum of Three Years batch no. 07 db **(91.5)** n22.5 t23 f23 b23 Anchors away for a full-bodied bourbon that gets the liquorice and spice mix pretty ship shape. 47.5% (95 proof).

COPPERWORKS Seattle, Washington.

⬦ **Copperworks American Single Malt Release No 44** minimum of 45 months in 8 casks. New American oak. Recipe pale malt, baronesse malt, genie malt & five malt db **(91.5)** n23 love the lurking, low key spice as the malt and oak cobble up some attractive ulmo honey tones between them; t23 diced fresh apple represents the malt if not with a plum, then certainly aplomb...; f22.5 the oils formulate towards the end giving a creamy toffee and mocha send-off; b23 one of those fascinating cross-pollinators where bourbon meets single malt. However, it is the fresh of the diced apple on delivery which really impresses. 50% (100 proof) 1,920 bottles

⬦ **Copperworks American Single Malt Release No 45** minimum of 36 months in 7 casks. New American oak & Manzanilla sherry. Recipe Fritz malt & pale malt db **(89)** n22 a double-sided grape attack offering softness and sharp fruit in equal measures. Light vanillas play second fiddle, though a weighty tannin-rich spice doesn't hang around...; t23 toffee raisin. The fruit is tart and salivating. The malt forms a a rich secondary layer; f22 just a little imbalance here and even late bitterness. But the vanillas stay the course; b22 last year Copperworks brought out a special

April Fools' bottling which offered no insight into the whiskey at all – which is far from the norm. As it happens, I always sample their whiskeys and try to read the clues on the nose and palate before I read the details of how it got there on the label: much more fun! Here I could easily recognise some kind of wine cask intrusion, though less than I thought as the Manzanilla takes up only 6% of the oak. It seems a lot more... 50% (100 proof) 1,681 bottles

⬩⬩ **Copperworks American Single Malt Release No 46** minimum of 36 months. New American oak. Recipe salmon safe genie db **(88)** n22 t23 f20.5 b22.5 A single malt which dominates with the malt rather than the deeper tannins. There are enough natural toffee notes harvested from the oak to ensure a silky consistency which, when coupled with the light heather honey and warming spices makes for a degree of agreeable complexity before the slightly bitter finish. 50% (100 proof) 2,033 bottles

⬩⬩ **Copperworks American Single Malt Release No 47** minimum of 3 years. Char#2 new American oak. Recipe baroness malt & five malt db **(94.5)** n23 I would not have been surprised had they informed me that chocolate malt was involved here: cocoa is playing an important part. As is the light liquorice; t23.5 such an impressive delivery: heather honey mixes in beautifully with the thick malt. But again the tannins have much to say as it veers in a liquorice and chocolate direction; f24 even now the spices, though there, are too lazy to make their mark and those chocolate tones become more mousse-like by the minute; b24 a single malt that needs a little bit of convincing that it's not actually a bourbon. In reality, it's a pretty tasty hybrid between the two and if you, like me, have a thing for whiskey in your plain chocolate mousse, then you are in for one hell of a pleasant surprise here. Delicious. 50% (100 proof) 1,415 bottles

⬩⬩ **Copperworks American Single Malt Craft Malt Week 2022** 30 months in new American oak cask 387. Recipe baroness malt, db **(94)** n23 the spices rocket on this one, a little maple syrup and liquorice holding back its excesses; t23.5 a shimmering collision between heather and ulmo honey guarantees a degree of rich vanillas and even old-fashioned fudge. The spices held back on the nose are momentarily unleashed, alongside a hickory fusillade; f23.5 long with a rich interplay between an intense maltiness which has suddenly found its voice, an even richer degree of vanilla and honey-ringed spice; b24 yet further proof that this distillery is very much improving on their cuts, this time keeping just enough oils in to make this as toothsome as possible without any unwanted tangs. A serious chewing whiskey of great depth and character. 60.45% (120.9 proof) 219 bottles

⬩⬩ **Copperworks American Single Malt Moscatel Cask** 3 years and 8 months in new American oak; finished 11 months in moscatel cask. Recipe pale malt db **(88)** n21.5 t22.5 f22 b22 A sweet, soft and strictly undemanding single malt which, seems content with its friendly toffee-raisin countenance. Some spices do, however, have a bit of the devil in them. 50% (100 proof) 336 bottles

⬩⬩ **Copperworks American Single Malt Special Release Finished In Jamaican Rum Cask** 3 years and 9 months in new American oak; finished 7 months in rum. cask. Recipe pale malt db **(77.5)** n19 t21 f18.5 b19 Over the years I have done a fair bit of work in Jamaica, visited and or worked at all the distilleries there and blended their rums. I have never once, though, come across the intense tobacco note which rips through this whiskey. Disappointing. 50% (100 proof) 289 bottles

⬩⬩ **Copperworks American Single Malt Special Release Hair of the Dog Adam Cask** 3 years and 3 months in new American oak; finished 7 months in HoftD cask. Recipe genie db **(83)** n20.5 t21.5 f21 b20 I'll be honest: I really struggle with a degree of hop in a whiskey. I know some people love this. But, for me, the balance has been completely compromised. This is one hoppy whiskey. If only it had some of the creamy sweetness of the Matt version which at least allows the malt to converse with the more eloquent vanilla tones. 50% (100 proof) 179 bottles

⬩⬩ **Copperworks American Single Malt Special Release Hair of the Dog Matt Cask** 3 years and 3 months in new American oak; finished 7 months in HoftD cask. Recipe genie db **(87)** n21 t22 f22 b22 Without glossing over this whiskey, I think I prefer the Matt finish... 50% (100 proof) 253 bottles

⬩⬩ **Copperworks American Single Malt Mystery Whiskey 2022 April Fools Release Aged Minimum of 48 Months** db **(90)** n22 the malt appears to have crystalised into Demerara...; t23 indeed, as the nose suggests, this is a brittle rendition, the oils playing second fiddle to barley sugar and spices which are super-salivating; f22 a lazy kind of hoppy note kicks in (or maybe that's the echo from another Copperworks whiskey from over an hour ago). Love the late spice razzle-dazzle; b22.5 not entirely a faultless bottling, but the high strength gives the malt full permission to do its thing. And my word...does it! 63.5% (127 proof)

DRY FLY DISTILLING Spokane, Washington.

Dry Fly Straight Triticale Whiskey Aged 3 Years db **(94)** n23 t24 f23 b24 just love triticale whiskey when made right. And this most certainly is and, indeed, I cannot remember it better mastered. What staggering complexity. One of the surprise whiskeys of the year. 45% (90 proof)

WOODINVILLE WHISKEY CO. Woodinville, Washington.

Woodinville Cask Strength Straight Bourbon bott code db **(94.5) n23** perhaps the most remarkable thing here is that among the frontrunners on the nose is clear, unmistakable malt barley which, considering the corn and oak involvement defies belief. But there it indubitably is... Keeping it company is a toffee apple sharpness dappled with oaky spices; **t24** this is very high-quality distillation. There are copper notes off the still giving the small grains a shimmering quality. Dense vanilla cascades in...the rye tones are now so fruity we are in sherry trifle country. Remarkable, though is the incessant salivating quality engineered by that mix if copper and crisp small grains; **f23.5** a chocolate cream cake, maybe slightly overcooked, and sweetened with Muscovado, dances around the palate again encouraged by that tangy copper element....; **b24** my heart skipped a beat when I opened the box to see it contained Woodinville. It had been a little while since I lasted tasted one of my favourite distilleries outside of Kentucky...and I was nervous as to whether they could keep their flag flying as high as the last time it passed my tasting room. That really would be a tall order. And although this may not be the equal of the last one I tasted, there is so much shimmering power, such intense flavours that you really want to shake the distiller by the hand... *56.62% (113.24 proof)*

Woodinville Straight Bourbon nbc db **(86.5) n22 t22 f21 b21.5** For those, like me, expecting a scaled down version of their cask strength bottling, prepare for a shock. To begin with, there is a quite peculiar aroma: a dried tea note in tandem with breast-beating oak. The delivery is muddled and confused, but by the midpoint has found a far more strident crystalline sugar and light cocoa thread. The milky finish, though, defies all comprehension when compared to what we know this distillery is capable of. *45%*

Woodinville Cask Strength Straight 100% Rye nbc db **(96) n24** the minty-chocolate note of the oak, the pulsing spices from the deeper tannins... just a framework for the sharp, acidic bite of the stone-fruit rye tones; **t24.5** for a moment or two you simply cannot move: the brain is too busy taking on board the raft of grain tones which capture rye at its most naked. There is a tartness which pushes salvation levels to danger red, the brittleness of the grain on imploding alert. And then, as all this keeps your tongue and taste buds on edge waiting for the next flavour explosion, there is a soothing milk chocolate mousse effect. Astonishing...; **f23.5** more relaxed now as the vanillas take the slack for a while. A lovely praline note soothed by caramel; **b24** good grief...! What have I just tasted? If you are looking for a rye where every atom of that grains unique and its intense character is captured and then displayed in its fullest form, then here you go. Sazerac, Pikesville, Wilderness Trail and now Woodinville: nailed it. All have their own unique characteristics and Woodinville certainly boasts that. In spades. *58.23% (116.46 proof)*

Woodinville Straight 100% Rye nbc db **(90) n22** surprisingly chalky, the rye has sacrificed a little of its expected dominance and sheen for an oaky dryness. Delicate and complex, nonetheless...; **t23** sharp, almost metallic in its countenance, the sugars are surprisingly flighty. Eye-watering at times with the middle occupied by dense tannin tones. Again, there is a metallic grip to this which does the grain little harm but increases the overall tartness and reduces the effects of the sugars; **f22.5** like the nose, chalky to a fault; **b22.5** when a whiskey is reduced by water, the oils are usually badly eroded and integrity whittled away. Woodinville seem to suffer this more than most as the differences are between their uncut and reduced whiskeys are as stark as you'll find anywhere in the US. That said, there is complexity enough to delight the most demanding rye lover. But the overexuberance of the drier chalkier vanillas at the cost of the overall story and, in Woodinville's case, beauty is worthy of consideration. Don't get me wrong, though: the final product here in its own right is highly complex and satisfying. But a very different animal to the nubile beast at cask strength... *45%*

Woodinville Straight Bourbon Finished With Toasted Applewood Staves nbc db **(88.5) n21.5 t22.5 f22.5 b22** A surprisingly muscular whiskey despite the huge caramel it is carrying. Although this amount of natural toffee usually results in a soft, enveloping whiskey, this is a much spicier dude with something approaching attitude. However, there is a secondary note in here which is not chiming quite as well as it might, especially on the nose. *50% (100 proof)*

Woodinville Straight Bourbon Finished In Port Casks nbc db **(87) n21.5 t22 f21.5 b22** There is momentarily a toffee raisin thread running through this yielding whiskey. As so often happens when a powering fruit note of wine casks meets high grade bourbon, the two main notes cancel the other out, and to a degree that has happened here. The good news is that the Port Cask is clean, not always the case. The spices take a little time to build but complexity makes way for that pleasant toffee raisin chorus. *45% (90 proof)*

Woodinville Straight 100 Rye Finished In Port Casks Harvest Release 2022 nbc db **(90) n22** the rye grain offers a diamond-hard bit which drills right into the Port with decent spice for back up. Perhaps not technically perfect, but fascinating; **t23.5** no shortage of flavour as the salivating rye again takes no prisoners. The result is a tart, two-toned fruitiness which oscillates in its texture as well as intensity of flavour; **f22.5** much more oak-induced caramel, as well as light grape off the Port; **b22** unlike the corn-dominated bourbon, the sharpness of the rye has the intensity and devilment to punch its way through the marauding grape. As whiskeys distilled from rye mash goes, this is an adventurous and entertaining version. The rye has no interest in joining forces with the grape: that has to hang on for dear life. 45% (90 proof)

◈ **Woodinville Straight Bourbon Finished In Ginjinha Casks** nbc db **(88)** **n22 t23 f21 b22** Well, that was different! Rare to encounter a brand new whiskey experience, but certainly managed that here. Ginjinha is an obscure liqueur with a unique flavour set, and I'm not sure I've ever encountered it outside its native Portugal. The cloves appear to have some kind of effect on the spices, just giving them an extra bite and warmth, especially on the finish. While the sharpness and contrary tartness of the bitter cherry certainly permeates from the moment it hits the palate. Struggles for balance at times and certainly has a rough time of it on the finish. Yet there are moments of this I enjoy more than I probably should... 47.5% (95 proof)

West Virginia
SMOOTH AMBLER Greenbrier County, West Virginia.
◈ **Smooth Ambler Founders' Cask Strength Series Straight Bourbon 2022 Aged 6 Years** batch 1 db **(92.5)** **n23** for a few moments I feared the toastiness might be too overwhelming. But then a cross section of balancing notes sweeps across the nose, including even a light saline feel to match the peppers. The red liquorice is superb, the kumquat is surprising but fits into the scene perfectly; **t23.5** what a sublime shew of heather honey from so early on. It is caught on the oily subtext of the corn and shews a prodigious degree of spice as the liquorice and hickory begin to find their place; **f22** slightly nutty and a petulant display of bitterness hooks onto the big vanilla; **b23** a bourbon which seems to swagger in its ability to hit just about every stereotypical bourbon note you can imagine. If that was my brand I'd be delighted, for its does exactly what it says on the tin. Soon they'll be able to do away with buying in: keep producing something this good and with a few tweaks they'll have quite a thoroughly deserved bourbon following. 61.8% (123.6 proof)

Wyoming
WYOMING WHISKEY
◈ **Wyoming Whiskey Double Cask** straight bourbon finished in sherry casks db **(89.5)** **n22** a tad flat, but the spiced sultanas are pleasant enough...; **t22.5** the bourbon has first dibs on the taste buds. But it is short (and medium sweet) before the fruit makes a far more telling contribution; **f22** ah, now it is talking: the bourbon tones are decidedly of the red liquorice persuasion. Pastel bonbons are offered, too.... but there is a very late furriness; **b23** have to say I was pleasantly surprised by this. Anything sherry finished has given me a Pavlovian complex and I am expecting to taste the worst, with sulphur creeping in. Is there any sign of the dreaded S word...? Well, very, very late on, yes and not in enough quantity to do any damage. A high-end sherry butt, one that has done a pleasing job here of not being so dominant that complexity is compromised to the point of extinction, as is so often the case. 50% (100 proof)

◈ **Wyoming Whiskey Outrider American Straight Whiskey** db **(92.5)** **n22.5** an excellent, punchy persona, marrying some fancy, dry tannin notes with a much more expansive red and black liquorice. Curiously creamy, too...; **t23.5** superb! An earthy vanilla note gangs with the spices to make for a wonderfully juicy kick off. A degree of maltiness plays off against the oak while a mix of ulmo and heather honey do a top job on the measured sweetening; **f23** dry, spicy and warming. The vanilla now has a far drier hue; **b23.5** absolutely love this. One of those whiskeys which keeps you guessing which direction it will next turn and never seems to make a false move. Deep vanilla and deeply satisfying. 50% (100 proof)

◈ **Wyoming Whiskey Single Barrel Straight Bourbon** db **(93)** **n23** ramps up the oaky amps from the first sniff. Dry, but some citrus has just enough whoomph to penetrate; **t23** surprisingly soft landing on the palate thanks to friendly oils. A momentary chocolate nougat flourish which heads gently towards a more lightly spiced hickory core; **f23** long, continuing that toasty chorus on the nose and then a chocolate-toffee finale which spices up by the second; **b24** a satisfying bourbon ticking all the right boxes and no slouch on the complexity front, either. Dishes out the tannins occasionally, too. Back home in Kentucky to taste the US whiskies for the 2024 Bible. This was a pretty good start. 48% (96 proof)

◈ **Wyoming Whiskey Small Batch Bourbon** db **(85)** **n22 t22.5 f19.5 b21** A bourbon of extremes: one minute it is riding high on a delightful heather honey crest. And then it slips at the end towards an unkempt bitterness. That is one amazing schism. 44% (88 proof)

American/Kentucky Whiskey Blends
◈ **Magnificent Beast Blend No. 1 (90.5) n22.5** lashings of spiced liquorice. A hint of maple, too...; **t23** super silky tannin: heather honey spread on slightly burnt toast; **f22** much drier, though

that suits that spiced liquorice again; **b23** as American blends go, this is as flavoursome as they get. The light whiskey is responsible for that chiffon feel on the palate while the Balcones ramps up the agreeable liquorice and honey. A big whiskey bursting with classic bourbon articulation and matching spices, get curiously glossed down. Lovely. *50% (100 proof)75% 3-y-o Malt distilled at Balcones, Texas, 22.2% 15-y-o light whiskey distilled at MGP, Indiana, 2.8% 2-y-o malt whiskey distilled at Real Spirits. Bottled by Crowded Barrel Whiskey Co.*

Whiskey Distilled From Bourbon Mash

⟳ **Bhakta Armagnac Cask Finish Bourbon Distilled 2013** bott code **(94)** n23 classically clipped nose associated with Armagnac cask secondary maturation: all the preferred bourbon signals are still there, especially the black liquorice and heather honey. But it is all tightly squeezed and disciplined; **t23** a silkier delivery than expected and sweeter, too. A compelling blend of ulmo and manuka honeys arrive early also seem to add a waxiness. Red liquorice and light hickory fill the drying midground; **f23** a typically shortish fade, as is the norm with brandy/cognac/Armagnac and rum cask finishes. What is certainly not the norm is the degree of lemon blossom honey breaking out just before the oak brings a firm but nutty curtain down; **b24** my general dislike of bourbon finished in wine casks is well known. However, if a bourbon cask must be finished in something then I admit I get far more enjoyment if the cask chosen is from a fellow spirit barrel. As it happens, the Armagnac cask chosen for this was way ahead of the norm and the complexity levels at work here were at times mesmerising, especially the variance in the honey tones. Today, as it happens, I learned there is honey style (of the many hundreds I have sampled worldwide) I had never encountered before. It is called Kentuckiana: a blend of Kentucky and Indiana honeys. Tomorrow I shall grab some, just to see if the wide variety found here matches up. *50.3% (100.6 proof) distilled in Indiana*

⟳ **Rock Town Column Still Collection Single Barrel Bourbon Whiskey Cask No 4 Aged 36 Months** **(81)** n21 t22.5 f18.5 b19 Some very good bourbon compromised by a less than brilliant sherry butt that is not entirely free of sulphur interference. Some great bourbon wasted. There should be a law banning old sherry butts from entering the US. *60% (120 proof) mash bill 79% corn 13% malted barley 8% wheat distilled in collaboration with Bardstown Bourbon Company*

⟳ **Three Chord Straight Bourbon Finished in Pinot Noir Barrels** batch no. 29 **(92.5)** n22.5 I'm guessing there is a rye grain contribution to this bourbon as the grape is reacting with some element within the whiskey to conjure up a black cherry boiled candy nose; **t23.5** and there we go again! The delivery is rock solid and the fruitiness of the crunchiest variety. So juicy and clean enough to give your teeth a polish; **f23** a beautiful behaved and polite finale with the fruit gently lingering; **b23.5** just shews you how paranoid I am these days with cask finishes. The last distilled from mash finish I tasted earlier today knocked my taste buds out for over two hours because of the sulphur content from the Port cask. When I saw "Pinot" I feared the worst and re-scheduled this as the last whisky of the day (well, night really). Had I read the bottle I would have seen that the Pinot casks are from California – so no need for alarm: not an off note to be had either by nose or mouth. This unusual experience is about as clean and precise a fruity edge you will find attached to what was once bourbon. The molten muscovado notes – and that persistent black cherry – accommodate the gathering oaky vanillas with ease. Such a pleasant surprise. *49.5% (99 proof) Distilled in Kentucky*

⟳ **World Whisky Society Classic Collection Cognac Edition Number 14 Aged 10 Years** **(94)** n23 nippy. Early spices, including coriander, some curious acetone, which would have worked well with their Doc Holiday brand, a little dried date and a blood orange-red liquorice; **t23.5** pleasingly mouth-filling with early corn oils. Then spices attack early and in earnest but soon peak to allow a powerful burnt butterscotch tart and muscovado sugar. Indeed, the sugars seem to hold sway...; **f23.5** stays on the burnt fudge theme. So much natural caramel, all within a toasty tannin and roast coffee frame; **b24** the World Whisky Society have to be the kings of distilled from bourbon mash whiskey! Another improbably complex whisky sourced, like their other 10-year-old from a distillery in Oklahoma with the same mash bill...but this time they have found in Cognac casks a far more sympathetic vessel for maturation. The depth to the roast coffee note on this is simply amazing.... *58.5% 352 bottles*

⟳ **World Whisky Society Couture Collection Aged 6 Years**, sherry oloroso barrels finish **(91)** n22.5 the huge corn oils are already fat. The oloroso thickens matters further with a grapey moist fruitcake layering. The spices are delicate but play a key role in ensuring this isn't too friendly...; **t23** the delivery is purely about the high quality oloroso which tub-thumps its grapey credentials to delicious effect. All the better for taking a more neutral bitter-sweet stance and initially keeping to a fruitcake demeanour. As the corn oils begin to wend their way into the mix, alongside the tannins, we are moved from fruitcake to cherry Victoria sponge, complete with castor sugar through the middle; **f22.5** back to the corn oils again which keep a tight hold on the ever-increasing tannin; **b23** seeing that the mash bill is 99% corn and 1% malted barley (required, among other things, to kick off the fermentation) it is hard to describe the spirit, distilled in Indiana, as originally being straight bourbon rather than straight corn. But for the sake of trying to avert confusion with the label, I'll put it in this section with other former bourbons. Of its type quite excellent with no bourbon character whatsoever. But they have chosen some outstanding oloroso casks – slightly sweeter than many – which have paid handsome dividends. 48%

⬩ **World Whisky Society Couture Collection Aged 10 Years**, finished in sherry Madeira barrels **(90) n23.5** whoever distilled this did a good job: this is a clean nose allowing both the small grains and the grape to work in tandem with the dry oaky vanilla to maximise complexity. The strands of honey alternate between heather and lemon blossom; **t23** the delivery certainly favours a honeyed grape persona. But then the wheat makes its spicy presence felt thick layers of molasses and grape ease the impact; **f21** there is a very vague furry note to the finale, though this doesn't entirely undo the delicate complexity between fruit, vanilla and spice; **b22.5** distilled in Oklahoma from a mash bill of 51% corn, 45% wheat and 4% malted barley, there is no doubting that this did, indeed, start life as a straight bourbon. Though exactly what "sherry Madeira" casks are completely beats me! No denying the impressive complexity to this, or the elegance to the layering. 48%

Whiskey Distilled From Rye Mash

⬩ **Door Knocker 7 Years Old Finished In Ex-Bourbon Barrel** bott code **(85.5) n21.5 t22 f21 b21** A very strange, extremely green whiskey with a little too much tang for its own good. The middle does, admittedly, yell rye from the rooftops. But this is just too much like hard work to properly enjoy. Obviously an experimental whiskey. And not all experiments work... 49% (98 proof)

⬩ **Smooth Amber Old Scout Straight Rye Finished in Port Casks Aged 7 Years** batch no 6 **(79.5) n22 t22 f17.5 b18** Trying to balance out something as sharp as rye with something as grapey as a port cask is always like trying to push a barrel uphill. The chances of finding full integration are slim: some things simply aren't meant to be. The nose is confusing: rye this sharp on one side isn't supposed to be this flat. While, on the palate, after an initial eye-watering but slightly confusing blast of green grain, the landscape is simply too monotonous, all the highs and lows normally prevalent with grain bulldozed into the same toffee-raisin flatness. And, to cap it all, a furry off-note (the type of which that badly did down the average quality of Scotch whisky for many years) from the port cask at the very death. Sigh... 51.5% (103 proof) distilled in Indiana

American Single Malt

⬩ **Big Moustache American Single Malt (90) n22.5** the thinnest liquorice tone drifts off the cask. The malt forages off the oak, with little snippets of demerara sugar in there to resolve any tensions...; **t23** beautifully distilled: the oils are perfectly in tune with the overall density of the flavour profile. The malts lurch about to be noticed; the oak is an immoveable constant, the tannins varying between classic, broad-brushed toastiness and flightier hickory. The sweetness is more evolved than on the nose thanks to a light heather honey tone which, like the spices, benefits from the oils; **f22** a much more simplistic array of toasty tannin and spices; **b22.5** it has been a long time now since I tasted an American single malt which doesn't burst with bourbony characteristics: indeed, off the top of my head I can think of only one in total. This gives a bold attempt to trump the malt over the tannin, but it doesn't quite come off. It's a slow burner but the tannins takes control early on and never release their grip. That said, delicious! 45% (90 proof) ncf BBC Spirits

⬩ **Clermont Steep American Single Malt Whiskey Aged 60 months** in new American oak nbc db **(86) n21.5 t22 f21 b21.5** A very curious single malt that's a bit green on the nose but compensates on the palate with a salad of oak-induced sugary tones. Not bad if you are looking for a flavourful oddity. A bit of a disappointment if you're looking for a high-grade single malt. 47% (94 proof) Jim Beam

Other American Whiskey

⬩ **Three Chord Bourbon and Corn Whiskey Finished in Honey and Toasted Barrels** batch no. 1 **(92.5) n23** the oak is doing far more interesting things than you might imagine: the layering of the vanillas is to be admired, as the degree of charring to the toffee. In the background a kind of burnt heather honey rumbles; **t23** thick and honeyed without the syrup mouth feel I feared. There is a Kentucky-made honey that fits the identikit, though it comes without those assuredly warming spices; **f23** wow! Just dig the intensity of that butterscotch; **b23.5** well, that was different! A strange kind of toasted honeycomb and marshmallow effect, geed-up with spices. The kind if whiskey I feel I shouldn't like, but actually do... 55.65% (111.3 proof)

Canadian Whisky

The vastness of Canada is legendary. As is the remoteness of much of its land. But anyone who has not yet visited a distillery which sits serenely on the shores of Lake Manitoba more or less bang in the middle of the country and, in early Spring, ventures a few miles out into the wilderness, has really missed a trick.

Because there, just a dozen miles from the remotest distillery of them all, Gimli, you can stand and listen to the ice crack with a clean, primeval crispness unlike any other thing you will have experienced; a sound once heard by the very first hunters who ventured into these uncharted wastes. And hear a distant loon call its lonely, undulating, haunting song, its notes scudding for miles along the ice and vanishing into the snow which surrounds you. Of all the places on the planet, it is the one where you will feel a sensation as close to nature - and your insignificance - as you are likely to find.

It was also a place where I felt that, surely, great whisky should be made. But in the early days of the Gimli distillery there was a feeling of frustration by the blenders who used it. Because they were simply unable to recreate the depth and complexity of the legendary Crown Royal brand it had been built to produce in place of the old, now closed, distilleries to the east. When, in their lab, they tasted the new Crown Royal against the old there were furrowed brows, a slight shaking of heads and an unspoken but unmistakable feeling of hopeless resignation.

To understand why, we have to dispense with the nonsense which appears to have been trotted out by some supposed expert in Canadian whisky or other who has, I have been

YUKON
▲ Yukon

BRITISH COLUMBIA

ALBERTA

MANITOBA

▲ Pemberton
Shelter Point ▲ Okanagan ▲ ▲ Alberta
Devine ▲ ●**Vancouver** ▲ Highwood **SASKATCHEWAN**
Sheringham **Calgary**
Macalonely's Caledonian ▲ Black Fox

▲ Palliser

Gimli

Vancouver:
Central City
The Liberty Distillery

Key	
●	**Major Town or City**
▲	**Distillery**

advised by quite a few people I meet at my tastings, been writing somewhere that Canada has no history of blending from different distilleries. Certainly that is now the perceived view of many in the country. And it is just plain wrong: only a maniac would write such garbage as fact and completely undersell the provenance of Canadian whisky. Crown Royal, when in its pomp, was a meticulous blending of a number of different whiskies from the Seagram empire and by far the most complex whisky Canada had to offer.

The creases in the furrowed brows deepened as the end of the last century approached. Because the key distilleries of LaSalle, Beupre and Waterloo were yielding the very last of their stocks, especially top quality pure rye, and although the much lighter make of Gimli was of a high standard, they had not yet been able to recreate the all- round complexity as when adding the fruits of so many great distilleries together. The amount of experimentation with yeasts and distilling speeds and cutting times was a wonder to behold. But the race was on: could they, before the final stocks ran dry, produce the diversity of flavours to match the old, classic distilleries which were now not just closed but in some cases demolished?

When I had sat in the LaSalle blending lab for several days in the 1990s and worked my way through the near extinct whiskies in stock I recognised in Beupre a distillery which, had it survived, probably might have been capable of producing something as good, if not better, than anything else on this planet. And it was clear just what a vital contribution it made to Crown Royal's all round magnificence.

So I have monitored the Crown Royal brand with interest, especially since Gimli and the brand was acquired by Diageo some 15 years ago. And anyone doubting that this really was a truly great whisky should have accompanied me when I visited the home of my dear friend the late Mike Smith and worked our way through his astonishing Crown Royal collection which showed how the brand's taste profile had evolved through the ages.

And, at last, it appears all that hard work, all those early days of experimentation and fine tuning at Gimli have paid off. For while the standard Crown Royal brand doesn't yet quite live up to its starry past, they have unleashed upon us a whisky which dazzles, startles and engulfs you in its natural beauty like an early spring morning on Lake Manitoba.

The whisky is called Crown Royal Northern Harvest Rye. It was Jim Murray's World Whisky of the Year 2016: batch L5085 N3 had redefined a nation's whisky.

The fact it should have achieved this at a time when Canadian whisky was at a nadir, with far too many brands dependent on adding too many unacceptable things as flavouring agents, is providential. It shows that keeping the grains at a maximum to be, with oak, the main source of flavour is the way to define a nation's whisky style: rye whisky by name, rye whisky by nature. So perhaps it is no great surprise that five years on Canada did it again and pulled off the Whisky Bible World Whisky of the Year for a second time with the 2021 edition. The closest whisky in style to Northern Harvest is Alberta Premium. And when they let this astonishing whisky loose at cask strength there was no stopping it. Sometimes by anything worldwide.

QUEBEC

ONTARIO

Glenora

Caldera ▲ NOVA SCOTIA

Valleyfield

● Quebec

● Montreal
Cirka

▲ Still Waters

Canada Mist ▲ ● Toronto
▲ Forty Creek
▲ Kittling Ridge

▲ Walkerville

Jim Murray's Whisky Bible Canadian Whisky of the Year Winners

2004/5	Seagram's VO
2006	Alberta Premium
2007	Alberta Premium 25 Years Old
2008	Alberta Premium 25 Years Old
2009	Alberta Premium
2010	Wiser's Red Letter
2011	Crown Royal Special Reserve
2012	Crown Royal Special Reserve
2013	Masterson's 10 Year Old Straight Rye
2014	Masterson's 10 Year Old Straight Rye
2015	Masterson's 10 Year Old Straight Rye
2016	Crown Royal Northern Harvest Rye
2017	Crown Royal Northern Harvest Rye
2018	Crown Royal Northern Harvest Rye
2019	Canadian Club Chronicles: Issue No. 1 41 Year Old
2020	Crown Royal Northern Harvest Rye
2021	Alberta Premium Cask Strength Rye
2022	Canadian Club Chronicles Aged 43
2023	Alberta Premium
2024	Sons of Vancouver 4

Canadian Distilleries
BLACK FOX FARM AND DISTILLERY Saskatoon, Saskatchewan. 2015.
SE Eleven Blended Whisky 2021 Quercus cask, serial no. 00152B, db **(86.5)** n21.5 t22.5 f21 **b21.5** This is one of the most exotically spiced whiskies I have encountered for a very long time. Despite the chocolatey sweetness, it is just too spicy on this occasion and gives just a little bit too much of the traditional English Bread Pudding feel for its own good. 48.2%

SE Eleven Cask Finish Single Grain triticosecale grain, oloroso cask, serial no. 00920, db **(90)** n22 flat juicy, clean grape, save for a few spicy peaks; t22.5 I'm almost thrown back in my chair by the intensity of the raisony sugars that combust on arrival. Salivating, thick with concentrated fruitcake and lashings of molasses; f23 dries slightly as the warming spices begin to take control. Some vanilla makes a welcome entry. The tannins do control the finale...; **b22.5** if you want to compare the difference between the effects of bourbon/virgin oak and sherry casks, here's a great example. The bottling below is one of the most complex whiskies I have tasted this year. This isn't. Pleasant, as this is a decent quality wine cask at work. But the layering and complexity has been massively compromised and the unique qualities of the grain muted. That said...I think you'll rather enjoy it...! 47.5%

SE Eleven Single Grain triticosecale grain, Quercus cask, serial no. 01206, db **(95)** n23.5 wow....! That is a unique nose for this year, one of the most questioning you'll find. The tannins from oak (Quercus), which includes black liquorice, practically throbs while the grain, seems both tight and relaxed offering a half fruit/half vegetable soupiness; t24 truly unique. Loads of bourbony tones with a mix of ulmo and heather honey alongside molasses, but then we cut down into a deeper level where the grains reside, partially spicy, semi-fruity and at once melting in the mouth and yet firm and rigid. The mouth feel. incidentally, is nigh on perfect...; f23.5 all as before, melded together and fading amid extra molasses; long with a toasty residue **b24** last time I tasted this it was given as virgin oak. Well, Quercus is oak, so I presume they mean this is virgin cask again. If so, they seem to have for the balance working much better this time to make the most of this hugely flavoured grain – a kind of wheat and rye cross - to make for one of the most distinguished Canadians this year. Not just beautiful...amazing, too... 47.6%

CENTRAL CITY BREWERS & DISTILLERS LTD. Surrey, British Columbia. 2013
Lohin McKinnon Chocolate Malt Single Malt Whisky Sauternes barrels db **(80)** n19 t23 f17 b21 Chocolate malt and Sauternes Barrels...? Sound like something straight out of the Glenmorangie blending lab. To taste, this is truly amazing: the closest thing to liquid Jaffa Cake

biscuits I have ever encountered. So orangey...so chocolatey... Sadly, the nose and finish tell their own tale: if you are going to use wine casks from Europe, make sure they have not been sulphur treated first. *43%.*

Lohin McKinnon Lightly Peated Single Malt Whisky oloroso sherry barrels db **(69.5) n17.5 t19 f16 b17** A polite tip to any micro distillery planning on using European wine casks. Just don't. Or you might end up with a sulphur-ruined disaster like this. *43%.*

Lohin McKinnon Muscat Wine Barrel Single Malt Whisky db **(78.5) n19 t21.5 f19 b19** A reminder, were it needed, that disappointing wine casks are not just restricted to Spain. *43%.*

Lohin McKinnon Niagara Wine Barrel Single Malt Whisky db **(87) n21.5 t22.5 f21 b22** If memory serves, it was these poor chaps who ended up with malt shewing the dangers of maturing whisky in sherry butts. They have wisely gone closer to home for their wine cask this time: Niagara. And this wasn't a barrel that fell over the Falls (well, I don't think so, anyway) but from one of the local vineyards. The result is a full-flavoured but eye-watering experience, certainly sulphur free, but with enough under-ripe gooseberry to keep your eyes watered for quite a while. Just needed an extra year or two in cask maybe for a more meaningful relationship between fruit and oak. Tart but very tasty. *43%.*

Lohin McKinnon Peated Single Malt Whisky db **(95.5) n23.5 t24 f23.5 b24.5** This is genuinely top rate, outstandingly distilled and matured peated whisky *43%.*

Lohin McKinnon Tequila Barrel Finished Single Malt Whisky db **(92) n23 t23 f22.5 b23.5** A fascinating and salivating addition to the whisky lexicon. *43%.*

Lohin McKinnon Wine Barrel Finished Single Malt Whisky finished in B.C. VQA Okanagan Valley Back Sage Vineyard Pipe wine barrels db **(90.5) n22 t23 f22.5 b23** Impressive balance here with the fruit doing enough but not too much. *43%.*

COPPER SPIRIT DISTILLERY Bowen Island, British Columbia.

◈ **Copper Spirit Wheat Whisky** db **(93) n23** Significantly cleaner distillate than their rye bottling which allows the wheat to display all its spicy charms in tandem with the light tannins. That fragile presence of vanilla ensures harmony; **t23.5** mmmm!!! Now that is superb! The sugars are a varied mix of heather honey and molasses, and they immediately react with the full-blown spice off the wheat. The vanillas are thick, too, offering a slightly cake-like feel to this; **f23** long - with the oak really trying to lay down a dryer, toastier phase to ensure a more docile fadeout. But those molasses notes refuse to be silenced and chip away, as do the spices...; **b23.5** the wheat is leaping from the glass like salmon from a remote British Columbian river. The mix of honey, molasses, wheat and deep, peppery spices is a mouth-warmer and heart winner. Cracking, beautifully sculpted whisky! My word, I'd love to see this one at cask strength...! *43% sc*

◈ **Copper Spirit Rye Whisky** db **(87) n22 t22 f21.5 b21.5** In this case for a Canadian whisky, when they say rye, they mean rye...as that is the only grain in use here. And it shows! Lots of newly baked rye bread on both the nose and throughout the middle of the delivery. And no shortage of muscovado sugars, too. But there is a muscularity to this whisky emanating from the oils from the cut which are apparent on the finish and give the rye an overall thickness of texture out of alignment with its strength. They have certainly rung out every last atom of rye flavour from the grain all the same... *43% sc*

DEVINE SPIRITS Saanichton, British Columbia. 2007.

Glensaanich Single Malt Whisky batch no. 4 db **(88) n22.5 t23 f20.5 b22** As the first bottling I encountered of this was superb and the second not so, I was curious to see what a pour from the bottle would bring forth this time. Well, something that sits somewhere between the two but with a character all its own. *45%.*

Glensaanich Quarter Cask Ancient Grains batch no. 1 db **(91.5) n23 t23 f22 b23.5** A beautiful little essay in complexity. The varied grains spelt, emmer, einkorn, khorosan and, of course, locally grown organic BC barley have been put together to delicious and fascinating effect. A real entertainer, especially when warmed for a while. *45%.*

FORTY CREEK Grimsby, Ontario. 1992.

Forty Creek Confederation Oak Reserve lot no. 1867-L, finished in Canadian wine barrels **(94) n23 t23.5 f23.5 b24** Forty Creek feel relaxed with this brand and seem to know how to pull the strings for near maximum effect. Very clean, too. *40%.*

Forty Creek Confederation Oak Reserve lot no. 1867-M, finished in Canadian wine barrels, bott code: BG/HL12447 **(94.5) n23.5 t24.5 f23.5 b24** Just so charming and elegant. It's the quiet ones you have to watch... *40%.*

Forty Creek Copper Pot Reserve bott code: DGIHC12074 **(89.5) n22.5 t23 f21 b23** They have remained very true to style since this brand first hit the shelves. The finish could do with a clean-up, though. *43%.*

Forty Creek Copper Pot Reserve bott code: DGIHK01391 **(95.5) n23 t24 f24 b24.5** Another stupendous Canadian from a distillery that has re-found its brilliance. This is the cheese to their Confederation oak chalk... And don't ye knock it all back at once... 43%.

Forty Creek Double Barrel Reserve lot no. 267, finished in once used American bourbon barrels **(87) n21.5 t22.5 f21 b22** Incredibly lush, but perhaps a tad too incredibly lush. Those caramel notes dominate with too much of a velvet fist, though it does briefly open out for some enjoyable oaky interplay, though all a little muffled. The finish is somewhat off key, alas. 40%.

Forty Creek Double Barrel Reserve lot no. 272, finished in once mellowed American bourbon barrels, bott code: DGIIA09007 **(91) n23 t22 f23 b23** Badly needs the Murray Method to get this one singing in harmony. When it does, just sit back, listen...and be entertained. 40%.

Forty Creek Premium Barrel Select bott code: DGIIB11069 **(88.5) n22 t22.5 f22 b22** A silky soft arrangement which ensures the fruity element always has pride of place and the juicy, marzipan sweetness is controlled. A little dull at the death, spices apart, but this is as friendly as a relatively rich whisky can get. 40%.

GLENORA Glenville, Nova Scotia. 1989.

Glen Breton Rare Single Malt Aged 10 Years nbc db **(86) n21 t22.5 f21 b21.5** Not quite as spick and span as the last GB 10 I encountered. Here someone appears to have experimented slightly with the cut and made it wider, piling on some bitter oils which dominate both the nose and finish. The midground malt does has a lovely biscuity sweetness to it, though. 43%

Glen Breton Rare Single Malt Aged 14 Years nbc db **(94.5) n23 t23.5 f23.5 b24** This is remarkable. I am going to ask the editor to keep the existing Glen Breton 10 notes in (as well as having the latest bottling). The reason is that over time obviously that great stock has moved on ten years. The tasting notes are near enough identical, except there is noticeably more oak on both the nose and the finish from the late middle onwards. Otherwise, it is pitch perfect! This so rarely happens. Wow, this really is sublime malt. And the emphasis is on malt... 43%

Glen Breton Rare Single Malt Aged 19 Years nbc db **(91) n22** some caramel has been leached from the oak giving the big barley and butterscotch tart a two- rather than three-dimensional feel...; **t23.5** ah, that is such a glorious delivery! The malt is on steroids while the natural gristy sweetness is underpinned by sharp, Corsican-style heather honey. Some lovely grapefruit tones, too...; **f22** a slight sign of tiredness on the cask as a little bitterness squeezes in; **b23.5** another magnificent malt bomb from Glenora. 43%

Glen Breton Rare Single Malt Aged 21 Years nbc db **(95.5) n23.5** oh, just grab the layering on this: the malt comes at you with at least three levels of intensity and sweetness, while I can spot a minimum two from the oak, one offering a lightly buttered toast, the other a bourbon-style spice; **t24** the delivery racks up top marks. The marriage of those perfect light oils and the citrus-spiked malt just makes you purr and grunt to yourself in undisguised pleasure. The oaks build a firmer structure through the middle, but as soon as one part is constructed, it is immediately overrun with marauding malt. The spice buzz is so warming, yet all the more impressive for knowing when to apply the brakes; **f24** very long, still with the malt in pole position...and just as on the nose, a slight bourbon-style note filters through...this time healthy hickory; **b24** everything works on this. It is blemish-free having been perfectly distilled and magnificently matured. Even the mouth feel offers a majestic insight into the most buttery of malts. Quite brilliant, by anyone's standards. When I'm working out Canadian whisky of the year for this year's Bible (WB24), two of the finalists will be this and Glenora's 16-year-old peated. That alone, will be one of a battle to decide because, at the moment, I just can't split them in quality... 43%

The Dark Glen Single Malt Aged 16 Years nbc db **(96) n24** the kind of peat that sings lullabies: so soft, so gentle in its smokiness. The phenols are understated but kiss and caress while a deeper layer of tannin proffers even shyer spices; **t24** absolutely adorable gristiness which is so rare on a malt of this relative antiquity. One of those delightful melt-in-the-mouth deliveries where the barley sugars leave rings of peat after they have dissolved. The oak, coupled with a pitch-perfect light oiliness ensures a matchingly genteel vanilla thread that offers further ballast. Salivating from the first moment and this fades only when the peat takes a slightly more ashy persona; **f24** the spices make almost a speech of apology for intruding on this delicate congregation of sweet peat and vanilla. Some very, very late mocha is perfectly aligned; **b24** this is triumph of elegance and balance. When a peat is this understated it is too easy for outside influences to wreck the storyline. However all the parts fall into place as though specially engineered. A Glenora to be in awe of... 43%

HIGHWOOD DISTILLERS High River, Alberta. 1974.

Highwood Distillers Centennial Canadian Rye Whisky db **(87.5) n21.5 t22 f22 b22** A much more even Canadian than the last time I encountered this. The tangy note which disrupted its natural flow has been replaced by a much more alluring oily-ulmo honey sweetness which sits attractively with the toffee, sultana, and delicate spice. 40%

Highwood Distillers Highwood Canadian Rye Whisky db (90) n22 the acacia honey and toffee is jazzed up gently with delicate spice; t23 silky cream toffee with delicate shards of vanilla; f22.5 the lightest sticky toffee pudding; b22.5 a quintessential Canadian rye. More to the point Highwood at its most Highwood... 40%

Highwood Distillers Liberator Canadian Rye Whisky db (90) n21.5 dull fruit and toffee; t23 brilliant! The delivery is a joy: an immediate mini explosion of spice perfectly counters the chewy cream toffee and vanilla thrust....; f22.5 a little citrus on the vanilla and toffee fade makes this surprisingly salivating very late on; b23 much more to this than the dull fruit and toffee nose promises. As Canadian as a punch-up at an ice-hockey match. Except here they are hitting each other with feathers... 42%

Highwood Distillers 'Ninety' 5-Year-Old Canadian Rye Whisky db (85) n21.5 t22 f20.5 b21 An undemanding Canadian rye where the toffee is ubiquitous. Just let down slightly by a degree of bitterness on the fade. 45%

Highwood Distillers 'Ninety' 20 Year Old Canadian Rye Whisky db (91) n22.5 fruity and fulsome, there is a curious salty, almost coastal feel to this...although the distillery is some 600 miles from the sea...; An unusual mix of apple and rhubarb tart, with an extra dollop of vanilla; t22.5 the immediately enveloping fruit is punctured by the strafing of peppers, which themselves seems to kick of a wonderful ulmo honey middle.. with toffee fudge for company. You are not going to find many 20-year-old whiskies this salivating; f22.5 the layering of the oak is polite and understated, while the spices still fizz slightly. A little bread and butter pudding on the finish, helped along by light molasses; b23.5 just had a horrible thought: the last time I visited this distillery, this 20-year-old whisky hadn't even been made. When this Covid nightmare is over is time to get out to the Prairies once more. Would love to see what else they have lurking in their warehouse! 45%

Canadian Rockies 17 Years nbc (95.5) n24 where did that mix of ripe and under-ripe gooseberry come from? Mingles with the vanilla and grain as if balancing a 12-inch ruler on your finger...; t24 with that gooseberry nose, the delivery could only be a mouth-watering affair. And now with a mix icing sugar, light butterscotch, and vanilla, all in tune with that singular fruity feature and an almost perfectly proportioned pinch of white pepper, we have a Canadian that is stunningly layered and constantly melting in the mouth; f23 the peppers persist. Though the fruit has vanished now, the vanilla remains unsullied and pure to the end; b24.5 this whisky has made a huge leap in quality since I last encountered it. I tried to count the layers after delivery...and gave up. Shows an elegance to win any heart. Magnificent. 50%

Canadian Rockies 21 Years nbc (92) n23 the oak enjoys room for a quiet solo while a fruit pastel sharpness lingers in the background with semi-sleeping spice; t23.5 a lush mouth-feel rather than flavour profile arrives first. But when the flavours do arrive, it is the ulmo honey which leads the way, just ahead of the vanilla which mix deliciously in the light oils; f23 chocolate vanilla wafer, with the vaguest hint of gooseberry; b24 Intriguing. Elegant. Delicious.... 46%

◌ **Canadian Rockies 28 Years Old** (94) n23.5 how pleasing is this...? The oak dominates but without a single hint of aggression or overexuberance. Instead, vanilla and butterscotch coo their presence with buttered acacia honey – even a hint of peanut butter – ensuring complexity and just-so sweetness: a lullaby of an aroma...; t23.5 melt-in-the-mouth what seems like corn and accompanying corn oil. Again, the sugars are delicate and melds perfectly with the gloriously subtle vanillas while the spices ping and flicker. The oils are close on perfect for weight; f23 there is the vaguest bitterness underlining the great age of this whisky but that sits perfectly with those elegant vanillas and persistent sprinkling of honey and (presumably) corn oil; b24 a whisky which carries its years effortlessly. Some whiskies prefer to plaster their personality all over the taste buds. This one just likes to seductively whisper them. 46% *Fountana Group*

LAST STRAW DISTILERY Vaughan, Ontario.

◌ **Last Straw Stout Whisky** Lot No SW001 db (90) n21.5 untidy with a little stale beer note disrupting the thicker, more attractive, oils...; t23 oh...! Now didn't expect this! The hop has vanished and instead we have a semi-bourbon kick of intense, flinty demerara and red liquorice. There is also a malty creaminess on display, too; f22.5 the spices which had begun their journey from the midpoint change in tone towards the end and become less pulsing and busier. The creamy dark sugars are also still in play, almost liqueur-like at times. The sugars have also changed tack, now less angular and more molten and in line with the prevailing creaminess...and a very late but friendly hop echo...; b23 the many regular readers of the Whisky Bible know that I am no great fan of whiskies matured in ex-beer barrels. The reason? The bitterness of the hop too often destroys the overall balance of the whisky...and tends to leave a nagging bitterness at the death which can ruin some good work which may have gone on before. Well, not so here.

Only the nose shews a degree of disharmony. However, from the first mouthful onwards we are in a delightful world of creamy sugars and even mocha. The hop certainly wasn't the last straw here.... 45% nc ncf

THE LIBERTY DISTILLERY Vancouver, British Columbia. 2013.

⬦ **The Liberty Distillery Trust Whiskey Ancient Grains** nbc db (94.5) n23.5 the latest batch of this has taken the nose on to a more honey-rich territory though the wonderfully pernickety grain and tannin interplay is still there to tantalise; t24 lovely mouth feel: clean, precise vanillas wrapped in a soft oil with a light mocha and spice development. Always busy, always working...; f23 lots of cocoa at play here – indeed not unlike a chocolate and vanilla ice cream in flavour; b24 really adore this style of whisky. This is grainy and bitty, the flavours just never standing still, and the variance of cocoa themes is quite amazing. Liberty has stepped up in class and now they have created a whiskey of this complexity which works so well, especially with the sugars being so understated and elegant, I hope they keep it exactly in this style as a core product. Superb. 44%

LUCKY BASTARD DISTILLERS Saskatoon, Saskatchewan.

Lucky Bastard Rye db (89) n22 a generous cut offers up heavy oils but the rye sneaks through for a sharp riposte; t23 about as truly comprehensive a rye delivery as you can hope for with the grain fragile, crisp and coated in Demerara sugars. Indeed, the sweetness takes some shifting and blends in adroitly with the growing vanillas. The texture is sensational, the sharpness of the grain penetrating...; f21.5 a little on the sticky, oily side with a few tell-tale bitter notes But those intense rye notes won't be denied, even now...; b22.5 thanks all at Lucky Bastard for sending me this bikini-clad lovely on the label. Certainly brought a smile. Glad you are doing well...and look forward to visiting to see your maturing stock and to discuss the vile hypocrisy which contaminates certain sections of the whisky industry. In the meantime, get those cuts a bit shorter...!! 62.65%

MACALONEY CALEDONIAN DISTILLERY Victoria, British Columbia. 2016.

Macaloney's Caledonian Dunivaig Peated Single Malt matured in Kentucky bourbon, recharred Portuguese, red wine & virgin American casks, db (93.5) n23 pork scratchings! Wonderful! The peatiness mimics a Dudley delicacy, while elsewhere the malt, still young, parades around confidently...; t23.5 stunning mouth feel. The most sensual of oils spreads ulmo honey-sweetened vanilla and dates. The smoke, however, plays a complex game, both pricking the oiliness, offering a drier phenol tone and a softening cloudiness, too...; f23.5 we are now back with the ulmo honey and vanilla, plus a little butterscotch. The smoke has dropped off the pace, save a playful prickling of spice; b23.5 a rather gorgeous young malt where the mouth feel is perfectly matched by the alure of the unique peaty tones. Should sell well in the Black Country of England, this. As it happens, I have probably tasted better in their warehouse, but not, so far, in bottled form. Superb! 46% nc ncf

Macaloney's Caledonian Glenloy Single Malt matured in Kentucky ex-bourbon, recharred red wine and sherry casks, batch no.3, bott Jun 2021, db (90.5) n22.5 the faintest over exuberance on the cut means a couple of half points are lost, but those feints might come in useful further down the line. Elsewhere the sugars are healthy and the oak firm; t23 genuinely fat and chewy where the malt get maximum game time. Very much how I remember the last batch, complete with the sticky toffee pudding and associated dates. Never less than lively and salivating...; f22.5 long with a slight nod towards moist date and walnut cake...; b22.5 further evidence that this distillery is coming along rather well. 46% ncf 1215 bottles

Macaloney's Caledonian Glenloy Island Single Malt Whisky Whisky Maker's Signature Expression Kentucky bourbon, re-charred red wine & sherry casks, bott Apr 20 db (90.5) n22 t23 f22.5 b23 When in my Canadian base, Victoria, after a day's tasting I'll settle down at my Club to dine on that prince of fish, the halibut, to allow its tender meat and exquisite flavours to massage my tired taste buds. As I was examining Victorian whisky today, but in Lockdown UK rather than British Columbia, I had a halibut here, instead, perfectly baked in enough tin foil to forge a coat of armour...and not allow a single atom of juice to escape. Tasting this malt both before and after the melt-in-the-mouth fish (but certainly not with) was an experience I can thoroughly recommend. This, is by far and away, the best thing from Macaloney's I have tasted this year. 46%. nc ncf. 1,276 bottles.

Macaloney's Caledonian Invermallie Single Malt matured in recharred Portuguese red wine barrique, cask no.60, bott Jun 2021, db (89) n22.5 t23.5 f20.5 b22.5 Oh my word! This has made a Herculean jump in quality from the last time I tasted it. Shame about that slight furriness. 46% ncf sc 352 bottles

Macaloney's Caledonian Invernahaven Single Malt matured in oloroso & PX casks, batch no.1, bott Jun 2021, db (89) n22 thick, sweet, grape; t22 grape, sweet, thick; f22.5 sweet, thick, grape. And spice!!!! **b22.5** well, if you ever want to do away with yourself with a sherry overdose, here's your weapon... *46% ncf 421 bottles*

Macaloney's Caledonian Kilarrow Peated Single Malt matured in Kentucky bourbon, recharred Portuguese red wine & sherry casks, db **(83) n20 t22 f20 b21** Flavoursome and chewy. But an overwhelming feeling that the spirit isn't up to the normal high standards. The result is too much bubble gum and an uncomfortable niggle of feints at key moments. A shame. *46% nc ncf*

Macaloney's Peated Mac Na Braiche Island Single Malt Spirit nbc, db **(81.5) n21 t22 f18.5 b20** A head-scratcher of a malt. Whatever happened to the character and personality? It has peat and it comes from a distillery I know, from having sampled from their maturing stock, is not short of characterful and good quality malt. But even allowing for the slightly wide cut, you expect more; instead you appear to get some kind of overwhelming flat-caramel rich fruitiness cancelling out the peat. A bemusing dram. Not unpleasant, save an obvious cask niggle on the finish. Just far, far too dull and ordinary elsewhere. *46%. nc ncf.*

Macaloney's Caledonian Skarrabollis Single Cask Peated matured in virgin American cask, db **(94) n22.5** layered butterscotch offers as much clout as the shy peat...; **t24** the all-round succulence and chewability languidly hits home first, then...Eureka! Out of nowhere the malt hits its straps, and the phenols engage with the honeyed tannins and my word! We're in business! Spices arrive, gently at first...then in force. The vanilla re-forms as ulmo honey, the light maltiness turns into concentrated grist...and at last the smoke decides it has a job to do and gently fills the mouth. The complexity is compelling, almost shocking...; **f23.5** a very long finale with the peaty spices buzzing, balancing out the thick, creamy vanillas; **b24** technically, a dream of a malt with faultless distillate merging beautifully with a very fine cask. The amazing thing is, at the beginning so little happens. It is a dropped intro of a dram... *46% nc ncf sc*

Macaloney's Caledonian Skarrabollis Single Cask Ex-Bourbon Peated matured in Kentucky bourbon cask, db **(95) n23.5** soft and comforting...peak reek carried on the wind from a croft; **t24** the nose had already announced that this is high quality malt. And the clarity of the flavours here reveals far better cuts on the still than had previously been found. The smoke almost oscillates dampened slightly by a fruit pastel sweetness and intensifying maltiness. The midground vanilla explosion almost makes you punch the air with delight; **f23.5** long, light ulmo honey, ultra-intense malt....and still that warming cloud of smoke to accompany the spices...; **b24** I think we can safely say that, on this evidence, Macaloney Caledonian has arrived on the world stage of great distillers. A little bit of mucking about and a few learning curves negotiated to get there. But if they can keep this up then they will be much admir'd and loved across the whisky-loving world. *46% nc ncf sc previously Peated Darach Braiche spirit*

Macaloney's Caledonian Skarrabollis Single Cask Red Wine Peated matured in recharred Portuguese red wine barrique, db **(89.5) n21.5 t23 f22.5 b22.5** An interesting drop off in quality from the Skarrabollis Kentucky barrel. Here the wine has managed to skew the balance and make for a much harder malt. Just a little too ragged at certain times. That said, this is big and flavoursome and still loads to get our teeth into. *46% nc ncf sc previously Peated Mac na Braiche spirit*

Macaloney's Caledonian Spirit of Kikinriola Single Cask Spirit triple distilled pot still, recharred Portuguese red wine barrique, db **(93) n23 t23.5 f23 b23.5** A weighty spirit despite having gone through the still thrice: the fruit offers both a Jammy Dodger biscuit to go with the Custard Creams. Excellent spices, in perfect sync. And the late chocolate and cherry cake is rather wonderful Superbly constructed. Seriously tasty and complex *46% nc ncf sc*

Macaloney's Caledonian Spirit of Kikinriola Single Cask Spirit triple distilled potstill, virgin American cask, db **(91) n22.5 t23 f22.5 b23** The kind of experience to almost leave you in a trance, so mesmerising is it. Borderline overly sweet to the point of liqueur. But far too complex to fall into that trap. The mouth feel is ridiculously lush without ever falling into th trap of being cloying. And though all kinds of sugars abound – golden syrup particularly - the winning formulae is achieved by the ridiculously complex layering of the virgin oak, taking us from red liquorice to black cherry. *46% nc ncf sc*

MAD LABORATORY DISTILLING Vancouver, British Columbia.

◈ **Madlab Single Malt Release # 7 Aged 42 Months** bottled 2023 db **(84) n21 t22 f20 b21** It is an interesting concept, distilling without copper. Which I presume is going on here as I can find little evidence of it being in the make-up. It is not like the early, undrinkable, editions of the malt from the Wilson Distillery in New Zealand of the 1980s where the impurities attacked at will and a sharp "green" note made your eyes water. That was an experience I'll never forget... This is much softer and on delivery the malt is uncommonly intense. But, for all-round depth, you'd hope they'd put some in the system somewhere. Lots of vanilla-toffee off the barrel to round out and soften any potential edges. Truly unique. *42%*

PEMBERTON DISTILLERY Pemberton, British Columbia. 2008.

Pemberton Valley Single Malt Whisky cask no. 1, 200 litre Four Roses ex-bourbon barrel, dist 20 Sept 10, bott 13 Mar 20 db **(88) n22 t23 f21 b22** A far slicker malt than their previous expressions over the years. Still a niggling degree of feint. But the barley gives full value for money with a confident and intense performance. Rather like the delicate hickory that flits around the nose and the midpoint. Enjoyable. *44%. nc ncf sc.*

Pemberton Valley Single Malt Whisky 120 litre French oak apple brandy cask, dist 22 Nov 14, bott 9 Mar 20 db **(85) n20.5 t22 f21 b21.5** Doesn't hold back on the flavours. Thick with malty, apple-ey nougat. The last note again underlines the weakness of the cut, but the influence of the oak – and the juicy properties of the barley – are first class. *44%. nc ncf sc.*

Pemberton Valley Single Malt Whisky 200 litre Woodford Reserve ex-bourbon barrel, dist 10 Jun 14, bott 9 Mar 20 db **(90) n21.5 t23.5 f22 b23** A much better, more beautifully balanced and rounded malt from Pemberton. Helped by starting off with a much superior spirit than usual. Not perfect, but the extra chocolate nougat notes from the cut fit in very comfortably with the beautifully intense barley. Chewy and delightfully weighted and paced, this is on a different level altogether to anything I have seen from them before. The extra tannin towards the end not only offers weight, but a charming spiciness and depth, too... *44%. nc ncf sc.*

SHELTER POINT DISTILLERY Campbell River, British Columbia. 2011.

Shelter Point Distillery Artisanal Cask Strength Whisky American oak, finished in French oak db **(91) n22.5 t23.5 f22 b23** Looks as though the law in Canada now says you even have to have the barrels from both English and French language... A beautifully complex and intense malt. *54.8%. 1,200 bottles.*

Shelter Point Artisanal Single Malt Whisky Distiller's Select db **(94.5) n23 t24 f23.5 b24** When I initially tasted this distillery's very first maturing cask quite a little while ago now, the evidence provided by the lightly yellowing spirit left me fully confident that they would, with great care, be capable of producing a very high class malt. They have not let me down. This is truly beautiful. *46%. nc ncf.*

Shelter Point Double Barreled Single Malt Whisky finished for 335 days in Quails Gate Pinot Noir cask, bott 2019 db **(89) n22 t23 f21.5 b22.5** Whisky from one of my favourite Canadian distilleries maturing in a barrel from one of my favourite Pinot Noir winemakers. Quails Gate is usually pretty dry and medium bodied, sometimes a tad heavier. Shelter Point malt is delicate. The balance, as might be expected is patchy. But when it works, it does so beautifully...; *50%. nc ncf.*

Shelter Point Double Barreled Whisky finished for 152 days in Quails Gate Old Vines Foch cask, batch no. 4, bott 2019 db **(86) n22 t21 f22 b21** Nowhere near the usual high standard of Shelter Point. The wine has overwhelmed the malt and seldom is there cohesion. Juicy in part with the odd cocoa note. But not an unqualified success. *50%. nc ncf. 1,644 bottles.*

Shelter Point Single Cask Quails Gate Old Vines Foch Reserve Finish bott 2019 db **(84.5) n22 t22.5 f20 b20** A hard, tight whisky which is unforgiving. The fruit seems detached and the whole metallic and tart. The big, juicy flavour delivery apart, fails to find happiness on the palate. *46%. nc ncf sc. 228 bottles. Single Cask Release no. 2.*

Shelter Point Smoke Point Whisky peat finished, bott 2019 db **(92.5) n23 t23 f23 b23.5** Even the healthy dose of peat injected into this with a high-quality finish can't entirely hide away the youthful nature of this malt. But when something is this fresh, mouth-watering and simply alive, then perhaps you don't want it to. Oh, for the vitality of youth... *55%. nc ncf. 1,044 bottles.*

SHERINGHAM DISTILLERY Sooke, British Columbia. 2015.

Sheringham Whisky Red Fife grain: Red Fife/barley, ex-bourbon cask, bott 2019 db **(86) n21.5 t22 f21 b21.5** Not technically a perfect whisky, but the initial produce of new distilleries very seldom are. The usual light feint at work here which adds on the extra oils and slight bitterness on the finish. But provides, also, an attractive chewability to the abundant sweet caramels extracted from an excellent ex-bourbon cask. A work in progress, for sure. But enough good points not to forsake this distillery from Sooke. *45%.*

SONS OF VANCOUVER DISTILLERY N.Vancouver, BC. 2015

⬦ **Sons of Vancouver Release Number 3 Caribbean Cask** bott 2022 db **(93) n23** a compelling nose, thumping out diverse but always fulsome tannins which combine seemingly by instinct with the crisp dark sugars. A gentle fruitiness quivers and sighs without ever making a statement; **t23.5** rather than flavour, it is a soft creaminess, the richness of the mouthfeel, which registers first. Probably because the nose itself hinted of none of this. As on the aroma, the tannins are bitty with the oak full on but beautifully assisted by those surreptitious sugars and delicate spices. The grains also come into play, at first cohesive, then far more individually but always high pitched; **f23** a dry, uncomplicated finale, long yet mostly free from oils but displaying some gorgeous chocolate tones. The rye and tannins continue their big-flavoured united front; **b23.5** the fact the finish is so clean after those initial oils on entry means that this is beautifully distilled spirit. Despite a degree of simplicity, the layering ensures complexity and there is no doubting the excellence of the barrels used in maturation. Highly attractive and singular in style. 53.5%

⟐ **Sons of Vancouver Release Number 4 Cask Strength** bott 2023 db (96) **n23** a much more brutalist nose than their Caribbean creation (although there is something distinctly Caribbean about the coconut at play), some serious esters pitching in in an attempt to soften. The sugars gang up to infuse a kind of toffee brownie touch to this, though the vanilla is no slouch, either. What happens next is likely to go one of only two ways: either it will be an insane flavour fest...or a massive disappointment....; **t24.5** wow! Impeccably mouth-filling and the explosion of flavours on about the third flavour beat remind you of an ammunition dump going off: first a small detonation followed, in this case, by one huge paroxysm of piquancy. The flavours that hit you are almost overwhelming – this really is something else besides. There must be some very deep charring here, as some of the flavour profile is Kentucky rye with knobs on: ultra-intense cocoa and hickory with a stunning background of soothing molasses. Better still, there is a buttery oiliness aiding the esters which both softens and controls the intensity, while at the same time ensuring it continues to slide majestically around the palate. Rye, incidentally, pulses from the first moment to the last...; **t24** it takes so long to get your brain away from that astonishing arrival, it is hard to focus and determine just where the finish begins. Late on we have a wonderful hickory and maple syrup combination, allowing the grain to still offer a juicy presence. The drier vanilla from the oak, along with even, warming spices makes for near perfect balance; **b24.5** make no mistake: this is an astonishing whisky. I'm not sure I will locate a more flavoursome one than this all year. Possibly the most estery bottling I've encountered for a year or two, but this seems to accentuate every sweet tone on display – and there are many – meaning the drier nuances offer the perfect countering pitch. 63.2%

SPIRIT OF YORK Toronto, Ontario. 2015.
Spirit of York 100% Rye db (93.5) **n24.5 t23.5 f22 b23.5** Whoever engineered this, their first-ever whisky bottling, must have been using the Lawrenceburg, Indiana, rye as its blueprint, including virgin oak casks. Matches its intensity and clarity in so many ways, though perhaps not at the death. For a first whisky from Toronto's famous and historic distilling district, the distillers from the Spirit of York should take a bow: this is memorable and authentic stuff distilled, romantically, in part of the old Gooderham and Worts Building...! Toronto is well and truly back on the whisky distilling map... 46% (92 proof).

STILLWATERS DISTILLERY Concord, Ontario. 2009.
Stalk & Barrel 100% Rye Single Cask Whisky (86.5) **n20 t23 f21.5 b22** Despite the light feintiness, this really does rack up some big rye notes. Rock hard from nose to finish – save for the oils from the wide cut – the delivery and afterglow offer a stupendous degree of grain and spice. Technically not perfect, but worth discovering just for the uncompromising ride. 60.2%. sc.

Stalk & Barrel Single Malt Whisky (84) **n19 t22.5 f21.5 b21** Full on malty, chocolate-laden spiced toffee nougat. Once past the so-so nose, becomes pretty enjoyable. 60.2%. sc.

TROUBLED MONK Red Deer, Alberta. 2018.
Grainhenge Meeting Creek Aged 40 Months Batch No. 01 #2 & #4 char new American oak db (94) **n22.5** the oak is hardly shy as it stretches out the tannins as far as they can go without fracturing. Very precise distillation means there is no oil pollution, leaving the tannins and barley a very clear target to find. It does take time, but the malt does finally make inroads into toasty oak; **t24** now that's much better! The explosive malt is not only first to arrive, but it's accompanied by silky oils that are nowhere to be seen on the nose. It means the sugars – crisp and with the lightest hint of heather honey - are first on the scene before relaxed barley sugar leads in the oak. The spices are, frankly, brilliant, timing their pulses of intensity perfectly and flickering around the roof of the mouth with the developing mocha. Just so many magnificent layers...; **f23.5** all kinds of cocoa notes which, when at the level of intensity, have been fashioned by both the oak and barley one suspects. Subtle and sophisticated; **b24** my word! What a start! The Troubled Monk should get some words of comfort from this Bible at least. Beautifully distilled, thoughtfully created and oozing class. A standing ovation. 56.7%. nc ncf. 450 bottles.

YUKON BREWING Whitehorse, Yukon. 1997.
⟐ **Two Brewers Yukon Single Malt Release 35** (92.5) **n22 t23.5 f23.5 b23.5** A fat and at times frantic mouth-filler, full of Yukon's usual big personality. Which is odd as the nose wasn't

quite chiming in time, perhaps over dependent on an Advocaat-style sweetness. But the eye-watering sharpness of the barley more than makes amends, while the intensity of the grain itself is majestic. This appears to be a form of malt concentrate, and with a light bite making a nonsense of the 46%. The tannins are also playing up to their highest game, the vanillas so rich and forthright and blending in so beautifully with the malt. The sweetness, beyond the barley sugars, are two-toned, one distinctly ice-sugar style, augmented by a far deeper muscovado type. But all this seems to add, like a pinch of salt, to the purity of the malt. The final moments give way to the tannins with the lightest hint of mocha...barley sweetened, of course. That is one substantial Canadian Malt whisky.... 46% Highfern

Canadian Single Rye
CIRKA DISTILLERIES Montréal, Quebec. 2014.
Cirka Premier Whisky 93/07 Québécois Réserve Paul Cirka 3 years in new American oak #3, 5 weeks in Oloroso sherry casks db (82) n22 t21.5 f19.5 b19 Fantastic to see a new distillery making 100% rye whisky in Canada. It warms the heart! Not so good, though, is to see the grain vanish without trace under an uncompromising blanket of fruit, so the rye's unique qualities cannot be heard and enjoyed. A smattering of sulphur from the oloroso butt does it no favours, either. Still, I look forward to seeing this distillery flourish. It deserves to. 46%. nc ncf.

Canadian Blended Whisky
Alberta Premium (95.5) n24 t25 f22.5 b24 It has just gone 8am and the Vancouver Island sky is one of clear blue. My windows are open to allow in some chilly, early Spring air and, though only the first week of March, an American robin sits in the arbutus tree, resplendent in its now two-toned leaves, calling for a mate, as it has done since 5.15 this morning, his song blending with the lively trill of the house finches and the doleful, maritime anthem of the gull. It seems the natural environment of Alberta Premium, back here to its rye-studded best after a couple I tasted socially in Canada last year appeared comparatively dull and restrained. I am tasting this from Bottle Lott No L93300197 and it is classic, generating all I expect and now demand. A national treasure. 40%

Alberta Premium Aged 20 Years db (72) n19.5 t20.5 f15 b17 Singularly the biggest disappointment of the year. A strange cold tea and tobacco note has infiltrated what is usually the most rock-solid rye in the business. This is my beloved Alberta Premium.... unrecognisable. They have got this so wrong... 42%.

Alberta Premium Cask Strength Rye bott code: L9212ADB013408:16 db (97.5) n24.5 t24.5 f24 b24.5 Truely world-class whisky from possibly the world's most underatted distillery. How can something be so immense yet equally delicate? For any whisky lover on the planet looking for huge but nearly perfectly balanced experience, then here you go. And with rye at its most rampantly beautiful, this is something to truly worship. Daily. 65.1%.

Bearface Aged 7 Years Triple Oak Canadian Single Grain ex-bourbon barrels, finished in French oak red wine barrels & Hungarian oak, bott no. H1418W1MH (88.5) n22 t22.5 f22 b22 About as soft as whisky gets. If they could find a way of tuning out some of the caramel, they'd definitely have a more satisfying whisky. 45.5%.

Bearface One Eleven Series batch no. 1, nbc (89) n22 t23 f22 b22 OK, this is one very weird Canadian whisky. But is it enjoyable? Well, anyone who says it isn't is telling you a Bearfaced lie... 42.5%. Ten parts Bearface cut with one part Agave Espadín.

Benjamin Chapman 7 Year Rye (86.5) n21.5 t23 f20 b22 Once you overcome the nose, which appears almost to possess a hoppy kick, we are on much more enjoyable territory. Incredible molasses and cocoa theme, especially on the glutinous delivery. The strange hop-like bitterness returns at the very death, alas. But such is the glorious richness of the delivery, this is well worth looking out for. 45% (90 proof) imported & bottled by 3Badge.com

Black Velvet (78) n18 t20 f20 b20. A distinctly off-key nose is compensated for by a rich corn and vanilla kick on the palate. But that famous spice flourish is a distant memory. Another big caramel number. 40%

Canadian Club 100 Proof (89) n21 t23 f22 b23. If you are expecting this to be a high-octane version of the standard CC Premium, you'll be in for a shock. This is a much fruitier dram with an oilier body to absorb the extra strength. An entertaining blend. 50%.

Canadian Club 100% Rye (92) n23 t23.5 f22.5 b23 Will be interesting to see how this brand develops over the years. Rye is not the easiest grain to get right when blending differing ages and casks with varied histories: it is an art which takes time to perfect. This is a very attractive early bottling, though my money is on it becoming sharper in future vattings as the ability to show the grain above all else becomes more easily understood. Just so wonderful to see another excellent addition to the Canadian whisky lexicon. 40% (80 proof)

Canadian Club 1858 Original bott code: L1019FFBB (**91**) **n22 t23.5 f22.5 b23** I'm always amused when I hear from single malt connoisseurs that Canadian Club is a neutral whisky. Gosh, if those peppers are neutral, I'd hate to see what they do when they should they ever go to war... 40%

Canadian Club Chronicles: Issue No. 1 Water of Windsor Aged 41 Years (**97**) **n24.5 t24 f24 b24.5** Have I had this much fun with a sexy 41-year-old Canadian before? Well, yes I have. But it was a few years back now and it wasn't a whisky. Was the fun we had better? Probably not. It is hard to imagine what could be, as this whisky simply seduces you with the lightness and knowledgeable meaning of its touch, butterfly kissing your taste buds, finding time after time your whisky erogenous zone or g spots ... and then surrendering itself with tender and total submission. 45% (90 proof).

Canadian Club Chronicles Aged 42 Years bott code: L19260IW (**96.5**) **n24 t24 f24 b24.5** I have just tasted one of the top ten whiskies of the year for absolute certain. Simply spellbinding. 45% (90 proof). Issue No. 2.

Canadian Club Chronicles Aged 43 Years bott code: L202311W11:20 (**95**) **n24.5 t23.5 f23 b24** This has certainly moved on, even from the 42-year-old and a long way from the 41. To truly understand this Canadian, the Murray Method is not just a suggestion, but essential. It opens up the nose to show one of the most complex and complete in the world this year, involving layering and subtle side plots which eventually mesmerise. By comparison, the experience on the palate is more simplistic, as is always the case when caramels begin to enter the conversation: had it been the equal of the nose, this would have been in the running for World Whisky of the Year... 45%. Issue No. 3 - The Speakeasy.

Canadian Club Premium (**92**) **n23 t22.5 f23 b23.5**. A greatly improved whisky which now finds the fruit fitting into the mix with far more panache than of old. Once a niggardly whisky, often seemingly hell-bent on refusing to enter into any form of complexity: but not now! Great spices in particular. I'm impressed. 40%

Canadian Mist (**78**) **n19 t20.5 f18.5 b20**. Much livelier than previous incarnations despite the inherent, lightly fruited softness. 40%

Century Reserve 21 Years Old (**91.5**) **n23.5 t23 f23 b22**. Quite beautiful, but a spirit that is as likely to appeal to rum lovers as whisky ones. 40%

Crown Royal bott code: 318 B4 2111 (**87.5**) **n22 t23 f21 b21.5** Carries on in the same style as above. But at least the finish is a lot happier now with welcome ulmo honey extending further and the spices also working overtime. Still a little residual bitterness shows more work is required but, unquestionably, keep on this course and they'll soon be getting there. 40%

Crown Royal Black (**85**) **n22 t23 f18.5 b21.5**. Not for the squeamish: a Canadian which goes for it with bold strokes from the off which makes it a whisky worth discovering. The finish needs a rethink, though. 45%

Crown Royal Black bott code: L9 337 N9 4:05 db (**87**) **n21 t22 f22 b22** Definitely an improvement from the last time I tasted this, which was something akin to being hit over the head by a branch falling from a maple tree. Sill it maintains its muscular façade, and the nose with its peculiar fruity barbs is still a little bit of a challenge; but now it offers something which before eluded it: layering. Chewier and sweet and sugars now seem to enjoy a pleasant toing and froing with the toasty oak and spice. Plenty to grapple with here. 45% (90 proof).

Crown Royal Bourbon Mash Bill bott code: L8 N04 N7 db (**94.5**) **n23.5 t23.5 f23.5 b24** Whiskies like this do so much to up the standing of Canadian whisky. 40% (80 proof).

Crown Royal Cornerstone Blend (**85.5**) **n21 t22 f21 b21.5**. Something of a mish-mash, where a bold spiciness appears to try to come to terms with an, at times, random fruity note. One of the most curious aspects of this quite different whisky is the way in which the weight of the body continues to change. Intriguing. 40.3% (80.6 proof)

Crown Royal DeLuxe (**91.5**) **n23.5 t23 f22.5 b22.5** Some serious blending went into this. Complex. 40% (80 proof)

Crown Royal Hand Selected Barrel (**94.5**) **n23.5 t24 f23.5 b23.5** If this is a single barrel, it boasts extraordinary layering and complexity 51.5% (103 proof)

Crown Royal Limited Edition (**87**) **n22 t22.5 f20.5 b22**. A much happier and productive blend than before with an attractive degree of complexity but the more bitter elements of the finish have been accentuated. 40%

Crown Royal Noble Collection 13 Year Old Bourbon Mash bott code: L8037 2S 00108:06 db (**96**) **n24.5 t24 f23.5 b24** It's Canadian, Jim: but not as we know it... Deliciously going places where no other Canadian has gone before... 45% (90 proof).

Crown Royal Noble Collection French Oak Cask Finished bott code: L9 086 2S 001 db (**88.5**) **n22.5 t23.5 f20.5 b22** Not quite the same tale of unalloyed joy at the last time I tasted this. This is an altogether tighter version with most of the fun restricted to the delivery which, when combined with a satin mouth-feel, makes for a gorgeous fruit-laced and spicy experience made all the chewer by the generous toffee. However, the finish is bitter, tangy, and completely out of sorts, undoing some of the earlier excellent work. Hopefully, the next bottling will be a little truer to type. 40% *(80 proof)*.

Crown Royal Northern Harvest Rye bott code L5085 N3 **(97.5)** n25 t24.5 f23.5 b24.5 This is the kind of whisky you dream of dropping into your tasting room. Rye, that most eloquent of grains, not just turning up to charm and enthral but to also take us through a routine which reaches new heights of beauty and complexity. To say this is a masterpiece is barely doing it justice. 45%

Crown Royal Northern Harvest Rye bott code: L8 353 N5 **(97)** n25 t24 f23.5 b24.5 Having spent a little while in Canada over the last year, I have had the pleasure of a few stunning Northern Harvest Ryes in that time. But I admit I did a double-take when this bottling turned up in my lab for the official sample tasting. It was by far the darkest example of this brand I had ever seen – and I admit that I feared the worst, as that can often mean the sharp complexity which is the hallmark of a whisky such as this can be compromised. I need not have worried: the glass is almost shattering from the enormity of vivid delights contained therein. A stunning whisky, as usual, but they will have to ensure that the colour returns to its lighter gold, perhaps with slightly younger casks, to guarantee the fresh style remains, as this could easily have become a dullard. This, though, is anything but. 45% *(90 proof)*.

Crown XR Extra Rare bott code: L9 257 2S 001 db **(94)** n23.5 t23.5 f23 b24 Complex and absolutely first rate. I had feared it would not live up to earlier glories. But the blender must take a bow: this is serious blending..! 40% *(80 proof)*.

Crown Royal XO (87.5) n22 t21 f22.5 b22. With an XO, one might have hoped for something eXtraOrdinary or at least eXOtic. Instead, we have a Canadian which carried on a little further where their Cask No 16 left off. Always a polite, if rather sweet whisky, it falls into the trap of allowing the Cognac casks a little too much say. Only on the finish, as the spices begin to find channels to flow into, does the character which, for generations, set Crown Royal apart from all other Canadians begin to make itself heard: complexity. 40% WB15/398

Gibson's Finest Aged 12 Years (77) n18 t20 f19 b20. Unlike the Sterling, going backwards rather than forwards. This is way too syrupy, fruity and toffee impacted. Despite the very good spice, almost closer to a liqueur than a true whisky style. 40%

Gibson's Finest Rare Aged 18 Years (95.5) n24 t24.5 f23.5 b23.5 So far ahead of both Sterling and the 12, it is hard to believe they are from the same stable. But make no mistake; this is pure thoroughbred: truly world class. 40%

Great Plains Craft Spirits 18-Year-Old Brandy Casks finished in Jerez brandy casks, bond date. 09 01 00, batch no.1 **(95)** n23.5 t24 f23.5 b24 Great Plains it may be. But there is nothing plane, or particularly Canadian, about this one-off blockbusting beauty. This is something completely different...and if you are not careful it will seduce you until you have tracked down every last bottle. Superb cask management married to a very impressive distillate results in a Canadian offering rare cadence. To say I'm impressed doesn't quite cover it... 54.5% *(109 proof)*

Heavens Door The Bootleg Series Canadian Whisky 26 Years Old 2019 finished in Japanese Mizunara oak casks **(96)** n24 t24 f23.5 b24.5 It thrills me when I see Canadian whisky take on this advanced form of complexity, rather than rely on the false promises of fruit juice. A standing ovation to those responsible for this delightful and star quality Canadian. 55.75% *(111.5 proof)*. 3,797 bottles.

the required sharpness. 40%.

J.P. Wiser's 18 Years Old bott code 54SL24 L16341 **(94)** n23 t24 f23 b24 Some great blending here means this is a slight notch up on the bottling above, though the styles are almost identical. Main differences here concern the fruit aspect: more prolific and spicier on the nose and then added moist date on the delivery. Significantly, there is more honey on the longer finish, also. Remains a deliciously rounded and satisfying whisky. 40%.

J. P. Wiser's 35 Year Old (96) n23.5 t24 f24 b24.5 Many, many years ago I tasted Canadian older than this in the blending lab. But I have never seen it before at this age as an official bottling. What I had before me on the lab table could not have engineered this style, so this is as fascinating as it is enjoyable. 50%. *Ultra-Rare Craft Series.*

J. P. Wiser's Dissertation (89) n22 t22 f22 b22.5 A distinctive and quite different style being handsome, a little rugged but always brooding. 46.1%.

J.P. Wiser's Double Still Rye (94) n23.5 t23.5 f23.5 b23.5 Big, superb rye: a genuine triumph from Wiser's. 43.4%

J.P. Wiser's Last Barrels Aged 14 Years (94.5) n24.5 t23.5 f23.5 b23.5 You don't need to be pulsing with rye to ensure a complex Canadian of distinction. 45%

J. P. Wiser's Rye 15 Year Old (89) n22 t22.5 f22.5 b22 Doesn't do too much. But what it does do, it does big... 40%.

J. P. Wiser's Rye Triple Barrel bott code L16331 54SL24 **(85.5)** n22 t21.5 f21 b21 Three types of toffee barrel by the looks of it. Pleasant but lacking complexity. 45%.

J. P. Wiser's Seasoned Oak Aged 19 Years seasoned 48 months, bott code L18114EW0814 **(87.5) n22.5 t23 ff20.5 b21.5** Some high-octane tannin trumps all, though some rich fruit – moist dates especially - rounds off the peppery oak. Enjoys a glossy, coppery but unravels somewhat at the death with a furry, off-key finale. Some lovely, lilting moments but the balance seems controlled. 48%. *Rare Cask Series. Exclusive to the LCBO.*

Lot 40 Cask Strength (88.5) n23.5 t24 f20 b22 At last! Lot 40 at full strength! You will not read this anywhere (or anything to do with my many whisky creations over the last 25 years as journalists can sometimes be a pathetically narrow-minded and jealous bunch disinclined to tell the true story if it doesn't suit their own agenda) but when I first created the style for Lot 40 a great many years back the first thing I proposed was that it should be a rye at cask strength. The idea was liked in principle but regarded way too radical for its time and dropped. So I helped come up with a weaker but still excellent rye. This is a different style to what I had in mind as the oak gives a slant I would have avoided. But it gladdens my heart to see it nonetheless. 53%. *Ultra-Rare Craft Series.*

Lot No. 40 Rye Whisky bott code 54SL24 L16344 **(96) n24 t24 f23.5 b24.5** Now this is very close to the rye I had in mind when first involved in putting this whisky together the best part of a couple of decades ago. Much more complex and satisfying than the previous re-introduced bottling I encountered...which in itself was magnificent. Here, though, the honey I had originally tried to lasso has been brilliantly recaptured. Happy to admit: this is better than my early efforts. There really is a Lot going on... Classic! 43%.

Masterson's 10 Year Old Straight Rye Whiskey batch no. 016 **(94) n23 t23 f24 b24** One of the most beautiful finishes to any whisky on the planet this year. 45% *(90 proof).*

Pike Creek French, Hungarian & American oak casks **(89) n23 t22.5 f21.5 b22** You know you have a great nose on your hands when a fly drowns in your whisky even before you get a chance to taste it... Decent stuff keeping your taste buds at full stretch. 45%.

Pike Creek 10 Years Old finished in port barrels **(80) n21.5 t22.5 f17 b19.** The delivery is the highlight of the show by far as the fruit takes off backed by delicate spices and spongy softness. The nose needs some persuading to get going but when fully warmed, gives a preview of the delivery. The furry finish is a big disappointment, though.40%

Pike Creek 10 Year Old Rum Barrels Finish bott code 54SL24 L16174 EW07:30 **(86.5) n22 t22.5 f20 b22** A far happier fellow than the Port finish, for sure – even though the slight furriness on the finale is a bit of a bore. Before reaching that point, though, there is a velvet revolution involving much honey. 42%.

Pike Creek 21 Year Old Single Malt Cask Finish (87.5) n21 t23.5 f21.5 b21.5 Pleasant and fruity. As silky as you like with a moist date and spiced theme. But, doubtless, through the cask finish, the age and accompanying complexities seems to have been lost in translation somewhere... 45%. *Ultra-Rare Craft Series.*

Revel Stoke Blended Canadian Whisky (87) n21 t22 f22 b22 Canadian at its softest and most friendly. Clean, unchallenging and happy to drift in its simple Demerara sugars and toffee. Pleasant. 40%

Rich and Rare Reserve (86.5) n19.5 t21 f23.5 b22.5. Actually does what it says on the tin, certainly as to regard the "Rich" bit. But takes off when the finish spices up and even offers some ginger cake on the finale. Lovely stuff. 40%

Sam Barton Aged 5 Years bott code: L814502B **(86.5) n21 t22 f21.5 b22** A much improved blend of late with a much studier structure after the clean, now classically Canadian nose. Good spice buzz and lots of easy charm. 40%. *La Martiniquaise.*

Seagram's Canadian 83 (86.5) n21 t22 f21.5 b22. A vastly improved blend which has drastically cut the caramel to reveal a melt-in-the-mouth, slightly crisp grain. There are some citrusy edges but the buttery vanilla and pleasing bite all go to make for a chic little number. 40%

Seagram's VO (91) n22 t23.5 f22.5 b23. With a heavy heart I have to announce the king of rye-enriched Canadian, VO, is dead. Long live the corn-dominant VO. Over the years I have seen the old traditional character ebb away: now I have let go and have no option other than to embrace this whisky for what it has become: infinitely better than a couple of years back; not in the same league as a decade ago. But just taking it on face value, credit where credit is due. This is an enjoyably playful affair, full of vanilla-led good intention, corn and complexity. There is even assertive spice when needed and the most delicately fruity edge...though not rye-style. Thoughtfully blended and with no little skill, I am impressed. And look forward to seeing how this develops in future years. A treat which needs time to discover. 40%

Signal Hill Whisky bott no. 181560932 **(82) n21.5 t21.5 f19 b20** There is no little irony that a hill which dramatically juts 470 feet out of the sea to present one of Canada's most startling and historical points should be represented by a whisky that is so intransigently flat... 40%. *ncf.*

Union 52 (90.5) n23 t23 f22.5 b23 A very different type of Canadian which is as busy as it gets. 40%.

Scottish Malts

For those of you deciding to take the plunge and head off into the labyrinthine world of Scotch malt whisky, a piece of advice. And that is, be careful who you take your advice from. Because, too often, I hear that you should leave the Islays until you have tackled the featherlight Speysiders and the bolder, weightier Highlanders. This is just complete, patronising nonsense. The only time that rings true is if you are tasting a number of whiskies in one day. Then leave the smoky ones till last, so the lighter chaps get a fair hearing.

I know many people who didn't like whisky until they got a Talisker from Skye inside them, or a Lagavulin to swamp their tastebuds with oily iodine. The fact is, you can take your map of malt whisky, start at any point and head in whichever direction you feel. There are no hard and fast rules. Certainly with over 1,600 tasting notes for Scottish malts here you should have some help in picking where this journey of a lifetime begins.
It is also worth remembering not always to be seduced by age. It is true that many of the highest scores are given to big-aged whiskies. The truth is that the majority of malts, once they have lived beyond 25 years or so, suffer from oak influence rather than benefit. Part of the fun of discovering whiskies is to see how malts from different distilleries perform to age and type of cask. Happy discovering.

LEWIS

Abhainn Dearg

Isle of Harris

SKYE

Isle of R

Talisker

Torabhaig

Ardnam

Tobermory

Ncn'e

MULL

Oban

ISLAY

Isle of

Isle of

Springbank
Glen Scotia
Glengyle

Islay

Bunnahabhain

Ardnahoe

Caol Ila

Kilchoman

Bruichladdich

Bowmore

Port Ellen

Laphroaig

Lagavulin

Ardbeg

ORKNEY ISLANDS

Highland Park
Scapa

Wolfburn

Pultney

Clynelish
Brora

Dornoch

Balblair
Glenmorangie
Dalmore
Invergordon
Teaninich

Glen Ord
GlenWyris
Royal Brackla
Banff ☦
Macduff

Speyside see page 24
Glenglassaugh

Knockdhu

Inverness ●
Glendronach
Glenugie

Glen Albyn ☦
Tomatin
Ardmore

Glen Mhor ☦
Glen Garioch

Millburn ☦

The Speyside Distillery

Royal Lochnagar

Aberdeen ●

Dalwhinnie

☦ Glenury Royal

Fettercairn

Blair Athol
Glencadam
Glenesk ☦

Fort William ●
North Port
Ben Nevis
Edradour
Lochside

Glenlochy
Aberfeldy
Arbikie

Lindores
Strathearn
Abbey
Dundee ●

Glenturret ☦ Perth
Aberargie
Daftmill
Tullibardine
Eden Mill
Kingsbarns

Deanston
Cameronbridge
InchDairnie

Glengoyne
Rosebank
Glenkinchie
St. Magdelene

Loch Lomond
Starlaw
Edinburgh ☦
☦ Dumbarton
North British

Interleven
Glasgow ●
Glasgow
☦ Littlemill
Strathclyde
Auchentoshan
Port Dundas ☦
Kinclaith ☦

Borders

Girvan
Ailsa Bay
Ladyburn ☦

Key
- ● **Major Town or City**
- ♦ Single Malt Distillery
- ♦ (*Italics*) Grain Distillery
- ☦ Dead Distillery

Annandale

Bladnoch

Speyside

Roseisle
Glen Moray
Elgin
Linkwood
Glenburgie
Miltonduff
Longmorn
BenRiach
Glenlossie
Mannochmore
Glen Elgin
Cardhu
Rothes
Macallan
Tamdhu
Dalmunach
Knockando
Imperia
Dailuaine
Aberlour
Glenfarclas
Glenallachie
Dalmunach
Benrinnes
Cragganmore
Ballindalloch
Allt-A-Bhainne
The Glenlivet
Tamnavulin
Balmenach
Tomintoul
River Spey
Braeval

Distilleries by Town	Mortlach	Glenrothes
Dufftown	Dufftown	Glenspey
Glenfiddich	Pittyvaich	**Keith**
Convalmore	**Rothes**	Aultmore
Balvenie	Speyburn	Strathmill
Kininvie	Glen Grant	Glen Keith
Glendullan	Caperdonich	Strathisla

SINGLE MALTS
ABERFELDY

Highlands (Perthshire), 1898. Bacardi. Working.

Aberfeldy Aged 12 Years bott code: L19032249021553 db **(78.5) n20 t20.5 f19 b19** Reduced to 40% and then rammed with caramel for colouring. And we are talking at this age, when tasted in good bourbon casks, one of Scotland's more delightful and effortlessly complex whiskies. Instead we are still presented with this absolute non-event of a bottling. Bewildering. 40%.

Aberfeldy Guaranteed 15 Years in Oak finished in red wine casks, batch no. 2919, bott code: L19291ZA8021209 db **(92) n22.5 t23 f23.5 b23** No easy task to create a whisky that is both exceptionally gentle and delicate but without being bland and uninteresting. They have pulled it off here! 43%.

Aberfeldy Aged 16 Years bott code: L16118ZA805 db **(83.5) n21 t21 f20.5 b21** An astonishingly dull whisky for its age. Sweet and soft for sure, but very little character as it appears to bathe in rich toffee. If you want a safe, pleasant whisky which says very little, here's your dram. 40%.

Aberfeldy Aged 21 Years bott code: L18092ZA803 db **(88) n22 t22.5 f21.5 b22** Poodles along pleasantly but feels like a Fiat Uno engine in what, for this distillery, should be Jaguar XK... 40%.

Aberfeldy Aged 25 Years db **(85) n24 t21 f19 b21.** Just doesn't live up to the nose. When Tommy Dewar wrote, "We have a great regard for old age when it is bottled," as quoted on the label, I'm not sure he had as many as 25 years in mind. 40%.

Gordon & MacPhail Connoisseurs Choice Aberfeldy Aged 25 Years first fill sherry puncheon, cask no. 4054, dist 6 Jun 93, bott 21 Jun 18 **(94.5) n23.5 t24 f23 b24** Don't know about Aberfeldy: almost Aberlour a'bunagh-esque in the intensity of its sherry attack. And make no mistake: this is high grape, faultless oloroso at work here. Except, this presents the fruit in a much more clear, untroubled form, making the power of the personality of the distillery, slowly work its way into the picture which it does thanks to its rich, malty chassis. 58.8%. sc. 444 bottles

ABERLOUR

Speyside, 1826. Chivas Brothers. Working.

Aberlour 10 Years Old db **(87.5) n22.5 t22 f21 b22.** Remains a lusty fellow though here nothing like as sherry-cask faultless as before, nor displaying its usual honeyed twinkle. 43%

Aberlour 12 Years Old Double Cask db (89) n22 t23 f21.5 b22.5 A delicately poised malt which makes as much ado about the two different oak types as it does the fruit-malt balancing act. 40%

Aberlour 12 Years Old Double Cask Matured db (88.5) n22 t22.5 f22 b22. Voluptuous and mouth-watering in some areas, firmer and less expansive in others. Pretty tasty in all of them. 43%

◇ **Aberlour 12 Years Old Double Cask Mature** American oak and sherry oak casks, bott code LKPT0298 2023/01/17 db (86) n22.5 t22 f20 b21.5 Well, the grape couldn't be more luxuriant on the nose if it tried: really moist sherry trifle. And it's no slouch on the palate, either, with the fruit directing operations with only minimal spice to aid it. But the finish is a let down by comparison, the bitterness revealing a sulphury weakness which lingers. 40%

Aberlour 12 Years Old Non Chill-Filtered db (87) n22.5 t22 f21 b21.5. There are many excellent facets to this malt, not least the balance between barley and grape and the politeness of the gristy sugars. But a sulphured butt has crept into this one, taking the edge off the excellence and bringing down the score like a cold front drags down the thermometer. 48%. ncf.

Aberlour 12 Years Old Sherry Cask Matured db (88) n23 t22 f21 b22. Could do with some delicate extra sweetness to take it to the next level. Sophisticated nonetheless. 40%

Aberlour 15 Years Cuvee Marie d'Ecosse db (91) n22 t24 f22 b23. This always was a deceptive lightweight, and it's got lighter still. It is sold primarily in France, and one can assume only that this is God's way of making amends for that pretentious, over-rated, caramel-ridden rubbish called Cognac they've had to endure. 43%

Aberlour 15 Year Old Double Cask Matured db (84) n23 t22 f19 b20. Brilliant nose full of vibrant apples and spiced sultana, but then, after a complex, chewy, malt-enriched kick-off, falls surprisingly flat on its face. 40%

Aberlour 15 Year Old Sherry Finish db (91) n24 t22 f23 b22 Quite unique: freaky, even. Really a whisky to be discovered and ridden. Once you acclimatize, you'll adore it. 43%

Aberlour 16 Years Old Double Cask Matured traditional oak & sherry oak casks, bott code: L N2 27 2019/05/14 db (88) n22.5 t22 f21.5 b22 None of the dreaded S word here, so well done sherry butts. But this is underpowered in this day and age for the kind of malt it could be. The lack of oils are crucial. 40%.

Aberlour 16 Years Old Double Cask Matured Batch AB16 1-21 db (92) n23.5 t23.5 f22 b23 Aberlour here shewing a touch of class without breaking sweat, as it once so easily did. The honey-copper combination sounds like a whisky writer taking the Mick, but in such excellent form this whisky is a Law unto itself. 40%

Aberlour 18 Years Old db (91) n22 t22 f24 b23 Another high performance distillery age-stated bottling. 43%

Aberlour 100 Proof db (91) n23 t23 f22 b23. Stunning, sensational whisky, the most extraordinary Speysider of them all...which it was when I wrote those official notes for the bottling back in '97, I think. Other malts have superseded it now, but on re-tasting I stand by those original notes, though I disassociate myself entirely with the rubbish: "In order to savour Aberlour 100 at its best add 1/3 to 1/2 pure water." 57.1%

Aberlour A'Bunadh Batch No. 61 Spanish Oloroso sherry butts db (95) n23 t24 f23.5 b24.5 Although matured in 100% sherry butts – and clean, sulphur-free ones at that – one of the most remarkable, and delicious, features of this malt is the bourbon-esque quality of the oak notes mixing in with the grape. Wow! 60.8%. ncf.

Aberlour A'Bunadh Batch No. 63 Spanish Oloroso sherry butts db (93) n23.5 t24 f22 b23.5 Slightly lighter than some A'Bunadhs, which holds out well and seemingly clean until trace bitterness arrives. But so much to savour here. 61%. ncf.

Aberlour Casg Annamh batch no. 0001 db (84.5) n21.5 t22.5 f19 b21.5 The nose is at first promising with nutty sherry tones dominating, then dry but with the most subtle countering muscovado and black cherry sweetness. Then comes the threat of the S word...which is confirmed on the rough, furry finish. The delivery starts with those sugars well into their stride, arriving early and mingling with the spice. Dates and figs represent the fruit with panache. 48%. ncf.

Cadenhead's Sherry Cask Aberlour Aged 9 Years oloroso sherry hogshead, dist 2011, bott 2020 (90) n22 moist cherry cake. No skimping on the malty vanilla, either...; t23 cherry drop candy bursts on to the palate like a firecracker. Profound demerara sugars and playful grist make unusual but compelling bedfellows; f22.5 at last the tannins arrive. But they are soon biffed up be belligerent fruitiness...; b22.5 vibrant, salivating, young and just damned good fun! 55.0%

ABHAINN DEARG

Highlands (Outer Hebrides), 2008. Marko Tayburn. Working.

Abhainn Dearg New Make db (92.5) n23 t23 f23.5 b23. Exceptionally well made with no feints and no waste, either. Oddly salty – possibly the saltiest new make I have encountered, and can think of no reason why it should be – with excellent weight as some extra copper from the new still takes hold. Given a good cask, no reason this impressive new born son of the Outer Hebrides won't go on to become something significant. *67%*

AILSA BAY
Lowland, 2007. William Grant & Sons. Working.

Ailsa Bay db (92.5) n23.5 t23.5 f22.5 b23 I remember years back being told they wanted to make an occasional peaty malt at this new distillery different in style to Islay's. They have been only marginally successful: only the finish gives the game away. But they have certainly matched the island when it comes to the average high quality. A resounding success of a first effort, though I'd like to see the finish offer a little more than it currently does. Early days, though. *48.9%.*

    Aerstone Land Cask Aged 10 Years peat dried, bott code L6G83001412 db (90) n23.5 agreeably pungent, worth a cattle byre ring to the phenols. Not in any way of the Islay style, this has a stand-alone kick; t23 holy smoked mackerel. This has one of the most acidic, biting phenolic punches anywhere in Scotland and genuinely creates something new so far as a Lowland malt is concerned. A peat freak's delight but the fabulous lilt to the barley sugar, juicy and full of muscovado intensity, will really wow even the whisky lover not usually attracted to big peaty malts; f21 such a disappointing finish. The oils have vanished, and we have bland toffee in its place; b22.5 I really do adore this malt. Having said that, I am so frustrated by the 40% abv which detracts so much from the overall experience as the oils drop out with alarming rapidity, thus reducing both length and complexity. Also, not sure if those toffee notes are intended or not, but they need muzzling. With bolder, more confident treatment, this could be one hell of a single malt. At the moment it is operating with only two of the four engines running. What potential! *40% William Grant.*

ALLT-Á-BHAINNE
Speyside, 1975. Chivas Brothers. Working.

Berry Bros & Rudd Allt-á-Bhainne 23 Year Old cask no. 125314, dist 1995, bott 2019 (95) n24 t24 f23 b24 I still smile when I think of conversations I held, long before this whisky was ever made, with blenders who preferred to use this distillery's malt at very young ages, especially 3- to 5-years-old because they felt it was a whisky not best suited to great age. This is coming up for nearly 25 years in cask, and there is not a wrinkle, not a single blemish. Superb! *52.7%. nc ncf sc.*

Chapter 7 Allt-A-Bhainne 2008 Aged 12 Years Coal Ila finish bourbon barrel, barrel no.169 (89.5) n22 t22 f23 b22.5 In many ways typical of this distillery in its fragility. Seen lightly peated A-A-B in the blending lab from time to time. In bottled form, quite a rarity. Limited complexity, but typically charming. *49.7% sc*

Old Malt Cask Allt A'Bhainne Aged 27 Years refill hogshead, cask no. 16942, dist May 92, bott Oct 19 (94) n23 t23.5 f23.5 b24 Class in a glass. *50%. nc ncf sc. 256 bottles.*

The Whisky Cask Company Allt-A-Bhainne 1992 bourbon cask, cask no. 1800472, Sep 1992, Jul2020 (94.5) n23.5 t23.5 f23.5 b24 I have to admit I was pretty dubious as to whether this malt could make it from one end of the tasting experience to the other without disintegrating: this is not a distillery built for great age. But, my word, it made it: taxed by the tannins, but, protected by the distinct, Clynelishesque waxy honey, you still feel there may have been another four or five years to spare with this one with careful handling... *49.2% nc ncf sc 272 bottles*

ANNANDALE
Lowlands, 2014. Annandale Distillery Company Ltd. Working.

    Annandale Founder's Selection Man O' Swords Smoulderingly Smoky STR ex-red wine cask, cask no 375, dist 2017, bott 2022, db (94.5) n23.5 this is a ten minute nose, minimum. Devotees of Ardmore will appreciate the subtlety of the smoke on this, arriving before and then disappearing behind a patchwork of delicate fruit tones. Heftier and more advanced than its five tender years, there is so much to savour...; t23.5 for a moment, forget the smoke. It is the excellence of the oils here which impresses from the off...and then the peat makes its elegant though spice-spluttering entry. The malt makes no effort to escape the riches of those pleasing oils, leaving the smoke and raspberry-jammy sweeter tones to create their own duet...; f23.5 as can often be the case with STR's, there is a charming outbreak of vanilla and light cocoa. These spices persist but, like the smoke, do so politely...; b24 not sure you can expect much more from a 5-year-old single Scotch malt than this. The shaving of the barrel has generated enough fresh tannin to age the malt ahead of its years, while the smoke is more decoration than declaration. As one has become to expect from this now great Lowland distillery: First Class Malt. *60.5%*

    Annandale Founder's Selection Man O' Words Smooth and Mellow STR ex-red wine cask, cask no 306, dist 2017, bott 2022 db (94) n23 conservative and non-committal at normal room temperature, a little warming has an immediate impact on the dry oak, giving a much sturdier countenance to the sweeter malt; **t24** a gorgeous, salivating assembly of concentrated malts, each facet framed by a deep oak shadow. The usual excellence of the oils adds to the all-round complexity and satisfaction. The impregnation of the tannins briefly give a slight bourbon depth to this one...; **f23.5** it took a little time for the humble berries to make their mark, but they got there in the end. Light rumbling spice, soft cocoa and still that oily, enigmatic barley lasts for a devil of a long time...; **b23.5** it was quite fitting tasting this on April Fool's Day. The wording of the brand, like Swords, is a continuous circular around the circumference of the bottle. Only a subtle change of colour reveals the actual identity of the bottle...well, that and the quill as opposed to a sword. Those who imbibe just a little too much of this without spitting – which would be a very easy thing to do – will be none the wiser. Because, just like this stunning whisky, it is teasing and subtle. And for a five-year-old without the aid of peat for extra substance.... just wow! 60.1%

Annandale Man O' Sword cask no. 100, dist 2014 db **(92.5) n23.5 t23 f21.5 b23.5** The strangest thing...I nosed this and thought: Jim Swan. This delightful style has the late, great whisky consultant's finger prints all over it. A young malt from a brand new distillery already punching way above its weight age-wise and in terms of complexity. Welcome to the whisky world, Annandale. And what a worthy addition you have already become. Now you just have to keep up this standard: no pressure at all... 61.6%. sc. 256 bottles.

Annandale Man O' Sword Smoulderingly Smoky once-used ex bourbon cask, cask no. 470, dist 2015 db **(96.5) n24 t24.5 f23.5 b24.5** Make no mistake: new distillery or no, this is fabulously and truly faultlessly made and brilliantly matured whisky which allows every last element of the distillery's personality to be seen. What a genuine treat! What an immense start to such a new distillery! 60.2%. sc. 271 bottles.

Annandale Man O' Words cask no. 140, dist 2014 db **(89.5) n22.5 t22.5 f22 b22.5** A malty delight. Had been meaning to take in Annan Athletic FC and Annandale Distillery over the last four years but my diary just wouldn't allow it. Somehow I have to make it happen. This distillery promises great things. 61.6%. sc. 273 bottles.

Annandale Rascally New Make Malt Spirit db **(93) n23 t23 f23.5 b23.5** Beautifully distilled, the impressive oiliness to the body helps massively ramp up the maltiness at the chewy finish. Earlier, spices abound, as does the coppery sharpness. Not exactly me-too new make with the distillery character easy to distinguish. 63.5%

Annandale Rascally New Make Peaty Malt Spirit db **(94.5) n24 t23 f24 b23.5** Just love the control of the phenols here, making this as friendly a peated new make as you could wish for. The aroma is particularly attractive thanks to the evenness of the grist and lack of showmanship. That quiet elegance spills over onto the palate which, though a little thin for the first flavour wave or two, builds equally in oils and confidence, ensuring the desired cocoa finish works particularly well with the peat. Scrummy! 63.5%

Annandale Vintage Man O'Words 2015 once used ex-bourbon cask, cask no. 150 db **(96) n24 t24 f23.5 b24.5** Considering this is a 5-y-o whisky only, I think we are going to have to consider the possibility that we have a truly world-class distillery in our midst... So beautifully made and matured, the age seems almost irrelevant. The malt is absolutely immaculate: no malt should be quite this good as this still tender age...! 61.6%. sc.

The Whisky Chamber Annandale 5 Jahre 2015 PX sherry hogshead **(87.5) n23 t23.5 f22 b19** OK, I admit it. There is nothing wrong with the sherry: no sulphur and clean. However, there is something wrong with the sherry: it is too big for the delicate 5-year-old malt it is smothering the life out of. Imagine a 300lb man's thick woollen overcoat draped over the shoulders of a five-year-old child. The coat still looks as though it is made from beautiful cloth, expertly cut, but its shape is lost as the child buckles and vanishes under its weight. And so we have this whisky. So, yes, the nose and delivery are enjoyable because this is very fine PX, radiating sweet, thick fruit and spices in more than ample quantities. But as the fruit detracts and dries, (and bitters slightly, as is so often the case with PX) where's the malt? Now there's the question... 56.1%. sc.

ARDBEG
Islay, 1815. Glenmorangie Plc. Working.

Ardbeg Guaranteed 8 Years Old For Discussion bott code 18/01/2022 db **(94.5) n23.5** the understated vibrancy of the phenols is either great work by the blender or someone waving a magic wand. There is a still a gristy freshness to this, as is highly desired, but the phenols gather like storm clouds which eventually send down a bolt of peat and pepper. Green and compelling; **t24** such balance: it is like a trapeze artist carrying the weight of the oils and phenols across a massive canyon without a single wobble before reaching the other side. Gloriously youthful and mouth-watering on delivery, even as those oils gush in and even as the phenol begin to add up in weight. But the light molasses and the intricate peppers ensure the sweetness and vivacity so vital to a young malt like this keeps the palate on a state of high alert...; **f23** the spices have a slightly testier countenance while a little cocoa mixes in with the smoke. Yet the oils ensure maximum silkiness... and length; **b24** there is nothing to discuss: this is simply superb Ardbeg shewing all the riches and lustre the 5-year-old steadfastly refuses to embrace. When smoke melts in the mouth, when the sugars are directly in equal proportion to the measured spices, when the mouth feel is enriched by oil but light enough to allow all the more delicate structures to stand unbowed after the tsunami of phenol...then you know this is Ardbeg being true to itself... *50.8% ncf*

◈ **Ardbeg Guaranteed Ten Years Old** bott code 19/08/2022 db **(94.5) n23.5** no Ardbeg 10 would be complete without a citrussy element to it. This one, though, absolutely bathes in a grapefruit and lime blend which does all in its power to lighten the impact of the smoke. Even by Ardbeg's bewilderingly enigmatic standards, this is possibly the most genteel 10-y-o nose from this distillery I have encountered either inside or outside of the lab, be it Ardbeg's or mine...; **t24** wow! I am quite blown away by this new-found lightness of touch. The milky-chocolate dovetailing with the phenols is a delightful touch, while the prominence of the light molasses and most delicate liquorice – giving a brief bourbon boost to this most quintessential of Scottish single malts – is an unexpected bonus of flavour intensity. The spices take a back seat while the vanillas are not shy coming forward earlier than of old. But all attention is drawn to the magnificence of the grist which melts on the palate like a candle below a peaty flame; **f23.5** a slightly annoying bitterness has crept in from somewhere (that somewhere being the oak). But the spices, as though aware of this incursion, have sprung to life and create a sublime diversion. The peat now pulses in smoky layers, intricately wrapped up in those gorgeous oils; **b24** there are so many things right with this, especially the melting of the peaty grist on the tongue and the overall layering which makes you want to kneel in the direction of Islay and bow in soul-embracing reverence. But there are equally some surprises on this one which stop you in your tracks, too. Especially the early depth of citrus and, in a rare negative trait: that later bitterness. For the latter problem these things happen during bottling, though it may have cost Ardbeg 10 an award in the 2024 Bible. My abiding memory of this bottling, though, and speaking as one with an emotional and professional attachment to this brand, is one of satisfaction. *46% ncf*

Ardbeg 10 Years Old db **(97) n24 t24 f24 b25** Like when you usually come across something that goes down so beautifully and with such a nimble touch and disarming allure, just close your eyes and enjoy... *46%*

Ardbeg 10 bottling mark L10 152 db **(95) n24.5 t23.5 f23.5 b23.5** A bigger than normal version, but still wonderfully delicate. Fabulous and faultless. *46%. Canadian market bottling in English and French dual language label.*

Ardbeg 17 Years Old earlier bottlings db **(92) n23 t22 f23 b24.** OK, I admit I had a big hand in this, creating it with the help of Glenmorangie Plc's John Smith. It was designed to take the weight off the better vintages of Ardbeg whilst ensuring a constant supply around the world. Certainly one of the more subtle expressions you are likely to find, though criticised by some for not being peaty enough. As the whisky's creator, all I can say is they are missing the point. *40%*

Ardbeg 17 Years Old later bottlings db **(90) n22 t23 f22 b23.** The peat has all but vanished and cannot really be compared to the original 17-year-old: it's a bit like tasting a Macallan without the sherry: fascinating to see the naked body underneath, and certainly more of a turn on. Peat or no peat, great whisky by any standards. *40%*

Ardbeg 19 Years Old db **(93) n23 t23 f23.5 b23.5** One of the sensuously understated Ardbegs that could be found in style (though with a different peat imprint) from time to time during the 1960s. *46.2%.*

Ardbeg 19 Years Old 2020 Release db **(89) n21** unusually untidy for Ardbeg. Attractive saline notes but the phenols are uneven to the point of being discordant; **t23** that's much better! A quite thick set malty-smokiness drifts off towards the toasty sugars. For a moment there is an air of Ardbeg normality as the light vanillas pulse; **f22.5** all understated and full of trickery. Vague minty notes blossom on the light heather-honey phenol. The oak sticks to that salty tang... and tang is the right word...; **b22.5** pretty much OK and enjoyable despite the slight mess on the nose and mildly odd landing. But not sure when just OK was acceptable for Ardbeg... *46%.*

Ardbeg 20 Something db **(96.5) n24 t24 f24 b24.5** Such mastery over the phenols...such elegance! It is though the whisky was distilled from gossamer... *46%.*

Ardbeg 21 Years Old db **(96.5) n24 t24 f24 b24.5** Tap into Ardbeg with great care, like someone has done here, and there is no describing what beauty can be unleashed. For much of the time, the smoke performs in brilliant fashion somewhere between the ethereal and profound. *46%*

Ardbeg 23 Year Old db **(93) n22.5 t24 f23 b23.5** A malt forever treading on eggshells, trying not to disturb the tannins. As a dram, makes a nervous wreck of you, as you spend the entire time waiting for the shallow truce to be broken and the oak to declare war and come pouring in. Thankfully, it never quite happens. As all whiskies, not to be taken with water. But, in this instance, a tranquilliser might not go amiss... *46.3%.*

Ardbeg 1977 db **(96)** n25 t24 f23 b24. When working through the Ardbeg stocks, I earmarked '77 a special vintage, the sweetest of them all. So it has proved. Only the '74 absorbed that extra oak that gave greater all-round complexity. Either way, the quality of the distillate is beyond measure: simply one of the greatest experiences – whisky or otherwise – of your life. 46%

Ardbeg 1978 db **(91)** n23 t24 f22 b22. An Ardbeg on the edge of losing it because of encroaching oak, hence the decision made by John Smith and me to bottle this vintage early alongside the 17-year-old. Nearly ten years on, still looks a pretty decent bottling, though slightly under strength! 43%

Ardbeg An Oa db **(95.5)** n24 t24 f23.5 b24 I'd never say "whoa" if someone poured me an Oa... 46%.

⋙ **Ardbeg An Oa** new charred oak, PX sherry and first fill bourbon casks. bott code 22/01/2022 db **(89)** n22.5 a dry, potash and intense peat head-to-head against a date and grape fruitiness; t23 much softer on delivery than on the slightly acidic nose. Indeed, too soft, with the big toffee and raisin flatness where the wine has its way. Until the fruit took over, the rolling of the malt on the palate had been rather lovely; f21.5 possibly the least interesting Ardbeg finish. Ever. Flatter than various upper parts of a witch...; b22 this is absolutely nothing like the Oa I remembered from the last time out – though that was a few years back, admittedly. Here the PX has thrown a grapey gown - actually more of a ClingOAn ClOAking device - over matters. 46.6%

Ardbeg Arrrrrrrdbeg db **(84.5)** n21.5 t21.5 f20.5 b21 For me, more aaarrrrggghhh! than arrrrrrr. For a start, I hardly recognise this as an Ardbeg in style. Since when did that old Bowmore character of Victory V cough sweets hickory been part of its DNA? And what is that weak, lily-livered finish all about. The sugars come and go as they please but without being part of a set plan while the phenols wobble. Yes, of course there are some pleasant (but short-lived) phases. But Ardbeg? Just nowhere near the mark. 51.8%.

Ardbeg Blaaack db **(92)** n22.5 t23 f23.5 b23 Still a different to feel to this than the Ardbegs of old. And though where once upon a time the move through the gears was seamless and this is just a little clunky at times, overall it works rather attractively. 46%.

Ardbeg Blaaack Committee Release db **(86.5)** n22 t22 f21 b21.5 Just way too dull for an Ardbeg. The wine is just a little too busy filing down the edges of the malt and peat to really offer anything constructive. The result is a malt which lurches about the palate with an ungainly countenance. The spices certainly give their all, but the phenols – following an impressive start - are never allowed to make the kind of complex and stunningly balanced contribution that usually sets Ardbeg apart. 50.7%.

⋙ **Ardbeg Corryvreckan** bott code 09/11/2021 db **(97)** n24 a curiously punchy nose with a distinct clove hit running right up against the profound smoke....which itself is a blend of hefty peaty and more acidic and assertive bonfires. The result is a massive iodine kick and a few choppy waves; t24 much easier sailing on delivery, which is absolutely top-notch. Unusually these days for Ardbeg, there is a rich salty seam to this, offering a complex coastal feel to the mix of phenol and molasses, given them a stark, three-dimensional feel. The drier tannins, with a powdery vanilla touch, really is a superb touch, too, and works particularly well against the still malty backdrop with its gristy sweetness, though stained now by deeper oaky notes; f24.5 the spices and sugars at the tiller here and steering the taste buds away from the more restless and agitated waters of those early intense phenols. That said, the smoke is lingering, and the acidity is far from nullified. The laying is labyrinthine and, frankly, mind-blowing to the very end...if that ever actually arrives...; b24.5 one of the things perhaps more noticeable about Ardbeg now than the past is the lack of salty seasoning. Well, that is not the case here where the sea salt appears to magnify the flavours especially and bring them to a rich crescendo. Corryvrecken is the world's third most powerful whirlpool and can be located – and best avoided – in the teeming seas between Islay and Jura. It nearly made 1984 into Orwell's Edwin Drood and was brought to life by the inimitable film-making talent of Powell and Pressburger in their 1945 classic *I know Where I'm Going*. Well, I certainly know where I'm going...to take this bottle home from my tasting lab for a fabulous late-night dram that I can enjoy with my computer switched off and my senses fully switched on... 57.1%

Ardbeg Dark Cove db **(86)** n22.5 t22.5 f19.5 b21.5. For whatever reason, this is a much duller version than the Committee Edition. And strength alone can't explain it, or solely the loss of the essential oils from reduction. There is a slight nagging to this one so perhaps any weakness to the sherry butts has been accentuated by the reduction of oil, if it has been bottled from the same vatting – which I doubt. Otherwise, the tasting notes are along the lines of below, except with just a little less accent on the sugars. 46.5%

Ardbeg Dark Cove Committee Edition db **(90.5)** n23.5 t23 f21.5 b22.5 Big sherry and bigger peat always struggle somewhere along the line. This one does pretty well until we reach the finale when it unravels slightly. But sulphur-free. And challenging. 55%

Ardbeg Drum db **(92.5)** n23 t23.5 f22.5 b23.5 Well! I wasn't expecting that! It is as if this is from some super-fine cut, with 20% of the usual heart each way being sent back re-distillation.

Scottish Malts

No idea if this is the case, but it is the only way I can think of creating a non-chillfiltered Ardbeg this clean and fragile. Quite extraordinary... 46%.

Ardbeg Grooves db (95) n24 t23.5 f23.5 b24 Groovy. 46%.

Ardbeg Grooves Committee Release db (95.5) n24 t23.5 f24 b24 Even groovier! 51.6%.

Ardbeg Guaranteed 30 Years Old db (91) n24 t23 f21 b23. An unusual beast, one of the last ever bottled by Allied. The charm and complexity early on is enormous, but the fade rate is surprising. That said, still a dram of considerable magnificence. 40%

⬦ **Ardbeg Hypernova** bott code 09/11/2021 db (96.5) n24.5 a nose that has just about stopped me in my tracks. If you can imagine a Jimmy Finlayson double take in a Laurel and Hardy film, then you have a pretty clear picture of my reaction after nosing this. This was so similar to pouring from a warehouse thief into my tasting glass a young Ardbeg from a second fill bourbon cask, it was uncanny. Only the strength was down. Otherwise, the three-dimensional clarity of the smoke, lightened by more than a squeeze of lime and then bolstered by magnificent layers of hickory, freshly ground pepper, Venezuelan medium roast cocoa, lemon blossom honey and, above all, ultra-delicate but perfectly peated grist was exactly, almost to an atom, of what was to be expected. It is, in two words, near perfection...; t24 gorgeous, salivating soft oils are matched by the dripping juiciness of the grist. The freshness of both the barley and citrus is epic. The juiciness is off the scale while the peat both cajoles and caresses as well as ensuring extra depth to compliment the limited oak input. Early in the midground there is also a butterscotch/ulmo honey...but all this is imparted on the glossiest of light oils...; f24 ah, some relative quiet as the smoke climbs down a peg or to, leaving the spices more room to make a noise. That butterscotch/vanilla/ulmo honey thread is in no hurry to go away...; b24 if, like me, Ardbeg has an extra special place not only in your heart but also soul and entire life, then the nose to this will strike a very deep and perfectly pitched cord. All Ardbeg labels these days have "The Ultimate" printed across them. On this occasion it is written with total accuracy. This is a young stunner of brain-popping complexity; one of the rarest treats for your senses. And, for the avoidance of doubt: yes, this is a sexy whisky: how can anything this sensual not be? And anyone who thinks it isn't, shouldn't be around whisky... 51%

Ardbeg Kelpie db (95) n24 t23.5 f23.5 b24 Beautifully crafted and cleverly – and intriguingly - structured. An understated Ardbeg for true Ardbeg lovers... 46%.

Ardbeg Kelpie Committee Edition db (94) n24 t24 f22.5 b23.5 As Burns might have said: I'se no speer nae to anither helpie o' Kelpie... 51.7%.

Ardbeg Provenance 1974 bott 1999 db (96) n24 t25 f23 b24. This is an exercise in subtlety and charisma, the beauty and the beast drawn into one. Until I came across the 25-year-old OMC version during a thunderstorm in Denmark, this was arguably the finest whisky I had ever tasted: I opened this and drank from it to see in the year 2000. When I went through the Ardbeg warehouse stocks in 1997 I earmarked the '74 and '77 vintages as something special. This bottling has done me proud. 55.6%

Ardbeg Uigeadail db (89) n25 t22 f20 b22. A curious Ardbeg with a nose to die for. Some tinkering - please guys, as the re-taste is not better - regarding the finish may lift this to being a true classic 54.1%

⬦ **Ardbeg Uigeadail** bott code 09/11/2021 db (93) n23.5 I never thought I'd see the day when I described an Uigeadail nose as "lazy" But, for all its peppery spikiness, this is lazy...; t23.5 after the nose hardly bothering to rise from is delightfully peaty stupor, here we see some activity...most of it oak induced. Perhaps the acidity to the nose is an indicator of what will happen once on the palate, but there is real bite and a sharpness attacked to tannin which in turn reacts to the sugary oils. Bizarrely, we are then thrown into a flavour doldrum where only vanilla lives....talk about odd...; f23 takes a little while for this to come back to life, but when it does the vanillas carry a very attractive degree of smoke, plus a surprise late hickory and spice backstory; b23 usually, an Ardbeg tells a story, or works with a set degree of evolution on usually the nose but certainly the palate. Not here. This is simply a random compilation of things, some expected, others not, happening on the palate. Delicious. But a bit like the Monty Python Confuse A Cat sketch...in Ardbeg form... 54.2%

Ardbeg Supernova 2019 db (92.5) n23.5 t23 f23 b23 A kind of sub-Supernova as it has now lost much of its old explosive oomph. 53.9%.

Ardbeg Traigh Bhan db (94.5) n24 t23.5 f23.5 b23.5 Ah, Traigh Bhan, the remote Singing Sands beach on Islay, if memory serves. Where back in the very early 1980s, before anyone had heard of Ardbeg – or hardly Islay whisky come to that matter - you could spend a day at the silent, deserted, unknown distillery and then return to Port Ellen. And as the sun thought about setting, but before the midges (teeth freshly sharpened) came out to play, walk past a herd of goats that could win a World Championship for flatulence, and on to the Singing Sands – Traigh Bhan - where I and the lady who was unluckily destined to be, for a short time, Mrs Murray would find a remote spot to try, but only providing we were upwind from the goats, and add to the Murray clan. It as an act that began and ended with a bottle top or two full of Ardbeg 10. Magical.... Maybe I should return to those sands with a bottle of this – which, fittingly, seems, older, softer, less energetic than the elixir Ardbeg I tasted of yore - and see what happens... 46.6%.

Ardbeg Wee Beastie Guaranteed 5 Years Old bott code: L2395911 22/06/2020 **(91)** n24 t23.5 f21.5 b22 A lovely whisky, make no mistake. But for a five-year-old Ardbeg, over 35 years of experience with this distillery had conditioned me to expect just a little more. Starts off with a mesmerically youthful lustiness full of the sunny joys of a blossoming spring. Ends in the grey of a foggy autumnal evening.... 474%. ncf.

Ardbeg Wee Beastie 5 Years Old bott code: 18/06/2021 db **(89)** n23 t23 f21 b22 Back in the days when no-one had ever heard of Ardbeg, when not a tourist made their way on the downhill path to this sleeping Cathedral of whisky; when the stills were silent and there was more noise from the owners ripping open quotes from companies in how much it would cost to level the old place to the ground then there was in the distillery itself, I would spend an entire day and see nobody, bar the brewer on his daily five minute march around silent grounds. And on certain days I would join him and walk up the stairs in his near condemned offices passing a little framed notice on a wall, dating from the 1920s or '30s which swore that Ardbeg reached perfection at 7 years. When I had managed to help save the distillery from planned destruction and the present owners brought me in as consultant blender, there was a big problem: they wanted a 10-year-old, but there was none around to bottle. Some very old, or very young. One of my suggestions was that we follow the saying of the 1920s and launch a 7-year-old. No, Glenmorangie wanted to make a statement: it had to be at least 10 years-old. So, I created the 17. And the other problem, which I pointed out while suggesting the 7-year-old would be that bring a malt out of that age, there would be less stock available for the 10 when that finally came of age. So the 7-year-old never happened, alas. Now, nearly 25 years later, they are promoting a 5-year-old. Enjoyable enough in its own way. But too tame and disappointing for me, lacking the salivating complexity that is possible at that age. Mind you, had to laugh at the tasting note saying it had the flavour of creosote. I hope whoever wrote that has never tasted that stuff as it is highly carcinogenic. Sadly, I have (when I was in my late teens, a chemist once made up a mixture to cure a very heavy cold I had, basing his prescription on creosote. He was later struck off...!) and can assure you, there is no creosote flavours involved here! 474%

✧ **Ardbeg Guaranteed 5 Years Old Wee Beastie** bott code 09/11/2021 db **(87)** n22.5 t23 f20 b21.5 As above 47.5% ncf

ARDMORE
Speyside, 1899. Beam Suntory. Working.

Ardmore 12 Year Old Port Wood Finish db **(90)** n21.5 t23.5 f22 b23 Here we have a lovely fruit-rich malt, but one which has compromised on the very essence of the complexity which sets this distillery apart. Lovely whisky I am delighted to say...but, dammit, by playing to its unique nuances it could have been so much better...I mean absolutely sensational...!46%. ncf.

Ardmore Aged 20 Years 1996 Vintage 1st fill ex-bourbon & ex-Islay casks, bott code: L723657A db **(89.5)** n22 t23 f22 b22.5 Slightly confused by this malt, for all its charm. At 20 years old this distillery projects, through its usual ex-bourbon cask portfolio of varied usages, a quite disarming complexity. To bolster it with extra oak and smoke slightly undermines the inherent subtlety of this malt which sets it apart from all others. Highly enjoyable, nonetheless. 49.3%. ncf.

Ardmore 25 Years Old db **(89.5)** n21 t23.5 f22.5 b22.5 A 25-y-o box of chocolates: coffee creams, fudge, orange cream...they are all in there. The nose may be ordinary: what follows is anything but. 51.4%. ncf.

Ardmore 30 Years Old Cask Strength db **(94)** n23.5 t23.5 f23 b24 I remember when the present owners of Ardmore launched their first ever distillery bottling. Over a lunch with the hierarchy there I told them, with a passion, to ease off with the caramel so the world can see just how complex this whisky can be. This brilliant, technically faultless, bottling is far more eloquent and persuasive than I was that or any other day... 53.7%. nc ncf. 1428 bottles.

Ardmore 1996 db **(87)** n22 t22 f21 b22. Very curious Ardmore, showing little of its usual dexterity. Perhaps slightly more heavily peated than the norm, but there is also much more intense heavy caramel extracted from the wood. Soft, very pleasant and easy drinking it is almost obsequious. 43%.

Ardmore Legacy bott code: L1 117 SB1 db **(91.5)** n23.5 t23 f22 b23 Now that's way more like it! I remember how underwhelmed I was when the first bottling of this came out. But year on year they have managed to get far closer to the soul of the distillery, which happens to be one of my favourites in Scotland. Indeed, the present owners have it in their portfolio because of me. But ssssshhhh: don't tell anyone. Still room for improvement, though. Get the colour down and the strength up slightly, and they will have a potential award-winner on their hands. 40%.

◈ **Ardmore Legacy** lightly peated, bott code L218200004673 db **(88.5)** n22.5 t22.5 f21.5 b22 Such a frustrating bottling! Still on an upward curve, but nowhere near where it should be – in the low mid 90s for Ardmore of this age from varied ex-bourbon casks. The Murray Method is not just an option here: it is essential. At ordinary temperature it sits dead in the glass. The MM stirs it not only back to life, but it rises like Lazarus to charm with intricate peat, especially on the nose and through the early and mid-parts of the delivery. The texture is pleasantly silky. But there is a wall of toffee which ensures a blandness through the late middle to the finish which I just don't see in casks I blend with. Extremely pleasant – and sweet in all the right places and you will enjoy it. But this is Ardmore (I was even instrumental in the present owners acquiring it!). This should be so much more of an exhibition. *40%*

Arcanum Spirits Private Release Ardmore Aged 10 years 1st fill St.Martinique rum barrels **(95)** n23.5 t24 f23.5 b24 even through a rum barrel that totally unique Ardmore persona is unmistakably present. No other distillery in Scotland has such a flourish to its signature phenols. Just....yes! *58.5% nc ncf sc 157 bottles*

Berry Bros & Rudd Ardmore 12 Year Old cask no. 800961, dist 2006, bott 2019 **(90.5)** n23 t22.5 f22 b22.5 One of the perennial joys of writing this book is happening across cask-strength bottlings of Ardmore being true to form. This one is slightly young for its age thinner in body than is usual. But still displays a wonderful degree of complexity even when not quite firing on all cylinders. *56.8%. nc ncf sc.*

Oxhead Classic Casks Ardmore 2009 **(94)** n23.5 one of the smokiest Ardmores I've encountered for a little while, the peat being loud, proud and distinctly floral, too; t23.5 classic soft oils and melting barley sugars before the peat begins to take slow but very firm hold. The tannins firm up with a slight buttery and banana flourish; f23 lovely chocolate mint amid the peat; b24 when they bought the malt in for this, they must have forgot it was around the 9ppm phenols and brought in a job lot from Laphroaig and mixed it in with existing stock...as this has to be in the 20s. The pedant in me wants to mark this down because it is not representative of a true Ardmore. However, the whisky lover in me cannot do anything other than sing its praises. *59.6%*

Single Cask Collection Ardmore 11 Years Old ex Laphroaig cask, cask no. 707531, dist 2008, bott 2019 **(92.5)** n22.5 t23 f24 b23 Another ex-Laphroaig which initially throws things out of sync momentarily with the extra peat and bite. But then more than amends with a superb and hugely satisfying finish. In an hour's time Scotland will be taking on Croatia, needing a win to stand any chance of qualifying or the last 16 of the European finals. If their forwards can finish as wonderfully as this, they are in with every chance. *61.1%. sc. 245 bottles.*

Single & Single Ardmore 2009 10 Year Old American oak **(91.5)** n22.5 t23.5 f22.5 b23 A totally fascinating bottling. The lack of input from the cask means we are able to see the sweet, malty machinations of the Ardmore up close. For decades I have been telling people that, in whisky, less is often more. Here is a beautiful case in point... *53.9%. sc. 257 bottles.*

Teacher's Highland Single Malt quarter cask finish db **(89)** n22.5 t23 f21.5 b22. This is Ardmore at its very peatiest. And had not the colouring levels been heavily tweaked to meet the flawed perceptions of what some markets believe makes a good whisky, this malt would have been better still. As it is: superb. With the potential of achieving greatness if only they have the confidence and courage... *40%. India/Far East Travel Retail exclusive.*

Valour Whisky Ardmore Aged 12 years bourbon barrel Cask No 708704 dist 08/12/2009 bott 10/06/2022 **(92.5)** n23 though the oak has made an indent, there is still something fresh-faced about this aroma, the malt not having lost all its youth. The lack of smoke is curious (it is there, but not in its usual quantity) but there are grape-fruity compensations; t23 warm, young, fat and just a shade anarchic at first. But the gathering of the molasses and slow-motion, atom-by-atom growth of phenol turns the mid-ground into a far happier and more compelling place; f23 ahhh! Now we have thick malt on which to chew, the smoke more detached and almost acidic now. The saw-dusty tannin contrasts beautifully with the barley and light mocha; b23.5 a particularly rugged Ardmore with the peat levels a little lower than normal. Gets off to a slow start, but gradually grows into something a little special. *59.1% 216 bottles*

The Whisky Chamber Ardmore 10 Jahre 2009 bourbon barrel **(93)** n23 t23 f23 b24 When it is possible to vat casks together of a certain age at Ardmore, then 10-year-old offers probably the best chance of shewing the distillery at the finest. Not so easy with a single cask, which is just a single fragment of that complex equation. Well, as it happens, this cask has most of the boxes ticked. *56.8%. sc.*

The Whisky Tasting Club Ardmore 12 Year Old bourbon oak first fill, cask no. 70386, dist Jul 2008, bott Dec 2020 **(94.5)** n23.5 t23 f24 b24 Well done, WTC!! This is just like heading into the old Ardmore warehouses and drawing spirit from one of the better condition bourbon barrels. Where it really stars though, is the playful aggression of the spices and spirit, which ensures this is never a simple luxuriant smoothie, but something you have to negotiate. Brilliant! *57.3% 180 bottles*

AUCHENTOSHAN

Lowlands, 1800. Morrison Bowmore. Working.

Auchentoshan 10 Years Old db (81) n22 t21 f19 b19. Much better, maltier, cleaner nose than before. But after the initial barley surge on the palate it shows a much thinner character. 40%

Auchentoshan 12 Years Old db (91.5) n22.5 t23.5 f22.5 b23 A delicious malt very much happier with itself than it has been for a while. 40%

Auchentoshan Aged 12 Years bourbon & sherry casks, bott code: L00007SB320081440 db (86) n22.5 t22.5 f20 b21 Being triple distilled, Auchentoshan is one of Scotland's lightest, most intricate spirits to start with. Therefore, to maximise its character it needs gentle handling and the malts given free reign. This, however, is essentially sherry dominated, except perhaps for on the nose where some attractive acacia honey filters through. The delivery also has moments of complexity and clarity, but they are fleeting before the grape and tannins take command for a surfeit of dryness. The growing furry tones on the finish confirms, as detectable on the nose, that not all the butts escape the dreaded sulphur candle. 40%

Auchentoshan 14 Years Old Cooper's Reserve db (83.5) n20 t21.5 f21 b21. Malty, a little nutty and juicy in part. 46%. ncf.

Auchentoshan 18 Years Old db (78) n21 t21.5 f17 b19. Although matured for 18 years in ex-bourbon casks, as according to the label, this is a surprisingly tight and closed malt in far too many respects. Some heart-warming sugars early on, but the finish is bitter and severely limited in scope. 43%

Auchentoshan 21 Years Old db (93) n23.5 t23 f23 b23.5 One of the finest Lowland distillery bottlings of our time. A near faultless masterpiece of astonishing complexity to be cherished and discussed with deserved reverence. So delicate, you fear that sniffing too hard will break the poor thing...! 43%.

Auchentoshan 1979 db (94) n23.5 t24 f23 b23.5 It's amazing what a near faultless sherry butt can do. 50.1%

Auchentoshan American Oak db (85.5) n21.5 t22 f20.5 b21.5. Very curious: reminds me very much of Penderyn Welsh whisky before it hits the Madeira casks. Quite creamy with some toasted honeycomb making a brief cameo appearance. 40%

Auchentoshan Blood Oak French red wine db (76.5) n20.5 t19 f18 b19. That's funny: always thought blood tasted a little sweet. This is unremittingly bitter. 48%. ncf.

Auchentoshan Classic db (80) n19 t20 f21 b20. Classic what exactly...? Some really decent barley, but goes little further. 40%

Auchentoshan Select db (85) n20 t21.5 f22 b21.5. Has changed shape of late, if not quality. Much more emphasis on the enjoyable juicy barley sharpness these days. 40%

Auchentoshan Solera db (88) n23 t22 f22 b21. Enormous grape input and enjoyable for all its single mindedness. Will benefit when a better balance with the malt is struck. 48%. ncf.

Auchentoshan The Bartender's Malt batch 01, bott code: L172249 db (94.5) n23.5 t24 f23 b24 Seeing as this was assembled by a dozen bartenders from around the world, namely Messrs Alvarado, Billing, Halsius, Heinrich, Jehli, Klus, Magro, Morgan, Schurmann, Shock, Stern and Wareing surely this is the Bartenders' Malt, not Bartender's Malt. Still, I digress. Good job, boys and (presumably) girls. Some might mark this down as a clever marketing ploy (which it may well be...). I'd rather record it as an exceptionally fine Auchentoshan. And by the way, bartenders, you have proved a point I have been making for the last 25 years: the finest cocktail is a blend of whiskies...even if from the same distillery...Now don't you go ruining this by putting ice, water, or anything else in it... 47%.

Auchentoshan Three Wood db (76) n20 t18 f20 b18. Takes you directly into the rough. Refuses to harmonise, except maybe for some late molassed sugar. 43%

Auchentoshan Three Wood bourbon & Oloroso & PX sherry casks, bott code: L9274SB323011209 db (88) n22 t23 f21 b22 Three woods there may be. But it's the PX that really counts. A semi-syrupy concoction with massive chewiness. The half-expected bitter finish offers a stark contrast. 43%.

Auchentoshan Virgin Oak db (92) n23.5 t23 f22.5 b23 Not quite how I've seen 'Toshan perform before: but would love to see it again! 46%

◇ **Valour Whisky Auchentoshan 27 Years Old** cask no 900655, dist 1995 (95) n23.5 charming display of marzipan mingling with light grapefruit and quietly intense malt; t24 oh... that is just one of the most engrossing deliveries of the year! The salivating malt has retained the richness displayed on the nose, but each increasing flavour wave doubles its intensity. There are light spices and more marzipan, too. But the mind is fully occupied with that outrageous malty lift off...; f23 slightly bitter as the oak rushes in on delicate ground. But the barley pushes back and there is now a degree of creaminess to the late vanilla and butterscotch; b24.5 this is a distillery which, at these kinds of years, can offer variable whisky, to put it kindly. However, when a nugget of a cask has been found it can offer extraordinary riches. Here is a such an example.

It is a half hour whisky, no less, to explore its myriad incarnations in the glass – using the Murray Method, of course... *52.1%*

◇ **Whisky Republic Auchentoshan** American Oak bourbon casks, bott code L2333 db **(88.5)** n22 t23 f21.5 b22 I find this the most curious dram. Anyone who knows me will vouch that I will back 100% ex bourbon casks over other types all day every day. Yet the fact they are using only first and second fill bourbon casks here – as announced on their label - baffles me. When I'm creating a whisky of this style, for me using a moderate percentage of third fill ex-bourbon is a must – on the grounds that it allows the malt to punch through the effects of the oak. This guarantees balance and extra personality. A strong toffee presence and the 40% means the finish has little chance to shine. But the pleasant nose is nutty with tickling spices, too. And the delivery is a belter: the malt filtering through in full (seemingly third fill) juiciness with an acacia honey sweetness as extra back up. But the fade is disappointingly dull. A bit of tinkering and they could have something rather wonderful on their hands. *40%*

AUCHROISK
Speyside, 1974. Diageo. Working.

Auchroisk Aged 10 Years db **(84)** n20 t22 f21 b21. Tangy orange on the nose, the malt amplified by a curious saltiness on the palate. *43%. Flora and Fauna.*

Fadandel.dk Auchroisk Aged 10 Years 1st fill oloroso hogshead, cask no.73, dist Dec 2010, bott Feb 2021 **(87)** n23.5 t20.5 f21.5 b21.5 Abounds in spice while the nose enjoys some high-quality Dundee cake moments. Pleasant enough, but the heat is a little too much to bear when so little is offered in malty body. Struggles to find a balance. Like the Port, a shame as the cask is faultless and some hard work gone into this: maybe a case of right cask, wrong distillery... If you do get a bottle, make sure you make the most of the nose; it is terrific! *58.7% sc 256 bottles*

Hepburn's Choice Auchroisk Aged 9 Years wine hogshead, dist 2011, bott 2020 **(82.5)** n21 t21.5 f20 b20 Young and pretty monosyllabic in its utterances. The wine cask has denuded the malt of its sugars at a time it needed them most. No off notes or anything untoward. But the balance isn't quite there, either. *46%. nc ncf 809 bottles.*

Hepburn's Choice Auchroisk 10 Years Old rum cask, dist 2009, bott 2019 **(87.5)** n22 t22.5 f21 b22 Usually a disappointing malt, it appears that the rum cask has used its sugary influence to hem in the more deliciously malty aspects to wonderful effect. The finish is typically weak, nonetheless. Even so, enjoy the early salivating crispness of the barley tinged with a superb outer coating of lightly spiced heather honey. *46%. nc ncf sc. 182 bottles.*

Old Malt Cask Auchroisk 21 (89.5) n22.5 t23 f21.5 b22.5 A beefed up Auchroisk, as weighty on the palate as the Old Malt Cask 20-year-old is light. This is full of peppers and coffee, too, making for a full-bodied treat which does unravel slightly before the tangy finish. *53%*

The First Editions Auchroisk Aged 23 Years 1997 refill hogshead, cask no. HL17814, bott 2021 **(87.5)** n22 t22.5 f21 b22 Seems very settled and comfortable in its malty simplicity. The finish is on the short side of a malt this age, but falls within the Auchroisk remit. The nose and delivery, though, charm – especially thanks to offering just the right degree of semi-gristy sweetness. *54.6%. nc ncf sc. 199 bottles.*

AULTMORE
Speyside, 1896. Bacardi. Working.

Aultmore 12 Year Old db **(85.5)** n22 t22 f20 b21.5. Not quite firing on all cylinders due to the uncomfortably tangy oak. But relish the creamy malt for the barley is the theme of choice and for its sheer intensity alone, it doesn't disappoint; a little ulmo honey and marzipan doff their cap to the kinder vanillas. *46% WB16/028*

Aultmore of the Foggie Moss Aged 12 Years bott code: L18135ZA903 db **(92.5)** n23.5 t23.5 f22.5 b23 A whisky purist's delight. So delicate you can see the inner workings of this fine malt. *46%. ncf.*

Aultmore 18 Year Old db **(88.5)** n22.5 t22.5 f22 b21.5 Charming, but could do with having the toffee blended out... *46%*

Aultmore of the Foggie Moss Aged 18 Years batch no. 481, bott code: L15244B100 db **(94.5)** n23.5 t24 f23 b24 It is so satisfying when the sweetness and spices of a malt combine for near perfect harmony. Flattens towards the finish, but this is high grade malt. *46%. ncf.*

Aultmore Aged 21 Years refill hogshead, batch no. 00107, bott code: L18281ZA501 db **(95.5)** n24 t24 f23.5 b24 When you get a very decent spirit filled into exceptionally good casks, the result – providing the whisky is disgorged neither too early nor late – is usually a positive one. The refill hoggies here must have been in fine fettle, for this a bit of a stunner. No, make that a classic! Potential gong material, this. *46%. nc ncf.*

Aultmore Exceptional Cask Series 21 Years Old 1996 db **(94.5)** n24 t23.5 f23.5 b23.5 There is age creaking from every pore of this whisky. The nose is magnificently sensual with its orange blossom honey theme, spicy toasty tannins lurking at every corner. And those tannins carry on their impressive work, yet at the same time allowing a delicious alloy of malt and sultanas to not only thrive but fully fill the palate. Toward the end we are back to those insistent tannins which, if anything display an age greater than its given years. A malt plucked at the very right time from the warehouse: it would never have made half as good a 25-year-old. 54%. Selected for CWS.

◈ **King of IB Aultmore 40 Years Old 1982** cask 3245 bott 2018 **(96) n24** classic may be an overused term but it is entirely appropriate here. Dream of how a 40-year-old malt bathed in faultless oloroso and emboldened by perfect degree of uncompromised oak should be: here you have it. The spices are respectful, refusing to dominate but doing their job of lightly prickling and alerting. The fruit is playing the dual role of lightening with its sweeter, grapier tones but also adding ballast with a formidable and delightful volley of dried dates; **t24** if the spices held off on the nose, then they were saving themselves for full deployment on delivery, though still refined enough to allow those gloriously rich fruit tones radiating from the salivating sherry to make a soft and soothing marker. At last, they move in with seemingly measured increments in intensity. Meanwhile, the softer oaks hum contentedly - happy to allow the residue sweetness of the grape and even, perhaps, towards the middle a few weathered shards of barley sugar. Subtle outbreaks of muscovado sugars keep the oak on course and the complexity levels ticking over...; **f24** we have moved into 80% dark chocolate territory here as the oak absorbs those intrinsic sugars. At times we have fruit and nut, thanks to the grape and walnut oils which add to in the increasing glossiness on the finish. Even so, it dries as it should and not with a hint of tiredness or bitterness along the way; **b24** by far the best whisky I have tasted from Aultmore. Remember: this cask was filled so that perhaps within four years, maybe six if lucky, and a dozen if it won the jackpot, it would be part of a blend. Especially as 1982 saw this distillery right in the middle of the Whisky Loch, with many neighbouring distilleries either mothballed or closed down altogether. Somehow it found itself occupying a warehouse for well over three decades longer than expected. And by the time it was bottled became one of the oldest-ever exemplars of this distillery. Standing proud and near faultless, it is assisted by a something of a miracle of that time: a sherry cask entirely untroubled by sulphur tainting. This is a throwback of a wine cask leading to some kind of award in Whisky Bible 2024. This is a thing of beauty. And near indescribable elegance. 52.6%

Single Cask Collection Aultmore 14 Years Old 1st fill bourbon cask, cask no. 306878, dist 2006, bott 2020 **(91) n22.5 t23 f22.5 b23** I have a soft spot for elegantly well-made and matured malts which do not try to show off. Here's classic example. 52.2%. sc. 209 bottles.

William & Co Spirits World Whisky Club Movie Series Aultmore 11 Years Old sherry oak octave cask finish, cask no. 9527869, dist Sept 08, bott Jun 20 **(92.5) n23 t23.5 f22.5 b23.5** perhaps it is supposed to be "Drambusters". But is more like "Ice Cold in Alex", as this is dry as crossing The Sahara. And, having done it once myself, I should know. In a day when sweet sherry casks are all the rage, it is a welcome and wonderful change to find one which is so proudly dry. This is pretty sophisticated stuff. But without the Murray Method in action, it will be hard to spot all the tessellations in this delicate mosaic. 54.3%. 102 Bottles.

BALBLAIR

Highlands (Northern), 1872. Inver House Distillers. Working.

Balblair 10 Years Old db **(86) n21 t22 f22 b21.** Such an improved dram away from the clutches of caramel. 40%

Balblair Aged 12 Years American oak ex-bourbon & double-fired American oak casks, bott code: L18/357 R18/5536 IB db **(87) n21.5 t22 f21.5 b22** There is no escaping a distinct tired cask tang to this. From the nose to the finale the oak pokes around with a little too much meanness of spirit. But it is the wonderful clarity to the barley – including a delicious citrusy freshness – which keeps the malt on course. I suspect the next bottling will be a whole lot better! 46%. nc ncf.

Balblair Aged 15 Years American oak ex-bourbon casks, followed by first fill Spanish oak butts, bott code: L19 079 R19/5133 IB db **(93) n23 t23.5 f23 b23** Ah, after the relative disappointment of the 12-year-old, so good to see we are right back on track here. Twenty years of very bitter experience has taught me to fear the worst and hope for the best so far as the use of sherry butts are concerned. But my hopes are rewarded: not 100% perfect, but close enough. 46%. nc ncf.

Balblair Aged 17 Years American oak ex-bourbon casks, followed by first fill Spanish oak butts, bott code: L19/057 R19/5097 IB db **(94) n23.5 t24.5 f22.5 b23.5** One of the best arrivals on the palate of any Scotch whisky I have tasted this year. 46%. nc ncf. Travel Exclusive.

Balblair Aged 18 Years American oak ex-bourbon casks, followed by first fill Spanish oak butts, bott code: L19/121 R19/5220 IB db **(83) n22 t23 f18 b20** Balblair's luck has run out on the sherry butts. A heftier expression than the 17-year-old and the sulphur ensures there is nothing like the degree of complexity. *46%. nc ncf.*

Balblair Aged 25 Years American oak ex-bourbon casks, followed by first fill Spanish oak butts, nbc db **(91) n23.5 t23.5 f21 b23** There has been hard work here to harmonise fruit and oak and allow the barley a say, too. But when sherry is this ripe, not the easiest stunt to pull off. Gets pretty close, though! *46%.*

Balblair 1975 db **(94.5) n24.5 t23.5 f23 b23.5.** Essential Balblair. *46%*

Balblair 1989 db **(91) n23 t23 f22.5 b22.5.** Don't expect gymnastics on the palate or the pyrotechnics of the Cadenhead 18: in many ways a simple malt, but one beautifully told. Almost Cardhu-esque in the barley department. *43%*

Balblair 1989 db **(88) n21.5 t22 f22.5 b22.** A clean, pleasing malt, though hardly one that will induce anyone to plan a night raid on any shop stocking it... *46%*

Balblair 1990 db **(92.5) n24 t23.5 f22 b23.** Tangy in the great Balblair tradition. Except here this is warts and all with the complexity and greatness of the distillery left in no doubt. *46%*

Balblair 1991 3rd Release bott 2018, bott code L18/044 R18/5054IB db **(94.5) n23.5 t23.5 f23.5 b24** A malt embracing its passing years and has aged, silver temples and all, with great style and panache. *46% nc ncf.*

Balblair 2000 2nd Release bott 2017, bott code L17/R121 db **(95.5) n24.5 t24 f23 b24** First encountered this malt at a tasting I gave in Corsica earlier in the year. It blew away my audience while equally seducing me. Sampled back in the tasting lab, if anything it is even more stunning. The stock of this under-appreciated distillery rises by the day... *46%. nc ncf.*

Balblair 2001 db **(90.5) n23.5 t23.5 f21.5 b22.5** A typically high quality whisky from this outrageously underestimated distillery. *46%*

The Whisky Barrel Originals Balblair 10 Years Old 1st fill oloroso hogshead, cask no. TWB1008, dist Sept 09, bott 2019 **(91.5) n23 t23 f22.5 b23** The cleanest sherry cask you could ever wish for. And lightest: a butterfly of a sherry cask. *57.6%. sc. 298 bottles.*

BALMENACH
Speyside, 1824. Inver House Distillers. Working.

Fadandel.dk Balmenach 7 Year Old 5 months finish in a 1st fill PX Octave, cask no. 430A, dist 17 Oct 12, bott 14 Apr 20 **(90) n22.5 t22.5 f22.5 b22.5** This is so outrageously ridiculous, it's actually very good. The youthful malt is in mortal combat with a grapey cask of gorilla strength. Bizarre! It is probably just a grape atom away from disaster. ... but so entertaining, too... *55.4%. sc. 75 bottles.*

Old Malt Cask Balmenach Aged 14 Years refill barrel, cask no. 16791, dist Dec 04, bott Jun 19 **(94.5) n23 t24 f23.5 b24** Glories in its complex malty freshness! A joy of a dram. *50%. nc ncf sc. 141 bottles.*

Old Malt Cask Balmenach Aged 14 Years refill hogshead, cask no. HL18196, dist Sept 2006, bott Feb 2021 **(89) n22.5 t22.5 f22 b22** Beautifully made and leaves you in no doubt of its Speyside credentials. *50%. nc ncf sc. 301 bottles.*

Old Malt Cask Balmenach Aged 14 Years refill hogshead, cask no. HL18695, dist Mar 2007, bott May 2021 **(91.5) n22.5** an enjoyable volley of sharp, youngish, quite salty barley tones; **t23** such a beautiful collection of crisp, salivating barley tones, accompanied by rich, gristy malt: a kind of double-edged sword...and one that has certainly been sharpened...; **f23** a lovely digestive biscuit fade; **b23** for whisky of its age, it thoroughly enjoys dishing out lighter, younger sweeter barley notes of a Balmenach some years younger. Malty and refreshing. A more confident, malt intense version than its sister cask. *50% sc 332 bottles*

THE BALVENIE
Speyside, 1892. William Grant & Sons. Working.

The Balvenie Double Wood Aged 12 Years European oak sherry casks, bott code: L8D 7738 2309 db **(82) n22 t21 f19 b20** Pretty standard but uninspiring fare with sharp fruit pinching the palate until the furry sulphur tang arrives. Oh, how I miss Balvenie in standard bourbon casks at this age or even a little younger which gives you a chance to see how amazingly brilliant this distillery actually is. *40%.*

The Balvenie DoubleWood Aged 12 Years bott code: L34E 4950 **(85.5) n22 t22.5 f20 b21** Every year I give this whisky (from one of my favourite distilleries) another crack, hoping it will at last heal my broken heart (broken still for the long lost and irreplaceable Balvenie 10). The fact that, at long last, I have found one without a major sulphur nag helps get the score up. That doesn't mean that there isn't sulphur, because, sadly, there is – right at the death. Though, thankfully the sulphur influence peaks at minor, rather than major. The great news is that the nose and delivery can be thoroughly enjoyed, light figs and dates on the aroma, a maltier infusion with toffee tones on delivery. The spices are a Godsend and stir things up which otherwise would have been a touch too linear, as soon as the cherry juicy has vanished. But the sulphur on the finish only moans rather than scolds. But until the sulphur is gone altogether, the distillery will remain underrepresented of its true astonishing capabilities. 40%.

The Balvenie 16 Year Old Triple Cask db (84.5) n22 t22.5 f19 b21. Well, after their single cask and then double wood, who saw this coming...? There is nothing about this whisky you can possibly dislike: no diminishing off notes (OK, well maybe at the very death) and a decent injection of sugar, especially early on. The trouble is, when you mix together sherry butts (even mainly good ones, like here) and first fill bourbon casks, the intense toffee produced tends to make for a monosyllabic, toffeed, dullish experience. And so it proves here. 40%

The Balvenie Caribbean Cask Aged 14 Years bott code: L8D 7263 1707 db (91.5) n23t23 f22.5 b23 A different kind of rum style from Balvenie to others they have done in the past, this working far better and despite a slight caramel overdose, more complexity this time round. 43%.

The Balvenie Double Wood Aged 17 Years db (84) n22 t21 f20 b21. Balvenie does like 17 years as an age to show off its malt at its most complex, & understandably so as it is an important stage in its development before its usual premature over maturity: the last years or two when it remains full of zest and vigour. Here, though, the oak on the bourbon cask has offered a little too much of its milkier, older side while the sherry is a fraction overzealous and a shade too tangy. Enjoyable, but like a top of the range Mercedes engine which refuses to run evenly. 43%.

The Balvenie Double Wood Aged 17 Years European oak sherry casks, bott code: L34D 50322808 db (95) n24 t23.5 f23 b24 Just fabulous to see this marriage between bourbon and sherry cask being such a happy one. Both sets of barrels are blemish-free while the weight and balance is exemplary. Luxurious in every degree and a magnificent example of the difference sulphur-free sherry butts can make to a whisky, especially as one as top drawer as The Balvenie... So deserves to be another three percent higher in strength, too... 43%.

The Balvenie Aged 21 Years Port Wood db (94.5) n24 t24 f23 b23.5 What a magnificently improved malt. Last time out I struggled to detect the fruit. Here, there's no escaping. 40%

The Balvenie PortWood Aged 21 Years finished in PortWood port casks, bott code: L34D 4498 1204 db (86) n23.5 t22.5 f19 b21 The gnawing sulphur fade is an unfortunate ending to a malt which starts so brilliantly well. So much fresh fruit abounding here, much of it of the sugar candy variety. Those incapable of picking up sulphur are in for a treat. 40%.

The Balvenie The Sweet Toast of American Oak Aged 12 Years finished in Kentucky virgin American oak barrels, bott code: L6D 6404 0603 db (87.5) n23 t22 f21.5 b21 Not anything like carefully balanced enough. Virgin oak has to be treated carefully and with respect: that is a lot of tannin being awoken and barley is no corn or rye. Needs rebalancing as this has the potential for greatness. But not in this form. 43%. Story No. 1.

The Balvenie Tun 1509 Batch No. 6 bott code: L34D 5015 2608 db (93) n23.5 t24 b23.5 This must be from Balvenie-by-the-Sea. Amazing salt levels here, especially on the nose and early delivery. Has all the hallmarks of blender David Stewart, one of the top three at layering Scotch whisky in living memory. Just a shame about the late tang, though not too much damage done. 50.4%.

The Balvenie The Week of Peat Aged 14 Years bott code: L6D 6432 1103 db (96) n24 t24 f23.5 b24.5 This could also, I suppose, be called a Weak of Peat as the phenols never really get anything like a head of steam. But, then, it never even attempts to and is quite right to concentrate on a subtlety which demonstrates the greatness of the this malt when matured in bourbon casks. One of those rare malts where the delivery and follow through on the palate is a match for a brilliant nose. Make no mistake: we have a true Speyside gem here. 48.3%. ncf. Story No. 2.

BANFF
Speyside, 1863–1983. Diageo. Demolished.

Gleann Mór Banff Aged Over 42 Years dist 1975 (91) n23 t23.5 f22.5 b22 This was distilled in the same year I visited my first distillery in Scotland...and that was a bloody long time ago. Not many casks have made it from then to today, and those that have are in varying states of quality: old age does not always mean an improvement in a whisky's fortunes...often the reverse. This is a classic example of a malt which should have been bottled a little time back. But it is still massively enjoyable, throwing up the odd surprise here and there and keeping to the malty script despite the militant oak. Quite an experience....41.1%.

BEN NEVIS
Highlands (Western), 1825. Nikka. Working.

Ben Nevis 10 Years Old 2008 batch no. 1, 1st fill bourbon, sherry and wines casks, dist 21 Apr 08, bott Sept 18 db (86.5) n21 t22.5 f21 b22 A robust, no holds barred malt which gets you both with the intensity of fruit and oak as well as the sheer power of the spirit itself! The varied wine casks don't perhaps gel as they might (not helped by a small sulphur note), though the intensity of the delivery may bring a pleasurable bead of sweat to the brow. 62.4%.

Ben Nevis Synergy 13 Years Old db (88) n22 t22 f21.5 b22.5 One of the sweetest Ben Nevises for a long time, but as chewy as ever! A bit of a lady's dram to be honest. 46%

Ben Nevis 32 Years Old 1966 dist Jun 66, bott Sept 98 db (95.5) n24.5 t23.5 f24 b23.5 Way back in 1998 some 1966 Ben Nevis was bottled for the US market as a "101" in 75cl bottles...but for some reason never got there. So for 20 years they slumbered peacefully in a warehouse at the distillery, entirely and blissfully forgotten, about until one day they were rediscovered by chance. That whisky, with a little softening from 20 years in glass, has now been re-consigned to 70cl bottles and at last put up for sale. What we have is a real blast from the past: a window into a Ben Nevis's distilling history, as a 32-year-old whisky bottled now from 1987 stock would certainly have a different feel. This reveals the distillery when it had the type of bite much favoured by blenders and which ensures a single malt with a singular personality. Just magnificent! 50.5%. Forgotten Bottlings Series.

Chapter 7 Monologue Ben Nevis 24 (90) n22 t23.5 f22 b22.5 can't say I've ever seen a Ben Nevis quite like this before. But I like it!! 53%

Fadandel Ben Nevis 25 Years Old (92.5) n22.5 t23.5 f23 b23.5 at once lofty and dense, in a way only Ben Nevis can be. Real knife and fork whisky. 55%

Hepburn's Choice Ben Nevis 9 Years Old bourbon barrel, dist 2011, bott 2020 (89.5) n22.5 the malt is piled so high on the nose, it positively pulses! The youthfulness is apparent, but the light but balancing strands of oak deserve respect, too...; t22.5 the nose forecasts the malty soup to come and the oils guarantee a real chewabilty to this; f22 light cocoa touch gives a certain Malteser candy quality to this; b22.5 just brilliant to see this distillery unplugged. A really fun ride, shewing just how beautifully distilled this malt was. 46%. nc ncf sc. 251 bottles.

⌦ **Vintage Bottlers Ben Nevis 26 Years Old** hogshead cask no 416, dist 29/03/97, bott 15/08/22 (91.5) n22.5 t23 f22.5 b23.5 By Ben Nevis' usual chunky standards, this is as flighty and citrussy as it gets. Absolutely thick with grist and barley sugar. And chimes as cleanly as the church bell reverberating to my right. The oak offers the only sizeable weight, and this arrives in a succession of intense layers of tannin, carrying with it well-judged spices. A malt which brilliantly sits astride the border of light and heavy whisky. 47.1% sc 252 bottles

BENRIACH
Speyside, 1898. Brown-Forman. Working.

The BenRiach Aged 10 Years Curiositas Peated Malt bourbon, toasted virgin oak & rum casks, bott code: 2018/10/11 LM11452 db (89.5) n22.5 t22.5 f22 b22.5 Unrecognisable from the original Curiositas and though the strength is back up to 46% abv, somehow the body has become lighter. Enjoyable but a head scratcher. 46%. nc ncf.

The BenRiach Aged 12 Years Matured In Sherry Wood db (95.5) n23.5 t24 f24 b24 Since previously experiencing this the number of instances of sampling a sherry wood whisky and not finding my taste buds caked in sulphur has nosedived dramatically. Therefore, to start my tasting day at 7am with something as honest as this propels one with myriad reasons to continue the day. A celebration of a malt whisky in more ways than you could believe. 46%. nc ncf.

Benriach 12 Year Old Port Pipe db (94.5) n23 t24 f23.5 b24 big, big, peat. But a very un-Islay or island style smokiness, thanks to the structure of the phenols which appear almost aloof. A cracking malt. And a classic for those who can remember its malty days from 30 years back. 59.7%

The BenRiach Aged 21 Years Classic bourbon barrels, virgin oak, PX sherry & red wine casks db (90) n22.5 t23 f22 b22.5 Rich textured and complex, there is a glorious clarity to the sugars and fondant vanillas. Even the spices seem happy to dovetail into the merry mix without creating too many waves. 46%. nc

The BenRiach Aged 21 Years Tawny Port Wood Finish db (87.5) n22 t21 f22 b21.5 I'm not sure if the cask finish was designed to impart a specific fruitiness profile or simply repair some tired old oak. In either case, it has been a partial success only. The intemperance of the tannin makes its mark in no small measure both on nose and delivery and it is only in the finish that the sugars bond strongly enough together to form a balance with the woody input. 46%.

The BenRiach Aged 21 Years Temporis Peated bourbon barrels, virgin oak, Pedro Ximenez & oloroso sherry casks db (87.5) n22.5 t22 f21.5 b21.5 Begins nobly with a fanfare of alluring acidic peat, but then strange (mainly orangey) fruit notes keeps chipping away at its integrity and ruining the song and balance. And so it also pans out on delivery, though the smoke is soon muzzled. For a flavour wave or two both smoke and fruit are in perfect harmony but it is fleeting and not worth the dull finish which follows. Enjoyable, but kind of irritating, too. 46%. nc ncf.

The BenRiach Aged 22 years Moscatel Wood Finish db (81) n21 t23 f17 b20 Not sure any wine finish I have tasted this year has thrown up so many huge, one might even say challenging, perfumed notes which score so highly for sheer lip-smacking effect. Had this cask not given the impression of being sulphur treated what an enormous score it would have amassed...! 46%.

The BenRiach 25 Years Old db (87.5) n21.5 t23 f21 b22. The tranquillity and excellent balance of the middle is the highlight by far. 50%

The BenRiach Aged 25 Years Authenticus db (91) n23 t23 f22 b23 Every moment feels as old as a Roman senator...who is eventually stabbed in the back by Oakicus. 46%.

BenRiach 35 Year Old db (90) n23 juicy dates and plums are tipped into a weighty fruitcake; t24 sit right back in your armchair (no..? Then go and find one...!!) having dimmed the lights and silenced the room and just let your taste buds run amok: those plums and toasted raisins really do get you salivating, with the spices also whipping up a mid-life storm; f21.5 angular oak dries and bitters at a rate of knots; b22 sexy fruit, but has late oaky bite. 42.5%

BenRiach Cask Strength batch 1 db (93) n22.5 t24 f23 b23.5 If you don't fall in love with this one, you should stick to vodka... 57.2%

The BenRiach Curiositas Aged 10 Years Single Peated Malt db (90.5) n23 t23 f22 b22.5 "Hmmmm. Why have my research team marked this down as a 'new' whisky" I wondered to myself. Then immediately on nosing and tasting I discovered the reason without having to ask: the pulse was weaker, the smoke more apologetic...it had been watered down from the original 46% to 40%. This is excellent malt. But can we have our truly great whisky back, please? As lovely as it is, this is a bit of an imposter. As Emperor Hadrian might once have said: "ifus itus aintus brokus..." 40%

The BenRiach Peated Cask Strength batch 1 db (95) n24 t23 f24 b24 Stunning whisky magnificently distilled and, though relatively young, almost perfectly matured. 56%.

BenRiach Peated Quarter Casks db (93) n23.5 there's a lot of peat in them barrels. The citrus is vital...; t24 a plethora of sugars and caramel leached from the casks make for a safe landing when the smoke and malt – with a slightly new make feel - arrive in intensive form; f22.5 the caramel continues, now with spice; b23 though seemingly youthful in some phases, works a treat! 46%

Birnie Moss Intensely Peated db (90) n22 youthful, full of fresh barley and lively, clean smoke; t23.5 juicy, fabulously smoked, wet-behind the ears gristy sugars; f22 some vanillas try to enter a degree of complexity; b22.5 before Birnie Moss started shaving... or even possibly toddling. Young and stunning. 48%. nc ncf.

BENRINNES
Speyside, 1826. Diageo. Working.

Benrinnes 21 Year Old ex-sherry European oak casks, dist 1992 db (83.5) n21 t22 f19 b21.5. Salty and tangy. Some superb cocoa moments mixing with the muscovado sugars as it peaks. But just a little too furry and bitter at the finish. 56.9%. 2,892 bottles.

Chapter 7 Benrinnes 2009 (87.5) n22 t23 f20.5 b22 Benrinnes is not the go to distillery for great single malt. However, I have to say that there are no great complaints from me here. An excellent oloroso cask here has been deployed to add not just dripping grape, but unexpected weight and massive spice. The thin finish is truer to form, but the journey there is a flavoursome one. 54%

The First Editions Benrinnes Aged 20 Years 2000 bourbon barrel, cask no. 18212, bott 2020 (82) n21 t21.5 f19.5 b20 The thinness of the malt is revealed in all its glory here, from the sharp acetate nose right through to quickfire finale. A good show of barley early on, but this soon burns out. 49.4%. nc ncf sc. 243 bottles.

Hepburn's Choice Benrinnes 9 Years Old wine hogsheads, dist 2010, bott 2020 (86.5) n21.5 t21 f22 b22 The lack of muscle from the malt allows the cask to dictate. That means it's fruit pastels all round...though low calorie ones as sugars remain at a premium. Not typically Benrinnes, though, as this has some chewing in it...and spice! 46%. nc ncf. 696 bottles.

Hepburn's Choice Benrinnes 10 Years Old wine cask, dist 2009, bott 2019 (83) n20 t21 f21 b21 Not a particularly bad wine cask. But the malt base is so feeble it is just incapable of making any kind of impression, or ensuring any degree of complexity. Not unpleasant, but a malt which goes precisely nowhere. 46%. nc ncf sc. 110 bottles.

Old Malt Cask Benrinnes Aged 24 Years refill hogshead, cask no. 17812, dist Sept 96, bott Dec 20 (85) n22 t21.5 f20.5 b21 A little extra body than the norm for a Benrinnes allows the malt and spice to congregate into something momentarily weighty, then salivating but ultimately a little stretched and overly simple. 50%. nc ncf sc. 316 bottles.

Scyfion Choice Benrinnes 2006 pomegranate Armenian wine cask finished, bott 2019 (91) n22.5 t23 f22.5 b23 This is very weird. I tasted their Bashta cask vatted malt earlier in the day and got pomegranates....!!! I'm assuming this is the same cask type here: if it is, I have just impressed if not amazed myself! Well, my last girlfriend, Judy, was half Armenian: I think I know what to get her for Christmas. Lots of character and personality here. 50%. nc ncf sc. 158 bottles.

Scottish Malts

Single Cask Collection Benrinnes 12 Years Old rum cask finish, cask no. 303890, dist 2008, bott 2020 (83) n20.5 t22 f20 b20.5 A very curious choice of cask for this particular distillery: I think I could have written the tasting notes even before nosing it and putting to my lips. Rum casks have a habit of imprisoning the malt with a crunchy sugar shell. It needs good body to pierce this shield... and Benrinnes would never, in a million years have that kind of weight and energy. So it proves. Not that it doesn't have moments to enjoy, especially though, the midpoint where some malt does seep through. But it is very short-lived. 55.7%. sc. 253 bottles.

Stronachie 18 Years Old (83.5) n21.5 t21 f20 b21. This is so much like the older brother of the Stronachie 12: shows the same hot temper on the palate and even sharper teeth. Also, the same slim-line body. Have to say, though, something strangely irresistible about the intensity of the crisp malt. 46%

The Whisky Chamber Benrinnes 20 Jahre 2000 bourbon barrel (89) n22.5 an excellently balanced affair: the nose and vanilla harmonise delightfully. Didn't expect that...! t23 and even better on delivery as the malt takes off with eye-wateringly sharp and salivating confidence: so rare to find a Benrinnes with this kind malty punch; f21.5 just begins to tire slightly. Dry and vaguely bitter; b22 now this is impressive. A Benrinnes which for once displays a body rich and fit enough to go on a mini malt marathon. 54.9%. sc.

Wilson and Morgan Benrinnes 2011 First Fill X Finish bott 2022 db (89.5) n23 have to say: the balance between barley and under-ripe green grape is just about perfect. Only trace sugary residue apparent; t23 much more intense here, as the muscovado sugars kick in early with a dash of molasses for good measure. The malts are grassy and juicy enough to cut through the restrained grape; f21 bitters out somewhat; b22.5 for the second time, a distillery that skimps, rather, on personality and for which there is no great expectation has received the W&M treatment and been raised a notch or two. The finish is typically weak. But the rest of the show is a vibrantly entertaining one. 46%

BENROMACH
Speyside, 1898. Gordon & MacPhail. Working.

Benromach 15 Year Old db (78) n20 t22 f17 b19. Some charming early moments, especially when the grape escapes its marker and reveals itself in its full juicy and sweet splendour. But it is too short lived as the sulphur, inevitably takes over. 43%

Benromach Aged 15 Years first-fill casks, bott code: 30/01/20 db (94.5) n23.5 t24.5 f23 b23.5 the last time I tasted this sulphur ruled, not OK. Not now. Upgrades to serious little charmer status. The extraordinary touch of this whisky on the palate, its kisses and caresses and its most subtle of flavour profiles...never shouting, just hints, whispers, promises and sighs. Apparently whisky isn't sexy. People have tried to, quite literally, destroy my career because I say it is. Well taste this, Murray Method and all, and tell me if you are being seduced or not...43%

Benromach Aged 15 Years bott code: 30/10/20 db (82) n23 t23 f17 b19 This was doing so well. The succulent, blood orange and lightly spiced nose. Then the labyrinthine kumquat and fruitcake interplay on delivery. Then...then...a slow but continued release of the S element. Sigh! When will these disappointments end...? 43% nc ncf

Benromach 21 Years Old db (91.5) n22 t23.5 f23 b23 An entirely different, indeed lost, style of malt from the old, now gone, big stills. The result is an airier whisky which has embraced such good age with a touch of panache and grace. 43%

Benromach 30 Years Old db (95.5) n23.5 t24 f24 b24 You will struggle to find a 30-year-old with fewer wrinkles than this.. Magnificent: one of the outstanding malts of the year. 43%

Benromach 39 Year Old 1977 Vintage db (94) n23.5 t24 f23 b23.5 Just love it when a whisky creaks and complains and lets you know just how old it is...but then produces the magic that keeps alive, well and captivatingly complex after all these years. 56%.

Benromach 1972 cask no. 4471 db (94) n23 t23.5 f23.5 b24 Has turned completely grey, but this is one sprightly malt. 55.7%. sc.

Benromach 1977 cask no. 1269 db (87.5) n22 t21.5 f22 b22 Plucked from the warehouse a little too late with its best days behind it. The oak is overlord here, the tannins aggressive enough to bring water to the eye, as does the grapefruit citrus kick. But by no means is all lost as the malt is proud, robust and rich and puts up a chewy rear-guard action. 49.6%. sc.

Benromach 2012 First Fill Sherry (89) n23 forget the grape. Even the firm wall of tannin. This is all about the deftness of the smoke. So charming...; t22.5 after such a rich nose, the initial youthfulness to the spirit comes as an eyebrow raiser. But it is short lived and soon the grape and smoke are back in harness and forming a thicker combination than on the nose; f21.5 lacks the balance of both nose and delivery. The tannins are aloof and full of bluster while the spices fizz briefly. Quite an austere finale, though; b22 a whisky which doesn't quite find its best rhythm but has enough going on with its impressive components to ensure character and entertainment. 59.4%

124

Benromach 100° Proof db (94) n23 t23.5 f23.5 b24 For any confused US readers, the strength is based on the old British proof strength, not American! What is not confusing is the undisputed complexity and overall excellence of this malt. 57%

Benromach 20th Anniversary Bottling db (81) n19 t22 f19 b21 Bit of a clumsy whisky never really feeling right on the nose or palate, though has its better moments with a big malt crescendo and a delicate minty-chocolate movement towards the late middle and early finish. 56.2%

Benromach Cask No. 1 dist 1998, bott 2018 db (89.5) n23 like a bunch of grapes you forgot you had in the bag...; t22 fat, oily slightly off-key start but corrects itself as a tart but attractive gooseberry notes arrives; f22 dry powdery mocha; b22.5 an unusual fingerprint to this and intriguingly haphazard in its development. 60.1%

Benromach Cask Strength 2001 db (89) n21.5 t23 f22 b22.5. Just fun whisky which has been very well made and matured with total sympathy to the style. Go get. 59.9%

Benromach Cask Strength 2003 db (92) n22.5 t23.5 f23 b23.5 Hats off to the most subtle and sophisticated Benromach I have tasted in a while. 59.4%

Benromach Cask Strength Batch 1 dist 2008, bott 2019 db (90.5) n23.5 t22.5 f22 b22.5 Some smoky malts terrify people. This, I suspect, will enjoy the direct opposite effect. As friendly a peated malt as you'll ever find. 57%

Benromach Heritage 35 Year Old db (87) n22 t21.5 f22 b21.5. A busy exchange of complex tannin notes, some backed by the most faded spice and caramel. All charming and attractive, but the feeling of decay is never far away. 43%

Benromach Heritage 1974 db (93) n23.5 t23 f23 b23.5 Made in the year I left school to become a writer, this appears to have survived the years in better nick than I... 49.1%

Benromach Heritage 1976 db (86.5) n21.5 t21 f22.5 b21.5 There are times when you can have a little too much tannin and this has crossed the Rubicon. That said, look closely on the nose for some staggering lime and redcurrant notes which escape the onslaught as well as the gorgeous butterscotch on the finish as the sugars fight back at the death in style. Some moments of genius in the oakiest of frames. 53.5%

Benromach Organic Special Edition db (85.5) n22 t21 f21.5 b21. The smoky bacon crisp aroma underscores the obvious youth. Also, one of the driest malts of the year. Overall, pretty. But pretty pre-pubescent, too... 43%

Benromach Organic 2010 db (95.5) n24 t24 f23 b24.5 Gentle, refined and exquisitely elegant. 43%

Benromach Peat Smoke Batch 3 db (90.5) n22 t23 f22.5 b23 An excellent malt that has been beautifully made. Had it been bottled at 46 we would have seen it offer an extra degree of richness. 40%

Benromach Peat Smoke 2008 db (85.5) n22 t22 f20.5 b21 Well, that was certainly different! The nose has the oily hallmark of a Caol Ila, though without the phenol intensity. The palate, those oils apart, is a very different tale. A unique flavour profile for sure: a kind of smoked toffee fudge which actually makes your tongue ache while tasting! And there is a bitterness, also. Normally I can spot exactly from where it originates...this one leaves me baffled...though I'd go from the distillation if pushed. 46%

Benromach Sherry Cask Matured Peat Smoke dist 2010, bott 2018 db (94.5) n23.5 t24 f23 b24 These type of whiskies so often fall flat on their face. This, by contrast, is a magnificent beast of a malt... 59.9%

Benromach Triple Distilled db (88) n23 the firmness to the malt has an almost Irish pot still quality: sharp, yet with a firm, brooding disposition; t22.5 salivating and ultra-clean. Gristy sugars melt into the mix with vanilla upping the weight; f21.5 a slight oak-sponsored bitterness from the more antiquated casks makes its mark; b22 the finish part, a really charming barley character pervades throughout. 50%

Benromach Vintage 1976 db (89.5) n23 t23.5 f21 b22 hardly complex and shows all the old age attributes to be expected. That said...a very comfortable and satisfying ride. 46%

Benromach Wood Finish 2007 Sassicaia db (86.5) n22 t22 f21 b21.5. Now back to the new distillery. Problem with this wood finish is that even when free from any taint, as this is, it is a harsh taskmaster and keeps a firm grip of any malty development – even on a dram so young. A brave cask choice. 45%

BLADNOCH
Lowlands, 1817. David Prior. Working.

Bladnoch 10 Year Old bourbon barrels, bott code: L18/8829 db (91) n22.5 t23 f22.5 b23 Just wonderful to see Bladnoch back in the market place again, and this time obviously receiving the kind of attention in warehouse and tasting lab it deserves. The 10-year-old was for years a Lowland staple before a succession of owners saw it all but vanish off the map. This 10-year-old suggests they have the nucleus of what can again become a much-prized dram. Though a ten-year-old, either some of the casks used in this were a lot older, or there has been heavy usage of first-fill bourbon somewhere along the line, because the tannins have an unusually significant say. The result...rather delicious and you get a hell of a lot for a ten-year-old... 46.7%. ncf.

Bladnoch 11 Year Old bourbon & red wine casks, bott code: L19 WB db **(87.5) n21.5 t23 f21 b22** Certainly no escaping the full- on juiciness of the delivery which broadcasts a full on vividness of the fruit. The malt, though, offers the more alluring backbone, though the two styles have problems integrating at the death. Would love to see this without the wine. 46.7%. ncf. First Release.

Bladnoch 15 Year Old Adela oloroso sherry casks, bott code: L18/8083 db **(91) n22 t23 f23 b23** I still feel a bit like Inspector Clouseau's boss, twitching at the mere thought of a sherry butt. But no need for alarm here: faultless oloroso influence here, indeed coming to the aid perhaps of an initial spirit which may not have been originally up to Bladnoch's excellent name. Surprisingly delightful. 46.7%. ncf.

Bladnoch 17 Year Old Californian red wine finish db **(87.5) n22 t23 f21 b21.5** At its zenith on both nose and delivery, both imparting boiled sweet fruitiness and lustre. After that, as well as spice, a non-sulphured bitterness seeps into the proceedings. 46.7%. ncf.

Bladnoch 27 Year Old bourbon cask finish db **(95) n24.5 t23.5 f23 b24** The best nose of a Lowlander I have encountered for a good number of years. A gem of single malt. 43%. ncf

⬧ **Bladnoch Classic Collection Alinta Peated Release** PX sherry & ex-bourbon casks bott code L23/8026 027 db **(91) n22.5** this is a nose as chunky as the bottle from which the whisky was poured. The cut on this has been very generous and the peat present may have been given a smoky screen to any excesses. Oh, and what peat!! Forget the soft Islay style: this is altogether another animal which revels in its anthracitic acidity and discharged the phenols with nose-nibbling intent. A soft molasses and spotted dog pudding undercurrent sooths when required...; **t23** possibly the fattest delivery of a Lowland whisky I have ever encountered. You need extra jaw muscles to chew your way through this one, with that friable peat caught in those massive oils, the acidic bite escaping the gravitational pull only in startling pulses while the heather honey and fruit which oscillates between a pleasing sweetness and even more delightful tartness; **f22** ultimately a tad untidy due to that generous cut, giving a distinct murkiness to the phenols. However, there is a charm to that intense fruitcake note which comes to the rescue...; **b23** hardly a malt that sits on the fence or lies back and thinks of The Lowlands... Huge in spectacularly un-Bladnoch style. Could do with those cuts being trimmed but you cannot other than simply gasp at the beauty of the peat and myriad sugar and spice tones performing all kinds of delicious antics on the palate. If your quest is the beefiest of Lowlanders, then look no further.... 47%

⬧ **Bladnoch Classic Collection Liora** bourbon and new oak casks nbc db **(92.5) n23.5** pleased to see the distillery has lost none of its citrussy countenance, even though there is a relatively heftiness to this. Though here it is sparkling with strands of acacia honey and inevitable spices considering the cask choices. Indeed, as the malt warms in the hand, the honey gains weight and moves into heather honey territory...; **t23** probably the oiliest delivery to a Bladnoch I have ever encountered. This cut off the stills has incorporated as much body as is possible, so the chewiness is profound. Those drier oils off the still have also impacted early on the sweeter tones gleaned from the oak, creating a complex power struggle between two contrasting styles. By the midpoint it is clear that those honey tones are winning and that a very healthy rich malt back up is moving the entire piece towards an agreeable sweetness; **f23** a very long finale for obvious reasons. Thin acacia honey has piggy-backed onto the denser barley while the vanillas begin to shew a degree of muscle; **b23** some 40 years ago, when I first visited this distillery, it was renowned then for producing probably the lightest of all the Lowland double-distilled single malts and possessed a chalkiness which mingled with the otherwise sweet and untroubled barley. My word: how times change! For a start, back then it would have been unthinkable to see it in bottle at more than 40% abv. This 52.2% partially virgin oak version is a whopper by comparison and almost beyond the realms of imagination a generation ago. The same can be said when about 25 years ago I remember capturing and releasing a barn swallow which had become trapped in the Bladnoch stillhouse. The fragile elegance of that beautiful, deftly coloured bird was a perfect synonym for the whisky itself; on this evidence, today it would have to be a buzzard... 52.2% ncf

⬧ **Bladnoch Classic Collection Vinaya** sherry and bourbon casks bott code L22/8427 285 db **(92.5) n23** a just a lovely fit between the farmhouse cake, the barley sugars and the acacia honey...so delicate and fragile...; **t23.5** the honey on the nose needs second invitation to lead the charge on the plate. Except no there is a fitting waxiness to the honey, too, while the vanillas and intense barley march forward in unison. The barley remains magnificently rich throughout; **f22.5** when a malt is this salivating even in its dying throes, you know you've found a pretty solid whisky. There is a slight, late niggle off a sherry butt, but nothing fatal; **b23.5** a much cleaner-distilled bottling which allows the honey to go about its business unmolested by oils. Really high class, enjoyable malt. 46.7% ncf

Bladnoch Samsara Californian red wine & bourbon casks, bott code: L18/8081 db **(87) n21.5 t23 f21 b21.5** Wine casks at work and not a sulphur atom in sight. However, there is no escaping a certain unscheduled bitterness or the fact that perhaps some of the malt was technically not the greatest ever distilled in Bladnoch's history. The result is a patchy experience, delicious in part, but bitty and bitter in others. Lush though on delivery and the plusses are big ones. 46.7%. ncf.

Bladnoch Talia 26 Year Old red wine casks nbc db **(89.5) n23.5 t22.5 f21.5 b22** Have to say, knowing Bladnoch as well as I do (and loving it even more intensely!) I was a little frustrated by the heavy-handedness of the grape which carries all before it. There is still a residual juiciness from the barley 44%. ncf. 2020 Release.

Bladnoch Single Cask 2020/01 California red wine hogshead, cask no. 38, dist Jan 08, bott Mar 20 db **(90) n22.5 t23 f22 b22.5** A very bold wine influence tends to wipe out the usual charming malt character offered up by Bladnoch at this age. But the wine cask is clean and clear in its design, ensuring a wonderfully flavoursome experience. Though if blind-tasted, I wouldn't have picked Bladnoch in 50 increasingly desperate guesses... 56%. nc ncf sc. 289 bottles.

BLAIR ATHOL
Highlands (Perthshire), 1798. Diageo. Working.

Blair Athol 23 Year Old ex-bodega European oak butts db **(90.5) n23 t23.5 f21.5 b22.5** Very often you think: "Aha! Here's an un-sulphur-treated sherry-matured malt!" And then find long into the finish that the taint turns up and sticks with you for another 20 minutes. Is there a slight trace on this late on? Yes. But it is one of the lightest and least concerning I have encountered this year. Which leaves you with plenty of luscious grape to enjoy... 58.4%. 5,514 bottles. Diageo Special Releases 2017.

Blair Athol Distillery Exclusive Bottling batch no. 01, refill, rejuvenated & American oak ex-bourbon casks, bott code: L9316DQ002 db **(94) n23 t24 f23.5 b23.5** A distillery that has come so far away from its days as a producer of fodder malt for Bells, when the spirit was thin and inconsequential, it is now a malt to be sought after and savoured rather than snubbed. This expression really underlines not just the high quality that this distillery is now capable of but also its depth of character. Delightful. 48%. 6,000 bottles.

Hepburn's Choice Blair Athol 10 Years Old bourbon barrel, dist 2010, bott 2020 **(91) n22.5** the malt shines, glittering with sugars; **t23** quite beautiful: not just the sublime intensity of the barley and the glorious backdrop of semi-bourbon style tannin and Demerara, but the mouth-feel, too...; **f22.5** much drier with late cocoa powder; **b23** the distillery feels very at home at this age and in excellent bourbon cask. Shews off the old-fashioned Perthshire sweetness to maximum effect. Adorable. 46%. nc ncf sc. 187 bottles.

Hepburn's Choice Blair Athol 11 Years Old wine hogshead, dist 2009, bott 2020 **(83.5) n20 t21.5 f21 b21** A very tight malt which seems to be clamped in leg irons. Very little sweetness escapes the dull fruit, though for one all too brief moment it does open up after delivery and relaxes. 46%. nc ncf sc. 383 bottles.

Old Malt Cask Blair Athol Aged 24 Years sherry butt, cask no. 17193, dist Jun 95, bott Sept 19 **(88) n21.5 t22.5 f22 b22** Fat and malty, the sherry butt makes no great impression, other than perhaps upping the viscosity slightly. Some lovely spices in action with the vanilla. Busy and satisfying. 50%. nc ncf sc. 294 bottles.

Old Malt Cask Blair Athol Aged 25 Years sherry butt, cask no. HL18205, dist Mar 1995, bott Feb 2021 **(89.5) n23** when the fruit is this clean an understated and the cask so confident yet naturally modest, the resulting marriage of styles usually charms and entices. This is no different...; **t23** superb mix of salivating barley even now, moistening the lush, though slightly pithy grape. A light butterscotch touch, too...; **f21.5** the cask tires slightly, but the spices keep the flame burning; **b22.5** not the perfect sherry butt but one good enough to cover the quarter century with something to spare and keep the complexity levels high. 50%. nc ncf sc. 293 bottles.

Old Malt Cask Blair Athol Aged 25 Years sherry butt, cask no.HL18688, dist Nov 1993, bott May 2021 **(90.5) n23** wonderfully complex if you give it ample time to come alive. At first it appears the wine has the exclusive rights on all aromas, but slowly the oak makes its mark and always in barely discernible layers. At the same time some aspects of the grape lightens and just becomes faintly crisper and more juicy; **t23** silky textured and muscovado sugared. The tannins hold medium weight while the dryness of the grape skin grows in importance; **f21.5** just a little bitter as the tiring oak takes a toasty turn; **b23** the Murray Method and 20 minutes of your times will show this in a light to pleasantly surprise you. 50% sc 197 bottles

Skene Blair Athol 2015 Southern Highlands Scotch Single Malt first-fill Oloroso sherry, cask no: 900093, dist: 2015, bott: 2020, db **(89.5) n21** dull, vaguely off key despite a attendant grapey sugars; **t23** a dull initial delivery...and then...whoomph! It just goes up in a flame of oak-spattered barely, surprising considering its age. But the layering is sublime, taking full advantage of the limited oil available. The malt pulses proudly but the spice and fruit hit the spot...; **f22.5** a lovely spiced fade with outline vanilla. Dries to a warm, chalky, finish; **b23** one of those rare malts where the nose lies. Totally lacking in inspiration when sniffed at, it comes alive in the glass to a delightful degree. *48% ncf, 246 bottles*

The Whisky Cask Blair Athol 12 Years Old Oloroso Sherry Finish dist 2007 bott 2020 oloroso finish db **(90.5) n23 t23 f22 b22.5** a massively graped-up Blair Athol where the fruit is ripe and sweet and salivation levels run high. *56.4%*

BOWMORE
Islay, 1779. Morrison Bowmore. Working.

Bowmore Aged 10 Years Spanish oak sherry casks & hogsheads, bott code: L172033 db **(92.5) n23.5 t23.5 f22.5 b23** A very happy marriage between some full on peat and decent sherry butts makes for the intense malt promised on the label. *40%*.

Bowmore Aged 12 Years bott code: L182208 db **(86.5) n22 t22 f21 b21.5** This is some surprise package. With the phenol level being markedly down on the last bottle of this I encountered and the oils wearing thin long before the end – not assisted by the 40% abv – this Bowmore never quite gets going. Perhaps the midpoint has something to latch on to and thoroughly enjoy where the peat and oils do find accord. But it is far too short-lived. *40%*.

⟜ **Bowmore Aged 12 Years**, bott code L2266SB3 db **(91.5) n22.5** the peat drifts through with a nudge and a wink rather than at full throttle. The vaguest ozone sharpness kicks in, too. But it is the deployment of the light seaweed and sea salt which impresses most; **t23** though a 12 year old, there is plenty of grassy malt to combine with the controlled smoke to make for an excellent delivery. A mix of muscovado and molassed sugars filter through alongside the peat, the sympathetic oils ensuring even extra softness; **f23** just love those spices which arrive like one of those argumentative types that must have the last word. Even at the death, though the malt is still present and pulsing out its low intensity toasty smoke; **b23.5** I'm always delighted when a malt surprises me for the better. The last few bottles of this I had tasted had been far from memorable. This, however, is an excellent representation of this great distillery. Would have been better still had the abv been up a notch or two. *40%*

Bowmore Aged 15 Years 1st fill bourbon casks, bott code: L172034 031 db **(88) n23.5 t22 f21 b21.5** This was going swimmingly until the caramel just went nuts. I know first-fill bourbon casks are at work here, but hard to believe that was all natural... *43%*.

Bowmore Aged 15 Years sherry cask finish, bott code: L172073 db **(91) n23 t22.5 f22.5 b23** A sherry influenced whisky outpointing a bourbon cask one....how often will you find that in this book...? *43%*.

Bowmore Aged 15 Years bott code: L9289SB323250923 db **(94) n23.5 t23.5 f23 b24** A joyful experience with the peat in expansive mode and the Victory V cough sweet adding the right kind of toasted sugars. An easily quaffable kind of 15-year-old...not something you normally associate with a whisky of this good age. I just love to see Bowmore in this kind of mood. *43%*.

Bowmore Aged 18 Years Oloroso & Pedro Ximénez casks, bott code: L172067 060 db **(82) n20.5 t22.5 f19 b20** A dirty old nose – and I don't just mean the peat – pre-warns of the furry finish. But there is no denying the sheer joy of the voluptuous grape grappling with the phenols on delivery and in the wonderful moments just after. *43%*.

Bowmore Aged 18 Years bott code: L9172SB322071130 db **(87) n21.5 t22 f21.5 b22** A grouchy, moody dram inclined to bite your head off. The nose is positively snarling with the peat offering no give whatsoever and happy to give you a bit of the old acid. While the delivery likewise gives your what for with a volley of dry, unforgiving, peaty expletives. The finish is no less harsh. Only a few curt molasses and hickory notes offer solace. *43%*.

Bowmore Aged 23 Years Port Matured db **(86) n22 t22 f21 b21.** Have you ever sucked Fisherman's Friends and fruit pastels at the same time, and thrown in the odd Parma Violet for good measure...? *50.8%*

Bowmore Aged 25 Years Small Batch Release db **(85.5) n21 t22 f21 b21.5.** Distilled at the very heart of Bowmore's peculiar and uniquely distinctive Fisherman's Friend cough sweet era. You will never find a more vivid example. *43%*

Bowmore Aged 30 Years db **(94) n23 t24 f23 b24** A Bowmore that no Islay scholar should be without. Shows the distillery at its most intense yet delicate; an essay in balance and how great oak, peat and fruit can combine for those special moments in life. Unquestionably one of the best Bowmores bottled this century. *43%*

Bowmore Black 50 Year Old db **(96.5) n25 t24 f23 b24.5** a little known fact: a long time ago, before the days of the internet and a world of whisky experts who outnumber the stars that puncture the sky on the very darkest of nights, I actually tasted the first Black Bowmore in their very basic blending lab and gave it the required seal of approval before they allowed it to hit the shelves. It wasn't a 50-year-old beast like this one, though. And it proves that though something may have reached half a century, it knows how to give pleasure on at least a par with anything younger ... 41%

Bowmore Black Rock oak casks db (87.5) n22.5 t22 f21 b22. A friendly, full bodied dram whose bark is worse than its bite. Smoked toasted fudge is the main theme. But that would not work too well without the aid of a vague backdrop cinnamon and marmalade. If you are looking for a gentle giant, they don't come more wimpish than this. 40% WB15/336

Bowmore Devil's Casks III db (92.5) n23 t23 f23.5 b23.5 a whisky created by Charles Williams, surely. So, at last...I'm in league with the devil...! Hawwwww-hhaaaa-haaaaaa!!!! 56.7%

Bowmore No.1 first fill bourbon casks, bott code: L172026 db (91.5) n23 t23 f22.5 b23 Bowmore was never the most peaty of Islay's malts. But here the phenols are at their shyest. Delicate and all a rather sexy tease... 40%.

Bowmore Small Batch "Bourbon Cask Matured" db (86) n22 t22 f21 b21. A big improvement on the underwhelming previous Small Batch from this distillery, then called "Reserve", though there appears to be a naivety to the proceeding which both charm and frustrate. The smoke, hanging on the grist, is very low key. 40%.

Oxhead Dram Addicts Bowmore 1997 db (94.5) n23.5 t23.5 f23.5 b24 When you catch the distillery in its friendliest mode, like now, you see there is far more than just peat to prize. The subtlety of the spice working in tandem with thinned, molten honeycomb and concentrated butterscotch is hard not to applaud. And then factor in the tantalising smoke, both as a background rumble and vaguely earthier base ...and you have before you a dram of quiet beauty... 43.2%

Valour Islay Single Malt Bowmore Aged 24 Years 2nd-Fill Sherry hogshead, cask no: 9002100, dist: 16/02/1997, bott: 14/05/2021 (93.5) t23.5 t24 f22.5 b23.5 Sherry influence without the damaging sulphur hit. Wonderful! A beautifully weighted malt shewing the distillery in lively fashion. Far from your standard Bowmore. 54.8% sc

Wemyss Malts Black Gold Bowmore 1989 30 Years Old hogshead (82.5) n20 t22.5 f19 b21 This malt technically fails on so many levels. Something over the 30 years or so has happened to this cask that is very odd. All kinds of strange notes (most of them metallic, but also a bit of the swimming pool on the nose), that, as a blender, I'd mark off and keep away from any whisky I'm working with. Yet, despite all that, despite its metallic tang, there is also something irresistibly attractive about this brute. 50%. nc ncf sc. 175 bottles.

Wemyss Malts Kilning The Malt Bowmore 1996 23 Years Old hogshead (94) n23.5 t23.5 f23 b24 If this were any more polite a malt, it'd do a curtsy before a-leaping onto your taste buds... 47.9%. nc ncf sc. 218 bottles.

Wilson and Morgan Bowmore 21 Years Old Oloroso Finish dist 2000 bott 2021 db (87.5) n24 t23.5 f18b22 once upon a time there were many who worked at Bowmore who believed that 21 years was the optimum age for this distillery. Who will argue on the early evidence of this bottling...? 56.5%

BRAEVAL
Speyside, 1974. Chivas Brothers. Working.

Skene Braeval American Oak 2014 Speyside Scotch Single Malt hogshead cask no: 9900153, dist: 30th Sept 2014, bott: Dec 2020, db (87.5) n21.5 t22.5 f21.5 b22 A skittish, underdeveloped malt of fascinating unpredictability. The thin nose shews a weakness or two and doesn't prepare you for the juicy, malty onslaught that is to come on delivery. The gristy sugars fare melt in our mouth as the spices ramp up the overall depth. The finish is predictably fragile, but still clings to enough malty citrus and spice to make for an enjoyable encounter. High octane, refreshing barley-water... 50% ncf 327 bottles

BRORA
Highlands (Northern), 1819–1983. Diageo. Closed.

Brora 34 Year Old refill American oak hogsheads db (88.5) n22.5 t22 f22 b22 The nose kinds of sums things up perfectly: skeletal fingers of age are all over this: citrus offers sinew and a little smoke the flesh...but time is catching up... 51.9%. 3,000 bottles. Diageo Special Releases 2017.

BRUICHLADDICH
Islay, 1881. Rémy Cointreau. Working.

Bruichladdich 2005 12 Year Old fresh sherry hogshead, cask no. 998, dist 20 Jul 05, bott 2018 db (92.5) n23.5 t24 f23 b22 There is virtually no balance to this whisky, yet it somehow works. A whisky every home should have: if you receive a bit of a surprise in your life, this will violently shake you back into the world... 60.4%. nc ncf sc. 372 bottles. Bottled for MacAlabur.

Bruichladdich Black Art 7 Aged 25 Years db (95) n23.5 t24 f23.5 b24 Have to say I do love this whisky. One of the most complex Bruichladdichs since its conversion back to a peaty distillery with a delivery that gives you something slightly different each time you taste it....as a genuinely great 25-year-old should be. 48.4%.

Bruichladdich Islay Barley Aged 5 Years db (86) n21 t22.5 f21.5 b21. The nose suggests a trainee has been let loose at the stills. But it makes amends with an almost debauched degree of barley on delivery which lasts the entirety of the experience. Heavens! This is different. But I have to say: it's bloody fun, too! 50%. nc ncf.

Bruichladdich The Laddie Eight Years Old American & European oak, cask no. 16/070 db (83) n21.5 t22 f19 b20.5 Doesn't chime anything like so well as the Classic Laddie, for instance. The sugars surge and soar in impressive manner, the mid-range smokiness benefiting. But there is a tightness which does very few favours. 50%.

Bruichladdich Laddie Classic Edition 1 db (89.5) n23 t23 f21 b22.5. You probably have to be a certain vintage yourself to fully appreciate this one. Hard to believe, but I can remember the days when the most popular malt among those actually living on Islay was the Laddie 10. That was a staunchly unpeated dram offering a breezy complexity. Not sure of the age on this Retroladdich, but the similarities almost bring a lump to the throat... 46%

Bruichladdich Scottish Barley The Classic Laddie db (78.5) n20 t21.5 f18 b19. Not often a Laddie fluffs its lines. But despite some obviously complex and promising moves, the unusual infiltration of some sub-standard casks has undone the good of the local barley. If you manage to tune out of the off-notes, some sublime moments can still be had. 50%. nc ncf sc.

⬥ **Bruichladdich The Classic Laddie Scottish Barley Unpeated** bott code 2019/02/27 (90.5) n22.5 super intense barley with a massive vanilla thread; t22.5 the vanilla and barley are playing power games from the moment they set foot on your palate. These manoeuvres aren't exactly subtle, but they are juicy and salivating; f23 now, that's better! The impressive oils offer a shooting sheen and allow the warring factions to at last find common ground. Some rather lovely, dried walnut and cocoa join the late-arriving spices; b22.5 plays out on the palate as boasting something nearer 60% abv than 50%, probably because of the intense battling between the malt and the vanilla elements, neither of which are initially willing to give way to the other. I remember 40 years ago when Laddie unpeated was easily the biggest-selling malt in Islay. That was as docile as a dram as this is feisty. 50% ncf

The Laddie Ten American oak db (94.5) n24 t23.5 f23 b24 This, I assume, is the 2012 full strength version of an Islay classic which was the preferred choice of the people of Islay throughout the 70s, 80s and early 90s. And I have to say that this is already a classic in its own right.... 46%. nc ncf.

The Laddie Sixteen American oak db (88) n22 huge natural caramels dipped in brine; t22.5 very even and gentle with a degree of citrus perking it up; f21.5 reverts to caramels before the tannins strike hard; b22 oak 'n' salt all the way... 46%

The Laddie Twenty Two db (90.5) n24 t23 f21.5 b22 Fabulous coastal malt, though the oak is a presence always felt. 46%

Octomore 7.1 5 Years Old ex-bourbon casks, cask no. 16/080 db (96) n23.5 t24.5 f24 b24 Fan-bloody-tastic...!! A kid of a whisky which sorts the men from the boys... 57%.

Octomore 7.2 5 Years Old bourbon & Syrah casks, cask no. 15/058 db (81.5) n21 t23 f18 b19.5 I love the fact that the sample bottles I have been sent under "education." Brilliant! An hilarious first. But here, if anything is to be learned by those who for some reason don't already know, is the fact that you don't piss around with perfection. Five-year-old Octomore in bourbon cask is a joy that has just about proved beyond description for me. Pointlessly add wine casks – and the sulphur which so often accompanies them – and you get a whisky very much reduced in quality and stature. Some superb moments on this, especially round the time of the warts-and-all delivery. But as it settles the faults of the Syrah casks slowly become clear. What a shame. And waste of great whisky. An education, indeed! 58.5%.

Octomore 10 db (95) n24 t24 f23 b24 When I am tasting an Octomore, it means I am in the home straight inside the stadium after running (or should I say nosing and tasting) a marathon. After this, there are barely another 20 more Scotch malts to go and I am closing in on completing my 1,200 new whiskies for the year. So how does this fare? It is Octomore. It is what I expect and demand. It gives me the sustenance and willpower to get to the crossing line. For to tell you guys about a whisky like this is always worth it...whatever the pain and price. Because honesty and doing the right thing is beyond value. Just ask David Archer. 50%.

Octomore Edition 10.1 Aged 5 Years PPM 107 db (95) n23.5 t24 f23.5 b24 We've been here before. Except maybe this one has a bit more vanilla on hand, as well as some sweetening oils.... 59.8%.

Octomore Edition 10.2 Aged 8 Years PPM 96.9 db (94) n23 t24.5 f23 b23.5 It's an interesting debate: is Octomore at its best when very young and peat has full control? Or when matured and the oak has had a chance to create a more nuanced whisky? I'd say from this evidence, and other Octomores I have seen over the years it is at is best when a little younger than this, as here the peat, despite the extraordinary complexity on the delivery, has just lost some of the power of its magic. *56.9%.*

Octomore Edition 10.3 Aged 6 Years PPM 114 db **(96.5) n**24 **t**24 **f**24 **b**24.5 Bloody hell...!! What peat...!!! Yes, we have been down this road before but this one has taken us into a sooty-dry cul-de-sac. Have you ever had an enormous whisky? Yes...? Well, that'll be a little minnow you'll need to throw back against this smoke-billowing beast. *61.3%.*

Octomore Edition 10.4 Aged 3 Years PPM 88 db **(95.5) n**24 **t**24 **f**23.5 **b**24 If you take this whisky for what it is: a very young hugely peated monster of a malt then you'll be very happy indeed. This is one crazy, mixed up kid. And one hell of a smoky one, too. More than great fun. It is a right of passage: for both the whisky and its consumer... *63.5%.*

Port Charlotte Aged 10 Years db **(95) n**23.5 **t**24 **f**23.5 **b**24 Very high quality and teasingly complex peated malt. *50%.*

Port Charlotte Heavily Peated db **(94.5) n**23 **t**24 **f**23.5 **b**24 Rearrange the following two words: "giant" and "gentle". *50%*

⟐ **Port Charlotte Heavily Peated Aged 10 Years** cask 3245 bott code 2022/01/20 db **(95.5) n**25 cattle byre earthy: farmyard pungent. Big, volumous, engulfing smoke with a little spearmint rubbed in. But, for all its enormity, for its ability to swallow you whole in its beguiling peaty vapour, it is just so disarmingly gentle with it....One of the great whisky noses of the year; of its type, perfect, in fact...; **t**23 after the cumulonimbus of a cloud of smoke on the nose, the subtext on the palate of a much more brittle delivery comes as a bit of a shock. Sandwiched between the phenols is a remarkable wave of mouth-watering gristy malt, just abounding with sugars; **f**23.5 the finish is outstanding. Just the right amount of oils allows this to hit the palate without ever becoming cloying and invites the peat to slowly make its exit with a series of bold, yet always charming, thrusts and counterthrusts with the spices rising and then fading in rhythm. Just a light dusting of cocoa towards the finish as the late vanillas make their mark, too; **b**24 as to be expected, there is plenty of the farmyard about this one, especially on the nose. And as someone when in England who, lives in the country...just wonderful...! On the nose, the malt resembles a gaseous planet of its own. But your exploring tastebuds finds that there is, after all, an outer crust to this giant. A huge malt and even though working to script, still full of surprises...and delights. *50%*

Port Charlotte Islay Barley 2011 Aged 6 Years db **(95) n**23.5 **t**24 **f**23.5 **b**24 There is a controlled intensity to this that is borderline frightening. A malt whisky of majestic beauty. *50%.*

Port Charlotte Islay Barley 2012 Aged 6 Years db **(92) n**23 a pretty abrasive, acidic kick to the phenol; **t**23.5 a softer body than the norm with more oils, contrasting vividly with the nose; **f**22.5 the peats have set leaving only an oily and vanilla-rich glow; **b**23 it has been a privilege, as well as great fun, to line up all three Port Charlottes together and compare their varying merits, their similarities, their divergencies. It has also been an education, because the beauty of whisky is that you learn from every mouthful – or should – no matter how long you have been in the game. *50%.*

⟐ **Vintage Bottlers Port Charlotte 21 Years Old** rum barrel, cask no 260, dist 18/07/01, bott 16/08/22 **(89) n**23 **t**23 **f**21 **b**22 The peat to this is so compact to both the nose and delivery, you are wondering what tools you may have in the shed to loosen it. It makes for a smokiness that is less than all its parts. That said, a mild eucalyptus note does draw into the phenol to the extent of making the eyes water. The oak contribution is a curious one, first offering that brief jolt is eucalyptus, then an almost American-stye hickory bent (doubtless through mingling with the peat) and then, finally, an off-key bitterness from some spent tannins. A mixed bag. *48.7% sc 259 bottles*

BUNNAHABHAIN
Islay, 1881. Burn Stewart Distillers. Working.

Bunnahabhain Aged 12 Years db **(85.5) n**20 **t**23 **f**21 **b**21.5. Lovers of Cadbury's Fruit and Nut will adore this. There is, incongruously, a big bourbony kick alongside some smoke, too. A lusty fellow who is perhaps a bit too much of a bruiser for his own good. Some outstanding moments, though. But, as before, still a long way removed from the magnificent Bunna 12 of old... *46.3%. nc ncf.*

Bunnahabhain 12 Years Old bott code: 1903372L512-1116327 db **(84) n**20.5 **t**23 **f**19 **b**21.5 Remains true to the new style of Bunna with its slightly skewed sherry notes on nose and finish compensated for by the fabulously sweet and rich ultra - grapey delivery. The sulphur does stick slightly at the death. Oh, how I would still Wester Home back to the great Bunnas of the early 1980s... *46.3%. nc ncf.*

Bunnahabhain Aged 18 Years db **(93.5) n**24 **t**24.5 **f**22 **b**23 Only an odd cask has dropped this from being a potential award winner to something that is merely magnificent... *46.3%. nc ncf.*

Bunnahabhain XXV Aged 25 Years db **(94) n**23 **t**24 **f**23 **b**24 No major blemishes here at all. Carefully selected sherry butts of the highest quality (well, except maybe one) and a malt with enough personality to still gets its character across after 25 years. Who could ask for more...? 46.3%. nc ncf.

Bunnahabhain 46 Year Old db (91) n24 t23 f21.5 b22.5 Needs a good half hour in the glass to open up and have justice done to it. Perishes towards the end, but the nose and build up to that are remarkably beautiful for a whisky which normally doesn't do age very well... 42.1%.

Bunnahabhain An Cladach bott code: 2001007L512:3719206 db (90.5) n23 t23.5 f21.5 b22.5 For those who prefer their island whiskies to be bold and fulsome. Quite an adventure. 50%. ncf. World Traveller Exclusive.

Bunnahabhain Ceòbanach db (87.5) n21.5 t22.5 f21.5 b22. An immensely chewable and sweet malt showing its years but much in character. A charming liquorice and acacia honey lead then a developing, dry smokiness. Great fun. 46.3%

Bunnahabhain Cruach-Mhòna bott code: 20009961515:2019169 db (89) n23.5 t23 f21 b21.5 Hard to concentrate until you have cleared the water from your eyes. It is not the strength: it is the extraordinary tartness! Technically not the greatest: the messy finish underlines that. But the nose and delivery are something else entirely. 50%. nc ncf. Travel Retail Exclusive.

Bunnahabhain Darach Ùr Batch no. 4 db (95) n24 t24.5 f23 b23.5 Because of my deep love for this distillery, with my association with it spanning some 30 years, I have been its harshest critic in recent times. This, though, is a stunner.. 46.3%. nc ncf.

Bunnahabhain Eirigh Na Greine bott code: 1979539L512:4919127 db (89.5) n23 t23 f21.5 b22 A sweet, spicy, complex Bunna but with a curiously thin shell. 46.3%. nc ncf. Travel Retail Exclusive.

Bunnahabhain Moine 7 Year Old Oloroso Finish db (85) n22 t23.5 f18 b21.5 The faults are apparent on both nose and finish especially. But the grape intensity of the delivery is, momentarily, something special. 60.1%.

Bunnahabhain Stiùireadair bott code: 1910838L514:1919015 db (83.5) n21 t22 f20 b20.5 Although the sherry influence is clear of any sulphur content, the grape never comes across articulately on this, either on the nose or delivery. There are some brief moments on arrival when the malt goes directly into delicious fruitcake mode but it is all too brief. From then on it never sits comfortably. The stiùireadair, the helmsman, has steered the wrong course... 46.3%. nc ncf.

⟡ **Bunnahabhain Stiùireadair**, bott code 24350S3L5 22336 db (84) n21 t23 f19.5 b20.5 I remember being a little perplexed the last time I tasted this – and a couple of years on I am still scratching my head. Maybe I'm hampered by remembering what kind of dram this was 40 years ago when I used to holiday in one of the original worker's cottages and drink the 12-year-old by the roaring peat fire as the wind rattled everything that wasn't nailed down. The entire spirit here feels different – wrong, even. The nose never finds harmony and even the posturing malt seems a little out of sorts. The delivery is monumentally mouth-watering: I'll give it that. The young barley is almost three dimensionally sharp and there are five or six seconds of unbridled joy as the malt digs deep to entertain. But then it flounders towards the finish, so we are back to untidy, discordant notes and even a little tang from the sherry. Still not the Bunna I so deeply love. 46.3% nc ncf

Bunnahabhain Toiteach A Dhà bott code: 1767068L510:0218253 db (86) n22 t22 f21 b21 A heavyweight malt which first thumps you as hard as possible with unreconstructed peat. And after you get up off the floor from that, you are rabbit punched by chunky fruit notes. Eschews subtlety and charm for impact. But have to say it is a great improvement on the earlier Toiteach. Just a slight technical flaw to this, evident on the finish in particular. 46.3%. nc ncf.

Bunnahabhain Toiteach Un-Chillfiltered db (75.5) n18 t21 f17.5 b19. A big gristy, peaty confrontation on the palate doesn't hide the technical fault lines of the actual whisky. 46%. ncf.

⟡ **Art Edition No 4 Bunnahabhain Aged 13 Years** sherry cask, dist 2009, bott 2022 (94) n23.5 the cleanest sultana. The most teasing of now you see it, now you don't spices. The most fragile of lemon blossom honey tones. The most intrinsic of vanillas...; t23.5 salivating and disarming on delivery, the fruit is fresher than on the nose and heavier, too. The spices arrive early and tease just as on the nose while the tannins start as merely a hint but by the midpoint are firmly established...; f23 ooh, much drier here with just a vague salty kick to briefly gee up both the malt and tannins. But dries with mounting vanilla and does so gracefully; b24 easily one of the most faultless sherry butts I have encountered for a good while. If anything, it is too good: the fruit almost devours all traces of the distillery's style until you reach the very end. Delightful. 53.2% nc ncf 60 bottles Whiskyjace

⟡ **Kingsbury Gold Bunnahabhain Aged 17 Years** cask no 3600, dist 2004 (95.5) n23.5 get those spices... get that intense malt... get that melted muscovado sugar... get the complexity of those tannins. And just get the way the raisins are draped all over it... rrrrrrrr!!!!! t24 now that is just unfair... You are just coming to terms with the way the elements have danced so seductively over your nose.... Now the malt uses all of the rich oils available to cling to every atom of your tongue and grind its malty body into your taste buds. The spices sizzle but are kept under control by outpourings of heather honey followed by sherry trifle; f24 ever so long and now heading into the realms of sophistication. The layering is exquisite with all the contours spotted earlier taking turns in pulsing their presence before the barley and vanillas sign off...; **b24** an admission: when I first saw this whisky and saw it had come from a turn of the century sherry butt, my heart sank, and I left this to the last tasting of the session...expecting sulphur to bring a miserable curtain down on a long day. How wrong could I be: this is faultless sherry at work, and it offers its fruity charm in a way that the barley. No such thing as a sexy whisky, eh? Sexist to say so, apparently. What utter rot: this is the epitome of a sexy malt, playing its erotic moves out on your tongue and palate with not a hint of shame. *62.8% sc 426 bottles*

⬩ **Kingsbury Gold Staoisha Bunnahabhain Aged 8 Years** cask no 1131, dist 2013 **(94)** **n23** adorably young, so the smoke has a green tinge to it. This freshness gives a wonderful clarity to the smoke, almost as though it is see-through, where on the other side can be found grassy, grapefruit tones; **t23.5** really lovely arrival on the palate with those citrus, grassy tones allowing the tastebuds to go into full salivating mode. The smoke offers what little weight is present, both in depth and from a phenolic pressure bearing down on the barley; **f23.5** long with light cocoa tones mixing with the barley and phenol tail. Late vanillas dry things a little; **b24** the kind of whisky which gives young malts a fantastic name. Stupendously refreshing, you'd be hard pressed to find a more beautifully appointed 8-year-old Scotch peated single malt this year... *59.6% sc 180 bottles*

Old Malt Cask Bunnahabhain Aged 27 Years refill hogshead, cask no. 17325, dist Nov 91, bott Oct 19 **(96.5)** **n24.5** **t24** **f23.5** **b24.5** Old school Bunna at its oldest! Love it! A truly exceptional cask that demands half an hour just to get to know. *50%. nc ncf sc. 209 bottles.*

Single & Single Bunnahabhain 2002 17 Year Old bourbon cask **(94.5)** **n23** **t23.5** **t24** **b24** A meticulously complex whisky and worthy 500th sample I have tasted this year in very trying circumstances... *54%. sc. 197 bottles.*

Wilson & Morgan Barrel Selection Bunnahabhain 18 Year Old sherry butt, cask no. 1432, dist 2001, bott 2019 **(90)** **n22.5** **t23.5** **f21.5** **b22.5** Bunna's history with sherry butts has not been the best over the last 30 years. So I feared the worst, to be honest. But this is a very decent and honest cask with no discernible off notes. The spices are x-certificate and its only weakness is over-active tannin. Otherwise a superb whisky experience. *59.7%. sc.*

Wilson & Morgan Barrel Selection Bunnahabhain Heavy Peat dist 2014, bott 2019 **(92.5)** **n23** **t23** **f23** **b23.5** Young and not the slightest attempt at subtlety. But when you have an Islay at this age, it isn't subtlety you are looking for.... *48%.*

⬩ **Valour Whisky Bunnahabhain 30 Years Old** cask no 5390, dist 25/11/91, bott 08/12/21 **(94)** **n23.5** a lovely, if unexpected, mix of digestive biscuit and ground walnut. The sugars are sparse but deft enough to make a difference...; **t23** the malt trundles through at the most leisurely pace, shaking hands here and there with the oak which has purpose from the first moment. The honey is likewise cautious but, just as on the nose, arrives in sufficient quality to make its mark; **f23.5** this is the highlight: so many super-subtle elements arriving together in unison. The heather honey has reduced but now teams up with thin golden syrup to weave intricate notes into the toasty tannin, frothing cocoa and niggling spices...; **b24** old school, unpeated Bunna which gives a glorious exhibition of piling on the pleasure. Starts slowly but builds into something of exceptional complexity. You don't see this distillery in this kind of mood very often. *50.1% sc 147 bottles*

CAOL ILA
Islay, 1846. Diageo. Working.

Caol Ila Aged 12 Years db **(89)** **n23** **t23** **f21** **b22.** A telling improvement on the old 12-y-o with much greater expression and width. *43%*

Caol Ila Aged 18 Years bott code: L9185CM008 db **(82.5)** **n21.5** **t22** **f19** **b20** Still improving – slightly. Certainly a little more sweetness early on to bolster the weak phenols. But the off kilter finish remains poor. Still one of the great mysteries of Scotch whisky in how they manage to make a bottling so unrepresentative of such a great distillery.... *43%.*

Caol Ila Aged 25 Years bott code: L71860M000 db **(95.5)** **n24** **t24** **f23.5** **b24** Even after all these years this malt can not only lay on its Islay credentials with its eyes closed, but does so with an almost haughty air, cocking a smoky snook at the passing quarter of a century... *43%.*

Caol Ila 30 Year Old refill American oak & European oak casks, dist 1983 db **(96.5)** **n24** **t24.5** **f24** **b24** Indisputably, one of the most complex, well-rounded and complete Caol Ilas I have tasted since they rebuilt the distillery... *55.1%. 7,638 bottles. Diageo Special Releases 2014.*

Caol Ila Moch db **(87)** **n22** **t22** **f21** **b22** I think they mean "Mocha"... *43%.*

Caol Ila Moch bott code: L9234CM009 db **(92.5)** **n23** light but uses its oils to lock in the ulmo and acacia honey with the sleepy peat; **t23** silky, lightly oiled but the spice lift is stunning. The smoke works in a similar upward projectory; **f23** long, the ulmo honey returns with a little banana. The smoke and vanillas have formed a late double act as the spices still tingle; **b23.5** this has upped its

133

game phenomenally. Nothing like the limp bottling I tasted last time, this one really does grab Caol Ila by the horns. The only complaint: should have been at 46%... 43%.

Abbey Whisky Caol Ila Aged 11 Years 2008 hogshead (93) n23.5 t24 f22.5 b23 So what we have here is Caol Ila naked as it were: in the prime of its life and in what it appears to be a Third-fill hogshead. This means you get little colour and only limited interference from the cask, though what is does offer is a beautifully consistent soft vanilla sub plot. This wins because we can see just how sexy this naked body is, with its voluptuous, oily curves and its peaty, scented magnetism. This is beautifully made whisky allowing the grist a free hit on juicy sweetness. This, ladies and gentlemen, is Caol Ila exactly as nature intended... 54.2%. sc. 120 bottles.

Art Edition No 3 Caol Ila 2008 (89.5) n22.5 Caol Ila at its most reflective: the smoke and the intense gristy barley are on equal terms, though, slowly mind, an acidic anthracite bite begins to emerge amid quiet semi-zesty tones; t23 the delivery is sharp enough to cut yourself on: both the spices and juicy citrussy tones are enough to make your eyes water! Then.... peace. Either it is a very long finish, or the midpoint is simply bathed in gentle, apologetic phenols; f22 just a tad bitter as all passion is spent and some of the more exhausted tannins take hold; b22 the delivery stands out like a volcano jutting from a calm sea. All the explosiveness is confined to the first three or four flavour waves, which has little sympathy for prisoners. The rest is the calm before and after the storm. 52.6%

Artful Dodger Caol Ila 9 Year Old 2008 (94) n23.5 t23.5 f23 b24 As a 9-year-old, Caol Ila displaying towards the top of its form with an almost improbably degree of gristy sugars on song. Particularly impressive, though, is the laid-back smoke – this distillery can come through a lot peatier than this – and revels in its slightly ashy, drier sub-plot. Makes a mockery of the strength, as this is a real softy. 63.4%. sc.

Chapter 7 Chronicle Caol Ila Small Batch 8 Year Old 1998 first fill bourbon casks, dist May 11, bott Mar 20 (93) n23.5 t23 f23 b23.5 A superb example as to why blenders love working with this malt from bourbon cask. Even at a relatively young 8-years-old you can see how the smoke dishes out power and softness in even doses. The house oils ensure a rounded quality but still lets the light mocha and spice notes off the oak have a good hearing. Not a sensational whisky, but simply one with a massive feel good factor. 49.2%. 893 bottles.

Chapter 7 Caol Ila 2011 Aged 9 Years bourbon barrel, barrel no.157 (92) n22.5 super soft with the peating levels seeming a little lower than the normal 35ppm. This gives the thin molasses a little extra chance to shine; t23.5 the youth of the malt works in its favour as this has the energy to fully concentrate all the peat it can find. The sugars displayed on the nose soon join in the action, too; f23 dry and powdery with a little cocoa and liquorice mixing with the smoke; b23 for a 9-year-old there is so much complexity and layering! 50.4% sc

Chapter 7 Caol Ila 2011 Aged 9 Years first fill bourbon barrel, barrel no.160 (91) n22 a little bubble gum and cream soda intriguingly mix with the smoke; t23 curious: a silky Caol Ila, yet not overly oil dependent. There is a sublime wave of ulmo honey and malt, quite apart from the phenols; f23 usually with this distillery the oils would hit a peak here. But, no! The usual oils have vanished, leaving a much more parched feel to the malt and peat...and still this very unusual intense Malteser candy malt and chocolate finale; b23 as ubiquitous as Caol Ila as independent bottlings may be, casks with this particular shape and personality are virtually unknown. A subtly distinctive and highly enjoyable version. Considering this is only three casks apart from another, quite different bottling, the intrigue can only grow. 52.2% sc

Chapter 7 Caol Ila 2012 Aged 8 Years bourbon hogshead, barrel no.325862 (88) n21 t22 f23 b22 Unusually for Chapter 7 cask, doesn't quite blow you away in the way we have now come to expect. The nose is cranky, aggressive and untidy, while the delivery is a shade too tart. However, as the oils mount so, too, do the soothing praline tones which gives the finish a far more distinguished feel than had once seemed possible. 51.4% sc

Fanandel.dk Caol Ila Aged 8 Years PX octave finish, cask no.301321, dist Feb 2013, bott Apr 2021 (87) n21 t23 f21 b22 Possibly only a PX cask could overcome and dumb down a full bloodied Islay malt. The nose has a strange creosote kick, though the delivery is rather wonderful. First the taste buds are almost massaged to death by the mesmerising hand of the grape; a little smoky blanket is there to keep you warm. But once the bullish peppers disappear, there is very little else to report, save some late milk chocolate. 54.2% sc 66 bottles

The Finest Malts City Landmarks Caol Ila Aged 11 Years bourbon barrel, cask no. 024, dist 2007, bott 2018 (93) n22.5 t23 f23.5 b24 An attractive, no-nonsense Caol Ila that lets the dog see the rabbit. Slightly drier nose than usual, allowing the peat to nip a little while the palate is massaged by a comforting sweetness that balances out the perfectly-weighted phenols. A lovely buttery flourish to the finale, too. Spot on for its age and cask type. 53.2%. nc ncf sc.

The First Editions Caol Ila Aged 8 Years 2010 refill hogshead, cask no. 16790, bott 2019 (92) n22.5 t23.5 f22.5 b23.5 The rough edges to this one act in its favour: complex and bitty, it keeps the taste buds guessing and fully entertained. 59.7%. nc ncf sc. 295 bottles.

The First Editions Caol Ila Aged 10 Years 2010 wine cask, cask no. 18211, bott 2020 **(76)** n19 t21 f17.5 b18.5 Tight, compressed and never for a moment relaxing its usual stride, I would never have recognised this as a Caol Ila. I'm sure some will celebrate the punchiness of the peat and love the all-round aggression. And the acerbic dryness at the death. But, sadly, I'm not one of them... 59.3%. nc ncf sc. 282 bottles.

Glenwill Caol Ila 1990 hogshead, cask no. 1481 **(96)** n24 t24 f24 b24 Exemplary. 53.9%.

Gordon & MacPhail Connoisseurs Choice Caol Ila Aged 15 Years first fill bourbon barrel, cask no. 302298, dist 10 Sept 03, bott 1 Feb 19 **(96)** n23.5 a beautiful controlled pungency to the peat with the tannins mingling to more than make up the numbers; salty and sooty, too; t24 the oils missing in the nose are soon apparent and offering a light gloss to the sweet phenols; a light molasses note sweetens the kippers; f24 the light spices which entered the fray early on stay the pace and add flair to the smoky chocolate; b24.5 classic in every sense. This is what you should expect from a Caol Ila at this age and from this type of cask...and wow! Does it deliver! Truly stunning. 55.7%. sc. 210 bottles.

Hepburn's Choice Caol Ila 8 Years Old refill hogshead, dist 2010, bott 2019 **(87)** n21.5 t21.5 f22 b22 A light rendition with the smoke fleeting and fragmented. Youthful and fresh, it takes a little time to hit its straps. 46%. nc ncf sc. 379 bottles.

Hepburn's Choice Caol Ila 10 Years Old bourbon barrels, dist 2010, bott 2020 **(93)** n23 gorgeously layered peat which retains a disarming humbleness to the obviously rich smoke. A sprig of mint and light butterscotch ups the complexity; t23.5 such a delight! A quiet magnificence to the delivery, the light oils helping to soften and spread the smoke so there is no aggression or crash landing...; f23 the delicate vanillas attached to the drier tannins mount a challenge while the spices remain polite and in tune...; b23.5 anyone with a love for a true, traditional Islay - when a 10-year-old was the standard age - will adore the timeless simplicity of this: beautifully made and beautifully matured. 46%. nc ncf. 369 bottles.

⬧ **Kingsbury Gold Caol Ila Aged 9 Years** cask no 807262, dist 2013 **(95)** n23.5 dense. The phenols seem a bit lower than the normal 35ppm but the tannins are certainly up. This should result in a significant spice pinch on the nose...and it doesn't disappoint. A little orange blossom honey lingers, too...; t24 beautifully mouth-filling delivery. But it is the intense marriage between the barley sugars, molasses and high-grade Venezuelan chocolate, beautifully crowned by a deep phenolic pulse and then rounded by the trademark Caol Ila oils which makes this such a fabulous delivery and then long follow-through. The slow growth of the spice is glorious...; f23.5 after the immaculate intensity of all that has gone before the finish, though deep in polished oak is relatively modest. However, the long mocha and spice finale keeps the attention; b24 for a 9-year-old from a barrel, the rich amber colouring of this malt is quite extraordinary: presumably a first fill cask at work. When cool this malt borders on the nondescript. The Murray Method unlocks almost incredible complexity. Caol Ila like you have rarely seen it before... For a 9-year-old...just...wow! 58.7% sc 261 bottles

Scyfion Choice Caol Ila 2010 Moscatel roxo cask finished, bott 2019 **(90.5)** n21 salty, phenolic...sweaty armpits...t23 the delivery is much more easy to negotiate: the distillery's oils in full spate and trapping the grape at its juiciest. The peat positively swirls...; f23.5 another Caol Ila where the tannins, smoke and grape have fixed up to present a form of chocolate raisin; b23 there will be those out there who will kick down doors to get hold of this and find no fault with it. My view is a little more reserved...perhaps as I had a problem getting past the sweaty armpit nose. But you are rewarded for forsaking the armpits for the body.... 58.9% nc ncf 246 bottles

The Single Cask Caol Ila Aged 6 Years cask no 311895 dist 15.05.13 bott 26.02.20 **(91)** n23 typical for its age Caol Ila bellicose smokiness, backed by nibbling spice and apologetic citrus. The oils allow all parties the usual degree of extra weight; t23 a thick layering of vanilla gives the peat something to hang on to. The midground does see a brief outbreak of muscovado sugar. But it is soon put down by the phenols...; f22 too young to have extended beyond the big peat and vanilla hanging onto the lingering oil; b23 a classic and delightful off the peg young Caol Ila, this one thoroughly enjoying life in an uncomplicated hoggy which allows it to stretch its youthful, peaty wings... 59.1% sc nc ncf 313 bottles

The Single Cask Caol Ila 2007 ex-bourbon barrel, cask no. 307362 **(94)** n22.5 t24 f23.5 b24 Lightly spiced, delicately honeyed and very satisfying. So beautiful... 57.8%. nc ncf sc.

The Single Cask Caol Ila 2008 PX sherry finish, cask no. 318690B **(94)** n23 now there's a miracle: the smoke pierces the grape with some ease. Not complex, but by no means unpleasant; t23.5 now I'm even more amazed: a PX cask giving the smoke and spices a free role. The muscovado sugars have plenty of smoke to contend with; the mouth feel lacks the usual oils and both grape and peat take the opportunity to have their sometime belligerent say. Gloriously salivating; f23.5 calms down now and concentrates entirely on the complexity. Close your eyes and spit the layering between the tannins, smoke, chocolate and almost barely discernible grape and you've got ten minutes to savour; b24 one of the true surprise whiskies of the year. I cannot remember the last time a PX cask was so forgiving...and even beneficial to a whisky. Stunning. *60.9% sc*

The Single Malts of Scotland Reserve Cask Caol Ila 10 Year Old (92) n23 t22.5 f23 b23.5 Anything but one dimensional as the peat performs circus acts here to entertain: from the high wire with an ethereal gristiness rich in molten sugar, to earthier, head in lion's mouth phenols that rumble a dull roar. And the delivery is a cannonball firing you some distance. The tannins hitch a ride on the malt's natural oils and an apologetic degree of vanilla. Oh, and did I mention the sublime late spices...? *48%.*

The Single Malts of Scotland Reserve Cask Caol Ila 11 Year Old (86) n21 t22.5 f21.5 **b21** Gristy, oily and fat. The smoke offers anthracite on the nose and little on the palate. Just not enough oak involvement and never quite gets going. *48%. nc ncf.*

The Whisky Embassy Bonn Caol Ila 11 Year Old hogshead, cask no. 300058 (93) n23 the oak hasn't bothered to turn up here, not least because this is possibly a third fill cask: it is all about the charm of the sweet peat; t23.5 all those luscious oil lines, mingling with the peat and acacia honey...; f23.5 the usual light cocoa slips in with the smoke, but the honey, uninterrupted by tannin, has stayed the course...; b23 there is an unfussy, naked simplicity to this that one can only applaud. Caol Ila seen stripped down to the basic....and it is a very beautiful experience. *58.6%. nc ncf sc.*

Wilson and Morgan Caol Ila 12 Years Old First Fill PX Finish dist 2009 bott 2022 db (94) n23.5 wow!! Just look at the layering of that peat. Rather than becoming one great stodgy mass on the nose, we can see the grape trapped between phenols. All very earthy and cattle byre at times...; t23.5 if round one on the nose was to the peat, then round two here is probably the grape on points. Certainly, the delivery is sharp as a knife as the fruit cuts a path through the smoke. But the phenols recover – with a buttery vanilla prop; f23 not often a PX finish allows the smoke to infiltrate to the end virtually unmolested, but here it is...; b24 great to see an Islay fending off the PX influence to still reveal its true personality. A beautifully weighted, classy and complex malt. *55.3%*

CAPERDONICH
Speyside, 1898. Chivas Brothers. Closed.

Gleann Mór Caperdonich Aged Over 23 Years (86) n22 t22 f20.5 b21.5 Some beautiful banana skins on the nose. But before it slips up on the clumsy finish, the malt and spice do have a few moments of unbridled glory. A slight failing on the cask, though, means the development is limited and always borderline tangy. *59.4%.*

CARDHU
Speyside, 1824. Diageo. Working.

Cardhu 12 Years Old db (83) n22 t22 f18 b21. What appears to be a small change in the wood profile has resulted in a big shift in personality. What was once a guaranteed malt love-in is now a drier, oakier, fruitier affair. Sadly, though, with more than a touch of something furry. *40%*

Cardhu Aged 15 Years bott code: L9207IX005 db (88) n22 t22.5 f22 b21.5 Still a bit of a slave to the toffee, which dominates too often in too many places. But a slight notch up from the last bottle I tasted as there is more heather honey at play now, which works well with the underlying, bitty spices. Yes, enjoyable. But the overall cream toffee theme, however, does this malt no favours at all. *40%.*

Cardhu 18 Year Old db (88) n22.5 t23 f20.5 b22 Very attractive at first. But when you consider what a great distillery Cardhu is and how rare stocks of 18 year old must be, have to say that I am disappointed. The fruit masks the more intricate moments one experiences on a Cardhu to ensure an acceptable blandness and accounts for a poor finish. Why, though, it is bottled at a pathetic 40% abv instead of an unchillfiltered 46% – the least this magnificent distillery deserves – is a complete mystery to me. *40%*

Cardhu Amber Rock db (87.5) n22 t23 f21 b21.5. Amber is the right colour for this: it appears stuck between green and red, not sure whether to go or not. The delivery, in which the tangerine cream is in full flow reflects the better elements of the nose. But the finish is all about being stuck in neutral. Not helped by the useless 40% abv, you get the feeling that a great whisky is trying to get out. The odd tweak and we'll have a winner. That said, very enjoyable indeed. Just even more frustrating! *40%. Diageo.*

Cardhu Gold Reserve bott code L12181X002 db (86) n21 t22.5 f21 b21.5 The last time I tasted this, maybe two or three years ago, it was a rather pale – or perhaps I should say overly dark – representation of one of Speyside's finest malts. As before, a wonderful flare on delivery as the spices light up the delicate honey tones. Then comes the caramel of doom... I had hoped that the owners, Diageo, had seen the error of their ways. They haven't. *40%*

Game of Thrones Cardhu Gold Reserve House Targaryen db (84) n20.5 t22 f20.5 b21 Not having a single television set in any of my three abodes dotted around the place, I have never seen Game of Thrones. Not once. I cannot tell you, even roughly, what the story is about. I have had Bibles to write, distilleries to visit, shows to perform, birds to watch. So I can't tell you whether Targaryen is a person, a place or some kind of fictional spice. Which means I cannot compare the whisky to the name to see if they somehow match. Sorry. However, if it means "a little flat with off-key fruit and plenty of toffee to chew on" then, bingo! They've nailed it. 40%.

CLYNELISH

Highlands (Northern), 1968. Diageo. Working.

Clynelish Aged 14 Years bott code: L7285CM008 db (86.5) n22 t22.5 f20 b21 Very strange. This is one of the world's true Super Distilleries, in the top five of the most beautifully complex in Scotland. Yet from this very subdued, relatively character-bypassed bottling it would be hard to tell. 46%.

Clynelish Aged 14 Years bott code: L9331CM007 db (95) n23.5 t24 f23.5 b24 The last time I tasted a bottle of this it was one of the biggest disappointments of the year. Make no mistake: Clynelish ranks among the best 10 distilleries in the world and is probably second only to Glen Grant on Scotland's mainland. With the supplies they have available, this should be knocking hard and loud on the door of the Whisky Bible's World Whisky of the Year every single Autumn. The fact it doesn't suggests they have taken a more commercial considerations into account than actually allowing Diageo's world-class blenders to fine tune this into the Lamborghini of a malt, seeming content to see it potter around like a top of the range VW Polo. At last, the style and shape is there to be seen...though there is still so much more to reveal... 46%.

Clynelish Distillery Exclusive Bottling batch no. 01, bott code: L9204DQ001 db (89) n23 t23 f21 b22 The first batch of a distillery exclusive bottling: this should be fun. Not bad, but the finale in particular is a tad tame by Clynelish's incredibly high standards while the honey notes – and this distillery probably does honey better than any other in Scotland – have been blunted a little. Look forward to the next batch hitting the 95 point mark, where this extraordinary distillery deserves to be... 48%. 3,000 bottles.

Game of Thrones Clynelish 12 Year Old House Tyrell db (89) n23 t23 f21 b22 Undone slightly by the finish, but that delivery...wow! 51.2%.

Acla Selection Summer Edition Clynelish 21 Year Old hogshead, dist 1996, bott 2018 (89.5) n23 t22.5 f21.5 b22.5 Even by Clynelish standards much of what to be found here is enigmatic, with the lightest ulmo honeys little more than trace elements over vanilla tones that are barely audible themselves. Underdone slight by a bitter note which creeps in from the late middle. But, elsewhere, salivates and caresses at just the right time in the right places. 45.7%.

The Single Malts of Scotland Reserve Cask Clynelish 8 Year Old (85.5) n22 t22.5 f20. b21 Clynelish ordinaire. Unaccountably bitter in the wrong places. 48%.

The Whisky Cask Company Clynelish 1995 sherry butt, cask no 8655, dist Sep 1995, bott Oct 2019 (91) n23 a peppery nose: a moist fruitcake with attitude...and no shortage of nuts, too...; t23.5 the extraordinary complexity to the malt comes to the fore here as few distilleries could see the barley at times battle through so much fruit after all these years. The insane salivation levels on entry are the highlight, though, especially when the orange blossom honey arrives so early; f21.5 just very slightly off-key and bitter, though some compensating chocolate balances well with the toasted raisins...; b23 nearly but not quite an outstanding butt. But forget that late lingering bitterness. The journey to that point really is the reason why we love great whisky with a passion. 49.6% nc ncf sc 590 bottles

COLEBURN

Speyside, 1897–1985. Diageo. Closed.

Gordon & MacPhail Private Collection Coleburn 1981 refill sherry hogshead, cask no. 476, dist 11 Mar 81, bott 14 Mar 19 (94) n25 t22.5; f23 b23.5 It is a strange and interesting fact that the reason this distillery closed down was because blenders didn't much care for the whisky. Back in the 1970s and '80s it built up a deserved reputation for producing a dirty "sulphurous" whisky which many blamed on the worm coolers used in the distilling process. It is curious that the degree of sulphur detected by blenders that made it a distillery non grata was a mere infinitesimal fraction of the degree of sulphur which totally screwed up so many scores if not hundreds of thousands of sherry butts. Yet the Scotch Distillers Association, obedient handbag dogs covering the tracks of their employers and baring their teeth and yapping and snarling at anyone who doesn't feed them, passed it off as just another unique flavour for whisky. And the imagination of egotistical troublemakers such as myself. Such nauseating humbug. The fact is, when well matured the Coleburns of this world produced a beautiful malt whisky, such as this. While whisky, from whichever distillery, sitting in sherry casks treated with sulphur candles are ruined and a pox on the industry no matter however long they remain in the warehouse. And no matter what garbage blow-hards like the SWA PR (Pernicious Rot) department tell you. 55.9%. sc. 101 bottles.

CONVALMORE

Speyside, 1894–1985. William Grant & Sons. Closed.

Convalmore 32 Year Old refill American oak hogsheads db **(96.5) n24 t24 f24 b24.5** Being 32 years old and bottled in 2017, these must be casks from among the very last production of the distillery before it was closed for the final time in 1985. The new spirit then, from what I remember, was not the greatest: thin and with an occasional tendency to be on the rough house side. Time, though, is a great healer. And forgiver. It has passed the last three decades turning from ugly duckling to the most elegant of swans. A sub-species, though, that is on the brink of extinction... 48.2%. 3,972 bottles. Diageo Special Releases 2017.

Gordon & MacPhail Rare Old Convalmore 1975 (94) n23 t24 f23 b24 The rarest of the rare. And in tasting, the flavour map took me back 30 years, to when I used to buy bottles of this from Gordon and MacPhail as a 10-year-old...probably distilled around 1975. The unique personality and DNA is identical on the palate as it was then; except now, of course, there is far more oak to contend with. Like finding an old lover 30 years further on: a little greyer, not quite in the same lithe shape as three decades earlier...but instantly recognisable and still very beautiful... 46%

CRAGGANMORE

Speyside, 1870. Diageo. Working.

Cragganmore 12 Years Old bott code: L9304CM005 db **(84) n21.5 t21.5 f20.5 b20.5** As Cragganmore darkened over the years its malty guile receded, finally to a speck before vanishing altogether. How I long for the days when this malt was first launched and it abounded with the sophisticated complexity that blenders drooled over; a malt that could link the other malts together with its charm and understated complexity. And, as a singleton, would keep you spellbound as you watched the fragile union between oak and grain plot its delicious, unusually dry course. I suspect that the all-powerful owners of this distillery have surrounded themselves with "experts" who will tell them how great this Classic Malt is. Grovel, grovel. I think they need to listen, instead, to a genuine friend who will tell them what, after a brief juicy delivery, a toffee-laden Classic Bore it has now become. 40%.

Cragganmore 15 Years Old 150th Anniversary American oak, bott code: L9116DQ004 db **(94) n23.5 t23.5 f23 b24** Cragganmore is, like most distilleries, at its very best in good American oak. Here the natural caramels have joined the tannins to create about as thick and singular a malty intrigue as you are likely to find. A big whisky, but one that is very easy to scale... 48.8%.

CRAIGELLACHIE

Speyside, 1891. Bacardi. Working.

Craigellachie 13 Year Old db **(78.5) n20 t22 f18 b18.5.** Oily and intense, it shovels on the malt for all it is worth. That said, the sulphur notes are its undoing. 46%

Craigellachie 17 Year Old db **(88.5) n22 t22.5 f22 b22** Technically falls flat on its face. Yet the whole is way better than the sum of its parts...46%

Craigellachie Aged 17 Years bott code: L19011ZA500 db **(94) n23 t23.5 f23.5 b24** This bottling is a great improvement on previous versions I have encountered. What an interesting and delicious dram, shewing the distillery at its best! 46%.

Craigellachie 23 Year Old db **(91.5) n23.5 t23 f22 b23.5** Expected a little house smoke on this (the malt made here in the early 1990s always had delicate phenol), but didn't show. The honey is nothing like so shy. 46% WB16/035

Craigellachie Exceptional Cask Series 1994 bott May 18 db **(91.5) n22.5 t23 f23 b23** How fascinating. Yes, a sherry butt and yes: there is sulphur. But this time it is not from the sherry, as the nose reveals a particular character from the condenser which does accentuate a mild sulphur character. Yet the clean wine casks tell a different, at once puckering yet juicy, story. Beautifully structured and a jaw-aching chewing malt with an unusual late salivation point. 54.8%. Bottled for Whisky L! & Fine Spirits Show.

Old Malt Cask Craigellachie Aged 14 Years sherry butt, cask no. HL18202, dist Aug 200, bott Dec 2020 **(88.5) n22 t23 f21.5 b22** Found myself fascinated by this one: on arrival this initially suggests boiled fruit candy. Then, within a few flavour waves, the sugars have dissipated and we are in dry whisky territory. The nose tingles, but those spices take a little time to arrive and stir the finale up when they do. Pleasant, malty and salivating in the exact spots you'd like them to be. 50%. nc ncf sc. 328 botles.

Scyfion Choice Craigellachie 2007 Saint Daniel wine cask finished, bott 2019 **(81.5) n19 t22 f20 b20.5** The wine and malt are at odds for this thin gruel of an off-key dram. I'm afraid the saints can't be praised on this occasion. 46%. nc ncf sc. 212 bottles.

The Single Cask Craigellachie 2012 oloroso octave finish, cask no. 800622A **(94) n23 t24 f23 b24** Faultlessly clean sherry makes the most of a lively young malt and some outstanding oak. Works a treat as this is one very complex malt. Brilliant! 56.8% sc

Whisky Illuminati Craigellachie 2011 Spanish oak sherry hogshead, cask no. 900328 **(85)**
n21.5 t22.5 f20 b21 Interesting to compare this with their Glentaucher's sherry offering. That
sparkles from first moment to last, while this is a stodgier affair, first with a nose shorn of balance
and then on the palate, the malt making no impact on the grape whatsoever. Unlike with the
'Tauchers. Good spices and pleasant chewiness plus sugary notes to enjoy. But never even hints
at greatness. 67.9%. sc. 100 bottles.

William & Co Spirits Master Life Club CGLH.1 12 Years Old sherry oak octave cask, cask
no. 7526913, dist Jun 08, bott Jun 20 **(86)** n21 t22.5 f21 b21.5 The nose is everything I wish I
could be: young, thin and a little fruity. Its performance on the palate has a lot more going for
it and the delivery is positively voluptuous. Both grain and fruit combine to create a rounded
whole, while the oak is surprisingly upfront. The limited finish, however, is a re-creation of the
nose. 55.3%. 102 bottles.

DAILUAINE
Speyside, 1854. Diageo. Working.

The First Editions Dailuaine Aged 12 Years 2007 sherry butt, cask no. 16641, bott 2019 **(84)**
n21 t22 f20 b21 Juicy on delivery, but very limited from then on. Too dry and austere, especially
in the gagged finish. 57.6%. nc ncf sc. 294 bottles.

Old Malt Cask Dailuaine Aged 12 Years sherry butt, cask no. 16640, dist May 07, bott Jun
19 **(88)** n21.5 t22.5 f22 b22 Makes a laudable attempt to get the into every square inch of
your palate. Ignore the slightly restrained nose and celebrate a very above average Dailuaine
where malt is not just in the centre ground, but works its way into every other aspect of the
experience. A surprise package – for all the right reasons! 50%. nc ncf sc. 271 bottles.

The Single Cask Dailuaine 1997 ex-bourbon barrel, sherry cask finish, cask no. 15563 **(85.5)**
n22 t21 f21.5 b21 A sclerotic malt, set in a grapey straight jacket in which it seems unable
to move. That said, it's a clean finish, the spices busy and entertaining. But all a little too stiff.
Though, as Dailuaines go, I have tasted a lot worse... 52.9%. nc ncf sc.

The Single Cask Dailuaine 2008 1st fill bourbon barrel, cask no. 301698, dist 13 Feb 08 **(91.5)**
n22.5 t23 f23 b23 This is one of those distilleries where the quality of the cask will make a huge
difference in the outcome of the whisky. The structure of this malt is so delicate that it comes
under undue influence from any weaknesses. Here, I'm happy to report there are none. Dailuaine
at its absolute finest. 57.3%. sc.

William & Co Spirits Jotun DLUA.1 11 Years Old sherry oak octave cask, cask no. 10926823,
dist Jan 09, bott Jun 20 **(87.5)** n22 t22.5 f21 b22 A very acceptable sherry cask offers an
attractively clean, fruity range across nose and delivery. For a brief moment or two, the malt is
able to meet the challenge on delivery and follow-through and does so deliciously. But on nose
and, more so, the finish it is found lacking. Good spices to chew on, though. 54.1%. 76 bottles.

Wilson and Morgan Dailuaine 23 Years Old Oloroso Finish dist 1997 bott 2020 db **(90)**
n23 for a Dailuaine nowhere near as unresponsive as usual and here thrusts its malty (and even
slightly smoky?) body at the high-grade grape. The result is complex and elegant; t23 salivating
and at times even eye-watering. Doesn't show its age, as the malt really is fresh and confident
while the tart fruit is the perfect riposte; f21.5 long-ish with a slight orange peel tang; b22.5 a
charmingly understated malt. Usually, Dailuaine would disappear beneath an oloroso cask and
vanish without trace. Not here. There is enough life in the malt to play pretty patterns with the
fruit. There is a mystery, though. I'm getting trace peat on the nose...I've isolated items in the lab...
and it's definitely from the whisky. That may explain the distillery's extra weight... 55.4%

DALLAS DHU
Speyside, 1899–1983. Closed. Now a museum.

Gordon & MacPhail Private Collection Dallas Dhu 1969 refill sherry hogshead, cask no. 1656,
dist 10 Jun 69, bott 12 Jun 19 **(96)** n24.5 t24 f23.5 b24 even in the early 1980s when I began
in earnest my journeys around Scotland seeking out their rarest drams, Dallas Dhu was among
the very hardest to secure. You might find the odd one here and there: indeed, if you did locate
one you bought it, no questions, as you knew it might be a year or two before another surfaced.
By the time I began writing about whisky full time, the distillery had been closed nine years and
even then its rare bottlings were commanding high prices, making it harder to sample. So it is for
that reason I have chosen this as the 1,250th whisky tasted for the Jim Murray Whisky Bible 2021.
It brought a thrill to find a bottle 40 years ago. That feeling has not remotely diminished in the
passing four decades. And the hour spent to understand this magnificently complex malt were
as enjoyable as any of the last four months I have spent tasting... Please nose and taste with the
reverence it deserves... If you open and taste immediately, it scores in the mid 80s. An hour or
so employing the Murray Method...and you'll have one of the whisky experiences of your life....
43.1%. sc. 176 bottles.

Scottish Malts

DALMORE
Highlands (Northern), 1839. Whyte and Mackay. Working.

The Dalmore Aged 12 Years American white oak and Oloroso sherry casks, bott code: L0029 09 29 P/011096 db **(87) n21.5 t23 f20.5 b22** A malt which has changed tack since I last tasted it. Then, as it had been for years, the malt was lost under a blanket of caramel. Now the barley is muzzled by fruit. Attractively at first as the sugars and grape elegantly and decisively make their mark. Sadly, a furry veil, thin but unmistakable, descends to given it a coarse and bitter finish. Glad to see far less toffee in the mix. But if sherry casks must be deployed, then a malt as potentially good as Dalmore deserves clean and faultless ones. 40%.

Dalmore 12 Years Old Sherry Cask (84.5) n21 t21.5 f21 b21 A flat whisky with precious little to say despite the busy spice. Pleasant in its own inoffensive way. But a dullard, nonetheless. 43%

The Dalmore Aged 15 Years American white oak and finished in Oloroso sherry casks, bott code: L0034 08 35 P/011099 db **(90.5) n23 t22.5 f22 b23** It speaks! Normally a whisky that has very little to say for itself. Like the Dalmore 12, looks like a malt in transformation here, though in this case with far more success. Where once, for all its years, it, like the 12, refused to offer little more than toffee, now the mouthfeel has altered and allowed the whisky itself to say a few lines. Just an odd mildly naughty sherry butt, but I suspect these will be frogmarched out for future bottlings... 40%

The Dalmore Aged 18 Years American white oak and Matusalem Oloroso sherry casks, bott code: L0030 04:17 P/011104 db **(88.5) n23 t23 f21 b21.5** There is a timelessness to the nose that takes some of us back to our first whisky experiences of the 1970s; and one presumes that it must have been enjoyed long before then, too. The fusion of malt, light kumquat and moist Dundee cake is truly classic. The mouthfeel, with its kissing oils and glistening sugars are also of noble antiquity. But from the mid-point onwards comes a wailing bitterness from the wine casks which would be better if not there. If only those sugars could be extended and the fruits happier, what a malt this would be! 43%.

The Dalmore 21 Year Old db **(88.5) n22 t23 f21.5 b22** fat, unsubtle, but enjoyable. 42%

The Dalmore 25 db **(88) n23.5 t22.5 f20 b22** The kind of neat and tidy, if imperfect, whisky which, were it in human form, would sport a carefully trimmed and possibly darkened little moustache, a pin-striped suit, matching tie and square and shiny black shoes. 42%.

The Dalmore 30 Year Old db **(94) n24 t24 f22.5 b23.5** A malt, quite literally for the discerning whisky lover. Essays in complexity are rarely so well written in the glass as found here... 45%

The Dalmore Aurora Aged 45 Years db **(90.5) n25 t22 f21.5 b22.** Sophisticated for sure. But so huge is the oak on the palate, it cannot hope to match the freakish brilliance of the nose. 45%

The Dalmore Candela Aged 50 Years db **(96) n25 t24 f23.5 b23.5.** Just one of those whiskies which you come across only a handful of times in your life. All because a malt makes it to 50 does not mean it will automatically be great. This, however, is a masterpiece, the end of which seemingly has never been written. 50% (bottled at 45%).

The Dalmore 1263 King Alexander III db **(86) n22 t22.5 f20 b21.5.** Starts brightly with all kinds of barley sugar, fruit and decent age and oak combinations, plus some excellent spice prickle. So far, so good...and obviously thoughtfully and complexly structured. But then vanishes without trace on finish. 40%

The Dalmore Ceti db **(91.5) n24 t23.5 f21.5 b22.5** A Ceti which warbles rather well... 44.7%

The Dalmore Cigar Malt Reserve Limited Edition db **(73.5) n19 t19.5 f17 b18.** One assumes this off key sugarfest is for the cigar that explodes in your face... 44%

The Dalmore Dominium db **(89.5) n22.5 t23 f22 b22** Like so many Dalmores, starts brightly but as the caramels gather it just drifts into a soupy lump. Still, no taint to the fruit and though the finish is dull you can say it is never less than very attractive. 43%. Fortuna Meritas Collection

The Dalmore Port Wood Reserve American white oak and Tawny port pipes, bott code: L0036 00 25 P/0111 db **(92) n22.5 t23.5 f22.5 b23.5** One of the most dry Port Wood bottlings I have ever encountered. If James Bond insisted on a whisky for his Martini, then it would probably be this. 46.5%.

The Dalmore Regalis db **(86.5) n22.5 t21.5 f21 b21.5.** For a brief moment, grassy and busy. Then dulls, other than the spice. The caramel held in the bottling hall is such a great leveller. 40%. Fortuna Meritas Collection

The Dalmore Valour db **(85.5) n21 t22 f21 b21.5.** Not often you get the words "Valour" and "fudge" in the same sentence. 40%. Fortuna Meritas Collection

The Dalmore Visitor Centre Exclusive db **(95.5) n25 t24 f22.5 b24** Not exactly the easiest distillery to find but a bottle of this is worth the journey alone. I have tasted some sumptuous Dalmores over the last 30-odd years. But this one stands among the very finest. 46%

The Dalmore Quintessence db **(91) n22 t23.5 f22 b23.5** A late night dram after a hard day. Slump into your favourite chair, dim the lights, pour yourself a glass of this, warm in the hand and then study, quietly, for the next half hour. 45%.

Deer, Bear & Moose Dalmore Aged 14 Years sherry butt, dist Oct 04, bott May 19 **(84.5)** **n19 t23 f20.5 b22** While the nose may be tight and unresponsive, the delivery is an orgy of golden syrup and spiced fruit. Pity the sulphur also reveals itself slightly on the finish, too... 57.4%. nc ncf. Flaviar & Friends.

⟫ **Whisky Republic Dalmore 29 Years Old** bourbon hogshead, cask no.84, dist 01/90, bott 06/19 **(89) n23** the sensual nose creaks with old age. We are in exotic fruit territory, but the tannins have added an extra oaky phalanx to the attack. The result is overcooked, sugar-free gooseberry tart to accompany those gentler fruits; **t22.5** beautiful structure on delivery, the mouthfeel bathing in the barley. But the promiscuous oak spotted on the nose makes its presence felt very early and the bitterness bites, the intense manuka fighting back for balance; **f21.5** slightly over-toasted Peruvian coffee at play, keeping in tune with the scorched earth style of the malt; **b22** this malt was probably at its zenith five or six summers back when I suspect a deeply honeyed Dalmore was sitting in the cask. Today it a much more bitter affair, shewing what happens when oak is given a little bit too much of a free hand. 56.4% sc 181 bottles

DALWHINNIE
Highlands (Central), 1898. Diageo. Working.

Dalwhinnie 15 Years Old db **(95) n24 t24 f23 b24** A malt it is hard to decide whether to drink or bath in: I suggest you do both. One of the most complete mainland malts of them all. Know anyone who reckons they don't like whisky? Give them a glass of this – that's them cured. Oh, if only the average masterpiece could be this good. 43%

Dalwhinnie Winter's Gold bott code: L1135CM db **(85.5) n21 t23 f21 b20.5** When I opened this I was fully expecting to nose and taste a potential Whisky Bible Award Winner. The last bottling I tasted scored 95 and was a sublime representation of a complex and truly underappreciated distillery. The nose amazed me right enough...though not for the right reasons. I'm all for the use of young whiskies, as they often have a charm, energy and vibrancy which are free from the occasional corruption of oak. This however, doesn't get the nose right at all, with far too many New Makey notes giving this a positively embryonic feel. Not many winters had passed for some of these casks, one felt. We are at least handsomely compensated on the delivery by the euphoria of toffee and heather honey in full embrace with the thick barley. But by the finish we are left with the toffee alone, save for a few dates. all of which passes by so quickly. One if the biggest disappointments of the year. By a long chalk. 40%.

Game of Thrones Dalwhinnie Winter's Frost House Stark db (87.5) **n22 t22 f21.5 b22** This is my fourth Game of Thrones whisky I have now sampled. And, having never seen the TV series, I am beginning to get the picture: the programme is about toffee, isn't it! Because, again, caramel is the dominating factor here, somehow flattening out the higher peaks from this mountainside distillery, which happens to be one of the world's best. The delightful burst of juicy barley just after the tame delivery is all too brief. 43%.

DEANSTON
Highlands (Perthshire), 1966. Burn Stewart Distillers. Working.

Deanston 10 Years Old Bordeaux Red Wine Cask Finish bott code: 1952859L511:2619164 db **(91) n22 t22.5 f23 b23.5** A cask type that seems to suit Deanston's singular style. Very attractive. Impressed with this one big time. 46.3%. ncf. Travel Retail Exclusive.

Deanston 10 Year Old PX Finish db **(83.5) n21 t22.5 f20 b20** Displays the uncompromising sweetness of a whisky liqueur. A must-have malt for those who like their sherry influence to be way over the top. The finish, like the nose, reveals minor a dry, furry element. 57.5%.

Deanston 12 Years Old bourbon casks, bott code: 17242991509:5018106 db **(84) n21 t22 f20 b21** All the fun is on the impact, where the barley is about as intense as anything else produced in Scotland. However, the weakness on both nose and finish points accusingly at the Deanston character of off-key feintiness. 46.3%. ncf.

Deanston 18 Year Old batch 2 db **(89.5) n23 t22.5 f22 b22** A soft treat for the palate... 46.3%. nc ncf.

Deanston 18 Years Old 1st fill bourbon casks, bott code: 1911691L511L:2618334 db **(89.5) n22 t23.5 f21.5 b22.5** An intense, highly enjoyable dram where the malted barley gangs up and gives the other characteristics only bit parts. 46.3%. ncf.

Deanston 20 Year Old db **(61) n15 t16 f15 b15** Riddled with sulphur. 55.4%. nc ncf.

Deanston 40 Year Old PX Finish db (87.5) **n22 t23 f21 b21.5** The PX is doubtless in use here to try and give a sugary wrap around the over-aged malt. Some success, though limited. This type of cask has the unfortunate habit of restricting complexity in a whisky by embracing it too tightly with its wealth of syrupy top notes. The aromas and flavours which do escape often seem brittle and clipped, and this is the case here: the whisky has no chance to tell of its 40 years in the cask – the period that counts most now is the time it has spent in PX. Love the spices, though, and the overall mouthfeel. Whatever its limitations, this still does offer a lovely dram. 45.6%.

Deanston Virgin Oak virgin oak casks, bott code: 1866939L512:4118241 db (**87.5**) **n22.5 t22.5 f21.5 b21** The overall lightness of Deanston's malt is emphasised by the lingering impact of the tannin towards the finish which knocks the early balance off kilter. An attractively complex nose, though, and the acacia honey on the barley concentrate delivery, followed by zonking spice, is to die for. 46.3%. ncf.

❖ **Deanston Virgin Oak**, bott code 2150179L5 db (**93**) **n23** attractively layered barley and vanilla. Not overly complex beyond the tessellated oakiness, but certainly effective...and promises much on the palate; **t23.5** clean, salivating and lively, the malt is pure and intense. Light shards of heather honey represent the new oak with breath-taking charm. The controlled spices through the middle are a treat and work well with the intensifying honey; **f23** for a Deanston, not only is this long, but it is also gorgeously formulated. The oils play a key role in ensuring both the barley and vanillas stay the course; **b23.5** I remember being underwhelmed by the last version of DVO I encountered. This is another matter entirely and one can bathe in the busy and rich middle which makes the most of the sugary compounds leached from those virgin casks. The best Deanston I've had in years and almost certainly working from better base malt spirit off the stills. Impressed. 46.3% ucf

Acla Selection Summer Edition Deanston 18 Year Old sherry hogshead, dist 1999, bott 2018 (**88.5**) **n22.5 t23 f21 b22** A busy malt, which though stretched towards the finish, underlining the fragile nature of the spirit, early on delights in a glorious mix of spice, barley and complex tannins. The vital citrussy sugars also impress. Enjoyable fayre. 49.3%.

Malt Vault Deanston 24 Year Old dist 1996 (**87.5**) **n22 t21 f22.5 b22** An usually perky Deanston which makes up for its lack of complexity with a distinctly impressive display on the malt front. The fact that the basic spirit lacked much depth is emphasised by the barrel being good enough to generate an attractive degree of bourbon character, on the nose especially. Harsh and hot in part, as one might expect, it is worth hanging on for the attractive, light chocolate conclusion. 51.4% 271 bottles

The Single Cask Deanston 1996 oloroso sherry finish, cask no. 271 (**86.5**) **n22 t22 f21 b21.5** A very safe malt where an attractive oloroso cask has ironed out the usual cracks in the Deanston armoury. It certainly allows the spices to forage around the taste buds unhindered and even, briefly, a little orange blossom honey to drift about the malt. 52.7% sc

DUFFTOWN
Speyside, 1898. Diageo. Working.

The Singleton of Dufftown 12 Years Old db (**71**) **n18 t18 f17 b18**. A roughhouse malt that's finesse-free. For those who like their tastebuds Dufft up a bit... 40%

The Singleton Dufftown Aged 12 Years European and American oak casks, bott code: L9039DM001 db (**79**) **n21.5 t21 f17.5 b19** Much improved from the last bottling I tasted. But still whisky ordinaire and my old comment about the taste buds being "Dufft up" still stands for the rough and ready finish. A little dried orange peel on the nose and a few moments of acceptable maltiness on the delivery really isn't good enough, though. 40%.

The Singleton of Dufftown Aged 15 Years bott code: L7149DM000 db (**84.5**) **n21.5 t22 f20.5 b20.5** Nutty and rich on delivery. Toffee-weighted, thin and boring elsewhere. 40%.

The Singleton of Dufftown Aged 18 Years bott code: L7094DM000 db (**86.5**) **n21 t22 f21.5 b22** To be honest, I was expecting a bit of a dud here, based on some 30-years-experience of this distillery. And though, for an 18-year-old, it can't be said really to hit the heights, it has – as so many less than brilliant distilleries over the years – mellowed enough with age to show a certain malty gentleness worthy of respect. 40%.

The Singleton Dufftown Malt Master's Selection blend ref. 1106, refill, ex-sherry and bourbon casks, bott code: L9149DM003 db (**83**) **n20.5 t21 f20.5 b21** The sherry and bourbon casks wipe each other out leaving a soft, occasionally malty sweetness. Absolutely nothing wrong with it, and better than some Dufftowns of times past. But I'm looking for more than flatline malt...and I don't find it. 40%.

❖ **The Singleton Dufftown Malt Master's Selection**, bott code L2261DM003 db (**85.5**) **n22.5 t22 f20 b21** A malt quite singular in its ordinariness. While the nose is quite promising for a Dufftown, showing some attractive strands of fruit to accompany the very young malt, the palate itself is noticeably inert, other than a spicy freshness. But that is way too short lived, and the malt quickly rolls downhill to a bland, uncomfortable toffee and fruit finale. 40%

The Singleton of Dufftown Spey Cascade db (**80**) **n19 t20 f21 b20**. A dull whisky, stodgy and a little dirty on the nose. Improves the longer it stays on the palate thanks mainly to sympathetic sugars and an ingratiating oiliness. But if you are looking for quality, prepare to be disappointed. 40%

The Singleton of Dufftown "Sunray" db (**77**) n20 t20 f18 b19. One can assume only that the sun has gone in behind a big toffeed cloud. Apparently, according to the label, this is "intense". About as intense as a ham sandwich. Only not as enjoyable. 40%. WB15/121

The Singleton of Dufftown "Tailfire" db (**79**) n20 t20 f19 b20. Tailspin, more like. 40%.

Kingsbury Gold Dufftown 12 Year Old dist 2008, cask no. 700208 (**84.5**) n22 t22.5 f20 b20 Even Kingsbury, who seem to conjure up well above average casks, can't get much of a tune out of this distillery. Expectations for this distillery are low at the best of times. Here we can enjoy some rollicking spices on delivery which momentarily have the key to the more attractive and juicy barley notes. But it is too short and let down by the typically off-key, personality-free finale. 56.1% sc 136 bottles

EDRADOUR

Highlands (Perthshire), 1837. Signatory Vintage. Working.

Edradour 13 Year Old 1st fill oloroso sherry butt, dist 4 Dec 95, bott 4 May 18 db (**95**) n24 t23.5 f23.5 b24 When this whisky was distilled it was made at, then, Scotland's smallest distillery. Well, that may be so, but there is no denying that this is one absolutely huge whisky. And not only that, one where no degree of understated enormity is out step with any other: it is a giant, but a beautifully proportioned one. The spicy, sherry trifle on steroids nose will entrap you. The staggering complexity of the sturdy tannin and muscular fruit will keep you there, spellbound. The chocolate on the finish is almost an arrogant flourish. This really is Edradour from the old school, where its old manager Puss Mitchell had laid down the law on the type of sherry butt the hefty malt had to be filled into. Were he with us now, he'd be purring... 54.2%. 661 bottles. Bottled for Whisky L! & Fine Spirits Show.

FALKIRK

Lowland, 2020. Falkirk Whisky Distillery Company Ltd. Working.

Falkirk Distillery New Make db (**94.5**) n24 t24 f23 b23.5 I must be one of the few remaining in the industry who can still remember the exquisite new make which gushed into the spirit safe of the Rosebank distillery before it closed in 1993. In fact, many years before that tragic year. From what I recall, that was a little chunkier than this, with more dry cocoa on the finish. This, however, retains the Falkirk tradition for inherent early sweetness. Indeed, the midground on this new make is nothing short of stunning, with concentrated barley sugar at its most agile and friendly. It backs up the nose which is clean but retains huge personality, again barley being at the forefront of all with enough oils to flatter but not too much to weigh down: the cuts are impressive. The arrival is sharp, as it should be, before exploding into that huge malt statement. The finish is curiously free of drier tones and even heads towards a light grapefruit citrus finale. Highly impressive new make which leaves us counting down the days with confidence to when it will be bottled as whisky. 63.5%

FETTERCAIRN

Highland (Eastern), 1824. Whyte and Mackay. Working.

Fettercairn Aged 12 Years bott code: L0044 15 45 P/011012 db (**88.5**) n22 t22.5 f21.5 b22.5 Well, I have to laugh. The battles with blender and dear friend Richard Richardson I have enjoyed over the last quarter of a century about the quality, or otherwise, of this malt have been ferocious though (usually) good natured. Here I have to doff my hat and give a nod to acknowledge credit where it is due. This exhibits all the distillery's normal languid nuttiness. But instead of then heading off on a tangent and into areas usually best left unexplored, as is normally the case, this actually embraces some very attractive heather honey notes which sits comfortably with both the juicier barley tones and light caramels. It all works rather well. Yes, I really rather enjoyed this one! 40%.

Fettercairn Aged 16 Years 1st Release 2020 bott code: L0124 08:22 P/0121/6 db (**91**) n21.5t23 f23.5 b23 It's Fettercairn, Jim. But not as we know it. Those chocolate malt notes enter this into an entirely new dimension. The best bottling from this distillery I can remember. Love it! 46.4%.

Liquid Treasures 10th Anniversary Fettercairn 10 Year Old rum barrel, dist 2008, bott 2019 (**80.5**) n21 t22.5 f17 b19 Malty but hot and aggressive in time-honoured tradition. As is the exceptionally thin and course finale...though that is a disappointment because there is a promising, though brief buttery but malt-rich oiliness early on. A very grim finish, indeed. 57.4%. sc. 136 bottles.

MacAlabur Fettercairn 12 Year Old bourbon barrel, cask no.4611, dist Oct 2008, bott Dec 2020 (**88**) n22 t23 f21 b22 After so many unpleasant and underwhelming encounters with Fettercairn over the last 30 to 40 years, it is almost bringing a tear to my eye to find a 12-year-old I have quite enjoyed. Indeed, blind-tasted I'm not sure I would have recognised this as the beast of Fasque at all: in fact, I'm sure I wouldn't. Certainly the degree of dull nuttiness has been trimmed on both nose and palate, and the clarity of the barley has been notably improved, especially on the delivery which now even has the confidence to indulge in a little muscovado sugar development. The finish bitters and disappoints after such a welcoming start. But, overall, a very decent malt. *57.8% 210 bottles*

Oxhead Classic Casks Fettercairn 2007 (86) n21.5 t22 f21 b21.5 Good old Fettercairn! You can trust this chap to provide a relatively monosyllabic speech and it does so with gusto. Yes, it's big malt all the way, though the usual gluey thin notes can be spotted on both nose and finish. Above average for the distillery for sure. *54.4%*

⟐ **Skene Fettercairn 31 Years Old** hogshead no 648086, dist 1990, bott 2022 (87) n23.5 t22 f20 b21.5 I very vividly remember the new make of Fettercairn from around 1990 and it wasn't a pretty sight. Over 30 years on and, naturally, it has changed course dramatically after three decades in oak. It still miss-fires and the finish stubbornly remains a bit of a wreck. But the nose has taken on a breath-taking elegance shewing a regal quality that would not have been out of place at my King's coronation at Westminster Cathedral earlier today. The marriage between heather honey and lemon curd tart is of the style associated with the better whiskies as they pass into old age. The mouthful on delivery also delights, as does the early three dimensional, delightfully fat malted barley. From there onwards things slip downhill in a way only Fettercairn can, becoming just a little acetate-driven along the way. The finish is, well...Fettercairn. *42% sc*

GLEN ALBYN
Highlands (Northern) 1846–1983. Diageo. Demolished.
Gordon & MacPhail Rare Vintage Glen Albyn 1976 (96) n22.5 t24.5 f24.5 b24.5 Wow! My eyes nearly popped out of my head when I spotted this in my sample room. Glen Albyns come round as rarely as a Scotsman winning Wimbledon. Well, almost. When I used to buy this (from Gordon and MacPhail in their early Connoisseur's Choice range, as it happens) when the distillery was still alive (just) I always found it an interesting if occasionally aggressive dram. This masterpiece, though, is something else entirely. And the delivery really does take us to places where only the truly great whiskies go... *43%*

GLENALLACHIE
Speyside, 1968. The GlenAllachie Distillers Co Limited. Working.
The GlenAllachie 10 Years Old Cask Strength batch 2 db (87.5) n21.5 t22.5 f21.5 b22 Never thought I'd say this of a Glenallachie: but I quite enjoyed this. Despite its strength, the distillery's old trademark flamethrower character didn't materialise. The malt remains intact throughout but it is the natural caramels and vanilla from the oak which seriously catches the eye. This has spent ten years in some seriously good oak. I'll even go as far as to say that the malt-dripping delivery is rather gorgeous. *54.8%. The GlenAllachie Distillers Company.*

The GlenAllachie 12 Years Old db (86.5) n21.5 t22.5 f20.5 b22 Whoever is putting these whiskies for Glenallachie together has certainly learned how to harness the extraordinary malt intensity of this distillery to its ultimate effect. Still a touch thin, at key moments, though, and the bitterness of the finish is purely down to the casks not the distillation. *46%. The GlenAllachie Distillers Company.*

The GlenAllachie 18 Years Old db (89) n23 t22.5 f20 b22.5 As friendly as it gets from this distillery. *46%. The GlenAllachie Distillers Company.*

The GlenAllachie 25 Years Old db (91.5) n23 t23.5 f22 b23 Around about the time this whisky was made, distillery manager Puss Mitchell, who then also had Aberlour and Edradour under his auspices, took me from time to time in his office and poured out samples of new make and maturing Glenallachie. The result, usually was a searing sensation to my mouth and a few yelps and cries from me (much to the amusement of Puss): it was then the most unforgiving – and thin - of all Scotland's malts. Indeed, when I wrote Jim Murray's Complete Book of Whisky in 1997, only one distillery in Scotland was missed out: it was Glenallachie. I had written the piece for it. But it just accidentally fell by the wayside during editing and the whisky was so ordinary I simply didn't notice. "It's a filler, Jim", said Puss as I choked on the samples. "This is for blending. It's too hot and basic for a single malt. This is no Aberlour." How extraordinary then, that the distillery now under new and focused ownership, has brought out the whisky from that very time. It is still a little thin, and on arrival it still rips into you. But the passing quarter of a century has mellowed it significantly, astonishingly. So now the sugars from the grist act as balm; the gentle tannins as peacemaker. This is, against all the odds, now a very attractive whisky. Even Puss Mitchell would have been amazed. *48%. The GlenAllachie Distillers Company.*

The Duchess Glenallachie 24 Years Old cask no. 23, dist 12 Dec 95, bott 13 Aug 20 (84.5) n21 t21.5 f21 b21 When this was distilled, it was a malt blenders would use sparingly if they could because of its thin, harsh tones. A couple of dozen years in a good cask has becalmed it and managed to highlight both the barley and barley sugars. But the thin, glassy texture ensures that its past never completely hidden. 55.1%. *Game & Wildlife Series.*

⬩⬩⬩ **Skene Glenallachie 32 Years Old** butt no100468, dist 1989, bott 2021 **(88.5) n22.5 t23 f21 b22** Like Fettercairn, Glenallachie was, during the late 80s and early 90s a malt shunned by blenders for its fiery nature and was even treated with kid gloves by the blenders of the company who owned it, Chivas. And, like Fettercairn, it is a malt that has improved with age, though still capable of revealing its fallibility at the death. The nose boasts that polished maltiness of a dram which was firewater in its early days. The delivery and follow-through, though, is a very evenly matched maltiness which pleases without becoming overly complex. The finish, though starting confidently, diminishes and the inherent gremlins strike. That all said, there is something rather wonderful by the unblinking intensity of that delivery and the crystal clarity of the barley. 43.2% sc

Valour Whisky Glenallachie Aged 30 years bourbon barrel cask no 602 dist 20/02/1992 bott 2022 **(89) n22.5** the thinness of the spirit is still apparent. But there is no denying the wonderful roast chestnut sweetness, capped by malty sugars; **t22.5** the underlying delivery is as hard as nails: the brittleness to the barley almost shocking. But the muscovado sweetness improves things tremendously, helped along by surprisingly delicate oils; **f22** a tad bitter, tangy and thin but those concentrated malty tones are everywhere; **b22** I'll be honest. Having just tasted the best flight of Scotch this year – all from Valour – I expected them to fall flat on their faces with this one. Glenallachie distilled in 1992 was not a malt blenders much fought over. I tasted plenty that year, and it was thin and was quite happy to rip your throat out. This, however, 30 years on, has a waxy feel unique to lesser whiskies which have improved marvellously in time – Littlemill offers similar markers. But in the three passing decades, it has taken on a new shape and personality. It is, by any standards, rather lovely. Though its obvious weaknesses are always apparent. 50.3%

GLENBURGIE
Speyside, 1810. Chivas Brothers. Working.

Ballantine's The Glenburgie Aged 15 Years Series No. 001 American oak casks, bott code: LKRM1245 2018/04/03 **(86) n21.5 t22 f21 b21.5** Clunking caramels clog up the nose and finish big time. But there are some interesting tannin-laden spice notes in full swing as well. 40%.

Gordon & MacPhail Connoisseurs Choice Glenburgie Aged 20 Years refill American hogshead, cask no. 4036, dist 22 Jul 98, bott 31 Jan 19 **(92.5) n23.5 t23.5 f22.5 b23** A single malt that will appeal to the bourbon-loving fraternity. Sweet and beautifully paced throughout. 55.3%. sc. 245 bottles.

Hepburn's Choice Glenburgie 10 Years Old rum barrels, dist 2009, bott 2020 **(94) n23.5 t23.5 f23 b24** The nose is very similar to some experimental casks I worked on years back, using those from Guyana. So many rum casks simply refuse to allow the malt to play. This is a genuine exception where everything falls into place. For a 10-year-old, it is just frothing with personality. A true classic of its type. 46%. nc ncf. 297 bottles.

GLENCADAM
Highlands (Eastern), 1825. Angus Dundee. Working.

Glencadam Aged 10 Years db **(95) n24 t24 f23 b24** Sophisticated, sensual, salivating and seemingly serene, this malt is all about juicy barley and balance. Just bristles with character and about as puckeringly elegant as single malt gets...and even thirst-quenching. My God: the guy who put this one together must be a genius, or something... 46%

Glencadam Aged 10 Years Special Edition batch no. 1, bott code: L1702608 CB2 db **(90.5) n22.5 t23.5 f22 b22.5** A weightier, oakier version of the standard Glencadam 10. Fascinating to see this level of oak involvement, though it further underlines what a delicate creature its spirit is... 48.2%. nc ncf. Special edition for The Whisky Shop.

Glencadam Aged 13 Years db **(94) n23.5 t24 f23 b23.5** Tasting this within 24 hours of Brechin City, the cheek by jowl neighbours of this distillery winning promotion after a penalty shoot out success in their play off final. This malt, every bit as engrossing and with more twists and turns than their seven-goal-thriller yesterday, is the perfect way to toast their success. 46%. nc ncf. 6,000 bottles.

Glencadam Aged 15 Years db **(90.5) n22.5 t23 f22 b23** The spices keep the taste buds on full alert but the richness and depth of the barley defies the years. Another exhibition of Glencadam's understated elegance. Some more genius malt creation... 46%

Glencadam Aged 17 Years Triple Cask Portwood Finish db **(93.5) n23 t24.5 f22 b24** A 17-year-old whisky truffle. A superb late night or after dinner dram, where even the shadowy sulphur cannot spoil its genius. 46%. nc ncf. 1128 bottles.

Glencadam Aged 18 Years db **(96.5) n24.5 t24 f23.5 b24.5** So, here we go again: head down and plough on with the Whisky Bible 2018. This is the first whisky tasted in anger for the new edition and I select Glencadam for the strangest of reasons: it is the closest distillery to a football ground (North British, apart) I can think of, being a drop kick from Brechin City's pretty Glebe Park ground. And why is that relevant? Well today is a Saturday and I should really be at a game but decided to start off a weekend when there are fewest interruptions and I can get back into the swing of things before settling into the rhythm of a six day tasting week. Also, Glencadam, though criminally little known beyond readers of the Whisky Bible, is among the world's greatest distilleries producing one of the most charming whiskies of them all. So, hopefully, it will be a little reward for me. And offering the bourbon cask induced natural, light gold - which perfectly matches the buzzard which has just drifted on the winds into my garden - this enticingly fills the gap between their 17- and 19- years old. Strikes me there is a fraction more first fill cask at play here than usual, ensuring not just a distinctively honeyed, bourbony edge but a drier element also. Distinguished and elegant this is a fabulous, almost unbelievable way to start the new Bible as it has the hallmarks of a malt likely to end up winning some kind of major award. Somehow I think the bar set here, one fashioned from gold, will be far too high for the vast majority that will follow over the next five months... 46%. nc ncf.

Glencadam Aged 19 Years Oloroso Sherry Cask Finish db (84) n21.5 t22 f19.5 b21. Mainly, though not quite, free of sulphur so the whisky after 19 years gets a good chance to speak relatively ungagged, though somewhat muffled. 46%. nc ncf. 6,000 bottles.

Glencadam Aged 25 Years db (95) n25 t24 f22 b24 Imagine the best-balanced team Mourinho ever produced for Chelsea. Well, it was never as good as this nose... 46%. nc ncf.

Glencadam Reserva Andalucía Oloroso Sherry Cask Finish sherry and bourbon casks, bott code: L20 06138 CB2 db (91) n22.5 t23 f22.5 b23 Glencadam is such a charming and fragile malt, it is to be seen at its best in bourbon cask. So I was intrigued to see how they would tackle a sherry cask finish on this. First the all clear: no sulphur. Secondly, they have done justice to the malt as they have not allowed the grape to grip too tightly. Not the same charisma as the bourbon bottlings. But hugely enjoyable still, at least because the young barley continues to hold the upper hand. 46%. nc ncf.

GLENCRAIG
Speyside, 1958. Chivas Brothers. Silent.

Cadenhead's Single Malt Glencraig 31 Years Old (92) n22.5 t23.5 f23 b23 Well done Cadenhead in coming up with one of the last surviving Glencraig casks on the planet. The feintiness shows why it was eventually done away with. But this is a malt with great distinction, too. 50.8%

GLENDRONACH
Highlands, 1826. Brown-Forman. Working.

GlenDronach 8 Year Old The Hielan db (82) n20 t22 f20 b20. Intense malt. But doesn't quite feel as happy with the oil on show as it might. 46%

The GlenDronach Aged 12 Years "Original" db (86.5) n21 t22 f22 b21.5. One of the more bizarre moments of the year: thought I'd got this one mixed up with a German malt whisky I had tasted earlier in the day. There is a light drying tobacco feel to this and the exact same corresponding delivery on the palate. That German version is distilled in a different type of still; this is made in probably the most classic stillhouse on mainland Scotland. Good, enjoyable whisky. But I see a long debate with distillery owner Billy Walker on the near horizon, though it was in Allied's hands when this was produced. 43%

The GlenDronach Aged 18 Years "Allardice" db (83.5) n19 t22 f21 b21.5. Huge fruit. But a long-running bitter edge to the toffee and raisin sits awkwardly on the palate. 46%

The GlenDronach Aged 18 Years Tawny Port Wood Finish db (94.5) n23.5 t24 f23 b24 A malt with not just an excellent flavour profile but sits on the palate as comfortably as you might snuggle into an old Jag. 46%.

The GlenDronach Aged 21 Years Parliament db (76) n23 t21.5 f15 b16.5 Red-hued, myopically one dimensional, rambles on and on, sulphur-tongued, bitter and does its best to leave a bad taste in the mouth while misrepresenting its magnificent land. Now, who does that remind me of...? 48%.

The GlenDronach 25 Years Old oloroso cask, cask no. GD#7434, dist 9 Jul 93 db (94.5) n23.5 t24 f23 b24 Had I any fireworks I would be setting them off outside now in celebration. I'm currently on my 1,058th whisky for the 2020 Bible and this is the first time I have tasted three sherry casks on the trot under 30-years-old that did not have a sulphur problem....and all Glendronach's. At least I don't think this has, though there is a very late, tantalising niggle. But I can forgive that because this is your archetypal fruitcake single malt, complete with burnt raisins and glazed cherries. Toasty, tingly and just wonderful... 54.2%. sc. Bottled for The Whisky Shop.

The GlenDronach 25 Years Old Pedro Ximénez cask, cask no. GD#5957, dist 21 May 93 db (88.5) n22 t22 f22.5 b22 I thought this may have been bottled for the Flat Earth Society.

Because the PX, as PX has a very annoying tendency of doing, has made this very flat, indeed. Pleasant, for sure. But the usual peaks and troughs have been obliterated by the unforgiving thick sherry, though the busy spices shews there is still plenty of signs of life. Also some attractive sticky dates at the very finish. Oh, 100% sulphur-free, too! 55.6%. sc. *Bottled for The Whisky Shop.*

The GlenDronach 26 Years Old oloroso cask, cask no. GD#77, dist 15 May 92 db (81) n19 t22.5 f19 b20.5 Strangely musty, dull and, late on, tangy. 50.3%. sc. *The Whisky Shop.*

Glendronach 26 Years Old 1993 (92) n23 if you are looking for layering in a nose, hunt no further: crisp dark sugars meld into the malt while a fruitcake element confirms unhurried but completed aging; t23.5 succulent, not least thanks to the early oils which help keep the barley intact. That is only brief, though, as the oaky fruit takes hold and becomes increasingly toasty – even suggesting something much greater than its years. The spices make a major impact halfway through and recede only slowly...; f22.5 buttered, slightly burnt toast with a light grapey undercurrent. Cocoa and warming spice are held in place by those excellent oils; b23 a malt that at times seems a lot older than its 26 years. This is a celebration of oak, though never an orgy. Instead, the sugars with their faint fruity undertones create a just-so fragility. The spices cap a fabulous display by the tannins. This is a malt which can give you an idea of how some whiskies a good dozen years older sometimes behave... 54.9%

The GlenDronach Traditionally Peated db (89.5) n21.5 t23 f23 b22 A curiously untidy whisky that somehow works. Maybe by the force of will of the intense peat alone. One of those curious drams where the whole is better than the individual parts. 48%.

GlenDronach Peated db (93.5) n23.5 t23.5 f23 b23.5 I rarely mark the smoky whisky from a distillery which makes peat as an afterthought higher than its standard distillate. But here it is hard not to give massive marks. Only a failing cask at the very death docks a point or so... 46%

Abbey Whisky Glendronach Aged 24 Years 1993 sherry butt, cask no. 652 (95.5) n24 classic old British Christmas cake drowning in rich fruit, molasses and brandy: simply sublime...; t24 oh, the layering! From the first moment there is a surprising hint of chocolate – though this soon falls prey to the re-emerging sultanas and plums; f23.5 long, increasingly toasty, with a burnt Dundee cake feel before that cocoa makes a gentle reappearance; b24 it would be only too easy to mistake this as a duplicate of the 27-year-old below. But it isn't: here the fruit and oak is far more measured and sophisticated. Exemplary... 60.6%. sc.

Abbey Whisky Glendronach Aged 27 Years 1992 PX puncheon, cask no. 5850 (92.5) n22.5 t23.5 f23 b23.5 I actually laughed out loud when I nosed this. It was like being back in my reporting days in Fleet Street again at El Vino's in the 1980s and tasting their Glendronach sherry matured malt: a massive, six-foot grapey overcoat drowning the apologetic frame of a five foot man. Once upon a time I used to dislike this whisky style because of its brash fruitiness without a trace a sympathy for the malt. Nearly 30 years on and I could almost dab at a damp eye of fondness. For this is a sherry cask without a blemish, in which sulphur is a stranger. So deep are the scars of the vile, unforgiving sulphur butts we have been forced to endure over the last three decades, today this is a whisky to be revered rather than, as it once was, mocked... 54.5%. sc.

Cadenhead's Cask Strength Glendronach Aged 30 Years fresh sherry hogshead since 2013, dist 1990, bott 2020 (96) n24.5 complexity doesn't even begin to tell the story here. The cask is a faultless one, free of sulphurous damage. It means the grape has all the muscovado sugars and toasted raisins needed to make its mark in the most impressive way possible...; t24 this is olde worlde whisky: pre-sulphur-ruined Highland malt at its most compelling. The slightly burned Dundee cake and molasses combine with an assured sub strata of malt and lashing of vanilla. The mix of dry cotton wool oak and spiced fruit and barley is something to savour...and savour again; f23.5 wonderful spices and an almost latent smokiness to that spice allows the malt to mingle with the last strands of the fruit to gain maximum complexity; b24 a malt hanging on by a threat. Another summer and the amazing loquaciousness if the barley-grape mix would be compromised The oak has really started to call the shots. But this remarkable distillery has something in reserve if the cask is good enough. And this is. Not a single sulphur note: it represents this distillery at this landmark age at its very best. One of the truly great bottlings of the year. And for a distillery as complex and hard to understand as Glendronach, one if the great bottlings of the last decade... 45.4% *Specially bottled for Cadenhead's Whisky Shop Vienna*

GLENDULLAN

Speyside, 1972. Diageo. Working.

Singleton of Glendullan 12 Years Old db (87) n22 t22 f21 b22. Much more age than is comfortable for a 12-y-o. 40%

The Singleton of Glendullan 15 Years of Age bott code: L7228DM001 db (89.5) n22 t23 f22.5 b22 Mixed feelings. Designed for a very specific market, I suspect, and really impossible not to like. But would the real Glendullan with all its intrinsic Speyside characteristics please stand up. 40%.

The Singleton of Glendullan 18 Years of Age bott code: L6186DM000 db **(89) n23 t22.5 f21.5 b22** A very pleasant if safe whisky where the real character of the malt is hard to unearth. 40%.

The Singleton Glendullan Classic bott code: L5288DM000 db **(91.5) n23 t23 f22.5 b23** Such an attractive freshness to this, the whole being a cross between barley sugar and fruit candy. 40%. *Exclusive to Travel Retail.*

Singleton of Glendullan Liberty db **(73) n17 t19 f18 b19**. For showing such a really unforgiving off key bitter furriness, it should be clamped in irons... 40% WB16/036

Singleton of Glendullan Trinity db **(92.5) n24 t23 f22.5 b23** Designed for airports, this complex little beauty deserves to fly off the shelves... 40% WB16/037

The Single Cask Glendullan Aged 10 Years PX Finished cask no 131 dist 10.Oct.10 bott 15.Oct.20 **(88) n22 t22 f22 b22** Sadly, the PX has put the dull into Glendullan. Not an off cask, but simply a mismatch between malt and grape. A clean cask at work, thankfully. So there are the spices to enjoy with the thick layer of grapey sugar. Pleasant, but far too linear for a Speysider like Glendullan. 60% sc nc ncf 262 bottles

GLEN ELGIN
Speyside, 1900. Diageo. Working.

Glen Elgin Aged 12 Years db **(89) n23 t24 f20 b22**. Absolutely murders Cragganmore as Diageo's top dog bottled Speysider. The marks would be several points further north if one didn't get the feeling that some caramel was weaving a derogatory spell. Brilliant stuff nonetheless. States Pot Still on label - not to be confused with Irish Pot Still. This is 100% malt... and it shows! 43%

Glen Elgin Aged 12 Years bott code: L007ICM002 db **(91) n22.5** the oak pounds rather beautifully on the nose, bringing with it some dried orange peel: the bitter-sweet/sharp-dry interactions are superb. Some dulling toffee does it few favours; **t23** a gorgeous texture, helped along by a mix of dark sugars and fizzing spices. The mid-ground is intense malt, but again the toffee tones just take the edge off the more expansive and complex moments. Just beyond the midway point a little bitter chocolate arrives with the dried orange peel...; **f22.5** fabulous spices add a little varoom to late honeycomb; **b23** I had long argued that Glen Elgin was so far ahead of Cragganmore that it should be considered Diageo's Speyside Classic Malt. Having just tasted the two side-by-side in my lab, the Glen Elgin is so far ahead of its once excellent sister brand it is almost to lap it... 43%.

Chapter 7 Monologue Glen Elgin 13 Years Old 2007 (87) n21.5 t22.5 f21 b22 These Chapter 7 bottlings have been bemusing me and exciting me in equal measure, presenting distilleries in a way they are rarely seen...even by me in the blending lab. This, however, is a disappointment. Glen Elgin is one of the undiscovered gems of Speyside but rather than seeing the malt in all its considerable splendour, the double wine cask influence has flattened too many peaks and troughs. Only on the delivery do we see a battle royale between the fruit and barley. The rest, alas, is simply too simplistic for greatness ...the finish especially. 52%

GLENESK
Highlands (Eastern), 1897–1985. Diageo. Demolished.

Gordon & MacPhail Rare Old Glenesk 1980 (95) n23.5 t24 f23.5 b24 What a charmer: better dead than when alive, some might argue. But this has weathered the passing three and half decades with ease and really does have something of an ice cream feel to it from beginning to the end...well I suppose the distillery was located close to the seaside...One of the most understated but beautiful lost distillery bottlings of the year. 46%.

GLENFARCLAS
Speyside, 1836. J&G Grant. Working.

Glenfarclas 10 Years Old db **(80) n19 t20 f22 b19**. Always an enjoyable malt, but for some reason this version never seems to fire on all cylinders. There is a vague honey sheen which works well with the barley, but struggles for balance and the nose is a bit sweaty. Still has distinctly impressive elements but an odd fish. 40%

Glenfarclas 12 Years Old db **(94) n23.5 t24 f23 b23.5** A superb re-working of an always trustworthy malt. This dramatic change in shape works a treat and suits the malt perfectly. What a sensational success!! 43%

Glenfarclas 12 db bott code 061120 **(87) n21.5 t22.5 f21 b22** A nutty version of this classic Speysider. The wine influence is a dry one - much more austere here than of old. The early mid delivery is the high point, when the grape is at its most succulent. But, late cocoa apart, there are influences here forcing an overloading of late extra dryness. 43%

Glenfarclas 15 Years Old db **(85.5) n21.5 t23 f20 b21**. One thing is for certain: working with sherry butts these days is a bit like working with ACME dynamite... you are never sure when it is about to blow up in your face. There is only minimal sulphur here, but enough to take the edge off a normally magnificent whisky, at the death. Instead it is now merely, in part, quite lovely. The talent at Glenfarclas is unquestionably among the highest in the industry: I'll be surprised to see the same weaknesses with the next bottling. 46%

Glenfarclas 17 Years Old db (94.5) n23.5 t24 f23 b24 When a malt is this delicate, it is surprising the difference that just 3% can make to the oils and keeping the structure together. A dram for those with a patient disposition. 43%.

Glenfarclas 18 Years Old db (84) n21 t22 f20 b21. Tight, nutty and full of crisp muscovado sugar. 43%. Travel Retail Exclusive.

Glenfarclas 21 Years Old db (83) n20 t23 f19 b21. A chorus of sweet, honied malt and mildly spiced, teasing fruit on the fabulous mouth arrival and middle compensates for the few blips. 43%

Glenfarclas 25 Years Old db (84) n20 t22 f20 b22. A curious old bat: by no means free from imperfect sherry but compensating with some staggering age – seemingly way beyond the 25-year statement. Enjoys the deportment of a doddering old classics master from a family of good means and breeding. 43%

Glenfarclas 40 Years Old db (95) n24.5 t23.5 f23 b24 A few moments ago an RAF plane flew low over my usually quiet cottage, violently shaking the windows, silencing my parrot and turning a great spotted woodpecker feeding in my garden to stone: it was too shocked to know whether to stay or fly. And I thought, immediately: Glenfarclas 40! For when, a long time ago now, John Grant paid me the extraordinary compliment of opening his very first bottle of Glenfarclas 40 so we could taste it together, a pair of RAF fighters chose that exact moment to roar feet above his distillery forcing the opened bottle from John's startled hands and onto the lush carpet...into which the initial measures galloopingly poured, rather than our waiting glasses. And it so happened I had a new sample to hand. So, with this whisky I made a fond toast: to John. And to the RAF. 43%.

Glenfarclas 40 Years Old db (94) n23 t23 f24 b24 Couldn't help but laugh: this sample was sent by the guys at Glenfarclas after they spotted that I had last year called their disappointing 40-year-old a "freak". I think we have both proved a point... 46%

Glenfarclas 50 Years Old db (92) n24 t23 f22 b23 Most whiskies cannot survive such great age. This one really does bloom in the glass and the earthy, peaty aspect makes it all the more memorable. It has taken 50 years to reach this state. Give a glass of this at least an hour's inquisition, as I have. Your patience will be rewarded many times over. 44.4%

Glenfarclas 50 Years Old III ex-Oloroso sherry casks db (88.5) n23.5 t21 f22 b22 You can actually hear it wheezing as it has run out of puff. But it is easy to recognise the mark of an old champion... 41.1%. ncf. 937 bottles.

Glenfarclas 105 db (95.5) n23.5 t24 f24 b24 I doubt if any restorative on the planet works quite as well as this one does. Or if any sherry cask whisky is so clean and full of the joys of Jerez. A classic malt which has upped a gear or two and has become exactly what it is: a whisky of pure brilliance... 60%

Glenfarclas £511.19s.0d Family Reserve db (88) n22.5 t22.5 f21 b22 Not the best, but this still ain't no two bob whisky, mister, and make no mistake... 43%

Cadenhead's Cask Strength Glenfarclas Aged 17 Years fresh sherry hogshead since 2017, dist 2003, bott 2020 (96) n24 now this sets a poser: are we talking Chelsea buns or Danish pastry? Whichever, the moist raisin will tempt you to death: this is fruity perfection...; t24 mouthfeel and fruity intent can't be bettered: salivation levels are just about manageable as the black cherry and muscovado sugars strike in cahoots with the spice. Oh, that spice... Then we have the layering oak, almost too labyrinthine to begin to full appreciate. But when you get an amazing marriage of French toast with Melton Hunt Cake, I knew we are onto something a little special. Did I mention the spices....? My God...!! The spices...!!! f23.5 sulphur...? No. Bitterness....? No. Tiredness...? No. Just more bloody near perfect marriage between ridiculously nubile grape and top rate malt, with God knows how many layers of near perfect tannin...? Yes... b24.5 exquisite. Absolutely, disgustingly, ridiculously exquisite... 52.3% Specially bottled for Cadenhead's Whisky Shop Campbeltown

GLENFIDDICH
Speyside, 1887. William Grant & Sons. Working.

Glenfiddich Our Original Twelve 12 Years Old Oloroso sherry & bourbon casks, bott code: L8D 8260 2611 db (82) n22 t22.5 f18 b19.5 Although they call this their "Original Twelve", I can clearly remember when Glenfiddich dispensed with their flagship unaged bottling, the celebrated fresh and juicy one that after a lifetime in ex-bourbon casks had conquered so many uncharted seas, and replaced it with a 12-year-old. And the original didn't have this degree of sherry involvement by any stretch of the imagination. The nose is attractively infused with fruit and the barley glides over the palate on delivery. It is the scratchy, bitter-ish, furry and off-key finish, revealing more of the olosoro influence than we'd really like to know, that brings the side down. 40%.

Glenfiddich Caoran Reserve Aged 12 Years db (89) n22.5 t22 f21.5 b23. Has fizzed up a little in the last year or so with some salivating charm from the barley and a touch of cocoa from the oak. A complex little number. 40%

Glenfiddich Rich Oak Over 14 Years Old new American & new Spanish oak finish db (90.5) n23 t22 f23.5 b22. Delicious, thoughtful whisky and one to tick off on your journey of malt whisky discovery. Though a pity we don't see it at 46% and in full voluptuous nudity: you get the feeling that this would have been something really exceptional to conjure with. 40%.

Glenfiddich 15 Years Old db (94.5) n23 t23 f24.5 b24 If an award were to be given for the most consistently beautiful dram in Scotland, this would win more often than not. This under-rated distillery has won more friends with this masterpiece than probably any other brand. 40%

Glenfiddich Aged 15 Years Cask Strength db (85.5) n20 t23 f21 b21.5. Improved upon the surprisingly bland bottlings of old, especially on the fabulously juicy delivery. Still off the pace due to an annoying toffee-ness towards the middle and at the death. 51%

Glenfiddich Aged 15 Years Distillery Edition American & European oak casks, bott code: L32C 4704 0908 db (95.5) n24 t24 f23.5 b24 A rumbustious malt which comes at you at full throttle. Big, muscular...but, deep down, a bit of a pussycat, too...Brilliant! 51%. ncf.

Glenfiddich 15 Years Old Solera bourbon, new oak and sherry casks, Solera vat finish, bott code: L8D 6980 2106 db (87) n22 t22.5 f20.5 b22 Have to say that this particular batch is pretty unrecognisable from the 15-year-old Solera I tasted (and helped in creating) in its first-ever form the best part of 30 years ago. The fault lines in the sherry can be detected, especially on the mildly furry finish. But this is thinner of body, too, which means the spices are a little too loud on the nose and struggling to find a counteracting partner on the palate. I do still love the oily drollness of the bitter-sweet delivery. But the middle empties rather than fills. The finish is out of sync and quarrelsome, leaving a disappointing finish to a whisky which once never disappointed. 40%.

Glenfiddich Aged 18 Years Small Batch Reserve Oloroso sherry & bourbon casks, batch no. 3231, bott code: L32D 4706 0606 db (91.5) n23 t23 f22 b23.5 One of those malts which, cleverly, is as much about the experience of the mouthfeel and texture as it is the flavour itself. A vague weakness on the finish but, otherwise, a celebration of lustre... 40%.

Glenfiddich Age Of Discovery Aged 19 Years Bourbon Cask Reserve db (92) n23.5t24 f22 b22.5. For my money Glenfiddich turns from something quite workaday to a malt extraordinaire between the ages of 15 and 18. So, depending on the casks chosen, a year the other side of that golden age shouldn't make too much difference. The jury is still out on whether it was helped by being at 40%, which means the natural oils have been broken down somewhat, allowing the intensity and richness only an outside chance of fully forming. 40%

Glenfiddich Age Of Discovery Aged 19 Years Madeira Cask Finish db (88.5) n22.5 t22.5 f21 b22.5. Oddly enough, almost a breakfast malt: it is uncommonly soft and light yet carries a real jam and marmalade character. 40%

Glenfiddich 21 Years Old db (86) n21 t23 f21 b21. A much more uninhibited bottling with loads of fun as the mouth-watering barley comes rolling in. But still falls short on taking the hair-raisingly rich delivery forward and simply peters out. 40%

Glenfiddich 30 Years Old db (93.5) n23 t23.5 f23.5 b23.5 a 'Fiddich which has changed its spots. Much more voluptuous than of old and happy to mine a grapey seam while digging at the sweeter bourbon elements for all it is worth. Just one less than magnificent butt away from near perfection and a certain Bible Award... 40%

Glenfiddich 30 Years Old European Oloroso sherry & American bourbon casks, cask selection no. 00049, bott code: L34D 4828120710 db (96.5) n24 t24.5 f24 b24 The move from 40% abv to 43% has made a huge difference, as little as it sounds. Taking that further step up to 46% could be a game changer for the distillery itself. Glenfiddich, 30 years ago the champion of the younger Speysider, has always been at its very best, and at its natural limit at the 18 to 21-year-old mark. This bottling reveals that things have fundamentally changed. For the better... 43%.

Glenfiddich 50 Years Old db (97) n25 t24 f24 b24 William Grant blender David Stewart, whom I rank above all other blenders on this planet, has known me long and well enough to realise that the surrounding hype, with this being the most expensive whisky ever bottled at £10,000 a go or a sobering £360 a pour, would bounce off me like a pebble from a boulder. "Honestly, David," he told my chief researcher with a timorous insistence, "please tell Jim I really think this isn't too oaky." He offered almost an apology for bringing into the world this 50-year-old babe. Well, as usual David Stewart, doyen of the blending lab and Ayr United season ticket holders, was absolutely spot on. And, as is his wont, he was rather understating his case. For the record, David, next time someone asks you how good this whisky is, just for once do away with the Ayeshire niceness instilled by generations of very nice members of the Stewart family and tell them: "Actually, it's bloody brilliant if I say so myself! And I don't give a rat's bollocks what Murray thinks." 46.1%

Glenfiddich Fire & Cane finished in sweet rum casks, bott code: L32D 4985 2608 db **(96) n24 t24 f23.5 b24.5** I think those of us in the industry who can now be described in the "veteran" category can only smile at the prospect of tasting a full blown peaty Glenfiddich: the distillery that once stood for the cleanest, least peat influenced malt in the whole of Scotland. But when you nose and taste this, you wonder why they didn't take this route from day one, for rarely do you find a distillery that creates a peaty malt so naturally to the phenolic manor born. This is not a gimmicky whisky. No, this is something to be respected and cherished for thing of beauty it actually is. 43%. Experimental Series #4.

Glenfiddich Grand Cru Aged 23 Years Cuvée cask finish, bott code: LA4D 9012 0210 db **(90) n22.5 t23 f23 b22.5** Cuvee, but not curvy. Even so, attractive and delightfully salivating in so many ways... 40%.

Glenfiddich IPA Experiment Experimental Series No 1 bott code: L34A4972141211 db **(86) n21.5 t22.5 f21 b21** IPA and XX...all very Greene King brewery of the early 1980s... An IPA is, by definition, extra hopped in order to preserve the beer on a long journey (to India, originally). I can't say I am picking out hop here, exactly, unless it is responsible for the off-key bitter finale. Something is interfering with the navigation and after an attractive early malty blast on delivery everything goes a little bland. 43%.

Glenfiddich Project XX Experimental Series No 2 bott code: L34B4041170207 db **(95.5) n24 t24 f23.5 b24** "20 minds, one unexpected whisky" goes the blurb on the label. And, in fairness, they have a point. It has been a long time since I have encountered a distillery-produced malt this exceptionally well rounded and balanced. All 20 involved should take a bow: this is Glenfiddich as it should be...xxellent, in fact! 47%.

Glenfiddich Reserve Cask sherry casks, Solera vat no. 2, bott code: L2D 6784 2904 db **(88.5) n21.5 t23 f21.5 b22.5** Glenfiddich, when on song, is one of my favourite distilleries: its malt can offer a clarity of flavour and effervescence that few distilleries in Scotland can match. Sherry influence has a tendency to negate that natural brilliance. However, the delivery reveals a delicious degree of that gorgeous house vitality, an effect which tapers as the grape and other influences slowly take control. A rather delightful malt with stupendous malty sweetness on delivery and an attractive softness which is entirely in keeping with the pace of the flavour development. A lovely malt, indeed. 40%. Travel Retail Exclusive.

Glenfiddich Select Cask bourbon, European oak and red wine casks, Solera vat no. 1, bott code: L2D 6836 0505 db **(85.5) n21 t21.5 f21.5 b21.5** With its heavy leaning on a safe, linear toffee-raisin simplicity, some people will call this smooth. Others, like me, will call it a bit of a dullard. 40%. Travel Retail Exclusive.

Glenfiddich Winter Storm Aged 21 Years Icewine Cask Finish Experiment bott code: LA3 C9009 2510 db **(95) n24 t24 f23 b24** With Storm Dennis on the warpath outside causing widespread flooding and mayhem to much of Britain, never is a whisky needed more than now. And how can you find one more fitting...? What better than to find Glenfiddich at its more juicy, crisp and alluring. Absolutely love it! Almost makes you look forward to the next storm to batter Britain... 43%. Experimental Series #3.

GLEN GARIOCH
Highlands (Eastern), 1798. Morrison Bowmore. Working.

Glen Garioch 8 Years Old db **(85.5) n21 t22 f21 b21.5.** A soft, gummy, malt – not something one would often write about a dram of this or any age from Geary! However, this may have something to do with the copious toffee which swamps the light fruits which try to emerge. 40%

Glen Garioch 10 Years Old db **(80) n19 t22 f19 b20.** Chunky and charming, this is a malt that once would have ripped your tonsils out. Much more sedate and even a touch of honey to the rich body. Toffeed at the finish. 40%

Glen Garioch 12 Years Old db **(88.5) n22 t23 f21.5 b22.**A significant improvement on the complexity front. The return of the smoke after a while away was a surprise and treat. 43%

Glen Garioch 12 Years Old db **(88) n22.5 t22.5 f21.5 b22.** Sticks, broadly, to the winning course of the original 43% version, though here there is a fraction more toffee at the expense of the smoke. 48%. ncf.

Glen Garioch 15 Years Old db **(86.5) n20.5 t22 f22 b22.** In the bottling I sampled last year the peat definitely vanished. Now it's back again, though in tiny, if entertaining, amounts. 43%

Glen Garioch Aged 16 Years The Renaissance 2nd Chapter bott code: L162292 db **(81) n21 t23 f18 b19** For a wonderful moment, actually two: once on the nose and then again on the delivery, you think you are heading towards some kind of Sauternes-type magnificence...

then it all goes wrong. Yes, there are fleeting moments of borderline perfection. But those dull, bitter notes have by far the bigger and longer say. Perhaps the biggest disappointment of the year... 51.4%.

Glen Garioch 21 Years Old db (91) n21 t23 f24 b23 An entirely re-worked, now smokeless, malt that has little in common with its predecessors. Quite lovely, though. 43%

Glen Garioch 30 Years Old No. 503 dist 1987, bott 2017 db (89) n22.5 t23 f21.5 b22 This is from the exotic fruit school of ancient whiskies, the oak's tannin now out-manoeuvering the fruit. Perhaps moved on a little too far down a chalky, tannin-rich route though a little smoke does cushion the blow. Ancient, but still very attractive. 47.1%. Selected for CWS.

Glen Garioch 1995 db (86) n21 t22 f21.5 b21.5. Typically noisy on the palate, even though the malty core is quite thin. Some big natural caramels, though. 55.3%. ncf.

Glen Garioch 1997 db (89) n22 t22.5 f22 b22.5 had you tasted this malt as a 15-year-old back in 1997, you would have tasted something far removed from this, with a peaty bite ripping into the palate. To say this malt has evolved is an understatement. 56.5%. Whisky Shop Exclusive.

Glen Garioch 1997 db (89.5) n22 t23 f22 b22.5. I have to say: I have long been a bit of a voice in the wilderness among whisky professionals as regards this distillery. This not so subtly muscled malt does my case no harm whatsoever. 56.7%. ncf.

Glen Garioch 2000 Bourbon Cask db (93.5) n23 t24 f23 b23.5 The distance this malt has travelled from the days when it was lightly peated firewater is almost beyond measure. A bourbony delight of a Highland malt. 57.3%. ncf.

⬩ **Art Edition No 7 Glen Garioch Aged 11 Years** dist 2011, bott 2022 (89) n22.5 the malt carries the usual Geery nip, though the oak appears to have a few teeth, too...; t22.5 mmmm! Supremely intense delivery with the malt initially in deep concentrated form. As the tannins kick in, there is a split between the light heather honey sitting with the malt and the bitterness slowly intensifying off the cask; f22 the bitterness, though dominating for a while eventually fades (quite unusual in a malt) allowing the malt to regain lost but now drier ground; b22 it surprises me that this distillery didn't return to its original peaty style, taking into account the demand for phenolic single malt. Certainly, the weight of the malt would have served the peat well. As it is, in its "new" style you are always left thinking there should be more to come. Attractive and chewy, nonetheless... 53.4% nc ncf 60 bottles Whiskyjace

GLENGLASSAUGH
Speyside, 1875. Brown-Forman. Working.

Glenglassaugh 30 Year Old db (87) n22.5 t23 f20 b21.5. A gentle perambulation around soft fruitcake. Moist and nutty it still has a major job on its hands overcoming the enormity of the oak. The buzzing spices underline the oak involvement. Meek, charming though a touch furry on the finish. 44.8%.

Glenglassaugh 40 Years Old Pedro Ximénez cask, cask no. GG#3060, dist 8 Dec 78 db (88.5) n22.5 t22 f22 b22 Despite the best efforts of the molasses and life-giving PX cask, you can't help getting away from the feeling that here is one pretty exhausted malt. Both the nose and delivery in particular reveal oak tones more associated with a spent whisky. Yet it is still breathing and has energy enough to reveal a delicate complexity and grapey charm unbothered by sulphur. Then the late spices arrive like the 8th cavalry when all seems lost. It has hung on in there. Just! 46%. sc. Bottled for The Whisky Shop.

Glenglassaugh Evolution db (85) n21 t22 f21 b21. Cumbersome, oily and sweet, this youngster is still evolving. 50%.

Glenglassaugh Nauticus 1st Anniversary 8 Years Old cask no. 288 db (91) n22.5 t23 f22.5 b23 Nauticus. But nice. 56.1%. sc.

Glenglassaugh Revival new, refill and Oloroso sherry casks db (75) n19 t20 f17 b19. Rule number one: if you are going to spend a lot of money to rebuild a distillery and make great whisky, then ensure you put the spirit into excellent oak. Which is why it is best avoiding present day sherry butts at all costs as the chances of running into sulphur is high. There is some stonkingly good malt included in this bottling, and the fabulous chocolate raisin is there to see. But I look forward to seeing a bottling from 100% ex-bourbon. 46%. nc ncf.

Glenglassaugh Torfa db (90) n23.5 t22.5 f22 b22 Appears happy and well suited in its new smoky incarnation. 50%.

Abbey Whisky Glenglassaugh Aged 7 Years 2012 Oloroso hogshead, cask no. 563 (86.5) n21.5 t21.5 f22 b21.5 Some enjoyable phases but this is a wild dog barking in the night. A beautiful creature, I'm sure, but with too many annoying traits and a distinctly mongrel feel with a vague smokiness and a vivid fruit. And with all that spice it bites, too.... 58.7%. sc.

Woolf/Sung The Hunter Glenglassaugh 40 Year Old 1972 sherry cask (90) n22 t24 f21.5 b22.5 Presumably came out of cask in 2012 and only just been bottled. Probably on the way its strength was heading south. Well, the well-founded fears I had of this being a Glenglassaugh sherried have been alleviated: this has not been topped up in a recent sulphurous sub-standard sherry butt, as is too often the case, but this appears to have lived in only the one wood – filled long before sherry butts and the whisky within them were ruined. That said, this a bit of a thin knave, though patience while holding on the palate will reward handsomely as both the complexity of the grape and the myriad tannin tones interplay with a something approaching an art form. The finish is nowhere near so accomplished but, overall, this is a malt which makes impressive play of its great age. 42.9%. sc.

GLENGOYNE
Highlands (Southwest), 1833. Ian Macleod Distillers. Working.

Glengoyne 10 Years Old db (90) n22 t23 f22 b23 Proof that to create balance you do not have to have peat at work. The secret is the intensity of barley intertwangling with oak. Not a single negative note from first to last and now a touch of oil and coffee has upped the intensity further. 40%

Glengoyne 12 Years Old db (91.5) n22.5 t23 f23 b23 The nose has a curiously intimate feel but the tasting experience is a wonderful surprise. 43%

Glengoyne 12 Years Old Cask Strength db (79) n18 t22 f19 b20. Not quite the happiest Glengoyne I've ever come across with the better notes compromised. 57.2%. nc ncf.

Glengoyne 15 Years sherry casks db (81) n19 t20 f21 b21. Brain-numbingly dull and heavily toffeed in style. Just don't get what is trying to be created here. Some late spices remind me I'm awake, but still the perfect dram to have before bed – simply to send you to sleep. Or maybe I just need to see a Doctor... 43%. nc. Ian Macleod Distillers.

Glengoyne 17 Years Old db (86) n21 t23 f21 b21. Some of the guys at Glengoyne think I'm nuts. They couldn't get their head around the 79 I gave it last time. And they will be shaking my neck not my hand when they see the score here...Vastly improved but there is an off sherry tang which points to a naughty butt or two somewhere. Elsewhere mouth-watering and at times fabulously intense. 43%

Glengoyne 18 Years first-fill sherry casks db (82) n22 t22 f18 b20. Bunches of lush grape on nose and delivery, where there is no shortage of caramel. But things go downhill once the dreaded "s" word kicks in. 43%. nc. Ian Macleod Distillers.

Glengoyne 21 Years Old db (90) n21 t22 f24 b23 A vastly improved dram where the caramel has vanished and the tastebuds are constantly assailed and questioned. A malt which builds in pace and passion to delivery a final, wonderful coup-de-grace. Moments of being quite cerebral stuff. 43%

Glengoyne 25 Year Old db (95.5) n24 t24.5 f22.5 b23.5 A beautiful sherry-matured malt from the pre-cock up sulphur days. Not a single off note of note and a reminder of what a sherry cask malt meant to those of us who were involved in whisky a quarter of a century ago... 48%

GLEN GRANT
Speyside, 1840. Campari. Working.

Glen Grant 5 Years Old db (89) n22.5 t22 f21.5 b23. Elegant malt which has noticeably grown in stature and complexity of late. 40%

Glen Grant Aged 10 Years db (96) n23.5 t24 f23.5 b24 Unquestionably the best official 10-y-o distillery bottling I have tasted from this distillery. Absolutely nails it! Oh, and had they bottled this at 46% abv and without the trimmings...my word! Might well have been a contender for Scotch of the Year. It won't be long before word finally gets around about just how bloody good this distillery is. 40%

Glen Grant Aged 10 Years db (96) n24.5 t24 f23.5 b24 This is the new bottling purely for the UK market without, alas for a traditionalist like me, the famous, magnificent white label. The bottle design may not be a patch on the beautifully elegant one that had served the distillery with distinction for so long, but the malt effortlessly stands up to all scrutiny. The only difference between this and the original bottling available world-wide is a slight reduction in the work of the sugars, the muscovado ones in particular, and an upping in the green, grassy, sharper barley. Overall, this is a little drier yet slightly tarter, more reserved and stylish. My one and only regret is that it is not yet upped to 46% so the people of Britain could see a whisky, as I have so many times in the private and privileged enclave of my blending lab, as close to perfection as it comes... 40%

Glen Grant Aged 10 Years bott code: LRO/GE01 db (95.5) n24.5 t24 f23 b24 Perhaps slightly fatter than one or two other bottlings of GG10. But still bang on course with my previous observations, other than the finish not having quite the same sparkle. One of those whiskies which seems delicate and fragile, but at the same time big and robust. Just how does it do that....? 40%

Glen Grant Aged 10 Years bott code: LRO/GD26 db (94) n23.5 t23.5 f23.5 b23.5 A malt which wears its heart on its sleeve, So delicate, so fragile and easily fractured that it has to be treated with extraordinary care. Just how delicate and fragile this whisky is, just how under threat unique and beautiful malts like these are, is revealed on both nose and delivery... 40%.

Glen Grant Aged 10 Years bott code: LRO/JCl7 db **(96) n24.5** one of the noses of the year: the layering of kumquats, grapefruit and melon suggests a Speysider double its years. But it is not as simple as that: with Glen Grant, it rarely is. This is exceptional because of the detail: it has the complexity of a mosaic, the fineness of a D'Angelo brush stroke and the fragility of the finest porcelain. Rarely do malt and oak harmonise so flawlessly after just ten years...; **t24** so soft and salivating on entry. The greeting is one of lightly zesty citrus, grist and acacia honey: the result is profound salvation. You await the layering...and here it comes. The malt is rich. The vanillas are uncluttered and precise. Which all sounds simple, except for the countless layers and hints of fruits, honeys of varied hue and oak-laced spices; **f23.5** maybe a hint of light toffee amid the butterscotch and spiced exotic fruit crumble. Even the thinnest layering of praline... **b24** last year I had worried that some of the sparkle had been drained from this classic Speysider as a 10-year-old. The fact it took me half an hour just to get through the nose tells you all you need to know. I have just looked at the label for the first time and smiled where it says that you will find "orchard fruits". Maybe. But certainly not any orchard found in Scotland. At this ridiculously young age it has taken on exotic fruit status, usually the domain of the great Speysiders of significant vintage. A whisky for those in search of perfection... 40%.

Glen Grant Aged 10 Years bott code LRO/KCl1 db **(94) n24** as always, one of the great noses of world whisky: just a swirl of apricot and apple crumble amid the sharp, grassy barley. Soft vanillas tease and caress; **t23.5** a rounder mouth feel than previously, perhaps, with a little more emphasis on fruit than before. But still the barley encircles the palate and clings to the oils while spices make almost apologetic noises; **f23** surprisingly short with a light fudge and raisin note melding with the barley; **b23.5** superb whisky, but not quite the refreshing salivating tone poem it once was with the dulling fruitiness wearing down the edges and helping to contribute towards a slightly shorter finish. That said, we are still talking of gentle excellence, the hallmark of this distillery. But if wine casks are involved here, perhaps they can be toned down a little to restore this malt back to its former brilliance. 40%

Glen Grant Aged 12 Years db **(95) n23.5 t24 f23.5 b24** Beautifully distilled, thoughtfully matured and deeply satisfying malt. 43%.

Glen Grant Aged 12 Years bott code: LRO/FE 03 db **(95) n24 t24 f23 b24** A slightly different slant to previous 12-year-olds but still within the expected and brilliant spectrum. Fabulous. 43%.

Glen Grant Aged 12 Years bott code: LRO/FK06 db **(94) n24 t23.5 f23 b23.5** Very similar to previous bottling, with no shortage of intensity. The only difference is a little less sweetness through the mid-range between delivery and finish and a slightly bigger caramel note, instead. 43%.

Glen Grant Aged 12 Years bott code: LRO/GE07 db **(92) n23.5 t23.5 f22 b23** A small step sideways from previous bottlings, not least because of the intensity of the malt and its relaxed attitude with the oaky vanillas then gives way to an surfeit of uncharacteristically dull toffee. Get the distinct feeling that this malt is performing well within its capabilities... 43%.

Glen Grant Aged 12 Years Non Chill-Filtered db **(91.5) n23 t23 f22.5 b23** In so many ways speaks volumes about what non-filtration can do to one of the world's truly great distilleries... 48%. *Exclusive to travel retail.*

Glen Grant Aged 12 Years bott code: LRO/GC19 db **(94.5) n23.5** light lychee and the most delicate barley grist; **t24** fizzes on delivery as the barley goes into salivation orbit. The vanillas and butterscotch arrive early, but so to the spices to ensure there is so much life! **f23** the spices still rumble, but, as you would expect from GG, the delicate nature of the barley, the mild honey notes and the kissing vanilla just makes you sigh...; **b24** that's much more like it: such balance, such dexterity..! The last time I sampled this, though delightful, it didn't quite yield the complexity I was expecting. This one is nearer expectation! 48%. *ncf.*

Glen Grant Aged 12 Years bott code: LRO/HI18 db **(94.5) n23.5 t24 f23 b24** My rule is to never look at the previous year's scores and notes and judge the whisky at it comes. So, interesting it matches the last bottling I tasted even, I now see, down to the sectional scoring. Can't quibble with the tasting notes, either, which are pretty much identical. 48%. *ncf.*

Glen Grant Aged 15 Years Batch Strength 1st Edition bott code: LRO/FG 19 db **(96.5) n23.5 t24.5 f24 b24.5** When I saw this was also 1st Edition, I thought it was the same whisky as I tasted last time. Except with a different bottling code. However, although the early personality is near identical, it really does change on the finish where the bitterness has now been eradicated. This not only improves the score to the finish, but the overall balance and performance. The entire journey is now faultless; and journeys don't often come better than this. 50%.

Glen Grant Aged 15 Years Batch Strength 1st Edition bott code. LRO/FG 21 db **(94) n23.5 t24 f23 b23.5** One of the maltiest malts of the year! Just a joy! 50%.

Glen Grant Aged 15 Years Batch Strength 1st Edition bott code: LRO/HI16 db **(97) n24.5 t24 f24 b24.5** What a malt this has now become! The fact that for two successive bottlings they have blown me off my tasting desk means they appear to have nailed the personality of this malt, and in so doing extracting and then displaying the extraordinary and unique charm of this distillery. *50%.*

Glen Grant Aged 15 Years Batch Strength 1st Edition bott code LRO/JH03 db **(96.5) n24** three-dimensional, crisp barley in the time-honoured Glen Grant tradition. Fresh for all its extra years, the trademark grassiness intact and thriving but with an accompaniment of apricot jam and thin acacia honey: glorious...; **t25** salivating from the kick-off – as any self-respecting Glen Grant should be. The malt is both lush and layered though the tannins make an earlier, charmingly polite entry, offering little more than a subtle weight change. The oils work wonders in both magnifying the malt and ensuring a consistency of intensity. Pleasing butterscotch tones meander through the plot...indeed, this is near perfect; **f23.5** drier as the tannins hind ground and the spices far more provocative than on the 10-year-old. But the barley still holds its head high...and well it might...; **b24** a deep sigh of satisfaction followed the tasting of this. Glen Grant is, unquestionably, the greatest distillery in Scotland at this moment and probably number two in the world. I had hoped that this new cask-strength bottling would be true to the Glen Grant tradition of keeping wine interference to an absolute minimum – or, preferably, none at all. And that it has done. A malt of sheer, unquestionable beauty and so wonderfully and endearingly true to the distillery. *50%*

Glen Grant Aged 18 Years Rare Edition db **(97) n24.5 t24.5 f23.5 b24.5** The most crystalline, technically sublime Speyside I have tasted in a very long time... I didn't expect to find a better distillery bottled Glen Grant than their superlative 10-year-old. I was wrong... *43%.*

Glen Grant Aged 18 Years Rare Edition bott code. LRO/EE04 db **(97) n24.5 t24.5 f23.5 b24.5** See tasting notes to the Glen Grant 18 above. A different bottling, but not a single alteration in character, other than maybe just a fraction extra spice at the very end. Another Glen Grant knocking on the door of perfection. *43%.*

Glen Grant Aged 18 Years Rare Edition bott code: LRO/EE03 db **(97) n24.5 t24.5 f23.5 b24.5** So, I have chosen this as my 1,200th whisky of the 2020 Bible...which means I have tasted the last 1,000 whiskies on average at 15 samples a day, day in day out – analysing, re-analysing and describing - from morning to late evening virtually every single day without a break. Here I look for faults and weaknesses; changes, shifts of emphasis, a variation of pace as the flavours come through. And can find none. Well, maybe the vaguest hint of bitterness at the death. But this, as usual, is sublime. Though perhaps it does have two new challengers now: the Glen Grant 15 and the Glen Grant Chronicles. Didn't think it possible. But this distillery has just upped its game... *43%.*

Glen Grant Aged 18 Years Rare Edition bott code: LRO/GB15 db **(92) n23 t23.5 f22.5 b23** A surprise bottling, this. Very unlike the Glen Grant 18s I tasted earlier in the year which were their usual bright, dazzling, mesmerising and heart-stopping selves. This is darker in colour, dimmer in flavour, full of malty riches but extra toffee, also, which appears to up the body but compromises the complexity, especially at the death. *43%.*

Glen Grant 18 Years-Old Rare Edition db **(96.5) n25** as near as damn it perfection. I have been nosing this for just coming up to 30 minutes now, and still not entirely sure where to start. The nose is a like a chorus trained not just pitch perfect but in precision timing, the breathing patterns inaudible. Even by Glen Grant's extraordinary standards this is exceptional, with the sharpness of the barley a beautiful – and almost impertinent – constant considering we are talking a malt aged 18 years. However, so many other delicate forces are at work here, almost imperceptibly, that that sharpness cannot dominate – it becomes just a factor. Warm slightly and release just the most teasing atom or two of smoke, though against such a flighty background it acts as a balance; it is the base. It is joined by the oak which plays many roles, from a weightier, vaguely bourbon red liquorice depth (just a hint, mind), to more purring, gentle ulmo honey sweetness, a little vanilla dabbing the honey dry here and there. Amazingly there are spices, tiny ones like houses for a model village. Everything is small scale. Intrinsic. But when added together becomes understatedly huge...and a thing of exquisite beauty...; **t24** you can safely say that what goes for the nose applies to the delivery and follow through. This is salivating, as the sharpness on the nose foretells but soon this is met by a slightly unexpected creaminess, the deft oils coating the palate to pleasing effect, allowing the vanillas and butterscotch to tumble around the mouth and stick.. The surprise, however, and the aspect which takes a massive leap from the nose is the energy of the spice; **f23.5** a whisky of such fragility cannot go too long without burning out the more complex aspects, leaving behind the more durable elements. This includes a very slight bitterness gleaned from the oak, though the now fragmenting honey does its best to counter. The spices now gently simmer...; **b24** you know that moment when the last notes fade of Vaughan-Williams' A Lark Ascending, or you are in a hilltop meadow and a real lark sings sweetly above your head for its mate before fluttering and parachuting back to its grassy home, and you sit there quietly pondering what you have just experienced. And so the nose, the best I have experienced all year, has the same effect here. Just as there is sometimes a trill of urgency to the lark, so there is a corresponding sharpness to the call of this Glen Grant nose. But, of course, being Gen Grant that sharpness would never be allowed to be the defining character: there are multiple layers at work to ensure that. It is the thinness and fragility of those layers which sets this distillery apart. Take this magnificent malt through the Murray Method for an almost kaleidoscopic view of this whisky, with it changing from one brilliant nose and flavour formation to the next. There just isn't really time enough in the world to do justice to this malt. But it is worth trying to create it. 43%

Glen Grant 40 Year Old db (83.5) n22.5 t21 f20 b20. Probably about ten summers too many. The nose threatens an oakfest, though there are enough peripheral sugars for balance and hope. Sadly, on the palate the cavalry never quite gets there.40%.

Glen Grant 170th Anniversary db (89) n23.5 t23.5 f20 b22. The odd mildly sulphured cask has slipped through the net here to reduce what was shaping to be something magnificent. Still enjoyable, though. 46%

The Glen Grant Arboralis bott code: LRO/HK 27 db (90.5) n23 t22.5 f22 b23 For a Glen Grant, this is dense stuff. One of the heaviest noses ever from the distillery I have encountered matched by a personality and flavour profile which is dark, tight, almost filled with angst. GG as I have never quite seen it before in the last 40 years. Enjoyable and stylistic but lacking that elegance, complexity and all-round finesse which sets the distillery apart from all others in Scotland and, indeed, the world. 40%.

Glen Grant Five Decades bott 2013 db (92) n24 t23.5 f21.5 b23 A nose and delivery of astonishing complexity. Hardly surprising the fade cannot keep up the pace. 46%

Glen Grant Rothes Chronicles Cask Haven first fill casks, bott code: LRO/HI23 db (96) n24 t24.5 f23.5 b24 Remains, as last year, one of the most significant and alluring of all Scotland's malts. Beautiful. 46%.

Chapter 7 Glen Grant 1998 (96) n24.5 lightly stewed gooseberries. And then a slow unravelling of light, tropical fruit. Classic...and very rare in this state...; t24 don't bother to count the layers...there are simply too many, and often too delicate. Even after all these years the barley still trills its highest notes – like a goldcrest invisibly from a fir. Then comes those slightly weightier fruits, though now gently adorned in vanilla. On another level we have salivating muscovado sugars mixing with slightly toasted toffee. Prissy spice and even red liquorice as a vaguely bourbon-esque note is hit; f23.5 the fruit has now been consumed. But all other complexities and treats remain on the table; b24 it is like finding the missing link. Here we find a Glen Grant just as it is in the process of transitioning from being a stupendously fine Speyside single malt into a noble dram showing every aspect of forthcoming greatness as it slips into antiquity. Go easy on the Murray Method: this peaks at the smallest fraction above room temperature for maximum tropicality and complexity. 51.1%

Gordon & MacPhail Speyside Glen Grant 1948 1st fill sherry butt, cask no: 440 (97.5) n25 I really am not sure the nose of a Scotch whisky can be better than this. It has everything you can wish for... and so much more. Indeed, where does one start? Well, I suppose it has to be the peat, the smoke, subtle but telling, reminding us that Speyside whisky was, on a daily basis made to a peatier theme than is the case in most our lifetimes. But it is the way it acts as a curtain to the play: pulling back so the scene is set for a dramatic lead by taught heather honey and the mystery of the spice offering countless levels of warmth and intensity, but all of them – miraculously – in sync with the other players. There is welcoming moist gingerbread where I had expected those tell-tale signs of great age: eucalyptus and menthol. The only nudge in that direction comes from discreet mint, but even that is eclipsed by crisp sugars. There is no severity to the tannins whatsoever and the residual fruit from the sherry has crystalised into a mix of Demerara sugar and, when warmed, a much drier grape skin intensity; t24 after 72 years, you'd be half expecting the oak to have routed all before it, taking no prisoners. When served cool, the oak remains withdrawn, happy to rumble in its infinite shade of complexity in the background, noticeable only if you concentrate your mind upon it. Only when warmed a little does the oak agitate and demand top billing. In either style (though particularly with the MM) the heather honey blossoms and when warmed offers a waxy texture which works rather brilliantly with the oak f24 with oak barrels these days not being what they once were, by now, you'd be expecting a bitterness to be biting into the finish. Well, you'll have a long wait: there is a not an atom of an off note to be found. This is an incredibly rare case of an impeccable malt filed into an impeccable cask finished in true harmony. The oils have been measured throughout, but here, no, they begin to collect...and that means a lengthy, tapering finale. The spices also build. But, intriguingly, we can see that this warming is a marriage of oak and the lightest smoke together. So even late on there is weight and complexity. But there needs to be sweetness, too. And here it comes...improbably, through late malt; b24.5 my lovely old father was 72 when we lost him way back in 1989. If only he had worn as well as this improbably magnificent malt, I think he would have been with us for many more years. This cask could have been kept on for a few more summers yet. But it has been plucked probably at the right time, when the smoke still plays an important role and the oak offers no admonishment, just complexity and joy. I tasted this whisky with two glasses side by side: one was at normal room temperature, the other warmed as in the Murray Method. And here we have a case of a whisky best left undisturbed and allowed to quietly go about its business. Too much excitement and it has a bit of a heart attack...or, rather, oak attack. Though a compensation is that it brings alive the fruit which, at a cooler temperature, had taken a far more sedate position and the honey which alters not only its countenance but texture. Really, to understand the true complexity of this malt may take another 72 years. I left this as the final whisky to taste for the 2022 Whisky Bible. Well, they do they say leave the best 'til last.... 52.5%

GLENGYLE

Campbeltown, 2004. J&A Mitchell & Co. Working.

Kilkerran 12 Year Old db **(90.5)** n22.5 t23 f22.5 b22.5 A malt far more comfortable at this age than some of the previous, younger, bottlings from a few years back. Has a fragile feel to it and the air of a malt which must be treated gently and with respect. 46%

Cadenhead's Authentic Collection Cask Strength Kilkerran Aged 11 Years bourbon barrel, dist 2009, bott 2021 **(89.5)** n23 a delightful mixture of nutty malt and delicate citrus. Possibly one of the most genteel noses I have encountered from Campbeltown. There is a curious, distant, smokiness to this, also, a kind of semi-weighty afterthought...making it softer still, though that hardly seemed possible...; t23 outstanding structure. There is a firmness to the milt missing on the nose, but this soon melts and the malt comes through in concentrated form with full on salivation; f21 a little bitterness is captured from the cask; b22.5 would have scored very high had it not been for the finish. Even so, the nose and delivery deserves mentioning in dispatches as this is a wonderful example of lots of not very much happening combining to make a whole lot... 56.5% 204 bottles

GLEN KEITH

Speyside, 1957. Chivas Brothers. Working (re-opened 14th June 2013).

Glen Keith 10 Years Old db **(80)** n22 t21 f18 b19. A malty if thin dram that finishes with a whimper after an impressively refreshing, grassy start. 43%

Glen Keith Distillery Edition bott code: db **(87.5)** n22 t22.5 f21 b22 The nose offers flighty malt in the company of weightier caramels. While on the palate excellent sweet/spice arrival on the palate, then a blossoming of barley. Simple vanillas and light tannin through the mid-ground. However, perhaps too toffee dependent on the finish, though the spices buzz contently. So, a malt which keeps true to Glen Keith's ability to remain on the more delicate side of the Speysiders, ensuring a gentle persuasion of malty tones rather than forcing itself upon the drinker. But could benefit from a little less caramel. 40%

⬧ **Glen Keith Distillery Edition**, bott code LKRT0584 2023/01/26 db **(86)** n21.5 t22 f21 b21.5 Glen Keith in unpeated form is one of the more delicate flowers of Speyside and here it has problems standing up to the over exuberance of the toffee. It certainly starts promisingly enough with a soothing array of malt on both nose and early delivery. But as soon as the toffee turns up in such force, it's game over. 40%

The First Editions Glen Keith Aged 26 Years 1993 refill barrel, cask no. 16784, bott 2019 **(93)** n23 t24 f22.5 b23.5 For an unfashionable distillery, this can sometimes come up with the odd cracker. And here is one! 56.7%. nc ncf sc. 162 bottles.

The First Editions Glen Keith Aged 28 Years 1993 refill barrel, cask no. HL18214, bott 2021 **(88.5)** n22 t22.5 f22 b22 Great to see a Glen Keith in fine fettle. Always on the lighter side of the Speysiders, this still has enough malty richness to absorb the oak without too much damage. Indeed, the slow arrival and burn of the oaky spice is a very attractive feature. Salivating and tart, blenders would have loved this in a 25-year-old blend to really give the malt section almost a third dimension. A light creamy cocoa signs off the experience attractively. 56.4%. nc ncf sc. 149 bottles.

Kingsbury Glen Keith 26 YO 1994 (93) n23 although showing its age, there are no wrinkles on this nose. The oak is abundant yet passive and the gentle nature even allows a molecule or two of peat to chug round; t23.5 where the tannin holds the nose, so to speak, the barley captures the palate from the very first moment, offering its signature Speyside grassy juiciness even after the passing of a quarter of a century. Stunningly juicy and still crisp with a thin sugary coating. The oak is content to let the spices do the talking; f23 tires a little but well within the scope of its age. But this was homed in a very good cask and had there been a fault, this light spirit would have betrayed it. There are none, so the gentle butterscotch holds sway; b23.5 this exudes a noble Speyside character at the very tip of its comfort zone age-wise. That a malt can be this grassy and alive so late into its life still amazes me. 57.3%

Liquid Treasures From Miles Away Glen Keith 27 Year Old bourbon barrel, dist Jan 93, bott Feb 20 (88.5) **n22 t22.5 f22 b22** The buyer for Liquid Treasures seems to have a thing for thin and malty malts. Just be thankful this is in a bourbon barrel for the barley can sparkles to maximum effect. In any other cask this would have vanished out of sight. But here, at least, we have some charming citrus notes which lifts the malt both on the nose and on delivery. Little meat but a lovely shape nonetheless. 58.4%. sc. 146 bottles.

GLENKINCHIE
Lowlands, 1837. Diageo. Working.

Glenkinchie 12 Years Old db (85) **n19 t22.5 f21.5 b22.** The last 'Kinchie 12 I encountered was beyond woeful. This is anything but. Still not firing on all cylinders and can definitely do better. But there is a fabulous vibrancy to this which nearly all the bottlings I have tasted in the last few years have sadly lacked. Impressive. 43%

Glenkinchie 12 Years Old bott code: L0016CM002 db (88.5) **n21.5 t22.5 f22 b22.5** A definite upgrade on the last 'Kinchie I sat down to properly study. Actually taken aback by the sharp nose which has more in common with new make than a 12-year-old. But soon relaxed into the malt and milky chocolate which makes for a pleasing if simplistic theme. Salivating in part, too, and seems to eke out as much honey as it can find. A tad too much toffee, but pleasant, nonetheless. 43%.

Glenkinchie The Distillers Edition Amontillado cask-wood, dist 2005, bott 2017, bott code: L7222CM000 db (91.5) **n23 t23.5 f21.5 b23** Now that is one very elegant whisky. 43%.

Glenkinchie The Royal Edinburgh Military Tattoo bott code: L9186CM005 db (93.5) **n23 t24 f23 b23.5** One of the most flavoursome Glenkinchies I've ever encountered, really making the most of its malty disposition. Many a Glenkinchie lover will have the name of expression of this tattooed somewhere about their person... Gorgeous! 46%.

THE GLENLIVET
Speyside, 1824. Chivas Brothers. Working.

⬦ **The Glenlivet 12 Years of Age** Double Oak matured European & American oak, bott code LKZS7959 2022/11/21 db (93) **n23** a cream sherry richness to the aroma with dual attack of sweetness coming from both the still visible, indeed sharpy fresh, malt and a sugary footprint of the oak; **t23.5** a truly delightful delivery. This is as thick and creamy on the palate as any Speysider you'll find this year and there is something of the Viennese Whirl about this, boasting as it does cream and jam amid a confident vanilla surround. The malt remains intense and proud while the spices happily run amok; **f23** no surprise that those peppers still rap out their warming beat. The impressive oils string along the malt, too, though now age is catching up and vanilla from the drier oak has a bigger say; **b23.5** a lovely malt boasting far more character than it did five or ten years ago and can now, on this evidence, be relied upon for a rich, long and intense experience. And astonishingly creamy, too. 40%

The Glenlivet 12 Years of Age bott 2017/03/30 db (92.5) **n23 t23 f23 b23.5** Probably the best Glenlivet 12 I have tasted for quite a while...lucky Americans! An extra few percentage points of first fill bourbon cask has gone a long way here. Excellent and satisfying. 40% (80 proof)

The Glenlivet Excellence 12 Year Old db (87) **n22 t21.5 f22 b21.5.** Low key but very clean. The emphasis is on delicate. 40%. Visitor Centre and Asian exclusive.

The Glenlivet 18 Years of Age bott code: 2017/02/02 LKPL0386 db (83.5) **n22 t22 f19 b20.5** This is a rather flat version of a usually rich malt. Has the odd honey-charmed moment and the spices aren't hiding, either. But way too much caramel has turned the usual undulations on the palate to something of pancake proportions. A little furry at the death, also. 43%.

The Glenlivet Alpha db (92) **n23.5 t24 f21.5 b23.** You get the feeling some people have worked very hard at creating a multi-toned, complex creature celebrating the distillery's position at the centre of Speyside. They have succeeded. Just a cask selection or two away from a potential major Bible award. Maybe for the next bottling.... 50%

The Glenlivet Archive 21 Years of Age batch no. 0513M db (95.5) **n24 t24 f23.5 b24** Less archive and more achieve. For getting so many honey tones to work together without it getting overly sweet or syrupy really is a major achievement. 43%

The Glenlivet Captain's Reserve finished in Cognac casks db (89.5) **n22 t23 f22 b22.5** A laid-back malt playing games being simultaneously spicy and super-soft. 40%.

⬦ **The Glenlivet Caribbean Reserve** finished in Caribbean Rum casks, bott code LKZS7738 2022/11/15 db (89) **n21.5** typically tight as some rum casks can be: the sugars appear crisp, burned and a little tart. Some spice nip in the offing; **t23** a truly delightful delivery. This is as thick and creamy on the palate as any non-wine cask Speysider you'll find this year and there is something of the Viennese Whirl about this, boasting as it does cream and jam amid a confident vanilla surround. As on the nose, spices bristle; **f22** we are back to that crisp burnt sugar dynamic found on the nose. Except the spices here really are very busy. The late mocha is welcome; **b22.5** many rum cask bottlings give little. This, by contrast, is uncommonly silky yet attractive. *40%*

The Glenlivet Cipher db **(96.5) n24.5 t24 f23.5 b24.5** It has taken over half an hour to distil these tasting notes into something that will fit the book: we have more new entries than normal and I'm running out of room. Few whiskies I taste this year, however, will compare to this. *48%*

The Glenlivet Conglass 14 db **(92.5) n22 t23 f23.5 b24** High quality. *59.8%*

The Glenlivet Distiller's Reserve bott code: 2019/04/01 db **(87) n21.5 t22 f21.5 b22** A soft, rotund malt designed to give minimum offence... and succeeds. Unless you are offended by the overstating of the caramels. *40%*

The Glenlivet Founder's Reserve bott code: 2017/04/04 LCPL 0591 db **(88.5) n23 t22 f21.5 b22** Anyone who can remember the less than impressive start to this brand will be pretty amazed at just how deliciously approachable it is now. *40%*

The Glenlivet Founder's Reserve American Oak Selection bott code: 2020/11/24 db **(83) n22 t21.5 f19 b20.5** One of those malts where you aren't always quite sure what you'll be getting. This one is at the lower end of the spectrum hampered by a little too much toffee flatness through the middle and then the double whammy of an untidy fuzzy dullness on the finish. Early on in the delivery the barley positively sparkles. But it is not enough from a distillery as good as this one *40%*.

⟫ **The Glenlivet Founder's Reserve American Oak Selection**, bott code LKZS7667 2022/11/09 db **(85) n21.5 t22.5 f20 b21** Although the accent on the malt has been increased in recent years – especially on the salivating delivery - this is still very much a conservative malt, kept in check from any excitement by the toffee which especially riddles the endgame. A very safe whisky. *40%*

The Glenlivet 15 Years of Age French Oak Reserve bott code: 2016/12/19 LCPK 2465 db **(93) n23.5 t23 f23 b23.5** Many years ago when this first came out it wasn't very good, to be honest. Then it was re-shaped, upped a gear and became a very enjoyable dram, indeed. Now, having apparently been steered on a slightly different course again, it is just excellent...An expression that has evolved slowly but quite beautifully. *40%*.

The Glenlivet The Master Distiller's Reserve bott code: 2016/10/04 LCPK 1866 db **(86.5) n22.5 t22 f20.5 b21** It is a shame the malty sparkle on the nose and delivery isn't matched by what follows. A pleasant, safe dram. But too toffee-rich and doesn't develop as this great distillery should. *40%*.

The Glenlivet The Master Distiller's Reserve Solera Vatted bott code: 2017/03/01 LCPL 0371 db **(89.5) n22.5 t23 f22 b22** Pretty much in line with the 2015 bottling above, except there is slightly more caramel here shaving the top off the higher notes. *40%*.

The Glenlivet White Oak Reserve bott code: 2019/03/01 db **(89) n23 t23 f21 b22** Starts promisingly but fades dramatically on the toffee. *40%*.

Gordon & MacPhail Connoisseurs Choice Glenlivet Aged 14 Years refill bourbon barrel, cask no. 800670, dist 10 Nov 04, bott 15 Jul 19 **(94.5) n23.5 t24 f23 b24** The Glenlivet in maximum honey mode. Brilliant! *64%. sc. 162 bottles.*

GLENLOCHY
Highlands (Western), 1898–1983. Diageo. Closed.
Gordon & MacPhail Rare Old Glenlochy 1979 (95) n23.5 t24 f23.5 b24 it has been many years since a bottle from this long lost distillery turned up and that was such a classic, I can remember every nuance of it even now. This shows far greater age, but the way with which the malt takes it in its stride will become the stuff of legend. I held back on tasting this until today, August 2nd 2013, because my lad David this afternoon moved into the first home he has bought, with new wife Rachael and little Abi. It is near Fort William, the remote west coast Highland town in which this whisky was made, and where David will be teaching next year. His first job after moving in, though, will be to continue editing this book, for he worked on the Whisky Bible for a number of editions as researcher and editor over the years. So I can think of no better way of wishing David a happy life in his new home than by toasting him with what turned out to be a stunningly beautiful malt from one of the rarest of all the lost distilleries which, by strange coincidence, was first put up for sale exactly 100 years ago. So, to David, Rachael & little Abigail... your new home! And this time I swallowed..*46%. ncf.*

GLENLOSSIE
Speyside, 1876. Diageo. Working.
Chapter 7 Glenlossie 2008 Aged 12 Years bourbon hogshead, barrel no.9603 **(91) n22** a little spicy celery amid the malt and vanilla; **t22.5** gorgeously silky arrival with acacia honey and

barley in deep conversation; **f23.5** the honey has receded slightly leaving a sawdusty dryness, but the waxiness returns with a little cocoa and liquorice in tow. Very refined, elegant and magnificently complex on the fade; **b23** a glossy 'Lossie... *51.1% sc*

Golden Glen Glenlossie Aged 22 Years hogshead, cask no. 7108, dist 26 Nov 97, bott 27 Nov 19 **(96.5) n24 t24 f24 b24.5** A fabulously complex individual, always popping up with the odd surprise each time you taste it. Even if you live by the Murray Method, as you should, you will be entirely forgiven for not spitting this one out. One of those whiskies that demands a leather chair on the spot for you to sink into, subdued lighting, peace and quiet, a clean atmosphere...and all the time in the world. If I were able, I'd mark this down as a 96.75...it is so closely pushing the magical 97 mark! *53.9%. 222 bottles. Bottled by The Last Drop for No. 23.*

The Single Cask Glenlossie 2008 oloroso octave finish, cask no 12477A **(89) n22** an attractive fudge and raisin lead with busy spices; **t23** lots of toffee before a burst of barley – hard to keep it down at this distillery! – though that soon vanishes as a weightier oaky mocha theme moves in; **f21.5** an annoying bit of bitterness at the end; **b22.5** some late arriving S off the oloroso rocks the boat slightly at the very death. Which was annoying, as I thought we'd got away with it. The journey up until that point was a delightfully pleasant one... *56.5% sc*

The Whisk(e)y Company The Spirit of Glenlossie Aged 22 Years hogshead, cask no. 7107, bott 2019 **(95.5) n24 t24 f23.5 b24** Keen-eyed observers will notice that this is the sister cask to the monumental Golden Glen bottling. This is also an essay in charm and sophistication, though lacking that almost unidentifiable charisma, that sheer magic, of its sister cask. Truly brilliant, nonetheless... *55.5%. sc. 234 bottles.*

GLEN MHOR
Highlands (Northern), 1892–1983. Diageo. Demolished.
Glen Mhor 1976 Rare Malt db **(92.5) n23 t24 f22 b23.5.** You just dream of truly great whisky sitting in your glass from time to time. But you don't expect it, especially from such an old cask. This was the best example from this distillery I've tasted in 30 years...until the Glenkeir version was unleashed! If you ever want to see a scotch that has stretched the use of oak as far it will go without detriment, here it is. What a pity the distillery has gone because the Mhor the merrier... *52.2%*

GLENMORANGIE
Highlands (Northern), 1843. Glenmorangie Plc. Working.
◈ **Glenmorangie The Original Aged 10 Years** bourbon cask finish, bott code L2448951 db **(94.5) n23.5** there is something almost comforting about that effortless interlocking between clean, pleasingly sharp malt and the more genteel vanillas leached unhurriedly from the oak. It is an aroma which in many ways actually defines single malt Scotch...; **t23.5** such a crisp and salivating delivery where the barley is beautifully defined, while though not actually being intense, and the lightest Demerara sugars underline a certain brittleness to their presence: the result is salivating and layered, especially when the delicate spices and rich vanillas promised on the nose arrive to ensure a delightfully intricate middle; **f23** the beautiful clarity of the base spirit shines through here as the malt and tannins stick around, as though preserved in aspic. Those spices, though never assertive, still hang on and build long enough for a pleasing late prickle; **b24** encountering the Glenmorangie 10 is like meeting up with a great and true old friend. Consistent, great company and always there for you. *40%*

Glenmorangie 15 Years Old db **(90.5) n23 t23 f22 b22.5** Exudes quality. *43%*

Glenmorangie 15 Years Old Sauternes Wood Finish db **(68) n16 t18 f17 b17.** I had hoped – and expected – an improvement on the sulphured version I came across last time. Oh, whisky! Why are you such a cruel mistress...? *46%*

Glenmorangie 18 Years Old db **(91) n22 t23 f23 b23** Having thrown off some previous gremlins, now a perfect start to the day whisky... *43%*

Glenmorangie 19 Year Old db **(94) n24 t23.5 f22.5 b24** Fruity or malty...? I can't decide...but then I don't think for a moment that you're supposed to be able to... *43%.*

Glenmorangie 25 Years Old db **(95.5) n24 t24 f23.5 b24** Every bit as statesmanlike and elegant as a whisky of this age from such a blinding distillery should be. Ticks every single box for a 25-year-old and is Morangie's most improved malt by the distance of Tain to Wellingborough. There is a hint of genius with each unfolding wave of flavours with this one: a whisky that will go in 99/100 whisky lover's top 50 malts of all time. And that includes the Peatheads. *43%*

Glenmorangie 30 Years Old db **(72) n17 t18 f19 b18.** From the evidence in the glass the jury is out on whether it has been spruced up a little in a poor sherry cask – and spruce is the operative word: lots of pine on this wrinkly. *44.1%*

Glenmorangie Allta db **(89) n22.5 t23 f21.5 b22** This is a very different 'Morangie: the Allta, could well be for Alternative. Because while the distillery is rightly famed for its cask innovation, there is no barrel style I can think of on the planet which can shape the malt in this unique way. So either grain or yeast is the deciding factor here – perhaps a mixture of both (and you can rule out water!). My money is on yeast, as the only ever time I've come across something quite like this was in a lab in Kentucky with some experimental stuff. The perfect Glenmorangie to confuse your friends by... 51.2%.

Glenmorangie Astar db (93) n24 t23.5 f22 b23.5 Astar has moved a long way from the first bottling which left me scratching my head. This is one of the maltiest of all their range, though the lightness of touch means that any bitterness can be too easily detected. 52.5%.

Glenmorangie Bacalta db (87) n22 t22.5 f21 b21.5. Unusually for a Glenmorangie the narrative is muffled and indistinct. Has some lovely moments, but a bit sharp and lacking in places. 46%

⟫ **Glenmorangie Barrel Select Release Amontillado Finish Aged 12 Years**, bott 08/22 bott code L2458870 db (95) n24 this is some nose where the term "subtle" barely does it justice. There is a spiciness, but one that refuses to bite or in any way take away from the deft nuttiness which mingles so assuredly with the malt. Just about the perfect balance between sweet and dry, you can at times pick out elements of both...and then settle that you can find neither, or at least one that is dominating. This nose alone is worthy of 15 minutes of anyone's time...; t24 as it happens, the delivery is far sweeter than the nose ever suggests might be possible with an intense sultana, red liquorice and Demerara sugar lead reaching an early and heart-stopping crescendo. As is so often the case with a 'Morangie, the malt travels hand-in-hand with the more elegant and even deposits of oaky vanilla; f23 relatively short, but we're back to that sweet/dry neutrality again. A little dried ginger mingles with the vanilla, but some molasses and raisin acts as the perfect foil; b24 this is a malt shewing more sophistication than a coach load of Leeds United supporters. Not a malt that can be tasted and understood immediately, the multi facets are fascinating. 46%

⟫ **Glenmorangie Barrel Select Release Cognac Cask Finish Aged 13 Years** bott 05/21, bott code L21421274 db (90) n22.5 the classic Cognac clipped maltiness: firm with the barley solid and the sugars angular and crisp...; t24 the nose reconstructed on the intense palate, the only addition is a softer, juicier malty thread which carries the vaguest hints of something grapey. But it is very vague and more like a muscovado type sugar surge...; f21 quite dry and allows just a thread of bitterness of the oak to slightly undo some of the balance; b22.5 this is one of those whiskies which is all about the delivery. Which is quite brilliant. 46% ncf

⟫ **Glenmorangie Barrel Select Release Malaga Cask Finish Aged 12 Years** bott 08/20, bott code L2397974 db (96) n23.5 faultless wine cask: so clean that each note hits the nose with a rare purity, especially the boiled candy lucidity which is clear enough to allow the malt to have an important, if understated, say also...; t24 just wow! The delivery is pitch-perfect grape, along with watermelon and a spiced maltiness sweetened by a spoonful of heather honey; f24 long with the honey staying the course and the malt becoming more and more dominant by the moment. However, those spices have no intention of going away. Even the finish is unbelievably clean and precise and the layering truly labyrinthine...; b24.5 if I described this as distilled pastel fruits, I really wouldn't be far from the truth. One of the most fruity, clean and refreshing malts I have tasted in a very long while and ticks more boxes than I have boxes. This really has a classic and cleanest fruit note of any whisky I have ever encountered. One of the greatest Glenmorangies of all time... 473%

⟫ **Glenmorangie Barrel Select Release Palo Cortado Finish Aged 12 Years** bott 08/22, bott code L2458741 db (89.5) n22.5 a non-committal aroma, there is a little bit of cancelling the other out between grape and grain The spices which filter through are clearly oak-derived, though a desiccated Brazil nut note does also make its mark; t23.5 oh, a much more forthright delivery, with the personality coming out of its (Brazil?) shell; to ensure instant salivation. Indeed, there is a surprising and disarming tartness to this which is semi-eyewatering, though by the midpoint this has settled more towards a blackcurrant pastry with the odd dollop of chocolate for good measure; f21 the cocoa lingers, though that original tartness is now a little strained and has become a tad tangy; b22.5 one of the odder sherry styles, I was wondering if it was going to offer an oloroso or amontillado take to the whisky. In the end it offers neither and something very much in its own imitable style. Something completely different. 46%

Glenmorangie Cadboll db (86.5) n21 t23.5 f20.5 b21.5 Every year a challenging new breed of Glenmorangie appears to be thrown into the mix, as though to fully test the taste buds. This is this year's offering: different again, with neither the nose nor finish quite up to par with the outstanding delivery – indeed, the finale is pretty bitter, indeed. But the texture and intensity of the barley on arrival is borderline brilliant, as is the most wonderful caramel which frames it with a buttery sweetness. 43.1%

⟫ **Glenmorangie The Cadboll Estate Single Barley Aged 15 Years** bourbon & amontillado sherry casks, bott code L2481242 db (94) n23 very much the old-fashioned style of sherried whisky, though here allowing just a tad more vanilla on the nose than is the norm. Hard to imagine a softer aroma...; **t23.5** now this isn't like a normal sherry-infused malt. For a start the delivery is both much sweeter and spicier than is the norm. And the barley gets a far bigger pitch to display its credentials than normal – and doesn't pass up the chance of making it happen; **f23.5** a wonderfully nutty finale – mainly diced hazelnuts – which melds into the oak-led vanilla effortlessly. The grape has a gentle overview, but this is shared almost exactly equally with the softest of malt statements; **b24** the land around the Cadboll estate is easy on the eye, sweet to the nose - especially in Spring or Summer when the crops are in full bloom - and easy on the ear with birdsong aplenty. It is also undulating and friendly, which very much sums up this genteel malt which is rounded in all the right place. A class act. 43%

Glenmorangie Dornoch db (94) n23.5 t23 f23.5 b24 A rare Glenmorangie which this time does not put the emphasis on fruit or oak influence. But this appears to concentrate on the malt itself, taking it through a routine which reveals as many angles and facets as it can possibly conjure. Even if the casks are from a central warehouse, at times a seascape has been created by a light salty influence – so befitting the whisky's name. A real treat. 43%

Glenmorangie Ealanta 1993 Vintage db (97.5) n24 t24 f24.5 b25 When is a bourbon not a bourbon? When it is a Scotch single malt...And here we have potentially the World Whisky of the Year. Free from the embarrassing nonsense which passes for today's sherry butt, and undamaged by less than careful after use care of second-hand bourbon casks, we see what happens when the more telling aspects of oak, the business end which gives bourbon that extra edge, blends with the some of the very finest malt made in Scotland. Something approaching one of the best whiskies of my lifetime is the result... 46%

◇◇◇ **Glenmorangie Extremely Rare 18 Years Old** matured oak casks, bott code L2483682 db (96) n24 the epitome of an even aroma: the malt is entire and yet relaxed - certainly relaxed enough to form an improbably genteel alliance with the fruitier tones, principally of lightly spiced dried dates and kumquat pith. Hard to imagine an aroma being so understated yet saying so much...; **t24** as on the nose, the balance is impeccable. The palate is bathed and kissed by the most rounded of malts which combine with its interlocking fruit to get the juices flowing from the very first moment. Now and then does it veer towards a deliberate sharpness to avoid the experience being just too comfortably soporific. Here we hit passion fruit territory which, with the gathering cocoa, hints at a high-grade liqueur; **f23.5** slightly more mocha now, though the malt still has a major presence amid the gathering oaky vanillas; **b24.5** the softness of the oils is balm; the juiciness of both the malt and delicate fruit is succour. When it comes to balance, this has to be the Lord of the Glenmorangies. 43%

Glenmorangie Global Travel Retail 12 Year Old db (89.5) n22 t23 f22 b22.5 Heavy duty Morangie with subtlety and dexterity giving way to full on flavour with a cream toffee mouthfeel. 43%.

Glenmorangie Global Travel Retail 14 Year Old db (84) n22 t22 f19 b21 A pretty straightforward offering by Morangie's normally complex standards but let down by the late furry bitterness on the finish. 43%.

Glenmorangie Global Travel Retail 16 Year Old db (94.5) n23.5 t23.5 f23.5 b24 I particularly love this as the distillery in question is never in doubt: had "Glenmorangie" running through it like a stick of Blackpool rock. Despite the light phenols... 43%.

Glenmorangie Grand Vintage 1996 db (95) n23.5 t24 f23.5 b24 Principally has a firm, glazed feel to this. But he intensity of the malt takes the breath away. Too beautiful... 43%.

Glenmorangie Grand Vintage 1997 db (95) n23.5 t24 f23.5 b24 Such glorious weight and counterpoint: a lesson in cask understanding. A classy vintage, indeed. 43%.

Glenmorangie Lasanta sherry casks db (68.5) n16 t19 f16 b17.5. The sherry problem has increased dramatically rather than being solved. 46%

Glenmorangie Lasanta Aged 12 Years sherry cask finish db (93) n23.5 t24 f22 b23.5 A delightful surprise: every bottling of Lasanta I'd ever tasted had been sulphur ruined. But this new 12-y-o incarnation has got off to a flying start. Although a little bit of a niggle on the finish, I can live with that in the present climate. Here's to a faultless second bottling... 43%

◇◇◇ **Glenmorangie The Lasanta Aged 12 Years** bourbon & sherry casks, bott code L2466231 db (93) n24 the peppers warming that heady mix of old fine wine cork, burnt plum pudding and dried dates is something to savour. Even the vaguest hint of mint... Just love that dryness combining with that reticent sweetness. This truly is a nose for the demanding...; **t23.5** a much silkier ensemble on delivery than ever hinted at on the nose. Though, following on from the aroma, the sugars take a little persuasion to relax, though when they do they give the buttery grape a far more joyous complexion. The spices are deep and profound while the oak isn't mucking about either...; **f22** there is just the vaguest tanginess to this, though it takes its time to decide to appear. Just love the lingering blood orange, spices and the most determined flakes of malt imaginable; **b23.5** this is one of those malts I also sample with a degree of trepidation:

over the passing years I have encountered both outstanding and slightly disastrous versions of this brand. This one gets the thumbs up. Not least because it has the demeanour of a malt a lot older than its given dozen years. *43%*

Glenmorangie Legends The Duthac db (**91.5**) n23.5 t23.5 f21.5 b23 Not spoken to their blender, Bill Lumsden, about this one. But he's been busy on this, though not so busy as to get rid of the unwelcome you-know-what from the wine casks. Educated guess: some kind of finish involving virgin oak, or at least first fill bourbon, and sherry, probably PX on account of the intensity of the crisp sugar. *43%. ncf.*

Glenmorangie Milsean db (**94**) n23 t23.5 f23.5 b24 A quite beautiful malt which goes out of its way to put the orangey in 'Morangie... *46%*

Glenmorangie Nectar D'Or db (**94.5**) n23.5 t24 f23 b24 I was told that this was different to the last Nectar D'or as it has no age statement. To be honest, I was never aware that it had! But it doesn't matter: it is always about the blending of the malt styles from the distillery and the pursuit of balance. And what I have said about this whisky before still perfectly sums it up: an exercise in outrageously good sweet-dry balancing... *46%.*

⬦ **Glenmorangie The Nectar D'Or Sauterenes Cask Finish** aged in American oak, finished in sauternes casks, bott code L2468349 db (**91**) n23.5 what is it about the Sauternes influence which manages to get such a delicate yet strangely intense sweet fruit note to slip in so comfortably among the rampant spices and more accommodating malts? t23 the usual silky evolution of the grape, though this time not as sweet or as sharp as some previous bottlings. But is here threading in a briefly rich grapey vein to the main vanilla and malt skeleton; f22 huge vanilla dominance – not unlike sucking several wafer biscuits; b22.5 it is a strange thing, but no matter which of the near 50 countries I have given whisky tastings in over the last 30 years, I am asked which type of wine finish is my favourite and which I think is the best exponent of that time. My answer has long been Sauternes as the most consistent and a style which most often works so beautifully in tandem with malt. And it is this Glenmorangie rendition I usually cite as the very best exponent of the type. For that reason I was nervous tasting this as, I as I worried that a gremlin may have entered the fray. I need not have worried as the Sauternes casks were faultless. This remains the epitome of bitter-sweet/sweet-dry complexity, though here the vanilla is perhaps a little too dominant at the expense of the fruit... *46%*

Glenmorangie Quinta Ruban 14 Year Old db (**87**) n22 t22 f21 b22 Something of the sweet shop about this with the sugary fruitiness. But doesn't quite develop in structure beyond its simple – though thoroughly attractive – early confines. *46%.*

⬦ **Glenmorangie The Quinta Ruban Aged 14 Years** bourbon & port casks, bott code L2487071 db (**95**) n23.5 a nose as delicate and fragile as they come. When coolish the malt and grape are pretty much on equal terms, but somehow it is lacking an anchor and though delightful is perhaps a little too flighty. Bring in the Murray Method, warm slightly, and suddenly the oak has boarded and while the grape and grain retain their charming dexterity, the oak has taken the whole experience up a gear, especially in the spice department; t24 the oils accompanying Glenmorangie malt are of the lightest in all Scotland. But here they play a telling part in binding together the gristy sweetness of the barley with the drier, more tannin grape skin element of the fruit. Also the mixing of gristy sugars with the heavier blend of muscovado and molasses really allows the grape a free hand; f23.5 long and remarkable for, those who remember this 1970s speciality, its sherry trifle effect. Or, perhaps in this case, spicy Port trifle...; b24 from the distillery which invented Port cask involvement in whisky – and the far-sighted blender, come to think of it – comes the one of most whisky alluring Port cask whiskies in the world. Mind-bending complexity...but the Murray Method and a half hour of your time is essential to fully understand the extraordinary heights and depths this malt reaches. *46%*

Glenmorangie Signet db (**94**) n23.5 t24 f23 b23.5 Ah, that's better! Faith and excellence has been restored! *46%.*

⬦ **Glenmorangie Signet** bott code L2465458 db (**95**) n23.5 for all its seeming softness, there is a subtle punchiness, too, with the oak busily jabbing away. The fruit is distinctly citric: kumquats to be far more precise, which add a slightly acidic nip. On the next table, a cup of Blue Mountain Jamaican coffee has just been poured...; t24 a much softer, more rounded delivery than of old with a fabulously initial hit, a lull, and then a slow but climatic build up of its complex contents. That wonderful early juiciness is a glorious combination of malt and clementine augmented by black cherry. The spices have not just heat by weight, also, and as we move towards the midpoint we are joined by a rich mocha note, the chocolate playing second fiddle to the coffee. A distinctive style of dense Corsican heather honey keeps the sugars on track; f23.5 amazingly, despite so many rich tones weaving in and out of this sample, the finish is still mainly defined by malt. There is a very slight dry tang at the very death as the spices still nibble; b24 Signet back to its very proudest. This is an unashamed essay in subtlety and sleight of hand with various elements vanishing and then reappearing or playing tricks in their degree of intensity. It is the pace of the flavour development of the whisky, with it moving from one phase to the next, which is most mesmerising. This is the last of a dozen from this distillery – the 12 single malts of Tain – I have tasted this year. And I have to say: Glenmorangie is in a very good place right now. 46%

Glenmorangie Signet Ristretto db (86.5) n22 t22.5 f21 b21 Not so sure about this one. Think I prefer my Signets non-Ristrettoed. Flies way too far towards unconstrained sweetness on delivery, but big sweetness on delivery often leaves a bit of a mess in its wake. And I have to admit I am no fan of the dishevelled, tangy finish. 46%.

Glenmorangie Taghta db (92) n23 t23 f23 b23 A curious Glenmorangie which, unusually, appears not to be trying to make a statement or force a point. This is an old Sunday afternoon film of a dram: an old-fashioned black and whitie, (home grown and not an Ealing, or Bogie or Edward G Robinson) where, whether we have seen it before or not, we know pretty much what is going to happen, in a reassuring kind of a way... 46%

Glenmorangie A Tale of Cake db (87) n22 t23 f20 b22 So rare for acacia honey to show so early on a 'Morangie, but there it is and does a great job in offering the delicate touch to the busier spices. Sadly, there is the dull throb of an off-key cask which gets a little too loud for comfort on the finish. There are those who won't spot it, but more who will and it is a distraction from an otherwise genteel dram. 46%.

Glenmorangie Tarlogan db (95) n24 t24 f22.5 b23.5 Interesting. I have just tasted three new Dalmore. Identical colour and some very similar toffeed characteristics. I allowed a whisky-loving visitor to taste them, without telling him what they were. He could barely tell them apart. Here, I have three new Glenmorangies. All of a different hue. I may not like them all; we will see. But at least I know there will be remarkable differences between them. This fabulous malt radiates the countryside in a way few drams have done before. As refreshing as an early morning dip in a Scottish pond... 43%

Glenmorangie Tayne db (87.5) n21 t22.5 f22 b22. Tangy back story. But also a curious early combination between butterscotch and Werther's Original candy. The malt – topped with a splash of double cream – is in the centre ground, though, as the star showing. 43%. Travel Retail Exclusive.

Glenmorangie Tùsail Private Edition db (92) n24.5 t23 f21.5 b23 Doesn't quite live up to the nose. But that would have been a big ask! From the Understated School of Glenmorangie.46%. ncf.

⟳ **X by Glenmorangie** db (90) n22 light but a maltfest, nonetheless, with the teasingly spiced tannins flexing greater muscle mass than might be expected; t23 deliciously malty from the get-go, the overt grassiness making the mouth respond to full salivation levels. The tone of the tannin chimes in perfect harmony with the malt, making for a satisfying overall pitch. Spices begin to dig in towards the middle, yet sublime strands of honey keep the sweetness at very moreish levels; f22.5 that tannin stands its ground without giving an inch. The spices rise and fall and a gorgeous layer of cocoa accompanies the lightly honeyed barley to the death...; b23 at first I thought this was a whisky created by Elon Musk. But can't remember the last time I saw a whisky so intent on talking itself down. "Made for Mixing" chirps the label, implying it isn't, well, quite up to sampling as a singleton. No! This is far better than that: a delicate, paradoxically complex malt which does the simple things to rather lovely, refreshing effect. Surprisingly impressed. 40%

GLEN MORAY
Speyside, 1897. La Martiniquaise. Working.

Glen Moray Classic 8 Years Old db (86) n20 t22 f21 b23. A vast improvement on previous bottlings with the sluggish fatness replaced by a thinner, barley-rich, slightly sweeter and more precise mouthfeel. 40%

Glen Moray 10 Years Old Chardonnay Matured db (73.5) n18.5 t19 f18 b18. Tighter than a wine cork. 40%

Glen Moray 12 Years Old db (90) n22.5 t22 f23 b22.5 I have always regarded this as the measuring stick by which all other malty and clean Speysiders should be tried and tested. It is still a fabulous whisky, full of malty intricacies. Something has fallen off the edge, perhaps, but minutely so. Still think a trick or two is being missed by bottling this at 40%: the natural timbre of this malt demands 46% and no less... 40%

Glen Moray 16 Years Old db (74) n19 t19 f18 b19. A serious dip in form. Drab. 40%

Glen Moray 20 Years Old db (80) n22 t22 f18 b18. With so much natural cream toffee, it is hard to believe that this has so many years on it. After a quick, refreshing start it pans out, if anything, a little dull. 40%

Glen Moray Aged 21 Years Portwood Finish db (95) n23.5 t23.5 f24 b24 As soft and yielding on the palate as any malt you'll ever find. But not short on the complexity front, either. A true entertainer. 46.3%. ncf.

Glen Moray Aged 25 Years Port Cask Finish dist 1988 db (88) n23 t22.5 f20.5 b22 Thought I'd celebrate Andy Murray's second Wimbledon victory, which he completed just a few minutes ago, by having another go at a Glen Moray 25-year-old (Moray is pronounced Murray). I remember last time being slightly disappointed with this expression. Well this later bottling is a little better, but nowhere near the brilliance Murray displayed in gaining revenge for Canada last year getting World Whisky of the Year. Curiously, if this is a 25-year-old and was distilled in 1988, then presumably it was bottled in 2013...the first time Murray won Wimbledon! *43%*

Glen Moray Aged 25 Years Port Cask Finish bourbon casks, dist 1994, bott code: L933659A db **(93) n24 t23.5 f22 b23.5** An exhibition of mind-blowing layering. The nose and delivery are a malt-lover's dream come true. *43%.*

Glen Moray 25 Year Old Port Cask Finish batch 2 db **(95) n23.5 t23.5 f24 b24** Some quite first rate port pipes are involved here. Absolutely clean as a whistle and without any form of off-note. A distillery I have a very soft spot for showing very unusual depth – and age. Brilliant. *43%. 3295 bottles.*

Glen Moray Aged 25 Years Port Cask Finish dist 1988, bott code L709759A 2017/04/07 db **(94) n23 t23.5 f23.5 b24** A lovely intense malt where the Port casks leave big fruity fingerprints at every turn. *43%.*

Glen Moray 30 Years Old db **(92.5) n23.5 t23.5 f22.5 b23** For all its years, this is comfortable malt, untroubled by time. There is no mistaking quality. *43%*

Glen Moray 1984 db **(83) n20 t22 f20 b21.** Mouthwatering and incredibly refreshing malt for its age. *40%*

Glen Moray 1989 db **(86) n23 t22 f20 b21.** Doesn't quite live up to the fruit smoothie nose but I'm being a little picky here. *40%*

Glen Moray Bourbon Cask 1994 cask no. 42/0, bott code. 25/04/17 170635 db **(93.5) n23.5 t23.5 f23 b23.5** For most people in England Glen Moray is a highly productive goalscorer for Brighton. But it would be great if the world woke up to just what lovely whisky can come from this much under-rated distillery. *56.4%. sc.*

Glen Moray Burgundy Cask 2004 Distillery Edition cask no. 213, bott code: L012257A 2020/05/01 db **(93) n23 t23.5 f23 b23.5** Curiously, the last few Burgundy casks I had tasted from distilleries around the world, if unmolested by candles, had shewn much more breast-beating spice at work than this relatively sedate chap. But don't get me wrong, this still has plenty of fizz and much to say...all of it worth listening to. *60.1%. sc.*

Glen Moray Chardonnay Cask 2003 Distillery Edition cask no. 7670, bott code: L012257A 2020/05/01 db **(95.5) n24 t24 f23.5 b24** If your thing is burnt fruitcake: smouldering, blackened raisins in particular, then I think I have just unearthed a single malt whisky just for you. A wine cask matured malt with no damaging sulphur whatsoever, which has been a rare thing this year and makes me want to cheer this bottling from the rooftops. However, there is no escaping the fact that this a form of trial by fire...or toasting to be specific. From the eye-watering, spicy and acidic nose to the honeyed finish you are offered something very different and bordering on genius. *58.9%. sc.*

Glen Moray Chenin Blanc Cask 2004 Distillery Edition cask no. 341, bott code: L012257A 2020/05/01 db **(75) n18 t23 f16 b18** If any wine industry was worse for sulphur-treating their casks than the Spanish, it was the French. Alas, in this case. Because the sweet and voluptuous beauty of the grape is there for all to see. *60.3%. sc.*

Glen Moray Classic db **(86.5) n22 t21.5 f21.5 b21.5.** The nose is the star with a wonderful, clean barley-fruit tandem, but what follows cannot quite match its sure-footed wit. *40%*

Glen Moray Elgin Classic bott code: L929657A 2019/10/23 db **(89) n23 t23 f21 b22** An Elgin Classic ....brushed with peat! Never thought I'd see the day. A delightful aroma of the gentlest nature. The finish, though, could do with a little less toffee. I say this as I am more than aware what a true Elgin Classic is: when my son was born in 1986 I took him to this distillery while he was just a few months old. And I had also bought him a Glen Moray 12 to open on his 21st birthday. Its colour was natural pale straw, as Glen Moray always, classically was. Some 35 years ago Gen Moray was synonymous with light natural colour and a full malty flavour. Wouldn't it be wonderful if it could be again... *40%.*

Glen Moray Elgin Classic bott code: 2021/07/07 db **(87) n22 t22.5 f20.5 b22** Have to admit that a greying eyebrow was raised when I nosed this: "bit young for an 8-year-old," thought I. But when I inspected the bottle, no sign of a number eight. Thankfully, youth serves this distillery well. This is a malty cove at the best of times. And when this young it is though you have a ripening barley field right there in your glass. Green, clean and refreshing nose and a startlingly new-makey, freshly cut grass delivery. Sadly, a big toffee effect starts to take hold, slightly bittering and dulling the finale. *40%*

 Glen Moray Elgin Classic, bott code L234857B 22/12/14 db **(89) n22** two-toned intense, clean, young malt...and toffee; **t23** how salivating is that! The barley is straining at the leash to make its mark with a hyperactive and juicy bite. Cream toffee takes over from the midpoint; **f21.5** more cream toffee but with spices quietly fizzing in the background; **b22.5** a young malt bursting at the seams with vitality and good intent. But perhaps a little subdued by some overindulgent toffee. More than pleasant, though. *40%*

Glen Moray Classic Port Cask Finish db (89.5) n21 t21.5 f23.5 b23.5 A malt which has to somehow work its way to the exit...and finally does so with supreme confidence and a touch of class along the way... 40%

Glen Moray Elgin Classic Cabernet Cask Finish bott code: L820057B 2018/07/19 db (88) n22 t23 f21 b22 Not normally a great fan of malt with this degree of dryness on the finish. But must say I enjoyed the sophisticated pathway to the finish, if not the eye-wateringly tight finale itself. But enjoy the seasoned moist fruitcake nose and the angular, juicy berry fruits – under-ripe gooseberries in particular on delivery. Then hold on tight... 40%.

Glen Moray Elgin Classic Chardonnay Cask Finish bott code: L822667C 2018/08/14 db (83) n21 t22 f20 b20 You know when you have a date with a rather attractive looker you have only just met. And make a reservation at a special restaurant where, with a sinking feeling of the heart, you find out over dinner that, no matter how well you prompt and cajole, how tightly you hang on to their every dull word, that person has nothing whatsoever of interest to say; and you have so little in common that you cannot wait for the evening to end as boredom sets in. Well, that, I'm afraid, was just like tasting this malt... 40%.

Glen Moray Elgin Classic Peated Single Malt bott code: L912557E 2019/05/06 db (88.5) n22 t23.5 f21 b22 Definitely a much better all-rounder than the last bottling of this I tasted. But still palpably at the wrong strength, allowing far too much chalky vanilla given free entrance to undo the great work of the peat and the outstanding distillate. Mesmerically soft on delivery and the house mega-maltiness is soon evident, to wholly delicious effect. But the way it crumbles away on the finish is a bit of a shame. This has the potential for a malt in the 93-94 range. As it is: quite lovely...but soooo frustratingly underpowered! 40%.

⤳ **Glen Moray Elgin Classic Peated**, bott code L301857A 2023/01/18 db (92.5) n23 highly attractive mix of peat reek and anthracite, the latter adding a degree of acidity. The youth is emphasised by the lemon drop quality to the barley; t23.5 the spices are more prominent than I expected, but they are blunted by the rich texture of the malt which offers its own sweet quality. The smoke puffs but cannot reduce the overall juiciness of the sherbet lemon. Elsewhere an oily butterscotch tart persona adds to the complexity; f22.5 long, with a light shadow of vanilla. The spices still pop, and the phenols still throb; b23.5 now that's more like it! The last time I tasted one of these the smoke could barely be seen for the toffee. Not this time. Hardly heavily peated, but because the malt is so light it appears smokier than it actually is. Quite charming and will satisfy those who love the weight of the peat to be more elegant than elephant. Complex and satisfying. 40%

Glen Moray Elgin Classic Port Cask Finish bott code: L922067B 2019/08/08 db (92.5) n22.5 t23.5 f23 b23.5 Another slightly underpowered malt, but it has to be said that the quality of these Port casks is exceptionally high. This is gorgeous malt at any strength. 40%.

Glen Moray Elgin Classic Sherry Cask Finish db (85) n21 t22 f20.5 b21.5. Must be a cream sherry, because this is one exceptionally creamy malt. A bit of a late sulphur tang wipes off a few marks, but the delicious grapey positives outweigh the negatives. 40%

Glen Moray Elgin Classic Sherry Cask Finish bott code: L9150570 2019/08/30 db (88) n22 t23 f20 b22.5 When the fruit gets into full stride it becomes quite a joy. The dangers of sherry butts though are always there as a reminder. 40%.

Glen Moray Elgin Heritage Aged 15 Years Oloroso sherry casks & ex bourbon American oak, bott code: L890127B 2019/08/14 db (90.5) n23.5 t23 f21.5 b22.5 Very curious how even though this is weaker than Signature, the characteristics of the casks comes through so much more brightly, mainly thanks to less toffee apparent. The off-key sherry finale, excepted, of course. 40%.

Glen Moray Elgin Heritage Aged 18 Years db (94) n23.5 t24 f23 b23.5 Absolutely true to the Glen Moray style. Superb. 47%

Glen Moray Elgin Signature Aged 12 Years American oak, bott code: L831157B 2018/11/07 db (86) n23.5 t22.5 f19.5 b21 Now here's a mystery. Bourbon casks...yet a dull fruity furriness on the finish. Until that point is blazed away with that stunning malty intensity that makes Glen Moray in bourbon cask a little bit special. 48%. ncf. Cask Collection Exclusive.

Glen Moray Elgin Signature Aged 15 Years American & sherry casks, bott code: L821157C 2018/11/07 db (89) n22.5 t22.5 f22 b22 Another Glen Moray cut off in its prime. Pleasant but goes for impact rather than complexity. 48%. ncf. Cask Collection Exclusive.

Glen Moray Elgin Signature Elgin Classic first fill American oak, bott code: L924157A 2019/09/23 db (90) n23 t23 f22 b22 Hmmm! Lovely malt from this brilliant distillery. Not sure about the finish, though, where toffee abruptly ends what had been such a satisfying experience. 48%. ncf. Cask Collection Exclusive.

Glen Moray Fired Oak Aged 10 Years db (90) n22.5 t23 f22 b22.5 Very attractive. But missing a trick at 40%: it is needing the extra oils to ramp up intensity and take into another dimension. 40%.

Glen Moray Madeira Cask Project 13 Years Old dist 26 May 06, bott code: L012557A 2020/05/04 db **(90.5) n23 t23.5 f21.5 b22.5** Even with a cask offering just a light sulphur touch, the bountiful and slightly unusual delights of the nose and delivery in particular make its sins very easy to forgive. 46.3%. nc ncf. UK Exclusive.

Glen Moray Mastery db **(89.5) n23.5 t22.5 f21.5 b22** Has an expensive feel to this, to be honest. But, though a huge GM fan, have to say that for all its very clean, attractive, unblemished fruit; for all its juiciness I'm afraid it's just a little bit too one-dimensional. No doubting its charm and elegance, however. 52.3%.

Glen Moray Peated Classic db **(87.5) n21.5 t22.5 f21.5 b22**. Really never thought I'd see this distillery, once the quintessential Speyside unpeated dram, gone all smoky... A little bit of a work in progress. And a minor word to the wise to their blenders: by reducing to 40% you've broken up the oils a shade – but tellingly - too much, which can be crucial in peaty whiskies. Up to 46% next bottling and I think you'll find things fall into place – and not apart... Some minor erotic moments, though, especially on the fourth or fifth beats, when the sugars and smoked vanilla do work well together. Too fleeting, though. 40%

Glen Moray Rhum Agricole Cask Finish Project Oloroso sherry casks & ex bourbon American oak, bott code: L921058A 2019/07/29 db **(94.5) n24 t23.5 f23 b24** A beautifully weighted malt that melts on the tongue. A highly unusual flavour profile and one that benefits from some top class blending. What a treat of a dram. 46.3%. ncf. UK Exclusive.

Glen Moray Sherry Cask Finish 1994 cask no. 904/57, bott code. 25/04/17 170636 db **(92) n23.5 t23 f22 b23.5** Old-fashioned, traditional dry oloroso influence in its most resounding form. A must find malt for those looking to broaden their positive whisky experiences.56.7%. sc

Acla Selection Summer Edition Glen Moray 28 Year Old barrel, dist 1990, bott 2018 **(91.5) n23 t22 f23.5 b23** A very similar experience to the OMC 28-year-old below. Except here the oak has a firmer grip, making the honey play an even more crucial role. 50.9%.

Cask Treasure Glen Moray 2008 (88) n22 t22.5 f21.5 b22 A well-made Glen Moray showing the distillery in its classic, malty light. Oak structure is limited, though even a well-used cask permits enough spice to give the oily finish a tingle. 59.2%

Fananddel.dk Glen Moray Aged 12 Years 1st fill oloroso quarter cask, cask no.28B, dist Jan 2008, bott Oct 2020 **(89.5) n22.5** healthy moist fruitcake territory; **t23** a Glen Moray without intense malt being at the heart of the delivery is always a shock to the system. Eventually the probity of the sherry wins through and the midpoint offers a delightful Garibaldi biscuit countenance; **f21.5** more toasted raisin and late bitterness...; **b22.5** it is always a bit of a shock to see Glen Moray in anything but a bourbon cask: that is what blenders demanded it to be in as this distillery was guaranteed to considerably multiply the pure barley feel. Thankfully the oloroso cask is essentially blemish free...but the malt struggles to make its normal impact. An enjoyably fruity experience, though the identity of the distillery is lost. 49.5% sc 135 bottles

The First Editions Glen Moray Aged 23 Years 1996 refill barrel, cask no. 18217, bott 2020 **(92.5) n23** seemingly simplistic malt at first. But slowly your nose acclimatises, and the oak comes into focus, forming wonderful patterns with the barley. Charming...; **t23** so, so wonderful! The malt is a tapestry of delicate honeys and sugars – none heavier than Demerara and heather honey – melting and then reinventing themselves in continuously delightful waves....; **f23** just adore the late grapefruit on the finish, ensuring there is more to this than implied by the malt and oak love in...; **b23.5** so wonderful when whisky gives all the outward appearance of something light and inconsequential, but on closer inspection offers so much... 55.9%. nc ncf sc. 135 bottles.

The First Editions Glen Moray Aged 25 Years 1994 refill hogshead, cask no. 16609, bott 2019 **(94) n23.5 t24 f23 b23.5** Another first class offering from the First Editions portfolio. 54.6%. nc ncf sc. 339 bottles.

Old Cask Glen Moray Aged 16 Years refill barrel, cask no. HL18197, dist Aug 2004, bott Feb 2021 **(87.5) n21.5 t22.5 f21.5 b22** Although the slightly sharp nose promises little, the delivery is an eye-opener...literally! Glen Moray is one of the maltiest whiskies in all Scotland and here it has it in shiels. Magnificently lucid on the palate, though after the brief injection of oils, the finish mirrors the thinness of the nose. 50%. nc ncf sc. 260 bottles.

Old Malt Cask Glen Moray Aged 16 Years refill barrel, cask no. HL18663, dist May 2005, bott May 2021 **(93) n23** malt breakfast cereal with a little molasses sprinkled on...; **t23.5** silky malt...then the sugars and spices arrive at the same instant to give everything a fabulous, mouth-watering jolt and surge; **f23** heather honey on toast. Has someone peppered it...? **b23.5** a model of malty Speyside respectability. Understated in its excellence. 50% sc 322 bottles

Old Malt Cask Glen Moray Aged 24 Years refill barrel, cask no. 18200, dist Feb 96, bott Dec 20 **(94.5) n23.5** this is brinkmanship: oak offering as much structure and weight as possible without tipping the scales and no longer allowing the malt to hold sway. A lovely grassiness pervades, sharpened further by a hint of lemon drops; **t23.5** the perfect translation on delivery from the story told on the nose. Lemon drops and concentrated barley hit an exact balance with the oaky spices which buzz from the first moment....and remind you of the vintage. So juicy and fresh despite the passing years; **f23.5** understated but effective oils stretch the barley and the profound juiciness to improbable lengths....; **b24** hard to find a more archetypical Glen Moray at this age than this cask. One of my favourite Speyside distilleries at its most delightful. *50%. nc ncf sc. 185 bottles.*

Scyfion Choice Glen Moray 2007 Areni Noir wine cask finished, bott 2019 **(85) n22 t23.5 f18.5 b21** A malt boasting a sublime delivery as the ripe fruits and spices gang together to let rip. Likewise, the follow-through is an outstanding display of layered fruit candy leading down to a small reservoir of malt. Just a little furry tang on the finale though that turns into gnawing sulphur. *50%. nc ncf sc. 132 bottles.*

Oxhead Classic Casks Glen Moray 2007 db **(92) n23 t23.5 f22.5 b23** It is harder than you think to find Glen Moray casks which sit comfortably beyond 12 years. Being a light malt, often blemishes can be easily spotted, or the oak has just begun to bully the barley. But here's a charmer, keeping its ultra-malty persona intact. And, better still, gives one of the most alluring, ultra-malty deliveries of the year. There is also a beautiful prickliness to the spices thanks to the excellent oak. Normally, this would be a great choice for an early evening dram. But this has enough about it to be that chewy, lingering one before bed, too. *56.9%*

Scyfion Choice Glen Moray 2007 Foursquare rum cask finished, bott 2019 **(91.5) n23.5 t23 f22 b23** It is perhaps ironic that the owner of the Foursquare distillery in Barbados shares my slight weariness of cask finishes (in my case because over 25 years I have tasted a disproportionately high number of unimpressive ones) yet here is one of his casks being used to finish a single malt. And, I have to say, doing a good job of it. *46%. nc ncf sc. 97 bottles.*

The Whisky Chamber Glen Moray 13 Jahre 2007 bourbon cask **(86.5) n22.5 t22 f20.5 b21.5** By no means a normal Glen Moray: much more burn and attitude to this fella, resulting in sharpness which is almost alien to the distillery. The usual high grade, concentrated malt is there. But hard to find among the foreground noise. *58.3%. sc.*

GLEN ORD
Highlands (Northern), 1838. Diageo. Working.
Glen Ord Aged 12 Years db **(81) n20 t23 f18 b20.** Just when you thought it safe to go back... for a while Diageo ditched the sherry-style Ord. It has returned. Better than some years ago, when it was an unhappy shadow of its once-great self, but without the sparkle of the vaguely-smoked bottling of a year or two back. Nothing wrong with the rich arrival, but the finish is a mess. I'll open the next bottling with trepidation... *43%*

Singleton of Glen Ord 12 Years Old db **(89) n22.5 t22.5 f22 b22** A fabulous improvement on the last bottling I encountered. Still possesses blood oranges to die for, but greatly enhanced by some sublime spices and a magnificent juiciness. *40%*

The Singleton of Glen Ord Aged 15 Years European & American oak casks, bott code: L8038DM003 db **(90.5) n23 t23.5 f21.5 b22.5** The fun of the label on many a bottle of whisky is just how far removed the described tasting notes are to what is actually poured from the bottle. Here, there are no quibbles from me: the promised ginger and chocolate come true! *40%.*

Singleton of Glen Ord 32 Year Old db **(91) n23.5 t23 f22 b22.5.** Delicious. But if ever a malt has screamed out to be at 46%, this is it. *40%*

The Singleton Glen Ord Distillery Exclusive batch no. 01, bott 2019, bott code: L9193DQ0002 db **(95.5) n24.5 t23.5 f23.5 b24** It is unfortunate that the Glen Ord distillery is not the easiest in Scotland to get to. But while they have this bottle in their shops, get plane, boat, go-cart, train, pushbike, helicopter, space hopper, parachute, pogo stick, glider, Harley- Davidson, horse, foot-scooter, paraglider, huskies, jet ski, cannon, roller skates, bobsleigh, canoe, Penny Farthing, Zeppelin, windsurf, camel, sedan, jet propulsion pack, elephant, raft, auto-rickshaw, lawnmower, crutches...absolutely bloody ANYTHING to get you there. Because this is the great Gen Ord unplugged, naked and as beautiful as you'll ever find it. *48%. 6,000 bottles.*

GLENROTHES
Speyside, 1878. Edrington. Working.
The Glenrothes 10 Years Old sherry seasoned oak casks db **(80.5) n19 t22.5 f19 b20** Neither a nose or finish I much care for: tight, a little tangy and out of sync. But I certainly approve the delivery which shows no such constraints and celebrates the voluptuousness of its maltiness. *40%. nc. The Soleo Collection.*

The Glenrothes 12 Years Old sherry seasoned oak casks db **(68) n17 t19 f15 b17** Sulphur addled. *40%. nc. The Soleo Collection.*

The Glenrothes 18 Years Old sherry seasoned oak casks db **(87) n22 t22.5 f21 b21.5** Nutty and hefty, there is always a slight tang to this which slightly reduces the intricate nature of the barley. The off-key finish confirms not all is well, but this being the truly brilliant distillery it is, an inner depth of barley and ulmo honey ensures there always something to treasure from this dram. 43%. nc. The Soleo Collection.

The Glenrothes 25 Years Old sherry seasoned oak casks db (86) n23 t22 f19.5 b21.5 The nose is the star turn here, shewing some of the complexity you might demand of a 25-year-old malt. The adroitness of the barley ripe Chinese gooseberry is particularly alluring. But after a surprisingly malt delivery and a volley of pleasant sultana, it is the finish (again) which reveals a furry weak link. 43%. nc. The Soleo Collection.

The Glenrothes Whisky Maker's Cut first fill sherry seasoned oak casks db (95) n23.5 t23.5 f24 b24 Unspoiled casks at work. An absolute must for sherry cask lovers. 48.8%. nc. The Soleo Collection.

Cadenhead's Glenrothes 18 Year Old port cask, dist 2001 (87.5) n21 t23.5 f21 b22 Having spent the last couple of decades running away from any Glenrothes matured in a wine cask, have to admit I took this whisky on with more than a degree of trepidation. The dry, penurious nose makes you start looking for the hills...when suddenly you are stopped in your tracks by the sheer voluptuousness, the honey-laden generosity of the delivery that makes delicious celebration of the stunning grape. There is little else to cling on to with any warmth after that – perhaps a little salty chocolate and spice maybe. But that delivery...just wow! 53.6%. 246 bottles. Cadenhead Shop Cask Series 2019 Baden.

Fadandel Glenrothes 8 Years Old (86) n21.5 t21 f22 b21.5 Technically, nothing wrong with this malt. It's just been plucked from the cask at a time when harmony was at a premium. They are all there: bruising tannins, big fruit, warming spice. But they are not talking to each other. Firm in body, though lush when lingering, it is pleasant enough without ticking the right boxes. 59.8%

◈ **Kingsbury Glenrothes 1997 Aged 24 Years** hogshead, cask no 19502 (86) n22.5 t23 f19.5 b21 The overdependence on sherry butts so far as Glenrothes is concerned means that it is all too rarely people get the chance to see the distillery in all its honeyed glory as it sits in the glass here. However, a nagging bitterness from the oak does its best to diminish the fineness of the structure of this dram. 62.6% 259 bottles

GLEN SCOTIA
Campbeltown, 1832. Loch Lomond Distillers. Working

Glen Scotia Aged 10 Years Peated first fill bourbon barrels db (94.5) n24 t23 f23.5 b24 This entire whisky style is a throwback to the very first peated whiskies I tasted 40 years ago. Indeed, anyone still alive and able to remember Glen Garioch when it was heavily peated through its own kilns will raise an eyebrow of happy recognition... One of the greatest Glen Scotias of all time. 46%. nc ncf.

Glen Scotia 11 Years Old 2006 cask no. 532, dist Dec 06, bott Apr 18 db (92.5) n22.5 t23.5 f23 b23.5 Absolutely typical Glen Scotia, proudly displaying its rugged charm. 55.6%. sc. 212 bottles. Bottled for The Whisky Shop.

Glen Scotia Aged 15 Years American oak barrels db (91.5) n22.5 t23 f23 b23 Great to see this rather special little distillery produce something quite so confident and complete. 46%. ncf.

Glen Scotia 18 Year Old American oak casks & first fill oloroso casks, bott code: L2/221/17 db (95) n24 t24 f23 b24 ,y Panama is doffed in grateful thanks for the excellent use of un-sulphured clean sherry butts which give this malt a genuine lustre. And as three dimensional as its sister PX bottling is just one... 51.3%. ncf.

Glen Scotia Aged 25 Years American oak barrels, bott 2017, bott code: L8/187/17 db (94) n23.5 t24 f23 b23.5 So beautiful! Truly adorable – and probably a Scotia as you have never quite seen it before. Incredibly rare to find a Scotch single malt so under the thumb of a bourbon character: this must have been filled into very fresh first-fill bourbon barrels to come up with this highly American effect. Trump that! 48.8%. ncf.

Glen Scotia 45 Year Old db (96) n24 one of those remarkable whiskies where the oak, revealing the odd grey hair (or is that revelling in...?), appears to be holding off to ensure the salty, exotic (or do I mean erotic...?) fruits are allowed the clearest run...; t24 immediate oak impact on delivery now. But a little maple syrup mingles with butterscotch and salted butter to ensure special things happen. Towards the mid-point orange blossom honey lands, and then melts in the mouth...; f23.5 light walnut cake complete with crème fondant; lots of intact barley and lighter red liquorice; b24.5 outrageously beautiful for its age with not even the hint of a beginning of a crack. Stupendous. 43.8%.

Glen Scotia 1999 refill bourbon barrel, cask no. 455 db (89) n22.5 a slight salty, grassy note; toffee apple; t22.5 eye-wateringly fresh barley, but the midground fills with fudge; f22 soft, linear caramels b22.5 really extracts every last caramel molecule out of the cask! 60.5%. sc. Bottled for Glenkeir Whiskies.

Glen Scotia 2008 Second Shop Bottling db (84) n22 t21 f21 b20 Too salty and bitter for its own good 56.3%. sc.

Glen Scotia 2015 db **(92) n22** highly unusual for a malt this young to boast such an oaky buzz: the spices are positively prickly! **t23.5** oh, how impressive is that?! The entry and immediate mouthfeel confirm that this is a very competently made spirit which is technically sound, yet rich enough to add a certain lustre of the fresh fruit imparted by the cask. For a youngster, this Scotia polishes up rather beautifully. Grapey, mouth-watering and succulent, there is joy with every chew; **f23** superb finish....and what a long one is offered, too. The spices remain on full parade, but all is muffled by that exquisite fruit. Light butterscotch adds a softness to the intensifying tannin; **b23.5** tasted blind, there is no way that this could be recognised as a Glen Scotia, such is the input from the wine casks. Equally, you would hardly believe its tender years, either. Precocious doesn't even begin to cover it... *55.8% TWC Exclusive.*

Glen Scotia Campbeltown 1832 American oak & Pedro Ximenez sherry casks, bott code: L2.186 19 db **(92.5) n23** suet pudding with extra dose of maple syrup; **t23.5** my word, that PX makes its mark early. But, such a rare thing to find, the malt is brought into play early on, thereby arresting the sweetness but allowing a magnificently beautiful duet to be played by the two main characters; **f23** balances out beautifully as the spices kick start late; **b23** one of the best malts using PX casks on the market today. Elegant and adorable. *46%. ncf.*

Glen Scotia Campbeltown Harbour first fill bourbon casks, bott code: 23 10 2018 db **(87) n22 t22 f21.5 b21.5** The best description of Campbeltown and its harbour was provided by 19th century whisky explorer Alfred Barnard. This malt hardly matches the whiskies you would have found of that time, and it doesn't quite match up to how you picture Campbeltown whiskies today, either. For this is very flat and far too caramel dependent, though the mix of saltiness and gentle sweetness is high attractive. The smoke unfurls at the very finish...but for all its easy attractiveness, it is still all a little too docile and tame. *40%.*

Glen Scotia Campbeltown Harbour first fill bourbon barrels, bott code: L20.111.20 db **(89.5) n22.5** a thin layer of peat smoke breaks up the monopoly of the citrussy tannin; **t22.5** lovely mouthfeel: soft with a few firming ribs. The malt shines briefly before the lightly spiced tannins take over; **f22** just a little bitterness; **b22.5** it is a very brave move to limit a malt to 100% first-fill bourbon cask, as this appears to have done, and reduce to 40% abv, because building structure and layering is almost next to impossible. Instead you are left with a take it or leave it type malt – though this does have plenty to take! Actually, I am being a little unfair because a degree of depth is supplied by the most delicate smokiness. But the scope remains restricted. *40%.*

⬧ **Glen Scotia Campbeltown Harbour** first fill bourbon casks, bott code L429122 18.10.2022 db **(90) n22.5** there is a rare oaky, toasty bite amid an obviously young maltiness: a fascinating paradox. More than a hint of French toast to this...; **t23** salivating from the first second. The barley is strikingly intense, the secondary vanilla capturing some excellent molasses tones. Beautifully layered; **f22** much drier as the sugars wear off, allowing the limited spices to bite into the thickening oils. Remarkably juicy even at the death with the vaguest hint of dark cherry and mocha: a slight nod to bourbon, there...; **b22.5** the last time I tasted this I was somewhat underwhelmed, pointing out that the best-ever description of Campbeltown harbour was painted by Alfred Barnard about 130 years earlier. There was nothing bland about his prose, which couldn't be said for the malt. That was about three years ago. Inspecting it again I see that some life has been breathed into this – despite playing the dangerous game of using first-fill ex-bourbon only: casks which have a tendency to overwhelm with vanilla and flatten out. There is an element of that here, but the intensity of the young malt saves the day: the richness of the barley sugars is wonderfully refreshing. *40%*

Glen Scotia Campbeltown Malts Festival 2019 rum cask finish db **(94) n23.5 t23.5 f23 b24** Too often rum casks can tighten a malt to the point of strangulation. Not here. Lively and outstandingly well balanced. *51.3%.*

Glen Scotia Campbeltown Malts Festival 2020 Tawny Port Finish Aged 14 Years Peated bott code: L4.078 20 db **(93) n23.5 t23 f23 b23.5** Such fun when a distillery employs cask that are 100% clean and sulphur free. Only then can you create a malt like this with so many hidden doors to discover... *52.8%. nc ncf.*

Glen Scotia Double Cask finished in American oak & Pedro Ximenez sherry casks db **(85.5) n22 t22 f20.5 b21.** When blending, I do not like to get too involved with PX casks, unless I know for certain I can shape the effect to further or enrich the storyline on the palate. The reason is that PX means the complexity of a malt can easily come to a sticky end. That has happened here with both the malt and grape cancelling each other out. Soft and easy drinking with an excellent early delivery spike of intensity. But a dull middle and finish. And dull has never been a word I have associated with this distillery. Ever. *46%. ncf.*

Glen Scotia Double Cask American oak barrels & PX sherry casks, bott code: L2.092.19 db **(88) n22.5 t23 f20.5 b22** "Rich and Spicy" pronounces the label...and they are not wrong. About as succulent as it gets on delivery and there is a golden magic moment as that spice crashes into the heather honey. Undone slightly, though, by a disappointing finish. *46%. ncf.*

Glen Scotia Distillery Edition No. 6 19 Years Old first fill bourbon cask, dist Jul 99, bott Aug 18 db (95.5) n23.5 t24 f24 b24 One of the most charmingly, disarmingly beautiful single cask malts I have tasted this year. 57.9%. sc. 195 bottles.

Glen Scotia Warehouse Edition 2005 13 Years Old recharred American oak, first fill oloroso sherry finish, dist Sept 05, bott Aug 18 db (87.5) n21.5 t23 f21 b21.5 Another salty offering which peaks on delivery with a huge malt and muscovado sugar burst. Flattens out thereafter and bitters out, too. 56.2%. sc.

Glen Scotia Victoriana db (89.5) n23 t23 f21.5 b22 An unusual malt for a cask strength. Beyond the nose there is limited layering, instead concentrating on the malt-toffee intertwangling. 51.5%

Glen Scotia Victoriana Cask Strength bott code: L4.053.19 db (94.5) n23.5 this has come out as gung-ho crushed hazelnut and barley. The subtlest hint of smoke makes you do a nasal double-take: is it there or not? It is...; t24 a fizzing display of ultra-lively, salivating tannins – a malt revelling in some sublime American oak. And if that isn't juicy enough, the barley pitches in to up the salivation score even further; f23 an elegant climb down. Drier, a little spice but some sexy cocoa notes moving towards praline; b24 as cheerfully bright and breezy a malt as you are likely to find and one bursting with deceptive complexity. If this is trying to depict your average bottle of whisky from Victorian Campbeltown, then it has failed miserably: it was never this good...! 54.2%. nc ncf.

Glen Scotia Vintage 1991 American oak barrels, bott code: L8 092 19 db (94) n23.5 t24.5 f22.5 b23.5 A very honest malt, brimming with the distillery's endearing character. Whilst tasting this whisky I was deeply saddened to learn of the death of a friend and Whisky Bible devotee, Fran Budd, a warm and charming lady who left us long before she should have done. I raise a glass of this excellent malt and toast your memory, Fran: I suspect you would have approved. 46.7%. nc ncf. Traveller Exclusive.

GLEN SPEY
Speyside, 1885. Diageo. Working.

Glen Spey Aged 12 Years db (90) n23 t22 f22 b23 Very similar to the first Glen Spey I can remember in this range, the one before the over-toffeed effort of two years ago. Great to see it back to its more natural, stunningly beautiful self. 43%

Old Malt Cask Glen Spey Aged 24 Years refill barrel, cask no. 18198, dist Sept 96, bott Dec 20 (89.5) n23 t23.5 f21 b22 Rarely found these days, Glen Spey was, a century ago, one of the first malts sold internationally as a singleton to promote the lighter Speyside style. Just the slightest tang on the finale apart, this is a wonderful example of a much underappreciated malt. 46.1%. nc ncf sc. 207 bottles.

GLENTAUCHERS
Speyside, 1898. Chivas Brothers. Working.

Ballantine's The Glentauchers Aged 15 Years Series No.003 traditional oak casks, bott code: LKRM0071 2018/02/13 (86) n22 t22 f21 b21 Alarm bells ring when confronted by the dull nose with a neutral fruit and caramel edge. When the palate offers something fat and glossy (that's a new one for 'Tauchers) with a dull spice development to accompany the vague fruit and caramel, the heart sinks and flashing lights join the ringing alarm. The big, boring caramel finish drives you to distraction.... If anyone on this planet has championed Glentauchers longer or louder than me, or with more heart-felt gusto, then I would like to meet them. For well over 20 years I have been telling anyone who cares to listen – and many who don't – that this is one of Scotland's finest distilleries worthy of its own proprietary bottling. It finally arrives, and instead of a malt which scores in the mid-90s, as it should (and so often has done with independent bottlings in Whisky Bibles past), we have before us something pleasant, bland and not instantly recognisable as a 'Tauchers. Frankly, it could be from any Scottish distillery as the blueprint for the nose and flavour profile is shared by many: too many. As I say, pleasant whisky. But, knowing just how good this whisky really is (using 100% bourbon cask, no colour, no chill-filtration) what a huge and crushing disappointment. A bit like going to see the Sistine Chapel and finding someone had whitewashed over it.... 40%.

⬦ **Art Edition No 5 Glentauchers Aged 13 Years** Bourbon cask, dist 2009, bott 2022 (95) n23.5 the malt is pristine. At times quite brittle, at others, when the vanillas rise, softer and dabbing its powdery sweetness on the barley; t24 that, ladies and gentlemen, is the perfect delivery: the malt could not be any more clean or precise, the sugars more gristy and the vanillas and spices more beautifully weighted to give the most erudite oaky presence. Salivating... Adorable...; f23.5 just a slight breath of citrus lightening the malty load even late on. But that barley still has much to say even though the dryness of the butterscotch tart is beginning to draw in...; b24 it is just too easy to overlook the beauty and delicate complexity of this malt: Murray

Method, please. A blender's dream and a malt lover's 20 minutes of naked pleasure. Faultless and technically perfect for its age. And if I was to take home a sample from 20 or so whiskies I have tasted today to savour for my own personal pleasure...this'd be it... And by a long chalk. *53.8% 60 bottles Whiskyjace*

Canongate Distilled at Glentauchers 24 Years Old ex bourbon barrel cask no 22069 filled 12/16/96 bottled 02/19/2021 **(95.5) n24 t24 f23 b24.5** There is always something magical and mercurial about Glentauchers in this kind of mood. One of those rare malts which sparkles at both ends of the Murray Method spectrum and launches a thousand possibilities into the mind of any bright-eyed blender. Delicate, complex and yet always boasting a fabulous presence. *46.2% ncf nc 239 bottles*

Fadandel Glentauchers 12 Years Old (95) n23 anyone who has crumbled Maltesers in their hands and smelt it, will know exactly what is in their glass here...; **t24** the pace, layering, the oils, the intensity... Glentauchers is one of the few distilleries able to pull this off. Mind-blowingly complex without even noticing it. Pure malt...with countless add-ons....; **f24** the subtle oils elongate the experience. This means the malt has to give way slightly to the vanilla. And a fragile praline note slips in for good measure; **b24** 'Tauchers in overdrive. Makes great malt whisky look so damned easy... And let's just say spitting this one was not that easy.... If you are looking for a 12 year old Speyside of breath-taking, star quality..then you've just found it. You know, I just can't find a single fault with this one... *58.1%*

The Great Drams Glentauchers 10 Years Old cask no. 700435, dist 24 Jun 09, bott 1 Oct 19 **(94) n23.5** a delicious cross between a banana sandwich and egg custard tart; **t23.5** it's the enigmatic sweetness on delivery that wins you over: just a light brushing of gristy sugars to help facilitate the drier, spicier tannins that hint of chocolate mint; **f23** almost sawdusty as a delicate mocha and vanilla theme lasts longer than might be expected; **b24** comes across as one of those whiskies where the distillery doesn't even seem to try, yet effortlessly conjures up something disarmingly stylish and complex. *48.2%. nc ncf sc.*

◈ **Valour Whisky Glentauchers 2007 Aged 15 Years** dist 29/11/07 bott 26/06/23 sherry butt cask no 900655 **(96) n23.5** what a stunning aroma: the malt is thick but takes turns with fabulous toasted raisins for world dominance...; **t24** wow! That toastiness is there from the very off: we are talking Melton Hunt Cake, complete with dark cherries, with an extra dollop of raisin and molasses. Working deliciously just below these inflamed flavours is a glorious and proudly rigid maltiness. But if those flavours aren't enough, the spices from the oak are rattling on the taste buds, using all the available weight from the hefty oils to make their presence keenly felt. The whole picture is one of constant movement and intensity; **f24** for the finish that intensity is dialled down slightly. But the continuous flavour turmoil continues. Still those raisins are toasted, though now joined with a little buttercream. The malt boldly and proudly holds its own, occasionally flaking off towards a softer vanilla tone while the spices are spent and allows the whisky to die, as it deserves, nobly and in peace; **b24.5** a Speyside whisky filled into a sherry butt in 2007....and not even the slightest hint of a sulphur note. That makes this bottling a collectors' item just for that amazing fact alone. Glentauchers is one of the great, underappreciated, virtually undiscovered distilleries of Scotland. And is one of the few that has the inner strength to dictate to a healthy, high grade sherry butt such as this, rather than the other way round. This is a peach of a bottling, the whisky almost shattering the glass with so much flavour and personality desperate to get out. The marriage between the powering barley and the muscular grape is of legendary dimensions. The kind of malt I find very hard to spit, however professional I may be. And for those who remember blended Scotch from 40 years ago, there is a rigidity to this that many will still recognise. Oh, and another point: this cask has been plucked from the warehouse and bottled at the very peak of its powers. To add water to this would be a crime against whisky.... *64.2% nc ncf 363 bottles*

GLENTURRET
Highlands (Perthshire), 1775. Edrington. Working.

Glenturret Aged 8 Years db **(88) n21 t22 f23 b22.** Technically no prizewinner. But the dexterity of the honey is charming, as this distillery has a tendency sometimes to be. 40%

The Glenturret Aged 10 Years db **(76) n19 t18 f20 b19.** Lots of trademark honey but some less than impressive contributions from both cask and the stillman. 40%

The Glenturret Fly's 16 Masters Edition db **(96) n24.5 t24 f23.5 b24.5** When I first found Glenturret some 30 years so ago, their whisky was exceptionally rare – on account of their size and having been closed for a very long time – but the few bottlings they produced had a very distinctive, indeed unique, feel. Then it changed as they used more Highland Distillers sherry butts which were, frankly, the kiss of death. Here, though, we appear to have reverted back to exactly how it tasted half a lifetime ago. Rich, kissed with copper and stirred with honey. It is, as is fitting to old Fly, the dog's bollocks... 44%. *1,740 bottles.*

Glenturret 30 Year Old db (94) n23 t24 f23 b24 The ultimate exhibition of brinkmanship, surely: hangs on to its integrity by a cat's whisker... 43.4%.

Glenturret Peated Drummond db (87) n21 t23.5 f21 b21.5 The wide cut from the small still means the odd feint creeps into this one; the peat is too much on the sparse side to paper over the cracks. However, the delivery is something that has to be experienced. A new make freshness can be found all over the show, but even that gives way as the golden syrup and smoke mingle for one of the briefest yet most beautiful star quality moments of the whisky year. 58.9%.

The Glenturret Peated Edition db (86) n19.5 t22 f21.5 b22. Pleasant enough, for sure, even if the nose is a bit rough. But in the grand scheme of things, just another peated malt and one of no special distinction. Surely they should concentrate on being Glenturret: there is only one of those.... 43%

The Glenturret Sherry Edition db (78) n19 t21 f19 b19. Not sure if this sherry lark is the best direction for this great distillery to take. 43%

The Glenturret Triple Wood Edition db (84) n20 t22.5 f20 b21.5. Not the happiest of whiskies, but recovers from its obvious wounds by concentrating on the juicy grain, rather than the grape. 43%

Art Edition No 1 Rhuadh Mhor 2010 bott 2021 (92.5) n23 t24 f22 b23.5 A quite excellent whisky (despite a light sulphur niggle) adorned on the bottle by a no less impressive painting by German artist Martin Pudenz, whose eclectic work features on all three Art Edition labels. This painting, at knee-height of a woman sitting in a short, revealing skirt with a large bouquet of flowers on her lap covering her torso and head is semi-erotic and would be appreciated by fans of Basic Instinct. I have yet to hear Britain's mouthy, hypocritical, puritanical, nauseatingly Woke whisky writers denounce this and try to force the artist and bottlers out of business. But then, I suppose, it is not in their self-interest, is it. After all, how can they be seen to denounce art? Then again, I always thought that writing was found under the umbrella of the arts, also.... Mind you, jealousy always was a very basic instinct... 52.6%

Fanandel.dk Ruadh Maor Aged 10 Years Moscatel Quarter Cask cask no.156A, dist Dec 2009, bott Jul 2020 (92.5) n23 t24 f22.5 b23 Just brilliant! A great example of a wine cask genuinely adding rather than subtracting from a peaty encounter. A minor classic, especially for this distillery which appears to be coming back to life quite impressively. 53.8% 178 bottles

◈ **Kingsbury Ruadh Maor Glenturret 2011 Aged 11 Years** hogshead, cask no 120 (88.5) n22 t23 f21.5 b22 A light young, "floaty" smoke aroma where the phenols drift and appear to pick up light mocha on the wind....and this theme continues on the palate. Unusually light-bodied for a Glenturret with a surprising lack of copper in its make-up, which translates to the thinnish finish. But enough sweet malty phenols doing the rounds for overall satisfaction. 62.6% 273 bottles

The Whisky Chamber Ruadh Maor 9 Jahre 2010 refill PX sherry cask (89.5) n23 t23.5 f20.5 b22.5 For years the sherry butts at Glenturret meant one thing: sulphur. Having been bought in under the Highland Distillers regime, the sherry bottlings stood no chance. This, however, is another story. Is it a perfect cask? Well, no it does have a little echo at the finish it could do without. But where this malt wins is in its rumbustious nature which old timers like me appreciate. Finish apart, this is old school. And very beautifully made, too. 56.2%. sc.

GLENUGIE
Highlands (Eastern). 1834-1983. Whitbread. Closed.

Deoch an Doras Glenugie 30 Years Old dist 1980, bott 2011 db (87) n22 t23.5 f19.5 b22. It is now 2017 and it has been six long years since this arrived in my tasting room - something I didn't expect to see again: a distillery bottling of Glenugie. Well, technically, anyway, as Glenugie was part of the Chivas group when it died in the 1980s. As far as I can remember they only brought it out once, either as a seven- or five-year-old. I think that went to Italy, so when I walked around the old site just after it closed, it was a Gordon and MacPhail bottling I drank from and it tasted nothing like this! Just a shame there is a very slight flaw in the sherry butt, but just great to see it in bottle again. 52.13%. nc ncf.

GLENURY ROYAL
Highlands (Eastern), 1868-1985. Diageo. Demolished.

Glenury Royal 36 Years Old db (89) n21 t23 f22 b23. An undulating dram, hitting highs and lows. The finish, in particular, is impressive: just when it looks on its last legs, it revives delightfully. The whole package, though far from perfect, is pretty astounding. 50.2%

Gordon & MacPhail Rare Old Glenury Royal 1984 (95.5) n23 t24 f23.5 b25 In the rare instances of the early 1980s I tasted a young Glenury, it was never this good and hardly looked up for 30 years in the cask. But this incredibly rare bottling of the malt, the best I have ever encountered from Glenury and distilled in the final days of its 117 year existence, stands its ground proudly and performs, unforgettably, the Last Post with magical honeyed notes... 46%.

HAZELBURN (see Springbank)

HIGHLAND PARK
Highlands (Island–Orkney), 1795. Edrington. Working.

Highland Park 8 Years Old db (87) n22 t22 f22 b21. A journey back in time for some of us: this is the original distillery bottling of the 70s and 80s, bottles of which are still doing the rounds in obscure Japanese bars and specialist outlets such as the Whisky Exchange. 40%

Highland Park 10 Year Old Ambassador's Choice db (74) n17.5 t20 f17.5 b19. Some of the casks are so badly sulphured, I'm surprised there hasn't been a diplomatic incident...46%

◈ **Highland Park 10 Year Old Viking Scars**, bott code L0096EL04 10/03 db (89) n23.5 nothing subtle about the peat on this HP. Where once it would have to be teased out, here it is up and standing to attention the moment your pour into the glass. The aroma is far from powerful, but those phenols project themselves sharply and the accompanying muscovado sugars are no less lucid; t23 initially melt-in-the-mouth before the spikey barley ramps up the salivation levels to red. Sublime chocolate fruit and nut in the midpoint which go well with that unusually crisp peat; f20 dull, bitter and disappointing; b22.5 a very different animal to the old Highland 10, this one having claws....or perhaps I mean swords. Try to ignore the finish, which is not worthy of the earlier, excellent entertainment. 40% nc

Highland Park Aged 12 Years db (78) n19 t21 f19 b19. Let's just hope that the choice of casks for this bottling was a freak. To be honest, this was one of my favourite whiskies of all time, one of my desert island drams, and I could weep. 40% WB16/048

Highland Park Aged 15 Years db (85) n21 t22 f21 b21. Had to re-taste this several times, surprised as I was by just how relatively flat this was. A hill of honey forms the early delivery, but then... 40%

Highland Park Loki Aged 15 Years db (96) n24 t24 f23.5 b24.5 the weirdness of the heather apart, a bit of a trip back in time. A higher smoke ratio than the bottlings of more recent years which new converts to the distillery will be unfamiliar with, but reverting to the levels regularly found in the 1970s and 80s, probably right through to about 1993/94. Which is a very good thing because the secret of the peat at HP was that, as puffed out as it could be in the old days, it never interfered with the overall complexity, other than adding to it. Which is exactly the case here. Beyond excellent! 48.7%. Edrington.

Highland Park 16 Years Old db (88) n23 t23 f20 b22. I tasted this the day it first came out at one of the Heathrow whisky shops. I thought it a bit flat and uninspiring. This sample, maybe from another bottling, is more impressive and showing true Highland Park colours, the finish apart. 40%. Exclusively available in Duty Free/Travel Retail.

Highland Park Thor Aged 16 Years db (87.5) n22.5 t22.5 t23.5 f19 b22.5. Now, from what I remember of my Norse gods, Thor was the God of Thunder. Which is a bit spooky seeing as hailstones are crashing down outside as I write this and lightning is striking overhead. Certainly a whisky built on power. Even taking into account the glitch in one or two of the casks, a dram to be savoured on delivery. 52.1%. 23,000 bottles.

Highland Park Ice Edition Aged 17 Years db (87) n22 t23 f21 b21. The smoke drifts around until it finds some spices. Frustrating: you expect it to kick on but it stubbornly refuses to. Caramel and vanilla up front, then bitters out. 53.9%.

Highland Park Aged 18 Years db (95.5) n23.5 t24 f24 b24 If familiarity breeds contempt, then it has yet to happen between myself and HP 18. This is a must-have dram. I show it to ladies the world over to win their hearts, minds and tastebuds when it comes to whisky. And the more time I spend with it, the more I become aware and appreciative of its extraordinary consistency. The very latest bottlings have been astonishing, possibly because colouring has now been dropped, and wisely so. Why in any way reduce what is one of the world's great whisky experiences? Such has been the staggering consistency of this dram I have thought of late of promoting the distillery into the world's top three: only Ardbeg and Buffalo Trace have been bottling whisk(e)y of such quality over a wide range of ages in such metronomic fashion. Anyway, enough: a glass of something honeyed and dazzling calls... 43%

Highland Park Aged 21 Years db (82.5) n20.5 t22 f19 b21. Good news and bad news. The good news is that they appear to have done away with the insane notion of reducing this to 40% abv. The bad news: a sulphured sherry butt has found its way into this bottling. 47.5%

Highland Park Aged 25 Years db (96) n24 t24 f24 b24 I am a relieved man: the finest HP 25 for a number of years which displays the distillery's unmistakable fingerprints with a pride bordering on arrogance. One of the most improved bottlings of the year: an emperor of a dram. 48.1%

Highland Park Aged 30 Years db (90) n22 t22.5 f23 b22.5 A very dramatic shift from the last bottling I tasted; this has taken a fruitier route. Sheer quality, though. 48.1%

Highland Park 40 Years Old db **(90.5)** n20.5 t22.5 f24 b23.5 Picking splinters from my nose with this one. Some of the casks used here have obviously choked on oak, and I feared the worst. But such is the brilliance of the resilience by being on the money with the honey, you can say only that it has pulled off an amazing feat with the peat. Sheer poetry... 48.3%

Highland Park 50 Years Old dist Jan 60 db **(96.5)** n24.5 t24 f24 b24 Old whiskies tend to react to unchartered territory as far as time in the oak is concerned in quite different ways. This grey beard has certainly given us a new slant. Nothing unique about the nose. But when one is usually confronted with those characteristics on the nose, what follows on the palate moves towards a reasonably predictable path. Not here. Truly unique – as it should be after all this time. 44.8%. sc. 275 bottles.

Highland Park Dark Origins db **(80)** n19 t23 f18 b20. Part of that Dark Origin must be cocoa, as there is an abundance of delicious high grade chocolate here. But the other part is not so much dark as yellow, as sulphur is around on the nose and finish in particular - and does plenty of damage. Genuinely disappointing to see one of the world's greatest distilleries refusing to play to its strengths and putting so much of its weight on its Achilles heel. 46.8%. ncf.

Highland Park Earl Haakon db **(92)** n22.5 t24 f22.5 b23. A fabulous malt offering some of the best individual moments of the year. But appears to run out of steam about two thirds in. 54.9%. 3,300 bottles.

Highland Park Einar db **(90.5)** n23 t23 f22 b22.5 A curious style of HP which shows most of its usual traits but possesses an extra sharpness. 40% WB15/328

Highland Park Freya 1st fill ex-bourbon casks db **(88.5)** n22 t23 f21.5 b22. The majestic honey on delivery makes up for some of the untidier moments. 52.10%.

Highland Park King Christian db **(83.5)** n22 t22.5 f18.5 b20.5. A hefty malt with a massive fruit influence. But struggles for balance and to keep full control of the, ultimately, off-key grapey input. Despite the sub-standard finale, there is much to enjoy with the early malt-fruit battles on delivery that offer a weighty and buttery introduction to the diffused molasses and vanilla. But with the spice arrives the Achilles heel... 46.8%

Highland Park Leif Eriksson bourbon and American oak db **(86)** n22 t22 f21 b21. The usual distillery traits have gone AWOL while all kinds of caramel notes have usurped them. That said, this has to be one of the softest drams you'll find. 40%. Edrington.

Highland Park Ragnavald db **(87.5)** n21.5 t22 f22 b22. Thickset and muscular, this malt offers a slightly different type of earthiness to the usual HP. Even the malt has its moment in the sun. But the overall portrait hangs from the wall at a slight tilt... 45.05%

Highland Park Sigurd db **(96)** n23.5 t24.5 f23.5 b24.5 Breathtaking, star-studded and ridiculously complex reminder that this distillery is capable of serving up some of the best whisky the world can enjoy. 43%

Highland Park Svein db **(87)** n22 t22 f21.5 b21.5. A soft, friendly dram with good spice pick up. But rather too dependent on a tannin-toffee theme. 40% WB15/318

Highland Park Viking Soul Cask 13.5 Years Old 18 month sherry seasoned quarter cask finish, cask no. 700066, bott 2019 db **(88.5)** n22 t23.5 f21 b22 The quarter cask finish is a brave move to make after over 13 years of normality. And the extra oak really does punch through, and not always in a way that feels particularly relaxed or natural. The fruitiness arrives in sugary waves and enjoys a delightful spice flourish. But for an HP, the most rounded of all Scotland's malts, it feels a tad frantic. No faulting the fabulous delivery, though, which appears to have had the cocoa rammed forward with the grape ahead of time... 55.4%. nc ncf sc. 159 bottles. Bottled for MacAlabur.

Artful Dodger Orkney Highland Park 14 Year Old 2004 ex-sherry butt, cask no. 18 **(86.5)** n22 t23 f20 b21.5 Less Artful Dodger than Jammy Dodger. The fruit envelops all aspects of this malt - on nose and delivery in particular. Deep vanilla tones hit back, as do the spices, but the dull finish brings an end to an intriguing passage of development. Perhaps by no means the worst sherry butt, but not the best, either. 58.8%. sc.

Cadenhead's Cask Strength Highland Park Aged 28 Years refill butt, dist 1992, bott 2020 **(95)** n23.5 by now, after 28 years, the light pettiness of this whisky should be hanging on by a thread. But such is this malt's fragile nature, it is the phenols leading the way. And they have picked up a little eucalyptus along the way to ensure the age is by no means overlooked. The honey of younger casks is missing, though, but compensated for by residual grist. Just so elegant...; t24.5 ridiculous! Heading for 30-years old and the delivery is salivating. And here's the bonus. That grist apparent on the nose is the first flavour to burst all over the taste buds. Soon followed by a light smearing of honey that was absent from the aroma. By the time you come to terms with the spices you realise it has the lightest touch of peat in its midst; f23 this is an old school sherry butt with minimum creaking and zero sulphur. The fade has none of the complexity of the delivery and follow-thorough. But, with plenty of vanilla apparent and still the softest peat breeze, it fades in style...; b24 when you get an HP of this vintage, you hope it will be a used sherry butt at work rather than first fill. It is, and you will be rewarded by seeing HP in its undiluted magnificence. 58.7% Specially bottled for Cadenhead's Whisky Shop Milan

❧ **Ferg and Harris Highland Park 2004 Aged 18 Years** finished in 2nd fill oloroso butt, cask no 4689, bott 2022 (89.5) n23 beautifully even temperament with a glorious spice nip and lazy smokiness to the sultana-studded heather honey; t23.5 exceptional mouth feel, the oils being absolutely perfectly weighted. The intensity of the heather honey is spellbinding, holding with it concentrated barley sugar, all which pulses alongside the spice. Light plum juice and a vague but attractive fig note stirs in the fruit; f21 bitters somewhat as the sherry butt kicks in a little sulphur to the determined honey; b22 hard to find HPs in oloroso from this period that isn't in some way sulphur affected. But the journey up to the point it kicks in is a quite stunning one with the oils being in total sync with the richness of the honey and the cleverness of the phenols. For those unaffected by the dreaded S word, this might be one of your whiskies of the year... 59.7% sc ncf Young Spirits

William & Co Spirits World Whisky Club Movie Series Highland Park 12 Years Old sherry oak octave cask finish, cask no. 5027113, dist Nov 07, bott Jun 20 (91) n23 t22 f23.5 b22.5 As enjoyable as I found this, I just felt there was a heaviness to the fruit which, for too long, diminished slightly the complexity of the HP itself. That said, weighty, chewable, entertaining and a malt that just gets better as it progresses. 54.7%. 102 bottles.

HOLYROOD

Lowlands, 2019. Rob Carpenter. Working.

Holyrood New Make 262 Days Cask 383 first fill Spanish oak db (88) n22 t23 f21 b22 Well, more new-ish make or malt spirit than new make. But let's not split hairs. Let's look at what they have on show. Well, for a start, a genuine standing ovation for cask choice: this is 100% sulphur free. Which gives their Maris Otter malt a chance to strut its stuff. And it doesn't need a second invitation. The barley is standing up proudly to the light sultana incursions and even after a short time the tannins begin to prod with a few light spices. The nose is dry-ish as the grape skin holds sway, a little surprising, perhaps. But the youthful delivery regains its malty feet and keeps them planted. Even so, this is light, very mildly off-key distillate which, perversely, needs a little cleaning as well as fattening – for in this state it will be prone to being easily bullied. 50% sc nc ncf

IMPERIAL

Speyside, 1897. Chivas Brothers. Silent.

Imperial Aged 15 Years "Special Distillery Bottling" db (69) n17 t18 f17 b17. At least one very poor cask, hot spirit and overly sweet. Apart from that it's wonderful. 46%

Chapter 7 Imperial 1998 Aged 22 Years bourbon barrel, barrel no.104355 (88.5) n22 t22 f22.5 b22 Along with Littlemill and others, Imperial holds the distinction of being a malt that was very poor when young, but one that holds a certain elegance in old age. Here we see Imperial at its glassy best: that glassy sheen to the body that, again, Littlemill boasts...though there is always a little resiny feel to it. With Littlemill that invariably arrives at the end. With Imperial it may arrive at any time. Here it is early. But as that light gluey element dissipates, then the sharp barley intensity becomes deeply attractive. Pretty one dimensional, admittedly – but that's one more than it had in its earlier life... 52.1% sc

Single & Single Imperial 1995 24 Year Old American oak (87) n22.5 t22.5 f20 b22 Very typically Imperial in a fine bourbon cask, the oak has laid a excellent foundation for the malt to free itself from the distillery's shackles and really let rip. Sadly, the poor original distillate catches up for a thin, gluey finish. 49.9%. sc. 204 bottles.

The Single Malts of Scotland Marriage Imperial 28 Year Old (80.5) n20.5 t21 f19 b20 For me, this is one of the most fascinating malts I will taste this year, 2020. Because 28 years ago I visited the chilly confines of this distillery quite often – and rarely found a new make that augured well for the future. The fact the distillery closed disappointed but didn't exactly surprise me. Here you can see why. The gluey nose is reminiscent of Littlemill in its last days, the delivery thin and tart. The finish, after it passes through some decent milk chocolate notes, is simply a wreck. This whisky may have soul, but there is no body...and that is why the blenders decided enough was enough. Usually the passing of three decades – or thereabouts – brings redemption to a failed distillery, Littlemill again being a case in point. Not here though. To be sampled simply as a whisky life experience rather than the expectation of great, or even particularly good, whisky. 40.88%.

INCHGOWER

Speyside, 1872. Diageo. Working.

Inchgower 27 Year Old db (93) n22.5 t24 f23 b23.5 Delicious and entertaining. Doesn't try to play the elegant old malt card. Instead gets stuck in with a rip-roaring attack on delivery, the fizzing spices burning deep and making the most of the light liquorice and molasses which has formed a thick-set partnership with the intense malt. The only hint of subtlety arrives towards the death as a little butterscotch tart allows a late juiciness from the barley free reign. Just love it! *43%. 8,544 bottles. Diageo Special Releases 2018.*

Deer, Bear & Moose Inchgower Aged 22 Years dist Sept 95, bott Dec 17 **(94.5) n23 t24 f23.5 b24** Inchgower in prime Jekyll and Hyde mode, at first the juicy, swashbuckling fruit pointing towards a malt half its age. Then, fascinatingly, a wave of tannins sweeps in bringing with it a salty, mildly earthy depth, as well as major spices... and suddenly the malt looks every bit its years. The layering on delivery is worth savouring, as it really relishes the old school griminess for a minute or two before moving into a sweeter marzipan richness with a seasidey saltiness burning into the piece. You never know what you are going to get from this distillery. But this is one of the most complete and complex versions for quite a while. A wonderful surprise. *52.1%. nc ncf sc.*

The First Editions Inchgower Aged 23 Years 1997 sherry butt, cask no. 18208, bott 2020 **(89.5) n22.5** the molasses which could be picked up on its sister cask 18203 here makes its mark much earlier, this time on the nose. Indeed, there is almost a touch if rum to this one...; **t22.5** fat, chewy and just a slight rumbling of something grapey to keep the spices company; just enough malt to fire up the salivation levels; **f22** the oak leaks though to give you a sense of decent age for the first time; **b22.5** a fuller, more characterful version of cask 18203..dare I say it: a little more like the old, traditional style! *55.6%. nc ncf sc. 264 bottles.*

Kingbury Gold Inchgower 20 Year Old hogshead, dist 2000, cask no. 2 **(92.5) n23 t23 f23 b23.5** Inchgower making a point of showing its considerable character. A must try bottling. *47.8% sc 209 bottles*

Old Malt Cask Inchgower Aged 23 Years sherry butt, cask no. 18203, dist Aug 97, bott Nov 20 **(88.5) n22 t22 f22 b22.5** For an Inchgower, this is a remarkably straightforward cove. Had I been tasting a 23-year-old Inchgower 23 years ago, my tastebuds would have been led merry dance as the oilier notes build up and thickened. A generation on, so to speak, we have a lighter, cleaner malt now, still with a little grime for old time's sake on the nose. But the clarity of the malt on the palate here, aided and abetted by the molasses through the middle keeps a little of the weight but a far brighter, enjoyable, better-balanced experience than of old. *50%. nc ncf sc. 294 bottles.*

INVERLEVEN
Lowland, 1938–1991. Demolished.

Deoch an Doras Inverleven 36 Years Old dist 1973 **(94.5) n24 t23.5 f23 b24** As light on the palate as a morning mist. This distillery just wasn't designed to make a malt of this antiquity, yet this is to the manor born. *48.85%. nc ncf. Chivas Brothers. 500 bottles.*

Gordon & MacPhail Private Collection Inverleven 1985 refill bourbon barrel, cask no. 562, bott 2018 **(96.5) n24 t24.5 f23.5 b24.5** I am still haunted by the day Inverleven distilled for the very last time, their manager telling me: "That's it, Jim. We're done." It was another shocking event: a great Lowland distillery which made a very consistent, malty, mildly fragile make and was absolutely excellent for blenders at about 5 years in decent second fill bourbons, and even better in firsts; and quite magnificent at about 8 years in both. Of course, the demise of Inverleven was the foretelling of the eventual closure of the unbettered Dumbarton grain distillery in which the malt complex was housed. But these were acts of whisky vandalism by a company, Allied Domecq, which never could get it right with the management of their single malts. This delicate and noble malt is a rare testimony to a distillery lost for all the wrong reasons. There is not a bum note, not a blemish. It is Lowland perfection and a whisky tragedy all rolled into one. *57.4%. 130 bottles.*

ISLE OF ARRAN
Highlands (Island–Arran), 1995. Isle of Arran Distillers. Working.

Isle of Arran Machrie Moor 5th Edition bott 2014 db **(91.5) n22.5 t24 f22 b23** A few tired old bourbon barrels have taken the score down slightly on last year. But the spirit itself is nothing short of brilliant. *46% WB16/049*

The Arran Malt 10 Year Old db **(87) n22.5 t22.5 f20 b22.** It has been a while since I last officially tasted this. If they are wiling to accept some friendly advice, I think the blenders should tone down on raising any fruit profile and concentrate on the malt, which is amongst the best in the business. *46%. nc ncf.*

The Arran Malt 12 Years Old db **(85) n21.5 t22 f20.5 b21** Hmmmm. Surprise one, this. There must be more than one bottling already of this. The first I tasted was perhaps slightly on the oaky side but otherwise intact and salt-honeyed where need be. This one has a bit of a tang: very drinkable, but definitely a less than brilliant cask around. *46%*

The Arran Malt Aged 14 Years db **(89.5) n22 t23.5 f21.5 b22.5.** A superb whisky, but the evidence that there has been a subtle shift in emphasis, with the oak now taking too keen an interest, is easily attained. *46%. ncf.*

The Arran Malt Aged 17 Years db (91.5) n23.5 t23.5 f21.5 b23 "Matured in the finest ex-Sherry casks" trills the back label. And, by and large, they are right. Maybe a single less than finest imparts the light furriness to the finish. But by present day sherry butt standards, a pretty outstanding effort. 46%. nc ncf. 9000 bottles. WB15/152

The Arran Malt Fino Sherry Cask Finish db (82.5) n21 t20 f21 b20.5. Pretty tight with the bitterness not being properly compensated for. 50%

Acla Selection Island Edition Isle of Arran 22 Year Old hogshead, dist 1996, bott 2019 (86.5) n22 t22 f21 b21.5 Punches slightly heavier than its strength and while the light heather honey tones impress, a dry, vaguely bitter, flourish to the oak detracts somewhat and closes down the conversation. 48.3%.

Golden Cask Arran Aged 21 Years cask no. CM240, dist 1996, bott 2017 (94.5) n23.5 t24 f23 b24 Impeccable Arran. 51.6%. sc. 254 bottles.

MacAlabur Isle of Arran 10 Year Old peated, first fill bourbon barrel, cask no.09/060, dist Sep 2009, bott Jan 2020 (94) n23.5 t24 f23 b23.5 When you get near distilled malt in a very fine cask there can be only one outcome. Curiously, exactly 25 years ago this week I sat Wembley Stadium with Arran's first-ever distillery manager Gordon Mitchell in the seat beside me, as we watched England beat Scotland 2-0 in the European Championships and, together, marvelled at Paul Gascoigne's legendary goal, our feelings at opposing poles. A few days ago an England team which performs better on its knees than its feet met at the same (updated) venue in the same competition for a joyless 0-0 bore draw. A quarter of a century ago Arran's then Chairman and founder, Harold Currie, also had huge football connections, having once been Scottish League St Mirran's Chairman and gave Alex Ferguson his first-ever senior managing position. When the distillery was being built, I suggested to Harold that he might want to take a peaty route, but his mind was set: "I want it to be as close to Macallan as we can get it. I really don't want it to be Islay style, even if we are on an island." And that was that. I know Gordon wouldn't have minded it being, for at least a few mashes a year, a peated malt. Instead he said. "Well, Jim we'll just have to be content that we get a little bit of peat off the water that runs off Loch na Davy" It is curious that as I watched England pathetic, passionless attempt against Scotland, my mind wondered back to those conversations, not least because neither Gordon Mitchell or Harold Currie are with us now. And then, just a day or two later, I found Harold Currie waiting for me in my tasting lab. It is excellent. As a 10-year-old I think even the great Harold Currie would be impressed with the elegant touch of the peat. 55.8% 241 bottles

Vintage Bottlers Isle of Arran 24 Years Old single sherry cask, dist 02/09/97, bott 11/01/22 (93) n23.5 t24 f22.5 b23 Always warms the cockles when you encounter a faultless sherry butt and one that has riches yet subtlety enough to make the nose a real beckoning finger: really does sit, with its sultana-laden fruitiness, very comfortably with the yielding oak and light and even and ever-thickening malt. The fact that on delivery it finds sugars enough to form a delightful grape and barley duet is better still, especially with the spices ensuring a third dimension. The finish may be duller but I dare you not to end this one with a smile on your face. Deeply satisfying and a rare sherry offering that allows so much malt to enjoy star billing. 51.6% sc 235 bottles

W.W. Club AR.1 Arran Aged 11 Years American oak cask, cask no. 19, dist Oct 05, bott Feb 17 (86.5) n21.5 t22.5 f21 b21.5 Plenty of rich, creamy honey on delivery. And no little succulent malt, too. But a little too much tang towards the finish, confirming a quaver on the nose. 57.7%. sc. 321 bottles. William & Co. Spirits.

ISLE OF JURA

Highlands (Island–Jura), 1810. Whyte and Mackay. Working.

Isle Of Jura Aged 10 Years db (79.5) n19 t22 f19 b19.5. Perhaps a little livelier than before, but still miles short of where you might hope it to be. 40%

Jura Aged 10 Years American white oak bourbon barrels, aged Oloroso sherry butts, bott code: L0143 07 59 P/012028 db (89.5) n22.5 soft malt, sweet and a little lemon sherbet; t22 follows the nose by taking the softie route...only here goes into ultra-soft mode. Perhaps a little too much sweetness and caramel early on, but as that clears a light vanilla and raisin combination filters through; f22.5 decidedly toasty and dry. A little light molasses helps balance things; b22.5 the best part of 40 years ago I used to travel annually to Jura and stop at the hotel, the owner of which also being a director of the distillery next door. And every year I would bring back one of his hotel bottlings, complete with its label portraying a stag, usually ex-bourbon and sweet as a nut. It would be great if they could revert more towards a bottling which shewed the character of the distillery as starkly as that old hotel bottling did, as this appears to be hiding a great many things. That said, a more enjoyable Jura 10 than in the recent past: definitely on the up and worth watching. 40%.

Jura Aged 12 Years American white oak ex-bourbon barrels, aged Oloroso sherry cask finish, bott code: L80205 00:43 P/005956 db (87.5) n22.5 t23 f20.5 b21.5 For the most part, this is an artful malt proudly portraying its coastal origins, with a sharp, malty saltiness creeping onto the nose and delivery in very respectable proportions. The mouthfeel is also a delight on entry, as is the rich chocolate fruit and nut middle. Just a shame that a rogue sherry cask has leaked some of the dreaded S element into the mix, which builds into a furry bitterness at the death. Mid Europeans devoid of the sulphur gene will devour this with joy. So much else to enjoy, though, especially that juicy delivery. I look forward to seeing the next bottling... 40%.

Jura Aged 14 Years American Rye Cask ex bourbon and American rye barrels, bott code 2022/06/11 L2131 db **(95.5) n24** brilliant! Now that is what I call a nose! There is a most subtle mintiness coming off the rye casks. There is also a fixed, firm honey tone, too, of the heather honey variety. All beautifully amalgamated with the tannins always challenging and asking questions. Fascinating....and behaves a lot older than its 14 years; **t24** after such an excellent nose, it would be easy for the delivery to be a let-down. But it isn't. Instead, we have a gentle oiliness softening the deep and powering tannins which offer a lightly overdone toast factor to the chocolate lime candy. I did not expect to pick up any rye notes on this...but they are unquestionably there via the rigid sugars; **f23.5** considering the shyness of the oils late on, the finish is pretty lengthy. The cocoa has melted out of the chocolate lime which the vanillas are now on overdrive; **b24** the mint coming off the rye casks is by no means an unknown phenomenon, but by no means guaranteed, either. This is complex, big on flavour while offering a subtle complexity as a degree of eucalyptus sneaks in. More remarkable, the delivery gives the feeling that something a lot older than 14 years has gone into this. The best Jura I have tasted in years – and in contention for a Whisky Bible award. Can't recommend this bottling enough. 40%

Isle Of Jura Aged 16 Years db **(90.5) n21.5 t23.5 f23 b23** A massive improvement, this time celebrating its salty, earthy heritage to good effect. The odd strange, less than harmonious note. But by far and away the most improved Jura for a long, long while. 40%

Jura Aged 18 Years American white oak ex-bourbon barrels and red wine casks, bott code: L0006 13:36 P/011235 db **(85.5) n21.5 t23.5 f19 b21.5** Although the nose is tight, almost mean, in its persona you are let half-fearing the worst, but wondering for the best. There is an outlandish outbreak of massive flavour on delivery, both the malt and fruit almost shrill in their proclamations of their intent. This is high juiciness in excelsis, the sugars crisp and full of grist and Demerara. And on the finish a slight chocolate note hovers, but then a degree of sulphur drifts in...as threatened by the nose. It is so frustrating when wine casks have needlessly and fatally been given the sulphur candle treatment. This has so many beautiful moments. But... 44%.

Jura Aged 21 Years Tide American white oak ex-bourbon barrels & virgin American oak casks db **(94) n23 t23.5 f23.5 b24** Not for the first time, caramel plays a big part in a Jura. But here to appears to be better weighted and structured thanks to greater tannin involvement. Pleasingly and impressively complex. 46.7%.

Jura Aged 21 Years Time American white oak ex-bourbon barrels & ex-peated malt casks db **(92) n23.5** the playful spice tweaks both your nose and that of the chunky tannin; the phenols offer an attractive deep base note; **t23.5** crystalised brown sugars formulate from the off, the tannins having a big say in matters. But it is those wisps of smoke that add structure and balance, seemingly tying together the crisper sweet notes and the earthier oakiness. Spices ping around with abandon; **f22** digestive biscuit dipped in mocha; **b23** alongside Tide, great to see Jura back offering us something that intrigues: a bit like the first Jura I ever tasted – on the island's hotel – nearly 40 years ago... 47.2%.

Jura 1988 bott 2019 db **(91.5) n22 t23 f23 b23.5** So unusually clean I wondered if this was a wine cask, almost certainly port, at work or just Demerara sugars off the oak working at their ultimate fruitiness. Or, most likely, both! 52.8%. nc ncf. 1,500 bottles.

Jura 1989 American white oak ex-bourbon barrels, bott 2019 db **(83.5) n21 t22.5 f19 b21** None of the glitz and little of the balance displayed by the Two-One-Two, below. Not the most enticing of noses , though the piece rallies briefly on delivery as the intense malt is steered into position by excellent spice. Then it all unravels... 53.5%. nc ncf.

Jura One and All Aged 20 Years db **(83.5) n21 t22 f19.5 b21** A metallic tang to this. Nutty with tart, fruity borders but nothing to get excited about. Doesn't quite add up. 51%. nc ncf.

Jura One For The Road Aged 22 Years Pinot Noir finish db **(89) n23 t23 f21 b22** Enjoyable though ultimately a bit too straight and, just like the single road on Jura, goes nowhere... 47%. nc ncf.

Jura Journey mature white oak ex-bourbon barrels, bott code L3019 db **(88) n22 t22 f21.5 b22.5** Apologetic smoke pops up mainly on the nose and forms no more than a barely discernible background noise on the palate. The early malt projection is decent, but rather melts into simplicity rather than complexity and gets lost once on the palate, especially as the vanilla and toffee blots all else out. One for Malteser lovers. 40%

Jura Special Wood Series French Oak American white oak bourbon barrels, French oak cask finish, bott code: L9108 02:36 P/008522 db **(89) n22.5** the French oak appears to have brought with it French heather honey – Bruyère – to smarten this up and give the spices something to bounce against; **t23** soft delivery with an immediate malty charge. The honey also slowly materialises, though the tannins appear to have a little of the devil about them; **f21.5** just a tad untidy here and bitter. But the honey has made way for molasses; **b22** so much to enjoy here, but feel this is understrength for what it is trying to achieve, the oils breaking down too quickly and making the transition at the end a little too rugged. But a full-flavoured Jura as you have never quite seen her before! *42%.*

⬩ **Jura Red Wine Cask Finish** matured white oak ex-bourbon with red wine cask finish, bott code L2054 db **(89) n23** clean, malty, a little salty and topped by a hint of mushed grape skin. If they were looking for complexity, they've found it...; **t23** astonishing three-dimensional fruit on delivery takes you aback. This is shooting off the charts so far as juiciness is concerned while as the fruit calms towards the middle, I am minded of my old mum's redcurrant jam from the 1960s...Incidentally, the malt is concentrated and clean...; **f20.5** just a little dullness creeps in with the vanilla; **b22.5** Jura these days appears to be making bold statements. And often they include broad brush strokes on a selected target: here it is the fruit. There is definitely an unfortunate niggle to the finish. But that is more than compensated by the beguiling nose and the vivid delivery and follow-through. Just...wow! *40%*

Jura Superstition db **(73.5) n17 t19 f18 b18.5.** I thought this could only improve. I was wrong. One to superstitiously avoid. *43%*

Jura Two-One-Two American white oak ex-bourbon barrels db **(90.5) n23** the tannins are embroidered neatly into the lush, citrus-tinged barley; **t22.5** busy on delivery – and even busier as the spices make their mark; again the oak holds all the cards and dictates, but the hickory and muscovado sugars work well together; **f22** just bitters vaguely on the fade; **b23** lets the tannins do the talking. And if anyone is buying this from a bar, say you'll have one, too... *47.5%. 6,000 bottles.*

⬩ **Jura Winter Edition** matured American white oak with Spanish sherry cask finish, bott code L2348 db **(89.5) n22.5** intricate and busy despite the caramel coating. Even a surprise hint of coconut at work here while friendly spices burble beneath the plum pudding; **t23** excellent kick off! So juicy with myriad layerings of subtly honeyed sweetness. Fresh, young and salivating the barley easily outstrips the laboured fruit; **f21.5** the toffee kicks in a little here and dampens the fun, though polite spices persist; **b22.5** goes easy on the sherry. Youthful and charmingly supple throughout. *40%*

The First Editions Jura Aged 14 Years 2007 sherry butt, cask no.HL18376, bott 2021 **(93) n23.5 t23.5 f23 b24** A pleasing, beautifully rounded bottling with a surprise gooseberry kick. Highly attractive and about as good as one might expect from this distillery. I'd say that this is as marvellous and inspirational as the very Paps of Jura, but I'd probably be denounced as sexist by some Woke thickie... *50.1% nc ncf sc 495 bottles*

ISLE OF RAASAY
Isle of Raasay, 2017. R&B Distillers. Working.
Isle of Raasay Hebridean Single Malt Moine 2-02 db **(91) n22.5** the hugely attractive peat is of that dry, ashy variety which generates a bit of acidity into the mix. There is a nip which has nothing to do with the alcohol. Below that is a softer smokiness which mingles more with the barley-sugars and rising but always shy vanillas. A few unexpected heavy oils are also lurking around; **t23** the first notes on delivery are ones which betray the extra generosity of the cut. But these are soon lost as the extraordinarily and deliciously sweet peat not only enters the fray but dominates it...though a gorgeous chocolate-mint middle impresses also; **f22.5** there are two distinctive buzzes at the death. One involves the smoke. The other, those extra oils...; **b23** for its obvious youth and despite the slight weakness of its wide-ish cut, this is immensely enjoyable malt and hopefully a pointer of great things to come from this new distillery. I wish them well. *46.4%*

KILCHOMAN
Islay, 2005. Kilchoman Distillery Co. Working.
Kilchoman 10 Years Old cask no. 150/2007, dist 20 Jul 07, bott 11 Jun 18 db **(96) n24 t24 f23.5 b24.5** Has controlled the oils beautifully. Class in a glass. *56.5%. sc. 238 bottles. Bottled for The Whisky Shop.*
Kilchoman 10 Years Old 100% Islay cask no. 84/2008, dist 6 Mar 08, bott 19 Mar 18 db **(91) n23.5 t23 f22 b22.5** Such is the high class of Kilchomen, even an exceptionally good malt on the whisky stage is not quite up to the distillery's normal performance. Not a bad place to be... *53.2%. sc. 239 bottles. Bottled for Loch Fyne Whiskies.*
Kilchoman 12 Years Old bourbon cask, cask no. 36/2006, dist 4 May 06, bott 21 Jun 18 db **(93.5) n23.5 t23.5 f23 b23.5** High grade malt taking a slightly different course from this distillery's normal style. *56.9%. sc. 228 bottles. Bottled for Loch Fyne Whiskies.*

⬧ **Kilchoman Cognac Cask 2023 Edition** (92.5) n23 that typically clipped smokiness you get from spending time in rum or cognac casks. A little lemon blossom honey softens the prevailing firmness; t24 now opens up in slow motion, like a blossoming flower. Those sugars garnered from the Cognac cask are first to display, initially seemingly impervious. Then that changes as a more tactile maltiness unfurls, the smoke at first barely discernible is now all the time putting on weight; f22.5 the unpeated aspect of the malt is still doing some major work. The tannins have a little bit of late attitude, but the creaminess literally smooths over any problems; b23 the 50ppm phenols – on a par with Ardbeg - have been muted here in part by the Cognac cask. But instead we are treated to the most sensational intensity on delivery and the fruit appears to capture the phenols before slowly releasing them into play. Really enjoyable – and with a fascinating slant. 50% nc ncf

⬧ **Kilchoman Fino Sherry 2023 Edition** (94) n23 a peppery spicy nibble accompanies thick and even peat; t23.5 superb delivery! The smoke bursts the door, but after that initial rumble of smoke, the shape changes and we are suddenly confronted by a phenolic, rock-hard boiled fruit candy: an astonishing change in tack. The salivation levels immediately explode in house style, while light oils smother the taste buds with peaty sultanas; f23.5 an incredibly long finale with those rich peat tones spread over a wide area. The Fino cask has a very slight late wobble, but amid so much going on it might be hard to notice; b24 another Kilchoman which works over the brain as hard as it does the taste buds, with its subtle changes of pace, intensity and emphasis. An easy dram to sit back and just enjoy - a real bugger to try and analyse and get to the bottom of! 50% nc ncf

⬧ **Kilchoman Loch Gorm 2023** db (95) n24 the smoke, the odd waft which appears to be of the intense, agricultural variety, appears to be a tapestry woven into the fabric of the tannin; t24 a deft, earthy delivery, keeping the full power of the peat under wraps, though it doesn't take too long to grow into something substantial. There is a dual textured middle: first a firm muscovado sugar, slightly fruity, crustiness pitching against the oilier phenols; f23.5 long, with lashings of butterscotch; b24 muscular, deep and unpredictable in its development: it certainly has a unique fingerprint. The Murray Method underscores the depth of that variance: when cold and then slightly warmed they are almost too different malts, Now that's what I call complexity... 46% nc ncf

KINCLAITH

Lowlands, 1957-1975. Closed. Dismantled.

Mo Ór Collection Kinclaith 1969 41 Years Old first fill bourbon hogshead, cask no. 301453A, dist 28 May 69, bott 29 Oct 10 (85.5) n22 t22 f20.5 b21. Hangs on gamely to the last vestiges of life, though the oak, without being overtly aggressive, is squeezing all the breath of out of it. 46%. nc ncf sc. Release No. 2. The Whisky Talker. 164 bottles.

KINGSBARNS

Lowland, 2014. Wemyss. Working.

Kingsbarns Dream to Dram db (94) n23.5 a mix of youthful charm and more relaxed maturity gives the malt a nuanced appeal. But the barley is so rich, you feel that you have just picked it from a field, dank after a late summer rain, and crushed it in your hands, even before malting. Green and clean; t24 salivating, but not in the sharp way I was expecting from the nose. Instead a mashing of icing sugars and fresh barley mix with the light oils from the distillate to provide a seemingly simple and beautifully effacing lead. But as you concentrate, you realise so much good is happening in there; f23 just a little tanginess as the casks and grain have not quite managed to align quite to perfection. But still no faulting the vanilla and barley fade; b23.5 just too ridiculously good for a new distillery. The malt really does make this a Dram of Dreams, too. And if this were not a single malt, blenders would be falling over themselves to use as top dressing in a blend. So simple. Yet sublime. 46%.

Kingsbarns Founder's Reserve #1 American oak bourbon barrel, dist 2015, bott 2018 db (93.5) n23.5 no age. But, my word! The intensity of the barley is startling and there is tannin enough to ensure this is no one horse race; t23.5 only excellent American oak can galvanise malt in this way, helping it to really ratchet up the intensity, so there is a stunning purity to help settle the semi-hidden sharp, metallic notes of a new still at work, f23 long with very beautifully judged oils from an excellent cut. The oak has grace enough to add a little vanilla and custard without taking away from the naked charm of the barley itself; b23.5 you really can't ask for much more from a three-year-old malt. There are no new makey signs here, though there is always the feel of a little youthful exuberance. Superbly distilled and excellently matured. And enough muscle around the spice to suggest this could have matured for a great many more years. A fledgling distillery heading in the right direction and certainly one to watch. And a perfect choice for the Whisky Bible 2021's 1,200th whisky of the year... 62.1%.

Kingsbarns Founder's Reserve #2 STR barriques, dist 2016, bott 2019 db **(93) n23.5 t23.5 f23 b23** As usual the STRs force their somewhat inelegant, abrasive but mouth-filling will on the whisky. Never match a great bourbon cask for sheer panache and heart-winning charm, but sometimes, like here, for eye-watering effect they have no equal. Oh, here's a little trick for you I have been carrying out for the last decade or so: to get the full flavour from STR-matured malt, leave in a tasting glass for three or four days with a watch lid over the top. This softens the whisky into a much more sensual dram and the malt – and therefore the base characteristic of the distillate - has a far bigger say in proceedings. If you add water very slightly to reduce strength and leave, you don't get anything like the same results or complexity. Try it. But as for this bottling... Wow! What fun! And such high class, too... 61.1%.

KNOCKANDO
Speyside. 1898. Diageo. Working.

Knockando Aged 12 Years bott code: L7229CM000 db **(82) n20 t22.5 f19 b20.5** My dear, late friend and mentor Jim Milne was for a very long time J&B blender and for decades this malt came under his clever jurisdiction. It was Jim who persuaded me, over a quarter of a century ago now, to publish my views on whisky, something I felt I was underqualified to do. He vehemently disagreed, so I took his advice and the rest, as they say, is history. I knew Jim's work intimately, so I know he would not be happy with his beloved Knockando in this incarnation. His Knockando was dry, making the most of the interaction between bourbon cask and delicate malt. This is sweet and, worse still, sulphur tarnished by the sherry: I doubt he would ever let grape get this kind of grip, thus negating the distillery's fragile style. Some lovely moments here for sure. But just too fleeting. 43%.

Knockando Aged 18 Years dist 1998, bott code: L9038CM001 db **(94) n23.5** malt. To the power of malt...; **t24** this barley boasts a malty intensity that is rare to match in pure atomic mass. Dense, intense, sharp, full...just sheer barley...concentrated...; **f23** still juicy to the end. Malty and spicy fade...; **b23.5** nowhere near the charm and complexity of the 21-year-old. But, my word! This has a malt intensity that is hard to match elsewhere. However, at this age you expect the casks to making a difference. But, no. The malt is in total control. Beautiful for sure. But nowhere near the overall complexity and joy of the 21-y-o... 43%.

Knockando Aged 21 Years Master Reserve dist 1994, bott code: L9081CM001 db **(96.5) n24 t24 f24 b24.5** Some 30 years ago I was on the original J&B training team and Knockando (I think as a 12-year-old) was used in the programme, where I would compare this against the peated malts of Islay. The Knockando I had known and worked with for many years was a bone-crushingly dry dram. Though older, this is alive and fresh. And, frankly, a delightful surprise. The 25-year-old, those three decades ago, had far more tannin per annum spent in cask in its make up and even drier...though I remember marching my students from the Craigellachie Hotel to the River Spey as the mid-summer solstice sun was rising to drink the whisky beside the fast-running waters with which it was rightfully associated. I still get letters and emails from those who experience that spectacular awakening of the whisky spirit in our souls to this very day... This is a much fresher incarnation of that reverential aged malt of the late 1980s and early '90s. And, I have to say...a little bit better,... Indeed, I am soon to embark on my 1,100th whisky of the 2021 Bible. And I cannot think of a better, more complete, single malt so far... 100% sulphur free..100% barley rich... 100% a treasure... 43%.

Knockando 1990 db **(83) n21 t22 f20 b20.** The most fruity Knockando I've come across with some attractive salty notes. Dry, but a little extra malty sweetness these days. 40%

KNOCKDHU
Speyside, 1894. Inver House Distillers. Working.

AnCnoc 12 Year Old db **(94.5) n24 t23 f23.5 b24.5** A more complete or confident Speyside-style malt you are unlikely to find. Shimmers with everything that is great about Scotch whisky... always a reliable dram, but this is stupendous. 40%

anCnoc 12 Years Old bott code: L19/051 R19/5082 IB db **(94) n23.5** green banana and lucid barley. Spices flicker and glimmer...; **t23.5** teeming barley, layered in both sweetness and intensity: there is a chewy fatness containing the juicier sugars, then a more gristy side mingling with the spice; **f23** malty to a fault, just a little duller than of yore. Heavier caramels mingle with the slightly bitter tannins; **b24** remains one of the truly beautiful, largely undiscovered great malts of Scotland. At 46% and with other minor technical adjustments, this could be a major award winner... 40%.

AnCnoc 16 Years Old db **(91.5) n22 t23.5 f23 b23** Unquestionably the spiciest AnCnoc of all time. Has this distillery been moved to the coast..? 46%

anCnoc 18 Years Old bott code: L19/052 R19/5084 IB db **(85) n22 t22 f20 b21** Even one sherry butt containing sulphur in a malt as delicate as anCnoc has consequences. And these can be found on the light furry nibble on the tongue towards the end. A shame, as I had selected this as sample number 1,100 on my home-straight for the 2021 Bible. Has plenty of its old zest and brilliance, for those biologically unable to detect sulphur. *46%.*

AnCnoc 22 Year Old db **(87) n22 t21.5 f22 b21.5.** Often a malt which blossoms before being a teenager, as does the fruits of Knockdhu; struggles to cope comfortably with the inevitable oakiness of old age. Here is such a case. *46%. Inverhouse Distillers.*

AnCnoc 24 Years Old db **(94) n23 t24.5 f22.5 b24** Big, broad-shouldered malt which carries a lot of weight but hardly veers away from the massively fruity path. For sherry loving whisky drinkers everywhere... *46%. nc ncf.*

AnCnoc 30 Years Old db **(85) n21 t23 f19 b22.** Seat-of-the-pants whisky that is just on the turn. Still has a twinkle in the eye, though. *49%*

AnCnoc 35 Years Old bourbon and sherry casks db **(88) n22.5t22 f21.5 b22.** The usual big barley sheen has dulled with time here. Some attractive cocoa notes do compensate. *44.3%. nc ncf.*

AnCnoc 1999 db **(95.5) n24 t24 f23.5 b24** I noticed as I was putting the bottle away that on their back label their description includes "Colour: soft, very aromatic with a hint of honey and lemon in the foreground" and "Nose: amber with a slight yellow hue." Which would make this malt pretty unique. But this is worth getting for far more than just the collectors' item typo: this is brilliant whisky – one of their best vintage malts for a very long time. In fact, one of their best ever bottlings...period.*46%. nc ncf. WB15/160*

AnCnoc 2002 bott Mar 17, bott code: L17/089 R17/5104 IB db **(86) n21.5 t23 f20.5 b21** Overall, it is enjoyable and well spiced, but a mushy, tangy, untidy finish shows up the failings of the odd cask used. This is a distillery whose spirit yearns for ex-bourbon so its stunning naked form can be worshipped, loved and salivated over. *46%.*

AnCnoc Barrow 13.5 ppm phenols db **(88) n22 t21 f23 b22** A quite peculiar Knockdhu. The usual subtle richness of texture is curiously absent. As are friendly sugars. The strange angles of the phenols fascinate, however. *46%. nc ncf. Exclusive to travel retail.*

AnCnoc Blas db **(67) n16 t18 f16 b17.** Blast! Great chocolate. Shame about the sulphur.... *54%. nc ncf.*

AnCnoc Black Hill Reserve db **(81) n20 t22 f19 b20.** The furriness threatened on the nose and realised at the finish does this great distillery no favours at all. *46%. nc ncf.*

AnCnoc Cutter 20.5 ppm phenols db **(96.5) n24 t24 f24 b24.5** Brilliant! An adjective I am far more used to associating with anCnoc than some of the others I have had to use this year. The most Ardbeg-esque mainland malt I have ever encountered. *46%. nc ncf.*

AnCnoc Peatheart batch no. 1, 40ppm, bott code: L17/301 R17/5394 db **(91.5) n22 t23.5 f23 b23** Won't be long before Peatheart becomes the peataholics' sweetheart. Curiously underperforming nose, but makes amends in style on the palate. *46%.*

AnCnoc Rùdhan bott code: L16/273 R16/5391 db **(94.5) n24 t23.5 f23.5 b24** Hard to imagine a mainland Scottish distillery producing a more complex, elegant and wholly ingratiating peated malt... What a gem this is! *46%.*

AnCnoc Rutter 11 ppm phenols db **(96.5) n24.5 t24.5 f23.5 b24** I remember vividly, at this great distillery's Centenary party exactly 20 years ago this summer, mentioning to the then distillery manager that I thought that the style of the malt produced at Knockdhu was perfectly geared to make a lightly malted peat along the lines of its neighbour, Ardmore. Only for a few weeks of the year I ventured. I'm pretty certain this malt was not a result of that observation, but it is heartening to see that my instincts were right: it's a sensation! *46%. ncf nc. WB15/320*

LADYBURN
Lowlands, 1966–2000. William Grant & Sons. Closed.

Mo Ór Collection Rare Ayrshire 1974 36 Years Old first fill bourbon barrel, cask no. 2608, dist 10 May 74, bott 1 Nov 11 **(89.5) n22 t23.5 f22 b22.5.** I had a feeling it'd be this distillery when I saw the title on the label... it couldn't be much else! Fascinating to think that I was in final countdown for my 'O' levels when this was made. It appears to have dealt with the passing years better than I have. Even so, I had not been prepared for this. For years during the very early 1990s Grant's blender David Stewart sent me samples of this stuff and it was, to put it mildly, not great. Some were the oakiest malt I ever tasted in my life. And, to compound matters further, the distillery's own bottling was truly awful. But this cask has re-written history. *46%. nc ncf sc. Release No. 4. The Whisky Talker. 261 bottles.*

LAGAVULIN
Islay, 1816. Diageo. Working.

Lagavulin Aged 8 Years bott code: L7285CM013 db **(95.5) n25 t23.5 f23 b24.5** Having gone from the colouring-spoiled Cardhu to this chardonnay-hued Lagavulin in all its bourbon cask nakedness, you have to wonder: why don't they do this for all their whiskies. This was the age I first tasted Lagavulin possibly the best part of 40 years ago. It was love at first flight, and my passions – with the whisky in this beautifully natural form, though not as heavily peated now as then – have not been remotely doused. 48%.

Lagavulin Aged 12 Years bott 2017, bott code: L7089CM000 db (94) n23.5 t23.5 f23 b24 When I first tasted Lagavulin at this age, the phenol levels were around the 50ppm mark and not the present day 35. That meant the finish offered just a little extra Islay. Even so, I challenge you not to adore this. 56.5%.

Lagavulin Aged 12 Years bott 2018, bott code: L8072CM008 db (96) n24 t24 f23.5 b24.5 Technically, from a distilling perspective, borderline perfection. From a maturation one, slightly weaker for, although the bourbon casks give you the clearest view possible of the brilliance of the spirit, a very slight late bitterness just breaks the spell. Even so, we are talking Islay at its most truly classic. 57.8%.

Lagavulin 12 Year Old refill American oak hogsheads db (96) n24.5 t24 f23.5 b24 I think whisky like this was invented by the whisky gods to be experienced at this full strength. Even people who do not regard themselves as peat lovers are likely to be seduced by this one. Talk about controlled power.... 56.5%. *Diageo Special Releases 2017.*

Lagavulin 16 Years Old db (95) n24 t24 f23 b24 Although I have enjoyed this whisky countless times socially, it is the first time for a while I have dragged it into the Tasting Room for professional analysis for the Bible. If anyone has noticed a slight change in Lagavulin, they would be right. The peat remains profound but much more delicate than before, while the oils appear to have receded. A different shape and weight dispersal for sure. But the sky-high quality remains just the same. 43%

Game of Thrones Lagavulin 9 Year Old House Lannister db (89.5) n22 t23.5 f21.5 b22.5 Lagavulin as I have never seen it before, the phenols being kept on a tight leash. 46%.

Cadenhead's Lagavulin 11 Year Old dist 2007 (96) n24 t24 f23.5 b24.5 If you are going to celebrate an anniversary, then why not pick one of the greatest distilleries in the world, choose a cask from one of its optimum ages and then make sure it is about as honest and accurate a picture of that distillery that a blender could hope for? Well, that's what's happened here. Just look at that the grist on that nose, yet as the phenols swirl around there is no mistaking the barley, either. Then, on the palate, the way in which the peat radiates around the mouth as though in slow motion, a burst of barley juice here, light liquorice there. And smoke, so stunningly controlled, everywhere. Congratulations on your anniversary. And also on this glorious, to-die-for Lagavulin. 45%. 348 bottles. *10th Anniversary of Cadenhead Switzerland bottling.*

LAPHROAIG
Islay, 1815. Beam Suntory. Working.

Laphroaig 10 Years Old db (90) n24 t23 f20.5 b22.5 Has reverted back slightly towards a heavier style in more recent bottling, though I would like to see that old oomph at the very death. Even so, this is, indisputably, a classic whisky. The favourite of Prince Charles apparently: he will make a wise king... 40%

Laphroaig 10 Year Old bott code: L80099MB1 db (94) n23.5 t23.5 f23.5 b24 An essay in voluptuousness. The oils speak volumes here, gathering the two-toned phenols and landing them in all corners of the palate and ensuring they stick there. The iodine kick off on the nose is like a salty trademark, the balance between the sootier phenols and juicer Demera notes a joy to experience. The finish is not so much enormous as controlled and long, with a sublime degree of mocha moving in for the last blissful moments. Glorious. Still, after all these years... 40%.

Laphroaig 10 Year Old bott code: L8 831 SB1 db (95) n24 t23.5 f23.5 b24 So consistent is the Laphroaig 10, that this is one of the whiskies I test myself each day with to check that my nose and palate are on song. Having done this for the last 15 years or so, I think I can recognise whether a particular bottling from this distillery is up to scratch or not. Just a word of caution: their back label recommends that you add a splash of cool water to this whisky. I thoroughly recommend you do absolutely nothing of the sort. Laphroaig is served best by the Murray Method when its untold brilliance can be seen in its myriad layers. As an experiment, I have added cool water as they suggest – and it shrinks the whisky dramatically and breaks up the oils and sugars which are then lost to us. Please, never murder this fabulous whisky so cold-bloodedly. Oh, and having tasted a few score of Laphroaig 10s over the last 40 years or so, have to say this is bang up there with the very best: it is certainly among the most complex. 40%.

Laphroaig 10 Years Old Original Cask Strength db (92) n22 t24 f23 b23 Caramel apart, this is much truer to form than one or two more recent bottlings, aided by the fresh, gristy sweetness and explosive spices. Wonderful! 55.7%

Laphroaig 12 Year Old 2005 bott 2017 db (91.5) n21.5 t23.5 f23 b23.5 Here we go: one of the exceptions in whisky that proves the rule. I have long wailed about the usage of PX cask and peaty malt together. And from the nose, you think your case will be won again, for here is another example of one giant nullifying another: both the smoke and fruit cancelling the other out. Yet, confound it, the delivery shows signs of proving me wrong and the finish continues in the same fashion. For once a PX cask is allowing the peat to breathe and sing. And what's more itself kick up a juicy encore. Beyond the nose a PX and smoky giant that walks tall. Who would have thought...? 55.3%. *Selected for CWS.*

Laphroaig 18 Years Old db (94) n24 t23.5 f23 b23.5 This is Laphroaig's replacement to the woefully inadequate and gutless 15-year-old. And talk about taking a giant step in the right direction. Absolutely brimming with character and panache, from the first molecules escaping the bottle as you pour to the very final ember dying on the middle of your tongue. 48%

Laphroaig Aged 27 Years dist Oct 88 to Nov 89, bott Mar 17, bott code: L7062VB1 db (96.5) n24.5 t24 f23.5 b24.5 The 27 passing years and the added interference of fresh ex-bourbon barrels and quarter casks has taken its toll on the potency of the peat. Instead of Laphroaig pulsing with its renowned style of sea-soaked phenols, we are now faced with a dram which is more than content to allow age and gentility to be the guiding hand; so now less febrile and more cerebral. Such an honour to taste whiskies of this extraordinary yet understated magnitude. I can think of no other presently available whisky which so eloquently demonstrates that you don't have to stand a spoon up in the peat for the phenols to have such a vital input. 41.7%. *ncf.*

Laphroaig Aged 30 Years db (94) n24 t23 f23 b24. The best Laphroaig of all time? Nope, because the 40-y-o is perhaps better still... just. However, Laphroaig of this subtlety and charm gives even the very finest Ardbeg a run for its money. A sheer treat that should be bottled at greater strength. 43%

Laphroaig Aged 40 Years db (94) n23 t24 f23 b24. Mind-blowing. A malt that defies all logic and theory to be in this kind of shape at such age. The Jane Fonda of Islay whisky. 43%

Laphroaig The 1815 Legacy Edition bott code: L7059VB1 2070 db (92.5) n24 t24 f21 b23.5 a sherry butt away from one of the best new whiskies of the year. 48%. *Travel Retail Exclusive.*

Laphroaig Au Cuan Mòr db (95) n24 t24 f23 b24 You don't need to squint at the back label to be told that first fill bourbon barrels are at work here: this is where Kentucky, Jerez and Islay merges with breath-taking ease and harmony. 48%. *Travel retail exclusive.*

Laphroaig Brodir Port Wood Finish bott code: L6157MB1 db (91.5) n24 probably one of the most old-fashioned Islay warehouse aromas I have ever encountered: that incomparable mix of smoke, oak and grape hanging thickly in a moist, salty air...; t22 the usual gristy sugars have been silenced by the intense, moody fruit; f23 much better balance late on as a little liquorice and treacle joins the clouds of phenols to ensure complexity; b22.5 this is a big Laphroaig at its most brooding and taciturn. Not for when you are at your most frivolous. 48%.

Laphroaig Four Oak bott code: L6327VB1 2359 db (88) n22 t22.5 f21.5 b22 Attractive, but the smoke seems a little in awe of the oak as it is unusually quiet. 40%. *Travel Retail Exclusive.*

Laphroaig Lore db (94) n23.5 t24 f23 b23.5 Seeing how much I adore this distillery – and treasure my near 40 years of tasting its exceptional malt and visiting its astonishing home – I left this to become my 750th new whisky for the 2016 Whisky Bible. "Our richest expression ever" the label promised. It isn't. Big, fat and chunky? Tick. Bounding with phenols? Yep. Enjoyable? Aye! Richest expression ever. Nah. Not quite. Still, a friendly beast worth cuddling up with. And, whatever they say on the label, this is a stunner! 48%. *ncf.*

Laphroaig Lore bott code: L7229VB1 db (96) n23.5 t24 f24 b24.5 Laphroaig how I've never quite seen it before – and we are talking some 40 years of intimately studying this malt: truly a lore unto itself... 48%.

Laphroaig PX Cask bourbon, quarter and Pedro Ximenez casks db (96) n23.5 t24.5 f24 b24. I get the feeling that this is a breathtaking success despite the inclusion of Pedro Ximenez casks. This ultra sweet wine is often paired with smoky malt, often with disastrous consequences. Here it has worked, but only because the PX has been controlled itself by absolutely outstanding oak. And the ability of the smoke to take on several roles and personas simultaneously. A quite beautiful whisky and unquestionably one of the great malts of the year...in spite of itself. 48%. *Travel Retail exclusive.*

Laphroaig Quarter Cask db (96) n23 t24 f24 b25 A great distillery back to its awesome, if a little sweet, self. Layer upon layer of sexed-up peatiness. The previous bottling just needed a little extra complexity on the nose for this to hit mega malt status. Now it has been achieved... 48%

Laphroaig Quarter Cask bott code: L8268 db (93) n23 t23.5 f23 b23.5 Laphroaig Quarter Cask: where is thy sting? Easily the most strangely subdued bottlings of this great malt I have ever encountered. Make no mistake: this is still a lovely dram in its own right, but just not what I expected – or now demand – from this Islay classic. 48%. *ncf.*

Laphroaig Select bott code: L1162SB1 db (94) n23.5 quite literally reeks of Laphroaig: an unmistakable aroma high on iodine and a sharp saltiness. With unusual mixed messages of young whisky and big, layered "red" oak; **t23.5** ah, I remember: this is the Laphroaig where a degree virgin American oak is deployed in maturation. That immediately makes sense of the follow through which is in contrast to the sublime young Laphroaig which pounds the taste buds with its unrelenting phenolic output. Despite being just 40%abv, the oils are excellent and help meld the smoke and ever-growing tannins into a glorious unit. The sugars are restrained but vital in keeping he balance intact; **f23** once the smoke begins to dissipate slightly, the effect of the oak helps raise the cocoa profile, sweetened by residual Demerara sugars. The spices are far more telling at the death as the smoke collects for a weighty and warming finale; **b24** this is a far better bottling than the last Select I tasted, which was among their earliest. They have obviously come to understand the whisky and the balance between young, vivacious peat and virgin oak that little bit better: the result is a substantial step upwards. Better use of young whisky here than Ardbeg's overly tame 5-year-old and if they could get the strength up six percentage points, this would hugely sweep quite a lot of awards – in the Whisky Bible, also. Absolutely delightful and a peat worshipper's wet dream.... 40%. nc

⬩ **Laphroaig Select** bott code L2251SB1 db **(90.5) n23** the youthfulness contributes to a sweet, minty outline to the soft but striking phenols. The vaguest outline of molasses gives a nod towards a gentle tannin influence; **t22.5** ah...not as I remember it. The delivery is much more muted than before with the vanilla easily on an even keel with the phenols. A lack of oils from the midpoint onwards does little to spread the meagre dark sugars. Complex, but always acting within itself; **f22** short, vanilla dominant with smoke and spice; **b23** this is Laphroaig at its most conservative and strictly on its best behaviour. While the peat is deep and meaningful on the nose, the same can't be said once it strikes the palate. Not quite the big, complex beast I remember from last time. 40% nc

William & Co Spirits LPHG.2 15 Years Old bourbon oak octave cask, cask no. 5627900, dist Sept 04, bott Jun 20 **(94) n23.5 t23.5 f23 b24** The enduring excellence of Laphroaig is helped along here by it having been kept in bourbon cask only, so the complex peaty story can be played out in its own time and without interference. A true peat lovers' dram to be savoured before bed. 53.2% 66 bottles.

LINKWOOD
Speyside, 1820. Diageo. Working.

Linkwood 12 Years Old db **(94.5) n23.5 t24 f23 b24** Possibly the most improved distillery bottling in recent times. Having gone through a period of dreadful casks, it appears to have come through to the other side very much on top and close to how some of us remember it a quarter of a century ago. Sublime malt: one of the most glittering gems in the Diageo crown. 43%

Berry Bros & Rudd Linkwood 12 Years Old cask no. 102, dist 2006, bott 2018 **(91) n22.5 t22.5 f23 b23** Crumbs! Plays the austere Speysider with panache. 46%. nc ncf sc.

Chapter 7 Monologue Linkwood 12 Years Old 2008 (90) n22.5 one of the chunkier Linkwood noses of recent years. There is a fruit and tannin pile on and seemingly something phenolic...though surely not...; **t23** multi-layered citrus, not least kumquat more associated with bourbon. Like on the nose, the tannins have a lot to say. Towards the end, barley makes itself heard; **f22** busy, spicy, warming and still generating barley; **b22.5** it's Linkwod, Jim. But not as we know it.... 50.3%

Kingsbury Sar Obair Linkwood 30 Year Old sherry hogshead, dist 1989, cask no. 6617 **(96.5) n24 t24.5 f24 b24** One fears that at any given moment this malt will crash and disintegrate as the age catches up with it, as the nose has already told you the oak is playing a blinding game and doing extraordinary things. Miraculously, it seems, this Linkwood keeps its shape throughout and never does drop over the end of a cliff. It is one of those old casks which leaves you not just satisfied but in complete awe... This, incidentally, will be an award winner of some type. If not, there really is no justice in this cruel world... 53.4% sc 242 bottles

The Single Malts of Scotland Reserve Cask Linkwood 12 Year Old (92.5) n23 t23 f23 b23.5 Linkwood at its fruitiest and flightiest, concentrating on a lightness of touch that sets out to charm – and does! Lime blossom honey abounds, mixing liberally with the grassy barley to accentuate the malt while giving the limited oakiness an extra boost, too. It is so light you can even pick a molecule or two of peat here and there, though to say weight is added is stretching the imagination. The salivating never lets up from first mouthful to finish, making this joyous malt perfect for summer evenings. A minor little classic, this. 48%

⬩ **Skene Dhu Linkwood 14 Years Old** European oak ex-oloroso cask, dist 2008, bott 2022 **(91.5) n23.5** a gem of a nose! This is all about subtlety, shadows and shades. The fruit is a mix between blood orange and crushed sultana but going easy enough on both to allow the barley a gentle wallow; **t23** that early meeting of concentrated malt and lightly muscled grape offers almost perfect synchronisation. Salivating and at times positively sharp; **f22** almost frothy in its application of the fruit...as though it has a head on it. But this passes and little bit of bitterness creeps in; **b23** you can see why blenders prize this malt, especially in this kind of condition. This enjoys wonderfully understated complexity, the fruit flickering in and out of play. The finish may have its weaknesses but, overall, a satisfying rendition. *48%*

LITTLEMILL
Lowland, 1772. Loch Lomond Distillers. Demolished.
Littlemill 21 Year Old 2nd Release bourbon cask db (**87**) **n22 t21.5 f21.5 b22.** So thin you expect it to fragment into a zillion pieces on the palate. But the improvement on this as a new make almost defies belief. The sugars are crisp enough to shatter on your teeth, the malt is stone hard and fractured and, on the finish, does show some definite charm before showing its less attractive teeth....and its roots... Overall, though, more than enjoyable. *47%. nc ncf.*

Littlemill 25 Year Old db (**92.5**) **n22 t24 f23 b23.5** Another example of a malt which was practically undrinkable in its youth but that is now a reformed, gentle character in older age. *52%*

Littlemill 40 Year Old Celestial Edition db (**90.5**) **n23.5 t23 f22 b22.5** As we all know, when this was distilled four decades back, the new make sprang from the stills as fire water. And for the first few years in the cask it roared at and incinerated the palate of any blender foolhardy enough to try it. And so, inevitably, the distillery died. In later years it is making up for its violent youth and here offers a serene maltiness about as far removed from its original character as is possible. Enjoy the dying rays of this once vituperative spirit, now so charming in its dotage. *46.8%. 250 bottles.*

Littlemill 1964 db (**82**) **n21 t20 f21 b20.** A soft-natured, bourbony chap that shows little of the manic tendencies that made this one of Scotland's most-feared malts. Talk about mellowing with age... *40%*

Littlemill 2017 Private Cellar 27 Year Old db (**93**) **n23 t23.5 f23 b23.5** How ironic and sad that the last casks of what were unloved – and unusable - firewater when distilled have now, after nearly three decades, calmed into a malt which is the matured embodiment of grace and finesse. *51.3%.*

Master of Malt Single Cask Littlemill 27 Year Old dist 1991 (**94.5**) **n23 t24 f23.5 b24** Another old Littlemill shewing genuine elegance in its twilight years. Kind of Malteser candy with benefits from the moment it hits the palate right through to the finale. A little bourbon-style tannin on the nose doesn't quite prepare you for the chocolatey maltfest which follows... Truly delicious. I promise you: no-one, and I mean no-one, could envision it would be this good in the days when it was working.... *47.2%. sc.*

LOCH LOMOND
Highlands (Southwestern), 1966. Loch Lomond Distillers. Working.
Loch Lomond Aged 10 Years Lightly Peated bott code: 10 01 2019 db (**86**) **n20.5 t22 f21.5 b22** Maybe I'm wrong, but this strikes me as being a vatting of distillation types (Inchmoan, Croftengea etc.) with their usual designated Loch Lomond straight and clean style. The result is a feinty beast, much heavier than any "Loch Lomond" I have before encountered, but buttressed with some major fudge and phenols: the Loch Lomond Monster... *40%*

Loch Lomond 10 Year Old 2009 Alvi's Drift Muscat de Frontignan Finish db (**96**) **n23.5 t24.5 f23.5 b24.5** One of those rare whiskies which is every bit as remarkable for its mouthfeel than it is for its flavour personality, which in itself borders on the unique. No, what the hell! This IS unique! A malt whose beauty you can only marvel at....I am truly blown away... *53.2%. Selected by Slijterij Frans Muthert & Dramtime.nl.*

Loch Lomond Aged 12 Years db (**93.5**) **n22.5 t23.5 f23.5 b24** Great to see they now have the stocks to allow this malt to really flex its muscles... *46%. ncf.*

Loch Lomond 12 Year Old The Open Special Edition 2020 db (**92.5**) **n24 t23.5 f22 b23** If anyone needs proof that superb whisky can be got from a relatively young malt (old when I started this game of writing about whisky in the 1980s!) just by the clever use of bourbon casks in particular, then here it is. *46%.*

Loch Lomond Aged 14 Years Inchmoan American oak casks, bott code: L2.080.20 db (**88.5**) **n21.5 t23 f21.5 b22.5** This is like watching Charlie Chaplin sloshing paint onto a wall, or glue onto wallpaper. Slap, slap! Here everything is slapped on: the feints, the barley, the sugars, the oak. Slap, slap, slap! Love it, but don't expect subtlety. *46%. ncf. Traveller Exclusive.*

Loch Lomond 15 Year Old db (**87.5**) **n21.5 t22 f22 b22** Spends a lot of its time waving its malty flag. But a slight tartness on both nose and on palate means it never quite settles into a comfortable narrative *46%.*

Loch Lomond Organic Aged 17 Years bott code: L2 120 18 db (**96.5**) **n24 t24.5 f23.5 b24.5** Organic...? Orgasmic, more like! A dram which will win the hearts, minds and souls of both bourbon and scotch whisky lovers. In fact, if you don't like this, whatever the cut of your jib, you might as well give up now.. *54.9%. nc ncf.*

Loch Lomond Aged 18 Years American oak casks, bott code: L2.234.18 db (95) n23 t24 f23.5 b24.5 Tasting the Loch Lomond whiskies this year has been such a pleasure. It is always heart-warming to find a distillery that uses American oak casks to best advantage and other types sparingly and with the distillery style in mind. Here is another case in point: the bourbon casks have been shaped to extract every last jot of honey out this expression, as well as complexity. I doff my Panama... 46%. ncf.

Loch Lomond The Open 18 Year Old Course Collection Carnoustie 1999 db (92) n23 t23.5 f22 b23.5 Decided to wait until the 2018 Open at Carnoustie was in full swing before checking to see if this is up to par. Well, it is beyond that: a true double birdie as rarely is Loch Lomond this clean and malt rich. Would grace any 19th hole... 47.2%.

Loch Lomond Aged 18 Years Inchmurrin American oak casks, bott code: L2.083.20 db (95) n23.5 t24 f23.5 b24 Have to say: this is Inchmurrin revealing all its pure naked beauty. And it's some sight to behold, believe me. At this age always a good dram. Now truly a great one. 46%. ncf. Traveller Exclusive.

Loch Lomond 21 Year Old db (89.5) n22.5 t22.5 f22 b22.5 Not sure if the oily style of the spirit made 21 years ago is quite as accommodating so far as complexity is concerned as most of the spirit which has come since. 46%.

Loch Lomond 25 Year Old Three Wood Matured Colin Montgomerie db (95) n24 t23.5 f23.5 b24 I have never met Colin Montgomery, though his car and my car once parked simultaneously nose to tail in Mayfair, London, our respective personalised number plates almost touching. Mr Montgomery, I noted, was quite a large individual so was not surprised that he could persuade a small rubber ball to travel a great distance with one well-timed thwack. This whisky, then, being of a delicate and fragile nature is very much, physically, his antithesis. No doubt Colin Montgomery found the rough a few times in his long career; he certainly won't with this. 46.3%.

Loch Lomond 30 Year Old db (86) n23.5 t23 f19 b20.5 When nosing, just sit there and contemplate the spices on that fruit pudding. Wow..! But on delivery, unusually for a malt this age it is the sugars which gets the first word in, a light golden syrup number moving serenely into position with the duskier plummy tones. The spices build as advertised. But then it all starts going Pete Tong as some major furriness grows on the finish. What a shame! Until the treatment of the sherry butts kick in from three decades back, we had been on a delightful journey of unusually polished balance. But, for better or worse, it is a whisky of its times... 47%.

Loch Lomond Classic American oak casks, bott code: 17 12 2018 db (84.5) n21 t22.5 f20 b21 Though called "Classic", the flat, chewy toffee middle and finish makes this pleasant but very un-Lomond like in character. Fudged in every sense... 40%.

Loch Lomond Cristie Kerr Vintage 2002 db (94) n23 the vaguest hint of smoky bacon adds what little weight there is to this gentle celebration of barley; t23.5 such a beautiful presentation of barley in all its heather-honeyed finery. Salivating, lightly oaked and perfectly spiced; f23.5 continues in the same form, but late on a little nuttiness appears, which moves towards praline; b24 Lomond at is malty best and cleanest. Someone in Toronto this year told me he had never found a Loch Lomond he'd ever enjoyed. I hope he discovers this minor classic... 48.1%.

Loch Lomond The Open Special Edition Distiller's Cut first fill bourbon and refill American oak casks, bott code: 12 03 2019 db (95.5) n23.5 t25 f23 b24 One of the finest Loch Lomonds I have ever encountered. No: the finest. The distillery will go up several notches above par for anyone lucky enough to encounter this one.... 46%. ncf. Chosen for Royal Portrush.

Loch Lomond Original American oak casks, bott code: L2.042 20 db (90) n22.5 t23 f22 b22.5 I think this was the malt a few years back I nearly fainted from because of the feints. Many... I pause at this point because after 21,000 different samples, that's well over 100,000 mouthfuls of whisky and over 100,000 times of picking up a glass and putting it down again to write over the last 17 years, I finally knocked a charged tasting glass over the computer, thereby killing it. Death by malt. Or, rather, it was at this point it died as it had happened two samples ago. A brand new Apple Mac bought just for the Whisky Bible 2021 edition dying in its line of duty. So now an old one – with the letters e r t o a h and n obliterated by a few years' pounding has been brought out of retirement to complete the last couple of hundred whiskies (this is number 969)... Anyway, back to the Loch Lomond Original. This now a feint-free maltfest which goes easy on complexity but is big on charm. 40%.

Glengarry 12 Year Old db (92.5) n22.5 t23.5 f23 b23.5 Probably the most intense malt on the market today. Astonishing. And stunning. 46%. ncf.

Inchmoan Aged 12 Years Peated recharred American oak and refill bourbon American oak casks, bott code: L4.295.19 db (85.5) n20 t22.5 f21.5 b21.5 Seems as though the whole world has gone slightly mad and changed beyond recognition since I last opened a bottle of this. The only thing that hasn't changed, it seems, is the feintiness on Inchmoan. A little sweeter now, maybe. And the peat now has the distinctively chocolate mint quality of the old Merlin's Brew ice lolly. Though that lost old classic would have this licked... 46%. ncf. *Loch Lomond Island Collection.*

Inchmoan 1992 Peated refill bourbon barrels db **(95) n23 t24.5 f23.5 b24** I do believe I was at Loch Lomond distillery in 1992 while they were producing the Inchmoan strand of their output. So to see it after all this time is astonishing. No less astonishing is the sheer excellence of the malt, which here is almost a cross between a light rye-recipe bourbon and a smoky island scotch. This is a true Loch Lomond classic 48.6%. ncf. *Loch Lomond Island Collection.*

Inchmurrin Aged 12 Years bourbon, refill and recharred casks, bott code: L2.248.18 db **(88.5) n21.5 t23 f22 b22** Best Inchmurrin I have tasted in a good number of years. The calibre of the malt is top-notch, allowing the barley a fabulously lively, intense yet even run. Well spiced, too. Inch by Inch, it is getting there. At this rate the next bottling will be hitting the 90-mark for the Bible, once an unlikely proposition. A little cleaner on the nose and it'll be there. A bit like the distillery: a real character. 46%. ncf. *Loch Lomond Island Collection.*

Inchmurrin Madeira Wood Finish bott code: L2.185.18 db **(93) n23 t23.5 f23b23.5** Well, a lush and beautifully clean Madeira cask is one way of negating any weakness on the nose. Trouble is, that fruit becomes a little too bossy...though this can be forgiven when the quality of the casks are this high. A real lip-smacking crowd pleaser. 46%. ncf.

Kingsbury Gold Inchfad 13 YO 2007 (88.5) n22 t23 f21.5 b22 One of those malts which, though constantly out of tune and struggling to find its rhythm, still manages to put together enough earthy barley of the rich and salivating variety to make this a dram worth investigating. Cleaner off the still than most Inchfads, it also has room to allow the oak to have a minor bourbon moment. A real brute of a malt with a bit of bite to it, too... 56.2%

Oxhead Classic Casks Croftengea 2007 db **(87.5) n22.5 t23 f20.5 b21.5** I remember well the last commercially bottled 2007 Croftengea I encountered...it had me hiding under my tasting desk for safety. This is a much friendlier fellow keeping on a malty track with some pleasant marzipan notes making the delivery and midpoint rather attractive, compensating for the thin, unconvincing, slightly bitter finish. 54.9%

The Single Cask Croftengea 2007 ex-wine cask, cask no. 71 **(81.5) n18 t21.5 f21 b21** Even at the best of times, sampling a Croftengea can be like trying to break in a particularly bloody-minded horse: you get thrown everywhere and can take one hell of a kicking. The fact that your saddle has been loosed by an unimpressive wine cask makes the job even more difficult. Hard to find a single positive about the nose but I suspect the inner masochist in me has a grudging respect for the wildness on the palate. 55.7%. nc ncf sc.

LOCHSIDE
Highlands (Eastern), 1957–1992. Chivas Brothers. Demolished.

The Whisky Agency Lochside 1981 butt, bott 2018 **(96.5) n24 t25 f23.5 b24** I suspect I must be one of the very last people still working in the whisky industry who visited this distillery in the days when it was at full throttle. I was horrified by its closure way back in 1992 and thinking back on it now still fills me with great sadness. Some distilleries were awful and deserved their fate. This never for a moment did. I remember once going to see Montrose play a home game and afterwards popped into the distillery to have a word with the staff on duty. The new make then, as every time I visited, was spot on (and very warming after perishing in the main stand). And here is a magnificent example of its stunning make spending the best part of 40 years in faultless sherry oak. The result, as I expected (and the reason I left this for among the final five whiskies for the 2021 Whisky Bible) is a study of single malt Scotch: a malt of astonishing and beguiling beauty. 48.6%.

LONGMORN
Speyside, 1895. Chivas Brothers. Working.

Longmorn 15 Years Old db **(93) n23 t24 f22 b24** These latest bottlings are the best yet: previous ones had shown just a little too much oak but this has hit a perfect compromise. An all-time Speyside great. 45%

Longmorn 16 Years Old db **(84.5) n20.5 t22 f21 b21.** This was one of the disappointments of the 2008 edition, thanks to the lacklustre nose and finish. This time we see a cautious nudge in the right direction: the colour has been dropped fractionally and the nose celebrates with a sharper barley kick with a peppery accompaniment. The non-existent (caramel apart) finale of yore now offers a distinct wave of butterscotch and thinned honey...and still some spice. Only the delivery has dropped a tad...but a price worth paying for the overall improvement. Still a way to go before the real Longmorn 16 shines in our glasses for all to see and fall deeply in love with. Come on lads in the Chivas lab: we know you can do it... 48%

Longmorn 23 Year Old db **(93) n23 t24 f23 b23.5** I can just imagine how this would be such rich top dressing for the finest blend I could concoct: as a single malt it is no less a delight. 48%. ncf.

189

Fadandel Longmorn 13 Years Old (91.5) n23 earthy as well as spicy, the polite intensity of the freshly baked fruitcake is superb; t23 when the fruit is so rich and malt so vibrant, and neither wish to give way, you know you are experiencing a sublime delivery. Naturally, they eventually settle down but it is the malt and midground cocoa which, surprisingly, outplays the fruit. All the while it remains sharp and fresh, though...a little younger than its years...; f22.5 lengthy, with a wonderful chocolate, nut and raisin depth; b23 another massively impressive cask from a company now establishing themselves as the bottlers of some of Scotland's most interesting malts...ones which reveal themselves in their natural attire. 55.2%

The First Editions Longmorn Aged 21 Years 1998 refill barrel, cask no. 17324, bott 2019 (96.5) n25 t24 f23 b24.5 Longmorn is a malt greatly prized by the better blenders. This bottling leaves you in no doubt why...one of the single casks of the year, for sure. 56.3%. nc ncf sc. 186 bottles.

Gordon & MacPhail Private Collection Longmorn 1966 first fill sherry butt, cask no. 610, dist 1 Feb 66, bott 22 Mar 19 (96) n25 t24 f23 b24 The colour of a greatly aged tawny port and enough oak for Henry VIII to build the biggest ship ever to set sail for Jerez and plunder as many sherry butts as he wished. Like a great wine, needs a good half hour minimum to breathe in the glass to open for best results and maximum complexity. 46%. sc. 398 bottles.

THE MACALLAN
Speyside, 1824. Edrington. Working.

The Macallan 10 Years Old db (91) n23 t23 f21.5 b23.5 For a great many of us, it is with the Mac 10 our great Speyside odyssey began. It has to be said that in recent years it has been something of a shadow of its former great self. However, this is the best version I have come across for a while. Not perhaps in the same league as those bottlings in the 1970s which made us re-evaluate the possibilities of single malt. But fine enough to show just how great this whisky can be when the butts have not been tainted and, towards the end, the balance between barley and grape is a relatively equal one. 40%

The Macallan Fine Oak 10 Years Old db (90) n23 t22.5 f21.5 b22 Much more on the ball than the last bottling of this I came across. Malts rarely come as understated or as clever than this. 40%

Macallan 12 Year Old db (61) n15 t16 f15 b15 An uncompromising and comprehensive essay in the present day sulphured sherry butt problem. 43% US tag CP981113

The Macallan Sherry Oak 12 Years Old db (93) n24 t23.5 f22.5 b23 I have to say that some Macallan 12 I have tasted on the road has let me down in the last year or so. This is virtually faultless. Virtually a time machine back to another era... 40%

The Macallan 12 Years Old Sherry Oak Elegancia db (86) n23 t22 f20 b21. Promises, but delivers only to an extent. 40%

The Macallan Fine Oak 12 Years Old db (95.5) n24 t24 f23.5 b24 A whisky whose quality has hit the stratosphere since I last tasted it. I encountered a disappointing one early in the year. This has restored my faith to the point of being a disciple... 40%

The Macallan Fine Oak 15 Years Old db (79.5) n19 t21.5 f19 b20. As the stock of the Fine oak 12 rises, so its 15-y-o brother, once one of my favourite drams, falls. Plenty to enjoy, but a few sulphur stains remove the gloss. 43%

The Macallan Fine Oak 17 Years Old db (82) n19.5 t22 f19.5 b21. Where once it couldn't quite make up its mind on just where to sit, it has now gone across to the sherry benches. Sadly, there are a few dissenters. 43%

The Macallan Sherry Oak 18 Years Old db (87) n24 t22 f20 b21. Underpowered. The body doesn't even come close to matching the nose which builds up the expectancy to enormous levels and, by comparison to the Independents, this at 43% appears weak and unrepresentative. Why this isn't at 46% at the very least and unambiguously uncoloured, I have no idea. 43%

The Macallan Fine Oak 18 Years Old db (94.5) n23.5 t24 f23 b24 Is this the new Fine Oak 15 in terms of complexity? That original bottling thrived on the balance between casks types. This is much more accentuated on a cream sherry persona. But this sample is sulphur-free and quite fabulous. 43%

The Macallan Fine Oak 21 Years Old db (84) n21 t22 f20 b21. An improvement on the characterless dullard I last encountered. But the peaks aren't quite high enough to counter the sulphur notes and make this a great malt. 43%

The Macallan 25 Years Old db (84.5) n22 t21 f20.5 b21. Dry with an even drier oloroso residue; blood orange adds to the fruity mix. Something, though, is not entirely right about this and one fears from the bitter tang at the death that a rogue butt has gained entry to what should be the most hallowed of dumping troughs. 43%

The Macallan Fine Oak 25 Years Old db (90) n22 t23.5 f22 b22.5 The first time I tasted this brand a few years back I was knocked off my perch by the peat reek which wafted about with cheerful abandon. Here the smoke is tighter, more shy and of a distinctly more anthracitic quality.

Even so, the sweet juiciness of the grape juxtaposes gamely with the obvious age to create a malt of obvious class. 43%

The Macallan Fine Oak 25 Years Old db **(89) n23 t23 f21 b22.** Very similar to the Fine Oak 18. However, the signature smoke has vanished, as I suppose over time it must. Not entirely clean sherry, but much remains to enjoy. 43%

The Macallan Fine Oak 30 Years Old db **(81.5) n22 t22 f18 b19.5.** For all its many riches on delivery, especially those moments of great bourbon-honey glory, it has been comprehensively bowled middle stump by the sherry. Gutted. 43%

The Macallan Millennium 50 Years Old (1949) db **(90) n23 t22 f22 b23.** Magnificent finesse and charm despite some big oak makes this another Macallan to die for. 40%

The Macallan Lalique III 57 Years Old db **(95) n24.5 t23 f23.5 b24** No experience with this whisky under an hour pays sufficient tribute to what it is all about. Checking my watch, I am writing this just two minutes under two hours after first nosing this malt. The score started at 88.5. With time, warmth, oxidation and understanding that score has risen to 95. It has spent 57 years in the cask; it deserves two hours to be heard. It takes that time, at least, not just to hear what it has to say to interpret it, but to put it into context. And for certain notes, once locked away and forgotten, to be slowly released. The last Lalique was good. But simply not this good. 48.5%

The Macallan 1824 db **(88) n24 t23.5 f19 b21.5.** Absolutely magnificent whisky, in part. But there are times my job is depressing...and this is one of them.. 48%

The Macallan 1824 Estate Reserve db **(90.5) n22 t23 f22.5 b23** Don't know about Reserve: definitely good enough for the First Team. 45.7%

The Macallan 1824 Select Oak db **(82) n19 t22 f20 b21.** Soft, silky, sometimes sugary... and tangy. Not convinced every oak selected was quite the right one. 40%

◈ **The Macallan A Night On Earth** db bott code 22/07 db **(83.5) n21 t22 f19 b20.5** What a dullard. If I have a night on Earth, I want it to be a damn sight more exciting than this one. The bourbon and sherry casks have cancelled each other out. The attractive slow build of intense – slightly too young – malt is negated by the vaguely off-key fruit. Also, seriously understrength for what they are trying to achieve. 40%

The Macallan Fine Oak Master's Edition db **(91) n23 t23 f22 b23.** Adorable. 42.8%

The Macallan Fine Oak Whisky Maker's Selection db **(92) n22 t23 f23 b24.** This is a dram of exquisite sophistication. Coy, mildly cocoaed dryness, set against just enough barley and fruit sweetness here and there to see off any hints of austerity. Some great work has gone on in the lab to make this happen: fabulous stuff! 42.8%. Duty Free.

The Macallan Gold sherry oak cask db **(89.5) n22 t23.5 f21.5 b22.5.** No Macallan I have tasted since my first in 1975 has been sculpted to show the distillery in such delicate form. 40%

The Macallan Ruby sherry oak cask db **(92.5) n23 t24 f22 b23.5.** Those longer in the tooth who remember the Macallan 10 of 30 years ago will nod approvingly at this chap. Perhaps one butt away from a gong! 43%.

The Macallan Sienna sherry cask db **(94.5) n23 t24 f23.5 b24.** The pre-bottling sample presented to me was much more vibrant than this early on, but lacked the overall easy charm and readily flowing general complexity of the finished article. A huge and pleasing improvement. 43%.

The Macallan Rare Cask Black db **(83.5) n21.5 t22 f19 b21.** Pretty rich and some intense, molasses, black cherry and liquorice notes to die for. But some pretty off-key ones, too. Overall, average fare. 48%

The Macallan Select Oak db **(83) n23 t21 f19 b20.** Exceptionally dry and tight; and a little furry despite the early fruitiness. 40%

The Macallan Whisky Makers Edition db **(76) n19 t20 f18 b19.** Distorted and embittered by the horrific "S" element... 42.8%

Heiko Thieme's 1974 Macallan 65th Birthday Bottling cask no. 16807 dist 25 Nov 74 bott Jul 08 **(94) n23 t23 f24 b24** This is not whisky because it is 38%abv. It is Scottish spirit. However, this is more of a whisky than a great many samples I have tasted this year. Ageism is outlawed. So is sexism. But alcoholism isn't....!! Try and become a friend of Herr Thieme and grab hold of something a little special. 38% 238 bottles.

◈ **Gordon and MacPhail Speymalt Macallan 2000** cask 3245 bott 2018 **(92.5) n24.5** the sherry influence is profound: moist dates mingling with salty sultanas and blood orange peel. The chunky tannins carry a distinct cocoa signature, the overwhelming picture when warmed slightly is elegantly rich Melton Hunt fruitcake. Together, they forge a nose that is off the charts amid contemporary Macallan barrels; **t24** sublimely silky on delivery helped along by a surprising degree of early spice. But it is the weight and gorgeously rotund nature of the mouthfeel which particularly wins the heart here. Muscovado sugars and molasses gloriously combine to balance out the drier sherry tones, while the grape skin proffers further depth and tannin to add to those already displayed by the oak; **f21** it is near impossible to find sherry-matured Macallan of this period – either direct from the distillery or independently bottled – to be entirely free of lingering sulphur, and this does display some. Even so, residual raisins and weighty vanilla plus modest dark chocolate do their best to compensate; **b23** as sherry-influenced Speyside noses go for the 21st century, this is about as good as it gets. The finish is a nod to the frailties of the late 20th and early 21st century sherry-influenced whiskies and in that respect escapes lightly. But there is more than enough for both the nose and delivery to ensure an experience to remember for a lifetime, for it is classic even by Macallan standards. *52.6%*

MACDUFF
Speyside, 1963. Bacardi. Working.

The Deveron Aged 10 Years bott code: L17 284ZAB03 2327 db **(94) n23.5 t23.5 f23 b24** Does the heart good to see a distillery bring their malt out as a ten-year- old – when so many think that such an age is beneath them. This shews the distillery at its most vivid and fresh, when the oak has had time to work its magic but not overstay its welcome; when the barley is still king. And, my word, its crown positively glitters gold here... *40%.*

The Deveron 12 Year Old db **(87.5) n22 t22 f21.5 b22.** Buttery and pleasant. But feels like driving a Ferrari with a Fiat Uno engine. Woefully underpowered and slightly too flat in too many places where it should be soaring. The trademark honey notes cannot be entirely defied, however. *40%*

The Deveron Aged 12 Years bott code: L172018700 db **(94.5) n23.5** retains its big malt personality, though there is far more citrus about now, the oak is weightier and brings into play delicate layers of acacia honey...; **t23.5** ...and it is the honey which lays the foundations for the dropped malty intro.. The mouthfeel is sexy and succulent, a light butterscotch note representing the oak; again, a citrus note hangs about, mainly lime; **f23** at last a little spice comes into play. But the continued complexity...just, wow! **b24** hi honey! I've homed in...! *40%.*

The Deveron Aged 18 Years bott code: L181168700 db **(93) n23 t24 f22.5 b23.5** Someone has started not to just fully understand this always badly underrated distillery, but put it on the map. *40%.*

Fadandel.dk Macduff 13 Year Old barrel, cask no. 8102355, dist 27 Nov 06, bott 28 Nov 19 **(92) n23 t23.5 f22.5 b23** Oh, thank god!! After a day of one sherry butt or wine cask finish after another at last I can taste malt...as in MALT whisky. How amazing is that! Just like the old days. And you know what...? Not only does it have personality, but it's bloody delicious! *54.2%. sc. 191 bottles.*

Old Malt Cask Macduff Aged 14 Years refill hogshead, cask no.HL18702, dist Apr 2007, bott May 2021 **(88.5) n22 t23 f21 b22.5** Great to see a MacDuff where both the nose and delivery trot out an impressive light honey barley theme which shows the malt in a golden light. However, this was filled into a slightly tired cask and the delicate nature of the malt doesn't have quite enough muscle to fully overcome the late bitter notes. The intensity of the delivery, though, is magnificent. *50% sc 282 bottles*

Old Malt Cask Macduff Aged 21 Years refill hogshead, cask no. 15147, dist May 97, bott May 18 **(78) n20 t20 f18 b20** Sticks out like a sore thumb for the other Macduffs in this family, presumably a poor cask undoing the good of the spirit. A duff Macduff... *50%. nc ncf sc.*

Saar MacDuff 2008 dist 14.02. 2008 bott 11.11.2020 **(92.5) n23.5** could nose this all day: the malt simultaneously bristles and glitters; **t23.5** a series of sweetened grapefruit and lemon notes form a stunning duet with the crystalline malt. Salivating, clean and expansive. The spices take their time to erupt but soon vanish once they do; **f22.5** some light vanilla nudges itself into the malty picture; **b23** just adore this. A very compliant cask which allows the distillery full voice and the malt every opportunity to display its charming wares. *53.9%*

Single Cask Collection Macduff 12 Years Old cask no. 11270, dist 2007, bott 2019 **(87.5) n22 t23 f20.5 b22** A placid Macduff which allows the full-blown malt only so much scope. There is a light fruit note to accompany the barley on the nose. The mouth feel is a much fatter affair and the malt takes off in an attractive if simplistic manner, a little ulmo honey adding to the sweetness and luxuriating effect. The finish is dull and tangy by comparison, however. *47%. sc. 374 bottles.*

TnT Casks MacDuff Aged 10 Years refill sherry butt cask no TNT900052 dist 23.01.12 bott 17.02.22 db **(92.5) n23** spiced cherry fruit cake with a perfectly spiced uplift to the vanilla. Still fresh and youthful, but old enough for wonderful depth and complexity; **t23.5** as on the nose, there is a freshness to the fruit, and now demerara sugar, too. And this results, with the aid of a huge spice burst, in maximum salivation. And as eager as the fruits are to please, there is still enough room for the barley to bloom; **f23** as the vanillas pick up, so the whisky dries. But the burnt raisin at the death is a perfect finish; **b23** no need to be charitable about this whisky: it is a rare genuinely unspoiled sherry butt bringing fruity excellence. A joy of a dram. *57.2% sc nc ncf bottled in aid of 2021 floods in Germany.*

MANNOCHMORE

Speyside, 1971. Diageo. Working.

Mannochmore Aged 12 Years db (84) n22 t21 f20 b21. As usual the mouth arrival fails to live up to the great nose. Quite a greasy dram with sweet malt and bitter oak. 43%.

Chapter 7 Mannochmore 2008 Aged 12 Years bourbon hogshead, barrel no.16612 (90.5) n22.5 t23.5 f22 b22.5 The majority of Mannochmores I have tasted over the years have failed to do justice to a distillery which blenders often enjoy for the lovely clarity of the barley. This is a rare example of its full effervescent quality on show, starting with a hint of it on the three-dimensional nose and really taking off on the juiciest of deliveries. Mannochmore is essentially a light spirit, and again this is true to type which means the cask does leave a few footprints at the finish. A superb dram and, in this form, a fine portrait of the distillery. 52.5% sc

MILLBURN

Highlands (Northern), 1807–1985. Diageo. Demolished.

Millburn 1969 Rare Malt db (77) n19 t21 f18 b19. Some lovely bourbon-honey touches but sadly over the hill and declining fast. Nothing like as interesting or entertaining as the massage parlour that was firebombed a few yards from my office twenty minutes ago. Or as smoky... 51.3%.

MILTONDUFF

Speyside, 1824. Chivas Brothers. Working.

Ballantine's The Miltonduff Aged 15 Years Series No.002 American oak casks, bott code: LKRM1193 2018/03/27 (88.5) n23 t22 f21.5 b22 Soft, spicy, attractive but far too much one-dimensional caramel for complexity or greatness. Some decent bourbon notes filter through, though. (The Murray Method brings out the caramels further – best enjoyed at cool bottle temperature). 40%.

Cadenhead's Whisky & More Baden Miltonduff 10 Year Old firkin cask (95.5) n23.5 t24 f24 b24 Firkin hell...!! This really isn't much interested in taking prisoners.! Instead it just wallows in its own swamp of spicy fruitiness and adds chocolate when required. The mouthfeel is as soft, chewy and rounded as any you'll find this year, with the accent on fat dates. As you know, I make no secret that there are some awful fruity whiskies about. This is the antithesis: a huge malt simply brimming with a fruity intensity and clarity to die for. The late mix of Venezuelan cocoa and spiced papaya is almost taking the piss. Magnificent hardly does this justice... 54.5%. sc.

Kingsbury Gold Miltonduff 21 Year Old hogshead, dist 1998, cask no. 10143 (94) n23 even at 21 years, the grassiness to the malt is endearing. The spices and vanillas seem perfectly matched; t24 a dangerous delivery: not one you can be content with just the once! This is the definition of malty complexity: the barley is multi-toned, ranging from almost eye wateringly sharp freshness through digestive biscuit and barley sugar; f23.5 not all the hogsheads Allied filled into were quite as healthy as this: no hidden bitterness, just more and more malt drifting on varied layers of intensity and sometimes spice; b23.5 when you taste one of the older Ballantine blends and wonder why there is such a rich and sturdy composition to the malt, now you know. A sublime example from a sublime distillery. 52.5% sc 233 bottles

Scyfion Choice Miltonduff rara Neagra wine cask finished, dist 2011, bott 2020 (88) n22 t23 f21.5 b21.5 A perfectly enjoyable and acceptable wine cask influenced malt. The trouble is, the influence is a little too much, therefore, after the spicey crescendo about five or six flavours waves in, we have a pretty monosyllabic grapiness taking us through to the bittering finish. Is this an improvement on Miltonduff left in its natural state? Almost certainly not. Too much is not always a good thing. 46% nc ncf 248 bottles

The Single Cask Miltonduff 1st fill bourbon barrel, cask no. 700988, dist 25 Jul 08 (93) n23 the crisp barley strikes against the nose like a wooden hammer on a piano string..; t24 just about faultless, as you might expect from this distillery. The slow build of barley intensity is magnificent enough as it is. Then add that spice in close on exact quantities and the complexity starts heading through the roof. So mouth-watering.... just so beautifully made...; f23 light chocolate layering, though the mild late bitterness is not intended; b23 another superb bottling from this entirely underrated distillery. I have at times argued that this distillery provides the world's most mouth-watering malt. This bottling does little to detract from my point. 59%. sc

The Single Cask Miltonduff 2009 sherry butt, cask no. 90030 (88.5) n22 t22.5 f22 b22 As sherry butts go, not too bad. Perhaps a little tight towards the finish, but forgivably so. Its strength is the intensity of the grape, which is uncompromising, making the integration of the spice and move towards cocoa much more interesting than usual...quite fascinating, even. Its weakness: the uncompromising intensity of the grape.... 64.5%. nc ncf sc.

William & Co Spirits Miltonduff 11 Years Aged sherry oak octave cask, cask no. 8327283, dist 18 Feb 09, bott 19 Jun 20 (94.5) n24 now, that is magnificent! Sherry unencumbered by any sulphur treatment, so there is a grape jam quality to this – such is the sparkling clarity of the fruit. And who cannot be blown away by that teasing heather-honey note sticking close to the oaky vanilla frame? A true joy of a nose....; **t23.5** Miltonduff has the propensity to offer just the right mouthfeel and here are the perfect conditions for it to do its stuff. There is no clunking overweight of oak, or engulfing fruit. Even the malt can be detected and this sits close to the tannins and fruit which behave with perfect grace and poise. A big, chewable malt...but you wouldn't really notice...; **f23** where its sister bottling fell away slightly, this cask sticks to the script. Only the spices stick their head above the parapet as a wonderful Jaffa Cake orange joins the grape before the dark cocoa takes over...; **b24** such a close relation to William and Co's Mingo bottling, I'm hardy surprised the cask numbers are so close. This, though, champions a cleaner grape and far more even development. My word I enjoyed this: sheer class. *53.8%. 89 bottles. Bottled for Nectar Spirit Selection.*

MORTLACH
Speyside, 1824. Diageo. Working.

Mortlach Aged 12 Years The Wee Witchie sherry & bourbon casks, bott code: L8284DM001 db **(92.5) n23** a lovely toffee and raisin theme with the barley lively enough to have a nibble at it; **t23** mouth-watering, fresh and sharp on delivery. Far more life on this than expected from the colour with the plum notes offering both depth and more salivating qualities; **f23.5** a pleasing spiciness amid the drier vanillas; **b23** clean, untainted sherry casks at work: rather lovely. *43.4%.*

Mortlach Aged 12 Years The Wee Witchie bott code: L9176DM006 db **(86.5) n21.5 t22 f21.5 b21.5** A competent full-bodied single malt but overladen and eventually overcome by too much toffee. The tannins cast an attractive spell and the malt stirs the cauldron impressively on delivery. But this is simplistic whisky and lacking in the complexity one feels it could so easily attain. *43.4%*

Mortlach Aged 16 Years db **(87) n20 t23 f22 b22.** Once it gets past the bold if very mildly sulphured nose, the rest of the journey is superb. Earlier Mortlachs in this range had a slightly unclean feel to them and the nose here doesn't inspire confidence. But from arrival on the palate onwards, it's sure-footed, fruity and even refreshing... and always delicious. *43%*

Mortlach Aged 16 Years Distiller's Dram ex-sherry casks, bott code: L8330DM004 db **(93.5) n23.5 t23.5 f23** soft vanilla and barley sugars – as well as a dry, pulsing spiciness representing age; **b23.5** after quite a long period in the doldrums, this distillery really does have the wind in its sails once more. Excellent whisky. *43.4%.*

Mortlach 18 Year Old db **(75) n19 t19 f18 b19.** When I first tasted Mortlach, probably over 30 years ago now, it really wasn't even close to this. Something went very wrong in the late '80s, I can tell you...*43.4%. Diageo.*

Mortlach 20 Year Old Cowie's Blue Seal db **(87) n22 t22 f21.5 b21.5** Pleasant, but apart from a little oak on the nose never gets round to displaying its age. The odd orange blossom honey money opens it up slightly but a shade too tame and predictable. *43.4%.*

Mortlach 25 Year Old db **(91.5) n23** just love the lemon grass alongside the liquorice and hickory; **t23.5** thick and palate-encompassing. The sugars are pretty toasty with a light mocha element in play; **f22.5** crisp finale with a return of the citrus, sitting confidently with the late spice; **b22.5** much more like it. The sugars may be pretty full on, but there is enough depth and complexity for a narrative to be told. Very much a better Mortlach on so many levels. *43.4%.*

Mortlach Rare Old db **(79) n20 t21 f19 b19.** Not rare enough... *43.4%. Diageo.*

Mortlach Special Strength db **(79.5) n20 t21.5 f19 b19.** Does whisky come any more cloyingly sweet than Mortlach...? Not in my experience.... *49%. Diageo.*

◈ **Art Edition No 6 Mortlach Aged 15 Years** Oloroso hogshead, dist 2008, bott 2023 **(87) n22 t22.5 f21 b21.5** Chunky, deep, oily and heavy. Pre-2010 Mortlach or I'm a ten-pound kipper! One of those occasions where I knew the whisky even before I had checked the sample bottle. Absolutely typical Mortlach from that era: a bruising heavyweight lacking elegance but certainly not substance. Though it has its technical faults, the depth of the malt is sometimes unfathomable. And before it descends into its final oily, tangy orgy, the brief kiss of cocoa is rather charming. For those who prefer their whisky in a dirty glass... *52.4% nc ncf 60 bottles Whiskyjace*

The First Editions Mortlach Aged 13 Years 2007 wine barrel, cask no.18375, bott 2021 **(93) n23 t23.5 f23 b23.5** Now and again a Mortlach appears that tends to surprise you with a puff of smoke. And here is one with the phenols most at home on the nose...mixed in with some acidic (or is it alkaline?) anthracite.... Thankfully that wine cask has left enough room for the malt to stretch its legs, especially on the nose. Though the grape arrives early on in delivery, alongside the reinforcing smoke. As the phenols tail off, the barley becomes cleaner and more dominant forming a superb team with the growing spices. First rate stuff: Mortlach at its absolute best! *50.2% nc ncf sc 118 bottles*

The First Editions Mortlach Aged 13 Years 2007 wine barrel, cask no.HL18664, bott 2021 **(84) n22.5 t22.5 f19 b20** One of those casks I find quite fascinating because of the polarisation in its personality. The nose is a tapestry of malt and spicy notes, reinforced with a thread of raisin. Likewise the delivery stops you in your tracks as your taste buds are given a delicious working over of light ulmo honey, muscovado sugars and salivating barley. The finish by comparison is harsh, dry and uncompromising: the exact opposite of the earlier, subtly sweet complexity. Mind you: that can be wine casks for you... *54.5% nc ncf sc 286 bottles*

Hepburn's Choice Mortlach 10 Years Old wine cask, dist 2009, bott 2019 (90.5) n23 t22.5 f22 b23 Youthfully fresh and malty. But it is the low rumble of smoke on the nose, delivery and finish in particular that genuinely intrigues! Refreshing and crisp, all the same. *46%. nc ncf sc. 375 bottles.*

Hepburn's Choice Mortlach 13 Years Old wine hogsheads, dist 2007, bott 2020 (78.5) n20.5 t20.5 f18.5 b19 Overall, a dull and bitter dram which enjoys an all too brief malty surge on delivery. *46%. nc ncf. 512 bottles.*

MOSSTOWIE
Speyside, 1964–1981. Chivas Brothers. Closed.
Rare Old Mosstowie 1979 (84.5) n21.5 t21 f21 b21. Edging inextricably well beyond its sell by date. But there is a lovely walnut cream cake (topped off with brown sugar and spices) to this which warms the cockles. Bless... *43%. Gordon & MacPhail.*

NORTH PORT
Highlands (Eastern), 1820–1983. Diageo. Demolished.
Brechin 1977 db (78) n19 t21 f18 b20. Fire and brimstone was never an unknown quantity with the whisky from this doomed distillery. Some soothing oils are poured on this troubled – and sometimes attractively honeyed – water of life. *54.2%*

OBAN
Highlands (Western), 1794. Diageo. Working.
Oban 14 Years Old db (79) n19 t22 f18 b20. Absolutely all over the place. The cask selection sits very uncomfortably with the malt. I look forward to the resumption of normality to this great but ill-served distillery. *43%*

Oban Aged 14 Years bott code: L9337CM005 db (88) n23 t22.5 f20.5 b22 So much better than the last Oban 14 I tasted, which had lost its identity totally. It here now has a far more bright and shimmering attitude on the nose, as was the case back in the day. Still heavier than of old with less fretwork to admire, but at least we are now blessed with honey and blood oranges, as well as pretty rounded maltiness. Likewise, the delivery is alive and salivating as the heather-honey kissed malt shews little inhibition...well, at first. However, the dull bitterness that creeps in at the midpoint is determined to last the course, alas. A long way from the magnificent Obans of its heyday, but this is much nearer the mark than in recent years. *43%.*

⬩⬩⬩ **Oban 14** bott code L2178 db (94.5) n24 peaches and cream with extra peaches....there is also the most delicate and fragile of peaty notes: a genuine classic this with just-so oils; t23 the layering of intense malt is impressive. The playful interlapping of spices is equally delightful...; f23.5 too ridiculously soft for words. Those phenols that aren't supposed exist to turn up early and make play with the heavy roasty tannins. The citrus notes carry on regardless. At the midway point some toffee caramels begin to interfere with the otherwise significant kumquats...; b24 don't even think about drinking this cold as I once saw some idiot influencer (who probably knows as much about whisky as I as I can tell you about the inner core of some barely known meteor) informs his victim public. This has to be warmed to body temperatures, and then magic happens. Perhaps the most underrated of Diageo's old "Classic Malt" range. *43%*

Oban The Distillers Edition special release OD 162.FX, dist 1998, bott 2013 db (87.5) n22.5 t22.5 f21 b21.5. Some attractive kumquat and blood orange make for a fruity and rich malt, though just a little furry towards the finish. Decent Demerara early on, too. *43%*

Oban Distillery Exclusive Bottling batch no. 02, refill, ex-bourbon and rejuvenated casks, bott code: L9337CM008 db (91.5) n23 t23.5 f22 b23 Who knew that one day they'd bring out an Oban this sweet? Usually a malt with an absent-minded, salty dryness that never did anything with great intention or seemingly with a game plan. Here, though, this has been set out to be as friendly as possible. And it has most certainly succeeded! *48%. 7,500 bottles.*

Oban Little Bay db (87.5) n21 t23 f21.5 b22. A pleasant, refreshing simple dram. Clean and juicy in part and some wonderful oak-laden spice to stir things up a little. Just a little too much chewy toffee near the end, though. *43%*

Game of Thrones Oban Bay Reserve The Night's Watch db (87.5) n22 t23 f21 b21.5 Starts promisingly, even offering a saltiness you tend not to see from this distillery these days. The intense grist on the malt makes for a beautiful delivery. But flattens fast and furiously as the caramels kick in. *43%.*

PITTYVAICH

Speyside, 1975–1993. Diageo. Demolished.

Pittyvaich 28 Year Old db (86.5) n22.5 t22 f20.5 b21.5 The nose is an attractive blend of malt and hazelnut. The delivery is sweet, gristy and promising. But it thins out fast and dramatically. So limited in scope, but pleasant in the early phases. *52.1%. 4,680 bottles. Diageo Special Releases 2018.*

PORT ELLEN

Islay, 1825–1983. Diageo. Closed.

Port Ellen 9 Rogue Casks 40 Year Old db (96) n24 t24 f23.5 b24.5 One of the great surprise whiskies this any many years. I didn't expect this bottling to display such astounding elegance and balance, but it does from the first moment to the last. It has taken me close on three hours to analyse this malt. Had I the space, my notes could probably take up a page of this book. But here I have simplified it over many temperatures and varying oxidisation levels. Those nine rogue casks must have been as beautifully seasoned as they come. Stunning. *50.9%.*

Port Ellen Aged 37 Years dist 1978 db (91) n24.5 t22.5 f22 b22 The bark is far better than the bite: one of the great noses of the year cannot be backed up on the palate as the oak is simply too demanding. An historical experience, but ensure you spend as much time nosing as you do tasting... *55.2%. 2,940 bottles. Diageo Special Releases 2016.*

Port Ellen 37 Year Old refill American oak hogsheads & refill American oak butts db (88) n23 t21.5 f22 b21.5 The oak scars the overall beauty of the malt. *51%. 2,988 bottles.*

Port Ellen 39 Years Old db (96.5) n24 t24 f24 b24.5 A malt which defies time and logic, and the short-sighted individuals who closed down this distillery and later, unforgivably, ripped out its innards (despite my one-kneed imploring). Tragically beautiful. *50.9%.*

PULTENEY

Highlands (Northern), 1826. Inver House Distillers. Working.

Old Pulteney Aged 12 Years db (90.5) n22 t23 f22.5 b23 A cleaner, zestier more joyous composition than the old 43%, though that has less to do with strength than overall construction. A dramatic whisky which, with further care, could get even closer to the truth of this distillery. *40%*

Old Pulteney Aged 12 Years bott code L15/030 R15/5046 IB db (91) n22.5 t23 f22.5 b23 Remarkably consistent from the bottling above. The salt continues to ensure lustre, though this bottling has a little extra – and welcome – barley gristiness. *40%. ncf.*

⬩ **Old Pulteney Aged 12 Years**, bott code L05/12/2022 db (92) n22.5 what appears to be a sub-currant of smoke occasionally burst into something a little more weighty and forceful. Pear-droppy citrus feels at home with comfortable vanilla and barley. Love the sweet-dry alternation...; t23 the fruit drops win, and we are treated to an intense juicy, fruity tick-tack candy, sharpness. The barley is bubbling underneath...while the smoke offers a surprise oiliness and depth; f23 late vanilla and mocha and still that gorgeous smoke depth; b23.5 had to double check the label on this one to see if this was some kind of peated version: no mention. Certainly the smokiest Pulteney 12 I've ever encountered, and the good news is that the phenols do not overly dominate this distillery's trademark complexity. But it does certainly maximise the weight and length. *40%*

Old Pulteney Aged 15 Years db (95.5) n24 t24 f23.5 b24 More than a night cap. One you should definitely take to bed with you... *46%.*

Old Pulteney Aged 17 Years bott code: L15/329 R15/5530 IB db (82) n20.5 t22.5 f19 b20 This is usually one of the greatest whiskies bottled anywhere in the world. But not even something of Pulteney 17's usually unfathomable excellence and charisma can withstand this degree of sulphur. Much greater care has to be taken in the bottling hall to preserve the integrity of what should be one of Scotland's most beautiful offerings to the world. *46%. ncf.*

Old Pulteney Aged 18 Years db (81) n19 t21.5 f20 b20.5 If you are going to work with sherry butts you have to be very careful. And here we see a whisky that is not careful enough as the sulphur does its usual damage. For those in central Europe without the "sulphur gene", then no problem as the fruit is still intact. *46%.*

Old Pulteney Aged 21 Years db (97.5) n25 t24 f24 b24.5 By far and away one of the great whiskies of 2012, absolutely exploding from the glass with vitality, charisma and class. One of Scotland's great undiscovered distilleries about to become discovered, I think... and rightly so! *46%*

Old Pulteney Aged 25 Years American & Spanish oak casks, bott code: L17/282 R17/5353 IB db (96) n25 t23.5 f23.5 b24 A quiet but incredibly complex reminder why this distillery is capable of producing World Whisky of the Year. Age is all around you, but degradation there is none. *46%.*

Old Pulteney 35 Year Old db (89) n23 t21.5 f22.5 b22 A malt on the perimeter of its comfort zone. But there are enough gold nuggets included to make this work. Just. *46%.*

Old Pulteney Aged 40 Years db (95) n23.5 t23.5 f24 b24 This malt still flies as close to the sun as possible. But some extra fruit, honey and spice now grasps the tannins by the throat to ensure a whisky of enormous magnitude and complexity 51.3%

Old Pulteney 1990 Vintage American & Spanish casks db (85) n21 t23 f21 b20. As you know, anything which mentions sherry butts gets me nervous – and for good reason. Even with a World Great distillery like Pulteney. Oddly enough, this bottling is, as near a dammit, free of sulphur. Yee-hah! The bad news, though, is that it is also untroubled by complexity as well. It reminded me of some heavily sherried peaty jobs...and then I learned that ex Islay casks were involved. That may or may not be it. But have to say, beyond the first big, salivating, lightly spiced moments on delivery you wait for the story to unfurl...and it all turns out to be dull rumours. 46%.

Old Pulteney 2006 Vintage first fill ex-bourbon casks, bott 2017, bott code: L17/279 R17/5452 IB db (93) n23 t23.5 f23 b23.5 A beautiful, lightly salted ceremony of malt with the glycerine feel of raspberry and cream Swiss rolls. Just so love it! 46%.

Old Pulteney Dunnet Head Lighthouse bourbon & sherry casks db (90.5) n22 t23.5 f22 b23 Loads to chew over with this heavyweight.46%. nc ncf. Exclusive to travel retail.

Old Pulteney Huddart db (88.5) n22 t22.5 f22 b22 Hopefully not named after my erstwhile physics teacher of 45 years ago, Ernie Huddart, who, annoyingly, for an entire year insisted on calling me Murphy rather than Murray, despite my constant correcting the mistake. One day he told me off for my not remembering some or other Law of Physics. When he finished berating me quite unpleasantly at high volume before my fellow classmates, I simply said: "Well, sir, that's fine coming from you. You've had a year to learn that my name is Murray and not Murphy, and still you failed!" He was so lost for words at this impudence I got away with it, though if his glare could have killed... Anyway, back to the whisky: this seemingly young, lightly smoked version shows all the hallmarks of being finished in peaty casks, as opposed to being distilled from phenolic malt, hence the slightly mottled and uneven feel to this. Odd, but attractive. Oh, and Huddart...? I think that's actually the name of the nondescript old street on which the distillery sits 46%.

Old Pulteney Navigator bourbon & sherry casks db (80) n19 t23 f18 b20. Sherry butts have clearly been added to this. Not sure why, as the sulphur only detracts from the early honey riches. The compass is working when the honey and cocoa notes briefly harmonise in beautiful tandem. But otherwise, badly off course. 46%. nc ncf.

Old Pulteney Noss Head Lighthouse bourbon casks db (84) n22.5 t22 f19 b20.5. If Noss Head was as light as this dram, it'd be gone half way through its first half decent storm. An apparent slight overuse of third and less sturdy second fill casks means the finale bitters out considerably. A shame, as the nose and delivery is about as fine a display of citrus maltiness as you'll find. 46%. Travel retail exclusive. WB15/327

Old Pulteney Pentland Skerries Lighthouse db (85) n21 t22 f20.5 b21.5. A chewy dram with an emphasis on the fruit. Sound, evens enjoys the odd chocolate-toffee moment. But a little sulphur, apparent on the nose, creeps in to take the gloss off. 46%. WB15/323

Gordon & MacPhail Connoisseurs Choice Pulteney Aged 19 Years first fill ex-bourbon barrel, cask no. 1071, dist 26 Aug 98, bott 21 Jun 18 (95.5) n23.5 t24 f24 b24 Malt from one of the world's very finest distilleries matured in a first- class cask. The result is inevitable. The interplay between oak and malt starts on the first molecules to hit the nose and ends only when the story is told. Can't ask any more of the spices, or their interaction with the liquorice and Manuka honey mix. Everything is perfectly paced and weighted, even the natural caramels that could so easily have tipped this towards a blander bottling. Toasty, sublimely complex and breath-taking. 57.5%. sc. 192 bottles.

ROSEBANK
Lowlands, 1840–1993. Ian Macleod. Closed- soon to re-open. (The gods have answered!)
Rosebank 21 Year Old refill American oak casks, dist 1992 db (95.5) n23.5 t24 f24 b24 Rosebank is at its very best at eight-years-old. Well, that won't happen again, so great to see it has proven successful at 21... 55.3%. 4,530 bottles. Diageo Special Releases 2014.

ROYAL BRACKLA
Speyside, 1812. Bacardi. Working.
Royal Brackla Aged 12 Years bott code: L18192B700 db (85) n22 t22 f20 b21 A definite improvement on previous bottlings but, coming from Bacardi's formidable stable, I had expected more. The finish is still dull as ditch water, with nothing other than toffee to find but there is an upping of fresh fruit on both nose and delivery. 40%.

Royal Brackla Aged 16 Years bott code: L18158B700 db (88) n22.5 light and zesty, a little spice flickers around the caramel; t22.5 soft, bordering luxuriant, there is a big malt and caramel hook up. But it is the all too brief, refreshing, zingy delivery which stars; f21 still a little too much on the dull-ish caramel side; b22 a very pleasant malt, but you get the feeling it is being driven with the handbrake on... 40%.

Royal Brackla Aged 21 Years bott code: L18297B701 db **(91.5) n23** maintains its unusual but delightful lychee sweetness, that sweetness now extending to maple syrup and fudge; **t23** delicate and salivating, initially shewing little sign of great age. It takes a while but the toastier tannins finally arrive; **f22.5** salty, with a chocolate fudge finale; **b23** where both the 12- and 16-years olds appear both to be tied to a vat of toffee, this beauty has been given its wings. Also, I remember this for being a malt with a curious lychee note, hence tasting it today. For yesterday I tasted a malt matured in a lychee liqueur barrel. Pleased to report no shortage of lychees here, either. 40%.

Fadandel Royal Brackla 13 Years Old (89) n22 though the cask is tiring, it still offers enough vanilla to frame the thick barley; **t22.5** what a salty beast this is! A particularly puckering delivery, especially when the barley goes into overdrive; **f22** huge malt but the cask shows a mild touch of tanginess as it tires; **b22.5** this is a flavour bomb that doesn't need much prodding before it detonates. Perhaps not entirely the ticket technically, but if ever you need a full-flavoured ultra-malty restorative...here it is!! 56.1%

The Single Cask Royal Brackla 2009 barrel, cask no. 304159, dist 24 Mar 09 **(94) n23 t24 f23.5 b23.5** One of my greatest disappointments on the scotch scene in recent years has been the lack of excellent bourbon cask bottlings to show distilleries at their very best. One of those which has suffered has been Royal Brackla. From this, you can see why I am a fan of this distillery presented in an oak which showcases its considerable charm. 57.2%. sc.

Whisky Republic Royal Brackla Aged 15 Years bourbon hogshead no 310835 dist 11/2006 bott 04/2022 **(92) n23.5** for all its years, celebrates a bright pear-drop quality which maximises the barley presence. Softly salty and deft; **t23.5** explosive barley which is surprisingly heavy on the Demerara sugar. The midground is a tapestry of complex and beautifully structured barley and oak tones, at times becoming quite biscuity in the process. Excellent oils allows the flavours to glide about the palate; **f22** flattens and simplifies a little thanks possibly to a well-used second or even third fill cask, which leaves the tell-take tangy residue; **b23** such a beautifully clean malt which wears its age with elegance and dignity. A quietly classy dram. 59.5% 314 bottles

William & Co Spirits Brackla 9 Years Old sherry oak octave cask, cask no. 9327879, dist 12 Apr 11, bott 22 Jun 20 **(91) n22.5** forget the obvious fruit and accompanying spices. Just listen to all that barley still belting through! Love it...; **t23** after a brief salute to a grape or two, all attention is paid to the barley which fills the mouth with a salivating freshness. The spices on the nose are even more active here and help make for a busy and delightfully structured piece. The waves of flavour crash thick and unusually fast, as though the whole, increasingly sweet, malt is in a hurry...; **f22.5** good quality oak act as a sound baseline for the increasingly youthful barley topping. So clean for a malt finish and retains its barley sugar sweetness to the very end...; **b23** it's always fun to find a malt under ten years old bottled when the barley still has a massive amount of life and energy to give. This makes for an essential pre-prandial dram, stirring the tastebuds up something chronic. 52.8%. 90 bottles. Bottled for Stir Cocktail Bar & Nectar Spirits Selection.

ROYAL LOCHNAGAR

Highlands (Eastern), 1826. Diageo. Working.

Royal Lochnagar Aged 12 Years db **(84) n21 t22 f20 b21.** More care has been taken with this than some other bottlings from this wonderful distillery. But I still can't understand why it never quite manages to get out of third gear...or is the caramel on the finish the giveaway...? 40%

Royal Lochnagar Aged 12 Years bott code: L9214CM003 db **(93) n23.5** superb! A sharp, copper-rich aroma going heavy on the esters. The malt forms a lovely outer shield. But it cannot entirely keep in all the exotic fruit, including pineapple and jackfruit which gives the core a delightful sharpness...; **t23** a succulent, salivating delivery, soft on arrival with the barley and light caramels melting first. Slowly that distinctive metallic tang builds, and with it the fruit – though now less from tropical climes but of a more prosaic grapiness; **f23** a pleasant farewell of vanilla, toffee, light ulmo honey, barley, Garibaldi biscuit and the very lightest liquorice: complex...; **b23.5** for the first time in some little while I have found a Lochnagar 12 which manages to underline the small still properties of this distillery with rich and intense dram true to its traditional style. For too long bottlings had been flat and lifeless and could have been mistaken as the ill-treated malts from anywhere. Not this time. This projects a delightful richness unique to Royal Lochnagar. It is like welcoming back a long lost friend. Queen Victoria, once this distillery's patron, would have been amused.... 40%.

Royal Lochnagar Distillery Exclusive batch no. 01, first-fill European oak and refill casks, bott code: L9302DQ0001 db **(82) n22 t23 f17.5 b19.5** Ultimately a dull, monotonous whisky after a promising and lively start. Love the fresh, salivating delivery and with some great spices, too. But the story ends by the midpoint. The European oak has done this no favours whatsoever, ensuring a furry, off-key finale. 48%. 5,004 bottles.

Game of Thrones Royal Lochnagar 12 Year Old House Baratheon db **(89)** n22 t22.5 f22 b22.5 Not sure when I last encountered a Lochnager of such simplicity. Friendly and impossible not to like. *40%*.

Old Malt Cask Royal Lochnagar 21 (91) n22.5 t23 f22.5 b23 From the first sniff we find a malt refusing to ruffle any feathers. Every aspect is carefully manicured and then capped if it looks like getting out of hand. So we have pristine barley on the nose, turned and honed by a sympathetic cask, uneager to invest too much of itself in the game. It is hardly surprising, then, that the delivery is mouth-watering, the barley finding few obstacles to the tastebuds. Only on the finish does a light, citrusy, chalky dusting of oak hover into view. An essay in genteel, unassuming elegance. *50%*

ST. MAGDALENE
Lowlands, 1798–1983. Diageo. Demolished.

Linlithgow 30 Years Old dist 1973 db **(70)** n18 t18 f16 b18. A brave but ultimately futile effort from a malt that is way past its sell-by date. *59.6%*

Gordon & MacPhail Private Collection St. Magdalene 1982 refill American hogshead, cask no. 2092, dist 1 Jul 82, bott 21 Mar 19 **(96)** n24 t24 l f23.5 b24.5 It has been eight long years since a new St Magdalene turned up in my tasting room and that, like this, was distilled just a year before the closure of the distillery itself. And I can tell you for nothing, when it was made never in a million years did any of those within the distillery believe for a second that it would finally be tasted nearly 40 years after the spirit was filled into a very good American oak barrel. For a start, this was a Lowland malt that, in its lifetime, was used exclusively for blending, most of it at three and five years old. It is light in structure and flavour and conversations I had with blenders in the 1980s confirmed that they didn't trust this malt to add sufficient body to the malt content for it to be used for older blends, though that didn't stop Diageo once bringing it out as a 23-year-old. Of all the St. Mag distillates I tasted from about 1970 through to 1983, I thought 1982 the finest of the bunch, so no surprise that it has held its head high and proud here, even displaying the same citrusy undercurrent that I thought made the 10-year-old so charming way back in 1992. I have in here, not just a throwback but a little whisky miracle in my glass. This malt has no right to be this good. But, my god it is...!! *53%. sc. 161 bottles.*

SCAPA
Highlands (Island–Orkney), 1885. Chivas Brothers. Working.

Scapa 12 Years Old db **(88)** n23 t22 f21 b22. Always a joy. *40%*

Scapa 16 Years Old db **(81)** n21 t20.5 f19.5 b20. For it to be so tamed and toothless is a crime against a truly great whisky which, handled correctly, would be easily among the finest the world has to offer. *40%*

Scapa Glansa peated whisky cask finish, batch no. GL05, bott Jul 18 db **(91)** n22 t23.5 f22.5 b23 A delightful whisky which could be raised several notches in quality if the influence of the caramel is diminished. *40%*.

Scapa Skiren db **(89.5)** n22.5 t22.5 f22 b22.5 Chaps who created this: lovely, you really have to power this one up a bit... *40%*

Gordon & MacPhail Connoisseurs Choice Scapa Aged 30 Years refill bourbon barrel, cask no. 10585, dist 2 Sept 88, bott 13 Sept 18 **(94)** n22.5 t24 f23.5 b24 One of those exceptionally rare occasions when the threatening tannins on the nose fail to materialise on the palate. Instead we have glorious display of varied honey tones far more usually associated with its neighbouring Orkney distillery. Stunning displays of light saltiness mixes brilliantly with the lime blossom honey before the spices and tannins set. A thing of beauty. *53.8%. sc. 148 bottles.*

SPEYBURN
Speyside, 1897. Inver House Distillers. Working.

Speyburn Aged 10 Years bott code: L16/303 R165434 IB db **(84.5)** n21 t21.5 f21 b21 Appears to celebrate and even emphasises its remarkable thinness of body. As usual, juicy with a dominant toffee character. *40%*.

Speyburn Aged 10 Years Travel Exclusive American oak ex-bourbon & ex-sherry casks, bott code L18/055 R18/5069 IB db **(89.5)** n21.5 t22.5 f22.5 b23 Really imaginative use of excellent sherry butts. An understatedly complex and delicious malt. *46%. ncf.*

Speyburn Aged 15 Years American oak & Spanish oak casks, bott code L1717/253 R17/5323 IB db **(91)** n22 t23.5 f22 b23.5 Well done: not an off sherry butt in sight, helping to make this an enjoyably rich and fulsome malt. One of the most inventive and sympathetic Speyburns of all time. *46%.*

Speyburn Aged 18 Years db **(86)** n22 t22.5 f20 b21.5 Nutty, malty and displaying a cocoa tendency. But the finish is a bit on the bitter side. *46%.*

Speyburn Aged 25 Years db (**92**) n22 t24 f23 b23. Either they have re-bottled very quickly or I got the diagnosis dreadfully wrong first time round. Previously I wasn't overly impressed; now I'm taken aback by its beauty. Some change. 46%

Speyburn Arranta Casks first fill ex-bourbon casks bott code: L16/097 R16/5130 IB db (**90**) n22 t23 f22 b23 Speyburn at its most vocal and interesting: rather beautifully constructed. 46%.

Speyburn Bradon Orach bott code: L17/039 R17/5048 IB db (**75**) n19 t19 f18.5 b18.5 Remains one of the most curious distillery bottlings on Speyside and one still unable to find either its balance or a coherent dialogue. 46%.

Speyburn Hopkins Reserve Travel Exclusive bott code R18/5066 IB db (**92**) n23 t23 f22.5 b23.5 The kind of ultra-simplistic raw, smoky Speysider that the distillery's founder John Hopkins would have recognised – and drooled over - over a century ago... 46%. ncf.

The First Editions Speyburn Aged 14 Years 2007 sherry butt, cask no.HL18373, bott 2021 (**94**) n23 t23.5 f23.5 b23.5 Not only could I easily drink this whisky...I could kiss it. Today I have suffered disappointment with three malts ruined or at least damaged by sulphur casks. This being a sherry butt, I was wary, to put it mildly. There was no need! Speyburn presented in a manner very rarely seen. And beautifully so. 50.2% nc ncf sc 32 bottles

THE SPEYSIDE DISTILLERY

Speyside, 1990. Speyside Distillers. Working.

Spey 10 Year Old port casks db (**87**) n22 t22.5 f20.5 b22 Soft and nutty, there is an attractive easiness to the fruit as it makes its salivating, bitter-sweet way around the palate. Just a little bit of a tang on the finish, though. 46%. nc ncf. 3,000 bottles.

Spey 12 Years Old limited edition, finished in new oak casks db (**85.5**) n21.5 t23 f19.5 b21.5. One of the hardest whiskies I have had to define this year: it is a curious mixture of niggling faults and charming positives which come together to create a truly unique scotch. The crescendo is reached early after the delivery with an amalgamation of acacia honey, barley sugar and butter notes interlocking with something bordering classicism. However, the nose and finish, despite the chalky oak, reveals that something was lacking in the original distillate or, to be more precise, was rather more than it should have been. Still, some hard work has obviously gone into maximising the strengths of a distillery that had hitherto failed to raise the pulse and impresses for that alone. 40%. nc. 8,000 bottles.

Spey 18 Years Old ltd edition, fresh sherry casks db (**82.5**) n19 t23.5 f19 b21. What a shame this malt has been brushed with sulphur. Apparent on nose and finish, it still can't diminish ir detract from the joy of the juicy grape on delivery and the excellent weight as the liquorice and treacle add their gentle treasures and pleasures. So close to a true classic. 46%. nc.

Spey Chairman's Choice db (**77**) n19 t21 f18 b19. Their Chairman's Choice, maybe. But not mine... 40%

Spey Fumare db (**90.5**) n22 t23.5 f22 b23 A very different type of peaty malt with some surprising twists and turns. As fascinating as it is quietly delicious. I am looking at Speyside distillery in a new light...46%. nc ncf.

Spey Fumare Cask Strength db (**93**) n23 t23.5 f23 b23.5 Unquestionably The Speyside Distillery in its prettiest pose. And this strength ensures perfect lighting... 59.3%. nc ncf.

Spey Royal Choice db (**87**) n21 t23 f21 b22. "I'll have the slightly feinty one, Fortescue." "Of course, Your Highness. Would that be the slightly feinty one which has a surprising softness on the palate, a bit like a moist date and walnut cake? But with a touch too much oil on the finish?" "That's the blighter! No ice, Fortescue!" "Perish the thought, Sir." "Or water, Forters. One must drink according to the Murray Method, don't you know!" "Very wise, Sir." 46%

Spey Tenné finished in Tawny Port casks db (**90**) n22.5 t23 f22 b22.5 Upon pouring, the handsome pink blush tells you one of three things: i) someone has swiped the whisky and filled the bottle with Mateus Rosé instead; ii) I have just located where I put the pink paraffin or iii) this whisky has been matured in brand spanking new port casks. Far from a technical paragon of virtue so far as distilling is concerned. But those Tawny Port casks have brought something rather magical to the table. And glass. 46%. nc. 18,000 bottles.

Spey Tenné Cask Strength db (**88**) n22.5 t22 f21.5 b22 Plenty of weirdness to this – and spicy fun, too! What magnificent (port?) casks they must have used for this...!! 59.5%. nc ncf.

Spey Trutina bourbon casks db (**90**) n22.5 t23 f22 b22.5 The best Speyside Distillery bottling I have encountered for a very long time. Entirely feint free and beautifully made. 46%. nc ncf.

Beinn Dubh db (**82**) n20 t21 f21 b20. Mountains. Dogs. Who can tell the difference...? I suppose to a degree I can, as this has for more rummy undertones and is slightly less inclined to layering than the old Danish version. 43%

Old Malt Cask Speyside Aged 25 Years refill hogshead, cask no.HL18698, dist Sept 1995, bott May 2021 (**86.5**) n22.5 t23 f20 b21 It is quite frightening to think that on a cold Sunday morning in a Glasgow warehouse I opened up the first-ever filled cask of Speyside to taste it on its 3rd birthday. The day Speyside distillery could claim that it made whisky, not just new make or malt spirit. Now here I am tasting it as a 25-years-old...so sobering amid all this alcohol. It would take a little bit of artistic licence to describe this as a great 25-year-old malt. It is certainly pretty good, especially if intense barley is your thing. But there is a bite and thinness to this which suggests the stills were a bit fierce the day the spirit safe was flowing. After a quite beautiful crescendo of concentrated barley and acacia honey, it moves towards an ever-bittering fade and there is not enough body to the malt to see off the excesses of the cask. Such a fascinating experience, though... *50% sc*

Valour Whisky Speyside Distillery Aged 26 years bourbon barrel Cask No 44000698 dist 25/06/1996 bott 27/06/2022 (**95**) **n23.5** crisp barley engulfed in even crisper acacia honey and light red liquorice to give a quasi bourbon-like feel now and again; **t24** fabulously fruity: juicy plums mixing in with sticky, honeyed barley. The tannins are mesmerising and totally in step, tune and weight with the other elements to offer an excellent whole. The slow build of the confident spice is not just required but perfectly executed; **f23.5** there is a glistening quality here of copper: the stills were obviously young and generous when this was distilled and 26 years on ensures a richness which is perfectly complemented by the drier vanillas and unspoiled barley; **b24** some malts from this region take on an exotic fruity hue at this age: not here. It is fruity from old age, right enough. But here we are more in the land of greengages and lemon blossom honey. A peach of a dram from the earliest days of this distillery before, for several years, their make became far less than impressive. This is how I remember the whisky in quality when I became the first person to taste it on its third birthday. Had only they stuck fast to this quality. A gold nugget of a dram – one for every serious collector to find...and savour. *54.3% 244 bottles*

SPRINGBANK
Campbeltown, 1828. J&A Mitchell & Co. Working.

Springbank Aged 10 Years db (**89.5**) **n22 t23 f22 b22.5.** Although the inherent youthfulness of the 10-y-o has not changed, the depth of body around it has. Keeps the taste buds on full alert. *46%*

Springbank Aged 15 Years db (**88.5**) **n22.5 t22 f22 b22.** Last time I had one of these, sulphur spoiled the party. Not this time. But the combination of oil and caramel does detract from the complexity a little. *46%*

Springbank Aged 18 Years db (**90.5**) **n23** busy in the wonderful Springbank way; delicate greengage and date; nippy; **t23** yummy, mouthwatering barley and green banana. Fresh with excellent light acacia honey; **f21.5** fabulous oak layering, including chocolate. A little off-key furriness from a sherry butt late on; **b23** just one so-so butt away from bliss... *46%*

Springbank Aged 21 Years db (**90**) **n22 t23 f22.5 b22.5** A few years ago I was at Springbank when they were bottling a very dark, old-fashioned style 21-year-old. I asked if I could take a 10cl sample with me for inclusion in the Bible; they said they would send it on, though I tasted a glass there and then just for enjoyment's sake. They never did send it, which was a shame. For had they, they most probably would have carried off World Whisky of the Year. This, though very good, is not quite in the same class. But just to mark how special this brand has always been to me, I have made this the 500th new single malt scotch and 700th new whisky in all of the 2015 Whisky Bible. *46%. WB15/096*

Springbank 22 Year Old Single Cask hogshead, cask no. 582, dist May 97, bott Jan 20 db (**95.5**) **n24 t24 f23.5 b24** It is rare these days for me to be genuinely taken aback by a whisky. But this managed it. The malt is pleasingly light in colour for its age, and certainly for a Springbank of this age. So second fill ex-bourbon, even third, possibly. Which when the tannins fire their broadside on the very first sniff...yes, there is reason to be taken aback. Of course, the trademark of this distillery is labyrinthine complexity. And though labyrinthine may be taking it a bit far here, you can still descend very deeply into this malt and have plenty of passages to explore. Certainly, I love to take the saline route here, which gives a delightful piquancy to tannin and sharpens the barley tones that float around it. So it is pleasing to see that this route can be followed on the beautifully soft delivery which just abounds in vanilla. But there is just as much thickset barley, too. This is magnificent malt which repays using the Murray Method for best results. But, as you will see, the nose is at its best at one temperature (relatively cool and the experience on the palate is at its zenith when warmed a little. Oh, and before I forget...look out for the fascinating strata of peat. Fair took me aback, it did... *55.4%. Bottled for HMMJ collection.*

Hazelburn Aged 8 Years bourbon cask, bott 2011 db (**94.5**) **n23 t24 f23.5 b24** A very curious coppery sheen adds extra lustre and does no harm to a very well made spirit filled into top grade oak. For an eight year old malt, something extra special. *46%*

Longrow Aged 10 Years db (**78**) **n19 t20 f19 b20.** This has completely bemused me: bereft not only of the usual to-die-for smoke, its warts are exposed badly, as this is way too young. Sweet and malty, perhaps, and technically better than the marks I'm giving it – but this is Longrow, dammit! I am astonished. 46%

Longrow 14 Years Old refill bourbon and sherry casks db **(89) n24 t23.5 f19 b22.5.** Again, a sherry butt proves the Achilles heel. But until then, a charmer. 46%

Longrow Aged 18 Years (94.5) n25 t23 f23 b23.5 If you gently peat a blend of ulmo, manuka and heather honey you might end up with something as breathtakingly stunning as this. But you probably won't... 46%. WB15/103

Artful Dodger Springbank 18 Year Old 2000 1st fill sherry hogshead, cask no. 646 **(96) n24 t24 f24 b24** For an 18-year-old Springbank has all the creaks and grey hairs of something a lot more than twice its age... The oak seems to date back to Robin Hood, the grape could have been from a wine shared by the disciples. This malt (some of them shewing the odd partiality to peat) bends and bows like a medieaval inn. But even so you have to say this: the balance and interplay between the delicate factions is a work of art to behold, The palate is not for a single moment molested as the tannins and gentle juices go about their business. This is a malt for that special occasion. A parent's 90th birthday perhaps; your own 60th. Your child's 30th. This is all to do with time and wisdom. And on the subject of time, less than an hour at the glass with this whisky will not do it any justice at all. The next time I taste this, it will be to celebrate the lockdown that keeps me imprisoned in the UK being lifted. It is a whisky for extraordinary moments in one's life. 45.9%. sc.

Kingsbury Sar Obair Springbank 28 Year Old oloroso sherry butt, dist 1991, cask no. 323 **(95.5) n24 t24 f23.5 b24** An incredibly salty dram. But just a little too good to sprinkle on your fish 'n' chips. Not sure that fabulous array of pastel-shaded fruit would go with it either. Come to think of it, this Springbank is a meal of its very own... 54.7% sc 185 bottles

STRATHISLA
Speyside, 1786. Chivas Brothers. Working.

Strathisla 12 Years Old db **(85.5) n21.5 t22 f21 b21.** A slight reduction in strength from the old bottling and a significant ramping up of toffee notes means this is a malt which will do little to exert your taste buds. Only a profusion of spice is able to cut through the monotonous style. Always sad to see such a lovely distillery so comprehensively gagged. 40%.

Hidden Spirits Strathisla 15 Year Old dist 2002, bott 2018 **(89) n21.5 t23 f22 b22.5** At times simplistic, at others attractively complex. 51.2%.

STRATHMILL
Speyside, 1891. Diageo. Working.

Strathmill 25 Year Old refill American oak casks, dist 1988 db **(89) n23 t22 f22 b22** A blending malt which reveals the kind of big malty deal it offers older brands. 52.4%. 2,700 bottles. Diageo Special Releases 2014.

⟨image⟩ **Skene Strathmill 32 Years Old** butt no.1635, dist 1990, bott 2022 **(90.5) n23.5** pretty stupendous. The respect and interplay between the rich malt and the raisiny, nutty fruitcake is sublime. Delicate citrus notes, mainly grapefruit, star, too... A hint of oak-induced spice, but no more...; **t23** in true Strathmill style, the malt is first out of the blocks and keeps its distance for some time from the chasing fruits.... though it is eventually caught. The stewing intensity of that malt – and the accompanying juiciness is something to behold. The midground is spiced up and showing signs of a cocoa influence; **f21.5** a little untidy at the death, as though with so much has happening before, they are now not sure how to end the gig. A bit dry and bitter at the very end, though...; **b22.5** oddly enough, just three days ago I was in Scotland creating a couple of new blended whiskies and I was mentioning to someone my regret how little Strathmill we see around today, either available as a young blending malt or in older form for single cask bottling. And then this turns up on my desk. 54% sc

TALISKER
Highlands (Island–Skye), 1832. Diageo. Working.

Talisker Aged 10 Years bott code: L0045CM001 db **(84.5) n22.5 t22.5 f19 b20.5** There is a more youthful stirring to the nose than the original old 8-year-old used to possess. Decent smoke and a vague spice prickle. A kind of caramelised version of a trusty old friend. Conversely, the attractive, silky delivery sees the smoke taking its time to make its mark though the barley is much livelier, at first offering a juicy start before the caramels take hold. But it's downhill rapidly for the finish which really dishes out the caramel before an untidy light furry touch. So, sadly, still nothing like the dashing Talisker of old (when they purposefully used only ex-bourbon casks for sharper impact and clarity), the one where as a party piece amongst friends I would buy them a double hit of this and then, after carefully nosing, taking the whole lot in one go, chewing slowly, and then let the insane spices do the rest. Just tried it: next to nothing. Just a polite buzz on delivery where once there was a nuclear explosion. Humungous amounts of toffee, though...and the later, irritating, buzz is not, alas, spice at all... 45.8%.

⌖ **Talisker Aged 10 Years**, bott code L2329CM001 db **(85)** n22 t22.5 f20 b20.5 Considering that, 48 years ago, this was the first distillery on the planet I ever visited, you can understand why its whisky has a special place in my heart. And why, even 25 years ago, I took a quiet proprietorial pride in its greatness: a malt fizzing with peppers, quality and complexity. So imagine my sheer misery when a couple of years back I had to give this once great brand a paltry 84.5 – at least ten points short of par. I was hoping this year's offering would show that that bottling was a freakish one-off. A blip. Sadly, not so. By Talisker's once great standards this remains obstinately bland with the toffees talking far more loudly than is good for it, especially on the nose and weak finish. The highlight is the delivery when the light spices and gentle peat join forces with the juicy barley for a punchy, salivating lift off. Then...phut...! That's yer lot. Yes, enjoyable in its own simplistic way. But by Talisker standards, just leaves you shaking your head. 45.8%

Talisker Aged 18 Years bott code: L0023CM001 db **(86.5)** n23 t22 f20 b21.5 Like the 10-year-old, not up to the same high standards of the last bottling I tasted. Starts promisingly as a deft smokiness drifts in and out a light heather honey and lightly-salted cucumber semi-freshness. But the delivery feels weighed down by far too much toffee while the finish is bitter and uneven. Some OK moments early on. But Talisker should be so much better than this. 45.8%.

Talisker Aged 25 Years bott 2017, bott code: L7023CM000 db **(96.5)** n24 t24 f24 b24.5 A malt of magnificent complexity that generously rewards time and concentration. So for some, it may not be easy to get through the forests of oak early on, but switching your senses on to full alert not only pays dividends, but is no less than this great old malt deserves or demands. 45.8%. 21,498 bottles.

Talisker 30 Years Old db **(93.5)** n23 t24 f23 b23.5 Much fresher and more infinitely entertaining than the 25 year old...!!! 45.8%

Talisker 30 Years Old db **(84.5)** n21 t21.5 f21 b21. Toffee-rich and pretty one dimensional. Did I ever expect to say that about a Talisker at 30...? 53.1%

Talisker 57 Degrees North db **(95)** n24 t24.5 f23 b23.5 A glowing tribute, I hope, for a glowing whisky... 57%

Talisker Dark Storm charred oak db **(92)** n22 t23.5 f23 b23.5 Much more like it! Unlike the Storm, which appeared to labour under some indifferent American oak, this is just brimming with vitality and purpose. 45.8%.

Talisker Neist Point bott code: L6067CM000 db **(87)** n22 t21.5 f22 b21.5 Not exactly Nil Points, but for people like me who adore Talisker (indeed, it was a visit to this distillery 43 years ago that turned my appreciation of whisky into a passionate love affair), it tastes like the malt has barely got out of second gear. Where is the fizz and bite of the peppery phenols on impact? The journey through myriad styles of smoke? The breath-taking and life-giving oomph? Not to be found in this pleasantly tame and overly sweet version, though the spices do mount to something towards the very end. It is like observing a lion that has had its teeth forcibly removed. 45.8%.

Talisker Skye (85) n21 t22 f21 b21. The sweetest, most docile Talisker I can ever remember with the spices working hard in the background but weirdly shackled. More Toffee Sky than Vanilla... 45.8% WB16/051

Talisker Skye bott code L1215CM011 db **(95)** n24 the smoke dazzles: sweet, minty and full on, it also digs out some hickory for good measure. The smokiest Talisker I have nosed possibly this century: one that means business, but never loses its taut elegance, either...; t24 I am almost in disbelief here. How long has it been since I tasted a Talisker and spices burned though with such a peppery intensity? Not like of 40 years ago, admittedly, or even 30. But certainly with more intent than we have seen in the last quarter of a century. The demerara sugars and gristy young malt also make a delightful mark in whisky which oozes quality from every poore; f23 the oils which had done such a magnificent job early on really build now and with the light caramels smother all but the soft, velvety vanilla and the jagged spice. Cut the caramel further this would be simply astonishing whisky...; b24 I had to smile how the label boasts that the distillery is the "oldest" on the island, now that it at last has company. So I am curious to see how they would respond. Of all island whiskies of Scotland, this is the one that has perhaps disappointed most in recent years, having lost the innate fire and zest that set it apart from not just any other distillery in Scotland, but the world. In other words, it had lost its way. But, my word...this is so much like Talisker of old, warming and comforting in equal measures. Talisker, in 1975, was the first distillery I ever visited and was introduced there to its secrets direct from the cask: a true life-changing moment. I, also, have spent a lifetime encouraging people to spit their whisky rather than swallow...but with one exception: Talisker. Indeed, nearly 30 years ago I had the fun of introducing Sir Michael Palin (oh, congrats on the "Sir", Mike!) to cask strength Talisker in my kitchen, the effect of which was not unlike me strapping him into an electric chair: the greatest experience of his drinking life, he called it as he staggered slightly, in shock, towards my front door... Since then, Talisker has declined to the point of insignificance: a flat whisky with a bit of smoke but too much caramel. Not now; not with this: at that younger age which always suited this distillery better than most. This great distillery, perhaps spurred on by local competition, has with Lazarus qualities returned to life. Don't spit. Don't sip. Gargle and swallow. At last here is a Talisker worthy of that most ancient tradition. 45.8%

🔹 **Talisker Skye**, bott code L2341CM004 db (89) n22.5 so young it's actually quite good. Punchy with nippy anthracite alongside a fresh-cut grassy maltiness. And the ubiquitous toffee...; t23 again, this youngster shows no fear and happily let's rip onto the palate: exactly how a Talisker should. Gorgeously salivating with concentrated, sharp barley. The peat is now more muffled... and then vanishes under the toffee; f21.5 disappointing because, rumbling peppery bite apart, this has far too much vanilla and toffee for any meaningful complexity; b22 not to be tasted after 7pm. A whisky so young it should be in its bed by then. Has some sublime moments on nose and delivery but eventually vanishes under the wight of the unforgiving caramel... 45.8%

Talisker Storm db (85.5) n20 t23 f21 b21.5 The nose didn't exactly go down a storm in my tasting room. There are some deft seashore touches, but the odd poor cask –evident on the finish, also - has undone the good. But it does recover on the palate early on with an even, undemanding and attractively sweet display showing malt to a higher degree than I have seen any Talisker before. 45.8%.

Talisker Storm bott code: L9249CM003 db (89.5) n23 much more salient peat than in earlier bottlings and though the normal bite of spice is now a gentle peck, the layering of the phenols, aided by light milk chocolate, is rather lovely; t21.5 there is a youthful attack to the arrival which is hinted at on the nose, but nothing like so obviously as can be found here. The midground gets lost in just little too much caramel; f22.5 the peat and cocoa reasserts itself just in the nick of time and the malt grows dramatically in quality from their involvement. The spices certainly begin to kick in as the light oils vanish; b22.5 what an improvement. Still none of the old Talisker fizz and more of a gentle breeze than the storm that was once guaranteed from any distillery bottling from this distillery. And though naggingly young, there is an attractive character and structure to this, especially on the nose and finish. 45.8%.

🔹 **Talisker Surge** db (92.5) n24 Talisker at its most eloquent: the smoke shews all the charm of the distillery in its youngest development. Earthy, crisp and at times toasty: quite superb...; t23 much smokier than many Taliskers have been in recent years. Quite brash, though not so much with the usual Talisker spices but its youth unfettered and raw; f22.5 quite a short finale. Though, naturally, the smoke is determined to make it through to the end; b23 a delightful combination of charm and determined brutality. Shame about the thinness and lack of development. But what it does, it does juicily and memorably. 45.8%

Old Malt Cask Talisker Aged 9 Years sherry butt, cask no. 17806, dist Dec 10, bott Dec 20 (87.5) n22.5 t21.5 f22 b21.5 Insanely saline on the nose with the peat having to battle its way through alongside the young grist. The sherry butt offers no negative connotations but the peat and spice – the usual foundation stone for this distillery – has gone AWOL. 50%. nc ncf sc. 411 bottles.

TAMDHU
Speyside, 1897. Ian Macleod Distillers. Working (re-opened 3rd March 2013).

Tamdhu db (84.5) n20 t22.5 f21 b21. So-so nose, but there is no disputing the fabulous, stylistic honey on delivery. The silkiest Speyside delivery of them all. 40%

Tamdhu Aged 10 Years oak sherry cask db (69.5) n17 t18.5 f17 b17. A much better malt when they stick exclusively to ex-bourbon casks, as used to be the case. 40%

Tamdhu Aged 18 Years bott code L0602G L12 20/08 db (74.5) n19 t19 f18 b18.5. Bitterly disappointing. Literally. 43%.

Tamdhu 25 Years Old db (88) n22 t22 f21 b23. Radiates quality. 43%

Tamdhu 2006 cask 2165 American oak sherry hogshead db (92.5) n23 such a pleasing marriage of clean grape and darting spice. The peel of blood orange adds a sharper note to the fruit; t23 sublime mouthfeel with an almost perfect degree of oiliness: not so much that it masks all else, but certainly enough to adequately coat the palate and last the course. Look out also for the layering of custard as the vanilla and barley combine; f23.5 as the fruit drops, the complexity elevates. Drier, yet still sweet enough for lemon blossom honey to succinctly have a say. A lovely, vaguely salty Digestive biscuit fade underlines the quiet elegance; b23 just heart-warming to find this distillery in such wonderful form. Impressive. 56.9%

The Whisky Chamber Tamdhu 13 Jahre 2007 port cask (88) n22 t22.5 f21.5 b22 Visually, hard to tell if this has come from a whisky cask or the local blood transfusion unit...I haven't spat out anything of this colour since I was last at the dentist's...This is one very different whisky! Nearer red in colour to the subtle pink many Port Cask whiskies become, it also has an incredible firmness to the palate: the red wall. Sometimes that can result in a brittle whisky; here it is solid. Even the nose offers no yield whatsoever with a piledriving brusqueness to the fruit. Sugars about early on, mainly of the muscovado variety found in Dundee cake. But then it solidifies once more, so both fruit and barley have a crunchiness. Salivating early on, you have to take your hat off an admit that this is something very different, indeed. *57.3%. sc.*

TAMNAVULIN
Speyside. 1966. Whyte and Mackay. Working.

⬡ **Tamnavulin Double Cask** sherry cask finish, batch 0308, bott code L3026 db **(90.5)** n23 heady, hefty and of the Dundee cake variety; t23 after a delightful blood range and barley lift-off comes a curious alternating sweet-dry grape skin middle; f22 chocolate orange plus a bit of bitter nagging on this shewing that the sherry butt didn't entirely escape treatment; b22.5 have we got 100% perfect sherry casks at play? No. Have we got 100% complexity? Absolutely. 40%

⬡ **Tamnavulin Red Wine Cask Edition No 1** French Cabernet Sauvignon finish, batch 001243, bott code L2284 db **(82)** n22 t22 f18 b20 Doesn't skimp on the fruit. And there is a real tart wine gum feel to this, too. But let down by the by the half-expected gnawing bitterness on the finish (the French are worse than the Spanish at this). 40%

⬡ **Tamnavulin Red Wine Cask Edition No 3** German Pinot Noir finish, batch 000164, bott code L2339 db **(88.5)** n22.5 t22.5 f21.5 b22 Rare to find pinot cask finishes quite this far in the mouth. The nose is equally plump with pretty even distribution between clean barley and raspberry jam on toast. The fruit tones it down somewhat on delivery with a charming vanilla and barley before the somewhat neutral finale. 40%

⬡ **Tamnavulin Sherry Cask Edition** Finished in three types of sherry cask, batch 30502, bott code L2334 db **(93)** n23.5 enduring and endearing, there is genuine complexity and layering to the fruit: not something that can often be said on a nose these days. Love how the fruit is both wispy and weighty and that's despite the heady density of the fruit; t23.5 sumptuous, rotund, salivating and stark. The grape is an ever-moving object, shape-shifting and varying in output and density. Mixes raisins with sultana with the odd, weightier hint of Melton Hunt Cake; f22.5 much drier now with the tannins playing a previously ignored roll. A slight burr of bitterness; b23.5 a magnificent bit of blending at work here to create such depth. Rarely seen on sherry-reliant malts these days. 40%

⬡ **Tamnavulin White Wine Cask Edition Sauvignon Blanc Cask**, batch 060808, bott code L2174 **(94)** n23.5 now, that is how to layer a nose. Absolutely nothing standing out alone, but this is all the better for the firmness which gives those Chinese gooseberry and acacia honey notes a step up..; t24 just a beautiful, melt-in-the-mouth arrival of watermelon and Cantaloupe melon alongside spiced sultana and treacle-treated coconut strands; f22.5 attractive spices become surprisingly warm. The vanilla has thickened from the mere hint it had earlier been. And a little green apple still salivates atop it all..; b23.5 what a sophisticated Tamna this is and one deserving of a standing ovation. Wine casks with NO sulphury payback allows you to indulge in its myriad intricacies and foibles. The type of whisky you treat yourself to at the end of a bastard day. Suddenly, after sinking into the richness of a mouthful of this, the world seems no less complicated. But a far, far better place. 40%

TEANINICH
Highlands (Northern), 1817. Diageo. Working.

Teaninich 17 Year Old refill American oak hogsheads & refill American oak barrels db **(90)** n22 t23 f22 b23 A distillery rarely celebrated in bottle by its owners. Here they have selected an age and cask profile which gets the mix between simple barley and far from taxing oak just about right. Minimalistically elegant. *55.9%. Diageo Special Releases 2017.*

Fandandel.dk Teaninich Aged 11 Years 1st fill oloroso quarter cask, cask no.700799B, dist Jan 2009, bott Aug 2020 **(91.5)** n22.5 the fruit has a curious punchy brevity to it: concentrated and tight, even after being stretched by the Murray Method. But it is constructed with intricacy and free from faults. The plum jam is mercifully under sugared; t23.5 much fatter than the nose, with the fruit unfurling with a salivating sharpness. This gives a glorious two-tone feel on the palate with a marked contrast between the earlier thick oils and the runny grape juice; f22.5 impressive late spice and vanilla; b23 quarter casks have a propensity to intensify everything... and this is no exception. Entirely sulphur free, the fruit is allowed to get on and do its job. And the way it handles both the oak and barley-rich honey and spice (from one of Scotland's heavier malts) it is certainly doing that! *56% 152 bottles*

Gleann Mór Rare Find Teanininch 1975 Aged 46 Years (94.5) n24 certainly the oak walks with a limp, has grey hair and when it sits down finds a rocking chair and something to knit. But in this case it is still knitting an intense malty theme into the tannins so we are mesmerised by the deftness of the light banana and butterscotch; t23.5 a crème brulee for starters, then a salivating layer of slightly tangy malt. Of course it is the oak pulling the strings and soon that is back in the cockpit generating countless layers of the most vaguely spiced vanilla; **f23** even after all these years, no off notes, no bitterness. Just quiet but active old age with the most gentle of vanilla-led farewells; **b24** when you consider that this whisky was made in the very first year I began my journey around the world's distilleries, all I can is that this amazing malt has negotiated the passing 46 years with less scars than I. This is hardly a distillery renowned for reaching great ages. But the oak was so much more reliant then than now and the malt has taken full advantage of that to stun us all. 45.1%

TOBERMORY

Highlands (Island–Mull), 1795. Burn Stewart Distillers. Working.

Tobermory 10 Years Old db (73.5) **n17.5 t19 f18 b19**. The last time I tasted an official Tobermory 10 for the Bible, I was aghast with what I found. So I prodded this sample I had before me of the new 46.3% version with all the confidence Wile E Coyote might have with a failed stick of Acme dynamite. No explosions in the glass or on my palate to report. And though this is still a long way short, and I'm talking light years here, of the technical excellence of the old days, the uncomplicated sweet maltiness has a very basic charm. The nose and finish, though, are still very hard going. 46.3%

Tobermory Aged 15 Years db (93) **n23.5 t23.5 f23 b23** A tang to the oils on both nose and finish suggests an over widened middle. But such is the quality of the sherry butts and the intensity of the salt-stained malt, all is forgiven. 46.3%. nc ncf.

Tobermory 42 Year Old db (94.5) **n23.5 t23.5 f23.5 b24** A real journey back in time. Wonderful. 47.7%

Ledaig 18 Year Old batch 2 db (71) **n16 t20 f17 b18**. There are many ways to describe this whisky. Well made, alas, is not one of them. The nose sets off many alarms, especially on the feinty front. And though some exceptional oak repairs some of the damage, it cannot quite do enough. Sugary, too – and occasionally cloyingly so. 46.3%. nc ncf.

Ledaig Dùsgadh 42 Aged 42 Years db (96) **n25 t24.5 f22.5 b24** It has to be about 30 years ago I tasted my first-ever Ledaig – as a 12 year old peated malt. This must be from the same stocks, only this has been housed in exceptional casks. Who would have thought, three decades on, that it would turn into some of the best malt bottled in a very long time. A smoky experience unlikely to be forgotten. 46.3%

Acla Selection Island Edition Tobermory 23 Year Old hogshead, dist 1995, bott 2019 (94) **n24 t23.5 f23 b23.5** One of the most gentle and elegant malts to comes from this island in a very long time. 49%.

Acla Selection Island Edition Ledaig 11 Year Old hogshead, dist 2007, bott 2018 (88.5) **n22.5 t22.5 f21.5 b22** The smoke offers a light, acidic fug on both nose and palate, though all the sweetness is confined to the delivery where the grist goes into overdrive. Spices are sprinkled evenly and the youth ensures the sharpness is very, very sharp! 52.6%.

Cadenhead's Authentic Collection Cask Strength Ledaig 11 Year Old ex-bourbon cask, dist 2008, bott Sept 19 (90.5) **n22 t23 f22.5 b23** If this malt was handed in as homework, it would probably be docked a few marks for being technically off the pace. But it would soon make them up again, as the oak this has been housed in perfectly matches the distillery's style, allowing a nuanced depth to the smoke and an impressive degree of barley to be seen. The nose hints at a lack of copper, and there is some evidence that the stills might have been operating slightly faster than they were comfortable with. But the nutty smokiness compensates for the thinness of body; the barley applauded for its salivating qualities. What great fun! 55.2%. sc.

Chapter 7 Ledaig 10 Year Old 2009 bourbon hogshead, cask no. 700493, dist May 09, bott Mar 20 (92.5) **n23.5 t23.5 f22.5 b23** Can't remember the last time I tasted a Ledaig so technically on the money as this. I've worked with many a cask of this over the years, in the blending lab as well as in the tasting room for The Bible. The nose is pure grist, the phenols reeking from the malt as though it had just come off the mill. Consequently, the malt simply melts in the mouth with a freshness that fair brings a tear to the eye. Slowly the tannins offer a vanilla alternative... Just beautiful. 51%. sc. 351 bottles.

Chapter 7 Ledaig 24 Year Old 1995 bourbon hogshead, cask no. 189, dist Sept 95, bott Mar 20 (91.5) **n23.5 t23.5 f22 b22.5** One of those peated whiskies where you aren't quite sure if the lightness of smoke is due to a lower phenol level or the passing of years. Here it is probably both. The lightly smoked butterscotch note is a treat, the delivery an exhibition of how mouthfeel plays such a vital role. Here it is fat, chewing malt...the longer you chew the slightly peatier it gets. Only a very late bitterness can be found in the deficit column... 51.6%. sc. 242 bottles.

⟫ **Ferg and Harris Ledaig 1995 Aged 27 Years** finished in 1st fill oloroso, cask no 147, bott 2022 (82) **n21.5 t22 f18.5 b20** Well, this one had me scratching my head. "It's an unpeated

Ledaig" I was told. Which, by definition, means it's a Tobermory – Ledaig is simply the peated version. That seemed unlikely, until I thought of the eccentric distillery manager of that time - which made all things possible. As for the whisky...I fear the finishing in the oloroso was a mistake as there are traces of sulphur all over this, making for a dry, slightly lumpy experience: the Germans will love it!!! *47.2% sc ncf Young Spirits*

Oxhead Classic Casks Ledaig 1995 (95.5) n24 t24 f23.5 b24 If you're looking for big smoke and even medium strength...don't bother. It ain't there. But, instead, we are gifted with a portrait of what time can do given the right circumstances: excellent spirit and high quality, blemish-free oak. This has been blessed enough to move into the exotic fruit category...and that means something rather special. The nose is adorned with diced mango, banana and peach...which is all held together by the faintest whisps of peat. By rights, the delivery should be super soft....and it is. It is a caress of oak-enriched oils, again the smoke going undercover to glue together the creamy butterscotch and mocha which hang around long enough even for some praline to form at the very death. This is the definition of great Scotch single malt. *48.6%*

Oxhead Classic Casks Ledaig 2009 (90.5) n23 t22.5 f22 b23 An elegantly dry Ledaig where, from the sooty peat on the nose to the chalky finale, gentle understatement is the order of the day. The delicate infusion of the citrus to add to the barley remnants does its bit for a brief juicy passage. Beautiful oils throughout. *56.4%*

Valour Whisky Ledaig Aged 15 years bourbon barrel Cask No 44000698 dist 25/06/1996 bott 27/06/2022 (96) n24 t24.5 f23.5 b24 One of the most remarkable things about this bottling is that it perhaps captures Ledaig better than any I have encountered for a very long time. It is, in effect, the distillery distilled. The fingerprints unique, clear and unmistakable. Oh, and it is also a Ledaig distilled to its top specs and matured in a perfectly fitting cask. A half-hour malt which builds on the palate with astonishing complexity and balance. Certainly the best single cask Scotch I have tasted so far this year and well in line for honours. Quite glorious. And bollocks to Covid: if it takes two weeks in quarantine to get to China to grab a bottle of this, then so be it... *54.3% 266 bottles*

The Whisky Barrel Originals Ledaig 11 Years Old 1st fill oloroso hogshead, cask no. TWB1006, dist Feb 08, bott 2019 (92.5) n23 t23.5 f23 b23 Bizarrely light for a first-fill oloroso: indeed, one of the lightest I have ever seen. But make no mistake: this is a heavyweight and there is no denying its smoky scrumminess. *63.4%. sc. 298 bottles.*

The Whisky Cask Company Ledaig 1997 sherry hogshead, dist Sep 1997, bott Oct 2019 (84.5) n23 t22.5 f19 b20 A very different Ledaig, even taking into account the substantial fruit input thanks to the sherry cask. This is hard whisky, as though distilled from marble rather than malt. Even the nose makes little attempt to befriend, let alone seduce. The acidity levels from the peat is way above the norm, as much sniffing burning anthracite, rather than the usual soothing phenols of the turf. However on the palate things actually become testing: there is a few moments where grape and smoke unite, but the remainder is a battle. Full of flavour, though never harmony. *55.6% nc ncf 264 bottles*

The Whisky Cask Tobermory 11 Years Old PX Sherry Finish dist 2008 bott 2020 oloroso finish db (84) n20 t21.5 f21.5 b21 A classic example of where a PX cask bludgeons the malt into submission. Certainly quaffable. Enjoyable, even, in a negated way. But a serious personality bypass here: save a momentary spasm of intense date, and a late flurry of chocolate, it is all too predictable. *56.4%*

The Whisky Embassy Bonn Ledaig 8 Year Old Bordeaux no. 16 (91.5) n23 t23 f22.5 b23 A disarmingly beautiful malt which makes the most of its tender years. *60%. nc ncf sc.*

Whisky-Fässle Ledaig 10 Year Old hogshead, dist 2008, bott 2018 (94) n23.5 t23.5 f23 b24 Just breath-taking. Had I tasted this blind, I might have marked it down as a vatting of Caol Ila and young Ardbeg. Can't see this lasting long on the shelves...or in the home cabinet.. *52.7% nc ncf*

TOMATIN

Speyside, 1897. Takara, Shuzo and Okura & Co. Working.

Tomatin 8 Years Old bourbon & sherry casks db (89) n22 t23 f21.5 b22.5 A malt very proud of its youth. *40%. Travel Retail Exclusive.*

Tomatin 12 Year Old finished in Spanish sherry casks db (91.5) n23 t23.5 f21.5 b23.5 For a great many years, Tomatin operated under severe financial restrictions. This meant that some of the wood brought to the distillery during this period was hardly of top-notch quality. This has made life difficult for those charged with moulding the stocks into workable expressions. I take my hat off to the creator of this: some great work is evident, despite the finish. *43%*

Tomatin 14 Year Old Port Finish db (92.5) n23 t24 f22.5 b23 Allows the top notch port a clear road. *46%. ncf.*

Tomatin 15 Years Old American oak casks db (89.5) n22.5 t22.5 f22 b22.5 A delicious exhibition of malt. *46%. Travel Retail Exclusive.*

Tomatin Aged 15 Years ex bourbon cask, bott 2010 db (86) n21 t22 f21.5 b21.5. One of the most malty drams on the market today. Perhaps suffers a little from the 43% strength as some of the lesser oak notes get a slightly disruptive foothold. But the intense, juicy barley trademark remains clear and delicious. *43% Tomatin Distillery*

Tomatin 15 Years Old bourbon barrels and Spanish Tempranillo wine casks db (88.5) n22 t23 f21 b22.5. Not free from the odd problem with the Spanish wine casks but gets away with it as the overall complexity and enjoyment levels are high. *52%*

Tomatin 18 Year Old db (82) n21.5 t22 f19 b20 Sadly some sulphur on the casks which makes the finish just too dry and off key. Underneath are hints of greatness, but the sherry butt doesn't give it a chance. *46%*.

Tomatin 21 Year Old db (94.5) n24 t23.5 f23 b24 One of those malts which looks as though It's not even trying, but just nonchalantly produces something rather delightful and of very high class. *46%. Global Travel Retail Exclusive.*

Tomatin 25 Years Old db (89) n22 t23 f21.5 b22.5. Not a nasty bone in its body: understated but significant. *43%*

Tomatin 30 Year Old European & American oak casks db (85.5) n21 t21 f22.5 b21. Unusually for an ancient malt, the whisky becomes more comfortable as it wears its aged shoes. The delivery is just a bit too enthusiastic on the oaky front, but the natural caramels soften the journey rather delightfully. *46%. ncf.*

Tomatin 30 Years Old bott 2018 db (93) n23 t22.5 f24 b23.5 Puts me in mind of a 29-year-old Springbank I have tasted for this Bible, which showed similar initial signs of wear and tear. But as the whisky warmed and oxidised, then so it grew in the glass and began to reveal previously hidden brilliance. This is not, perhaps, up to those gargantuan standards but what is achieved here shews the rewards for both patience and the use of the Murray Method. Patience and care are most certainly rewarded 46%.

Tomatin 36 Year Old American & European oak db (96.5) n24 t24.5 f23.5 b24.5 The difference between old oak and the newer stuff is brilliantly displayed here. Make no mistake: this is a masterpiece of a malt. *46%*

Tomatin 40 Years Old Oloroso sherry casks db (87.5) n21.5 t23 f21 b22 One of those malts which offers a graceful peep at the past, when sherry butts were clean and offered nothing to fear. But no matter how good the cask time takes its toll and the intense chalkiness reveals tannins that have got slightly the better of the barley. Thankfully the grape is still intact and brings us a beautiful raisin and date depth before the chalk returns a little more determined than before. *43%. Travel Retail Exclusive.*

Tomatin 1995 Olorosso Sherry db (82) n21 t22 f19 b20 You can peel the grape off the malt. But one of the sherry butts wasn't quite as spotless as one might hope for. The inevitable tang arrives towards the finish. *46%*.

Tomatin Amontillado Sherry 2006 Aged 12 Years Old db (82) n21 t22 f19 b20 You'd think from the score that sulphur plays a part here. And you'd probably be right. Just bitter and dull in all the places it shouldn't be. Those incapable of detecting sulphur will love the rich sultana delivery. *46%*.

Tomatin Cabernet Sauvignon 2002 Edition db (82) n21 t22 f18 b21 Surprising degree of weight to this one. The fruit is not quite flawless with a little bit of a buzz on the nose and finish especially. But the rich mouthfeel and a pleasant, lush Garibaldi biscuit effect does ensure some very satisfying phases. *46%*.

Tomatin Caribbean Rum 2007 Edition db (89.5) n22 t23 f22 b22.5 Beautifully clean malt though, as is their wont, the rum casks keep everything tight. *46%*.

Tomatin Caribbean Rum 2009 Aged 10 Years Old db (90.5) n22.5 clean barley with a light liquorice and Demerara sugar outer casing; t23.5 I think the old term: "pure malt" would be the perfect description for this; f22 the rum casks do their job and lock in the sugars for a slightly fast finish; b22.5 as is so often the case, the rum cask has encased the malt in crisp sugar, limiting development slightly. But it also ensures the malts are at their maximum intensity. *46%*.

Tomatin Cask Strength db (80) n19 t22 f19 b20 Stunning malt climax on delivery. But always undone by a dull, persistent off note from the cask. *57.5%*.

Tomatin Decades II db (91.5) n23 t23 f22.5 b23 Tomatin does intense malt as well as any distillery in the world. And here they give an object lesson. *46%*.

Tomatin Five Virtues Series Earth Peated Malt refill hogshead oak casks db (88) n22 t22.5 f21.5 b22 Can honestly say I have never seen Tomatin in this kind of shape before: enjoyable once you acclimatise... *46%*.

Tomatin Five Virtues Series Fire Heavily Charred Oak de-charred/re-charred oak fired casks db (94) n23.5 t24 f23 b23.5 High class malt with a sweet bourbon drizzle. *46%*.

Tomatin Five Virtues Series Metal Bourbon Barrels first fill bourbon barrels db (95) n24 t24 f23 b24 There's metal enough in the "Earth" bottling. Was wondering where the metal comes into things here. As these are first fill bourbon casks, wonder if it was the type of warehouse they came from in Kentucky... Anyway, talking metal: this is pure gold... 46%.

Tomatin Five Virtues Series Water Winter Distillation sherry butts & bourbon barrels db **(72)** **n18 t20 f16 b18** A small degree of molassed chocolate escapes the grim sulphured tightness of the sherry. 46%.

Tomatin Five Virtues Series Wood Selected Oak Casks French, American & Hungarian oak casks db **(90)** **n22.5 t23 f21.5 b23** A Franco-Hungarian truce means the malt and bourbon casks can work their magic...Some truly brilliant and unique phrases here. 46%.

Tomatin Highland Legacy db **(88)** **n22 t22.5 f21.5 b22** Clean, nutty malt but beyond that unremarkable. 43%.

Tomatin Warehouse 6 Collection 1977 db **(96)** **n24.5 t24 f23.5 b24** A tale of exotic fruit. Which in turns means a story of great antiquity. Truly old school. And truly magnificent. Do not open the bottle unless you have a good half hour to study this work of art. And the Murray Method will reward you handsomely... 49%.

Cù Bòcan Signature bourbon, oloroso sherry & virgin oak casks db **(82)** **n21.5 t21 f20 b20.5** A virgin defiled amid brimstone. 46%.

Fadandel.dk Tomatin Aged 10 Years 2nd fill oloroso octave finish, cask no.1837B, dist Apr 2009, bott Feb 2021 **(88.5)** **n22 t22.5 f22 b22** An impressively neat and tidy dram with the required sugars spic and span. Only briefly do those many sugars find enough depth and confidence to speak up loudly enough to be heard. Otherwise it is a series of excellent spice and dry cocoa notes interrupted by a hint of dried grape skin here and there, the tannins never for a moment out of place. For once with this distillery the barley is notably subdued. Elegant enough to be one for the Martini set. 59.9% 69 bottles

The First Editions Tomatin Aged 25 Years 1994 sherry butt, cask no. 18213, bott 2020 **(94)** **n23.5** something of the bakery about this: a freshly created Chelsea bun with a gorgeous mix of raisin and icing sugar. Of course, after 25 years there is more: the oak opens up different, deeper channels with the vanilla also enjoying a delicate toast chestnut sweetness, too...; **t23.5** just a brilliant entry, as still salivating after all these years. The softness of the oils do not detract from the crisper elements of the barley itself, though the midground luxuriates in a mix of spice and very lightest sultana touch. Below all this rumbles the aged oak....; **f23** long, thanks to those delicate oils, and the pastry sugars seem to linger with the vanilla; **b24** for a Tomatin the barley refuses to dominate like usual and even the sherry butt play an understated game. Instead we have a malt of exquisite balance and charm. Unalloyed beauty. 47.9%. nc ncf sc. 402 bottles.

The Single Cask Tomatin 2006 ex-bourbon barrel, PX sherry octave finish, cask no. 5777B **(87)** **n22 t22.5 f21.5 b21** An even malt where the PX has a surprising degree of influence. As the problem can often be with PX involvement, any bitterness present is amplified by the sugary wine. Some spices relieve the slightly one-dimensional feel. Pleasant enough, but never quite feels comfortable. 53.7%. nc ncf sc.

◈ **Skene Tomatin 32 Years Old** hogshead no 10140, dist 1989, bott 2022 **(90)** **n22.5** concentrates on a simplistic symphony of barley sugar and undemonstrative tannins. Surprisingly grassy and fresh even after all these years; **t23** house style malt belts it out, at first in a juicy fashion, befitting the grassy nose, and then a drier one as the chalky tannins seek egality; **f22** the cask is tiring now and begins to bitter slightly, though a little cocoa compensates; **b22.5** Tomatin, like Glen Moray and Strathmill is prized for its intensely malty personality. Here it doesn't disappoint and the grassy quality to the barley, now in its fourth decade, is remarkable. 44.9% sc

The Whisky Cask Tomatin 12 Years Old Chateau Margaux Cask dist 2009 bott 2021 oloroso finish db **(89)** **n22.5** talk about austere! The dry grape skins try to suck every last atom of sweetness from the game barley. Certainly complex...; **t23** at last, the grape bursts into life with a brief fusion with the barley sugars for a truly brilliant delivery. But soon it reverts to type, with sombre tannins from both the grape skin and the oak; **f21** I'll be generous and describe it as dry and sophisticated...; **b22.5** Tomatin, being one of the most malty whiskies on Earth, is one of the few that would be able to inject a grainy personality over a cask like this. My experience with First Growth Bordeaux wine barrels and whiskies has not been one that warms the heart. The French are even more enthusiastic at waving sulphur candles in casks than the Spanish. Thankfully, this didn't knock me sideways with sulphur, as most from that region do. But there is also a miserly dryness which allows only certain aspects of the malt to flourish. I know some people will declare this their whisky of the year. But if only that dryness hadn't been quite so thorough! 54.8%

TOMINTOUL

Speyside, 1965. Angus Dundee. Working.

Tomintoul Aged 10 Years bott code: L16 02149 CB2 db **(84.5)** **n20.5 t22 f21 b21** A very consistent dram but far too much emphasis of the chocolate toffee rather than the big malt you feel is bursting to break free. 40%.

Tomintoul Aged 12 Years Oloroso Sherry Cask Finish db (73.5) n18.5 t19 f18 b18. Tomintoul, with good reason, styles itself as "The Gentle Dram" and you'll hear no argument from me about that one. However, the sherry influence here offers a rough ride. 40%

Tomintoul Aged 12 Years Oloroso Sherry Cask Finish bott code: L17 02772 CB2 db (74.5) n20 t19 f17.5 b18 A slightly cleaner sherry influence than the last of these I tasted, but the ungentle sulphur makes short work of the "gentle dram". 40%.

Tomintoul Aged 14 Years db (91) n23.5 t23 f21.5 b23 This guy has shortened its breath somewhat: with the distinct thinness to the barley and oak arriving a little flustered and half-hearted rather than with a confident stride; remains a beautiful whisky full of vitality and displaying the malt in its most naked and vulnerable state. But I get the feeling that perhaps a few too many third fills, or under-performing seconds, has resulted in the intensity and hair-raising harmony of the truly great previous bottlings just being slightly undercooked. That said, still a worthy and delicious dram! 46%. nc ncf.

Tomintoul Aged 15 Years Portwood Finish db (94) n23 t23.5 f23.5 b24 So rare to find a wine finish which maximises the fruit to the full without allowing it to dominate. Charming. And so clean. Probably a brilliant whisky to help repair my damaged palate after tasting yet another s******ed sherry butt. I'll keep this one handy...46%. nc ncf. 5,820 bottles.

Tomintoul Aged 15 Years With A Peaty Tang bott code: L17 02975 CB2 db (89.5) n23 t23 f21.5 b22 Being a bit older than their original Peaty Tang, the phenols here are less forward. But, then, it calls itself "The Gentle Dram" and on this evidence with good reason. 40%.

Tomintoul Aged 16 Years db (94.5) n24.5 t23.5 f23 b23.5 Confirms Tomintoul's ability to dice with greatness. 40%

Tomintoul Aged 25 Years db (95) n25 t24 f23 b23.5 A quiet masterpiece from one of Scotland's criminally under appreciated great distilleries. 43%

Tomintoul Aged 40 Years db (86) n22 t21 f21.5 b21.5. Groans every single one of its 40 years. Some lovely malty moments still, as well as butterscotch. But the oak has just jogged on past the sign that said 'Greatness' and carried straight on into the woods... 43.1%. nc ncf.

Tomintoul Cigar Malt Oloroso sherry casks, bott code: L20 07917 CB2 db (92) n23 t23 f22.5 b23.5 As someone who has never smoked so much as a cigarette, let alone a cigar, in my entire life, perhaps I am the last person who can judge this whisky or the purpose it was intended. However, as a judge of the whisky as...well, as whisky, then I have no problems. Perhaps most noticeable is an overwhelming impact of the under-ripe fruit, flattening out and filling in the nooks and crannies. The combined imprint of the grape skin and the vanillas make for a malt in search of its sweet spot, which is finally extinguished when the light trace of ulmo honey alongside the grist gutters and vanishes after too brief a life. A serious whisky... to be taken seriously.... 43%.

Tomintoul With A Peaty Tang db (94) n23 t24 f23 b24. A bit more than a tang, believe me! Faultlessly clean distillate that revels in its unaccustomed peaty role. The age is confusing and appears mixed, with both young and older traits being evident. 40%

Old Ballantruan db (89.5) n23.5 t23 f21 b22 Profound young malt which could easily be taken for an Islay. 50%. ncf.

Old Ballantruan Aged 15 Years bott code: CBSC4 02976 db (95) n23.5 t24 f23.5 b24 A Tomintoul classic. 50%. ncf.

TORABHAIG

Isle of Skye, 2017. Mossburn Distillers. Working.

Torabhaig Legacy first-fill bourbon cask, cask no. 307, dist Jan 17, bott 9 Nov 20 db (92.5) n23 t23.5 f22.5 b23.5 A marvellous moment. My first visit to a whisky distillery came 46 years ago when I visited the Talisker distillery. And now the Island of Skye boasts a second single malt whisky. At Talisker back in 1975 I was given whisky direct from the cask, truly a life-changing experience. Nearly half a century on, I can still taste it today and remember those sensations, as though it were yesterday.... This beautifully made malt, exceptionally fine for 3-year-old - is a different character: then Talisker was wild, a far more explosive dram than is being made at the same distillery today. This, for all its pleasing smoke and full-on spice does not match the Talisker of yore. But why should it? This is a distillery in its own right, doing its very own thing with its very own personality. And though it maintains the island tradition, its lightness of touch really is something to be admired...and fully savoured. Back in 1975 I had to take an aged, barnacle-clad old puffer across to the distillery. Today I can drive there over a bridge. I genuinely look forward to doing so: some people need congratulating for this excellent addition to the Scotch Malt Whisky lexicon... 61.67%. sc.

Torabhaig Legacy first-fill bourbon cask, cask no. 300-600, dist Jan 17, bott 9 Nov 20 db (89.5) n22.5 t22.5 f22 b22.5 Such an attractive whisky for a malt so young. This is all about elegance and fragility which is carried off with panache. 46%. sc.

TORMORE

Speyside, 1960. Chivas Brothers. Working.

Tormore 12 Years Old db (75) n19 t19 f19 b18. For those who like whisky in their caramel. 40%

Chapter 7 Tormore 1990 Aged 31 Years bourbon barrel, barrel no.325862 (94.5) n24.5 t24 f22 b24 Tormore, as a standard malt, is a plain Jane. Oops being "sexist"! Let's put a few more of my staff out of work as punishment. Sorry, I meant an inert Bert, a grim Jim, an ordinary Joe. But after three decades we see Tormore produce a nose that it would be hard to believe possible. Jane or Jim, Bert or Bertha, Joe or Jo...it is quite stunning, an experience of rare beauty. And the most teasing experience on the palate for threatening to go over the age edge, but always coming back to safety. 50.2% sc

TULLIBARDINE

Highlands (Perthshire), 1949. Tullibardine Ltd. Working.

Tullibardine Aged 12 Years first fill bourbon casks, bott code: 21/0016 db (92.5) n23.5 t23 f23 b23 Really quite excellent. Should definitely be out at 46% to let the extra oils stretch the tannins and sugars even further. Some malts cannot handle 100% ex-first fill bourbon and lose their personality. This appears to be one which thrives, deliciously, in an oaky climate. 40%

Tullibardine 15 Year Old db (87.5) n22 t23 f21 b21.5 Starts quite beautifully but stubbornly refuses to kick on. Just adore the nuttiness on both the nose and delivery, as well as the lilting malt in the early stages which is both juicy and barley intense. There is even a light orange blossom honey note soon after...then just fades under a welter of dulling vanilla and caramel tones. Not far off being a little beauty. 43%

Tullibardine Aged 20 Years db (92.5) n22.5 t24 f22.5 b23.5 While there are whiskies like this in the world, there is a point to this book...43%

Tullibardine Aged 25 Years db (86.5) n22 t22 f21 b21.5. There can be too much of a good thing. And although the intricacies of the honey makes you sigh inwardly with pleasure, the overall rigidity and fundamentalism of the oak gives a little too far. 43%

Tullibardine 1970 db (96.5) n25 t24.5 f23 b24s I am a professional wordsmith with a very long time in whisky. Yet words, any words, can barely do justice... 40.5%.

Tullibardine 225 sauternes cask finish db (85) n20 t22.5 f21 b21.5. Hits the heights early on in the delivery when the honey and Lubeck marzipan are at full throttle. 43%

Tullibardine 228 Burgundy cask finish db (82) n21 t22 f18 b21. No shortage of bitter chocolate. Flawed but a wow for those looking for mega dry malt. 43%

Tullibardine 500 sherry cask finish db (79.5) n19 t21 f19 b20.5. The usual problems from Jerez, but the grape ensures maximum chewability. 43%

Tullibardine Custodians Collection 1962 52 Years Old db (87.5) n22 t22 f21.5 b22 This oldie has gallantly fought in the great oak wars of 1987 to 2014 and shows some serious scars. Thankfully a little exotic fruit and citrus makes some impact on the austere tannins on the nose, but they aren't around to reduce the excesses of the finale, though a little chocolate does go a long way. The silky delivery doesn't quite hide the mildly puckering, eye-watering aggression of the tannin but butterscotch does its best to add a limp sweetness, as does the unexpected wave of juicy barley. Some fascinating old timer moments but, ultimately, a tad too ancient for its own good. 40.1%.

Tullibardine The Murray Cask Strength dist 2007, bott 2019, bott code: 19/0067 db (94.5) n23.5 t24 f23 b24 while touring China at the back end of 2019, I met a couple of people who told me they had bought previous bottles of this brand thinking that it was related to me, and therefore must have my seal of approval. Please let me reiterate: this whisky has nothing to do with Jim Murray, a name which is itself Trademarked. I make no financial gain from this whisky, nor do I allow any whisky in the world to be named after me. I make no profit from the individual sales of whisky and, though I am a consultant blender, do not make money from the sales of any brand; nor do I have any shares in any whisky company. The only recommendation I can make for this brand is confined to my independent review of it here. 56.6%. The Marquess Collection. Sixth edition.

Tullibardine The Murray Double Wood Edition matured in bourbon and sherry casks, dist 2005, bott 2020, bott code: 21/007 db (95.5) n24.5 t24 f23 b24 The finest example of The Murray I have tasted yet. The balance on the layering is simply exquisite. If you haven't done all your chores for the night: chickens fox-proofed, dog taken for walk, kids in bed, partner safely watching something on tv/reading book/out for the night...then don't bother cracking open this bottle. This is a malt that needs a good hour's peace and quiet...time to concentrate without interruption. The nose alone will eat into half an hour at least.... Don't say you haven't been warned...Oh, and I refer my honourable readers to the appendage of the tasting notes for this brand I did last year... 46%

Tullibardine The Murray Marsala Cask Finish dist 2006, bott 2018, bott code: 18/0167 db (86) n22 t22 f20.5 b21.5 A dry and heavy dram, very much the opposite of the standard sweet, gristy, malty affair from bourbon cask. Lots of frisky bite and nibble of delivery as the plummy fruit gets into full swing. But the tightness of the cask arrests further meaningful development. 46%. *The Marquess Collection.*

Tullibardine Sovereign bourbon barrel db (89.5) **n22.5 t23 f21.5 b22.5** Beautifully salivating despite the intricate oak notes. 43%

WOLFBURN

Highlands (Thurso), 2012. Aurora Brewing Ltd. Working.

⬥ **Wolfburn 10 Years Old** Oloroso sherry casks, bott 2023 db (94) **n23.5** mixed fruit tones: dried grape skin against a more open raisin fruit cake; the oak leaves no doubt that it has something serious to say by dealing out both spices and fruit-infused vanilla in measured abundance. All the spices have a specific tannin kick...; **t23.5** mmm! Just adore that texture! The perfect cut means just enough oils are trapped to give a gloss to both the rich malt and the delicate plummy fruit. Just a sub-current of sweetening ulmo honey; **f23** drier, as those tannins take a grip again. But there are enough sugars still on the win to easily cope; **b24** a malt which carries its ten years with aplomb: has stocked up enough oak to give an air of maturity, but still allows both the malt and fruit enough canvas to paint whatever picture they desire. Elegant, surprisingly juicy and quite delicious... 46% *nc ncf*

Wolfburn Aurora sherry oak casks db (91.5) **n22.5 t24 f22 b23** Early days at a distillery and still finding their feet with the still. The cut on this was wider than on the previous bottling I sampled, but there is no faulting the use of the 100% sulphur-free sherry butt. There is the odd aspect of genius attached to this dram, for sure. For the record: just vatted this with some OTT oak-hit sherry-cask 1954 malt in need of the kiss of life, or like a vampire in need of a virgin's blood: I suspect the first time a Wolfburn has been mixed with a 60-year-old Speysider. Result? One of the most complex and complete experiences of the last couple of months – a would-be award winner, were it commercially available! Stunning! 46%. *nc ncf.*

Wolfburn Aurora Sherry Oak db (91.5) **n23** gooseberry tart. Buttery tannin and then further shades of grapefruit and grist; **t23.5** much, much sweeter on delivery than the nose would lead you to believe. For the first flavour wave or two we have a lovely oak/grist balance, all melt-in-the-mouth style, then a much more intense and exaggerated muscovado sugar volley. The fruit remains restrained, very much down the apricot and fig route rather than heavy grape; **f22** slightly bitter again but now with a firmer tannin skeleton on which the apricot hangs; **b23** an elegant sherried malt which seems happy to use anything other than grapes in its fruit cocktail. Still a light nagging bitterness. I'd so much love this distillery to bottle something that is 100% bourbon cask so we can see this outstanding malt in its most naked form. I suspect it might get a few Wolf whistles... 46%

⬥ **Wolfburn Aurora Sherry Oak** db (86) **n22.5 t23 f19 b21.5** The creamiest Aurora I have yet encountered but one that shews a degree of sulphur interference on the finish, alas. Until then this had been its typical Wolfburn charmer full of lusty maltiness and polished by delicate raisins. The weight, also, is exemplary making this a first-class chewing malt on delivery. It was all going so well... 46% *nc ncf*

Wolfburn Langskip bott 27 May 19 db (94) **n23 t24 f23 b24** Rich, full bodied, intense, unforgiving. A whisky that doesn't just dip its toe in the outgoing surf... 58%. *nc ncf.*

Wolfburn Langskip db (94.5) **n23.5** such a gorgeous mix of bright barley and marshmallow. A little citrus points towards youth but also ensures there is limited sharpness to the softest of aromas; **t24** ...and it's those citrus tones which arrive first, providing a bite missing from the nose. But the malt teems forth, wave upon wave in the most magnificent fashion. This has now become chewing whisky, with the texture thickening by the moment. A little ulmo honey and the odd dab of golden syrup balances out the drier oak-induced vanilla; **f23** just a mild hint of bitterness towards the finale, though the malt still provides an uncanny intensity so late on; **b24** the house style as the whiskies get older appears to be towards a thick, gently oiled maltiness and the various avenues that are taken from there. Again, just a vague bitterness has crept in, but fails to disrupt the overall excellence. 58% *nc ncf*

⬥ **Wolfburn Langskip** db (94.5) **n23.5** fascinating: I don't remember any phenols last time I tasted this, but there is a definitely a shadow of something smokey lurking beneath the malty-citrussy waves; **t24** wow! I do remember this explosive citrus, though! As malt explosions go, this is TNT quality. Incredibly refreshing and salivating, the oils, like the nose, appears to suggest some loitering phenols...which in turn ramps up the weight and intensity overall; **f23** the fade is left to the predictable vanillas, the well-mannered spices...and again, that slight hint of chocolatey phenol; **b24** this distillery seriously impresses me. Their core malt really is of very high standard: not only is it intensely malty, but it has personality and character, too. An absolute treat of a dram. 58% *nc ncf*

Wolfburn Latitude bott code: LATITUDE-0001 db (95.5) **n24 t23.5 f23 b24** Lattitude has put Wolfburn well on course for whisky greatness. From their earlier bottlings I had hoped that they would be slowly building towards a whisky of such excellence. Even more remarkable considering that age plays no part other than to perpetuate the freshness. But age doesn't always matter if you get the balance right. And that they have certainly achieved here. Just imagine a malt like this, this well balanced and in tune, with time on its side. My taste buds quiver in anticipation... *46%. nc ncf.*

Wolfburn Lightly Peated Cask Strength Aged 7 Years Limited Release sherry and bourbon casks db (95) n23.5 the label may say "lightly peated". The nose suggests something a little more striking on the phenol front when taking into account the gentleness of the surrounding vanilla and barley. Light crushed sultana is as modest as the barley; t24 salivating, as any seven-year-old scotch should be. But, like the nose, the body, for all alcoholic might, is an essay in understatement. It's the mouthfeel which is the initial triumph: beautifully oiled without ever becoming slick, the peat providing earthiness but no Islayness. The fruit, encased in milk chocolate, is a counterweight to a brief tannin surge; f23.5 at last a little spice comes into play... and decides to linger seemingly forever. Most remarkable, though, is the light molasses which cling to the delicate smoke; b24 well, I wanted to get my tasting day off with a bang. And a positive. So couldn't have chosen better than this. Must say, I don't often comment about labels. But just love this one: so striking! As for the whisky...well, far too complex to decide over from a single tasting alone. The Murray Method is vital for stirring the pot and maximising complexity and, especially, getting those sugars going. Some very serious thought went into creating this masterpiece from the far north... *58.2% nc ncf 1840 bottles*

Wolfburn Lightly Peated Morven db (90.5) n23 for a wolf, this is just so alluringly gentle. Delightful butterscotch and vanilla mingles with the wispy smoke, a little citrus here and there lightening the rich texture; t23.5 lovers of Caol Ila will appreciate this oiled, delicately smoked texture. And the way the peat accumulates to hang, suspended on the palate. Ulmo honey dabs a gentle sweetness onto the tastebuds; f21.5 a nagging bitterness at the death ties in with late spice; b22.5 plenty of malt to chew on, and a delicate morsel of peat for good measure. But the failure to entirely control the late bitterness steers this bottling away from the greatness it deserves... *46% nc ncf*

Wolfburn Morven db (91.5) n23 t23 f22.5 b23 Confirmation, were it needed, that lightly peated malt is a brilliant way of getting a distillery's whiskies out at a young age without the lack of development becoming too clear. This is a delicious and refined amble on the taste buds. *46%. nc ncf.*

◈ **Wolfburn Morven Lightly Peated** db (95) n24 a surprise, a drier nose than the last Morven I encountered with a semi-Port Ellen style gristiness. They really have got the peat levels on the money here, so it balances so beautifully with the delicate vanilla. But as the peat concentrates, it heads towards a far more farmyard style cattle byre pungency....which I rather adore...; t23.5 so much gristy sugars beefed up by a thin layer of molasses and heather honey. The oils only really come up to scratch when the Murray Method is applied: cooler and they happily hide. The spices are playful and relevant; f23.5 peated chocolate...; b24 it is almost impossible to describe how Wolfburn's peaty version has risen over the last couple of years from excellent to truly outstanding. Most astonishing is the diversity in personality even within the smokiness. Almost uniquely, it is three-toed: first shewing a degree of shy dryness, then a gristy sweetness and then, as it merges with the oils, an altogether more agricultural persona. This is quite simply brilliant. *46% nc ncf.*

Wolfburn Northland db (88.5) n22.5 t22 f22 b22 Limited complexity but maximum charm for one so young. *46%. nc ncf.*

Wolfburn Northland db (89.5) n22.5 a lovely mix of young, citrus-light malt and slightly sturdier oak; t22.5 clotted barley! Thick and creamy malt with a dash of heather honey; f22 still fat, but a tad tangier than it might be...; b22.5 a year or two since I last tasted this. Then I felt it needed some muscle on its young bones...and it certainly provides it here. A beautifully gristy dram which celebrates barley with a mouth-watering rejoice but now a little extra oil keeps it longer on the palate. *46% nc ncf*

◈ **Wolfburn Northland** db (89.5) n22.5 t23 f21.5 b22.5 Talk about consistency! Practically a complete re-run of the last time I tasted this, even with the slightly bitter kink at the finale. Just apply the notes above and you'll be spot on. *46% nc ncf*

Wolfburn Single Malt Scotch Whisky db (91.5) n23 t23 f22.5 b23 This is a very young malt showing an intriguing wispy smokiness, its evenness more in line with having been matured in ex-Islay casks than using low phenol barley. Still, it might have been, and, if so, perhaps reveals a style that would not have been entirely unknown to the people of Thurso when they last drank this during Victorian times. It is probably 30 years ago I was shown to a spot in the town where I was told the original distillery had been. Now it is back, and eclipses Pulteney as the producers of the most northerly mainland Scottish whisky. For all its youth, its excellence of quality glimmers from the glass: a malt as beautifully flighted as a cricket ball delivered by the most crafted of spinners. And offers a delightful turn on the palate, too. The building of a new distillery, no matter how romantic its location or story, does not guarantee good whisky. So I am delighted for those involved in a project as exhausting as this that a very good whisky is exactly what they have on their hands. *46%. nc ncf.*

Wolfburn Small Batch Release No. 155 first fill ex-bourbon barrels, finished for six months in fresh port hogsheads db (**93**) **n23 t23.5 f23 b23.5** My word! This may be a new distillery. But they don't half produce some serious whisky... *46%. nc ncf. 5,300 bottles.*

Wolfburn Small Batch Release No. 204 first fill ex-bourbon barrels, finished for six months in Madeira hogsheads db (**90**) **n23 t23 f21.5 b22.5** A young malt which takes full advantage of the elegance provided by the Madeira casks. *46%. nc ncf. 5,800 bottles.*

Wolfburn Small Batch Release No. 270 half-sized first fill ex-bourbon barrels db (**92**) **n23.5 t22.5 f22.5 b23.5** You'd think from the lighter colour to Wolfburn 128 this would be less developed and offering fewer flavour options. Curiously, the reverse is true, the flavours more even, satisfying and elegant. *46%. nc ncf. 6,000 bottles.*

UNSPECIFIED SINGLE MALTS (CAMPBELTOWN)

Cadenhead's Campbeltown Malt (**92**) **n22 t24 f23 b23**. On their home turf you'd expect them to get it right... and, my word, so they do!! *59.5%*

UNSPECIFIED SINGLE MALTS (HIGHLAND)

Arcanum Spirits Avalon 12 Year Old Whisky Edition No.4 1st fill ex-bourbon barrel, dist Nov 2008, bott Nov 2020 (**92**) **n22 t23.5 f23.5 b23** Reaps the benefit of an excellent 1st fill bourbon cask, upping the delicate honey notes magnificently. Beautiful malt. *58.9% sc*

Asda Extra Special Highland Single Malt bott code: L6B 8127 1511 (**84.5**) **n21.5 t22 f20 b21** Nutty and lush. But the degree of toffee on show makes this almost closer to being a candy liqueur than a Highland malt. Perfect...if you like toffee! *40%.*

Compass Box Myths & Legends I (**96**) **n24.5 t24 f23.5 b24** I quite literally have no idea which distillery this is from. But those who are slightly in love with Clynelish in bourbon cask – one of the greatest experiences available in Scotch single malt whisky – will appreciate this. It may not be Clynelish, but the apples and honey make for a very creditable impersonation. By the way, I think Compass Box founder John Glaser suggests you can take ice with your whisky. Anyone adding ice or water to this deserves never to taste spectacularly great whisky again. Murray Method all the way for astonishing results... *46%.*

Glen Marnoch Highland Single Malt bott code: L12 12 18 (**91**) **n22 t23 f23 b23** A beautifully even and satisfying Highlander. No great age, but so much charisma. *40%. Produced for Aldi.*

Glen Turner Cask Collection Rum Cask Finish bott code: L907357A (**90.5**) **n23 t22 f23 b22.5** A very well-manicured malt. *40%. La Martiniquaise.*

Glen Turner Heritage Double Cask Port Cask Finish bott code: L834657A (**94**) **n23.5 t24 f23 b23.5** An impressive piece of cask finishing where the speech by the port is pretty and important, but the microphone has not been turned up too loudly. *40%. La Martiniquaise.*

Glen Turner Malt Legend Aged 12 Years bott code: L832557C (**87**) **n21 t23.5 f21 b21.5** A fat, velvety malt with an attractive, lush fruitiness but just a little too much sharpness out of the oak. Plenty to enjoy. *40%. La Martiniquaise.*

Glenwill Highland Single Malt rum cask finish (**88**) **n22 t22 f21.5 b22.5** An easy malt where the sugary shell of the rum comes into play infrequently. *40%. Matisse Spirits Company.*

Glenwill RV rum cask finish (**80**) **n21 t21 f19 b19** Mainly toffeed, characterless and just zzzzzzzzz..... *40%. Quality Spirits International.*

Glenwill S = 1 sherry butt finish (**73**) **n19 t21.5 f16 b17.5** S = Sulphur. *40%. Quality Spirits International.*

Highland Queen Majesty Classic bott code: 21/0043 (**86**) **n21.5 t22 f21.5 b21** Her Majesty has turned from Highland Queen to Highland Princess. Notably younger than the last time I looked, the nose makes an exhibition of its new makeyness. Harsh if nosed cool, soft and gristy when slightly warmed. The mouth feel may be silky but the firmness of the young malt itself is striking. Calmed by a little toffee. *40% Tullibardine Ltd*

Highland Queen Majesty Aged 12 Years bott code: 21/0044 (**89**) **n22.5 t22 f22 b22.5** A better balanced malt than of before: the Queen wears her crown just a little more carefully. There is still a little toffee lurking round, but doesn't play the court jester as it once did. *40% Tullibardine Ltd*

Highland Queen Majesty Aged 14 Years Sherry Cask Finish bott code: 21/0045 (**90.5**) **n22** very pleasant, though the plummy fruit leaves it feeling a little flat; **t22.5** a curious delivery. Although 14, and despite a hefty touch from the sherry cask, the delivery is a little thin, young in character and salivating thanks to the abundant rich malt: far from what I was expecting. But there is no doubting its alure on the palate as the tannins and spices kick down the doors to make their dramatic entry; **f23** long, spicy, silky fruits – mainly blueberries – drift on the palate to unite some time; **b23** takes a little while to get the measure of this. But persistence pays off. More complex and rewarding that it first seems. That mix of fruit and spice is rather lovely while the understated malt is heroically brilliant. *40% Tullibardine Ltd*

UNSPECIFIED SINGLE MALTS (ISLAND)

Fadandel Orkney 14 Years Old (88.5) n22.5 t22 f22 b22 Fragrantly malty with a pleasing topping of light smoke to add both personality and weight. Has that feeling of a well-used cask, so not too much vanilla to add to the party or gee up the complexity. Well made, refreshing and salivating. But it is the intensity of the barley which sticks in both palate and memory. *60.8%*

Oxhead Classic Casks Secret Orkney 2005 (93) n23 t23.5 f23 b23.5 Secret Orkney, by which I assume they mean Highland Park. Both HP and Scapa share a honeyed signature at times but the lazy smoke on this probably points to the former. Not sure where this has been warehoused, but there does appear to be some briny, seaweedy notes on the nose, which is an unexpected bonus. The body is racked with salted honey and waves of intense barley. A little tiredness on the finish, perhaps. But the soft spice and delicate cocoa make amends. A beautifully sculpted malt. *58%*

Whisky-Fässle Orkney 17 Years Old butt, dist 2002, bott 2019 **(89.5) n23 t23 f21.5 b22** The oils and fruit on this ensure a long, increasingly toasty and bitter finish. But the nose is an essay of age, charm and balance with the vanilla and barley in harmony with the spiced spotted dog pudding. The delivery, meanwhile, is a festival of varied sugar and honey tones – and malty ones at that – missing on the nose and finish. *49.1%. sc.*

Whisky-Fässle Orkney 12 Years Old hogshead, dist 2007, bott 2020 **(89) n22 t23 f22 b22** An exceptionally dry malt, the salt adding to the eye-watering qualities. It's a HP, devoid of both trademark smoke and honey. But still beautifully made and the deft barley interacts with the tannins and spice with a relaxed countenance. Quietly elegant and refined. *51.3%. sc.*

UNSPECIFIED SINGLE MALTS (ISLAY)

Arcanum Spirits Private Reserve Islay Whisky Edition No 5 dist 10/05/2011 bott 25/05/2022 db **(95) n23.5 t24.5 f23 b24** French wine casks, especially from the better châteaux, tend to be the kiss of death for Scotch: in that part of the world, they are even more insane in their use of sulphur than the Spanish. Not this time. A wonderful wine cask working wonders and finding harmony with a high-class Islay leading to a delivery and follow through of exquisite texture and complexity. Fabulous. And well played France. *58.9%*

Bruadaradh Lochindaal 9 Years Old dist 1 Sept 09, bott 6 Nov 18 **(86.5) n22.5 t22.5 f20.5 b21** The saltiness of the nose, combined with peat reek on the breeze talks Islay to you. But there is a nip on the nose, too, which suggests the cask has a little issue. Thankfully, this doesn't fully arrive until the finish when the burn and bitterness fair grabs you. But until then, enjoy the vanilla, natural caramel, heather honey and ultra-light phenol serenade... *634%. nc ncf sc.*

Bruadaradh Lochindaal 9 Years Old dist 1 Sept 09, bott 17 Nov 18 **(90.5) n22.5 t23 f22 b23** A much more docile bottling than their other one (above) with far fewer stumbling blocks. The mintiness to the peat on the nose tends to give a feeling of greater age - though they are twins. As before, the smoke is shy and happy to hide behind the more militant elements. Though little is particularly militant here with the ulmo honey and light spice really making a wonderful pairing. There is still a little bitterness to negotiate at the end here, but the malt and smoke do some great repair work. *50%. nc ncf sc.*

Demijohn Islay 10 Year Old (95) n23.5 t24 f23.5 b24 A faultless Islay: beautifully distilled and matured just the right number of years in an absolutely brilliant bourbon cask. Whoever selected this cask should take a bow. Hebridean nectar... *58.1%*

Finlaggan Cask Strength Islay Single Malt (88) n22.5 t23 f21.5 b21 A massive peated malt which that phenolphiles will lap up. But for its all its big Islay muscle, struggles to come together and balance out as even as might be hoped. *58%. The Vintage Malt Whisky Company.*

Finlaggan Eilean Mor Islay Single Malt (88.50) n22 t22.5 f22 b22 Oily Islay with a pleasant if limited disposition. *46%. The Vintage Malt Whisky Company.*

Finlaggan Old Reserve Islay Single Malt (91) n23 t23f22.5 b23 No great age I suspect. But the intensity and charm are profound. Unmistakably Islay! *40%.*

Finlaggan Port Finish Islay Single Malt (92.5) n23 t23.5 f23 b23.5 Huge peat at work, dry and almost coal dust-like. But its wings are initially clipped by the port before it takes off once more...to profound effect. *46%. The Vintage Malt Whisky Company.*

Gleann Mór Rare Find Islay Aged 15 Years dist 2006 **(88.5) n22 t23 f21.5 b22** Was doing so well until the bourbon cask began to bitter out at the end, though the nose did forewarn. However, this is beautifully peated and rounded – true classic Islay style. A little Granny Smith apple gives it a degree of tartness, too. *52.1%*

Peat's Beast bott code: L 07 08 17 **(92)** n22.5 t23 f23.5 b23 Nosing this whizzed me back to the late 1980s and my old office in a national newspaper in Fleet Street where, by night, I was taking my first tentative steps into the then unknown and practically non-existent medium of whisky writing. And I remember opening up a Bowmore 5-years-old bottled by Oddbins. I'm not saying this is a Bowmore, but so many features on display in that landmark bottling 30 years ago are also to be found here... 46%. ncf.

Peat's Beast Twenty Five bott code: L1 1409-2017 11 **(88.5)** n23 t23 f20 b22.5 There are far more beastly Islay whiskies than this out there – a quarter of a century in the cask means the teeth have been blunted, the claws clipped. And if you must "tame it" further, for God's sake ignore the daft advice on the label about adding water. Please use the Murray Method described on page 9. That will keep the thing alive while making it purr at full decibels... And this is so lovely (well, finish apart), it is worth listening to at full volume...which isn't very loud. 52.2%. ncf.

Port Askaig Islay Aged 12 Years Spring Edition ex-bourbon hogsheads, dist 2006 & 2007 **(95.5)** n24 t24 f23.5 b24 Only a bourbon cask can allow the phenols to play and galivant with such fun and abandon. You get the feeling that the casks were plucked from the warehouse at exactly the right time. Fabulous! 45.8%. nc ncf. 5,000 bottles.

Port Askaig 14 Year Old Bourbon Cask dist 2004 **(95)** n24 t23.5 f23.5 b24 For those who prefer their peat to caress rather than kick. Elegant and so beautifully sensual. 45.8%.

Port Askaig 15 Years Old sherry cask **(87.5)** n22.5 t22 f21.5 b21.5 I know, I know: I have a blind spot for this kind of whisky. Rather, not blind, but not an over developed appreciation of the big smoke notes slugging it out with and then being neutralised by equally big, occasionally eye-wateringly sharp, fruit ones. At least the sherry is clean and extra marks for that. But, for me, this is just too much of a tit-for-tat malt leaving a neutral toffee fruitiness to claim the big prize. Pleasant, I grant you. But I want it to be so much more.... 45.8%.

Port Askaig 25 Years Old (91) n23 t23.5 f21 b22.5 Bottled at the right time – another year or two would have seen a dramatic slide. But as it is, so much to quietly savour. 45.8%.

Port Askaig 28 Years Old (92.5) n23.5 t23.5 f22 b23.5 Classically understated. 45.8%.

Port Askaig 33 Years Old Single Cask (95) n23.5 t24.5 f23 b24 Islay at its most coastal. Shews its age with rare elegance. Sublime. 50.3%. sc.

Port Askaig 45 Years Old (90.5) n23 t23 f22 b22.5 Even in my scaringly long career, I can probably count the number of peated malts that made it to this kind of age and then into a commercial bottling on one hand. Certainly by the end it is showing every year that has passed, but for an unexpected period the malt hangs together...sometimes surprisingly deliciously. 40.8%.

Port Askaig 100 Proof (96.5) n24 t24 f24 b24.5 Just exemplary, high quality Islay: a must experience malt. If you find a more beautifully paced, weighted and elegant Islay this year, I'd like to hear about it... 57.1%.

Port Askaig 110 Proof (91.5) n23 t23 f22.5 b23 Beautifully made and elegantly matured. An excellent Islay. 55%.

Saar Single Malt Islay Whisky Edition 3 11 Years Old dist 7.10.2010 bott 14.10.2021 **(93)** n23.5 the full-on phenol promises menace, but all the time acts like a large sleeping dog determined to lick you to death. Some lovely sub notes of lemon and custard; t23.5 shows a little youthfulness in the delivery, confirming that a used bourbon cask is allowing the malt unfettered access to all parts of the palate. The smoke drifts with intent; f22.5 relatively short....perhaps the downside of the well-used cask, though the lingering oils stretch the phenols as far as they are willing to go; b23.5 a pretty faultless cask. Add to that that this has been perfectly distilled and it all adds up to a delightful Islay experience. Great cask picking, somebody...! 52.2% 223 bottles

Saar Single Malt Islay Whisky Edition 5 11 Years Old dist 7.10.2010 bott 16.11.2021 **(89)** n23 the smoke here is denser than edition 3, with much more spice invested; t22.5 again, the phenols are to the fore and in no mood for prisoners. Punchy and powdery with a pleasantly spiced molasses backdrop; f21.5 just falls away into a peated bitterness; b22 fascinating. From the same run as Edition 3, being distilled on the same date. But an inferior cask means the high value spirit has to work overtime and pull out the stops to ensure this retains an overall level of quality commensurate with the original distillate. On the plus side for some, the result is far more muscular phenols. 53.6% 223 bottles

Valour Whisky Distilled At An Islay Distillery Aged 11 years bourbon hogshead cask No 22000002 dist 17/10/2010 bott 10/06/2022 **(95)** n23.5 fabulously coastal, with sea spray and ozone nudging into the prickly phenols. A gratifying degree of passing a field of cows in an open-top Jag XK...; t24.5 for a 10-12 year-old south coast Islay (which this surely must be) the deportment of the smoke and raging gristy sugars is outstanding and hits the spot. Spices rises early to add to the controlled phenolic mayhem, then a surprisingly early but wonderful thick strata of cocoa joins the fray. All the time there is a sub-current of youth...; f23 a little lazy towards the end, as though it feels it had worked hard enough earlier. But it remains surprisingly fat and chewy, cocoa and marzipan joining the lingering smoke; b24 you instinctively know when you've encountered high quality Islay picked at the very apogee of its smoky but balanced intensity. And on this occasion your instincts would be right... *54.3% 353 bottles*

◇ **Valour Whisky An Islay 30 Years Old** bourbon barrel, dist 11/90, bott 04/22 **(92.5) n23.5** purringly classic. Iodine levels are pleasingly high while a soft saltiness graphs the softer phenols and so accentuates the minty sweetness; **t23.5** oak not apparent on the nose is soon here! Tannins outmuscle the phenols early on, though the gang warfare nature of the peat works in wresting back control. While that little scuffle is being enacted on your palate, a gorgeously smoke-infused ulmo honey note settles on the tongue to guarantee balance; **f22.5** that oak really is persistent. But so, too, are those beautifully soft phenols The added mocha and vanilla and even a slight, very late, hint of lemon blossom honey; **b23** a massively satisfying old un which has taken the oak influence as far at it could go before any negativity could kick in. The phenols, which tend to reduce in influence with the passing years, have kept their end up exceptionally well. *51.4% 150 bottles*

◇ **Vintage Bottlers Secret Series 3 Islay 32 Years** Old dist 20/11/90 **(95.5) n24 t24 f23.5 b24** I'm afraid some distilleries just can't keep secrets, and Laphroaig is one of them. I'm not sure how many nanoseconds it took to identify the distillery by the nose alone, I doubt if it was many. When at around 30-years-old, only one Islay gives this particular shade of purple heart candy on the nose, especially when coupled with that particular type of anthracite for company. Or this sweet, silky phenolic thumbprint around the 30-year-old mark. But don't make the mistake this is just about flavour. It is also supremely tactile, too, and the touch, the caress of the palate is about as good as anything I have tasted so far this year. The silky texture is the definition of sensuality, and the joy is intensified by the extraordinary interplay between the manuka honey, light molasses and pulsing smoke. Some will have you believe that you cannot say that a whisky is sexy. Well, those idiots shouldn't be in the whisky industry if they can't recognise that a malt as sensual as this is as sexy as it gets... *52.1% sc 242 bottles*

The Whisky Chamber Buair an Diabhail Vol. XVIII bourbon cask **(86.5) n22 t22 f21 b21.5** It may be swamped in more smoke than a 1950s London pub, but there is something unmercifully metallic about this malt. Especially on the rigid finish. Plenty of molasses to sweeten the impact, but a whisky that is hard to embrace. *574%. sc.*

The Whisky Chamber Teagmháil Leis an Diabhail Vol. II 10 Jahre 2009 bourbon cask **(92.5) n23.5 t23.5 f22.5 b23** If Covid means you can't get to a Scottish beach this year, here's a chance to let it come to you... *58.2%. sc*

UNSPECIFIED SINGLE MALTS (LOWLAND)
Tweeddale Single Lowland Malt Scotch Whisky 14 Years db **(89) n21.5 t23.5 f22 b22** busy, bustling, elegant and old-fashioned...like a small borders town. *62%. nc ncf sc.*

UNSPECIFIED SINGLE MALTS (SPEYSIDE)
A.D. Rattray Cask Speyside 10 Year Old db **(89) n22 t22.5 f22 b22.5** An elegant and lightly smoked malt which would double as either a pre-prandial dram, or one for the wooden hill... *46%.*

Angels' Nectar Aged 11 Years Cairngorms 2nd Edition (92) n22.5 t23 f23.5 b23 Though a collector of First Editions, I tend to think that this 2nd has some slight amendments to ensure extra depth and entertainment. Having said that, there will be times when my mood would take me to the more fighty and fragile First edition. Two very impressive Angels. *46%. sc. 146 bottles.*

◇ **Angels' Nectar Cairngorms 4th Edition (91.5) n22.5** well, just look at you! All done up in that refined maltiness and prodding your citrus notes in all directions...; **t23.5** I just adore those gristy-sherbet-lemon experiences where the sugars dissolve and the salivation levels go nuts. The tannins offer a degree of spice, but lots more vanilla. Light heather honey thickens things with a refined sweetness; **f22.5** just a slight bitterness creeps in, but nothing major: the malt is there still in droves...; **b23** I love this kind of cask: unspectacular, even and honest, it is the definition of an unpretentious whisky. Just so beautifully distilled and housed in a top-rate cask which has exploited every nuance in those complex malty tones. Brilliant. *46% sc 371 bottles*

Asda Extra Special Speyside Single Malt bott code: L6A 8226 1412 **(81) n20 t21.5 f19 b20.5** Pleasant, soft and sweet and briefly delicious on delivery...but entirely linear. As it develops, devoid of character or personality as the big dollop of caramel and tired casks has taken its toll. *40%.*

Compass Box Myths & Legends II (95) n24 t23.5 f23.5 b24 Incredibly lively malt on the palate. The delivery is one of the most memorable this year, aided and abetted by sublime bourbon casks allowing the malt to reveal all its naked beauty.. *46%.*

Creag Dhu Speyside aged in sherry casks, bott code: L151220 **(92) n23 t23.5 f22.5 b23** Malts like this help point towards a recovery from the sulphur problem to hit Scotland's sherry casks. This is almost faultless and the only complaint is that, at barely over 40%abv, too much body has been lost by reduction: this screams out to be cask strength. *40.2%*

❖ **Ferg & Harris Speyside Aged 12 Years** Pedro Ximenez 1st Fill bourbon barrel, 6 months PX hogshead finish **(94) n23** such a sublime inter-reaction between heavy duty fruitcake and hairy-chested tannins. Even a spiced up, peppery, gingery buzz in there, too...superb..; **t23.5** wow! An immediate dip into heather honey on delivery thanks to a fabulous volley of intense barley sugar augmented by first a molasses and muscovado sugar mix and then a plum jam plus a lighter fruity shade of figs and pear juice. However, the constant rattling from the spices, keeping up the great work on the nose, really is something; **f23.5** it may calm down, but the complexity remains undiminished. Echoes of all the earlier starring features, except now with a vanilla shadow beautifully representing the oak. The spices tone down accordingly..; **b24** such a mesmerically harmonious Speyside. It is big and bold in so many places. Yet the parts fit so seamlessly, there is so little jarring as its myriad parts meld, its enormity is so easily overlooked. Excellent. 55.7% ncf Young Spirits

Scyfion Carron Burns staraya Shalanda cask finished, dist 2008, bott 2019 **(78.5) n19 t21 f19.5 b19** Some whisky finishes work, some don't. This don't. 50% nc ncf sc 172 bottles

❖ **Vintage Bottlers Secret Series 2 Speyside 29 Years Old** dist 21/05/92 **(94.5) n23.5 t23.5 f23.5 b24** Whoever selects Vintage Bottlers' casks certainly has a penchant for intensely malty single malt. This would be another blender's delight, as the clarity to the barley is quite superb and would provide a fair top dressing. As a singleton, it does not try to overburden the drinker with complexity. However, it is perhaps the nose which comes closest to setting questions, as at times it is difficult to know exactly where the oaky vanillas end and the firmer malts begin. The delivery itself is as simple as it gets: intense malt with a sweetening butter-biscuit trail. The vanilla wafer finale is relatively dry, but a perfect ending. Just faultless, gorgeously natural progression throughout. Truly satisfying. 44.8% sc 266 bottles

UNSPECIFIED SINGLE MALTS (GENERAL)

❖ **Angels' Nectar Oloroso Sherry Single Cask Edition (84.5) n21.5 t22 f20 b21** There is much to commend with the singular Melton Hunt Cake thrust and pitch of the burnt grape. But equally, there is a roughness to this, finalised by the off-key finish, which I have long avoided in sherry butts. Though, doubtless the central Europeans will be clambering over themselves for a bottle of this.... 57.9% sc 181 bottles

❖ **Angels' Nectar Oloroso Sherry Cask Edition (88) n22 t22.5 f21.5 b22** Not too many problems with this sherry butt (save a slight niggle at the very death) which ensures the grape dominates from first to last. Silky textured, the tannin has a slightly burnt toast feel to it. Malt is barely detectable until very late on. As for the spices: beautifully pitched, they absolutely steal the show! 46%

Compass Box Myths & Legends III (95.5) n23.5 t24 f24 b24 It is noticeable that Compass Box have, by and large, reigned back on the over oaking and are back to allowing the whiskies themselves to do the talking. Another exceptionally beautiful malt from them using bourbon casks that allows the personality of the malt to come through in all its gentle but complex beauty. I just wish more blenders would take note of this. 46%.

Kingsbury Gold Kilbride 14 YO 2006 (90.5) n23 thumping peat: salt and full of farmyard intensity; **t23** sharp delivery with biting barley. The oak helps ramp up the peat which, like on the nose, refuses to hold back from going the full phenols...; **f22** perhaps a little on the thin and hot side. But the barley sweetness persists to the end; **b22.5** gosh! I feel that I have just been flattened by a peat cutter. Subtle it isn't. Phenolic fun...? You bet! 55.7%

Kingsbury Mhaine Baraille 19 YO 2001 (95) n23.5 cherry cake and chocolate chips. Incredibly even and docile, but there is a monster lurking; **t24** silk was hinted on the nose....and it is delivered here effortlessly. A light molasses sweetness thickens further as the vanilla and barley become entangled in the oils. The spices, like all else, are big yet refuse to bite, contentedly nibbling on the senses instead. The fruit tones seem embedded in equal measure with the tannin and malt: remarkable; **f23.5** we are back to cherry and chocolate. So sticky and rich, it is like a dessert; **b24** a brooding dram with the weight of the world on its shoulders. But if you have ever wondered what I mean about the palate being "caressed", then this whisky is the definition. This is very high-class malt, indeed. 45.6%

Kingsbury Ruine 13 YO 2007 (87) n21.5 t22.5 f21 b22 Despite the rumbling and highly attractive peat, there is just a constant niggle from the oak which undoes the obvious potential. I won't say it was Ruined, simply because the delivery is such a multi-layered treat, especially when the smoked chocolate biscuit arrives. But neither the nose nor tangy finish are quite what they should be. 56.5%

M&S Speyside Aged 12 Years bott code: L031220 **(81.5) n22 t21 f18.5 b20** For its age lacks complexity, other than a brief spell on the nose where the malt and oak appear to be gently cajoling the other. But the performance on the palate, if initially pleasant and malty, flattens alarmingly before finishing in overly bitter fashion. 40%

Matisse Single Malt Aged 19 Years (91) n23 t22.5 f22.5 b23 A malt that operates by stealth, seemingly wanting to go unnoticed. However, perseverance will pay off for the taster. 40%. Matisse Spirits Company.

Peat's Beast bott code: L 20 02 19 (89) n22 t23 f22 b22 A very safe malt by heavily peated standards, determined not to offend. 46%. ncf.

Peat's Beast Batch Strength Pedro Ximenez sherry wood finish, bott code: L 18 10 19 (89.5) n22.5 t23 f22 b22 If this whisky was comedy it would be pure slapstick. 54.1%. ncf.

William & Co Spirits 11 Years Aged cask no. 8327273, dist 2009, bott 2020 (91.5) n23 wonderful fruit and nut combination offers richness and promise; t23 the barley still has much to say despite the weighty fruit presence. So, the start is mouth-watering and deft. The weightier grape and spices surge with confidence, the oils offering a perfect platform to show the growing depth. The midpoint layering is profound and reverts to the fruitcake suggested on the nose, but the oaky toastiness gives it an attractively burnt quality; f22 not quite as on-song as the earlier rounds. But the tannins still have much to say, the spices in particular; b23 Miltonduff is one of the most dexterous of all Speyside malts and boasts personality enough to handle both oak and fruit infusion in its stride. The relatively young age of the malt is never in question. But the muscle it has developed is mightily impressive. 54.4%. 108 bottles. Bottled for Mingo Cocktail & Whisky.

Scottish Vatted Malts
(also Pure Malts/Blended Malt Scotch)

Angels' Nectar Islay Rioja Cask Edition 7 Years Old (91) n22.5 if you are not concentrating fully when you put this to your nose, the glass will demand your full attention. This is a head turner and nose-twitcher of the highest order: the peat is as firm and well-chiselled as any you will find, and the flintiness of the grape is the perfect match; t23 one of those rare malts which is simultaneously hard as nails and, elsewhere on the palate, a silky, gently oiled teddy bear. Salivating, especially when the unpeated malt and the grape manage to unite...and never loses its youth; f22.5 long, in that Caol Ila-style of oiliness with sublime layering and sticky peat. The grapey tones are crisp but fleeting. The spices begin to make a noise; b23 an outrageous, fun Islay plucked from the warehouse at a tender age and reeking not just of peat but Rioja, too. No off notes; superbly made and one to give your tastebuds a thorough working over. 46%

Angels' Nectar Cairngorms 12 Years Old 3rd Edition (90) n22 the barley offers an attractive simplicity, concentrating on delicate vanillas and diced apple; t22.5 every bit as salivating as the nose suggests, again with the barley at full volume. Just a slight suggestion of oaky vanilla here and there, underlined by the gentle spices; f22.5 so good to find a bottling this delicate free from late bitterness! Drier, naturally, but there are still malty remnants to keep the chalky vanilla company; b23 I have a weakness for beautifully distilled and sympathetically matured, clean single malts like this. I wish there were more around. 46%

Art Edition No 2 (95) n23.5 any wine casks used here are free from fatal interference: the layered, clean grape is given free rein to seduce, delight, astonish and simply entertain at will. All kinds of fat sultana and plums at play here, but never to the cost of the oak, which offers a spicy riposte well within the desired boundaries. Somewhere or other some acacia honey and marmalade offer the attention-seeking sweetness to fill in any cracks; quite simply, a joy...; t24 it is the combination of both the mouthfeel and the layering of the flavours which leave you floating on some kind if grapey cloud. Chocolate raisin presents itself early in the piece and unmistakable barley pops up in almost concentrated form to ensure this isn't a one-way fruity street. As for the layering...you'll lose count...! f23.5 long and languid, the oils now have an important say and it spreads the Malteser-like chocolate and vanilla to all corners; b24 in a word: brilliant! A masterpiece! This is an artform in itself... 45.2%

Ben Bracken Blended Malt Aged 12 Years (85.5) n22.5 t21 f21 b21. Quite a tight malt with a predominantly toffee theme. 40%

Berry Bros & Rudd Islay Blended Malt bott code: L18/8215 (90.5) n22 t23 f22.5 b23 An endearing vatting which sums up the island's whiskies without any drama but still highly attractively and with no wrong turns. 44.2%. The Classic Range.

Berry Bros & Rudd Sherry Cask Matured Blended Malt Whisky bott code: P/001036 (84) n22 t21.5 f20 b20.5 Despite the early muscovado sugars which ooze all over the delivery, this turns into one of the most strangely bitter malts I have tasted in a very long time. Like a fruitcake that has been incinerated in the oven and syrup poured over it so no-one might notice... Odd! Though I'm certain there are types who will fight to the death for a bottle of this. A whisky, let us say, to divide opinion. 44.2%.

Berry Bros & Rudd Peated Cask Matured Blended Malt bott code: L18/8214 (92) n22 t23 f23.5 b23.5 Gentle and evenly paced. 44.2%. The Classic Range.

Chapter 7 Anecdote Blended Malt 24 Year Old 2 bourbon hogsheads, dist Jul 95, bott Mar 20 (93.5) n23 t23.5 f23.5 b23.5 Tells a quietly delicious tale. 47.9%. 424 bottles.

Chapter 7 Williamson 2010 Aged 9 Years bourbon barrel, barrel no.907 **(95.5) n24 t24 f23.5 b24** Magnificent: there is no other word. 53.9%

Chivas Regal Ultis bott code LPNK1759 2016/09/16 **(89.5) n22.5 t23 f21.5 b22.5** This vatted malt is the legacy of Chivas' five master blenders. But to pay real respect to them, just remove the caramel from the bottling hall. The whisky will be light coloured, for sure, but I suspect the flavour profile will blow us all away... 40%. Chivas Brothers Ltd.

Compass Box The Circle bott May 19 **(94.5) n23.5 t24 f23 b24** If a malt whisky this year proves no great age is required to create something of great beauty, then here it is. A wonderful crossover between lemon blossom honey and pear drops on the nose helps focus the attention on the clarity of the malt. Such a nose demands a delivery of great malty complexity...and you won't be disappointed. The bourbon casks add their own magic spell to proceedings, intertwingling both vanilla and butterscotch with pipette-measured exactitude and ensuring the spices play an important but never over-dominant role. Simple. Yet not. A real treat of a dram. 46%. nc ncf. 6,151 bottles.

Compass Box No Name bott Sept 17 **(92.5) n23 t23 f23 b23.5** I'll give it a name: Compass Box Bleedin' Delicious! 48.9%. nc ncf. 15,000 bottles.

Compass Box No Name, No. 2 bott Feb 19 **(93.5) n23 t23.5 f23.5 b23.5** Think a lightly oiled Islay whisky where the peat is powering, but totally in sync with the overall balance of the piece. And where a light heather honey note ensures there is no bitterness and the phenols never get too acrid or sooty. Spot on wood management with this fella. 48.9%. nc ncf. 8,802 bottles.

Compass Box The Peat Monster bott code: L 11 12 18 **(94.5) n23.5 t23.5 f23.5 b24** This is the most complete Peat Monster I've encountered for a little while. It's all about the balance and here it manages to allow sheer enormity to come through loud and clear, but not at the expense of tact and complexity. 46%. nc ncf.

Compass Box The Peat Monster Cask Strength **(89) n23.5 t23 f20.5 b22** Plenty of peat between your teeth but deserving of some better oak. 57.3%

Compass Box The Peat Monster Reserve **(92) n23 t23.5 f22.5 b23.** At times a bit of a Sweet Monster...beautiful stuff! 48.9%

Compass Box The Spice Tree French oak head & American oak body hybrid casks, bott code: L 28 11 18 **(96) n23.5 t25 f23.5 b24** Don't know about The Spice Tree...Honey Tree more like.. So strikingly beautiful! 46%.

Compass Box The Story of The Spaniard 48% aged in Spanish wine casks, bott Jun 18 **(90.5) n23 t23 f22 b22.5** Often Compass Box lets the oak do the talking, occasionally too loudly. Here the tannin has a dry edge, but fits into the scenario perfectly. 43%. nc ncf.

Copper Dog batch no. 16/0673, bott code: L8127IY001 **(89) n22 t23.5 f21.5 b22** A whisky which first saw the light of day at the fabulous Craigellachie Hotel in Speyside, where I gave my first whisky lectures over a quarter of a century ago and in the 1990s wrote many chapters of my various books. The number of vatted malts we created from the whiskies in the bar...far too many to mention, though none then capable of shewing this kind of finale. 40%.

Cutty Sark Blended Malt **(92.5) n22 t24 f23 b23.5.** Sheer quality: as if two styles have been placed in the bottle and told to fight it out between them. What a treat! 40%.

Deerstalker Blended Malt Highland Edition **(94) n23.5 t23.5 f23 b24** A quite beautiful whisky by any standards. 43%

◈ **Distiller's Choice Aged 5 Years**, bott code L318122 **(88) n22 t23 f21 b22** A real pudding of a dram. Way too heavily weighed down with toffee bordering treacle, the finish is an untidy mismatch. But the delivery, for all its lack of guile, is definitely entertaining for its chewy spiced plum pudding. A huge, if unsubtle, malt. 40% Wm Morrison

Fadandel.dk Isla Blended Aged 10 Years In Memory of Bessie Williamson hogshead barrel, cask no.LAP224, dist May 2011, bott May 2021 **(94) n23.5 t23.5 f23 b24** Trying to think why this reminds me so much of a very decent standard barrel of 10-year-old Laphroaig. Answers on a postcard, please. By the way, if you want to experience malt whisky being perfectly made, then here's your bottle... 58.4% sc 323 bottles

The First Editions Hector Macbeth Aged 24 Years 1997 bourbon barrel, cask no.HL18662 **(92.5) n23.5 t24 f22 b23** Those for a penchant for whisky distilled by bees had better buzz off and find a bottle... 51% nc ncf sc 333 bottles

The First Editions John McCrae Aged 23 Years 1995 refill hogshead, cask no. 16643, bott 2019 **(86.5) n22 t22.5 f20.5 b21.5** A decent enough vatting in part. But there is perhaps a little too much tang, to reveal tiring oak. 44%. nc ncf sc. 246 bottles.

The Gladstone Axe American Oak bott code: B2061099 **(91.5) n22 t23 f23.5 b23** a deeply pleasing blend. It does what a blend should do: offer succulence and complexity in a way you can barely notice...unless you really look. Unostentatious, but highly impressive. 41%

The Gladstone Axe The Black Axe peated malts with touch of smoke, bott code: B2031092 **(88.5) n22.5 t22 f22 b22** Pleasant whisky but with a much duller and less tantalising persona than its sister blend, American Oak. Slightly too much emphasis on the spice this time round which seems to make up for the lack of smoke I had been expecting. The nose apart, much drier, less emphasis on the sugars but still with a late satisfying sweep of milky chocolate. Rich toffee, though, can be found in every crevice. 41%

Glen Turner Heritage Double Wood Bourbon & Madeira casks, bott code. L311657A **(85.5)** n21.5 t22 f21 b21. A very curious amalgamation of flavours. The oak appears to be in shock with the way the fruit is coming on to it and offers a bitter backlash. No faulting the crisp delivery with busy sugar and spice for a few moments brightening the palate. 40%.

Glen Turner Pure Malt Aged 8 Years L525956A **(84)** n20 t22 f22 b20. A lush and lively vatting annoyingly over dependent on thick toffee but simply brimming with fabulously mouth-watering barley and over-ripe blood oranges. To those who bottle this, I say: let me into your lab. I can help you bring out something sublime!! 40%

Hogwash Blended Malt Scotch Whisky Blend No. 08 bott code: LBB 3C 4353 **(85.5)** n21.5 t22 f21 b21 Juicy in part. And if you are looking for a gentle, soft, refined, complex, gentleman of a vatted malt...this isn't it. 40%. *Produced for Aldi.*

Johnnie Walker Green Label 15 Years Old (95) n24 t23.5f23.5 b24. God, I love this stuff... this is exactly how a vatted malt should be and one of the best samples I've come across since its launch. 43%. *Diageo.*

Johnnie Walker Green Label Aged 15 Years bott code: L9076DN002 **(91)** n23 t23.5 f22 b22.5 Really lovely malt, but would dearly like to see the degree of toffee reduced on this as you feel there is so much going on that can't quite be heard. 43%.

◈ **Kingsbury Mhaine Baraille 2003 Aged 19 Years** hogshead, cask no 33 **(89)** n22 genteel if slightly unresponsive malt fattened out by tannin; t23 ah, that's better. The barley appears to possess some attitude, if only short lived. But for a second it flexes its slightly salty muscles and allows the Digestive biscuit chewiness to linger on the oils; f22 dry, slightly spiced tannin; b22 a whisky remarkable for its unremarkableness. The malts and vanillas appear in harmony but seem determined to do nothing particularly interesting. Instead, you can just suck contentedly on the biscuity big barley and let the light tannins bring up the rear. 46% 289 bottles

Kingsbury Sar Obair Mhain Baraille 40 Year Old hogshead, dist 1979, cask no. 57 **(95)** n23.5 t24 f23.5 b24 Age pours off this whisky like sweat from a long distance runner. And this really has come a long way over 40 years, impressively notching up more and more complexity as each year passes. Truly great whisky. 56.4% sc 173 bottles

Le Gus't Selection X Speyside Blended Malt 39 Years Old sherry cask, cask no. 4 **(94.5)** n23.5 t24 f23 b24 Truly Xcellent. 60.4%. sc. 109 bottles.

Le Gus't Selection XI Speyside Blended Malt hogshead, cask no. 403 **(91)** n22.5 t23 f22.5 b23 Appears to have good age to this and a little bit of class. 49.7%. sc. 262 bottles.

MacNair's Lum Reek 12 Years Old (89) n22 t22.5 f22 b22.5 Interesting chimneys they have in this part of Scotland, which appears to reek marzipan and apple blossom where you might expect, coal, peat or wood...! 46%. *The GlenAllachie Distillers Company.*

MacNair's Lum Reek 21 Years Old (91) n22.5 t23 f22.5 b23 A wild malt tamed it seems to me and certainly not lacking in personality 48%. *The GlenAllachie Distillers Company.*

MacNair's Lum Reek Peated (88.5) n22 t22 f22 b22.5 Has the consistency of a nail file wrapped in velvet. Enough edges to this to draw blood. But the modest smoke soothes and kisses better. The salivating maltiness is another surprise. Not quite like any other vatted malt I have before encountered. And have to admit: I kind of begrudgingly like it, though McNair's appear to always include a malt that can pick a fight with itself in a 5cl miniature...! 46%. *The GlenAllachie Distillers Company.*

Matisse 12 Year Old Blended Malt (93) n23.5 t23 f22.5 b23. Succulent, clean-as-a-whistle mixture of malts with zero bitterness and not even a whisper of an off note: easily the best form I have ever seen this brand in. Superb. 40%. *Matisse Spirits Co Ltd.*

Mo'land (82) n21 t22 f19 b20. Extra malty but lumbering and on the bitter side. 40%.

Monkey Shoulder batch 27 **(79.5)** n21 t21.5 f18 b19. Been a while since I lasted tasted this one. Though its claims to be Batch 27, I assume all bottlings are Batch 27 seeing as they are from 27 casks. This one, whichever it is, has a distinctive fault found especially at the finale, which is disappointing. Even before hitting that point a big toffeed personality makes for a pleasant if limited experience. 40%. *William Grant & Sons.*

Morrison Mac-Talla Islay Single Malt Terra Classic Islay bott code 21/081 db **(93.5)** n23.5 so much grist sweetening the already lightly lemony air. The smoke hangs evenly around in thick, oily clouds; t23.5 finds its stride immediately. Both the melting castor sugars and the phenols seem to simply melt together. From nowhere a sudden eruption of drier phenols and spices... but soon all is peaceful again...; f23 the vanillas are late, but arrive And with them comes the warming spices. The oils make for a long finale; b23.5 those with a bent for exceptionally clean, gently oiled Caol Ila-style Islays will be thrilled with this one. It is not just the Terra – the land and

Scottish Malts

surroundings – which maketh the malt. So, too, does the cask. And this is exceptional and entirely blemish-free. A treat of a dram. *46% nc ncf*

Old Perth Blended Malt 23 Years Old dist 1994, bott code: 18/182 **(95) n24 t23.5 f23.5 b24** Creakier than a haunted mansion. But full of much more welcoming spirits. This shows its oaky age with the same pride a veteran might display his war wounds. Not even a hint of a single off note: amazing! *44.9%. nc ncf.*

Old Perth Cask Strength Matured in Sherry Casks bott code 21/085 **(92.5) n23.5** wonderful raspberry jam and grape jelly mixed and spread on lightly buttered toast and a plethora of shy spices, make for a stunning starting point. When the vanilla pods make themselves heard, we are really heading into top territory; **t23.5** a delivery to die for: the mouthfeel is the epitome of sensuality while the slow evolving of varied strands of fruit of differing intensity, sweetness and sharpness is spellbinding; **f22.5** drier here as the vanillas and barley at last have their say and fruit falls away; **b23** how rare to find a 100% sherry cask vatted malt as pure as the driven Highland snow. No great age, but old enough to reveal desired complexity. Hats off to Morrison's. Old-school distillers and blenders producing old-school Scotch. And that is something we could do with a lot more of... *58.6% nc ncf*

Old St. Andrews Aged 10 Years Twilight batch no. L3017 G2716 **(91) n22 t23.5 f22.5 b23** Takes a different course from the previous batch, eschewing the sharper tones for a more rumbling, deeper and earthier character. Very much above par. *40%.*

Old St. Andrews Aged 12 Years Fireside batch no. L2927 G2716 **(93) n23 t23 f23.5 b23.5** Returns to its usual high quality brand which usually makes the cut. *40%.*

Old St. Andrews Aged 15 Years Nightcap batch no. L2976 G2716 **(86) n22 t21.5 f21 b21.5** Well, this certainly is a nightcap: I fell asleep waiting for something to happen. Pleasant honey at times and chewy toffee but a bit short on the charisma front. *40%.*

Perfect Fifth Two Sisters Blended Malt cask no 4563 ex-bourbon hogshead filled 1 Nov 1989 bott 19 Feb 2021 **(93) n23 t23.5 f23 b24** Fuultless Speyside malt here from Balvenie but spoon-fed with a drop of a sister Grants single malt. This is just about the perfect pre-prandial dram, being long and salivating and teasing your tastebuds into a state of expectation. Such a charmer! *49.2%*

Poit Dhubh 8 Bliadhna (90) n22.5 t23.5 f21.5 b22.5. Though the smoke which marked this vatting has vanished, it has more than compensated with a complex beefing up of the core barley tones. Cracking whisky. *43%. ncf. Pràban na Linne.*

Poit Dhubh 12 Bliadhna (77) n20 t20 f18 b19. Toffee-apples. Without the apples. *43%. ncf. Pràban na Linne.*

Poit Dhubh 21 Bliadhna (86) n22 t22.5 f21 b20.5. Over generous toffee has robbed us of what would have been a very classy malt. *43%. ncf. Pràban na Linne.*

Royal Salute 21 Year Old Blended Malt (88.5) n23 t22 f21.5 b22 Malt and caramel-themed throughout. *40%.*

Shackleton Blended Malt bott code: L8123 11:52 P/004904 **(85.5) n22.5 t22 f20 b21** An old-fashioned dusting of smoke plus a layering of Demerara ensures a certain gravitas is maintained through this vatted malt, starting at the come-to-me nose and continuing throughout the broad body on the palate. Falls away at the end, though, when too much bitterness sneaks in. *40%.*

◈ **Shackleton**, bott code L2356 **(93.5) n23.5** an outstanding nose, not least because of the marriage between butterscotch and lemon blossom honey which gives a gravitas to the sweetness. Phenols are of the now you see it, now you don't variety...all adding to the teasing complexity; **t23.5** the only time the Murray Method works in favour with an intense amalgam of spiced sweet malts bristling with tannin and full-on oils. At lower temperatures there is a crisp barley sugar punch to this, the spices more aloof and oils move in later with a balanced measure of oak and barley; **f23** long (do I hear the siren call of murky Fettercairn at the death?) with the sugars still battling with the drier tannins. Excellence depth to the fade, either way...; **b23.5** Scottish vatted (or Blended) Malt is an area which often underwhelms. Here though I may well have discovered an award-winner for this year. This has moved on apace and is some distance from the first bottlings. A whisky which doesn't aways benefit from the Murray Method, it is arguably at its best at cool room temperature (Shackleton would have approved!) as the intricate malts are then seen at their sparkling best with other aspects muted. *40%*

Shetland Reel Finished in Shetland Blended Malt Whisky ex-sherry casks, bott code: 248/19 **(79) n20 t20 f19 b20** Tight, dry and doesn't sit very prettily... *47%.*

Son of a Peat batch no. 01 **(91) n23.5 t23 f22 b23** Peaty, but not just for peat's sake... *48.3%. nc ncf. Flaviar.*

Valour Speyside Blended Malt Aged 27 Years sherry butt, dist Jan 1994, bott Mar 2021 **(95.5) n24 t24 f23.5 b24** This is brilliantly distilled whisky that has spent 27 years in an unspoiled, top-end sherry butt. The fact that it was distilled on the same date, comes in one cask and yet still is a blended malt should put the Whisky Sherlock Holmes out there on the trail of what this whisky

222

actually is. Single malt or blend, from sherry cask and from 1994...well, it just doesn't come any better.... It will take one hell of a whisky to see this off as Vatted malt of the year. A glorious whisky to hunt down and savour... not least because you are slipping back in style and quality to 25-30 years old sherry cask whiskies found 30 years ago. 55.2% nc 628 bottles

◈ **Valour Whisky 30 Years Old Blended Whisky Cask 9 (89.5) n23 t23 f21.5 b22** A whisky truly on its metal. An extremely curious degree of copper gives this a late sharpness, as though one of the distilleries involved here had either just had a new still fitted or had major repair work done to an existing one. Irrespective of that, there is a major malt (indeed, the grain is conspicuous by its absence) and toffee tang to this, though the later bitterness from the oak are an unwanted distraction. 50.8% 570 bottles

◈ **Valour Whisky 30 Years Old Blended Whisky Cask 10 (92) n23.5 t23 f22.5 b23** Don't know about 30 years old. The aroma takes me back nearer 60 years to butterscotch tart at Cotswold Road Primary School in Belmont, Surrey. Both the butterscotch and malt are monumental on the nose and is in keeping with a whisky that has glided past three decades without breaking sweat. The aging process has come naturally, with little drama as the oak makes its inevitable intervention. Indeed, the dovetailing of the chalkier tannins and the firm, slightly metallic but pleasingly honeyed malt. This has successfully avoided the bitterness found on Number 9 and shews far more at a vatted style malt than a traditional malt and grain blend, the effects of the grain being quite invisible... 51% 580 bottles

Water Proof batch no. 001 **(86) n21.5 t22.5 f20.5 b21.5** A toffee and raisin style malt which certainly hits a crescendo with the caramel and the sugars have a distinctively grapey quality. But, as pleasant as it is, it is just a little too one-paced and single threaded in style. Also a slight niggle on the finish which matches the bright yellow label... 45.8%. Macduff International.

Wemyss Malts Family Collection Flaming Feast Blended Malt batch no. 2018/04 **(87) n21.5 t23 f21 b21.5** Pleasant enough. Juicy in part, malty and spicy. But from the mid-point onwards, just too flaming dull. 46%. nc ncf. 6,000 bottles.

Wemyss Malts The Hive Blended Malt Whisky batch no. 002 **(91.5) n23 t23.5 f22 b23** A malt greatly bolstered by the upping of the strength since its last bottling, which makes the honey positively buzz... 55.5%. ncf. 9,000 bottles.

Wemyss Malts Nectar Grove Blended Malt Madeira wine cask finished, batch no. 001 **(95) n23 t24.5 f23.5 b24** Just blown away by this. Nectar, indeed...! 54%. nc ncf.

Wemyss Malts Spice King Blended Malt batch no. 002 **(89) n21.5t23 f22 b22.5** I remember last time out with this vatted malt I felt a little swizzed by the lack of spice. No such complaints this time: a real rip-roaring malt! 58%. ncf. 9,000 bottles.

Wemyss Malts Velvet Fig Aged 25 Years Blended Malt sherry casks **(87) n22.5 t22.5 f21 b21** No off notes. Sadly, just one of those occasions when the casks married together here have not gelled quite as one might have hoped. Attractively soft delivery and for a few moments the fruit apparent has a genuinely complex moment or two. But then it falls apart slightly as various strands fail to tie or simply find dead ends. I do love the mouthfeel on delivery, though. 42.3%. nc ncf. 5,000 bottles.

SCOTTISH RYE
ARBIKIE

Highlands, 2013. Working.

Arbikie Highland Rye Aged 4 Years Cask Selection Single Grain Scotch charred American oak, Armagnac barrels, cask nos. 3, 5, 13 & 14, dist 2015 db **(89) n21.5 t23.5 f21.5 b22.5** A massive lurch upwards in character and quality from their initial bottling, this time the grain is given a platform to perform and entertain. And doesn't it take the opportunity with both hands! A dense rye, still slightly thick from the wide cut. But the sugars are profound and delicious. So much personality – and still room for improvement as their experience increases. Exciting times! 46%. nc ncf. 1,220 bottles.

Arbikie Highland Rye 1794 Edition Single Grain Scotch new charred American oak db **(88) n21** a really hefty tobacco note on this from that ultra-generous cut should destroy any hope of a comeback. But the rye is in there in firm, sweet and determined mood; **t22.5** there you go! The intensity of the rye is borderline brutal....and just so beautiful. For a moment those feints attack with gusto. But such is the crispness and classic lines of the pitch-perfect rye, the grain wins in the most impressively salivating manner...; **f22.5** long, with the oils nibbling away. But a wonderful chocolate-toffee note determined to dominate; **b22** now here is a whisky which probably doesn't benefit from the Murray Method, which kicks up more of the heftier feints on show. This is best served at room temperature where the rye retains a charming crispness which salivates the taste buds as a truly great rye should. You know, had the cut been better than this, this would have been one of the top ryes I had tasted this year. This is so close to being a little bit special. Talk about the Beauty and the Beast... 48%.

Scottish Grain

It's a bit weird, really. Many whisky lovers stay clear of blended Scotch, preferring instead single malts. The reason, I am often told, is that the grain included in a blend makes it rough and ready. Yet I wish I had a twenty pound note for each time I have been told in recent years how much someone enjoys a single grain. The ones that the connoisseurs die for are the older versions, usually special independent bottlings displaying great age and more often than not brandishing a lavish Canadian or bourbon style.

Like single malts, grain distilleries produce whisky bearing their own style and signature. And, also, some display characteristics and a richness that can surprise and delight. Most of the grains available in (usually specialist) whisky outlets are pretty elderly. Being made from either maize or wheat helps give them either that Canadian or, depending on the freshness of the cask, an unmistakable bourbony style. So older grains display far greater body than is anticipated.

That was certainly underlined in most beautiful and emphatic style by last year's Scotch Grain Whisky of the Year. The Last Drop Dumbarton 1977 had all that you should demand from a magnificent grain and more.

The fact that it was from Dumbarton was significant. For years, right up until its tragic and unnecessary closure in 2002, this distillery made the core grain for the Ballantine's blends and it was, following the closure of Cambus, without question the producer of the highest quality grain in Scotland. I had worked with it many times in the blending lab and it was as though I had the finest marble to sculpt from.

Dumbarton and Cambus have long been my two favourite grain distilleries, not least because both are thick with character. So no great surprise, then, that the Jim Murray Whisky Bible 2021 Single Grain of the Year was from Cambus.

And so it was again for 2023. In 2021 it was Perfect Fifth who came up with the goods, this time Chapter 7. This year there have been noticably fewer Single Grains bottled, probably because of the extraordinary prices these are now fetching in the market place. Often bottlers would rather spend the cash on a malt. Sometimes, though, they are overlooking untold quality. Thankfully, the ever-impressive Valour didn't.

Jim Murray's Whisky Bible Scottish Grain of the Year Winners	
2008	Duncan Taylor Port Dundas 1973
2009	The Clan Denny Dumbarton Aged 43 Years
2010	Duncan Taylor North British 1978
2011	The Clan Denny Dumbarton Aged 40 Years
2012	The Clan Denny Cambus 47 Years Old
2013	SMWS G5.3 Aged 18 Years (Invergordon)
2014	The Clan Denny Dumbarton 48 Years Old
2015	The Sovereign Single Cask Port Dundas 1978
2016	The Clan Deny Cambus 25 Years Old
2017	Whiskyjace Invergordon 24 Year Old
2018	Cambus Aged 40 Years
2019	Berry Bros & Rudd Cambus 26 Years Old
2020	The Last Drop Dumbarton 1977
2021	The Perfect Fifth Cambus 1979
2022	Whisky-Fässle Invergordon 44 Year Old
2023	Chapter 7 Cambus 1998
2024	Valour 35 Years Old

Single Grain Scotch

CALEDONIAN Lowland, 1885. Diageo. Demolished.

The Cally 40 Year Old refill American oak hogsheads, dist 1974 db **(88.5) n23.5 t23 f20 b22** This poor old sod is tiring before your nose and taste buds. But it hangs on grimly to give the best show it can. Quite touching, really..we are witnessing first hand the slow death of a once great distillery. *53.3%. 5,060 bottles. Diageo Special Releases 2015.*

The Sovereign Caledonian 35 Years Old refill hogshead, cask no. 14271, dist Feb 82, bott Oct 17 **(87) n22 t22 f21 b22** Caledonian MacBrayn? Caledonian Canal? Caledonian Sea? Amazingly salty and coastal, more so than any grain I have encountered before. Has its unique and oddly delicious charm,but runs out of legs well before the finale. *46.9%. nc ncf sc. 154 bottles.*

CAMBUS Lowland, 1836. Diageo. Closed.

Cambus Aged 40 Years dist 1975 db **(97) n24.5 t24 f23.5 b25** I chose this as my 600th whisky for Bible 2018: a tragically lost distillery capable of making the finest whisky you might expect to find at 40 years of age. And my hunch was correct: this is flawless. *52.7%. 1,812 bottles. Diageo Special Releases 2016.*

Chapter 7 Cambus 1998 (92) n24 t23 f22.5 b22.5 There is something almost noble about that nose. Though soft and yielding it also stands erect and proud. The custard tart sweetness isn't something normally associated with nobility, admittedly. But so pure is it, so unwavering are those notes, it leaves you captivated. The delivery likewise fills the palate with a rich, dessert-like sweetness, with a little citrus ensuring a non-spiced bite. The mid-ground and finish never quite hit the complexity levels hoped for, despite the best prodding by the light spice, though that is more the failing of the cask than the spirit, one suspects. *47.6%*

Berry Bros & Rudd Cambus 26 Years Old cask no. 61972, dist 1991, bott 2018 **(96.5) n24 t24 f24 b24.5** Few whiskies this year have displayed so many beguiling twists and turns: a true gem of a grain, though always a bit of a rum do. I can imagine my dear friend of nearly three decades, Doug McIvor, leaping from his seat when he unearthed this sample....something as rare as any kind of satisfying Charlton Athletic experience... *55.1%. nc ncf sc.*

The Cooper's Choice Cambus 1991 refill sherry butt, cask no. 61982, bott 2018 **(90) n23.5 t24 f20.5 b22** A very good whisky from the Swedish Whisky Fed which will probably make it to the quarter finals of any whisky competition – and then lose to an English malt... *58.5%. sc. Bottled for the Swedish Whisky Federation.*

The Perfect Fifth Cambus 1976 cask no. 05916, dist 27 Oct 76 **(93) n23.5 t24 f22 b23.5** An impressive example of the what then was arguably the finest grain distillery in Scotland. The structure is sound and the Canadian style of whisky is exactly what should be expected of a fine corn Cambus of this age. There is a slightly nagging bitterness caused by the tiring oak, but the inherent sweetness controls this well. The sugar-spice balance is pretty near perfection. Has the odd fault, but the complexity of the sweet riches outweigh those slightly bitter failings. *57.6%. sc.*

The Perfect Fifth Cambus 1979 cask no. 900003 **(96.5) n23.5** just classic. The corn oils and ulmo honey are in a love clinch...; **t24.5** now I'm in one...with the glass...! The ulmo honey spreads around your palate like your lover on a rug before a log fire... And now the oak is gorgeously embedded into the corn. So the mouthfeel gains an equal role to the flavours...and they are luxurious and delicate in the extreme. A fragile blend of acacia and heather honey on one higher pitch, ulmo honey on a deeper, and here even with a light coconut touch...; **f24** no bitter notes, which so often happens at this age and after so much honey on display. Just a slow sunset of corn oils, still the ulmo honey and now a wonderful but measured degree of pattering spice...; **b24.5** given the right cask and the right time, Cambus is as good as anything distilled in Scotland. Here we see it in sublime form: no major faults from the cask...and certainly not the distillate. How many varying forms and densities of sweetness can you find on one whisky? Well here's your chance to find out...get counting...! *53.2%. nc ncf sc.*

Sansibar Whisky Cambus 1991 bott 2019 **(88) n22** almost rum-like with sweet estery qualities; **t23** incredibly sweet delivery, but spices arrive early to harmonise. No shortage of golden syrup; **f21** bitters out as the cask gives way...; **b22** a rather weak bourbon cask has done this no favours. Some superb moments. *47.7%.*

The Sovereign Cambus 29 Years Old refill hogshead, cask no. 15010, dist Sept 88, bott Apr 18 **(86) n22 t22.5 f20.5 b21** Lots of fat and bubble gum at play here. Some superb moments on the corn, but never feels entirely at ease with itself, thanks to some stuttering oak. *45.6%. nc ncf sc. 299 bottles.*

The Sovereign Cambus 30 Years Old refill hogshead, cask no. 14857, dist 1988 **(94) n23.5 t24 f23 b23.5** A good hundred years ago, this grain was bottled and marketed as an equal to a single malt. If the distillery was still alive today a similar campaign would not bring in many complaints. A beauty! *45.2%. nc ncf sc. 313 bottles. Exclusive to The Whisky Barrel.*

The Whisky Cask Company Cambus 27 Years Old bourbon barrel, cask no. 286, dist 24 Sept 91, bott 29 Nov 18 **(95.5) n24 t24 f23.5 b24** ridiculously beautiful. *57.6%. sc. 286 bottles.*

CAMERONBRIDGE Lowland, 1824. Diageo. Working.

Artful Dodger Cameronbridge 35 Year Old bourbon barrel **(94.5) n23.5 t24 f23 b24** Soft and succulent all the way, this is a masterclass in how to ramp up the natural caramels without losing shape or interest. Light traces of ulmo honey also generate controlled sweetness but it is what feels like corn oil that makes a huge difference, stretching the narrative further than originally seemed possible and allowing the delicate spices and sweeter vanillas plenty of room and time interact. Burnt fudge towards the finish underscores the age. Ridiculously charming. *52.2%.*

Liquid Treasures From Miles Away Cameronbridge 38 Year Old bourbon barrel, dist Feb 82, bott Feb 20 **(94.5) n23.5 t23.5 f23.5 b24** Textbook grain whisky seemingly made from corn as there is a Canadian-style corn oil and vanilla richness to this which really extracts the last nuance out from the syrupy sugars. Lush, lengthy and benefitting from a sublime bourbon barrel which ensures a perfect measure of sugars adds to the depth. When these older Cameronbridges are on form they are really something to behold. And this is a faultless stunner. *48.6%. sc. 140 bottles.*

Old Particular Cameronbridge 26 Years Old refill hogshead, cask no. 12233, dist Oct 91, bott Dec 17 **(93) n23 t23.5 f23 b23.5** A Scotch that wanted to be a bourbon when it grew up... *51.5%. nc ncf sc. 569 bottles.*

The Sovereign Cameronbridge 26 Years Old refill butt, cask no. 14752, dist Oct 91, bott Feb 18 **(79) n19 t22 f18 b20** Sweet and fruity but curiously tight on the nose and finish. *56.9%. nc ncf sc. 481 bottles.*

The Whisky Barrel Originals Cameronbridge 37 Years Old refill bourbon barrel, cask no. TWB1005, dist Feb 82, bott 2019 **(86.5) n22 t23.5 f20 b21** As you'd expect from a C'Bridge of this vintage, there is plenty to involve your taste buds and enjoy. But, equally, there is a little frustration of the dustiness on the nose and emaciated body towards the finish – something not normally expected. That essentially leaves the delivery and follow through to enjoy – and it doesn't let you down, the ulmo honey and spices forming a delightful partnership and not without a Canadian feel. The remainder disappoints. *51%. sc. 164 bottles.*

World of Orchids Cameron Brig 1991 26 Years Old bourbon cask, cask no. 031 **(94.5) n23.5 t23.5 f23.5 b24** Truly faultless. Cameron Bridge must have had a hell of a bee invasion back in 1991...! *56.4%. sc.*

CARSEBRIDGE Lowland, 1799. Diageo. Demolished.

The Sovereign Carsebridge 44 Years Old refill hogshead, cask no. 14189, dist May 87, bott Sept 17 **(90) n22.5 t23 f22 b22.5** Very attractive, but about as sweet as you'd like a whisky to go. *50.9%. nc ncf sc. 150 bottles. The Whisky Barrel 10th Anniversary bottling #7.*

DUMBARTON Lowland, 1938. Pernod Ricard. Demolished.

Fadandel.dk Dumbarton 30 Years Old cask no. 25241, dist 18 Mar 87, bott 27 Mar 17 **(86) n22 t22.5 f20 b21.5** A clumsy grain festooned with honey and spice, but little ability to bring them happily together. Delicious early on but bitters out as the oak finally cracks. *57.2%. sc. 168 bottles.*

The Last Drop Dumbarton 1977 cask no. 140000004 **(97) n24.5 t24.5 f23.5 b24.5** Last Drop have been and done it again. They've only gone and found a near faultless barrel from what was once, before it was needlessly destroyed, a near faultless grain distillery. Nothing unusual you'd say, except that this spent 42 years in oak, giving it plenty of time to go wrong. Nothing did, so you have a pristine example of a grain distilled in the year I returned to the UK having hitch-hiked through Africa. And in my flat in Melton Mowbray, which also housed my Press Agency, would always sit a bottle of Chivas Regal...a very different, lighter and more delicate blend than you see today. And this barrel, most likely, was filled to be added to another bottling of Chivas, 12 years on. Instead, it remained in a warehouse seeking perfection...and as near as damn it finding it. *48.7%. sc.*

Scotch Malt Whisky Society Cask G14.5 31 Year Old 2nd fill ex-bourbon barrel, dist 1 Oct 86 **(96) n24 t24 f23.5 b24.5** The confident solidity of this grain stands out like Dumbarton Rock... one of the great whiskies of the year, anywhere in the world. *50.6%. sc.*

Single Cask Collection Dumbarton 30 Years Old bourbon barrel **(96) n24 t24.5 f23.5 b24** Taste a whisky like this and you'll fully understand why I regard the destruction of this distillery as one of the greatest criminal acts ever perpetrated against the Scotch whisky industry by the Scotch whisky industry. *52.1%. sc.*

The Sovereign Dumbarton 30 Years Old refill barrel, cask no. 14247, dist Mar 87, bott Sept 17 **(92) n23 t23.5 f22.5 b23** Beautiful stuff and those who appreciate Canadian will particularly benefit. But a little tiredness to the oak reminds you of its great age. *55.3%. nc ncf sc. 160 bottles. The Whisky Barrel 10th Anniversary bottling #6.*

The Sovereign Dumbarton 30 Years Old refill barrel, cask no. 14327, dist Mar 87, bott Oct 17 **(94) n23.5 t24 f23 b23.5** Practically a re-run of the Single Cask Dumbarton 30, except not all the dots on the sugars are joined. That said, still a whisky work of art. *50.2%. nc ncf sc. 135 bottles.*

The Sovereign Dumbarton 31 Years Old refill hogshead, cask no. 15477, dist 1987 **(92) n22.5** a light lavender note introduces a bourbon weightiness; **t23.5** ah....the trademark stiff spine delivery. Rock hard sugars are surrounded by more forgiving corn notes. A slight oiliness to fill the mouth, but the spice-sugar battle is the main attraction through to the finish...; **f23** ....and more of the same...! **b23** Dumbarton's style stood alone among Scotland's grain distilleries: its idiosyncratic style is in full spate here. *50.5%. nc ncf sc. 207 bottles. Exclusive to The Whisky Barrel.*

The Sovereign Dumbarton 31 Years Old bourbon barrel, cask no. 15801, dist Mar 87, bott Feb 19 **(86.5) n22 t22.5 f20.5 b21.5** Unusually grassy and fresh for a Dumbarton. The firmness arrives later than normal, though with it an unfortunate bitterness from the cask. *43.5%. nc ncf sc. 186 bottles.*

The Whisky Barrel Dumbarton 30 Year Old barrel, cask no. 13436, dist 1987 **(96.5) n24 t24.5 f24 b24** Dumbarton at anything from 21to 30 is about as good as grain whisky gets (hence why Ballantine's can be sensational), providing it has lived in the right cask. And this is the right cask...*56.7%. sc. 197 bottles.*

GARNHEATH Lowland, 1964. Inver House Distillers. Demolished.

The Cooper's Choice Garnheath 48 Year Old dist 1967, bott 2016 **(96) n24 t24 f24 b24** It is an honour to experience a whisky both so rare and gorgeous. Perhaps not the most complex, but what it does do is carried out close to perfection. A must find grain. *41.5%. nc ncf sc.*

GIRVAN Lowland, 1963. William Grant & Sons. Working.

The Girvan Patent Still Over 25 Years Old db **(84.5) n21.5 t21.5 f20.5 b21.** A pretty accurate representation of the character these stills were sometimes quietly known for at this time, complete with some trademark sulphury notes – presumably from the still, not cask, as I do pick up some balancing American white oak character. *42%. nc.*

The Girvan Patent Still No. 4 Apps db **(87) n21.5 t22 f21.5 b22.** A first look at probably the lightest of all Scotland grain whiskies. A little cream soda sweetens a soft, rather sweet, but spineless affair. The vanillas get a good, unmolested outing too. *42% WB15/369*

Berry Bros & Rudd Girvan 12 Years Old cask no. 532388/9, dist 2006, bott 2018 **(94) n23 t24 f23 b24** If you wondered why Grant's blends have been so good for so many years, then try out this straight down the line example of their 12-year-old grain. If I were asked in a tasting to describe what I should expect from this distillery at this age, then really this bottling has completely nutshelled it! This is when average equals excellence. *46%. nc ncf sc.*

Chapter 7 Girvan 1991 Aged 30 Years bourbon barrels, barrels nos 54689 & 54969 **(93) n23** the grain and oaky vanilla make for a lush partnership. A little golden syrup makes it friendlier still; **t23.5** unsurprisingly, a honey tone makes the first move – both in terms of texture and flavour. This is a heather- and ulmo honey mix, supplemented by a light build of warming spice. Slowly the oils from the grain get a foothold, and with it comes the layered vanilla; **f23** a little bitterness tries to make a case, but those honey notes are in no mood to give way; **b23.5** slick and sweet, this is Girvan in overdrive. Few whiskies enter their fourth decade with so many sugars still in pristine nick: this could almost do as a dessert whisky.... Delicious. And remarkable. *49.6%*

Fadandel.dk Girvan 13 Year Old barrel, cask no. 532404, dist 11 Jul 06, bott 30 Aug 19 **(86.5) n22.5 t23 f20 b21** Characteristic fatness surrounded by friendly sugars and marzipan makes for a delicious nose and opening. Sexy spices, too. But not the best finish I've seen from this distillery, being a tad bitter and generally askew. *61.2%. sc. 203 bottles.*

The First Editions Girvan Aged 38 Years refill hogshead, cask no. 14749, bott 2018 **(95) n23.5 t24 f23.5 b24** Wears its age and gravity lightly: this is wonderful grain whisky. *50.3%. nc ncf sc. 302 bottles.*

The Great Drams Girvan 11 Years Old cask no. 300609, dist 27 Jun 07, bott 27 Feb19 **(91.5) n22.5 t23.5 f22.5 b23** Any softer or more shy and this grain would barely escape from your glass. But with some cajoling you end up with a very accurate representation of this distillery for its age. *46.2%. nc ncf sc.*

Lady of the Glen Girvan 1991 cask no. 54459 **(89.5) n22.5 t23 f22 b22.5** Though seemingly soft and yielding, the sturdy subplot maximises the otherwise limited oak influence. Good spice prickle while late sugars are able to counter the encroaching bitterness. *43.2%. sc.*

Liquid Treasures Entomology Girvan Over 28 Years Old ex-bourbon barrel, dist 1989, bott 2018 **(86.5) n23 t22 f20.5 b21** A typical pea-souper of a Girvan, thick on the nose with sugary promise and no shortage of oak-encouraged vanilla depth then eye-smartingly sweet delivery with golden syrup mixing in with the oils. A warming sub plot as the spices build but a little disappointing as the oak gives way to bitterness. *52.7%.*

Old Particular Girvan 27 Years Old refill hogshead, cask no. 12191, dist Dec 89, bott Nov 17 **(91)** n24 t22.5 f22 b22.5 It's all about the amazing nose, yesiree...! *51.5%. nc ncf sc. 148 bottles.*

Scyfion Choice Girvan 2006 Islay whisky cask finished, bott 2018 **(92)** n23 t23.5 f22.5 b23.5 An intriguing concept brilliantly executed! *46%. nc ncf sc. 90 bottles.*

William & Co Spirits Girvan Aged 13 Years cask no. 2127889, dist 22 Jun 20 **(79)** n20 t20 f19 b20 The fate of many grain whiskies over the last 15-20 years is that they have been stored in old sherry butts treated in sulphur from the days when there was little restraint on those accursed candles. It is the sad reason the overall standard of blended scotch has dipped notably. Here we have a Girvan whose charms are lost by an elementary mistake all those years ago, save an attractive sultana/marzipan undercurrent. The good news is that there are those, especially in central Europe, who will want to buy this by the case-load, reading the sulphur for smoke. It is all up to the individual's DNA. *53%. 69 Bottles. Bottled for the 2nd Anniversary of Juyin Café.*

INVERGORDON Highland, 1959. Emperador Distillers Inc. Working.

Cave Aquila A Knight's Dram Invergordon 44 Years Old cask no. 20, dist Dec 72, bott Mar 17 **(95)** n24 t24 f23.5 b23.5 You almost want to give the spices a standing ovation... *46.7%. sc.*

The Cooper's Choice Invergordon 1974 43 Years Old (91) n24 t23 f21.5 b22.5 If the delivery and finish can't quite live up to the nose, that is hardly surprising. This is the aroma of all talents, offering a small grain bourbon type leathery sweetness together with a more genteel vanilla-clad Canadian of high quality. The immediate delivery has a good stab at matching that, and at first succeeds, especially with the depth of the maple syrup and honeycomb. But it understandably fades, then tires late on as the bitterness evolves. *46.5%. nc ncf sc.*

Fadandel Invergordon 15 Years Old (91.5) n22.5 a very light touch of olive amid the almost Canadian-style vanilla sweetness; t23 game from the start, there is salty sharpness closer to malt than grain. A cascade of molten white sugars before the gentle tannins arrive; f23 lingering chocolate wafer; b23 not the most complex of grains. But a whisky that makes the most of its energy and freshness. Charming. *62.7%.*

The Finest Malts City Landmarks Invergordon Aged 46 Years bourbon barrel, cask no. 32, dist 1972, bott 2018 **(93.5)** n23.5 gentle vanilla and corn oil. Uncomplicated but very alluring and effective...; t23.5 simplistic white sugars dissolve on impact forming a juicy frame in which gentle layers of vanilla form and intertwine. Plenty of natural caramels; f23 Curiously for a grain, there is almost a profound maltiness to this; a very slight bitterness of the oak, but nothing drastic; b23.5 time appears to be lost on this one. No great bowing and scraping to the oak. Good age is apparent, but only if you really think about it...Such elegance. *49.9%. nc ncf sc.*

MacAlabur Invergordon 28 Year Old hogshead, cask no.77737, dist Jul 1991, bott Nov 2019 **(91.5)** n23.5 Invergordon at its most relaxed: allows the lightly sweetened vanilla a free hand. Curiously spiceless and docile; t23 excellent vanillas coat the palate, even offering a degree of ever-ripe banana. Perhaps even a little moist marzipan, too; f22 very slightly overdoes the bitterness as the oak gives way slightly. A little demerara sugar helps compensate, as do the oils; b23 buckles a little late on under the strain of age. But the nose and delivery are absolutely top notch. *570% 220 bottles*

Single & Single Invergordon 1974 45 Years Old (94.5) n23 t23.5 f24 b24 Just how you want an old grain to be. Still full of life after all these years... *46.6%. sc. 156 bottles.*

Single Cask Collection Invergordon 26 Years Old rum barrel finish **(87)** n22 t22.5 f21 b21.5 Soft and sweet in the time-honoured Invergordon tradition. But with this amount of sugar at work, it needs to breathe and evolve. Rum casks have a tendency to clip a whisky's wings so, though a very decent and soothing grain, the fun comes to a slightly premature and bitter end. *574%. sc.*

The Sovereign Invergordon Aged 25 Years refill barrel, cask no. 18167, dist May 1995, bott Mar 2021 **(92.5)** n23 just wonderful when a whisky shews not just very good age but a lemon sherbet fizz to underline that this grain is still green and blossoming; t23 a beautiful, if simplistic, mix of salivating lime-blossom honey and sturdy vanilla; f23 a little cocoa powder envelops any lingering sweetness; b23.5 a beautiful cask at work has ensured a charming evenness. Delightful. *42.0%. nc ncf sc. 63 bottles.*

The Sovereign Invergordon 30 Years Old refill hogshead, cask no. 15012, dist May 87, bott Apr 18 **(88)** n23 t23 f20.5 b21.5 Promises so much, but the oak can't quite match the deal. *51.6%. nc ncf sc. 314 bottles.*

Whisky-Fässle Invergordon 44 Year Old bourbon barrel, dist 1972, bott 2017 **(95.5)** n24.5 where scotch meets Kentucky: the influence of the oak married to the corn offers a distinctive soft bourbon burr with matching delicate spice. But we are talking very well-aged bourbon here where the heather honey has made its mark and the lightest liquorice add colour. A ten minute nose minimum....no, make that 15...Unquestionably one of the greatest noses I'll encounter this year; **t24** this, as the nose promises, melts on the tongue allowing the slow dispersal of honey and praline. Strands of red liquorice act as a further bind as the sugars and tannins dovetail gloriously, the spices pricking and soothing, pricking and soothing again; **f23** dries and rumbles its spices more quietly as the praline divests itself of its sugars and nuts but retains the cocoas; **b24** a potential grain of the year for sure. A faultless cask offering a bourbon style grain...but a bourbon that cannot presently be offered from Kentucky. Because at the moment no 44-year-old bourbon has matured this slowly to allow the very softest of integrations. It doesn't just nose and taste brilliantly, but the entire feel is something that has to be experienced. Truly great whisky that would be admired both sides of the pond. 46.9% nc ncf

LOCH LOMOND Highland, 1966. Loch Lomond Group. Working.

Loch Lomond Single Grain db **(93) n23** crisp sugars are willing to absorb the vanilla; **t23.5** indeed, the sugars on the nose are indicative of a sweet grain, for the delivery centres around the maple syrup lead. The oak is something like most anchors at work: barely visible to invisible; **f23** the oaks do have a say, though you have to wait a while on the long finale. A little spice arrives, too; **b23.5** elegant grain; keeps the sweetness controlled. 46%

Loch Lomond Single Grain Peated db **(91) n22** more like bonfire smoke, rather than peat. But smoky it is and with a real acidic nip to it, too...; **t23.5** surprisingly, the delivery isn't as soft and oily as their usual mouthfeel for LL Grain. This has a more clipped personality and that includes the Demerara sugars. But just love that flavour explosion shock waves in when the smoke and spices suddenly seem to wake to the fact they are there – and really let you know about it....! **f22.5** settles down a smoky rumble with a light vanilla and muscovado sugar accompaniment; **b23** different, intriguing...and beautifully weighted. Love it! 46%.

LOCHSIDE Highland, 1957. Pernod Ricard. Demolished.

The Cooper's Choice Lochside 44 Year Old dist 1964, bott 2015 **(92.5) n23.5** not unlike a bourbon-Canadian blend (yes, I have encountered such a thing) where a muscular coconut-honey candy theme dominates the subservient vanilla; **t24** salivating and soft, corn oils drift among the obliging sugars without a care in the world; you can hear the tannins knocking, but only the spices gain entry; **f22** back to a coconut toffee thread; bitters late on; **b23** it's hangs on in there, giving in to its age only in the final moments... 41.2%. nc ncf sc. The Vintage Malt Whisky Co.

NORTH BRITISH Lowland, 1885. Diageo & Edrington. Working.

Gordon & MacPhail Connoisseurs Choice North British Aged 28 Years first fill sherry puncheon, cask no. 73847, dist 23 Oct 90, bott 29 Nov 18 **(82.5) n21 t21.5 f21 b19** Huge grape, under which the distillery and grain vanishes entirely. Delicious as in part it may be, you might as well get a bottle of sherry. 61%. sc. 181 bottles.

The Sovereign North British 32 Years Old refill hogshead, cask no. 18166, dist 1988 **(95) n23.5** such a gorgeous buttery edge to this: reminds me of my old mum's bowl in which she used to make the cakes...and I would help myself to when she'd finished with it so I could dutifully lick it clean as any self-respecting 8-year-old lad would...; **t24** oh, good Lord! That is ridiculous. Near perfect weight on the corn oil, rendering this halfway between Canadian and Bourbon. Then such delicate layers of lime blossom honey, harmonising with the softest vanillas imaginable; **f23.5** just a slight bitterness off the cask, but gentle fruits compensate; **b24** North British at its very finest: this is faultless grain whisky. Amazingly, so gentle it is spice free... 51.1%. nc ncf sc. 199 bottles.

Single Cask Collection North British 28 Years Old cask no. 20013, dist 1991, bott 2019 **(92.5) n22.5** one of those brilliant noses that reminds you more of the actual warehouse than the spirit contained in the barrel. A little saltiness sharpens the nose buds...; **t23** mouth-filling with soft oils and a slight banana take on the vanilla. The spices are in fast, peppery and warmer than an irritated wife's ear lashing....; **f23.5** now the sugars take on a beautiful blend of ulmo and heather honey as the vanillas add depth and slightly dry proceedings; **b23.5** actually spilling over with flavour. "Neutral whisky"? Pull the other one. 50.1%. sc. 180 bottles.

The Whisky Gallery The Magician North British Aged 5 Years oak barrel, cask no. 291, dist 2006, bott 2019 **(94) n22.5 t24 f23.5 b24** Beautifully distilled and really well matured in a barrel which allows the grain to reveal its full character: with North British, that means a lot. Though young there is still marzipan on the nose and sublime heather honey on delivery. A little grassy, too, while the late spices are superb. Any blender would give his right arm to work with a grain of this quality in a 5-year-old blend. Indeed, good enough to mix in with some of your better non-sherried malts up to the age of about 15-year-old as you could create something very interesting with this chap, especially with that light oiliness which means a little of this goes a long way. 49%. sc. 242 bottles.

NORTH OF SCOTLAND Lowland, 1957. North of Scotland Distilling Co. Silent.

The Pearls of Scotland North of Scotland 1971 dist Dec 71, bott Apr 15 **(95.5) n25 t23.5 f23 b24** What a beautifully elegant old lady...and one with virtually no wrinkles... 43.6%

PORT DUNDAS Lowland, 1811. Diageo. Demolished.

The Cooper's Choice Port Dundas 1999 18 Years Old Marsala finish **(87) n21.5 t22.5 f21 b22** Pleasant enough, especially on delivery with the big grape and delicate spice interplay. But otherwise I don't get it. Grain whisky isn't full-bodied enough to react with wine casks and offer any serous complexity. And this is a lost distillery here being overwhelmed with its unique character is lost. That said, if you are looking simply for delicious, muscular spiced fruit, here's your dram! 53%. nc ncf sc.

The Sovereign Port Dundas Aged 31 Years refill hogshead, cask no. HL18165, dist Feb1990, bott Mar 2021 **(93) n23** superb density to this: not dissimilar to melted demerara sugar atop a bowl of porridge. The oak ensures an excellent tingle factor with the subtlest spice; **t23.5** immediately mouth-filling and soft, again with the oils on early duty. There is even room for an early juiciness. The vanillas open gently but with no little confidence and slowly soak up the sweeter elements; **f23** dries and spices as the age begins to shew its toasty credentials; **b23.5** pretty much spot on Port Dundas. Not at its most complex, but wonderfully intact and coming through here at the creamier end of its normal spectrum. A chewy, three-course meal of a grain... 48.2%. nc ncf sc. 239 bottles.

STRATHCLYDE Lowland, 1927. Pernod Ricard. Working.

Glasgow Gardens Festival 30th Anniversary Strathclyde 30 Year Old 1988 cask no. 62125, dist 9 Jun 88, bott 10 Jun 18 **(87) n22 t23 f20.5 b21.5** I think I remember Hunter Laing bringing out a 30-year-old Strathclyde last year which surprised me with its gentle good manners. This time probably much closer to what I was expecting, with the rough edges of the distillery at that time clearly on display here, despite a flurry of superb golden syrup notes on delivery. 54.3%. sc. Exclusive to The Whisky Barrel. 138 bottles.

Old Particular Strathclyde 11 Years Old sherry butt, cask no. 11952, dist Nov 05, bott Jul 17 **(91) n22 t23.5 f22 b23.5** Not just a sherry butt! But a clean, 100% untainted, entirely sulphur-free sherry butt! Fabulous! 55.5%. nc ncf sc. 638 bottles.

The Sovereign Strathclyde 28 Years Old refill barrel, cask no. 15804, dist Aug 90, bott Feb 19 **(90) n22.5 t23 f22 b22.5** Looks like Strathclyde were still going through a corn mash at this time, so soft, sweet and oily is this. Very un-Strathclyde for the era in its untroubled shifting through the gears. 51.1%. nc ncf sc. 198 bottles.

The Sovereign Strathclyde 30 Years Old refill hogshead, cask no. 14448, dist Sept 87, bott Nov 17 **(90) n22 t22 f23.5 b22.5** It is as though the grain has fallen asleep after 30 years and finally wakes up late in the day. 50.7%. nc ncf sc. 175 bottles.

That Boutique-y Whisky Company Strathclyde 30 Year Old batch 1 **(87.5) n22 t22.5 f21 b22** A grain that gives you a right punch in the throat on delivery. The sugars are profound but without structure and of very limited complexity. 53.1%. 228 bottles.

UNSPECIFIED SINGLE GRAIN

Borders finished in Oloroso sherry casks **(66) n15 t18 f15 b18.** Finished being the operative word. Has no-one been listening regarding the total mess sherry butts are in. I wonder why I bother sometimes. Jeez... 51.7%. nc ncf. R&B Distillers.

Haig Club toasted oak casks **(89) n21.5 t23 f22.5 b22** When I first saw this, I wasn't quite sure whether to laugh or cry. Because 25 years ago bottles of single grain whisky were the unique domain of the flat cap brigade, the miners and other working class in the Kirkcaldy area of Scotland. Their grain, Cameron Brig, would be drunk with a splash, mixed with Coke or ginger, even occasionally with Irn Bru, or straight and unmolested as a chaser to the ubiquitous kegged heavy, McEwan's lager or a bottle of Sweetheart stout. When I suggested to the hierarchy at United Distillers, the forerunners of Diageo, that in their finer grains they had a product which could conquer the world, the looks I got ranged from sympathy for my lack of understanding in matters whisky to downright concern about my mental well being. I had suggested the exquisite Cambus, now lost to us like so many other grain distilleries in those passing years, should be brought out as a high class singleton. It was pointed out to me that single grain was, always had been and always will be, the preferred choice of the less sophisticated; those not wishing to pay too much for their dram. Fast forward a quarter of a century and here sits a gorgeously expensive bottle in a deep cobalt blue normally associated with Ballantine's and a very classy, heavyweight stopper. In it is a grain which, if the advertising is to be believed, is the preferred choice not of the back street bar room idlers carefully counting their pennies but of its major ambassador David Beckham: it is the drop to be savoured by the moneyed, jet-set sophisticates. My, oh my. Let's not call this hype. Let's just say it has taken some genius exec in a suit half a lifetime – and probably most of his or hers - to come around to my way of thinking and convince those in the offices on the floor above to go for it. Wonder if I qualify for 10 percent of profit for suggesting it all those years back...or, preferably, five percent of their advertising budget. Meanwhile, I look forward to watching David pouring this into some of his Clynelish and Talisker. After all, no-one can Blend it like Beckham... 40%. WB15/408

Haig Club Clubman bourbon casks, bott code: L90860U002 **(87.5) n21 t22.5 f21.5 b22** Once you get past the caramel on both nose and finish it is easy to be drawn into enjoying this sweet grain which seems to glisten with acacia honey influence. 40%.

⟨⟩ **Haig Club Clubman** bourbon casks, bott code L3027DU002 **(88.5) n22 t22.5 f22 b22** Pleasant enough. But still a lazy dram, far too dependent on a chorus of toffee. The mouth feel is a success and the more salivating aspects of the sugar-oak-vanilla combo. A step up from recent bottlings, especially with the latent mocha finale. Though too little to propel this to perhaps where it should be, I hope it keeps travelling in this upward direction. 40%

The Tweeddale Grain of Truth Highland Single Grain bott code: L2.282.19 09.10.2019 **(92.5) n23 t23.5 f23 b23** You could imagine some dour Victorian minister of the kirk, lashing his congregation for being the sinners, without a single hope of salvation, he believes them to be over a miserable two hours on a relentlessly grey, rain-sodden, windswept Sunday morning somewhere up in the bleakest Highlands. And when he says there can be no drinking on the Sabbath, he means all alcoholic drink...with the exception of a dram or two of Tweeddale's Grain of Truth... Aye, that should finish them off, he'd be thinking...This is distilled from a mash bill of half wheat and half peated malt. The result is uniquely sombre and austere grain which, it has to be said, is captivating in its unique and fascinating, smoky bleakness. Love it! 50%. nc ncf.

The Whisky Works Glaswegian 29 Year Old Single Grain (92) n23.5 t23.5 f22 b23 Not often you get ginger on the nose of a grain whisky, butW this one obliges. Signs of a mis-spent youth here, as this shows all the classic signs of a roughhouse whisky when young, a bit of the Gorbals, and though still shewing the odd scar or two, now has a real touch of polished old school, debonair recalcitrance about it. 54.2%. nc ncf. 1,642 bottles.

WoodWinters The Five Distinguished and Rare Aged 39 Years (93) n22.5 t24 f23 b23.5 A grain of marvellous pedigree and integrity, at least equal to the vast majority of single malts whiskies you will find...51%. sc. 330 bottles.

Vatted Grain

Angus Dundee Distillers Blended Grain 50 Year Old (91.5) n23 t23.5 f22 b23 Just champion..! 40.1%.

Compass Box Hedonism first fill American oak casks, batch no. MMXIX-A, bott 28 Feb 19 **(91) n23 t23 f22.5 b22.5** After suffering at the hands of so many sulphurous sherry casks over the last month, I have sought sanctuary in John Glaser's Hedonism, a safe wine cask-free zone. It was a sensible choice... 43%. nc ncf.

Compass Box Hedonism Maximus (93.5) n25 t22.5 f23 b23. Bourbon Maximus... 46%

Compass Box Hedonism The Muse bott Feb 18 **(89) n23 t23 f21 b22** A fruit fly landing in a whisky while it is waiting to be tasted is always a good sign: these things know where to find sweetness. 53.3%. nc ncf.

Compass Box Hedonism Quindecimus (88.5) n22.5 t22 f22 b22 Sweet and refreshingly ordinary grain. Well made and unspectacularly delicious. 46%

⟨⟩ **Valour Whisky Blended Grain 35 Years Old** cask nos 16 & 37, dist 12/87, bott 12/22 **(95) n24** so much younger than half its three score year and ten, this is a real softy on the nose, light honey vanilla mingling with toffee; **t24** melt-in-the-mouth creamy toffee made all the sweeter for the liquid muscovado and icing sugars; **f23** chocolate toffee with a slow butterscotch build; **b24** the grains used here were of the softer enveloping style. A simple, uncomplex composition it may be, but it makes for a dangerously easy-drinking blend. Were it not a whisky it'd be a feather pillow... 55.2% 487 bottles

William Grant & Sons Rare Cask Reserves 25 Years Old Blended Grain Scotch Whisky (92.5) n23 t23.5 f23 b23. A really interesting one, this. In the old days, blenders always spent as much time vatting the grains together as they did the malts, for if they did not work well as a unit it was unlikely harmony would be found in their blend. A long time ago I was taught to, whenever possible, use a soft grain to counter a firmer one, and vice versa. Today, there are far fewer blends to choose from, though 25 years ago the choice was wider. So interesting to see that this grain is soft-dominated with very little backbone at all. Delicious. But screams for some backbone. 47%. Exclusive to The Whisky Shop.

Scottish Blends

If any whisky is suffering an identity crisis just now, it must be the good old once ubiquitous Scottish blend.

For so long the staple, the absolute mainstay of the Scotch whisky industry it has seen its market share increasingly buried under the inexorable, incoming tide that is single malt. But worse, the present-day blender has his hands tied in a way no previous generation of blenders has had before.

Now stocks must be monitored with a third eye, one that can judge the demand on their single malt casks and at increasingly varied ages. Worse, the blender cannot now, as once was the case, create blends with subtly shifting textures - the result of carefully using different types of grain. So many grain distilleries have closed in the last quarter of a century that now most blends seem remarkably similar to others. And there is, of course, the problem of sherry butts which has been fully documented over the years in the Whisky Bible.

For Jim Murray's Whisky Bible 2018 I tasted or re-tasted 128 blends in total, a quite significant number. And there is no doubt that the lack of choice of grain for blenders is beginning to pose a problem for the industry. What was particularly noticeable was the number of blends which now lack a crisp backbone and have softened their stance, making them chewy and pliable on the palate but often lacking the crispness which can maximise the complexity of the malts on display. By the time you add in the caramel, the results can sometimes be just a little too cloying.

Naturally, it was the bigger blenders - those possessing by far the largest stocks - who best escaped this narrowing down of style among the younger blends in particular, and recently it was that thoroughbred blend known even by our grandparents and great-grandparents, White Horse, which really caught the eye...and palate.

As I have at long last re-started my travelling across the world following the international Covid close-down, it has been interesting to hear how blended whisky, Scotch in particular, has often been brought up in conversation among whisky enthusiasts. Perhaps because their interest has been aroused with the single malts they are finding with different cask styles being blended together, ever more questions are being asked of me about standard blends involving malt and grain. Yet among the distilers themselves this interest does appear to be only mutedly matched, though Chivas have impresssed with their much improved 13 year old, carrying off the 2024 Blend of the Year title.

Jim Murray's Whisky Bible Scottish Blend of the Year Winners	
2004/5	William Grant's 21 Year Old
2006	William Lawson Aged 18 Years
2007/8	Old Parr Superior 18 Years Old
2009	The Last Drop
2010	Ballantine's 17 Years Old
2011	Ballantine's 17 Years Old
2012	Ballantine's 17 Years Old
2013	Ballantine's 17 Years Old
2014	Ballantine's 17 Years Old
2015	The Last Drop 1965
2016	The Last Drop 50 Years Old
2017	The Last Drop 1971
2018	Compass Box The Double Single
2019/20	Ballantine's 17 Years Old
2021	Ballantine's 30 Years Old
2022	Ballantine's Finest
2023	Cutty Sark Aged 12 Years
2024	Chivas Regal Extra Aged 13 Years

Scottish Blends

100 Pipers bott code LKVK2677 2016/07/01 **(74) n18 t19 f19 b18** These 100 Pipers deserve an award. How can they have played for so many years and still be so off key and out of tune? It is an art form, I swear. I feel like giving the blend a special gong for so many years of consistent awfulness. 40%. *Chivas Brothers Ltd*

Aberdour Finest Piper Blend Scotch Whisky bott code: L18024 **(86.5) n21.5 t22 f21.5 b21.5** An attractive, grain-led blend with just the right sweetness at just the right moments. The very lightest of toffee and vanilla finishes, though it is the spice which excels late on. 40%

Aberdour Finest Piper Blend bott code L19066 **(88.5) n22 t22 f22.5 b22** A solid blend with a little extra weight and padding than before and some lovely juicy moments, too. Satisfying with an impressively long finish in which the spices sparkle. 40 %

Artful Dodger Blended Scotch 41 Year Old ex-bourbon hogshead **(95.5) n24 t24 f23.5 b24** Now and again, one of those ultra-sensuous whiskies turns up in my tasting room...and you melt into the glass as you sample it. Here's one such occasion where the blender, either 41-years-ago, or now, has understood how the grains can layer and structure a blend, and how the malt can fuse with the tannins and more caramelised elements. The result is a blend that you would chew, except it dissolves before you get the chance. The grain-malt ratio looks to be pretty spot on, as is the spice which nibbles and harries warmly, but without a hint of aggression. Just ahhhhhh.... 494%. *sc.*

The Antiquary bott code L 02 08 16 **(86) n20 t22 f22 b21** Appears to be going along the present day trend of spongy, super soft grain which doesn't always do the best of favours to the obviously high quality malt in here. Pleasantly sweet and chewy with an attractive base note. 40%. *Tomatin Distillery.*

The Antiquary Aged 12 Years bott code L 17 12 15 **(87.5) n21.5 t22 f22 b22** The smoke I so well remember from previous bottlings appears to have dispersed. Instead we have an ultra-lush blend dependent on molasses and spice to punch through the major toffee. 40%.

The Antiquary Aged 21 Years bott code 2016/02/29 LK30215 **(92.5) n23 t23.5 f23 b23** If you are not sure what I mean by a beautifully paced whisky, try this and find out. 43%.

The Antiquary Aged 35 Years bott code L 24 08 15 **(96.5) n24 t24 f24 b24.5** Enjoy some of the grains involved in this beauty: their type and ability to add to the complexity is, tragically, a dying breed: the hardest whisky I have found so far to spit out...and I'm on dram number 530....! Antiquary's late, great blender, Jim Milne, would shed a tear of joy for this creation of unreconstructed beauty and brilliance, as this was just out of his school of elegance. 46%.

Ballaglass Blended Scotch Whisky (85) n21 t22 f21 b21. Perfectly enjoyable, chewy – but clean – blend full of toffee and fudge. Very good weight and impressive, oily body. 40%.

Ballantine's 12 Years Old (87) n21 t22 f21 b23. The kind of old-fashioned, mildly moody blend Colonel Farquharson-Smythe (retired) might have recognised when relaxing at the 19th hole back in the early '50s. Too good for a squirt of soda, mind. 40%. *Chivas Bros.*

Ballantine's 17 Years Old (97.5) n24.5 t24 f24 b25 Now only slightly less weighty than of old. After a change of style it has comfortably reverted back to its sophisticated, mildly erotic old self. One of the most beautiful, complex and stunningly structured whiskies ever created. Truly the epitome of great Scotch. 43%.

Ballantine's Aged 21 Years (94) n23.5 t24 f23.5 b24 Even though the strength has been reduced, presumably to eke out rare stocks, the beauty of this blend hasn't. 40%

Ballantine's Aged 30 Years (95.5) n24.5 t24 f23 b24 A fascinating malt, slightly underpowered perhaps, which I have had to put to one side and keep coming back to see what it will say and do next... 40%.

Ballantine's Aged 30 Years bott code LKRK1934 2016/05/16 **(96) n24.5 t24 f22.5 b24** Practically a replay of the bottle I tasted last year, right down to that very late, barely perceptible furriness. Simply one of the world's most sensual drams... 40%. *Chivas Brothers Ltd.*

❖ Ballantine's Finest, bott code LKYT0041 **(89) n23** the smoke has a more delicate hue these days, though a simplistic fruitiness is not to be sniffed at...or, rather, is. Grain is a little more prominent, which shews a slight lack of sync with the malts. Even so, very attractive and alluring; **t22.5** early firm grain dominance before the oils kick in, bringing with it a hint of smoky kipper and a brief yelp of something particularly malty and sweet; **f21.5** not quite the Ballantine's finish of yore: this has a few too many rough edges and the grain's call is too often left unanswered; **b22** not quite the smoky cove it once was, the grains are pretty well accentuated here giving it a particularly austere finish in particular. 40%

Ballantine's Finest bott code: 2021/08/03 **(95) n24 t24 f23 b24** Very much on course to meet last year's bottling in quality. Still a blend which just seems to marry its smoky credentials with the grains and tannins with consummate ease – though I know the truth will be very different: what magnificent mixing this is. One of those whiskies which is just too easy to dismiss as just another blend. Try the Murray Method and just watch this grow in the glass...

and count the flavour layers and cleverness of the smoke: for a no-age statement blend, you can ask for little more. Remains one of my preferred whiskies when relaxing. Brilliant. *40%*

Ballantine's Hard Fired (86.5) n22 t22 f21 b21.5. Despite the smoky and toasty elements to this, you're left waiting for it to take off...or even go somewhere. Perhaps just a little too soft, friendly and grain indulgent. Decent, enjoyable blend, of course, but a little out of the Ballantine's usual circle of high class friends. *40%*

Ballantine's Limited release no. A27380 (96) n24 t24.5 f23.5 b24 Each Limited release has a slightly different stance and this one holds its posture with more debonair, lighter-on-foot poise. The vague furry note of recent bottlings is missing here or, rather, is of the least consequence. The fruit, also, is more of a sheen than a statement more room for the malt and vanilla to play and the spices to impart age. It may be soft on both nose and palate – especially the delivery – as the grains have obviously been vatted to create minimum traction, but it is a blend of quiet substance. Another Ballantine's brand this year hitting the 96 or more mark. Astonishing, absolutely astonishing...more a case of Ballantine's Unlimited... *40%*.

◈ **Bell's Original**, nbc (90.5) n23 very attractive strata of malt aided by yielding grain. Soft, slightly toffeed but with just enough depth to compliment the delicate muscovado sugars; t22.5 silky mouth feel and highly attractive spices. Again, the grain is doing a great job in propping up the sweeter aspects of the malt, especially the thinned golden syrup. Surprising degree of maltiness detectable; f22 a little grain bite late on, but molten golden syrup on chalky vanilla ensures entertainment; b23 only last Saturday I was tasting Bell's in the Stoke City boardroom after the game with Millwall. The Bell's there was smokier than this with a few extra layers of honey. I said at the time that the most consistent thing about Bell's is its inconsistency – and I actually meant that as a compliment, as the odd surprise here and there does no harm and keeps you on your toes. An impressive and satisfying blend. *40%*

Bell's Original bott code: L1109CK012 (84) n21 t22 f20.5 b20.5 Having casually tasted Bell's from time to time, it dawned on me that its character was changing. And that I hadn't given it a full review for some little while. The most significant thing I had noticed, and fully confirmed here with this bottle before me, is that the smoke which had been brought back a decade ago to breathe the extra life and weight into the bend had now completely vanished. Also, the grains have a different mouth feel and are far more prominent. If you are looking for a silky blend with a strong grain character, here you go. The old complexity has simply disappeared. The old Bell's just doesn't ring as sweetly as it once did. *40%*

Bell's 8 Years Old (85) n21.5 t22.5 f20 b21. Some mixed messages here: on one hand it is telling me that it has been faithful to some of the old Bells distilleries – hence a slight dirty note, especially on the finish. On the other, there are some sublime specks of complexity and weight. Quite literally the rough and the smooth. *40%. Diageo.*

Berry Bros & Rudd The Perspective Series No.1 21 Year Old bott 2019 (90) n22.5 t22.5 f22 b23 One of those highly unusual blends where the influence of the grain takes a back seat. *43%. 6,300 bottles.*

Black & White (91) n22 t23 f22.5 b23.5 This one hasn't gone to the dogs: quite the opposite. I always go a bit misty-eyed when I taste something this traditional: the crisp grains work to maximum effect in reflecting the malts. A classic of its type. *40%. Diageo.*

Black Bottle bott code 2038310 L3 16165 (94.5) n23.5 t23.5 f23.5 b24 Not the byword for macho complexity it was 15 years ago but after a lull in its fortunes it is back to something that can rightfully boast excellence. Brilliant. *40%.*

◈ **Black Bottle**, bott code 2408123L3 (90) n22.5 the peat, without being flamboyant, nibbles and nips like the smouldering embers of a turf fire. The grain also has a bit to say, too... and that roughs things up a little...; t23.5 brilliant oils make for a gorgeously chewy delivery, the smoke meeting the grain to forge a rugged and quite fabulous partnership; f21.5 the smoke has burned out, though spices now dance in its place, and the oils have dissipated, accentuating a surprising thinness; b22.5 another blend, like Ballantine's Finest, which has slightly toned down the smoke since its days of plenty. Even so, there remains an attractive rock pool phenol kick which impresses. Excellent chewing whisky. If they could sort the finish out and extend it, this could be back amongst the Whisky Bible awards. *40% Gordon Graham*

Black Bottle 10 Years Old (89) n22 t23 f22 b23 A stupendous blend of weight and poise, but possessing little of the all-round steaming, rampaging sexuality of the younger version...but like the younger version showing a degree less peat: here perhaps even two. Not, I hope, the start of a new trend under the new owners.

Black Dog 12 Years Old (92) n21 t23 f24 b24. Offering genuine sophistication and élan. This minor classic will probably require two or three glass-fulls before you take the bait... *42.8%*

Black Grouse (94) n23 t24 f23 b24. A superb return to a peaty blend for Edrington for the first time since they sold Black Bottle. Not entirely different from that brand, either, from the Highland Distillers days with the smokiness being superbly couched by sweet malts. *40%*

The Black Grouse Alpha Edition (72.5) n17 t19.5 f17 b18. Dreadfully sulphured. 40%

Black Hound (83) n21 t21.5 f21 b20.5 Here's to Max! Max grain in this but no complaints here as the relatively limited caramel doesn't spoil the enjoyment of what feels like (though obviously isn't) a single distillery output. Crisp at first, then succulent, chewy cream toffee. 40%. Quality Spirits International.

Black Scott 3 Years Old bott code: 3L08460154 (85.5) n20.5 t22 f21.5 b21.5 Pretty standard, though not unattractive fare. The nose is a bit of a struggle but relaxes on delivery and even entertains with a spicy blitz. 40%. Toorank Productions BV.

Black Stripe (77) n19 t20 f19 b19 Untidy without character. 40%.

Blend No. 888 bott code L15/8185 (84.5) n21 t22 f20.5 b21 Light, breezy and sweet, this is grain dominant and makes no effort to be otherwise. Soft, untaxing and pleasant. 40%. House of MacDuff.

Boxes Blend (90) n22.5 t23.5 f21 b23. A box which gets plenty of ticks. 40.9%. ncf.

Buchanan's De Luxe 12 Years Old (82) n18 t21 f22 b21. The nose shows more than just a single fault and the character simply refuses to get out of second gear. Certainly pleasant, and some of the chocolate notes towards the end are gorgeous. But just not the normal brilliant show-stopper! 40%. Diageo.

Buchanan's Master bott code: L7313CE001 (94.5) n24 t23.5 f23 b24 Some 40-odd years ago I was in love with Buchanans: it was one of the truly sophisticated blends from which I learned so much and this pays homage to the legacy. On the down side the grains are nowhere near so complex and the vague furry bitterness at the end tells its own tale. But I doff my Panama to blender Keith Law in genuine respect: works like this don't just happen and this is a blended Scotch worthy of the name. 40%.

Castle Rock (81) n20 t20.5 f20 b20.5. Clean and juicy entertainment. 40%

Catto's Aged 25 Years bott code RV9499 (94.5) n23 t24 f23 b24.5 A far better experience than the last time I officially tasted a Catto's 25 seven or eight years ago. Both malts and grains are of the charming style once associated with Catto's Rare : so jaw-droppingly elegant... 40%. International Beverage Holdings Ltd.

Catto's Deluxe 12 Years Old bott code L 18 03 16 (86.5) n21.5 t22 f21.5 b21.5 A safe, sweet and sumptuous blend which places major emphasis to the molasses. Won't win any beauty contests but there is a weighty earthiness, also. 40%. International Beverage Holdings Ltd.

Catto's Rare Old Scottish bott code L 25 01 16 (83) n20.5 t21 f20.5 b21 Once fresh as dew on morning grass, this has changed in recent years with a different grain profile which no longer magnifies the malt. Adopted a rougher, more toffeed approach from its once clean cut personality: not even a close approximation of the minor classic it once was. 40%. International Beverage Holdings Ltd.

Chapter 7 Blended Scotch 26 Year Old 1993 sherry butt, dist Dec 93, bott Mar 20 (77) n22 t22 f16 b17 A blend, by definition, should be about layering and complexity and, if desired, not allowing any single trait dictate to the rest. So this blend fails because although the sherry cask is rich and sweet but, sadly, nowhere near sulphur free, the story is fruit and grain. And then sulphur. A lot of sulphur, in fact... Which after the malts have matured for 26 years minimum is a bit sad. A Chapter that needs serious re-writing. 44.9%. sc. 618 bottles.

The Chivas 18 Ultimate Cask Collection First Fill American Oak (95.5) n24 t23.5 f24 b24 Immeasurably superior to any Chivas 18 I have tasted before. A true whisky lover's whisky... 48%. ncf.

Chivas Regal Aged 12 Years bott code 2021/07/21 LKX R3996 (94) n23.5 t23.5 f23 b24 Does the heart good to see that Chivas have kept the standard of their 12 high, after too long in the doldrums. This is a complex, magnificently structured blend. Sill not with the finesse which put it in a league of its own during the 1970s. But way, way better than it had been for far too long. In a period when standard blends up to 12-years-old are going through a rough patch, Chivas 12-year-old is exactly what it says on the tin: Regal. 40%

⟐ **Chivas Regal Aged 12 Years**, bott code LKXS7352 2022/11/11 (89) n22.5 some extra apple fruitiness to this (not unknown in the Chivas of the late 1970s), this is still a little weighed down by toffee alongside the tannins; t23 salivating and determined to display its trademark Speyside malts, which salivate profusely, the grains are a little aggressive by comparison; f21.5 still grain heavy and a tad bitter, too. Some toffee lingers. Just a little off key at the death; b22 so much is right with this blend – but a little too much wrong for greatness. When the Speyside malts are in full sail, we have a glorious exhibition of charm and balance. But other factors dig in to force a tangy weightiness which doesn't quite fit in. 40%

Chivas Regal Extra Aged 13 Years bott code: 2021/05/24 (89) n23 t23.5 f20.5 b22 One of those frustrating whiskies which starts rather well but tapers off a little. 40%.

⟐ **Chivas Regal Extra Aged 13 Years** Tequila cask selection, bott code LKXT0011 23/01/10 (95) n23.5 those who can recognise it will pick up the tequila tang early on. It appears to sit comfortably with the crisp grain. The malt, clean and sweet, stirs only in the background. The most endearingly subtle phenol at play completes an impressive cast; **t24** the best and most complete delivery of any mainstream blend I have tasted this year. Not only is there immediate weight and impact, but the salivation levels are also off the charts. Wonderful esters give the malts on board a lustre while the grains are firm and ensure structure; **f23.5** long, with low levels of teasing spice helping to keep those salivation levels high. Vanilla from the oak plays a major part here while the grains still maintain an excellent rigidity. There is also a boiled sweet fruitiness at play here before those spices really do take final command; **b24** you get the feeling that the blender has moved on significantly with this brand, not only understanding better its unique dynamics but making better casks being available for an overall upgrade in class. Don't be surprised if this wins a major gong in the 2024 Whisky Bible: this is a belting blend. *40%*

Chivas Regal Aged 15 Years finished in Grande Champagne Cognac casks, bott code: 2018/07/19 **n23 t22.5 f22 b22.5** Can't quite escape the over-zealous caramel. But there is an undoubted charm to this and extra clever use of the sweeter elements to good effect. Probably one of the softest and most moreish whiskies launched in the last year or so. *40%.*

Chivas Regal Aged 18 Years bott code LKRL0346 2017/01/30 **(86) n22 t22 f21 b21** A great improvement on the last bottling I encountered with a pleasing chewiness and understated spiciness. But this remains far too dependent on a big caramel surge for both taste and structure. *40%. Chivas Brothers Ltd.*

Chivas Regal Aged 18 Years Gold Signature bott code 2022/05/03 **(82.5) n21 t22.5 f18.5 b19.5** Such a disappointment. This should be on a different plane entirely from the dullard that's before me in this glass. There is caramel at every turn, especially on the nose and finish. Only when on maximum Murray Method warming do we begin to get some kind of structure on the nose, with an orchestrated blast of Speyside. And this structure does blast through the toffee on the palate, too, to deliver an all-too-briefly charming opening salvo. But soon it succumbs to the massive caramel one final time – the only thing to break ranks being a niggling sulphur note.... *40%*

Chivas Regal Aged 25 Years bott code 2017/03/01 LPML0373 **(95.5) n24.5 t24.5 f22.5 b24** This is quite brilliant whisky. Maybe just one sherry butt away from what would almost certainly have been among the top three whiskies of the year... *40%. Chivas Brothers Ltd.*

Chivas Regal Extra (86) n20 t24 f20.5 b21.5. Chivas, but seemingly from the Whyte and MacKay school of thick, impenetrable blends. The nose may have the odd undesirable element and the finish reflects those same trace failings. But if chewy date and walnuts in a sea of creamy toffee is your thing, then this malt is for you. This, though, does show genuine complexity, so I have to admit to adoring the lush delivery and early middle section: the mouthfeel is truly magnificent. Good spice, too. Flawed genius comes to mind. *40%*

Chivas Regal The Chivas Brother's Blend Aged 12 Years bott code 2016/04/12 LPEK0613 **(81.5) n21 t21.5 f19 b20** Oh, brother! Fabulous texture but a furry finish... *40%.*

Chivas Regal Mizunara bott code: LPBM0253 2018/02/06 **(89.5) n22.5 t23 f22 b22** For years the Japanese copied everything the Scotch whisky industry did, not quite realising – or perhaps willing to believe – that many of their indigenous whiskies were of world class standard deserving respect and discovery in their own right. Now the Scots have, for the first time I'm aware of, openly copied the Japanese– and celebrated the fact. The Japanese oak used within the marrying process does appear to have given an extra impetus and depth to this blend. Definitely offers an extra dimension to what you'd expect from a Chivas. *40%.*

Clan Campbell bott code LR3 1047 13/09/05 **(89) n21.5 t23 f22 b22.5** Amazing what happens when you reduce the colouring Last time I tasted this I could barely find the whisky for all the toffee. Now it positively shines in the glass. Love it! *40%. Chivas Brothers Ltd.*

Clan Campbell rum barrel finish, bott code: 2018/04/04 **(90.5) n22 t23.5 f22 b23** This blend is all about impact and staying power. All kinds of rum and caramel incursions, but a really lovely broadside on the palate. *40%.*

Clan Campbell Dark rum barrel finish, bott code 2017/03/29 LPHL 0570 **(89.5) n22 t23 f22 b22.5** Putting my rum blender's hat on here, can't think which barrels they used to get this degree of colour and sweetness. Still, I'm not arguing; it's a really lovely, accommodating dram. *40%. Chivas Brothers Ltd.*

Clan Gold 3 Year Old (95) n23.5 t24 f23.5 b24. A blend-drinkers blend which will also slay the hearts of Speyside single malt lovers. For me, this is love at first sip... *40%*

Clan Gold Blended 15 Years Old (91) n21.5 t23 f23.5 b23 An unusual blend for the 21st century, which steadfastly refuses to blast you away with over the top flavour and/or aroma profiles and instead depends on subtlety and poise despite the obvious richness of flavour. The grains make an impact but only by creating the frame in which the more complex notes can be admired. *40%*

Clan Gold 18 Years of Age bott code L6X 7616 0611 **(95) n24 t24 f23 b24** Nothing like as juicy and cleverly fruity as it once was, yet marriage between malt and grain seldom comes more happy than this... *40%. Quality Spirits International.*

Clan Gold Finest bott code L10Z 6253 1902 **(83) n20 t21 f21 b21** Sweet, silky, soft and caramel heavy. Decent late spice. 40%. *Quality Spirits International.*

Clan MacGregor (92) n22 t24 f23 b23 Just gets better and better. Now a true classic and getting up there with Grant's. 43%

Clan Murray bott code L9X 7694 1411 **(86) n20 t22.5 f21.5 b22** For the avoidance of doubt: no, this not my blend. No, I am not the blender. No, I do not get a royalty from sales. If I could have had a tenner for each time I've had to answer that over the last decade or so I could have bought my own island somewhere, or Millwall FC... Anyway, back to the whisky. Far better nose than it has shown in the past and the delivery has an eye-watering bite, the finish a roguish spice. Rough-ish but very ready. 40%. *The BenRiach Distillery Co. Ltd.*

Clansman (80.5) n20.5 t21 f19 b20. Sweet, grainy and soft. 40%. *Loch Lomond.*

Clansman bott code L3/170/15 **(84) n21 t22 f20 b21** More to it than of old, though still very soft, the dark sugars and spice have a very pleasant input. 40%. *Loch Lomond Group.*

The Claymore (85) n19 t22 f22 b22. These days you are run through by spices. The blend is pure Paterson in style with guts etc, which is not something you always like to associate with a Claymore; some delightful muscovado sugar at the death. Get the nose sorted and a very decent and complex whisky is there to be had. 40%. *Whyte & Mackay Distillers Ltd*

Claymore bott code: L90049/007412 **(89.5) n22.5 t22.5 f21.5 b23** No longer called The Claymore, it seems. And in losing the "The" it appears to have lost a lot of weight, too. This is a much more elegant version than yore, which was a bit of a weighty beast and overly dependent on caramel. This, is without so much caramel in the mix to flatten the content, which I much prefer. Lots of very attractive personality to enjoy. And the perfect whisky for soccer lovers with a touch of romance in their souls. The Claymore was a whisky brand which advertised extensively in London football grounds, such as Millwall and West Ham during the 1910s and 1920s and if you find old film of London-based games during that period on Youtube, watch out for their ubiquitous adverts. Indeed, in the Millwall programme of 100 years ago, there was always a Claymore ad next to the team line-ups. My preferred dram for when watching football...before diving and ridiculous football kits became the fashion. 40%

Cliff Allen db **(92.5) n23 t23.5 f23 b23** Oddly enough, this is a heartier fellow than the 42% version with far more peat involvement. Beautifully weighted, excellent presence on the palate and you can hardly ask for more from a standard blend. I could easily make this my pre-bed dram... 40%

Cliff Allen batch L20239 **(88) n22.5 t22 f21.5 b22** A little while since I last encountered this fellow: and he's changed. Certainly started smoking, not heavily, but enough to overcome the old graininess....at least on the nose. Light citrus tones also make inroads into the dominant vanillas. More complex than before. 42% 4,000 bottles

Co-op Aged 3 Years bott code: LL1147P/015640 **(84) n19.5 t22 f21 b21.5** A sweet, chewy, caramel-rich blend which keeps simplicity to a fine art. The nose is a bit of a mess. And the inevitable bitter burn notes of the caramel is detectable at the finish. But pleasant enough its own undemanding way. 40%

Coachbuilt Build No 001 (92.5) n22.5 a slight over-emphasis on caramel undermines the subtlety of the fruit and vanilla which should have been the over-riding theme; **t23.5** not faulting the suspension of this vehicle: beautifully soft and undulates in all the right places. A tidal wave of tannin thumps the palate, for a moment giving a mildly bourbon quality to this Scotch. The midpoint of an almost tart chocolate liqueur is complimented perfectly by the fizzing, pleasantly salted spice: beautifully crafted; **f23** plenty of slick Belgian chocolate to the finish with a lovely vanilla wafer. The caramel sticks its head back in when not needed and slightly over-dries things at the death; **b23.5** not a whisky for those going on the wagon...a single glass of this full-bodied beauty will invariably lead to another. If they could play down the part of the tannin-rich caramel in this, this'd be a First-Class carriage all the way. Very impressed with this rarity: a blend that entertains and keeps you guessing. 46%

Compass Box Delilah's XXV American oak & sherry casks **(82) n20.5 t22.5 f18 b21** A blend with an astonishing degree of natural caramels in play, giving the whole piece a soft, chewy feel with both sugars and spices coming off at a tangent. Sadly, the sherry input is distracting on the nose and distinctly tangy and furry towards the end. 46%. nc ncf.

Compass Box The Double Single bott Mar 17 **(97) n24.5 t25 f23.5 b24** By no means the first time I have encountered a single malt and grain in the same bottle. But I am hard pressed to remember one that was even close to being this wonderful...This is Compass Box's finest moment... 46%. nc ncf. 5,838 bottles.

Compass Box Great King St. Artist's Blend (93) n24 t23 f22.5 b23.5. The nose of this uncoloured and non-chill filtered whisky is not dissimilar to some better known blends before they have colouring added to do its worst. A beautiful young thing this blend: nubile, naked and dangerously come hither. Compass Box's founder John Glaser has done some memorable work in recent years, though one has always had the feeling that he has still been learning his trade, sometimes forcing the issue a little too enthusiastically. Here, there is absolutely no doubting that he has come of age as a blender. *43%. nc ncf.*

Compass Box Great King Street Experimental Batch #00-V4 bott Sept 13 **(93) n22.5 t24 f23 b23.5.** A blend combining astonishing vibrancy with oaky Russian roulette. Not a dram to do things by halves... *43%. 3,439 bottles.*

Compass Box Great King Street Experimental Batch #TR-06 bott Sept 13 **(92) n22 t23.5; f23 b23.5** I think this one's been rumbled... *43%.*

Compass Box Great King Street Glasgow Blend (88.5) n22 t23.5 f21 b22 Just the odd note seems out of place here and there: delicious but not the usual Compass Box precision. *43%*

Compass Box Great King St Glasgow Blend batch no. GB 209, bott 8 Aug 19 **(89) n23 t23.5 f20.5 b22** Perhaps a rogue cask away from an award. *43%. nc ncf.*

Compass Box The Circus bott Mar 16 **(93) n23 t23.5 f23 b23.5** Scotland's very own Clown Royal... *49%. nc ncf. 2,490 bottles.*

Compass Box This Is Not A Luxury Whisky bott Aug 15 **(81) n20 t21.5 f19.5 b20.** Correct. *53.1%. nc ncf. 4,992 bottles.*

Compass Box Rogue's Banquet (94.5) n23.5 t23.5 f23.5 b24 Quite a different tack from Compass Box, really concentrating on the daintiness a blend might reveal despite the sometimes voluptuous body. Helped along by sublime cask selection. Gorgeous. *46%.*

Consulate (87) n21.5 t22 f22 b21.5 I assume this weighty and pleasant dram was designed to accompany Passport (whose chewiness it now resembles) in the drinks cabinet. I suggest, if buying them, use Visa. *40%. Quality Spirits International.*

Crawford's (83.5) n19 t21 f22 b21.5. A lovely spice display helps overcome the caramel. *40%*

Crag and Glen Aged 3 Years bott code: L1175P/016087 **(85.5) n21 t21.5 f21.5 b21.5** Even deploying the Murray Method, the uneven grain and toffee mix on the nose won't trouble the drinker for long. Though there is a half decent marriage of the two styles on the palate, to give a sweet, silky and long ride, though complexity never quite enters the equation. The sweetness to the whisky is never lost. *40% Sainsbury's*

Cutty Black (83) n20 t23 f19 b21. Both nose and finish are dwarfed and flung into the realms of ordinariness by the magnificently substantial delivery. Whilst there is a taint to the nose, its richness augers well for what is to follow; and you won't be disappointed. At times it behaves like a Highland Park with a toffeed spine, such is the richness and depth of the honey and dates and complexity of the grain-vanilla background. But those warning notes on the nose are there for good reason and the finish tells you why. Would not be surprised to see this score into the 90s on a different bottling day. *40%. Edrington.*

Cutty Sark (78) n19 t21 f19 b19. Crisp and juicy. But a nipping furriness, too. *40%*

Cutty Sark Aged 12 Years bott code: L11330759A **(95) n23.5 t24 f23.5 b24** Some 30 years ago when devising the Murray Method of tasting, I found that Cutty was one of the few whiskies that didn't benefit from being warmed slightly. It was always at its best when at its sharpest in the glass as the Speysiders seemed to cut through the grain with a grapier sharpness, so it would dance, almost angularly on the palate and causing maximum salivation levels when doing so. This is still a wonderful experience when at room temperature and by drinking it thus you will be rewarded in countless ways. However, the blend has evolved over the last three decades and although the nose is still inferior when warmed (I have given the nose score when cool), the overall experience when using the Murray method is far more complete. Either way, this is one very elegant classic. *40%*

Cutty Sark Aged 12 Years (92) n22 t24 f23 b23 At last! Cutty 12 at full sail...and blended whisky rarely looks any more beautiful! *40%. Edrington.*

Cutty Sark Aged 15 Years (82) n19 t22 f20 b21. Attempts to take the honey route. But seriously dulled by toffee and the odd sulphured cask. *40%. Edrington.*

Cutty Sark Aged 18 Years (88) n22 t22 f22 b22 Lost the subtle fruitiness which worked so well. Easy-going and attractive. *43%*

Cutty Sark Aged 25 Years (91) n21 t23.5 f22.5 b23 Magnificent, though not quite flawless, this whisky is as elegant and effortlessly powerful as the ship after which the brand was named... *45.7%. Berry Bros & Rudd.*

Cutty Sark Prohibition Edition American oak, bott code L0401W L4 11/18 **(91) n21.5 t25 f20 b24.5** Probably the best label and presentation of any whisky in the world this year: sheer class. On the back label they use the word authentic. Which is a very interesting concept. Except authentic whisky sent to the USA back in the 1920s wouldn't have that annoying and debilitating rumble of sulphur, detectable on both nose and finish. And I suspect the malt content would have been higher – and the grain used showing far more of a corn-oily character. That all said, I doubt the blender of the day would have achieved better delivery or balance: indeed, this delivery has to be one of the highlights of the whisky year. You will not be surprised to discover my resolve cracked, and I swallowed a full mouthful of this special blend. And, gee: it was swell, bud... 50%. Edrington.

Cutty Sark Storm (81.5) n18 t23.5 f19.5 b20.5. When the wind is set fair, which is mainly on delivery and for the first six or seven flavour waves which follow, we really do have an astonishingly beautiful blend, seemingly high in malt content and really putting the accent on ulmo honey and marzipan: a breath-taking combination. This is assisted by a gorgeous weight to the silky body and a light raspberry jam moment to the late arriving Ecuadorian cocoa. All magnificent. However, as Cutty sadly tends to, sails into sulphurous seas. 40%. Edrington.

Demijohn Finest Blended Scotch Whisky (88) n21 t22 f23 b22 OK, now that's spooky. You really don't expect tasting notes written ten years ago to exactly fit the bill today. But that is exactly what happens here: well maybe not quite exactly. Ten years ago I wrote the "wonderful firmness of the grain" where today, like 90% of all blends, it is much more yielding and soft than before. Thankfully, it hasn't detracted from the enjoyment. 40%

Demijohn Finest Blended Scotch Whisky (86) n22 t21 f21.5 b21.5 Soft, undemanding blended with a light juiciness. Big on the toffee, though. 40% Specially blended by Adelphi

Dew of Ben Nevis Supreme Selection (77) n18 t20 f20 b19. Some lovely raspberry jam Swiss roll moments here. But the grain could be friendlier, especially on the nose. 40%

Dewar's Aged 12 Years The Ancestor bott code: L17338ZA80109:20 **(87) n21.5 t22 f21.5 b22** A welcoming blend, relying mainly on softer grains which suck you in and caress you. A little orange peel and tart tannin helps give the blend vibrancy, but there is always a slight murkiness hanging around, too, which becomes more apparent at the death. 40%.

Dewar's Aged 15 Years The Monarch bott code: L18340ZA800 1326 **(81) n21 t21.5 f18 b20.5** Sweet and chewy in part, but the fuzzy finish abdicates. 40%.

Dewar's Aged 18 Years The Vintage bott code: L19030ZA8051642 **(96.5) n24 t24.5 f23.5 b24.5** This is how an 18-year-old blend should be: complex, noble and both keeping you on the edge of your seat as you wonder next what will happen, and falling back into its furthest recesses so you can drift away on its beauty... A blend that upholds the very finest traditions of the great Dewar's name. 40%.

Dewar's Aged 25 Years The Signature bott code: L18081ZA8011034 **(96) n24 t24 f24 b24** A 25-year-old blend truly worthy of that mantle. Always an honour to experience a whisky that has been very cleverly sculpted, not haphazardly slung together: a blender's blend. I doff my Panama to the blender. 40%.

Dewar's Double Double Aged 21 Years Blended Scotch Whisky finished in oloroso sherry casks, bott code: L19106ZA500 **(88) n23.5 t23.5 f18.5 b22.5** Another blender's blend. Or would have been 30 years ago. But doesn't seem to quite take into account the Russian roulette decision to add extra oloroso into the mix – Russian roulette with only one empty chamber that is... 46%.

Dewar's Double Double Aged 27 Years Blended Scotch Whisky finished in Palo Cortado sherry casks, bott code: L19106ZA501 **(96.5) n24 t24 f24 b24.5** A blend not scared to embrace its peaty side. And sherry butts free from sulphur. A double miracle at work. And one of the best new blends I have tasted for a year or two. Superb. 46%.

Dewar's Double Double Aged 32 Years Blended Scotch Whisky finished in PX sherry casks, bott code: L19107ZA501 **(86.5) n21.5 t24 f20.5 b20.5** I clocked the PX influence before I was aware it was officially finished in that cask type. After the staggeringly beautiful and vivid 27-year-old, this is very much a case of following the Lord Mayor's show. Yes, the sherry influence is pristine and untainted by sulphur, and the spices do a grand job. But to put a 30 year old blend into PX is like restoring an Old Master with a nine inch brush dipped into a gloss finish. Lovely in places (the astonishing delivery shews just how much sublime complexity was originally around)...but could have been so much more... 46%.

Dewar's Illegal Smooth Mezcal Cask Finish Aged 8 Years bott code: L20027ZA8002254 **(88) n23 t23 f20 b22** There is not the remotest doubt in my mind that of all the blending companies of Scotland, it is Dewar's that in recent years have upped their game most and returned to their once given place amongst the greats. This is probably just a cask away from adding to their rich tapestry of sublime blends. But, sadly, a little sulphur has entered the fray here – not a massive amount, but enough to dull the glitter from a potentially 24 carat blend. With the muscular grape sparring with the crisp grain and fulsome malt, at first this was going rather well, especially with the lightly spiced undertone. Look forward to seeing the next bottling... 40%.

Dewar's White Label bott code: L18241ZA204 2203 **(82) n20 t21 f20 b21** A great improvement on the last White Label I tasted (though nowhere near my great love of the 1970s!) but some murky grain still apparent. Definite layering and structure here, though. 40%.

Dhoon Glen (86) n21 t22 f21.5 b21.5 Full of big flavours, broad grainy strokes and copious amounts of dark sugars including chocolate fudge and now a little extra spice, too. Goes dhoon a treat... 40%. Lombard Scotch Whisky Ltd.

Dimple 12 Years Old (86.5) n22 t22 f21.5 b21. Lots of sultana; the spice adds aggression. 40%.

Dimple 15 Years Old (87.5) n20 t21 f24 b22.5. Only on the late middle and finish does this particular flower unfurl and to magnificently complex effect. The texture of the grains in particular delight while the strands of barley entwine. A type of treat for the more technically minded of the serious blend drinkers among you. 40%. *Diageo.*

Dimple Golden Selection (84.5) n21 t22 f20.5 b21 A clumsy, untidy bottling with a little too much bitterness on both nose and finish. The odd heather honey note drifts about and some saving busy spice, too. But too easily the honey turns to burnt honeycomb, especially noticeable on the dry finale. Certainly the caramels add to the ungainly narrative. 40%.

Eternity Diamond Reserve Old Premium Blend Oloroso sherry cask finish (86) n21 t22 f21.5 b21.5 Enjoy the chocolate notes which pop up at regular intervals and the chewy mouthfeel which accommodates them perfectly. Just not sure about those gin notes which appear to pepper this blend...and may have cost points. 40%.

Eternity Royal Reserve Noble Blend ex-bourbon casks (89) n22.5 t22 f22.5 b22 Determined to stay on the delicate side of the tracks, has both a pleasing sweetness, weight and mouthfeel throughout. Sometimes, though, it reminds me of a Geneve... 40%.

Fadandel Blended Scotch (86.5) n20 t21.5 f22.5 b22.5 The nose is worth ignoring, Murray Method or not, as there is something of the citrus-softened floor cleaner about this. However, it improves on delivery remarkably with an early volley of salivating fresh malt towards the finish. It is there that things begin to gel, and we enter the realms of complexity without ever reaching the centre. Good late oils give a real polish to that intense, spicy malt. 47.5%

The Famous Grouse bott code L4812TL1 25/08 (88.5) n22.5 t23 f21 b22 Changed its stance a few years back from light blend to a middle-weighted one and has worked hard to keep that position with thoughtful use of the phenols. Unlike many other brands it has not gone colouring mad and the little toffee apparent does nothing to spoil the narrative and complexity: I doff my hat. 40%

The Famous Grouse bott code: L4001DL13 (87.5) n22 t23 f20.5 b22 I had held back a year or two from re-tasting this as I wanted to see if they had managed to get the sulphur out of their system. Not quite, but there is definitely a vast improvement from some Grouse I tasted on the road (not in the lab) before Covid hit. Still pretty tight on both nose and finish, although at least the aroma does contain a degree of malt sparkle. But I have to say the delivery is a sheer joy and one of the few blends where the layering is at times quite dazzling with the malts having an input big enough that you can actually pick them out, having their own debate, amid the firm grains. An unusually crisp blend for these days. Just need to get that last sulphur out of the mix...and perhaps re-instate a little smoke, which appears to have been lost: not entirely, but significantly. 40%

⟐ **Famous Grouse**, bott code L4021EL012911 (87) n21.5 t22 f21.5 b22 A much cleaner blend than it has been for a while. Still a little too emphatic on the grain which shouts a little too loudly and punches a touch too hard. The malt, in salivating barley sugar form, is fleeting but effective. The finish, though, has a little too much tang. 40%

The Famous Grouse Gold Reserve (90) n23.5 t23 f21.5 b22 Great to know the value of the Gold Reserve is going up...as should the strength of this blend. The old-fashioned 40% just ain't enough carats. 40%. *Edrington Group.*

The Famous Grouse Married Strength (82.5) n19 t22 f20 b21.5. The nose is nutty and toffeed. But despite the delightful, silky sweetness and gentle Speyside-style maltiness which forms the main markers for this soft blend, the nose, like the finish, also shows a little bitter furriness has, sadly, entered into the mix. Not a patch on the standard Grouse of a decade ago. 45.9% WB16/019

The Famous Grouse Mellow Gold sherry & bourbon casks (85) n20 t23.5 f20 b21.5. While the nose and finish tell us a little too much about the state of the sherry butts used, there is no harm tuning into the delivery and follow though which are, unquestionably, beautiful. The texture is silk normally found on the most expensive lingerie, and as sexy as who you might find inside it; while the honey is a fabulous mix of ulmo and orange blossom. 40%

The Famous Grouse Smoky Black (87) n22 t22 f21 b22. Black Grouse by any other name. Flawed in the usual tangy, furry Grouse fashion. But have to say there is a certain roughness and randomness about the sugars that I find very appealing. A smoky style that Bowmore lovers might enjoy. A genuinely beautiful, smoky, ugly, black duckling. Sorry, I mean Grouse. 40%

The Famous Grouse Smoky Black bott code: L02860 (94) n23 a strange nose: smothered in peat, though the grains dominate....; t23.5 now that is rather lovely: the delivery is a sweet, Bowmore-style smokiness drifting amid more Speyside-style malt before the grains begin to get amongst them. Salivating and lively....; f23.5 long, with the oils bathed in smoke and even late on barley gets in on the act, nestling amid the light tannins and toffee...and late arriving spice; b24 what a transformation, Last time I tasted this, sulphur was in the system and undermined what looked like a potentially excellent blend. Here, we are talking 100% sulphur-free blended whisky...

and the result is glorious. A little on the sweet side, perhaps. But forgivable with such an elastic mouth feel and a smoky disposition to keep you warm and contented on the coldest night...or on the chilliest grouse moors... 40%.

◈ **Famous Grouse Smoky Black**, bott code L0421E L04 (94) n23.5 one of those rare blends where the powering grain is actually an attraction: the complexity of the phenols ensures that. Stirring, lively, nippy and gorgeously peated; t23.5 textbook delivery with myriad cushions of peat further plumped up by some silky grains to emphasize a lovely balance of textures; f23 a late emphasis on vanilla amid a smoky, lightly spiced sub-plot keeps the narrative going. A pleasingly long finish thanks to the extra oils; b24 so impressed with this. A knife and fork blend with an array of textures ensuring a kaleidoscopic ensemble of sweetness and smoke. Deeply satisfying whisky. 40%

Firean blend no. 005, bottling line. 003, bott code. L17066 (91.5) n23 t23.5 f22 b23 Does the heart grow older to encounter a blend so happy to embrace its smokier self. Deliciously impressive. 40%. Burlington Drinks

Firean Lightly Peated Old Reserve Small Batch Blend No 5 L10123 (91.5) n23 subtle, smoking embers of peat darting around the nose like flies over a lake; gentle fronds of lemon drizzle cake wave on the smoky breeze; t23.5 just brilliant! Smoked acacia honey...; f22 the grains begin to move into view...and so do the lightly smoked spices; b23 high class blending with top rate layering. Amazingly well structured and silky towards the end. 43%

For Peat's Sake bott code: L20 07581 CB2 (94) n23.5 t24 f23 b23.5 Anyone can add peat to a whisky. It doesn't guarantee balance or success. But this is a triumph simply because the blend has been careful to keep a shape and structure beyond peat. It is magnificently complex and skilfully weighted. What an absolute treat of a blend. A dram which just doesn't Peater out... 40%

Fort Glen The Blender's Reserve Aged 12 Years (88.5) n21.5 t23 f21.5 b22.5 An entirely enjoyable blend which is clean and boasting decent complexity and weight. 40%

Fort Glen The Distiller's Reserve (78) n18 t22 f19 b19. Juicy, salivating delivery as it storms the ramparts. Draws down the portcullis elsewhere. 40%. The Fort Glen Whisky Company.

Gleann Mór Blended Whisky 18 Year Old (87) n21.5 t23 f20.5 b22. A few passages in this are outstanding, especially when the delicate honey appears to collide with the softest smoke. A slight bitterness does jar somewhat, though the softness of the grain is quite seriously seductive 43.9%

Gleann Mór 40 Year Old Blend (94) n23 t23.5 f23.5 b24 Some 52-year-old Carsebridge makes up about a fifth of this blend, but I suspect the big oak comes from one of the malts. A supreme old whisky which cherishes its age. 44.6%

Glen Brynth (70.5) n18 t19 f16 b17.5. Bitter and awkward. 43%

Glenbrynth Premium Three Year Old (82) n19 t21 f21 b21 An enormously improved, salivating, toasty blend making full use of the rich muscovado sugars on display. Good late spice, too. 43%. OTI Africa.

Glenbrynth 8 Year Old (88) n21.5 t22 f22.5 b22. An impressive blend which improves second by second on the palate. 40%. OTI Africa.

Glenbrynth Pearl 30 Year Old Limited Edition (90.5) n22.5 t23.5 f21.5 b23 Attractive, beautifully weighted, no off notes...though perhaps quietened by toffee. Still a treat of a blend. 43%. OTI Africa.

Glenbrynth Pearl 30 Year Old bott code L8V 7410 28/11/11 (88) n22.5 t22.5 f21 b22 A genuinely strange blend. Not sure how this whisky was mapped out in the creator's mind. A hit and miss hotchpotch but when it is good, it is very good... 43%. OTI Africa.

The Glengarry bott code L3/301/15 (80) n19 t21 f20 b20 A brand that would once make me wince has upped its game beyond recognition. Even has the nerve to now possess an attractively salivating as well as silky disposition. 40%. Loch Lomond Group.

Glen Lyon (85) n19 t22.5 f22 b21.5. Works a lot better than the nose suggests: seriously chewy with a rabid spice attack and lots of juices. For those who have just retired as dynamite testers. Unpretentious fun. 43%. Diageo.

Glen Talloch Choice Rare & Old (85.5) n20.5 t22.5 f21 b21.5. A very pleasing sharpness to the delivery reveals the barley in all its Speyside-style finery. The grain itself is soothing, especially when the caramel notes kick in. 40%. ncf.

Glen Talloch Gold Aged 12 Years (85) n21 t22 f21 b21. Impressive grain at work insuring a deft, velvety caress to the palate. Mainly caramel speaking, despite the age, though there is an attractive spice buzz towards the thin-ish finish. 40%

Glen Talloch Peated (77) n18 t20 f20 b19 The awful tobacco nose needs some serious work on it. The taste is overly sweet, mushy and shapeless, like far too many blends these days. Requires a complete refit. 40%. Boomsma Distillery.

Glory Leading Aged 32 Years (88.5) n22.5 t22.5 f21.5 b22 At times a little heavy handed and out of sync. But the overall experience is one of stunningly spiced enjoyment. 43%

Scottish Blends

Glory Leading Blended Scotch Whisky 30 Years Old American oak casks (93) n22.5 t23 f23.5 b24 a big, clever, satisfying blend which just gets better and better... though not too sure about the Crystal Palace style eagle on the label. Even so, love it! 43%

Golden Piper (86.5) n22 t21 f22 b21.5. A firm, clean blend with a steady flush through of diverse sugars. The grain does all the steering and therefore complexity is limited. But the overall freshness is a delight. 43%. Whisky Shack.

Goldfield bott code: L1805078CB2 (87) n22 t22 f21 b22 High grain on show it may be, but when the grain is this good – and this firm, something of a collectors' item in itself – all can be forgiven. Above average icing sugar involvement, too, to keep you going to the late spice. Forget about malt complexity and all that stuff. Brilliant, unsullied young scotch grain at its best. 40%

Goldfield (85) n20.5 t22 f21 b21.5 It is something when you recognise a whisky just from its mouthfeel rather than its taste. But that is the case here, as Goldfield as the grains involved are diamond hard: a bit like old White Bush Irish but without the confrontational attitude. Softens with toffee in the right places. But slightly undone on this bottling with a lazy juniper note which has crept in. 40%

Grand Macnish 12 Years Old (86) n21 t22 f21.5 b21.5. A grander Grand Macnich than of old with the wonderful feather pillow delivery maintained and a greater harmonisation of the malt, especially those which contain a honey-copper sheen. 40%. MacDuff.

Grand Macnish Black Edition charred Bourbon casks, bott code L15 8863 (94.5) n24 t23.5 f23 b24 A blended whisky classic. 40%. MacDuff International Ltd.

Grand Macnish Double Matured Aged 15 Years Sherry Cask Edition ex-bourbon barrels, Jerez Oloroso sherry butt finish, batch no. 002, bott code: P/000837 (94) n23.5 t23.5 f23 b24 Delighted to report that the sherry involvement is without blemish. This Grand Macnish is very grand, indeed. 43%. Macduff International.

Grant's Aged 12 Years bott code: L6X 6682 1305 (96) n24 t24 f23.5 b24.5 There is no doubting that their 12-year-old has improved dramatically in recent years. Doubtless better grain than their standard blend, but also a slightly braver use of phenols has paid handsome dividends. Sits proudly alongside Johnny Walker Black as one of the world's must have 12-year-old blends. For me, the perfect daily dram. 40%

Grant's Cask Editions No. 1 Ale Cask Finish bott code: L1X 7354 1809 (91) n22.5 t23 f22.5 b23 A much cleaner, more precise blend than when this was first launched, with less noticeable beer character: impressive. 40%.

Grant's Cask Editions No. 2 Sherry Cask Finish bott code: L3Z 7760 0211 (84.5) n21.5 t22 f20 b21 A lovely fresh, fruity and salivating edge to this even boasting an early honeyed sheen. Complexity has been sacrificed for effect, however. 40%.

Grant's The Family Reserve bott code: L3A 8017 1711 (85) n21 t22 f21 b21 What was once the very finest, most complex nose in the entire Scotch whisky lexicon is now, on this evidence, a mushy shadow of its former self. Where once there was a judicious mix of softer and firmer grain to ensure the malts could make the most eloquent of speeches, now there is just a spongy sweetness which shouts loud enough to silence the poetry. If you like your blend fat, sweet, chewy, softer than quicksand and boasting a bitter, vaguely off-key finale here you go. But for those of us who once revered Grant's as the greatest of all standard blends, a whisky whose artistry once gilt-framed the very finest Scotland had to offer, this will not be a glass of cheer. I cannot blame the blender: he can work only with what he has available. And today, after a succession of nonsensical grain distillery closures (nonsensical to anyone who understands whisky, but not the soul-less bean counters who haven't the first clue) the choice in his lab is limited. It would be like blaming the manager of Bradford City for being a third tier football club because they won the FA Cup in 1910. Times change. And not, sadly, always for the better... 40%.

Grant's Signature bott code: L1Z 7468 1609 (79) n19 t22 f18 b20 Smudged. 40%

Grant's Stand Fast Triple Wood bott code L3F 6365 28022124 (86.5) n21.5 t22.5 f20.5 b22 For years one of the great things about Grant's blends was how beautifully integrated the grains and the malts were, making them usually among the most complex all Scotland had to offer. Here you get the feeling that the grains want far too much say, though the malts do dissolve into the mix with a delightful grassy, Speyside touch making the middle ground a delight. You also fear that the grain had been held in once sulphured sherry butts, because the finish is weakened by a distinctive, nagging furriness. The Murray Method does up the oils significantly and help reduce the negative effects. Pleasant enough. 40%

◈ **Grant's Stand Fast Triple Wood**, bott code L00171331701 (91.5) n23.5 a beguiling degree of complexity, allowing all aspects – maturation, grain and malt – to have a pretty even say. Layered with a bitter-sweet balance highly unusual in blended Scotch today; t23.5 acacia honey forms a formidable stratum with a deft vanilla and plum jam backup. The grain soothes against the building spice. f21.5 still fruity with spices refusing to back down. Surprising degree of tannin, but toffee, too; b23 remains the quintessential, super busy, highly complex blend which, when on form, keeps top youngish blends at the forefront of great whisky. Some bottlings I have tasted on my travels have been blighted by the odd sulphury note. This one sitting on my blending table also has a vague sulphur nibble late on but is hardly blighted. This stands fast. 40%

The Great Drams Blended Cask Series 7 Years Old batch no. 2, bott Feb 20 (89.5) n22.5 t23 f22 b22 An exceptionally bright and clean blend to be applauded. But it was like listening to the violins without a single cello to be had. 46.2%.

Guneagal Aged 12 Years (85.5) n21 t22.5 f20.5 b21.5. The salty, sweaty armpit nose gives way to an even saltier delivery, helped along by sweet glycerine and a boiled candy fruity sweetness. The finish is a little roughhouse by comparison. 40%. William Grant & Sons.

Haddington House (81) n20 t21 f20 b20 Good grief! This has changed since I last tasted it over a decade ago. Gone is its light, bright juicy character and in its place a singularly sweet, cloying blend due, I suspect, to a very different grain input. 40%. Quality Spirits International.

Haig Gold Label (88) n21 t23 f22 b22 What have before been pretty standard stuff has upped the complexity by an impressive distance. 40%. Diageo.

The Half Century Blend batch no. 4 (95) n24 t24 f23 b24 A rich malt making an absolute nonsense of its age statement. A fruitcake theme then moves into far maltier territory, but it is the sheer beauty of the lush mouthfeel which blows you away. Dark summer cherries and chocolate Maltesers melt into the other while light spices offer a third dimension. The is even a Farley's Rusk moment, though totally in keeping with the narrative... Oh, and look out for the flawless, teasingly understated seem of ulmo honey, too. Stunning. For its age: breathtaking. 45.6%.

Hankey Bannister (84.5) n20.5 t22 f21 b21. Lots of early life and even a malt kick early on. Toffee later. 40%. Inverhouse Distillers.

Hankey Bannister 12 Years Old (86.5) n22 t21.5 f21 b22. A much improved blend with a nose and early delivery which makes full play of the blending company's Speyside malts. Plenty of toffee on the finish. 40%. Inverhouse Distillers.

Hankey Bannister 21 Years Old (95) n23.5 t24 f23.5 b24 With top dressing like this and some obviously complex secondary malts, too, how can it fail? 43%.

Hankey Bannister 25 Years Old (91) n22.5 t24 f21.5 b23 Follows on in style and quality to 21-year-old. Gorgeous. 40%

Hankey Bannister 40 Years Old (89) n22 t23 f22 b22. This blend has been put together to mark the 250th anniversary of the forging of the business relations between Messrs. Hankey and Bannister. And although the oak creaks like a ship of its day, there is enough verve and viscosity to ensure a rather delicious toast to the gentlemen. Love it! 44%. Inverhouse.

Hankey Bannister 40 Year Old (94) n23.5 t23.5 f23 b24. Pure quality. The attention to detail is sublime. 44.3%. Inverhouse Distillers.

Hankey Bannister Heritage Blend (92) n23 t24 f22 b23 Just so soft and sensual...46%.

Harveys Lewes Blend Eight Year Old batch 4 (93) n23.5 t23 f23 b23.5 First tasted this in the front parlour of legendary Harvey's brewer Miles Jenner's home just after Christmas. It tasted quite different from their previous bottlings – and quite superb. Nosed and tasted now several months on in the cold analytical light of a tasting room...helped along with that deft addition of subtle peat, it still does. Superb! 40%

Hazelwood 18 Year Old (88) n23.5 t22.5 f20.5 b22 Until the final furry moments, a genuine little, understated, charmer. 40%. William Grant & Sons.

Hazelwood 21 Year Old (74) n19 t20 f17 b18. Some decent acacia honey tries to battle against the bitter imbalance. 40%. William Grant & Sons.

Hazelwood 25 Year Old (89.5) n22 t23 f22 b22.5 Distinctly chunky. 40%. WG & Sons.

High Commissioner bott code L2/305/16 (87.5) n21.5 t22.5 f21.5 b22 Boasts an unusually well balanced disposition for a young blend, not at all cowered into being a one trick caramelled pony. Instead, we are treated to a fulsome array of huskier and duskier notes, especially the molasses mixing with a hint of phenol. Delicious. 40%. Loch Lomond Group

High Commissioner bott code: L111021 (91) n22 t23 f22.5 b23.5 An attractively complex blend, one of the few these days where the malt (and I think even a certain distillery) can be detected. The grain used for this blend is especially lush, but that doesn't prevent some delightful barley notes push the salivation button. Superb layering with outline vanilla and tannins ensuring an excellent chewiness. Rare to find such top notch layering in such a relatively low budget brand. Deserves better recognition for its excellence. 40%

High Commissioner Aged 7 Years Lightly Peated bott code: 22 06 2018 (89) n22.5 t22 f22 b22.5 A seemingly simple malt with a lot of complexity if you want to find it. 40%.

Highland Baron (88.5) n22 t22.5 f22 b22 Has seriously upped the smoke and honey ratio in recent years. Deserves its Baronetcy. 40%. Lombard Scotch Whisky Ltd.

Highland Bird bott code L9Z 6253 2302 (83.5) n21 t21 f20.5 b21 I've had a few of these over the years, I can tell you. Glasses of this whisky, as well. As for the blend, this is by far and away the cleanest, enjoyable and most well-balanced yet: a dram on the up. 40%. QSI.

Highland Harvest Organic Scotch Whisky (76) n18 t21 f19 b18. A very interesting blend. Great try, but a little bit of a lost opportunity here as I don't think the balance is quite right. But at least I now know what organic caramel tastes like... 40%

Highland Mist (88.5) n20.5 t23 f22.5 b22.5 Fabulously fun whisky bursting from the bottle with character and mischief. Had to admit, broke all my own rules and just had to have a glass of this after doing the notes... 40%. *Loch Lomond Distillers.*

Highland Piper (79) n20 t20 f19 b20. Good quaffing blend – if sweet - of sticky toffee and dates. Some gin on the nose – and finish. 40%

Highland Pride (86) n21 t22 f21.5 b21.5. A beefy, weighty thick dram with plenty to chew on. The developing sweetness is a joy. 40%. *Whyte & Mackay Distillers Ltd.*

Highland Queen bott code L12 356 (87) n22.5 t22.5 f20.5 b21.5 If the caramels on this could be reduced slightly what a brilliant blend we'd have on our hands here. As it is, the nose is a hotbed of complex intrigue with earthier and lighter honeyed notes combining sublimely while the delivery allows the sugars, vanillas and spices room to make their cases. Bar the spices, just all dies off a little too soon. 40%. *Tullibardine Ltd.*

Highland Queen Aged 8 Years bott code L15 071 (89.5) n23 t22.5 f21.5 b22.5 A classy blend showing great character and entertainment value. 40%. *Tullibardine Ltd.*

Highland Queen Aged 12 Years Blended Scotch Whisky (87) n22 t22 f21 b22. A polite, slightly more sophisticated version of the 8-year-old...but without the passion and drama! 40%

Highland Queen Aged 12 Years bott code L15 071 (90) n23 t22.5 f22 b22.5 A much weightier blend than it used to be, displaying excellent pace of flavour development on the palate. Decent stuff! 40%. *Tullibardine Ltd.*

Highland Queen Sherry Cask Finish bott code L16 201 (81.5) n19 t22 f19 b21.5 The sherry isn't exactly free from sin, and the grape easily overpowers the nuances of the blend itself. So, attractive to a degree, but... 40%. *Tullibardine Ltd.*

Highland Queen 1561 bott code L16/80 28.01.16 (94) n23.5 t23.5 f23 b24. As it happens, I have a home where on a living room wall is an old oil painting of Fotheringhay, where the life of Mary Queen of Scots, the Highland Queen, ended on an executioners' block in 1561. Indeed, the house is quite close by and sits near the River Nene which passes through Fotheringhay. The village itself is quiet, particularly fragrant during Spring and Summer and with an unmistakable feel of history and elegance. Not at all unlike this excellent and most distinguished blend. 40%. *Tullibardine Ltd.*

Highland Queen 1561 30 Years Old bott code LF13017261 261 (88.5) n23.5 t23.5 f19.5 b22 Shame about the finish. Until then we had one of the sweetest yet gentle blends of the year. 40%.

Highland Reserve bott code B154 (80) n19 t21.5 f19.5 b20 An easy quaffing, silky and profoundly grained, toffee-enriched blend. 43%. *Quality Spirits International.*

Highland Warriors (82) n20 t21 f20.5 b20.5 This warrior must be wanting to raid a few grain stores... 40%. *Quality Spirits International.*

The Highland Way (82.5) n20 t21 f21 b20.5 Grainy, with a big sweet toffee middle which makes for a slightly juicy dram of a class barely distinguishable from so many other standard blends. 40%. *Quality Spirits International.*

The Highland Way bott code B445 (83.5) n20 t21.5 f21 b21 More Milky Way than Highland Way... Very similar to the 40% version, except some extra milk chocolate at the finish. 43%.

HM The King (89.5) n23 t22 f22 b22.5 So majestic to find a blend these days not swamped by artificial colouring. Royalty, indeed! 40%. *Branded Spirits USA.*

Islay Mist Aged 8 Years bott code: L20 06871 CB2 (93.5) n23.5 t23.5 f22.5 b24 Too often their 8-year-old versions have been more a case of Islay Missed than Mist. Not this time: bullseye! I could enjoy that any evening! 40%. *Macduff International.*

Islay Mist Aged 8 Years Amontillado Napoleon Cask Finish bott code L16/8826 (76) n19 t20 f18 b19 For those of you not carrying the sulphur recognition gene, I suspect this will be a delight. For those of us that do, well sorry: but not tonight, Napoleon. And this sulphur is a bit of a carry on, MacDuff... 43%. *MacDuff International Ltd.*

Islay Mist Aged 8 Years Manzanilla La Gitana Cask Finish bott code L15/8293 (85) n21.5 t22 f20 b21.5 Lots of phenolic cough sweet properties but the fruit and smoke form a tight, enclosed union with little room for scope. The finish is rather too bitter. 40%.

Islay Mist Aged 8 Years Palo Cortado Wellington Finish bott code: CBSC4 06075 05.08.19 (81) n20 t22 f19 b20 Tight, eye-wateringly sharp and fights against friendly integration despite the big lime marmalade theme. The niggling sulphur doesn't help at all. This Wellington has met a Napoleonic-type Waterloo... 43%. *Macduff International.*

Islay Mist Aged 10 Years bott code: L20 07001 CB2 (94) n23.5 t23.5 f23 b24 A rare blend where the emphasis is squarely in the malt. One glass of this is a near impossibility.... 40%. *Macduff International.*

Islay Mist Aged 12 Years bott code: L19 06053 CB2 (86.5) n21.5 t22.5 f20.5 b22 The grains are far more prevalent here than the 10-year-old, giving the blend an attractive softness at the price of complexity. Love the salivating delivery which makes up for the dull, slightly nagging finale. *40%. Macduff International.*

Islay Mist Aged 17 Years bott code L15/8826 **(96) n24 t24 f23.5 b24.5** A truly brilliant blend that should have no water added and be spared as much time as you can afford. *40%. MacDuff International Ltd.*

Islay Mist Aged 21 Years bott code: L20 07315 CB2 **(94.5) n24 t23.5 f23 b24** The blender should take a bow. Jolly well played: this is quite superb! *40%. Macduff International.*

Islay Mist Deluxe bott code L16/8283 **(87) n22 t22 f21.5 b21.5** A charmingly brazen blend, offering young peat to you with far less reserve than it once did. More an Islay Fog than Mist... *40%. MacDuff International Ltd.*

Isle of Skye 8 Years Old (94) n23 t24 f23.5 b23.5. Where once peat ruled and with its grain ally formed a smoky iron fist, now honey and subtlety reigns. A change of character and pace which may disappoint gung-ho peat freaks but will intrigue and delight those looking for a more sophisticated dram. *40%. Ian Macleod.*

Isle of Skye 21 years Old (91) n21 t23.5 f23 b23.5 What an absolute charmer! The malt content appears pretty high, but the overall balance is wonderful. *40%. Ian Macleod.*

Isle of Skye 50 Years Old (82.5) n21.5 t21 f20 b20. Drier incarnation than the 50% version. But still the age has yet to be balanced out, towards the end in particular. Early on some distinguished moments involving something vaguely smoked and a sweetened spice. *41.6%*

The Jacobite (78.5) n18 t18.5 f22 b20. Neither the nose nor delivery are of the cleanest style. But comes into its own towards the finish when the thick soup of a whisky thins to allow an attractive degree of complexity. Not for those with catholic tastes. *40%. Booker.*

James Alexander (85.5) n21 t21.5 f21.5 b21.5. Some lovely spices link the grassier Speysiders to the earthier elements. *40%. Quality Spirits International.*

James Buchanan's Special Reserve Aged 18 Years bott code: L7237CE001 **(89) n22.5 t24 f20.5 b22** A blend I have known and admired a very long time. Since indeed, my beard was black and I carried not an ounce of weight. And I am still, I admit, very much in love with, though she has betrayed me with a Spanish interloper... *40%.*

James Buchanan's Special Reserve Aged 18 Years bott code: L0003CE001 **(95.5) n24 t24 f23.5 b24** So understatedly complex and as always when free from any off-key sherry casks – as this is – sheer class...!!! *40%.*

James King Aged 5 Years (84) n19.5 t21 f21.5 b21.5 While the nose never quite gets going, things are quite different on the palate. And if you find a more agreeable chocolate fudge blend this year, please let me know. *43%. Quality Spirits International.*

James King Aged 8 Years (86) n21 t21 f22 b22 A far better constructed blend than of old, with the grains far more able to deal with the demands of the caramel. Fresh and salivating early on, despite the lushness, one can even fancy spotting the odd malt note before the spiced fudge takes command. *43%. Quality Spirits International.*

James King 12 Years Old (81) n19 t23 f19 b20. Caramel dulls the nose and finish. But for some time a quite beautiful blend soars about the taste buds offering exemplary complexity and weight. *40%. Quality Spirits International.*

James King Aged 12 Years bott code B289 **(84.5) n21 t22 f20.5 b21** The malt has a far grander say than the 40% version, chipping in with an elementary Speyside note on both nose and delivery. It doesn't take long for the fudge-rich grain to take command, though. Easy, un-taxing whisky. *43%. Quality Spirits International.*

J&B Jet (79.5) n19 t20 f20.5 b20. Never quite gets off the ground due to carrying too heavy a load. Unrecognisable to its pomp in the old J&B days: this one is far too weighty and never properly finds either balance or thrust. *40%. Diageo.*

J&B Reserve Aged 15 Years (78) n23 t19 f18 b18. What a crying shame. The sophisticated and demure nose is just so wonderfully seductive but what follows is an open-eyed, passionless embrace. Coarsely grain-dominant and unbalanced, this is frustrating beyond words and not worthy to be mentioned in the same breath as the old, original J&B 15 which, by vivid contrast, was a malty, salivating fruit-fest and minor classic. *40%. Diageo.*

J&B Rare (88.5) n21.5 t22.5 f22 b22.5 I have been drinking a lot of J&B from a previous time of late, due to the death of their former blender Jim Milne. I think he would have been pretty taken aback by the youthful zip offered here: whether it is down to a decrease in age or the use of slightly more tired casks – or both – is hard to say. *40%. Diageo*

Jock MacDonald Blended Whisky bott code: L20 Cb3 07469 **(88) n22 t22.5 f21.5 b22** A charming, sweet, surprisingly malty (well, early on) blend which sets its stall out to offer the gentlest of rides. High grade grain and a light smattering of lemon blossom honey at the start makes up for the thinner, but spicier finish. Limited in scope, but enjoyable. *43%.*

John Barr Reserve Blend bott code: L9287 09:38 P/010214 **(84) n21 t22 f20 b21** Never quite gels in the way I am now coming to expect from Whyte and Mackay blends. Lurches about both nose and palate as though unsure of which direction to take. The nose is a little raw, the finish bitter and lightly furry. The nuttiness between does have some attraction, though. *40%.*

Johnnie Walker Aged 18 Years bott code: L7276DN001 **(92) n23 t23.5 f22 b23.5** "The Pursuit of the Ultimate 18 year old Blend," says the label under the striding man. Well, they haven't reached their goal yet as, for all its deliciousness, this falls short of true Johnnie Walker brilliance thanks to an overly soft grain usage, when it was crying out for a variation which included a firmer, ramrod straight grain for extra mouthfeel complexity, and give something for the malts to bounce off. That said, the extra but by no means over enthusiastic use of phenols ensures impressive depth to a genuinely lovely whisky. *40%.*

Johnnie Walker Black Label 12 Years Old bott code: L8217CA003 **(95) n23.5 n24 f23.5 b24** Just another example of this blend being in tip-top form and showing a consistency which could almost make you weep with delight. The teasing phenols coupled with its salivating properties make for something rather special. *40%*

Johnnie Walker Black Label Aged 12 Years bott code L1198CA003 **(95) n23 t24 f24 b24** as I have mentioned elsewhere, blended whisky isn't quite where it should be quality-wise. However, Black Label 12 has made no compromise in quality. And although, for the first time since I first wrote the Whisky Bible in 2003 Chivas 12 has come close to matching it for sheer elegance and élan, still the long stride of Johnnie Walker was able to see it over the finishing line. *40%*

◈ **Johnnie Walker Black Label Aged 12 Years**, bott code L2343CA006 **(90.5) n22.5** where's the subtle smoke? Where is that sub strata of heather honey? Both AWOL and we instead have an unexpected, though by no means unattractive, essay of spice (where there was once peat) and toffee vanilla (where there was once honey); **t23.5** brilliant recovery on delivery. It is the texture which seduces, the almost corn oil type glycerine gliding over the tase buds, bringing with it a charming mix of barley sugar and lemon blossom honey; **f22** alas and alack, too thin. The vanilla and tannins have a big say here with a little butterscotch, too. But the spices play it alone with little body to cling to; **b22.5** the first time in years I have tasted a JW Red and Black side by side...and the Red won hands down. By no means a bad blend, it just lacks the Black Label traits of smoke and honey, and we are left with a much lighter creation. *40%*

Johnnie Walker Black Label Triple Cask Edition bott code: L8327CB009 **(92.5) n23 t23.5 f22.5 b23.5** Strange this should be in under the Black Label banner as it lacks the associated weight and delicate smokiness. Still silky and seductive, but much more naked grain on show. *40%.*

Johnnie Walker Blue Label (88) n21 t24 f21 b22 What a frustrating blend! Just so close to brilliance but the nose and finish are slightly out of kilter. Worth the experience of the mouth arrival alone. *43%. Diageo.*

Johnnie Walker Blue Label (89) n22.5 a cleaner nose than of late concentrating on the honey rather than the fruit - which had long been a mistake. Outstanding heather-honey and tannin interplay, but still a little fuzziness lurks; **t23.5** a much smokier delivery than is apparent on the nose, the peat and spices rushing headlong into the fray. The honey remains a little detached; **f21** excellent honeycomb towards the end. That furriness on the nose reignited here, sadly...; **b22.** Very decent, but still far from perfect. The furriness points to one weakness. Another is the 40% breaking up the oils, weakening the structure. If only this was at 46%... *40%.*

Johnnie Walker Blue Label The Casks Edition (97) n24.5 t24.5 f23.5 b24.5. This is a triumph of scotch whisky blending. With not as much as a hint of a single off note to be traced from the tip of the nose to tail, this shameless exhibition of complexity and brilliance is the star turn in the Diageo portfolio right now. Indeed, it is the type of blend that every person who genuinely adores whisky must experience for the good of their soul...if only once in their life. *55.8%.*

Johnnie Walker Blue Label Ghost & Rare bott code: L8277DN006 **(96) n24 t24 f23.5 b24.5** There is nothing new about using dead distilleries within a blend. However, finding them in one as good as this is a pretty rare occurrence. This just creaks of old whiskies all over the show. And what a marvellous show this is...for me, far more entertaining than the standard Blue Label thanks to less sherry influence, allowing the whiskies themselves to show their talents fully. *43.8%.*

Johnnie Walker Double Black (94.5) n23 t23.5 f24 b24. Double tops! Rolling along the taste buds like distant thunder, this is a welcome and impressive addition to the Johnnie Walker stable. Perhaps not as complete and rounded as the original Johnnie Walker Black...but, then, what is? *40%.*

Johnnie Walker Double Black bott code: L9320CA008 **(94) n23.5 t23 f23.5 b24** A kiss-and-tell blend with the softness of the grains making this among the most gentle of the blend on the market today, with all its attributes, even the peat, no more than a caress... *40%.*

Johnnie Walker Explorers' Club Collection The Gold Route (89) n23.5 t24 f19.5 b22. Much of this blend is truly the stuff of golden dreams. Like its Explorer's Club stable mate, some attention has to be paid to the disappointing finish. Worth sending out an expedition, though, just for the beautiful nose and delivery... *40%. Diageo.*

Johnnie Walker Explorer's Club Collection 'The Royal Route' (93) n24.5 t24 f21.5 b23 A fabulous journey, travelling first Class most of the way. But to have discovered more, could have been bottled at 46% for a much more panoramic view of the great whiskies on show. 40%. *Diageo*

Johnnie Walker Gold Label Reserve (91.5) n23 t24 f22 b23. Moments of true star quality here, but the finish could do with a polish. 40%. *Diageo.*

Johnnie Walker Gold Label Reserve bott code: L9214DN005 (91) n23 t24.5 f21.5 b22 A mixed bag of a bottling, with far more highs and lows than you'd normally find. Even so, the highs are of Everest proportions; 40%.

Johnnie Walker King George V db (88) n23 t22 f21 b22 One assumes that King George V is no relation to George IV. This has genuine style and breeding, if a tad too much caramel. 43%

Johnnie Walker Platinum Label Aged 18 Years (88) n22 t23 f21 b22. This blend might sound like some kind of Airmiles card. Which wouldn't be too inappropriate, though this is more Business than First... 40%. *Diageo.*

Johnnie Walker Red Label bott code: L8329T5001 (86) n21.5 t22 f21 b21.5 Seeing as I spend half my life travelling around the globe – or at least did until Covid-19 happened along – I probably get to taste Johnnie Walker Red more than any other blend as it is a staple of the world's Airline Lounges. And I must say it is rare to find two the same as the smoke levels can differ dramatically from one bottle to the next, sometimes peat-less, at others seemingly not far off a thinned out Caol Ila. So I must say the Striding Man has become a bit of a friend and travelling companion to me. Which makes it all the more odd and ironic that the first time I actually sit down with a bottle of Red for the Whisky Bible for a year or two this is the first to display a furry note and tang. I have noticed that for the last year it had improved impressively, more often than not with a pleasing smoky rumble and on average from the dozen or so different bottles I've sampled from around the globe, a score something like an 89 world be nearer the mark. Only moderate peating to this and the caramels are just a little too enthusiastic: it is reminiscent of when the blend went through a wobble a couple of years back.... Bet you when I'm back travelling again, the first JW Red will be a belter....! 40%.

⟫ **Johnnie Walker Red Label**, bott code L2337T5002 (94.5) n23.5 adorable spices emphasise the art played by the smoke in gingering up the relaxed grain. Busy, complex and rewarding; t23.5 mouth-filling and salivating in one fell swoop. The malts galivant around the palate with abandon, slowly giving way to the more robust grain and smoke mix. Almost an estery sweetness: unusual in a blend these days; f23.5 long, lush and still the smoke has much to say, bringing in the spices with a clever build up; b24 you have to doff your top hat to this Striding Man. Weakened only by a surfeit of toffee, this is otherwise a charming reminder of just how easily effective a well-balanced blend can - and should – be. High quality grain perfectly accompanied by genteel malts...though with a pleasing degree of smoke to offer both higher and more base tones. Seriously impressive. 40%

Johnnie Walker Select Casks Aged 10 Years Rye Cask Finish (90) n22.5 t23 f21.5 b23 With the use of first fill bourbon casks and ex-rye barrels for finishing, hardly surprising this is the JW with the most Kentuckian feel of them all. Yet it's even more Canadian, still. 46% (92 proof).

Johnnie Walker X.R Aged 21 Years (94) n23.5 t24 f23 b23.5. How weird: I nosed this blind before seeing what the brand was. My first thought was: "mmm, same structure of Crown Royal XR. Canadian??? No, there's smoke!" Then looked at what was before me and spotted it was its sister whisky from the Johnnie Walker stable. A coincidence? I don't think so... 40%.

Kenmore Special Reserve Aged 5 Years bott code L07285 (75) n18 t20 f19 b18. Recovers to a degree from the poor nose. For those who prefer their Scotch big-flavoured and gawky. 40%

Label 5 Aged 12 Years bott code L515467C (90) n23 t22.5 f22 b22.5 One of the easiest drams you'll find this year with just enough complexity to lift it into the higher echelons. 40%.

Label 5 Extra Rare Aged 18 Years bott code L5301576 (87.5) n21.5 t22.5 f22 b21.5 You have to say this is pleasant. But from an 18-year-old blend you should be saying so much more. Salivating and at times fresh and juicy, other than the late spice little gets the pulses racing in the vanilla and sugar morass. A tad too much toffee, alas. 40%.

Label 5 Classic Black bott code L403055D (87) n22 t22 f21 b22 A malt famed for its indifferent nose now boasts an aroma boasting complexity, layering and spice. The mix of spice and muscovado sugars elsewhere is no less appealing, though the mouthfeel is a little too fat and yielding. But what an improvement! 40%. *La Martiniquaise.*

Label 5 Gold Heritage (92) n22.5 t23.5 f22 b24 A very classy blend very skilfully constructed. A stunningly lovely texture, one of the very best I have encountered for a while, and no shortage of complexity ensures this is a rather special blend. I'll even forgive the dulling by caramel and light milkiness from the tired bourbon barrel. The overall excellence outweighs the odd blemish. 40%

Label 5 Premium Black bott code: L720856A (84.5) n21 t22 f20.5 b21 An, at first, luscious, then later on ultra-firm blend with the accent decidedly on the grain and caramels. 40%.

Langs Full & Smoky (89) n22.5 t22.5 f21.5 b22.5 Light and smoky would be a more apt description. But a pleasant peaty blend all the same. 43%. Ian Macleod Distillers.

Langs Rich & Refined (90) n23 beautiful structure to this: nutty and warming, vaguely spiced vanillas – offering both weight and lightness of touch simultaneously; t22.5 the grains perhaps have the braver say even on delivery, but they are assisted by a glossy oiliness which bigs up the light thread of acacia honey. The midpoint has a distinctly Mars Bar feel of nougat, chocolate and caramel working in unison; f22 mainly spices carried on the oils; b22.5 a thoughtfully crafted, quietly complex blend. 46%. Ian Macleod Distillers.

Langs Smooth & Mellow (88.5) n22.5 t22.5 f21.5 b22 No quibbling with the name of this brand! Most of the action is on the graceful nose and honey-flecked delivery which is briefly chewy. The dry and slightly bitter finish, though, doesn't try to compensate for the obvious lack in weight. That apart, agreeably easy going. 43%. Ian Macleod Distillers.

The Last Drop 1965 American Standard Barrel (96.5) n24 t24.5 f23.5 b24.5 Almost impossible to imagine a blended whisky to be better balanced than this. If there is a cleverer use of honey or less intrusive oak in any blended whisky bottled in the last year, I have yet to taste it. An award winner if ever I tasted one. Magnificent doesn't quite cover it... 48.6%. Morrison Bowmore. The Last Drop Distillers Ltd.

The Last Drop 1971 Blended Scotch Whisky 45 Years Old (97) n24.5 t24 f24 b24.5 Even though I now know many of the people involved in the Last Drop, I am still not entirely sure how they keep doing it. Just how do they continue to unearth whiskies which are truly staggering; absolute marvels of their type? This one is astonishing because the grain used is just about faultless. And the peating levels can be found around about the perfect mark on the dial. Like an old Ballantine's which has sat and waited in a cask over four decades to be discovered and tell its wonderful, spellbinding and never-ending tale. Just mesmerically beautiful. 47%.

The Last Drop 50 Year Old Sherry Wood (97) n24 t24.5 f24 b24.5 You'd expect, after half a century in the cask, that this would be a quiet dram, just enjoying its final years with its feet up and arms behind its head. Instead we have a fairly aggressive blend determined to drive the abundant fruitiness it still possesses to the very hilt. It is backed up all the way by a surprising degree of warming, busy spice. There is a hell of a lot of life in this beautiful ol' dog... 51.2%

The Last Drop 56 Year Old Blended Scotch Whisky (96.5) n24.5 t24.5 f23.5 b24 Just one of those whiskies there is not enough time in the day for. One to share with your partner...when the lights are low and you are on your own... 47%.

Lauder's bott code L 08 10 14 4 BB (78.5) n19 t20 f19.5 b20 For those who like whisky with their cream toffee. Decent spice fizz, though. 40%. MacDuff International Ltd.

Lauder's Aged 15 Years bott code L16/8189 (93) n23 t23.5 f22.5 b24 Not the big fat sherry influence of a decade ago...thank heavens...!! This is a gorgeous blend for dark, stormy nights. Well, any night really... 40%. MacDuff International Ltd.

Lauder's Aged 25 Years bott code: P001434 2020/03/18 (91) n23 t23 f22 b23 After two months of incarceration in my British cottage, I moved my tasting room into the garden where the air was still and the whiskies seemed to be more at home: at one with nature. In the cloudless sky a pair of swifts danced for their prey above my garden, one, its head bleached white as it faced the setting sun; the other, as it twisted and turned, reflected the powerful, dying rays off its coal-black wings. To my left a pair of great tits flew to and from their secret chamber in "Mum's" ancient apple tree on their thankless task of feeding their brood. While, just 30 feet away, a crow sat atop a fir, bellowing his mastery over all he surveyed. Meanwhile, a blackbird chinked its evening alarm, much in the way robins do at home in Frankfort. So it was when Archibald Lauder created his first blend in the first half of the 19th century; and so it is now. The finest things in life never change... 42%. Macduff International.

Lauder's Oloroso Cask bott code L 25 01 16 4 BB (86.5) n21.5 t24 f19 b22 A magnificent blend for those unable to nose or taste sulphur. For those who can, a nearly whisky as this is borderline brilliant. Yes, both nose and finish especially have their weakness, but the narrative of the delivery, not to mention the brilliance of the mouthfeel and overall weight and pace of the dram is sublime. Before the sulphur hits we are treated to a truly glorious Jaffa cake mix of controlled fruity sweetness as good as any blend I have tasted this year. 40%. MacDuff International Ltd.

Lauder's Queen Mary bott code L 04 11 14 4 BB (86.5) n22.5 t21.5 f21 b21.5 The sweet oily aroma of Angel Cake and even some roast chestnut: the nose is certainly highly attractive. This almost translates through the body of blend when the caramel allows, the grains showing an oily strain and a slightly malty kick here and there. 40%. MacDuff International Ltd.

Liquid Treasures From Miles Away Taraansay 12 Year Old bourbon barrel, dist Apr 07, bott Feb 20 (92) n22.5 t23 f23 b23.5 A very pretty, flawlessly structured blend which milks every last degree of juiciness from mix of ulmo honey and light maple syrup which have been liberally sprinkled with spice. Not big on complexity, but knows how to maximise on effect, using the full body and delicate oils with aplomb. So lovely. 59.5%. sc. 249 bottles.

The Loch Fyne (89.5) n22 t23 f21.5 b23. This is an adorable old-style blend....a bit of a throwback. But no ruinous sherry notes...just clean and delicious. Well, mainly... 40%

Loch Lomond Reserve db (86.5) n21.5 t22 f21.5 b21.5. A spongy, sweet, chewy, pleasant blend which is more of a take as you find statement than a layering of flavour. 40%

Loch Lomond Signature bott code L3/306/15 (86) n22 t21.5 f21 b21.5 Not quite the malty force it can be, though the sugar almonds are a treat. Succulent and gently spiced though the caramel has just a little too much force towards the end. 40%. Loch Lomond Group.

Lombard Gold Label (88) n22 t22 f22 b22 after evaluating this I read the tasting notes on the back of the label and for about the first time this year thought: "actually, the bottlers have the description pretty spot on. So tasted it again, this time while reading the notes and found myself agreeing with every word: a first. Then I discovered why: they are my tasting notes from the 2007 Whisky Bible, though neither my name nor book have been credited... A gold label, indeed... 40%.

Long John Special Reserve bott code: 2017/08/10 (87.5) n21.5 t22 f21.5 b22 An honest, non-fussy blend which makes a point of stacking the bigger flavours up front so it hits the ground running. The grains and toffee shape all aspects, other than this rich delivery where the malt offers both weight and a lighter, salivating quality also; an even a gentle thread of honey. The type of blend that an offer for a refill will be seldom refused. 40%.

Lord Elcho (83.5) n20 t22 f21 b20.5 Such a vast improvement on the last bottling I encountered: this has lush grain at the front, middle and rear that entertains throughout, if a little one dimensionally. A little bit of a tweak and could be a high class blend. 40%. Wemyss Malts.

Lord Elcho Aged 15 Years (89.5) n23.5 t22.5 f21.5 b22 Three or four years ago this was a 15-year-old version of the Lord Elcho standard blend today. So, small mercies, this has moved on somewhat and now offers up a genuinely charming and complex nose and delivery. One is therefore surprised to be disappointed by the denouement, taking into account the blend's history. Some more clever and attentive work on the middle and finish would have moved this into seriously high quality blend territory. But so much to enjoy as it is. 40%. Wemyss Malts.

Lord Scot (77.5) n18.5 t20 f19.5 b19.5. A touch cloying but the mocha fudge ensures a friendly enough ride. 40%. Loch Lomond Distillers.

The Lost Distilleries Blend batch 9 (91) n23 t23.5 f22.5 b23 The distilleries may be lost to us, but on the palate they are especially at home. 52.1%. 476 bottles.

Mac Na Mara bott code L 25 08 14 2 07 48 BB (84) n21.5 t22 f19.5 b21 As usual, a glass of tricks as the flavours come tumbling at you from every direction. Few blends come saltier and the dry vanilla forges a fascinating balance with the rampant caramel. A fraction furry at the death. 40%. Pràban na Linne Ltd.

Mac Na Mara Rum Cask Finish bott code L 23 05 16 3 BB (86) n22.5 t22 f21 b21.5 Lost a degree of the sugary crispness normally associated with this brand and after the initial rum embrace resorts far too quickly to a caramel-rich game-plan. 40%. ncf. Pràban na Linne Ltd.

Mac's Reserve bott code: L9C 7908 0711 (84) n21 t21.5 f21 b20.5 Perfectly acceptable, easy going soft and sweet whisky. But if they really want to pay tribute to cooper Jimmy Mackie, the Mac in question, then they should drop the toffee and let the oak do the talking. 40%.

MacArthur's bott code L16/L31 R16/5192 IB 1735 (87.5) n21.5 t22 f21.5 b22.5 Not quite the tricky and cleverly smoked blend of a few years back. But still a weightier chap than a decade ago, not least because of the softer grain type. The malts do come through with just enough meaning to make for a well-balanced and thoroughly enjoyable offering. 40%.

MacQueens (89) n21.5 t22.5 f22.5 b22.5. I am long enough in the tooth now to remember blends like this found in quiet country hotels in the furthest-flung reaches of the Highlands beyond a generation ago. A wonderfully old-fashioned, traditional one might say, blend of a type that is getting harder and harder to find. 40%. Quality Spirits International.

MacQueens of Scotland Aged 3 Years (86) n20.5 t22 f21.5 b22 Rare to find a blend revealing its age at 3 years, though of course many are that.... and a day. Enjoyable, with attractive weight and even an ulmo honey note to partner the spices which, combined, makes it distinctively a cut above for its type. 40%. Quality Spirits International.

MacQueens of Scotland Aged 8 Years (78.5) n18 t21.5 f19 b20 A little furry and off key. 40%. Quality Spirits International.

MacQueens of Scotland Aged 12 Years (89.5) n23 t22.5 f21.5 b22.5 Some outstanding malts have gone into this charming blend. 40%. QSI.

Master of Malt Blended 10 Years Old 1st Edition (84.5) n21.5 t22.5 f20 b20.5. A pleasant enough, though hardly complex, blend benefitting from the lovely malty, then silky pick-up from delivery and a brief juicy barley sharpness. But unsettled elsewhere due, mainly, to using the wrong fit of grain: too firm when a little give was needed. 47.5%. ncf. WB15/353

Master of Malt 30 Year Old Blended Scotch Whisky (86) n21.5 t23 f20 b21.5 Typical of Master of Malt blends it is the delivery which hits fever pitch in which myriad juicy notes make a mockery of the great age. Sadly, on this occasion both the nose and finish are undone by some ungainly oak interference, and latterly quite a tang. 47.5%.

Master of Malt 40 Year Old Blended Scotch Whisky batch 1 (93.5) n24 t23.5 f22.5 b23.5 Some outstanding oak at play here. For a blend the grains and malts appear a little isolated from the other, but the overall effect is still wonderful. 47.5%.

Master of Malt 50 Year Old Blended Scotch Whisky (92.5) n24 t23.5 f22 b23 Hard to keep all the casks of over 50 years in line. But so much else is sublime. 47.5%.

Master Of Malt St Isidore (84) n21 t22 f20 b21. Sweet, lightly smoked but really struggles to put together a coherent story. Something, somewhere, is not quite right. 41.4%

Matisse db (90) n22 enticing pink grapefruit juice offers extra freshness; t23 soft and salivating from the start there is a sparkle both to the light citrus tones and muscovado sugars. Such satisfying weight and surprising depth with the barley showing through excellently; f22.5 vanilla and spice; b22.5 a superb every-day blend of no little charm and complexity. 40%

Matisse Aged 12 Years (88.5) n22 t22 f22 b22.5 Creamy and pleasant, the extra tannins appear to blot out the barley which impresses so well on my standard blend, making the grain here that little bit starker. Extra spice, naturally, with the age and depth. But not quite the same elegance. 40%. Matisse Spirits Company.

Matisse Aged 12 Years (89.5) n22 t23 f22 b22.5 A good deal of fruit can be found on both nose and delivery, though always on the light, ethereal side. Indeed the aroma has a lot of freshly cut green apple and cucumber while lime blossom honey accounts for the satisfying sweetness on delivery. Some really good spices at play, too. Light, elegant and always broadcasting an alluring charm. 40%

Matisse Aged 21 Years (80.5) n22 t22.5 f17 b19 The sulphur rumble on the finish does a dis-service to the chocolate raisin preamble. 40%. Matisse Spirits Company.

Matisse Aged 21 Years (88) n22 t23 f21 b22 Although toffee and grain are poking through from every direction there is enough malt to ensure depth. The highlight, though, is the resounding, thick, honey-laden delivery, bolstered by beautifully weighted spice. The slightly untidy finish is not in keeping with the excellence of the delivery, though. Bold, chewy and always on the hefty side: a substantial blend. 40%

Matisse Old Luxury Blend (92.5) n23 t23 f23 b23.5 ONe of those very classy blends you'd rather not spit out... At 46% would probably go up a point or two. 40%. Matisse Spirits Company.

Matisse Old Luxury Blend (86) n21.5 t23 f20.5 b21.5 All the luxuriating comes in the brilliant delivery and follow through which is sumptuous and creamy, sweet and oily like the filling in a Swiss roll. The finish is a little threadbare and tangy by comparison and the nose grain reliant. But that delivery....wow! 40%. Matisse Spirits Company.

Matisse Royal (81) n19 t22 f20 b20. Pleasant, if a little clumsy. Extra caramel appears to have scuppered the spice. 40%. Matisse Spirits Co Ltd.

McArthurs (89.5) n22 t22.5 f22 b23 One of the most improved blends on the market. The clever use of the peat is exceptional. 40%. Inverhouse Distillers.

McKendrick's 3 Years Old (71) n18 t20 f16 b17 "Supple, Strong and Silky" boasts the label. Unsubtle, standard 40% abv and silky says the whisky. Cloying to a degree and with a little sulphur off note late on, presumably from the ex-sherry grain casks. Not Asda's finest. 46%. Asda

Monarch of the Glen (81) n20 t21 f20 b20 A youthful grainfest wallowing in its fat and sweet personality. 40%. Quality Spirits International.

Monarch of the Glen Aged 8 Years (82.5) n19 t20.5 f21.5 b21.5 The initially harsh grain takes time to settle but eventually finds a decent fudge and spiced mocha theme. 40%. QSI.

Monarch of the Glen Aged 12 Years (82) n22 t22.5 f22 b22 I always enjoyed this for its unusual fruity nature. Well, the fruit has gone and been replaced by chocolate. A fair swap: it's still delicious! 40%. Quality Spirits International.

⟐ **Morrison's Aged 3 Years**, bott code L100823 (88.5) n22 t22.5 f22 b22 A young blend it may be, and a supermarket one at that. But there is nothing wrong with this silky soft offering. Plenty of sweetness on the palate, perhaps toffee here and there. But just the lightest trace of smoke, especially on the nose, also ensures some unexpected and delightful depth. 40%

Muirhead's Blue Seal bott code L15 138 780 21 (84.5) n21.5 t21 f21 b21 A clean, uncluttered and attractive blend with heavy emphasis on grain and no shortage of caramel and spice. A distinct wisp of malt can be located from time to time. 40%. Tullibardine Ltd.

The Naked Grouse (76.5) n19 t21 f17.5 b19. Sweet. But reveals too many ugly sulphur tattoos. 40%.

Nation of Scots (92.5) n23 t23 f23 b23.5 Apparently, this is a blend designed to unite Scots around the world. Well, I'm not Scottish but it's won me over. If only more blends could be as deliciously embracing as this. 52%. Annandale Distillery.

Oishii Wisukii Aged 36 Years (96) n24.5 t23.5 f24 b24 Normally, I'd suggest popping into the Highlander for a pint of beer. But if they happen to have any of this stuff there...break his bloody arm off: it's magnificent! 46.2%. *The Highlander Inn, Craigellachie.*

Old Masters G (93) n24 t23 f23 b23 A high quality blend with enough clarity and complexity to suggest they have not stinted on the malt. The nose, in particular, is sublime. Thankfully they have gone easy on the colouring here, as it this is so delicate it could have ruined the artistry. 40%. *Lombard Scotch Whisky Ltd.*

Old McDonald (83.5) n20 t22 f20.5 b21. Attractively tart and bracing where it needs to be with lovely grain bite. Lots of toffee, though. 43.%. *The Last Drop Distillers. For India.*

Old Parr 12 Years Old (91.5) n21.5 t23.5 f23 b23.5 Perhaps on about the fourth of fifth mouthful, the penny drops that this is not just exceptionally good whisky: it is blending Parr excellence... 40%. *Diageo.*

Old Parr Aged 15 Years (84) n19 t22 f21 b22. Absolutely massive sherry input here. Some of it is of the highest order. The nose, reveals, however, that some isn't... 43%

Old Smuggler (85.5) n21 t22 f21 b21.5. A much sharper act than its Allied days with a new honeyed-maple syrup thread which is rather delightful. Could still do with toning down the caramel, though, to brighten the picture further. 40%. *Campari, France.*

Old St. Andrews Clubhouse batch no. L2997 G2716 **(87.5)** n21.5 t22 f22 b22 Just a little extra grain bite to this one means the usual juiciness is down, though the slow spice build is pretty sexy. Lots of coffee-toffee tones to chew over. 40%.

Outlaw King bott code: L19 199 PB **(90)** n23 t22.5 f22 b22.5 More of an Outlaw Queen with a delicate but shapely body like this. And, indeed, once upon a time blends displaying this degree of naked peatiness were outlawed. Blenders veered away from smokiness after the Second World war to concentrate on lighter, softer creations. With smoke very much back in vogue it is great to see a blend shewing so little reserve in its peaty intent. 40%.

Passport bott 2019/08/11 **(83.5)** n20 t21.5 f21 b21 Just a fleeting moment after the delivery when Jimmy Laing old masterpiece flashes onto the scene only to be quickly eviscerated by the uncompromising caramels. 40%

Parkers (78) n17 t22 f20 b19. The nose has regressed, disappearing into ever more caramel, yet the mouth-watering lushness on the palate remains and the finish now holds greater complexity and interest. 40%. *Angus Dundee.*

Pure Scot bott code: L 08 02 17 **(87)** n21.5 t22.5 f21.5 b22 The grain is both yielding and profound while the malt notes mostly are lost in a toffee swirl. Mid to late arrives spices, but complexity is at a premium and the structure perhaps a little too soft. That said, a little acacia honey goes a long way and the overall experience is very satisfying indeed, especially with the sugars always slightly ahead of the game. 40%. *Bladnoch Distillery.*

Pure Scot Virgin Oak 43 virgin oak cask finish, bott code: L18/89.7 **(93)** n23 23.5 f23 b23.5 A sensational little blend worth finding. Not particularly complex as to regards malt and grain layering, but the integration of the tannins for a blend is a rare joy. 43%. *Bladnoch Distillery.*

Queen Margot (85.5) n21.5 t22 f21 b21. A clean, silky-textured, sweet and caramel-rich blend of disarming simplicity. 40%

Queen Margot Aged 5 Years (89) n22 t22.5 f22 b22.5 A very attractive blend with a most agreeable level of chewability. The chocolate orange which bolsters the yielding grain appears to suggest some good, clean sherry influence along the way. 40%

Queen Margot Aged 8 Years (85) n21 t22 f21 b21. Pleasant, untaxing, with a hint of oaky vanilla after the sugary crescendo. 40%

Robert Burns (85) n20 t22.5 f21 b21.5. Skeletal and juicy: very little fat and gets to the mouthwatering point pretty quickly. Genuine fun. 40%. *Isle of Arran.*

The Royal & Ancient (80.5) n20 t21.5 f19 b20. Has thinned out dramatically in the last year or so. Now clean, untaxing, briefly mouth-watering and radiating young grain throughout. 40%

Royal Salute 21 Years Old bott code LKSK2858 2016/07/13 **(96)** n24 t23.5 f24 b24.5 Elegant, sensual and the epitome of great blending. What else would you expect...? 40%. *Chivas Brothers.*

Royal Salute 21 Year Old The Lost Blend (95.5) n24 t24 f23.5 b24 Lost Blend...? Panic over, chaps: discovered it in my Whisky Bible tasting lab....!! And well worth finding, too.... 40%.

Royal Salute 21 Years Old The Polo Collection bott code 2017/04/25 LPNL0722 **(95)** n23.5 t23.5 f24 b24 A significantly different RS21 to the last standard bottling I came across, this being very much meatier – which is rather apt seeing that horses are involved. Mixes suave sophistication with a certain ruggedness: not unlike polo, I suppose. Not a dram to chukka away under any circumstances... 40%. *Chivas Brothers Ltd.*

Royal Salute 21 Year Old Polo Collection 3 (92) n23 t23.5 f22.5 b23 As soft as a velvet polo jumper... 46.5%.

Royal Salute 25 Year Old The Signature Blend (93) n24 t23.5 f22.5 b23 A curious blend which both underlines its age, yet with the lightness of touch, then proceeds to hide it, too. 40%.

Royal Salute 32 Years Old Union of the Crowns bott code 2017/01/17 LPNL0102 **(96.5)** n24 t24.5 f24 b24 I trust Nicola Sturgeon has given The Union of Crowns, this truly outstanding and worthy Scotch blend to celebrate the joining the kingdoms of England, Scotland and Ireland, her seal of approval and she will help promote it fervently as a great Scottish export... 40%.

Royal Salute 38 Years Old Stone of Destiny bott code 2016/12/20 LPNK2479 **(93.5)** n24 t23.5 f22.5 b23.5 Knowing the blender and having a pretty educated guess at the range of stocks he would have to work from, I tried to picture in my mind's eye how this whisky would nose and taste even before I opened the bottle. In particular, I tried to pre-guess the mouthfeel, a character vital especially in older blends but often overlooked by those who eventually taste it, though it actually plays a significant role without the drinker realising it. Well, both the nose and mouthfeel were just as I had imagined, though some aspects of the finish were slightly different. An engrossing and elegant dram. 40%. Chivas Brothers Ltd.

Royal Salute 62 Gun Salute (95.5) n24.5 t24 f23 b24 How do you get a bunch of varying whiskies in style, but each obviously growing a grey beard and probably cantankerous to boot, to settle in and harmonise with the others? A kind of Old People's Home for whisky, if you like. Well, here's how...43%. Chivas.

Royal Salute The Diamond Tribute (91) n23.5 t23 f21.5 b23. Ironic that a diamond is probably the hardest natural creation, yet this whisky is one of man's softest... 40%. Chivas.

Royal Salute The Eternal Reserve (89.5) n23 t23.5 f21 b22 One of those strange whiskies where so much happens on the nose and delivery, but much less when we head to the finish 40%

Royal Silk Reserve Aged 5 Years (92.5) n23 t23 f23 b23.5 I was lucky enough to be the first person outside the tasting lab to sample this whisky when it was launched at the turn of this century. It was quite wonderful then, it still is so today though the grains aren't quite as brittle and translucent as they were back then. Still, I admire beyond words the fact that the current blenders have eschewed the craze for obscuration by ladelling in the colouring as though lives depended on it. What we can nose and taste here in this heart-gladdeningly light (both in colour and personality) blend is whisky. As an aside, very unusual for a blend to hide its age away on the back label. 40%.

Royal Warrior (86) n21 t22 f21.5 b21.5. An entirely pleasant grain-rich, young, old fashioned blend which masters the prevalent sugars well when they appear to be getting out of hand. Extremely clean and beautifully rounded. 40%

Sandy Mac (76) n18 t20 f19 b19. Basic, decent blend that's chunky and raw. 40%. Diageo.

Scots Earl (76.5) n18 t20 f19 b19.5. Its name is Earl. And it must have upset someone in a previous life. Always thrived on its engaging disharmony. But just a tad too syrupy now. 40%.

Scottish Collie (78) n18 t20 f20 b20 I thought I heard you saying it was a pity: pity I never had any good whiskies. But you're wrong. I have. Thousands of them. Thousands of them. And all drams.... 40%. Quality Spirits International.

Scottish Collie (80) n20 t21 f19 b20 A greatly improved blend with a far more vivacious delivery full of surprising juiciness and attractively controlled sweetness. Not as much toffee influence as had once been the case, so the spices cancels out the harsh finish. 43%. QSI.

Scottish Leader Aged 12 Years bott code P037533 L3 09.18 16082 **(89.5)** n22 t23 f22 b22.5 A vast improvement on the last Leader 12 I encountered, this really finding a relaxed yet intriguing style. 40%.

Scottish Leader Original bott code P03 555 L 08.35 16342 **(83)** n19 t22 f21 b21 Had this been the "original" Scottish leader I tasted 20 or so years ago we'd have a lighter coloured, less caramel heavy, more malt sparkling whisky. As it is, overcomes a cramped nose to offer some excellent complexity on delivery. 40%.

Scottish Leader Signature bott code P038914 L316256 **(90.5)** n22 t23.5 f22 b23 Thoroughly enjoyable and beautifully constructed blend in which thought has clearly gone into both weight, texture and flavour profiling: not a given for blends these days. The nose and delivery are waxy with a vague honey richness; the delivery uses that honey to full effect by offering a growing firmness and then busy interplay between light oak, spices and weightier malts. Had they gone a little easier on the dumbing-down toffee, this might have bagged an award. 40%.

Scottish Leader Supreme bott code P039255 L3 14.21 16278 **(77)** n18.5 t20 f19 b19.5 Sticky, sweet and overly simple. 40%.

Scottish Piper bott code L17033 **(82)** n20 t20 f21.5 b20.5 Continues its traditional toffee drone, though with a spicier finale than before. 40%. Burlington Drinks

Scottish Piper Blended Scotch Whisky bott code: L20205 **(88)** n22 t22.5 f21.5 b22 A light smoke accompaniment drones long into the delivery like the bagpipes depicted on the quaint label. These phenols are easily detected on the nose, too, ensuring a satisfying weight and a malty countenance to balance out of the firm young grain. Might be stretching it to say this is complex, but it is still very highly satisfying... 40%

Scottish Prince (83.5) n21 t22 f20 b20.5. Muscular, but agreeably juicy. 40%

Sia Blended Scotch Whisky (87) n21 t22.5 f21.5 b22. Rare to find a blend that's so up front with its smoke. Doesn't scrimp on the salivation stakes or sheer chewiness, either. *43%*

Sir Edward's Aged 12 Years bott 18-09-2018, bott code: L826170-00150 **(87.5) n22 t22 f21.5 b22** Worth having around the house for the charming 1930's-style label alone. They make big play of the brand having been around since 1891 – the year of my maternal grandmother's birth! – and even have 1891 included in the mould of the bottle. But an unnecessary over-reliance of caramel takes the score down. There is enough evidence on the early clarity and texture of the grain that this blend could hold its own and entertain thoroughly in its natural state. Rather lovely spices counter the sweetness impressively. Simple, but genuinely enjoyable whisky. *40%. Bardinet.*

Sir Edward's Aged 12 Years Blended Whisky bott code: L104670 15/02/2021 **(88) n22 t23 f21 b22** A slight improvement on the last bottling, mainly through a very slight injection of smoke into a blend that appears predisposed towards phenols. Again, the caramel brings the score down slightly. But when you add the light saltiness together with the heather honey on delivery, plus spice and additional smoke, you cannot but conclude that this is a more than satisfactory blend. *40%.*

Sir Lawrence Original (88.5) n22 t22.5 f22 b22 A simple and thoroughly enjoyable blend which wrings as much character out of the grain as possible and marries it with the most playful barley notes which peak just after delivery. Vanilla and toffee are in abundance but, thanks to the outstanding fitness of the grain, are unable to alter the overall contoured shape of the blend. Excellent spices, too. Simple, but satisfying. *40%*

Sir Lawrence Original bott code: L2007792CB1 **(87) n21.5 t22.5 f21.5 b21.5** A little malt has gone a long way here, perhaps reflecting the excellence of the grain at work. A little toffeed, perhaps, but the vanilla impresses mightily, as does the early jam doughnut sweetness. Clean and lip-smacking. *40%*

Sir Edward's Finest Blended Whisky bott code: L027272-025111 **(83.5) n20.5 t21.5 f20.5 b21** Doesn't quite reach the heights as their very acceptable 12-year-old either in finding its balance or narrative. Nothing wrong with the delivery, though, which makes the most of a satisfying mouth feel. *40%*

Sir Edward's Smoky Blended Whisky nbc **(93) n23** I admit it: this is a far better nose than I expected. Very good grain means minimal interference and maximum softening of the gentle phenols that steadily build in depth; **t23.5** brilliant! A near perfect match between the peat and young grain means the phenols literally melt in the mouth on arrival while the smoke is followed by the most pleasing Demerara sugars. And what a delivery! Sweet, fresh and salivating...just too rare in blended whisky these days; **f23** a longer finish than it first seems: once more the grains are top notch, ensuring a lulling softness and an unrestricted view of the light oak. The slow build of spice is rather glorious and more than enough to make do with... **b23.5** it is quite amazing what some judiciously added peat can do to an otherwise standard blend. I doff my hat here: the phenol levels are exactly where they need to be to maximise complexity and balance. Excellent. *40%.*

Something Special bott code LPFK 1116 2016/06/30 **(90) n22 t22.5 f23 b22.5** One of the few blends that has actually improved in recent years. Always been an attractive, interesting if non-spectacular blend which I have enjoyed when meeting it at various bars with friends around the world. Now there is personality enough to punch through the toffee and leave you wanting more. *40%. Chivas Brothers Ltd.*

Something Special Legacy (92) n23 t22.5 f23 b23.5 Good, solid blender is David Boyd. And here he has married substance with subtlety. Lovely stuff. *40%*

The Sovereign 45 Years Old Blended Scotch cask no. 15894, dist Dec 73, bott Mar 19 **(94.5) n23.5 t23.5 f24 b23.5** Falls under the luxuriant heading for a blended scotch. Soft, silky and unravels at the most gentle of paces. *51%. sc. 300 bottles. Bottled for The Whisky Barrel.*

⋙ **Special Reserve**, bott code L2347 **(92.5) n23** pretty taken aback by the depth of the smoke here which puffs out like an old steam engine. Light kippery lead with a squeeze of lemon. The grain cuts in with firm hands, but always perfectly in tune; **t23** substantial oils meet the crunchy muscovado sugars head on. The smoke both billows gently and adds to the zingy spices. That thin layer of zesty grapefruit juice goes a long way...; **f22.5** long with an attractive vanilla tail. But the oily smoke clings on for even more depth; **b23.5** an attractively smoky blend enlivened by a surprise citrus thread that is especially prominent on the nose and finish. Impressive mouthfeel and chewability, salivating and sure-footed. One of the best basic supermarket blends I have tasted for a good decade or more. *40% One Stop*

Stag Hunter (79) n19 t20 f20 b20 Hard to get past the gin-type nose. Not sure if this is a bottling hall issue, or if we have a blend that celebrates a botanical-style personality. *40%*

Stag Hunter L17039 **(79) n20.5 t20 f19 b19.5** A very basic blend which struggles to get past the grain and toffee. The bitterish finish leaves a little to be desired. *40%*

Teacher's Aged 25 Years batch 1 **(96.5) n24 t24.5 f23.5 b24.5** Only 1300 bottles means they will be hard pushed to create this exact style again. Worth a go, chaps: considering this is India bound, it is the Kama Sutra of blended scotch. *46%. Beam Inc. 1300 bottles. India & Far East Travel Retail exclusive.*

Teacher's Origin (92) n23 t23 f23 b23 Almost brings a tear to the eye to taste a Scotch blend that really is a blend. With a better grain input (Dumbarton, say),this perhaps would have been one of the contenders of World Whisky of the Year. Superb! *40%*

Teacher's Origin (88.5) n22 t23.5 f21 b22 A fascinating blend among the softest on the market today. That is aided and abetted by the exceptionally high malt content, 65%, which makes this something of an inverted blend, as that, for most established brands, is the average grain content. What appears to be a high level of caramel also makes for a rounding of the edges, as well as evidence of sherry butts. The bad news is that this has resulted in a duller finish than perhaps might have been intended, which is even more pronounced given the impressive speech made on delivery. Lovely whisky, yes. But something, I feel, of a work in progress. Bringing the caramel down by the percentage points of the malt would be a very positive start... *42.8%. ncf.*

Tesco Special Reserve Minimum 3 Years Old bott code L6335 16/04171 **(83.5) n19 t22 f21.5 b21** Improved of late. Now unashamedly in the date and walnut school of blends, where before it had only dabbled; thick, uncompromisingly sweet and cloying but with enough spice and salivation to make for pleasant and characterful bit of fun. *40%.*

⬙ **Uhuru Batch Number Two** virgin oak barrel, dist 01/06/2010, bott 05/09/2022, bott code YS3404-2 **(89) n21.5** incredibly light and youthful for a virgin oak cask. Plenty of new makey sharpness leavened only by light vanillas; **t22** soft and salivating with the grassy barley ramping up the thin acacia honey. Not so impressive when cool but a dose of the MM sends it into mouth-filling raptures; **f23** ah, now some more complex structure as the tannins move in – though still not in the way normally associated with virgin oak. At the very death we have a glorious mocha moment or two with a molasses and heather honey nod towards that virgin cask...; **b22.5** distilled at 55.2589 degree north and 04.8349 west, which suggests we have tea-spooned Ailsa Bay from Girvan. If so, it is somewhat different to any other I have before encountered. I had expected a brash dose of tannin from the virgin cask – and more honey. Instead, the malt is youthful and fragile at first but finally settles into a dram which gives up its rich, honeyed depths with a degree of reticence. Murray Method essential. *55% ncf Young Spirits. Vatted Malt.*

Ushers Green Stripe (85) n19 t22.5 f21.5 b22. Upped a notch or two in all-round quality. The juicy theme and clever weight is highly impressive and enjoyable. *43%. Diageo.*

Walton Royal Blend Deluxe Reserve (91.5) n22.5 t23 f23 b23 It's amazing what a dose of good quality peaty whisky can do to a blend. Certainly ensures it stands out as a deliciously chewy – and smoky – experience.*43%*

Waitrose Three-Year-Old bott code: L1089P/015330 **(87) n21.5 t22 f21.5 b22** A very friendly whisky which is rounded in all the right places and fills the mouth with sugars and spices in a pleasing manner. Definitely too caramel dependent, but beyond the toffee – and attendant coffee – there is a delightful sweet-dry interplay. Perfectly enjoyable. *40%*

Waitrose 8 Years Old Aged in Bourbon Casks bott code: L120121 **(89) n22.5** light smoke drifts above the noisy toffee; **t23** brilliant delivery with phenols upfront and giving weight to a silky, grain-led arrival which offers growing complexity as the malts arrive; **f22** the dates and walnut finish is typical of an overly darkened blend...a little in the old Whyte & MacKay style, though more smoke and spice evident on this blend; **b21.5** cut the caramel and this would be a stupendous blend. Sadly, the complexity can barely be found for toffee. Even so, still a thoroughly enjoyable dram. But so frustrating when it could so easily be on another level altogether... *40% In partnership with Ian MacLeod*

Whisky Works Quartermaster 11 Year Old Blended Scotch 2019/WV02./MX bott code: L9263 09:08 P/010456 **(89) n24 t24 f19 b22** There is malt, malt, juicy to a fault, in the blend, in the blend....there is grain, grain, that proves to be a pain, in the Quartermaster's Blend. My eyes are dim, I cannot see, I'm glad I brought my nose with me. I'm glad I brought my nose with me... *46.4%. nc ncf. 1,593 bottles.*

White Horse (94.5) n24 t23.5 f23 b24 A masterclass in how to use peat with precision to both raise the profile and complexity of a blend giving it both weight and gravitas, but never allowing it to pompously govern or overwhelm the myriad little other battles going on in the glass. A real old school blend which, I admit, is one I am drawn to when watching old black and white British movies. A charming taste of true tradition. *40%*

White Horse Aged 12 Years (86) n21 t23 f21 b21. Enjoyable, complex if not always entirely harmonious. For instance, the apples and grapes on the nose appear on a limb from the grain and caramel and nothing like the thoroughbred of old. Lighter, more flaccid and caramel dominated. *40%. Diageo.*

White Walker bott code: L8282KS002 **(80) n19 t22.5 f19 b20.5** Pouring from the top. As you might expect, there is no nose when frozen, other than the vaguely discernible, ultra clean tip of the grain. The big surprise is that there is a decent degree of flavour on delivery – again the grains at work and carrying a presentable amount of Demerara sweetness and here's the real shock...a very thick, chewable, oily body. So, early on, much more character than I expected. But the finish is as non-specific as I had feared and trails off with a certain bitterness. OK, that was it unshaken, and pouring from the top:

Whyte & Mackay bott code: P/011524 01:36 L0049 **(88.5) n22 t22.5 f21.5 b22.5** Very few things in life don't change over time. But I have to say the extraordinary lushness of character of a Whyte and MacKay is one of them. Maybe I'm imagining things, but it seems to have taken its foot off the caramel slightly, allowing the malts and grains in particular to showcase their wares with a little extra confidence. The result is a subtly sweeter dram, the date and walnut cake – the blend's signature tune – still there in all its glory, but the extra vanillas of the grain in particular, slightly extra succulence of the malt both making their mark. Toasty and tasty at the finish, this is a blend that is moving almost imperceptibly towards sunnier ground. The dullest of sulphur notes on the finish prevents this from scoring even more highly: my guess it is from old sherry butts used to store the grain. But I refuse to let that spoil the overall enjoyment of this blend, of which there is much. 40%.

◈ **Whyte & Mackay Triple Matured**, bott code L3013 **(91.5) n22.5** serious depth: a honeyed buffer softens the impact of the grain, which is young but not without personality; **t23** the softness on the nose is multiplied on delivery where the grains boast of silky, massaging qualities, and allow for the spices to arrive and make themselves fully heard. Excellent layering with barley in the frame; **f22.5** long and thoughtful finish. Some toffee does build but still those spices tingle and the malt lingers but all within the confines of the luxuriant grain; **b23.5** the toffee seems to have abated, and with it the weight. We are left, instead, with a rather well appointed and manicured dram which allows the spices full play. The grains are still the boss but acts as the umbrella in which impressive complexities unfold. 40%

Whyte & Mackay Aged 13 Years bott code L6334 14//04116 **(89.5) n22 t23.5 f22 b22** Like the standard Whyte and Mackay...but thirteen years old and a little lighter... 40%.

Whyte & Mackay Aged 50 Years (96) n24.5 t24 f23.5 b24 Age issues from every pore of this blend like sweat from a long-distance runner. And this certainly has travelled a distance, as I get the feeling some of the whiskies here are well beyond their 50th birthday. A classy blend which give you the feeling of the great age like a sports car fills you with sensations of power and speed. 44.6%. 175th Anniversary.

Whyte & Mackay Triple Matured bott code 16//04120 L6329 **(86.5) n21 t23.5 f20.5 b21.5** The kind of blend you can not only stand your spoon up in but your knife - table or carving - and fork – table or pitch - as well. The nose suggests something furry is in the offing which, sadly, the finale confirms. But the delivery really is such wonderful fun! Thick with intense toffee, which shapes both its flavour and mouthfeel, and concentrated date and walnut cake. Roasty yet sweet thanks to the molasses this is about the chewiest blend on the market today. 40%.

William Cadenhead's 20 Year Old Blend batch no. 3 **(91.5) n23 t23.5 f22 b23** There are a depressingly withering number of us who used, each year, to head to Campbeltown not to visit the distilleries - you couldn't then gain access – but to find the Cadenhead blends which had a truly unique character and offered something no other blend could get remotely near to. Indeed, I remember driving back once not with a boot full or Springbank but blended malt that I knew would get my whisky loving friends to see this type of whisky in an entirely new light. So my heart skips a beat at the sight of Cadenhead blend in a way few others these days might – we are talking close on 40 years of memories here. The grains on this one are sublime, offering both softness and rigid backbone (a style now criminally rare) but 35 years ago there was no sulphur to worry about on the sherry butts. Here a little has crept in, visible on the finish. A shame, as biting freshness on the grape early on is a salivating joy; the determined firmness of the grain to control it, a whisky lovers delight. 46%.

William Lawson bott code: L19182ZA80 **(87) n21.5 t22 f21.5 b22** A heady, honeyed dram which puts far more emphasis on weight than most blends out there these days. The caramels do gang up momentarily, but the overall score boasts harmony...and even more honey...!! 40%.

The Woodsman freshly built oak casks & double-scorched bourbon barrels, bott code: L0118 22:04 P/011830 **(92.5) n23 t23 f23 b23.5** One of the things so often overlooked in a whisky is the mouthfeel. The label of this blend talks much about the wood types. But the reason they work so well is because they have created a structure to the whisky which allows you to explore those flavours to their maximum. A kind of Whyte and MacKay, but with extra depth. Very impressed! 40%.

Irish Whiskey

Of all the whiskies in the world, it is Irish which probably causes most confusion amongst both established whisk(e)y lovers and the novices.

Ask anyone to define what is unique to Irish whiskey - apart from it being made in Ireland and the water likewise coming from that isle - and the answer, if the audiences around the world at my tastings are anything to go by, are in this order: i) it is triple distilled; ii) it is never, ever, made using peat; iii) they exclusively use sherry casks; iv) it comes from the oldest distillery in the world; v) it is made from a mixture of malted and unmalted barley.

Only one of these answers is true: the fifth. Though other countries are now paying the compliment of aping this style. And it is this type of whiskey, Irish Pot Still, which has dominated the Irish Awards in the Whisky Bible for the past two decades, not to mention the minds and palate of whiskey lovers. I well remember in the 1990s Irish Distillers actually turning their backs on this profound and purest form of Irish, regarding it too big in style for the marketplace; and had actually withdrawn Redbreast, leaving only an old Irish wine merchant to carry the style with their Green Spot brand, which I happily championed around the world to wake people up to what they were missing. Also, I managed to get Irish Distillers to ensure Jameson restore the Pot Still character that had been lost since at least the 1960s. The irony is that now there is a range of magnificent Pot Still whiskeys that can be found, perhaps to furnish this new and grateful market, Jameson has again lost the fabulous Pot Still backbone which had made it an essential whiskey to have about the home: certainly for one reason or another, it is nowhere near as telling as it once was. My Irish eyes aren't smiling...

Jim Murray's Whisky Bible Irish Whiskey of the Year Winners

	Irish Whiskey	Irish Pot Still Whiskey	Irish Single Malt	Irish Blend
2009	Jameson 07	N/A	N/A	N/A
2010	Redbreast 12	N/A	N/A	N/A
2011	Dun Leire 8	N/A	N/A	N/A
2012	Powers John's Lane	N/A	Sainsbury's Dun Leire 8	N/A
2013	Redbreast 12 Year Old	Redbreast 12 C.Strength	Bushmills Aged 21	Jameson
2014	Redbreast 12 C.Strength	Redbreast 12 C.Strength	Bushmills Aged 21	Jameson
2015	Redbreast Aged 21	Redbreast Aged 21	Bushmills Aged 21	Jameson
2016	Midleton Dair Ghaelach	Midleton Dair Ghaelach	SMWS 118.3 Cooley 1991	Powers Gold Label
2017	Redbreast Aged 21	Redbreast Aged 21	Bushmills Aged 21	Jameson
2018	Redbreast Aged 21	Redbreast Aged 21	Bushmills Aged 16	Bushmills Black Bush
2019	Redbreast 12 C.Strength	Redbreast 12 C.Strength	Bushmills Aged 12	Bushmills Black Bush
2020	Redbreast 12 C.Strength	Redbreast 12 C.Strength	Bushmills Aged 21	Jameson
2021	Midleton Barry Crockett	Midleton Barry Crockett	Bushmills Port Cask Reserve	Bushmills Black Bush
2022	Bushmills 30 Year Old	N/A	Bushmills 30 Year Old (SC)	Bushmills Black Bush
2023	Redbreast 12 C.Strength	N/A	Hinch Aged 19 Years	Storehouse Special
2024	Natterjack Cask Strength	Blackwater Dirtwater	Hyde No. 11	Natterjack Cask Strength

Pure Pot Still
BLACKWATER DISTILLERY

Blackwater Dirtgrain Mash Bill 08 bourbon cask; 50% malt, 35% barley, 15% oat, cask no BLA00085 db **(93) n23 t23.5 f23 b23.5** Light, clean and refreshing, the oak has its biggest say on delivery when its unique sweetness clings to the outside of the tongue. Good oils make this a clingy proposition despite the otherwise light character. The spices play an intriguing part being nippy yet effusive on the nose and much more relaxed and delicate representative of the limited oak on the palate. The mix of heather and ulmo honeys stars, though especially when working with the intense malt. Superb – and proper for its type – soft/hard mouthfeel, all signed off with attractive mocha. *45.3% sc 1000 bottles*

Blackwater Dirtgrain Mash Bill 15 rye cask; 40% barley, 30% malt, 15% oak, 12% wheat, 3% rye, cask no BLA00047 db **(95) n24 t24 f23 b24** This is one complex, deeply absorbing pot still whiskey. It may be a little drier than the others, but what it loses in honey it makes up in labyrinthine complexity. If this were Bourbon, we'd be calling the nose "bitty small grains", where the diverse grains are both shewing up individually and melding together to form delightful associations. This is not just true on the nose but also the delivery. Even the finish lasts for ever and the palate seems to be busy sorting out the sweet from the sharp, the soft from the brittle. The sugars go only so far as to provide a muted, high almond content marzipan. The speck of rye in this recipe makes an improbable mark alongside the barleys, a sharpening agent from which the barley benefits: those are the crunchy tones. The oat leads the softer front. An absolute and instant Irish classic. *44.2% sc 1000 bottles*

Blackwater Dirtgrain Mash Bill 38 apple brandy cask; 40% barley, 40% wheat, 20% malt cask no BLA00051 db **(91.5) n22.5 t23 f23 b23** Any lover of Weetabix will be all over this. It is the wheat which dominates both on nose and arrival and the delivery really does conjure up the breakfast cereal in very stark form. Not as spicy as I had expected given the mash bill, except at the very end when the oak gets more heavily involved. Very well made with the complexity levels rarely bothering to get out of third gear. *47.1% sc 1000 bottles*

Blackwater Dirtgrain Mash Bill 93 sherry cask; 46% barley, 35% malt, 15% oat, 4% peated malt, cask no BLA00003 db **(88) n22 t23 f21 b22** Strangely enough, the least interesting and enjoyable of the four Blackwater Dirtgrains, though I suspect the cask is to blame here rather than the mash bill. There is a tanginess here that is not helpful, especially at the death, while some of the more complex moments are cut off in their prime...again though seemingly an outside interference. The delivery and oaty chewiness early on, touched by light ulmo honey, is the highlight. From then on, it's downhill... 43.1% 1000. Bottles

DINGLE County Kerry. 2012. Porterhouse Group.

Dingle Pot Still Third Release db **(93.5) n23.5 t23.5 f23 b23.5** This is a very impressive pot still whiskey, by which I assume they mean there is unmalted barley. Truly wonderful and can't wait to see this mature into something rather special... 46.5%. ncf. 3,400 bottles.

KILBEGGAN County Westmeath. 1757, recommenced distilling 2007. Beam Suntory.

Kilbeggan Single Pot Still Irish Whiskey bott code: L19130 05/12/19 db **(89.5) n23** though the cut is generous, the honeys arrive in force – heather honey leading the pack. There is even a sweetened eucalyptus note, as well as an underlying earthiness; **t22.5** the oils from that cut gang-up early to giving that earthiness flavour form. Again, the heather honey makes an impact, especially with the thick oils, then a blossoming maltiness takes hold; **f21.5** some caramels filter through and dampen But the oils buzz and the malt and honey duet can still be heard above the background hubbub; **b22.5** the closest Pot Still to the last days of the old Jameson Distillery in Dublin I have ever tasted: this could be Redbreast from the late 1980s. 43%.

MIDLETON County Cork. 1975. Irish Distillers.

Green Spot bott code L622831252 db **(95) n23.5 t23.5 f24 b24** A slightly different weight, pace and sugar emphasis to this bottling. But remains a true classic. 40%.

Green Spot bott code: L921031490 db **(94) n24 t24 f23 b23** What a beautiful whiskey. If they could cut down on the pointless over-emphasis on the caramel and up the strength, they'd have a contender for World Whisky of the Year... 40%.

Green Spot Château Léoville Barton finished in Bordeaux wine casks, bott code L622331248 db **(79) n20 t22 f18 b19** I'd so desperately like to see this work. But, once again, far too tight and bitter for its own good. The damaging sulphur note is worthy of neither the great Green Spot or Leoville Barton names... 46%.

Green Spot Chateau Montelena Zinfandel wine cask finished, bott code: L719331280 db **(88) n23 t23.5 f19.5 b22** There is something fitting that Green Spot, an Irish Pot Still whiskey brand created many generations back by Dublin's Premier wine merchants, should find itself creating new ground...in a wine cask. Any European whisk(e)ys matured in American wine casks are thin on the ground. That they should be Chateau Montelena from Napa Valley makes this all the more remarkable. Does it work? Well, yes and no. The unique style of Irish Pot Still is lost somewhat under a welter of fruity blows and the fuzzy, imprecise finish is definitely off key. But there is no denying that it is a whiskey which does possess the odd magic moment. 46%.

Green Spot Chateau Montelena finished in Zinfandel wine casks, bott code: L921931293 db **(89.5) n23 t23.5 f21 b22** Pleasant enough, for sure. But a slight gripe that the unique Pot Still character has been over-run by the exuberance of the grape... 46%.

Method and Madness Single Pot Still bourbon & sherry barrels, finished in Acacia wood, bott code: L91931458 db **(95) n23.5 t23.5 f24 b24** A Pot Still creation that just gets better and better the linger you taste it. A brilliant and quite adorable exhibition of one-upmanship and profile development. 46%. ncf. Bottled exclusively for Celtic Whiskey.

Method and Madness Single Pot Irish Whiskey bourbon barrels, finished in Virgin Hungarian oak **(94) n23 t23.5 f23.5 b24** Now there was a nose! One that took me back almost 25 years to when I was visiting the Czech whisky distilleries soon after the fall of the communist regime. That whisky was matured in local oak, offering a near identical aroma to this Irish. 46%.

Method and Madness Single Pot Still bourbon & sherry barrels, finished in wild cherry wood, bott code: L919831459 db **(96) n24** the cherry wood oozes from every molecule. Significantly, though, so too does the Pot Still. This is the type of clean nose, that could happily spend an hour with if I had the time. Or make love to, had I energy...Sexy, sexy stuff...; **t24** rigid Pot Still – just like the old days!!! So wonderful when the Pot Still personality isn't slaughtered in the sacrificial slab of sherry. Barley crunches its way through the gears, as does a lovely Demerara undercurrent; **f24** long, distinguished, increasingly well spiced and the cherry wood won't be outdone as here is a now telling tannin note, something quite apart from oak. Still, though the crunchy sugars and barley grains to their thing. Method. Madness. Majestic...; **b24** one of the most flavoursome whiskies of the Whisky Bible 2021. A true joy to experience: Billy Leighton, I could give you a kiss! I may well have just tasted Irish Whiskey of the Year... 46%. ncf.

Method and Madness Single Pot Still Irish Whiskey sherry & American barrels, finished in French chestnut casks db **(88) n22 t23 f21 b22.5** Ah...memories of the late 1970s or perhaps very early '80s. Walking in the lonely autumnal forests surrounding the tiny French village of Evecquemont, taking my girlfriend's family's soppy Alsatian for long walks, during which I would hoover up wild sweet chestnuts by the score. Never then figured it playing a part in whisky, especially Irish. Not sure it is the perfect marriage, but certainly adds to the whiskey lexicon. 46%.

Midleton Barry Crockett Legacy American bourbon barrels, bott code L623631258 db **(95)** **n23.5 t24 f23.5 b24** Thank God for my dear old friend Barry Crockett. One of the top three most knowledgeable whiskey/whisky people I have known in my lifetime, you can at least be relieved that his name is synonymous with a truly great spirit. Fittingly, his whiskey is free of sherry butts, so I can just sit back and enjoy and not be on tenterhooks waiting for the first signs of a disastrous sulphur note to take hold. Indeed, the only thing that takes hold of you here is the Pot Still's stunning beauty... 46%. ncf.

Midleton Barry Crockett Legacy American bourbon cask, bott code: L918431409 db **(96.5)** **n24 t24.5 f23.5 b24.5** It has been my privilege and honour to have known Barry Crockett slightly over 30 years now. He, 'I and the late, much missed blender Barry Walsh championed Irish Pot still at a time when it had very much gone out of favour and the higher powers within the industry did not care one way or another if it vanished altogether. These were in days when all the Irish Pot still being used came from casks entirely free from sulphur treatment and the unique grain could be seen in all its naked glory...and what a gorgeous, passion rising stunner it was. There is now a generation within the industry who have never tasted wholly clean, unspoiled Pot Still and (from conversations I have had with them around the world) think that a tangy, bitter finish is part of its natural profile. It isn't and here you can see a style not entirely unknown three decades back. Though of the many samples of Pot Still I looked at with Barry Walsh, I don't remember any coming from bourbon that had this degree of fruitiness. Murray Method style of tasting essential here to maximise sweetness, as the sugars are the key to this easily underrated Irish. 46%. ncf.

Midleton Dair Ghaelach Grinsell's Wood Ballaghtobin Estate American bourbon barrels, finished in Irish oak hogsheads, batch no. 1, tree no. 7, bott code L504031020 db **(97.5) n24 t25 f24 b24.5** What we have here, if I'm not very much mistaken, is a potential World Whisky of the Year. Rarely these days am I given an entirely new flavour profile to chew on. Not only do I have that, but I am struggling to find any faults at all. Ireland is not known for its mountains: well, it certainly has one now. 57.9%. ncf.

Powers Aged 12 Years John's Lane Release bott code L623731261 **(96) n23.5 t24.5 f23.5 b24.5** A slightly different slant on the toffee and fudge – and now has a degree of rye-recipe bourbon about it - but firmly remains the go to Pot Still of quite staggering beauty. 46%. ncf.

Powers John's Lane Release American oak casks, bott code: L920631479 db **(83) n21 t22 f19 b21** Ah, great!! Matured in American oak. So, for once, no sulphur then. I taste there and there, on the finish (confirming what I hadn't wanted to believe on the nose), unmistakably the grim reaper of whiskey itself: sulphur notes. How come? Grabbed the bottle and read the blurb. Not just American oak. But Iberian, too. I must teach my staff to read the small print. With whiskey, like in life, there are many catches to be found... Hold on for a toffee and sulphur ride all the way. 46%. ncf.

Powers Signature Release bott code L433231240 **(87.5) n21 t23 f21.5 b22** A much lazier version of this excellent Pot Still than I have become used to. Far too much fudge at play here, undermining the layering and complexity. Sexy and chewy for sure and a must for those into dried dates. But the usual Pot Still character is a little masked and the usual slightly off key sherry butt turns up at the very last moment. 46%. ncf.

Powers Three Swallow Release bott code L617031171 **(83.5) n21 t21 f21.5 b20** Pleasant. No off notes. But vanishes into a sea of toffee. The fact it is pure Pot Still, apparently, is actually impossible to determine, In the last six months I have seen three swallows: a barn swallow, a Pacific and a Wire-tailed. Wherever I saw them in the world, India, The Philippines, my back garden, they all swooped and darted in joyous abandon. This Three Swallow by Powers has, by vivid contrast, had its wings clipped. 40%. ncf.

Powers Three Swallow Release American bourbon barrels & Oloroso sherry casks, bott code: L920631483 db **(84.5) n22 t21.5 f20.5 b20.5** Death by chocolate? Nope: death by toffee. Slow strangulation. If that doesn't get you, the boredom will. A fanfare for the brief burst of pot still on delivery. But it is soon ruthlessly silenced. 40%. ncf.

Redbreast Aged 12 Years bott code L634031413 db **(88.5) n22.5 t23 f21 b22** By far the flattest Redbreast I have tasted since...well, ever. Far too much reliance on obviously first-fill sherry, which had flattened out and virtually buried the unique personality of the Pot Still itself. Enjoyable, for sure. Beautiful, even, in its own way. But it should have been far more than this... 40%.

Redbreast Aged 12 Years bott code: L927731644 db **(93) n23.5** a light smothering of orange blossom honey on deep vanilla. The oakiness possesses a little church pew dustiness...; **t23** probably the softest Redbreasts delivery of all time, a restrained fruitiness taking its time to warm up and get going. A little starchy Pot Still makes its presence felt, and spices immediately after; **f23** a Cadbury's chocolate fruit and nut finale with the grain being surprisingly reticent...; lots of toffee and vanilla late on; **b23.5** one of the most docile and pacific Redbreasts I've encountered in the last 30-odd years. Lovely, though. *40%.*

Redbreast Aged 12 Years Cask Strength batch no. B1/18 db **(96) n24.5 t24.5 f23 b24** Probably one very slightly sulphured cask from World Whisky of the Year. Both nose and delivery is blarney-free Irish perfection. Worth hunting this bottle down for something truly special... *56.2%. ncf.*

Redbreast Aged 12 Years Cask Strength batch no. B2/19, bott code: L921931501 db **(95.5) n24 t24 f23.5 b24** Just like the last time I tasted this, there is just the very faintest sulphur echo. But it is miniscule and apparent only very late into the experience...and after two or three mouthfulls. Pot still at its potiest... *55.8%.*

Redbreast Aged 15 Years bott code L624931266 db **(84) n21 t22 f20 b21** When you have this much sherry influence on a whiskey, it is likely that one day you will fall foul of the odd furry butt, as is the case here. *46%. ncf.*

Redbreast Aged 15 Years bott code: L930431724 db **(80) n19 t22 f18 b21** A few too many sulphured casks for its own good. *46%.*

Redbreast Aged 21 Years bott code L612731109 db **(97) n24.5 t24 f24 b24.5** The mercifully restrained fruit and absolute total 100% absence of sulphur allows the Pot Still to display its not inconsiderable beauty unmolested and to the fullest extent. One of the world's most beautiful and iconic whisk(e)ys without doubt. The fact that so many facets of this whiskey are allowed to say their piece, yet never over-run their time and that the tenets are equally divided makes this one of the truly great whiskeys of the year. *46%. ncf.*

Redbreast Aged 21 Years bott code: L918331405 db **(94) n24** layered fruit. A little ginger pays a surprise visit and the oak is likewise laid in distinctive strata...; **t23.5** silky and spicy for the very first moments, the grain barely recognisable by flavour but by the stiffness of spine only; the salivating qualities early on seems to run hand-in-hand with the juiciest grape; **f23** a dull toffee-vanilla-grapey fade ...where is the enlivening barley...? **b23.5** this is perennially one of the contenders for the Bible's World Whisky of the Year, and once was only a single sulphured cask away from winning it. This year sulphur isn't a problem but, ironically, the sherry is. For the grape here is a little too boisterous, meaning the balance has been compromised. Lovely whisky, for sure. But when the grape dominates – and flattens - so much greatness will elude it... *46%.*

Redbreast Aged 27 Years ruby port casks, batch no. B1/19, bott code: L933633750 db **(93.5) n23.5 t25 f21.5 b23.5** If tragic can be applied to a whiskey, then it can here One minute the perfect exhibition of a wondrous whiskey type. The next, faulty obliteration... if I'm permitted a scream...... Arrrrrrggggghhhhhhh!!!!! *54.6%.*

Redbreast Aged 32 Years Dream Cask db **(96.5) n24 t24.5 f23.5 b24** A fabulous pot still very comfortable in its ancient clothes. Marvellous! *46.5%.*

Redbreast All Sherry Single Cask db **(73.5) n17 t23.5 f15 b18.** I mean: seriously guys....??? A single cask pure pot still whiskey and you bottle one with sulphur fingerprints all over it? I don't have the number of what cask this is from, so I hope yours will have come from clean sherry. If you have, you are in for a treat, because the sheer brilliance and magnitude of this whiskey was able to blot out the sulphur for a good seven or eight seconds as it reached heights of near perfection. A bowl of raspberries now and a 20 minute break to help cleanse my palate and relieve my tongue which is still seriously furred up. So frustrating, as I could see a clean butt of this getting Single Cask Whisky of the Year ... *59.9%. sc.*

Redbreast Dream Cask Aged 28 Years ruby port casks, cask no. 400295, bott code: L933633750 db **(96) n24.5** the depth and layering of this made a liar of the label straight away – or at least the front of it. It is obvious there is more going on here than ruby port alone and an inspection of the small print reveal that oloroso and bourbon casks are at play here, too. Perhaps the cleverest, yet most easily over-looked aspect is the spice. Not just some sizzling random spice. But one that is measured and integrated. As is the fruit which varies from a cream sherry-type pillow softness to a more lusty plum pudding. There is an intrinsic toastiness, too, which mirrors the spice in its careful weight and disposition. This a 15-minute minimum Murray Method nose. And, unquestionably one of the finest in the world this year..; **t24.5** talk about cream sherry on the nose.... The marriage of oloroso and ruby port has generated the most classic cream sherry landing on the palate. But, as on the nose, it is the delicate and intricate layering which sets this apart from the rest and takes this into true world class territory. There is a clever acidic touch which comes and goes, allowing the dark, salivating sugars pride and place from time to time., This is all about weight and counterweight: old-fashioned blending at its finest..; **f23** ah!...and to the Achilles heel. Toasty and an element of chocolate truffle. But that dull, bitter echo of sulphur from, presumably, the sherry butt. Not loud, but the mild furriness is indelibly there..; **b24** until the finale, this was on course for World Whisky of the Year. But that will never be won with a whiskey blemished by sulphur and, though the mark is small, it is, alas, there.... Tragic, as this is as much an art of work as it is a whiskey... *40%. 915 bottles.*

Redbreast Lustau Edition Sherry Finish bott code: L930531725 db **(95)** n23.5 t24 f23.5 b24 Faultless sherry casks at work. And the Pot Still is firm and decisive. Who can ask for more....? Well, I could ask for the toasted almonds promised on the label, being exceedingly partial to them. The fact they never turn up is compensated for by the overall excellence...and the chocolate... 46%.

Red Spot Aged 15 Years bourbon, sherry & marsala casks, bott code: L829131516 db **(83)** n21 t22 f19 b21 Oh, what I'd give for the days when you could taste the actual magic of the Pot Still itself, such as in the original Green Spot, rather than some lumbering fruit casks, and slightly sulphured ones at that. 46%. ncf.

Yellow Spot Aged 12 Years bourbon barrels, sherry butts & Malaga casks, bott code L622431250 db **(87)** n22 t22 f21 b22 My previous comments stand for this, too. Except here we have a persistent bitterness towards the finish which reveals a weakness with one of the butts. An exceptionally bitty whiskey that does have its moments of soaring high, especially when the varying citrus note correlate. 46%. ncf.

Yellow Spot Aged 12 Years bourbon barrels, sherry butts and Malaga casks, bott code: L929031680 db **(92.5)** n24 t24 f21.5 b23 I thought the first bottlings of this were a tad out of sorts, the balance proving elusive. I backed blender Billy Leighton to crack this one eventually... and he has. This has moments of pure whiskey paradise. But the garden of Eden has a snake... and thy name is Sulphur... 46%. ncf.

ROYAL OAK DISTILLERY

◇ **The Busker Single Grain** bott code L2106534 db **(88.5)** n22.5 t22.5 f21.5 b22 A very young grain for a singleton that is anything but neutral. The intense peppery tones on the nose makes it pretty unique among grain distilleries on the British Isles – and it is great to see another one join the Irish firmament where for too long there were too few. The mouth feel is soft and yielding and for the odd moment or two some deft honey notes sing sweetly. The finish is a little brash by comparison, however. But, overall, for a youngster this isn't half bad and shews that by the time it reaches 10- or 12-years-old, it will be quite a treat for sore taste buds. And, also, as the creator and blender of Ireland's first-ever all-grain bottling, I'm so delighted to see another one out there. 44.3%

◇ **The Busker Single Malt** bott code L2139336 db **(90)** n22.5 lots of copper giving this a sharp tang on the nose, though this is softened by the rich barley. The lightest heather honey notes fleetingly wander through the Dundee cake; t23 now that honey (acacia) really takes on a sublimely soft delivery. The malt is gloriously rounded and intense and spreads the spices evenly, and even some tannins towards the middle; f21.5 there is a residual nagging to the finish, shewing that one of the sherry butts had, at some stage in its life, been sulphur treated. It just about gets away with it thanks to the sheer excellence of the distillate and the honey tones which have decided to hang around with the barley and spice to the very end; b23 the Royal Oak distillery shewing that it really can conjure up some magical whiskey. But really does deserve better wine cask to look its best. Very promising, though, and from little acorns.... 44.3%

◇ **The Busker Single Pot Still** bott code L2107260 db **(86.5)** n22 t23 f20 b21.5 Another Busker which is somewhat off key. I have no doubt their basic spirit is fine and there is a degree of firmness to this Pot Still Whiskey which ticks all the right boxes. But I get the overwhelming feeling the sherry casks deployed were not up to the quality of the distillate and have trimmed some of the more complex nuances I would have expected from the whiskey itself. At times peppery and spikey, at others salivating and rich, the dull, aching bitterness tells you why the finish doesn't work. Frustrating, as in the right casks this could have been belting whiskey. 44.3%

◇ **The Busker Triple Cask** bott code L2139347 db **(89)** n23 a soft, deeply attractive nose concentrating on a mix of fruit and vanilla for its most disarming moments. This is as gentle as any Irish blend gets, attractively punctuated by the most delicate essence of lychee and kiwifruit (especially when cooler)...wow! t22 super silky mouth feel thanks predominantly to the yielding grain. The midpoint shews some light tannin from the oak, but the fruits now have a more pastel candy persona; f21.5 a slight bitterness at the death, though the vanillas, light caramels and almost apologetic spice ensures a comfortable landing; b22.5 the nose, especially before slightly warming, was a real surprise...and a very pleasant one: that was one impressive fruit cocktail. The work on the palate is a little more standard and a slight bittering blemish on the finish is a bit of a shame. But, overall, one of the easier Irish blends you might encounter. 40%

UNSPECIFIED

◇ **Blackwater Shenanigans Edition Single Pot Still (87)** n23.5 t22 f20 b21.5 I could almost weep: a superb distillate obviously containing a fascinating and complex recipe which delivers the goods until a tired cask spoils things somewhat. On the nose this really goes to town on the unmalted barley which gives a sublime honeyed glow to gristier malt. Fresh and even offering a degree of bourbon-style sweetness. The green apple fruitiness is totally in sync. It takes only a moment on the palate to confirm this was obviously superbly distilled, the distillate is clean but guaranteeing extra intensity from the soft oils which cling to the varied sugars. However, the late bitterness is unfortunate and points accusingly at the cask rather than the product of the still. A better cask and this would have been a high scorer. *40%*

⬧ **Curraghmore First Release (94.5) n24** both the French virgin oak and the oloroso cask contribute willingly to a busy yet deft aroma. Below the higher, peppery, spicy notes is a softer level entirely, where the unmalted barley has worked beautifully in tandem with the bourbon cask to offer an endearing light peach, pawpaw and acidic passionfruit theme, topped with vanilla and sweetened with genteel lemon blossom honey. Not what I was expecting...; **t24** after that nose it was highly unlikely the delivery would be anything other than salivating...and there are no disappointments. Simply melts in the mouth on delivery...the malt involved playing an important gristy game here. There is a brief flash of those fragile fruit tones again before the virgin French oak reconnects with a comparatively weighty tannin thrust; **f22.5** a very slight dry furriness, added to a mild bitterness on the finish gives me reason to doubt the sherry butt involved. But there are still enough honey tones filtering through, as well as a light lychee and mangosteen flourish, to cope; **b24** a beautifully distilled Pot Still which overcomes the potential obstacle of tender years with a complex amalgamation of delightful and mostly delicate flavour tones. Great work by my (very!) old mate, fellow blender Noel Sweeney. Noel is a man with a voracious appetite, and he has succeeded in turning a couple of four-year-old casks and a five-year-old into a five course feast for the nose and palate, most of them involving exotic fruit. Absolutely superb. *46% distilled at The Great Northern Distillery*

⬧ **Hyde No 12 Pot Still Cask 1893** bott 01/22, bott code L02723 L2 **(88.5) n22 t23 f22 b21.5** A true Pot Still Irish even containing oats, as well as both malted and unmalted barley. But there is a huge toffee character to this downplaying the intricacies on the nose and finish in particular. However, there is so much good going on with the delivery - with a plethora of busy, mouth-watering notes bursting out around the palate - that there are truly moments of greatness. Just need a way to keep them coming, perhaps by finding a way of stifling the overly enthusiastic caramel. Do love the milk chocolate finale, though. *46% ncf 5000 bottles*

⬧ **Lakeview Single Estate Coming of Age Edition 2 (73.5) n19 t18.5 f18 b18** Interesting link: Single Estate is usually thought of in regard to Jamaica rum, where there were plantations. And plantations used to be found in Ireland...some circular thinking there. As for the whiskey itself. I believe that this was from a new distillery and the first effort I viewed last year was more than satisfactory. However, they should have got their cuts right before committing a barrel to bottle. Simply off key and out of alignment from first sniff to the last tangy and oily ember. It is, as so aptly put by its owning company, Wayward.... *46%*

⬧ **Portmagee Single Pot Still Barbados Rum Cask Finished** cask no 3, bott 2022 **(86) n23 t22 f20 b21** An intriguing, delicate nose leading with apricot and marzipan. There is a secondary, slightly heavier tone thanks to a generous cut. Even so, the pulsing, malty, delivery is surprisingly heavy and slick considering that nose and the grains take the lead, though those oils are close behind. There is a quite a bready, doughy feel to the mid-point but the finish, bittering by the second, is definitely out of alignment with the rum cask and accompanying spices working overtime to form a coating to bring things back into line. A very late flourish of grape juice does some good, but one still gets the feeling that we have a work in progress here. *40% sc ncf 352 bottles*

Single Malt
COOLEY County Louth. 1987. Beam Suntory.

Connemara bott code L9042 db **(88) n23 t22.5 f20.5 b22.** One of the softest smoked whiskies in the world which, though quite lovely, gives the impression it can't make its mind up about what it wants to be. *40%*

Connemara Aged 12 Years bott code L9024 db **(85.5) n23 t21.5 f20 b21.** The nose, with its beautiful orange, fruity lilt, puts the shy smoke in the shade. *40%*

Connemara Cask Strength bott code L9041 db **(90) n21.5 t23 f22 b22.5.** A juicy negative of the standard bottling: does its talking on the palate rather than nose. Maybe an absence of caramel notes might have something to do with that. *57.9%*

Connemara Peated Single Malt Irish Whiskey bott code: L19109 03/10/149 db **(89) n23 t22.5 f21.5 b22** I'm afraid I'm old and ugly enough to have been around to taste the very first ever batch of Connemara - at Cooley distillery, as it happens - after it came off the bottling line. Then the peat was rich and unhindered. Since then it has gone through a chequered career with phenols levels rising and falling like the tides at nearby Carlingford Lough. That must have been close on 30 years ago now... Pleased to say the peat is back to it old confident self...well, early on at least. But I don't remember the toffee dampening its natural spontaneity as it does here... *40%*.

Tullamore Dew Single Malt 10 Years Old db (**91.5**) **n23 t23 f22.5 b23**. The best whiskey I have ever encountered with a Tullamore label. Furtively complex and daringly delicate. If only they could find a way to minimise the toffee... 40%. *William Grant & Sons.*

The Tyrconnell Single Malt Irish Whiskey Aged 16 Years Oloroso & Moscatel cask finish, bott code: L19020 07/02/19 db (**94**) **n23.5 t23.5 f23 b24** So rare to find a sherry-matured Irish whiskey that isn't benighted by sulphur. An absolute treat. 46%.

The Whisky Cask Company The Poplar Tree 2002 PX sherry cask, dist May 2002, Bott Jul 2020 (**92**) **n23 t24 f22 b23** The Sherry Tree, surely. Should be "poplar" with anyone with a sweet tooth.... and a taste for delicious, highly intense whiskey. 52.9% 301 bottles

The Wild Geese Single Malt (**85.5**) **n21.5 t21 f22 b21.** Just ignore the Wild Goose chase the labels send you on and enjoy the malt, with all its failings, for what it is (and this is pretty enjoyable in an agreeably rough and ready manner, though not exactly the stuff of Irish whiskey purists): which in this case for all its malt, toffee and delicate smoke, also appears to have more than a slight touch of feints - so maybe they were right all along...!!! 43%. *Cooley for Avalon.*

DINGLE County Kerry. 2012. Porterhouse Group.

Dingle Single Malt Whisky batch no. 3 db (**87**) **n21 t22 f22 b22** Young, much closer in personality to new make than seasoned whiskey. In fact, reminds me of the blending lab when I'd come across a barely three-year-old Dailuaine, a Scottish Speysider which, at this juncture of its development, is its closest flavour-type relative. Lovely, though, if you an looking for a taste of unspoiled, gently oiled maltiness – and a piece of Irish whiskey history. Clean and beautifully made. 46.5%. ncf. 13,000 bottles.

Dingle Single Malt Whisky batch no. 4 db (**84**) **n20 t22 f21 b21** I always prefer to discover that a distillery makes gin because I have been there or been briefed about it. Not through sampling their whiskey. And I'm afraid there is juniper quite strongly on the nose here and few other odd flavours hitting the palate. Despite the mega dry finish, lots of malt on show and seemingly otherwise well made. 46.5%. ncf. 2,000 bottles.

Dingle Single Malt Whisky batch no. 5 db (**88.5**) **n22 t22.5 f22 b22** Genteel malt shewing no great age but certainly celebrates an uninhibited maltiness which charms and possesses no pretentions of grandeur. Just a slight background apple cider feel to the nose, and a vague feintiness to the body. The barley is all over this, but melts towards a soft butterscotch tart finish. 46.5%. ncf.

Dingle Single Malt Whisky Cask Strength batch no. 5 db (**92**) **n23 t23.5 f22.5 b23** The extra oils work a treat on this: there is a chasm between this expression and the 46.5 version, the cask strength bottling here allowing full amplification to some otherwise understated components. 59.3%. ncf.

HINCH Ballynahinch. 2016. Dr Terry Cross OBE

Hinch An Chead Dun New Make (**95**) **n23.5 t24 f23.5 b24** Absolutely top-rate new make brimming with character. Pretty flawless: no feints and no burn from running the stills under a whip. This is the epitome of relaxed distillation, allowing the barley full expression on both nose and palate. The nose itself is a gentle caress of malt with just enough oils retained to ensure a soft landing. The barley sugar is profound on delivery and becomes even more salivating as the flavour waves progress. Excellent light oils on the finish keeping the barley in action for the maximum length of time with no bitterness present, even late on, with the late usual cocoa perfectly sweetened by the lingering barley. Most likely a spirit big and characterful enough to see this ensuing whiskey into ripe old age. Hard to ask for much more. Exemplary: a blender's dream. 63.5%.

MIDLETON County Cork. 1975. Irish Distillers.

Method and Madness Single Malt Irish Whiskey bourbon barrels, finished in French Limousin oak casks db (**92**) **n22 t23.5 f23 b23.5** A very different Irish which is quietly uncompromising and seriously tasty... 46%.

OLD BUSHMILLS County Antrim. 1784. Casa Cuervo.

Bushmills Aged 10 Years matured in two woods db (**92.5**) **n23 t23 f23 b23.5.** Absolutely superb whiskey showing great balance and the usual Antrim 19th century pace with its flavour development. The odd bottle of this I have come across over the last couple of years has been spoiled by the sherry involvement. But, this, as is usually the case, is absolutely spot on. 40%.

Bushmills Single Malt Aged 10 Years bott code: L8270 IB 005 db (**92.5**) **n23 t23 f23 b23.5** A very consistent Irish benefitting again from faultless sherry butts. 40%.

Bushmills Aged 12 Years Single Malt Aged in Three Woods oloroso sherry & bourbon casks, Marsala cask finished, bott code: L9102IB 001 db (**89.5**) **n23.5 t23 f21 b22** Slightly lumpy in style, but there are some beautiful moments in there. 40%. *Exclusive to Taiwan.*

Bushmills Distillery Reserve Single Malt Aged 12 Years bott code: L8170 IB 002 db **(95) n23.5** beautiful stratum of cocoa, apricot, heather honey and the chalkiest malt in the British Isles...; **t24** very unusual for a Bushmills of any era to kick off with a sweet delivery. But that's what you are presented with here as that heather honey kicks in, followed by layers of greengages and exploding white grape. The malt and sawdusty oak form layers alongside the toffee; **f23.5** not technically perfect, but all is forgiven as this has legs despite the lack of oils. The chocolate toffee takes over, with just a slight sultana kick here and there; **b24** what a stunning example of Bushmills this is. 40%

Bushmills Aged 16 Years db **(71) n18 t21 f15 b17.** In my days as a consultant Irish whiskey blender, going through the Bushmills warehouses I found only one or two sulphur-treated butts. Alas, there are many more than that at play here. 40%

Bushmills Single Malt Aged 16 Years Rare Matured in Three Woods Oloroso sherry, bourbon & port casks, bott code: L9249 IB 002 db **(90.5) n23 t23.5 f21.5 b22.5** Until the late finish barely a single off note thanks to some superb casks in use here. If only they could bring the toffee element down slight to allow a far clearer view of the excellent fruit and malt tones in play 40%.

Bushmills Aged 21 Years db **(95.5) n24.5 t24 f23.5 b24** An Irish journey as beautiful as the dramatic landscape which borders the distillery. Magnificent. 40%

Bushmills Single Malt Aged 21 Years Rare Matured in Three Woods Oloroso sherry, bourbon & Madeira casks, bott 2019, bott code: L9085 IB 003 db **(82) n21 t21.5 f19.5 b20** A very disappointing malt. Obviously the light dusting of tongue-numbing sulphur affects the nose and finale but some damage is already done before on the palate with a stark toffee effect that keeps complexity to a minimum. The odd honey tone here and there, and a slight saltiness, too. But, from this distillery, we should be having a whiskey in the mid-90s points-wise... 40%.

Bushmills Port Cask Reserve ruby port pipes, bott code: L8170 IB 001 db **(95.5) n24 t24 f23.5 b24** This Steamship does First Class only... 40%. The Steamship Collection.

Bushmills Rum Cask Reserve first fill Caribbean rum casks, bott code: L9130 IB 001 db **(94) n23.5 t23.5 f23 b24** The blender has really called this one right. Brilliant usage of rum casks to enrich the notoriously slight maltiness of Old Bushmills. A malt that is in full sail... 40%. The Steamship Collection.

Bushmills Sherry Cask Reserve Oloroso sherry butts, bott code: L9078 IB 002 db **(90.5) n22.5 t22.5 f22.5 b23** Clean, unsullied casks make for an easy-drinking, super-rounded Irish with an untaxing complexity. Very pleasant, indeed. 40%. The Steamship Collection.

Bushmills Single Malt The Steamship Collection #3 Bourbon Cask db **(95) n24.5 t23.5 f23 b24** This steamship is sailing in calm seas of complexity...Take your time over this one: it is deceptively brilliant. 40%.

The Whisky Cask Company Bushmills Capall 26 Years Old 1st fill bourbon barrel, cask no, 8391, dist 16 Oct 91, bott 26 Mar 18 **(94.5) n22.5 t24 f24 b24** Had the nose been as sensational as the experience on the palate some kind of award for this whisky would have been a certainty. Magnificent. 50.5%. sc. 175 bottles.

The Whisky Cask Company Bushmills Madra 26 Years Old 1st fill bourbon barrel, cask make the most of their older casks, methinks. 494%. sc. 156 bottles.

WEST CORK DISTILLERS County Cork. 2003. West Cork Distillers.

West Cork Irish Whiskey Bog Oak Charred Cask Matured db **(88.5) n23 t22 f21.5 b22** A little known fact: I own a 100 to 125 year-old portable Irish pot still made entirely of copper with brass handles, once owned by a Victorian or Edwardian illicit distiller. Which would explain as to why it was found in an Irish bog over 20 years ago and has been in my possession ever since. Anyway, it is extremely unlikely it ever produced a spirit which ended up quite so heavy in natural caramels... 43%. West Cork Distillers Limited.

West Cork Irish Whiskey Glengarriff Peat Charred Cask Matured db **(90.5) n23 t22.5 f22 b23** Well, Ireland is on the way to Kentucky from here... 43%. West Cork Distillers Limited.

Mizen Head Cask Strength Single Malt Irish Whiskey Bodega sherry casks db **(90.5) n22.5 t23.5 f22 b22.5** Well done chaps! Until the very death, barely a sulphur atom in sight! But such is the power of this distillery's love of caramel character, it even overtakes the fruit...which takes some doing! 60%. West Cork Distillers Limited.

UNSPECIFIED SINGLE MALTS

Currach Single Malt Irish Whiskey Atlantic Kombu Seaweed Cask ex-bourbon casks, finished in seaweed charred virgin oak casks, batch no. 1, bott Mar 20, bott code: 07220 **(83) n20.5 t22 f20.5 b20** Probably a whisky for the Swansea or Japanese market, where seaweed is held in high esteem. However, as a whisky in its own right I'm afraid this hits rough waters immediately, with the malt lurching around the palate as though in a gale. The sweet spot lasts far too briefly, a vague honey note well into the delivery but the tang on finish isn't one that is easy to savour. Salt is conspicuous by its absence, oddly enough, in the Whisky Bible 2020, I noted that Ireland had produced 29 different finishes in the previous year alone. This was not included amongst them. *46%. ncf. Origin Spirits Ireland.*

The Dublin Liberties Copper Alley 10 Year Old Single Malt sherry cask finish, bott no. L16 280 W3 **(94.5)** n23 t24 f23.5 b24 Well done, chaps! You have picked yourself a first class sulphur-free cask! What a rare treat that is this year! *46%.*

The Dubliner 10 Year Old Single Malt bourbon casks, bott no. L17390-179 **(89)** n22 t23 f21.5 b22.5 'The real taste of Dublin" warbles the label in time-honoured Blarney tradition. Of course, the true, historic taste of Dublin is Irish Pot Still, that beguiling mix of malted and unmalted barley. But, in the meantime, this juicy little number will do no harm. *42%.*

Dunville's VR Aged 12 Years Single Malt finished in ex-Pedro Ximénez sherry casks **(87)** n23 t22.5 f20 b21.5 The success story here is on the nose: despite its Spanish inquisition, there is a profound Kentucky note leading the way, a sharp almost rye-like note with its fruity crispness. The delivery also has its moments, the riot of date and molasses in particular. The rest of the tale, much of it bitterly told, doesn't go quite so well, alas. *46%. ncf.*

Egan's Single Malt Fortitude Pedro Ximénez casks bott code: L18 003 264 **(79)** n19 t22 f19 b19 Bitter and off-key. *42% (92 proof). ncf.*

Egan's Single Malt 10 Aged Years bott code: US001 244 **(90)** n22.5 t23.5 f22 b22.5 Rich, rounded and puts the "more" into this Tullamore-based bottler...*47% (94 proof). ncf.*

Fitzwilliam Single Malt American oak db **(92.5)** n23 clean as a whistle: the phenols are vibrant and true and edged with mild spice. Again, the house-style citrus tone plays an important, balancing part; t23 salivating barley grows into something far weightier as the smoke makes its considerable mark. Some very light oils help thicken the phenols; f23 just a little mocha as the spices grow and the peat growls; b23.5 a beautifully crafted young peated Irish. Delightful. *43%*

Fitzwilliam Single Malt Imperial Stout Cask Finish Grain db **(88)** n21.5 t22.5 f22 b22 Considering I am no fan of hopped whisk(e)y, there was much here to enjoy. Certainly, the intense chocolate on the finish was a surprise, though the early citrus on delivery – grapefruit especially – wasn't. But one of the most refreshing beer cask whiskeys I have tasted in years. *46%*

Fitzwilliam Single Malt Cider Cask Finish double distilled db **(90)** n22 fresh malt. Even fresher apple...; t22.5 when tasted cool, before the Murray Method, the apple is so in your face you almost recoil in shock. When warmed slightly, this is a far better prospect with both the malt and vanillas from the oak offering a soothing balance; f23 hits its stride now with a light golden syrup sweetness sitting very comfortably with the clear malt and spice; b22.5 I have lost count of the number of cider cask finishes I have tasted over the years. None, though, have offered such a sharpness to the mix. Still the perfect whiskey for Apple employees: something to be enjoyed at home... *40%*

Glendalough Single Malt Irish Whiskey Aged 17 Years American oak bourbon cask, Japanese Mizunara cask finish **(89.5)** n21.5 t23 f22 b23 Quite a cerebral whiskey, and one with a unique fingerprint. But could have done without the juniper. *46%. ncf.*

Glendalough Single Malt Irish Whiskey Aged 25 Years Tree #2 Jack's Wood American white oak bourbon cask, Spanish oloroso cask & virgin Irish oak finish **(95)** n23.5 t24 f23.5 b24 No discernible problems from the oloroso, other than the very faintest long-distance buzz. Which means this is one hell of a malt. *46%. ncf.*

Hinch Peated Single Malt nbc **(87)** n22 t22 f21.5 b21.5 So rare to find a slightly feinty note in Irish, but here it is on the peaty nose and, big delivery and quarrelsome finish. A unique character, that's for sure...and what a character! Technically not quite at the races, but the peat is taking few prisoners and the oils from that wide cut ensures that the big smoke goes nowhere in a hurry. An odd whiskey, it has to be said. Knives and forks ready for this one: tuck in to enjoy... *43%. The Time Collection.*

Hinch Single Malt Chateau De La Ligna Grand Reserve Finish Aged 19 Years **(94)** n23.5 t24 f23 b23.5 The delivery and various other moments hit the highest heights. This is a malt of extraordinary lustre and depth. About as friendly an Irish as you'll find this year. As it happens, my friend Chris Heaton-Harris, the Secretary of State for Ireland, today met up with our new monarch and whisky lover King Charles III, just days after the sad and heart-rending demise of our much-loved and glorious Queen Elizabeth II. Chris has long wanted to learn about whiskey. I'll fittingly start him off on this... *48%*

Hyde No.1 President's Cask Aged 10 Years Single Malt sherry cask finish **(85.5)** n23 t22 f20 b20.5 Pleased to report the sherry butt(s) used here offer no sulphur, so a clean malt with an outstanding fruity aroma. But it does quite literally fall flat because after the initial juicy, malty entry things go a bit quiet – especially towards the middle and finish where a dull vaguely fruity but big toffee note clings like a limpet. A wasted opportunity, one feels. *46%. ncf.*

Hyde N0.10 Banyuls Cask Finished Single Cask Singe Malt first fill bourbon, finished first fill banyuls gran cru cask, bott Jun 2020, bott code: 31420 **(87.5) n22 t22 f21.5 b22** Beyond the citrus on the nose, there is a husky-voiced wine cask influence. A rasping, deep resonance to the fruit but slightly undone by a shortage of sugars. Dry and dusty, the bourbon cask influence appears to have been airbrushed out while the warming, pinching, white pepper spice will come as little surprise. Far from standard fare and always entertaining. *43% ncf 390 bottles*

⬧ **Hyde No 11 The Peat Cask 1949** bott 07/21, bott code L29322 **(92.5) n22.5** if you can imagine peat with its feet up on a chair and dozing, then you just about have a picture of the comatose attitude of these phenols. Smoky for sure, but only half-heatedly so, allowing the youthful, non-peated malt to dig in deep with some sharp grassy tones. There is a light vanilla filling in there, too; **t23.5** attractively youthful by nature, there is quite a surprise as the oils gird their loins. There was little evidence of much fatness on the nose, but here it is, coating the mouth and bringing with it a gorgeous chocolate mint. The melted Demerara sugars also trickle about the palate to ensure sweetness is maintained; **f23** thins out and spices up. But the vanillas bulk up and along with the retained chocolate mint has a bit of an ice cream feel to this; **b23.5** says on the tin that it is sweet and peaty. And it doesn't lie. But there is so much more with a surprise attack of oil which gives this malt many extra dimensions...and the ability to reach parts of the palate very few Irish can. Chewy and truly delicious, this is easily one of the most entertaining and enjoyable Hydes I have yet encountered. Superb. *43% ncf 5000 bottles*

The Irishman Aged 12 Years first fill bourbon barrels, bott 2017 **(92) n23.5 t23 f22.5 b23** Old Bushmills like you have never quite seen her before in bottle. Works a treat. *43%. ncf. 6,000 bottles.*

The Irishman 12 Years Old Florio Marsala Cask Finish cask no. 2257 **(90) n22 t23 f22.5 b22.5** A clean, unsullied cask but the grape allows the malt little room for manoeuvre. Very pleasurable though, and definitely a whisky rather than a wine.; *46%. ncf sc. 320 bottles.*

The Irishman Aged 17 Years sherry cask, cask no. 28657 **(94.5) n24 t24 f22.5 b23.5** It's the hoping that kills you. After 20-odd years of tasting sherry casks ruined in Jerez, you view every whisky from sherry butt, be it a full term maturation or partial, with suspicion. You hope...but sadly, that hope is terminated by grim disappointment. Here, though, we have a happy experience. Is it 100% perfect sherry butt? No. Does it damage the whiskey? Not really. This is a full-on sherry influenced Irish celebrating the grape with style. The finale shews the slightest of weaknesses, but in light of what is out there it is forgiveable (well, not quite forgiveable enough for it not to be robbed of an award in the Whisky Bible!) and forgettable. *56%. ncf sc. 600 bottles.*

Jack Ryan Single Malt Irish Whisky Aged 12 Years bourbon cask **(92.5) n23.5 t23 f22.5 b23.5** Deft, very clean malt whisky where decent bourbon wood adds all kinds of beautifully paced complexity. Not even a hint of an off note. Impressive. *46%*

Kinahan's Heritage 10 Year Old Single Malt (93) n23 t23.5 f23 b23.5 A beautifully constructed whiskey where, very rare for a single malt these days, you can actually taste the malt itself... A treat of a whiskey. *46%.*

Kinahan's Special Release Project 11 Year Old Armagnac finish, cask no. 48 **(95.5) n23 t24.5 f23.5 b24.5** This isn't good whiskey. Or even very good whiskey. It is truly great Irish whiskey. *58.9%.*

Lambay Whiskey Single Malt finished in Cognac casks, bott code: L4329718 **(92.5) n23.5 t24 f22 b23** I've always thought that Bushmills at about 7-years-old has a special esprit de coeur (as opposed to corps!) which allowed the distillery to be seen at its freshest, most fulfilling and most true to the distillery's style. There is more than a touch of this evident here as this malt, whoever made it, boasts extraordinary verve and dash. Magnificent up until the point of the late finish when things become a little too bitter for their own good. That apart, stunning. *40%. ncf.*

Liquid Treasures Summer Dram 2018 Irish Malt Over 26 Years Old ex-bourbon barrel, dist 1992, bott 2018 **(90.5) n23.5 t23 f21.5 b22.5** the oak has taken control, here but in an entirely benign manner, bringing the barley into play here, dishing out spices there, standing back and allowing the ulmo and heather honeys to do their things at other times. Complex and beautifully paced, just shewing a degree of weariness at the finale. But don't we all...? *48.3%. sc.*

Mourne Dew Single Malt Irish Whiskey (87) n21.5 t22.5 f21.5 b21.5 The barley has all the blarney on delivery, making itself soft, sultry, salivating and finally, thanks to the oak, spicy. Just a niggling juniper-type kink to the nose and finish veers it slightly off course. *43%*

⬧ **Mourne Dew Single Malt Irish Whiskey** nbc **(86) n21.5 t22 f21 b21.5** The malt pours over the tastebuds like water from a burst dam and is beautifully refreshing with its young grassiness in full spate. But I have a problem with the hop note on both the nose and gathering at the midpoint for its beery finish. Hop is bitter and can cause all kinds of problems in a whiskey, especially one as delicate as this. If you love hop-heavy whisk(e)y, then this'll be a hit for you. I'll just try to concentrate on the barley itself, which is salivating and moreish. Mon Dieu! *43% ncf*

Quiet Man Single Malt 8 Years Old db **(91.5) n23** fabulous malt boasting a disarming freshness and citrussy gloss which showers the nose with icing sugar and permits a hint of spice. All hush-hush, all low-level...; **t23.5** not often the remarks of the nose can be repeated verbatim for the taste, but you'd get away with it here. The only thing to add is the mouth-cleaning juiciness of the malt...and now an extra dose of grapefruit juice for sharpness; **f22** a lack of oils means the finish is a little short. And we have butterscotch now where there was once barley; **b23** now this takes me back. Crawling through certain warehouses in Ireland selecting specific casks to blend together. I must have tasted over 500 barrels of this age and of this well-used bourbon cask type...and I never tired of it. Just a quietly magical whisky...though I do wish it had been bottled at least 50% abv for the real sparkle and magic to be discovered by an unsuspecting public. 40%

The Quiet Man 8 Year Old Single Malt Irish Whiskey bourbon casks **(89) n22 t23 f21.5 b22.5** Had the finish not dulled quite so quickly this would have scored a lot higher. Nothing less than pleasant throughout. 40%

The Quiet Man 8 Year Old bourbon cask, bott code L18080088 **(88.5) n23 t23 f20.5 b22** Forget the finale: salute, quietly, the nose and delivery! 46%. ncf sc. 385 bottles.

The Quiet Man 8 Year Old oak bourbon cask **(88) n21.5 t22.5 f22 b22** Sssshhhh! Keep your voices down when telling people this: but this is mouth-watering, malty cove helped along with some oaky spices. Short on complexity slightly, but big of chewy texture and creamy toffee. 40%

The Quiet Man 12 Year Old Kentucky bourbon casks **(93) n23 t23.5 f23 b23.5** Odd, isn't it? The owner of this brand named this whisky The Quiet Man in memory of his father, John Mulgrew, who was known by that epithet. Yet, coincidentally, it was Maurice Walsh, the grandfather of one of the greatest Irish whiskey blenders of all time, Barry Walsh, who wrote the novel The Quiet Man from which the film was made. I feel another movie coming on: The Silence of the Drams. But sssshhhh: don't tell anyone... 46%. ncf.

The Quiet Man 12 Year Old Sherry Finished bourbon casks, finished in oloroso sherry casks, bott code: L17304295 db **(73) n18.5 t20 f16.6 b18** Ah. Sadly, the sulphur isn't quite as quiet as one might hope. 46%. ncf.

The Quiet Man "An Culchiste" 12 Year Old Kentucky bourbon cask **(93) n23 t23.5 f23 b23.5** So incredibly similar to the last Quiet Man 12. Riveting, insanely intense malt which pricks every nerve on the palate. Find the original tasting notes from a couple of years back and be impressed by the consistency. This really puts the malt in single malt....!!! 46%

The Sexton Single Malt batch no. L71861F001 **(91) n23 t23.5 f22 b22.5** Unmistakably malt from The Old Bushmills Distillery, and seemingly from sherry cask, also, as that distillery probably enjoys an above average number unsullied by sulphur. 40% (80 proof).

Teeling Whiskey Single Malt Vol V Revival Aged 12 Years cognac & brandy casks, bott code: L18 001 088 **(90.5) n23.5 t23.5 f21 b22.5** Sharper than a newly whetted knife. 46%. nc ncf.

Tullamore D.E.W. Single Malt Aged 14 Years four cask finish: bourbon, oloroso sherry, port & Madeira, bott code: L3 5009TD 08/01/2018 **(76) n23.5 t20 f15.5 b17** Vividly reminds me of the early 1990s when I was regularly in the tasting lab of my dear old friend the late, great Barry Walsh, going through his most recent efforts to try and perfect the balance on his embryonic Bushmills 16. This works wonderfully on the nose but is immediately fragmented on delivery, a problem Barry had to battle with for a good many months, in fact the best part of a year, before things clicked into place. But, also, in those days with a malt of that age there was no such thing as a sulphur problem, either, which there is here and wrecks the finish entirely. 41.3%.

The Whistler Aged 7 Years The Blue Note Oloroso Finished (87) n22 t22 f21.5 b21.5 The great news: no sulphur! A clean sherry butt, which is a shock in itself. The less good news: the malt was a little too young and lacking in body to really be able to much more than a vehicle for the grape. Enjoyable, rich sultana with attractive spice. But lacking in whisky-ish structure and complexity: just too much like a straight sweet sherry! 46%. nc ncf.

The Whistler Aged 10 Years How The Years Whistle By Oloroso Finished (92.5) n23 t23.5 f22.5 b23.5 A fabulously clean sherry butt which is much more at home with a broader-spectrumed malt... 46%. nc ncf.

Writer's Tears Red Head Oloroso sherry butts **(86) n21 t22.5 f21 b21.5** There are so many good things going on here: the gentle, salty orange-blossom honey which drifts across the nose; the voluptuous embrace of the malt on delivery, offering such a happy marriage between barley and spotted dick pudding. At times mouth-watering and alive. But, as on the nose and late on the finish, a dull ache of sulphur. A shame. But, still, the positive points are worth concentrating on... 46%. ncf.

Irish Vatted Malt

The Liberator Irish Malt Whiskey Tawny port finish, batch no. one nbc **(85.5) n21.5 t22 f21 b21** A big, unwieldly malt with, I have to say, a character unmatched by any Irish whiskey I have before encountered. I can't say this is technically on the money as there appears to be a number of feinty issues bubbling around from nose to finish: not something I have often encountered with Irish malt. And at times the fruit and malt characters appear to wish to spar rather than harmonise. But.... The gristy sugars and a light molasses note does make for the odd fluting and even salivating moment and the spices give some welcome pep. Though of course, those heftier feint notes do gather, as they always tend to do, for an uncomfortable finish. A malt that certainly tells a tale... 46%. 700 bottles. Inaugural Release.

The Liberator Malt Whiskey Tawny Port Finish ex-bourbon, batch no.2 (89) n21.5 t22 f23 b22.5 Not sure how, but a confusing, then complex whiskey which gets there in the end! At first, thought it was going the same way as their last off-beam offering, but the turn round was remarkable. 46%

◈ **The Liberator Tawny Port Finish** batch no.5 (91) n23 this is high calibre Port at work offering the most even and delicate fruitiness. Frail spices appear to be the representatives of the cask while a vague ulmo honey and butterscotch sweetness does its bidding for the slightly unusual malt; t23.5 so lush, the creaminess of the joint grape and malt form the perfect foil for the juicier, more salivating younger element. The mid-point has a milky Malteser thrust before the fruit shuffles back into play; f21.5 there is a little bit of a vaguely feinty tang which the spices, so quiet on the nose, now run riot against in self-defence; b23 some aspects, especially on the delivery, are of an old-fashioned cream sherry sparkling with a rich malty inflection. When I created a vatted Irish whiskey some 25 years back, I suspect the malts I used were different to the ones I am experiencing here. But I certainly didn't use – or have access to – Port casks of this clean, understated excellence, either. Enjoyable and something truly unique. 46%

Single Grain
COOLEY County Louth. 1987. Beam Suntory.

Hyde 1916 No.3 Áras Cask Aged 6 Years Single Grain bott Feb 16 (87) n22 t23 f20.5 b21.5 Cooley grain probably ranks as the best being made right now, with the loss of Dumbarton and Port Dundas in Scotland. Sadly, as deliciously rich as this is, far too much toffee on the finish rather detracts from its normal excellence. Highly enjoyable, but the flag flies nowhere near full mast. By the way: the 1916 on the label doesn't represent year of distillation or bottling. Or is there to celebrate the year of my dad's birth. No, it is something a little more political than that. 46%. ncf. 5,000 bottles.

Kilbeggan Single Grain Irish Whiskey American oak casks, bott code: L18099 24/09/18 db (85.5) n22 t22 f20.5 This is one of the finest grain distilleries in the world: certainly the best in Ireland and a match for anything at the other end of the Irish Sea. The unmistakable mouthfeel and early volley of sugars confirms that this is Cooley: there is nothing quite so beautiful. But yet again, I'm tasting a Kilbeggan brand with a massive toffee footprint. I wondered at first if it was the oak. But, no, never on a grain like this. This is caramel, as in the colouring stuff. Please, kindly, will you desist from killing your own brilliant whiskey stone dead! Thank you. 43% (86 proof).

MIDLETON County Cork. 1975. Irish Distillers.
Method and Madness Single Grain Irish Whiskey bourbon barrels, finished in virgin Spanish oak casks db (89.5) n22 t22.5 f22 b23 About time they brought out another bottling, but with a little less sherry than this. 46%.

WEST CORK DISTILLERS County Cork. 2003. West Cork Distillers.
Skibbereen Eagle Single Grain Irish Whiskey Bodega sherry casks db (88.5) n21.5 t23 f22 b22 As frictionless as the post Brexit border between Britain and Ireland shall be... 43%. West Cork Distillers Limited.

UNSPECIFIED SINGLE GRAIN
Fitzwilliam Single Grain American oak db (91.5) n22.5 citrus and spice with background vanilla; t23 sumptuous and silky, light tannins spread osmotically through the body with spices on their tail. Light smattering of muscovado sugars throughout; f23 melts away leaving residual sugars and tannin; b23 beautifully made and citrus-laden, this is as soft a grain as Midleton's is brick hard... 43%

Glendalough Double Barrel Irish Whiskey first aged in American bourbon casks, then Spanish oloroso casks (88.5) n22.5 t23 f21 b22 A very pleasant malt but rather vague and at times a little dull. 42%

Glendalough Single Cask Irish Whiskey Grand Cru Burgundy Cask Finish cask no. 1/BY19 (87.5) n22.5 t24 f20 b22 Strikes me more of a grain than a malt whisky this, not least because of the gorgeous velvety mouthfeel. The honeys on delivery are sublime: predominantly ulmo honey but a little acacia slipping in, too. There is a light fruitiness getting on the act. But the finish is undone slightly by the furry tang of a naughty wine cask. A real shame, for otherwise this would have been one hell of a score... 42%. ncf sc. 366 bottles.

Teeling Whiskey Single Grain wine casks, bott Mar 17, bott code: L17 004 075 **(94)** n23 t24 f23 b24 What a beautiful grain whisky this is. Thankfully the wine casks don't interrupt the already spellbinding narrative. 46%. ncf.

Single Rye
KILBEGGAN County Westmeath. 1757, recommended distilling 2007. Beam Suntory.

Kilbeggan Small Batch Rye Irish Whiskey bott code: L18094 20/09/18 db **(85.5)** n22.5 t22 f20.5 b20.5 Quite brilliant to see rye whiskey coming out of Ireland: long may it continue. However, for the next batch I'd like to see it up its game considerably, as this is surprisingly tame. Certainly the rye momentarily brightens up the nose like the sun peering through a cloud to unveil the rich colours of a country garden. But then it hides behind a cloud again, in this case one of unbudging caramel with no silver lining whatsoever. The fact that it feels that there is no finish to this, so anaemic has it become, means this whiskey is not yet aligned as it should be: something is blocking the glory of the rye. And we know it is there, for on delivery it shimmers like a pearl before disappearing through your fingers and into the depths. 43% (86 proof).

Blends
Bushmills 12 Years Old Distillery Reserve db **(86)** n22.5 t22.5 f20 b21. This version has gone straight for the ultra lush feel. For those who want to take home some 40% abv fruit fudge from the distillery. 40%

Bushmills 1608 400th Anniversary (83) n21 t21.5 f20 b20.5. Thin-bodied, hard as nails and sports a peculiarly Canadian feel. 46%. Diageo.

Bushmills 1608 db **(87)** n22 t23 f20 b22. A blend which, through accident, evolution or design, has moved a long way in style from when first launched. More accent on fruit though, predictably, the casks aren't quite what they once were. Ignoring the furriness on the finish, there is much to enjoy on the grape-must nose and how the fruit bounces off the rigid grain on delivery. 46%

Bushmills Black Bush (91) n23 t23 f21.5 b23.5. This famous old blend may be under new management and even blender. But still the high quality, top-notch complexity rolls around the glass and your palate. As beautiful as ever. 40%

Bushmills Black Bush (95) n24 a teasing singing of the crisp fruit notes and far from shy and tender malt: sexy and disarming; t24 supremely rich, making the most of the rock hard grain to fully emphasis both the juicy barley and lusciousness of the grape influence; f23 dries, allowing the caramel to take a bow. But the spices up their tempo to compensate b24 a blend that just feels so right on the palate. Remains a true work of Irish art... 40%.

Bushmills Black Bush bott code L6140IB001 **(95)** n23.5 t24 f23.5 b24 Of all the famous old blends in the British Isles, this has probably bucked the trend by being an improvement on its already excellent self. The warehouses of Bushmills distillery boast the highest quantity of quality, unsulphured sherry butts I have encountered in the last 20 years, and this is borne out by a blend which has significantly upped the wine influence in the recipe but has not paid a price for it, as has been the usual case in Scotland. Indeed, it has actually benefitted. This is a belter, even by its normal own high standards. Truly classic and should be far easier to find than is normally the case today. 40%.

Bushmills Black Bush Sherry Cask Reserve bott code: L1047IB **(94)** n23 t24 f23 b24 As majestic and gloriously structured as always, and vividly salivating, too. But annoyingly loses a point for the faintest furry niggle from a sherry butt on the finish. 40%.

Bushmills Original (80) n19 t21 f20 b20. Remains one of the hardest whiskeys on the circuit with the Midleton grain at its most unflinching. There is a sweeter, faintly maltier edge to this now while the toffee and biscuits qualities remain. 40%

Bushmills The Original bott code: L1175IB **(92)** n22.5 t23 f23 b23.5 Last year, for the very first time I noticed that the steel rods which for 40 years reinforced this blend had softened. Not on the nose. But, intriguingly, on the palate. Normally it would be two years before I'd look again. But, intrigued, I couldn't wait. And yes, that transformation was not my imagination. Welcome to the new, super-soft, friendly, mouth-watering and quite delicious White Bush. Words, incidentally, I never thought I would ever write. 40%.

Bushmills Red Bush bourbon casks, bott code: L7161IB001 db **(92)** n22 t23.5 f23 b23.5 A beautifully balanced and erudite blended Irish fully deserving of discovery. And after the preponderance of wine-finished Irish from elsewhere, it was great to taste one that hadn't already set my nerves jangling in fear of what was to come. A worthy and beautiful addition to the Bushmills range. I always knew I'd be a little bit partial to a Red Bush. 40%.

Bushmills White Bush bott code: L8185 IB 02S **(85)** n21 t22 f21 b21 For decades this was the toughest blend in all Ireland, the one you not so much cut your teeth on, but broke them. The grain was hard enough to make ships from in the dockyards and you drank this not so much for the pleasantries, but the effect. In recent years it has yielded a little to finer tastes, and though the nose still gives away absolutely nothing – except toffeed grain – at least the delivery on the palate is both clean and salivating. No off notes from second rate sherry butts. Just a sweet toffee firmness that has now also done away with the old aggressive finale. Surprisingly pleasant. 40%. *Known as "White Bush" due to the white label.*

Clonakilty Irish Whiskey batch no. NEBC002. bourbon cask, Imperial Stout Trooper cask finish **(88.5) n21.5 t22.5 f22.5 b22** Just love the brightness on the delivery, especially the initial burst of malt. Beer cask finishes have embittered me over the years, but pleased to report that there is no hop interference and residue here and those strikingly juicy tones on delivery carry through unmolested. Decent cocoa at the death, too. 50.2%. ncf. 1,400 bottles. *Bottled for New England Brewing Co.*

Clonakilty Port Cask Finish batch no. 0012 **(90) n22 t23 f22 b23** A whiskey where you're between a rock and a soft, fruity place... 43.6%. ncf. 1,000 bottles. Cask Finish Series.

Clonakilty Single Batch batch no. 003/2018 **(86) n21 t22 f21.5 b21.5** Clean and salivating, this is a hard as nails, simplistic Irish dependent on toffee as its principal flavour profile. 43.6%. ncf.

Clonakilty Single Batch The Gentle Cut batch no. 012 **(86) n22 t23 f19.5 b21.5** Starts rather beautifully, with the rigid grain allowing the sugars scope to bring forward the sugars and spices out into the open. The finish, though, is dry and off balance. 43.6%. ncf. 1,500 bottles.

The Dead Rabbit Aged 5 Years virgin American oak finished, bott no. L18001-011 **(93) n23 t23.5 f23 b23.5** The rabbit is dead: long live Dead Rabbit...! Oh, Murray Method to take this from a decent to a truly excellent Irish, by the way. 44%.

The Dublin Liberties Oak Devil bott no. L17 048 W3 **(94) n23.5 t23.5 f23 b24** The Cooley grain at work here is of superstar status. So beautifully balanced and the word "lush" hardly does it justice... 46%.

The Dubliner Bourbon Cask Aged batch no. 001, bott no. L0187F252 **(87.5) n21.5 t22.5 f21.5 b22** A soft, clean attractive blend which peaks on delivery with a lilting juiciness which works brilliantly with the grain which is as yielding as a feathered silk pillow. Vague spices plot a course towards the bitter lemon finish. 40%.

The Dubliner Master Distiller's Reserve bourbon casks, bott no. L17718-320 **(91) n23.5 t23 f22 b22.5** Refreshing and tender. A bit of an understated treat. 42%.

Dundalgan Charred Cask Irish Whiskey db **(87) n21.5 t22 f22 b21.5** This is an interesting one: you have a spirit that produces a fair chunk of oil. You then char a cask, which produces caramel. The only result possible is a thick whiskey on both nose and palate with limited scope to develop. So although the end product is the antonym of complexity, the flavours and mouthfeel are attractive and satisfying, especially if you are into malt and toffee. There are even some very late spices to stir things up a bit. 40%. West Cork Distillers Limited.

Dundalgan Irish Whiskey db **(84) n21 t21 f21 b21.5** Pleasant, inoffensive, toffee-dominant and bland. 40%. West Cork Distillers Limited.

Dunville's Three Crowns (80) n19 t22 f19 b20 Three casks and Three Crowns. So three cheers for the return of one of the great names in Irish whiskey! Somewhere in my warehouse I have a few original bottles of this stuff I picked up in Ireland over the years and at auction. None I opened tasted quite like this. Have to say that, despite the rich-lip-smacking delivery, certain aspects of the tangy nose and finish don't quite gel and are a little off key. The coronation remains on hold... 43.5%.

Dunville's Three Crowns Peated (94.5) n23 t24 f23.5 b24 Even people purporting not to like peaty whisk(e)y will have a problem finding fault with this. This is a rare treat of an Irish. 43.5%.

Egan's Centenary finished in French Limousin XO Cognac casks nbc **(94) n23 t23.5 f23.5 b24** So wonderful to find an Irish where both the spirit and the oak is in such deep harmony. A subtle Irish where the blender has carefully listened to what the casks are telling him. Superb. 46%. 5,995 bottles.

Éiregold Irish Whisky Special Reserve bourbon cask matured **(84.5) n20.5 t22 f21 b21** Curious that when I had whiskey a column in one of the quality Irish publications back in the 1990s, I was gently admonished for using the term Eire, for Ireland, in my copy. But here we are... The grain dominates this particular blend, in the Irish style that came to prominence in the 1960s, with toffee not far behind. Bit lost by the descriptor on the back (which I read, as always, after tasting this) as the cinnamon and cloves that they promise is always sign of great age. I get neither note either on nose or taste on this young whiskey, but the sweet toffee-vanilla theme is pleasant enough if not particularly demanding. 40%

Feckin Irish Whiskey (81) n20 t21 f20 b20. Tastes just about exactly the feckin same as the Feckin Strangford Gold... 40%. The Feckin Drinks Co.

Flannigans Blended Irish Whiskey (87.5) n21.5 t22.5 f21.5 b22 About as mouth-watering and easy going a blended Irish as you'll hope to find. Excellent sugars and velvety body ensure the most pleasant, if simple, of rides. Even a little spice peps up the flagging finish. 40%.

Great Oaks Cask Strength Irish Whiskey db **(90.5)** n22 t23 f22.5 b23 A joyful whisky brimming with personality. 60%. West Cork Distillers Limited.

Great Oaks Irish Whiskey db **(87)** n22 t22 f21.5 b21.5 Easy going, full of its signature caramel chewy sweetness. Pleasant and non-threatening. 46%. West Cork Distillers Limited.

Great Oaks New Frontiers Irish Whiskey db **(94)** n23.5 t24 f23 b23.5 Very high class and inventive Irish. West Cork have seriously raised their game here and have entered a new quality dimension. 59%. West Cork Distillers Limited.

Hinch 5 Years Double Wood ex bourbon casks & virgin American oak barrels, bott code: 16919 **(93)** n23 t23.5 f23 b23.5 A malt which works very well indeed, and deserves to. And even more so if at a greater strength and non-filtration. Impressive and highly enjoyable Irish which gives you minimum blarney and the truest flavour profile. 43%. The Time Collection.

Hinch Aged 10 Years Sherry Cask Finish bott code: 23519 **(89)** n21.5 t23 f22 b22.5 An, at first confused and later more relaxed, Irish that offers plenty of enjoyment. So many memorable moments, but a little more care with these casks would have brought a lot more. Still, that's my blender's perfectionist hat on. Just enjoy it! 43%. The Time Collection.

Hinch Small Batch Bourbon Cask bott code: 16919 **(93)** n23 t23.5 f23 b23.5 The bourbon casks make such a difference here. A blend which is allowed to shew both its sweeter and richer nature. 43%. The Time Collection.

Hinch Craft & Casks Irish Whisky Imperial Stout Finish bott code: L1098H001 **(86)** n20 t23 f21 b22 I know that beer cask finishes are all the rage but forgive me if I don't become a fully paid-up member of the Supporters' Club. When the nose smells something a lot closer to an empty glass of Guinness that has been left standing on the bar-room table for an hour two than actual whiskey, you start to lose me. I agree, without the use of thumb screws, that after the tap room delivery the middle is brilliant: the texture is attractive, the creaminess to a vague, sweet chocolatey maltiness is a tasty flavour combination in particular; and there are even the odd bursts of honey. But the finish wanders off course again...though I'm pleased to report there are no technical off notes with the casks themselves. I suspect those, the stout-hearted, who have a penchant for this kind of whiskey will be in paroxysms of hoppy delight...and power to your elbow. Yes, there are aspects of this I seriously enjoy, but others...I just have to grin and beer it. 43%

Hinch Distillery Exclusive 2008 bott 31/8/2022 db **(92)** n24 the tannins make no secret that they are in control here: from the bizzy, pinging, nippy spice to the old, polished oak, there is a feeling of controlled antiquity to this. There is even an earthy smokiness in there, too, without being exactly peaty. There's a heather honey tinge to the dried dates. Bejabbers, this is seriously complex....; t23.5 just so wonderfully fat and mouth-filling from the very first moment. We are talking over-ripe figs here, plus a little melon. Then we get to something deeper and far more difficult to unravel. The spices, initially more gentle than the nose suggests, lead the way and again it is oak dominant. With a wonderfully contrasting chalky, dried liquorice tone completely at odds with the deft oils coating the palate; f21.5 now this is an odd one. Unlike any other finish I have before encountered – anywhere. I originally thought the dreaded 'S' word had snuck in with the developing bitterness. But it can't be as that vanishes within the life of the favour profile – something sulphur never does. It is as though the pips and skin of the grape have dried out on the palate and the honey has exhausted itself...; b23 a blended Irish truly like no other. Not sure about that bewildering finish. But the nose and delivery to get there is a journey of undiluted joy. 56.4%

Hyde No. 6 President's Reserve 1938 Commemorative Edition sherry cask finish, bott May 17 **(77)** n18 t22 f18 b19 Lush grape for sure. But the very last thing I'd commemorate anything in would be a sherry cask: unless you want sulphur to give you a good Hyding.... 46%. ncf.

Hyde No.8 Heritage Cask 1640 stout cask finish, bott Nov 2020 **(92.5)** n22 t23 f24 b23.5 I admit it: I feared the worst, as is always the case when beer barrels are involved. But, in truth, the cask adds no hoppy transgression to this while the texture does at least give a nod towards oatmeal stout. An absolute surprise package: I am shocked...for all the right reasons. Far better than I could possibly imagine. 43% ncf 5000 bottles

The Irishman Founder's Reserve Caribbean Cask Finish rum cask, cask no. 9657 **(93)** n23 t23.5 f23 b23.5 This brings to an end a run of tasting six consecutive Irish whiskies, each tainted by sulphur. This, naturally, has not an atom of sulphur as, sensibly, no sherry cask was used anywhere in the maturation (three hearty cheers!). Frankly, I don't know whether to drink it, or kiss it.... 46%. ncf sc. 318 bottles.

The Irishman Founder's Reserve Florio Marsala Cask Finish cask no. 2786 **(82.5)** n21 t23.5 f17.5 b20 A nipping, acidic, biting nose: borderline aggressive. But, momentarily, all is forgiven! The fruit is as lush as any delivery in the world this year, helped along by a thin maple syrup sweetness and balancing vanillas. Shame, then, about the very late sulphur tang. Whoever put the sulphur candle in this cask wants shooting: this would otherwise have been real stunner. 46%. ncf sc. 204 bottles.

The Irishman Superior Irish Whiskey bott code L6299L059 **(93)** **n23 t23 f23 b24**. What a quite wonderful blend: not of the norm for those that have recently come onto the market and there is much more of the Irish Distillers about this than most. Forget about the smoke promised in the tasting notes on the label...it gives you everything else but. 40%.

Jameson (95) **n24.5 24 f22.5 b24** I thought I had detected in bottlings I had found around the world a very slight reduction in the Pot Still character that defines this truly classic whiskey. So I sat down with a fresh bottle in more controlled conditions...and was blown away as usual. The sharpness of the PS is vivid and unique; the supporting grain of the required crispness. Fear not: this very special whiskey remains in stunning, truly wondrous form. 40%

Jameson bott code L701012030 **(87)** **n22 t22.5 f21 b21.5** Now, isn't that the way it always happens! Having tasted crisp, characterful true-to-form Jamesons around the globe for the last year or so, the one I get here for a re-taste is the "other" version. Suddenly the sexiest Irish on the market has become a dullard. Where it should be soaring with Pot Still it is laden with toffee. And a little sulphur nagging on the finish doesn't help, either. Does tick the other boxes, though. But hardly representative. 40%.

Jameson bott code: L108512 **(86.5)** **n22 t22.5 f21 b21** Oh dear. For another year the once great Jameson has slipped back from a master of complexity to a decent but ultimately toffee-riddled blend. I had hoped that last year's fall from grace was temporary. But the pot still character I had managed to instal into the blend back in the 1990s appears to have been stripped away. Not entirely, as the delivery shews a little pot still at work. And there is some lovely spice-centred complexity through the middle, though this is a brief burst compared to of old. This finish, though, is deadly dull as caramel exclusively takes hold. 40%

Jameson 18 Years Old bott code L629231345 **(91)** **n22 t23 f23 b23** Definitely a change in direction from the last Jameson 18 I analysed. Much more grain focussed and paying less heed to the oak. 40%.

Jameson Black Barrel double charred bourbon barrels, bott code: L932431768 **(93)** **n23 t23 f23.5 b23.5** Probably the softest Irish whisky I have encountered in over 40 years. But the complex sexing up by the spice raises the standard to another level. 40%.

Jameson The Blender's Dog bott code L608231059 **(91.5)** **n22.5 t23 f23 b23** A very slight variance on the previous sample (above) with the grain whiskey a little more dominant here despite the softer mouthfeel. All the usual tricks and intrigues though a little less orange blossom honey a tad more maple syrup, which helps lengthen the finale. 43%.

Jameson Bold bott code L617431172 **(93)** **n24 t23.5 f22.5 b23** Absolutely spot on with the tasting notes above. Only changes are slightly more fudge through the centre ground and a degree less bitterness on the finish, though still there. Crucially, however, the honey has a bigger late say. 40%. *The Deconstructed Series.*

Jameson Caskmates **(91.5)** **n23.5 t23 f22 b23** Some serious elements of Jameson Gold involved in this, especially the acacia honey thread. Delightful. 40%

Jameson Caskmates Stout Edition bott code L629315085 **(93)** **n22 t23.5 f24 b23.5** A very different experience to the Teeling equivalent. Here, the beer is far less prevalent on nose and taste, but makes a significant, highly positive, contribution to the mouthfeel. A super lush experience. 40%.

Jameson The Cooper's Croze bott code: L929031684 **(94.5)** **n23.5 t24 f23 b24** After a spate of pretty soul-destroying sulphur-riddled and spoiled Irish whiskeys, I could almost weep for coming across a bottling that is just as beautiful as when I tasted it last. Magnificent whiskey. 43%. ncf.

Jameson Crested bott code: L933631800 **(85.5)** **n22 t22 f20 b21.5** Unquestionably dulled since its release – or re-lease, if you count the classic old Crested 10 brand. A little barley sneaks through on the nose but the degree of toffee seems to have increased exponentially. A slightly furry grape kick towards the finale, but not too untoward. Incredibly far removed from the Crested 10 I used to regularly drink over 30 years ago. Unrecognisable, in fact. 40%.

Jameson The Distiller's Safe bott code L60331023 **(93)** **n24 t24 f22 b23** This brand's safe, too...at least for another bottling! As near as damn it a re-run of the last bottle I tasted, though here the butteryness kicks in sooner and there is a vague bitterness on the now chocolate-flaked finale. Still a stunner. 43%. *The Whiskey Makers Series.*

Jameson Gold Reserve (88) **n22 t23 f20 b22.** Enjoyable, but so very different: an absolute re-working with all the lighter, more definitively sweeter elements shaved mercilessly while the thicker oak is on a roll. Some distance from the masterpiece it once was. 40%

Jameson Round bott code L625831239 **(93.5)** **n22.5 t24 f23.5 b23.5** Just such a sensual whiskey... 40%. *The Deconstructed Series.*

Jameson Signature bott code L617531177 **(93)** **n24 t23.5 f22.5 b23** No longer Signature Reserve, though every bit as good. This, though, like some other Jamesons of late appears to have an extra dose of caramel. Bring the colouring down and whiskey – and the scores here - will really fly! 40%.

Jameson Signature Reserve (93) n23.5 t23.5 f22.5 b23.5. Be assured that Signature, with its clever structuring of delicate and inter-weaving flavours, says far more about the blender, Billy Leighton, than it does John Jameson. 40%. *Irish Distillers.*

Kilbeggan Traditional Irish Whiskey bott code: L19113 16/10/19 db (88) n22 t22.5 f21.5 b22 A really lovely Irish blend, making best use of some prime grain whisky which allows the barley present to ramp up the complexity and oak likewise with the spices. Just a shade too much toffee at the death. 40% (80 proof).

Kilbeggan 15 Years Old bott code L7048 db (85.5) n21.5 t22 f21 b21. My word! 15 years, eh? How time flies! And on the subject of flying, surely I have winged my way back to Canada and am tasting a native blend. No, this is Irish albeit in sweet, deliciously rounded form. However, one cannot help feeling that the dark arts have been performed, as in an injection of caramel, which, as well as giving that Canadian feel has also probably shaved off some of the more complex notes to middle and finish. Even so, a sweet, silky experience. 40%. *Cooley.*

Kilbeggan 18 Year Old db (89) n23 t21.5 f22.5 b22. Although the impressive bottle lavishly claims "From the World's Oldest Distillery" I think one can take this as so much Blarney. It certainly had my researcher going, who lined this up for me under the Old Kilbeggan distillery, a forgiveable mistake and one I think he will not be alone in making. This, so it appears on the palate, is a blend. From the quite excellent Cooley distillery, and it could be that whiskey used in this matured at Kilbeggan... which is another thing entirely. As for the whiskey: apart from some heavy handedness on the toffee, it really is quite a beautiful and delicate thing. 40%

Kinahan's Heritage Small Batch Blend (87.5) n22 t23 f21 b21.5 All aboard for the plush delivery, a gorgeous mix of briefly intense malt but overwhelmingly soft, sweet and embracing grain. The weak link is the tart and rough-edged finale, undermined further by a slight bitter note. But earlier there is plenty of fun to be had with the vanilla and spices. 46%.

Kinahan's KASC Project B. 001 hybrid cask (Portuguese, American, French, Hungarian & chestnut) (86) n20 t22 f22 b22 Well, that is different. The wood has the biggest say here, especially on the nose where the spirit is left bullied, quivering and unnoticed in some inaccessible corner. While the flavour profile is very pleasant, it certainly didn't ring true and when I later spotted the chestnut inclusion, the sensations immediately made sense. Intriguing, though. 43%.

Lakeview Single Estate Irish Whiskey db (88.5) n22 t22.5 f22 b22 A tad on the new-makey side, as witnessed on both nose and finish. But there is compensation aplenty as the sugars and spice begin to dig in and play games with the free-flowing grapey notes. Young and almost tempestuous in its ladling out of the spices. Great fun and bodes well for the future of this distillery. 46%

Lambay Whiskey Small Batch Blend finished in Cognac casks, bott code: L4732519 21/11/19 (92) n23 t23 f22.5 b23.5 The uncomfortable landing on the finish apart, this is a blend to savour with high quality malt making the most of a very sympathetic grain. Some really beautiful moments... 40%. ncf.

⬦ **The Liberator Small Batch Double Port Finish** batch no.2 (91) n23 one of the driest Port finishes I have yet encountered – despite the fruit and despite the light gristy maltiness which is still apparent. The effect is more like another Portuguese wine, the finest from the Douro region with its dry grape skin eloquence; t23 the subtlest sugars carry the maltiness far. The oaky tannins pitch in with a vanilla thread that seems to carry the thinnest jammy edge; f22 just a vague offkey note nibbles at you, but this is overcome by continued excellent laying of apologetic sugars and firmer, drier oaks; b23 a beautifully weighted, disarmingly complex blend where the Port, thankfully, doesn't over-sweeten and allows the varied aspects and vistas of this whiskey to be inspected and cherished to their fullest. 46%

Midleton Very Rare 30th Anniversary Pearl Edition db (91) n23.5 t24 f21 b22.5 The nose and delivery will go down in Irish whiskey folklore... 53.1%

Midleton Very Rare 1984 (70) n19 t18 f17 b16. Disappointing with little backbone or balance. 40%. *Irish Distillers.*

Midleton Very Rare 1985 (77) n20 t20 f18 b19. Medium-bodied and oily, this is a big improvement on the initial vintage. 40%. *Irish Distillers.*

Midleton Very Rare 1986 (79) n21 t20 f18 b20. A very malty Midleton richer in character than previous vintages. 40%. *Irish Distillers.*

Midleton Very Rare 1987 (77) n20 t19 f19 b19. Quite oaky at first until a late surge of excellent pot still. 40%. *Irish Distillers.*

Midleton Very Rare 1988 (86) n23 t21 f21 b21. A landmark MVR as it is the first vintage to celebrate the Irish pot-still style. 40%. *Irish Distillers.*

Midleton Very Rare 1989 (87) n22 t22 f22 b21. A real mouthful but has lost balance to achieve the effect. 40%. *Irish Distillers.*

Midleton Very Rare 1990 (93) n23 t23 f24 b23. Astounding whiskey: one of the vintages every true Irish whiskey lover should hunt for. 40%. *Irish Distillers.*

Irish Whiskey

Midleton Very Rare 1991 (76) n19 t20 f19 b18. After the Lord Mayor's Show, relatively dull and uninspiring. 40%. Irish Distillers.

Midleton Very Rare 1992 (84) n20 t20 f23 b21. Superb finish with outstanding use of feisty grain. 40%. Irish Distillers.

Midleton Very Rare 1993 (88) n21 t22 f23 b22. Big, brash and beautiful – the perfect way to celebrate the 10th-ever bottling of MVR. 40%. Irish Distillers.

Midleton Very Rare 1994 (87) n22 t22 f21 b22. Another different style of MVR, one of amazing lushness. 40%. Irish Distillers.

Midleton Very Rare 1995 (90) n23 t24 b21 b22. They don't come much bigger than this. Prepare a knife and fork to battle through this one. Fabulous. 40%. Irish Distillers.

Midleton Very Rare 1996 (82) n21 t22 f19 b20. The grains lead a soft course, hardened by subtle pot still. Just missing a beat on the finish, though. 40%. Irish Distillers.

Midleton Very Rare 1997 (83) n22 t21 f19 b21. The piercing pot still fruitiness of the nose is met by a countering grain of rare softness on the palate. Just dies on the finish when you want it to make a little speech. Very drinkable. 40%. Irish Distillers.

Midleton Very Rare 1999 (89) n21 t23 f22 b23. One of the maltiest Midletons of all time: a superb blend. 40%. Irish Distillers.

Midleton Very Rare 2000 (85) n22 t21 f21 b21. An extraordinary departure even by Midleton's eclectic standards. The pot still is like a distant church spire in an hypnotic Fen landscape. 40%. Irish Distillers.

Midleton Very Rare 2001 (79) n21 t20 f18 b20. Extremely light but the finish is slightly on the bitter side. 40%. Irish Distillers.

Midleton Very Rare 2002 (79) n20 t22 f18 b19. The nose is rather subdued and the finish is likewise toffee-quiet and shy. There are some fabulous middle moments, some of flashing genius, when the pot still and grain combine for a spicy kick, but the finish really is lacklustre and disappointing. 40%. Irish Distillers.

Midleton Very Rare 2003 (84) n22 t22 f19 b21. Beautifully fruity on both nose and palate (even some orange blossom on aroma). But the delicious spicy richness that is in mid launch on the tastebuds is cut short by caramel on the middle and finish. A crying shame, but the best Midleton for a year or two. 40%. Irish Distillers.

Midleton Very Rare 2004 (82) n21 t21 f19 b21. Yet again caramel is the dominant feature, though some quite wonderful citrus and spice escape the toffeed blitz. 40%.

Midleton Very Rare 2005 (92) n23 t24 f22 b23. OK, you can take this one only as a rough translation. The sample I have worked from here is from the Irish Distillers blending lab, reduced to 40% in mine but without caramel added. And, as Midleton Very Rares always are at this stage, it's an absolute treat. Never has such a great blend suffered so in the hands of colouring and here the chirpiness of the pot still and élan of the honey (very Jameson Gold Label in part) show just what could be on offer given half the chance. Has wonderful natural colour and surely it is a matter of time before we see this great whiskey in its natural state. 40%

Midleton Very Rare 2006 (92) n22 t24 f23 b23. As raw as a Dublin rough-house and for once not overly swamped with caramel. An uncut diamond. 40%

Midleton Very Rare 2007 (83) n20 t22 f20 b21. Annoyingly buffeted from nose to finish by powering caramel. Some sweeter wisps do escape but the aroma suggests Canadian and insufficient Pot Still gets through to make this a Midleton of distinction. 40%. Irish Distillers

Midleton Very Rare 2008 (88.5) n22 t23 f21.5 b22. A dense bottling which offers considerably more than the 2007 Vintage. Attractive, very drinkable and without the caramel it might really have hit the heights. 40%. Irish Distillers.

Midleton Very Rare 2009 (95) n24 t24 f23 b24. I've been waiting a few years for one like this to come along. One of the most complex, cleanest and least caramel-spoiled bottlings for a good few years and one which makes the pot still character its centre piece. A genuine celebration of all things Midleton and Barry Crockett's excellence as a distiller in particular. 40%.

Midleton Very Rare 2010 (84) n21 t22 f20 b21. A case of after the Lord Mayor's Show. Chewy and some decent sugars. But hard to make out detail through the fog of caramel. 40%

Midleton Very Rare 2011 (81.5) n22.5 t20 f19 b20 Another disappointing version where the colour of its personality has been compromised for the sake of the colour in the bottle. A dullard of a whiskey, especially after the promising nose. 40%. Irish Distillers.

Midleton Very Rare Irish Whisky 2012 db (89.5) n22 t23 f22 b22.5. Much more like it! After a couple of dud vintages, here we have a bottling worthy of its great name & heritage. 40%.

Midleton Very Rare Irish Whisky 2014 db (78.5) n20.5 t22 f17 b19. Must say how odd it looks to see Brian Nation's signature scrawled across the label and not Barry Crockett's. Also, I was a bit worried by this one when I saw the depth of orange hue to this whiskey. Sadly, my fears were pretty well founded. Toffee creaks from every corner making for a mainly flat encounter with what should be an uplifting Irish. Some lift at about the midway point when something, probably pot still, throws off the shackles of its jailer and emerges briefly with spice. But all rather too little, especially in the face of a dull, disappointingly flawed, fuzzy finale. Midleton Very Rare should be, as the name implies, a lot, lot better than this safe but flabby, personality bypassed offering. The most frustrating aspect of this is that twice I have tasted MVR in lab form just prior to bottling. And both were quite stunning whiskeys. That was until the colouring was added in the bottling hall. 40% WB15/416

Midleton Very Rare 2016 (87.5) n22 t22.5 f21.5 b21.5 The grain, not exactly the most yielding, has the clearest mandate to show its uncompromising personality A huge caramel presence softens the impact and leads to a big show of coffee towards the finish. But between these two OTT beasts the Pot Still is lost completely soon after its initial delicious impact on delivery. 40%.

Midleton Very Rare 2017 (90.5) n22 t23.5 f22 b23 Slightly less toffee than there has been, but still a fraction too much. But superb complexity levels nonetheless and one of the most attractively sweet MVRs for a little while. 40%.

Midleton Very Rare 2018 bott code: L826431444 (88.5) n22.5 t23 f21 b22 All about understatement. But like many an Irish at the moment, just weakens towards the finish. 40%.

Midleton Very Rare 2019 bott code: L925431568 db (92) n23 t23.5 f22 b23.5 One of the better Midletons for a while and really going full out for maximum meltdown effect. Classy, if slightly flawed. 40%.

Mizen Head Original Irish Whiskey Bodega sherry casks db (87.5) n21.5 t22.5 f21.5 b22 Maybe this was a bit unlucky, in that I have just come from tasting Glenfarclas sherry casks of the 1980s to this. No damaging sulphur (though a little forms late on the finale), so some Brownie points there. But the lack of body to the spirit and shortage of complexity on the grape, beyond a delicious cinnamon spice, doesn't help the cause. Enjoyable, but thinner than you might expect or desire. 40%. West Cork Distillers Limited.

Mourne Dew Irish Whiskey (89) n22 t22.5 f22 b22.5 Clean as a whistle and sharp as a knife. This blend positively trills its intentions of allowing the grain to join the malt in cleaning out the palate with its crystalline, cutglass citrussy sugars. Don't expect all kinds of complexity. The spices amid the light tannins towards the end apart, this is all about simplicity...and doing simple things well. 40%

◇ **Mourne Dew Premium Irish Whiskey** nbc (90.5) n22.5 a squeeze of lime on the sweetened vanilla-barley mix; t22.5 youthful, clean and salivating with a wonderful effervescence striking through the midpoint. Grapefruit juice and intense vanilla and butterscotch form a delicious combo; f22.5 such distinguished spices amid the remaining vanilla and citrus; b23 a silky blended Irish just full of citrus fruity vitality. A real tastebud cleanser. A palate igniter that is almost the perfect pre-prandial Irish. 40% ncf

◇ **Natterjack Blend No 1** virgin American oak finish, bott code 22023-305 (89.5) n22 almost a light tobacco note to the rock-solid, uncompromising grain...; t22.5 just love the two-toned attack on the palate here: the sumptuous, chewy oils and toffee, both weighted down yet lightened by a molasses sweetness and the rock-hard uncompromising spine running through this; f22.5 silkier at the death and aided now by a sharper (and quite unexpected) lemon blossom honey note; b22.5 this Natterjack has less of a softer belly than the last bottling of this I tasted and makes a point of digging in hard with the grain. This is much about the character on the palate as it is about the flavour profile. 40% Gortinore Distillers & Co

◇ **Natterjack Irish Whiskey Cask Strength** virgin American oak finish bott code 22025-308 (95.5) n23.5 surprising degree of castor sugar and vanilla here. The spices from the oak plays an important part of shaping this; t24 sublime mouth feel on delivery: truly faultless. Bites like a playful lover, showers the taste buds with the sweetest kisses of sherbet lemon and orange blossom honey. The oils are simply perfect and the layers available to chew almost infinite; f24 much more simplistic with a toffee-coffee theme...with some late very busy spices for balance; b24 a compete role reversal from last I tasted this brand: then the 40% bottling outperformed the cask strength version. This time, though, the cask strength has come on leaps and bounds to turn into a truly excellent Irish. Riveting...this is one sexy toad. 63% Gorinore Distillers

Paddy bott code: 20/04/21 (76) n20 t19 f18 b18 A blend I have never much cared for...and still don't. Hard, uncompromising, bitter and lacking balance. A kind of Hillman Imp but without the trimmings. You'll probably find the landlord serving it you at some remote Irish village inn a whole lot friendlier and better company. Even the blasted cap doesn't screw back on...! 40%

◇ **Portmagee Barbados Rum Cask Finished** bott code L01/0808 (87.5) n22 t21.5 f22 b22 Despite a clean, sprightly lemon sherbet-tinged nose, the formidable hardness of the Middleton-style grain is uncompromising. Curiously, rum casks usually add an extra crispness to a whisky but here it does appear to soften, certainly on the nose and also on the finish. At its best, when the Murray Method is deployed, the grassy juiciness is brought to maximum level with light cocoa coating sprinkling for the finale. 40% ncf

⟡ **Portmagee Barbados Rum Cask Finished Aged 9 Years** cask no 9, bott 2023 **(90.5)** n22.5 drier, aged tannins from the oak bathe in a surprisingly fruity sweetness. Attractive waves of butterscotch seep into the mix, alongside muscovado sugars; **t22.5** on warming those harder grain tones break down to allow a beautiful lift of vanilla and even more than a hint of Advocaat, aided by its now creamy texture. But a brief wave of maltiness before the tannins really get to town...; **f22.5** an attractive, complex finish that is particularly well balanced. The sugars possess the crispness expected from an ex-rum cask while the vanilla is fresh enough to add a slight sweetness as well as its usual drying nature...; **b23** a thoroughly enjoyable, mildly complex blend which offers a vague and very brief non-specific fruitiness before moving on to a much more compelling battle between delicate sugars and high-grade vanilla. Very satisfying. 40% 442 bottles

Powers Gold Label (96) n23 t24.5 f24 b24.5 A slightly different breed. This is not all about minute difference in strength...this is also about weight distribution and flavour pace. It is a subtly different blend...and all the better for it...Make no mistake: this is a truly classic Irish. 43.2%

Quiet Man Blended db **(88.5) n22 t22.5 f21.5 b22.5** A Quiet Man by name. And a Quiet Whisky by nature. The grain rolls about the palate gathering sugars and vanillas along the way and depositing them evenly with a charming citrus sigh as it does so. Perhaps one of the most pleasantly natured and easy-drinking whiskeys on the planet. 40%

Quiet Man "An Culchiste: 12 Years Old Eifel bourbon casks db **(87) n22 t22 f21 b22** Curious how the 8-year-old sparkles by comparison to its spicier older brother. The delivery is promising enough with all kinds of malty statements made. But then it flattens out to become one-paced, dry and a little tangy. Pleasant, but the 8-year-old has spoiled me...!! 46% ncf

The Quiet Man Superior Irish Whiskey Blend bourbon cask matured **(86.5) n21.5 t22 f21 b22** A very quiet whiskey: beyond the charming, delicately sweet cream toffee it has little else to say. Though, to many, it will be quite enough... 40%

Roe & Co bourbon casks, bott code: L9227NB001 **(90.5) n22 t23.5 f22.5 b22.5** A silky, sexy massively-flavoured blend where the complexity is not only given room to thrive but the bourbon casks ensure an extra degree of rich, honey depth, too. If they could just kill the un-needed caramel, this would be such a big scorer. 45%. ncf.

⟡ **Roe & Coe (87) n21.5 t22 f21.5 b22** A silky Irish determined not to over tax the taste buds. Lots of toffee upfront, especially on the nose. And plenty of firm, biting grain at the death. 45% ncf

Samuel Gelston's bott code: 05/07/2021 **(86.5) n21 t22.5 f21 b22** This appears to have taken over from White Bush as the quintessential hard-nosed, unyielding blend with a grain solid enough to demolish houses. A welcome lack of caramel does ensure that the malt positively explodes on delivery, bringing with it an excellent juiciness. A little icing sugar and spice for a lovely vanilla-rich midpoint, especially with those spices buzzing noisily. The finish returns to its rock-solid self. Kind of old school White Bush but with a sweeter, almost marshmallow-style flourish. 40%.

Slane Irish Whiskey Triple Casked bott code: L34638 **(86.5) n22 t22.5 f20.5 b21.5** Soft and supine, this whisky is all about softness and mouthfeel: that feeling of a soothing friend by your side. Could do with a bit more personality on the flavour front so the simple sugars don't over dominate as they have a tendency to do here. Excellent spices slowly grow at the finish to offset the furry bitterness of, presumably, a sherry butt or two at work here. Pleasant and promising whiskey. 40%.

Storehouse Special Port 'n' Peat Single Cask batch 3 db **(94) n23.5 t23.5 f23 b24** I deliberately nosed this after experiencing Penderyn's outstanding Peated Portwood. Can it live in the same exulted company? Easily! 46% 404 bottles. The Liberator.

Storehouse Special Malt x Moscatel Finish batch 1 db **(90.5) n23** the grape is firm. The grapefruit juice is flimsier...; **t23** a real palate cleanser if there ever was one. The fruit is light in body but intense in action. Spices nip, but only half-heartedly; **f22** super-soft now with the main players missing; **b22.5** such a clean malt I feel that my teeth are already sparkling after tasting this. The lack of body is mildly disconcerting, especially when the fruit is so full of promise. A lovely experience all the same. 56.7% nc ncf. The Liberator.

Teeling 15 Years db **(87.5) n21.5 t23 f21 b22** A highly perfumed and richly spiced malt, this benefits from still having a significant and attractive malt presence after all these years. The nose is a one off, a mix between ground roast chestnut and talcum powder. A svelte mouthfeel assists the sugars to calm down the growing spice but only to a degree. However, the finish is dry...and we are back to that talc again. Attractive in part. But wholly odd. 58.7%

Teeling Whiskey Barleywine Small Batch Barleywine finish, bott Sept 18, bott code: L18 016 270 **(84.5) n21 t21.5 f21 b21** Well, that's a new flavour profile after all these decades in the business! Am I big fan? Well, not really. Love the cream soda texture, I admit. And the suffused sweetness But there is a lurking semi-bitterness which seems to tighten everything about it. I'm sure there are those out there, though, that will worship it. Just not me. 46%. ncf.

◈ **Titanic Distillers Premium Irish Whiskey 401** bott code 22017-214 (93.5) n23.5 the sturdiness of the grain could almost be threatening, but the countering gentleness of the thinned lemon blossom honey works elegantly. And we have smoke...; t23.5 the delivery alternates between a macho hardness and shimmering, genteel molten Demerara sugar and lemon sherbet. Again, as on the nose, the peat creeps in while you are not looking...; f23 less room here for complex pleasantries. Dry, firm, chalky...and stealthily satisfying; b23.5 a blended whiskey as sturdy as the dockyards which were responsible for the most famous ship ever built. There is a hardness to this which reminds me of the grains used in White and Black Bush, but the surrounding malts are soft, salivating and juicy almost to a fault and offered extra gravitas by a thin mist of phenols. I lost several great uncles who were stokers in the Battle of Jutland in WWI. My Irish grandfather was a stoker from the Great War who survived: he would have so appreciated this whiskey. I doff my blender's hat to whoever put this one together... Love it! 40%

Tullamore D.E.W. bott code: L1 5297TD 30/11/2018 (81.5) n21.5 t21 f19 b20 When you are using a grain as hard as this you have to be careful of the caramel as it amplifies its effects. Lots of toffee followed by a dull buzz. Still a very dull Irish. 40%. William Grant & Sons.

Tullamore D.E.W. Aged 12 Years bourbon & oloroso sherry casks, bott code: L3 5294TD 22/11/2018 (91.5) n23 t23 f22 b23.5 When a whiskey is this good, you wonder what the other two Tullamore blends are all about. 40%. William Grant & Sons.

Tullamore D.E.W. Caribbean Rum Cask Finish bott code: L1 5184TD 23/07/2018 (80) n21 t20 f20 b19 Sweet, soft and a dullard of the very first order. Far more effect from the caramel than the rum casks. There may have been exotic fruit in the tasting lab. But it vanished once it entered the bottling hall. So massively disappointing. 43%. William Grant & Sons.

Untamed (92) n23 t23.5 f22.5 b23 Sometimes simplicity works a whole lot better than over-indulgence. Beautifully crafted and reaps the rewards of such naturally high strength, especially when it comes to those delightful citrus notes which ensure the palate is constantly aroused. A little big dram. 60%

West Cork Bourbon Cask db (87.5) n22 t22.5 f21 b22 No-one does caramel like West Cork, and even in their blend – in which their own grain has attractively thinned their hefty malt, it comes through loud and clear. Indeed, had I not known the distillery, I would have marked this down as a Canadian or a young, unfulfilled bourbon. Wonderfully soft and proffers some seriously lovely moments. 40%. West Cork Distillers Limited.

The Whistler Oloroso Sherry Cask Finish bott code: L19/34018 141 (83.5) n20 t22 f20 b21.5 Too much sulphur on the sherry kicks it out of tune. A shame, as some outstanding heather honey and raisin notes deserved better. 43%. nc ncf.

The Wild Geese Classic Blend Untamed (90) n22.5 t23 f22 b22.5 Appears to shew high grain content, but when that grain happens to be excellent then there are no moans from me. 43%.

The Wild Geese Rare Irish (89.5) n22 t23 f22 b22.5 Just love this. The Cooley grain is working sublimely and dovetails with the malt in the same effortless way wild geese fly in perfect formation. A treat. 43%. Cooley for Avalon.

Writers Tears (93) n23.5 t24 f22 b23.5 Now that really was different. The first mix of pure Pot Still and single malt I have knowingly come across in a commercial bottling, but only because I wasn't aware of the make up of last year's Irishman Blend. The malt, like the Pot Still, is, I understand from proprietor Bernard Walsh, from Midleton, but the two styles mixed shows a remarkably similar character to when I carried out an identical experiment with pure pot still and Bushmills the best part of a decade ago. A success and hopefully not a one off. 40%.

Writers' Tears Copper Pot Florio Marsala Cask Finish Marsala hogshead, cask no. 3150 (84.5) n22.5 t22 f20 b20 Starts brilliantly, promising so much... but then falls away dramatically at the end...And how ironic and fitting is that? I decided to taste Irish whiskeys today as it looked very likely that Ireland would beat England at Lords in their very first Test Match against them, and here was a chance to toast their historic victory. And, after skittling England out for an embarrassing 85 on the opening, incredible morning an extraordinary victory looked on the horizon. But while tasting this, Ireland themselves were blasted off the pitch and comprehensively routed, when they were all out for just 38 – the seventh lowest score in Test history. Irish writers' tears, indeed... 45%. ncf sc. 336 bottles.

Writers' Tears Double Oak American oak barrels from Kentucky & French oak Cognac casks, bott code: L9106L2273 (89.5) n23.5 t23 f21 b22 Does really well until the last leg. 45%.

Poitín

Mad March Hare Irish Poitín bott code: L16 001 021 (86) n20 t22.5 f21.5 b22 Full flavoured, oily and sweet there is plenty of icing sugar here to help make for an easy experience: perhaps too easy for a poitín! The nose suggests a bit more copper might not go amiss, though. And, seeing as It's poitín, why not go for a full strength version while you are at it.. 40%.

Japanese Whisky

How fitting that in the age when the sun never sets on where whisky is produced it is from the land of the Rising Sun that the finest can now be found.

A few years back Japan, for the first time ever, won Jim Murray's World Whisky of the Year with its insanely deep and satisfying Yamazaki Sherry Cask(s) 2013, a result which caused predictable consternation among more than a few. And a degree of surprise in Japan itself. The industry followed that up by commanding 5th spot with a very different but truly majestic specimen of a malt showing a style unique to Japan. How impressive.

It reminded me of when, some 30 years ago, I took my old mate Michael Jackson and a smattering of non-friends on a tour of the great Yoichi distillery on Hokkaido, pointing out to them that here was a place where a malt could be made to mount a serious challenge to the best being made anywhere in the world. While there, a local journalist asked me what Japanese distillers could learn from Scotland. I caused a bit of a sharp intake of breath – and a pathetically gutless but entirely characteristic denial of association by some whisky periodical executive or other who had a clear idea which side his bread was buttered – when I said it was the other way round: it was more what the Scots could learn from the Japanese.

The reason for that comment was simple: the extraordinary attention to detail and tradition that was paid by Japanese distillers, those at Yoichi in particular, and the touching refusal to cut costs and corners. It meant that it was the most expensive whisky in the world per unit of alcohol to produce. But the quality was astonishingly high – and that would, surely, eventually reap its rewards as the world learned to embrace malt whisky made away from the Highlands and Islands of Scotland which, then, was still to happen. Ironically, it was the Japanese distillers' habit to ape most things Scottish – the reason why there is a near century-old whisky distilling heritage there in the first place - that has meant that Yoichi, or the magnificent Hakushu, has yet to pick up the Bible's World Whisky of the Year award I expected for them. Because, sadly, there have been too many bottlings over the last decade tainted by sherry butts brought from Spain after having been sulphur treated. So I was also pleasantly surprised when I first nosed – then nosed again in near disbelief – then tasted the Yamazaki 2013 sherry offering. There was not even the vaguest hint that a single one of the casks used in the bottling had been anywhere near a sulphur candle. The result: something as close to single malt perfection as you will have found in a good many years. A single malt which no Scotch can at the moment get anywhere near and, oddly, takes me back to the Macallans of 30 years ago.

Japanese custom of refusing to trade with their rivals has not helped expand their export market. Therefore a Japanese whisky, if not made completely from home-distilled spirit, will instead contain a percentage of Scotch rather than whisky from fellow Japanese distillers. This, ultimately, is doing the industry no favours at all. The practice is partly down to the traditional work ethics of company loyalty an inherent, and these days false, belief, that Scotch whisky is automatically better than Japanese. Back in the late 1990s I planted the first seeds in trying to get rival distillers to discuss with each other the possibility of exchanging whiskies to ensure that their distilleries worked economically. So it can only

Chita

White Oak 🔺 Yamazaki

● Osaka

Togouchi 🔺

● Fukuoka

Key
● Major Town or City
🔺 Distillery

278

	Jim Murray's Whisky Bible Japanese Whisky of the Year Winners
2004	Pure Malt Black
2005	Nikka Coffey Grain Whisky 1991
2006	The Cask of Hakusha 1989
2007	Nikka Coffey Grain Whisky 1992
2008	Hanyu King of Diamonds
2009	Nikka Coffey Grain Whisky 1992
2010	SMWS 116.4
2011	Karuizawa 1967 Vintage
2012	Hibiki Aged 21 Years
2013	Hanyu Final Vintage 2000
2014	SMWS Cask 116.17 (Yoichi) 25
2015	Yamazaki Sherry 2013
2016	Yamazaki Mizunara
2017	Yamazaki Sherry 2016
2018	Nikka Coffey Malt Whisky
2019	The Hakushu Paul Rusch
2020	Nikka Taketsuru Pure Malt
2021	Yoichi Apple Brandy Wood
2022	The Kurayoshi 18 Pure Malt
2023	Nikka Coffey Grain Whisky
2024	The Matsui Sakura Cask

be hoped that the deserved lifting of the 2015 Jim Murray's Whisky Bible World Whisky of the Year crown, and the hitherto unprecedented international press it received has helped put the spotlight back on the great whiskies coming from the east. Because unless you live in Japan, you are likely to see only a fraction of the fabulous whisky produced there. The Scotch Malt Whisky Society should have a special medal struck as they have helped in recent years with some memorable bottlings from Japan, single cask snapshots of the greatness that is still to be fully explored and mapped.

Yet Jim Murray's Whisky Bible has provided a double-edged sword for the Japanese whisky industry. The amazing news for them was their World Whisky of the Year award precipitated sales worth billions of yen. And, consequently, a near exhaustion of stocks. The Hibiki 17 and Hakushu 12 vanished as brands altogether. But it means that, at long last and deservedly, whisky drinkers around the globe finally recognise that Japanese single malt can be second to no other. Their problem now is how to satisfy the thirst for Japanese whisky and knowledge on what it has to offer: at the moment they cannot. But Forsyths, the Speyside-based Scottish still manufacturers, are working overtime to supply more distilling equipment for the Land of the Rising Sun.

279

Single Malts

AKKESHI 2016. Kenten Co., Ltd.

The Akkeshi New Born 2019 Foundations 4 Malt and Grain Spirit bott Jul 19, bott code: IGZHS **(83.5) n21.5 t21.5 f20 b20.5** The rawness to this transgresses new make alone and enters into territory where not enough copper has been leached into the system to give this the required depth and roundness. Plenty of slightly oily malt doing the rounds but balance is at a premium. 48%.

The Akkeshi Single Malt Whisky Peated bott 2020, bott code: AJOJUJD **(90.5) n22** though more heavily peated, a flatter nose than the Lightly-Peated version (below); **t23** fat and intense, the spices waste no time getting to work on the tongue and roof of mouth. This isn't too bothered about subtlety: its single-minded purpose is to ram young, juicy peaty barley at you and see if you can cope...... A little lemon does soften some of the aggression; **f22.5** just slightly out of alignment with the delivery, a few odd notes start filtering through. But the peat-vanilla combination still does a job; **b23** a malt with a distinctive bite, this whisky has teeth! It's at times like this you'll learn to appreciate the Murray Method. 55%.

The Akkeshi Single Malt Whisky Sarorunkamuy Lightly-Peated bott Jan 20, bott code: JAXHS **(88.5) n22 t22.5 f21.5 b22.5** Not quite what I was expecting following some more rounded bottlings from this distillery in the past. Much thinner in body than anticipated, the smoke playing a playful game and attractively flirting with the busy, peppery spices. A little molasses and cocoa towards the end, but you feel a spine is missing for the gutsier notes to attack. A slightly strange but enjoyable malt nonetheless. 55%.

The Akkeshi Single Malt Whisky Sarorunkamuy Lightly-Peated bott Jun 20, bott code: AFMQV **(93) n22.5** young it may be, but the shy phenols offer a unique fingerprint. Slightly astringent, as though a little CO2 is in the air, the sweetness is strictly grist-based; **t23.5** brilliant delivery! The subtlest but most telling of oils ensures both the softest of deliveries and maximum length, too. Doesn't do the intensity much harm, either, which is formidable for the first five or six flavour waves. The main theme is chocolate, but first there is a fizzing mouth-watering quality which rocks you back in your seat...; **f23.5** chocolate pudding with smoke and spices at the very edges. Long, complex "bitty" notes quite similar to the finish of younger 1792 bourbon whiskies; **b23.5** one of the most exciting things about my job is when you locate a new distillery whose whisky offers something different. Akkeshi is one such distillery, and in this form generates a sharpness to its malt which guarantees lashings of intensity and personality. 55%

BS Fuji X The Akkeshi Single Malt Whisky cask no. 465, dist 2017, bott 2020 **(94) n23** the distiller has done a cracking job here: the cut is right on the bullseye, allowing the barley to show both a green fruitiness and green grassiness in its gloriously fresh delivery; **t24** the genteel smattering of peat emboldens the barley further. Now we have weight to complement the flightier fresh tones of succulent grass. The sugars a succession of melting grist notes...; **f23.5** long, poutingly spiced, and clean enough to allow both the smoke and vanillas to come through at their own pace...**b23.5** beautifully distilled, this is malt on maximum revs. No great age, but sensuous and classy. Note to self: once Covid is contained, an overdue visit to this distillery is essential...! 58%. sc. 800 bottles.

BENIOTOME

FUK Single Grain Whisky Aged 3 Years bott 2020 **(85) n21.5 t22 f20 b21.5** Oh well. Another whisky name to get me into trouble. Doubtless by including this whisky in here, I'm even more of a sexist than some warped idiots claim I am. The nose is thin, clean, and offering a little sliced cucumber. Perhaps there is a hint of a lack of copper, too, and this is later confirmed by the tangy finale. But I do love the salivating freshness of the delivery which generates a series of lemon sherbet and light acacia honey notes. 40%.

Miyabi Single Grain Whisky Aged 3 Years bott 2020 **(88) n22 t22.5 f21.5 f22** A fatter, more robust grain that the FUK with far greater confidence in its handing of its sugars, perhaps thanks to an attractive spiced counterweight. Again, the finish lacks firmness and structure, but the marshmallow and spice theme, accompanied by some outstanding vanilla tones is exceptionally pleasant. 40%.

CHICHIBU 2004. Venture Whisky.

Chichibu 2012 Vintage refill hogshead, cask no. 2089 db **(96) n24 t24.5 f23.5 b24** Is there anything more likely to make you sigh in delight that a beautifully made peated cask-strength malt that has spent sufficient years in non-wine casks for the light tannin and sensible phenols to marry, live happily in each other's company and have begotten myriad little flavour babies? Well, that is what has happened here with the malt even having its own little room for quiet as the smoke drifts contently about elsewhere. Simplicity and excellence. Some other distillers around the world should try this sometime. They'd be surprised just what a mind-blowing treat that can be.

Only a light bitterness towards the end prevents this from picking up a major Whisky Bible award. Because the delivery and first half dozen layers of follow-through has to be nigh on perfection. *60.8%. 349 bottles. Exclusive to The Whisky Exchange*

Cadenhead's World Whiskies Chichibu Aged 6 Years peated, bourbon barrel **(93) n24 t24 f22 b23** Another great whisky from Japan. If there was an award for delivery alone, this would probably be somewhere around the winner's rostrum. *59.0% 180 bottles*

EIGASHIMA 1919. Eigashima Shuzo co. ltd.

Dekanta Eigashima The Kikou Port Ellen cask, cask no. 11055, dist 2011, bott 2018 **(92) n22.5 t23 f23.5 b23** Forget the Port Ellen cask. That is just a red herring – or, rather, a smoked herring. This is all about the barley which is thick and intense, the extra depth coming late on from the tannins and, very belatedly, from very light peat. Beyond that, the phenols barely register – which is just as well, as you don't want anything to take away from the dense purity of the malt itself. *58.4%. sc.*

FUJI GOTEMBA 1973. Kirin Distillers.

The Fuji Gotemba 15 Years Old db **(92) n21 t23 f24 b24.** Quality malt of great poise. *43%.*

HAKUSHU 1973. Suntory.

The Hakushu Single Malt Whisky Aged 25 Years db **(93) n23 t24 f23 b23.** A malt which is impossible not to be blown away by. *43%*

HANYU 1941. Toa Shuzo Co. Ltd.

Ichiro's Malt Aged 23 Years (92.5) n23 t23.5 f23 b23. A fabulous malt you take your time over. *58%*

KARUIZAWA 1955. Mercian.

Karuizawa Pure Malt Aged 17 Years db **(90) n20 t24 f23 b23.** Brilliant whisky beautifully made and majestically matured. Neither sweetness nor dryness dominates, always the mark of a quality dram. *40%*

KURAYOSHI DISTILLERY 2015. Matsui Shuzo.

The Matsui Single Malt Mizunara Cask nbc db **(95) n24 t24 f23 b24** I cannot emphasise enough the brilliance and bravery of this distillery. The Asian market puts a high price on dark whisky. Yet here is a unique malt: young, entirely naked with no caramel work to hide any fat or blemishes. This is as natural and purely Japanese as Onsen. Except this is to be taken without water... *48% nc ncf*

⬥ **The Matsui Single Malt Mizunara Cask** nbc db **(94) n23.5** the spice tone to this is like no other on the planet. To be accurate, it is two-toned...one offering a nip, the other a warming rumble. This sits so comfortably with a vanilla and blancmange sweetness that is boosted by thick malt; **t24** I could taste this all day: the clarity of the barley is off the scales while the unique tannin pitch actually helps intensify the sharpness of the grassy barely; **f23** long, excellently oiled, thus maintaining that sexy, tactile feel this malt offers from the very first moment. The vanilla now really is at maximum revs...and still the barley clings on. A late bitterness pops up where it has never been before; **b23.5** Japanese whisky of the highest order which fully exploits the adroit charms of the mizunara casks. Would love to see this at cask strength: what an experience that would be... *43% ncf*

The Matsui Single Malt The Peated nbc db **(89.5) n22 t23 f22 b22.5** A typically idiosyncratic style of peating from this distillery, though the smoke often battles with the sugars as well as the tannin. Not quite as well balanced and rewarding as their extraordinary Sakura and Mizunara cask bottlings. Incidentally, I have just spent half an hour playing around with vatting the three styles together using instinct as my guiding light: some of the results were spectacular... *48% nc ncf*

⬥ **The Matsui The Peated** nbc db **(90) n22.5** a lovely chocolate mint amid the stiff, mildly acidic phenols...; **t23** a gristy sweetness makes for a wonderfully salivating arrival. The smoke is reserved but builds while the sweeter, unpeated section of the barley is no less confident and hands on; **f22** in come the tannins. The vanillas continue to have a barley sugar edge. While the peat rumbles with a spicy hit **b22.5** that's more like it! The last one I had of these never quite got its act together. This has and has learned its lines perfectly. *43% ncf*

The Matsui Single Malt Sakura Cask nbc db **(95.5) n23.5 t24.5 f23.5 b24** Forget about discreet sips. Take healthy mouthfuls and chew and allow the splendour of the complexity, complete with those mysterious hints of phenol, to unravel on your tantalised taste buds. So gentle. So genteel... Yet so understatedly enormous...yet so sprightly. A treat and a paradox of a whisky. *48% nc ncf*

❖ **The Matsui Singla Malt Sakura Cask** nbc db **(95.5) n23.5** cakey egg yolk and the most pathetic hint of something smoky drifting across the barley. Intriguing...; **t24.5** Wow! Never experienced a delivery of a Sakura cask quite like this before. Intense with the oak having a very early say and mixing in thickly with the rich barley. The strands of heather honey are sublime. Again, smoke appears on the radar...; **f23.5** a delicate smoky-spice mingles effortlessly with the tangled tannin and barley offering depth plus banana and custard softening and sweetening. Busy, long and deeply satisfying...; **b24** I have no idea if that delicate smattering smoke is in there by accident or design. But it certainly lifts this brand to previously unheard of heights. Magnificently complex from the structure of the mouth feel to the pulsing intensity on the middle and long complex finish, everything is right about this... *43% ncf*

KIRIN 1969. Kirin Group.

Kirin 18 Years Old db **(86.5) n22 t22 f21.5 b21.** Unquestionably over-aged. Even so, still puts up a decent show with juicy citrus trying to add a lighter touch to the uncompromising, ultra dense oak. As entertaining as it is challenging. *43%. Suntory.*

MIYAGIKYO (formerly Sendai). 1969. Nikka.

Miyagikyo Peated Single Malt Bottled in 2021 bott code 6/14A521023 db **(94.5) n23.5** the peat drifts effortlessly over the nose: dry, a little flaky and patchy in part, but always happy to allow both the sweeter malts and the more chalky vanillas to dive in and out of the picture at will...; **t23.5** just the most fragile and elegant of deliveries. No screaming or aggressive peat throwing its weight about. Just a measured smokiness adding to the wonderfully relaxed opening, the sugars noted on the nose now much more confident and mingling with perfect oils. Both the peat and vanilla combine for a much drier background....; **f23.5** those extra oils making themselves at home on delivery now extend to ensure a long finish as unhurried and charming as the rest of the experience. A few spices now to warm on a winter's evening. But everything remains calm, delicate, elegant...and very lazily smoky...; **b24** complex for all its apparent simplicity, this is a peated whisky for those who prefer their phenols to kiss and caress, rather than attack and strangle. Mesmerizingly beautiful. *48%*

Miyagikyo Single Malt Grande Non-Chill Filtered bott code: 6/24A341336 db **(88) n22 t22.5 f21.5 b22** A noticeably youthful display in the glass, starting with the fresh, malty nose and continued through on the eye-watering delivery. Lovely barley abounds, but so too does an extra degree of fruitiness which perhaps, overall, plays down this distillery's natural energy and gaiety. Likewise, the finish is very slightly bitter and dull – again not quite playing the Sendai's natural strengths. That said, a pleasant experience overall. *47%*

Nikka Single Malt Miyagikyo bott code: 6/04A041143 **(91.5) n22.5 t23.5 f22.5 b23** Will I ever taste a particularly bad Japanese again? Not in a month of Sendais, it seems. Only a little too much caramel prevents this from a much higher score. So effortlessly delicious, though.... *45%*

Nikka Whisky Single Malt Miyagikyo Apple Brandy Wood Finish bott 2020, bott code: 6/02J161349 db **(88.5) n22 t23 f21.5 b22** So fascinating to compare this with the Yoichi matured in the same cask type. The Hokkaido distillery's far greater quality and versatility shines through at every level. Indeed, how can you compare against genius? It is not a fair match. This, oddly enough, struggles to make the most of the apple while the cask appears to give this malt a particular firmness which towards the end is a little wearing. That said, I really adore the delivery on this which allows the malt to let rip and pulse out some startlingly intense barley notes. But beyond the midway point it becomes a little glassy, simple and even a tad metallic. But there's no denying that big barley statement. *47%.*

SENDAI 1969. Nikka.

Scotch Malt Whisky Society Cask 124.4 Aged 17 Years 1st fill butt, dist 22 Aug 96 **(94) n24 t24 f23 b23** If there is a complaint to be made, it is that, at times, one might forget that this is a whisky at all, resembling instead a glass of highest quality oloroso.*60%. sc.*

SHINSHU MARS 1985. Hombo Shuzo Ltd

Mars Komagatake Single Malt Limited Edition 2019 nbc db **(83) n21 t21.5 f20 b20.5** The nose lifts the red flag to warn of problems ahead and they don't hang about on arriving. The malt manfully battles for its usual place transferring from taste buds to heart, but the tang of the oak is a loud, continuous nagging. And the finish, sadly, is bang off key. *48% ncf*

Mars Komagatake Single Malt Limited Edition 2020 nbc db **(95.5) n23.5** the layering between the oak vanilla and the delicate nature of the malt is as clever and intricate as you are likely to find. A little gristy despite the weight. Just a little gooseberry juice at play, too; **t24** the second flavour wave is almost too wonderful to be able to concentrate on writing the tasting notes...! Just like the nose, it is the fragile quality of the malt which so delights, and the delicate spectrum of sugar tones that this brings about. That and the near perfect texture: lightly oily for maximum depth but not too oily to allow the gentlest favour breeze to blow. On a deeper, rumbling level comes the vanilla and the first spices notes. But it is like watching clouds moving about the sky: shapes slowly being formed slowly, almost imperceptibly...; **f23.5** just more of the same...though with the spices now a little clearer and warmer; **b24** I have tasted some great whiskies from this distillery over the years, though this is their first batch to reach me for a little while. Has their quality in any way diminished? Not remotely! The delivery and follow-through is almost bewildering in its beauty, though the Murray Method of tasting is essential for maximum effect. Having been to Japan many times and someone who has birded there in some if its remote mountains, I am more than aware that this country is capable of natural drama and beauty. And few whiskies come more naturally beautiful than this... *50% ncf*

Mars Komagatake Single Malt Double Cellars Bottled 2019 nbc db **(94) n23** an unusual slight saltiness the thick malt; **t23.5** amazing how the first moments on delivery seem slightly thin...then malt concentrate crashes down on the taste buds with remarkable power. Some superb light heather honey just gives a momentary extra sweetness; **f24** now we are back to a far softer, more even fade of that unique malt this distillery dispenses....and it never seems to end...; **b23.5** there is a good case for calling this single cellars Double Malt. Once again, the maltiness is deliciously profound. *47%*

Mars Komagatake Single Malt Tsunuki Aging Bottled 2018 nbc db **(92.5) n22.5** young, nutty and markedly clean. A touch of the Murray Method ramps the malt up massively; **t23.5** such is the incredible effect of the malt, you actually find yourself laughing as the intensity grabs every nerve ending on your taste buds, gives them a good shaking and then overwhelms them with tender kisses; **f23** keen malt works through to the end. The sugars are perfectly dispositioned to maximise the malty intensity. But a sub plot of dry cocoa powder acts as the perfect foil; **b23.5** youthful it may be, but the beauty of the malt leaves you gobsmacked. Like most Mars bottlings... *57% ncf*

Mars Komagatake Single Malt Tsunuki Aging Bottled 2019 nbc db **(91) n21.5** slightly more austere on the nose: a crisper tone to the sugars, while the outline of a butyric nose just hampers the complexity slightly; **t23.5** completely back on track on delivery with a breathtaking and eyewatering explosion of intense barley, fortified by citrus, hammers with peppery spice into the taste buds. The usual outstanding delicate oils enhances the mouth feel. Once again, the intense tones of the malt – something like concentrated Maltesers candy – just leaves you purring with delight; **f23** still spicy and relentlessly malty; **b23** this distillery appears to specialise in three-dimensional malt. *56% ncf*

Mars Komagatake Single Malt Yakushima Aging Bottled 2020 nbc db **(94) n23.5** the driest of Mars noses. The tannin offers dusty leather and hickory, the malt is but a squeak...; **t23** first it is the mouth feel that grabs you. The oils, intense – sort of. But does the job of adhesive sticking the liquorice and toasty tannins to the mouth. Slowly the malt moves from back seat to front...and the spices begin their erotic dance; **f24** the malt, having found its voice, sings now as beautifully as it has ever done, harmonising with the cut glass tannin. This is some duet...; **b23.5** usually: think Mars, think Malt... Not this time. Where normally the tannin is little more than a helpful bystander, here it grabs the steering wheel and drives the experience. The malt is for the earliest stages a hapless passenger. But not for long. Pretty good, though. In fact, just brilliant! *53% ncf*

WHITE OAK DISTILLERY1984. Eigashima Shuzo.

◈ **Akashi Cask Strength Bourbon Cask 2010** cask no 1355 db **(94) n23** quite green, but there is a wonderful vanilla current which carries the barley neatly and effortless; a soupçon of something smoky; some oily cashew nut, too; **t23.5** after the launch of unfettered, salivating barley, heather honey abounds, nobly textured, too, sticking to the roof of the mouth. A light leathery quality for a moment or two backed by a waxier tannin. The spices are sweeping in now but with no regression, just confidence; **f23.5** a surprise molasses kick blends in perfectly with that florid barley tone plus a little milk chocolate with walnut flakes; **b24** absolutely love it; no shy, shrinking violet, this. Has something to say and does so with broad brush strokes and backs it up with clever, intricate patterns of varied honeys. Beautifully distilled, excellently matured and a complex joy to experience. A must experience for those who enjoy a healthy dollop of whisky in their honey.... *56.9%*

YAMAZAKI 1923. Suntory.

The Yamazaki Single Malt Aged 18 Years db **(96) n23 t24.5 f24 b24.5** for its strength, probably one of the best whiskies in the world. And one of the most brilliantly and sexily balanced, too... All told, one glass is equal to about 45 minutes of sulphur-free satisfaction... *43%*

The Essence of Suntory Whisky Yamazaki Distillery sherry cask, dist 2008, bott 2019, bott code: LL9BNH db **(95) n24 t24 f23 b24** I'm not sure anyone in the world is doing sherry whisky better than Yamazaki right now. Here's another unreconstructed masterpiece from them. *53%.*

The Essence of Suntory Whisky Yamazaki Distillery Spanish oak, dist 2009, bott 2019, bott code: LM9BLO db **(92.5) n23.5 t23.5 f22 b23.5** take the finish out of the equation and this is a snorter. *56%.*

TSUNUKI MARS 2016. Hombo Shuzo Ltd

Mars Tsunuki The First dist 2016/17, bott 2020, nbc db **(95) n23.5 t24 f23.5 b24** When it comes to Japanese whisky, you expect thoroughness and attention to detail. Had they bottled their first-ever whisky scoring less than 89 points, I would have been both disappointed and surprised. What I certainly didn't expect was a malt of such depth and opulence Not to mention complexity and charm. This is a ridiculously good malt where the cuts from the still and cask usage just about embrace perfection. They have set themselves a very high bar from their very first bottling. Incidentally, the Murray Method is vital if you want to see what all this distillery has to offer. *59%*

YOICHI 1934. Nikka.

Nikka Single Malt Yoichi bott code: 6/60A061414 **(93) n23 t23.5 f23 b23.5** Well, I suppose you can blame me for this. I make no apology for helping the world fall in love with Japanese malt, though the consequences are, as we see here, younger malts used than a few years back. No matter: this is top quality distillate and gives the whisky lover a chance to see just how brilliantly constructed Japanese whisky is. Especially a distillery like Yoichi, which I have, for the last 25 years, been banging a gong for as one of the world's top distilleries. This shews exactly why. *45%*

◆ **Yoichi** batch 6/22E db **(89) n22.5** the youthful barley sings with unabandoned joy....the softest of smoke caresses; **t23** just ridiculously complex despite the obvious limited time in the cask. The barley intertwingles with the vanillas, taking turns to out-point the other. Not sure if you'll find a meltier middle in the world this year. As on the nose, the softest of smoke caresses; **f21.5** hasn't quite found its legs this far into the journey: the first nibble of something out of sync. But the phenols carry on caressing...; **b22** last time I tasted a Yoichi this young was in their blending lab 25 years ago. Even though this is not yet old enough to shave and still talks with a high-pitched voice, the apple-thinned peat warms from nose to finish. When away from destructive sherry casks, what a great whisky this distillery produces....still the best in Japan. *45%*

Yoichi Non-Peated Single Malt Bottled in 2021 bott code 6/14A541112 db **(93.5) n23.5** peatless. But certainly not joyless. The malt could hardly be more active on the nose if it tried. The tannins are also playing a blinder, offering a rich seam of spiced, seemingly freshly sawed oak. Elsewhere, moist butterscotch tart goes into overdrive. The whole thing appears to be three dimensional and alive...; **t23** now, that is odd. Only limited sign of oil on the nose...but it is wallowing in the stuff on delivery. Which in turn thickens the pristine barley, adding dollops of vanilla and ulmo honey to the party in carefully measured doses; **f23** long, malty...but enlivened by wispy strands if tannin, also bourbon-like in their refrain; **b24** malty and intense. A whisky hiding its light under a bushel of malt...*47%*

Yoichi Single Malt bott code 6/24A141259 db **(95) n24** perhaps the most understated and elegant nose I have encountered this year: certainly, among the top three. Not a single facet talks above a whisper and even the peat needs a little searching before it is found. When located, it grows, atom by atom to something a little farmyardy. Thinned heather honey and, initially, even thinner phenols, but there is also a fruit note there, so delicate, so almost imperceptible, its fault is that you are trying to work out what it is rather than just bathe and luxuriate in the overall bigger picture; **t23.5** now I'm laughing...it is that mystery fruit note which arrives first on delivery which captures both your attention and palate. How did it do that...? As on the nose, the peat is there – actually, far more confident than in the aroma - but still steadfastly refuses to dominate. This is partially because of the alliance forged by the malt and the structured tannins which ensure a vanilla-dominant undertone; **f23.5** long. Actually, ridiculously long. And now the peat has built into something including muscle, as there's a depth to this which before could not be found. Once more, the tannins play a supporting role with the vanillas, with a late interplay between crisp refined and delicate demerara sugar and more confident vanilla; **b24** as I sit here tasting and worshipping this spectacularly eloquent Japanese whisky in the heart of some of England's most beautiful countryside, I have just noticed that my small village has just been invaded by a team of Morris Dancers in full traditional regalia. How perfectly incongruous. As for the whisky, the peat, for some, will be more of a question than a statement. This is sublime whisky by any standards. Even for those incurable whisky snobs who blindly denigrate all Japanese, irrespective of quality in favour of Scotch. Arrogant idiots. *45%*

Yoichi Single Malt Grande Non-Chill Filtered bott code: 6/24A341124 db **(90) n23** charmingly complex with such a teasing smokiness amid the citrus; **t22.5** much more weight on juicy and malty delivery, though still the peat plays peak-a-boo...though not so much now with the playful fruit but the more confident tannins which rap out a dry-vanilla beat; **f22** dry and delicately spiced. For all intents and purposes, the phenols are now finished; **b23** something of an inscrutable malt, cards being kept close to the chest and aromas and flavours shown only when they need to be. One of the most understated whiskies of the year. *47%*

Vatted Malts

Kamiki Blended Malt Whisky Sakura Wood finished in Japanese cedar casks, bott code: 2020 11 **(93) n22.5 t23.5 f23 b24** This is strikingly brilliant! I thorough enjoyed their last bottling. This has gone up several notches and just explodes about the palate with the most magnificently balanced flavours. What a real eye-opener! And one of the most dangerous whiskies on the market today: one glass will never be enough of this... *48%*

⟡ **The Kurayoshi Pure Malt Whisky** nbc **(91) n23** fresh youthful malts. Lemon sherbet effervescence compliments the grassy barley; **t23** as mouth-watering as it is mouth-filling, this is malt at its most nubile. The barley sugars blend beautifully with that lemon sherbet; **f22** plenty of vanilla, but just a little bitterness of the oak, too...; **b23** a reviving malt for those who like an early morning whisky. The freshness on the nose and delivery gets all the senses going. *43% ncf*

⟡ **The Kurayoshi Pure Malt Whisky Aged 8 Years** nbc **(93.5) n23.5** love the light-heavy-light-heavy fluctuations. When the malt dominates, we are in lighter mode. Then the oak pulses and all is much weightier. The house honey style here is of the acacia variety...; **t23.5** that is such an impressive delivery. The malt is not just intense. It actually offers itself in varying degrees of concentration, though all of them of a sweet variety, the most subtle being a sweetmeat biscuit style; **f23** suffers from lack of oils (and strength) to take advantage of the sugars and tannins on offer. The light vanillas do an excellent job, though...; **b23.5** this malt has taken a massive step in the right direction from when I last tasted it. Sweet malts everywhere...but oh, how I would love this to be at 46% or beyond... *43% ncf*

⟡ **The Kurayoshi Pure Malt Whisky Aged 12 Years** nbc **(88.5) n21.5 t22.5 f22 b22.5** Absolutely nothing wrong with this whisky. The sugars and spices play their parts well and there are no surprises from tired casks. But this is just a little too flat (especially on the dull nose), even and non-commital for greatness, though it would take a daft person to say no to a second glass... *43% ncf*

⟡ **The Kurayoshi Pure Malt Whisky Aged 18 Years** nbc **(95.5) n24** just fabulous. A clever blend of heather and manuka honeys dovetail epically with the oaky tannins. The sticking plaster is the malt which, after nearly two decades, still has much to say. So complex....; **t24.5** yesssss! That delivery...oh, wow!!!! It's absolutely alive and just blows the mind with that intricate mosaic of varied honey tones and complex tannins. The spices pulse, the barley somehow offers an improbable degree of freshness and life...and elsewhere, honey...; **f23** the oak does revel. Little bitterness. But still there is so much honey flowing through this piece that it really doesn't matter. Amazingly, the barley stays on to complete the journey; **b24** probably the best malt under 46% in the world...and beautifully distilled by bees. *43% ncf*

⟡ **The Kurayoshi Pure Malt Whisky Sherry Cask** nbc **(78) n19 t20 f19 b20** Sadly, sulphured. *43% ncf*

⟡ **The Kyoto Purple Label** bott code 104284 **(83.5) n21 t22 f19.5 b21** Some very young malt whisky at play here, its lack of weight augmented by toffee. Certainly malty and salivating on delivery, even with a surprising salty slant. There even appears to be the odd phenolic note here and there. Better than previous bottlings, though the finish still lacks the back-up needed to last or particularly impress. Some very decent chewing early on, though. *43%*

Nikka Taketsuru Pure Malt bott code: 6/06J341519 **(94) n24 t23.5 f23 b23.5** Such an elegant malt. *43%*

Nikka Taketsuru Pure Malt bott code: 6/24A121324 db **(88) n23.5 t22.5 f19 b22** Even though I lived with a Japanese girlfriend for three years, I still cannot swear in her native tongue.... and I so wish I could. The nose and delivery are so complete. The essence of smoke drifting with such a fabulous disregard to care. The malt offering such sensuality in its layering. And then, tragically such a late, harsh sulphur-like curtain to the finish which brings the wind out of its sails. For a normal malt this would have scored in the high 70s or low 80s. But such is the magnificence of all that has gone before, it still scores highly. If your DNA is of a certain type, you will regard this a masterpiece. *43%*

The Shiki Malt Whisky (86) n22 t22.5 f20 b21.5 This is as exceptionally young as it is malty. Virtually no tannins can be detected on the nose but we are compensated by the youthful, citrussy call of undisturbed barley. Just how juicy and intense this barley is, is witnessed on delivery where, at the midpoint, some tannins do move in to add a drying balance. The Achilles heel is the finish which appears to lack a coppery depth and, with little oaky resistance, becomes tangy. A real curate's egg. And one that was hatched a little too early... *43%*.

Japanese Single Grain
CHITA 1972. Suntory.
The Chita Single Grain bott code L1610R db **(91.5) n23 t23 f22.5 b23** Spot on Corn Whiskey-type grain: could almost be a blueprint. Simple, but deliciously soft and effective. 43%.

KUMESEN 1952.
Makoto Single Grain Whisky Aged 23 Years bourbon cask, bott 2019 **(95.5) n24 t24 f23.5 b24** The more I taste of this grain distillery, the greater I am impressed. What a thoroughly charming, beautifully integrated whisky. Not a single false step or off note. Unquestionably one of the friendliest and most genteel whiskies of the year. Ignore this one at your peril...it is an absolute gem. 42%. *Bushido Series.*

TOYONAGA 1894.
Kangakoi Single Grain Whisky Aged 7 Years oak sherry casks **(86.5) n23 t22 f20 b21.5** The nose is exceptionally fine, full of delicate charm. Indeed, the aroma of succulent fruit carries a lightly honeyed sweetness, too. The complexity is nowhere near so abundant on delivery and the thin body may offer an attractive fragility, but means it does not have weight enough to counter the growing bitterness on the finish. 40%.

MIYAGIKYO 1969. Nikka.
Nikka Coffey Grain bott code: 6/24A341034 db **(95.5) n23.5** still coffey by name and nature. White coffee, this time with accent on Java. A gorgeous sub-plot of light molasses and mumbling spices confirms all is right with the world...; **t24** super-soft delivery in place with sweetness and sharpness set to exactly the correct levels. The sugars are hard to define exactly; perhaps a blend of thinned down ulmo honey and icing sugar. But it melts in the mouth exactly as it should...and is met with the perfect response of ever-arming spices...; **f24** I'll just repeat about the finish exactly what I wrote last year....because nothing has changed: it is identical...; **b24** every year I look at the latest bottling of this astonishing grain, searching for a weakness here, a failing there. But no. Guaranteed consistency: it is like a song you know the words to and can sing along with. I had always linked silk with China...until I found this whisky all those years back. And it is as soft and luxurious now as it has ever been. Wonderful. 45%

Blends
Kaigan 100% Japanese Blended Whisky db **(92.5) n23.5** simply magnificent. This is back to how young Japanese blends 30 years ago used to be: amazingly complex with myriad layering, with every other layer involving acacia honey. Malt plays a big part but so does vanilla with just the odd hint of toffee here and there; **t23** after all that honey on the nose it is hardly surprising that that is the driving force on delivery also. The light spices generate a little heat, but it is that marriage between the malts and honey which forms the main thrust; **f22.5** spicier now with a vanilla wafer holding a delicate mocha cream; **b23.5** 100% Japanese whisky that 100% is at its best using the Murray Method. A real top-notch beauty. 43%

The Kyoto Aka-Obi red belt nbc **(86.5) n21.5 t22.5 f20.5 b22** A near miss of a whisky: a blend that is so close to being a cracker, but the odd out of sync note takes it away from where it might have been – especially on the bitter finish. The timbre of the vanillas are a delight...but the bittering out was avoidable. It is at times like this I miss the fact I can't get on a plane with my blending hat on and sort out an easily avoidable problem... 40%

The Kyoto Kuro-Obi Black Belt nbc **(94.5) n23.5 t24 f23 b24** Like the Red Belt, this appears to have a textile label: superb...and unique so far as I can remember in 45 years of whisky tasting. And as for the whisky...? Worthy of the label. The mouth feel, texture and bourbon and spice combination work a treat, as does the toastiness of the sugars. Perhaps the greatest compliment is that, mouth feel apart, the grains are barely discernible. It is the malt and oak which create the storyline and structure. And beauty. 46%

◇ **The Kyoto Black Label** bott code 030805 **(94) n23.5** a busy nose, some spices chirping while the malt is far from shy; **t23.5** just brilliantly salivating from the very first moment! A plethora of light sugars and even deft ulmo honey hold their ends up against the toffee tones which are weightier in this bottling than previous bottlings. The spices, as on the nose chip and chirp away; **f23** there are dark, oaky tones revealing some age at work here. Any Japanese who visited England and ever tasted dark or burnt fudge would instantly recognise the finale; **b24** still a gorgeous blend, but a warning: very close to the edge so far as the toffee is concerned and just a thimbleful more might well have tipped this from complex and delicate to monosyllabic. Fine lines can determine a fine whisky... 46%

◇ **The Kyoto Red Label** bott code 104248 **(88.5) n22 t22.5 f22 b22** An improved brand with a much sharper tone especially on delivery which very much lives up to the tradition of

Japanese blends. This is undone slightly by the degree of toffee which slightly overcompensates on the singularity of the softness and results in a masking of complexity. However, the maltier tones do still manage to shine though. Easy going and enjoyable. *40%*

Nikka Days bott no. 6222H261103 **(89) n22.5 t22 f22 b22.5** Unquestionably the softest, least aggressive whisky I have tasted for the 2020 Whisky Bible. *40%.*

Nikka Whisky From The Barrel db **(91) n22.5 t23 f22.5 b23** I have been drinking this for a very long time – and still can't remember a bottle that's ever let me down. *51.4%*

The San-In Blended Japanese Whisky nbc **(89) n22 t23 f21.5 b22.5** A silky, grain-rich blend which is quite beautifully-made and shows its sugar-spice charms to its fullest extent. *40%*

The San-In Blended Japanese Whisky ex-Bourbon Barrel nbc **(94.5) n23.5 t24 f23 b24** This is truly magnificent. The label promises fruit that doesn't arrive. But it doesn't need it. It's a show-stopper in its own right. *43%*

⟐ **The San-In** nbc **(87.5) n21.5 t22.5 f21.5 b22** The massive juniper hit on the nose comes as a real surprise. Some busy malts try to make amends on the palate with light muscovado sugars adding extra juiciness. Fantastically full flavoured on delivery with the toffee just having a trace effect. Lovely creaminess to this, too. But that juniper does still linger. *40%*

⟐ **The San-In** ex-Bourbon Barrel nbc **(88.5) n22 t22.5 f22 b22** More Tann-in than San-in: a much chunkier, sweeter blend than I remember previous San-Ins, with the emphasis decidedly on toffee and oak. This really does impress when it comes to chewing: the oils are sufficient to ensure a very long finish with those spices darting around kicking up some serious entertainment. A brief moment of toffee apple, but it needed a slightly sharper touch from the barley for balance to be satisfied. *43%*

Suntory Toki bott code: LEX1DEY **(95) n23.5 t24 f23.5 b24** When I first visited Japan some 30 years ago, I lamented how Japanese blends were more or less exclusively confined to the borders of their islands. The industry was convinced that these blends were inferior to Scotch, which they treated as a liquid god, and therefore not worthy of marketing anywhere other than in their own home markets. I strongly disagreed. Since I awarded World Whisky of the Year to a Japanese malt – also from Suntory – the world perception of Japanese has markedly changed and supermarket buyers are now looking to include Japanese on their shelves where once they were far more reserved and if they did, it would normally be a single malt. So, it is heart-warming to see Toki gain a wide market. And even more wonderful that this blend shews the singular finesse and lightness of touch which enabled me to fall in love with this style some three decades ago. *43%.*

Tenjaku Blended Whisky bott code: BAL43B003439 db **(88) n22 t23 f21 b22** Tenjaku means "skylark" in Japanese. That is a bird I oft watch and photograph, especially in the breeding season, as where detract from those more gristy tones, though. A handsome if uncomplex blend. *40%*

The Tottori Blended Japanese Whisky nbc **(91.5) n23 t23 f22.5 b23** Elegant, light, and sophisticated, this blend would be the perfect welcome home moment for when we are finally able to return from a day in the office.... *43%*

⟐ **The Tottori** nbc **(91) n22.5** gorgeously delicate with the malt forming a seamless ensemble with the vanilla-rich grains. So lovely...; **t23** salivating and fresh, the softness on the nose now envelopes the palate. Lovely citrussy tones embellish the vanilla; **f22.5** still silky with spice and tannin now to the fore; **b23** an endearingly gentle malt, less toffee-rich than other Japanese blends and much the better for it. *43%*

⟐ **The Tottori** ex-Bourbon Barrel nbc **(86.5) n21.5 t22 f21.5 b21.5** A much more bitter blend than of yore with some eye-watering elements battling against burnt fudge. This bottling settles on simplicity, rather than the old style of gentle surprise. *43%*

Other Japanese Whisky

⟐ **World Whisky Society Reserve Collection Japanese Single Malt**, Mizanura oak cask finish, cask no H2457-H2487, bott 7.10.22 **(86.5) n21.5 t23 f20.5 b21.5** Right. Keep the bottle, as the goth design is one of the best I have ever seen. But perhaps change the whisky for Edition No 2. This particular bottling struggles to find rhythm and balance and from the offbeat greenness on the nose to the untidy bitterness on the finish it never really finds its stride. There is a memorable malty intensity through the middle which does work well with the natural caramels off the oak. But there is always a background murmur of discord. Such are the fines lines between greatness and slight disappointment. *43% nc 6900 bottles*

English & Welsh Whisky

Year	England	Wales
	Jim Murray's Whisky Bible English and Welsh Winners	
2010	No winner	Penderyn Port Wood SC**
2011	The English Chapter 9	**Penderyn Madeira**
2012	Hicks and Healey Cornish 2004	**Penderyn Bourbon Matured****
2013	Hicks and Healey Cornish 2004	**Penderyn Portwood Swansea City****
2014	The English Chapter 6	**Penderyn Portwood**
2015	**The English Chapter 14****	Penderyn Portwood
2016	The English Whisky Chapter 16*	**Penderyn Portwood**
2017	**The English Chapter 14****	Penderyn Vintage 2003
2018	**The English Norfolk Parched****	Penderyn Icons Bryn Terfel*
2019	**Norfolk Farmers Single Grain****	Penderyn Tawny Portwood
2020	The English Triple Distilled	**Penderyn Single Cask M75-32****
2021	The English Aged 11 Years	**Penderyn Rhiannon**
2022	The English Vintage 2010	**Penderyn 15 Years Old**
2023	Cotswolds Bourbon Cask	**Penderyn Madeira Malvasia**
2024	Cotswolds Charred Virgin Oak	**Penderyn Ex-Rye 6 Years Old.**

Higher ranked bottling in bold.
** Denotes European Whisky of the Year (2010 -2021)
* Denotes European Whisky of the Year Runner-up (2010 -2021)

ENGLAND
ADNAMS Southwold, Suffolk. 2010. Working.
Adnams Rye Malt Whisky French oak casks, bott code: L17269 db **(90.5)** n22.5 t23.5 f21.5 b23 Almost an immeasurable improvement on this distillery's early offerings. This has some serious charisma and amplifies the home-grown rye rather beautifully. 47%. ncf.

Adnams Single Malt Whisky French oak casks, bott code: L18039 db **(85.5)** n22 t22 f20; b21.5 Technically not quite the ticket. But there is no faulting the big malt. 40%.

Adnams Triple Malt Whisky American oak casks, bott code: L18103 db **(91)** n22.5 t23.5 f22 b23 Considering malted barley, wheat and oats have all gone into the mash, there is hardly any surprise that the nose and flavour profile is starchy and busy. Indeed, the oats have the biggest say here (a little bit of oat can go a long way in whisky!) in both aroma and on the palate; and the added sweetness from the cask gives a distinctive porridge-like feel to the delivery. But the cut is a tad wide, so the oils are a bit on the tangy side. Even so, a stylised and stylish whisky well worth experiencing, not least for that fabulous porridge delivery. A whisky to start the day with... 47%. ncf.

BIMBER DISTILLERY London. 2015. Working.
Bimber Distillery Single Malt London Whisky re-charred American oak casks, batch no. 01/2019 db **(95.5)** n23.5 t24.5 f23.5 b24 It almost defies belief that a distillery seemingly operating for little over five minutes can come up with a whisky of such depth, magnitude, balance and all-round stunning beauty. The distillate here was of better quality than for their first bottling, and from that all else blossomed. Yet another brilliant whisky distillery is added to the already impressive English catalogue. The good people of Bimber have every right to be proud of such a malt whisky. 51.9%. nc ncf. 5,000 bottles.

COPPER RIVET DISTILLERY Chatham, Kent. 2016. Working.
Dockyard Distilled Masthouse Column Malt ex-bourbon ASB 1st & 2nd fill vintage 2018, db **(90)** n22.5 t23 f22 b22.5 Beautifully refreshing malt whisky with a delightful lime sharpness to it from beginning to end. Obviously to reduce scurvy.... 45%. nc ncf.

Dockyard Distilled Masthouse Single Malt Vintage 2017 cask nos.2017/07-08-09-10-18-19-20-21, dist 2017, bott Dec 20 db **(88.5)** n23 t22 f21.5 b22 A very promising start from a fascinating distillery found in one of the most historical parts of England. Just need, I think, to carefully weed out the odd cask or two to try and bring the finale back into line when they bottle next. With the right casks there is no doubt that they will produce a fulfilling malt – and increasingly so with older whisky used - with their own unique and intriguing stamp. Meanwhile, in a little under five hours' time England will be taking part in their first football cup final since 1966. So, I thought it was only right that today I should taste both English and Italian whisky, Italy, of course, standing in the way of the European Champion trophy. I chose Chatham to represent England for two reasons today: firstly, because it is a town linked with the very earliest known competitive football in southern England, their club even being founder members of the Southern League in 1894 – which had been formed to run as a counter League to the all-powerful Midlands and Northern-based Football League. The second was more personal: my mother's father was stationed and trained at Chatham during World War 1 (I still have all his papers), serving the British navy until 1918. He survived. Three of my maternal grandmother's brothers didn't: they were also trained at Chatham but were lost in the Battle of Jutland. Which rather puts today's football final into perspective. And also makes one wonder why, when you consider the hardships and sacrifices our forefathers went through all those years ago, not least those who passed through Chatham Dockyards, why so many idiotic, tiny-minded people today deliberately want to make western society such a bloody intolerant and nasty place in which to live. 45%. nc ncf.

COTSWOLDS DISTILLERY Shipton-on-Stour, Warwickshire. 2014. Working.
⋇ **Cotswold Single Cask Charred Virgin Oak** cask no 1672, dist 28/8/17, bott 14/11/22 db **(95)** n23.5 you might expect just a gentle degree of bourbon on the nose, and you'd be right. Most intriguing, though, is the style of sugar compounds busy working with and against the malt. Golden syrup leads the way – and always with an intense malty edge – but red liquorice and heather honey are also in the mix. With the more earthy tannins also on view, this is far more complex than it originally looks; t24 oh...wow...!!! That is a brilliant delivery. I have to say there are some slight signs of sweet cod liver oil on display early on, but the spices arrive to warm and help salivate. Although the vanillas are in concentrate form, the union of malt and heather honey ensures the flavours available are huge; f23.5 long and lingering, as you might expect from virgin oak, some butterscotch tones turn to vanilla as it dries; b24 as you might expect from a virgin oak cask, this is all about the tannins. And to be more precise, it is all about the sugars extracted from them. In this case the result has been remarkable, with a far more comprehensive display of

sugar variances than might reasonably be expected. The cod liver oil caused the greatest shock, not least because I can count on one hand the number of times over the last 30 years that I have encountered that particular profile. But my word: it works...! *54% nc ncf 275 bottles*

 Cotswold Single Cask Oloroso Spanish Oak cask no 2289, dist 9/5/18 bott 12/12/22 db **(95.5) n23.5** Melton Hunt Cake just out of the oven. The raisins are toasty but not burnt, the molasses is deep and thick set. Black cherries offer their dusky sweetness; **t24** confirmation on the palate of the clarity of this sherry cask. The oloroso radiates a glorious toasty sweetness. Despite it all, you can swear that the odd strand of malt makes it through all the fruit. The midpoint offers a wonderful treacle pudding intensity; **f24** what a finale! The silkiness of the fruit meets the gentle oils to ensure the finish is of epic length. Often with sherry butts a long finish means disaster, but not here. Indeed, it simply confirms that this is a faultless cask, and the dark cherries meet with the heather honey; **b24** this is about as close to pre-sulphur cask sherry butts as you are likely to get. Stunningly clean and rich. Finding a sherry butt this clean is like digging up a gold ingot among your potatoes.... Just about the definition of distilled Melton Hunt Cake: toasted raisins, nutty, lashing of molasses (some latter day recipes include muscovado sugar, but old man Dickinson of Dickinson and Morris fame who have made it since the 1850s, told me in the 1970s that molasses was the key sugar). *54.2% nc ncf 340 bottles*

 Cotswold Harvest Series Whisky No.2 (91) n23 t23.5 f22 b22.5 Cotswold concentrating on their malt here which in its clarity and richness underscores the high resolution of the distillate. Excellent quality, though complexity has been compromised slightly by the monosyllabic stance of the vanillas off the oak. Though not before an eye-watering, fruity crescendo is reached just after delivery. That said, excellent all the same... *53.6%*

 Cotswold Hearts & Crafts Banyuls Cask Matured batch no 01/23 db **(95) n23.5** matured in dessert wine casks...and it shows! The sweetness positively squawks at you but does so in a particularly sharp and clipped manner. Once the spices get in on the act we are talking a striking, fulsome aroma with a heather honey-dark liquorice moment or three that is not dissimilar to well-matured bourbon; **t24** immediately salivating and not for a moment does it even consider taking time out to rest: it just ploughs on with an intense, super-sharp fizzy fruit candy persona. Incredibly puckering and raw and when those spices kick in to their fullest.... wow! **f23.5** after the sweetness comes the balancing bittering moments – this drawing out all the toastiness from the oak it can muster. A thin background presence of molasses and manuka honey arrests any further bitterness while the spices, nowhere near as startling as the midpoint crescendo, still have plenty of work to do...; **b24** good grief! This whisky has some personality and is about as tart a single malt you'll find this year. Thrashes your taste buds until your eyes water. And you'll love every second...!!! *55.1% nc ncf 1510 bottles*

EAST LONDON LIQUOR COMPANY Bow Wharf, London. 2014. Working.

East London Liquor Company Whisky London Rye new French oak, ex-bourbon & PX finish db **(88.5) n22.5 t22.5 f21.5 b22** A bewildering first bottling from this new distillery. As gingery as ginger liqueur, as dry as a gin, as confusing as a rye whisky matured in French, American and Spanish oak, one of which carried PX. It is almost impossible to say under all that what the actual spirit itself is like, though pleased to report not a single off note on both nose and finish. I really do hope they also bottle some whisky which gives us a chance to savour the grain. And remember that, in whisky, a little less can give you so much more. *46.8%. 269 bottles. Inaugural release.*

HENSTONE DISTILLERY Oswestry, Shropshire

 Henstone Single Malt Ex-Bourbon Casks batch 16, bott 18/04/23 db **(90.5) n23** crisp malt flickers on the nose, providing a flirting sweetness which draws you in. The tannin notes of the oak are bang in tune, shewing a two-toned attack: one is delicate vanilla, the other is much more throaty and raw almost as though in the early throes of bourbonhood. As well as the underlying gristy malt sweetness there is a much diluted but vital lemon blossom honey sweetness; **t23** the delivery reveals a comparative fatness from the cut only mildly hinted at on the nose. But that is soon forgotten as the salivation levels rise exponentially as the malt comes into clearer focus. The tannins growl with resiny bass notes for extra depth: this works so well...; **f22** ah, now that slightly wider cut does make itself known as the tannins revert to a light vanilla and malt becomes drier and nuttier; **b22.5** whichever bourbon cask they had used here had never spent more than four years in any Kentucky warehouse, and even then, only at the lower levels. Hence this relatively young whisky is able give an earthy backbone to the trilling malt without becoming boorish and claiming overall dominance. This is an impressive offering from this English distillery close to the Welsh borders and the really good news is there will be better to come as they master their stills and offer an even cleaner spirit. Really loved this for its malty honesty and the beautiful pairing of the oak. I must make the near three hour drive up the A5 to, at long, long last, visit the town which was responsible for me getting my NUJ (National Union of Journalists) card back in 1978. On this evidence another great English whisky distillery has arrived – and I have turned full circle in my long writing career... 43.8%

LAKES DISTILLERY Cockermouth, Cumbria. 2014. Working.

The Lakes The Whiskymaker's Reserve No. 5 db (94.5) n23 a hefty nose, quite aquiline in contour. Not quite classic and proud, but certainly interesting and characterful with a strange droopiness to the phenols but an enriching fattiness at play. The sweet/dry perspective is faultless, as is the distillate; t24 an abundance of sugars well up early on, the muscovado ones imparting a light fruitiness to the picture. Sticky and fat in mouthfeel, there is much chewing to be done. But, vitally, it is also salivating and malty – as you would want it to be ...; f23.5 thins slightly at the end as the fats dissipate. But malt, delicate tannin and citrus remain constituent parts...; b24 an essay in layering. Such a vast improvement on the early Lake malts I encountered. This really is classy... 52%

SPIRIT OF YORKSHIRE DISTILLERY Hunmanby, Filey. 2016. Working.

Filey Bay Yorkshire Single Malt Whisky First Release db (95) n23.5 t24 f23.5 b24 I know it seems like an inappropriate thing to do when tasting the first-ever whisky bottled by a distillery, but I feel I have no option but to compare it with a distillery elsewhere. However, the Whisky Bible lives by its honesty. And I have to say that the first thing that flashed through my mind on tasting my first mouthful was: Glenfiddich! And that same thought kept recurring throughout this delightful experience. None of the whiskies you can find from that celebrated Speyside distillery today. No, I'm talking about the classic non-age statement version, for years its trademark brand, that was sadly lost a great many years ago to make way for the 12-Year-Old, one of two drams I miss most from the early days of the Malt Whisky Revolution. When you taste this, you'll see why. It is the sheer élan, the fabulous brightness of this whisky that both wins your heart and takes you back the best part of a couple of decades: youthful, fun, stunningly well made, the malt coming at you in varying intensities, never for a moment sitting still on the palate – always somewhere to go, something to do: fresh and massively satisfying. For a first-ever bottling this is right up there with the very best I have encountered. Of course it is youthful, but the tannins have presence and complexity enough to make that no issue at all. If it does, it is to make it to its own advantage. Why, this newby even has the temerity to be an identical colour to the famed old Glenfiddich. 46%. nc ncf.

Filey Bay Yorkshire Single Malt Whisky Second Release db (93) n23 t23.5 f23 b23.5 Another quite beautiful malt, but just lacking that priceless, enigmatic sparkle of the first bottling... 46%. nc ncf.

THE ENGLISH DISTILLERY Rowdham, Norfolk. 2006. Working.

The English Single Malt Aged 11 Years batch 003 db (94) n23.5 a more fruity nose than their previous bottlings, with the accent on fresh apple pie. Spices have been carefully added to give this gentle essay of an aroma a prod while the thinner notes have a decidedly grapefruit segment nip. Charming; t23.5 the mouthfeel is far fatter than the nose and fills early with rich, concentrated malt. As the tannins slowly enter the fray the saltiness rises and all becomes a little sharper and more vivid. There are excellent gristy sugars right through the piece; f23 a bit of tang and toffee as it reverts to a simpler, more butterscotch-led, finale. Late on, though, a delicate mocha note signs off; b24 I taste this an hour or so prior to England's women's football team playing Germany in the Final of the Women's Euros at Wembley. And toast their success, which will be achieved if they can repeat their semi-final form. If you harmonise as well as this malt, then there will be no problems... 46% 4,300 bottles

The English Single Malt Whisky 'Lest We Forget' 1914 - 1918 nbc db (95.5) n24 t23.5 f24 b24 Probably the most touching of any whisky label I have ever encountered, it is a British Tommy silhouetted against the flag of St George. "Lest We Forget" are, of course the words used to remember those who died during the 'Great War'. Rather than taste this in my lab, I am outside in my garden to sample this, late on a warm summer's evening. At the going down of the sun I tasted....and remembered...and it gives me the chance to pay my respects to my Grandmother's three brothers who were lost in the Battle of Jutland in May 1917 (just two months after the birth of my father). A whisky worthy of their memories... 43%. 1,499 bottles.

The English Single Malt Original batch L0522 db (82.5) n22 t22.5 f18 b20 If there is a bigger advocate and champion of The English Whisky Company than I on this planet, then I would like to meet them. And then shake their hand. But, equally, I cannot be anything other than honest: it is simply not in my nature. And I have to say that this bottling is way wide of the mark expected. The nose is loaded with light, young malt and is initially charming.... but not without its warning signs as a bitter off note lurks. The delivery does big up on the huge barley signature.

But then...an off-key bitter finish which I suspect is cask induced (and not unlike a sub-standard sherry cask at that) comprehensively spoils the party. Pretty amazed: not sure what happened there as this distillery normally avoids these pitfalls. *43% ncf*

The English Single Malt Whisky Small Batch Release Rum Cask Matured dist Mar 14, bott Mar 20, batch no. 01/2020, nbc db **(94) n23 t23.5 f23.5 b24** So simple. Yet so complex. Just fiendishly brilliant. *46%. 1,985 bottles.*

The English Single Malt Whisky Smokey bourbon casks, batch no. 001 19, nbc db **(92) n23.5 t23.5 f22 b23** One of those, warm sultry malts, where the peat acts as a pillow and blanket you can snuggle into. *43%. ncf.*

The English Single Malt Whisky Smokey bourbon casks, batch no. L00419, nbc db **(92.5) n23.5 t23 f22.5 b23.5** A far more complex and confident version of the last Smokey I tasted from St George. At 46% this could be a revelation... *43%. ncf.*

The English Single Malt Smokey batch L0222 db **(92.5) n23** the peat positively twitters and sings from the glass like a finch tucked away in the safety of a bush and burbling contently to itself. Nothing extravagant, nothing flash. Just pleasant, tuneful and entirely in keeping with the background oak; **t23** here we go again: the peat, gristy and always dissolving, gently potters about the palate, in charge yet as if it can't be bothered. The background vanilla and butterscotch is every bit as relaxed; **f23** could have been longer, but could hardly be better balanced. The phenols morph slightly into mocha while the butterscotch stays the course; **b23.5** I'm sure I've written before about this superb whisky that it could really benefit from being at 46% strength... and make no apology if I have. A sleeping giant which never quite wakes up. *43%*

The English Single Malt Smokey Virgin batch 01/2022 filled Oct 2012 bott Feb 2022 db **(95.5) n24 t24 f23.5 b24** I shall say nothing about the name of this particular brand. Though, doubtless, had I described a whisky like this in the Bible, a pile-on from my talentless detractors with an entirely warranted inferiority complex would have ensued and I would have been Cancelled. Again. But so far as the whisky is concerned, it is the perfect name for it. The tannins mount up on the nose and make no attempt to lessen on the palate, while the smoke drifts around as a gentle peacekeeper. Big, but so easy to enjoy and appreciate: this is a classic, not just amongst English but world whiskies. And, for me, touchingly evocative... *46%*

The English Single Malt Whisky Small Batch Release 1st fill American oak, bourbon cask matured, batch no: 03/2021, bott: May 2021, nbc db **(92.5) n23 t23.5 f22.5 b23.5** You know when a magician pulls off a trick and you can't help smiling or laughing to yourself. That's the effect this whisky had on me: five years old, matured in England – hardly up there with Kentucky or India in the hot summers league. And yet there it was: a malt absolutely spilling over with mouth-watering charm and personality. *46%, 1806 bottles*

The English Single Malt Small Batch Release Matured In Sherry Butts batch 01/2022 db **(93) n23** black cherry and spiced Melton Hunt Cake...sans marzipan. The oak has taken up a leading position, too; **t23.5** sultry and super-sensual on delivery, light custard cream biscuits make an immediate impact on the fruit and nut cake. The spices tingle and tease while light molasses dip in and out the increasing warming raisins; **f23** long, oily with far more accent now on the butterscotch and vanilla. The raisins are now toasted to the point of being burnt. Meanwhile, the spices have gained attitude and nip. It's the way a malt like this should end...; **b23.5** so delighted to report 100% sulphur-free casks. Wonderfully structured, so just pick those ripe grapes and enjoy! *46%*

The English Single Malt Whisky Triple Distilled batch no. 01/2019, dist Jun 11, bott Jun 19 db **(96) n24 t24 f23.5 b24.5** Malt whisky of this super-delicate type are rarely found better than this. *46%. 1,462 bottles.*

⟡ **The English Sherry Butt Heavily Smoked Small Batch Single Malt** filled Jun 2011 bott Jan 2023 bott code db **(95) n23.5** now that is so heady. The peat is of the thicker Islay-style. And, if that wasn't enough, the sherry matches it molecule for molecule. Unusually, rather than battling each other, as is so often the case with whiskies of this type, they immediately harmonise. Even more interesting is that the grape offers two distinct personalities: one that is thick and weighed down with smoke. The other, which is freshy and fruity...; **t24** so rare...but the arrival and development is almost a word-perfect re-run of the nose with the smoke and grape seemingly joined at the hip. The only difference is the missing juiciness of the fruit which has now taken on a far deeper fruitcake-style role. Even so, slightly thinner bodied than the nose suggests, but certainly no lack of weight on the chewy flavour profile. And no lack of complexity and layering either...; **f23.5** this must have been a very high PPM phenol because that peat is refusing to let go. And it sits beautifully with the delicate hickory and coffee which, like the spice, blossoms at the very death; **b24** yet another very high-quality bottling from Norfolk. On first viewing you might be forgiven for thinking that if you were looking for a complex, delicate whisky, this wouldn't be it. But certainly worth re-visiting because you will realise that is one gentle giant you have in your glass. *46% 2,132 bottles*

⬦ **The English Virgin Oak Small Batch Single Malt** filled Nov 2013 bott Jun 2023 batch No SB-3-23 db **(94.5) n23** there is only one thing matching the intense toffee-vanillas off the oak and that is the barley concentrate. As on the grain bottling, the white pepper is busy...; **t24** the spices on the nose need no second invitation to kick things off on the palate. A glorious blend of ulmo and heather honeys is accompanied by a delicate liquorice and lightly molassed second wave of intensity, while the third brings a back now more way honey: just wow! On top of that had such an intense vanilla backbone which holds the still busy spices in place; **f23.5** like on the earlier delivery, still there are innumerable layers of drier vanillas played up against a subtle sweetness. But it is that faultless, resolute, indefatigable vanilla which impresses most; **b24** there I something irresistible about big yet perfectly weighted whiskies which in their unfolding come across as delicate. And this really is big with the most impressive vanilla theme you'll find anywhere in the world this year, especially the way it takes those warming spices in its stride. Magnificent. *46% 2,800 bottles*

⬦ **The Norfolk Popcorn Single Grain Whisky Vintage Cask Vatting** virgin oak batch No NW-01-23 bott Mar 2023 db **(94) n23.5** a little warming in the hand brings the honey up to heart-winning levels. Though super-soft with the vanilla as gentle as the honey, some spices do ping off the oak to stop you from simply melting into the aroma; **t23.5** having done its job by injecting both honey and spice into the nose, the virgin oak now goes about the palate in a similar manner, though never so heavily as to prevent the gorgeous juiciness which rises early and fixes on an impressive red liquorice and pepper midground. The vanillas, likewise, are clean and powerful and set the tone for the finale; **f23** long, pleasing, speckled with spice but ultimately soothed by creamy, drying vanilla; **b24** no doubt about the virgin oak deployed here. Having done its stuff by injecting a spiced honeyness into the fray, it even provides the background vanilla guarantees the consistency. Could taste this all day... *45% ncf 1,500 bottles*

The Norfolk Single Grain batch 01/22 db **(91.5) n22** youthful, fresh and more than a passing resemblance to freshly picked spring grass and new mown hay. The lack of oaky interference is a surprise; **t23.5** much oilier than the nose depicts, and this works in its favour. The midground is magnificent: salivating yet with an ever-growing intensity of spiced tannin, which dry and increase in weight. And warms while the grains remain very alive. Operating on a slightly different level are those juicy grasses...and melt-in-the mouth icing sugars; **f23** grassy still...and then a light spiced chocolate sign-off; **b23** again, we have that unbeatable combination of great distillation and magnificent maturation to thank for the full-flavoured display. Perhaps younger in style than this brand normally conveys. *45%*

The Norfolk Single Grain Parched db **(96.5) n24.5 t24 f23.5 b24.5** A classic Irish "mod pot" style Irish pot still whiskey...from Norfolk! Nosed this when it was just a few months old... and it has moved on magnificently; indeed, beyond hope and expectation. Only the cat's bowler on the label and a green bottle seems to give the faintest hint towards anything Irish... For the record, by far the best Pot Still I have ever encountered made outside Ireland's shores... *45%. nc ncf sc.*

M & S Norfolk Distilled English Whisky **(94) n23.5 t23.5 f23 b24** This is a straw-coloured classic. Not often can you walk into a supermarket – in this case M&S in the UK – and pick up from the shelf such a technically outstanding and beautifully made whisky which simply aches of gloriously uncluttered gristy barley. For those of you who still don't trust English – which is a shame, because much of it is every bit as good as Scotch and, in the case of this distillery, usually very much better - think in this instance high class elegant and charmingly fragile Speyside. Youthful, but understatedly glorious. And just about the perfect pre-prandial whisky. *43% nc*

THE FOREST DISTILLERY Macclesfield. Cheshire. Working

⬦ **Forest Whisky Single Malt Cask No 1** db **(92.5) n23** a young, virile malt, very cleanly distilled and making the most of the healthy, nutty fruit offered from the cask. Though youthful, the tannins still make quite an attractive noise, especially when the glass warms and the spices come alive to compliment the delicate liquorice. Complex, well weighted and pleasingly well-balanced; **t23.5** excellent, juicy mouth feel. Much oilier than the nose suggests. But the entanglement between that thick grape and ever-increasingly chocolatey-style tannin is superb... especially when the malt, having bade its time, finds the opportunity to steal in for maximum impact thus giving a second mouth-watering wave after the initial fruity impact. The spices nibble throughout now but never with the same bite as on the nose; **f22.5** drier, vaguely bitter with the spiciness now a little grizzled despite the still obvious cherubness to the malt; **b23.5** applying the Murray Method to this whisky is the only way you can do it full justice. Only on the fifth time round did the full scale of the complexity of this malt become fully apparent...and did I spot the clever integration of the cocoa which is game changer so far as complexity is concerned? For such a small distillery, I am taken aback by its quality. This is a rare bottling worth finding if you can. *48%*

English & Welsh Whisky

THE OXFORD ARTISAN DISTILLERY Headington, Oxford. 2017. Working.

Exploratory Flask Series Rye batch. 1, English oak medium char db **(89.5) n21 t23 f22.5 b23** Now this is much more like it! Still not quite technically on the money, but the happy marriage of rye and cocoa – presumably courtesy of the English oak. For all its faults I adore this. And I suspect future bottlings could get a lot better yet, if they can iron out the wrinkles. 40.5%.

Oxford Pure Rye Spirit batch. 5, new American oak casks db **(83) n20 t22.5 f20 b20.5** The tobacco notes radiating from this shows that they are still a long way from really having where they want this still to be for a high-class malt of the general English style. We have something far more of the central European mould, which is briefly attractive– especially on the third and fourth waves when the rye has shaken off its oily marker to make an intense appearance. But those unwanted oils stick to the dry and untidy finish. 40%.

Oxford Rye Distiller's Edition new American oak cask, cask no. 101 db **(76.5) n18 t20.5 f19 b19** It is very hard to get past the unhappy, butyric-type note – both on nose and palate. It is my nature to be kind to new distilleries, if always honest. But a lot is being asked of me here... I will say, though, that just after the delivery there is a very attractive ultra-malty-nutty note which is enjoyable. But it is constantly under pressure. 45%. sc. 388 bottles.

Oxford Rye Very Special Inaugural Edition new American oak cask, cask no. 3, dist Nov 17 db **(88) n22 t22.5 f21.5 b22** Full-flavoured and chewy, this is a rye that has decidedly nougat tendencies. But it also veers at odd times towards kumquat and molasses. There is no rhyme nor rhythm to this spirit but, for all its anarchy, it certainly deals a few aces on the flavour profile. The rich chocolate as the oak gets more involved is also to be celebrated. Technically, not one for the purist. But for the flavour junkie, this has to be a big hit... 53.4%. ncf sc.

SACRED DISTILLERY Highgate. London

◇ **Sacred Peated English Whisky** Pedro Ximenez casks, nbc **(95) n23.5** sublime peating gives off just that perfect degree of acidity to set the nose twitching. Easy to overlook the healthy display of intense barley which runs parallel. Peat lovers will simply melt into the glass...; **t24** faultless. Magnificently made, the oils coat the palate with a buttery, honeyed, lightly spiced glow of intense malt. But the peat holds centre ground and throbs beautifully...; **f23.5** the Demerara sugars and heather honey found earlier survive until the very end, with the spiced phenols on an oily dais. Long and satisfying...; **b24** this is outrageously good whisky. Brilliantly distilled and helped by faultless cask selection. Frankly, I am quite staggered at just how good this is. Having just driven through Highgate (on the way to Millwall) just two days ago, should perhaps call this whisky "20mph" or "Kahn's Revenge". Look forward to this whisky being a regular in my old haunt, The Flask, or maybe The Spaniard. Easily good enough to become permanent fixtures in both houses. As well as yours... 48%

WESTWOOD DISTILLERY Kelsall, Cheshire. Working

◇ **The Cheshire First Release** db **(90) n22** a biting, acidic nose. Falls somewhere between anthracite and freshly cut pineapple, allowing the barley to slowly grow in stature. There is, duty demands I report, a vague butyric note. But a disarming injection of vanilla soon covers this up and magnifies the increasingly rampant barley; **t23.5** mouth-filling and just so full of flavour! The lushness doesn't quite hit full fat mode. But there is also a sublime fruitiness not unlike chewy fruit candy before the barley erupts in full-on grassy fashion. For a first bottling...just wow! **f22** slightly tangy from the wobble spotted on the nose. But the oak is muscular and powerful enough to hold up the now sturdier malt for inspection too; **b23** an extremely promising first bottling of the first-ever whisky from Cheshire, a county in which I once lived. This is brimming with personality, especially in the fruit department, helped along by some judicious cask selection. Goes big on the barley, too... For a first bottling, way above expectation. 46% nc ncf

WHARF DISTILLERY Towcester, Northamptonshire. 2011. Working

Wharf Rye New Make 100% rye db **(87) n21 t22 f22 b22** Rye white dog is usually fruity. Sometimes firm and fruity. Well, Wharf's triple-distilled rye is fruity all right. Except there is an apple note to this which I have not located anywhere else in the world. Fully flavoured and tangy towards the finale which quits, positively, on a chocolate note. Different, and not entirely technically perfect, and it will be interesting to see how this pans out after a few years. 61.3%

Wharf Fyr Drenc Grain Spirit db **(89) n22 t22.5 f22 b22.5** Wharf does like to reveal its own fingerprints whenever possible. And the nose here is particularly singular, revelling in a half Victory V cough sweet and half sharp love-heart candy persona – a kind of 1990s Bowmore, but without the peat. The malty delivery is much more traditional with a grassy freshness at first. But the Victory V returns for the bitter-sweet fade. Super soft and enjoyable. 40%

Wharf Solstice db **(91.5) n23 t23 f22.5 b23** The first time I clapped eyes on this distillery was when it was located a field away from the A5, just across the road from The Super Sausage, Britain's

294

most outstanding traditional café and deservedly the winner of a plateful of national awards. I used to sit outside, tucking into my heaven-made sausage sandwich (no cooking back in my tasting lab, so warm food had to be supplied - and this being as magnificent as it got - and still is - worth the 25-minute drive along Britain's most ancient highway. And I would contentedly gaze west across the road at the distillery, wishing they would not just make gin but see the light and turn their hand to whisky. That must have been in about 2016, because my mum, in her late 90s and painfully frail, was still with us then, and a few morsels of the Super Sausage's mashed potato was the only food she would eat. Well, sadly, my mum has gone. And so has that distillery across the road. But, thankfully Wharf distillery is not only still with us but now a fully-fledged whisky one which moved to Towcester, still just off the A5, but closer to me. And as for Northamptonshire's first-ever whisky? Just too easy and simple for safety: this is charming quaffing malt. 43.2%

Wharf Cattle Creep Madeira Cask Whisky db (80.5) n20.5 t21.5 f18.5 b20 Not remotely in the same class as Solstice. Undone by tobacco notes and a failure to marry up the wine influence with the grain. So, a malt which never finds a rhythm, fails to maintain the brief sweet spot and struggles for balance. The bitter finish doesn't help, either. Well, if you are going to get a whisky wrong, you might as a well be hung for some cattle as a lamb... 58.8%

WHITE PEAK DISTILLERY Ambergate, Derbyshire. 2016. Working.
◇ **White Peak Wire Works** Caduro bourbon STR cask db (95) n23.5 a 20-minute nose. Don't make the mistake of thinking this is just a rich malt aroma. Close inspection reveals uncanny complexity to the barley tones, the oaky vanilla playing its part. There's even some kind of phenol thing going on but, though minor, also appears to play a part. The butterscotch subtext is also ultra-delicate; t24 if you want a display of faultless layering of barley, come and give this the once (or twice) over. Simply cannot fault the structure of the malt and its range, the barley sugars responsible for a salivating higher note while the deeper malt and oak interplay never seems to settle on a single level of intensity. There is even a momentary gooseberry sharpness kicking in...; f23.5 long, with the oak-barley integration carrying on indefinitely...; b24 someone knew what they were doing when they were let loose on the stills. This malt has been distilled to a remarkable degree of craftmanship, hitting the g spot between being clean and keeping in oils enough to make for a richly textured lingering malt. So, another new English distillery turning out something that is truly remarkable. The intensity of the malt, as well as its purity, deserves some kind if award...and the quality and complexity is of a grade many a Scotch distillery would kill for to match. 46.8% ncf nc 5582 bottles
◇ **Wire Works Double Oak Port**, nbc db (91.5) n22.5 a very salty nose bringing out the higher tones of both the vanilla and the grape; t23.5 another brilliantly mouth-watering delivery from White Peaks. These guys know how to make an entrance: the timing of the explosive grape with the salty tannin is choreographed to near perfection. Just below those two powering notes comes the barley, its shirt ripped off and as muscularly naked as a malt can be; f22.5 lovely oils settles on the malt, through the spiced and salted sultana; b23 where is the salt coming from? The River Derwent or the Cromford Canal, which both sit close to the distillery? Well, it can't be the sea which is about as far away as you get it from any point in the UK. This distillery certainly knows how to salivate! 52.5%
◇ **Wire Works Necessary Evil Finish**, nbc (89.5) n22 youthful and with a slight vegetable note, the malt - with a vague smokiness attached - still comes out fighting...; t23 eye-wateringly intense and salivating the malt could hardly be any more intense. The midground offers more entertainment than a year on the BBC, the perfect oils and sharpening barley leading to a rhubarb tart and barley sugar crescendo – with some mocha and light smoke on the decline; f22 more mocha and vanilla as the oak holds ground; b22.5 have to say, the name of the whisky did make me chuckle to myself. Not technically ticking all the boxes, this still has enough personality to make for a delightful whisky. The delivery alone is worth the entrance fee. 51.3%

WALES
ABER FALLS DISTILLERY Abergwyngregyn, Llanfairfechan.
◇ **Aber Falls Single Malt** bott code L2304HA1 db (86.5) n22.5 t22 f20.5 b21.5 A young, pleasing malt with heavy emphasis on the barley. Suffers from the 40% abv as it has insufficient structure to take on the dilution and oils are at a premium from first to last. There is also a toffee note which subtracts rather than adds. But this is cleanly made and when clearly visible the malt has legs, thought the spicy ginger adds an extra crutch. Youthful – even very new makey here and there – but promising. But they need to get the strength up to do an obviously very decent malt justice. 40%

DÀ MHÌLE DISTILLERY Glynhynod Farm, Llandysul. 2012. Working.
◇ **Da Mhile Organic Single Grain MMXXII** Bourbon quarter cask db (88) n23 everything about this nose is firm and uncompromisingly solid: the only give is a surprise phenolic twist.

But elsewhere both the grain and oak are scarily rigid. The sugars, conservative to say the least, are of the flinty Demerara variety: seriously complex and alluring; **t22.5** ah...a little yield on the palate as the oils of the distillate meet with the softer vanilla tones to ensure a safety net. But those grains (barley?) really do clatter about the teeth. Again, the sugars are in short supply save a vague gristiness. There is no shortage of warming spices, though; **f21** slightly disappointing with some bitterness escaping off the oak; **b22** a very confident spirit settling out for a flinty, grainy character and it succeeds, especially on that compelling nose. Just a shame about that late bitterness. *46% ncf 400 bottles*

⬥ **Da Mhile Organic Single Malt MMXXII** Madeira cask, cask no MM1607 db **(85.5) n22 t22.5 f20 b21** Again, a niggling finale with some bitterness forcing its way onto the arena, though this time the nose warned that it would be on its way. But there is nothing wrong with the Madeira influence which provides a sweet fruity gloss over the whole, though its reaction with that bitter character is a bit odd. *46% sc ncf 246 bottles*

PENDERYN Penderyn, Aberdare. 2004. Working.

⬥ **Penderyn Amontillado** Sherry cask 5155 db **(95) n23.5** now, on the Murray Method only, this is one extraordinary nose: the most beguiling array of sweet-dry grape tones you'll expect to locate in a whisky glass. The trick, though, is that none are aggressive or all-persuasive. Just a delicate and - at times - quietly assertive grape diaspora. However, it is the drier layers which score the higher points; **t24** this is sheer class. The delivery on one hand is heavy and plummy-grape laden...and then you immediately find an alternative shrill, eye-watering tone, no less fruity but operating at an entirely different pitch. As we hear the middle, the oak comes out of its shell with a welter of vanilla-rich blows. The spices nip and bay...; **f23.5** at last the creaminess arrives that we often associated with Amontillado...and this is the perfect time for its gently oiled display. That cream gives the vanillas an Advocaat-style texture, with extra sweetness creeping in from the malt; **b24** by far the most satisfyingly complex of all Penderyn's sherry offerings I've encountered this year. This is an essay in nuance and layering. *59.5% sc bottled for China Duty Free Group*

⬥ **Penderyn Brandy Blood Tub** cask no B3 db **(95.5) n23** cherry drop candy...but framed in some pretty serious oak; **t24** so many layers on that delivery...where do you start? It would be all too easy to home in on those varied spices. But, for me, it is that glorious interaction between the ultra-concentrated malt and the elegant oak which distribute vanilla and butterscotch with breath-taking exactitude. I'm getting a headache just trying to keep track with the layering; **f24** so complex, hard to quite work out where the middle ends and the finish begins. If anything, the malt is now even more confined and intense...though as the vanillas spread, so too does the malt into a far more relaxed state; **b24.5** gets everything right that the Ruby Port Blood Tub got wrong: the Blood Tub method has corralled the malt into the most concentrated and pure form it is possible to imagine. Stunning. *58.9% sc exclusively for Hard to Find Whisky*

Penderyn Celt bott code 201422 db **(89.5) n22.5 t22.5 f22 b22.5** A relatively simplistic Celt compared to, say, the 503 bottling. One of the lightest peated malts you'll ever encounter. *41% nc ncf*

Penderyn Celt bott code 202966 db **(81) n21 t22.5 f18 b19.5** A slightly off kilter cask can do some damage to a delicate malt, and it has here. Some pleasant early smoky moments, but the bitterness at the end undoes a lot of the good... *41% nc ncf*

Penderyn Celt bott code 202466 db **(91.5) n22.5 t23 f23 b23** Think they should re-label this one and call it Spot The Peat. It is there...but your senses have to be on full alert to find it. Even so, it is gorgeous whisky with lashings of delicious malt to savour. *41% nc ncf*

⬥ **Penderyn Celt** bott code 220625 db **(90) n22** a very simple malt and vanilla duet. The peat is detectable, though barely; **t23** a charming outpouring of gristy sweetness. The tannins were hard to lay a straightforward vanilla counter and offer up spices, too; **f22.5** what little peat detectable has now vanished, allowing the tannins to have a bigger, spicier, more toasty and drier say; **b22.5** a drier, slightly more austere version of Celt where the tannins offer just a little extra bitterness, and the smoke never gets going. That said, still a pleasing whisky. *41% nc ncf*

⬥ **Penderyn Celt** bott code 222135 db **(94) n22.5** spot the peat! Yes, it is there, but makes you work to find it amid the grists and pleasing tannins. Instead, a teasing gooseberry jam comes into play; **t24** such a difficult whisky to spit! Despite the lower strength, the oils on the delivery are usefully rich and do a wonderful job corralling the light phenols and allowing them to intensify. But as the smoke gathers, so do the balancing sugars and malt; **f23.5** takes the foot slowly off the pedal and the intensity drifts and instead breaks down into complex constituent parts, to the extent that we can see that some mint and cocoa was tied in with the gentlest of phenols; **b24** the consistency of Penderyn's whisky is now comparable with any distillery on the planet. Here we go again with another faultless and fascinating bottling. The slow grow, the ever-developing intensity makes this bottling a minor classic. *41% nc ncf*

Penderyn Celt bott code 213895 db **(95) n23.5** possibly the maltiest of all Penderyn's cast, the barky three dimensional despite the playful smoke and soothing vanilla present; **t24** so, so sexy.

The way the smoke plays around the mouth, kissing and caressing and teasing to the max...just, wow! **f23.5** so great to find honey arrive so late in the day: this is not entirely divorced from a rare but magnificent provincial Belgium style. A slight nagging off-bitterness at the very end; **b24** just ridiculously pleasurable whisky. Beautifully distilled, perfectly matured and comes together a satisfyingly as a jigsaw. *41% nc ncf*

Penderyn Celt no bott code db **(93.5) n23 t23.5 f23.5 b23.5** Very similar in style to bottling 213895, though the peat is slightly more awkward and sharp. The silky honey still plays a glorious game, ensuring excellent riches. *41% nc ncf*

Penderyn Club rich Madeira finish, bott code 93101 db **(93.5) n23.5 t24.5 f22 b23.5** It noses with the elegance of Swansea City (in its Premier League days). *50%. nc ncf.*

Penderyn The Head Liner Icons of Wales No 9 Jamaica Rum and Ruby Port Casks db **(93) n23** wonderfully sweet and counter-dry nose, the oak pushed up early into the fray, leaving the spices and Demerara sugars to alternately arm-wrestle or hug. Unique and fascinating; **t24** a rare delivery to die for. The grape is succulent and looks as though it will immediately expand, but almost at once it is caught in a sugary grasp, making for a sublime soft/hard complexity. The malts have a brief shout before the light toffeeness of the cask begins to win through. Quite literally a rum and raisin middle...; **f22.5** although there is a definite weakness to the finale (and most probably the Port cask) there is still so much charm and interplay, that you cannot stop concentrating on this for a moment; **b23.5** now, I have to say that that is a fascinating vatting of casks. Though the Port has a weakness, perhaps in the same way Lloyd George had one for women. But Lloyd George was a complex being, and this malt reflects him perfectly. Lots of depth and surprises. And no little passion. *46%*

Penderyn Hireath Icons of Wales bott code 211682 db **(95) n24** rose gardens on balmy evenings. Light lemon sherbet entwined with mesmerising oaky vanilla tones of increasing confidence – even to the point of revealing a slight bourbon undertone; **t24** the barley arrives in myriad guises, predominantly light, grassy and salivating but the slow build of ulmo and lemon blossom types of honey really has to be experienced to be believed. The spices remain friendly, but always let you know they are there. Melt-in-the-mouth and multi-layered, yet always with that ulmo honey/vanilla countenance somewhere in the background; **f23** far more restrained as the oak takes a keener interest. Dries, but some persistent Demerara sugar and vanilla retain balance; **b24** for a whisky which sounds like an Indian opening batsman, it certainly has the ability to bowl you over. Some brave and elaborate cask management here ensuring, certainly on the nose and delivery, a malt of incredible delicacy. *46% nc ncf*

Penderyn Legend bott code 213354 db **(94) n23** dry, elegant and lightly graped. The oak is conservative and playing a blinder...; **t23** fattens up only when the Murray Method is applied and then becomes an excellent ping-pong match between deft vanillas and richer fruit; **f23.5** brilliant finish. Those oils have kept the ball in play and we are going into extra time with ulmo honey-sweetened light fruitcake. The spices tingle perfectly; **b24** it's a rare whisky which is this light and yet just gets better as it goes along. *41% nc ncf*

Penderyn Legend bott code 211626 db **(89.5) n22.5** a charming light mintiness to this one, before the delicate fruits kick in; **t23** refused to be anything other than fresh and malt dominant; **f22** simplistic but effective butterscotch and barley. A little toasted raisin here and there, but keeps everything simple, though there is a slight, late niggle; **b22** just one of those whiskies which isn't too fussed about making a big noise. But accentuates the malt whenever possible. *41%*

Penderyn Legend bott code 13 db **(89) n22.5** the usual dry, slightly saw-dusty aroma but with a boiled candy fruitiness giving it a lift; **t23** after the thin ulmo honey start, much busier than normal with the malt playing delicate games of strength with the raisin and apricot; **f21.5** malty, dry but slightly bitter, too; **b22** never the greatest fan of those dry finishes. But all points leading there offer fascinating malt and fruit interplay. *41%*

⟫ **Penderyn Legend** bott code 220811 db **(93.5) n24** gosh! Don't look now, but a few phenolic atoms are drifting about, accentuated by the lightness of the mango and lemon found alongside the vanilla. Had I the time, I could nose this all day...; **t23.5** peachy and salivating, the oils stir only when warmed and offer a lushness missing when cool; **f22.5** pretty non-committal when cool but a different proposition when gently warmed with the malt planting root and that vague phenol tone reappearing late on; **b23.5** a malt which appears to have fragility down to a fine art. This one, surprisingly, offers a little extra earthy weight, especially when the Murray Method is applied. A Legend that thinks it's a Celt... *41% nc ncf*

⟫ **Penderyn Legend** bott code 221006 db **(91) n23** a tale of vanilla-led oak harmonising with malt and broadened by the lightest dab of citrus: a whispered nose....; **t22** an early flash of cocoa reveals how the oak is gently controlling things here. The malt comes through with a surprising degree of light oil; **f23** unusually, the real complexity finally breaks out at the finish where citrus joins the quiet crowd of vanilla and barley; **b23** what a steady ship this is. No drama. Just an elegant and eloquent stream of gentle vanilla and malt consciousness. *41% nc ncf*

◈ **Penderyn Legend** bott code 222566 db **(92)** n23 the gentle fruits expected take a back seat on this one and give way to extra sawdusty vanillas; t23 ooh, a light outbreak of bourbon underscoring that oaky influence. Just love that slow build of mocha....; f23 lovely barley sugar with light hickory bent...and more mocha; b23 a vaguely bourbony theme to this, the oak offering a little toast and even the odd hint of hickory throughout. Dryer, but sweetened in the right places by barley sugar and mocha. A sophisticated charmer. 41% nc ncf

Penderyn Legend Women Who Whiskey 10th Anniversary Bottling bott code 210631 db **(93.5)** n23 such a lovely malt and marmalade overlap; t23.5 wow! After such a delicate nose, the intensity of the delivery comes as a surprise. The fruit blasts off juicily and indiscriminately before being calmed by intense malt and growing vanilla; f23 was expecting a chalky dryness, instead, I got some first-class barley. It does dry, though, with vanillas leading the way, though some chocolate intervenes; b24 for such an ostensibly light whisky, this bottling really does pack in the flavours... 43% ncf nc

Penderyn Madeira Finish bott code 200219 db **(89)** n23 t23 f21 b22 A very different, dark-coloured Penderyn, heading towards full amber. The dryness of the oak is vaguely severe at the finish, but still a malt that is fascinating in its layering. 46%. ncf.

Penderyn Madeira Finish bott code 203085 db **(94)** n23.5 t23.5 f23 b24 Lighter in both colour and in its footstep than the 219. The complexity levels seem to rise dramatically as a consequence. And although seemingly easy going both depth and length are magnificent... Talk about less being more....! 46%. ncf.

Penderyn Madeira Finish bott code 203383 db **(91)** n23 a distinct doughiness, the spices and raisins pointing towards a fruitcake mix; t23 aaah, that malty juiciness....!!! Wow! Excellent barley sugars in the background, too, lingering on the oils. The fruit has a much more fragile role than normal. Outstanding spices, too...; f22 the spices dominate an otherwise simplified finale... the vanilla and barley still easy to identify and enjoy b23 even lighter in colour and character than the 085. But doesn't boast the same mesmerising proportions, for all its considerable charm. Very high-quality fare. 46%. ncf.

Penderyn Madeira Finish bott code 202684 db **(94.5)** n23.5 here we go: this is much nearer in style to traditional Penderyn, the chalkiness and pithy grape harmonising in that unique Welsh way; t23.5 and the same goes for the flavour profile and mouth feel on delivery: pure, unalloyed Penderyn. Also beautifully warmed with the busiest of spices. Oh, but that malt-vanilla-grape harmony.... unmistakable; f23.5 long, lush thanks to superb oils, controlled spice, a sprinkling of cocoa and even some late orange blossom honey...gosh! b24 vaguely youthful, yet still Penderyn at its Penderynist. 46%. ncf.

Penderyn Madeira Finish bott code 2003312 db **(91.5)** n23 a spiced, sugar-coated fruitiness is etched into a disarming bourbon backdrop. Genteel and soft...; t23 every bit as crisp and salivating as the nose promise, but now with a serious blast of barley to add to the intensity and completeness; f22.5 superb spice working in tandem with a distinct Kentucky kick. The hallmarks of very high-quality wood at work in this improbably long finish; b23 what a ridiculously satisfying whisky. On a slightly different level to the very earliest Penderyns with an estery residue that makes this particular bottling seem never-ending... 46% ncf.

Penderyn Madeira Finish bott code 200581 db **(94)** n23.5 the lightest touch of peach is the only nod towards sweetness. All else is a subtle, dry chalkiness, delicate tannin, and teasing spice. It is as though the grist has no sugars. Peculiar...but also mesmerising; t23.5 a wonderful interplay between much drier tannins and almost enigmatic sweetness: you pick up on its barley sugar outline, but when you look for more...it vanishes. The tannins dance with a vague roastiness – not quite the usual Penderyn style, but this fits in with its surroundings perfectly; f23 such a distinguished finale: a little barley has glided its way through and joins forces with drier grape skin and a light rumbling spice; b24 a typically multi-layered offering from Penderyn, though with the fruit element a little quieter than usual. Less silky, estery and soft as their last bottling, this is far more complex and relentlessly elegant. A great whisky deserving of time and exploration. 46% (92 proof) ncf. Exclusively imported by ImpEx Beverages, Inc.

Penderyn Madeira Finish bott code 212466 db **(94)** n23 enjoys the pithy style almost to excess...; t23.5 wow! Didn't quite expect that malt surge quite so early in the game. Or the chocolate fondant middle; f23.5 takes time for a few burnt raisins to filter through, but they get there to ensure magnificent balance and depth; b24 it dawns on you only slowly just how fabulously weighted and subtly complex this whisky is. Penderyn at its most endearing and subtly complex. 46% nc ncf

Penderyn Madeira Finish bott code 213474 db **(93)** n22 dry, almost pithy with crushed grape seeds and skin; t23.5 an immediate outburst of sugars on delivery fits sublimely with the growing oils and spices; f23.5 such a gorgeously even and surprisingly long finish. The grape has plenty of juice, but the late combination of thick malt and spiced tannin works so well to balance matters; b24 yet another effortlessly classy act from Penderyn. Once they struggled to find this kind of harmony: now it happens along quite naturally. Has all the guile and penetration of a Briton Ferry attack...and that is some compliment... *46% nc ncf*

✣ **Penderyn Madeira Finish** bott code 220427 db **(88.5)** n22.5 t22.5 f21.5 b22 For all its profound maltiness, this is as dry and austere as a sermon in an Aberdare chapel on that grim last day in October 1926, the morning after Athletic had been beaten at home by Merthyr in Division Three South. *46%*

✣ **Penderyn Madeira Finish** bott code 221365 db **(94)** n23 like 220427 there is plenty dry toast. But this one has a little bit of oily marmalade to spread on it; t23.5 ah...! That's more like it. The gentle oils are in full swing, the malt is deep and entrenched. And the fruit makes just the right noises, in just the right places alongside just the right spices....; f23.5 wonderful fade of countering vanilla and light cocoa with that persistent fruit jelly; b24 one of those super-elegant ultra-intricate malts where the flavours appear to have been added by pipette. *46% ncf*

✣ **Penderyn Madeira Finish** bott code 221735 db **(94.5)** n23 mocha and spice in the slipstream of that fragile malt-grape mix; t24 just love that double layering of malt: one thick and oily, the second thinner and more even. There is a light sultana entanglement as well as an impressive volley of spice. The oak really is making its mark, but the malt accompanies it all the way. The crispness of the Demerara sugars is a luxury; f23.5 measured and malty, that mocha adds to that night-drink feel; b24 what is so intriguing is that this bottling is so similar to 221365... yet at the same time so very different. As intriguing as it is complex as it is delightful. *46%*

✣ **Penderyn Madeira Finish** bott code 222275 db **(89)** n22.5 back on its drier course the malt is carrying less gristy sugars while the fruit is of the dry grape skin variety; t23.5 lush with an intense maltiness adjacent to some serious grapefruit tones: pretty citrussy; f21 undone by a little bitterness at the death; b22 a misbehaving bourbon cask at fault for the finish: a shame. Until then, things had been more than entertaining, especially with that concentrated malt kick off. *46%*

Penderyn Myth bott code 200292 db **(95.5)** n24 super complex malt: multi-layering at the highest level. The malt and vanilla appear to be in cahoots and almost indistinguishable; gentle phenol notes hangs around like a ghost while the sugars just hint their presence and no more...; t24 I am purring with delight: a light saltiness has raised the voices of the malt and tannins above a whisper. The thinned ulmo honey hangs on the surprisingly oily body...and, as though in slow motion, the alt not only comes into view but intensifies majestically; f23.5 malt---cocoa... spice...all in hushed tones. And forever and a day...; b24 a malt beautifully weighted and complex lends one to think that we have encountered here a distillery that has mastered the whisky in its charge. This is cask selection at the highest level. And a contender for British Whisky of the Year. Not for its drama and noise.... for quite the opposite. Even if not the best, it will almost certainly be among the most elegant. *41%. nc ncf.*

Penderyn Myth bott code 90644 db **(94)** n23 the malt leaves a trail of smoke as light tannin and spices loop the loop; t23.5 mouth-watering and tart, this is thinner than most Penderyns these days. This means the barley and light biscuit and honey ones thump against the taste buds with more dramatic impact. About halfway in ulmo honey starts to make its mark, quietly, but with great effect; f23.5 drier now, but with more light smoke and spice; b24 a very different Myth to the previous bottling, this is using its meagre smoke resources to full effect thanks to the drier make up. Another malt for those who prefer their whisky complex and sophisticated rather than being a drama queen. But if you want to know how to maximise low-level smoke, rich barley and delicate honey, here is your go-to whisky. Even more beautiful than a leg of Welsh lamb...and that, believe me, is saying something... *43% (86 proof) nc ncf. Exclusively imported by ImpEx Beverages, Inc.*

Penderyn Myth db **(93.5)** n23 probably the lightest Penderyn nose of them all: the barley drifts a little listlessly, the vanillas are powdery and delicate but the charm is in the fragility of the sweet/dry balance, as well as the throw-away lime note; t23.5 without the Murray Method, this is a little too light. When warmed, the oils makes their play and perfectly captures the fresh fruits and darker tannins; f23 just a little cinnamon on the apple pie late on. Light sticky chocolate pudding, too....; b24 The Murray Method of tasting was invented for whiskies like this. A little limp and docile at normal temperature, but when warmed becomes an animal with both teeth and fallibility. Enormous complexity when aroused and not lacking in Fox's Biscuits chocolate mix superiority late on...; *43% nc ncf Imported by ImpEx Beverages San Francisco.*

Penderyn Myth bott code 212167 db **(91)** n22 the vanilla, always shadowed by vague fruit, grunts out its intent; t23.5 now it hits the rhythm missing on the nose, especially when the spices and molten barley gell. Some wonderful complexity and balance at work at the very same moment; f22.5 a little uncomfortable at the death as a dry, crabby fruitiness – think sloe straight off the tree, and then that fruit turned into a preserve – grabs hold; b23 a very fat variant of the Myth family, though perhaps with a little extra marmalade bitterness especially towards the fade. Fascinating, as you are never quite certain where it will take you next... *43% nc ncf*

Penderyn Myth db **(94.5)** n23 youthful, more than vaguely smoked and malty. A real live-wire on the nose; t23.5 a genuine orgy of malt: the youthfulness and lack of fruity extra allows the barley full width to expand...and the peat has no hesitation in also taking up the invitation; **f24** silky, spiced peat...but the barley still comes through with effortless clarity. Then a fabulous chocolate liqueur finale...; **b24** possibly the lightest Myth in colour I have yet encountered. But it doesn't suffer for it: the malt is splendidly alive and juicy. And the peat kicks in and gives just the right degree of weight and sweetness. Truly superb. *43% nc ncf with collar still intact*

Penderyn Myth db **(89) n23** tannins bite: this is heavy...; **t23** rounded, fat and sweet, there is a lardy spotted dog start to proceedings...before the oaky tannins really kick in and nibble with very sharp teeth. A vague raisin-stye fruitiness emerges, almost fruitcake-style, but the malt clings to the lard; **f20.5** grrrr...a slight sulphury nibble to this, though the spices do their best to divert; **b22.5** by no means the perfect Welsh whisky with a little late sulphur muddying the waters. Yet there is so much character afoot, it is hard not to succumb to its earlier unruffled charms. *43% nc ncf collar off*

◈ **Penderyn Myth** bott code 220187 db **(92) n22.5** oak is relatively full on here, offering the toast on which the marmalade is spread. No butter, though...; **t23.5** what a stunning delivery. The delicate nature of the heather honey is sublime, the weightier style of honey guaranteed by the forceful of the oak. Elsewhere juicy, jammy tones – a little raspberry in the midst of a little blood orange. Most surprising are the oils: there really is weight to this...and the malts get a good look in, also; **f22.5** malt, mocha and raisin offers a superb exit. Some very late bitterness; **b23.5** this is Penderyn's fruity regular and here it appears to be in bitter orange mode. Some profound tannins at work, too. Quite a big boy for something usually so delicate. *41% nc ncf*

◈ **Penderyn Myth** bott code 22372 db **(93) n23** light on the tannin, allowing the crushed Malteser and fruit candy a free hand...; **t23.5** distilled fruit bonbons. Lovely spices. But the barley sugar really makes an impact here and intensifies as delicate ulmo honey develops; **f23** at last the tannins begin to speak, though slightly bitterly. The malt and fruit, though without degree of forcefulness, still hold the upper hand; **b23.5** this bottling is the definition of understatement. Just so fruity, malty and yummy... *41% nc ncf*

Penderyn Peated bott code 200421 db **(91) n22.5** even on full volume the smoke is sparse, teasing almost. A light lemon zestiness biffs up the complexity; **t23** the adorable mouth feel is equalled by the sublime heather honey. Even now the smoke feels no more than chewing on the fumes of a distant haystack fire; **f22.5** a tad thin but the apologetically smoked mocha works well to maximise the finish; **b23** with the Murray Method the peat comes through loud and clear. Without it...happy hunting! *46% (92 proof) nc ncf. Exclusively imported by ImpEx Beverages, Inc.*

Penderyn Peated bott code 90162 db **(93) n23 t23.5 f23 b23.5** Youthful, exuberant and among the most teasingly-weighed peated Penderyns. *46%. ncf.*

◈ **Penderyn Peated** bott code 2200672 db **(95) n23.5** the smoke is no more than carefully located fingernails down the back: a pleasing, sensual tease leaving you wanting more...; **t24** grist melting on the tongue greets you. Then a slow ensemble of phenols, clutching onto rafts of oak. But the gristiness is sublime, the sugars melting on the tongue, the light embers of liquorice extolling the virtues of the deft tannins; **f23.5** long, thanks to lythe oils which glue together the spices and smoke. But in the background that intense malt refuses to be silenced; **b24** I remember the days when I was able to criticise Penderyn and give them modest or low scores. Ten whiskies into Penderyn's 25 and I haven't been able to drop one below 90. Their excellence is almost monotonous. In the same way as the fragility of this peat is totally disarming. This really is wonderful whisky, even by Penderyn's exacting standards... *46%*

Penderyn Portwood bott code 203071 db **(84.5) n21 t22 f20 b21.5** The tightness on the nose signals trouble ahead, and it doesn't lie. Sulphur, sadly, has leaked into this one – though those lucky ones who can't pick that up can enjoy a feast of muscular fruit and black pepper instead. *46%. ncf.*

Penderyn Portwood bott code 203371 db **(84) n21 t22 f20 b21** Another Port in a storm. Again, this is a tight cask with a vaguely sulphury edge. Big fruit through the middle, but the sweetness is nipped in the bud and balance compromised. *46%. ncf.*

Penderyn Portwood bott code 211682 db **(94) n23** incredibly weighty, the whole engulfed by heady grape skin. Some lovely vanilla and greengage jam does break out to make a game of it...; **t24** mouth-filling and chewy from the very first moment. The oak takes up a lot of room, but the fruit breaks free...again with a distinctly plummy hue. That profound dryness, which sets itself on another level, never quite goes away, but molassed (not an adjective) fruit cask compensates adequately; **f23** irresistible peppers work splendidly with the heavy-duty plummy fruit which lingers longer than expected. Just a little mocha plays out at the death; **b24** a big malt painted with a broad brush and inclined to make even broader statements on the palate... *46% nc ncf*

◈ **Penderyn Portwood** bott code 220592 db **(94) n23.5** unlike most of Penderyn's fruit-inspired noses, this one offers a jagged, nuggety semi-bite on the intensity. Such a wonderful crisp, demerara sugar sweetness on display, too. The oakiness is deep and earthy; **t23.5** not sure the oils could be more beautifully proportioned. Weight without fat, dexterity of fruit without decadence. The interplay between the sharpness of the sugared fruit and roundness of the rumbling vanilla is a treat; **f23** the spices really do zing here as the plummy, thick grape skin works so well with those persistent oils; **b24** an exhibition of balance and counterbalance as the crystalised fruit and oils slug it out. So much weight, so much flavour, so much élan... *46% ncf*

⬧ **Penderyn Portwood** bott code 222202 db **(87) n21.5 t23 f20.5 b22** Nothing majorly wrong with this malt as such. But at times relatively monosyllabic with the intensity of the fruit linking with the grape to extinguish development elsewhere. However, I thought I detected a weakness on the nose (which made me decide to make this the last whisky of the day) and this has been confirmed on the finish with a tell-tale furriness. However, central Europeans – and others less pernickety and demanding than me - will adore the fruity frothiness. *46% ncf*

Penderyn Rhiannon sherrywood Grand Cru finish, bott code 91852 db **(96.5) n23.5 t24 f24.5 b24.5** A cerebral whisky playing games and tricks. Near enough perfectly balanced and different enough to set this apart from any whisky before. Few whiskies ever reach this level of complexity... *46%. Icons of Wales No. 7.*

Penderyn Rich Oak bott code 200561 db **(93)** A lot of understated whisky in one small glass... *46% (92 Proof). nc ncf. Exclusively imported by ImpEx Beverages, Inc. 1 (250) 634 2276*

Penderyn Rich Oak bott code 200563 db **(95.5) n23.5 t24.5 f23.5 b24** This at times strays into high class Bourbon territory, while always keeping its malty credentials. Simply brilliant! One of the great whiskies of the year. *46%. nc ncf.*

Penderyn Rich Oak bott code 202812 db **(89) n22 t23 f22 b22** Very pleasant fayre, there is no doubt and rich. But lacking the complexity which normally wins the heart. *46%. ncf.*

⬧ **Penderyn Rich Oak** bott code 221402 db **(94.5) n23.5** the spices, transported on a sombre heather honey note arrives like so many bee stings. The tannins are exceptional, shewing deftness of touch yet extra weight when required. Elsewhere Demerara sugars forms a degree of countering crispness; **t24** pure silk! Natural caramels meld with the intense Malteser candy and ever-sharpening Demeraras. The layers of tannin actually pound as the spices arrive. Hard to describe the flavour lets: kind of pulsing but always half a notch below intense, so you are always aware of the complexity of the varying flavours on display; **f23.5** such a sumptuous exit of rich malt and deft ulmo honey. Light hickory lingers with the oils, as do the vanillas as the oak moves up a gear or two. The spices remain on contract to the very last flavour wave; **b23.5** must say, it is near impossible not to worship this particular whisky when in such magnificent form. Such a charmingly erudite display of malty vanillas which is perfectly pitched and paced. To turn down a second glass of this would be considered something beyond comprehension. If there is a fault, just a little underpowered... *46% ncf*

Penderyn Sherrywood bott code 200932 db **(93) n23 t23 f23.5 b23.5** A blemish-free sherry butt at work here allowing the full scope of this complex and superbly weighted whisky to be enjoyed unhindered. *46%. ncf.*

Penderyn Sherrywood bott code 203221 db **(89.5) n22.5 t23.5 f21 b22.5** Maybe a semi-feeble blemish at the end, but at least the journey was panoramic. *46%. ncf.*

⬧ **Penderyn Sherrywood** bott code 220544 db **(93) n23** that boiled cherry candy note Penderyn does so well has pole position. A delightful malt subplot drifts through unencumbered; **t23.5** exceptional mouth feel: this is so well distilled that the oils off the still really do an extraordinary job of magnifying the impact of the malt grist. The grape is a little less fulsome but offers enough dry pithy depth to make a difference. The spices oscillate; **f23** so much drier. The pounding spices underline the work of the oak but those oils and grists combine again to throw the malt right back into the lead role...; **b23.5** didn't quite expect to enjoy this as much as I did or find so many avenues being explored by the rich malted barley as it tries to escape the confines of the grape. *46% ncf*

⬧ **Penderyn Sherrywood** bott code 221714 db **(84) n22 t22 f19 b21** Not only doesn't sing anything like so well as 220544, towards the end it develops a bit of a wayward croak. Flat and uninspiring in Penderyn currency, even when the fruit and spices do get going, there is more than enough off-key niggle from a sub-standard sherry butt. *46% ncf*

Penderyn Single Cask bourbon cask, cask no. 182/2006, bott 11 Jul 19 db **(96.5) n24.5 t24.5 f23.5 b24** This is one of those rare, magical whiskies that is not about tasting notes but the shape, depth and overall experience. Which, has to be said, is pretty close to as good as it gets... *62%. ncf sc. Selected by Harrods.*

Penderyn Single Cask bourbon cask, cask no. 2/2006 db **(95.5) n23.5 t23.5 f24.5 b24** Massively tasty, but a curious Penderyn, all the same. The precise and eye-wateringly sharp grapefruit acts as a juicy diversion away from the barley, which slowly composes itself to mount to compelling challenge. This celebrates maltiness in the same way a sex addict revels in a threesome. A malt which simply refuses to leave the taste buds alone until they finally submit. *56.8%. ncf sc.*

Penderyn Madeira Malvasia Single Cask cask 1347/2017 dist June 2017 bott July 2022 db (96.5) **n24** now this is how a Madeira nose should be: a confection of fruity tones, taking us right across a salad of spiced dried dates, diced pomegranate, voluptuous fig and British plums. All this augmented by vanilla pods and cherry and walnut cake. Just amazing...; **t24** such a firm and dazzling delivery. Despite the elegant onslaught of fruit, barley plays a big part in the original juicy lift-off. But slowly the toasted raisins take a hand, along with the dates which are now a little juicier than on the nose. The spices are punchy but even while the oils gather in density; **f24** intense Paynes Poppets chocolate raisin, spiced of course, (for those old enough to remember them) and soft mocha before vanilla brings things to a quiet finale; **b24.5** simply faultless. A cask provided by the gods... 60.7% ncf

Penderyn Single Cask Ex-Olorosos Cask cask no. S76, dist Feb 2012, bott Aug 2020 db (94.5) **n23.5 t23 f24 b24** A nutty cask that has cracked it. Not a single off note and not so powerful as to dominate ruthlessly. More sorcery from the Welsh mountains: magic and majestic... 60.7% sc. *German selection by Schlumberger.*

Penderyn Single Cask Ex-Purple Moscatel Cask, cask no. W21, dist Feb 2021, Aug 20 db (93.5) **n23.5 t23 f23.5 b23.5** What a fun whisky! One of those malts that refuses to give your taste buds a moment's respite. 58.7% sc. *German selection by Schlumberger*

Penderyn Ex-Rum Single Cask 7 Years Old cask RB db (96) **n23.5 t24 f24 b24.5** So many disappointments when tasting malt matured in rum casks, the sugars closing down meaningful development. But not here. Unquestionably the best rum cask whisky I have ever tasted...I doff my hat to blender Aista Phillips. Please take a bow... 59.9% ncf

◈ **Penderyn Ex-Rye Single Cask 6 Years Old** cask 685/2016 db (96) **n24** buckle up: the spices are coming after you.... just Wow! Under those leading pepper tones comes a custardy sweetness. Custard, that is, overlaying some concentrated malt. The result is a sweet custard cream cookie dunked in coffee...; **t24** those oils...those oils...!!! Just yes...!!! Absolutely perfect weight to extract the most from that insane malt thrust. The spices, though controlled, never let up. However, the true complexity is found in the measured sweetness, with ulmo honey mixing in with a scoop of molasses and deft maple syrup. In the background the tannins, offering a light roast Java thread, merrily grumble...; **f23.5** the oils ensure maximum lingering properties. The spices still tingle, the sugars still spoil you rotten and the embers of the roast Java are still perculating...; **b24.5** needs full on Murray Method for best results here....and what results! A half hour tasting required to get to know this fellow and the intricacies of its sugary fingerprint. So magnificently complex! Actually, just so magnificent...full stop. 60.7% sc US exclusive ImpEx Beverages Inc

Penderyn Ex-Sweet Portuguese Moscatel Single Cask cask M6/2 dist Nov 2013 bott March 2019 db (92) **n22.5** for sweet Moscatel, this is one eye-watering dry nose...; **t23** the delivery does what it says on the tin: sugared grape, initially fat and full...then mysteriously thinning out as the spices arrive in droves; **f23** rather wonderful blackcurrant jam tart...slightly overcooked, of course...; **b23.5** for those who prefer there malts spicy and enormously fruity...come and get it! 60.9% nc ncf

Penderyn Single Cask 15-Year-Old Bourbon Cask cask no. B105/2005 db (96.5) **n24 t24 f24.5 b24** How fascinating to see a 15-year-old Welsh whisky. Curiously, in style it reminds one of a 12 or 13-year-old top-rank Bushmills filled into first fill bourbon. As much as I hate to compare distilleries from different countries, there is no getting away from it...it is uncanny. And while we are at it.... What about the Glen Grant strains from the midpoint to the finish. Indeed, from midpoint onwards we are in entirely unrecognisable ground so far as Welsh whisky is concerned: the barley has retreated behind a gorgeous coppery vanilla/honey mix, and we are luxuriating in the chocolate liqueur of the elite. What an absolutely cracking cask, doubtless set aside for this special day. And if anyone now doesn't recognise Welsh as being among the Grand Cru of the world's whiskies, then let's see what they have to say after spending half an hour with this masterpiece 59% sc. *Specially selected and imported by ImpEx Beverages, Inc.*

◈ **Penderyn Ruby Port Blood Tub** cask PT408 db (87) **n23 t21.5 f21.5 b21** Bloody hell! This is a bit of a one-off and make no mistake. Starts well enough on the nose with a huge bourbon-style tannin kick with red liquorice and toasted oak at the double. The fruit, though, is something else: a bit like my old mum's heavily sugared home-gown and baked redcurrant tart back in the day. But on delivery, one is thrown headfirst into a sticky wrestling match, the Ruby Port overpowering and pinning down any evidence of the Penderyn itself. Having said that, the tannins really are game, too. The half linctus, half demented Ruby Port finish is a shock to the system. A little liquorice from the oak makes a late attempt at complexity. Bloody hell! From a whisky that's redder than the Welsh government, one of the sweetest single malts you'll encounter this or any year. And perhaps the closest whisky I've ever encountered to cough syrup. I'll need to clean my teeth twice tonight, I think... 59% sc bottled for Whisky Leiden 2023

◈ **Penderyn Ruby Port Blood Tub** cask no PT412, dist 03/18, bott 05/23 db (95.5) **n23.5** as with its sister bottling, the bourbon-oak kick is profound. Much drier with less flighty fruit; **t23.5**....

whoomph! Those spices go up like a Porsche set on fire by anarchists in central London over 30 years ago – and, believe me, covering the Poll Tax riots I've had my beard singed by such a spectacle....; unlike PT408 where the sugars turn matters into some kind of liqueur-fest, the fruit here is sanguine and controlled, happily trading intensity with those off the wall tannins. The fruit jogs on with a light Melton Hunt Cake intensity as the oak really drives in; **f24.5** this is possibly its greatest moment of the experience as the sugars, with their heather-honey background, the molasses and the deeply intense muscovado sugars trade caresses with the boiled sugar candy fruit and magma-deep bourbony tannins. The delicate oils get involved, as do the spices and there never appears to be a conclusion to this smorgasbord of flavour complexity; **b24** the extra depth of oak makes such a vital difference on balance and complexity compared to Blood Tub PT408. And keeps those marauding sugars in check, too. Of the 25 Penderyn whiskies I tasted this year; this took the longest to fathom: an hour and 22 minutes to be precise. This is one very serious whisky. *59% sc ncf exclusively for Hard to Find Whisky*

⬦ **Penderyn Tawny Port Small Batch** db **(95) n23.5** stewed plums in a crusty tart. Simple, but so marvellously effective...; **t23.5** so pleasing on arrival. A lovely mix of Demerara sugars and light molasses form the framework by which all else can relax into. But better still the soft oils cling to every crevice while the spices tingle. The jammy build up is slow but purposeful...; **f24** what a finish...! If you love chocolate raisin, then here is your dream dram. The spices and sugars continue to sparkle. Even better, though, it is choreographed with perfect timing and poise: remarkable so late on; **b24** one of the most pleasing finishes I've encountered anywhere in the world this year. If you've got a thing for chocolate mousse or fruit and nut chocolate bars, then this is the one you won't be sharing with your guests. I know which whisky will be sitting on my bedside table tonight... *50% ncf 600 bottles Specially selected by La Maison du Whisky*

⬦ **Penderyn PX Sherry cask** no 974/2015 db **(89.5) n23** the devoutly rich grape lands like punches to the solar plexus...and nose...; **t23** very single minded supremely intense grape with a fabulous spice backing; **f21.5** the finish is pleasant enough and is bolstered by a faultless cask... but just so annoying one-dimensional...; **b22** nothing wrong with it, as such. And there is plenty to admire, especially on the delivery. But beyond that complexity levels really are at a premium. *59.4% sc ncf bottled for China Duty Free Group*

⬦ **Penderyn Small Batch Release – France Autumn 2022** db **(89.5) n23** some real breast-beating grape on shew here: ensures some niggling spices fits in with the tough guy nose; **t23** the most beautiful of nutty deliveries: diced walnut and macadamia, chiefly. But of course, the fruit makes the most telling contribution, chiming in with a mix of dry and juicy date – fitting well with the nuts. All this lifting by wonderfully warming spice and then a surprise, juice blast of malt; **f21.5** loses a mark for its light furry bitterness. But the dry Valpolicella fruitiness still does a job; **b22** a slightly disappointing wine cask has slightly smudged the overall picture late on. But until then, that fruit and nut interplay had me on the edge of my glass. Flawed excellence. *50% ncf 1030 bottles bottled for France*

British Blend

⬦ **Forest Whisky Blended Number 25** Oloroso cask finish **(92) n23.5** an adorable nose: as delicate as a forest bluebell, the fragility centres around the complexity of the malts which celebrate their will-o-the-wisp nature. That there are oats involved doesn't surprise me either. What is very different, though, is the stye of the tannin which sets out to be harsh, but then re-adjusts and falls into line with the grains in it whispering nature. Similarly, spices which threaten never seem to materialise...; **t24** have I just been transported to Japan? Because anyone who knows the type of Japanese sold principally in its home market will recognise this shimmering style immediately. The mouth-watering joy on arriving is head-noddingly delightful, and this is soon backed up by stellar layering of vanilla assorted malt styles, though all insisting on sticking to a genteel persona. The oils gather and help fix the growing spices in position; **f22** a very slight bitterness creeps in from old casks (and only after writing this do I discover that some of oloroso casks are over 50 years old. Bad news for letting through a few tired tannins, but good news for ensuring there is no sulphur at play)...; **b23** the most Japanese style whisky I have ever encountered outside the land of the Rising Sun, complete with the beautiful Wade ceramic bottle. But far from being the Rising Sun, we are in the land of the Cat and Fiddle, a pub I used to frequent as a stopping off point between my national newspaper office in Manchester and my home in Melton Mowbray. And many a pint of Robinsons did I sup over three years as I made my weary way home. Who, back in the 1970s, would believe that this loneliest of roadside Inns, with its moor s mists or summit snow, would 40 years on become a distillery. Certainly not me. Or the assorted cloth-capped farmers who would congregate with their pipes to form an engulfing blue haze. Well, there's nothing wrong with the whisky, that's for sure. Indeed, this is quite magnificent, despite its slight weakness on the finish. Now need to get back to check that they still keep the Robinson's Best Bitter in good nick... *47% nc ncf 400 bottles*

Australian Whisky

Jim Murray's Whisky Bible Australian Whiskies of the Year	
2024	**Belgrove Rye 8 Years Old**
2023	**Heartwood 2nd Moment of Truth**
2022	**Tin Shed Flustercluck**
2021	**Adams Distillery Cask Strength**
2020	**Bakery Hill Peated Malt Cask Strength**
2019	**Belgrove Peated Rye**
2018	**Limeburner's Dark Winter**
2017	**Heartwood Any Port in a Storm**
2016	**Heartwood Port Cask 71.3%**

Jim Murray's Whisky Bible 2024 Australian Whisky of the Year by State	
South Australia	Tin Shed Iniquity Gold Label
Tasmania	Belgrove Rye 8 Years Old
Victoria	Kinglake Full Noise Single Malt
Western Australia	Limeburners Darkest Winter Single Malt
New South Wales	The Aisling Boilermaker Series 2 Apera Cask

Key
● Major Town or City
▲ Distillery

Adelaide
Adelaide Hills
Tin Shed Disilling Co.

Fannys Bay

Hellyers Road

Launceston
Launceston Distillery
Adams Distillery

Cradle Mountain

TASMANIA

Nant Distillery

Belgrove Distillery
Old Kempton Distillery
Shene Estate & Distillery

Spring Bay

Nonesuch

Hobart

Killara

Hobart
Devil's Distillery
Lark Distillery
Old Hobart
Sullivans Cove

AUSTRALIA
ADAMS DISTILLERY Perth, Tasmania. 2012. Working.

◈ **Adams Tasmanian Single Malt Bourbon Cask Peated** cask no AD:211 db **(95.5) n24** they've done it again. I remember last year's peated sherry nose and how that one went box ticking. This version, sans grape, has a drier edge but still retains that delightful anthracite, acidic bite to go alongside the soft barnyardy aroma. Glorious...; **t24** quite distinguishably distilled and beautifully barrelled. The key is the soft oils off a near perfect cut which allows the smoke to cling to the palate – and roof of the mouth in particular – while sweeter, gristier tones ensure balance and a pleasing degree of intense barley to sit alongside the peat itself. Spot on layering depth and developing spice; **f23.5** warmer now thanks to that spice having been at work for a while. There is a brief cocoa note which takes off and vanishes after briefly touching down, allowing a drier nuttier note to take its place...; **b24** Adams do peat noses as good as anyone outside Scotland: theirs is a phenolic phenomenon. And this really is one that simply makes you go weak at the knees. 64.8% ncf 30 bottles

◈ **Adams Tasmanian Single Malt Peated Pino Slow Gin and Rum Cask** cask no AD:456 db **(93) n23** easy to overlook the grape on this and instead concentrate on the heavyweight oak and the lurking phenols. But look carefully and there is the fruit, rounding up the sweeter elements of the nose for vital balance; **t23.5** brilliant delivery of the most complex kind: the peat spreads from an initial source point into a far wider, almost spider's web of a framework, from which hangs those chunky tannins and associated spices and the most delicate fruity incursions. At the centre of the web is a dollop of chocolate. Can't get away, either, from an occasional cough syrup feel to this one...; **f23** the cocoa holds ground and sees off a brief gin-type assault. The spices, smoke and light fruit all register at varying levels of intensity; **b23.5** that is one bewildering history for a cask and I genuinely feared for this malt. But, thankfully, the sloe gin kicked only briefly into view very late on and makes a point of not hanging around. The result is a predictably complex whisky, but not one this rounded and even. Oh, and with a very big tannin statement for good measure. The Pinot cask has a very grapey say on this one. Not ostentatiously so. But injects the fruit into vital areas at key times. A quiet little wallflower of a whiskey this most certainly isn't... 54.9% ncf 36 bottles

◈ **Adams Tasmanian Single Malt French Oak Pinot Noir** cask no AD:0406 db **(93.5) n23.5** wow! The muscles on the tannins have muscles. And the grape is hardly of the swooning variety. The two styles are happy to slug this one out...with only a delicate lemon blossom honey happy to be the go-between...; **t23.5** for all the macho nose, the delivery is one that is couched in pure silky. Exceptional oils off the still combine with that honey off the malt - and when combining with the sweeter aspects of the oak creating a more heather honey tone. But that French oak makes no bones about its attitude and carried on with its chocolate and light liquorice assault. The fruit, meanwhile, is hanging on for dear life...; **f23** spicier, softer and for the first time even a degree of vanilla; **b23.5** this is a big, brawny malt whisky and, what's more, I don't think the creators had much intent to make it anything other than that. But at no time is it less than delicious. *49.1% ncf 49 bottles*

⬧ **Adams Tasmanian Single Malt Signature Series 2** nbc db **(87) n21.5 t22 f21.5 b22** A odd cove, this. Lots of malt dancing about, but there is almost a randomness to the way the honey and odd tobacco note, especially on the nose, make their mark. Distinctly hit and miss. *42% ncf*

⬧ **Adams Tasmanian Single Malt Signature Series 2** nbc db **(89) n22.5** a much sturdier aroma than the 42% version with the acacia honey holding its own against a more compact malt and tannin double act. Even a fleeting hit of cinnamon and Muscovado sugar amid the fuller spices; **t22.5** big tannin bite on delivery, followed by a whoosh of molten muscovado; **f21.5** like the 42% version, the finish doesn't sit quite right, and the odd unhappy tobacco-type note filters through; **b22.5** the greater oils help generate a bigger impact for the impressive honey at play. But there is a degree of nagging tang which undoes some of the better work. *59% ncf*

⬧ **Adams Tasmanian Single Malt Original Sherry Cask** multiple casks French oak ex Sherry cask db **(89) n22** quite a thin grape investment here and we are left to the oak to provide maximum drive; **t22.5** ah, there we go! The missing fruit is found on delivery with a silky, surprisingly sweet rush. For a moment or two there is even something slightly cough syrupy about this, especially when the spices engage. But the midground is spectacularly busy and bursting out with all kinds of intense, warming tannin; **f22** the fires abate, the fruity sugars remain...; **b22.5** not sure if they should be selling this as whisky or as a cough mixture. A malt that's as good for your lungs as it is your tastebuds: this is some experience! *47% 160 bottles*

⬧ **Adams Tasmanian Single Malt Original Peated Sherry** multiple casks ex-sherry cask peated slosh db **(94.5) n23.5** not quite the same peating levels as their last bottling of this and the phenols have made way for the far more intense tannins. Even so, it is a happy mix, especially when the grape finds a space to make its sweet statement; **t23.5** mouth-watering to a fault, there is a fascinating bourbonesque hickory note contending with the peat for top phenol dog. The silky grape acts like a buffer between the two. Textbook layering and with the spices now wriggling around, massive complexity; **f23.5** the softness of texture on the delivery is matched by the finish, even though the oak has plenty of voltage; **b24** the layering on this is, as to be expected, exquisite. It is curious how the peat has gained energy from the oak to perform at its most alluring, though, curiously, had the smoke not been there the tannins may have been a little too forthright for their own good. So soft...so powerful...What a belter! *44.8% 260 bottles*

ADELAIDE HILLS DISTILLERY Nairne, South Australia. 2014. Working.

78 Degrees Australian Whiskey db **(92) n23** roasted hazelnut and unusually layered barley: genuinely complex; **t24** toasted honeycomb from the get-go. Most surprising is the silky oiliness which spreads a complex array of elegant barley, some of it quite toasty around the palate and a slow build of cocoa; **f22** bitters out a little, though the spices rise; **b23** a very different take on malt on whisky, with the barley being both prominent yet offered in a form almost unrecognisable. The chocolate and honey elsewhere forms a beautiful platform from which all else can perform. Unique. *44%*

THE AISLING DISTILLERY NSW. 2014. Working

⬧ **The Aisling Boilermaker Series 1 Tawny Cask** db **(88) n22 t23 f21 b22** One of the drier noses to be found on a Tawny Port matured whisky and doles out its biting, nagging nature with a degree of severity. The delivery and first half dozen flavour waves are an altogether different matter with the body benefitting from the silky-lush grape which still has composure enough for the malt to have its say. The finish, though, returns to the brooding uptight nature of the nose. Not without some elements of chocolatey charm from the tannin. But the tang and roughness of the finale is a disappointment. *49% 1000 bottles*

⬧ **The Aisling Boilermaker Series 2 Apera Cask** db **(94.5) n23.5** sublime Cox's apple freshly bitten into...; the sharpness of the fruit does eventually allow a little malt into the mix, too; **t23.5** brilliant! The delivery is every bit as lively and refreshing as the nose. Again, the sugars – a kind of heather honey lightened with castor sugar – don't dominate but calm the sharper tones of the apple and fuller riches of the malt. The midground sees the oak beginning to open and the spices make their mark; **f23.5** perhaps a little more oil would have helped lengthen the sugars on the finish, but I am being greedy. Instead, it concentrates now on the elegance thanks to the beautiful texture of the dry oak allowing those apple tones to bid a delicate farewell, while the spices scuttle and warm the cocoa notes become substantial; **b24** many Apera casks can slightly overdo it on the sweetness. Not this one, which balances out sweet and dry with textbook complexity. And when at its sharpest, almost apple-fresh. Sheer class. *51% 1000 bottles*

⟳ **The Aisling Whiskycrafter Cnoc Neamh 2022 Reserve Edition** db **(91.5) n23.5** quite astonishing: sweetened lavender, primroses and lightly sugared lemon curd tart, plus grated macadamia nut, makes for a staggering and quite unexpected aroma. Among the most delicate and fragile, vaguely liqueur-ish, Australian nose I have ever encountered; **t23.5** just a whole bunch of sugars racing to melt in the mouth. The first is, not unexpectedly, barley sugar. But then we have a succession of lighter, muscovado and icing sugars alongside a thin, early season heather honey tone. There are some oils off the still sticking to the roof the mouth offering a deeper, vaguely bitter balance; **f22** a much less flavoursome finish with the lethargic grains and the growing tannins happy now to take control, but oils enough to keep things running yet awhile; **b22.5** the bourbon cask is the truth oak: it allows you to see the workings of the distillery like no other. And in this case, it just leaves you scratching your head: this has a singular personality and a disarming lightness despite the growing oils. It does not act like a single malt – and a pre-tasting scrutiny of the labels on the bottle does not confirm it is, either. Cannot wait to see where this distillery is going to take us. *51% 600 bottles*

⟳ **The Aisling Whiskycrafter Preimhe Shiraz Baraille Royalty Special Edition** db **(94) n23** I have stuffed my nose in a bag of Jelly babies, surely...? The softness of the fruit, the dryness of the sugars certainly points that way. Then the most subtle of spices, almost gentle enough to miss if you are not concentrating. Beguiling...; **t23.5** the perfect delivery: the mouth feel is sumptuous without ever being remotely cloying while the fruits tantalises without ever dominating. A wonderfully healthy thread of barley runs through the piece both emphasising the juiciness and holding everything together. The spices also make their play from the very first moment, forever flitting, but are kept in check by the intensity of the vanilla; **f23.5** long and rounded, still there is a pastel fruit quality to this. A lovely chocolate nut and raisin finish gets another thumbs up; **b24** a very happy whisky where the constituent parts come together almost effortlessly. Rounded and lush, the sweetness is beautifully refined, always steering towards the red current and plummy fruits. Deeply satisfying. *50% 850 bottles*

⟳ **The Aisling Whiskycrafter Tale of the Oak Royalty Special Edition 2nd Edition** db **(86) n22 t22.5 f20.5 b21** Oh! A bit of a step down from the previous Royalty Edition. Same lush grape early on, but there is also a grouchy, drying bitterness I hadn't expected to find. The nose offers the first warning; what follows confirms. A pity, for the when the grape breaks free, it is glorious. *47% 850 bottles*

ANIMUS DISTILLERY Kyneton, Victoria. 2012. Working.

Animus Distillery Alpha Whisky db **(90.5) n23 t23.5 f22 b22.5** Impressively forceful and confident it is helped by the clean, unsullied spirit. *54.5%*

ANTHROPOCENE

VI Anthropocene First Release Single Malt Port/bourbon cask **(91) n23 t23 f22 b23** Cheers to a new Ozzie distillery, and I toast its success with its first bottling. Like so many other whiskies from Australia, it is not exactly shy and just bursts onto the palate with a melee of intense – sometimes slightly too intense – flavours. Certainly knows how to grab your attention. But this is one bucking bronco of a dram. Fasten your seat belts, folks... *54.4%*

VI Anthropocene Second Release Single Malt sherry cask **(85.5) n21 t22 f21 b21.5** The cuts just aren't right on this fellow, allowing too many underlying feints to get a foothold. The grape itself is intense and means business. And for a while there is so much fruit to conjure with. Pleasant in part, but too many fault lines. *50.45%*

VI Anthropocene Small Reserve Release 01 Single Malt Port cask **(86) n21.5 t22 f21 b21.5** Attractively succulent thanks to another outstanding Port cask this distillery seems to be able call upon at will, though some stewed cabbage can be detected on the nose. A charming pastiche of plum and cherry jams intertwanging with the bedrock of firm malt. A little hot late on as per the house style. But perhaps a little too much vegetable where sugars should be. *46.2%*

VI Anthropocene Small Reserve Release 02 Single Malt Port cask **(83.5) n21.5 t21 f20 b21** The wide cut on this gives the grape very little leeway. Never quite finds its rhythm or purpose. *46.2%*

VI Anthropocene Small Reserve Release 03 Single Malt bourbon cask **(91.5) n22.5** a wide cut, but just on the right side of decency. A hint of nougat, delicate hickory and ginger, but malt and heather honey are well represented, also; **t23** that fatness on arrival comes as absolutely no surprise, as the cut has lassoed some oils into the frame. It is the honey, however, which holds court...a kind of moist honey-laden ginger cake; **f22.5** after the sweetness invariably on wide cuts, comes the bitterness, though more of a contrarian moan rather than anything negative or aggressive; **b23.5** if the cut is slightly generous, then the honey to be found on this is positively philanthropic... 47.2%

BAKERY HILL North Bayswater, Victoria. 1999. Working.

Bakery Hill Classic Malt Single Malt Whisky db (88) n22 t22 f22 b22 A straight as a die malt which makes little attempt to veer away from its cream toffee theme. 46%. ncf.

Bakery Hill Classic Malt Cask Strength Single Malt Whisky db (94) n23 t23.5 f23.5 b24 Because of the lack of oils present on Baker Hill malt, it can suffer slightly when reduced. Here the whisky, oils and all, is intact we get the malt in full glory. "Classic Malt" says the label. You hear no quibbles from me... 60.5%. ncf.

Bakery Hill Death or Glory db (94) n23 t23.5 f23.5 b24 Oh, my! Get the complexity on this fella! As minty as it is malty, on the nose especially, this has a colossal amount of development between the sweeter tones, mint included, and the drier oaks which act as anchor. Right in the middle of all this is sublime malt, salivating and sharp on one level, and almost biscuity and salty on another. One of those 15 minutes malts using the Murray Method to unlock a true beauty. When a malt is this on song, surely it should be called "Tunes of Glory"... 48%.

Bakery Hill Double Wood Single Malt Whisky db (90) n22 t23 f22.5 b23 A busy, attractive and quite full bodied Bakery Hill. 46%. ncf.

BELGROVE DISTILLERY Kempton, Tasmania. 2010. Working.

◈ **Belgrove Oat Whisky Rum Cask** date bottled 13.7.23 db (90) n23 one of the most forceful noses I have ever encountered of any oat whisky made anywhere in the world. Usually a silky, porridgey softness, we instead have a firm oatiness contained within a typical rum outer sugary shell. But, oddly, there is a mystery grapey fruit note, too, winging in from somewhere. To say this is intense is like saying that north Queensland is a little bit warm...; **t23** woooofffff! The oats crash land on the palate with a surprise peppery kick most likely off the oak and then several forceful shock waves of the rock-hard sugars off the rum cask. This is powerful medicine. And highly complex with various plots and sub plot at work regarding not just flavours but even texture...; **f21.5** bitters untidily on the finale and, as on the nose, there are shades of things grapey at work as the silk oat and busy spice play happily together elsewhere...; **b22.5** oddly enough, earlier this week I was in Scotland talking to a distiller about the pros and cons of oat whisky. And one of the pros I pointed out was the grain's unique and powerful flavour...and that one of the cons is that very few distilleries have been able to distil it successfully. Well, here's a successful, full-flavoured example and, highly unusually, in a rum cask to give solidity to a very soft whisky style. At times delicious.... but always intriguing. 60.2%

◈ **Belgrove Rye Whisky** cask PB074 bottled 16.5.19 db (88.5) n22 t22.5 f22 b22 One of those déjà vu moments: "hang on", I thought. "Haven't I tasted this one before?" And then a search back in the records shewed that I had...yet hadn't. Belgrove bottled part of this barrel in the April. And then bottled the remainder a month later! Well, it obviously hadn't changed much for the alert to go up. Curiously, I scored it the same as back then though find a little less tobacco and more staccato on the rye. Enjoyable, but not in the same league as their Wholly Shit Rye, which is a near perfection of rye distillation. 62.4%

◈ **Belgrove Rye Whisky 8 Years Old** cask PB057 bott 24.8.2023 db (96.5) n23.5 what a blistering nose: the rye is two-toned, ranging from sharp and eye-wateringly intense to deep and even a tad earthy once they link arms with the tannin. At times you could swear some eucalyptus is stalking it...; **t24.5** OK...no-one warned me for this. Certainly, their last rye bottlings didn't. But this is near perfect in delivery. Rye richness levels peak at 100% and stay the course. Despite healthy tannins it remains crisp and refreshing, as it should be, and there is evidence of a little mint...as there should be. Fabulous mouthfeel with the oils clinging to the roof of the mouth amplifying the faux fruitiness of the grain. The salivation levels remain attractively high with spices now aiding the sharper grains, the satisfaction levels on another scale entirely...; **f24** long – implausibly long – thanks to those oils with immeasurable strands of rye meeting an acidic blood orange note, and then met with a hint of cocoa (of course!). The spices remain controlled throughout and even now appear to only show alongside the still fragile and brittle remnants of the now oak-rattled grain...; **b24.5** hell's teeth! The flavours...!!! No-one is equipped with enough taste buds to fully take this one on. Easily the very best rye whisky I have ever tasted from outside North America. Simply mind-blowingly majestic and fearsomely flavourable. There are well-known distilleries in Kentucky who can't get their rye quite this pure, intense and punchy. And here's the rub: the pre-bottled sample I was sent – free from the heavier tannins – was even better still. I am blown away.... 67.2%

◈ **Belgrove Wholly Shit Rye Whisky** bottled 13.7.23 db (95.5) n24 ah....sheep shit! Not any old sheep shit, but carefully cured sheep shit...; **t24** I really cannot fault the delivery: absolutely everything about it works. The mouth feel is exactly how you want perfectly cut rye spirit to be with a salivating crispness of its own, complete with friendly Demerara sugars...and then a gorgeous smokiness ballooning all around it, thus ensuring a magnificent two-tone attack on the palate that just sways with perfectly accented flavours and layered smoke; **f23.5** at first a tangy fruitiness – not entirely unlike Chinese gooseberry – hits hard. As this vanishes the smoke moves back into place, though a more conforming demerara sugar keeps the sweeter end up. Light spices are sprinkled on the smoke...which lingers and lingers and lingers....; **b24** one of the great mouthfeels of this year with the most extraordinary combination of rock hard and yielding you're ever likely to meet. The phenol levels are also hitting near perfection. If I remember correctly, the sheep faeces used in the smoking of this comes from animals who have been fed on the draff coming directly from the distiller, making this the ultimate recycled smoked whisky on the planet. And damned good shit to boot... *57%*

🔹 **Belgrove Wholly Shit Rye Whisky** bottled 1.7.2023 db **(95.5) n24** ah....more sheep shit...! What I love is that teasing prickle which seems to bind all those smokey layers together. A slight shish kebab meatiness, too... (well, it has to be lamb...)...; **t24** as near as damn it to the other cask as makes no difference. Perhaps a light smattering of extra spice; **f23.5** again, same as its sister cask, except a little roast coffee moves into view. And not any old coffee bit civet coffee....; **b24** a pretty impressive re-run of its sister cask. Other than spice, the main difference being the distinctive late civet coffee component. But then, knowing how civet coffee is produced, as well as the peat, it really had to be.... *56.8%*

BLACK GATE DISTILLERY Mendooran NSW. 2012. Working.
Black Gate Distillery Port Cask Solera Batch No. 3 db **(87) n21.5 t22.5 f21 b22** A neat and comfortable malt, if not technically in the same league as their peated cask bottling, that seems as though it doesn't want to ruffle too many feathers. The port acts as a silky base but also ensures development and complexity is limited. *46.8%.*

CALLINGTON MILL Oatlands TAS. 2020. Working
Callington Mill Entropy Single Malt Tawny and Aperera casks – finished in Tokey, Muscat and Muscadelle casks db **(96) n24 t24.5 f23.5 b24** We are here in the realms of very serious whisky. Not only is it complex, it is almost perfectly structured, with the flavour rich yet still able to allow complexity full scope. Hard to imagine anything beating this to Australian Whisky of the Year: this is glorious. *52% ncf organic*
Callington Mill Sherry Fusion Single Malt Apara casks finished in PX and Oloroso casks db **(89) n22.5 t23 f21 b22.5** A big, yet even malt where the PX has been brought out like a roller to flatten any bumps in the wicket. *46% nc organic*

CHIEF'S SON DISTILLERY Somerville, Victoria. 2014. Working.
Chief's Son 900 Pure Malt db **(88) n22.5 t23 f20.5 b22** Much more to celebrate on the nose now with the vanilla and muscovado sugars at full throttle. This directly translates to a rich malt and honey delivery with the sugars working overtime to enhance complexity. Sadly, the tangy finish lets the side down. *45%*
Chief's Son 900 Pure Malt db **(89) n23.5 t23 f20.5 b22** Pity about the finish. But the extra strength helps bring out the star quality of the bourbon-style sweetness. At times absolutely delicious. *60%*
Chief's Son 900 Standard db **(92) n22.5 t23 f23 b23.5** A beautiful malt which from the first moment appears to put balance before all else. Excellent length on the finale rounds this off wonderfully, too. *45%*
Chief's Son 900 Standard db **(94) n23 t23.5 f23.5 b24** Just one of those annoying drams that it would be far too easy spending too much time drinking. Big...and beautiful. *45%*
Chief's Son Single Malt Cask Expression dark beer barrel batch CX-R4 db **(87) n22 t22.5 f20.5 b22** A far better experience than my last encounter with one of their beer-barrel matured malts. The hop, sadly, is discernible but not to the extent as before. And when it's not, the distillery's super-creamy texture goes into overdrive to get the heather honey and muscovado sugars working overtime with the stubborn barley. A slog for the purists, perhaps, but not on this occasion without merit... *4785%*
Chief's Son 900 Sweet Peat db **(92.5) n22.5 t23.5 f23 b23.5** This has unquestionably gone up a gear. Here's a poser, though: the stronger a spirit, the tighter the bubbles formed when shaken and the longer they remain. Yet do this trick with this whisky, the stronger version's bubbles disappear long before the weaker ones. But the intensity of the whisky experience confirms and underlines the difference in strength. Like water disappearing anti-clockwise down the plug hole, things are the opposite in Australia.... *60%*
Chief's Son The Tanist db **(84) n21.5 t22.5 f20 b20** Unbelievably fat in texture. The delivery wallows in a muted cream soda sweetness with barley and marshmallow through the middle. The finish though is a tad bitter despite a chocolatey intervention. A pretty idiosyncratic offering, but feels it loses its balance at about the halfway point as the bitterness creeps in. *43%*

COBURNS Burrawang NSW

⟨◆⟩ **Coburns Adonis** db (86.5) n21 t22 f21.5 b22 Adonis was a good-looking sort of chap by all accounts. If he was anything like this rendition, he was pretty beefy, too, and carrying a fair bit of fat. The vaguely wide cut is evidenced on both nose and finish. And delivery, come to think of it. But the jammy ripeness of the plum pudding does its best to colour over these mortal frailties, so if you are willing to overlook the odd hint of feint a sweet and juicy time is to be had. 61.2%

⟨◆⟩ **Coburns Ambrosia** db (91.5) n23 t23 f22.5 b23 Ambrosia indeed! A far better distillate at work here: cleaner and far more accommodating of both the rich fruity vibes and the conspicuous oak. There are fascinating spices at play here, especially on the nose where the oaky tannin is at its most prominent. It's those tannins which ensure that the fruitiness remains a mixed bag of sweet and dry. Still not perfectly distilled, but much better now with a cask in full alignment. 56.12%

⟨◆⟩ **Coburns Aphrodite** db (85) n21.5 t22 f20 b21.5 A bit like Adonis, this Aphrodite isn't all she's cracked up to be. Feinty she may be, at least her cloak of grape does a pretty good job of hiding the warts. Good spices, too. Adonis' perfect mate. 53.09%

⟨◆⟩ **Coburns Apollo** db (91) n22.5 t23.5 f22.5 b23 Now, I like this Apollo bloke as he's the God of Truth, something I've been purposely damaged for because I have fought for it all my career. And, truthfully, I have to say this a really enjoyable malt. Better distilled than some of its fellow gods, the mix of rich dates and lightly spiced plum pudding makes for, at times, quite a salivating joy. The light molasses on the full-bodied delivery works superbly. If I remember my Classics, wasn't Apollo also the God of Archery? If so, he didn't quite get the gold bull, but certainly nicked the blue and red. 55.05%

⟨◆⟩ **Coburns Athena** db (89) n21.5 t23 f22 b22.5 After the full-on delivery from Apollo, I was expecting the feinty bouncer from Athena...a pattern is developing here. Thankfully the feints are under better control here, though struggling a bit on the nose, while the fruit much more deft here than previously and bolstered by early spices. The finish is a little untidy, granted. But the overall picture is a fascinating one boasting excellent bitter-sweet balance. 56.74%

⟨◆⟩ **Coburns Calliope** db (94) n23 t24 f23 b24 How fitting that Calliope is linked with poetry as, so far, this whisky is speaking to me far more beautifully and romantically than any other in this set. She was also a pretty famous muse, too, which might upset some of the braindead whisky writers determined to destroy rather than create. For a start we are dealing with relatively spot on distillate, where barely an atom of feint can be found and a wine cask which offers heather honey to accompany the redcurrant tart. There is also a unique half peppery-half ginger spiciness in play which stirs up the tastebuds further. A grandiloquent offering at times, it is the multi-layering which offers the real poetry and elegance. This can be my muse anytime... 59.15%

⟨◆⟩ **Coburns Clio** db (87.5) n21.5 t22.5 f21.5 b22 The first whisky ever to be named after a French automobile. Misfires on the slightly feinty nose but picks up speed once it gets its fruity gears going. Never quite shrugs off its over-zealous cut, though the pithiness to the fruit is attractive, as is the late oaky surge. Not sure what Papa would make of it if bought for him on Father's Day. 55.16%

⟨◆⟩ **Coburns Cybele** db (94) n23 t24 f23.5 b23.5 As Cybele was getting on a bit in real immortality, I was expecting this to be caked in oak. And, as it happens, I wasn't to be disappointed as tannin plays a key role in both the nose and finish. And it also acts as the anchor for the fruits to fire into orbit on delivery. That under-ripe gooseberry melding with the blackcurrant tart really is a brilliant signature while the mix of thin golden syrup and molasses really does special things as we lead into that oaky finale. A beautifully made and matured whisky which offers delicious entertainment all the way. 55.1%

⟨◆⟩ **Coburns Dionysus** db (79.5) n20 t21 f19 b19.5 Dionysus was the god of wine making, unless I'm mistaken. But certainly not whisky making. He is also the god of feints... 56.7%

⟨◆⟩ **Coburns Gaia** db (93) n23 t23.5 f23 b23 Alphabetically going along this set, this was the first god I had to look up. Oh yes: the mother of the sky (Uranus) and the Earth in goddess form. Forgot all about her, to be honest. Well, this whisky is lot more memorable: chunky, salivating and copiously spiced. Though a little bitterness tags along at the death, this is clearly oak at work. As is the house style, the fruit dominates over the grain, though here the latter does get a work in edgeways. Love that delicate honey-liquorice time, too... 59.05%

⟨◆⟩ **Coburns Hermes** db (87.5) n22 t22.5 f21 b22 In British mythology Hermes is the god of delivering broken things to your back garden or two doors away. Even when you are in. Here things aren't broken exactly, but a bit crushed. Spices are just a tad out of control, a huge tannin note thumping everything out of its way as it races to the front. There is a wide cut, but those spices – not unlike German Christmas cake - do everything in their power to point your taste buds in a different direction entirely. 58.45%

◇◇◇ **Coburns Oceanus** db (89) n21.5 t23 f22 b22.5 A bit of humour here from the distillers: Oceanus spends his time bossing water around...and this bottling has more water in it than any other in their classic set. This thins out the feints slightly but doesn't do too much damage to the intense vanilla-tannin. The sugars on delivery are almost crystalline, as is the eye-wateringly sharp plum and raspberry fruitiness. Not a bad drop of Oceanus. *48.43%*

◇◇◇ **Coburns Pegasus** db (92.5) n22.5 t23 f23 b24 A bit like Pegasus, this whisky has the hallmarks of a thoroughbred and possesses uncanny balance. The mouth feel is sensual, making the most of the thick - but not fatally thick - cut. The fruit, not unlike pastille sweets, creates a glistening sheen. While, without for a moment letting up, the oak is present and toasty. Just gets better and better on the palate and wonderfully complex thanks to the rhythmic tannins. *58.1%*

◇◇◇ **Coburns Perseus** db (94) n23.5 t23.5 f23 b24 Named after my parrot, Perseus. Better known to all as Percy. Percy, being a Myers, is resplendent in turquoise, green, yellow, brown and grey. This (presumably) Port pink tinge in the glass doesn't enter into things. Tannins tumble from the glass, giving this big weight from the very start while the fruit - a kind of cross between pear and grape - only plays around the edges. Probably the most complete delivery and follow through of the entire range thanks to the stunning harmony between the fruit, spices, big tannin and background barley sugar. A very pretty boy. *55.27%*

◇◇◇ **Coburns Zeus** db (94.5) n23.5 t23.5 f23.5 b24 Somewhat perverse that the second weakest of all whiskies in this set should be Zeus, the top honcho of the Gods. If you are expecting fire and brimstone to be hurled at you, forget it. This malt is singularly about elegance and understatement. In many ways this is the one that has been most carefully tended to ensure complexity. And if that was the plan, then they have succeeded. Rather than this god being chiselled and hewn into a ceremonial statue, this is a tapestry of a malt, the fruit at its sharpest and most precise, the background barley sugar soothing, the spices creating rhythm and depth. Complex and satisfying, the fruit piquant and zesty, this really is, fittingly, Coburns' god of the gods... *51.09%*

CORRA LINN DISTILLERY Relbia, Tasmania. 2015. Working.
Corra Linn Fumosus Aqua Vitae Single Malt Whisky db (87) n21.5 t22.5 f21.5 b21.5 A particularly dry malt with a busy cross section of seasoning. The tannins bite a bit while a strange, meandering semi-fruitiness pitches up here and there, as does a lagging phenolic tone. An oddball malt which never quite settles on the direction it wants to take. Plenty of flavour and certainly intriguing. *56.2%*.

CRADLE MOUNTAIN WHISKY PTY LTD Tamr, Tasmania. Working.
Cradle Mountain A Walk In The Woods Single Malt batch 2009 db (95) n23.5 t24 f23.5 b24 Yet another absolutely First Class malt from Tasmania. And another that accentuates the chocolate for maximum yumminess. Superb. *60%*

DEVIANT DISTILLERY Sandy Bay, Tasmania. 2017. Working.
◇◇◇ **Deviant Medium Peated Single Malt** ex wheated bourbon cask, cask DD0019 db (91) n22 a mixed bag of boiled fruit candy rolls of the nose, leaving the smoke to clammer for attention; t23 candy...? Not 'alf! One of the sweetest deliveries of the year, absolutely choc-full of fruity juiciness. The malt also has a bit of a splurge at the midpoint before the oak lays down some earthier roots even ahead of the barley; f23 Jaffa cake orangey-chocolate makes for an unusually sweet finish with the apologetic malt latching on the vanilla as it goes into smoky walnut cake mode; b23 I wasn't too sure about this at first. Left it and returned later – giving two sessions of the Murray Method. In conclusion, this is deceptively complex with the spices working wonders. The peat is almost a distraction to the idiosyncrasies of the lightly fruity sugars. A thought-provoker... *50%*

◇◇◇ **Deviant Heavily Peated Single Malt** ex Tasmanian brandy cask, cask DD0001 db (94.5) n23 not overly impressed with the strange apricot fruit kick that tries to undermine the fledgling phenols; t24 ah...excellent! The peat has shaken off the fruit that has hampered the nose and builds in intensity with a wonderful degree of decorum. A surge of molasses really does let the medium roast Java/Brazil coffee blend beautifully and this in turns sparks off the spices; f23.5 again, so much molasses on the finish, the coffee and peat merging beautifully. Some vanillas try to get into the act, but make only a little headway; b24 now, that's much more like it. For a heavily peated malt, it is cumbersome in taking off and at times looks as though it is not going to make it. But, once airborne, it glides beautifully and impressively around the palate and then builds into magnificent domination. If you find a better coffee to peat ratio in a malt this year, let me know...please! *55%*

◇◇◇ **Deviant Unpeated Single Malt** ex bourbon & honey spirit casks, casks DD0010+DD0020 db (88.5) n22 t22.5 f22 b22 A pleasant, perhaps underpowered, malt looking for a balance between a malty theme and a honeyed charm. It finds it in the most part, though it spends time keeping clear of the bitter rocks of oak that at times threaten. Not exactly a challenging dram, I don't for a moment think it was supposed to be. Instead, it concentrates on clever variations of malty sweetness and here it succeeds without ever exerting itself. 46%

DEVIL'S DISTILLERY Hobart, Tasmania. 2015. Working.

Hobart Whisky Tasmanian Dark Mofo 2019 Winter Feast Exclusive ex-bourbon cask, rum maple finish, bott 25 Apr 19 db **(82.5)** n20 t22 f20.5 b20 Not sure what to say about this. Far more a liqueur than a whisky in character with the maple dominating the aroma to the cost of all else and the muscular sugars, though attractive, decidedly OTT. 59.1%.

Hobart Whisky Tasmanian Single Malt Batch 19-002 ex-bourbon cask, pinot noir finish, bott 25 Apr 19 db **(94)** n23 t24 f23.5 b23.5 Like being hit by the waves of a tropical storm, one flavour smashing into you after another. Just brilliant...! 57.5%.

Hobart Whisky Tasmanian Single Malt Batch 19-003 French oak port cask finish, bott 25 Apr 19 db **(93.5)** n23 t23.5 f23.5 b23.5 More beautifully intense than a harem... 46.4%.

Hobart Whisky Tasmanian Single Malt Batch 19-004 bott 25 Apr 19 db **(93)** n23 t23.5 f23 b23.5 How the Devil do they make their bourbon matured malt so buttery...? 55.5%.

Tasmanian Moonshine Company Tasmanian Malt Barrel Aged New Make port cask db **(91.5)** n23 t23 f22.5 b23 Big almost jammy fruit. But that is only half of it: a huge injection of hefty tannin has ensured backbone to the plummy muscle. And as for the spices....? Wow! A huge dose of flavours: this youngster isn't mucking about! 50%.

FANNYS BAY DISTILLERY Lulworth, Tasmania. 2014. Working.

Fannys Bay Single Malt Tasmanian Whisky Shiraz cask, cask no. 61 db **(93)** n22 t24 f23 b24 The nose may be surprisingly non-commital. But the same can't be said once it hits the taste buds. Wow! This malt packs a fruity punch! 63%. sc.

FLEURIEU DISTILLERY Goolwa, South Australia. 2004. Working.

Fleurieu Distillery The Rubicon ex-Seppeltsfield Port barrels db **(89)** n22.5 t22.5 f22 b22 A muscular whisky with some big flavour egos at work. When they gel, there are some magical moments. 55%. 500 bottles.

HELLYERS ROAD Havenview, Tasmania. 1999. Working.

Hellyers Road Single Malt Whisky 12 Year Old Original db **(84.5)** n19 t22 f21.5 b22. Forget the nose and get stuck into the massive malt. 46.2%.

Hellyers Road Original Aged 15 Years db **(92.5)** n23.5 t23.5 f22.5 b23 Almost, literally, a peach of a whisky from Hellyers...the most deft whisky ever from this distillery. 46.2%.

Hellyers Road Original Aged 16 Years db **(90.5)** n22 t23 f22.5 b23 Put on your tin hats for this one – there is shrapnel everywhere... Carnage...and it's delicious..! 66.8%. Master Series.

Hellyers Road Peated db **(91)** n22.5 t23.5 f22 b23 Hellyers offers a unique character in its own right. Put some pretty full-on peat into the mix and you are left with one of the most idiosyncratic whiskies in the world. And a sheer, if at times perplexing, delight...! 46.2%.

Hellyers Road Peated Aged 14 Years db **(87.5)** n22 t23.5 f21 b21 Despite the enormity of the peat, the sheer chutzpa of the strength and sweetness for a brief few moments have you at a point of near ecstasy, the technical gremlins are still there and make themselves heard at the finish. But, my word! What a ride!!! 63%. Master Series.

Hellyers Road Slightly Peated Aged 10 Years db **(91.5)** n23 t23 f22.5 b23 Hellyers Road has come of age in every sense: the lack of copper in their system that held them back for so long has now been mostly overcome by a mix of peat and extremely high quality oak. This is a quietly spoken little beaut. Congratulations all round: it has been a long journey... 46.2%.

HUNNINGTON DISTILLERY Kettering, Tasmania. 2017. Working

Hunnington Triple Distilled Single Malt sherry cask filled 12.12.2019 bott 23.4.2022 db **(90)** n23 t23.5 f21 b22.5 The type of single malt the German market in particular adores. Those who have become used to a syrupy PX style will be in for a shock with this elegant creature. 45.3% 65 bottles

KILLARA Kingston, Tasmania. 2016. Working.

Killara Distillery KD03 ex-sherry barrel db **(90.5)** n23 t23 f22 b22.5 A genteel and understated whisky. 46%.

KINGLAKE DISTILLERY Kinglake Central, Victoria.

◈ **Kinglake Single Malt** dist 14/8/19 bott 13/12/22 ex-bourbon barrels three malts grown in NSW and one from Scottish Borders batch OC12 db **(91)** n22 an unusually thin nose for Australia with oils AWOL until significantly warmed and the barley being unceremoniously shoved around by the brooding tannins. Clean to a fault with cascading vanilla at every turn. No surprises that spices are nibbling at will...; **t23.5** again, a very curious lightness – even momentary flavour pause – on delivery when cool, though this is rectified by the Murray Method. Then a delightful dovetailing of heather honey and vanilla and even a delicate bourbon character of light liquorice; **f22.5** the honey keeps its shape with spiced butterscotch for accompaniment; **b23** an incredibly fragile malt badly in need of the Murray Method of warming to get the very best from. Once it is prodded into action it moved from a thin, docile creature into something much richer and with a delightfully honeyed disposition. *46% 540 bottles*

⬩ **Kinglake Full Noise Single Malt** dist 24/9/19 bott 20/4/23 ex-bourbon barrels three malts grown in NSW and one from Scottish Borders batch 161/137 db **(95) n23.5** huge oak interference here...but of the very best kind. The barley may be intense in its own right but the spices fired into it from the casks agitate matters wonderfully. But to keep things in check, the vanillas also stretch into ulmo honey to complete a very satisfying performance on the nose...; **t23.5** such succulence: it is like sucking on an alcoholic throat lozenge. Early on there are some mild bourbon messages being sent, mainly around red liquorice and vague hickory. But, again, it is the honey which stars, catching on to the oils and spreading purposefully around the palate, keeping a close eye on those busy spices; **f24** just ridiculous layering on a finish which seems very reluctant to end. The spices carry on their profound work. But, as earlier the ulmo honey – now thickened by a heather honey back up – is more than compensating. But neither can stop the odd pulse of barley which perfectly fits the bill. An astonishingly beautiful fade...; **b24** Kinglake could have called this "Full Racket" is in Sybil Fawlty's interpretation of Brahms' Third Racket. Because without going into cliches, this really is a symphony. And, from a technical standpoint, so interesting when compared to their standard single malt above. There, there have been too meticulous with their cuts and edited out some of the oils that would help on the finish especially. Here the cut was fractionally wider, but still perfectly clean, and it has made an extraordinary difference. For a new distillery and I think my first tasting from them, I am quite blown away. And, what's more, they have turned a deaf ear to the siren of a wine cask and allowed the ex-bourbon barrels to shew just how magnificent their base malt whisky is. Stupendous. *60% 145 bottles*

LARK DISTILLERY Hobart, Tasmania. 1992. Working.

Lark Distillery Sherry Matured & Sherry Finished db **(95) n24 t23.5 f23.5 b24** I know Bill Lark abhors sulphur-treated sherry butts as vehemently as me. Which is why this is the only double sherry-matured whisky I picked up this year without fear that it would fail...And, of course, it didn't. It's a beaut! *50.8%.*

LAUNCESTON DISTILLERY Western Junction, Tasmania. 2013. Working.

Launceston Distillery Cask Strength Bourbon Cask Tasmanian Single Malt batch no. H17:18, db **(96) n23.5 t24 f24 b24.5** for a long time I have been pleading with distilleries to cut out the fancy stuff and bottle from ex-bourbon, so the true personality of the distillery is there to be seen. Well, this shews Launceston in a light I hoped but dare not believe they'd reach. Their last bottling from Bourbon cask I sampled was a bit undercooked. This is what happens when great spirit and great oak combine. Sublime: the richer textured Glen Grant of Oz. I think I've just tasted the Australian Whisky of the Year *61% 242 bottles*

LIMEBURNERS Albany, Western Australia. 2014. Working.

⬩ **Limeburners Darkest Winter Single Malt** db **(96) n24** the smoke billows, but with varied depth of peat. A lightly salted mixed diced nut works well with the vanilla. The evenness of all the parties involved is exceptional, the dovetailing and interplay unbelievable. But it is the sweet gristiness, almost like a peated ice cream cone, which just blows you away...; **t24** what a delivery! In the odd moment or two it reaches perfection with the peat and the grist harmonising. The sugars are improbably complex, running from that familiar gristiness to a delicate manuka and ulmo honey blend; **f24** fabulous milky mocha. We are back to dry ice cream cones and powdery smattering of peat...; **b24** this will brighten even the darkest winter day. This is just how a full-bodied single malt should be. Deceptively smoky and joyously enriching, this is one hell of a whisky: an absolute beaut! If this isn't Australian whisky of the year, then the one beating it will definitely be worth finding... *62.05%*

⬩ **Limeburners Heavy Peat** db **(91.5) n23** chunky, no prisoners taken, tightly knitted, pleasantly acidic phenols...; **t23.5** full bodied delivery with an early shewing of golden syrup. This sweetness is the perfect foil for the pounding peat which wings in on full charge. Good balance despite the degree of difference between the two elements. It is the richness of the Malteser-style malt which perhaps impresses above all; **f22** a surprisingly short finish which concentrates on the vanilla and lingering malt; **b23** typical Limeburners doing exactly what it says on the tin Heavy peat it may be, but not too heavy for this malt not to be bathed in a sweet gristiness. *61%*

◇ **Limeburners Port Cask Single Malt** db **(95) n23** endearing fruit levels: not too over the top but intense enough to represent a plum pudding. The subtlest, barely discernible nutmeg and pepper makes a huge difference; **t24** a sharp and salivating delivery soon reverts to a full-on battle between dark chocolate and Turkish delight. Unusually for a malt, the salivation levels increase, rather than the reverse as the fruit becomes sharper and spicier; **f23.5** although not overly oily, the finish lingers. The fruit remains true and clean, the tannins even and undemonstrative, the malt sweet and the spices acting almost like the drums of a band, keeping their composition on track; **b24** yet another glorious whisky form Limeburners whose quality really is now reaching unbelievably high levels. It is the attention to detail that pays off for them and their ability to match complexity with charisma. Magical. *61%*

◇ **Limeburners Tigersnake Mixed Grain Sour Mash** db **(95) n23** a mottled grainy effect, with an eye-watering sharpness which promises so much. Grassy with what appears to be a shimmering rye note trilling the loudest; **t24** if a delivery deserves a standing ovation, this is it: crisp, salivating, there is a vibrant apple fruitiness to the fore. But some spectacularly pulsing oak is soon at work to offer the perfect counterbalance. On warming the degree of heather honey mingling with some malt is astonishing; **f24** for a moment you wonder if there is a finish...because it never seems to end! The spiced coffee notes (and we are broadly talking a semi-heavy roast Java). The spices are almost too polite and refined; **b24** Limeburners once again digging into their inner Kentucky, y'all. It isn't anything like a bourbon in style, even if so in composition, but there is no stinting on the flavours. Indeed, it is as though someone has turned the flavour amp up to full volume. A wonderful, lively and inventive assault on the taste buds. Oh, and using the Murray Method, this has one of the widest ranges of noses and flavours from cool to warm I have experienced for the last year or two...*62.1%*

◇ **Limeburners Tigersnake Rye** db **(88) n22.5 t23 f20.5 b22** Absolutely no mistaking which grain is starring here. Attractively sharp in just the right places, it also displays a mouth-watering, fruity countenance and no shortage of spice. The finish is a bit flaccid and out of rhyme but, that apart, this is no mean rye. *55%*

McHENRY DISTILLERY Port Arthur, Tasmania. 2010. Working.

McHenry Singe Malt Whisky 200L ex-bourbon American oak cask, barrel no. MD55, dist 23 Sept 15, bott 26 Jan 21 db **(94) n23.5 t23.5 f23 b24** Now that is what I call a single malt whisky! Their last offering, though matured in bourbon, had a peculiar grapey quality which confused and distracted. No such problem here. This is first class distillate matured is high quality American oak and plucked from the warehouse at a very interesting period in its development. Hearty congratulations all at McHenry. Now let's just hope that some idiot doesn't complain that it sounds too much like a Scotch... *50%. sc.*

MT. UNCLE DISTILLERY Walkamin, Queensland. 2001. Working.

Watkins Whisky Co. Single Malt Whisky nbc db **(87.5) n22.5 t22.5 f20.5 b22** A distinctive malt, though one with a bit of multiple personality disorder. The nose certainly owes far more to a rum style than malt, as the esters are belted out. And there is even a hint of rye on the crisp and chipper fruitiness o the early flavour waves that follows the delivery. All this, of course, is down to an over the top cut which certainly glues up the finale. But after a number of pretty run of the mill whiskies today, this one has certainly got my nerve endings fired up. Lots of heather honey at work, too, though some of that comes from the wide-ish cut. All this care of Mark Watkins, head distiller: The Man From Uncle. And this is a very solo whisky... *43%.*

NANT DISTILLERY Bothwell, Tasmania. 2008. Working.

Nant Distillery Single Malt Whisky White Oak Cask cask no. 951 db **(94.5) n23 t24.5 f23 b24** Some of the passages in this malt as good as any Australian malt you are likely to taste. Just brilliantly distilled. *43%. sc.*

NEW WORLD WHISKY DISTILLERY Melbourne, Victoria. 2007. Working.

Starward Left-Field Single Malt bott code: 200824 **(94) n23 t23.5 f23.5 b24** How wonderful to find an Australian whisky which has escaped the considerable gravitational pull of its own country. Nothing like as beefy or chunky as many of its fellow Australians...and a bit of a rarity to find one at 40%abv, too! But what it lacks in traditional Ozzie Ooomph it makes up for with an attractive, oaky complexity. This is a considerable step up in quality from earlier bottlings I have had from this distillery. Indeed, not just a step up, but a journey to another world. This quite brilliant and a softer side of Australian whisky we have never quite seen before. *40%*

NONESUCH DISTILLERY Hobart, Tasmania. 2007. Working.

◇ **Nonesuch Single Malt PX Sherry**, cask no 69 db **(92.5) n22.5** even and easy-going. A surprise hint of cucumber and mint amid the fat, relaxed grape...how curious...; **t23.5** grape and dates exude fruitiness while the texture lives up to the fatty promise on the nose. The fourth and fifth flavour waves peak with maximum lightly spiced grape which fits in beautifully with the natural breakfast grape jelly persona. The oak has kicked in early, though, to ensure some culture and balance; **f23** surprisingly dry with most of the oils now spent. The vanilla builds up steam. But the fruit persists with a delightful trickle of sharp, under-ripe grape notes; **b23.5** a delightful, almost coy whisky where the PX shows subtlety and complexity incredibly rare in this type of cask. Full of surprises and tricks this is a malt which will delight. *45% 72 bottles*

⬧ **Nonesuch Single Malt Pinot Noir Cask**, cask no 90 db **(93) n23** just a little salt is sprinkled on the moist Dundee cake: just love that light nutty thread; **t24** spot on! Varying grape intensity and shifting degree of sweetness makes this a complex critter from the off. But, as on the nose, it is as though someone has sprinkled in a little salt to maximise the flavours with the grape at times reaching concentrated levels; **f22.5** time for the oak to kick in and it obliges. A very slight bitterness, perhaps, but within range. But a little chocolate and dry ginger cake makes for a pleasant finale; **b23.5** the last Pinot I tasted from Nonesuch was sulphur tainted. This isn't. The result is a far more accessible and compelling bottling. One of the Australian deliveries of the year on the palate with its eye-watering, three dimensional fruit. *50.5% 40 bottles*

⬧ **Nonesuch Triple Grain American Oak**, cask no. 88 & 91 db **(90.5) n23.5** something distinctly American about this – no surprise! But it is the corn oils which are the key, holding in place the tell-tale acacia honey notes off the virgin casks (I had now better check that there is virgin oak used and corn in the recipe, or I'm going to look a bit stupid...). The subtlety of spice is breathtaking. The pace, elegance and overall beauty of this nose is charming... (and yes there is corn, but only one virgin oak cask, so close...) ....; **t23.5** a kind of bourbon light. Or maybe light bourbon. Again, we have the corn making a statement, the mix of heather and lemon blossom honey kicking in with the malt to make for salivating complexity. And those oils are so sticky: maybe something off the stills as well as the corn...; **f21** there had been a background bitterness trying to gain entry earlier, but the honey had seen it off. With the sweeter tones dissipating, that slight bitterness has grabbed the headlines a bit; **b22.5** while the finish maybe not quite perfect, it would take a right old misery-guts to do anything other than savour the nose and delivery. Some outstanding moments. *48% 81 bottles*

⬧ **Nonesuch Triple Grain Pedro Ximenez Sherry Cask**, batch ND68 **(87.5) n22.5 t22.5 f21 b21.5** When PX comes along this thick and lush and as well-appointed as this, it is far too easy for the grains and tannins to put their feet up and let the grape do all the work...what is what has happened here. The slight bitterness to the finish hasn't helped, but I just wish those grains, which vanish after their shy but playful appearance on the nose, had more of an input. Even so, there is no problem with the grape itself which is clean and succulent. *45%*

OLD HOBART DISTILLERY Hobart, Tasmania. 2007. Working.
Overeem Single Malt Whisky Port Cask cask no. OHD-178 db **(94.5) n23.5 t24 f23 b24** one of those rare malts where a lot happens, but does so organically and with every shift in the gears getting the taste buds revving. *60%. sc.*

OLD KEMPTON DISTILLERY Redlands, Tasmania. 2013. Working.
Old Kempton Distillery Single Malt Tokay cask, cask no. RD023 db **(91) n22.5 t23 f22.5 b23** So many Tokay casks through the years have been wasted in the whisky world through being sulphur treated. No such worry here as the fruit gets a free hand to weave its intense, almost citrusy, magic on this malt. Just love the creaminess to this whisky and the busy, prattling spices which prevent things becoming a little too comfortable. A very satisfying experience. *46%. sc.*

SHENE ESTATE DISTILLERY Pontville, Tasmania. 2014. Working.
Shene Mackey Trinity Tasmanian Single Malt nbc db **(90.5) n23 t24 f21 b22.5** If you are not seduced by this full-on delivery, nothing will win your heart! *49% ncf*

SPRING BAY DISTILLERY Spring Beach, Tasmania. 2015. Working.
⬧ **Spring Bay Single Malt Cabernet Sauvignon - American Oak Cask** bott 5/23 db **(93) n23** thick, clean and muscular, this sports a classical fruitcake – rich in sultanas and molasses – sharpened with that coastal peck of salt; **t23.5** so much sweeter on delivery than the nose. Again, that salt is early into play ramping up the flavour profile and ensuring a degree of acerbity into the apple, gooseberry and rich grape theme. The tannins form an impressive spine, while the spices kick in with intent. The deft malty undertones help keep the sweetness levels high; **f23** long, spicy with that heather honey still clinging to the fade; **b23.5** another impressive innings from Spring Bay, finding a surprising degree of silky sweetness particularly from the malt. Satisfying whisky. *48%*

⬧ **Spring Bay Single Malt Tawny Port Cask** db **(93.5) n23** just love the way the grape has attached to the oak here giving it a firm resonance that sits well with the flightier barley. The star ingredient thought, is the saline drip which sparks extra sharpness into all aspects. Hints of rock pools here...; **t23.5** wow! Tangy and zingy, again the product of that sprinkling of sea salt. From the grapey-ness of the nose, this has a more intrinsic sweetness with a little heather honey weighing in on the fatter banana and passionfruit lead. The subtext of ultra-intense malt is true Spring bay style; **f23** the oaky tanginess wears away to be left with a rich malt, cocoa and vanilla fade; **b24** easily the most coastal in style of any Australian whisky, shewing a remarkable degree of briny freshness on both nose and delivery. Incidentally, I always taste some Australian whiskies when the Aussies are in town for the Ashes series. Today they are at Edgbaston, Birmingham, just over an hour's drive from my tasting lab. It is the final day and the lads in green and gold are pinned down on 128-4, needing another 153 runs to win the first Test. Play has not long started after stormy weather; it is warm and close outside and having been both a reasonably successful swing bowler in my day, as well as an opening bat, I know which of the two I would rather be in these conditions. What a pity I don't have the time to sit with this nuggety malt and watch play come to its fascinating conclusion. Because the game is as finely balanced as this whisky. *46%*

SULLIVANS COVE DISTILLERY Cambridge, Tasmania. 1995. Working.

Sullivans Cove Old & Rare American Oak cask no. HH0296, filled 9 May 00, bott 10 Sept 19 db (93.5) **n23 t24 f23 b23.5** A delightful and unusual whisky which concentrates solely on the intensity of the barley. The delivery is something to savour. *49.2%. sc.*

TIMBOON RAILWAY SHED DISTILLERY Timboon, Victoria. 2007. Working.

Timboon Single Malt Whisky Bourbon Expression dist 14 Feb 14, bott 13 Feb 20 db (92) **n23 t22 f24.5 b22.5** Takes its time to get there, but one of the best finishes of the year – anywhere on the planet! *71.1%.*

TIN SHED DISTILLING COMPANY Adelaide, South Australia. 2013. Working.

⬦ **Iniquity Den's Dram Lazy Daze** db (89) **n22** just the hint of a hint of feints. But here this seems to add to the oily richness of the bitter-sweet grains; **t23** despite the strength (or lack of it, to be precise), I'm really bowled over by the delivery which ramps up the malt to, at times, exquisite levels. Spices tingle while the tannins growl a bit; **f22** lovely butterscotch fade with the crust being just slightly singed; **b22** Lazy Daze sitting in my lab, how am I going to work off all this flab? Tasting Den's Aussie malt, looking to see if there's a fault... *40%*

⬦ **Iniquity Gold label batch 007** (94.5) **n23** the grape is brimming over the side of the glass: I think we are in for one colossal delivery on the palate. Despite all this fruitcake richness, the malt has found room for a major say, too...; **t24** a nose like that never lies! Just beautiful from so many angles, but not least the way the heather honey infiltrates the grape at key moments to ensure a lightness of touch to the weight of the fruit. Healthy strands of malt can be picked out at regular intervals, but the closer to the middle you go the plummier this becomes; **f23.5** such an elegant and well-manicured finish. The fruit, previously gushing, is now neat and tidy to fit comfortably with the deeper tannins. The spices remain low but present, but the final notes are one of plum jam on toast; **b24** when they picked a Port cask for their whisky, did they pick one hell of a Port cask! One of the best I have tasted this year. Couple that with some excellent distillate and what we have is a brilliant all-round performance.... *56%*

⬦ **Iniquity Silver Label Batch 23** db (84) **n20 t22 f21 b21** No doubting this is a bit of a full-flavoured character, all right. But just a little too feinty for me, with not enough of the usual Iniquity magic coming through to compensate – save perhaps a massive volley of malt soon after delivery. Very much silver to their gold... *40%*

TRIA PRIMA Mount Barker, South Australia. 2018. Working

⬦ **Bruxa Rebis Release** tawny cask, cask no TP014, dist 11/18, bott 06/22 db (91) **n23** pretty pungent in a Porty kind of way, but flat also. Mainly toffee raisin...; **t23.5** typical Adelaide Hills: the delivery is stunning! Well made and for a short while intensely malty; there is a first-class wall of grape to get through. The sugars are of the Demerara variety, and these hold up against the healthy spice; **f22** strangely flat by comparison with the Port cask being just a little too domineering for too long. There is a delicate toffee note but the complexity is limited. The spices are heroically busy, though...; **b22.5** oddly enough, this is probably the most beautifully distilled of the three Adelaide Hills whiskies I tasted this year. And there is nothing wrong with the Tawny port cask. Except, perhaps, it is ultimately too dominant to allow the expected nuances to develop. But I am being a perfectionist. This is still such a lovely melt-in-the-mouth, fully flavoured whisky. Great stuff! *59.2% sc 153 bottles*

⬦ **Bruxa Traditional Release** tawny cask, batch no.2 db (92.5) **n23** placid grape with a surprisingly delicate gristiness not even hinted at in the Rebis version. Really lovely...; **t23.5** soft, intensely malty...even gristy; toffee raisin and heather honey welcome the spices; **f22.5** long, slightly bitter...but those gorgeous malty notes have decided to go nowhere; **b23.5** unlike the Shaman Traditional Release, which was like a watered down version of the Rebis, this Bruxa Traditional has entirely different landscape to the full strength version. Where that was dropping in grape, this concentrates on beautifully distilled malts with the fruit coming in a distant second. Great stuff. *46% nc ncf*

⁂ **Enchantress Rebis Release** apera cask, cask no TP028, dist 07/19, bott 07/22 db **(94) n23** one of the drier noses from an apera cask I have found for some while. This is going down the delicate route, despite its strength. It picks up the oak tones effortlessly and they land with barely a murmur...; **t23.5** pleasingly silky delivery, the grape spreading slowly across the palate, like oil landing on water. The malt remains true enough to form a firm background note until the tannins start to grab onto the ladder...; **f23.5** so impressive! Long, and here transferring to a concentrated dried grape but with an understated manuka honey thread just offering enough sweetness for balance keeping in with the toasted oak and other dusky nuances of this malt; **b24** funny how flavours trigger memories. In mid-taste, I was suddenly taken back to Speyside in about 1986 or '87 and a warehouse where we dipped into an oloroso butt and tasted a 12-year-old old Tomatin. My word, the similarity is extraordinary... *61.2% sc 148 bottles*

⁂ **Shamen Rebis Release** bourbon cask, cask no TP018, dist 12/18, bott 07/22 db **(90.5) n23** pounding barley lifted by spices and eloquent acacia honey; **t23** big, salivating lift off with a malt and vanilla core. The spices erupt in conjunction with intensifying malt. The honey hums throughout; **f22** a surprisingly glossy finish with a metallic sheen keeping guard over that lengthy malt; **b22.5** doesn't bother too much with complexity but doesn't really have to. This is all about angles, sharp ridges and intensity, which it does rather well. *61% sc 107 bottles*

⁂ **Shamen Traditional Release** bourbon cask, batch no.1 db **(86) n22 t22 f20.5 b21.5** Significantly thinner than the Rebis edition, as to be expected, with vanillas dominating, though with a dusty dryness. As on the nose, the honey appears to have been removed from this version, so a chippy, metallic theme seems to offer the balance to the momentarily intense malt. The finish is a little too flakey, though, and the oils from the cut have nowhere to hide. *46% nc ncf*

UNSPECIFIED SINGLE MALT

⁂ **Heartwood The Best of Times Cask Strength**, dist Jan 2012, bott Jul 22 **(91) n23** quite faultless sherry: the oloroso dominates while white peppers nip and bite; **t23** while the Fino struggles to make any impact on the nose, it makes a brilliant effort of sharpening the lush grapes on arrival into something far more intense and interesting about half the way through. At first the malt appears to have been sacrificed under this avalanche of salivating grape but very slowly it begins to see daylight. Meanwhile that big spice kick on the nose really kicks in immediately on impact. The sum total is rather beautiful; **f22** long, increasingly malty and with a surprising degree of butterscotch finding its voice towards the death. The spices throb, though with less malice now, while the fruit offers a shallow softness to erase a little rubbery-ness at the death; **b23** I'm thrilled to taste a malt dedicated on the bottle to Lyn Lark on the very day the mother, indeed, the Grande Dame to be, of Australian whisky at last (and way behind time) inducted into the Australian Distillers Hall of Fame. Lyn is someone once met never forgotten. Not sure I can say quite the same about this whisky. But, like Lyn, it certainly makes its mark with a rich, enveloping character. I raise a glass of this to you, Lyn: hearty congratulations! *55.1% 195 bottles*

VATTED MALT

⁂ **Tasmanian Independent Bottlers The Blend, Oat + Malt + Peat Tib, Blend 2** bott Sept 22 **(92) n23** just where are those spices coming from? Deep, almost pungent, it has to be a showering of phenols reacting most unusually with semi-aggressive tannin. The oats offer a curious viscosity to the fruit. The overall picture is one of spicy jam tarts; **t23.5** Wow! A chew-athon of an Aussie with stand-your-spoon up fruit on Derbyshire oak cake. It's the spices, though, which grab you, buffeting the taste buds with warming intent. The midpoint becomes surprisingly dry, despite some molasses, as something akin to coriander makes its mark; **f22.5** the oils burn off relatively quickly here and there is a delicate bitterness, too. Fragmented phenols hang-on as the vanilla's up their game at long last; **b23** as time goes on, I find it harder and harder to discover new nose and flavour profiles in whisky....even when blending. Well, I've certainly uncovered one here: the oats leap from the glass and make, when working in tandem with the wine casks, for a very profound statement on the palate, especially in their mouth feel. The spices have much to say for themselves, too, and in many ways steer the course of the whisky. The peat is spasmodic but makes its mark when it feels like it. A unique and deeply attractive whisky experience. *53.4% 183 bottles*

European Whisky

Jim Murray's Whisky Bible 2024	
European Whiskies of the Year By Country	
Austrian Whisky of the Year	Broger Burn Out
Belgian Whisky of the Year	Belgian Owl Intense Cask Strength Cask 7172240
Czech Whisky of the Year	Svach Old Well Czech Single Malt Lightly Peated
Danish Whisky of the Year	Mosgaard Organic Single Malt Peated Bourbon Cask
Finnish Whisky of the Year	Kyro Wood Smoke
French Whisky of the Year	Meyer's Hohwarth Blend Superieur Finition Pinot Noir
German Whisky of the Year	Feller Single Malt Torf PX Sherry Cask Strength
Italian Whisky of the Year	Retico Finest Italian Single Malt Aged 7 Years Limited Edition
Portuguese Whisky of the Year	Venakki Woodwork Rare Portuguese Cask Batch 2
Slovakian Whisky of the Year	Nestville Single Cask Virgin Oak
Slovenian Whisky of the Year	Broken Bones Single Malt Aged 4 Years Batch 1/22
Swedish Whisky of the Year	Granum Single Grain Batch 1
Swiss Whisky of the Year	Säntis Malt Single Malt Edition Dreifaltigkeit lot No 9

European Previous Winners

	European Whisky Multiple Casks	European Whisky Single Cask
2010	Santis Malt Highlander Dreifaltaigheit	Penderyn Port Wood Single Cask
2011	Mackmyra Brukswhisky	The Belgian Owl Aged 44 Months
2012	Mackmyra Moment "Urberg"	Penderyn Bourbon Matured SC
2013	Penderyn Portwood Swansea	Hicks & Healey 2004
2014	Mackmyra "Glod" (Glow)	Santis Malt Swiss Highlander
2015	English Whisky Co. Chapter 14 N.P	The Belgian Owl '64 Months'
2016	English Whisky Co. Chapter 16	Kornog Chwee'hved 14 BC
2017	English Whisky Co. Chapter 14	Langatun 6YO Pinot Noir Cask
2018	Penderyn Bryn Terfel	The Norfolk Parched
2019	Nestville Master Blender 8YO	The Norfolk Farmers
2020	Thy Whisky No. 9 Bøg Single Malt	Penderyn Single Cask no. M75-32
2021	PUNI Aura Italian Single Malt	Braeckman Single Grain Aged 12 Years
2022	Kornog St Erwan	Belgium Owl 15 Year Old
2023	Belgian Owl 11 Years Old	Mosgaard Single Malt Black Peat

AUSTRIA
BROGER PRIVATBRENNEREI Klaus. Working.

◈ **Broger Burn Out Heavily Peated Malt Whisky** bott code LBO-13 db (95) n23.5 peat just doesn't come drier and more ashen as this: highly acidic – a bit like cleaning out the peat fire in a crofter's cottage the morning after a cold night and then the soot getting up your nose. This aroma has one message and message alone...; t24 the unexpected sweetness which marches onto the palate has a powerful hickory dimension, not unlike Victory V cough sweets...and as the phenols bite it becomes a little more like Victory V joined by Fisherman's Friend sucked and chewed at the same time. There is also barley sugar at work here, too. And after that nose, that is one hell of a surprise...; f23.5 the finale remains friendly, with that marauding smoke always seemingly toping with icing sugar. Amazingly long...yet always balanced...; b24 there are peat maniacs who might gasp at the nose of this one. But they will equally gasp in amazement of how sweet it becomes on the palate by comparison with the austere, sooty dryness on the nose. In some ways quite bizarre. In all ways, rather beautiful. 42%

◈ **Broger Hoamat Gerste bott code LGE-15** db (94.5) n23 intense malt topped with custard tart; t24 the most profound maltiness imaginable. Imagine concentrated malt...concentrated again. Then a secondary layering of creamy tannin-fed vanilla infused with the shyest spice...; f23.5 only at the death does the oak move put from hiding behind the most massive malty skirt imaginable. A little welcome roughage as the spices nip and some deeper tones make their mark; b24 malt whisky at its very maltiest. The delivery is the fabric of dreams. Remarkable. 42%

◈ **Broger Hoamat Roggen** bott code LRO-16 db (89.5) n22 well-made and decent maturation evident. But the rye is most remarkable for its reticence to dominate; t22.5 the Murray Method will kick those dozing rye notes into action and ones stirred, the grain makes a sweet fist of it and, at the point of delivery, fire all its salivating guns in one huge volley. From then on the buttery vanilla sees itself as the rye's equal; f22.5 tame butterscotch with a rye sub-plot. Delightfully easy going and attractive...especially when the marzipan kicks in with the delicate spice; b22.5 a well-made, pleasant rye with some characterful phrases especially early on. But maybe a tad disappointing as the vanilla off the oak has over-dominated the grain somewhat, certainly by comparison to their spectacular malt version. Murray Method essential for most rewarding results. 42%

◈ **Broger Hoamat Weizen** bott code LWZ-15 db (89) n22.5 some of that nip on the lemon blossom honey and bread rather suggests wheat...; t22.5 layered marzipan over an oily spiciness; f22 lashing of vanilla and butterscotch. The black pepper is still bubbling away. Loses a mark for a little late bitterness off the oak; b22 some weizen whiskies shout very loudly and beat their chests. Then you find one like this, just quietly going about its business but still offering. Peppery sting. Get the feeling this is a whisky asking perhaps to be let loose at something above 42%. 42%

◈ **Broger Jubiliaums Edition 30 Jahr Brennerei 15 Jahre Whisky** bott code LJU-23 db (94.5) n24 if I had 50 madeira casks ahead of me, still sloshing about with their very finest wine and I had to pick one...it'd be something that nosed rather like this. Half a point lost because there is an atom or two of sulphur, but most central Europeans would never find that in a million years. But that layering of grape and black pepper, all reinforced with sturdy oak....just wow! t24 it's not just the purity and dexterity of the grape – which at once is eye-wateringly tart, sweet and lush – it is the oaky nuances on the deeper layers below, giving the perfect balancing dryness to the huge juiciness. And the variable intensities of the spices, seemingly blowing hot and cold. I have consumed many an enormously flavoured Melton Hunt cakes with less fruitiness on display than this...; f23 there was almost an inevitability there would be a light sulphur niggle on this. But such is the continued richness of the fruitcake on hand, the blemish is only a minor one...; b23.5 if this was only a matter of high-quality Madeira which is bouncing out of the glass, the score would be high, but not this high. What makes this so special is the proud richness of the tannin from which the fruit makes is heady, spicy dustbowl. Penderyn-like in its Madeira-emblazoned glory... 46%

◈ **Broger Medium Smoked Rauchmalz-Whisky** bott code LMS-13 db (91.5) n23.5 this is as delicate and layered as the Burn Out is uncompromisingly one-dimensional and in your face. The smoke this time lacks acidity and plays the role of chaperone to the gentle vanillas rather than a guard determined to keep them out...; t23 if this were a plane landing, you wouldn't feel the touch down, let alone a bounce. Effortlessly delicate despite the width of the spectrum of smoke, which ranges from dry and precise, to silky sweet and anchoring. There is even a curious, palate-cleansing citrus note blowing through, before the creamy hickory arrives; f22 a very quiet finale. The oils have congregated now. A light milky praline note is caressed by the remaining genteel smoke...; b23 I nosed this side by side Burn Out to gauge the variance in smoking levels. By comparison this is slightly nearer light than medium but there are still phenols enough to ensure that weight and depth are maintained throughout. What you don't get is the almost insane variance between sweet and dry, the sugars here much more of a muscovado style, this generating a light fruity note through the piece. Delightful. 42%

DESTILLERIE WEIDENAUER

Weidenauer Dinkel Whisky code L13 db **(91.5) n23** the spices buzz in early for this intensely wheaty nose. Just love that non-committal sweetness; **t23** mind-bogglingly intense delivery, and no letting up, even as the sugars and vanillas come out to play. This grain specialises in concentrated form...and here it is super-concentrated...; **f22.5** superb layering between the grain and the oak. As on the nose, the sweetness is almost disguised. Digestive biscuit-like...without the chocolate...; **b23** perhaps of all Europe's distilleries, you can trust this one to extract every last atom of flavour from its grain...especially the rarer ones. The oils give this an unusual tenderness, too. Worth finding for experiencing something very different....and as authentically Austrian as a Wiener schnitzel... 42%

Weidenauer Dinkelwhisky Oloroso Sherryfass 4 Jahre code L2013 db **(84) n22 t22.5 f18.5 b21** Something is lost in translation here, I think. I suspect that this is a 9-year-old whisky in which the last four years were spent in a first fill sherry cask. This is pretty easy going at first but then the wine seems determined to stamp its authority over every aspect of the whisky, like an over-assertive bride's mother issuing must-be-obeyed orders about a forthcoming wedding reception. For some, that leaves a bitter taste in the mouth. And so it does here as a little too much sulphur creeps in. 44%

Weidenauer Dinkelmalz Pedro Ximenes code L13 100% dinkel 2/3 malzdb 3 years PX finish **(94) n23** hardly a subtle arrival by the wine, which is at its grapiest and the oak at its most persuasive. Excellent, drier, spiced up notes, too. Well balanced with the malted spelt just about holding its own; **t23.5** thick enough to stir with a spoon. The grape exudes all the PX characteristics you could imagine, especially its viscosity.... but the spices are so quick off the blocks, they almost take your breath away. The sweetness is pretty profound, too, considering the age. This is juicy from the off and unnervingly sure-footed...; **f23** ahh...some lovely chocolate arrives from nowhere. Anyone who remembers and had a tooth for Payne's Chocolate Raisin Poppets will be a very happy whisky drinker by now...; **b24** malted spelt grain maturing in a PX cask. Not something one happens upon every day. My natural, Pavlovian instincts were to fear the worst. But the sherry cask proves not just to be clean but of exceptional quality, so the malt comes out unscathed. And anyone tasting this will have had their whisky knowledge broadened...myself included. One of the best PX-led whiskies I have tasted for a year or two. 44%

Weidenauer Hafer Whisky Single Malt code L11 db **(86.5) n21 t22.5 f21.5 b21.5** Their oak whisky is the speciality of the house. Here, though, it's not quite as on song as usual. The cut is a little wider than normal, resulting in a loss of complexity and balance. Absolutely no faulting the startingly tart oat delivery which leaves your hairs standing on end, though. 42%

Weidenauer Hafermalz 10 Jahre code L12 first fill kleines sherryfass db **(85.5) n21.5 t22 f20.5 b21.5** The mix of slight feintiness and eye-watering grape on the palate means this never quite settles down and gels as it should. 42%

Weidenauer Hafer Whisky code L11 db **(94.5) n24** the clarity of the cut here does as much for the tannin as it does the oat. Big mix of toasted (and slightly burnt) yam, black pepper and golden-syrup-laced porridge makes this the best nose of my day. And certainly the most unique...; **t23.5** the golden syrup wasn't a mirage: it is the first to settle, though creamy oats are not far behind. The tannin filter through in shimmering layers; **f23** light oils carry the oats far further than they first seemed capable of going. The syrup and spice create a complimentary duet while those tannins yield both drier elements and tangy, toastier ones. It is all very well matched...; **b24** my word! That's much more like it. Beautifully distilled and old enough to ensure that the tannins ramp up maximum complexity...!!! This is the one I'll be having a little glass of at the end of my very long tasting day... 42%

Weidenauer Hafer Whisky Tawny Port Finish code L97-02 db **(96) n24** beguiling. If you can tell me which of the oats, the tannin or the grape holds sway, then you are a better man (or woman) than I. This is layering almost at its ultimate, with the chattering spices the warmed icing on the cake...; **t24** a whisky so old and so fragile. Of course, there is a rich, spiced fruitcake feel to this...a kind of oaty Melton Hunt Cake. But this goes very much deeper thanks to the pulsing flavour profile of the varying ingredients shining and then vanishing. Underpinning all this is a shadowy, but telling, layer of molasses. Genius...; **f24** long, lingering, the fruit now entering fried date territory, the tannins mixing between butterscotch and mocha, the oats being...well oats... again mixing with the remaining molasses; **b24** after two disappointing sherry Weidenauers, I decided to turn to any Port in a storm. And this Tawny did the trick: it is, frankly, sensational. The 1997 whisky – from roughly the first time I visited the distillery – shows remarkable depth. This whisky is a lesson in layering. It is almost mesmeric, the way in which the grain, the fruit and tannin seem to take turns in dominance and then simply blend together for a few moments of intensity before the process starts again. And, remarkably, it applies to both the nose as well as palate. This is one of the great whiskies of the year and in the running for a European gong at least. Sublime. And improbably complex. 46%

Weidenauer Hafer-Dinkel Malt Whisky Blend Pedro Ximenes Finish 10 Jahre code 2012 db (85) n21.5 t22.5 f20 b21 Wonderfully busy and luxuriating arrival on the palate, the PX obviously fattening up the beast. But both nose and finish tend towards dullness and not of the usual Weidenauer excellence. A little dirty on the finish, too. 44%

Weidenauer Special Dark Hafer-Dinkel Fasstarke Sheeryfass code 2013 100% malz db (87) n20 t23.5 f21.5 b22 At cask strength this really accelerates on the palate into something quite enormous. The nose is a mess, threatening disruption down the line, but the bits it gets right are staggering. By far the most chocolate imbued of all Weidenauer's whiskies, and when the grape gets going, it feels like a like a spiced, molten Mars bar chockful of raisins and sultanas. Definitely a bipolar whisky. 53.4%

DACHSTEIN DESTILLERIE Radstadt. Working

Mandlberggut Rock Whisky Single Malt 5 Years db (91) n22.5 supremely clean with the unmolested barley sparkling on the nose; t23 gorgeously creamy delivery, the barley whipped into a paste with a delightful walnut fondant accompaniment; f22.5 impressive finish. Long, with textbook bitter-dry interplay. A sharp, salivating late fruit note probably has more to do with a burst of fresh tannin; b23 the feintiness which dogged this distillery is nowhere to be seen here in an exhibition of outstanding distilling. All the flavour profiles – and there are many in this complex malt – are not overburdened by unwelcome oils. Juicy and fulfilling. 41.1%

DESTILLERIE FARTHOFER Öhling. Working.

◇ **Farthofer Bio-Gerste 2018 Single Malt** db (90.5) n22.5 sumptuously rich nose on two levels, offering both spotted dog and plum pudding. Delicate spices and well-mannered malts wait their turns for recognition...; t23.5 that is just one magnificent delivery! Gorgeous cream sherry type mouthfeel carries on with heather honey and grape in thickish form. Some hefty oils off the cut have contributed. The spices tickle gently; f22 the oils from the daring cut gather now and the bite confirms this...; b22.5 a very brave piece of distilling has paid off here where the hint of feints have combined with the fruit to make a large and ultimately rich malt. This could have gone either way... but this has definitely ended up on the right side of delicious...! 43% ncf 500 bottles

◇ **Farthofer Bio-Mais 2017 Single Grain** cask LbMW117 db (89) n22 big and brooding. This looks like a moody whisky, thick in oil and rich in corn. The oak is refusing to be ignored, as well, so the spices nibble from behind the dark tannins; t23 the usual wide cut again and once more the flavours not only hitch a ride but manage to up their game in the process. The corn offers its own oils, and these enjoy a lovely fruit-inspired ulmo honey sweetness, sharpened significantly by the fizzing spice; f22 chewy with multi-oak components adding further weight to the selected feints. Lots of vanilla on display late on; b22 wow! These days Farthofer are really specialising in full-on flavour and this type of corn whisky is adorned with countless honey and spice tones. Still would love to see them get those feints down a tad to do the whisky full justice.... 43% sc ncf

◇ **Farthofer Braugerste 2014** db (92.5) n22.5 you really do get pears (one of my favourite fruits) on the nose of this. Usual tannins and spices...but those pears!!! t23.5 house style enormity. And very much its thumbprint pears at work, incredibly overripe ones which explode with juice which runs down your hand when you bite into it: that kind of juice...; f23 this is where the complexity kicks in. Again, another house style with the spices deep and busy with a tannin rumble. The very vaguest hint of something feinty but doing no damage. Retains a salivating character until pretty late on; b23.5 another Farthofer whisky you can stand your spoon in. The pear wine casks used in this whisky is unique to Farthofer distillery and here that particular fruit is on full display to give the whisky a truly unique style. Indeed, there is enough pear here for a partridge to hide in... Must admit, just love it! And probably at its best at room temperature. 43%

DISTILLERY ZWEIGER Mooskirchen. Working.

Zweiger Smoked Prisoner bott code SH/L0601/17 db (89) n22 t22 f22.5 b22.5 Probably not the whisky of choice for officials of the European Court of Human Rights. 44%.

EDELBRENNEREI FRANZ KOSTENZER Maurach, Working.

Selektion Franz Single Malt 6-Year-Old batch no. L2/2013, db (90) n23 t23 f21.5 b22.5 Wonderful to have a glass of whisky from a distillery I haven't tasted for a year or two. I've missed their wonderfully distinctive style. Though I have to say the distillate now is of higher quality than it once was, with the cuts doing far more favours. 52.2%

KUENZ NATURBRENNEREI Gödnach. Working

◇ **Rauchkofel Single Malt Sherry Cask Finished Batch IX** db (89) n22 little scraps and hints of gooseberry and grape, but a slightly wide cut does drown the more subtle tones; t23 brilliantly mouth-watering start with no little honeydew melon getting in on the act. Big malt surge, but again the oils interfere towards the finish; f21.5 just a little bitterness amid the stewed gooseberry and vanilla; b22.5 so many things to enjoy here, the delivery in particular. A little cleaner spirit would have made a huge difference to what would have been an elegant and charming malt: when a whisky goes for this amount of delicacy the cuts have to be on the mark. However, a distillery obviously capable of excellence: I look forward to their next bottlings. *43% 1932 bottles*

⬩ **Rauchkofel Single Malt Port Cask Finished Batch III** db (93) n23 a pithy fruitiness makes for an overall dry nose, especially when the chalky vanillas start to make themselves heard; t23.5 doesn't hang around reaching a crescendo: the fruit is out of the traps in nanoseconds and combines with the salivating barley to ensure there is a depth to the screeching fruit. From that moment we are in slow descent, the spices leading the way as the oak dovetails at first equally with the grape before taking control...; f23 ticks all the right boxes; b23.5 so beautifully made. Hard to expect much more from a Port cask finish with the fruit making a mountain of a delivery before making way for subtlety. Impressive for so many reasons. *49.1% 452 bottles*

LAVA BRÄU Feldbach. Working.

⬩ **Bio Brisky Lava Bräu Single Malt Eiche Rum Fass Jg 2015** bott code: H 4 15 db (91.5) n22.5 t23 f23 b23 So unusual for a rum cask. None of the firmness and cult de sacs a rum cask can often bring you. But lots of fruit and gentle grist. What a joy of a dram... 40.8%.

Brisky Lava Bräu Single Malt Eiche JG 2007 bott code: B 04 07 db (87) n21.5 t22.5 f21.5 b22 the wide cut has generated a moist gingerbread persona to this – slightly so on the spiced nose but especially to the finish. Thick, weighty, chewy and salivating and not afraid to get the oils working, too. 40.1%.

Genesis Rare Cask Single Malt JG 2012 bott code: H 3 12 db (90.5) n23.5 t23 f21.5 b22.5 I have met many a distiller in Kentucky who comes from German stock. This single malt appears someone has decided to take the return ticket. 47.2%.

LEBE & GENIESSE Lagenrohr. Working

⬩ **Bodding Lokn Single Malt Special Edition Single Cask**, fassnr.22, dist 2017, bott 2022 db (86.5) n20.5 t22 f22 b22 There is no escaping the feint on the nose – unusual for this distillery – though the uniquely bitter-sweet punch to the malt and oak does last out to make amends. Most intriguingly, about halfway through there is a squirt of passionfruit liqueur, complete with plain chocolate. Brief and distinctive it sets the taste buds on full alert. Though winning no awards technically, the later entertainment value remains high. 47%

⬩ **Bodding Lokn Single Malt Double Cask Sherry Finish**, fassnr.18, dist 2016, bott 2022 db (89.5) n23 almost ridiculously intense barley: the oils are thick, as are the sugared grape, and have intensified further to make a barley porridge of a nose. Overtly sweet but the vanillas play an interesting drying game...; t22.5 even more thick and lush on delivery than the nose – and I wasn't sure that was possible. Again, the malt has been caught up in the intense oil and toffee-raisin theme, with the spices becoming increasingly busy and warm; f21.5 just a tad over oily now with a slightly bitter, cloying fade. Again, the malt is everywhere; b22.5 Wow! This is a heavy duty single malt where both the oils from the cut and the syrupy sugars off the grape try to stifle growth. Both fail, thankfully, allowing some complex depth to win through. 46%

⬩ **Bodding Lokn Single Malt Single Cask Classic**, fassnr.17, dist 2018, bott 2022 db (90.5) n22.5 beautifully toasty and almost smoky in its depth but lightened by a lemon curd sweetness; t23 exceptionally firm and becomes far more approachable when the Murray Method has maximised the oils. Then the vanillas begin to kick in, alongside a salivating malt and citrus double bill. The spices tingle; f22.5 dries appreciably, allowing the cocoa to take command. The spices stay busy; b22.5 quite a young brute when samples cool. But changes character dramatically – and very much for the better – once warmed. Limited complexity, but what there is, is carried out impressively. 43%

MARILLENHOF DESTILLERIE KAUSL Mühldorf. Working.

Wachauer Whisky M43 Double Oak bott code L:WD01 db (80.5) n21 t21.5 f19 b19 This is the 1,137th whisky I have tasted for the 2020 Bible, but none of the previous 1,136 have given me quite the shock this has done. I cannot say exactly what kind of oak this has been in, other than to admit that I would not be surprised if one was a vat of cough syrup. Well, it certainly made me cough... There appears to be a huge, bitter, tannin kick, as well as sweet cherry juice. But you just can't get away from the cough mixture. A whisky to be taken three times a day after meals... 43%.

PETER AFFENZELLER Alberndorf in der Riedmark. Working.

Peter Affenzeller Blend dist 2011, bott code: L-1117105 db (89.5) n21.5 t22 f23 b23 A whisky with no backbone whatsoever. Softer than any bathroom essential that people have been fighting for all over the world. While there might be a slight vegetable note on the nose, the array of syrupy sugars on delivery and beyond make the aroma an irrelevance. 42%.

Peter Affenzeller Single Malt 6 Years Old bott code: L-1903207 db (92) n22 t23.5 f23 b23.5 One of those unusual whiskies where the nose puts you on your guard, but the overall performance simply seduces you. 42%.

PFANNER Vorarlberg. Working.

Pfanner Single Malt Single Barrel 2011 first fill sherry oak cask, cask no. 5, dist 16 Jun 11, bott 09 Oct 17 db (93.5) n23 t23.5 f23 b23.5 Delightful whisky benefitting from an entirely clean sherry cask. 56.2%. sc. 412 bottles.

REISETBAUER Axberg, Thening. Working.

Reisetbauer 15 Year Old Single Cask Single Malt Whisky dist 2001 db (86.5) n20 t21.5 f23 b22 From the earliest days of this distillery, the technical flaws of the distillate are obvious. However, the malt has reacted favourably with some high class oak. The result is a whisky that grows in confidence as it goes along, like the girl who thought she was too plain to go to the ball, only to find she was as pretty as many. Late on the mix of chocolate nougat and treacle tart is rather compelling and worthy of drinking from a glass shoe.... 48%. sc. 500 bottles.

WALD4TLER GRANIT-DESTILLLERIE Hollenbach. Working.

Mayer Granit Moar Whisky Gluatnest Torfrauh-Gerstenmalz bott code: L/15 db (88.5) n22 t22 f22.5 b22 One of those typically central European tight peated malt whiskies. Absolutely no give on this one, either on the nose or the palate: this is rock hard and rather than gently spreading the smoke around seems intent on giving you a prescribed dose of it. That said, impossible not to enjoy, especially when the molasses melt and feel it safe to come out and play. 44%.

Mayer Granit Whisky Goldader Dinkelmalz bott code: L/13 db (92) n22 t23.5 f23 b23.5 You are left nodding your head with approval at this one. A real touch of Austrian aristocracy at play. 44%.

Mayer Granit Whisky W4 Blended bott code: L/15 db (88) n21.5 t22.5 f22 b22 Light and fully entertaining, the cut is cleaner and its personality relaxed, allowing a gentle meandering of acacia honey and ginger to add sweetness and warmth in just-so quantities. Enjoyable. 42%.

WHISKY-DESTILLERIE J. HAIDER Roggenreith. Working.

◇ **JH Dark Rye Malt 6 Jahre** gelagert 100% roggenmaltz, dunkel gerostet bott code L215 db (87) n21 t22.5 f21.5 b22 Well, the nose might be a bit squiffy and warped. But there is no doubting the trademark J Haider flavour explosion on delivery. Here, though, we have much more oak making an impact than its older Rare Dark Rye brother. The tannins stabilise the over-zealous oils from the cut, the rye coming through as an insurance policy to keep those flavours rolling. By no means technically perfect, as evidenced by the nose and finish, but so typically for a Haider, there is no skimping on the bigger flavours. 41%

◇ **JH Rare Dark Rye Malt 8 Jahre** 100% roggenmaltz, dunkel gerostet bott code L2R14 db (90) n21.5 a little nougat – plus a hint of a milk chocolate side dish - tries but fails to contain the vigorous grain...; t23.5 kaboom! It's blast off for the rye for the moment it impacts on the palate. Both sharp and biting and also, thanks to the oils, fruitier and soothing. There is a hint of nougat still, though now surrounded by a light layer of minty chocolate; f22.5 very long. The rye has a much juicier disposition now. But that lovely chocolate mint remains...; b22.5 where I am sitting to taste this is about 10 yards from the very spot a German V2 rocket landed during the Second World War, causing a rather big hole in the ground. I doubt if the explosion caused that day was much larger than the flavour explosion once those ryes went to town on the palate. When it comes to uncompromising flavours, Haider is the distillery.... 46%

◇ **JH Rare Single Malt & Jahre** 100% gerstenmaltz, dunkel gerostet bott code L4R14 db (92) n22.5 the malt and oak are pretty equally matched. However, it is the oak which is providing the warmer notes for a freezing early August day...; t24 the house style oils are much reduced here, allowing the barley sugar to build and intensify almost linearly. For the inevitable JH crescendo, we are talking concentrated Maltese candy...; and we are talking sheer deliciousness...; f23 the fact the still intense malt is flanked by spicy oak really makes this a bigger and weightier experience than you might first have expected. The final strains are recognisable chocolate mint; b23.5 technically, in a different – far higher - league than their rye bottlings. Much cleaner distillate off the still and the malt intensifies to levels that hit unadulterated magnificence. Late on even the house stye of chocolate mint has infused into the fun. 46%

Waldviertler Original Rye 8 Jahre roggen/gerstenmalz db (90) n22.5 proud, clean rye singing its usual crisp song, even with a touch of lavender; t23 the grain is intense on landing and pings out a salivating volley. The tannins are close behind and towards the middle they meet for a juicy, spicy and honeyed hug; **f22** just dries and bitters slightly as the oils gather; **b22.5** an unmistakable style from Austria's kings of crystalline rye. 41%

Waldviertler Original Rye 15 Jahre roggen/gerstenmalz db **(94) n23** on similar lines to the 8-years old, though now the lavender has blossomed into menthol; delightfully crisp and intense: there are distilleries in Kentucky who would be proud to sport a nose like this to their rye; **t24** so brilliantly well rounded is this, there even appears to be a degree of smokiness ensuring softness. It might just be a trick of the casks but there is no mistaking the sheer nakedness of the rye when that powers through **f23** a wonderful flotilla of spices and other classy oaky tones. The rye, of course, is still hanging around...as is that mystery smokiness; **b23.5** the great Waldviertler distillery at its very best. Hugely flavoursome, and every flavour hits the bullseye. 46%

Waldviertler Rye Malt 15 Jahre 100% roggenmalz db **(95) n23.5** initially, a rare case of the almost bourbon-like tannins outflanking a malted rye. Though the rye regrouping and saving something striking to say about that as the nose progresses. Wonderfully clean and concentrated once that rye gets going: this has been perfectly distilled; **t24** so many layers of grain, where do you start counting? Rye revealing itself like so many petticoats. But together they grow into something sharp and statement-making; **f23.5** stupendous chocolate joins in the rye-rich fun. The oaky spices hang around, too...; **b24** if a whisky was built for the Murray Method, this was it. I created at least five very different versions of this whisky through subtle warming. The difference in oak to rye ratio is breath-taking. I prefer the midpoint when they are evenly matched, but the moment those ryes are in control has all the makings of a winner. Magnificent distillation. 46%

Waldviertler Rare Blended Malt 6 Jahre db **(91) n22.5 t23 f22.5 b23** The fruit is unmistakable – and at times has a distinct grapefruit juice feel, especially on the nose. Clean, cleansing, sweet and most un-Waldviertler-like, save perhaps the fruit and chocolate finish wrapped in growing oils. 46%

Waldviertler Blended Malt 7 Jahre db **(86.6) n21.5 t23 f21 b21** A typically charming and mouth-watering ending from this distillery. Lacking in its usual weight and passion, perhaps, the nose is a little untidy with a curious smokiness. While that doesn't quite work on the nose, it adds a binding sweetness to the overall performance on the palate. The finish, however, is also on the tangy, uneven side. 42%

Waldviertler Dark Single Peated 10 Jahre db **(92) n23** Peat. With all kinds of craggy peaks...; **t23** a much more inclusive delivery (did I just say "inclusive"? How appallingly Woke of me...wash my mouth out...) with molasses and barley working in tandem to forge a delicious framework. Then the smoke muscles in, a little more gently and kindly than the nose makes it appear capable of; **f22.5** gorgeous mocha works brilliantly with that peat which has now reverted to type and positively hisses at you with intensity; **b23.5** the last whisky from them I unpacked... and it certainly explains now why I may have been getting a degree of smokiness on a couple of their other whiskies. There are swan-like Islay-style whiskies which drift effortless and gracefully around the palate. And then there are clunky ones, acidic and spitting with frizzled intent. This is proudly one of the latter. 46%

BELGIUM
THE BASSETS CRAFT DISTILLERY Rulselede

The Bassets Craft Distillery Good Old Charles Collection Peated Cask Single Malt Release 1 Oct 2023 db **(91.5) n22.5** although peated, the first note to strike home is a fresh apple/pithy tone, with the phenols very much coming second; **t23.5** a much better integrated delivery. The smoke is upfront here, ensuring the softest possible landing for those fruitier outlines which set the tastebuds salivating. The malt is also an intense presence: no great age and merrily adding to the fruit's ability to salivate; **f22.5** a much thinner finale with the smoke ganging up towards the end as those apple notes, now bathed in vanillas, still have their say; **b23** the first time I've encountered this Belgian distillery and I'm impressed. Well-made distillate with a slightly unusual personality, but when it gets into its stride a big and memorable one. I hope they can keep this standard going – and improve upon it in time – over the forthcoming years. 46%

The Bassets Craft Distillery Good Old Charles Collection Peated Cask Single Malt Release 2 Nov 2023 db **(93) n23** wow! The tannin has muscled in bigtime here to set up camp with that fruit and now much peatier smoke. Not only big, but pretty sexy and enticing, too...; **t23.5** this is every bit as big on landing as the nose promises. The smoke has not throttled back in any way and lands its punches cleanly and unmistakably. Even better, there is enough smoke to spare to join forces with that lurking fruit to ensure intensity levels start to climb off the scales.... especially with all those oak splinters around. Oh, and all this done with the softest mouth feel imaginable...; **f23** the smoke recedes and spices move forward...warmingly...; **b23.5** well, that improvement has already started. This is a denser, more complex whisky than Release 1 and certainly makes the most of both the smoke and tannins. Delicious. Just a pity it is not at cask strength. Now what a journey that would have been.... 46%

◈ **The Bassets Craft Distillery Good Old Charles Collection Cognac Cask Finish Single Cask Malt Okt 2023** db (89.5) n22.5 mesquite...? Surely not! Certainly some kind of phenolic occurrence here of a sweet and acidic kind, though the firm sugary band offered by the Cognac cask - acting like a rum one – ensures a countering crispness to the quicksand-like softness which otherwise envelops the nose; t23 this is an incredibly sweet and friendly single malt, the barley sugars and molasses uniting with an over-sugared, burnt raisin fruitcake...; f22 you can guarantee that when the main thrust of a whisky is sweet, the finish, as the sugars burn out, will be quite bitter by comparison. And so it proves...; b22 forget the Cognac Cask finish. I thought for a moment that I wasn't in Belgium tasting the European whiskies, but in Kentucky working on the mesquite smoked concerns. A remarkable, massively tasty if not always perfectly-balanced malt. 46%

◈ **The Bassets Craft Distillery Good Old Charles Collection Pedro Ximenez Sherry Wood Finish Nov 2023** db (84.5) n19 t22 f21.5 b22 I'll say this for the PX cask: not an atom of sulphur, absolutely highest quality and does a great job glossing over what the nose suggests was far from excellent distillate. I may be wrong, but I'd take a guess and say this was one of their earlier distillations when the odd mistake on the cuts was made. The PX has carried a magnificent recovery job. 48%

◈ **The Bassets Craft Distillery Cigar Malt Release 2023** bourbon cask finish Nov 2023 db (94.5) n23 that diced apple note appear to have become a bit of a signature of this distillery. As does the rich tannin involvement. Here, though, we all have honey, too, of the acacia variety, which is ensuring a deft sweetness as well as varied spices. Sure, I got the odd phenol atom or two drifting about like fine rain on the wind....; t24 some malts simply melt on the palate...and here is one of them. An absolute spitting image of the nose, the honey is key here as it binds the maltiness into that gathering tannin-led vanilla. Again, a little smoke drifts about. Ridiculous but wonderful amounts of bourbon liquorice fill the palate; f23.5 some delightful oils ensure depth and now the honey has absorbed some heftier tones and moved towards a waxy heather honey style which pitches its tent right up against the far more assertive spice; b24 again we are seeing some fabulous whisky out of Belgium. This really is a delight and if you want to ruin the complex brilliance of this whisky by puffing a cigar against it and destroying those precision-tooled points of balance and counter-balance then, well... that's your choice. A distillery that, should they concentrate more on whisky, will doubtless be giving Belgium Owl and Braeckman a good chasing over the forthcoming years. What fun! 50%

THE BELGIAN OWL Grâce-Hollogne. Working.

◈ **Belgian Owl Identity Aged for 36-41 Months** bott code LJ036048 db (92.5) n23 textbook Belgian Owl nose, ensuring that the citrussy/bordering on exotic fruit is at the forefront of all the activity. Fragile, even by this distillery's own delicate standards; t23.5 clean but curiously intense malt joins forces with the oak in nanoseconds to ensure maximum weight. The simplistic sugars are gristy and juicy and helped along with some confident oils; f22.5 just a shadow of bitterness off an oak cask here, though this does move towards a lightly spiced cocoa tone by the very end. The malt mingles still with the vanillas; b23.5 it is hard to imagine how a malt whisky can be so gossamer light yet mouth-filling all at the very same moment. Complex, salivating and intricate throughout. 46% nc ncf

◈ **Belgian Owl Evolution Aged for 48-59 Months** bott code LJ048044 db (94) n23 some of that spice nibble wouldn't be out of place in Kentucky... The tannins are heady without being overly heady. For a while I thought the citrus was missing...but late on spotted the grapefruit; t23.5 fat and chewy from the get-go, like on the nose it is the spice which springs into action earliest and with greatest intent. As the oak calms the malt begins to make very confident inroads, momentarily upping the juiciness...; f23.5 fabulous finale with spices galore and a glorious mocha thread; b24 outstanding balance here with some big players but none dominating – well not at least for a significant time. At some time or other either the oak, the barley, the spices or the mocha is in control but never long enough to make for oversimplification. The only thing missing is a dominance in the citrus-fruity department...a marginally extra dose of oak has seen to that. 46%

◈ **Belgian Owl Passion Aged for 42-47 Months** cask no 7172215 db (89) n22 as quiet as I have known any BO to be: clean, but a dull cloud of toffee and malt; t22.5 repeats the dose on the nose. But at the midpoint finds a charge of copper which briefly sharpens and salivates; f22 returns to its earlier quiet ways, though with a pinch of spice now...; b22.5 this is about as docile as this particular owl ever gets. The dominating factor is caramel which forms a friendly layer on top of the malt for an enjoyable but strictly non-taxing experience. 46% sc nc ncf

◈ **Belgian Owl Passion Aged for 42-47 Months** cask no 7172216 db (93) n23 a more pronounced nose than 215 with the barley certainly displaying a cutting edge; t23.5 immediately salivating as the barley really makes a song and dance on delivery. The midground sees the oak slowly assert itself with some sweet butterscotch tart; **f23** excellent spices warms the palate. Even slightly nutty on the fade; **b23.5** the understated excellence continues. *46% sc nc ncf*

◈ **Belgian Owl Passion Aged for 42-47 Months** cask no 7172217 db **(95) n23.5** superb layering with the oak tones found on two levels: the first is mid-depth and beautifully anchors the singing malt. The second proffers a degree of hazelnut and vanilla for surround sound; **t24** the silkiness of the oils combining with the stark nudity of the malt is breath-taking: incredibly mouth-filling and salivating with that busy oak up front earlier to ensure oscillating spices give a beat to the rhythm of the flavour development; **f23.5** improbably sweet, thanks mainly to the intense late gristiness capturing the friendlier elements of the vanilla. The layering of waxy, ulmo honey guarantees a long and pleasing finish; **b24** this really is malt whisky at its most entertaining. The varied styles of sweetness, when tempered by those precise spices make for a whisky to be enjoyed when the lights are low and you want to spend a good half hour giving your tastebuds an evening to remember... *46% sc nc ncf*

◈ **Belgian Owl Passion Aged for 42-47 Months** cask no 7172218 db **(90.5) n23** the oak for once blots out the majority of the barley's charms; **t23** this is principally about the mouth feel: the oils are just-so, ensuring a sugary coating which at first brandishes the barley and copper and then some bittering spice; **f22** still a little bitter at the death. The malt has cast off the shadow of the oak as displayed on the nose, though there is a fruit pastry finale...sans fruit; **b22.5** a bit of a garbled malt which can't make up its mind as to where it exactly wants to go. But some of the little byways it finds are quite charming. *46% sc nc ncf*

◈ **Belgian Owl Passion Aged for 42-47 Months** cask no 7172219 db **(95) n23.5** hugely intense malt...; **t24** insanely intense malt (with a bewildering proliferation of sugary gristy tones); **f23.5** ...back to hugely intense malt...and relax...; **b24** one of the maltiest whiskies I have tasted for a very long time. A kind of a Tomatin meets Glen Moray...with knobs on.... Oh, oils, spices, light copper involvement, ulmo honey.... all in near perfect qualities. A bit of a freak. And a bottle which if you see...grab it! *46% sc nc ncf*

◈ **Belgian Owl Passion Aged for 42-47 Months** cask no 7172220 db **(92.5) n23** an aroma that is no stranger to an early morning bakery, just after the pastries have left the oven...; **t23.5** the layering of the malt works well with the intermittent involvement of the spices. The oak ensures a degree of biscuit-like solidity...; **f23** some outstanding gristy sugars meets high grade marzipan. Still the oils and malt thrive.... the dryness of the very last embers are a tad unusual...; **b23** a comfortable whisky doing all within its power to offer an even and gentle experience. despite a degree of spicy involvement, it succeeds... *46% sc nc ncf*

◈ **Belgian Owl Vintage No 08 First Fill Bourbon Cask 11 Years** cask no 4712312 db **(94) n23** the oddest thing about this is that despite its eleven years, despite the indefatigable maltiness, there is also a green apple effect which renders the nose less than half the age it actually is: a kind of Peter Pan aroma...; **t23.5** concentrated malt...in concentrate. Wow! What a delivery that is: the oils are borderline thick, the spices are borderline steaming, the sugars are borderline honey. The apple aroma on the nose plays some part here, too, as the silky maltiness displays a sharp fruity edge; **f23.5** so much spice, but so evenly balanced between the oaky and malty factions. Salivating even to the very last...; **b24** the first thing that flicks through my mind is that this would have been far better had it been bottled at cask strength, as it is obviously that even at 46% some of the tannins have been pulled apart by reduction and become drier than they might have been. But I'm being a perfectionist. This still has a whole legion of things going on that makes not just for tasty tasting, but a fascinating encounter, too. *46% nc ncf 400 bottles*

◈ **Belgian Owl Thematic Series: Coffee 5 Years** coffee spirit cask finish nbc db **(94.5) n23.5** a fascinating nose: weighty and mildly earthy without any phenolic interference. The malt and oak are pretty much bound together and in harmony. Neither sweet nor dry, what sweetness does waft through is of an unusual but highly attractive milky molasses variety; **t24** the mouth feel is perfection on delivery. An oily chap which spreads and hugs every contour of the palate; a lackadaisical maltiness...and then, suddenly, something very different: an explosion of Demerara sugar and intense spice, the blast neutered by a silky, milky Brazilian middle roast coffee note. It's the subtlety of this development which really wins you over; **f23.5** just a hint of bitterness. But those sugars work hard to correct the balance. The elegant, teasingly indistinct coffee wafer biscuit note very late on melts perfectly; **b23.5** not quite the sensation created by Belgium Owl's sublime Saffron bottling last year. But certainly a malt which treats the tastebuds to a flavour profile unique in the 23,000 whiskies I have tasted for the Whisky Bible. A relaxed, satisfying and very subtle experience, indeed. *46% nc ncf 1,000 bottles*

◈ **Belgian Owl New Make Barley Spirit** bott code LI000151 db **(94) n23.5 t23.5 f23 b24** The kind of new make that is a blender's delight, as he knows that three, five, seven, ten years hence, given the right barrel, a higher than average quality whisky will be available to him. As for the whisky lover of today... well, this isn't whisky, of course. But it is a new make shewing some blistering malt intensity with a gristy sweetness heightened by just so oils and metal. Even the spices wait for their moment near the end to ensure balance. Who needs gin...? 46%

◈ **Belgian Owl Intense Cask Strength Aged for 36-60 Months** cask 7172240 db **(95.5)** n23 the oak is husky-voiced and full, certainly not shy of spice. The malt forms a thick well of moderate sweetness; t24 one of the deliveries of the year with the malt exploding into every crevice on the palate, the oils helping to coat it with a gristy sweetness. The result is salivation levels off the chart, and this only goes further into overdrive when the oak despatches the spices to cause further delicious mayhem; f24 settles down to a lovely malt and butterscotch theme, sweetened by a delicate glossy coating of demerara sugars. Some excellent oils ensure the final fade is a long time coming...; b24.5 if it is at all possible to overdose on malt, then don't take this intravenously. One of the maltiest coves it has ever been my pleasure to encounter. Oddly, the decent oak on show frames it rather beautifully and seems to concentrate the effect of the malt even more... 69% sc nc ncf

◈ **Belgian Owl Intense Cask Strength Aged for 36-60 Months** cask 7172241 db **(89.5)** n22.5 a little citrus has slipped into the barley, strangely accentuating the otherwise modest oak. The lingering sweetness of an empty biscuit barrel...; t23 sharp and salivating, there is a nip to this that has little to do with the strength and more to do with age. Very young in all its malty actions and the intensity of the gristy sugars backs this up...; f22 just a tad lazy on the finale with the oak barely bothering to complete what it started. Dry nonetheless; b22 a malt which promises much, delivers plenty but by no means all of its capabilities. Still, enjoyably zesty. 69% sc nc ncf

◈ **Belgian Owl Intense Cask Strength Aged for 36-60 Months** cask no 7172243 db **(91.5)** n22 pretty hazy caramels at work here. Mind you, intense barley is budding all around the fringes. The spice nip isn't backwards coming forwards; t23 unusually light-textured early on for a BO, the palate is cleansed initially before a slow build up begins, first of barley, then toastier oaks and finally a far friendlier form of tannin as the toffee grows into something formidable; f23.5 what a fabulous finale with the malt now spreadeagled across the palate and the butter toffee cream mixing with the oak for the kind of finish usually found in a pastry shop; b23 with no colouring added, this is a wonderful exhibition of caramels being extracted from the oak to give a softening and soothing effect. 69% sc nc ncf

◈ **Belgian Owl Intense Cask Strength Aged for 36-60 Months** cask no 7172244 db **(95)** n23 another stunner where the malt could not be more perfectly aligned with the delicate oaky tones. There are spices but this is just background noise to the prominent gristiness which offers the most delicate of sugars that appear to dissolve on the way to the nostril... So delicate and elegant...; t24 from a malt perspective, pure perfection, so this is hitting maximum salivation, too. The spices have just enough devil to ensure that the palate-hugging barley doesn't get too comfortable while the oak pounds out butterscotch tart much earlier than is the norm; f24 that unspoiled malt has staked its claim even this late on and is in no mood to give up its land. Just a slight hint of ulmo honey ensures the sweetness continues longer than it has any right; b24 I have just crumpled into a sated heap before my computer. It will be almost impossible to find a level of malt so beautifully tailored as this for the remainder of the research for this Bible. The kind of single malt I could drink all day every day. And when I say "malt" I'm really not joking...! 69% sc nc ncf

◈ **Belgian Owl Intense Cask Strength Aged for 36-60 Months** cask no 7172245 db **(93.5)** n23 this nose should be trademarked by Belgian Owl: that unique and unmistakable combination of intense malt and accommodating vanilla; t23.5 hard to imagine a whisky more salivating than this. The malt is not only in concentrated format, but it is seemingly set up to give your taste buds maximum interference. The range of the sugars are intriguing, from concentrated grist through to layered demerara and icing sugars, with the vaguest but telling hint of acacia honey; f23 long, sticky malt with. Lovely interplay of young green, grassy barley and more complex chalky vanillas; b24 there are times when tasting a Belgian Owl at cast strength is like having a bucket of freezing cold water throw into our face to bring to you to your full cognisant ability: this malt wakes up your senses like no other! 69% sc nc ncf

BIERCÉE DISTILLERY Ragnies

◈ **Witches Single Cask Whisky 5 years** Sauternes casks, bott 2023 db **(86.5)** n21.5 t21 f22 b22 Good grief! Well, I didn't expect that. A malt brimming with aggressive citrussy notes absolutely refusing to take prisoners – which is ironic because, come to think of it, my Grandfather was a prisoner of war in Belgium in WW1. They certainly have a yeasty and vaguely feinty pitch to them on the nose and the delivery is equally as unsettling...however...poof! By magic, suddenly the strangeness vanishes at around the midpoint when everything settles down for a delicious, if still unconventional meeting of barley and zesty marmalade. The spices on the finish are an unexpected bonus. Weird, certainly. But, behind the barbed wire, I bet my Grandad wouldn't have said no to a second glass... I look forward to watching how this distillery develops. *48% sc nc ncf*

BRAECKMAN GRAANSTOKERIJ Oudenaarde. Working

Braeckman Belgian Single Grain Whisky Oloroso Sherry Aged 13 Years first fill bourbon barrel, finished oloroso sherry butt, cask no. 284, dist 2007 db **(90.5)** n22.5 t23.5 f22 b22.5 This must have been finished in a first fill sherry butt...because this is just dripping in the stuff! For those who like a little whisky with their sherry...Oh, and this orgy, this white-knuckle ride of under-ripe fruit is about as far removed from their previous bottlings as could possibly be...! *60.2%. nc ncf sc. 796 bottles.*

Braeckman Belgian Single Grain Whisky Single Barrel Aged 12 Years first fill bourbon barrel, cask no. 97, dist 2007 db **(95.5)** n23 t24 f24.5 b24 The equivalent bottling was last year's European Single cask Whisky of the Year, and deservedly so. This one is also superstar status. Not quite up to the overall near perfection of last year's offering, due mainly to a slightly shy or lazy nose. But it certainly confirms that last year's winner was no fluke: this is quite brilliant in its own right. What a treat... *62.9%. nc ncf sc. 215 bottles.*

Braeckman Belgian Single Grain Whisky Single Barrel Aged 13 Years first fill bourbon barrel, cask no. 101, dist 2007 db **(92)** n23 t23.5 f22.5b23 Another beautiful whisky from Braeckman. Doesn't have the heart-stopping drama of their bottling which won the awards in last year's Bible...and there appears to have the handbrake – or do I mean handbraeck? – on. But, as you'd expect from this distillery, the charm offensive works. *64.9%. nc ncf sc. 218 bottles.*

BROUWERIJ PIRLOT Zandhoven. Working.

Kempich Vuur Single Malt Aged 3 Years Laphroaig quarter casks, cask no. L5, bott 24 Jan 17 db **(91)** n22 t23 f23 b23 Well, those quarter casks weren't wasted! What a joy of a malt! *46%. sc.*

DISTILLERIE WILDEREN Wilderen. Working.

Wild Weasel Single Cask Single Malt cask no. 37, bott 9/11/20 db **(87.5)** n21.5 t22.5 f21.5 **b22** from the very first sniff the house style kicks in with its truly unique fruity, scented aroma. The brain is in a whirr trying to work out exactly what that aroma may be...and you come to the conclusion the one and only time you have ever found it before was when nosing a Wild Weasel. Whisky, that is – not the furry alternative. Maybe there is another time I have spotted this nose – back to my childhood Christmases and dipping into the tin of Roses chocolates. There is a soft centre on the ultra-malty middle once on the palate, too... *46%. nc ncf sc*

Wild Weasel Single Malt Red Port Cask Finish dist May 2014, bott 9/11/20, cask no. 36 db **(88)** n21.5 t22.5 f22 b22 Big and spicey with some mean tannin at work here. But doesn't quite work as well as the White Port Cask bottling (below). The fruit is more game here, fuller and fatter while the sugars and spices are more random and less controlled. Makes a point of being as rich and full on as possible. Not a Wild Weasel to lay down and be tickled *46% nc ncf sc*

Wild Weasel Single Malt Sherry Cask Finish dist Apr 2015, bott 9/11/20, cask no. 33 db **(88)** n22 t22.5 f21.5 b22 Easily the most simplistic Weasel I've encountered yet. A safe sherry butt essentially fee from taint. But, equally, the least complex of this year's bottlings I've sampled, happy as it is to pulse a friendly, mildly fruity, lightly honeyed message. A very safe whisky. *46% nc ncf sc*

Wild Weasel Single Malt White Port Cask Finish dist May 2014, bott 9/11/20, cask no. 35 db **(92.5)** n22.5 t23.5 f23 b23.5 Good Lord! This whisky makes some statement. And the grammar and diction are superb. Not so much silky as pure ermine. Oh, and a word of warning: these peculiarly shaped, interesting and explosive bottles are not to be opened anywhere near a computer, trust me... *46% nc ncf sc*

WATERLOO DISTILLERY Waterloo. Working

◈ **Waterloo The Brancardier Single Grain** batch no II db **(88.5)** n22.5 t22 f22 b22 A "single grain", but I could swear I'm picking up malt on the nose. Alongside much lighter melon and quite a perfumy pepperiness. However, the body is perhaps a little too soft, for all its delightful vanilla, and could do with some extra weight. When the label told about how the whisky was distilled from their beer, my heart sank a little as I envisioned a distillation wrecked by hops. Delighted to report no such disaster awaited. Quite a jolly whisky which rumbles along in its own unique manner, even at times upping the juiciness levels. *40%*

◈ **Waterloo The Nurse Single Cask Grain** batch no II db **(93)** n23.5 adorable smoke on the nose here: not gunpowder as might have been smelt at this distillery 208 years ago...but unmistakable soft peat, boasting an Ardbegian citrus strain. Delicate to the point of crumbling before your very nose...; **t23** just like on the Brancardier, I could swear I'm picking up malted barley....and with that level of chocolate-rich peat I'm sure I must be. Also, how else do I get that intense Malteser candy middle dissolving on the tongue? The middle is laced with genteel oak; **f23** the finale at last sees the peppers arrive with a quiet determination to add a bit of threat into the malt and vanilla fade....and one serenaded by such comforting phenol...; **b23.5** a nurse with a glass-side manner that is impeccable. The peat level could not be more disarming. Remember how I mentioned lack of bod on the Brancardier? Well, those phenols have certainly made the difference. *42%*

⬧ **Waterloo The Surgeon Single Cask Malt** batch no I db (**85.5**) **n20 t22 f21.5 b22** Not the surgeon I'd like to have sticking a knife into me. Sorry, but just feel the nose doesn't work: too much going on not whisky-related...and certainly not malt whisky-related. To taste, the barley intervention is welcome and for all its later weaknesses the odd Demerara sugar and coconut milk note works quite well... *46%*

⬧ **Waterloo The Surgeon Single Cask Malt** batch no II db (**89**) **n22** quite a malty outbreak here. There is a note there which would be better off elsewhere. But the massive barley intervention is welcome...and required; **t22.5** again, there is a bitter niggle. But the barley sugar is huge; **f22** next time, hopefully, that restraining bitter note will have been eliminated. And that the gorgeous, super-rich and spiced-up barley note is much increased...; **b22.5** you get the feeling that lessons were quickly learned from the disappointing Batch I and here the accent is very much on the malt. And a very sexy accent it is, too.... *54%*

CORSICA
DOMAINE MAVELA Aléria. Working.
P & M Tourbé Corsican Single Malt Whisky bott code L1682 db (**92**) **n22.5 t23 f23 b23.5** A beautifully paced, gentle malt which always carries a threat on the peaty wind. *42%. nc ncf.*

P & M Aged 13 Years Corsican Single Malt Whisky bott code L2984 db (**95.5**) **n23.5 t24 f24 b24** Enough oak to make a Corsican nuthatch sing with happiness. This has swallowed up the years with ease and maximised complexity. World class whisky. *42%. nc ncf. 217 bottles.*

CYPRUS
LAMBOURI WINERY Kato Plates. Working
Lion Spirit Malt Whisky Aged in Commandaria Cask 2016 barrel 01 db (**94**) **n24** a nose steeped in both the sweet, velvety tones of Commandaria wine as it is history. Stunningly bitter-sweet in this case, as the oak has been exploited over the last six years to add a just-so degree of tannin sharpness. An effortlessly delightful nose with far more complexity than first meets the nostril...especially when you spot the spices working undercover and heather honey offering an extra degree of weight; **t24** just...wow! Like the dessert wine, it is lush, sumptuous and fulsome. Unlike Commandaria it doesn't retain its high-pitched sweetness. Here, instead, the sugars - actually, slightly heavier honey - meet head on with the intensity of the oak and then a secondary, in betwixt, brief maltiness – though that soon subsides as mighty spices from the oak move in; **f23** I was expecting a reprise of the honey/sugars. But it never quite comes. Instead, we can concentrate on the semi-dry, gently warming nutty tannins...helped by that sheen unique to the wine and even a late hint of chocolate liqueur; **b23.5** I saved this unique whisky, the first ever from Cyprus to be my 750th and theoretically last whisky of the 2023 Whisky Bible. Well, it is the 750th, but I hear will probably not be my last! In recent years I was lucky enough to have had a charming girlfriend who had close ties to Cyprus, though we never got out there. Through Judy, seven or eight years ago, I first learned of Commandaria dessert wine and had always wanted to visit where it was made, not least because its history dates back close on 3,000 years to the times of the ancient Greeks. To find that Cyprus' first-ever whisky had been matured in a vintage Commandaria cask was just too good to be true: this was something special. I was even fortunate enough to be able to taste the whisky at cask strength from that first-ever barrel – a style which I really hope they are able to bottle at a later date as the intense apricot and fig mix doesn't reveal itself in quite the same way when reduced....which, curiously, reverts on delivery something much closer to the aloof sweetness of the original wine. In a number of ways the most fascinating newcomer of the year: distilled beautifully with no off notes. And matured in a wine cask like no other. It is deserving of a special award all of its own. Congratulations to all concerned. And, Theo Paphitis, my old friend: I'm in....!!! *42.3% uf*

CZECH REPUBLIC
Single Malt
PRÁDLO DISTILLERY Plzen. Closed.
Prádlo 18 Years Old Czech Single Malt db (**96**) **n24** this is deep and sophisticated. It seems like Czech oak at play with phenols lingering, too, though from this distance of time it is hard to confirm them as peat-derived. Most stunning, though, is a dense kumquat tone which straddles the tannin and phenol and keeps you guessing just how sweet or dry this really is...it is a moving

target and almost impossible to gauge; **t24** an adorable, salivating coppery shell on delivery cracks to allow a sublime banana/vanilla frontispiece to the more profound and toasty tannin wave which sweeps in. The lightest liquorice and molasses imprint gives a fleeting touch of Kentucky, but we are brought back to central Europe as the firmer, heftier tannin reclaim the ground. All the time, though, the barley, juicy and forthright, will not be denied...; **f23.5** are those phenols, or just extra dark tannins – something extracted like never before from Bohemian oak – that is causing delicious confusion on the palate? Certainly no mistaking the light indigenous cocoa tones (indeed, anyone who remembers early 1990s Czech chocolate will raise a smile at that one..) and even a little black cherry...though no idea where that has come from. Most sensual, though, are those lingering, slightly nutty oils...; **b24.5** I take particular pride that in 1997 I brought to the attention of the world for the very first time the malt whiskies of the Czech Republic, although even then it felt as though I was disappearing behind the Eastern Bloc to do so. The country, when I visited a couple of years earlier, was still tied in many ways to the practises of communist Russia and of all the distilleries I have ever discovered, those that had made malt in the former Czechoslovakia seemed the greatest revelation of them all. And though I tasted every whisky then housed in the country's warehouses, I never came across an 18-year-old. This is a gem, believe me. Any serious whisky connoisseur must locate this to add not just to their lexicon of malt, but their knowledge. There is no other whisky on the planet, quite like this. I, for one, feel honoured to have experienced (and thoroughly enjoyed) it. Bravo..! *42.7%*

RUDOLF JELÍNEK DISTILLERY Vizovice. Working.

Gold Cock Single Malt Whisky 2008 Virgin Oak Czech oak barrels, dist Feb 08, bott Mar 17 db **(96) n24 t24 f24 b24** Not often you get gold cocks and virgins mentioned in the same sentence in a drinks guide. Or anywhere else, come to that. Equally few rampant cocks can crow so loudly; no virgin give so passionately. A consummate whisky consummated... *61.5%. nc ncf sc. 270 bottles.*

SVACH DISTILLERY Mirkovice. Working.

⬧ **Old Well Czech Single Malt Lightly Peated** Kagor cask finish bott code db **(94.5) n23** the smoke is adorable: soft, floaty yet boasting an inner intensity. The malt flicks around offering an extra degree of sweetness while the fruit hides, allowing the tannins space to sing their distinctive central European or even Moldovan song...; **t24** what a superb two-toned delivery. The very first moments are a glorious marriage of malty peat and sharp tannin. Next and within a nanosecond comes a second, detached avalanche of silky, spiced fruit...at times plummy, sometimes displaying overripe fig and adroitly sweetened further by lemon blossom honey. But as we reach the mid-point the peat has intensified into something significant and the spices highlight this...; **f23.5** a vanilla intense fade, though a middle cocoa and peat make things interesting; **b24** a beautifully distinctive malt which the taste buds tell you is most probably using Czech or some other rare oak, which imparts its own unique dose of vitality. The smoke however, is also a charmer. And here, though they claim to be lightly peated is, by most European standards, at least medium peated. A very elegant experience giving you a unique flavour profile, and one that has you soon refilling the glass... *46.3%*

⬧ **Svach's Old Well Golden Rose Original Single Malt Bohemian Whisky Single Cask** aged in bourbon and sherry casks bott code db **(86) n21.5 t23 f20 b21.5** Have to say it: this is a rather dull nose where the sherry has neutralised most else around it. And while it picks up superbly on delivery, the grape shewing an impressive versatility spreading from marmalade though to acacia honey, the finish has the furry feel of sulphur at work...which also accounts for the dullard nose. Some great moments, but some disappointments, too... *54.2%*

Svach's Old Well Single Malt Bohemian Whisky Peated aged in Laphroaig barrel, 2nd release, db **(90) n23 t22.5 f22 b22.5** Would struggle to call this complex, but what it does, it does rather well the use of the phenols is rather lovely. *46.3% nc ncf sc*

Svach's Old Well Single Malt Bohemian Whisky Peated aged in Bourbon and Porto barrels, 2nd release, db **(87.5) n22.5 t22 f21.5 b21.5** A slightly muddled malt. Hefty and smoky, the fruit grapples with both the phenols and tannins rather than plays along with them. Again, as is the house style, very dry and missing some much-needed honey, especially on the finish. have to say I do love the sooty dryness of the peat on the nose. Classy. *46.3% nc ncf sc*

Svach's Old Well Single Malt Bohemian Whisky Peated aged in Bohemian virgin oak barrels db **(94.5) n23.5 t23.5 f23.5 b24** Now what do we have here? The Czech Republic's first-ever 101 whisky...? Seems to be an excellent strength for this particular distiller and, compared to last year's peated offering, appears to have far more going for it with altogether better harmony. The extra oils from the higher strength definitely help, though I think the virgin native oak barrels will always out-display French wine casks. Appliance of the Murray Method is crucial in order to see the complex magnitude of the malt. You are inspecting a unique whisky fingerprint here... something that is almost primitive. *50.5%*

Svach's Old Well Single Bohemian Whisky Malt Unpeated aged in Bourbon and Pineau Des Charentes barrels, 2nd release, db (94) n23.5 t23.5 f23 b24 Was it the peat in the other bottlings which was hiding he sugars? Elegant, oily and complex, a malt which is complimented by the higher strength. A true delight to sample and the gently burning beacon to illuminate this distillery... 51.9% nc ncf sc

Svach's Old Well Single Bohemian Whisky Malt Me and Whisky Gang Peated bourbon and Sauternes barrels, dist 2017, db (89) n23 t23.5 f20.5 b22 Worth an extra 5 points just for being the first whisky label in the world to state: "fuck covid". I'll drink to that.... 50.8% 465 bottles

Svach's Old Well Single Malt Bohemian Whisky Silver Rose Peated db (94) n23.5 t23 f23.5 b24 Where their 50.5% peated malt was angular and disjointed to a degree bordering brilliance, this has taken a different, less bumpy route. Wow! This distillery has certainly discovered flavour...!! The secret, however, is that their base distillate is absolutely faultless. 53.5%

DENMARK

BRAENDERIET LIMFJORDEN Øster Assels. Working.

Lindorm Danish Single Malt Whisky 2nd Edition db (94) n23.5 t23.5 f23 b24 An incredibly sure-footed and complex whisky for a distillery so young. Wonderful stuff! 46%. ncf. 537 bottles.

BRAUNSTEIN DISTILLERY Køge. Working.

Braunstein Danish Single Malt Cask Edition no. 2 db (94) n23.5 t23.5 f23 b24 Seriously high quality distillate that has been faithfully supported by good grade oak. Complex, satisfying, and for its obviously tender years, truly excellent malt. A welcome addition to the Scandinavian – and world! – whisky lexicon. 62.4%

COPENHAGEN DISTILLERY Copenhagen. Working.

Copenhagen Single Malt Refined Edition Cask Strength Batch No 1 db (95) n24 t23.5 f23.5 b24 In a year of remarkable whiskies endlessly knocking on the door of the unknown, a very late entry from Denmark (stuck in Customs for a month) took me once again to territory new. I am quite used to seeing the blending of grain profiles – especially in the US – and fruits from differing wine casks. But this is one of the very few times where I immediately recognised a whisky created as a blend of varying tannin tones to take the lead role. Indeed, every role. So another malt that took a long time to unravel. And in whisky there is little more exciting than exploring unknown lands; and here we are in the densest forest without a map or compass. Quite a challenge. But well worth the effort as this, I guarantee, is a malt you will never quite get to the bottom of. Brave. Unique. 54.9% 422 bottles

Copenhagen Single Malt Raw II db (94) n23.5 t23.5 f23 b24 The last Copenhagen Raw had the odd technical gripe. Not this time. A fascinating mish-mash of youth and precocious tannin make for a sometimes sedate, occasionally rip-roaring experience. 51.4%

Whisky Raw Edition Single Malt 2020 batch no.1, db (91.5) n21.5 t24 f22.5 b23.5 A compellingly delicious malt. While the nose never quite gets going, things certainly do once the whisky has crossed the lips. And then you are in for a five-course malt. Another memorable bottling from this new distillery. 61.1% 300 bottles

Whisky Rare Edition Single Malt 2021 batch no.2, db (91) n21.5 t23 f23 b23.5 Denmark is rightly famous for its pork, its marzipan, its divorce rate, its beards, and its goalkeepers. But not until now, silk. On this evidence it soon will be. I have to admit that I feared the worst when I learned that aged gin casks had been used here. But I shouldn't have worried. After from a brief salute on the nose, the juniper vanishes. Still would like to see the distillate just a little finer in the cut. Must say, though, that the oils have been put to jolly good use. 49% 100 bottles

FARY LOCHAN DESTILLERI Give. Working.

⋙ Fary Lochan Distillers Choice No 4 bourbon & PX sherry casks, dist 4/12, bott 12/22 db (91) n22.5 bunches of grapes hang off the weighty nose; t23 the fruit is disarmingly delicate at first, but this is just a ruse: the fruit gangs up and becomes as lush as a thick piled carpet. But those spices, alongside some toasty oak really does ramp up the amps; f22.5 just a little bitterness from the tannin, though it does possess a certain cocoa element. But that fruit is still busy working, though all earlier sugars now are spent; b23 a musclebound malt thick in PX, but beneath the sultry fruit comes an excellent spice and vanilla curve. Not exactly one for the fairies... 53.3%

⋙ Fary Lochan Sweet and Spicy Muscatel No.1 bourbon & muscatel casks, dist 02/16, bott 03/23 db (88.5) n23 t23 f20.5 b22 The attractiveness of the blend of ulmo and acacia honey intertwangling with the deft malt is there for all to see. And the way the fruit, a kind of exploding sultana, adds extra salivating quality on the ultra malty palate is sublime. But it does a lose a few Brownie points for the nagging and deepening bitterness off the oak late on. But when this one is good, it's a stunner. 56.5%

KNAPLUND DESTILLERI Tarm. Working.

Knaplund Whiskey Batch One dist 2018 bott 2022 bourbon mash db **(94)** n23.5 I could be in Kentucky at work nosing and tasting the local produce... But I'm not: I'm in Germany sampling a Danish whisky. Bizarre. The marriage between corn oil and tannin is exemplary and delicate. Red.... then black liquorice and vanilla-sweetened spice is drifting enticingly from the glass; **t23.5** as on the nose, the corn oils make this easy. Their oils coat the palate and keep the Demerara sugars - and later heather honey - close. The vanillas form into something of almost ice-cream intensity - with a butterscotch topping. The spices are less nippy than on the nose but quietly play their part; **f23** just the briefest moment of bitterness, but it soon passes as the vanilla and banana take advantage of the remaining corn oils; **b24** seeing as this is the first whiskey ever distilled at the Knaplund distillery, this is not just history...but truly extraordinary. Unquestionably the best bourbon-style whiskey I have ever tasted that has been made outside of the United States. It is not only technically sound but filled in virgin American oak, the authenticity of the style is complete. A relatively young "bourbon" still and would have benefitted with doubling its age in the barrel. But the quality of the original distillate must have been pretty flawless as the cut was neither too heavy or light, but just right to pick up the intricacies of both the grain and the oak. I could not be more impressed. Or, frankly, surprised... 50% (100 proof) 390 bottles

MOSGAARD DISTILLERY Oure. Working.

⟡ **Mosgaard Cask Experiment Series No 3** bott 03/05/23 db **(84.5)** n22.5 t23 f19 b20 Rich and overly ripe, there is almost a peppered fatness to the nose and then followed by an unusually tart delivery – in both senses being both fruity and eye-wateringly sharp. So this whisky certainly gets off to a singular and very attention-seeking start. But the finish is off beam and nags, undoing much of the earlier magic. The overall effect is confusing. It's flavour profile peaks about four flavour-waves into the delivery when a true magic spot is reached, the lusciousness of the plummy fruit combining beautifully with the elegant spices and deep vanillas. Elsewhere, however, balance is at a premium and it is downhill from those brief dizzy heights. 56.1% 380 bottles

⟡ **Mosgaard Organic Single Malt Amontillado Cask** bott 10/22 db **(94)** n23 the nip on the nose has nothing to do with the strength: there are spices pouring out from somewhere. But they are couched in lush rich, over-ripe plums and juicy dates, too...; **t24** yikes! The top layer of my palate is being skinned! The spices could be used to fuel one of Elon Musk's trips to Mars. However, the velvet-gloved caress of the plum and Melton Hunt Cake fruitiness certainly compensates. At times eye-wateringly sharp..which perfectly fits in with the persona; **f23** although stone-fruit dry at the end, the little chocolate raisin phase it passes through is just-so..; **b24** you'll have to strap on your seatbelt to withstand this spice attack: it's been a long time since I received such a warming introduction on the palate: this is a warming dram. Just as well the surrounding fruits are so lush to help counter the blast. If you are looking for a feeble, simple malt, drenched in toffee to give it a dark look and a friendly feel around the palate....then you've come to the wrong whisky. This one has hairs on its chest....and was probably consumed by Vikings before setting sail... 58% sc 250 bottles

⟡ **Mosgaard Organic Single Malt Oloroso Cask** batch 1818, bott 04/23 db **(90)** n22.5 pretty simplistic by Mosgaard standards, the creamy toffee raisin dominating; **t23** some trickery on the palate: you are initially lulled into thinking this is going to be a bit if a toffee-dominated lump. Then...varoom! In come those penetrating spices out of nowhere. A few molasses and muscovado notes don't go amiss, either. Retains a degree of fatness throughout; **f22** slightly bitter, burnt toast. A smidgeon of cocoa; **b22.5** another spicy cove but perhaps a little on the bitter and dull side by comparison with the enormity of this distillery's best. 46.2%

⟡ **Mosgaard Organic Single Malt Palo Cortabo Cask** batch 3918, bott 04/23 db **(87.5)** n22 t22.5 f21 b22 Shares very similar traits to the oloroso bottling, especially with the toffee and spice. But the finish here is untidy, not helped by a distinct shortage of sugars which has plagued the piece throughout. Have to admire those spices, though. And though there is a degree of sophistication to the dryness of the theme, too often it feels like gears being scrunched as it tries to move forward. 53%

⟡ **Mosgaard Organic Single Malt Peated Bourbon Cask** batch 2218, bott 01/05/23 db **(96.5)** n24 living in the countryside as I do, that cattle shed bite attaching to the phenols is an aroma common around here. And just the perfect fit for this malt which has stretched the tannins into every corner. Perfectly balanced and gloriously earthy and rich; **t24.5** the one thing missing on the nose was honey. Well, no shortage here as the heather honey mounts its charge on the very first moment of the juicy and vaguely oily delivery and then sticks limpetlike to every flavour thrust which follows. The peat, as on the nose, is uncommonly even and retains that sublime earthiness throughout, as well as adding a few extra base tones. The tannin is profound, if a tad salty, deep in toasty vanilla and always, whatever it does, haunted by that sublime honey tone.... Some 250 whiskies in and this is easily one of the best experiences I have encountered this year on the palate as yet...; **f23.5** retains that toastiness, but also vanilla and toffee. And very late in is a surprise package: two or three waves of intense malt; **b24.5** a faultless cask offering a peaty-honeyed-vanilla bomb that is way beyond excellent. Talk about a honey cask. Almost freakishly perfect. 48.4%

NYBORG DESTILLERI Nyborg. Working.

Nyborg Destilleri Danish Oak Isle of Fiona batch no. 167 db **(93) n23 t23.5 f23 b23.5** Denmark is by far and away the least forested of all Scandinavian countries. So finding an oak tree to make a barrel from must have been a major achievement in itself. It was well worth the effort, because this is a stunner and the impact of the tannin is the least assertive of any European oak I have encountered outside of Spain. The balance of the nose is spot on with lazy harmony between grain and light toasty tannin with a little orange blossom honey as the buffer. The grist is on overdrive on the palate, the oak providing a slightly salty back up. With its Jaffa Cake sub-strata, there is much to celebrate here. 46%. nc ncf.

SMALL BATCH DISTILLERS Holstebro. Working

Small Batch Distillers Hjerl Hede Nr. 1 Dansk Produceret Single Malt 2019 db **(88.5) n22 t23 f22 b21.5** Young and bristling with malty tendencies. Eye-watering in its salivating properties, a gristy sweetness is never far away. 59%. nc ncf

SOLVOGEN BRÆNDERIET LIMFJORDEN Ruslev. Working.

Solvognen Single Malt (89) n22.5 a honey-rich breakfast cereal note to this one. Hefty, with a vanilla back-story to remind you of the oak; **t23** dense and intense: like entering a tangled thicket of rich honey tones and having to cut your way through. The oils tingle with accompanying spice while a buttery shortbread biscuit tries to dampen the honey's enthusiasm, but with limited success; **f21.5** a little gnawing feint clings to the tongue and palate while butterscotch keeps the sweetness alive; **b22** toasted honey is the theme of this easily quaffable whisky. Strikingly similar to Lawson's 12-year-old blend of many moons ago (and that is a great compliment!), but with a much wider cut giving extra oils. A good choice for those wishing to skip breakfast and go straight onto a decent whisky... 46%

STAUNING WHISKEY Skjern. Working.

Stauning Kaos Triple Malt Whisky batch no. 1-2020 db **(86) n22.5 t22.5 f19.5 b21.5** The thing about Kaos, is that you never quite know – as the name implies - what you are going to get. Sometimes it works magnificently. Other times it stumbles over itself, never quite able to find a rhythm or even a reason. Here we have a bottling which appear to be a succession of dead ends; at times intriguing, others you find yourself in dark alleyways. The slight feint kick doesn't work too much to its advantage here as it lets in a slightly over-bittered finish. Soupy honey notes liven things with rye but is then shut off. Some short bursts of excellence. But too short. Taking the nature of the beast into account, the next Kaos will be brilliantly chaotic...you just never know 46%.

Stauning Peat Single Malt Whisky batch no. 1-2020 db **(88.5) n22 t22 f22 b22.5** Very young grains at work here. Which means the phenols still have an edge to them. A wide, oily cut at work here. But that slight error is forgivable as it helps stoke up the thick intensity of the barley sugar and smoked honey. Never quite manages to disrobe from its cloak of youth. But just sweetly charms you to death... 47%.

Stauning Rye Whisky New American oak barrels, batch no. 1-2020 db **(94.5) n23.5 t24 f23 b24** Probably no grain on the planet offers a flavour kick like malted rye. It has an intensity and richness all its own, though the results can vary wildly from distillery to distillery. The best I have ever encountered is found at Alberta. Stauning has a different persona, retaining some of the sharper elements of unmalted rye, too. And from this evidence it is taking a quite unique and now magnificent shape. As it was I who suggested they produce rye whisky when Stauning was still but dream in its founders' eyes, I always take proud interest in their rye bottlings. This isn't a mile off what I had in mind... 48%. ncf.

THY WHISKY Snedsted. Working.

Thy Danish Whisky Distillery Edition Aged 4 Years ex-oloroso, cask no: 61-62, dist 2016, bott 2020 db **(93) n23.5 t23 f23 b23.5** The difference to a whisky a faultless sherry butt can make. Oddly enough, although 4-years-old, the youthfulness is more pronounced here than most of their 3-y-o bottlings. A treat of a bottling from one of the best exponents of young malt whisky in the world. 61.7% ncf

Thy Danish Whisky No. 10 Fjordboen Aged 3 Years ex-Oloroso cask, dist Jan 16, bott May 19 db **(91)** n23 t23 f22.5 b22.5 Should you ever need to discover what is meant by a dry oloroso finish to a whisky, here's your bottle! Youthful, but elegant. *49.9%. 1,005 bottles.*

Thy Danish Whisky No. 11 Stovt Aged 3 Years ex-port, ex-bourbon, ex-stout casks, dist May 16, bott Oct 19 db **(87)** n21.5 t22.5 f21 b22 I hadn't looked at the cask make up of this bottling before I nosed it. But I certainly did once I took my first sniff: hops! Now, the one thing I am no fan of is hops and whisky together. Rarely a comfortable combination, as the hop is a natural bittering agent and that plays havoc with the balance of a whisky. However, here an old Port cask has come to the rescue by offering a silky, fruity sheen to the heather-honey of the malt and bourbon cask. However, the heads and tails of soft hop give a strange persona. The middle, though, is a beautiful, creamy experience. *48%. 831 bottles.*

Thy Danish Whisky No. 12 Kornmod Aged 3 Years ex-Oloroso and ex-bourbon casks, dist Mar 17, bott Apr 20 db **(96)** n24 t24 f23.5 b24.5 Such magnificence for a whisky so young: the complexity and the layering are almost off the charts. Beautifully distilled and, for its age, just about perfectly matured. What a thrill to encounter oloroso influence this faultless. When this distillery gets it right, they get it very right. Simply wonderful whisky, irrespective of its age. *52.5%. 1,486 bottles.*

Thy Danish Whisky No. 13 Stovt Aged 3 Years bourbon, oloroso, PX and stout casks, dist Jan-Oct 2017, bott Nov 2020 db **(80)** n21 t21.5 f19.5 b18 What it is they say about too many cooks...? Ditto casks styles, sometimes. Had to smile when I saw they had pitted the ultimate sweetener, PX casks, against the ultimate bitterer... beer. The hops win in the pretty unattractive nose, then the PX kicks in to act as a kind of eraser. But instead, everything is flattened, except some uncontrolled spice and the late hop bitterness. Hopefully an experiment not to be repeated from this great distillery. *51.0% ncf 1825 bottles*

Thy Danish Whisky No. 14 Bøg Aged 3 Years oloroso cask,dist Apr-Dec 2017, bott Mar 2021 db **(94)** n23 t23.5 f23.5 b24 A prickly smokiness reminds me a little of the bacon Denmark is so rightly famed for. Not for stuffy Islay-style peat purists. But certainly, one for those who love it when high-class peat racks up the weight and complexity and a faultless sherry butt is on hand to soothe! *574% ncf 1627 bottles*

Thy Distillery Edition Aged 4 Years cask no 69 db **(89)** n22 something odd about this one... Right, just checked the bottle: the malt has been beechwood smoked. Let's just say it has the ability to make the nose curl a bit: this is sharp! t22.5 ah...that's a lot better! The deliver boasts an exhibition of varied sugars – ranging from ulmo and Brazilian rainforest honeys right through to toasted molasses. This indulges in the oils and punchy vanillas which abound; f22 after such a mind-blowing delivery – especially one so sweet – the finish will always tend towards relative bitterness; b22.5 well, this bottling has taken me somewhere on the whisky flavour map I had no idea existed. An exhausting malt, as you get worn out trying to work out what is happening to your nose and palate! Definitely worth a top-up, though, once acclimatised... *60.5% sc*

Thy Rex Organic Single Malt No 16 db **(88.5)** n22 t22.5 f22 b22 The strange feeling of history repeating itself. Takes me back over 30 years when the world's first-ever organic whisky, Da Mhille, was distilled at Springbank in Campbeltown for a Welsh organic farmer. I was the first-ever to taste this – I even wrote their little booklet for the malt's launch – but the weakness was that in trying to produce as much spirit as possible from the limited organic barley available, the cut was made just a little wider than it should have been and the quality suffered. And here we have the same problem. A little trick to improve it is to put the glass in very warm water for a little while and allow the heat to evaporate the heaviest of the spirit (something I was taught at a distillery the best part of 50 years ago). Do that on this and you raise the honey, malt and overall levels incredibly...and the score. And you create a beautiful chocolate finish, too. The score above is after three minutes' warming. The score straight from the bottle: (84.5) 21.5-22-20.5-20.5. *49.5%*

Thy Spelt-Rye db **(90)** n22 the tannins burst through very early and keep their ground. Meanwhile the rye is sharp and outperforms the spelt. All this drifting around on earthy oils; t23 and it is that oil which impacts first on the palate. It appears to hold the sugars in a vice-like grip, refusing to allow them to go anywhere. Lovely interplay of muscovado and molasses – again confirming that earthy quality - before the rye slowly begins to emerge as the grain champion; f22.5 hefty oils again from a generous cut wash up at the finale with cocoa for company. Amazingly, the rye still has a voice...; b22.5 another massively chunky offering from Thy. They seem determined at the moment to go for whisky heavyweights, and here is another three-course meal to tuck into. *479%*

Thy Stoft No 17 db **(94.5)** n23.5 full Murray Method and we are in uncharted territory: beechwood smoke mingling with dull manuka honey and chocolate...with the softest, most apologetic creamy hop im aginable...for those who remember milk stouts, you'll be at home...; t24 possibly qualifies as the softest whisky in the world. It is somewhere between a Sam Smith's oatmeal stout and Mackeson's milk stout in texture...and, for a moment or two, taste. Except here there is a gentle spiciness in tandem with a stirring of molten Demerara sugars. I absolutely adore this...; **f23** so long and so much slowly gathering chocolate. Molasses drips off this and still those dark, creamy stout notes but with barely a hop. Amazing...; **b24** I'm deliberately not looking at first to see how this whisky is composed, to keep my brain and senses on full alert. This one totally confuses me...though on the nose I'm certain there is some beechwood-smoke malt in there somewhere. Though not as much as before. The cask influence is very different, too, and I think I can detect distant hop...so distant I'm semi-doubting myself. Most unusual. It's no use...I'm going to have to look before I fill in the actual tasting notes, as this is a very, very singular and intriguing malt.... Right, now tasted: beautifully distilled with the cuts spot on, there is hop but so soft and fruity and the most sleek and luxurious sweetened stout effect you'll ever encounter. This is a beauty...and just how they happened to put all these eclectic facets together to make this work, I'll never know... *60.5%*

Thy Stoft No 18 db (88) n21.5 t22.5 f22 b22 The aroma is nutty, thick and oily. The oiliness on the palate proves the nose doesn't lie and the malt is intense; long (thanks to the generous cut) with the malts delving into Bakewell tart territory. Rich, simplistically yet intensely malty, sweet and exceedingly friendly. *473%*

Thy Stoft No 19 db (85) n21 t21.5 f22.5 b20 I don't even have to look at the bottle here. This is a dripping wet, fresh PX cask at work and an exceptional example where the super-sweet grape has strangled all else around it so it may live. Towards the finish there are some remarkable fruit notes – a kind of mix of passion fruit and mango, with grape juice thrown in for good measure. But elsewhere, moderate spices aside, all is sterile. The PX cask has won. The malt has been extinguished. Exterminated. Which means the world's PX nutters will be fighting tooth and claw to find the last bottle of this, the most PX heavy of all PX whiskies on the planet...a collectors' item. *59.1%*

Thy Distillery Edition db (90) n22.5 the oak is thumping its chest here. Yet the intense malt won't be cowered; **t23** not sure you'd be able to get a thicker and more complete maltiness if you tried. Works beautifully with soft spices; **f22** a plethora of dark sugars and thin heather honey attaches to the fading malts as the oils return; **b22.5** another big 'un with the tannins really upping the toastiness. The malt powers through here and there – well, there, there and there, too. *60.5%*

Thy Distillery Edition 4 Years Old Cask 164 db (87) n22 t22.5 f21 b21.5 Another hefty offering, full of big oils. A charming smokiness manages to keep everything in shape early on, both on nose and delivery. But as the sugars wear off, the gorgeous barley sugar ones in particular, the bitterness on the finish becomes a tad too overbearing. Oddly enough, I was even reminded of akavit by this one, especially on delivery. *58.3%*

Thy Distillery Edition 4 Years Old Cask 230 db (88.5) n22.5 t22.5 f21.5 b22 Presumably PX at work here. The nose is thick with sweet grape and the delivery isn't far behind. Spices pop and percolate but such is the influence of the wine cask that not much else gets a meaningful word in. Another bitter finish, though a little cocoa does join the raisin to even things out... *59.7%*

TROLDEN DISTILLERY Kolding. Working.

⬦ **Trolden Nimbus Cumulus VII Single Malt Peated Edition** ex-merlot cask db (94) n23.5 the grape is clean and significant, not least in blunting the teeth of those aggressive phenols...; **t23** probably the sharpest peated malt you'll taste this year. If the grape doesn't make your eyes water, the phenols will. When they join forces...good grief! Light melon softens and sweetens gently; **f23.5** really lovely layering here, with three significant styles working their magic. Firstly, there is the very simply, fruity grape. The next layer is acidic aloofness from the peat. Then a third layer where offshoots of the two have merged to form an intense united front.... Oh, late on there is a fourth: spice and lashings of it...; **b24** for a whisky this big, this chewy, this intense the complexity is surprisingly simple... *56% 45 bottles*

⬦ **Trolden Nimbus Stratus Single Malt Batch No 9** db (89) n22 the youthfulness emphasis just how the oak gouges into the clean barley; **t22.5** the malt is timid in its display, but at least ensures it gets the barley up there and noticed. The oak, on the other hand, barks and nibbles; **f22** the finish is quite short...well so far as the barley is concerned. The oak, as ever, bullies its way around with a passive-aggressive display of bitter-sweet tannin; **b22.5** the oak has all the major lines in this one act play. The malt has only a supporting role. *46% nc ncf 300 bottles*

⬦ **Trolden Nimbus Stratus Single Malt Peated Batch No 1** db (95) n24 just love this style of phenol caught somewhere between smoky bacon and anthracite. This nose has a bite, and it means to. Rock-hard even in the non-peated aspects, especially the leaking Demerara sugars and mid-ripe bananas which coats the piece; **t23.5** at first, it looks like those Demerara sugars on delivery don't stand a chance. In comes the smoke, flint-like in substance and envelopes the sugars, seemingly crushing them underfoot. But there is a delightful fight back and the sheer magnitude of the salivation levels confirms how effective it is. The smoke becomes more fragmented, but the acidity never lets up; f23.5 that marked acidity never quite goes away. But the tannins now make a drier statement, bringing the spices far more into play. The late oils also appear to cling to some malty remnants...; **b24** an exceptional single malt. Not only has this been outstandingly distilled, they have eschewed the softer Islay-style peat for a much more stylistic, acidic and taunting smokiness. *46% nc ncf 200 bottles*

Danish Non-Whisky

Arbejd 9 Days (86) n21 t22 f21.5 b21.5 This Islay tribute spirit brings a smile to the face for its pure impudence alone. The nose is far too thin, despite the peat reek, to amount to much. But about five or six flavour-waves in, the oak and phenols have united with enough combined weight to offer a genuinely pleasant run-in to the short-ish finish, the complexity gaining momentum all the time. A very light fruit note offers a degree of calm to the peaty turbulence. Surprisingly attractive (when Murray Method applied) and occasionally full on, despite its limitations. *47%*

Atlantis 6 Days (81) n20 t21.5 f19.5 b20 To quote the back bottle blurb: "Smooth corn-based bourbon infused with cocoa nibs, ultrasonic brewed coffee and a hint of warming nutmeg". You can draw your own conclusions. Mine is that, whatever you call this, it doesn't quite work, though the spices from the tannins do a good job of keeping the tastebuds alive. Perhaps more of a liqueur. *45%*

Hafnium 9 Days Old PX Sherry (86.5) n21.5 t22 f21 b22 That so much oaky spice abounds after just nine days is astonishing. This malt spirit is bathed in the voluptuousness of the PX cask and makes the point the moment it hits the palate. The finish may be over-dry, but overall a pleasant, untaxing ride with no off notes. *42%*

White Forest 14 days old (88) n22.5 t21.5 f22 b22 Well it certainly isn't white oak forest, as the wood on display here is cedar and chestnut. That alone is responsible for a memorably pungent nose...and that is even before you realise there is significant peat aboard here. If you suspect the delivery will be a confused mishmash of chest-beating flavours, then you are right: a free for all of peat and powering tannin, though the silky mouthfeel helps. Only on the finish does it all finally settle down into a genuinely delightful, layered composition, the smoke acting as the catalyst for more measured tones. Whisky it may not yet be. But it is certainly a unique and enjoyable experience! *47%*

ESTONIA
MOE DISTILLERY Moe. Working.

Tamm & Rukis 100% Rye Malt Whisky virgin American oak for 3 years, distilled from Sangaste winter rye, batch no. 1, bott 2019 db (89) n23 t21.5 f22.5 b22 Seeing as Estonians helped colonise America as far back as the very early 17th century, perhaps it should be no surprise Moe have decided to give this whisky a very Kentuckian slant, evident on both nose and palate. And very attractive it is, too. A fascinating and entertaining introduction by a new country to whisky. Or do I mean whiskey....? *44%.*

FAROE ISLAND
EINAR'S DISTILLERY Working.

⬨ **Einar's Single Malt Cask Strength Batch 6** db (91) n22.5 thinner nose than B5, trace phenols giving way to the very young barley: that "New Make" fingerprint is still found all over this. Grassy with a little grapefruit emphasising the lightness and youth. The smoke is enigmatic, though for the first time the ballast is now being supplied by delicate tannins as the oak makes a gentle play; t23.5 the effervescent freshness of the barley strikes from the very first moment; salivating, especially as the barley gangs up. As on the nose the smoke is enigmatic. Spices are refined, the midpoint highlight being the interplay between shy oak and bold barley while, again, the fruitiness is of the the sharp, citric variety; f22 tad too short for its own good: both the oils and smoke required for extra time are missing; **b23** exuding quality throughout, that fresh spirit feel is becoming a trademark. *56.5%*

⬨ **Einar's Single Malt Cask Strength Batch 7** db (92) n22.5 the weightiest nose yet with a pulsing, dry fruit lead thumping against the first signs of sturdy oak; t23.5 the mouthfeel grabs you before the flavours. The yielding softness unmasks oils in top form while the interference of the cask is benign. Salivating barley, ensuring the sweetness missing on the nose, hits first before a more genteel fruit and tannin involvement unobtrusively adds layers of depth; f23 the oils hold their nerve to ensure a pleasantly long finish. A youthfulness returns late on after the heftier fruit and oak have played out, leaving on the spice...; **b23** pleasing on so many levels. From nose to finish both distillate and barrel are in fine fettle. A malt brimming with character and ever-increasing depth. The youth is never far away, but we are now on the first rungs of genuine sophistication. *47% 575 bottles*

❧ **Einar's Single Malt Cask Strength Batch 8** db (92.5) n22.5 youthful as ever, though the sweetness of the barley is now matched by the drier elements of the cask, including grape skin. Countering signs of mixed age and youth, the saltiness also hinting at the passing of time. The shadowy smoke on B6 has been replaced by something a tad earthier; t23.5 adorable! The key is the oils which soon coat the palate to ensure a soft, velvety entry which carries barley in spades...or do I mean shiels...? Spices amid the chalk and marmalade while the barley is profound; f23 an unexpected bourbon-style flourish at the death. The cocoa dryness if almost inevitable but it is the layering and length which wins the heart; b23.5 a malt which always noses and tastes younger than it looks. But what a technically gifted, fascinating and entertaining whisky this is, despite its tender countenance. 52% 1,600 bottles

❧ **Einar's Single Malt Cask Strength Batch 10** db (94.5) n23 some age playing a key role. A dollop of acacia honey surprises but underlines the tannins. The fruit is fragmented, its sharp bitty-ness slightly distracting from the more relaxed honey and tannins; t24 now, that is just one brilliant delivery. Zinging with mouth-watering, fresh, expressive juiciness augmented by sublime and very warming spices. The barley sometimes powers through to add to the favour frenzy but perhaps most remarkable are the excellent oils clinging to the roof of the mouth and offering a silky texture in stark contrast to the exploding fruit, spice and oak below; f23.5 a quieter saner finish, a little shorter than the delivery would have you expect. But those oils do linger, and with them honey traces with the spice So terribly polite and orderly compared to the earlier moments...; b24 the busiest, most entertaining and salivating malt imaginable on the palate, making the most of its youthful freshness. Never stands still, always foraging and asking questions, the fruit brisk and brusque at the vanguard. Brilliant interplay between constituent parts, fabulous cask selection gives this bottling a sense of age. Adorable. 59.8% 451 bottles

❧ **Einar's Single Malt Cask Strength Batch 11** db (89) n22.5 deeper colour than B10, but more youthful with plenty of new makey gusto punching out a malty theme. Carried on the wind are striking, at times dry, grape skin notes and only on warming slightly do we see the charming presence of deft muscovado sugars. The tannins appear to be more wine accented than oak, and with it arrives attractive complexity; t22.5 the initial dryness on delivery apes the nose, though a barley-sugar rush soon follows. There is never a clear amalgamation between grape and grain and though both flitter and float around, neither match complexity of the previous batch; f22 very dry and accentuates the missing oils with its shortness. A few rumbling malt notes an austere, astringent fruitiness, while mildly warming spices wish to be heard; b22 honey has given way to dried grape skin, and oak to youth. But in typical Einar stye, there are always complicated little games being played out on the palate, often keeping you guessing the direction it takes next. 49% 1,460 bottles

❧ **Einar's Single Malt Cask Strength Batch 12** db (94.5) n23.5 at lower temps there is a vague vegetable note but once warmed this vanishes and we witness a beautiful amalgamation of delightfully pure maltiness and almost apologetic grape-juice sweetness. Custardy vanilla acts as the glue...; t24 stunning! One of the maltiest deliveries I have tasted so far this year. The clarity of the barley, aided by intense and busy spices, make for a salivating delivery. Oils are borderline perfection: neither too cloying or half-hearted to make an impact – it is if they have been precisely measured. The tannins form a delightful spine on which the low resonance fruit can hang – but the malt is just so clean and consistent; f23 spices now take command, pulsing its existence as the other factors quieten, even though the barley lasts the pace. But as it dries, vanillas take control...; b24 in many ways the most accomplished malt yet from this distillery. The closest malt to this in character is the Speysider Strathmill, once the key component to the J&B blend...and that is very high praise, indeed. 55%

❧ **Einar's Single Malt Cask Strength Batch 13** db (90) n22.5 a young malt embracing all the drier aspects of a sherry cask without yet having found a route to the sugars to be had off the oak. The result is an austere aroma I encountered only in the chilliest warehouses in the coldest parts of Speyside. At its best when warmed slightly, the movement of the molecules releasing in unequal measures the lightest of honey tones and busiest of spices; t23.5 that dry nose soon translates to an austere delivery. Again, the MM reveals previously hidden sugars off the grist, and alters the surface tension sufficiently to soften the mouthfeel from its determined hardness. It also creates complexity with a delightful mouth-watering quality including several waves of trim barley; f23 when cool still dry, accenting on the grape skin. When warmed a notch or two we have a far happier whisky which flourishes in subtlety and complexity. Malt controls the finale expanding further into a delicate lemon blossom honey and. Distinctive citrus tang. The sweet-dry layering at the end is mind-blowingly long...; b23 one for those who prefer their Martinis extra dry. If not and you prefer balanced and complex, deploy the Murray Method. 51 %

❧ **Einar's New Make** db (91) n22.5 t23.5 f22 b23 If I were blending a Scotch and this was sent as a sample of new make to be matured, I'd be marking this down as a very decent filler behind the two or three personality marking leads. It would be used for impact early on, making the most of malt intensity on delivery. And in this form as a dram of its own plenty to enjoy with the spice and rich oils. 47%

FINLAND
THE HELSINKI DISTILLING COMPANY Helsinki. Working.

Helsinki Whiskey 100% Rye Malt Release 17 Virgin American oak New French oak db (87) n21 t22 f22 b22 Even a wide cut cannot hide the presence of the major honey which ripples through this enormous whiskey. The rye never quite finds the right place to land and seems to be in a state of perpetual motion. Untidy in so many ways. But hardly a shrinking violet. 47.5%

⬦ **Helsinki Whiskey 100% Rye Malt Release #17 American Virgin Oak Ex Bourbon Ex Rye** db (86) n20 t22 f22 b22 This is the whisky that was very nearly never tasted for the Whisky Bible. The reason: I saw it said "Release 17"....and I remember last year tasting the Release 17... so thought it had been sent by mistake. But not so, although the same Release number, this had been matured in ex-bourbon and rye casks as well as virgin oak. Last year's was virgin oak and new French oak. I can't say I was overly enamoured with last year's offering, and I'm certainly not on the nose of this which has a distinct vegetable kick. But the taste itself reminded me of a Ukrainian spirit distilled from horseradish and not stinting on the sugars leeched from the virgin oak, either. A long way from being a great whiskey, but the flavour profile is pretty fascinating. 47.5%

Helsinki Whiskey Rye Malt Release 18 American virgin oak Peated Islay cask finish db (93) n23 the nose is solid, no give whatsoever: just stark rye and chipper peat. Needs warming for a while for maximum effect; t23.5 the delivery, though, is astonishing. Yes, a little wide on the cut, for sure, but that meeting of the crisp, salivating, fruit rye and the most distinct peat, which rumbles over the piece like not-too-distant thunder is glorious. The sugars are almost three dimensional...; f23 the oils are doing their job to ensure great length and spotlight the multi-layered rye complexity. Delicate spice, too, arrives late on...; b23.5 just.... wow...!!! This is a singular single malt in every sense. Peat and malted rye...two of the biggest flavours within whisky found combined in one bottle. The result is memorable, to put it mildly. It is also one of the hardest and most brittle whiskeys I have yet encountered, perhaps only the grain from the Midleton distillery in Ireland matching this whiskey for firmness. A unique, must-experience whiskey with plenty of quality and entertainment value. 47.5%

⬦ **Helsinki Whiskey 100% Rye Malt Release #18 American Virgin Oak Islay Whisky Finish** db (87.5) n21.5 t22 f22 b22 Hardly a paragon of faultless distillation but both the grains and the phenols open up sufficiently to make life attractively interesting. On the nose a tobacco note catches the peat off guard but it eventually sharpens up with the rye to offer a far more picturesque path to follow. On arrival the rye appears to have been stung into action now and delivers an incredibly crisp sugar and red liquorice note. On the finish we enter a more minty-chocolate territory, with a little molasses for afters. Still a slight niggle though, and it is that niggle that is the problem...; 47.5%

Helsinki Whiskey Rye Malt Release 20 Virgin American oak; ex-bourbon db (90.5) n22 the nose profits from a slightly cleaner cut from the still. The rye remains firm and muscular but the oak has a bigger say now and offers a citrus edge to the layered vanilla; t23 a fat arrival, not just from the oily cut, but from the sheer weight of the grain. However, it is the slow opening of the rye flavours, like the petals on a summer rose, which makes this a stand-out whisky. A slight accompaniment of heather honey; f22.5 gorgeous chocolate works beautifully with that lingering and still enormous rye; b23 these casks give the rye every opportunity to shine. And, my word! It doesn't need a second invitation. Massively flavoursome. 47.5%

⬦ **Helsinki Whiskey 100% Rye Malt Release #20 American Virgin Oak Ex Bourbon** db (91) n22.5 just like last year's bottlings, Release 20 gives a far better view of the grain thanks to a more precise piece of distillation. Over-ripe banana strikes home with the powering vanilla, and then grapefruit for balance. At times the tannin reveals the odd thought of world dominance...; t23 wow! The fabulous rye delivery is of the eye-watering type. The sugars are crisp and intense while the sub story seems to involve vanilla and milky cocoa; f22.5 whichever feints get through the net congregate here, though never to the overall detriment of the whiskey. Instead, the finish is thick, chewy and long, the rye giving a fruity taughtness amid the silky soft backdrop. It is about the only non-wine cask matured whisky that has ever conjured up sherry trifle on the finish...; b23 a strikingly flavoursome whisky which benefits in so many ways from the much cleaner distillate. At times the messages are a bit confused. But the overall story is one of deliciously fascinating originality. 47.5%

Helsinki Whiskey Rye Malt Single Cask Release 21 Virgin American oak db (91) n22 feinty nougat and concentrated rye; t23.5 admittedly, those feints turn up early. But they remain within the realms of acceptability. And then, with the aid of the incredibly intense rye, we are catapulted into almost unknown territory. A blend of ulmo and heather honeys ensure that a beautifully distributed sweetness works gloriously with the hazelnut and vanilla; f22.5 long, with lugubrious molasses interlinking with the vanillas and oils for a satisfying finale; b23 entirely understand why this was chosen as a single cask. Packed to the rafters with deliciously intense flavours. 53.2.5%

Helsinki Whiskey Rye Malt Release 22 Virgin American oak; Oloroso cask db (94) n23 the excellence of the oloroso is apparent with every sniff. The rye punches through with an irregular bite. So intense...! t23.5 just gorgeously rounded thanks to the wonderfully sculpted oils mixing with sticky acacia and heather honey blend. The midpoint is simply pure, concentrated rye. All this framed by semi-succulent grape. Spices filter through as the tannins magnify; f23.5 the oils hang around for the finish. But now we have a wonderful chocolate Flake candy death. But loitering is that delicious mix of concentrated rye and fresh grape; b24 an absolute stunner. Remarkable what a clean distillate and an even cleaner sherry butt can do. Intense and complex...and just so yummy...!! 53.2%

KYRÖ DISTILLERY COMPANY Isokyrö. Working.

◇ **Kyro Malt** batch no 160323 db (87.5) n21.5 t22.5 f21.5 b22 I'll have a bit of a wild stab here: I'm guessing that some of the older whiskies are in use because there is no mistaking the feints, especially when they nibble on the nose and then gnaw away on the palate late on. Choc-a-bloc with rich, rye-intense goodies, there is so much to enjoy about the praline theme from about a third of the way in, complimenting the feinty but nutty nose. 47.2% 100% rye malt

◇ **Kyro Malt Oloroso Sherry** batch no 111122 db (91) n22.5 that's one profound nose: the moist fruitcake mixing with some Yorkshire Parkin Cake for good measure. Some Jaffa cake orangey-chocolate completes the cakey triumvirate...; t23 splendidly mouth-filling! Yes, a few of the fabled Kyro feints slip in – and helps give that sprinkling of ginger by so doing. But, astonishingly, on top of the eye-wateringly intense malted rye, those other two cakes turn up in abundance...; f22.5 the spiciest Kyro I've encountered yet. A real chocolate and toasted fudge pudding late on; b23 despite the obvious distilling flaws apparent, the introduction of a high-class, sulphur-free sherry barrel has really whipped up the flavour profile. Impure entertainment... 47.2% 100% rye malt

◇ **Kyro Peat Smoke** db (85) n21 t22.5 f20.5 b21.5 This really is a head-scratching distillery, for sure. The feintiness of old is back which guarantees thick oils working untidily with the light phenols on the nose. Much better on delivery when the sugars kick in in near syrupy form and when the fifth flavour wave arrives the smoke peaks alongside the spice to register a degree of deliciousness. Surprisingly thin and disgruntled on the finish. A work in progress, I think is the term... 47.2%

◇ **Kyro Wood Smoke** alder smoked, batch 101022 db (94) n23 beautifully distilled. A fabulous clarity to this with a shimmering, sugary sheen to the charming, vaguely acidic and perkily spiced smoke; t23.5 wow! Those sugars spotted on the nose arrive at the very first beat on the palate. The phenols tuck into crevices it might find and in conjunction with the noble rye peaks early with a thick but mouth-watering and teasingly spiced crescendo. Good oils carry the vanilla; f23.5 thins out, as is this distillery's fashion. But the rye keeps its place on the palate and the salivation continues for an impressively long time. Just love those late heather-honey tones...; b24 what a difference a feint-free Kyro is! The rye here is intense and the smoke wonderfully sympathetic, making its mark but never over-dominating. Such an enjoyable, richly-flavoured whisky brimming with a unique personality. Superb! 47.2% 100% rye malt

TEERENPELI Lahti. Working.

Teerenpeli Aged 10 Years matured sherry & bourbon cask, batch no. 1/20, db (91) n23 t23 f22.5 b22.5 A well-balanced, essentially malty whisky which, like other Teerenpeli, is not done any favour by the relatively low bottling strength. 43% nc ncf

Teerenpeli Single Malt Aged 10 Years batch 1-22 db (91) n23 gooseberry that's fit to explode, kissed by lemon blossom honey; t23.5 the silly arrival melts in the mouth. The oak offers up vanillas to die for...and then a sherry fruitiness is absorbed into it; f21.5 dries and bitters thanks to a slight niggle on a wine cask; b23 this has more sherry trifle quality than some sherry trifles I've had! Quite lovely but could have done with being around the 46-50% abv mark for this to really hit its straps. As it is, a slight fault on the finish apart, this is simply brilliant. 43%

Teerenpeli Kaski Single Malt aged in sherry cask, batch no. 3/20, db (94.5) n23.5 t24 f23 b24 It is though one is tasting this remarkable whisky through a prism, with all its pure colours of flavour split into sharp, deeply attractive tone poems. Clarity on the palate rarely happens along by chance: someone has done some outstanding distilling and used to-die-for casks. 43% nc ncf

Teerenpeli Kaski batch 1-22 sherry and bourbon casks db (85) n22 t22 f20 b21 What a shame! Usually a joy to experience, this version has been weakened by a niggle on the finish not uncommon with sherry casks. 43%

Teerenpeli Kulo Single Malt aged in sherry cask, batch no. 2/20, db **(86) n23 t23 f19 b21** As modern classic sherry casks go, it's pretty classic...even to the extent of the distinct weakness on the finish... A shame as the nose has many of the grapey traits that once made sherry cask whisky so seductive. *50.7% nc ncf*

Teereenpeli Kulo Aged 7 Years batch 1-22 sherry casks db **(94) n23.5** black cherry and intense, well-aged, slightly overcooked fruitcake. But the spices....my word...the spices!!!! **t24** a firm layer of dry oak plants itself at the seat of the delivery. But not even that can prevent the grape from unravelling with toasty intent, raisins to the fore, dates – both succulent and dried – following behind and then the return of the black cherry. It is that thin layer of heather honey and marzipan on which all this sits which guarantees the complexity; **f23** as usual, the oak waits its turn to soberly dry things a little, though the honey remains. But even now, the fruit chivvies and harries...; **b23.5** a pure, full-on orgy of sherry. If you like some whisky in your grape this chap is for you. Super-succulent and warming. And not an off-note to be found... *43%*

Teerenpeli Palo batch 1-22 db **(90) n23** moist fruitcake, burnt raisin and all, softened by dry, ashy phenols; **t22.5** immediate sugary impact, then a ballooning of smoke. The fruit takes time to re-establish itself...; **f22** much drier with lazy hints of chocolate mixing in with the raisin. Delicate spices flicker; **b22.5** a strangely hesitant whisky with none of the key constituents wishing at any time to take command. But that does mean extra, mildly anarchic, complexity... *46%*

Teerenpeli Portti Single Malt Distiller's Edition batch 1-18 db **(88.5) n23 t22.5 f21 b22** A massively mouth-watering rendition that is about as sharp and tart as any Scandinavian whisky I have ever encountered. Light smoke tries to dampen down the intensity, but with only limited success. Bowles along quite idiosyncratically, but undermined at the death by a slight bitterness. *43% nc ncf*

Teerenpeli Savu Single Malt peated, batch no. 1/21, db **(89) n23 t21.5 t22.5 b22** What a nose! A gently peated whisky even more gently delivered. Again, lapsed into a style, unlike its last bottling, that could do with upping the strength to at least 46% (preferably 50%) because in this guise the oils are slightly too broken up to give both the fuller body and length of finish it deserves. There are fine margins in getting this whisky at its best at this strength. *43% nc ncf*

Teerenpeli Savu batch 1-22 db **(94.5) n24** this type of sensuality on the nose with peat should be licensed. One of the sexiest peat noses on the planet. Sweet with just a hint of hickory amid the phenols...; **t23.5** there's the hickory again...some sweetened Fisherman's Friend for the Fins. The smoke drifts like peat reek from a crofter's chimney. Spices gather, warm and then retreat as the barley sugar gathers pace; **f23** the heftier sugars kick in relatively late, very much of the Demerara variety. A blend of vanilla and barley sugar does make a passing appearance before the smoke returns for the finale; **b24** a distillery that has lived by the sheer clarity of its magnificent distillate is reaping dividends here as the beauty of this whisky unfurls on the palate. Sublime. *43%*

FRANCE
Single Malt
DISTILLERIE ARTISANALE LEHMANN Obernai. Working.

Elsass Whisky Single Malt Whisky Alsacien Premium db (86) n20.5 t21.5 f22 b22. This is about as close as you'll get to an abstract single malt. The early discordant notes of the distillate are thrown against the canvas of the malt, and then fruit is randomly hurled at it, making a juicy, then spicy, splash. The overall picture when you stand back is not at all bad. But getting there is a bit messy. *50%. ncf.*

DISTILLERIE DE LAGUIOLE Laguiole. Working.

Esprit De Twelve Malt Spirit Peat Project port cask db (92.5) n23 t23.5 f23 b23 Beautifully distilled and massively impressive, at times having a touch of the Islays about it. Very youthful, of course, but where it is impresses most is the way the high phenol content appears controlled without losing any of its impact. And the clever way the sugars emerge from the smoke. The wine causes a slight wobble on the balance front, especially on immediate impact. But this beast has time in its favour. A great way to start the tasting day. *65%. sc.*

DISTILLERIE DE PARIS Paris. Working.

Distillerie De Paris Whisky Paris Single Malt db (89) n21 t23 f22 b23 Usually distilleries are named after remote hamlets or villages, located as they are in the countryside where modest streams provide the cooling water and just enough people live roundabout to be employed there. Calling yourself Paris Distillery is another way of doing it....if you want to make a statement! And the whisky seems to reflect this mode of thought as this is big, earthy stuff which pumps its chest out early and is determined to make its way in the whisky world. A distillery to keep a watchful gaze upon... *43%.*

DISTILLERIE DES MENHIRS Bretagne. Working.
Eddu Brocéliande pure buckwheat aged for 5 years in French oak, bott code: L2052, db (**86**) **n21 t22 f21.5 b21.5** As clankingly heavy and ungainly as their Ed Gwenn is as clean, delicate, and fragile: the opposite end of this distillery's spectrum. The wide cut gives nutty and chewy personality to this, as does the unwieldly molasses 43%

Eddu Gold pure buckwheat aged for 10 years in French oak, db (**95.5**) **n24 t24 f23.5 b24** And when they say Gold, they aren't joking. The whole structure of this whisky, from nose to finish is like a house of cards... Magnifique! 43%

Ed Gwenn Whisky D'orge distilled from pure barley aged for 4 years in French and American oak casks, bott code: L2121, db (**91.5**) **n23 t23.5 f22.5 b22.5** The colour of Riesling, this promises a juicy barleyfest...and there are no disappointments. The cleanest, juiciest French whisky of the year. Beautifully made...and bravely matured! 45%

Eddu Silver pure buckwheat aged for 5 years in cognac casks, bott code: L2113, db (**89.5**) **n21.5 t22.5 f22.5 b23** Not the great Edu Silvers I have enjoyed in times past. But still, plenty of entertainment value, if a little clumsy in its execution. 43%

DISTILLERIE DU PÉRIGOLD Sarlat. Working.
Lascaw Blended Malt Whisky Aged 12 Years finished in Perigord truffle flavoured speciality oak barrels, bott 10/12/2019, bott code: L 65752/05/00 db (**91.5**) **n23.5 t22 f23 b23** Usually I get my truffles when breakfasting at Claridge's in London, their delicate tones emanating from my stupendous Eggs Benedict. I have to confess that I cannot be certain if what I get on the nose is that rare and celebrated fungus. But what I cannot deny is that this malt does have a certain je ne sais quoi, ensuring far above average complexity and grace. Mind you, at 46% this would be so much better... 40%

DISTILLERIE ERGASTER Passel. Working.
ER 2015 Single Malt Whisky Tourbé No. 001 db (**94**) **n23.5 t23.5 f23 b24** Magnifique! A stunning first bottling from Ergaster. Very much their own style of peatiness...and what style! Encore! 45%. 1,900 bottles.

DISTILLERIE GILBERT HOLL Ribeauvillé. Working.
Lac'Holl Vieil Or 10 Years Old Single Malt Whisky db (**92.5**) **n22.5 t23.5 f23 b23.5** A malt which gives one's taste buds a real working over. Superb balance. 42%

Lac'Holl 15 Years Old Single Malt Whisky db (**90.5**) **n23.5 t22.5 f22 b22.5** Such a rare display of barley and gristy sugars. Very impressive malt. And fabulously refreshing. 42%

DISTILLERIE GLANN AR MOR Larmor-Pleubian. Working.
Glann ar Mor Single Malt Bourbon Barrel bott 2021, db (**87**) **n22 t22.5 f21 b21.5** Still a long way from the honeyed greatness that this brand for so long exhibited. The extra width on the cut has ensured a little toffee-nougat is mixed in with the massive malt. Much more chewy, cumbersome and, finally, bitter than had long been its trademark, but at least doesn't stint on the malt. 46%

Glann Ar Mor American cask db (**88.5**) **n21.5 t22.5 f22 b22.5** By this distillery's standards, a pleasant, though relatively limited incarnation. Don't get me wrong: a perfectly serviceable and quaffable malt, bursting with Demerara sugars and spices. But amid the spikes come a lot of flat lines, especially on the nose. Excellent pre-prandial whisky, nonetheless, to get the tastebuds moving. 52%

Glann Ar Mor Double Maturation Cognac Cask db (**95.5**) **n23.5** the lightness of touch from the smoke is, well...I have to say it...just so sexy!! Such a tease of a nose with the healthy vanillas operating as the perfect foil; **t24** mouthfeel, the degree of sweetness to smoke...the lot... exemplary. This is magnificent spirit, clean and feint-free allowing the peat to play out unmolested, but with the ulmo honey marrying with both the intense malt and the highly strung vanillas from the cask to hit the heights; **f24** no chance of a quick fade here. This is a whisky, thanks to its superb oils and healthy use of phenols, that has decided to stay the course. Just more of the same...for a long time. Finally, the smoke subsides, the vanillas increase and it dries elegantly; **b24** everything comes together here...everything. The weight, the degree of oils, the clarity of the ulmo honey...and, of course, the smoke which is neither heavy nor light but appears to be administered in exact portions when and where required. A true classic even by this distillery's high standards. 52%

Glann ar Mor Single Malt Pedro Ximenez Finish 2021 bourbon barrel, PX cask finish, bott 2021, db (**92.5**) **n23 t23.5 f23 b23** Once more, this distillery has managed to find an absolutely top quality PX cask – vitally, without even the faintest hint of sulphur. It is absolutely taint free... so rare! Being a finish, the malt itself has had time to build up enough weight and body to carry the grape without being crushed by it. Silky, fruity, and always thoroughly enjoyable. Massively impressed by this. 56.3% sc

Kornog Coteaux du Layon 11 Years Old 2021 db (91) n21.5 delicate fruit, apricot in particular, but pretty tight and enclosed; t23 opens up beautifully on delivery. A classic example of a whisky charming by waves, the majority of them being a mix of sugars and fruit. The apricot is confirmed from the nose and helped by dark muscovado sugars rather than honey found in other whiskies from this distillery. Spices find a constant route through the piece, always changing their degree of intensity; f23.5 ah...now we have serious complexity: the surviving oils stretch out the fruit from the pith, the latter ensuring a drier persona more commensurate with the malt and increasing tannin; b23 a very different Kornog ultimately making a lie of the unpromising nose and treating the palate to a complex and lengthy examination. Classy and elegant. 50%

Kornog Single Malt Pedro Ximenez 2020 peated, sherry PX butt, bott 2020, db (95) n23.5 t23.5 f24 b24 PX and peat. Nearly always less a tale of harmony as one of open warfare. And though it may be on the nose, certainly by the mid-arrival weapons have been down and compromise has been reached. So rare do I find a PX cask which is involved with complexity. And yet here one is. For this is very, very complex, indeed... 56.2% sc

Kornog Single Malt Roc'h Hir 2021 peated, bourbon barrel, bott 2021, db (94) n24 t23.5 f23 b23.5 Under new ownership this distillery may be – and even found now with a change of name – but the exceptionally high quality of the Glann Ar Mor it was distilled as has not been remotely compromised. Excellent. 46%

Kornog Single Malt Sant Erwan 2021 peated, bourbon barrel, bott 2021, db (95.5) n24 t24 f23.5 b24 A growling, heavyweight of a malt which shows the peat in full muscular fashion. And with no shortage of hairs for good measure. However, it is the clever control of the honey that sets this one apart and ensure that this is a heavyweight with a gentle touch. Just brilliant. 50% sc

Kornog Saint Erwan 2022 db (94) n23 not quite as slick as the Saint Ivy or so willing to allow the grist to play a part. Here we have uncompromising phenols showing a degree of belligerence; t24 far more relaxed on delivery...at first. That's thanks to some early oils softening the way. As these dissipate, the phenols again gang together and dry. The midground does conjure up some complexity thanks to a light butterscotch thread linking with light mint; f23 dries fast and simplistically, leaving vanilla, smoke and a nagging spice buzz in its wake; b24 an admirably rough and ready type peated malt which rolls up its sleeves and is happy to do battle on the palate. 52%

Kornog Saint Ivy 2021 db (95) n23.5 even the peat muscles have peat: make no mistake... this is phenolic. You know when the peat is serious: it goes past that malty sugary phase and heads towards powdery dryness. And here you have it...; t24 as mouth-filling as it is mouth-watering, the is pulsing out the peat in tandem with glorious, gristy sugars, plus a light Love Heart candy. But just magnificent is the salivating barley which swirls around the palate like a free spirit; f23.5 long and continues to celebrate the depth of both the peat and barley and, increasingly, the vanilla...; b24 a pretty close relation to the Glann ar Mor Cognac cask, though with much bolder peat. Stunning, gristy freshness to this that reminded me of relatively young Port Ellen before it was needlessly and brainlessly murdered. 57.6%

Oloroso 21 DM db (96) n24 the grape tries to take a foothold. But the smoke seeps from every direction: huge and wonderfully controlled. Forget the alcohol: this is intoxicating from the enormity of its personality alone...; t24 the peat and sherry marriage on delivery is like sinking back in a huge leather chair. You are at once consumed and at the same time comforted...while always slightly in awe. Neither the peat nor grape is overly cooked. But one appears to bolster the other, so even the light spices which scurry around like field mice are nothing more than background. A word, though, for the intricate mix of molasses and manuka honey which thicken, soften, balance, cajole and delight...magnifique...! f23.5 long, but with far more vanilla on the fade than was shown previously, with a little ulmo honey amid the spices; b24.5 less a taste of whisky. More a life experience. Too often peat and sherry cancel the other out. Not here. This is the definition of harmony. 57.6%

DISTILLERIE GRALLET-DUPIC Rozelieures. Working.
G.Rozelieures Whisky De Lorraine Single Malt Whisky bott code: L446 db (87) n21.5 t22.5 f21 b22. Exceptionally nutty. The blossoming of the sugars on delivery is always attractive, as are the complex nougat/caramel/cocoa tones. Though the feints are always a threat, the genteel pace and softness of the malt makes it well worth a look. 40%

DISTILLERIE HEPP VUM MODERTAL Uberach. Working.
Authentic Whisky D'Alsace Whisky Single Malt Doble Fût No. 7 db (87) n21 t23 f21 b22 A much more complete malt than their No.6. The nose is a tad austere and, again, the

finale requires a fire extinguisher as the degree of burn increases. But there is no doubting the beauty and integrity of the delivery, a kind of malt and chocolate bonbon, even with a Milky Way element. My word it's hot, though. 40%. ncf.

DISTILLERIE J.ET M. LEHMANN Obernai. Working.

Lehmann Rendezvous Single Malt Peated bott code: L6604122 db **(90)** n22.5 if you have never encountered a soothing peaty nose before, well you have now...the delicateness to the phenols is remarkable, as though blended in with vanilla for extra gentility; t23 incredibly thick and chewy. There is a light cream soda touch to this, though the smoke soon drifts in alongside some pretty rich malt; f22 remains thick and malty, with the peat adding just a degree of extra depth. Playful muscovado sugars hang on 'til the death; b22.5 just noticed on the bottle that the notes suggest a finish of "tobacco leaves". So glad they are not to be found on this bottling as nine times out of ten that is a sign of a technical fault with the whisky. This is a much more lush, creamy affair with a delicate sweetness to accompany the gentle phenols. 40%

Lehmann C'est La Vie! Blended Whisky bott code L5505622 db **(86)** n21 t22 f21 b21.5 A very soft blend which operates between expansive vanilla, toffee and a tight, dry fruitiness with a furry, pithy orange peel tang. 40% ncf

Lehmann Coup de Foudre Single Malt db **(87.5)** n21.5 t22.5 f21.5 b22 A charmingly delicate malt which makes great play of the sweet gristiness of the barley and its intermingling with soft ripe greengage and gooseberry. A slight feintiness, noticeable on both nose and finish, and other extra oils reveal a wide cut, which makes the gentle caressing of the barley all the more remarkable. 40%

Lehmann Elsass Single Malt Gold db **(85.5)** n20 t22.5 f21.5 b21.5 If memory serves, I think I once described Lehman's whisky as "abstract", which the last four samples I've tasted today appears to confirm. This, briefly, is far more of the romantic school with a tradition and craftsmanship around the intense malt which is the centre of this study. Still the nose remains a challenge, as does the late finish. But all else is focussed on powering barley and some attractive spices. 40%

Lehmann Elsass Single Malt Origine db **(85)** n21.5 t22 f20.5 b21 The nose is pretty earthy and intense with a lot of dried kumquat peel at work, too. The highlight is the delivery, where the malt and its accompanying acacia honey goes into overdrive. The remainder is not quite the happiest of tales, with a bitterness digging in. Untidy despite the odd flash of joy. 40%

Lehmann Premium (92.5) n23 a deep, labyrinthine nose, though we appear to be swimming in a sea of heather honey to get to the bottom. The oak pulses on the nose...; t23.5 my word! The sheer viscosity of this malt takes the breath away: I swear I could stand a spoon in this stuff! The assembly of varied sugars and honeys is astonishing: ulmo honey in cahoots with heather honey on one hand, while a slightly lighter combination of fruitier muscovado and demerara sugars flit about on another. On a deeper level, the full oils from the cut rumble with thick vanilla to signify passing summers in the cask. The spices are present but tame...; f23 long and forever drier in personality, the vanilla refusing to give way; b23 the wide cut is forgiven here, taking into account the sheer deliciousness of its results. Sweet but, thankfully, never cloying and complex in both its build up and denouement. 50%

Lehmann Rendezvous (89.5) n22 heady spices (perhaps from a generous cut) lead the way with creamy-honeyed notes not far behind: not unlike rice pudding with a blob of acacia honey splodged in the middle; t23 a change in the pecking order: honey first, then spices and cream neck and neck just behind. Those oils ensure a suitably sensuous feel, while the layering at the midpoint is excellent; f22 highly attractive and lingering burnt honeycomb and butterscotch, then a thickening of the oils; b22.5 no problems having a rendezvous with this whisky any time. Not technically perfect, but the generosity of the honey more than makes amends. Oh, and I'd like to dedicate this whisky to my old school classmate from 50 years ago, Pendered, and his never-to-be-forgotten contribution to our in-English game of Call My Bluff. If he reads this, I need say no more... 40%

DISTILLERIE MERLET ET FILS Saint-Sauvant. Working.

Coperies Single Malt French oak barrels db **(89)** n21.5 lurking small still coppery oils but dulled by dry toffee; t23 now there's a transformation! The oils really are significant and on delivery soon capture and then amplify the gorgeous heather honey. The tannins press slightly with a delicate spice. Copper abounds, but the sharper vanillas are overcome by duller caramel...; f22 dries again, just as on the nose and though the copper sparkles still, that toffee returns, dulling the effect until a little bitterness creeps in; b22.5 a rich single malt in which both the alembic and the French oak play significant parts. The nose is a relatively simple affair and the finish battles with a little, out-of-sync late bitterness. But between those two points is a whisky of great charm, depending heavily on a delightful heather honey core, backed by major copper involvement and on-the-money oils: this was not made in a large still! Indeed, there is indubitably something of the Royal Lochnagars about this single malt. A little too much toffee dulls some of the complexity. If they could restrain those toffee notes and get the strength a little higher, what a whiskey this could become.... 40%

DISTILLERIE MEYER Hohwarth. Working.

Meyer's Pur Malt bott code L2313096 db (88.5) n21.5 t22.5 f22 b22.5 Tasting this on the mainland continent, rather than in Britain as I normally do, I shall have to report back to Percy, my Meyer's parrot, that there is a distinct improvement on the bread and butter malt of his favourite distillery. The nose is still revealing a weakness of the still but on the palate there is a far more impressive array of positive malty tones than was once the case. Some of them, I swear, carry a degree of smoke, too....and a hint of Werther's Originals And that has done no harm to the overall longevity of the richer tones. Oh, and the gristiness is also making a statement, making this a sweeter fellow than of old bar far. On the cusp of being a cracker.... 40%

Bourbon By Meyer's bott code L2303798 db (90.5) n22.5 a little weakness, perhaps, very similar to the Pur Malt, but the barley makes its mark as does a more marzipan-stye sweetness; t22.5 that's such a silky texture with a fruity corn oil subtext. That marzipan isn't going anywhere....; f23 a sticky if occasionally bitter ending. Once more, though, it is the outrageously full-on depth to that flavour profile, including the varied sweetness of the sugars, that keeps you spellbound. The vanillas are just as diverse, though the pulse of the spice is far more rigid; b23 one thing you can guarantee about Meyer's is that their whiskies really do generate enormous flavour and interest on the palate. Pretty neutral and non-committal when cold. Far more intense and colourful on both nose and palate when slightly warmed. Just adore the sweetness to spice ratio on this and the small grain charm. Having just returned from Kentucky, I can't say that this reminds me of any of the over 250 bourbon and other American whiskeys I tasted over there. But this is deserving to be enjoyed in its own right anyway. 40%

Meyer's Hohwarth Blend Superieur bott code L2318495 db (86) n21.5 t22.5 f21 b21 You never feel quite relaxed with this one or sure where it is going. On the nose that distinctive Pur Malt aroma clings to blend like an inexpensive perfume. Things improve with that unmistakable silkiness of the Hohwarth on the palate and this year enjoys just an extra degree of malty salivation. There is a subtle fruit strata which never yields, but the oils are pretty intense. The midpoint, though, is doused in sheer, hairy-chested malt because it comes to its chalky dry conclusion despite the best efforts of the Sauternes. A bewildering whisky. 40%

Meyer's Hohwarth Blend Superieur Finition En Fut De Bourgogne bott code L2303195 db (92) n22.5 curiously beefy with a lightly phenolic, meaty depth. Not exactly what I was expecting. Attractively full-bodied though, that's for sure....!! t23 another surprise! Where did all that sweetness come from after that nose...? Massive muscovado sugar kick, fruity and intense with the expected spices holding back behind a curtain of vanilla. Only now does the Sauternes involvement become apparent, not just with the juiciness but also a degree of grape skin depth, too; f23 satisfyingly complex, even now this bend refuses to let down its silky guard. Still the malts can be picked out and still those spices buzz. And the fruit keeps a watchful eye; b23.5 one of those blends you can either sit down on your own and be caressed by. Or with friends, occasionally calling a halt to the conversation for this whisky to have a very quiet but deeply interesting word with you. 40%

Meyer's Hohwarth Blend Superieur Finition Pinot Noir bott code L2312395 db (92.5) n23 the full crispness of the Pinot Noir grape has rarely been so apparent in a whisky as it is on this nose. But, because of its rigidity, there is room enough for the malt to encircle it to superb effect. So satisfying...and promising...; t23 no disappointment on delivery. That concentrated grapey firmness remains. But there is so much more, including plums, figs, black cherry and yellow raspberry jam with a mix of vanilla and thinned heather honey for even more glory. All this topped by just-so spicy seasoning off the oak...; f23 long, the oil concentrating now, as does the honey as the fruit recedes. No off notes, no bitterness, no tiredness from the cask....just silky remnants of all that was good...; b23.5 how can a whisky, so solidly hard in its fruit with the pinot, be so seducingly soft on the palate. And, what's more, so pitch perfect with the silkier, more yielding aspects, too. A fruit salad which never loses sight of the fact that it's a whisky... Quite lovely...with the exception of the hint of the dreaded S word.... 40%

DISTILLERIE MOUTARD Buxeuil. Working

Distillerie Moutard Whisky Bio finished in Chablis Grand Cru Les Clos db (89) n22.5 green apples all over this very young, fresh aroma. Gently metallic but hidden hints of a generous cut, too...; t22 youthful, malty and screaming "small still" from the glass as the delicate copper shimmers. Salivating, the delicate barley intermingles with that persistent windfall diced apple. The spices are busy, consistent but never loud; f22 vanillas try to settle but are upstaged by a tart fruitiness, at times perhaps a touch too tart; **b22.5** one of the rare organic whiskies anywhere in the world that has not been weakened by too wide a cut. That doesn't mean to say the spirit is perfect, as there is evidence that its hearts are just a little too generous. But the slight eccentricity of the grape influence from the cask covers over most of the damage while the malt at times also has its moments. But it is the influence of the copper from the still which gives this particular character. And one, when tied in with all those other factors, which makes the profile of the whisky quite unique. *45% sc*

M Whisky Bio 3 Years Old lot: WB*23821 db **(87) n21.5 t22.5 f21 b22** While it is a well-known fact that I don't pop my cork for every whisky I see, I also have to say that in 30 years of professionally tasting whisky no cork has ever popped more loudly than when I opened this bottle: my ears are still ringing...! As for the whisky sealed by that cork...well it is typically young, as is this distillerie's wont. That means the grains have full permission to make maximum impact, which they need no second invitation to do. The nose is a mixed, inconclusive, bag; fruity in a vague way with tannins giving weight but not helping in direction. The piece de resistance is the delivery, a pandora's box of grassy, grainy salivation, softened only by a little orange-blossom honey. After a brief flirtation with cocoa the finish dries and, ultimately, feels a tad too austere for its own good. *45%. sc.*

M Whisky Fumé 3 Years Old lot: WDER1*12521, bott 05 May 21 db **(91) n22** young, but a fascinating interplay between freshly diced crisp, green apple and an apologetic phenol, nonetheless: a genuinely unique and charming signature; **t23.5** now, this is the business. That is a fabulous delivery making the most of the whisky's tender years to ensure juiciness and quite enormous presence. The smoke rumbles around like clothes in a washing machine, exploring all avenues of the palate and forms a wonderful counterweight to those grassy, heather-honeyed higher tones of the grain. The mid-point, a welter of crashing waves, is quite a thing! **f22.5** relatively calm with the oak at last getting not just a foothold but taking charge for the house's usual dry finale; **b23** my French not being perhaps what it once was, I thought for a minute that this might reek of cigarettes! But, no, it is gently earthy and impressively adroit. Most enjoyable and at times pretty classy. *45%. sc.*

⟡ **Moutard 5 Ans Vieillissement Prolonge single cask** db **(91.5) n22.5** toffee apples at their very crunchiest alongside powerful tannin tones from the oak; **t23** silky and perfectly balanced from the very first mouthful. There are melt-in-the-mouth Demerara sugars working alongside the butterscotch, spices and ever-deepening tannin to ensure this never becomes aggressive and the right side of entertaining. Comforting, even...; **f23** just love the way the late chocolate builds so subtly into praline. Beautifully structured and complex; **b23** great to see a Moutard shewing the odd grey hair. And while some aspects remain youthful, the complexity levels are deeply satisfying as is the overall cask involvement. Whisky tres satisfaisant. *45%*

UNSPECIFIED

⟡ **Baron Denis Triple Cask** sherry, bourbon and banyuls casks **(89.5) n23** an uplifting deftly sweet, gently fruity aroma baring not the hint of a tooth. Creamy with a sprinkle of spice and just a hint of chewy fruit candy...; **t23** pure velvet! The fruit purrs over the palate, the highest notes having a kind of pink grapefruit stir to them. The sugars play an important part, mainly muscovado in style but with a little ginger and spice stirred in for good measure; **f21.5** bitters out with just a little too much enthusiasm. Good spice recovery, though...; **b22** soft and serene, this is a malt determined to serenade the palate. And succeeds... *40%*

Brenne matured in French oak **(89) n22.5** different.... very different! Indeed, unique! Just how Seville oranges have ended up in this I'll never know, and there is more than a touch of Jaffa Cake here, including the dark chocolate. The malt is in there somewhere, but hard to pinpoint. Those tannins and semi-liqueur-ish fruit notes are astonishing...; **t23** the initial taste profile comes as no surprise, but the tactility of the mouthfeel perhaps does. This is clinging and melt-in-the-mouth fare, all caresses and devoid of conflict. Those unique fruit notes are upfront again; **f21** the contrasting bitterness from the oak is perhaps something that needs to be tamed and controlled further down the line. It is a little out of place with the earlier performance; **b22.5** for each Whisky Bible there are maybe only three or four times I sit up and realise I'm in unchartered territory. Here is one such instance. Extremely fruity and perhaps a stepping-stone for those who think they don't like whisky but love liqueurs... *40%*

Maison Benjamin Kuentz Aux Particules Vines Edition 5 Blended Whisky finished in Lafon-Rochet barrels **(89) n22** malt and butterscotch combine quite sensually; **t22.5** super-soft delivery. Young, a little aimless at first but settles on exactly the same path as the nose with a some cocoa thrown in for good measure; **f22** warming with a late jammy flourish; **b22.5** pleasant and salivating, the spices are just kept in check by the fresh fruitiness. *46%*

Maison Benjamin Kuentz Aux Particules Vines Edition 6 Single Malt finished in red wine barrels **(86.5) n22.5 t22 f20.5 b21.5** On the nose the grape takes advantage of the light clean body. While on delivery there is sweet, succulent boiled fruit candy. Light tannins add a backbone and weight, The midpoint is not unlike the old sherry trifles of long ago; Finishes with aggressive spices and cherry. These whiskies have their own very unusual foibles. So many enjoyable outlines, but never seems to connect up to a main body. Great fun, though. *52%*

Maison Benjamin Kuentz Aveux Gourmands Single Malt finished in Rayne-Vigneau barrels **(88) n22 t21 f23 b22** Sometimes, as seriously as I take my work, you sometimes just have to laugh. Just recovering from the ploughing my tastebuds had received from the fish on their Cognac cask version, we now travel 180 degrees to a whisky which struggles on delivery, but positively massages your taste buds at the finish into whimpering, ecstatic submission. When I say, "struggles on delivery", what I mean is that the mouth feel on arrival is so uniquely slick and oily, that the mouth is momentarily thrown into confusion, and you have problems registering the actual taste. The nose is a little different, too: a vague maltiness mixed with an earthy-vegetable note. After the confusion of the delivery, the malt stakes its claim and builds up with a deliciously concentrated gristiness. You can certainly depend on Maison Benjamin for broadening your whisky horizons... *46%*

Maison Benjamin Kuentz Fin de Partie Single Malt ex cognac, bourbon, PX, oloroso and new oak barrels **(94) n23 t24 f23 b24** Someone has done a truly exceptional job in bringing all these cask types together and creating a malt as exceptionally balanced as this. Usually, such ventures are more likely to end in tears of disappointment than delight. Not this time. The nose has great fund bowling out various grapey sugars in tandem with a pasty, thick maltiness. At times you wonder, even, if some phenol has crept in from somewhere or whether it is a freak by-product of mixed tannins. But it is the delivery and follow-through which stuns: woven silk of salivating grape and malt purring through with varying levels of intensity. There is a hotness which reflects not so well on the distillate itself. But still the tastebuds are worked over by a chocolate milkshake of the British school and then a maltshake of the American, which fruitier sugars ping around like a British NHS ap. Wonderfully flawed. But the price to pray for such brilliant balance. *46%*

Maison Benjamin Kuentz Inouïe Mélodie Single Malt finished in red wine barrels **(87.5) n22.5 t22.5 f21 b21.5** Despite the house hotness and bite on delivery, the remainder of the story lacks many thrills and spills. Very warm whisky which is worth a go just for that astonishingly tart fruit explosion on delivery. Have a hanky on hand to dab away a tear. *46% sc*

Maison Benjamin Kuentz Spicy Nauba Single Malt (86.5) n22 t23 f20 b21.5 A very different kind of malt whisky with some elements that almost border on a liqueur. One is reminded of coconut from time to time, without that element ever really coming to the fore. The vanilla is certainly in full flow, both on nose and delivery and helps shape a silky mouthfeel which is greatly enriched by ulmo honey. But there is always a weakness to the structure: it is hinted at on the nose and confirmed on the somewhat metallic finish. Until that point, those with a sweet tooth will be fully satisfied. *45%*

Maison Benjamin Kuentz Tohu-Bohu des Terres Single Malt (92) n23 a joyous amalgamation of confident but by no mean arrogant peat and a sublime walnut subplot. Weighty, outwardly youthful, but never less than elegant; **t23** superb, lightly oiled mouthfeel from the very start allows the peat to have a two-dimensional aspect, sticking to the palate to ensure an earthy countenance, and then a much lighter smokiness which swirls around giddily. There is a light lemon-sherbet fizz to this, too, underlining a certain youthfulness, while guaranteeing balance both in flavour and weight; **f22.5** smoky peating bolstered by background spice...and some major tannins arriving very late in the game; **b23.5** impressively constructed malt where the peat has been used cleverly so not to drown out the various intrigues and sub-plots elsewhere. Rather lovely. *56.2%*

Maison Benjamin Kuentz Vegetal Musette 3 Year Old Single Malt aged in cognac barrels **(87.5) n22.5 t22 f21 b22** An outline feintiness gets the oils all in a dither. These work better on the nose, where a sticky gently spiced kumquat note quite impresses, than on the ultimately austere palate. Once past the chewy and intense malt on delivery – which appears to have a monopoly on the sugars - we are into slightly roughhouse territory. Still, the one thing that can't be levelled at this malt is dullness. Nor technical perfection. *45%*

Vatted Malts

Bellevoye Bleu Whisky Triple Malt Finition Grain Fin bott code: A18184A **(87.5) n21.5 t22 f22 b22** Goes pretty hefty on the tobacco note on both nose and delivery. But the wide cut delivers impressively on the chocolate nougat and even, surprisingly, a degree of chewy date alongside the malt. *40%.*

Bellevoye Blanc Whisky Triple Malt Finition Sauternes bott code: A18199A **(82.5) n20 t21.5 f21 b20** I am tasting in the near dark here for maximum sensory effect – and this one nearly knocked me off my chair. Certainly one of the strangest malts I have tasted this year with the most vividly citrusy nose on a Sauternes finish I have ever encountered – almost like washing up liquid. To say this whisky has a clean nose would be an understatement... Malty on the palate, but never quite feels right. *40%.*

Bellevoye Rouge Whisky Triple Malt Finition Grand Cru bott code: A18200A **(83)** **n21.5 t22 f19.5 b20** Despite the Grand Cru, there Smoke Blue as a tobacco element makes an undesired contribution. The fruit is sweet and intense, though. The finish a bit of a mess. *43%.*

GERMANY
ASCAIM EDLE DISTILLATE

⬥ **Tassilo Finest Munich Buckwheat Whisky** virgin oak barrels fasselageiung 2020-2023 lot no 8 db **(89)** **n22** punchy grain with ulmo honey and vanilla trying to keep a handle on the more muscular spices; **t22.5** wow! Just massive! The spice splinters everywhere, literally as the oak bulges around the palate. A little honey tries to calm things but gives up when the buckwheat itself catapults itself back into the fray: exhausting! **f22** very long with a little late cocoa taking on the outlandish oak and spice; **b22.5** buckwheat rarely plays games and it has no intention here, either. The oak has certainly installed some charming ulmo honey into the mix, mainly on the nose and to a lesser degree on the delivery. The huge flavour pile-up through the middle, with the buckwheat and spices trading blows, really does get the taste buds salivating. Very much a non-conformist whisky, this makes a point of broadcasting the individual flavours as loudly as possible, though one not always in tune with the other. That said, just love the whisky's bold, outgoing personality and flavour intensity. Would love to see this at cask strength...! Hold on to your hats if they ever do... *43%*

BIMMERLE PRIVATE DISTILLERY Achern. Working.
Everman Wilhelm Black Forest Double Distilled Single Malt db **(88.5)** **n22 t23 f21.5 b22** One of the most intensely malty whiskies to come out of Germany this year, this distillery makes absolutely no apology for making the barley the centre of attention.... despite its remarkable barrel policy of seven different types of casks. Even so, the barley is ably supported by a confident yet sympathetic oak assembly all the way, so the overall theme is never less than mouth-filling and deeply attractive. The highlight is the delivery, where the tastebuds are bombarded and then over-run by intense, creamy malt. The downside is light feintiness, most prevalent on the nose and finish, which is little helped by the aggressive aspects of the European oak deployed. But to forgive is easy when you get an exhibition of barley like this. *42%*

Everman Theo Black Forest Double Distilled Blended Whisky db **(90.5)** **n21.5** much lighter and far less maltier than their single malt. There is a little bickering tannin...; **t23** ah, much more like it. One fraction of the malty intensity found on their single malt. But the overall softness helps facilitate the complexities of the tannins which play a far more important part here; **f23** long, creamy, still plenty of flickering malt. But amid the vanilla, butterscotch and ulmo honey we find brilliant strands of German tannin which ensure a controlled, spiced tanginess, setting this whisky apart from others; **b23** in the single malt version, the seven cask varieties clashed long before the end. Here we see far more harmony, as it works wonders for the bitter-sweet balance. A blend you'll not quite master until maybe the fifth or sixth glass. A surprisingly complex cove. *40%*

BIRGITTA RUST PIEKFEINE BRÄNDE Bremen. Working.
Van Loon 5 Year Old Single Malt Whisky batch 2012 db **(85)** **n21.5 t22 f20 b21.5** Usually, a little extra strength will greatly enhance a complex whisky - if given time in the glass. The exception is when the cut is already a little too wide, resulting in a lumpy, ultimately bitter effort. Where this does benefit is in the richness of the fruit and the light mocha effect. *55%.*

BLACK FOREST WHISKEY Neubulach. Working
⬥ **Doinich Daal Black Forest Single Malt Baurahaib Batch No 06** db **(93)** **n23** such beautifully tapered heather honey. Starts expansively as it gels with the malt. But then slowly reduces its effect as the oaky vanillas kick in...; **t23.5** so fat and chewy. There is a degree of boiled candy sweets to this - a mix of barley sugar and cherry drops - but that doesn't detract from those all-encompassing oils and gathering spices; **f23** spiced vanilla with a competitive degree of malt even late on. The very late note of mocha is welcome; **b23.5** beautifully made and etched. Slightly underpowered perhaps, but its charm is never in doubt. *40% ncf*

⬥ **Doinich Daal Black Forest Single Malt Lochsaag Batch No 07** db **(85.5)** **n22.5 t23 f19 b21** Quite a brash young whisky, slopping all those grapes around early on. And with that little extra molasses and fruitcake effect, not to mention those semi-explosive spices, for a while this worked beautifully. But from about a third the way in and then with that late bittering, balance is compromised and the dreaded S word creeps in. Still, plenty to enjoy early on. *50% ncf*

⟐ **Doinich Daal Black Forest Single Malt Pfaffarrauscher Batch No 07** db (94.5) n23 there is almost a degree of playfulness to the citrus as it uplifts the malt and impressive oaky vanillas which have combined in impressive form. As for the spices? Wow! Could they be any more tingling? **t24** oh, what a mouth feel...what a delivery! Certainly 100 out of a possible 100 for that delivery which teams with the most ridiculously complex array of barley notes, of so many hues. Not just in tones of flavour but also intensity. But that isn't all: the overall viscosity of the oils simply cannot be bettered. As perfection subsides into just delightful brilliance, the malt keep their place at the table and the spice enjoy an extra course or two...; **f23.5** like chocolate wafers? Then you'll certainly love this. Especially if your passion is for delicately spiced ones...; **b24** the delivery offers the best opening seven or eight seconds on the palate of any whisky you'll taste this year. At times this is majestic. Your palate will rarely take a more enjoyable walk in the Black Forest. 48% ncf

BRENNEREI AM FEUERGRABEN Achern. Working.

⟐ **Salamansar Oloroso 10 Jahre First Fill Oloroso**, sherry butt finish db (92) n23 not sure I remember this much oak on a Salamansar bottling...and it is no worse for it. That builds the perfect dais from which the grape makes a very confident speech, though never trying to talk over the biscuity vanilla; **t24** so fat and lush on delivery. But the real fun begins when the monumentally spiced fruit carries with it a Jaffa cake chocolate and orange sweetness which peaks as a glorious triumph. Sensational...; **f22** long yet nowhere near as startling at the delicious apogee. We are back now to delicate vanillas and butterscotch with the fruit a fading memory...; **b23** hearty congrats to the distillers. They have made an indelible mark with their ten-year-old as the climax of this malt is among the best I have tasted from Europe this year. 50.4% ncf

⟐ **Salamansar Single Malt Acham 10 Jahre** 10% peated malt, sherry butt finish db (85) n21 t21.5 f21 b12.5 Even when warmed and cajoled, this remains a tight whisky throughout: shy, clinging on to its secrets with a mildly bitter backbone which congregate at the finish, though softened slightly by a modicum of cocoa. The oils offer an illusion of co-operation, as do some sparse sugars. Genuinely a unique flavour profile. 49% sc ncf

⟐ **Salamansar Single Malt Sherry Butt 4 Jahre** db (89.5) n22.5 quite a creamy feel to this blueberry pie; **t23** excellent delivery with plenty of muscovado sugars meeting a delicate maltiness. The oak is quite gruff and distributes its vanillas quite randomly and thickly...; **f22** that delightfully textured maltiness sticks to its guns and refuses to let the oak take command; **b22** a pleasing, profoundly malty youngster which, beyond the nose, has little to say in the wine department. Lovely mouth feel, too. 50.2%

BOSCH-EDELBRAND Unterlenningen. Working

Whisky Stube Spirit Of The Cask Gelber Fels Whisky French limousin oak, dist Oct 2014, bott Nov 2020, bott code: L01B11R20 (85.5) n20.5 t22.5 f21 b21.5 Not the first and won't be the last European whisky to fail slightly on the nose due to an over-exaggerated cut...and then blow you away with the enormity on the palate. The grain is not only intense, it appears to double up and come back at you again, this time bringing with it a light dose of acacia honey. With a wide cut comes the inevitable untidy finish. But a shrinking violet this is not... 60.9%

BRENNEREI FELLER Dietenheim-Regglisweiler. Working

⟐ **Feller Single Malt Torf PX Sherry Cask Strength** los 2911, dist 03/03/16 db (95.5) n24 the phenols have a very different temperament to the Islay style and a stark acidity that makes you leap upright in your seat. The tannins from the oak are also at fever pitch. Curiously, the grape hardly makes a mark. Wow...; **t24** can't really ask more of a central European peated malt than this. Clean from an excellent distillation, malty and underlined by the intrinsic sweetness which permeates throughout. The PX has a little input here with a busy sugary bluster throughout. But the most telling tones are those struck by the biting peat and the fresh oakiness. The overall picture is astonishing; **f23.5** long and partially languid, the phenols flop around on one hand and then join forces with the tannins for a more penetrating attack with the other. There is a vague fruitcake score which can be heard, but this vanished under drying embers of phenol and chocolate; **b24** you have to hand it to these Fellers: they go out of their way to make distinctive, memorable, highly enjoyable whisky. And, once again, they have succeeded. I mean, 40 parts per million phenols (thats above Laphroaig, Lagavulin and Caol Ila) and at full cask strength. That's the way to do it...! And, better still, they have created their own distinctive style: this is not me-too Scotch style copy. This bares its very own, deeply distinctive hallmark. Fabulous, Fellers...! 62.4% sc nc ncf

⟐ **Feller Single Malt Torf PX Sherry Los 2911**, dist 03/03/16 db (91.5) n23 reduced, the peat is more idiosyncratic and less willing to join forces with the tannins for balance. Here the acidity off the phenol is almost overly aggressive; **t23.5** the fabulous phenols tumble over the palate ahead of all else...then a blast of thin honey before the tannins attack with pointed teeth;

f22 a shade bitter as the tannin has been exposed thanks to the reduction of oils. The smoke all but disappeared long ago. A little heather honey lasts the course; b23 here we have the junior, soft ball version of Feller's spellbinding Torf/PX cask strength bottling. And it underlines just how water breaks up the oils of a whisky, destabilising its structure. A really lovely whisky, of course, but palls by comparison with the glorious, unedited 62.4% version. 46% nc ncf

◈ **Feller Signature 12 Single Malt Amarone Cask Los 575**, dist 22/03/10 db (95) n23.5 mesmerising mix of fruit and nut. The fruit is represented by an ensemble of stewed plum, diced apple and a raisin-heavy fruitcake...all the perfect accompaniment to that distinctive walnut sub-plot. And the subtlety of those spices.... just brilliant! t23.5 the house style of controlled intensity is in full flow from the very first mouthful. The fruit is not only prominent, but it also lets you know it. The rising of the spices, beaming like a full moon over the horizon, is stunning. Not least because it appears to intensify the depth of those plums and raisins, and momentarily, a little quaver of malt itself; f24 a faultless finish. The oils are so perfectly weighted, the sugars now favouring a molasses-style disposing and the fruit veering to sharper under-ripe fig and over-ripe lime. The tannins add further ballast while the spices hum contently. One of the finishes of the year...; b24 I think we are seeing the work of a distillery that, year by year, becomes more confident in all it does and is able to display the benefits of ever-improving whisky at full volume. There is no doubt now that Feller has become one of Europe's stellar distilleries so far as quality is concerned. And this is another classic they can add to their ever-growing number. Oh, and if you want to do something wicked, try blending the full strength peated with the Signature 12. Oh...my....word....!!! 57.5% sc nc ncf 116 bottles

BRENNEREI HENRICH Kriftel, Hessia. Working.
Gilors Single Malt Islay Cask Finish ex Islay fass, dist Jul 2013, bott Oct 2019, db (86) n21 t21.5 f22 b21.5 Pleasantly malty. But the disjointed nose and slightly over enthusiastic oils limits promise and growth. 45%

Gilors Single Malt Peated Fassstärke bourbon fass, dist 2012 & 2013, bot May 2021, db (88.5) n22 t22.5 f22 b22 There is no doubting the singular style of the peat to this distillery's whisky: not the kind of phenol to lull you into a smoky comfort zone; more one bite acidly into both the nose and palate. This is especially true on the stark aroma, though the eye-watering delivery leaves you in no doubt that you are in the presence of malt with little inclination to take prisoners. A butterscotch-barley note – perhaps sweetened by thin ulmo honey - settles down the fuss somewhat. 54.9%

Gilors Single Malt Peated Madeira Madeira fass, Dist Dec 2016, bott May 2021, db (90) n22.5 t23 f22 b22.5 A better distillate than in previous years takes this malt up another gear. Most enjoyable – and not a gremlin to be found. 45.3%

Gilors Single Malt Portwein Fass dist Nov 2015, bott Jan 2021, db (86.5) n20 t23 f21.5 b22 Once you get past the nose it is plane sailing. The aroma simply doesn't work, but the malt rallies charmingly on delivery which enjoys a lovely cherry candy fruitiness. A little Jekyll and Hide it might be. But the good moments are very good... 43%

Gilors Single Malt Sherry Duett PX fass & olorosso fass, dist 2013 & 2014, bott May 2021, db (89) n21.5 t23 f21.5 b23 I have often been asked if I'd like some nuts with my sherry. And here I been presented with it as a fete accompli. The nose isn't the easier work. And there is a slight niggle to the finale, too. Nut such as the thoroughness of the barley, such is the understatement of the molasses, such is the purity of the strands of fruit...it all works rather well. And it looks like it was that nuttiness that cracked it... 46.4%

BRENNEREI ZIEGLER Freudenberg, North Württemberg. Working.
Freud Whisky Distillers Cut Malt Whisky chestnut & ex-bourbon casks, matured old plum casks, bott code: L:W 2321 A db (88.5) n22 t22.5 f21.5 b22.5 With a name like Freud, you'd expect it to be complex... and this is very complex, make no mistake! The malt is always playing catch up and fighting for its ground. It certainly finds it about four or five flavour waves in, where the barley rides the waves of tannin with juicy aplomb. Or in this case, maybe, a plum. Toasty, spicy and very dry at the death this is perhaps a little too much about the casks, though the lovely chocolate waves found in the late middle seem to be universal. 41.5%

DESTILLERIE ARMIN JOBST E.K. Hammelburg. Working.
Jobst Grain Whisky 9 Jahre Madeira Cask A7 6 Jahre Barrique fass, 3 Jahre Madeira fass db (92.5) n22.5 t23.5 f23 b23.5 At last! An indisputably excellent bottling from Jobst after so many attempts that one way or another fell at one of the hurdles. Here it clears all the fences with something to spare (well, maybe on the nose the back hooves clip something). But off this one trots to the winners' enclosure, unquestionably a thoroughbred. How can you not applaud the measured resonance of the fruit and the way the tannins interlink with almost effortless

grace. The house nutty style is there in force, but this time isn't cracked with a sledgehammer cut and even allows the grains to have some kind of say in the matter. What superb balance and character this filly has. Definitely worth a flutter on.... 50%. sc.

DESTILLERIE & BRENNEREI MICHAEL HABBEL Sprockhövel. Working

Hillock 8 Year Old Single Malt Whisky 82 monate in ex bourbon fässern, 14 monate zum finish in ex Recioto fässern, bott code: L-2118 db **(87) n22 t22 f21.5 b21.5** A soft, friendly malt determined not to upset any apple carts, but in so doing rather lays too supinely at the feet of the dominant toffee. Malt and spices apparent and, overall, quite pleasant in the German style. 45.3%.

DESTILLERIE RALF HAUER Bad Dürkheim. Working.

◇ **Saillt Mór Jamaican Rum Finish** lot no 0123, bott 05/23 db **(92) n23** very clean PX, not even an outside hint of sulphur. The rum cask has done a stupendous job of keeping myriad fruit and mocha tones tightly controlled. Very attractive...; **t23** such a superb delivery. The fruit is dripping off the tongue from the very first moment. But those tight sugars ensure, just as on the nose, that there is a disciplined resonance throughout. Warming spices need no second invite to make their mark, but the most remarkable aspect is the eye-watering sharpness of the grape... not something often seen when PX is involved...; **f22.5** a slight bitterness is picked up from the oak. But the mocha apparent on the nose now opens up and what little sugar there is is lightly molassed and hell-bent on keeping the balance; **b23.5** when I saw the cask management for this whisky, I gasped. When something has spent six years in PX the last thing you expect them to finish it in would be Jamaican rum, which usually guarantees a sugary crustiness – so in this case sugar on sugar...! But that wasn't how it ended up for the nine years had allowed the tannins to really get to grips and ensure a wonderful toing and froing...and balance. One of the most uniquely shaped and eye-opening whiskies I will taste this year. 57.5%

◇ **Saillt Mór Madeira Finish** lot no 0223, bottled 05/23 db **(89) n22.5** a real pudding of an aroma - plums and suet lifted by a light thread of drift orange blossom honey; **t23** magnificently mouth-filling. Brilliant, seat of pant distillation because maximum oils have been extracted with only the most distant hint of a rubbery feint. This makes for a swamp-like thickness to the fruit and grain but with the oak pulsing in all the right places; **f21.5** a surprisingly dry yet salty finish with the spices working overtime; **b22** those oils really are borderline, but just get away with it, encouraging the spices to buzz at full volume: one of those whiskies where so much can be so easily overlooked on first inspection. So glutinous and complex is this, that little secrets hide away until discovered. Forget the first and second mouthful. They are the warm-up act. Only on the third – and by using the Murray Method – does the full depth and range of this extraordinary whisky come clear. Happy discovering. 58%

◇ **Saillt Mór Pfälzer Eiche** barrel no 91+92, lot no 0522, bott 05/22 db **(90) n22.5** huge oak presence rifles up the blood orange fingerprint. Distant ginger cake, too...; **t23** that is some delivery. Any whisky displaying this amount of muscular tannin has no right to be quite so mouth-watering, yet it is....especially when those muscovado sugars go nuclear. The spices do an excellent job, also...; **f22** I was expecting a potential bitterness from this. But it arrives more as a mild Columbian medium roast coffee than aggressive tannin; **b22.5** a macho whisky which prides itself in pulling no punches yet has a genuine softness of touch as it shifts gears. Don't have the information to hand but feels like a mixed grain offering as the underlying complexity points to something more than straightforward malt. A very different – and delicious - whisky. 46%

DESTILLERIE RIEGER & HOFMEISTER Fellbach. Working.

◇ **Destillerie Rieger and Hofmeister Schwabischer Rye Malt** bott code 13112 db **(89) n23** the rye announces its presence with a loudhailer. This is a very thick cut, but the intensity of the rye itself almost makes it impossible to spot for its pure density. Slowly you can pick out the grain strands and then more easily identify its semi-fruity, Demerara-chiselled riches; **t22.5** initially it is the dull oils of the thick cut which registers first. But soon that is brushed aside as those insanely intense rye tones hammer their presence home; **f21.5** again that wide cut returns, making for an untidy finish. The spices are impressive, though; **b22** good grief! This is rye sent careering into the taste buds at full throttle. The cut is unsubtle, but I suspect helps fashion the extraordinary intensity of the grain. 42%

◇ **Destillerie Rieger and Hofmeister Schwabischer Whisky No 4 Sherryfass Finish**, bott code 010322 db **(89.5) n21.5** a touch prickly, the busy spices don't entirely detract from the crispness of the fruit or the slight feint; **t23** such a surprising delivery quite out of character with the nose. The fruit has a Chardonnay-type juiciness joining forces with a wave or three of highly intense malt for a very salivating delivery. The spice prickle doesn't let up, either, making this massively flavoursome from the moment it enters the mouth until the finish begins to appear;

f22 the spices have no thoughts about giving up ground; **b23** while the warming nose may be a little alarming, there is something mesmerically attractive about the depth of the malt on this one and its slow evolution on the palate. A wide cut may cause a slight blemish on the nose but ensures maximum flavour explosion once in the mouth. A huge whisky for its strength. 42%

⁂ **Destillerie Rieger and Hofmeister Schwabischer Single Malt Portweinfass Finish**, bott code 310123 db **(83.5) n20 t22 f20.5 b21** I've tasted probably more Port cask finishes than any other living being. But nothing quite like this one. Not sure the initial spirit was quite up to the distillery's usual standards, offering a slightly milky note on the nose. This appears to be mirrored on the unkempt finish. It's saving grace is the concentrated maltiness through the middle and the playful spices, all couched in a soft, almost butter and jam, padding. But, as a whole, it doesn't quite come together as might be hoped and proves a little too warm and tangy for its own good. 40%

⁂ **Destillerie Rieger and Hofmeister Schwabischer Malt Rauchmalzwhisky**, bott code 100222 db **(94) n24** what an impressive, quite adorable mixture of rumbling smoke and no less earthy tannins from the oak. Dense, inviting, curiously salty and leavened by the subtlest splash of heather honey: oddly coastal; **t23.5** again, a salty flush to the delivery and smokiness unlike the usual Scottish style but more subtly infused into the tannins. The heather honey has a wonderfully waxy shell peppered by some warming, gritty spices; **f22.5** that waxiness remains but appears to be the product now of the slightly wider cut. Drier vanillas are eked out at the end; **b24** I really don't think I can better sum this whisky up than the last time I reviewed it: "The harmony of this beautiful whisky reminded me of a Sunday morning in a German village, the ancient church bells calling. To an English ear, it strikes slightly out of tune. But possesses a charm which captures the country with a disarming vibrancy." Well, this bottling still does and, on this occasion, has a little extra honeyed sparkle to add to the more insistent phenols. 45%

DESTILLERIE THOMAS SIPPEL Weisenheim am Berg. Working.
Palatinatus Single Malt Whisky Single Cask German Oak 2014 db **(94) n23.5 t23.5 f23 b24** Profound whisky so beautifully distilled (not something I have always said about Palatinatus). It appears that German oak bests suits this German malt. Neat! 45%. sc.

EDELBRÄENDE-SENFT Salem-Rickenbach. Working.
Senft Whisky Edition Herbert dist 2014 bott code: L-WE552 **(87.5) n21 t22.5 f22 b22** For all intents and purposes, a near re-run of bottling L-WE551. The feints deny this whisky glory, but the amazing mouthfeel through the mid-stretch, encompassing a quartet of praline, chocolate, hazelnuts and spice, really is quite brilliant. 45%

Senft Whisky Edition 83 dist 2014 bott code: L-WE183 **(87) n21 t22 f22 b22** A mind-bogglingly dense whisky very much in the feinty house style but here taking nuttiness almost to an extreme. Though there are obvious technical faults, they are of a type which will offer flavoursome compensation at the midpoint, and so it proves. About as chewy as any whisky gets there is toffee and hazelnut in concentrated form, and barley, too, thick enough to ladle into the glass. The late cocoa is inevitable, though the light accompanying mint is a bonus. Should be a bit of a failure, yet stubbornly entertains. 45%

Senft Whisky Edition Torf dist 2014 bott code: L-WT551 **(89) n22** the smoke takes its time to get any kind of head of steam. Tannins seem far more interested in leading. Some light muscovado sugar offers a delicate fruitiness to the picture; **t23** the oils arrive early and more thickly than the nose suggests. Those muscovado sugars prove to be more than just aromatic, sweetening the ground on which the peat finally dares to tread; **f22** the light nougat confirms this was still a wide-ish cut but those oils hold the late smoke and spice in place. Very buttery towards the end; **b22** technically, way better than its sister bottlings as the cut has been more precise and feints just about eradicated, though this is about as oily as any distillery should accept. Those looking for peat, though, might need to bring along a microscope as it is not immediately obvious and takes a bit of searching. A big whisky, nonetheless. 45%

EDELBRENNEREI BISCHOF Wartmannsroth. Working.
Bischof's Rhöner Whisky Grain Whisky Aus Rhöner Weizen Single Cask bott code: L-9 db **(85) n21 t22.5 f20.5 b21** Not as neat and tidy as the last bottling I enjoyed from them, the feints knocking things askew here. That said, it does have its tender moments especially when the particularly nutty character softens and moves towards a light praline, even vaguely coconut hue. Spices gather, but the balance dissipates. 40%. sc.

EDELBRÄNDE PREISER Stuehlingen. Working
Whisky Stube Sulmgau Whisky Single Malt acacia & chestnut wood, dist Dec 2016, bott Jan 2021 bott code: L0121 **(88.5) n20.5 t23.5 f22 b22.5** For fun, I often nose a whisky from pouring

blind just to try and guess what is coming next. And as I sniffed at this I said under my breath: "chestnut!" Which was, indeed, the case, though a degree of feints tries to disguise the wood type...and much else. And here's a question: does acacia wood help instal a degree of acacia honey into a malt. Well, if this is anything to go by, the answer is "yes". Because as uncomfortable the nose might be, the delivery is pure barley stirred into a honey pot. Another thing I expected was bitterness on the finish. And though it arrives it is nothing like so destructive as I feared. So with spices joining the fading remnants of the barley-honey mix there is so wonderful many layers to get through. Different. And truly delicious. 47%

EDELBRENNEREI DIRKER Mömbris. Working.

Dirker Whisky Aged 4 Years Sassicaia cask, bott code L A 16 db **(80.5) n18.5 t22.5 f19 b20.5.** A deeply frustrating whisky. This is one exceptionally beautiful cask at work here and - in the mid ground - offers all kinds of toffee apple and muscovado-sweetened mocha. Sadly, the initial spirit wasn't up to the barrel's standard. This really needs some cleaning up. 53%

EIFEL DESTILLATE Koblenz. Working.

Eifel Ahrtaler Pinot Noir Fass Single Rye db **(86) n21.5 t23 f20 b21.5** You know when you have bought a suit and, in the shop, thought it was comfortable and expansive....and then got home and found it was tight and occasionally pinched where it shouldn't. Well here you go. The Pinot cask is certainly a double-edged sword... 46%

Eifel Hones Venn PX Fass Malt and Peat db **(94.5) n23.5 t24 f23.5 b24** A profound, no holds-barred malt. A super-high quality PX cask was selected here: clean and faultless...and the peat must have had some muscle to make such an impact. A towering Eifel, so to speak and almost as good as anything I've ever experienced from this distillery.... 46%

Eifel Scheifel Malaga Fass Rye and Peat db **(92.5) n23 t23.5 f22.5 b23.5** One of the fun things about the samples I receive from this distillery, is that the bottles are numbered at the back... so I can taste them and try and work out their composition before the reveal. A muted pat on the back here as I finally worked out this was peated rye...though not before my fifth, possibly sixth, taste. A deeply unusual whisky style, made all the more baffling by the wine. But, miraculously, all the thrusts and counter thrusts work out well and harmonise. No mean feat with a whisky like this. My genuine congratulations to the distillers and blenders at Eifel: there were so many ways this could have gone wrong. 46%

Eifel Vulkaneifel Port Fass Single Malt db **(84.5) n22.5 t23 f18.5 b20.5** Before we reach the faulty finish, the delivery is even fruitier than the nose - which hardly seemed possible. It is certainly sweeter with a degree of blackberry honey found in the mix. A little barley finds its way into the midground mix along with the ever-warming spices, but it's all too brief. Ultimately, a lovely malt compromised by over reliance on the Port effect to the detriment of the grain and, therefore complexity. And finally, sadly, a late, gnawing bitterness which reveals a sub-standard cask. 46%

Eifel 746.9 Moscatel Fass Single Peated Malt 10 Jahre db **(92.5) n22** this distillery specialises in firm, bold, dry peaty noses...and this is as dry as that particular style stretches. Almost a green vegetable note to mingle with the dried grape skin..; **t23.5** the muscatel makes a major impact on delivery, a secondary barley note running alongside, kicking up the juiciness. The peat is detached, firm and almost severe in its countenance. However, a stratum of heather honey comes to the rescue; **f23** the spices buzz now as the tannins make their mark and suggest excellent aging. The peat-grape-honey triangle can still be heard but now relatively muted; **b24** for a malt which starts off shouting the odds and being as loud as possible, its transformation to a whispering whisky is a charming one. Complex and deeply satisfying. 46%

Eifel 746.9 Madeira Fass Single Malt 12 Jahre db **(95) n24** rich, intense and meaningful, though the grape has a greater depth than normal, even that has gorgeous layering. The spices dazzle, the heather honey is at its most cavernous; **t24** the heather honey reveals first. But, as on the nose, it has subterranean qualities, unusually a base among tenors. This isn't shy to reveal its good age, either, as the oak pitches in with toastier notes, too. All the time, the fruit offers a plum jelly but with limited sugars; **f23** medium length with the drier vanillas now dominant; **b24** elegant and endearing. Great to see spices in a soothing rather than aggressive manner. Superb distillate and a very good Madeira cask can only lead to excellence. This is deep stuff. 46%

Eifel 746.9 Malaga Fass Single Rye 12 Jahre db **(93.5) n23** unmistakable firmness to the grain leaves no doubt we're working with excellent base rye. The deep, chunky fruit rides the grain like a jockey on a thoroughbred.... The spices pinch and nip until we are in German Christmas biscuit territory here..; **t23.5** a fabulous, oily, salivating delivery. Apple strudel dominates; **f23.5** long, much drier and still we have that apple note alongside the persistent oils which keeps the entertainment alive. The grain rekindles for one last juicy thrust; **b23.5** they would be proud of a base rye like this in Kentucky. But actually finding a wine cask to complement it...now that takes some doing. They've done it before...and they've done it again.. 46%

Eifel The Peat Bell 2015 Moscatel Quarter Cask db (93) n23 t23.5 f23 b23.5 An outrageous whisky which sets out to make a statement – and succeeds. A great decision to make this cask strength to accentuate the richness of the grains in particular. Justice is served. 51.5%

Eifel The Rye Malt Bell 2014 Malaga Quarter Cask db (95) n23.5 t24 f23.5 b24 After working my way through this one, I am mentally and physically exhausted. I'm not sure the human sensory system was quite designed to withstand and fully evaluate something quite like this. Thank God they didn't add peat, as I'm pretty certain I wouldn't have survived. Anyone who hasn't experienced this must consider their whisky journey incomplete... 53%

ELCH WHISKY Gräfenberg. Working.
Elch Torfduet db (94) n23.5 peat smoke and heather honey...; t23.5 peat smoke and heather honey x 10...; f23 lots of peat smoke...and some heather honey....; b24 if you like heather honey. And you like peat smoke. And you prefer it when they are put together. Well, here's your whisky... 50.6%

FARO WHISKY DISTILLERY Schretstaken. Working.
Faro Feingert German Craft Whisky cask 214 local oak dist 4/2011 bott 11/2021 db (87.5) n21 t23 f21.5 b22 Distilled a decade ago when they probably hadn't quite got their cuts where they wanted them to be, there is no escaping the fact that certain facets of this whisky are pure gold. The heather honey which builds on delivery and then mingles with the malt is something to savour. And the fascinatingly tight beat of the local tannin is also pretty special. The finish, like the nose, reveals the weaknesses. But looking forward to seeing their later bottlings: if they can maintain the purity of that core honey, they are onto a winner... 42%

FESSLERMILL 1396 DESTILLERIE Sersheim. Working.
Mettermalt American Style Whisky batch L141 db (86.5) n22 t22 f21 b21.5 After tasting European whisky solidly for the last several days, I had just about forgotten what a 40% abv whisky felt like. Indeed, this is becoming a threatened species outside of mainstream brands. This strength means the maximum breaking down of oils, which in turn often results in short, vanilla-influenced finishes. Same for this, but the vanilla sets to work a lot earlier. Lovely light ulmo honey lift off on arrival as well as the nose, but lives a soufflé-like existence 40%

Mettermalt Classic batch L123 db (86) n22.5 t21.5 f20.5 b21.5 Certainly classic for this distillery in its lightness and overall gentleness. Icing sugars which melt in the mouth, a hint of grist and vanillas offering a degree of depth but still no great weight, and a tad bitter, too. Pleasant, fleeting whisky. 40%

Mettermalt Wacken Whisky batch L666 db (88.5) n22 t22.5 f22 b22 With a bottling or batch number of 666, you'd expect this to have the devil in it. But instead, we have Fesslermill's usual polite and gently endearing style which wouldn't say boo to a bat, even if the strength has been upped slightly. Once more we have to doff our caps to the chalky vanilla, relieved this time by a slight squirt of citrus. Attractively clean malt, though, has some particularly attractive moments, especially on the nose. Charming, but perhaps a little too charming for the local music festival...! 42.6%

Mettermalt Fools Garden batch LF1 db (89) n22 t23 f21.5 b22.5 A section of Mettermalt sticks gamely to a malt and vanilla theme. This is among the best of that ilk as this is by far and away the sharpest, most intense and confident in projecting the style. A little cask-induced bitterness at the end, though. 43%

Mettermalt Pur Whisky batch L1PUR db (90.5) n22.5 t22.5 f22.5 b23 A gentle malt which just glides over the palate like a breeze through the roses. Clean, softly gristy and the simple vanillas even out the thin barley sugars. As expected, some pleasing citrus notes skip in and out of the piece. Quite delightfully made and matured and altogether charming. 40%

Mettermalt Angelo Negro Single Nebbiolo Cask Roggen Whisky batch L150 db (82.5) n20.5 t21 f20.5 b20.5 Absolutely no problem with the integrity and effect of the grape. Or the part played by the spices. But the feinty quality of the original rye distillate leaves a little to be desired... 42.6%

Mettermalt Cask Strength Baurerlander Spelz Whisky batch L148 db (89) n21 t23.5 f22 b22.5 Massively intense spelt whisky which doesn't start too brightly with a distinct bubble-gum signature on the nose. But this one comes entirely into its own on delivery, starting with little oaks but then growing into stunningly heather-honeyed acorns. A little bitter at the death, alas, but a small price to pay for that salivating crescendo. And a little late chocolate compensates, anyway. 51.5% sc

Mettermalt Deltetto Single Arneis Cask batch L149 db (87) n22.5 t22 f21 b21.5 A lumbering, slightly heavy-handed whisky where random fruit notes are daubed onto a flimsy frame. The vanillas do a great job holding things together. But more spices at work here than is normal for this distillery, sometimes overt, occasionally overt. And it is they which lift both the tempo and the complexity considerably. 44.5%

Mettermalt Cask Strength Emmer Dinkel Whisky batch L143 db **(92)** n23 t23.5 f22.5 b23 Sharp, under-ripe fruit (including Chinese gooseberry and kiwi) stings the nose in perhaps the most agile of Fesslermill's bottlings. The grain is having a great time, too, punching out with a lovely abandon and mixing easily with the nutty vanilla from the oak. The spices heighten phases when they need to. Salivating, complex, excellently made and great entertainment in the glass. 52.4% sc

FINCH WHISKYDESTILLERIE Nellingen, Alb-Donau. Working.

Finch Schwäbischer Hochland Whisky Barrique R 19 bott code: L19130 db **(92)** n23 t23 f22.5 b23.5 The model of a beautifully balanced whisky able to contain any minor lurking feints. 42%.

GUTSBRENNEREI JOH. B. GEUTING Bocholt. Working.

J.B.G Munsterlander Single Malt Aged 8 Years sherry PX cask, cask no JBG87, dist 21.03.14, bott 13.10.22 **(92.5)** n23.5 I didn't even have to check the bottle to see what kind of casks are at work here: this is akin to sticking your nose in a moist, fresh PX cask. The back story of firm tannin and rounded malt is as charming as it is complex; t23.5 impossible to ask for more from a PX cask. The grape may be profound, and it may be sweet. But, as on the nose, the oak really makes an impact here, and not just with its busy and very warming spices. There are layers of vanilla and butterscotch apparent, even as the grape is busy at work. While the subplot of malt is never shaken. Not sure you'll find a better sweet-dry balance than this; f22.5 as if nutmeg has been stirred into a melted chocolate raisin bar. The oils are at maximum now, as the cut was quite wide, but the PX covered many of the tracks; b23 this is impressive. I'm not the world's greatest PX fan. But I have no problems singing the praises of this cask as it sets about ramping up complexity rather than flattening all before it, as so many PX casks have a tendency to do. A livewire, complex malt that's as chewy as they ever come. 61.4%

HAMMERSCHMIEDE Zorge. Working.

Hercynian Elsburn Single Malt Aged 11 sherry hogsheads PX Finish bott 30.05.23 bott code L2173 db **(93)** n23 oh my word: PX with bells on! The malt slips through only in the faintest of ways and is soon extinguished when it does. This is all about the grape...; t24 well, succulent would be one descriptor. As well as thick. Jammy. On top of the fruit comes a remarkable treacle tart kick, complete with associated spices. If you can imagine PX on steroids, I think you have the picture; f22.5 for a moment or two I had dared hope that we would get through to the end without an upset. But there is an unmistakable sulphur buzz here, though thankfully only a light one and completely overwhelmed by the sticky fruity which is no hurry to part; b23.5 only one type of cask on the planet can offer such richness of colour and such sweet intensity of fruitiness. It is quite dark where I am tasting and I won't be able to see the details of the cask involved until tomorrow morning. But I'll tell you this: it is a PX cask. And I'll tell you more, it was still dripping wet with the sweet sherry when it was filled...though before departing Jerez it had ever so briefly been in contact with a sulphur stick. Please to relate that the sherry and almost hidden malt is of such an excellent quality, the damage is absolutely minimal. One for PX freaks to absolutely drool over and tell their grandchildren about... 45% 79 bottles

Hercynian Willowburn Single Malt Sherry Octave No V14-01 bott 4/8/23 bott code L2178 db **(86.5)** n23.5 t22 f20 b21 Well, that was a bit of a swizz! After that amazing build up on the nose, I was expecting a fruity fiesta throughout. No such luck. The aroma was offering an intense mix of blackcurrant and blackberry jam with exploding plums, fig and juicy dates right up there with them. Fruity...? Not 'alf...! But then the sulphur came, like storm clouds on a sunny day... 61.7% 76 bottles

Hercynian Willowburn Single Malt Sherry Octave No V14-02 bott 4/8/23 bott code L2177 db **(93.5)** n23.5 a much nuttier, far less profound nose – even to the extent of walnut cake at play. The fruit is much lighter than their 61.7% version, drawing far more from dried dates – which go rather well with the walnut. When warmed some unripened greengages. In the background, the tannins mutter...; t23.5 didn't expect that sharpness of underripe grapes and gooseberries to be spread across all temperatures. This is eyewatering and palate cleansing all at once. There is also a very surprising depth to the grape once the oak stops muttering on the nose and joins forces with the fruit with a very clear speech; f22.5 yes, there is a slight weakness to the finale, but it really is minor. But there is nothing weak about the way the molasses go about their business so late on...; b24 you know when you've read a book a little too fast and a third the way in you spot something rather clever...and then you have to go back to see if the author has been repeating the dose from the start...and you find that he had. Well, this is one of those whiskies which if you take your eye off the ball, you might just pass off as another sherry-shaped offering. But is rather a lot cleverer than that. Very, very astute use of the sharper fruit tones here... *61.9% 75 bottles*

◇ **Hercynian Elsburn The Journey Single Malt** matured in fortified wine casks bott code L2167 db **(90.5) n22.5** a sharp fruit note seem to trigger a counteractive gooseberry sun plot. Fruity, but doesn't make a big thing about it...; **t22.5** not that sharpness takes off on the delivery, the gooseberries being determinedly underripe; **f22.5** superb strands of acacia honey dovetailing with the at last confident malt...; **b23** well, they started this journey with a slightly underpowered engine. A compensation is that the whisky hasn't been undermined by a sulphur-treated cask, so we get an opportunity to see this high-quality distillate without a negative interruption. Still would have liked to have seen the alcoholic content starting with a 5.... By the way, as I write this, somewhere between two and three hundred swifts, the entire combined population around the Liege area, are before me, above me and behind me in my hillside retreat gathering for their journey back to Africa. This is such a perfect whisky to toast their farewell... *43%*

◇ **Hercynian Elsburn Wayfare Single Malt** batch no 003 bott 2023 bott code L2170 db **(94.5) n23.5** this nose so gloriously celebrates the beauty of balance: not a hint of a sulphur atom gets you prepped hopefully for something rather special...and the spices begins to show, unlike many Hercynian bottlings, that this is not all about the fruit...this one is all about the oak...ad how the malt can provide a delicate side-line. The tannins are providing a spectrum of sugar tones, including maple syrup...; **t24** the creaminess of the delivery offers a curious counterpoint to the sweetness of the nose. As on the aroma there is an unspoken fruitiness. At first. Then, slowly, an apricot and lychee dept and sweetness grows. But, parallel to this, are a series of rampant sugars, mainly Demerara-style but topped off with healthy vanilla. The spices are rampant, though, and screech about the taste buds with abandon; **f23** the finale is surprisingly low key: even the spices have been quietened and we are back to delicate vanillas mingling with healthy malt...and then the odd bleat of fruitcake...; **b24.** a Hercynian cask at full strength with not a single blemish either from distillation or maturation. In this fettle, this is a whisky that is astonishing to behold, especially when the salivation levels go through the room. Possibly my favourite experience of Hercynian whisky: as much a German classic as Beethoven's 7th... *58.2% nc ncf 3840 bottles*

◇ **Hercynian Elsburn Single Malt Distillery Edition Matured In Best First Fill Sherry Casks** bott 2023 batch 004 bott code L2165 db **(89.5) n22.5** any more gentle and fragile you'd be terrified to pick the glass up; hazelnut dominates and we have here what remains of a fine old dry sherry wanting to be noticed. Not convinced the original distillate was bang on form...; **t23** confirmation the distillate is not on point here. But the slow build of the blackcurrant, molasses and continued nuts more than compensates; **f21.5** a little bit of a sulphur rumble, but the vanilla nuttiness does its best to make amends...; **b22.5** after all those in-your-face Hercynian bottlings, how rewarding it is to find a supremely delicate offering that requires some time and patience to appreciate fully. *45.8% nc ncf bottles 78*

◇ **Hercynian Elsburn Single Malt Aged 11 Years** sherry hogsheads; oloroso finish dist 11.2011 bott 14.06.2023 bott code L2175 db **(94.5) n23.5** huge plum and over-ripe dates...and that's just the starters. Sniff gently but more deeply and after catching an impressive oaky backbone, more fruit appears in the disguise of toffee raisin candy; **t24** that oloroso butt must have been dripping wet when it was filled for finishing: the grape has moved on from the nose into a far more succulent mode. Lightened molasses joins the apple and redcurrant introduction before a tart middle champions the worthiness of unripened greengages and gooseberry. When your eyes have stopped watering you'll notice a more weighty blackcurrant and hickory formulation that will tantalise and soft oils that will sooth...; **f23** at least we move away from the fruits – well not quite all of them – and the heather honey and marzipan combine sublimely while the red liquorice and trailing redcurrant aren't too shoddy, either. At the very tail...a dull, nagging, tongue-tingling sulphur appearance: a thousand curses on you, you ill-rendered element...; **b24** when you get sherry hogshead from around 2010 and then a secondary sherry finish, you expect some degree of ruination. Well, yes, there is the very vaguest sulphur atom flitting about here and there, especially at the death. But certainly not in the kind of concentrations that will do damage. And certainly no damage to whisky this rich and unashamedly celebrating its huge fruity existence. Actually, there was a third wood used: the one to house the bottle. I can understand why... *53.2% 282 bottles*

◇ **Hercynian Emporer's Way Peated Single Malt Amontillado** single sherry hogshead cask no 1167 dist 05.12.2018 bott 14.06.2023 bott code L2176 db **(95) n24** have you ever seen Islay-style peat seemingly apologise to the fruit for being in its presence...? Well, that's the effect you get here. The dryness of the grape and grapefruit giving a withering cuff around the ear to those pesky but frankly stunning phenols...; **t23.5** now we are in the realms of full-blown complexity: the peat shews first and well, backed up by a mix of barley and muscovado sugar. The spices retain a refined elegance and refuse to dominate above their station. This allows the vanillas to ramp up in intensity, while a non-specific fruitiness lingers and salivates; **f23.5** soft mocha, yet ever-increasing vanilla. But always there is that unseasoned fruity bite refusing to give way entirely. The big question: where the hell are those phenols now, unless somehow lost in that mocha...? **b24** an exhausting whisky to taste: so much is going on and you are forever trying to work out where the whisky is taking you. In the end you realise it's a malt determined to screw with your senses, the persistent under-ripe fruitiness never letting up and queering the pitch, the peat playing peak-a-boo once at its early zenith. The biggest red herring is the smokiness on the nose and delivery, which is never remotely matched anywhere else on the palate – even at the finale where, usually, the phenols assemble. But for overall understated beauty...just wow! A gobsmackingly beautiful malt, a potential European Whisky of the Year, and one determined to break all the laws of whisky. And your brain. 60% 270 bottles

HARDENBERG DISTILLERY Nörten-Hardenberg. Working

Beverbach Double Oak Aged Single Malt Whiskey aged in American & French oak casks, bott code: L08320073 db **(90) n21.5 t22.5 f23 b23** Ignore the nose. I was fearing the worst – and shouldn't have bothered. This is one of the most intensely malty whiskies from the whole of mainland Europe to be found this year... So impressed! 43%

KLEINBRENNEREI FITZKE Herbolzheim-Broggingen. Working.

◇ **Derrina Dinkelmalz Single Malt** bott code L5518 **(89) n22** rich and bready. A nose found, if you are lucky, in special bakers..; **t22.5** delicate, malty sugars shew early, aided by some rolling, soft oils. The grain is firm and offers up some charming ulmo honey; **f22** the oak kicks in quite hard late on but the thin honey stays the course as the oils increase; **b22.5** that's much more like it! The last of these I had was hampered by a feinty side show. They are still vaguely visible on the finish, but now you have to go looking for them. Instead, you can now enjoy a full-flavoured spelt whisky. 43%

◇ **Derrina Einkorn Single Grain** bott code L11218 **(94) n22.5** profound. Hard as nails, toasted Hovis. Surprising lack of sugars here: the grain and tannin have melded together to form quite a serious face...; **t24** brilliantly exuberant in its delivery, launching any number of flavour waves of brown bread delicately sweated with a light layer of ulmo and heather honey mixed in. The oil weight is perfection...; **f23.5** glorious echoes of the incredibly rewarding delivery and middle. More tannin now, but this is friendly fire adding to the overall excellence...; **b24** anyone who knows anything about straight wheat whiskey from Kentucky will immediately pick up the tell-tale signs of this grain. Fabulously fulsome in its flavour profile – complete with delicate strata of honey – the rigidity of the nose poses something of an enigma... 43%

◇ **Derrina Emmermalz Single Malt** bott code L6818 **(86.5) n22 t22.5 f20.5 b21.5** Fascinating comparing one wheat whisky (the Einkorn) directly with this other form. Considering that this is malted, I would have expected the Emmermalz to come out on top. But whisky is never quite that simple... Still, love the digestive biscuit nose, though that salty, coastal aroma is a bit of a surprise. On the palate, always seems to be on the thin side and under par. The flavours are diverse and confusing, ranging from early golden syrup to late black tea, including a heavy tannin finish. Bit of a crazy, mixed-up kid... 43%

◇ **Derrina Gerstenmalz Torfrauch "Stark" Single Malt** bott code 13119 **(90.5) n22.5** a mix of a slightly heavy cut and the unique peat style gives the delivery a pretty specific fingerprint. A delicate creosote note underlines the phenols as the dominating factor...; **t23** fat, chewy and romps in its marriage of liquorice and peat; **f22.5** light hickory with a little spice keeping those phenols relevant; **b22.5** what a fascinating, one-off peated style this is. Distinctive and even a little daring... 43%

◇ **Derrina Purpur Rotkorn Ur-Weizen Single Grain** bott code L14018 **(93) n23.5** this is quietly intense and, so often for this distillery, unique. The grain offers a pleasing bite, but the subtlety is astonishing...; **t23.5** full-frontal salivation from the first moment. The grains appear encrusted in muscovado sugars while the oak serenades with beautifully balanced vanilla; **f23** those grains work overtime to keep their shape and pulse out their charm. The vanillas are more skittish now as the tannins take hold. But still hugely flavoursome, even late on; **b23** over the years when I see this distillery has bottled a grain as opposed to a malt whisky, I get excited. Sample this unique whisky and understand exactly why. A very different and bold flavourfest. 43%

◇ **Derrina Reis Single Grain** bott code L10317 **(90) n22.5** oily on the nose like corn whisky, a mix of heather honey and golden syrup blends in with heady tannins. The most delicate of spices, too...; **t23** those honey tones expand across the palate, regularly fluctuating in intensity. A mix of German coffee-style biscuit and brusque tannin embolden the middle. Still we have first-class oil involvement...; **f22** gentle vanillas, but those oily honey tones hang on gloriously despite the rising bitterness...; **b22.5** it has long been argued that there could never be such a thing as a rice whisky. Well, there is now. And, what's more, it is no shrinking violet. Corn whiskey lovers would approve... 43%

◇ **Derrina Triticale Single Grain** bott code L10418 **(90.5) n22.5** the sharpness of the triticale is blunted a little by the firm oak and then soothed by a elegant ulmo honey; **t22.5** a soft custardy-marzipan arrival dries and even the spices a little, the oak here really playing a big part in the character building; **f22.5** a lovely interplay between drier vanillas and sweeter toffee. The grains sharpness has staying power; **b23** one of the distillery's more subtle and surprising bottlings. A classic case of where no particular personality trait dominates. It is curious because this grain - a kind of hybrid between wheat and rye - acts like neither, nor offers up either of those grains normal contributions to a whisky's make up. *43%*

⟐ **Derrina Weizenmalz Single Malt** bott code L5719 **(86) n21 t22.5 f21 b21.5** Massive flavours on delivery - most of it with a distinctive dark sugar accent. But, overall, just a little too feinty and bitter for its own good. *43%*

KORNBRENNEREI J.J. KEMPER Olpe. Working.

Whisky Stube Spirit Of The Cask Roggen Whisky American white oak barrel, dist Jun 2015, bott Nov 2020, bott code: L01B11R18 **(94) n23.5 t23.5 f23 b24** Absolutely top rate. The intensity is matched only by the delights of the semi-bourbon kick. No feints to worry about here: beautifully made and distilled. A triumph of a whisky... *61.23%*

KYMSEE WHISKY DESTILLERIE Grabenstätt

⟐ **Kymsee Single Malt Jerez Brandy Finish Cask Strength** db **(92) n23** gorgeously intact: the barley is dominant but attaches itself keenly to to the most delicate of dry, grape skin nuances...which in turn appear to cling to the firm oaks and spices. Really lovely...; **t23.5** again the malt is in super-concentrated form. But, yet again, just like on the nose, the fruit acts as a countering drying agent to the sweetness of that barley sugar. Add to the fact that there is enormous weight to this, and the spices and tannins are constructively active, and this then is a wonderfully chewable experience; **f22.5** long, plenty of heather honey but a slight bitter drone off the oak; **b23** quite beautifully distilled, packed with intense malt and steered to the finish by one of the rarest and most intriguing whisky styles - Jerez brandy - I have encountered in recent years. What's not to like...? *53.6%*

⟐ **Kymsee Single Malt Sherry Cask Finish** db **(90) n22.5** more garibaldi biscuit than fruitcake, the malt still manages to hold its shape; **t23** super-soft with a quick build of spice, the malt remains intense despite the gathering grape; **f22** long, understated but still lots of biscuity sugars at play...; **b22.5** a relaxing, easy-going malt where the sherry does its best not to dominate. Feels just a little underpowered at 42%. A delightful late night dram nonetheless. *42%*

⟐ **Kymsee Single Malt Quarter Cask Finish Cask Strength** db **(88) n22 t23 f21 b22** There is no mistaking the enormity of the concentrated malt - almost like an old-fashioned English barley wine. And with that, especially on delivery, comes a sublime shimmering of golden syrup and heather honey. Sadly, the quarter casking appears also to have caused an overdose on the oaky tannin, which ultimately leads to an accentuated late bitterness. A malt very much of two very conflicting halves. *54.4%*

LANTENHAMMER Havsham. Working

Sild Heritage 28 Lantenhammer Bavarian Pure Malt db **(90.5) n23** distinct banana and custard confirms a sweet lightness to this before juicy sultanas make their mark; **t23** ahhh! The malt has a voice and sings lustily and sweetly on arrival. The style remains almost fragile, the vanilla becomes mildly heavier as time progresses; **f22** still malty, but a light tartness creeps in from somewhere; **b22.5** not often you find German whiskies as understated as this these days. Goes for subtle messages rather than bold statements. *42% (125.3 proof)*

MARDER EDELBRÄNDE Albbruck-Unteralpfen. Working.

⟐ **Marder Black Forest Pure Single Malt Aged in Amarone Casks**, dist 01.2015, bott 11.2021 **(89.5) n23** the oak is punchy here, weighted significantly enough to stand shoulder to shoulder with the bitter-sweet fruit; **t22.5** delightfully creamy delivery, not entirely unlike a Bristol Cream sherry. Though, of course, the oak and malt make a significant input here. The sugars are firmly wrapped around the grape at first, then loosen to produce a more ulmo honey-vanilla style. Just love those spices buzzing from the oak; **f21.5** just a little on the bitter and austere side; **b22.5** a couple years back, I think it was, I tasted a peated malt from this distillery which lives long in the memory, teasing and tantalising every taste bud in my mouth to death. I cannot say that their Amarone cask offering has quite the same spellbinding effect and ability to seduce. But the creaminess of the fruit backed by some beautifully paced oak-induced spice does more than enough to make for a very attractive experience. *44.8%*

MÄRKISCHE SPEZIALITÄTEN BRENNEREI Hagen. Working.

DeCavo Single Malt Höhlenwhisky 5 Jahre fass-nr. L19 db **(93.5) n23 t23.5 f23 b24** The best whisky I have encountered from this distillery, by far. Few German whiskies come maltier than this! *58.3%. sc.*

MOONSHINE DISTILLERY Limburg. Working.

‡ **Moonshine Single Still Whisky Ex-Bourbon Barrel Vol. 1** lightly peated, dist 26/10/19, bott 15/12/22 db (**90.5**) **n22** young, surprisingly crispy malt, soothed by a feather-tickle of peat...; **t22.5** silky delivery but also referring a sharp, metallic tang which both waters the eye and kicks off full salvation mode...; **f23** really hits its stride very late on as the intense malt has settled with both the smoke and copper output and natural oils to maximise length and depth. The intensity of malt so late on is truly remarkable; **b23** thoroughly entertaining whisky notable for the intensity of the unpeated malt while the smoke, elsewhere, lingers and anchors. This distillery can truly say it has created a pretty unique trademark house style. 52.3%

‡ **Moonshine Single Still Whisky Ex-Bourbon Barrel Vol. 2** Ximenez-Spinola finish, dist 26/10/19, bott 15/12/22 db (**88.5**) **n22 t22.5 f22 b22** This distillery does manage to find some excellent PX casks free from sulphur taint. However, in some ways the PX is simply too true to type as the intense, almost vulgarly sweet creamy richness of the grape obliterates the outstanding malt which is dying to make its usual oration but cannot get a word in edgeways. A malt which will be much admired by the sherry-ultras out there. 52.3%

‡ **Moonshine Single Still Whisky Ex-Bourbon Barrel Vol. 3** lightly peated, dist 12/10/19, bott 23/04/23 db (**94.5**) **n23.5** the oak is out of the blocks ahead of both the peat and the barley sugar. Indeed, the tannins are making a statement here, and some of it sounds almost bourbonesque in accent. When the peat does finally establish its foothold, it impresses with both a firmness and contrary yielding quality: brilliant...; **t23.5** exceptional delivery where the malt makes up lost ground and simply pours over the tastebuds in the most gloriously intense manner. The peat drifts around with a benign countenance, while the barley sugars are supplemented by quite rich ulmo honey and vanillas...; **f23.5** long, waxy and returns to that bourbon-style oakiness hinted at on the nose. Wonderful layering and the pithy spices add to the late complexity; **b24** a much more complex fellow than Volume one: the oak has been let go to do its best and its interplay with the concentrated malt is nothing short of excellent. 52.3%

‡ **Palatiner Whisky Clan Daemon's Cut Ex-Bourbon Barrel Vol. 1** dist 12/10/19, bott 12/05/23 db (**92**) **n22.5** doesn't even try for complexity: just happy with the youngish spirit ramping up the malt intensity and seeing if the oak can cope: it can...; **t23.5** beautifully fat mouth feel: this has been excellently distilled allowing maximum oils without impinging on the overall quality of the spirit. This means the malt has every opportunity to go for maximum intensity...and it succeeds. The sugars are covered by a gristiness on steroids; **f23** long with much more telling involvement from the tannins now, ensuring a drier, toastier fade. The malt, however, refuses to stand down completely; **b23** this is one hell of a malty whisky: devilishly good. 66.6%

NORDPFALZ BRENNEREI Höning. Working.

Eagle Bow Pfälzer Börben Aged 6 Years matured American oak, finished chestnut barrel, bott code: L1836-1, db (**89.5**) **n22 t22.5 f22.5 b22.5** For the second day in a row, one sniff told me we were looking at chestnut casks – one of the most distinctive aromas in whisky – and by no means least attractive. 42.7%

Paltarmor 5 Years Old Blended Malt aged in American oak, oloroso sherry and Old Forester peated casks, bott code: L-SHH-666 (**91**) **n23 t23 f22 b23** Best quality distillate I have yet encountered from this distillery. To achieve such an intensity of malt takes some doing. A highly pleasurable whisky experience. 47.7% *distilled by Thomas Sippel, Bernhard Höning & Ralf Hauer*

Taranis Pfälzer Single Malt Never Surrender Edition 2020 port cask finished, dist Seot 2013, bott code: L-1836-8, db (**88**) **n22 t23 f21 b22** A niggardly Port cask, spoiling for a fight. Doesn't appear to want the sugars to thrive...but the barley and tannins ensure otherwise. Complex. 46.5% *229 bottles*

Taranis Pfälzer Single Malt Never Surrender Edition 2021 oloroso sherry cask and bourbon barrel, dist Dec 2014, bott code: L-1836-9, db (**93**) **n23 t23.5 f23 b23.5** A whisky of great confidence and character. What a great oloroso cask on show here. 52.7%

NORTHOFF FEINBRENNEREI Lippetal. Working

The Westfalia German Single Malt 2016 Cask TW123 ex-Cragganmore bourbon barrel bott 2022 db (**89**) **n22.5** very clean despite the drifting light phenols which came as a surprise; **t22.5** yep, no mistaking the peat which forms a thick body to this delicately oiled dram; malt unencumbered by smoke provides extra juiciness; **f22** extremely light and thin-bodied but the residual smoke is very pleasing. Slightly warming on the finale; **b22** a classic example of a malt which improves dramatically with the Murray Method. Quite thin and fiery at normal temperature, a little loving and warmth brings out some surprising and delightful depth. 50.5%

The Westfalia German Single Malt 2013 Cask TW68 ex-Laphroaig bourbon barrel bott 2022 db (**94.5**) **n24** magnificent nose: the phenols are on first sniff, massive – but entirely controlled and in step. A ten minute nose...just for the sheer pleasure..! **t23.5** the light body is at odds with the flavour profile. Just a charming churning of delightfully smoke-laden malt with delicate ulmo honey supplying the just-so sweetness; f23 drier – even quite chalky. Quite simplistic vanilla, then a return to the phenols...with a little cocoa and marzipan thrown in for good measure; b24 truly brilliant. Even people not particularly into peaty whisky are in danger of being seduced by this one. Everything understated but the whole ends up a lot bigger than you might think. However, it is the nuanced vanilla, chocolate and honey which really wins the day here. 51.1%

The Westfalia German Single Corn Whisky 2016 Cask TW115 American new oak barrel bott 2021 db (92.5) n23 t23.5 f22.5 b23 I am presuming that the corn in question is maize, as the oiliness does tend to offer that degree of richness. Grandiose honey alongside those oils makes this a beauty. 52.4%

The Westfalia German Single Rye2016 Cask TW127 American new oak barrel bott 2021 db (92) n23 t23.5 f22.5 b23 Not quite like an American rye...it has certainly forged its own character. The sugars impress as does the cut-glass character of the grin on delivery. Lots to get on with here. Improves massively using MM. 54.8%

The Westfalia Peated German Single Malt 2013 Cask TW32 ex-Springbank Port Cask bott 2021 db (88.5) n23.5 t22 f21 b22 Westfalia certainly know how to make peat talk the talk. Another whisky which needs a good ten minutes nosing to understand its myriad properties. On the palate, however, the smoke and fruit don't quite dance so well in step together. 50.5%

The Westfalia Peated German Single Malt 2017 Cask TW201 ex-PX Sherry octave bott 2022 db (89.5) n23 the usual thick, sticky smokiness you get when PX and peat collide. Except this perhaps is a lighter skeleton on which all the fat hangs and younger barley also has a part to play; t22.5 quintessential PX: hugely intense sugars, glutinous barley and smoky golden syrup; f22 by now the peat is exhausted – in both senses. A little bitter as the sugars run thin, too...; b22 a real free-for-all between two enormous forces. They seldom come together harmoniously – and they have struggled here, too. That said, well, you can't not enjoy the sheer enormity of it all... 59.3%

The Westfalia German Single Malt 2016 Cask TW121 ex-Tobermory sherry hogshead bott 2022 db (91) n23 t23 f22 b23 The initial arrival on the palate is quite startling – real raised eyebrows stuff. But this is great chewing whisky with the grape and barley on equal terms. 52.9%

The Westfalia Crazy Cask Experiment German Single Corn 2016 Cask TW134 ex-Old Pulteney sherry hogshead bott 2021 db (93) n23 easily the most spiced nose encountered in the Westfalia portfolio: sharp-toothed nibbling despite the chunky grape; t23.5 superb delivery. About as rich as can be hoped for, yet with the sweetness elegantly muted so although a little muscovado sugar comes into play, we are more down the line of sherry trifle that's a bit short on sugar...but not sherry...; f23 long, with the accent on the vanilla, and a few juicy sultanas hanging around; b23.5 a gorgeously constructed malt where the sherry appears to enjoy playing games regarding both intensity and sweetness. But that fat mouthful of a delivery is to die for... 55.8%

The Westfalia German Single Grain Whisky 2013 Cask TW46 ex-Longmorn sherry hogshead bott 2022 db (94.5) n23.5 t24 f23 b24 Sensational...in the true sense of the word. A lesson in complexity. Impossible not to be both impressed and blown away by this. 52.1%

NUMBER NINE SPIRITUOSENMANUFAKTUR Leinefelde-Worbis, Working.

⬧ **Nine Springs Singe Malt Single Cask Selection Ex-Bourbon** cask no.1128 db (91) n22.5 such a delicately light nose where the clean barley and gentle oak appearing to be left to just get on with it. It's lightened even further by a squeeze of citrus; t23 the delivery and follow-through follow the same pattern as the nose. Except a layer of acacia honey springs an intense sparkle to both the barley and oak; f22.5 a lovely, sweet butterscotch fade, but there is still a hint of citrus even this late on; b23 not the most complex malt whisky you'll encounter. But sometimes it doesn't have to be, as long as it does well what it sets out to do you are onto a winner. And if you are looking for a malt that is malt and shewing oak which is balanced and just the right degree of honey to make it ultra-accessible, then you're there. 46% sc

⬧ **Nine Springs Single Malt Triple Cask** db (84.5) n20.5 t22.5 f20.5 b21 I deeply suspect the ex-Bordeaux cask has been up to its tricks here. Hard to find Bordeaux casks that haven't had sulphur treatment somewhere along the line and the nagging, dulling bitterness overshadows what had initially been a busy and fascinating, promising and honey-soaked delivery. The nose does pulse out a warning, though. 46%

SAUERLÄNDER EDELBRENNEREI Ruthen-Kallenhardt. Working.

Thousand Mountains McRaven Single Malt Fassstärke db (89.5) n22.5 t22.5 f22 b22.5 Remembering what a Feintfest this was when I first encountered this distillery, absolutely delighted how this has progressed. Not even a hint of feint now: the intense, unsullied malt dominates quite beautifully. 59.8%

SCHRAML - DIE STEINWALD - BRENNEREI E.K. Erbendorf. Working.

Stonewood 181 (90) n22 t23.5 f22 b22.5 Perfectly serviceable near new make which is well bodied and full without being remotely feinty. The high-point comes shortly after delivery when the grains build into a rich acacia honey-tinged mass, but that sweetness seems to put extra emphasis on the late bitterness of the finish. 45%

Stonewood Smoky Monk (91.5) n22 t23.5 f23 b23 Genuinely impressed with this. The smoke is controlled at all times, from the nose which, though a little untidy, offers smoky bacon to the much more intense delivery and follow-through. This is complex, despite its tender years, helped along by the wonderful addition of cocoa and mint, which even gives a cooling effect to the mouth as it enters the finish. A little tannin can be detected on the satisfying finale. 40%

Stonewood Dra (91) n22 t23.5 f22.5 b23 Begins with a nose which has you scratching your head. Some good, honeyed points showing age, but also something less desirable, has crept in there. The delivery, though, is true to house style. They like deceptively big at this distillery and that is just what is offered here. Most impressive, though, is the layering of varied honeys, with heather honey in pole position and lemon-blossom offering the more trilling notes. The finish has that same feel as an unwanted invader trying to spoil things, but so excellent are the good points, which sign off with bourbon cream biscuits. 43%

SLYRS Schliersee-Neuhaus. Working.

Slyrs Bavarian Single Malt Aged 12 Years batch LD1007 db **(95)** n23 t24 f24 b24 Hurrah! The last 12-year-old Slyrs I sampled was a bit fuzzy around the gills. This one ticks boxes with almost arrogant aplomb. Way beyond excellent, this will be in the taste off for European Whisky the Year. And this really is a Slyrs Classic, perhaps their best bottling ever... 43%

Slyrs Single Malt Classic batch LH18381 db **(91.5)** n22.5 a couple of slices of tinned peach slip effortlessly into the malt and tannins make their presence felt; **t23** the malt, like in previous incarnations, is truly cosmic. Like cramming an entire bag of almost chocolate-free Maltesers into your mouth. I say "almost" as there is also a definite hint of milk chocolate amid the spiced hickory and honey-flacked vanilla; **f23** long, at times not entirely fault free, but the enormity of the malt carries through to the death; **b23** one of the most intensely malted whiskies I have encountered outside of Speyside. Take a bow, Slyrs... 46%

Slyrs Single Malt Port Cask Finish batch C0163 db **(91.5)** n22.5 a lovely layering of relaxed spice watches over the happy marrying of malt with boiled fruit candy; **t23.5** salivating and satisfying from the first moment, the light oils from the distillate are on the perfect wavelength of the succulent grape. Barley sugar and Werthers Originals make a great combination to represent the malt-oak duet; **f23** long, lightly spiced and persistently grapey for a much greater time than you'd think possible; **b23** a superb choice of Port cask, free from sulphur, ensures that we have a Slyrs that thumps out the flavours like a Baroque orchestra belts out Handle.. 46%

Slyrs Rye batch B03718 db **(88.5)** n20 t23.5 f22.5 b22.5 Rye and oat whiskies are the hardest of the grains to properly master. And we see here that Slyrs are on the way with their rye. Maybe the cuts aren't quite ideal, a common problem. But they are not far off and for a few golden moments soon after arrival on the palate, that unique fruit intensity of the rye goes into concentrated overdrive, before melding with the highly intense tannins. The sub-current of heather honey is also quite stunning. The outline of something special here. 41%

Slyrs Single Malt Rum Cask Finish batch E1978 db **(87.5)** n22.5 t22.5 f21 b21.5 As is so often the case, a rum cask has given this malt a tough exoskeleton. There is a crisp sugariness throughout, but also a residual tang which is uncomplimentary to the hard-working but overpowered malt. Spices buzz, though, and there is no escaping the fruit pastille undercurrent which has attached itself to this intriguing but slightly eccentric malt. 46%

Slyrs Single Malt Oloroso Cask Finish batch C0863 db **(84.5)** n21 t22.5 f20 b21 I have tasted a series of outstandingly good Slyrs whiskies today, some of them outrageously good, the odd one or two memorable for all the right reasons. Sad to end on a slightly down note as the oloroso cask(s) deployed here have not done this distillery justice and furnished their malt with a lumbering dryness and late tanginess which I, for one, don't particularly appreciate. Never mind: these days there are a multitude of magnificent others Slyrs to get stuck into... 46%

SPREEWOOD DISTILLERS GMBH Schlepzig. Working.

Stork Club Single Malt Whiskey ex-bourbon, ex-sherry & ex-Weißwein casks, lot no. 008543 L002 db **(88.5)** n22.5 t22.5 f21 b22.5 Not a faultless sherry butt. But one that offers more ticks than crosses. 47%. ncf.

ST. KILIAN DISTILLERS GMBH Rüdenau. Working.

Bud Spencer Der Blinde & Der Blonde Jorgo & Marcus Limited Edition db **(87)** n21.5 t22.5 f21 b22 It may not tick all the boxes technically, but you'll be hard-pressed to find a whisky more behind the vanilla cause. Soft and too delicate to cover any blemishes. Pleasant, though. 47%

Bud Spencer The Legend Rauchig Single Malt Batch No 2 db (94.5) n23.5 one of the most attractive Islay-style noses yet produced in Germany with the peat standing to attention, ready to take on all comers...but still being gentle enough to accept a lilting citrus and honey secondary layer; t23.5 silky mouthfeel, the barley landing gamely and immediately setting off a salivating response, before the peat begins to gently do its stuff. Spices jab away happily; f23.5 so often in Europe, the finish doesn't match the glory of what came before. But not this time. The excellently measured oils have done their job and reel the smoke in at the death. The honeyed chocolate ensures no late bitterness creeps in; b24 a malt with a punch to it, as you might expect. But, as noticed, it is the spices which do the most jabbing. The intense smoke is content to shadow box the sweeter barley and vanilla elements. Genuinely a knockout single malt... 49% ncf nc

St Kilian Bud Spencer The Legend Single Malt Batch No 1 db (83.5) n20.5 t21.5 f20.5 b21 As far removed from their astonishing Rauchid - smoky - batch two as can be imagined. Not just because of the lack of gentle peat, but the simple fact that the base distillate isn't even in the same league, possessing a few feinty edges. Absolutely no doubting the sanctity of the malt, though.... 46%

St Killian Kiliani Edition Gosbert Single Malt db (87) n22.5 t22.5 f20.5 b22 On nose and body, this just exudes St Kilian's beautifully soft honey which is now becoming their trademark. The nagging bitterness on the finish, though, reveals an off cask or two undermining the great work of the distillate... 46%

St Kilian Terence Hill The Hero db (88.5) n22 t22.5 f22 b22 A delightfully relaxed wander through clean and refreshing citrus and malt tones which have the rare honour of working their way through from the nose to still doing their stuff at the vanilla-drying finale. 46%

St Kilian Terence Hill The Hero Rauchid db (91.5) n22.5 t23.5 f22.5 b23 Someone has done their homework on how to make a peaty whisky non-aggressive or threatening to the uninitiated. Maybe it is the powerful praline note that acts as the phenol's partner throughout. They make a beautiful and very sexy couple. Such well behaved spice, too... 49%

St Killian Single Malt Signature Edition "Eight" casks 43% ex-rye, 27% ex-bourbon 19% ex-rotwein Rioja, 9% Pfalzer Eiche, 2%Akazie, Peated 54% ppm dist 2017/2018 bott 2021 db (95.5) n24 stunning...just jaw-droppingly stunning. Not just because it is peaty. But the layering defies belief...the best peated nose this year. The enigmatic sweetness amid the drier phenols and tannins just about hits genius level...; t24.5 there is no let up on delivery, either, as the smoke and myriad tannins get busy and immediately confound the palate. The "bittiness" and "busyness" to this is matched only by the small grains working in the finest bourbons. Here we have a to-die-for delivery, salivating yet deep...indeed labyrinthine with countless tunnels from which honey, barley sugar, spices and vanillas pop up from and disappear back into...; f23 if there is an Achilles heel, it is a slight niggle on the finish, but even that is easily lost amid the granular feel of the peat and vanilla; b24 there is no doubting now. On this evidence, St Kilian has arrived among the world's great whiskies and one more than capable of producing the best in Europe. Rarely do I encounter a whisky of such complexity, harmony and sensuality. Had the finish been in keeping with its earlier unbelievable high standards, an award would have been on its way. Even so, if there are 8,888 bottles of this out there, make sure that is reduced to 8,887... 53.8% nc ncf 8,888 bottles

St Killian Single Malt Signature Edition Ten ex-bourbon and ex-rum casks 81.6% Munchner malz, 12.2 Pilsener malz, 2.6% caramunch, 2.2% melanoidmalz, caraaroma 1.4% dist 2016/2017 bott 2022 db (89.5) n22.5 ah.... a slightly wider cut gives a little extra oil but doesn't prevent the malt making a big, moderately sweet statement; t23 now this really takes off. A glorious buttery feel to the honeyed barley with gathering grapefruit as things progress; the spices hit early but then taper off, making way for tangy vanilla; f21.5 quite a buzz to this finish as the remaining spices and those heftier oils make their mark. Still tangy at the death; b22.5 a lively malt which uses the inherent honey as a decoy to the busy flavour-changes which rip through this bottling. The heavier oils also play an important factor. 49.5%

St Killian Single Malt Ex-Sherry PX Cask no 1527 dist 25/10/2018 bott 19/7/22 db (90.5) n22.5 a veritable swamp of a nose, a black hole from which nothing can escape the incredible pull of the thick peat and grape; t23.5 good Lord! The most eye-watering, brain seizing moment after when this thuds into the palate: You are momentarily winded and in shock. There is initially a lull, a moment of sherry-filled silence and then....kaboom! The whole thing erupts and does so with little or no warning. What happens then is open to interpretation. But there is some kind of mess involving big spice and exploding, under-ripe grape; f22.5 to say it settles down is too much of a simplification. But let's just say it cools and controls itself a little. Though what those varying popping and biting notes are, I have no idea. The wonderful news is that this is 100% sulphur-free...; b22 simply one of those incomprehensible whiskies which is, technically from a cask perspective, a nightmare – PX and peat are rarely harmonious bedfellows, and they certainly aren't here – yet the stuff of wet dreams for those whisky thrill seekers who prefer to surf the waves of the most anarchic whiskies in town... *60.2%*

STEINHAUSER GMBH Kressbronn. Working.

Brigantia Aged 8 Years db (88.5) n21.5 t22.5 f22 b22.5 The cut is wide, meaning a little heavyweight oils leaks into an otherwise delicate malt. The delivery is s celebration of stone fruit, wild plums in particular. These work rather well with the chocolate and spices which eventually make their presence felt. Rather enjoyable whisky which would benefit with slightly more precision on the cut itself, thus denying the more tangy notes entry into would could be something rather excellent. *44%*

Brigantia Classic db (89) n21 t23 f22.5 b22.5 After the stop-start nose and delivery, we enter another world altogether, one where the malts reigns supreme. Love those spices, too. *43%*

Brigantia Cognac Single Cask db (91) n22.5 t23.5 f22 b23 Forget about having this for a nightcap. So vivid is this on the palate, it'll wake you up completely. *57% sc*

Brigantia Gin Cask Finish db (80) n21 t20 f19 b20 Gin is gin. And whisky is whisky. And never should the two twains meet. Grim. *46%*

Brigantia Single Malt Rum Cask Finish db (91) n22.5 t23 f22.5 b23 A sweeter, oilier version than their last bottling. Such is the ruminess of this, I poured what I thought was the Cognac cask version, nosed it and instantly realised I had the wrong sample! It doesn't come much rummier than that! A tad bitter at the death, though spices compensate. *46%*

Brigantia Schwaben Single Malt db (89.5) n22 this distillery doesn't specialise in noses: they certainly are never a pointer to what will be happening next. Some pleasant apple notes; t23 impressive malt coming through with light apple and pear just giving a gentler air; f22 lovely vanilla; b22.5 comprehensively malty and clean... *45%*

Brigantia Sherry Cask Finish db (89) n21.5 t23 f22 b22.5 A bold, assertive fruitiness to this malt sets it apart. Far from technically faultless, but highly enjoyable, nonetheless. *46%*

SYLT DESTILLERIE Sylt. Working.

Sild Triple Cask Bavarian Pure Malt Aged 5 Years db (80) n20 t22 f18 b20 My Pavlovian response to seeing three types of wine cask is one of trepidation. On this occasion it was entirely justified as the sulphur creeps all over the malt, the finish in particular. *44%*

WALDHOMBRENNERIE KLOTZ

❖ **Waldhombrennerie Buchenbach** Oloroso Sherry and Jamaica Rum cask, dist 10/2016, bott 10/2022, bott code L01B10R22 db (90.5) n21.5 the chunky cut means a distinct nuttiness (mainly walnut oil) runs through this while the fruits are hard at work filling the open spaces. The rum guarantees the experienced firmness countering the softer oils. A vague phenol note circulates; t22.5 now this comes together with a fabulous flavour explosion. Still fatty from the wide cut, but the precipitous spices dazzle; f23.5 what a brilliant finish. We go full mixed nuts here with the walnut joined by macadamia and pecan. This leads to a sensuous praline kick towards the death with just the odd strand of raisin interjecting here and there. Ultra-complex, multi-layered and highly rewarding; b23 it is odd when a slight misreading of the cut off still leads to something that may be even better than had the hearts been pure. There is a slightly feinty note, but it appears to capture the best of the two casks at work to ensure a single malt of exceptionally high complexity. A real flavour orgy that makes any weakness forgivable. *54.66% Spirit Of The Cask*

WHISKY DESTILLERIE LIEBL Bad Kötzting. Working.

Coillmór Single Malt Whisky Bavaria x Toscana II Caberlot Rotwein Cask Finish cask no. 687, destilliert 08 Jun 10, abgefüllt 13 Feb 19 db (80.5) n18.5 t23 f19 b20 A fantastic cask which radiates high quality grape from the moment it hits the palate. But even that struggles against the feints from the distillate. *46%. sc. 364 bottles.*

WHISKY DESTILLERIE BLAUE MAUS Eggolsheim. Working.

❖ **Blaue Maus Jubilaums-Abfullung 2023 Single Cask Malt 15 Years Old** fass Nr 1 dist 04/2008 db (88.5) n21.5 t22.5 f22 b22.5 A very dense malt making the best of its thick cut off the still. Too many entangling bitter tones for this to ever be great. But, equally, too many fascinating strands – like the marmalade and vanilla - for it not to be entertaining. *43.8%*

❖ **Blaue Maus Jubilaums-Abfullung 2023 Single Cask Malt 30 Years Old** fass Nr 1 dist 05/1993 db (94) n23.5 not often heather honey arrives straight off the bat of any whisky. But there it unmistakably is, helping to maximise the density of the malt in the process. Add to this those adorable spices and the result is a quite beautiful German nose....Oh, and one that could be mistaken for a Kentuckian one, too...; t23.5 high copper content on delivery – shows the working of a relatively new still. With rich red liquorice and a few other bourbon phrases, especially around the dark sugar and honey content interjecting with the vanillas and we are talking some serious complexity at work...; **f23** the generous oils, the sharp copper tones and the huge build-up of vanillas certainly makes the finish a long one. Those darker sugars hang about, as does a spicy liquorice development; **b24** this is much more like the Blaue Maus I know and love! A malt festooned with honey and nibbling and whispering at the taste buds with al kinds of secrets and tasty tittle-tattle. Complex and entertaining to a fault! Truly beautiful. 42.2%

☙ **Blaue Maus Jubilaums-Abfullung 2023 Single Cask Malt 35 Years Old** fass Nr 1 dist 04/1988 db **(91) n22** technically not quite as well-tuned as the 30-year-old. There is the odd smell of liniment – in Britain we called it Germolene – an antibacterial cream to help aid the repair of cuts to the skin. A first for any whisky I have encountered...and I admit I love it! **t23.5** wow! So much copper here, this must have been distilled in slow motion! There is no escaping the width of the cut, but, equally, you can't ignore the glory of that honey, too...; **f22.5** very tangy thanks to the copper and the generous oils. Never quite finds a happy medium, but impossible not to like those spiced vanillas, either, or the ultra-dry tannins; **b23** hard to believe that when this whisky was distilled I was putting the finishing touches to my first-ever book and my beloved club, Millwall, were on the cusp of winning promotion to the top tier of English football for the very first time in their history. And as for history with this distillery: well for a start you cannot taste this without tasting the 30-year-old by comparison. And here is a classic example of a distiller in the passing five years getting a far better understanding of just how his stills work and how to extract the maximum benefit out them. Happy Anniversary Blaue Maus! 41.2%

☙ **Blaue Maus Spinnaker Single Cask Malt Port Cask Edition** fass Nr 1 dist 09/2014 db **(86.5) n21.5 t22 f21.5 b21.5** Wow...Blaue Maus has kind of discovered "yoof". In some respects this is such a young whisky, in others there is big oak age statement. The colour confirms Port cask harassment, but the spirit didn't appear to be in the cask long enough to take instruction in just how the flavours should progress. The odd honey notes flashes though, as does malt but never quite managing to hit a rhythm. 43.3%

☙ **Blaue Maus Spinnaker Single Cask Malt Rum Cask Edition** fass Nr 1 dist 09/2014 db **(87) n21.5 t22 f21.5 b22** Very different for a Blaue Maus, this bottling seemingly being very young and one the nose it still proudly possesses the blush of new make. As such it is refreshing on delivery and malt stands head and shoulders above all other elements. It certainly seems untroubled by the rum cask. 43.3%

☙ **Blaue Maus Spinnaker Single Cask Malt Sherry Cask Edition** fass Nr 1 dist 09/2014 db **(89.5) n22** a hint of nougat joins forces with a simple malt tone. The fruit has bolted into a mousehole...; **t22.5** a super-light body and much more delicate than your average sherry-influenced malt. And, as on the nose, it is the malt doing the loudest squeaking...; **f22.5** once more the malt dominates alongside the caramels...without really trying to. You do fancy a little raisin is joining the spice to ensure depth to the late chewiness. Mmmm...now a last second coating of mocha...; **b22.5** a perfectly clean sherry butt to help this become a very comfortable toffee-raisin experience. 43%

WHISKY-DESTILLERIE MEW Neuried. Working.

☙ **MEW 12 Years Old** cask no 1, bott 10/05/23 db **(90) n23** heavyweight oak dried further by a pithy fruitiness. The spices are inevitable; **t23** a succulent delivery with the richness of the malt not only matching the fruit input but actually trumping it. The interplay is delightful; **f22** just a tad bitter from the oak but good oils to keep the vanillas and light sugars in play; **b22** not quite in the same league a MEW's Mizunara oak offering, but the Port cask used here is of seriously good quality to ensure a beautifully rounded whisky. 41% sc ncf

☙ **MEW Rare Cask Mizunara Oak** bott 11/12/23 db **(95) n23.5** honeydew melon mixing it with fresh oak shavings and peppery spices. Complex, sophisticated, charmingly understated and always striking the right balance...; **t24** that is such a wicked delivery with an extraordinary exhibition of Lubek marzipan joining with a sweet gooseberry fondant and a gently spiced heather honey...; **f23.5** remains sticky and spicy, a mild bitterness from the oak doing nothing to spoil the prevailing honey tones; **b24** have to say that this year the whiskies from Europe have been as high in quality as I can ever remember...and, so far, this is sitting just about on top of the pile. Perhaps the perfect exhibition of controlled sweetness... Majestic. 53.5% sc ncf 111 bottles

ICELAND
EIMVERK DISTILLERY Gardabaer. Working.

Flóki Icelandic Single Malt Whisky Double Wood Reserve 3 Year Old primary cask smoke no.171, secondary cask meed no.2, bott 2020 db **(86.5) n21 t21 f23 b21.5** You know how frustrating it can be when a corner kicks fails to clear the first defender. Well, this whisky is a bit like that with the peat. You get all ready for the phenols to come floating in, but it doesn't clear the slightly hefty feints, first on the nose and then the delivery. However, there is a delicious frothiness to this once established on the palate. And from this light honey and chocolate tones emerge. Just about finds some kind of balance. I can't wait to see how this malt develops when they've sorted those cut points out. It is obvious from the complexity on the finish that his distillery has the capability to progress. *45%. sc.*

Flóki Icelandic Single Malt Whisky Sheep Dung Smoked Reserve 3 Year Old ex-Flóki Young Malt casks, cask no. 10 bott 2020 db (87.5) n20 t23 f22 b22.5 Again badly needs the Murray Method to make it sing and bring out the considerable honey on tap. Very much a mood whisky and distinctly in the Marmite category. But the tobacco/hoppy/dungy kick may at times prove a little too much. A whisky that takes time to warm to but, once you become accustomed and the honeys start having their say, there is no denying this is not only huge, but hugely complex. *47%. sc.*

ISRAEL
GOLLANI DISTILLERY Qatsrin. Working.
Gollani Distillery Israeli Single Malt Whisky Unicask dessert wine cask dist 7/17 bott 10/20 db (85.5) n23 t22.5 f19 b21 One of the most remarkable things about this is that the nose and delivery is almost identical to the first single malt Indian whiskies I tasted in the late 1980s, though a style that no longer exists there now. This is well made. And the first signs on the nose are not only sympathetic, but complex. A slight pear-drop sharpness works well on both nose and delivery – and in the mouth, the malty follow-through is also attractive. But doubts about the quality of the cask as there is a furry bitterness spoiling things at the end. Would be interesting to see this in ex-bourbon. *62.5%*

LEGENDS DISTILLERY Ella Valley. Working.
Slingshot Kentucky Barrel Proof Batch no 2 db (81.5) n19.5 t21.5 f20 b20.5 Familiar signs of a new distillery still coming to terms with their equipment. The feinty nose confirms that they still haven't yet narrowed the cut points to a range which will ensure clarity and a free ride for the grains. That said, the delivery is momentarily excellent, the oils overcome by the sheer power of the sugary small grains and early tannins and even a light hickory echo. But it isn't too long before the feints again unfurl to create a foggy, confused middle and finish. The good news is that the early explosion of Demerara sugars point to a potentially bright future. First, though, someone has to be far more strict with those stills. I look forward to seeing future batches. *57.3%*

THE MILK & HONEY DISTILLERY Tel Aviv-Yafo. Working.
Milk & Honey Classic Single Malt Whisky db (92) n22 t23.5 f23.5 b23 A dry malt which keeps the sugars under control at all times. The result is a complex dram where the barley plays an ever-increasing part in the overall flavour structure, especially when it finds it has muscle enough to accept the growing oak without for a moment losing its poise. Reminds me of some old malt whiskies from Scotland that could be found in the early 1980s where intense malt met equally full-on oak but had personality enough to ride the storm. Loses a mark for a hint of juniper on the nose: I didn't know they made gin at this distillery. I'd any money now that they do. Chaps, please be more careful in your bottling hall. Otherwise, absolutely delicious. *46%.*

ITALY
L. PSENNER GMBH Tramin an der Weinstrasse. Working.
◇ **Retico Finest Italian Single Malt Aged 5 Years** aged in grappa and sherry casks bott code L23150 db (84) n20 t21.5 f21.5 b21 What's the Italian for déjà vu....? Picking up exactly the same weaknesses and strengths as last year, sadly with the weaknesses winning by a distance. Identical nougat style nose despite the best attentions of the sherry butt which works manfully to pull this round. Lots of dull toffee enlivened only by the raisin. The only difference I remember this time is a bit of extra bitterness leaking through at the death. *By the way it's 'gia visto!'. 43%*

◇ **Retico Finest Italian Single Malt Aged 7 Years Limited Edition** aged in grappa & gewurtraminer casks bott code L23149 db (94.5) n23.5 quite unexpectedly there is actually a grappa note bursting through on this: the first for any whisky I've nosed, at least so far as I can remember. There is also a nugget chocolate and marzipan doing the rounds, as well as a more unconventional grapiness. Or maybe I mean grappaness...; t23.5 what a delivery... Crisp, machine precise, crumbling under the weight of muscovado sugars. And German-style Christmas cake; then, pitched right in the middle of all this, a huge dollop of intense malt, as close to faultless as you could ever wish for. Even better, there is a significant backbone of intense tannin to keep the rigidity in place and the spices growing...; f23.5 long with a fabulous fig jam and and heather honey flourish. Still that malt powers through, though softer now with a forceful whisper replacing a proud bellow...; b24 47%

PUNI WHISKY DISTILLERY Glurns, Bozen. Working.

Puni Arte Batch 2 db **(91)** n22.5 t23 f22.5 b23 Soft and satisfying with an engaging sweetness which at times turns to a sultry sexiness. *46%*

Puni Arte Batch 3 db **(94.5)** n23 t24 f23.5 b24 This has to be high grade sherry at work here. The samples I have contain no details, other than name, rank and serial number.... I get those later. But faultless sherry doing what faultless sherry long ago once did. Anything but a puny Puni... *50%*

Puni Aura Cask Strength Batch 2 db **(89.5)** n23 another unashamed fruit fest. But there are some older tannins biting deep, too; t23.5 a two-tone whisky with a layering of well matured tannin which appears to have integrated with the grape. And a secondary level, younger, sharper more aggressive.... And in no hurry to mingle; f21 those younger fruits remain sharper for longer, taking on a kiwifruit persona. Not sure about the integrity of at least one of the casks, though; b22 the last Aura I tasted had a...well, aura. This one is huge but hamstrung by an unfortunate niggle on the finish. *63.5%*

LIECHTENSTEIN
TELSER DISTILLERY Triesen. Closed.

Telser Liechtenstein Annual Release No. 1 Double Grain triple cask db **(92)** n22.5 t24 f22 b23.5 Just incredible mouthfeel to this. And to add to the joy, the sugar profile is just about unique, the lion's share of the flavour profile dedicated to a beautifully lush malt concentrate. Liquid ulmo honey fills in the gaps. Something very different and simply brilliant. *44.6%. sc.*

THE NETHERLANDS
ZUIDAM BAARLE Nassau. Working.

Millstone Dutch Single Malt Whisky Aged 10 Years American Oak bott code: 0378ZU db **(92.5)** n24 t23 f22.5 b23 Bang on the money with the honey and the malt. Love it!! *43%*.

Millstone Dutch Single Malt Whisky Aged 10 Years French Oak bott code: 2927 ZU db **(88.5)** n22 t22 f22.5 b22 A surprise malt, this. French oak normally belts out a bit more bite and tannic pungency. Here it seems to be happy to go with the malty flow. *40%*.

Millstone Dutch Single Malt Whisky Oloroso Sherry bott code: 0328ZU db **(81)** n19 t23 f18 b21 Make no mistake: this is a fabulous, faultless sherry butt at work here. And the delivery offers grapey bliss. But, sadly, the underlying structure of the spirit itself throws up a few question marks. *46%*.

Millstone Dutch Single Malt Whisky Oloroso Sherry bott code: 0580ZU db **(84.5)** n21 t21.5 f21 b21 Eye-wateringly tart. *46%*.

NORWAY
AURORA SPIRIT DISTILLERY AS Lyngseidet. Working.

Bivrost Niflheim Artic Single Malt Whisky triple cask matured db **(88.5)** n22 t23 f21 b22.5 So Norway proudly joins the roll call of world whisky nations, and with this first-ever bottling also completes the Scandinavian set. It is certainly a creature hewn from its land, as this is a malt that matches the country's rugged geology with an awe-inspiring delivery, full of peaks and valleys, inlets and fjords: it is not an easy whisky to navigate. The nose is far from perfect, revealing a feinty nature which you know will return on the finish. The Murray Method will help you burn some of those oils off and release more of the lime blossom honey that is dying to escape and reveal something a lot more enticing, sexy even. The delivery, though, is about as rugged as it comes thanks again to those big oils, but also the malt which is fighting its corner frantically. Again the honey comes up for air, but it's frantic stuff - especially when the feints make their predictable return. So, a wonderful choice for my 1,000th sample for the Whisky Bible 2021. A King amongst Scandinavian malts and an experience you can't afjord to miss... *46%. 1,622 bottles.*

MYKEN DESTILLERI AS Nordland. Working.

Myken Artic Single Malt Whisky Octave Symphony 2020 4 Year Old db **(95)** n23.5 t24 f23.5 b24 this is actually far better than the last eight scotch single malts I tasted: not a sulphur molecule in sight. "Robert Louis Stevenson, Robbie Burns, Robert The Bruce, Bonnie Prince Charlie, Alec Salmond, Sean Connery, The Loch Ness Monster vi har slått dem alle sammen, vi har slått dem alle sammen! Nicola Thatcher can you hear me? Margaret Sturgeon... your distilleries took a hell of a beating! Your distilleries took a hell of a beating!" *47%*.

PORTUGAL
VENAKKI DISTILLERY Alpiarça. Working.

Venakki Moonshine Single Cask Cask No 6 **(93)** n23.5 t23.5 f23 b23 When is a whisky not a whisky? When it is just weeks away from being three years old and tastes as good as this. The nose alone can have you in a trance as you try to work out its distinctive but fabulously attractive mix of mallow, marzipan and a kind of soft, creamy cedarwood: a truly unique aroma in the whisky world. Very unusually, the delivery is the nose now in taste form, those semi-pungent tannins becoming, immediately, the source of the spice. But it is the soothing oils, spreading both warmth and an almost orangey sweetness across the roof of the mouth, making a fool of the spirit's non-whisky status. Precocious? Not half!!! And how I'd love to see the aroma of this Moonshine as a soap... *50% Moonshine Ltd*

◇ **Venakki Woodwork Rare Portuguese Cask** Portuguese malt and grain whisky batch no 2 **(96) n23.5** the malt is not just first out of the blocks. But second, third and fourth. But lumbering around in the slower lanes is an oily nuttiness and some pretty toothless spices. The vanillas, though, are a tad more confident and effective; **t25** swoon...! Yes, that is 25 out of 25. It is not a typo. I am stone cold sober and in full control of my faculties... I cannot fault this in any way, shape or form. You simply cannot find a more pristine version of intense malt sweetened only by barley sugars. And then thickened by a butterscotch and buttercream mix. Even the oak, as it pops into view at first offers tannins, but within seconds is melting under the omnipotence of the malt. As the oaks gather, so do the spices...; **f23.5** a warming, peppery finale. But it will take more than that for the intense malt to disengage..We are now also in the world of heather honey, butterscotch, Werther's Originals and the very lightest of molasses...; **b24** damn! This is good! Bloody good! Whatever the grain is doing, it is doing absolutely nothing to in any way negate the stunning beauty and intensity of that flawless malt. My guess, it is I know this distillery well. And have never had a doubt about the quality they were capable of producing. But did I ever expect anything of this breath-taking brilliance. Frankly, no. As the French would say, your mouth has been kissed by angels... *50.5% nc ncf*

SLOVAKIA
NESTVILLE DISTILLERY Hniezdne. Working.
◇ **Nestville Aged 12 Years Reminiscence of Vanilla**, bott code L25230105LB **(94) n23** very much in the house style, the oak puffs itself up and billows out dandelion seeds on the wing; **t24** any more rounded and we'd have the perfect orb. The gentleness of the oils is a caress, the peck of the tannins is a kiss. Such a sensual touch to the red liquorice and caramel theme. But perhaps most beguiling is the immediacy and intimacy of the spices which arrive even before the first flavour wave lands. The interplay between the darker, drier, tannins and the light molasses is something to cherish...though the spices never quite let go; **f23** "reminiscence of vanilla" claims the label, boldly. And they are not wrong... But they could have added "cocoa", too...; **b24** Nestville have gone and created their own style of whisky which has been on the burner for some while and finally exploded onto the worldwide attention in last year's Bible. Again, we have a whisky (they pointedly don't call it a single malt) which is astonishing in its silkiness: it is as though the taste buds are being caressed by a lightly spiced mink coat. 40%

◇ **Nestville Single Cask Virgin Oak** cask no 13291, dist 27/06/16, bott 05/05/23 db **(95.5) n24** so impressive: the heather honey tones have just the right weight to attach to the tannin ballast which combine to offer the lightest of bourbon coatings. The malt is present but thin. However, this is not about the malt: this is about gloriously spiced intonations. Beautifully distilled and matured: for what it is, not sure how it can be improved upon; **t24** the early oil levels come as a surprise: much more gloss on delivery than expected and this coating helps thicken the intensity of the creamy molten molasses and gorgeously toasty tannin with black liquorice building through the middle. Perhaps most startling, though, is the juiciness, which works sublimely with the natural caramels...thus giving a toffee apple effect. Meanwhile, the spices are exquisite; **f23.5** soft oils plus the odd spasm of malt amid the assembly of sweet and dry tannins; **b24** this distillery really does punch out some exceptional single malt. The tannins offer extraordinary depth and richness, here, without ever going over the edge. That is some feat: the initial distillate is delicate and easily damaged. A must-taste for those who savour oak at its most engrossing and complex. 45%

SLOVENIA
BROKEN BONES DISTILLERY Ljubljana. Working.
◇ **Broken Bones Single Malt Aged 4 Years** batch 1/22 db **(96) n24** a year old and weightier than previous bottlings I have encountered; I was expecting freshly fallen apple and instead served with rhubarb tart with custard. There is a sharper note in there, also – a kind of cross between barley sugar, a bale of newly cut grass and custard cream biscuits. I really adore this understated, fragile complexity. And my word! This really is complex...; **t24** so clean....so delicate....and, eventually, salivating. The sugars are at the forefront, most of them gristy and melting on impact. But there is the most glorious blend of ulmo and heather honey, too, ensuring a subdued vanilla-led sweetness. On a level below, the tannins make polite noises...; **f24** not sure

how something this light, this delicate can be quite so long on the finish. There doesn't appear to be heavy oils at play, but something is keeping those hinted fruit tones and more compelling vanillas going. And those newly discovered spices rumbling...; **b24** what can you say? For a 4-year-old, this is too outrageously good. Fabulous distillation with the stills run slowly, the cuts near perfection and the cask choice exquisite: this is rapidly becoming one of the greatest malts on mainland Europe and one with an unmistakable Glen Grant-ish characteristics There is both simplicity and complexity in equal measure. And, because it is flawlessly made and matured, you can just sit back and enjoy without the worry of any nasty surprises. Let the most delicate of malts wash over your palate and enjoy the whispered tale beautifully told... 46%

⟐ **Broken Bones Single Malt Peated Aged 4 Years** batch 2/22 db **(94.5) n23 t23.5** the apple missing on the non-peated version had emigrated to here while the smoke – a mix of peat and more acidic anthracite - has been bolstered from the days when this was a three-year-old and offers the perfect balancing weight. Ironically, though peated shews its youth more than the non-peated version...; **t23.5** the phenols though confidently up front are first on the scene but arrive layered and introspective. A secondary tier of unpeated barley salivates and mingles with the gentle tannins to offer a biscuity frame; **f23.5** a little oilier than the unpeated version but, curiously, slightly less spicy. Instead, a smoky mocha sweetened with Demerara sugars gives the finish a rounded and friendly feel; **b24** like their non-peated bottling, this has moved up a couple of gears since a three-year-old. The peat is more telling now and though this could have moved off into muscular mode, there is always a gentler refrain keeping matters civil and gentlemanly: this is one the most politely peaty whiskies you'll encounter this year. It is also the 777th and final whisky I will taste for the Jim Murray Whisky Bible 2024. I had purposely left the Broken Bones whiskies to the very last as I find them one of the most fascinating distilleries in the world. I had hoped they would end my whisky sojourn for 2024 off with an elegant flourish. As it happened, they exceeded expectation. This is a distillery to watch and all I have to do now is meet them for the first time and persuade them to up their production. 46%

SPAIN

DYC Single Malt Aged 10 Years db **(86) n23 t22.5 f19 b21.5** Initially, the best DYC I've tasted for some while. Look forward to getting my lips around it again soon. Pity about the sulphur on the finish, though, after such an arousing, fruity nose and delivery. 40%

DESTILERÍAS LIBER Granada. Working.

Whisky Pura Malta Embrujo De Granada bott code: Lote 21/049 db **(92.5) n23.5 t23.5 f22.5 b23** A dramatic variation from their last bottling with a highly attractive degree of salt giving this malt a distinctly coastal air, despite it being somewhat inland from the southern coast of Spain. My Fair Whisky...(Incidentally, the Murray Method lifts this whisky onto a far higher level than when served cool or chilled.) 40%

SWEDEN
HIGH COAST DISTILLERY Bjärtrå. Working.

High Coast Distillery Archipelago Baltic Sea 2019 bott Dec 2018 db **(95) n24 t23 f23 b24** Nautical...but nice! A deep whisky...and deeply impressive. 54.5%. nc ncf. 1,000 bottles.

MACKMYRA Gästrikland. Working.

Mackmyra Brukswhisky art nr. MB-004 db **(95.5) n24 t23.5 f24 b24** Having just tasted a succession of Scotch whisky brands each spoiled at the end by the unmistakable and unforgiving pollutant of sulphur; and after giving my poor, duffed-up taste buds a rest of over an hour during which time strawberries and crisps were consumed to try and neutralise the deadening effect on my palate, I have deliberately re-started my tasting day with a whisky I know to be as clean yet entertaining as can possibly be found. Was this a wise choice? You bet! Carrying a little more weight than some previous bottlings but still a real Scandinavian beauty... 41.4%.

Mackmyra Intelligens A1.01 db **(95) n23.5 t23.5 f24 b24** For Mackmyra this is pretty heavy duty. The oils are confident, bold even. The fruitiness is at times dense, occasionally subtle. Altogether a malt which gets your brain as well as your taste buds working overtime. However, it is the incredibly clever use of the peat which is worth a standing ovation. A true classic. 46%

Mackmyra Vintersol art. nr. MC-013, ex-port wine casks db **(74) n22 t20 f15 b17** Nope! After the promising (and threatening nose) becomes flat as a witch's tit and casts a less than pleasant spell on the finish. Poor casks like this are so un-Mackmyra-ish. 46.1%.

NORDMARKENS DESTILLERI AB Arjang

⟐ **Expecto II Single Malt** oloroso sherry cask bott code db **(92) n22.5** good grief! Aquavit! Those delightful Scandinavian spices certainly rumble around the nose. And there is an oloroso cask at work here. But the grape (clean and wonderfully sulphur-free) plays only second fiddle...; t23 once again, the first notes that hit me are those of their national juice. The grape flows in softly soon after and obliterates those early spices with a silky fruitiness weighed down with oaky vanilla; f23 just a little coffee early on, but that dissipates as the grape really gathers momentum towards the end while a lovely butterscotch tart subtext offers delicate sweetness; b23.5 now here's an odd thing. Sometimes I nose a whisky in the dark without having any clue what it may be. And then try to work it out: just having some professional fun. Well aquavit and ancient Stockholm bars immediately came to mind here...and I had indeed poured myself a Swedish whisky. Though its local character was the last thing I was expecting from a wine cask. But the sherry butt is flawless and helps ensure one of the softest whisky journeys you'll make this year... 50%

◈ **Granum Single Grain** batch 1 oloroso sherry cask db (94) n23 very clean with even the grape keeping a low profile, though definitely registers, in the same way raisins do in a Dundee cake, aided it seems by some muscovado sugars. Those aquavit notes on Expecto certainly don't bother to turn up here...; t23.5 that's one beautiful delivery! The oloroso is of the sweeter variety and the grain of the most humble and least troublesome. Salivating, lightly oiled and full of juicy sultana; f23.5 the grain still seems to be flying a white flag, leaving it to the tannins to offer up some delightful, very lightly spiced marzipan with a little plum jam for company...; b24 were I to award "Softest Whisky of the Year" there would be no contest. This really is the definition of silk on the palate. And benefits beyond belief from an outstanding oloroso cask which imparts so sweet and fragile fruitiness from beginning to end. Usually I can pick up the grains involved, but here I am stumped as they play only a background role of non-committal elegance. Exceptional: a whisky quite unlike any other... 52% nc ncf

NORRTELJE BRENNERI Norrtälje. Working.
Roslagswhisky Eko Single Cask batch: Sherry olorosfat 43-250, dest Apr 16, bott 31 Jan 20 db (91) n22.5 t23 f22.5 b23 Oh, so much better! A cleaner, more precise distillate ensures there are no luring feints around to take the edge of the charm and complexity which abounds here. An excellent sherry cask offers a grapey gloss on the intense vanilla and muscovado sugar mix. Layered, relaxed and the slow build of the spice and its salivating consequences cannot be faulted. Now they have found the right path, I hope they can stick to it. 48.7%. nc ncf sc.

SMÖGEN WHISKY Hunnebostrand. Working.
Smögen 100 Proof Single Malt Whisky (96) n24.5 t24 f23.5 b24 I'm almost certain that if I slipped this into one of my tastings anywhere around the world and told people this was a south coast Islay, not a single person would dispute my word. However, few casks even from Islay are as faultless and so magnificently weighted as this. A landmark malt. 57.1%. Highfern

SPIRIT OF HVEN DISTILLERY Sankt Ibb. Working.
Spirit of Hven Charlies Wagon Single Malt Whisky bott code: 82T015 1333 db (79) n20 t22 f18 b19 I have to say that I am a big fan of this distillery, and it usually scores exceptionally well in the Bible: it has set its own bar very highly. But this malt is far from Hvenly, being off balance, at times too sweet at others too bitter and overall, off key – especially towards the end. Very disappointing. 47.1%.

SWITZERLAND
DISTILLERIE BRAUEREI Locher Appenzell. Working
◈ **Säntis Malt Single Malt Edition Dreifaltigkeit Lot No 9** db (95) n24 the kind of smoky infusion whish just makes you purr with happiness. One of my favourite peat styles: a kind of mix between cattle sheds and bacon frying in the pan... Beneath that are deep plummy tones and a little dried date to inject a vague sweetness; t23.5 fabulously distilled, keeping in the essential oils but still offering a clarity to the malt which lightens the fruity load. All the time the smoke both rumbles and billows offering a dual purpose. Molasses, alongside heather honey knits into that intense plummy fruit and ensures balance. Thick, chewy and, frankly, magnificent...; f23.5 such a long finale. The smoke pulses, the spices tingles and the fruit allays with the barley and growing oak for a deeply pleasing sweet-dry interplay...; b24 Santis back to its most brilliant. My word: when this distillery pushes the right whisky buttons the result is sensational. So far, the best whisky I have tasted this year where the big, muscly elements work together like clockwork taking turns to dominate and then relax. Incredibly long with complexity values that fly off the charts. If you see a bottle grab it and ask questions later.... 52% ncf nc

◈ **Säntis Malt Single Malt Golfer's Birdie Water Aged 6 Years** nbc (89) n22 t23 f22 b22 All I can do is refer you to my tasting notes (above) to the previous tasting I did of this whisky a few years back. Nothing has changed, except slightly more honey on the finish, maybe. Otherwise, this remarkably consistent malt is word perfect to its previous bottling. 46% nc ncf 2,000 bottles

❖ **Säntis Malt Snow White No 10** prune finish, 2022 db (**91.5**) n23 my word! That fruit really does come out at you and means business. As sweet as...a prune. Love the grumbling spices, too...; t23 the nose promises a right fruity chewathon, and that's exactly what you get. There is a niggling bitterness – either hop or oak induced. But the rich fruit is accompanied by a molassed sugar presence and copes easily. The spices are warming and in superb harmony with the fruit, which takes on a bit of a soft-centred boiled candy feel; f22.5 that bitterness tries to grow but some mocha moves in to see off any potential damage; b23 I had no idea the Swiss were famous for prunes. They are now... 48% 2000 bottles

❖ **Säntis Malt Single Malt Edition Alpstein edition XIX**, sherry finish, bott 16/05/22 db (**86.5**) n22.5 t23.5 f20 b21 Fabulous sherry trifle on the nose and a marvellously confident delivery makes for a storming start to this flavoursome malt. Indeed, despite the healthy sherry influence on the delivery, the malt makes its presence felt in both flavour and texture. However, the bitterness on the finish, almost rubbery at times, compromises the overall balance. That said, the nose and delivery combo is sublime. 48% 2200 bottles

❖ **Säntis Malt Single Malt Edition Liechtenstein edition X**, pinot noir finish db (**89.5**) n23 stunningly rich: astonishingly floral with lashings of crystallised heather honey...; t23 succulent delivery with a near perfect mouthfeel so far as the oils are concerned. The malt and honey dovetail deliciously; f21.5 dry with a healthy smattering of cocoa amid the vanilla. An annoying late bitterness docks it a mark or so...; b22 another showing some irritating late bitterness. Until then we had a colourful display of honey and chocolate. So much to like... 53% 501 bottles

❖ **Säntis Malt Single Malt Edition Himmelberg** matured oak beer casks, finished red wine barrels, lot no 8 db (**94**) n23.5 such an attractive, seductive nose. Everything is based on a fragility and vulnerability: the fruit is so delicate its sems the oak may break through any moment. Or a rush of intense malt might happen along. But it doesn't: it has a nose of clarity, poise and calmness...; t23.5 a sublime redcurrant freshness to that coats the palate. Muscovado sugars act as an anchor keeping the barley, fruit and charming oak in place, though by the mid-ground some chocolate fruit and nut has started to make it presence felt; f23 light spices prickle while the oak is now outpacing the slightly creamy fruit and barley; b24 unquestionably the most elegant malt I have tasted from this distillery. The perfect pre-prandial whisky, even when given the full Murray Method of tasting, its growth in the glass always remains studied and perfectly balanced. Such charm. 48% nc ncf

❖ **Säntis Malt Single Malt Single Cask Exploration** pinot noir cask, cask no 1330, bott 02/02/23 db (**93**) n23 just love the light peppers which raises both the oak and grape above the barley; t23.5 another of the lighter styles of Säntis, with the barley working in tandem with the grape to produce a juicy delivery. As the grape skin become entangled with the tannin from the oak, the weight shifts though never enough to completely obliterate that sublime barley-grape juice duet...; f23 long with an almost inevitable cocoa intervention mingling delightfully with the fruity tannins; b23.5 a competent, well made and enjoyable malt which refuses to overindulge in the Pinot influence but extracts from the fruit all that is required to ensure a complex and deeply satisfying experience. 50.4% sc nc ncf 516 bottles

❖ **Säntis Malt Single Malt Edition Sigel** matured oak beer casks, lot no 5 db (**92**) n23 the ghostly shadow of past hops seem to vanish in a malty haze. Bitter-sweet...with the accent on the sweet; t23.5 a doubt anyone will remember the British cream stouts of the 1960s. Well, I just about do (I managed to help myself to Mackeson when my parents weren't looking) ...and this is the closest whisky I have yet encountered to it. The malt is in super-concentrated form and the sugars are a blend of muscovado and demerara, but with a vague milkiness of the barrels, ensuring that cream stout quality; f22.5 still creamy, vaguely spiced and a healthy dollop of vanilla to compliment the butterscotch; b23 it is well known that I am no advocate of beer barrel matured whisky, not least because the bitterness of the hops can cause havoc with the overall balance. Säntis, though, are in a league of their very own – especially when it appears to create a creamy hop-less stout like this with sugars appearing from every angle. 40% nc ncf

DISTILLERIE ETTER Zug. Working.

❖ **Johnett Single Malt Single Cask No 97** Pinot Noir barrel, dist 08/11, bott 05/23 db (**87**) n22 t22 f21 b22 A super-soft addition to the Johnett family. But the Pinot cask doesn't quite add the right balance for me, offering too much of a dampening grapiness to allow the malt to breathe. Indeed it is the lack of layering after the initial malty blast which leaves one frustrated most. When you consider that this is one of the least offensive whiskies to be found on the European mainland this year – with excellent distillate mingling with a wine cask with not a single blemish, it sounds like I'm being a bit curmudgeonly. But there is no getting away from it: this is a little bland. 53.8% ncf 182 bottles

❖ **Johnett Single Malt Single Cask No 113** Pinot Noir Barrel, Islay finish, dist 05/10, bott 05/23 db (**94.5**) n23.5 a single malt aroma that would not be out of place in the Highlands of Scotland, let alone mountains of Switzerland. Slightly saline kick to this, giving the grape extra piquancy. The smoke is humble but telling when it needs to be; the oak dank. There is a fabulous, timeless warehouse aura to this...; **t23** that really is an eye-watering introduction on the palate. Tangy, vibrant fruit finds the oak digging in equally as deeply and with it comes shafts of barley sugar, the malt lightening the grapey gloom. The phenols remain modest and content with their anchoring role. Spices buzz, fencing at the blood orange to prick its domination. All is delightfully interwoven; **f23** the Murray Method stirs some otherwise lazy oils and sugars into action; **b24** a real blast back in time, for some reason: reminds me of some of the casks I first nosed at Talisker in 1975 held in old sherry butts with that non-committal peat adding to their tantalising weight. A malt whisky never gives up its secrets on first encounter and only to a limited degree on second and third. However, the Murray Method really does prod those sugars into life and, with it, comes a wonderful balance. 64.48% ncf

⁂ **Johnett Single Malt Single Cask No 132** dist 02/12, bott 05/23 db **(94) n23.5** what a nose! Chocolate and diced Brazil nut. Just lightly topped with maple syrup and a few shards of barley; **t23.5** such a glorious exhibition of tannin from the very first moment but tracked every inch of the way by vivid dark sugars. There is also a semi-stickiness to the oils which helps boost the weight even further. But this is also a juicy chap which brings out the more salivating qualities of the malt at every opportunity; **f23** long, though softens considerably as the vanillins off the oak take shape. But maintains that busy juiciness, aided now by even more quixotic spices and a slow fade of mocha...; **b24** if I was tasting this blind, I might, certainly on delivery, momentarily mistake this for a bourbon...and pretty decent one at that. This is a magnificent shewing of what great oak and outstanding distillate can do. Faultlessly made and matured, this is a wonderfully bold workout for the taste buds... 61.59% ncf 203 bottles

LANGATUN DISTILLERY Langenthal, Kanton Bern. Working.

Langatun Single Malt Aged 10 Years Priorat Cask Finish cask no 634 dist Sept 2011 bott Okt 2021 db **(89) n22.5 t23 f21.5 b22** A malt which needs the Murray Method to tease out the balancing sugars for what would otherwise be an unusually dry wine influence. 49.12% nc 478 bottles

Langatun Marsala Cask Finish Single Malt dist Aug 2012, Mar 2021, Lot no. B01/03/21, db **(87.5) n22.5 t22 f21 b22** To nose, the wine is in concentrated concentrate form: tight, almost earthy, acidic. Can fair take the breath away...; a youthful malt punches out from beyond the fruit. To taste, the new make cocks a malty snook at the fruit, which then retaliates by landing a series of intense fruity blows on the taste buds. Irritatingly, the finish is quite bitter and tingly; this doesn't go quite according to plan by Langatun standards. An unusual minty cool finale. So despite the eight years in the cask this still boasts a very young persona on both nose and delivery. The Marsala cask, meanwhile, works like the devil to make amends... 49.12% nc

Langatun Old Bear (89.5) n22.5 t23 f21.5 b22.5 Definitely a different direction here for this distillery. 46%. Highfern

Langatun Old Deer (93.5) n22.5 t24 f23.5 b23.5 Old Deer? This is a 16 point stag of a malt.... 46%. Highfern

Langatun Single Malt Old Deer Classic Whisky batch 592/02/21 db **(89.5) n23 t24 f19.5 b23** Such brilliant whisky, save for the unfortunate nagging finish. But with evidence of Chelsea buns and Danish pasty, as well as the fruits of Eccles, who says that making great whisky isn't a piece of cake...? 46% nc

Langatun Rioja Cask Finish Single Malt dist 2014, bott 17/11/2020, cask no. 433, db **(92.5) n23.5 t23.5 f22.5 b23** Never sure why unsulphur-treated Rioja casks like this aren't more widely used. I have encountered only a handful over the years, and they have usually been above average. This probably boasts the best nose of them all.. 49.12% nc sc 467 bottles

Langatun Single Malt Old Crow peated, batch no. 309/10/20, db **(95.5) n23 t24 f24.5 b24** Well, I've tasted a few Old Crows in my time, but nothing like this new edition from Langatun. No traditional bourbon here. This is a whisky which stretches its malty, peaty muscles like a crow extends its wings in flight. If there was an award for the intense smoky chocolate malt of the year, no other whisky would get close. Caw! 59.7% nc

Langatun Single Malt Old Crow Peaty Whisky batch 308/12/21 db **(93.5) n23 t23.5 f23 b24** A superb whisky which boasts all the balance the Old Wolf was missing. As good as it was, it was still something to howl about. This is something to crow about... 46% nc

Langatun Single Malt Old Wolf Smoky Whisky batch 419/02/22 db **(90) n22.5** young, but a sweet nuttiness mingles attractively with the pleasingly delicate smoke and noisier fruits. A bolder sweetness comes through, too, giving the impression of a moist and smoky Melton Hunt cake; **t23.5** molasses and golden syrup burst out before the fruit has a chance to breathe. Extremely plummy, greengages especially, and some sublime fat flavour waves stroking the palate; **f21.5** reverses back into its shell slightly and bitters a tad. Spices assemble around the vague smoke; **b22** lots of impact but struggles for balance. The individual flavours are impressive and some of the sweeter ones border on astonishing. But as lovely as it is, never quite gets the story to unfold as it might. *46% nc*

❖ **Langatun Single Malt Port Cask Finish** dist 2016, bott 2022 **(89) n22.5** a kind of hefty, grumpy grapiness refusing to do much under the line of the pleasant fruit itself; **t23** chunky delivery which, when the malts gets going, really fills the out with a spectacular liquid Garibaldi biscuit; **f21** annoyingly off-centre, the raisins have a distinctly burnt feel to them; **b22.5** from one of the best distilleries in mainland Europe comes a Port cask finished whisky which doesn't quite fizz and captivate as I have come to expect. Excellent, delightful whisky for sure, especially on the magnificent delivery. But just allowing the intensity of the cask to overshadow the magic of the distillery itself. This is the price of setting their own bar so high... *49.12%*

Langatun Swiss Single Malt Whisky Aged 10 Years 2nd Release, Pinot Noir cask, cask no. 132, dist 2010 **(84.5) n21.5 t22.5 f20 b20.5** Pleasant enough. But a rare misfire by Langatun standards, the Pinot Cask not being up to the quality of the distillate. A little untidy sulphur at the end (and nose), but no problem as it slips though the honey-laden gears on delivery. *49.12% sc*

SEVEN SEALS DISTILLERY AG Schweiz, working.
Seven Seals Peated Double Wood (95) n23.5 t24 f23.5 b24 Massively impressive whisky, and manner from heaven for the peat freaks. So rare to find a peat as heady as this which seems to instinctively know when and when not to strike. Probably the best whisky I have ever encountered from this distillery...

Seven Seals Port Wood (86) n21.5 t22 f21 b21.5 A pleasant enough malt, but one which shows up a few weaknesses on the distilling side with feints being spotted from nose to finish. Lots of light butterscotch and vanilla, though.

Seven Seals Peated Port Wood Finish (88.5) n21.5 t22.5 f21.5 b22 The laid-back oak on the nose doesn't quite see eye to eye with the fruit: relaxed but out of sync, too. While on delivery a quite extraordinary exhibition of vanilla grips your attention. You expect fruit...but no...it's vanilla. And lashings of it, to the extent that when that expires we are back to a malty outline but also an off-kilter finish as a weakness from the distillate is exposed.

Seven Seals Peated Sherry Wood Finish (93) n23 t23.5 f23 b23.5 A faultless sherry cask has been deployed here to compliment rather than obliterate or do battle with the most delicate of peat influences. This works rather beautifully...

Seven Seals The Age of Aquarius Single Malt (87) n21.5 t23 f21 b21.5 Age of Aquarius must mean smoked fish... Better than last year's offering, though the finish still has a little bumbling sulphur hanging round, unfortunately, though nothing too devastating. Equally, the nose also offers a curious juniper kick. Where there is no problem whatsoever is the delivery which is a complex and busy array of smoked honey tones and salt which is quite aloof from the nose and finish. A curious shoal of sensations, indeed. *49.7%. Highfern*

Seven Seals The Age of Leo (94.5) n22.5 t23.5 f23.5 b24 The kind of whisky that makes you exhale with pure contentment, if not with a roar. Life is always full of pleasure when it is this whisky... *49.7%*

Seven Seals The Age of Pisces Oloroso Sherry Finish (78.5) n19 t22 f18 b19.5 Unfortunately, despite the obvious rich sweetness which attempts to swamp both the nose and palate, the sulphur from the sherry cask has a little too much to say for itself. *49.7%*

Seven Seals The Age of Scorpio Single Malt (90.5) n22 t23 f22 b23 I well remember last year's bottling, which was serious rough-house whisky determined to battle out World War 3 on your palate. This is an altogether more timid affair where your taste buds are at least given a sporting chance to work out what is happening on your palate. The answer is some surprisingly sweet and genteel, the delivery in particular likely to win your heart ... *49.7%. Highfern*

Seven Seals The Age of Taurus (93) n23 t23.5 f23 b23.5 A beautifully even malt where the smoke acts as both comforter and, at times, warlord when that acid bites. A really lovely, beautifully manicured experience. *49.7%*

WHISKY CASTLE Elfingen. Working
Whisky Castle Single Malt Doublewood cask no.508, db **(86.5) n20 t23 f21.5 b22** Plenty of toffee and malt on display, and there follow through on delivery pits spice against sweetened liquorice is a rather delicious way. But the wonky nose and slightly skewed finale takes this away from the distillery's usual assured excellence. *43% sc*

Whisky Castle Edition Käser cask no.504, db **(91.5) n22.5 t23.5 f22.5 b23** Once upon a time, castles - or the fortress settlements that stood as castles - were built with wood, often sturdy oak, before they got round to stone fortifications. This is as though one of those great wooden structures has been distilled down: the tannin almost outmuscles the fruit. Youthful, strapping stuff. *62% sc*

Deciphered and Distilled. The Bible's European Guide to Whisky Labels

English	German	French
Malt	Malz	Malt
Grain	Getreide	céréales
Wheat	Weizen	blé
Barley	Gerste	orge
Rye	Roggen	seigle
Spelt	Dinkel	épeautre
Corn	Mais	maïs
Oat	Hafer	avoine
Peated	getorft	tourbé
Smoked	geraucht	fumé
Organic	biologisch	biologique
Cask	Fass	fût
Matured in/Aged in	gereift in	vieilli en
Finish	Nachreifung	déverdissage
Double Maturation	Zweitreifung	deuxième maturation
Oak	Eiche	chêne
Toasted	wärmebehandelt	grillé
Charred	ausgeflammt, verkohlt	carbonisé
Years	Jahre	ans
Months	Monate	mois
Days	Tage	journées
Chill Filtration	Kühlfiltration	filtration à froid
Non Chill Filtered	nicht kühlgefiltert	non filtré à froid
No Colouring	nicht gefärbt	non coloré
Cask Strength	Fassstärke	brut du fût
Single Cask	Einzelfass	single cask
Cask No.	Fass-Nummer	numéro du fût
Batch	Charge	Lot/charge
Distillation Date	Destillations-Datum	date de distillation
Bottling Date	Abfüll-Datum	date de mise en bouteille
Alcohol by Volume/abv	Volumenprozente/% vol.	teneur en alcool/abv
Proof (American)	amerikanische Einheit für % vol.	unité américaine

Danish	Dutch	Swedish
Malt	Gerst	Malt
Korn	graan	säd
hvede	tarwe	vete
byg	gerst	korn
rug	rogge	råg
spelt	spelt	speltvete
majs	mais	majs
havre	haver	havre
tørv	geturfd	torvrökt
røget	gerookt	rökt
organisk	biologisch/organisch	ekologisk
fad	vat	fat
modning i	gerijpt in	mognad på/lagrad på
finish	narijping/finish	slutlagrat
dobbelt modning	dubbele rijping	dubbellagrat
egetræ	eik	ek
ristet	getoast	rostad
forkullet	gebrand	kolad
år	jaren	år
måned	maanden	månader
dage	dagen	dagar
kold filtrering	koude-filtratie	kylfiltrering
ikke kold filtreret	niet koud gefilterd	ej kylfiltrerad
ikke farvet	niet bijgekleurd	inga färgämnen
fadstyrke	vatsterkte	fatstyrka
enkelt fad	enkel vat	enkelfat
fad nr.	vat nummer	fatnummer
parti/batch	serie/batch	batch
destillations dato	distillatie datum	destilleringsdatum
aftapnings dato	bottel datum	buteljeringsdatum
volumenprocent	alcoholpercentage/% vol	volymprocent/% vol.
Proof	amerikaanse aanduiding voor % vol	Amerikanska proof

World Whiskies

BRAZIL
LAMAS DESTILARIA Matozinhos. Working

◇ **Lamas Amburana Single Malt** ex-bourbon cask, finished in Brazilian amburana wood cask finish db (88.5) n21.5 t23 f22 b22 The kind of whisky which leaves you scratching your head. It is a like a football team with a couple of internationals doing all kinds of magical things, while the rest of the team are journeymen lumbering around. When it's good, it's fabulous. When it isn't, it is distinctly average. That said, would love to use this in a blend. 43%

◇ **Lamas Angico Single Malt** ex bourbon cask finished in Brazilian angico wood cask db (93.5) n23 tannins all the way. Spices start soberly enough but ramp up the more you sniff, this going hand-in-hand with the input of the wood. The sugars are light, yet impeccably well-mannered and malty. And, in this case, essential for balance; t23.5 enjoys the house style softness on delivery: again, this is really beautifully made distillate with just the right oils. Barley spreads itself around the palate luxuriantly with acacia honey melding with the malt. Ripples of chocolate and vague citrus tones also drifts through. The spices begin cordially but slowly and stealthily builds in intent and execution; f23 lots of toffee and cocoa early into the finish, drying as the toastiness from the tannin increases. The spices by the end offer quite a nip, but never less than a pleasant one. This boasts probably the longest of all Lamas finishes....; b24 woah! This is one spicy fellow! Those tannins are on the attack from the first moment and, like a dog with a bone, refuses to let go. For those who like a whisky with a distinct attitude. Important to note: this is not a whisky that is hot from being distilled too fast: indeed, the distillate appears to be in a very fine shape. No, this is about a tannin attack of rare intensity. The mouthfeel, by the way, is truly first-class. Really enjoyable...and different. And revels in its understated complexity. 43%

◇ **Lamas Cumaru Single Malt** ex-bourbon cask finished in Brazilian cumaru wood cask db (93) n23.5 the outline is sweet and estery, almost in rum-like fashion. Only on warming do the tannins begin to emerge with any conviction, led by nibbling spice. Among a cluster of herbal/ spicy notes is one that is indefinable, other than being akin to a certain Brazilian biscuit being baked. But this is one very relaxed nose: light muscovado sugars linger on soft oils to ensure a friendly, welcoming aroma; **t23** the delivery is as impressive as the nose. The sugars are rammed early on, a mix of heather honey and golden syrup leading the way. But this is met and invaded by some warming spices which buzz and bite as loudly as the sugars sweeten. At the cusp where the tannins start to hold sway, there is a little confusion....; **f23** this dries somewhat surprisingly, the sugars spent much earlier than the nose and the delivery suggest. But we have complexity, too, with the tannins now layered and more dependent of the spice than the sugars. Oddly, even later and with the usual sweetness, there is some salivation, perhaps prodded by the spices. Now, that's very unusual...; **b23.5** talk about intriguing! The early sugars set this malt off in the right direction. For a moment or two the tannins begin interceding and there is a degree of untidiness. But although the sugars eventually lose way, the malt rights itself with an impressive display of spice and tannin. Very different. And seriously enjoyable. 43%

◈ **Lamas The Dog's Bollocks II Single Malt** 80% peated barley, 20% malt; ex-bourbon cask finished ex-moscatel seasoned cask db **(95) n23.5** such a relaxing breeze of scotch-style smoke. It rumbles on the nose like the sound of distant highway traffic: sometimes a little louder one moment than the next, not quite dominating...but always there. There is a saline nip upping the pungency, though on this one I am picking up a slight rubber note: must be from the tyres on the motorway. Slightly more spice and that sharp tweaking of the nose has not lost any of its devil...a delicate touch of Demerara sugar ensures balance; **t24** fabulous, salivating delivery. The oils both soften and ensure depth in equal measure. This is old-fashioned chewing whisky with multiple layers of wonderfully earthy malt moving into a more intense degree of tannin than I previously remember. But the barley stays big and adorable manuka give the phenols a less swarthy persona. Layered and busy; **f23.5** magnificently long, the spices have held back until we are in the early finish and then let rip. The tannins are more militant now, although they have appeared to have made an earlier entry than DB I; **b24** this is a class act. Some very superficial changes to the last offering with the tannin perhaps displaying a duller role from an earlier point. But still smoky, beautifully balanced, playfully sweet when need be, malty and, overall, deeply satisfying whisky. 46%

◈ **Lamas Eucalipto Single Malt** ex-bourbon cask, finished in Brazilian eucalipto wood cask db **(92.5) n23** concentrates on the tannins, though here are delicate yet builds into an intensity that blocks out the sharper attributes of the barley. The sweetness is quite powdery, not unlike that found at the bottom of a biscuit barrel; **t24** adorable delivery. Gristy, with the concentrated barley simply melting on arrival with those sugars cascading around the palate. The vanilla and butterscotch back-up grows slowly in spicy depth. Glorious weight, poise and pace to all the different facets at play: just impossible not to adore this; **f22** a slightly shorter finish than hoped for. Once again, restrained if slightly sharp tannin notes drift in, this time leaving a slight tang. The spices, inevitably, building into something conspicuously hot; **b23.5** for the most part, the subtlest of whiskies the flavours ghosting into place. And although this is as fragile as it gets the spices are perhaps overdone slightly at the death. But until then prepare to be charmed within an inch of your life. Wonderful....and quite unique. 43%

◈ **Lamas Red Stone Grain Whisky** ex-bourbon cask matured, new American oak barrel finished db **(89) n21.5** a light rubbery aroma, not dissimilar to some distillates from Loch Lomond in Scotland, gives this a distinct weightiness. Tasty tannins form a significant secondary background; **t23** corn oils envelop the mouth with sweet acacia honey. The sweetness is a pleasant surprise after the dullness of the nose, and those same oils ensure these sugars are fixed in orbit around the palate for the duration. Excellent weight with a slightly spicy intervention and a massive reveal of vanilla towards the middle; **f22** long, thanks to those oils. A very mild bittering, pleasantly offset by a now toastier style of sugar and softer vanillas. That light rubbery note prevalent on the nose returns at the death: quite dry despite the battling sugars; **b22.5** a less spicy affair than many Lamas malts. Distinctive but seemingly of slightly lesser quality despite the degree of outstanding sweetness through the middle. 43%

◈ **Lamas Sassafras Single Malt** ex bourbon cask finished in Brazilian Sassafras wood cask db **(94) n24** a beguiling nose. An unidentified phenol note hangs around ensuring the base notes are covered and that there is an anchor to the sensational complexity of the creamed vanilla topped by the subtlest blend of ulmo and heather honey...and dried coconut. Also, something not dissimilar to muscovado sugar melts atop a bowl of creamy porridge. Unique, ridiculously sensual and sexy and the epitome of elegance; **t23.5** if we have just experienced the whisky version of melt-on-the-nose, we now have a melt-in-the-mouth delivery on the palate. A fabulous combination of light honey tones melds with the grassy barley to give a slight impression of young adulthood rather than full maturity. Spices strum and, after a pause to allow the malt maximum effect, gets louder as the tannins begin to bare down with increasing weight. There is also a curious glazed lime candy note offering a controlled sharpness; **f23** warming and a little shorter than expected with, not for the first time, certain shapes and forms to the tannins I simply can't identify but fit in perfectly with the overall picture. It is the spices which linger, though....; **b23.5** another sample where alien flavours grow in stature, though this time part of the desired balance. And once more it is the interplay between the sugars and spices which grabs the attention, though on this occasion their symbiotic nature makes one want to purr with delight. What happens to that delicate mystery phenol note detected on the nose, it is impossible to say. Though, most likely, it is simply an idiosyncratic characteristic of the tannin. *43%*

⟣ **Lamas Sky Single Malt** peated barley, ex-bourbon cask, ice wine seasoned barrel finish db **(92) n23** though lightly smoked, significant esters give this a distinctive sheen and roundness. Charming in its balance between good weight and a more delicate touch. The smoke itself is a curious mix of peaty phenols and smouldering bonfire with a few tree branches added for a softening effect. Even so, there is a substantial presence to this....; **t23.5** the distinctive honeyed delivery comes as no surprise with those esters doing such a fine job on the nose. Halfway-house between pure silk and fine chewing malt thanks to the significant spice infusion. About a third through the piece, it slowly dawns that there is no great age here, but the tannins arrive in force, nonetheless. The phenols are layered: less muscular than on the nose, but beautifully weighted ensuring a full body to the mouth feel; **f22.5** considering those esters I keep finding and celebrating, the finish – though long – is definitely on the thinner side than the delivery would lead you to expect. Some lovely vanilla tones offer a comforting crutch for the weak phenols to limp along on; **b23** distinctively schizophrenic in its polarised complexity. A malt which offers you both a kissing, soothing, gently embracing sweetness throughout its lightly honeyed core and a far more tastebud-slapping phenolic lilt which incorporates a spiced-up bite. The finish, though pleasant enough, suffers by comparison as it feels a little bare after all that has gone on before. Fascinating and deeply entertaining. *47%*

⟣ **Lamas Smoked II Single Malt** 50% peated barley ex-bourbon cask and ex-stout oak cask db **(93) n23.5** ah! Those esters again, though this time more subtly displayed in a beautifully layered caress of the nose. There is a playful youthfulness despite the quaint peaty depth. The heather honey comes in strings and strands with a lazy phenolic note, melding with a delicate strawberry jam tone. Offering less smoke and more in the way of toasted oak, this is very complex and handsomely repays extra study; **t23.5** big on salivation early on, again the youth of this malt is underlined. The peat is far more vociferous here, though, just as on the nose there is an enormous amount of layering – which here results in extra chewing! Impressively, the malt in action throughout, the juiciness tinged here and there by the very fleeting fruitiness which soon burns out; **f22.5** at last those puzzling phenols really make their mark. They form a beautiful duet with the tannins which now are decidedly intense; **b23.5** along with the total lack of hop, the balance is the key to this malt. It is always big, occasionally hefty. But some aspects are also young, and it is fascinating in the way that more muscular tones are able to absorb these fresher aspects to generate a degree of verve into the mix. The tannin is particularly interesting: instead of being a rumbling base note, it is pitched high and therefor more easily detectable – quite an unusual aspect. A big whisky that is massively enjoyable. *47%*

CHINA
GOALONG DISTILLERY

⟣ **Goalong Single Malt Whiskey Bourbon Cask Aged 5 Years** nbc **(93) n23** such a pleasing display of vanillas and malt: the oak standing firm without even considering domination. A breath of fresh air..in more ways than one..; **t23.5** salivating, fresh barley very competently backed by a beautifully even degree of tannin. The citrussy gristiness of this five-year-old is unspoiled, the sweetness unsurprisingly of a barley sugar variety. The oils really are nudging perfection allowing that stunningly deft malt the widest possible canvas; **f23** retains its intricate malt values. Spices at last assemble late on, though, in keeping with the style, refuses to kick up too much of a storm; **b23.5** so, at last Chinese whisky – or whiskey as Goalong prefer, so I'll go along with it – in bottled form. And this really is impressive. I know some people like to have a Scotch whisky comparison to give some idea. The closest here is 100% ex-bourbon cask Cardhu, where the salivating, delicate, clean malt cascades over the sawdusty oak. The definition of an elegant, gentle malt but massively impressive nonetheless. *40% BBC Spirits*

⟣ **Goalong Single Malt Whiskey Small Batch Bourbon & Brandy Cask Aged 5 Years** nbc **(95) n23.5** an unapologetic display of hard boiled sugar fruit candy and barley sugar; **t24** fabulously crisp delivery, the sugar as crunchy as the malt. But what happens next is sensational: rather than tapering off to give way to the oak, the barley streams away in diverse directions, still retaining their malty bite but one line taking on more citrus, another thickening in its barley richness, another really dosing up on that fragile fruitiness. Thickly salivating for a very long time..; **f23.5** at last those expected vanillas arrives. And again, as appears to be the house style, the spices begin to make themselves known..; **b24** blown away by this. Helped by the stronger abv, which keeps those oils intact, the complexity of this whiskey after its initial arrival on the pallet is off the scale. This, make no mistake, is absolutely top-quality single malt whisky. 48% *(BBC Spirits)*

⬧ **Goalong Blended Whiskey** nbc **(87.5) n21 t22.5 f22 b22** A thin, toffee-rich whiskey, there is an attractive silkiness to the texture and things improve further as a shaft of thick malt opens up the juicier aspects. Overall, quite simplistic but still pleasantly attractive and easy going. 40% *BBC Spirits*

INDIA
AMRUT DISTILLERY Kambipura. Working

⬧ **Amrut Single Malt batch No 187** Aug 2022 db **(89.5) n23** as intense as the malt is, there is plenty of room left over for the rich banana-clad vanillas and firmer oaky tones to make their very attractive mark. Anyone who loves opening a fresh pack of McVitie's Digestive biscuits will certainly enjoy getting their nose over a glass of this...; **t22.5** mouth-filling with attractive oils...and then the malt goes into overdrive, intensifying with each passing flavour wave; **f21** the malt initially stands its ground, but this a little thinner and sharper than in previous years, meaning we have a shot and unceremonious finale; **b23** an enjoyable Amrut, though the silky and distinguished middle thread means the limited finale comes as a bit of a surprise... 46%

⬧ **Amrut Single Malt Cask Strength** batch No 125 Aug 2022 db **(95) n23.5** the essence of bourbon shimmers through the opening gears to this. The massive malt is pouched somewhere safe and initially away from the oaky thrust before setting itself free to mingle delightfully. Even so, light liquorice and fringe molasses make their mark, as does the heather honey. A borderline 24 for this impressive nose...; **t24** where bourbon may have been first to show on the nose, it is the malt which gangs up on delivery. And how! The barley is almost solid in its intensity, and sweet, too, thanks to a little heather honey interference. Slowly however, almost by osmotic effect, the tannin begins to seep into the mix and in come those distinctive bourbon-style tone with red liquorice and molasses laying down the markers. The spices, which began as a faint rumble and by the midpoint rather more than that....; **f23.5** sublime oils ensure the finish lingers. There is that now trademark thin sharpness so prevalent on the 46% version But, at full sail, the finale benefits from tapering the malt ...; **b24** Amrut at its very malty best. This batch is barley in concentrate...but with plenty of oak and sugars to ensure a long and complex ride. Super-impressive. And carries its bourbony charm with an effortlessness bordering on arrogance...; 61.8% nc ncf

⬧ **Amrut Fusion** batch No 103 db **(91) n22.5** such a young nose with the smoke nipping on the wing...; **t23** intensely juicy but there is a bit of bite and attitude to this also. Apple and pear juice join the sluicing barley on one hand, the layered smoke offers a more stabilising depth on the other. But throughout, there is bite nip and agitation...; **f22.5** two-toned. That oily roughness from the younger malts on one hand and a roast chestnut-sweetened, lightly smoked depth to the other. The late hickory is a welcome surprise...; **b23** welcome back for me for an old friend which, for one reason or another, I haven't tasted for three or four years. More simplistic than in days of yore. And occasionally a brawling roughhouse, too. But still very worth a gander at. Especially when warmed... 50%

⬧ **Amrut Master Distiller's Reserve Ex-Stout Cask** cask 4862 db **(91) n23** rich and creamy, I'm relieved to say no hop is apparent on the nose. Rather, an agreeable apple note integrates beautifully with the healthy barley; **t23** both muscular and fat on impact again with the barley really dishing out all its malty intent. Quite a swathe of muscovado sugar and spice to wade through but the oak really puts its foot down here and demands to be heard; **f22.5** frothy and creamy, it is long but just a little disjointed. The vanilla and malt remain as thick as thieves; **b22.5** I'm always a touch nervous with beer barrel-matured whisky as the bittering hop can cause havoc. No such problem here, though at times you know something is interfering with the whisky's natural progression... 50%

⬧ **Amrut Master Distiller's Reserve Ex-Stout Cask** cask 4863 db **(88) n22.5 t22.5 f21 b22** A sharper, slightly more aggressive version, this twin cask to 4862 concentrates on the youth of the malt, rather than the creaminess injected by the barrel. Indeed, though silky in part, a bitterness – doubtless hop induced - does creep into the mix, especially late on. Though not before a highly unusual lime candy note makes quite an impact. 50%

⬧ **Amrut Peated Single Malt** batch No 117 Apr 2022 db **(91.5) n23** not often one comes across smoked toffee apple...but I appear to have located it here...; **t23** fat, oily, warming and smoky...all in one immediate hit. Quite soon this malt comes alive with a blistering array of hickory and phenol tones which complement the other quite well. Some crunchy Demerara sugars meet the juicier malty notes head on...; **f22.5** excellent oils, warming spices; **b23** the Murray Method – or a balmy Indian evening – will do the trick for this malt. Too cool and things refuse to happen. Warmed gently in the hand and the malt comes to life with the peat the epitome of cooing softness. Technically, you know there is something on the finish a little imperfect. But there is no denying the attractiveness of the sensations offered. 46%

⟐ **Amrut Peated Single Malt Cask Strength** batch No 63 db **(96) n24** truly classic peaty whisky, offering a glorious alignment of varied smoky tones, ranging from subtle, distant crofter's reek to more acidic peat soot and even the odd hint of something a touch agricultural: just gorgeous. At times quite youthful, mind...; **t24** wow! This batch provides one of the most salivating deliveries to any peated malt in the marketplace today. The malt, quite apart from the peat, shimmers while the smoke wades in armed with peppery spices. Hickory makes an impressive bow...; **t24** a tad rough around the edges towards the finale but it is comfortable for all that. The hickory persists, topping in some extra Demerara sugars along the way, while the smoke billows and pounds; **b24** I remember a style not dissimilar to this a few years back with a standard strength Amrut Peated which lost control of balance thanks to a younger malts being used being out of sync. This carries similar traits, but the sheer natural power of this malt blasts through the problems as though they weren't there. I'll tell you this, though. If I can find some old timers in the industry and poured them a drop of this, they'd swear it was a young barrel of Glengarioch from the 1980s....a dead ringer. Forget about this being a smooth operator and all that malarky: this becomes rougher as it goes along, like an engine running short on oil...and combined with the uncompromising peat and juicy youth...it's just wonderful! 62.8%

⟐ **Amrut Rye Single Malt** batch db **(91.5) n23.5** the malted rye is mutedly sharp yet intense and has no qualms about dominating. The accompanying vanilla is a willing sidekick. Quite lovely...; **t23** a unique delivery. The sharpness, normally associated with the grain is coming from that unique malted rye trait. When the rye joins in, too, it becomes incredibly mouth-watering; **f22.5** an unusual but powerful finale of blackcurrant pastels; **b22.5** well! Didn't expect to see this, I have to admit. Though glad I did. No mistaking the grain, which is intense and deep. But Amrut have certainly carved their own personality on to this which is similar to some better North American ryes, Alberta being the closest. But there is a barely perceptibly slant away from that into wholly new territory. 50%

JOHN DISTILLERIES Cuncolim. Working

⟐ **Paul John Bold** db **(95) n23.5** the starring part of this whisky has always been the refined elegance of the smoke: nothing aggressive, just a caress and at most a gentle massage. The tannins act as an impressive skeleton which allows the peat to wrap itself around... It's the layering, though. Wow, that layering....! **t24** the smoke is every bit as gentle on delivery as it is on the nose. And now a little magic begins as thin and fragile acacia honey begins to melt into the phenols, first as a hint and then as pleasing act of quiet unity. An additional walnut note fills out the middle. Somehow, long into this ride, the malt remains juicy...; **f23.5** it would be so easy for this malt to just die off and enjoy a non-committal ending. But it doesn't. Instead, it rounds up the phenols one last time and sends them off on varying tastes ranging from deep, almost hickory-rich anchor roles but many more flitting and lighter palate cleansing duties once it has affiliated with the late molasses. The smoky coffee very late on is almost an inevitability; **b24** the peat is bold. But, essentially, it is not even close to being pushy, meaning that so much else happens around the smoke. This really is one of the most delicately and most complex layered peaty whiskies on the planet. A whisky that would be a crime to hurry. 46% nc ncf

⟐ **Paul John Brilliance** db **(94) n23** the malt melts towards a Werther's Originals sweet vanilla. Crushed pecan nut alongside a bready yeastiness gives this nose an unusual, come-hither attraction; **t23.5** a semi-youthful vibrancy ups the barley sugar sweetness. The salivation levels rise dramatically as the barley chimes as clear as a tolling church bell...; **f23.5** a delicate spice has risen, though now has to deal with weightier tannins and much drier, slightly spent malt. The very late custard cream biscuit certainly wasn't part of their first-ever bottling of this... but it's not at all out of place; **b24** a sparkling malt where the barley shews its most brittle sugary side to keep the juices flowing. A malt which benefits from the Murray Method to reveal its impressive range as it moves through the temperatures. The more you taste it, the more complex and classy it becomes... 46% nc ncf

⟐ **Paul John Classic** db **(96.5) n23.5** crushed honey-roasted nuts is not a common aroma to a whisky. But this is not a common whisky. The barley also has a Maryland Cookie thread to it, too, while the faintest hickory melds into thin liquorice...; **t24** the double whammy on the palate of gloriously honeyed barley and near perfect oils makes this a delivery to blow your socks off. The barley appears in concentrate, almost thick on the palate. But escorting its every move is that blend of ulmo and heather honey, which intensifies further as the molasses and liquorice comes into play; **f24.5** there was a kind of inevitability about the chocolate making its bow on the finish. The question was: cocoa, praline or mocha? It's mocha. And don't think the honey has finished with you yet. The heather honey has a few more tricks up its sleeve, especially as the spices begin to dance. The length defies both expectation and reason and it may be the finish which determines this as the best Indian Whisky for Bible 2024; **b24.5** as an unpeated, cask strength Paul John, it would be too easy to pass this off as Brilliance with Brawn. My word, this is so much more than that. At times it heads towards the heady world of high-end bourbon, but such is the integrity of both the barrel and the barley we head instead towards a honey fest of unambiguous beauty. There is not a single malt lover in the world who would not just sit back and sigh at this with rarely achieved contentment. And there might be the odd bourbon lover or a million who might join them. *55.2% nc ncf*

◇◇◇ **Paul John Edited** db (96) **n24** the smoke is playing games. One moment there standing on a peaty ridge, the next in a furrow hidden by crisp barley dipped in lemon-blossom honey. The most impressive aspect is the smoky gristiness not unlike a Port Ellen used to be between 8 years and 12...; **t24** very unusually, it is the mouth feel which first gains the attention - even before the flavours. Because the oils on this are sublime. And crucial. Then comes one of the most sensual battles in the current whisky world as the peat and naked barley gently manoeuvre for domination. There are no winners, but the mingling and counteractions between the two entertains for seemingly ever. Usually, chocolate evolves at the end. Here, though t appears to be an early by-product...and a spot-on deliciously one at that...; **f24** the spices have taken some persuading to make a contribution...but they are at last here, giving a lightly warm buzz to the higher phenols. The barley seems to have transmogrified into a pretty little essay on ripe greengages and fat, dark cherries. The final moments, though, are a slow flyover of smoke and honey...and the malt in league with the vanilla. Stunning...; **b24** I remember when, in their earliest days, Paul John launched Bold, Brilliance and Edited. All three were excellent but had the difficulty of coping with the distillate of brand-new stills...always a challenge. The malt made there now is better than then, but I always feared for Edited because it was such a complex, knife-edge malt needing very careful monitoring and weeding to ensure the peat composition was never too low or, equally dangerous, too dominant. Well, I needn't have feared. This is absolutely bang on the money: the very definition of a beautifully balanced and complex whisky. Magnificently Edited, in fact.... By the way. I chose this is my 750th and potentially final whisky of the 2024 Whisky Bible. Partly because I hadn't seen what I have long thought as one of the most underrated bottlings for a little while; and also because today India landed a rocket on the moon. That, however, is child's play. It is nothing to also having one of easily the top ten distilleries in the world. And keeping such a complex whisky as this bang on track... *46% nc ncf*

Paul John Mithuna db (97) **n23.5 t24 f25 b24.5** The end of the experience is like after you have just made love...and you are unable to speak or move while your senses get back into some kind of normality. If Mithuna means "Ultimate", then it is the perfect name. Or maybe Mithuna means "Perfect", then it is pretty close. Whichever, this is a kind of Indian version of a William Larue Weller, shewing that same extraordinary intensity, complexity and beauty. It is that very rarest of things. And, if nothing else, announces Paul John distillery on the world stage of truly great distilleries. This is a whisky to devour...while it devours you. Almost certainly destined for a top three spot in the Whisky Bible 2021. *58%. ncf.*

◇◇◇ **Paul John Nirvana** batch 01 L22269 db (91) **n23** a sweeter nose than when I last enjoyed this: glace cherry meets acacia honey and drier Lubeck marzipan: complex and delightfully paced. The barley sugars support the deeper malt tones. A relative degree of youth, too...; **t23** super-soft delivery with the malt again having the early upper hand. Not quite as full-bodied as most Paul Johns but the vanillas leached from the oak are also on the sweeter side and do nothing to undermine the honey and peaches. From about the midpoint attractive spices begin to call; **f22** perhaps one of the shortest finishes of any JP whisky, which is why the spices can now take centre stage. Love that German caramelised biscuity sweetness which flickers for a few moments before the very end; **b23** can't help thinking that we have a Jaguar XK with the engine of a Ford Anglia. In some ways the lighter strength works, as it ensures a continued gentleness. But some of those more beautiful tones could also do with a little amplification, as this is almost too delicate. But I am clutching at straws here: this is unashamed elegance. *40% nc ncf*

◇◇◇ **Paul John Oloroso** db (90.5) **n23** pretty much the perfect nutty oloroso nose. The barley, however, is nowhere to be seen...; **t23** confirmation of the cask's excellence: the grape is thick and of the sweeter variety for oloroso. Normally spices are upfront at this point, but here they are conspicuous by their absence. You will have to make do with very moist Melton Hunt Cake, lacking in the usual dark sugar intensity, perhaps, though an excellent toastiness does drift in at round the midpoint. The mouthfeel is sublime as the grape is thin enough to allow the tannins and some very late barley to find a spot; **f22** only late on do the spices stir, but there is also a modest degree of bitterness for the fruit to battle against; **b22.5** not an entirely blemish-free bottling, but most won't notice. Sherried whisky lovers will rip this one from the shelves. *48% nc ncf*

◇◇◇ **Paul John Peated** db (95) **n23.5** the peat is raring to go. But it is being held back, chained by thick grape. So, instead, we are getting a muted, if slightly acerbic smokiness with an attractive degree of nose nibble. Look closely an even a hint of hickory in there...; **t24** the mix of the rich fruit and bold, almost acidic peat, is eyewatering with only a little muscovado sugar trying to play things down a little. It is also completely tastebud-drowning...this is immense! It is the succulence which is impossible to ignore as there is a mix of juiciness and creaminess in one, the salivation levels upped by tannin-enriched spice. Then stratum of fruit and peat which eventually melt into one gloopy and delicious one; **f23.5** controlled spices now and a triggering of molasses and even blood orange peel. The smoke now is defused...; **b24** for a peated malt this strength, for the type of cask used, too...; this s a very noble whisky which insists of grace over gargantuanism. A pleasing and satisfying malt in so many respects: a true gentle giant. *55.5% nc ncf*

⟐ **Paul John PX** db **(89)** n22.5 thick, uncompromising, though delicately spiced, grape...; **t23** boom! It is though you have been hit by a barrel of sugary grapes! After the initial shock, things calm down for a moment, lightening a little with a salivating salvo of lychee and mango to briefly offer refreshment. Then it is back to the heavier grape; **f21.5** hmm: a tad bitter and out of sync; **b22** sometimes you just have to laugh when tasting PX. With some whiskies, it is though they have been painted with the finest brush, each stroke making a barely perceptible addition to detail....which perhaps perfectly summarises the majority of Paul John's outstanding output. Here it is as though the character has been sploshed on with a paint roller. Entertaining, the ending apart. *48% nc ncf*

RAMPUR DISTILLERY Rampur. Working

⟐ **Rampur Asava** Cabernet Sauvignon, American bourbon barrels and Indian red wine casks db **(90.5)** n23 such a gorgeously aligned nose with the ripe red berries working busily with both intense malt and rich tannin to find an excellent driving line...; **t23** a salivating and intensely malty kick off, this is one of the lighter Rampurs I have experienced through the years. The fruit makes no effort to add any more wight than the malt does and goes about its work with a shrill sweetness; **f22** slightly rubbery tang – and element vaguely apparent on the nose - and even a tad hot, there is a lovely chocolate-berry finale to soothe things; **b22.5** one of the things I was most curious about was how Rampur kept consistency in the glare of the Indian sun when in a matter of weeks a barrel can change direction dramatically. Well, for sheer quality and complexity on nose and delivery they have certainly maintained standards. The finish is a little rougher and more unsettled than the last I tasted a couple of years ago but still has colossal character. *45% ncf*

⟐ **Rampur Double Cask American** bourbon barrels & European oak sherry casks, batch no 1031, bott 08/22 db **(92.5)** n23 a spicy, breast-beating nose which, though weighty, has room enough for the malt and grape to take turns in muscular domination; **t23.5** rich, fat, sweet and spicy, the delivery leaves nothing to chance. The malt invades any unclaimed territory, ensuring complexity is the key. Yet for all its weight, salivating to the last, too...; **f22.5** long and oily, there is a slight warmth suggesting overly excited stills at some point. But the barley-vanilla theme works some late magic...; **b23.5** genuinely impresses with both the quality and integration of the sherry butts. A slightly slower distillation rate would probably have kicked this up into the 94 mark as the grumpiness on the finish is slightly out of tune with the overall excellence of the cask management. A throat-rattling whisky to savour after a long trip, or a drive through the New Delhi traffic... *45% ncf*

⟐ **Royal Ranthambore Royal Crafted Luxury Whisky** batch 1144, bott 29/9/22 **(88.5)** n22 t22.5 f22 b22 Old school Indian blend of the pure silk variety. Lots of toffee adds to the genteel, satisfying nature, but there are malts afoot, too, and they offer layering and salivation in equal quantities. Lovely stuff! *42.8%*

NEW ZEALAND
CARDRONA DISTILLERY WANAKA

⟐ **Cardrona Full Flight Single Malt** Pedro Ximenez sherry butt, cask no 114, dist 16/01/2016, bott 19/01/2023 db **(93)** n23 PX...!! It telegraphs the grape before you get within an inch of the glass. But the sweet fruit doesn't have all its own way as the oak manages to deliver a searingly warm spicy message; **t23.5** PX...!! The first moment on the palate is so sweet. And salivating, too, especially when the malt starts to get amongst the action. But then ramps up the sharpness momentarily before focussing its attention on the chocolate fruit and nut middle; **f23** the bitter aftermath often seen with a PX isn't spared here. But there is also a Garibaldi biscuit moment or two to impress; **b23.5** I noticed the New Zealand Falcon depicted on the label, and that turns out to be the distillery's bird of identity and the inspiration for its brand names. When I first visited New Zealand's then only distillery back in 1994, I took the opportunity to tour the country birding and experienced some indelible, life-memory moments, especially with a pair of mating tui which thrilled both myself and my then 8-year-old son with the most elaborate and breath-taking mating dance I have ever seen, involving the caldera of an extinct volcano and what appeared to be a synchronised plummet to their apparent doom. The NZ Falcon was far less a dramatic find, which I still recall sitting on a post with a quiet, confident elegance as it looked out for its next meal. That same elegance can be found with this whisky: no break-neck dives into volcanos here. I am not normally much of a fan of PX matured malt. But you have to give a nod of approval when something works well, as this does. *62.7% sc ncf nc 1131 bottles*

⬥ **Cardrona Growing Wings Single Malt** sherry & bourbon cask db **(95.5) n24** astonished; my first-ever nose of this new New Zealand distillery and what do we have? A faultless nose confirming beautifully distilled malt with not even a rumble of a hint of an off note. Some shimmering, nimble tannins and the influence of a sublimely (and ultra-rare) clean sherry cask or two. The fruit has the slight dominance when cool and offers a quiet nip to the grape. But when warmed, the tannins and barley have far more to say for themselves while the fruit dries into pithy mode; **t24.5** salivating to the nth degree, the malt here could not be any more intense and complete even if it had a total malt transplant. Meanwhile the grape – presumably PX with that outlandish sweetness – appears to be pulled back from the cask's usual arrogant dominance by a secondary, drier, date-like fruitiness. Quite amazing in its make-up, because it is an almost back-to-front malt where things happen far earlier than you might expect. For instance, there is a glorious cascade of mocha and raisin. Normally you would have to wait patiently until it arrived at the death. Not here. Up front and personal, that mocha concentrate works in tandem with the outrageously chewy malt to offer and delivers a middle unreplicated anywhere else in the world; **f23** much more bitter and bitty at the end, for a moment both the tannin and grape skin get into a bit of a tangle. But as both the malt and tannins resurface equilibrium is restored; **b24** happy marriages seem to be a bit of a rarity these days. But here's one. The way the bourbon and sherry casks have integrated is a match made in heaven. I at least, for one, am in love... This is a quite extraordinary whisky for a distillery so new...whichever part of the world you may find it. *64.6% ncf nc*

POKENO WHISKY CO.

⬥ **Pokeno Origin Single Malt** First fill bourbon casks, bott code 2220716 db **(92.5) n23** the intensity of the first fill-cask is stamping all over the youthfulness of the malt. Indeed, it finds a surprising degree of harmony. But most impressive in the cleanliness of the malt: this has been beautifully and very carefully made...; **t23** light-bodied and silky the malt builds and builds in its riches. But the tannins are always on the scene, though thankfully never dominating; **f23** milk chocolate Maltesers are an almost inevitable outcome of this barley-tannin mix. The cocoa is soft as the oils finally make their mark while some Demerara sugars represent the high point of the tannins; **b23.5** a very pleasant and impressive single malt which makes a virtue of its youth by ramping up the intensity of the smalt to beautifully mouth-watering levels. For a whisky that has been matured in exclusively first-fill bourbon, this has a surprising complexity and depth to its oaky layering – one usually brought about by introducing second fills. So, some fears I had have been allayed. If they could get this up to 46%, and make a non-chill filtering and non-colouring statement, this brand could go far...and I mean about 12,000 miles... *43%*

⬥ **Pokeno Revelation Single Malt** first fill bourbon and NZ red wine barrels, bott code 221921 db **(94) n23** youthful but this has weight and something to say: where the barley is lightly honied yet bold, the fruit is dry and lightly spiced, not unlike drying grape skin. At times surprisingly floral; **t23.5** a loud round of applause for the stunning delivery. Sharp and pugnacious, the barley is vivid and salivating, as one might expect from a young malt, seemingly further whetted by fleshy fruit. The spices are sublime, as is the dark chocolate Malteser middle and fade; **f23.5** yet more plain chocolate Malteser...with knobs on. A vague heather honey sweetness arrives surprisingly late, though the tannins gang up to counter; **b24** some 30 years ago, when I visited a local distillery for the first time, the head of sales for Seagram took me to the home of a relation who, on his farm, was producing the first high quality New Zealand red wine in the country. That wine was dry, chalky, immensely deep and complex and not unlike some of the finer Greek wines that used to be specially retained to go with lamb: I can smell and taste its memory even now. I also remember joking that one day he should sell his casks to the distillery for maturation...and here we have a New Zealand single malt influenced by native New Zealand red wine barrels. It does the heart good... for this is a joy of a young single malt. Brilliant! Oh, and the Revelation comes after tasting this using the Murray Method as opposed at room temperature... *43%*

⬥ **Pokeno Discovery Single Malt** first fill bourbon and sherry casks db **(89) n22** the malt is young, the tannins are feisty, and the fruit is thick. Big vanilla and spice sub-current...; **t23** fat and fulsome delivery with a huge surge in flavours, especially the malt, giving a wonderful all-round mouthfeel. As on the nose, the spices come in tandem with the thick vanilla. Veins of fruit pulse; **f21.5** untidy and just bitters out very slightly as balance is compromised. Late cocoa and that persistent spice helps to stabilise; **b22.5** was doing quite beautifully until it reached the finale where it lost its way somewhat. Even so, the delivery and rumbling flavour-waves thereafter are to be cherished. *43%*

⬥ **Pokeno Prohibition Porter Single Malt** first fill bourbon barrel aged in Porter, cask no 0051, dist 13.06.19, bott 02.08.22 db **(94.5) n23.5** the malt is brittle and profound. In the background, though, the pleasant acidic nip of something a little burned...; **t23.5** what a delivery! Unique! And truly delicious. Myriad barley tones fizz at the taste buds, ranging from an almost

Irish pot still unmalted hardness, through concentrated, sweet barley and finally reaching something far more toasty and eye-watering. In the meantime the structure of the whisky itself changes and becomes increasingly oily to the point of outright creaminess...almost like an old-fashioned milk stout...; **f23.5** and now we're back to that burnt malt character again...but so much more. The cream brings with it some latent cocoa and even some Seville orange from gawd knows where. The final embers though are those of intense malt and chalky vanillas: complex; **b24** OK, OK, I admit it! Experience has taught me to fear the worst with beer accented whisky: the hop bitterness has ruined many a promising distillation. So, I feared the worst. Not here, though. The main characteristic from the Porter is a prevailing roastiness, with a chocolatey sub-plot. Thankfully the hop makes no appearance whatsoever. Creamy and complex, it belies its years with an assured performance, surprising for a new distillery...A minor classic, it has to be said. And for a three-year-old...simply ridiculously good... *46% nc ncf 363 bottles*

⬧ **Pokeno Single Cask Single Malt PX Sherry Cask Finish**, cask no 0412, dist 30.04.19, bott 10.08.22 db **(92) n23** soft, friendly, moist fruitcake; **t23** this distillery really does know how to do excellent mouth feel. And the delivery is no exception. Perhaps lacks complexity thanks to the thick coating of PX, but the buzzing of the spice and building of the vanilla is a delight while the late heather honey hitting the midpoint offers yet another surprise; **f23** more hefty grape but the tannin and spice keeps the taste buds working. A late, surprising, explosion of date and chocolate raisin; **b23** another Pokeno which reacts wonderfully to the Murray Method. At cooler temperatures the PX holds far too firm a grip. However, on taking it through its paces, this malt certainly hits its straps as first the honey and then the cocoa makes profound contributions. This will be one of the better PX finishes I encounter this year. And for a three-year-old, I doubt if I'll experience better. *46% nc ncf 880 bottles*

THE SPIRITS WORKSHOP Sydenham, Christchurch

⬧ **Divergence Five Single Malt Whisky** db **(93) n23** there is a positive, attractive aroma on here which I last encountered, I feel, somewhere between 20 or 30 years ago.... maybe even more. I cannot place it – yet. And it will mither me all day. But the marriage between black cherry and blackcurrant...that's it...!!! Just came to me: my old mum's blackcurrant jam and tarts made from our garden blackberries in the 1960's... there is also a creamy grapiness, too. Super soft and super fruity. Of the malt itself...there is no trace...; **t23.5** incredibly rich cream sherry delivery. And though this is pretty monosyllabic early on, it soon thins sufficiently for some outstanding layering to shine. First comes the oak which is spicy and chest-thumping. Next, we have a succession of welcome citrus tones, ensuring the fruit is multi-faceted. These fruits are bolstered by an almost salty deep cherry tone which now mingles with the oak; **f23** impressively long, the cherry intensifies while there is a very (and I mean very) light unscheduled buzz on the tongue...; **b23.5** normally I grizzle when I'm unable to pick out the malt in a malt whisky. But so outlandishly complex are the fruit tones at play here, I can let that one pass. There is a very slight cask fault at the death – a certain tanginess will be detected – but I'll let that one go, too. A whisky this determined to entertain deserves to have the odd blind eye turned. My word, New Zealand whisky has come a long way since Lammerlaw... *46% nc ncf 216 bottles*

⬧ **Divergence Port Wood Single Malt Whisky** db **(89) n20.5** lots of toffee on this nose. But, otherwise, the spirit and port cask haven't rubbed up too well on each other: dull with precious little positive harmony. Even a touch of juniper...; **t22.5** now, I didn't expect that! An impressive recovery with the grape injecting a wonderful sharpness which managed to get the taste buds salivating. Again, toffee is a theme, seemingly steaming in off the tannins. That peculiar juniper note plays hide and seek, but we have such a gorgeous outpouring of molten toffee raisin - and even a smattering of barley – that it is easy to forget about it; **f23** maximum complexity now with a sharp tangerine note offering a kind of cursory Jaffa cake thread. The spices pulse almost inaudibly; **b23** I can't remember when a distillery last decided to make its mark with so many huge, tub-thumping whiskies. Here's the third in the batch, and no more a shrinking violet than the others. I feared the worst after the disappointing nose. But the recovery is delicious! *46% nc ncf*

⬧ **Divergence Virgin French Oak Single Malt Whisky** db **(90) n22.5** setting aside a niggling minor feint note, the tannins make their mark in a dreamy and creamy kind of way, molasses and muscovado sugars injecting a fruity illusion. Apart from the spirit, where that degree of creaminess is coming from has left me scratching my head; **t23** wow! Did I say creamy...? What a brilliant delivery: a kind of crème brulée meets sherry trifle. But, again, just where is that thick fruit note coming in from? The feints are present, but you have to look for them, rather than them finding you...; **f22** at last some malt enters the action, something akin to a chocolate malt at that, and surprisingly confidently, too. And still in creamy fashion...though the bitterness does overgrow, though more likely from the spirit than the cask; **b22.5** I have experienced quite a few virgin French oak cask matured whiskies over the years – not just in bottle for the Bible, but also as I crawl around various warehouses around the world, as well as in my blending lab. The cross-section of quality is surprising. But something they all have in common is the refusal to take prisoners: they are huge, tannin-stonking whiskies all. This one, though huge and tannin-stonking, is different. It is softer and kinder and peculiarly fruity in its own idiosyncratic way, though the wider cut off the still hasn't done the cask the service it might best appreciate. *46% nc ncf*

SOUTH AFRICA
JAMES SEDGWICK DISTILLERY Wellington. Working
⬩ **Three Ships Premium Bourbon Cask** bott code LW9 13B23 db (88) n22.5 t23 f20.5 b22
It is quite remarkable that a blended whisky which makes a virtue of its bourbon cask usage has so many constituent parts on the palate that one would normally identify with sherry! Fruit abounds, especially with its marmalade and apricot thrust. But the malts are pretty thick, too, and early on this ensures a delicious and complex delivery. The nose is also quite charming, kicking up vanilla with light lemon blossom honey holding out against the lightly spiced tannin. The finale is not so endearing, however, and the late bitterness is to be regretted. Even so, overall an enjoyable whisky which rewards you for not taking its advice of adding ice or water. Easily at its best when straight at hand temperature when the oils are seen to full advantage. 43%

TAIWAN
KAVALAN DISTILLERY Yuanshan. Working
⬩ **Kavalan Ex-Bourbon Oak** db (90.5) n22.5 t23 f22 b23 Also bottled in 2014, this ex-bourbon Kavalan can also be found at the Solaire Hotel, Manilla. I've included it simply because it gives the rare opportunity for whisky lovers to compare a 46% ex-bourbon from multiple casks against a selected cask strength version from a then fledgling distillery. This is still full of tub-thumping barley of extraordinary depth and clarity. But underlines how reducing in strength weakens the finish and makes for a chalkier persona when vanilla is in town. 46%
⬩ **Kavalan Solist Cask Strength Ex-Bourbon Cask** cask BO9102300A db (96) n23.5 playful vanillas hold back the intense barley, diced apple and freshly plucked, tender grass...but only for so long. Beautifully bright...; t24 just a fabulous delivery hitting all the right spots. The oils begin relaxed but begin to build. But the explosion of intense barley is as remarkable as it is delicious....; f24 just about the perfect finish for this type of whisky with the barley now crisp and radiating all kinds of brown sugars alongside the persistent grape. The oils are totally in tune and carry the sugars on a perfect pitch...; b24.5 a perfection of lip-smacking, juicy, intense malty grassiness. Although bottled in 2014, I found these still available at the Solaire Hotel in Manilla, who must have bought virtually the entire barrel. Almost worth a trip to the Philippines just to experience the mouth-watering classic of controlled intensity. Blew the crowd away when I included it in the line-up of a few tastings there, being voted top dog on one occasion. 56.3% 192 bottles

NANTOU DISTILLERY Taichung. Working
Nantou Distillery Omar Cask Strength Bourbon Cask cask no. 11140804, dist May 14, bott 25 May 17 db (96.5) n24 t24.5 f23.5 b24.5 Beautifully distilled; beautifully matured. Simply stunning! One of the single casks of the year, not least for its unique and almost exhaustingly delicious style. 56%. sc. 248 bottles.

CROSS-COUNTRY VATTED WHISKIES
⬩ **Knaplund High Rye Whiskey Aged 5 Years** batch 2 (92) n22 unquestionably the most rounded rye-effected noses in the marketplace today, despite a vague weakness off the distillation. Lacks the usual sugary bite of a rye or even high rye bourbon but we are gifted instead an avalanche of genteel but attractively layered vanilla; t23.5 where the nose sits on the fence, there is no such conservativism on the palate: the delivery is spiked with huge flavour. Again, there is a salty punchiness to this as there are all Knaplund whiskeys, but this really does appear to pique those sharper tones, amid which the Demerara sugars call loudest. But with just a little warming we ae back to those vanillas rolling about the palate like waves across the Atlantic...; f23 perhaps the softest finale to a rye I've tasted for a year or two. The vanillas are standing their ground, but there is also a minty call to this, too which sits beautifully with the slightly milky chocolate and very late and super-relaxed spice...; b23.5 a wonderful whiskey so laid back at times it seems it can scarcely be bothered to give you the grand tour of its charm. But with patience you get there, and it is well worth the prompting. This, incidentally, is a blend of Knaplund Danish whiskey and one distilled in the US. These were the first distillations of two distilleries, it should be riddled by faults. Well, apart from a very minor one on the nose, this is plain sailing... 50%

Slàinte

One of the things that has made working in the worldwide whisky industry for the last 31 years so enjoyable is the extraordinary number of fabulous people I have met in those three transformative decades.

Lifelong friendships have been forged with people within and without the industry, but connected by the common, deliciously golden thread of whisky itself. These fine, loving folk, both men and women, have been especially kind to me in the last few years as they saw me battle the extreme hatred which is peculiar to jealousy, intolerance and cold, warped ideology and so destructive when mixed together. Indeed, it is the very matter from which the evil of Cancel Culture is created.

Thank you all, both long term friends and the many tens of thousands of readers of the Whisky Bible I am still yet to meet around the world. Indeed, the words I wrote last year, which I repeat below, are as true now as they were then:

I am also indebted to the many people in the industry who saw straight through the shenanigans, understood the unpleasant game that was being played, and welcomed me back to their distilleries, or even to them for the first time. And also individuals from the bigger distilling concerns that are still keeping an arm's length, despite my obvious public support. Their arms around my shoulders and unstinting encouragement despite their positions within their companies has been a source of great comfort.

At times all your kind words have been overwhelming. I have, as they say, been feeling the love.

And again, I reiterate that I shall fight for freedom of expression and thought. It is also gratifying that in the last year, aware of universal misjustices, mine included, people have been waking up to the chilling threat that Wokery brings. One now just hopes that the new owner of Twitter will be able to clean that seething cesspit of lies and intolerance. As Orwell warned, keep repeating a falsehood enough times and fast enough and a lie becomes the truth. And that is what so many of us have experienced with a weaponised social media.

The battle against intolerance and injustice continues. Free thought and speech must prevail.

As ever, there are people who have gone to extraordinary lengths to help me keep the Whisky Bible on track and up to date. Or simply just kept me sane in the testing times created by pressures of hitting such a demanding deadline. This year these include a A-Z of truly wonderful people such as Julie Barry, Birgit Bornemeier, Daren Burney, Philip Cheng, Richard Cohen, David Hartley, Gill Hind, Eric Hocepied, Charlie Jones, Peter and Linda Mayne, Shaun Murphy, Cole Tomberlain, Angela Traver, Nicky Wall and Big John Waterfield. To each and every one I am truly indebted.

But there has to be an extra special mention for Heiko Thieme for, well.... just being Heiko Thieme. And, of course, Jane Garnett my long-suffering and quite wonderful PA who is always there by my side. Except on her days off.

Among those I would like to shake by the hand is Steve Jackaman, long ago the creator of the Glasgow font used since the very first edition of the Whisky Bible was assembled in 2003 and now still in place 20 years on....but only thanks to his great kindness which averted a disaster.

And as a way to a man's heart is invariably through his stomach, I'd also like to gratefully extend my credit card towards Mr and Mrs Murray for maintaining The Super Sausage at Towcester as Britain's very finest Café and providing the best sausage sandwich known to mankind; and the staff at the Main Street Diner in Frankfort, Ky, whose steak and eggs are the very building blocks of a whisky writer's life. Without these two celebrated establishments it is likely I may have starved to death long before this book was completed.

And finally, I'd like to thank Dave Sandlin at the quite brilliant and inspiring House of Commons whiskey bar in Frankfort, Kentucky, for not only providing me with the most amazing blast from the past with an Ancient Ancient Age 10-Years-Old, but access to some of the bourbons I hadn't yet found under my own steam. I wish this charming and much needed establishment the success it fully deserves.

Oh and please remember the motto of Jim Murray's Whisky Bible: The Truth: always and above all.